PHRYGIA
MINOR
sive
TROAS
Ilium
sive
Troja
Tenedus I.
ÆOLIS
IONIA
Colophon
Propr
tum

THE LANDMARK

FREE PRESS
New York London Toronto Sydney

THUCYDIDES

A COMPREHENSIVE GUIDE TO THE PELOPONNESIAN WAR

A Newly Revised Edition of the Richard Crawley Translation with Maps, Annotations, Appendices, and Encyclopedic Index

Edited by Robert B. Strassler

With an Introduction by Victor Davis Hanson

The editor gratefully acknowledges permission to use illustrations from various souces, as follow: 1.1: Courtesy of the Royal Ontario Museum, Toronto. 1.90: Ostia Museum. Photo Gabinetto Fotografico. 1.132: Deutsches Archäologisches Institut, Istanbul. 1.135: American School of Classical Studies at Athens, Agora Excavations. 1.144: Copyright British Museum. 2.22: Photograph by David Finn. 2.44: Alinari/Art Resources. 2.69: Epigraphic Museum, Athens. 2.84: Paul Lipke/The Trireme Trust. 3.48: American School of Classical Studies at Athens, Agora Excavations. 3.86: Copyright British Museum. 4.41: American School of Classical Studies at Athens, Agora Excavations. 5.47: Epigraphic Museum, Athens. 6.54: Epigraphic Museum, Athens. 6.61: American School of Classical Studies at Athens, Agora Excavations. 8.7: Copyright British Museum. 8.8: Courtesy of Thames & Hudson Ltd. Photograph by Peter A. Clayton. Appendix G: The Trireme Trust. Illustration by John F. Coates.

Free Press
A Division of Simon & Schuster, Inc.
1230 Avenue of the Americas
New York, NY 10020

This Free Press trade paperback edition February 2008

FREE PRESS and colophon are trademarks of Simon & Schuster, Inc.

For information about special discounts for bulk purchases,
please contact Simon & Schuster Special Sales at 1-800-456-6798
or business@simonandschuster.com

Designed by Kim Llewellyn
Maps by Anne Gibson

Manufactured in the United States of America

10 9 8 7

Library of Congress Cataloging-in-Publication Data

Thucydides.
[History of the Peloponnesian War. English]
The landmark Thucydides : a comprehensive guide to the Peloponnesian War / edited by Robert B. Strassler; introduction by Victor Davis Hanson.
p. cm.
"This edition uses the translation by Richard Crawley (1840–93) published in 1874"—CIP front matter.
Includes bibliographical references and index.
1. Greece—History—Peloponnesian War, 431–404 B.C. I. Strassler, Robert B., 1937– II. Crawley, Richard, 1840–1893. III. Title.
DF229.T55C7 1996
938'.05—dc20 96-24555
ISBN-13: 978-1-4165-9087-3
ISBN-10: 1-4165-9087-0

TO THE MEMORY OF
SAMUEL A. STRASSLER

CONTENTS

TRODUCTION

n, wrote the history of the war" is the first pronouncement
Var (1.1.1). Unfortunately, the merest glimpses of our
romising initial revelation of his name, nationality, and call-
nexpected places in his chronicle does Thucydides disclose
imself. He announces, for example, that he once suffered
that struck Athens between 430 and 427 (2.48.3),[a] the
es and thousands of his fellow Athenians (3.87.3).

des, in the third person, matter-of-factly enters his own
unt of the successful Spartan attack on the northern Greek
He tells us that:

> ad come from Athens to defend the place, sent to the
> Thrace, Thucydides son of Olorus, the author of this
> ne isle of Thasos, a Parian colony, half a day's sail from
> 4)

)lorus," is probably Thracian and royal, suggesting both a
edigree. Thucydides confirms that standing and prestige
was called to Amphipolis precisely because "he possessed
gold mines in that part of Thrace, and thus had great influ-
of the mainland" (4.105.1).

e Amphipolis from the shrewd Spartan general Brasidas
brunt of Athenian popular indignation:

> be an exile from my country for twenty years after my
> olis; and being present with both parties, and more
> eloponnesians by reason of my exile, I had leisure to
> losely" (5.26.5).

c. Numbers in paren-
pter, and section

Later Roman and Byzantine biographies, their anecdotes and gossip unproved but not necessarily always fanciful, add a few more intriguing personal details about Thucydides' life: formal philosophical and rhetorical training, aristocratic connections, a violent death, and burial at Athens. But beyond his own admitted survival of disease, battle, and exile, Thucydides tells us little else about his experience in the war years other than that he lived "through the whole of it, being of an age to comprehend events" (5.26.5). We should conclude that he was near thirty when the fighting broke out (431) and probably died in his sixties or early seventies in the mid-390s, with his history apparently left uncompleted.

ii.

Besides an intrinsic interest in learning more about the author of the finest history of the ancient world, we search for the elusive historical Thucydides in hopes of learning something of the man's outlook, his role in the events of his time, his association with the eminent figures of the fifth century—indeed, anything that might shed some additional light upon the intention, disposition, and outlook of the author of *The Peloponnesian War.* Given that he was an Athenian during the city's greatest age; a man of some wealth, property, and important family connections; and once an official of the government with a sizable command, important friends, and apparently numerous enemies at Athens, a few inferences are in order.

Like his contemporary the Athenian playwright Euripides, Thucydides was familiar with, but did not necessarily approve of, the sophistic and rhetorical movements that were spawned by the bounty of this Athenian century. Nor does Thucydides' own participation in the expanding regime of Athens suggest his agreement with an imperial democratic culture that grew out from the vast possession of subject states. Despite opportunity for profitable overseas concessions and military repute, wealthier Athenians like Thucydides probably felt more at home with a past timocratic[a] government that had once been the private domain of property owners. As moderate oligarchs, then, they were skeptical of unpredictable democrats and any others who championed a more radically egalitarian agenda that might diminish the power of Athens' upper classes (8.97.2).

For a man of Thucydides' experience and upbringing, democracy worked best when nominal and under the control of a single great man like Pericles (2.65.6–13). Less responsible demagogues and politicians, like Cleon and Hyberbolus, were both unpredictable and unreliable and so to be feared (3.36.6; 8.73.3). Their stock-in-trade was the agitation of the Athenian *demos,* an always fickle and sometimes quite dangerous rabble (2.65.4; 2.65.10–11; 3.36.4; 6.24.2–4).

In contrast, by the latter fifth century conservative Athenians of piety and virtue were odd men out. A particular Thucydidean example of this is the very rich Athenian statesman Nicias, who failed to arrest the folly of the Athenian mob, and for his troubles ended up dead at the end of the ill-fated Athenian expedition to Sicily (7.86.2–5). It is no accident that there is little naïveté, much less idealism and inno-

I.ii.a A timocratic government is one in which political power is directly proportional to property ownership.

the black-and-white history of Thucydides (2.35.2; 3.44.4; ust remember, was above all a man of action, an elected offi-, and a pragmatic intellectual, a successful combatant against :, hardbitten and intimate with both privilege and disgrace, a and outlived most of the greatest men of his age.

War

ch is to win applause of the moment, but as a possession 22.4).

ıtly writes of his own historical aims. We are warned early on ucydides gives us no exact title of his work—is to be more nt of the events of his age, momentous and portentous as arly, he believed that the war between Athens and Sparta at the poles of human and not just Greek experience, at and assumptions for a brief time ripped open by organized d left exposed for autopsy by the bewildered but curious lanation and instruction. For the diagnostician Thucydides, nd was constant and predictable, the story of civilized man nd repetitive, and thus his account of these events surely of er and reflective men not yet born (1.22.4–5; 2.48.3).

age "for all time" appears in elaborate antitheses of thought ual words, entire sentences, even whole episodes. Nature deed, pretext and candor lead to larger corollaries of land oligarchy and democracy, commerce and agriculture, wealth a purpose. The war between Athens and Sparta offers edge in the extreme variance between what a man says and 34.3), between the jealousy of ambition and the contempt 1.4), between the dream of a people and the reality of their .75.6–7; 7.87), between innate discomfiture with the good ion toward the base (2.64.4–65.11; 3.36.6; 4.21.2–22.2; : burdens and responsibilities of power and the necessary npotence (5.85–116), between democracy at home and 62.2–64.3; 6.17.2–18.7), between the Athenian thesis that reluctant players in a brutal cosmic order, and the Spartan ch hinges on the gods' punishment of the guilty and aid of 21–124; 2.60–62; 5.104–106). Athens and Sparta are states are also metaphysical representations of opposite ways of :, whose corollaries are often emphasized in a variety of

So the majestic Funeral Oration of Pericles (2.35.1–46.2) is to be placed immediately before the horrific plague (2.47.3–54.3), in the same manner as the Athenians' butchery of the hapless Melians (5.116.2–4) is a formal prelude for their own brutal extermination to come in Sicily (7.84.2–85.2). More concretely, the magnificent navy of Athens is to be contrasted with the invincible hoplites of Sparta (1.18.2–3; 1.142.5–8). The capital of Athenian imperialism is a match for the agrarian industriousness of the Peloponnesians (1.141.2–6), as the majestic Pericles towers over subsequent weaker successors (2.65.8–12) like Cleon and Alcibiades.

In his interest in formal polarities of thought and action, Thucydides is not always, I think, a more astute recorder than Herodotus (who lived c. 484–25), a near-contemporary historian, and therefore our most natural object of comparison. That Herodotus was less critical of sources and motive, more interested in ethnography, anthropology, myth, and yarn does not make him any less of a historian—or in turn Thucydides any more the biased theoretician, eager to select, omit, manipulate, and distort data according to his own preconceived and refined notion of what constitutes important and unimportant lessons of human behavior.

Rather, the differences between the two historians lie more in approach, method, and the generations in which they lived. Herodotus' travel mosaics of exotic tales, alien characters, and oddities of experience are all to be sorted out by the reader himself to form an overall picture of why a past generation of free Greeks triumphs over an oppressive and autocratic Persia, of who lies and who tells the truth, of what is believable and what not, of what is wisdom and what folly. So Herodotus, the itinerant Dorian, relies mostly on and is comfortable with an oral tradition. He feels no need to assess—at least in any systematic or formal way—the accuracy of what he hears, and provides little idea how all these reports join and fit into a unified whole. In some ways Herodotus is the most modern of historians, providing raw data and documentation without the intrusion of personal interpretation or explication.

In contrast, the younger Thucydides lives the history of the war that he writes, an account verifiable by eyewitnesses still alive (1.22.1–3). His prose is to be accepted or rejected by contemporaries in Athens with keen interests in rhetoric and style, a generation well acquainted with the logic of Socrates, the realism of Euripides, and the arguments of the Sophists. The influence of contemporary medical writers also offered to Thucydides the methodology of symptomatology, diagnosis, and prognosis that could be applied outside the realm of pure science: history is also a scientific discipline with its own proper set of rules and procedures (1.21–22; 2.48–49; 3.82–84). He cannot often, then, like Herodotus, say simply, "It is said . . . ," because the late-fifth-century Athenian audience of his history knows better and wants more. In any case, Thucydides feels the way to understanding is not through the sheer aggregate of examples, from which a few great notions of fate and chance might be freely deduced. The historian instead believes that the truth requires his own interpretation of the events he presents. It demands that he deem some occurrences not worthy of inclusion into his narrative, while others must take on unusual importance. If Thucydides' historical material is less rich and enchanting of Herodotus, his carefully chosen military episodes and mselves explicitly reveal cause and effect (1.97.2), follow a (5.20.2–3), and often lead to more profound and general perience (3.82–84; 5.85–116). And perhaps most impor- red through a war (5.26.5) far more lengthy, brutal, and reeks' noble defense of their country a half century earlier, t in some part account for his bleaker conclusions that uncontrollable and inevitable.

odotus also are the composition, style, and organization of ow Thucydides assembled *The Peloponnesian War* and not really ascertainable. His history has come down to us , but we do not know whether these divisions, or the chap- , derive from Thucydides himself or (far more likely) from ho worked centuries after his death. He seems instead to ry more as a chronicle of consecutive yearly military pters of related episodes. So after Book 1 has set the stage, with the spring warring season of the first year of the war, ate events in sequence through midwinter of 411. But then has no speeches), the history ends abruptly in midsentence his proposed twenty-seven-year account (5.26.1) are left

e either (1) composed his history without revision year by ressed; (2) begun writing the narrative from his notes only ted in 404; or (3) written and revised on and off from 431 his death—or perhaps simple frustration—cut short his he summer of the year 411, and prevented completion of the whole. The third possibility seems most likely, for here entire account Thucydides reveals knowledge of the war's and thus the approximate role his characters and events unity and theme of his work—if it had been completed.

e clearly divides into roughly two parts. The initial half the first ten years, the so-called Archidamian War from a formal preface (1.1–118.3) and seems to conclude with onnesian War ended in stalemate with the Peace of Nicias

resumption of hostilities in a variety of theaters in 421 equent Athenian disaster at Sicily (415–13), Thucydides something like a second introduction at 5.26. At some must have envisioned an integral and continuous twenty- se cohesive chronicle might now be brought all the way of Athens' Long Walls in 404. This continuation, clearly incomplete and less revised, is extant from 415 to 411 (from Book 5.26 to Book 8.109).

iii.

There is little argument that Thucydides' prose is difficult, and at times nearly incomprehensible. Yet its inherent abstruseness, its lengthy clauses and antitheses, and its deliberate understatement can still be moving. Thucydidean language often translates into English in a way more memorable than the direct and accessible expression of near-contemporary writers such as Xenophon or Lysias:

> "Revolution thus ran its course from city to city, and the places where it arrived at last, from having heard what had been done before carried to a still greater excess the refinement of their inventions, as manifested in the cunning of their enterprises and the atrocity of their reprisals. Words had to change their ordinary meanings and to take those which were now given them. Reckless audacity came to be considered the courage of a loyal supporter; prudent hesitation, specious cowardice; moderation was held to be a cloak for unmanliness; ability to see all sides of a question incapacity to act on any. Frantic violence became the attribute of manliness; cautious plotting a justifiable means of self-defense. The advocate of extreme measures was always trustworthy; his opponent a man to be suspected. To succeed in a plot was to have a shrewd head, to divine a plot a still shrewder; but to try to provide against having to do either was to break up your party and to be afraid of your adversaries" (3.82.3–5).

Thucydides' use of abstract nouns, his preference for constant variety in vocabulary, his fondness for archaic and even poetic expressions, and his often dramatic inversion of normal word order all ensure that his Greek is as complex as is his method of historical inquiry. Yet bear in mind that very little Attic prose was written before Thucydides. Nearly all of what was composed has been lost. Therefore we are not sure whether Thucydides' perplexing language is unique or typical, whether it reveals an entirely original method of expression, or simply mirrors the spirited intellectual ferment and experimentation of the times. Does the need to create ex nihilo words and phrases to match the depth of his abstract and conceptual thinking explain his singular literary technique? Or is Thucydidean style simply one with a peculiar, mostly lost, and now unrecoverable Athenian rhetorical florescence?

iv.

At Book 1.21–22 Thucydides clearly outlined his own methods of historical inquiry, offering a self-conscious candor rare in ancient narrative writing. He did not trust first impressions, he says, not even his own. But through inquiry and cross-examination of witnesses ("tried by the most severe and detailed tests possible"), autopsy,

on of written documents, Thucydides claims an objective
me some labor." His later admission that his own exile
careful investigation, "especially with the Peloponnesians"
mage of a careful and nonpartisan note taker, eager to hunt
emselves—both Athenian and Spartan—who took part in
owledge of Spartan custom and tradition (1.20.3; 4.80;
this confident assertion.

n fashionable to see this statement of principles at 1.21–22
of sorts, a sham to hide biased fiction packaged as "objec-
dern cynicism rings mostly false for a variety of reasons.
cydides' narrative is highly stylized and focused deliberately
als who best illustrate the author's own ideas about fate,
erience, elsewhere he is clearly aiming to be accurate, objec-
.

questioned (6.55.1), oracular pronouncements investigated
5), poets and prose authors both consulted and rejected
iptions on stone noted and copied (5.18.2–19.2; 6.54.7;
ial remains of buildings and walls explored and analyzed
4–6). Even the contents of graves are examined and
istorical hypotheses (1.8.1). Often such detail can appear to
(6.2.1–5.3), near-trivial (6.54.1–59.4), or even irrelevant, as
follow up on his earlier promises of completeness, regard-
ved. Thucydides himself said such research "cost me some
onder he despaired that "the absence of romance in my
ct somewhat from its interest" (1.22.4).

forty-one speeches in the history, presented in both direct
Because of the sheer number and variety of these addresses,
eneral of formal speeches in ancient historical and rhetorical
es' own enigmatic comments about his rules of usage
over their degree of veracity. There are, I think, four possi-
he speeches are accurate and nearly verbatim reproductions
er read, himself heard, or was told by others; (2) they are
de up by the author himself; (3) they are greatly elaborated,
sions of what men probably said; or (4) the one hundred
ot uniform and so vary according to the above categories.

both the historians Herodotus and Hecataeus, like the
es mostly as literary and dramatic fictions to interrupt and
ment of the narrative. But Thucydides' own characteriza-
.22.1 suggests a much different approach, one that warns
rture from past practice, and so should solve for us the
ty:

> "With reference to the speeches in this history, some were delivered before the war began, others while it was going on; some I heard myself, others I got from various quarters; it was in all cases difficult to carry them word for word in one's memory, so my habit has been to make the speakers say what was in my opinion demanded of them by the various occasions, of course adhering as closely as possible to the general sense of what they really said."

This careful declaration, however, has led only to more controversy. Does not Thucydides admit to two contrary agendas: contrivance ("to make the speakers say what was in my opinion demanded of them") and historical exactitude ("adhering as closely as possible to the general sense of what they really said")? Has he not entered that most controversial and irreconcilable of arguments—so popular once again now in academic circles—the cleft between "objective" and "subjective" truth?

Apparently, Thucydides is envisioning two very different circumstances for setting down speeches in his history: well-known addresses in which he was more or less able to find out what was really said, and other instances in which something probably was spoken, but went unrecorded or was forgotten. The latter orations had to be reconstructed more or less according to Thucydides' own particular historical sense of what was likely, appropriate, and necessary. How, then, can the exasperated reader determine the degree of authenticity of any given speech in the history?

He cannot. But surely he can rely on common sense to learn which addresses are more likely to have been spoken as recorded in the text of the history. Is there evidence—a large audience, an annual festive occasion, an official government proceeding—to suggest a speech was actually communicated, recorded, and subject to verification by Thucydides' readership? How conceivable is it (considering the place and time) that Thucydides could have either heard a speech himself or learned of its contents from others? Does an oration confirm a personal imprint, in line with the speaker's apparent nature and personality? Or does it seem instead stereotyped, designed by the historian himself to illustrate general and universal themes and so sometimes attributed to minor and otherwise unknown if not anonymous characters? And what are the preface and the reaction to a speech? Does an oration logically follow a course of events and in turn have an immediate effect on the conduct of subsequent actions in the narrative?

vi.

Succeeding generations of Greeks and Romans credited Thucydides with establishing objective history. His considerable skill in presenting that doctrine in formal prose left an undeniable mark even on his immediate literary successors, who likewise saw history as largely the unromantic story of political and military affairs. Indeed, many inquirers—Xenophon, Cratippus, and Theopompus—began their accounts where Thucydides had left off in 411. It is no surprise, then, that subse-

were judged largely by the degree to which they followed
y and integrity established by Thucydides. Xenophon
faulted for his failure to consult sources other than his own
blindness to the larger meaning of the very events he
that his histories were not much more than one personal
ntury chronicler Ephorus (405–330), also unlike Thucyd-
le and naive in his uses of sources, and lacks a workable
ore erudite Theopompus (b. 378) is found too bitter in his
distance and even the presumed air of objectivity of Thucyd-
War.

ymous Oxyrhynchus Historian, the mostly lost Hieronymus
the later and extant Polybius (200–c. 118) have often won
precisely because they are didactic and strive to teach the
abstract lessons from the near-endless wars and coups they
ause and effect, the employment of a strict chronology, and
urpose predominate. And like Thucydides these historians
they hear and read. Often they must outline formally the
to sort out rumor from fact. Even their speeches, embroi-
hey are, lend explication and sense to larger issues beyond
hus appear as "Thucydidean" rather than as mere fancies or
al expertise.

I[illegible]en Athens and Sparta

tory while confidently believing that

> war, and more worthy of relation than any that had
> ief was not without its grounds. The preparations of
> were in every department in the last state of perfection;
> rest of the Hellenic race taking sides in the quarrel;
> ing so at once having it in contemplation. Indeed this
> ement yet known in history, not only of the Hellenes,
> the barbarian world—I had almost said of mankind."

T[illegible] classical culture bears out Thucydides' judgment that the
P[illegible] twenty-seven-year nightmare that wrecked Greece.

y, the Greek *poleis* (city-states) had been unusually isolated
fr[illegible]Mediterranean history. Free to form their own customs and
tr[illegible]dreds of poleis nevertheless shared a common and venera-
b[illegible] and political culture. Most were broad-based oligarchies
th[illegible]nded aristocracies or had inherited power from intermedi-

ary tyrannies. The citizenry of hoplite yeomen, each owning and farming about ten acres of land, formed up as heavily armed infantry (*hoplites*) in the phalanx to battle neighboring Greek communities over disputed strips of borderland (1.15.2). From the seventh to the fifth centuries, there was a steady, if sometimes slow, advancement of Greek material and intellectual culture (1.13.1), as the protective practice of timocratic government and near-ritual infantry fighting prevented most political upheavals and limited the damage caused by frequent wars. The fifth century changed all that (1.1.2–3; 1.18.2–3; 1.23.1–6).

After the repulse of the Persians (in 490 and again in 480–79), the insular Greeks were faced with unforeseen military and political responsibilities in the Aegean and the Mediterranean at large, which were largely antithetical to the landed capital, infantry exclusivity, and smug isolationism of the traditional city-state (*polis*) (1.91.4–7; 1.93.3–7; 1.96.1). Unfortunately, as early as 478, the two most atypical and powerful of the city-states, Athens and Sparta, could not agree on joint leadership of the Greek alliance that had been so successful against the Persians (1.18.2–3; 1.95.7–97.1). Oddly, both poleis, although in diametrically opposite ways, rejected much of the traditional culture of the city-state—pitched battle by amateur militias, government by yeomen peers, economic reliance on citizen-worked farms, absence of satellites and tributaries. The antagonism set the stage, as Thucydides saw, for a horrific war like none other in the Greek past (1.1.1–3; 1.23.1–2).

The leadership of the maritime Greek federation against Persia fell to the Athenian navy (1.18.2; 1.73.4–75.3). Far from dismantling an oppressive imperial hierarchy, the Athenians throughout the mid-fifth century refined the Persian system of empire, and channeled the tribute to solidify and enlarge their own democratic culture at home while seeking tyrannical aggrandizement abroad (1.89.1–1.117.3). The enfranchisement and enrichment of those Athenians without money and land (2.37.1), together with the freedom and capital to wage war both imaginatively and continuously (2.39.2–3), meant that the past limiting protocols of the polis did not apply to an increasingly restive Athens (1.80.3–81.6; 1.142.1–144.3) In the process, Thucydides says, Pericles and the Athenian intelligentsia craft an apology for their oppression. It becomes a determinist, Hobbesian doctrine which explains that power—and hence justice—always and rightly accrues to the strong (2.64; 5.97).

Sparta offers both a material and a philosophical contrast. Her unique enslavement of nearly a quarter of a million rural indentured servants, the Helots, excused an armed elite from working their own plots. Rejecting the traditional Greek practice of free agriculture, Spartan society gradually institutionalized a complicated and harsh system of apartheid that called for constant surveillance of an enormous productive underclass (1.101.2–103.3; 1.132.4–5; 4.41.3). The result was the creation of the first true militaristic culture in the West, where all Spartiate males from the age of seven embarked on a vigorous course of military training (2.39.1–2; 5.66.2–4). The ensuing expertise would ensure a professional army (1.18.2; 4.40.2; 5.66.2–72.4), able to put down murderously at a moment's notice any hint of domestic insurrection (4.80.2–4) or, if need be, to march out to absorb and consolidate nearby territory in the Peloponnesus (1.19.1; 1.76.1). Inward, blinkered, [illegible] the sea, Sparta's self-interested conservatism takes on the [illegible] Athenian philosophical system, in which most Greek states [illegible] to practice justice under absolute canons of Hellenic law [illegible]

[illegible] ultimate confrontation between these two remarkable soci- [illegible] evitable and terrible (1.23.2; 2.11.6–9; 2.12.3); inevitable, [illegible] able antitheses between land and sea, autocracy and liberal- [illegible] try and broader Ionian commerce; terrible, because there [illegible] o powers neither an adherence to the past restrictions on [illegible] sufficient common political ground to negotiate a lasting [illegible] once and for all might arbitrate their contrasting views of [illegible] e.

[illegible] e navy fueled by overseas tribute, had no need to engage [illegible] in pitched battle (1.143.4–5; 2.13.3–8). Athens' biggest [illegible] cklessness of its own democratic government (1.144.1). A [illegible] citizenry, urged on and incensed by clever demagogues, [illegible] out military forces in unnecessary and exhausting adven- [illegible] 1–5).

[illegible] ually invade Athens (2.21.1–23.3). But for what purpose? [illegible] ative policy of simple challenges to pitched battle, coupled [illegible] agricultural devastation of Attica, could never bring a [illegible] knees (1.143.4–144.3; 2.65.11–13). Peloponnesian victory [illegible] nking and a veritable change in Spartan character itself [illegible] o cut off the tribute of Athens, spread insurrection among [illegible] cquire a navy of her own (1.121.2–5; 1.142.2–143.3)—all [illegible] n reactionary and inbred culture (1.69.4–70.8; 1.84.1–4), [illegible] otion that there are gods who punish an imperial power's [illegible] reek states.

[illegible] he struggle between a sea power and a land power meant [illegible] flict like the border fights of the past, but a long-drawn-out [illegible] ventually it became apparent that Sparta must man ships [illegible] n land. Maritime states loyal to Athens through contribu- [illegible] nanpower were to be lured away (1.81.3–4; 1.122.1); [illegible] oponnesian League must know that war by land might be [illegible] doorstep (1.142.4; 2.25.1–5). Homicidal revolution [illegible] ilization of serfs and slaves (4.80.5; 7.57.8), drawn-out [illegible] 34–116), mass murder and execution (5.116.3–4), and [illegible] (7.29.4–30.3)—all these were for Thucydides the expected [illegible] opposites, who would become ever more desperate and [illegible] progressed, as they learned that innovative and murderous [illegible] for absolute victory.

Thucydides suggests, I think, that the legacy of the Peloponnesian War would not be the victory of Spartan authoritarianism and the repudiation of the imperial democratic culture of Athens. No, it would be the irrevocable exhaustion and bankruptcy of the Greek city-state itself. The polis was, after all, an egalitarian but closed and static institution that could not adapt well to the military, economic, and political challenges of the wider Mediterranean world, changes initiated by the Persian invasion at the beginning of the fifth century, but dramatically and tragically elaborated by the virulent war between its most distinctive representatives, Athens and Sparta. And even if the Athenians are right about the universal relativity of justice and the amorality of power, we sense that such belief is nevertheless explicatory of their own destruction—and the demise of the *polis* itself. Our historian, it seems, does not necessarily like what he knows may be true.

IV. The Credibility of Thucydides

i.

Naturally, when the careful political and military tenets of centuries were cast out, Greeks turned toward superstition and religious fervor to explain both natural (earthquake, flood, eclipse, volcanic eruption, plague) and human (war, political extremism, revolution) calamity. This rise of concern with supernatural exegesis during the fighting held an obvious psychological interest for Thucydides. The gods and the haunts of the gods—Delphi, Delos, Olympia—appear frequently within *The Peloponnesian War* (1.25.1; 1.103.2; 1.134.4–135.1; 3.104.1–4; 5.1.1; 5.105.1–3; 5.49.1–50.4). But this fascination with the divine or unusual (1.23.3) does not seem to have clouded the author's own historical objectivity (2.28.1; 3.89.5). Nor does it suggest that Thucydides himself held deep religious beliefs, much less approved of the proliferation of oracles and prophecies. Again unlike Herodotus, he does not detect a divine motif in the unfolding of human events and surely does not write his history to confirm the sins of irreverence, hubris, and impiety.

On the contrary, Thucydides seems to see popular religion as more a social institution, valuable for inculcating and maintaining traditional conservative values. In that regard, superstition bereft of formal religious piety and restraint could only cloud human reason (2.8.2–3; 2.54.3–5; 7.50.4), and so add to the general cultural and intellectual decay unleashed by the war.

ii.

Of more interest are the occasional discrepancies and inconsistencies of Thucydides. They have caused alarm, understandable given the historian's vaunted pledge of accuracy. As in any great history, there are a few omissions (see note 8.5.5b), distortions, and mistakes in *The Peloponnesian War*, and they must be understood both in the context of the times and in light of the author's own historical aims and particular political outlook. Yet to perceive a personally engaged and emotional Thu-

ferences in his selection of material, is not necessarily to
n of objectivity. An historian, remember, can (and should)
ionated, but he is not necessarily unfair or biased—if, as in
his evidence and method of inquiry are stated candidly for

give an economic and social history of the Peloponnesian
example, only an abbreviated list of Athenian financial
ore lamentably, only occasional glimpses are given of the
constant fighting (2.16.1–2.17.1; 4.84.1–4), for this was
rity of the Greek population lived and suffered during the
chologically and emotionally, on the people who provided
war is omitted, primarily because Thucydides is writing a
e of the Peloponnesian War, not a cultural or agrarian
ury Greece. In this regard, Herodotus is by far the more
hnography and anthropology, and proves the more sensi-
re plays in a people's political and military conduct.

heroes and villains in Thucydides' history. To a modern
behavioral and social sciences, Thucydides can appear to
temperament, concentrating instead on "objective" and
timidity and heroism or recklessness versus self-control. In
is not predicated on or explained by one's specific envi-
but instead directed by the play of chance, fate, and hope
onditions universal to all and particular to no man.

n's thought and intent is scarcely appreciated in the histo-
d strokes of character. Intention counts for little; action is
oroughly majestic (2.65.5–9), and Cleon is violent and
21.3–4.22.2)—period. Most Spartans predictably conform
unimaginative stereotypes (1.86.1–1.87.6; 5.105.4), as if
Spartans of unquestioned dash and audacity, like Gylippus
as especially (2.25.2; 4.11.4–4.12.1; 4.81; 5.6.3–5.11.5).
ibiades is as un-Periclean (6.15.2–4) as the conventional,
Nicias. Admiration for men of action like Hermocrates of
; 6.72.2–5) and the Athenian general Demosthenes
ghs their occasional failures and errors in judgment
7.44.1–8).

dides' very limited angle of vision. Slaves and women are
from snippets in Thucydides' own text it is clear that
es during times of sieges (2.4.2; 3.74.2), and must have
the loss of male providers and especially during the great
Athens (2.45.2; 2.51.2–5). From Thucydides and other
es provided at least some of the power for the triremes on
numbers was felt by all to have deleterious effects on their
5; 8.40.2). More mundanely, no hoplite army could easily
aggage corps, who carried both equipment and supplies

(7.75.5). Yet again, both the unfree and the women remain virtually unknown, as Thucydides' history deals almost exclusively with the free male citizenry of the Greek city-states, a group that constituted perhaps no more than a quarter of the adult resident population.

Thucydides' concentration on political and military affairs is not to suggest that even he could possibly have given a comprehensive account of those events during the twenty-seven-year war (3.90.1). Both Plutarch and Diodorus, and extant official documents written on stone, all suggest that more went on than what we are told by Thucydides. No inkling, for example, is given about the transference of the Delian treasury to Athens (454), which marked the formal rise of Athenian imperialism. The purported "Peace of Callias" between Persia and Greece (449),[a] the important Athenian colony at Brea (445), and the reassessment of the Athenian tribute[b] (425) all help explain the rise and nature of Athenian power but are ignored by Thucydides. Events critical to an understanding of war itself are often scarcely mentioned or absent altogether, such as the "Megarian Decree" (the Athenian sanctions against Megara in 432) and the important treaties between Athens and Sicilian Egesta (418–417?).[c] Yet even that list of oversights is small, and it pales beside the information found only in *The Peloponnesian War*, completely unknown to later sources and undiscoverable from extant archaeological and epigraphic remains.

iii.

In the final analysis, what stands out about Thucydides is not his weaknesses but his strengths as a historian. We note his omissions, but no account of the Peloponnesian War or of fifth-century Greece in general is more complete. Some scholars worry over his cut-and-dried heroes and villains. But is there much evidence to suggest that these assessments were fundamentally wrong? Others argue that his speeches are biased distortions, but no one can prove that any are outright fabrications. At times Thucydides may be clearly mistaken in both detail and interpretation, but the extent of his accuracy and analysis astounds in a world where travel was difficult, written sources rarely available, and the physical obstacles to the writing of history substantial. For all the contributions of archaeology, epigraphy, and the wealth of Athenian literature, without Thucydides' singular history we would know very little about fifth-century Greece

Even more extraordinary is Thucydides' ability to use that knowledge to reach a higher wisdom about the nature of human behavior, whether it be unveiled by plague (2.53), revolution (3.82–84), or war (5.103). And never forget that Thucydides was much more than an accurate recorder, more even than a keen judge of human character and the role that natural law and chance play in men's affairs (3.45.5–7; 3.84.1–3). He was a profound literary artist as well, emotional and

IV.iia See Appendix E, The Persians, §5, and Appendix B, The Athenian Empire, §8.
IV.iib See Appendix B, The Athenian Empire, §11.
IV.iic If the correct date for this treaty is 418/7. Thucydides was either unaware of the recent treaty or felt it unnecessary or even antithetical to his explanation (6.6.8) of of the relationship between Athens and Egesta.

urprising occasions. The trapped Athenians who died in the
ot anonymous unfortunates, but irreplaceable patriots "all in
the best men in the city of Athens that fell during this war"
Mycalessus are tragically and ironically butchered in their
rbarians hired by democratic Athens to fight in Sicily, but
te, were sent home for reasons of economy and instructed
injure the enemy" on the way. The disaster on Sicily was
oss of triremes and infantry, more even than a warning about
l chauvinism and intellectual arrogance. It becomes in the
ter all,

> he victors, and most calamitous to the conquered. They
> oints and altogether; all that they suffered was great; they
> the saying is, with a total destruction, their fleet, their
> vas destroyed, and few out of many returned home."

des, a man of empathy and passion, was proud that he had
t as an essay which is to win the applause of the moment, but
ime (1.22.4)," *The Peloponnesian War* turns out to be no dry
ause and effect. No, it is above all an intense, riveting, and
g and weak men, of heroes and scoundrels and innocents too,
l circumstances of rebellion, plague, and war that always strip
ure and show us for what we really are.

Victor Davis Hanson
Professor of Greek
Department of Foreign Languages
and Literatures
California State University, Fresno

EDITOR'S NOTE

[illegible] ides' history over the last two thousand four hundred years
[illegible] ble in that his text has long been characterized by those who
[illegible] en assigned to read it) as difficult, complex, and occasionally
[illegible] written detailed commentaries—and excellent ones too—to
[illegible] hending its compressed and abstruse Greek, to discuss inter-
[illegible] roblematic sections, and to clarify the sometimes confusing
[illegible] which Thucydides describes simultaneous events. Yet almost
[illegible] e a knowledge of the ancient Greek language and a familiar-
[illegible] and mechanisms of Thucydides' world that today's student
[illegible] ot be expected to bring to the text. Some very fine transla-
[illegible] available, but in unhelpful editions that contain little besides
[illegible] ve uneven appendices, sparse indices, few if any explanatory
[illegible] f such poor quality as to be downright useless. As one reads
[illegible] cult to remember what year it is at any given point in the
[illegible] work's own system of consecutive year dating). Since Thucyd-
[illegible] x political and military history of a protracted war that took
[illegible] wide expanse of territory, it is not surprising that the general
[illegible] e of maps, specific dates, or knowledge of many practices,
[illegible] nditions of the time—is often puzzled by the text and unable
[illegible] struction from it. Indeed, without the guidance of a teacher,
[illegible] background knowledge from other sources, most readers
[illegible] hend—let alone appreciate—many of Thucydides' observa-
[illegible] and actions of his characters.

[illegible] dition is to fill that lacuna: to develop and employ a set of
[illegible] an be used with any text of Thucydides—the original Greek
[illegible] n in any language—so that students or general readers will
[illegible] nt themselves both geographically and temporally, and thus
[illegible] d the narrative. Beyond an introduction to Thucydides and
[illegible] includes over one hundred maps embedded in the text, a
[illegible] ding information on the date and location of the narrative,
[illegible] f the text of each chapter, explanatory footnotes, a thorough
[illegible] x, an epilogue, a glossary of terms, a regional and chronolog-

ical outline of events by book and chapter, and a few relevant illustrations. Finally, it contains a number of short technical appendices that provide background information about those aspects of life in ancient Greece that Thucydides did not think required explanation for readers of his time, but that will not be commonly known by readers today. This edition attempts by itself to provide sufficient textual assistance, geographic information, and background material for the general reader to understand and enjoy the marvelous work of one of humanity's first, and very best, historians.

Some elaboration is needed on a few of the important features mentioned above.

Maps of every significant episode are located in the text within that episode. Thus, every city, town, river, mountain, or other geographic feature that is important to the narrative and mentioned in a given episode is referenced to a location on a map found nearby in the text. For complex maps with many labels, a simple grid system permits footnotes to identify sites with map coordinates so that readers will know where to direct their attention on the map and thus minimize the time and effort required to locate a specific site. In the interest of clarity, each map displays the names of only those features that appear in the surrounding text: thus the reader is not forced to turn to a map section elsewhere in the book or a general map crowded with names drawn from the entire work. If the location of a place is unknown, the footnote admits this. If we moderns are not sure of its location, our uncertainty is mentioned in the footnote and indicated on the map with a question mark.

To orient the reader, a locator map with longitude and latitude coordinates appears in the outside margin of the page. It identifies the location of the main map by a rectangular outline placed in the larger, more easily recognizable regional setting. A few locator maps show outlines of two main maps to illustrate action occurring in widely separated locations. Some of the main maps show outlines of an additional inset map that displays particularly relevant areas at an enlarged scale. In the example on the following page, the area of the main map (Boeotia and Attica) is outlined on the locator map to the right, and the main map itself displays the outline of a detailed inset map of the Athens-Piraeus area, which is placed to the left. Figures containing more than one map are usually designed to be read from the outside inward on the page as map scales increase.

All maps display rudimentary scales in miles and kilometers and depict major topographical or cultural features cited in the text, such as mountains, rivers, roads, temples, defensive walls, and the like. A key to all map symbols used in this volume is located on page xxxii. The basemap used displays the modern positions of coastlines, major rivers, and major inland bodies of water, but the location and even the existence of some of these current features may be quite different from what existed in classical times. Significant differences in ancient and modern coastlines and bodies of water have been approximated using a narrow vertical stripe pattern.

Three reference maps showing all important sites named in the text are placed after the Index, at the very end of the book, where the reader can easily find them.

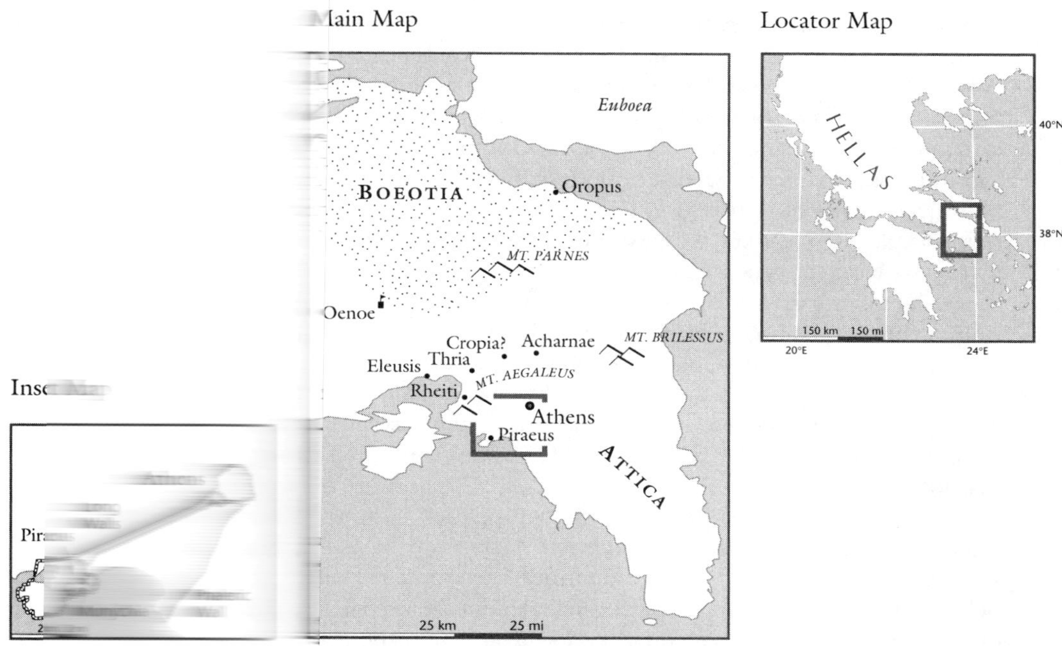

MAP 2.19 ATHENS AND ITS DEFENSES

convention, water and other natural features, such as islands
eled with italics to distinguish them from cultural features
Centers of population are indicated using small dots and
lettering, while regions are labeled using several sizes of
signed to approximate their relative sizes and degrees of
w exceptions, specific regional boundaries have not been
borders are not known or at best only partially known, and
to fluctuate over time. This lack of precision sometimes
range regions in a hierarchy of importance, or to classify
, a city, a fortress, a battle site, or a religious center, because
ht fit one or more of these categories at any given time, or

y refer place-names in the text to nearby maps, but also
odes of regional narrative that are separated by Thucydides’

treatment of historical simultaneity. Since his method is to describe all the events that take place in a given season throughout the Greek world before moving on to the events of the next season, he cannot provide the reader with any sustained or continuous regional narratives. Events of the winter of 426/5,[1] for example, are described serially for such regions as Sicily, Acarnania, and Attica, and this set of episodes is then followed by another sequence of regional episodes for the next time frame: the summer of 425. Thus regional narratives are broken up and extremely difficult for the reader to follow. This edition connects the regional episodes by footnote, specifying at the end of one such episode the book and chapter where the narrative returns to that region and, at that return, citing the location of the previous episode. Readers are thereby assisted to pursue a continuous regional narrative if they so wish. Footnotes are also used to mention and to discuss briefly some of the major points of scholarly controversy over interpretation, translation, or corruption of the text, and to indicate some of the more important connections of Thucydides' narrative with other ancient sources.

The reader who reads discontinuously, who casually dips into the history as time permits, is well served by the repetition of certain useful footnotes, usually at least once in each of the eight books. Map data are also frequently repeated for the same reason.

A **running header** is placed at the top of each page in order to help the same intermittent reader to reorient himself each time he returns to the work. The sample header displayed below identifies the book to which the particular page belongs (Book Six), the date by our calendar (416/5), the date by Thucydides' own system (16th Year/Winter), the location where the action takes place (Sicily), and a brief description of the narrative (*Settlement of Other Hellenic Cities*).

Book Six 416/5 16th Year/Winter Sicily *Settlement of Other Hellenic Cities*

More information is displayed in notes placed in the outside page margin at the beginnings of the hundred or so chapters into which each of the books is divided. In the sample marginal note shown on the next page, the first line identifies the book and chapter number (Book Four, Chapter 67). This identification is always aligned with the beginning of the new chapter, which usually, but not always, occurs at a new paragraph. The second line in the sample note, 424, is the date by our calendar; the line below that gives the date by Thucydides' own system (8th Year/Summer).[2] The fourth line describes where the action is taking place (Megara), and the final section briefly describes the action covered in the adjacent narrative. The text of each chapter contains section numbers in square brackets [2] to mark the divisions into which scholars have traditionally divided the text for ease of search, analysis, and discussion.

1 Classicists today use the virgule (/) to denote the winter season that crosses our year terminations—e.g., 426/5 is the winter season that begins after the Fall of 426 and ends before the Spring of 425. The numbers 426–25 would signify the entire span of the two years 426 and 425. All dates in this edition are B.C., unless otherwise specified.

2 Note that Thucydides' dating system is not included in the running headers and the marginal side notes of Book One because the war, whose years it measures, did not begin until the opening of the war in Book Two.

The Athenians, after plans had been arranged between themselves and their correspondents both as to words and actions, sailed by night to Minoa, the island off Megara, with six hundred hoplites under the command of Hippocrates, and took a position in a ditch not far off, out of which bricks used to be taken for the walls; while [2] Demosthenes, the other commander, with a detachment of Plataean light troops and another of *peripoli,* placed himself in ambush in the precinct of Enyalius, which was still nearer. No one knew of it, except those whose business it was to know that night. [3] A little before daybreak, the traitors in Megara began to act. Every night for a long time back, under pretense of marauding, and in order to have a means of opening the gates, they had been used, with the consent of the officer in command, to carry by night a rowboat upon a cart along the ditch to the sea and to sail out, bringing it back again before day upon the cart and taking it within the wall through the gates in order, as they pretended, to baffle . . .

istory ends abruptly in mid-war, mid-episode, and almost itten a short **Epilogue** in an attempt to satisfy the general ow the war ended. It addresses the often-asked question of dvantage from it and outlines what happened to the main next eighty years until the rise of Macedon ended this

ces written by a number of scholars is intended to provide ound information that would be necessary or useful to These essays provide limited discussions of such topics as nt, the Athenian Empire, the Spartan government, the Pelo- Persians in Thucydides, hoplite warfare, trireme warfare, ps in Thucydides, religious festivals, classical Greek money, ndars and dating systems. The introduction by Victor Davis is known of Thucydides' life, aspects of his work, and his place among ancient historians. Where appropriate, the introduction and the appendices are cross-referenced by footnote to relevant places in the text.

To assist the reader in finding passages or subjects within the text, this edition offers a more thorough and full **Index** than can be found accompanying any other translation. As a quick reference tool, and to display more clearly the relationship between many simultaneous but serially described events, the reader can also consult a matrix **Theaters of Operation in the Peloponnesian War.** There are, in addition, a **Glossary** and two **Bibliographies,** one concerned with ancient sources (more or less contemporary with Thucydides) and the other addressing modern books about Thucydides and his work. Finally, a number of **illustrations** have been chosen that bring to life places and objects that are contemporary with or prominent in the text: for example, Illustration 4.41 (located in Book Four, Chapter 41)[3] is a picture of the Spartan shield (now on display in the Agora Museum at Athens) that was captured by the Athenians at Pylos and taken to Athens, where it was discovered some years ago in an abandoned well in the Athenian *agora* (central square and marketplace).

This edition uses the translation by Richard Crawley (1840–93) published in 1874, which remains one of the two most widely read translations today—a testament to its fidelity to the text and its power as English prose. It was necessary, however, to update some of Crawley's Victorian English usages, to revise his outdated punctuation, and to replace terms he used whose meaning has shifted or been lost entirely. For example, I have substituted "trireme" (with an explanation of that term) for Crawley's "galley," a word that no longer means an oared warship so much as a nautical kitchen or a publisher's proof. After much deliberation, I decided in the interests of clarity to break up a few of Crawley's longest and most complex sentences (which often mirror the original Greek). I have also discarded the artificial and unhelpful titled segments into which Crawley divided his text.

On the whole, however, other than to americanize Crawley's British spelling, revisions are few and minor. Almost no changes were made to the speeches themselves, as these are the most outstanding and powerful feature of Crawley's work. Perhaps because he was educated at a time when oratory was still valued as a useful skill, and was systematically studied and taught in the schools, his translated speeches employ rhetorical devices in an expert and natural manner akin to the Greek usage itself. In this way, he achieves an eloquent rhythm and cadence that far surpass the speeches in all other translations that I have read—and which, sad to say, we rarely find in speakers today. Crawley's Pericles, for example, is truly grandiloquent and perhaps even purposefully a bit pompous, but never commonplace, wordy, or banal. Indeed, it has been a pleasure to work with Crawley's prose, and during the compilation of this edition my admiration and respect for his writing and diction skills have grown immensely.

Many of the best elements of this edition derive directly from the wonderful counsel and assistance I consistently received from many friends and colleagues,

3 This is the chapter in which Thucydides completes his description of the battle of Pylos.

[illegible] dge elsewhere. But since I did not in every case follow the
[illegible] stand behind and be responsible for all errors of omission
[illegible] ch I can only hope that there are not too many. At the least,
[illegible] d and assembled the useful features of this edition, so that
[illegible] r be undertaken again. There is an unbroken string of read-
[illegible] us to Thucydides himself—more than one hundred genera-
[illegible] espite many obstacles, have derived pleasure and instruction
[illegible] o ensure that it did not become lost, as were so many liter-
[illegible] world. It is thanks to these readers that Thucydides is still
[illegible] d there must have been moments in time when there were
[illegible]

[illegible] on is intended to increase the number of general readers of
[illegible] and in the future, by assisting them to appreciate his great
[illegible] consider the nature of historiography itself, and to learn
[illegible] world of ancient Greece—from which our own still derives
[illegible] dition's focus on the non-scholar, I believe that the scholar
[illegible] unique set of features quite useful. If this edition expands
[illegible] readers who tackle Thucydides and extends their grasp and
[illegible], or if it even marginally increases the number of professors
[illegible] de to incorporate Thucydides in their curriculum and to
[illegible] his text that they include in their course work, I will rest
[illegible] permitted "to compare small things with great" (4.36.3), it
[illegible] y of maps, notes, appendices, and indices will also become "a
[illegible] (1.22.4)—admittedly a minor and derivative one, but one
[illegible] ove useful to future readers of this marvelous history for as
[illegible] ad.

R.B.S.

Key to Map Symbols

Area of greater detail

Cultural features

- settlements
- fortified place
- temple
- battle site
- miscellaneous place
- anchorage
- road
- walls
- urbanized area (larger scale)
- regional boundary or extent (approximate)

Natural features

- mountain; mountain range
- cliff

- river

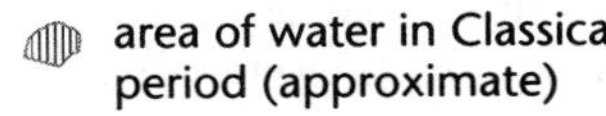

- area of water in Classical period (approximate)
- marsh

Calendar of the Peloponnesian War

Modern Date	Season	Location by Book and Chapter
431	End of summer	2.33
431/0	End of winter	2.47
430	End of summer	2.69
430/29	End of winter	2.70
429	End of summer	2.93
429/8	End of winter	2.103
428	End of summer	3.19
428/7	End of winter	3.25
427	End of summer	3.87
427/6	End of winter	3.88
426	End of summer	3.103
426/5	End of winter	3.116
425	End of summer	4.50
425/4	End of winter	4.51
424	End of summer	4.88
424/3	End of winter	4.116
423	End of summer	4.133
423/2	End of winter	4.135
422	End of summer	5.12
422/1	End of winter	5.25
421	End of summer	5.36
421/0	End of winter	5.39
420	End of summer	5.51
420/19	End of winter	5.51
419	End of summer	5.55
419/8	End of winter	5.56
418	End of summer	5.76
418/7	End of winter	5.81
417	End of summer	5.82
417/6	End of winter	5.83
416	End of summer	5.115
416/5	End of winter	6.7
415	End of summer	6.62
415/4	End of winter	6.93
414	End of summer	7.9
414/3	End of winter	7.19
413	End of summer	8.1
413/2	End of winter	8.6
412	End of summer	8.29
412/1	End of winter	8.60
411	End of summer	8.109

BOOK ONE

Illustration 1.1 Bust of Thucydides

1.1
ATHENS
Thucydides explains why he decided to write his history.

Thucydides,[1a] an Athenian, wrote the histor[illegible]ne Peloponnesians and the Athenians, beginning [illegible] broke out, and believing that it would be a great [illegible]f relation than any that had preceded it. This belief [illegible]unds. The preparations of both the combatants w[illegible]t in the last state of perfection; and he could see th[illegible]race taking sides in the quarrel; those who delaye[illegible]ing it in contemplation. [2] Indeed this was the gr[illegible]own in history, not only of the Hellenes, but of a l[illegible]an world—I had almost said of mankind. [3] For t[illegible]emote antiquity, and even those that more imme[illegible] could not from lapse of time be clearly ascertainec[illegible]h an inquiry carried as far back as was practicable [illegible]t to the conclusion that there was nothing on a grea[illegible]r in other matters.

1.2
The Archaeology[1a]
HELLAS
Thucydides offers an anthropological analysis of primitive life, noting that Attica's poor soil led to overcrowding and the establishment of colonies.

Fo[illegible] that the country now called Hellas had in ancie[illegible]ulation; on the contrary, migrations were of frequ[illegible]eral tribes readily abandoning their homes under[illegible]r numbers. [2] Without commerce, without freed[illegible]either by land or sea, cultivating no more of their [illegible]ities of life required, destitute of capital, never planti[illegible] could not tell when an invader might not come[illegible] when he did come they had no walls to stop him),[illegible]sities of daily sustenance could be supplied at one p[illegible]hey cared little about shifting their habitation, and c[illegible]t large cities nor attained to any other form of

1.1.1a [illegible] a discus- [illegible] life of [illegible]

1.2.1a [illegible] com- [illegible] pters of Book 1 (2–23) in which Thucydides seeks to contrast the greatness of the Peloponnesian War with the pettiness of previous history.

greatness. [3] The richest soils were always most subject to this change of masters; such as the district now called Thessaly,[3a] Boeotia,[3b] most of the Peloponnesus[3c] (Arcadia excepted),[3d] and the most fertile parts of the rest of Hellas. [4] The goodness of the land favored the enrichment of particular individuals, and thus created faction which proved a fertile source of ruin. It also invited invasion. [5] Accordingly Attica,[5a] from the poverty of its soil enjoying from a very remote period freedom from faction, [6] never changed its inhabitants. And here is no minor example of my assertion that the migrations were the cause of there being no correspondent growth in other parts. The most powerful victims of war or faction from the rest of Hellas took refuge with the Athenians as a safe retreat; and at an early period, becoming naturalized, swelled the already large population of the city to such a height that Attica became at last too small to hold them, and they had to send out colonies to Ionia.[6a]

1.3
HELLAS
Long ago, men in Hellas did not call themselves Hellenes, as proved by Homer's account of the Trojan war.

There is also another circumstance that contributes not a little to my conviction of the weakness of ancient times. Before the Trojan war[1a] there is no indication of any common action in Hellas, [2] nor indeed of the universal prevalence of the name; on the contrary, before the time of Hellen son of Deucalion, no such name existed, but the country went by the names of the different tribes, in particular of the Pelasgian. It was not till Hellen and his sons grew strong in Phthiotis,[2a] and were invited as allies into the other cities, that one by one they gradually acquired from the connection the name of Hellenes; though a long time elapsed before that name could fasten itself upon all. [3] The best proof of this is furnished by Homer. Born long after the Trojan war, he nowhere calls all of them by that name, nor indeed any of them except the followers of Achilles from Phthiotis, who were the original Hellenes: in his poems they are called Danaans, Argives, and Achaeans. He does not even use the term barbarian, probably because the Hellenes had not yet been marked off from the rest of the world by one distinctive name. [4] It appears therefore that the several Hellenic communities, comprising not only those who first acquired the name, city by city, as they came to understand each other, but also those who assumed it afterwards as the name of the whole people, were before the Trojan war prevented by their want of strength and the absence of mutual intercourse from displaying any collective action.

Indeed, they could not unite for this expedition till they had gained increased familiarity with the sea.

1.4
CRETE
Minos is said to have been the first king to rule by sea power.

And the first person known to us by tradition as having established a navy is Minos.[1a] He made himself master of what is now called the Hellenic

1.2.3a Thessaly: Map 1.3, AX.
1.2.3b Boeotia: Map 1.3, AX.
1.2.3c Peloponnesus: Map 1.3, BX.
1.2.3d Arcadia: Map 1.3, BX.
1.2.5a Attica: Map 1.3, BX.
1.2.6a Ionia: Map 1.3, AY. See Appendix H, Dialects and Ethnic Groups, §4–5, 7–8, for information on the Ionians and the colonization of Ionia.
1.3.1a Troy, site of the Trojan war: Map 1.3, AY.
1.3.2a Phthiotis: Map 1.3, AX.
1.4.1a Minos is the probably mythical ruler of Minoa, a legendary seafaring culture based on the island of Crete; see Map 1.3, BY.

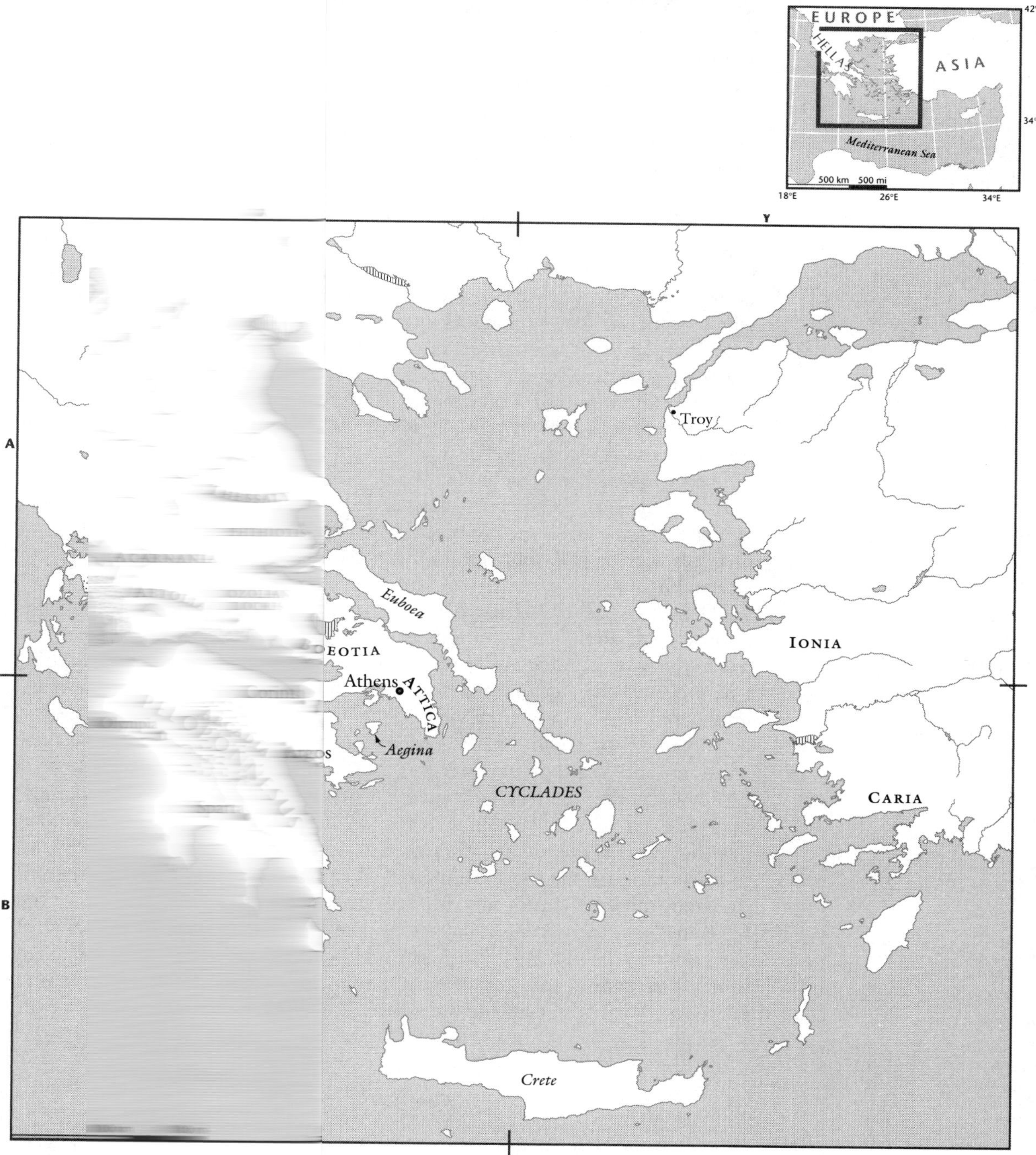
EUROPE
HELLAS
ASIA
Mediterranean Sea
500 km 500 mi
42°N
34°N
18°E
26°E
34°E
Troy
Euboea
EOTIA
Athens
ATTICA
Aegina
IONIA
CYCLADES
CARIA
Crete

MAP 1.3

sea, and ruled over the Cyclades,[1b] into most of which he sent the first colonies, expelling the Carians[1c] and appointing his own sons governors; and thus did his best to put down piracy in those waters, a necessary step to secure revenues for his own use.

1.5
HELLAS
Piracy was common and not entirely dishonorable in the past.

For in early times the Hellenes and the barbarians of the coast and islands, as communication by sea became more common, were tempted to turn pirates, under the conduct of their most powerful men; the motives being to serve their own greed and to support the needy. They would fall upon a town unprotected by walls, and consisting of a mere collection of villages, and would plunder it; indeed, this came to be the main source of their livelihood, no disgrace being yet attached to such an achievement, but even some glory. [2] An illustration of this is furnished by the honor with which some of the inhabitants of the continent still regard a successful marauder, and by the question we find the old poets everywhere representing the people as asking of voyagers—"Are they pirates?"—as if those who are asked the question would have no idea of disclaiming the imputation, or their interrogators of reproaching them for it. [3] The same pillaging prevailed also on land.

And even at the present day many parts of Hellas still follow the old fashion, amongst the Ozolian Locrians[3a] and the Aetolians,[3b] for instance, and the Acarnanians[3c] and that region of the continent; and the custom of carrying arms is still kept up among these mainland peoples from the old piratical habits.

1.6
HELLAS
Former practices can still be seen in remote parts of Hellas. Athens was the first polis to adopt luxurious habits; Sparta originated modern styles.

The whole of Hellas used once to carry arms, their habitations being unprotected, and their communication with each other unsafe; indeed, to wear arms was as much a part of everyday life with them as with the barbarians. [2] And the fact that the people in these parts of Hellas are still living in the old way points to a time when the same mode of life was once equally common to all. [3] The Athenians[3a] were the first to lay aside their weapons, and to adopt an easier and more luxurious mode of life; indeed, it is only lately that their rich old men left off the luxury of wearing undergarments of linen, and fastening a knot of their hair with a tie of golden grasshoppers, a fashion which spread to their Ionian kindred,[3b] and long prevailed among the old men there. [4] On the contrary a modest style of dressing, more in conformity with modern ideas, was first adopted by the Spartans,[4a] the rich doing their best to assimilate their way of life to that of the common people. [5] They also set the example of contending naked, publicly stripping and anointing themselves with oil in their gymnastic exercises. Formerly, even in the Olympic games,[5a] the athletes who con-

1.4.1b Cyclades, Aegean islands: Map 1.3, BY.
1.4.1c Caria: Map 1.3, BY.
1.5.3a Ozolian Locris: Map 1.3, AX.
1.5.3b Aetolia: Map 1.3, AX.
1.5.3c Acarnania: Map 1.3, AX.
1.6.3a Athens: Map 1.3, BX.
1.6.3b See Appendix H, Dialects and Ethnic Groups, §4–5, 7–8, for more on the Ionians.
1.6.4a Sparta: Map 1.3, BX.
1.6.5a These contests, the ancestor of the modern "Olympic Games," took place at the shrine of Olympia (Map 1.3, BX); see Appendix I, Religious Festivals, §5. Such festivals often included athletic and cultural contests.

tendec[illegible] middles; and it is but a few years since that the pr[illegible]y among some of the barbarians, especially in Asia, v[illegible]and wrestling are offered, belts are worn by the co[illegible]e are many other points in which a likeness might [illegible]ife of the Hellenic world of old and the barbarian [illegible]

Wit[illegible], later on, at an era of increased facilities of naviga[illegible]y of capital, we find the shores becoming the site of [illegible]thmuses being occupied for the purposes of comm[illegible]a neighbor. But the old cities, on account of the gre[illegible]were built away from the sea, whether on the islands [illegible]still remain in their old sites. For the pirates used t[illegible]nd indeed all coast populations, whether seafaring [illegible]

1.7
HELLAS
Because of piracy, cities were first built away from the sea.

The[illegible]reat pirates. These islanders were Carians[1a] and Pl[illegible] most of the islands were colonized, as was proved [illegible]t. During the purification of Delos[1c] by Athens[illegible]ves in the island were taken up, and it was found [illegible]nates were Carians: they were identified by the fas[illegible]d with them, and by the method of interment, [illegible] the Carians still follow. [2] But as soon as Minos [illegible]ommunication by sea became easier, [3] as he col[illegible]nds, and thus expelled the evildoers. The coast [illegible] to apply themselves more closely to the acquisi[illegible]heir life became more settled; some even began [illegible]lls on the strength of their newly acquired riches. [illegible]ould reconcile the weaker to the dominion of the [illegible]ssion of capital enabled the more powerful to red[illegible] subjection. [4] And it was at a somewhat later st[illegible]t that they went on the expedition against Troy.[4a]

1.8
AEGEAN ISLANDS
Thucydides cites evidence from graves that early islanders were Carians. After Minos expelled the pirates, cities expanded, accumulated capital, and built walls to protect themselves.

Wh[illegible] to raise the armament was more, in my opinio[illegible]ngth, than the oaths of Tyndareus, which bound [illegible]m. [2] Indeed, the account given by those Pelopo[illegible] the recipients of the most credible tradition is this. [illegible]ving from Asia[2a] with vast wealth among a needy [illegible]ch power that, stranger though he was, the countr[illegible]and this power fortune saw fit materially to increas[illegible]descendants. Eurystheus had been killed in

1.9
PELOPONNESUS
Thucydides describes how Agamemnon inherited his great power, which included naval power.

1.8.1a [illegible], BY.
1.8.1b [illegible]
1.8.1c [illegible]tion is [illegible]
1.8.4a Troy: Map 1.11, AY.
1.9.2a "Asia" here means Asia Minor, corresponding to the Asian territory of modern Turkey; see Map 1.11, locator.

Attica[2b] by the Heraclids. When Eurystheus set out on his expedition (to Attica), he committed Mycenae and its government to Atreus, his mother's brother, who had left his father on account of the death of Chrysippus. As time went on and Eurystheus did not return, Atreus complied with the wishes of the Mycenaeans, who were influenced by fear of the Heraclids—besides, his powers seemed considerable and he had not neglected to seek the favor of the populace—and assumed the rule of Mycenae and of the rest of the dominions of Eurystheus. And so the power of the descendants of Pelops came to be greater than that of the descendants of Perseus. [3] To all this Agamemnon succeeded. He had also a navy far stronger than his contemporaries, so that, in my opinion, fear was quite as strong an element as love in the formation of the expedition. [4] The strength of his navy is shown by the fact that his own was the largest contingent, and that of the Arcadians was furnished by him; this at least is what Homer says, if his testimony is deemed sufficient. Besides, in his account of the transmission of the scepter, he calls him

Of many an isle, and of all Argos[4a] king.

Now Agamemnon's was a continental power; and he could not have been master of any except the adjacent islands (and these would not be many), if he had not possessed a fleet.

And from this expedition we may infer the character of earlier enterprises. [1.10.1] Now Mycenae[1a] may have been a small place, and many of the cities of that age may appear comparatively insignificant, but no exact observer would therefore feel justified in rejecting the estimate given by the poets and by tradition of the magnitude of the armament. [2] For I suppose that if Sparta[2a] were to become desolate, and only the temples and the foundations of the public buildings were left, that as time went on there would be a strong disposition with posterity to refuse to accept her fame as a true exponent of her power. And yet they occupy two-fifths of the Peloponnesus[2b] and lead the whole, not to speak of their numerous allies outside. Still, as the city is neither built in a compact form nor adorned with magnificent temples and public edifices, but composed of villages after the old fashion of Hellas, there would be an impression of inadequacy. Whereas, if Athens were to suffer the same misfortune, I suppose that any inference from the appearance presented to the eye would make her power to have been twice as great as it is. [3] We have therefore no right to be skeptical, nor to content ourselves with an inspection of a city without con-

1.10
HELLAS
The size and magnificence of a city's ruins do not necessarily indicate its power: witness Sparta and Athens. Homer's description of the armada against Troy indicates its small size relative to current fleets.

1.9.2b Attica: Map. 1.11, BY.
1.9.4a Argos: Map 1.11, BX.
1.10.1a Mycenae: Map 1.11, BX.
1.10.2a Sparta: Map 1.11, BX.
1.10.2b Peloponnesus: Map 1.11, BX.

sideri[illegible]y safely conclude that the armament in question s[illegible]st as it fell short of modern efforts; if we can here [illegible]y of Homer's poems in which, without allowing f[illegible]hich a poet would feel himself licensed to emplo[illegible]as far from equaling ours. [4] He has represente[illegible]elve hundred vessels; the Boeotian[4a] complement [illegible]undred and twenty men, that of the ships of Philo[illegible]nceive, he meant to convey the maximum and the m[illegible]t any rate he does not specify the amount of any o[illegible] the ships. That they were all rowers as well as warri[illegible]unt of the ships of Philoctetes, in which all the men [illegible]Now it is improbable that many who were not memb[illegible] we except the kings and high officers; especially [illegible]e open sea with munitions of war, in ships, more[illegible] but were equipped in the old piratical fashion. [[illegible]e average of the largest and smallest ships, the numb[illegible]ill appear inconsiderable, representing as they did, t[illegible]

1.11 TROY A lack of money forced the Greeks at Troy to disperse their force, reduce siege efforts, and forego a quick victory.

Ar[illegible]much to scarcity of men as of money. Difficulty [illegible]e invaders reduce the numbers of the army to a p[illegible] live on the country during the prosecution of the[illegible]ctory they obtained on their arrival—and a victor[illegible]en, or the fortifications of the naval camp could[illegible]—there is no indication of their whole force havin[illegible]e contrary, they seem to have turned to cultivati[illegible] and to piracy from want of supplies. This was w[illegible]Trojans to keep the field for ten years against them;[illegible]enemy making them always a match for the detac[illegible] If they had brought plenty of supplies with them,[illegible] the war without scattering for piracy and agricu[illegible]e easily defeated the Trojans in the field; since [illegible]own against them with the division on service. [illegible]ck to the siege, the capture of Troy[2a] would have [illegible] less trouble. But as want of money proved the w[illegible]itions, so from the same cause even the one in qu[illegible]an its predecessors, may be pronounced on the ev[illegible]plished, to have been inferior to its renown and t[illegible] about it formed under the tuition of the poets.

1.10.4a [illegible]
1.11.1a [illegible]
1.11.2a [illegible]

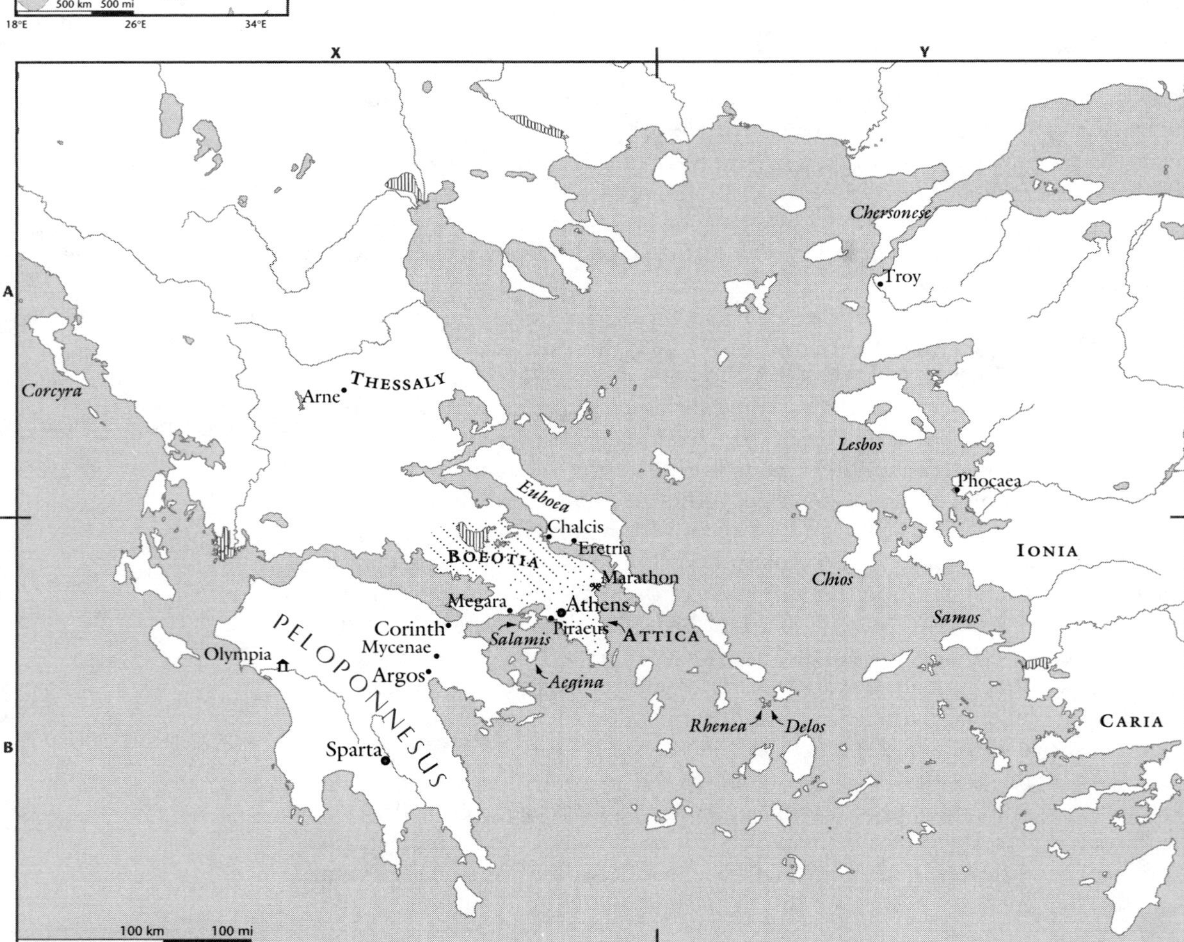

MAP 1.11 THE AEGEAN BASIN

Ev[illegible] Hellas was still engaged in removing and settling, [illegible]in to the quiet which must precede growth. [2] T[illegible]llenes from Ilium[2a] caused many revolutions, and fa[illegible]erywhere; and it was the citizens thus driven into e[illegible]ties. [3] Sixty years after the capture of Ilium the m[illegible] driven out of Arne[3b] by the Thessalians,[3c] and settle[illegible] the former Cadmeian land; though there was a divi[illegible]re, some of whom joined the expedition to Ilium. [illegible] Dorians and the Heraclids became masters of the Pe[illegible]ch had to be done [4] and many years had to elapse [illegible]tain to a durable tranquillity undisturbed by remov[illegible] send out colonies, as Athens[4a] did to Ionia[4b] and m[illegible] the Peloponnesians to most of Italy[4c] and Sicily[4][illegible] rest of Hellas. All these places were founded subse[illegible]Troy.

1.12
HELLAS
Migration and turmoil occurred in Hellas after the Trojan war. When tranquillity returned, Ionia, the islands, Italy, and Sicily were colonized.

Bu[illegible]s grew, and the acquisition of wealth became more [illegible]ues of the states increasing, tyrannies were establ[illegible]—the old form of government being hereditary m[illegible]rerogatives—and Hellas began to fit out fleets and a[illegible] to the sea. [2] It is said that the Corinthians were [illegible] modern style of naval architecture, and that Corin[illegible]n Hellas where *triremes*[2b] were built; [3] and we ha[illegible]thian shipwright, making four ships for the Samia[illegible]d of this war, it is nearly three hundred years ago t[illegible] Samos.[3a] [4] Again, the earliest sea fight in histor[illegible]thians and Corcyraeans;[4a] this was about two hundr[illegible]dating from the same time. [5] Planted on an isthm[illegible] been a commercial emporium; as formerly almos[illegible]tween the Hellenes within and without the Pelop[illegible]overland, and the Corinthian territory was the highw[illegible]raveled. She had consequently great money resou[illegible]epithet "wealthy" bestowed by the old poets on th[illegible]d her, when traffic by sea became more common, [illegible]d put down piracy; and as she could offer a marke[illegible]e trade, she acquired for herself all the power which [illegible]s. [6] Subsequently the Ionians[6a] attained to great [illegible]gn of Cyrus, the first king of the Persians, and of his [illegible]while they were at war with the former com-

1.13
HELLAS
As the cities of Hellas grew in wealth and power, traditional monarchies gave way to tyrannies. Corinth developed triremes.

1.12.2a [illegible]: Map [illegible]
1.12.3a [illegible]
1.12.3b [illegible]
1.12.3c [illegible]
1.12.4a [illegible]
1.12.4b [illegible]dix H, [illegible]7–8, for [illegible]ians.
1.12.4c [illegible]
1.12.4d [illegible]

1.13.2a Corinth: Map 1.11, BX.
1.13.2b *Triremes* were the standard warships of this period; see Appendix G, §4–7.
1.13.3a Samos: Map 1.11, BY.
1.13.4a Corcyra: Map 1.11, AX.
1.13.6a Ionia: Map 1.11, BY.
1.13.6b Cyrus the Great founded the Persian kingdom and ruled from 550 to 530. Cambyses ruled from 530 till 521. See Appendix E, The Persians, §1–2.

manded for a while the seas around Ionia. Polycrates also, the tyrant of Samos, had a powerful navy in the reign of Cambyses with which he reduced many of the islands, and among them Rhenea,[6c] which he consecrated to the Delian Apollo. About this time also the Phocaeans,[6d] while they were founding Marseilles,[6e] defeated the Carthaginians[6f] in a sea fight.

1.14
HELLAS
Navies deploying many triremes developed just before the conflict with Persia.

These were the most powerful navies. And even these, although so many generations had elapsed since the Trojan war, seem to have been principally composed of the old fifty-oars and long-boats, and to have counted few triremes among their ranks. [2] Indeed it was only shortly before the Persian war and the death of Darius the successor of Cambyses, that the Sicilian tyrants and the Corcyraeans acquired any large number of triremes. For after these there were no navies of any account in Hellas till the expedition of Xerxes; [3] Aegina,[3a] Athens, and others may have possessed a few vessels, but they were principally fifty-oars. It was quite at the end of this period that the war with Aegina and the prospect of the barbarian invasion enabled Themistocles to persuade the Athenians to build the fleet with which they fought at Salamis;[3b] and even these vessels had not complete decks.

1.15
HELLAS
Even the small navies of the past were instruments of real power.

The navies, then, of the Hellenes during the period we have traversed were what I have described. All their insignificance did not prevent their being an element of the greatest power to those who cultivated them, alike in revenue and in dominion. They were the means by which the islands were reached and reduced, those of the smallest area falling the easiest prey. [2] Wars by land there were none, none at least by which power was acquired; we have the usual border contests, but of distant expeditions with conquest the object we hear nothing among the Hellenes. There was no union of subject cities round a great state, no spontaneous combination of equals for confederate expeditions; what fighting there was consisted merely of local warfare between rival neighbors. [3] The nearest approach to a coalition took place in the old war between Chalcis[3a] and Eretria;[3b] this was a quarrel in which the rest of the Hellenic world did to some extent take sides.[3c]

1.16
HELLAS
Persia conquers Ionia and the islands.

Various, too, were the obstacles which the national growth encountered in various localities. The power of the Ionians[1a] was advancing with rapid strides, when it came into collision with Persia, under King Cyrus, who, after having dethroned Croesus[1b] and overrun everything between the Halys[1c] and the sea, stopped not till he had reduced the cities of the coast; the islands only being left to be subdued by Darius and the Phoenician[1d] navy.

1.13.6c Rhenea: Map 1.11, BY.
1.13.6d Phocaea: Map 1.11, AY.
1.13.6e Marseilles: Map 1.14.
1.13.6f Carthage: Map 1.14.
1.14.3a Aegina: Map 1.11, BX.
1.14.3b Salamis: site of the decisive naval battle between the Greeks and Persians in 480; see Map 1.11, BX, and Appendix E, The Persians, §4.
1.15.3a Chalcis, Euboea: Map 1.11, BX.
1.15.3b Eretria, Euboea: Map 1.11, BX.
1.15.3c Thucydides here refers to the "Lelantine war" of the late eighth century B.C. between Chalcis and Eretria of Euboea (Map 1.11, AX).
1.16.1a Ionia: Map 1.11, BY.
1.16.1b Croesus, king of Lydia (Map 1.14), conquered by the Persians in 546. See Appendix E, The Persians, §2–3.
1.16.1c Halys River: Map 1.14.
1.16.1d Phoenicia: Map 1.14. The Phoenician fleet was a major component of Persian naval power.

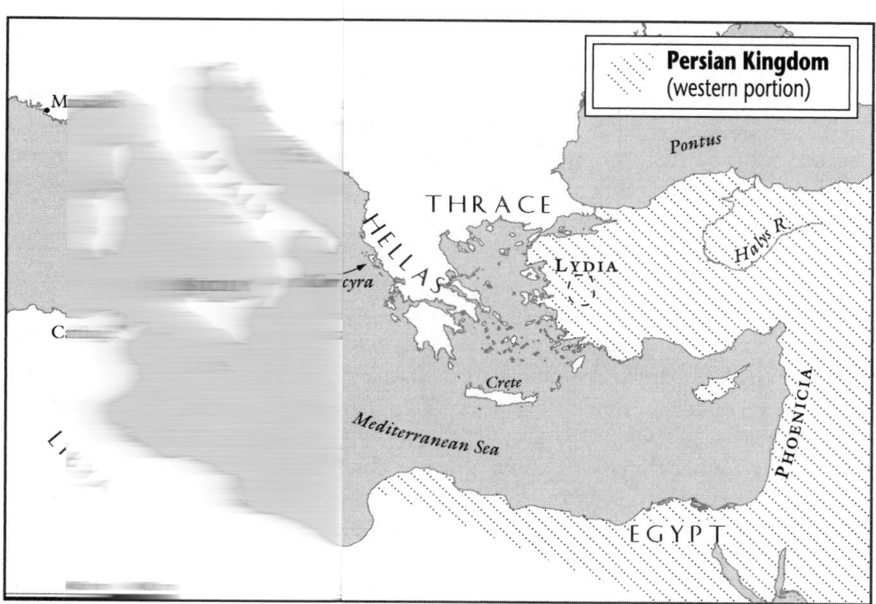

Map [illegible] Sea

1.17
HELLAS
Tyrants in Hellas itself, unlike those in Sicily, did not greatly extend their power.

A[illegible]re tyrants, their habit of providing simply for them[illegible] to their personal comfort and family aggrandizem[illegible]eat aim of their policy, and prevented anything great [illegible]; though they would each have their affairs with [illegible]ors. All this is only true of the mother country, for in [illegible] very great power. Thus for a long time everywher[illegible]causes which make the states alike incapable of comb[illegible]ational ends, or of any vigorous action of their own.

1.18
HELLAS
Sparta put down Hellenic tyrants and led Greek resistance to Persia. After the Persians' defeat Athens and Sparta quarreled.

B[illegible]when the tyrants of Athens and the far older tyran[illegible]as were, with the exception of those in Sicily, once [illegible] Sparta;[1a] for this city, though after the settlement [illegible]ent inhabitants, it suffered from factions for an unpa[illegible]still at a very early period obtained good laws, and [illegible] tyrants which was unbroken; it has possessed the s[illegible]t for more than four hundred years, reckoning

1.18.1a [illegible]

to the end of the late war, and has thus been in a position to arrange the affairs of the other states.[1b] Not many years after the deposition of the tyrants, the battle of Marathon was fought between the Medes[1c] and the Athenians. [2] Ten years afterwards the barbarian returned with the armada for the subjugation of Hellas. In the face of this great danger the command of the confederate Hellenes was assumed by the Spartans in virtue of their superior power; and the Athenians having made up their minds to abandon their city, broke up their homes, threw themselves into their ships, and became a naval people. This coalition, after repulsing the barbarian, soon afterwards split into two sections, which included the Hellenes who had revolted from the King,[2a] as well as those who had shared in the war. At the head of the one stood Athens, at the head of the other Sparta, one the first naval, the other the first military power in Hellas. [3] For a short time the league held together, till the Spartans and Athenians quarreled, and made war upon each other with their allies, a duel into which all the Hellenes sooner or later were drawn, though some might at first remain neutral. So that the whole period from the Median war to this, with some peaceful intervals, was spent by each power in war, either with its rival, or with its own revolted allies, and consequently afforded them constant practice in military matters, and that experience which is learnt in the school of danger.

1.19
HELLAS
Thucydides describes the different policies of the Spartan and Athenian alliances.

The policy of Sparta was not to exact tribute from her allies, but merely to secure their subservience to her interests by establishing oligarchies among them;[1a] Athens, on the contrary, had by degrees deprived hers of their ships, and imposed instead contributions in money on all except Chios[1b] and Lesbos.[1c] Both found their resources for this war separately to exceed the sum of their strength when the alliance flourished intact.

1.20
ATHENS
Thucydides notes that people accept traditions that are clearly in error, for example, the tale about Harmodius and Aristogiton.

Having now given the result of my inquiries into early times, I grant that there will be a difficulty in believing every particular detail. The way that most men deal with traditions, even traditions of their own country, is to receive them all alike as they are delivered, without applying any critical test whatever. [2] The Athenian public generally believe that Hipparchus was tyrant when he fell by the hands of Harmodius and Aristogiton. They do not know that Hippias, the eldest of the sons of Pisistratus, was really supreme; that Hipparchus and Thessalus were his brothers; and that Harmodius and Aristogiton, suspecting on the very day—indeed at the very moment fixed for the deed—that information had been conveyed to Hippias by their accomplices, concluded that he had been warned. They did

1.18.1b See Appendix D, The Peloponnesian League, §6.

1.18.1c The battle of Marathon (Map 1.11, BY) was fought in 490. See Appendix E, The Persians, §4. The Greeks regularly referred to the Persians as "the Mede," or "the Medes," and to the Persian wars as the "Median wars," although the Medes and Persians were distinct peoples. See Appendix E, The Persians, §1.

1.18.2a The term "King" is capitalized throughout this edition when it signifies the great King of Persia to distinguish him from all others carrying that title. See Appendix E, The Persians, §2.

1.19.1a See Appendix D, The Peloponnesian League, §6.

1.19.1b Chios: Map 1.11, BY. See Appendix B, The Athenian Empire, §2, 5.

1.19.1c Lesbos: Map 1.11, AY.

not at [illegible] ing to risk their lives and be apprehended for nothi [illegible] archus near the temple of the daughters of Leos [illegible] arranging the Panathenaic procession.[2a] [3] There [illegible] ded ideas current among the rest of the Hellenes, [illegible] ontemporary history which have not been obscu [illegible] ce, there is the notion that the Spartan kings have t [illegible] being that they have only one; and that there is a m [illegible] e, there being simply no such thing. So little pains [illegible] e investigation of truth, accepting readily the first st [illegible]

1.21 HELLAS Thucydides believes his conclusions to be reliable, and notes that this war was much greater than earlier ones.

On [illegible] he conclusions I have drawn from the proofs quote [illegible] be relied upon. Assuredly they will not be disturbe [illegible] a poet displaying the exaggeration of his craft, or by [illegible] he chroniclers that are attractive at truth's expen [illegible] at of being out of the reach of evidence, and time [illegible] hem of historical value by enthroning them in the re [illegible] from these, we can rest satisfied with having proce [illegible] data, and having arrived at conclusions as exact [illegible] matters of such antiquity. [2] To come to this war; [illegible] ition of the actors in a struggle to overrate its impor [illegible] over to return to their admiration of earlier event [illegible] the facts will show that it was much greater than t [illegible] it.

1.22 HELLAS Thucydides discusses the speeches in his text. He says it lacks romance because he intends it to be "a possession for all time."

Wi [illegible] eeches in this history, some were delivered befor [illegible] while it was going on; some I heard myself, other [illegible] rters; it was in all cases difficult to carry them word [illegible] ry, so my habit has been to make the speakers say w [illegible] emanded of them by the various occasions, of cours [illegible] possible to the general sense of what they really [illegible] rence to the narrative of events, far from permittin [illegible] om the first source that came to hand, I did not e [illegible] sions, but it rests partly on what I saw myself, partly [illegible] me, the accuracy of the report being always tried [illegible] detailed tests possible. [3] My conclusions have [illegible] the want of coincidence between accounts of the s [illegible] ferent eyewitnesses, arising sometimes from imper [illegible] s from undue partiality for one side or the

1.20.2a [illegible] is [illegible] 54–59.

1.22.1a [illegible] or discussion [illegible] dides.

other. [4] The absence of romance in my history will, I fear, detract somewhat from its interest; but if it be judged useful by those inquirers who desire an exact knowledge of the past as an aid to the understanding of the future, which in the course of human things must resemble if it does not reflect it, I shall be content. In fine, I have written my work, not as an essay which is to win the applause of the moment, but as a possession for all time.

1.23
HELLAS
Thucydides compares the Persian war and the much longer Peloponnesian War, and states that the latter's true cause was Spartan fear of the growth of Athenian power.

The Median war, the greatest achievement of past times, yet found a speedy decision in two actions by sea and two by land. The Peloponnesian War went on for a very long time and there occurred during it disasters of a kind and number that no other similar period of time could match. [2] Never had so many cities been taken and laid desolate, here by the barbarians, here by the parties contending (the old inhabitants being sometimes removed to make room for others); never was there so much banishing and bloodshedding, now on the field of battle, now in political strife. [3] Old stories of occurrences handed down by tradition, but scantily confirmed by experience, suddenly ceased to be incredible; there were earthquakes of unparalleled extent and violence; eclipses of the sun occurred with a frequency unrecorded in previous history; there were great droughts in sundry places and consequent famines, and that most calamitous and awfully fatal visitation, the plague.[3a] All this came upon them with the late war, [4] which was begun by the Athenians and Peloponnesians with the dissolution of the Thirty Years' Peace[4a] made after the conquest of Euboea. [5] To the question why they broke the treaty, I answer by placing first an account of their grounds of complaint and points of difference, that no one may ever have to ask the immediate cause which plunged the Hellenes into a war of such magnitude. [6] The real cause, however, I consider to be the one which was formally most kept out of sight. The growth of the power of Athens, and the alarm which this inspired in Sparta, made war inevitable. Still it is well to give the grounds alleged by either side, which led to the dissolution of the treaty and the breaking out of the war.[6a]

1.24
435
IONIAN GULF
Beset by civil strife, the commons of Epidamnus solicit aid from their "mother city," Corcyra, but she refuses them.

The city of Epidamnus[1a] stands on the right of the entrance of the Ionic gulf.[1b] Its vicinity is inhabited by the Taulantians, an Illyrian[1c] people. [2] The place is a colony from Corcyra,[2a] founded by Phalius son of Eratocleides, of the family of the Heraclids, who had according to ancient usage been summoned for the purpose from Corinth,[2b] the mother country. The colonists were joined by some Corinthians, and

1.23.3a This is a much debated passage for what it indicates about Thucydides' attitude toward religion. See the Introduction (sec. IV.i).
1.23.4a The Thirty Years' Peace treaty of 446; see 1.115.1.
1.23.6a It has been argued that section 6 here was written by Thucydides at a substantially later time than section 5, and may represent a radical change of mind about the causes of the war.
1.24.1a Epidamnus: Map 1.26, AX.
1.24.1b Ionic (Ionian) Gulf (the modern Adriatic Sea): Map 1.26, locator.
1.24.1c Illyria: Map 1.26, locator.
1.24.2a Corcyra: Map 1.26, AX.
1.24.2b Corinth: Map 1.26, BY.

other [illegible] [3] Now, as time went on, the city of Epi-
damn [illegible] populous; [4] but falling a prey to factions
arisin [illegible] ar with neighboring barbarians, she became
much [illegible] considerable amount of her power. [5] The
last a [illegible] he expulsion of those in power by The People. [illegible] the barbarians, and proceeded to plunder
those [illegible] and; [6] and the Epidamnians finding themselves [illegible] ambassadors to Corcyra beseeching their
moth [illegible] w them to perish, but to make up matters
betw [illegible], and to rid them of the war with the barbarians. [illegible] eated themselves in the temple of Hera[7a] as
suppl [illegible] bove requests to the Corcyraeans. But the
Corc [illegible] t their supplication, and they were dismissed
with [illegible] hing.

1.25 435 IONIAN GULF After consulting the oracle at Delphi, Epidamnus seeks and obtains promises of Corinthian help. Corinth had long resented Corcyra's contempt for her.

W [illegible] und that no help could be expected from Corcyra, [illegible] about what to do next. So they sent to Delphi[1a] [illegible], whether they should deliver their city to the
Cori [illegible] obtain some assistance from their founders.
The [illegible] was to deliver the city, and place themselves
unde [illegible] [2] So the Epidamnians went to Corinth, and
deliv [illegible] obedience to the commands of the oracle.
They [illegible] nder came from Corinth, and revealed the
answ [illegible] begged them not to allow them to perish, but
to as [illegible] Corinthians consented to do. Believing the
colo [illegible] themselves as to the Corcyraeans, they felt it
to be [illegible] rtake their protection. Besides, they hated the
Corc [illegible] pt of the mother country. [4] Instead of meeting w [illegible] orded to the parent city by every other colony
at pu [illegible] precedence at sacrifices, Corinth found herself
treat [illegible] power, which in point of wealth could stand
comp [illegible] en the richest in Hellas, which possessed great
milit [illegible] sometimes could not repress a pride in the
high [illegible] nd whose nautical renown dated from the days
of its [illegible] haeacians.[4a] This was one reason for the care
that [illegible] eet, which became very efficient; indeed they
bega [illegible] a hundred and twenty triremes.

1.26 435 IONIAN GULF When Corinthian settlers arrive at Epidamnus, Corcyra decides to support the Epidamnian exiles and besieges Epidamnus.

Al [illegible] Corinth eager to send the promised aid to
Epid [illegible] was made for volunteer settlers, and a force of

1.24.7a [illegible] (Map [illegible] ligarchs [illegible]
1.25.1a [illegible]
1.25.4a [illegible] s *Odyssey*, [illegible]

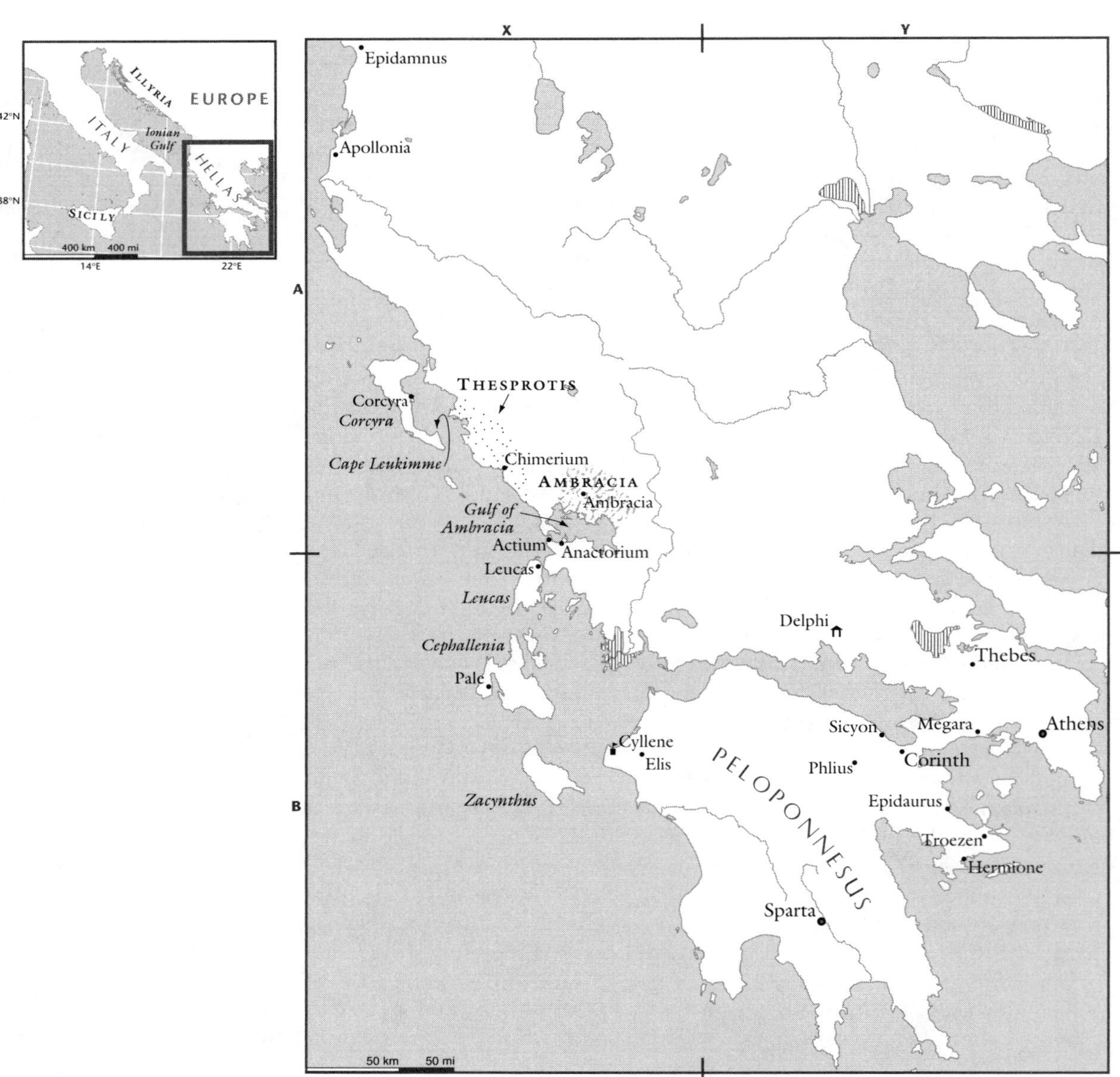

MAP 1.26 THE CORINTHIAN EXPEDITION

Ambr[illegible] and Corinthians was despatched. [2] They
march[illegible][2a] a Corinthian colony, the route by sea being
avoid[illegible]ean interruption. [3] When the Corcyraeans
heard [illegible]ers and troops in Epidamnus, and the surrender of [illegible] they took fire. Instantly putting to sea with
five-a[illegible] were quickly followed by others, they inso-
lently [illegible]nnians to receive back the banished party (it
must [illegible]pidamnian exiles had come to Corcyra, and
pointi[illegible]their ancestors, had appealed to their kindred
to res[illegible]niss the Corinthian garrison and settlers. [4]
But t[illegible]ans turned a deaf ear. Upon this the Cor-
cyraea[illegible]ons against them with a fleet of forty ships.
They [illegible]es, with a view to their restoration, and also
secure[illegible]llyrians. Sitting down before the city, they
issued[illegible]ffect that any of the Epidamnians that chose,
and o[illegible]epart unharmed, with the alternative of being
treate[illegible]efusal the Corcyraeans proceeded to besiege
the cit[illegible]thmus; [1.27.1] and the Corinthians, receiving in[illegible]ent of Epidamnus, got together an armament
and ca[illegible] to a colony at Epidamnus,[1a] complete political eq[illegible] to all who chose to go. Any who were not
prepa[illegible] by paying down the sum of fifty Corinthian
drach[illegible] colony without leaving Corinth. Great numbers t[illegible] proclamation, some being ready to start
directl[illegible]quisite forfeit. [2] In case of their passage
being [illegible]eans, several cities were asked to lend them a
convo[illegible] accompany them with eight ships, Pale in
Cepha[illegible]idaurus[2c] furnished five, Hermione[2d] one,
Troez[illegible] and Ambracia eight. The Thebans[2f] and
Phliasi[illegible]ney, the Eleans[2h] for unmanned hulls as well;
while [illegible]d thirty ships and three thousand *hoplites*.[2i]

1.27
435
IONIAN GULF
Corinth organizes a large force to colonize and rescue Epidamnus from Corcyra.

Wh[illegible]rd of their preparations they came to Corinth
with e[illegible]icyon,[1a] whom they persuaded to accompany
them, [illegible] garrison and settlers, as she had nothing to
do wit[illegible]wever, she had any claims to make, they were
willing [illegible]o the arbitration of such of the cities in the
Pelop[illegible]osen by mutual agreement, and to accept that
the c[illegible]th the city to whom the arbitrators might

1.28
435
IONIAN GULF
Corcyra offers to submit the dispute to arbitration or to the god at Delphi.

1.26.1a [illegible]
1.26.1b [illegible]
1.26.2a [illegible]
1.27.1a [illegible]
1.27.1b [illegible] See [illegible]ency, §3.
1.27.2a [illegible]
1.27.2b [illegible]n that [illegible]
1.27.2c [illegible]
1.27.2d Hermione: Map 1.26, BY.
1.27.2e Troezen: Map 1.26, BY.
1.27.2f Thebes: Map 1.26, BY.
1.27.2g Phlius: Map 1.26, BY.
1.27.2h Elis: Map 1.26, BX.
1.27.2i *Hoplite* is the Greek word for a heavily armed infantryman; see Appendix F, Land Warfare, §2.
1.28.1a Sicyon: Map 1.26, BY.

assign it. They were also willing to refer the matter to the oracle at Delphi. [3] If, in defiance of their protestations, war was resorted to, they should be themselves compelled by this violence to seek friends in quarters where they had no desire to seek them, and to make even old ties give way to the necessity of assistance. [4] The answer they got from Corinth was, that if they would withdraw their fleet and the barbarians from Epidamnus, negotiation might be possible; but, while the city was still being besieged, going before arbitrators was out of the question. [5] The Corcyraeans retorted that if Corinth would withdraw her troops from Epidamnus they would withdraw theirs, or they were ready to let both parties remain where they were, an armistice being concluded till judgment could be given.

1.29
435
CORCYRA
Corinth refuses Corcyra's proposals, declares war, and sends a fleet. It is defeated. Epidamnus surrenders.

Turning a deaf ear to all these proposals, when their ships were manned and their allies had come in, the Corinthians sent a herald[1a] before them to declare war, and getting under weigh with seventy-five ships and two thousand hoplites, sailed for Epidamnus to give battle to the Corcyraeans. [2] The fleet was under the command of Aristeus son of Pellichas, Callicrates son of Callias, and Timanor son of Timanthes; the troops under that of Archetimus son of Eurytimus, and Isarchidas son of Isarchus. [3] When they had reached Actium[3a] in the territory of Anactorium,[3b] at the mouth of the gulf of Ambracia,[3c] where the temple of Apollo stands, the Corcyraeans sent on a herald in a light boat to warn them not to sail against them. Meanwhile they proceeded to man their ships, all of which had been equipped for action, the old vessels being tightened[3d] to make them seaworthy. [4] On the return of the herald without any peaceful answer from the Corinthians, their ships being now manned, they put out to sea to meet the enemy with a fleet of eighty sail (forty were engaged in the siege of Epidamnus), formed line and went into action, and gained a decisive victory, [5] and destroyed fifteen of the Corinthian vessels. The same day had seen Epidamnus compelled by its besiegers to capitulate; the conditions being that the foreigners should be sold, and the Corinthians kept as prisoners of war, till their fate should be otherwise decided.

1.30
435
IONIAN GULF
The Corcyraeans now control the Ionian Gulf, but Corinth organizes a new fleet to challenge them again.

After the engagement the Corcyraeans set up a *trophy* on Leukimme,[1a] a headland of Corcyra, and slew all their captives except the Corinthians, whom they kept as prisoners of war. [2] Defeated at sea, the Corinthians and their allies returned home and left the Corcyraeans masters of all the sea about those parts. Sailing to Leucas,[2a] a Corinthian colony, they ravaged

1.29.1a Heralds, already a venerable Greek institution in Thucydides' day, operated under the protection of the god Hermes and were easily identified by the staff they carried. They alone could travel unmolested between states or armies during wartime in order to deliver messages, take back replies, and make perfunctory arrangements.

1.29.3a Actium: Map 1.26, AX.

1.29.3b Anactorium: Map 1.26, AX.

1.29.3c Gulf of Ambracia: Map 1.26, AX.

1.29.3d Like all triremes, these older ships required internal torsion ropes that pulled the bow and stern of the vessel together, strengthening the ship against wave action by tension and preventing joints from opening. For more information about naval battles, see Appendix G, Trireme Warfare.

1.30.1a Cape Leukimme: Map 1.26, AX. After a battle in ancient Greece, the victorious side raised a *trophy*, usually a set of captured armor, arranged on a pole at or near the battlefield; see Appendix F, Land Warfare, §6.

1.30.2a Leucas: Map 1.26, BX.

their [illegible] lene,[2b] the harbor of the Eleans, because they
had f[illegible] y to Corinth. [3] For almost the whole of the
perio[illegible] le they remained masters of the sea, and the
allies [illegible] ssed by Corcyraean vessels. At last Corinth,
rouse[illegible] r allies, sent out ships and troops in the fall of
the [illegible] an encampment at Actium[3a] and about
Chi[illegible] for the protection of Leucas and the rest of
the f[illegible] orcyraeans for their part formed a similar station [illegible] party made any movement, but they remained
conf[illegible] e end of the summer, and winter was at hand
befo[illegible] d home.

1.31 433 ATHENS Alarmed by Corinthian threats, Corcyra sends envoys to Athens to ask for help. Corinth also sends envoys to Athens to present her position.

C[illegible] he war with the Corcyraeans, spent the whole
of th[illegible] nent and that succeeding it in building ships,
and i[illegible] to form an efficient fleet; rowers being drawn
from [illegible] the rest of Hellas by the inducement of large
bour[illegible] ans, alarmed at the news of their preparations,
bein[illegible] n Hellas (for they had not enrolled themselves
eithe[illegible] he Spartan confederacy), decided to appeal to
Athe[illegible] alliance, and to endeavor to procure support
from [illegible] hearing of their intentions, sent an embassy to
Athe[illegible] raean navy being joined by the Athenian and
her [illegible] he war according to her wishes being thus
impe[illegible] convoked, and the rival advocates appeared:
the [illegible] ows:

1.32 433 ATHENS Speaking to the Athenian assembly, the Corcyraeans acknowledge that their past policy of avoiding alliances has now left them dangerously isolated.

[illegible] eople that have not rendered any important
se[illegible] ir neighbors in times past, for which they
m[illegible] d, appear before them as we now appear
b[illegible] r assistance, they may fairly be required to
s[illegible] conditions. They should show, first, that it
is [illegible] e to grant their request; next, that they will
r[illegible] e kindness. But if they cannot clearly estab-
li[illegible] hey must not be annoyed if they meet with
a [illegible] rcyraeans believe that with their petition for
a[illegible] give you a satisfactory answer on these
p[illegible] erefore despatched us hither. [3] It has so

1.30.2[illegible]
1.30.3[illegible]
1.30.3[illegible] ap 1.26, [illegible] mond, [illegible] h Channel [illegible] *l of Hel-* [illegible]
1.31.1[illegible] e drachma [illegible] for a day's [illegible] ecially [illegible] ighly [illegible] l a bonus; see note 6.31.3b. Also see Appendix G, Trireme Warfare, §12.
1.31.3a Assembly: see Appendix A, The Athenian Government, §5–8.

happened that our policy as regards you, with respect to this request, turns out to be inconsistent, and as regards our interests, to be at the present crisis inexpedient. [4] We say inconsistent, because a power which has never in the whole of her past history been willing to ally herself with any of her neighbors, is now found asking them to ally themselves with her. And we say inexpedient, because in our present war with Corinth it has left us in a position of entire isolation, and what once seemed the wise precaution of refusing to involve ourselves in alliances with other powers, lest we should also involve ourselves in risks of their choosing, has now proved to be folly and weakness. [5] It is true that in the late naval engagement we drove back the Corinthians from our shores single-handed. But they have now got together a still larger armament from the Peloponnesus and the rest of Hellas; and we, seeing our utter inability to cope with them without foreign aid, and the magnitude of the danger which subjection to them implies, find it necessary to ask help from you and from every other power. And we hope to be excused if we forswear our old principle of complete political isolation, a principle which was not adopted with any sinister intention, but was rather the consequence of an error in judgment."

1.33
433
ATHENS
The Corcyraeans argue that because they are the second greatest naval power in Greece, their offer of alliance is an extraordinary opportunity for Athens, particularly since Sparta will surely start a war against Athens soon.

"Now there are many reasons why in the event of your compliance you will congratulate yourselves on this request having been made to you. First, because your assistance will be rendered to a power which, herself inoffensive, is a victim to the injustice of others. Secondly, because all that we most value is at stake in the present contest, and by acceding to our request under these circumstances you will give unforgettable proof of your goodwill and create in us a lasting sense of gratitude. [2] Thirdly, yourselves excepted, we are the greatest naval power in Hellas. Can you conceive a stroke of good fortune more rare in itself, or more disheartening to your enemies, than that the power whose adhesion you would have valued above much material and moral strength, should present herself self-invited, should deliver herself into your hands without danger and without expense, and should lastly put you in the way of gaining a high character in the eyes of the world, the gratitude of those whom you shall assist, and a great accession of strength for yourselves? You may search all history without finding many instances of a people gaining all these advantages at once, or many instances of a power that comes in quest of assistance being in a position to give to the people whose alliance she solicits as much safety and honor as she will receive. [3] But it will be urged that it is only in the case of a war that we shall be found useful. To this we answer that if any of you imagine that the war is far off, he is grievously mistaken, and is blind to the fact that

th[illegible] you want war, and that Corinth is influen-
tia[illegible] remember, that is your enemy, and is even
no[illegible] as a preliminary to attacking you. And this
sh[illegible] becoming united by a common enmity, and
he[illegible] hands, and also to insure getting the jump
or[illegible], either by crippling our power or by mak-
in[illegible] [4] Now it is our policy to preempt her—
th[illegible]e an offer of alliance and for you to accept
it;[illegible]rm plans against her instead of waiting to
de[illegible] against us."

1.34
433
ATHENS
The Corcyraeans report that Corinth has attempted to dominate Corcyra and refuses Corcyra's offer of arbitration.

[illegible]you to receive a colony of hers into alliance
is [illegible] that every colony that is well treated hon-
or[illegible]ecomes estranged from it by injustice. For
co[illegible]n on the understanding that they are to be
th[illegible]main behind, but that they are to be their
eq[illegible]nth was injuring us is clear. Invited to refer
th[illegible]nus to arbitration, they chose to prosecute
th[illegible]ather than by a fair trial. [3] And let their
co[illegible]e their kindred be a warning to you not to
be[illegible] nor to yield to their direct requests; con-
ce[illegible]nly end in self-reproach, and the more
str[illegible]e greater will be the chance of security."

1.35
433
ATHENS
Claiming that their alliance with Athens will not breach existing treaties, the Corcyraeans argue that Athens should prevent their naval power from becoming subject to a potential enemy of Athens.

[illegible]ur reception of us will be a breach of the
tre[illegible]u and Sparta, the answer is that we are a
ne[illegible] one of the express provisions of that treaty
is [illegible] any Hellenic state that is neutral to join
wh[illegible] [3] And it is intolerable for Corinth to be
all[illegible]her navy not only from her allies, but also
fro[illegible] small number being furnished by your own
sul[illegible]e excluded both from the alliance left open
to [illegible]ny assistance that we might get from other
qu[illegible] accused of political immorality if you comply[illegible] On the other hand, we shall have much
gre[illegible]of you, if you do not comply with it; if we,
wh[illegible]o enemies of yours, meet with a repulse at
yo[illegible] who is the aggressor and your enemy, not
on[illegible]nce from you, but is even allowed to draw
ma[illegible] dependencies. This ought not to be, but
yo[illegible]er enlisting men in your dominions, or you
sh[illegible]lp you may think advisable."

[illegible]cy is to afford us open approval and sup-
po[illegible]is course, as we premised in the beginning
of[illegible]We mention one that is perhaps the chief.

1.35.2a [illegible]y of [illegible]

Could there be a clearer guarantee of our good faith than is offered by the fact that the power which is at enmity with you, is also at enmity with us, and that power is fully able to punish defection. And there is a wide difference between declining the alliance of an inland and of a maritime power. For your first endeavor should be to prevent, if possible, the existence of any naval power except your own; failing this, to secure the friendship of the strongest that does exist."

1.36
433
ATHENS
Reminding the Athenians of Corcyra's strategic location on the route to Italy and Sicily, the Corcyraeans conclude by warning that if Athens refuses alliance now, she may well confront combined Corcyraean and Peloponnesian fleets in a future war.

"And if any of you believe that what we urge is expedient, but fear to act upon this belief, lest it should lead to a breach of the treaty, you must remember that on the one hand, whatever your fears, your strength will be formidable to your antagonists; on the other, whatever the confidence you derive from refusing to receive us, you will be the weaker and less terrifying to a strengthened enemy. You must also remember that your decision is for Athens no less than for Corcyra, and that you are not making the best provision for her interests if, at a time when you are anxiously scanning the horizon that you may be in readiness for the breaking out of the war which is all but upon you, you hesitate to attach to your side a place whose adhesion or estrangement is alike pregnant with the most vital consequences. [2] For it lies conveniently for the coast navigation in the direction of Italy and Sicily,[2a] being able to bar the passage of naval reinforcements from there to the Peloponnesus, and from the Peloponnesus to there; and it is in other respects most suitably positioned. [3] To sum up as shortly as possible, embracing both general and particular considerations, let this show you the folly of sacrificing us. Remember that there are but three considerable naval powers in Hellas, Athens, Corcyra, and Corinth, and that if you allow two of these three to become one, and Corinth to secure us for herself, you will have to hold the sea against the united fleets of Corcyra and the Peloponnesus. But if you receive us, you will have our ships to reinforce you in the struggle."

[4] Such were the words of the Corcyraeans. After they had finished, the Corinthians spoke as follows:

1.37
433
ATHENS
The Corinthians accuse Corcyra of having pursued a policy of isolation so as to use their geographic position to abuse the many ships forced to put into Corcyra.

"These Corcyraeans in the speech we have just heard do not confine themselves to the question of their reception into your alliance. They also talk of our being guilty of injustice, and their being the victims of an unjustifiable war. It becomes necessary for us to touch upon both these points before we proceed to the rest of what we have to say, that you may have a more correct idea of the grounds of

1.36.2a The geographical relation between Corcyra and Italy–Sicily is displayed in Map 1.14. See Appendix G, Trireme Warfare, §7, for an explanation of why military vessels (triremes) were forced to follow coastlines and rarely ventured, like merchant vessels, into the open sea.

ou [illegible] cause to reject their petition. [2] According [illegible] icy of refusing all offers of alliance was a
pol [illegible] vas in fact adopted for bad ends, not for
goo [illegible] ct is such as to make them by no means
des [illegible] esent to witness it, or of having the shame
of [illegible] . [3] Besides, their geographical situation
ma [illegible] f others, and consequently the decision in
cas [illegible] lies not with judges appointed by mutual
agr [illegible] selves, because while they seldom make
voy [illegible] , they are constantly being visited by for-
eig [illegible] pelled to put in to Corcyra. [4] In short,
the [illegible] e to themselves in their specious policy of
co [illegible] to avoid sharing in the crimes of others,
but [illegible] of crime to themselves—the license of
out [illegible] compel, and of fraud wherever they can
elu [illegible] of their gains without shame. [5] And yet
if t [illegible] en they pretend to be, the less hold that
oth [illegible] e stronger would be the light in which
the [illegible] honesty by giving and taking what was
just [illegible]

1.38
433
ATHENS
The Corinthians claim that Corcyra has always treated them with inappropriate disdain that now at Epidamnus has become open hostility.

[illegible] n their conduct either toward others or
tow [illegible] our colony toward us has always been one
of [illegible] w one of hostility; for, say they, 'We were
not [illegible] ed.' [2] We rejoin that we did not found
the [illegible] by them, but to be their head, and to be
reg [illegible] pect. [3] At any rate, our other colonies
hor [illegible] much beloved by our colonists; [4] and
clea [illegible] satisfied with us, these can have no good
rea [illegible] n which they stand alone, and we are not
acti [illegible] g war against them, nor are we making
war [illegible] having received severe provocation. [5]
Bes [illegible] wrong, it would be honorable in them to
give [illegible] d disgraceful for us to trample on their
mo [illegible] le and license of wealth they have sinned
aga [illegible] and never more deeply than when Epi-
dan [illegible] which they took no steps to claim in its
dist [illegible] to relieve it, was by them seized, and is
nov [illegible]

1.39
433
ATHENS
The Corinthians argue that Corcyra offered arbitration only after she began to fear Corinthian retaliation, and that her fear also motivates her request for an Athenian alliance.

[illegible] hat they wished the question to be first
sub [illegible] is obvious that a challenge coming from
the [illegible] commanding position cannot gain the

credit due only to him who, before appealing to arms, in deeds as well as words, places himself on a level with his adversary. [2] In their case, it was not before they laid siege to the place, but after they at length understood that we would not tamely suffer it, that they thought of the specious word arbitration. And not satisfied with their own misconduct there, they appear here now requiring you to join with them not in alliance, but in crime, and to receive them in spite of their being at enmity with us. [3] But it was when they stood firmest that they should have made overtures to you, and not at a time when we have been wronged and they are in peril; nor yet at a time when you will be admitting to a share in your protection those who never admitted you to a share in their power, and will be incurring an equal amount of blame from us with those in whose offenses you had no hand. No, they should have shared their power with you before they asked you to share your fortunes with them."

1.40
433
ATHENS
The Corinthians threaten enmity and retaliation if Athens should ally with Corcyra, and remind the Athenians of Corinth's past support for them against rebellious Samos.

"So then the reality of the grievances we come to complain of and the violence and rapacity of our opponents have both been proved. But that you cannot equitably receive them, this you have still to learn. [2] It may be true that one of the provisions of the treaty is that it shall be competent for any state, whose name was not down on the list, to join whichever side it pleases. But this agreement is not meant for those whose object in joining is the injury of other powers, but for those whose need of support does not arise from the fact of defection, and whose adhesion will not bring to the power that is mad enough to receive them war instead of peace; which will be the case with you, if you refuse to listen to us. [3] For you cannot become their auxiliary and remain our friend; if you join in their attack, you must share the punishment which the defenders inflict on them. [4] And yet you have the best possible right to be neutral, or failing this, you should on the contrary join us against them. Corinth is at least in treaty with you; with Corcyra you were never even in truce. But do not propose the principle that those defecting from others are to be welcomed. [5] Did we on the defection of the Samians record our vote against you, when the rest of the Peloponnesian powers were equally divided on the question whether they should assist them?[5a] No, we told them to their face that every power has a right to punish its own allies. [6] Why, if you make it your policy to receive and assist all offenders, you will find that just as many of your dependencies will come over to us, and the principle that you establish will press less heavily on us than on yourselves."

1.40.5a If the Peloponnesian League debated the question of helping Samos in 441/0, Sparta probably proposed that such help be given. The revolt of the island of Samos from the Athenians took place in 441/0 and is described by Thucydides in 1.115–17. See Appendix D, The Peloponnesian League, §5. Samos: Map 1.11, BY, and Map 1.115.

1.41
433
ATHENS
The Corinthians demand gratitude for their help in Athens' war with Aegina and the revolt of Samos.

lenic law entitles us to demand as a right.
Bu offer and claims on your gratitude, which,
sin f our injuring you, as we are not enemies,
an does not amount to very frequent inter-
co e liquidated at the present juncture. [2]
Wh of ships of war for the war against the
Ae rsian invasion, Corinth supplied you with
tw turn, and the line we took on the Samian
qu ne cause of the Peloponnesians refusing to
ass o conquer Aegina,[2a] and to punish Samos.
An ses when, if ever, men are wont in their
eff es to forget everything for the sake of victor o assists them then as a friend, even if thus
far him who opposes them then as a foe, even
if h iend; indeed they allow their real interests
to ng preoccupation in the struggle."

1.42
433
ATHENS
The Corinthians call upon the Athenians to return past favors and not incur Corinth's enmity to secure a naval alliance.

iderations, and let your youth learn what
the and let them determine to do unto us as
we nd let them not acknowledge the justice of
wh ts wisdom in the contingency of war. [2]
No path generally speaking the wisest; but the
co the Corcyraeans have used as a specter to
pe is still uncertain, and it is not worth while
to o gaining the instant and declared enmity
of , wise to try and counteract the unfavor-
abl conduct to Megara[2a] has created. [3] For
kin wn has a greater power of removing old
gri of the case may warrant. And do not be
sec a great naval alliance. Abstinence from all
inj powers is a greater tower of strength than
any d by the sacrifice of permanent tranquillity
for advantage."

1.43
433
ATHENS
The Corinthians conclude by telling the Athenians that their best interests lie in rejecting Corcyra.

benefit by the principle that we laid down
at r has a right to punish her own allies. We
no same from you, and protest against your
rev g you by our vote by injuring us by yours.
[2] n us like for like, remembering that this is
tha e who lends aid is most a friend, and he
wh . [3] And for these Corcyraeans—neither
rec in our despite, nor be their abettors in

1.41.2a gina of
,

1.42.2a some
the
.1, 1.140.3–4, and 1.144.2), and therefore date it prior to mid-433, most take it as a reference to Corinth's hatred for Athens caused by the defection of Megara to the Athenian alliance in about 460; cf. 1.103.4.

crime. [4] So do, and you will act as we have a right to expect of you, and at the same time best consult your own interest."

1.44
433
ATHENS
The Athenians vote with a view toward a Peloponnesian war, noting Corcyra's large fleet and her position on the route to Italy and Sicily.

Such were the words of the Corinthians.

When the Athenians had heard both out, two assemblies were held. In the first there was a manifest disposition to listen to the representations of Corinth; in the second, public feeling had changed, and an alliance with Corcyra was decided on, with certain reservations. It was to be a defensive, not an offensive, alliance. It did not involve a breach of the treaty with the Peloponnesus: Athens could not be required to join Corcyra in any attack upon Corinth. But each of the contracting parties had a right to the other's assistance against invasion, whether of his own territory, or that of an ally. [2] For it began now to be felt that the coming of the Peloponnesian War was only a question of time, and no one was willing to see a naval power of such magnitude as Corcyra sacrificed to Corinth; though if they could let them weaken each other by mutual conflict, it would be no bad preparation for the struggle which Athens might one day have to wage with Corinth and the other naval powers. [3] At the same time the island seemed to lie conveniently on the coasting passage to Italy and Sicily.[3a]

1.45
433
ATHENS
Athens enters a defensive alliance with Corcyra and sends ten triremes to assist her.

With these views, Athens received Corcyra into alliance, and on the departure of the Corinthians not long afterwards, sent ten ships to their assistance. [2] They were commanded by Lacedaemonius son of Cimon, Diotimus son of Strombichus, and Porteas son of Epicles. [3] Their instructions were to avoid collision with the Corinthian fleet except under certain circumstances. If it sailed to Corcyra and threatened a landing on her coast, or in any of her possessions, they were to do their utmost to prevent it. These instructions were prompted by an anxiety to avoid a breach of the treaty.

1.46
433
CORCYRA
A Corinthian fleet sails to Chimerium, near Corcyra.

Meanwhile the Corinthians completed their preparations, and sailed for Corcyra with a hundred and fifty ships. Of these Elis[1a] furnished ten, Megara[1b] twelve, Leucas[1c] ten, Ambracia[1d] twenty-seven, Anactorium[1e] one, and Corinth herself ninety. [2] Each of these contingents had its own admiral, the Corinthian being under the command of Xenocleides son of Euthycles, with four colleagues. [3] Sailing from Leucas, they made land at the part of the continent opposite Corcyra. [4] They anchored in the harbor of Chimerium, in the territory of Thesprotis,[4a] above which, at some distance from the sea, lies the city of Ephyre,[4b] in the Elean district. By this city the Acherusian lake pours its waters into the sea. It gets its name from the river

1.44.3a The geographical relation between Corcyra and Italy–Sicily is displayed in Map 1.14.
1.46.1a Elis: Map 1.46, BX.
1.46.1b Megara: Map 1.46, BY.
1.46.1c Leucas: Map 1.46, BX.
1.46.1d Ambracia: Map 1.46, AX.
1.46.1e Anactorium: Map 1.46, AX.
1.46.4a Chimerium: Map 1.46, inset. Thesprotis: Map 1.46, AX and inset (according to N.G.L. Hammond; see note 1.30.3b.
1.46.4b Ephyre: Map 1.46, inset.

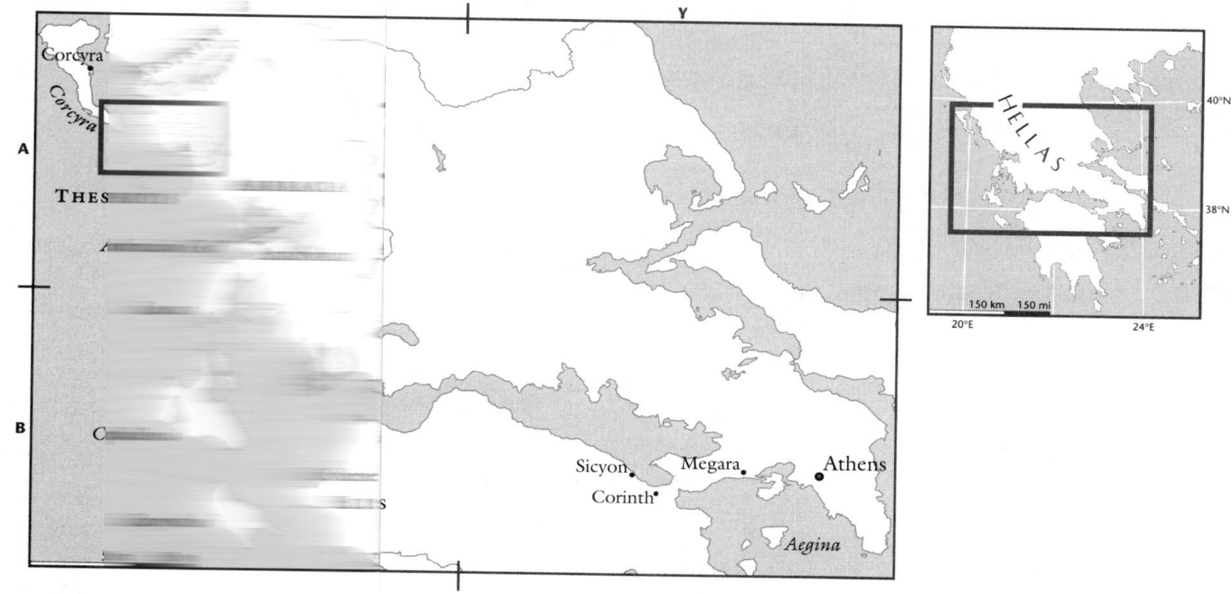

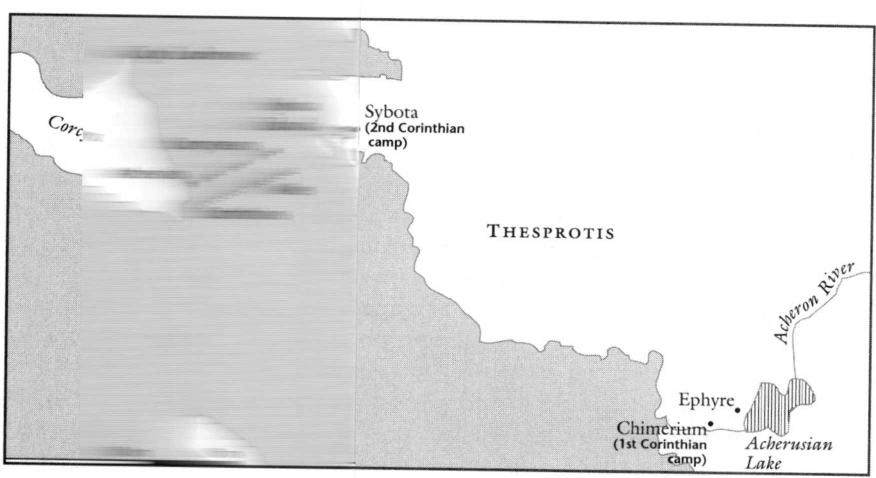

MAP 1.46 THE BATTLE OF SYBOTA

Acheron which flows through Thesprotis and falls into the lake. There also the river Thyamis flows, forming the boundary between Thesprotis and Kestrine, and between these rivers rises the point of Chimerium. [5] In this part of the continent the Corinthians now came to anchor, and formed an encampment.

1.46.4c Acherusian Lake/River Acheron: Map 1.46.

1.46.4d Thyamis river, possible location: Map 1.46, AY.

1.46.4e Kestrine: Map 1.46, AX.

1.47
433
CORCYRA
Corcyra deploys her fleet and army.

When the Corcyraeans saw them coming, they manned a hundred and ten ships, commanded by Meikiades, Aisimides, and Eurybatus, and stationed themselves at one of the Sybota isles[1a]; the ten Athenian ships being present. [2] On point Leukimme[2a] they posted their land forces, and a thousand hoplites who had come from Zacynthus[2b] to their assistance. Nor were the Corinthians on the mainland without their allies. [3] The barbarians flocked in large numbers to their assistance, the inhabitants of this part of the continent being old allies of theirs.

1.48
433
CORCYRA
The two fleets form up for battle.

When the Corinthian preparations were completed they took three days' provisions, and put out from Chimerium by night, ready for action. [2] Sailing with the dawn, they sighted the Corcyraean fleet out at sea, and coming toward them. [3] When they perceived each other, both sides formed in order of battle. On the Corcyraean right wing lay the Athenian ships, the rest of the line being occupied by their own vessels formed in three squadrons, each of which was commanded by one of the three admirals. [4] Such was the Corcyraean formation. The Corinthian was as follows: on the right wing lay the Megarian and Ambraciot ships, in the center the rest of the allies in order. But the left was composed of the best sailors in the Corinthian navy, to encounter the Athenians and the right wing of the Corcyraeans.[4a]

1.49
433
CORCYRA
In a long unskillful battle, each side's left wing is victorious. The Athenian ships at first abstain from joining the battle, then intervene tentatively, then fight hard to prevent a Corcyraean rout.

As soon as the signals were raised on either side, they joined battle. Both sides had a large number of hoplites on their decks, and a large number of archers and javelin throwers, the old imperfect armament still prevailing. [2] The sea fight was an obstinate one, though not remarkable for its science; indeed it was more like a battle by land. [3] Whenever they charged each other, the multitude and crush of the triremes made it by no means easy to get loose; besides, their hopes of victory lay principally in the hoplites on the decks, who stood and fought in order, the ships remaining stationary. The maneuver of passing through the line was not tried: in short, strength and pluck had more share in the fight than science.[3a] [4] Everywhere tumult reigned, the battle being one scene of confusion; meanwhile the Athenian triremes, by coming up to the Corcyraeans whenever they were pressed, served to alarm the enemy, though their commanders could not join in the battle from fear of their instructions. [5] The right wing of the Corinthians suffered most. The Corcyraeans routed it, and chased them in disorder to the continent with twenty ships, sailed up to their camp and burnt the tents which they found empty, and plundered the stuff.[5a] [6] So in this quarter the Corinthians and their allies were defeated, and the Corcyraeans were victorious. But where the Corinthians themselves were, on the left, they gained a decided success; the scanty forces of the

1.47.1a Sybota isles: Map 1.46, inset.
1.47.2a Cape Leukimme, Corcyra: Map 1.46, inset.
1.47.2b Zacynthus: Map 1.46, BX.
1.48.4a Map 1.46, inset, shows a reconstruction of the battle location and formations from J. S. Morrison and J. R. Coates, *The Athenian Trireme* (Cambridge: Cambridge University Press, 1986), 63. They follow N.G.L. Hammond, "Naval Operations in the South Channel of Corcyra, 435–433," *Journal of Hellenic Studies,* 65: 26–37.
1.49.3a For these maneuvers, see the Athenian commander Phormio's speech in 2.89.8, and Appendix G, Trireme Warfare, §5.
1.49.5a For naval "stuff" at shore bases, see Appendix G, Trireme Warfare, §8.

Corcy[illegible]akened by the want of the twenty triremes absent[illegible]ng the Corcyraeans hard pressed, the Atheni-ans be[illegible] them more unequivocally. At first, it is true, they r[illegible] any ships; but when the rout was becoming obviou[illegible]were pressing on, the time at last came when every [illegible]ction was laid aside, and it came to this point, that th[illegible]nians raised their hands against each other.

1.50 433 CORCYRA The victorious Corinthians massacre survivors, gather up the dead, and tow off hulks. Returning to battle, they sight approaching Athenian reinforcements and retire.

Aft[illegible]ans, instead of employing themselves in lash-ing fas[illegible] the hulls of the triremes which they had dis-abled, [illegible] to the men, whom they butchered as they sailed [illegible]much to make prisoners. Some even of their own fr[illegible], by mistake, in their ignorance of the defeat of the [illegible] number of the triremes on both sides, and the dis[illegible]ered the sea, made it difficult after they had once j[illegible]etween the conquering and the conquered; this ba[illegible]than any before it, any at least between Hel-lenes, [illegible]els engaged. [3] After the Corinthians had chased [illegible] land, they turned to the wrecks and their dead, [illegible]ceeded in getting hold of and conveying to Sybota [illegible]he land forces furnished by their barbarian allies. [illegible]n, is a desert harbor of Thesprotis. This task over, t[illegible] sailed against the Corcyraeans, [4] who on their p[illegible]em with all their ships that were fit for ser-vice an[illegible]ccompanied by the Athenian vessels, fearing that th[illegible]ing in their territory. [5] It was by this time getting [illegible] had been sung for the attack, when the Corint[illegible]o back water. They had observed twenty Atheni[illegible]h had been sent out afterwards to reinforce the ten[illegible]ans, who feared, as it turned out justly, the defeat [illegible]the inability of their handful of ships to pro-tect th[illegible]ps were thus seen by the Corinthians first. They s[illegible] from Athens, and that those which they saw were n[illegible]re more behind; they accordingly began to retire. [illegible]anwhile had not sighted them, as they were advanci[illegible]hey could not so well see, and were wonder-ing wh[illegible] backing water, when some caught sight of them, [illegible] were ships in sight ahead. Upon this they also ret[illegible]ing dark, and the retreat of the Corinthians had sus[illegible] Thus they parted from each other, and the

1.51 433 CORCYRA Twenty additional Athenian triremes join the Corcyraeans at Leukimme.

1.50.3a [illegible]

1.50.5a [illegible]assical [illegible]ey [illegible]brated [illegible]

battle ceased with night. [4] The Corcyraeans were in their camp at Leukimme,[4a] when these twenty triremes from Athens, under the command of Glaucon son of Leagrus and Andocides son of Leogoras bore on through the corpses and the wrecks, and sailed up to the camp, not long after they were sighted. [5] It was now night, and the Corcyraeans feared that they might be hostile vessels; but they soon recognized them, and the ships came to anchor.

1.52
433
CORCYRA
The Corinthians fear that the Athenians will try to prevent their departure.

The next day the thirty Athenian vessels put out to sea, accompanied by all the Corcyraean ships that were seaworthy, and sailed to the harbor at Sybota, where the Corinthians lay, to see if they would engage. [2] The Corinthians put out from the land, and formed a line in the open sea, but beyond this made no further movement, having no intention of assuming the offensive. For they saw reinforcements arrived fresh from Athens, and themselves confronted by numerous difficulties, such as the necessity of guarding the prisoners whom they had on board, and the want of all means of refitting their ships in a desert place. [3] What they were thinking more about was how their voyage home was to be effected; they feared that the Athenians might consider that the treaty was dissolved by the fighting which had occurred, and forbid their departure. [1.53.1] Accordingly they resolved to put some men on board a boat, and send them without a herald's wand to the Athenians, as an experiment.[1a] Having done so, they spoke as follows: [2] "You do wrong, Athenians, to begin war and break the treaty. Engaged in chastising our enemies, we find you placing yourselves in our path in arms against us. Now if your intentions are to prevent us sailing to Corcyra, or anywhere else that we may wish, and if you are for breaking the treaty, first take us that are here, and treat us as enemies." [3] Such was what they said, and all the Corcyraean armament that were within hearing immediately called out to take them and kill them. But the Athenians answered as follows: "Neither are we beginning war, Peloponnesians, nor are we breaking the treaty; but these Corcyraeans are our allies, and we are come to help them. So if you want to sail anywhere else, we place no obstacle in your way; but if you are going to sail against Corcyra, or any of her possessions, we shall do our best to stop you."

1.53
433
CORCYRA
The Athenians tell the Corinthians that the treaty is still valid, that they may not attack Corcyra, but that they may otherwise sail where they wish.

1.54
433
CORCYRA
Both sides erect trophies claiming victory.

Receiving this answer from the Athenians, the Corinthians commenced preparations for their voyage home, and set up a trophy in Sybota, on the mainland; while the Corcyraeans took up the wrecks and dead that had been carried out to them by the current, and by a wind which rose in the night and scattered them in all directions, and set up their trophy in Sybota, on the island, as victors. [2] The reasons each side had for claiming

1.51.4a Leukimme, at the northern end of Cape Leukimme on Corcyra: Map 1.46, inset.

1.53.1a For the significance of the "herald's wand" here, see note 1.29.1a.

the vic [illegible] rinthians had been victorious in the sea fight until n [illegible] een enabled to carry off most wrecks and dead, t [illegible] f no fewer than a thousand prisoners of war, and ha [illegible] nty vessels. The Corcyraeans had destroyed about [illegible] e arrival of the Athenians had taken up the wrecks [illegible] they had besides seen the Corinthians retire before [illegible] sight of the Athenian vessels, and upon the arrival [illegible] o sail out against them from Sybota.

1.55
433
CORCYRA
The Athenian role at Sybota was the first Corinthian complaint against Athens.

The [illegible] age home took Anactorium, which stands at the mo [illegible] lf.[1a] The place was taken by treachery, being comm [illegible] yraeans and Corinthians. After establishing Corint [illegible] retired home. Eight hundred of the Corcyrean [illegible] ey sold; two hundred and fifty they retained in capt [illegible] great attention, in the hope that they might bring c [illegible] rinth on their return; most of them being, as it happ [illegible] position in Corcyra. [2] In this way Corcyra mainta [illegible] ce in the war with Corinth, and the Athenian ves [illegible] was the first cause of the war that Corinth had ag [illegible] ely, that they had fought against them with the Co [illegible] y.[2a]

1.56
433
CHALCIDICE
Athens takes measures against Corinthian influence at Potidaea.

Alm [illegible] is, fresh differences arose between the Athenians [illegible] d contributed their share to the war. [2] Corint [illegible] for retaliation, and Athens suspected her hostilit [illegible] inhabit the isthmus of Pallene,[2a] being a Corint [illegible] y allies of Athens, were ordered to raze the wall o [illegible] the city, to give hostages, to dismiss the Corint [illegible] future not to receive the persons sent from Corint [illegible] em.[2b] It was feared that they might be persuaded [illegible] Corinthians to revolt, and might draw the rest of [illegible] hrace[2d] to revolt with them.

1.57
433
CHALCIDICE
As Perdiccas plots with the Spartans, Chalcidians, and Bottiaeans, Athens sends a fleet to Macedonia.

The [illegible] he Potidaeans were taken by the Athenians immed [illegible] Corcyra. [2] Not only was Corinth at length openly [illegible] on of Alexander, king of the Macedonians, had fr [illegible] ly been made an enemy. [3] He had been made [illegible] ians entering into alliance with Philip his brother [illegible] e allied in opposition to him.[3a] [4] In his alarm [illegible] try and involve the Athenians in a war with the Pel [illegible] ndeavoring to win over Corinth in order to bring a [illegible] ea. [5] He also made overtures to the Chal-

1.55.1a A [illegible] 46, AX.
1.55.1b T [illegible] their [illegible] 7.13.2, [illegible] Warfare, [illegible]
1.55.2a T [illegible] o Cor- [illegible]
1.56.2a I [illegible] ne [illegible] BX.
1.56.2b T [illegible] strates [illegible] able comment on the nature of the Athenian Empire at that date.
1.56.2c Perdiccas was the king of Macedonia (Map 1.60, AX).
1.56.2d Thrace: Map 1.60, AY. The Athenians referred to the member states of their empire to the north of the Aegean as "the places in Thrace," though Thrace itself lay largely where Bulgaria is today.
1.57.3a Derdas is thought to have possibly been king of Elymiotis, in upper Macedonia.

cidians[5a] in Thrace, and to the Bottiaeans,[5b] to persuade them to join in the revolt; for he thought that if these places on the border could be made his allies, it would be easier to carry on the war with their cooperation. [6] Alive to all this, and wishing to anticipate the revolt of the cities, the Athenians acted as follows. They were just then sending off thirty ships and a thousand hoplites to Perdiccas' territory under the command of Archestratus son of Lycomedes, with four colleagues. They instructed those in command of the ships to take hostages of the Potidaeans, to raze the wall, and to be on their guard against the revolt of the neighboring cities.

1.58
433/2
CHALCIDICE
When Potidaea fails to placate Athens, and Sparta promises to invade Attica, Potidaea revolts. The Chalcidians move from their coastal cities to Olynthus.

Meanwhile the Potidaeans sent envoys to Athens on the chance of persuading them to take no new steps in regard to them; they also went to Sparta with the Corinthians to secure support in case of need. Failing after prolonged negotiation to obtain anything satisfactory from the Athenians; being unable, for all they could say, to prevent the vessels that were destined for Macedonia from also sailing against them; and receiving from the Spartan authorities a promise to invade Attica if the Athenians should attack Potidaea, the Potidaeans, thus favored by the moment, at last entered into league with the Chalcidians and Bottiaeans, and revolted. [2] And Perdiccas induced the Chalcidians[2a] to abandon and demolish their cities on the seaboard, and settling inland at Olynthus,[2b] to make that one city a strong place: meanwhile to those who followed his advice he gave a part of his territory in Mygdonia[2c] round Lake Bolbe[2d] as a place of abode while the war against the Athenians should last. They accordingly demolished their cities, moved inland, and prepared for war.

1.59
432
CHALCIDICE
The Athenian fleet attacks Macedon.

The thirty ships of the Athenians, arriving in the Thracian[1a] area, found Potidaea and the rest in revolt. [2] Their commanders considering it to be quite impossible with their present force to carry on war with Perdiccas, and with the confederate cities as well, turned to Macedonia, their original destination, and having established themselves there, carried on war in cooperation with Philip, and the brothers of Derdas, who had invaded the country from the interior.

1.60
432
CHALCIDICE
Corinth sends volunteers and mercenaries to Potidaea.

Meanwhile the Corinthians, with Potidaea in revolt and the Athenian ships on the coast of Macedonia, alarmed for the safety of the place, and thinking its danger theirs, sent volunteers from Corinth, and mercenaries from the rest of the Peloponnesus, to the number of sixteen hundred hoplites in all, and four hundred light troops. [2] Aristeus son of Adimantus, who was always a steady friend to the Potidaeans, took command of the expedition, and it was principally for love of him that most of the men from Corinth volunteered. They arrived in Thrace forty days after the revolt of Potidaea.

1.57.5a Chalcidice: Map 1.60, BY.
1.57.5b The Bottiaeans are believed to have then inhabited Bottica (Bottike) in central Chalcidice, as shown on Map 1.60, AX (Simon Hornblower, *A Commentary on Thucydides* [Oxford: Clarendon Press, 1991], 1:101).
1.58.2a The title of the Chalcidian League was "the Chalcidians," a term that Thucydides always employs save for one moment, after the Peace of Nicias, in which Athens sought the dissolution of the league (5.39.1).
1.58.2b Olynthus: Map 1.60, BX.
1.58.2c Mygdonia: Map 1.60, AX.
1.58.2d Lake Bolbe: Map 1.60, AY.
1.59.1a Thracian area: see note 1.56.2d.

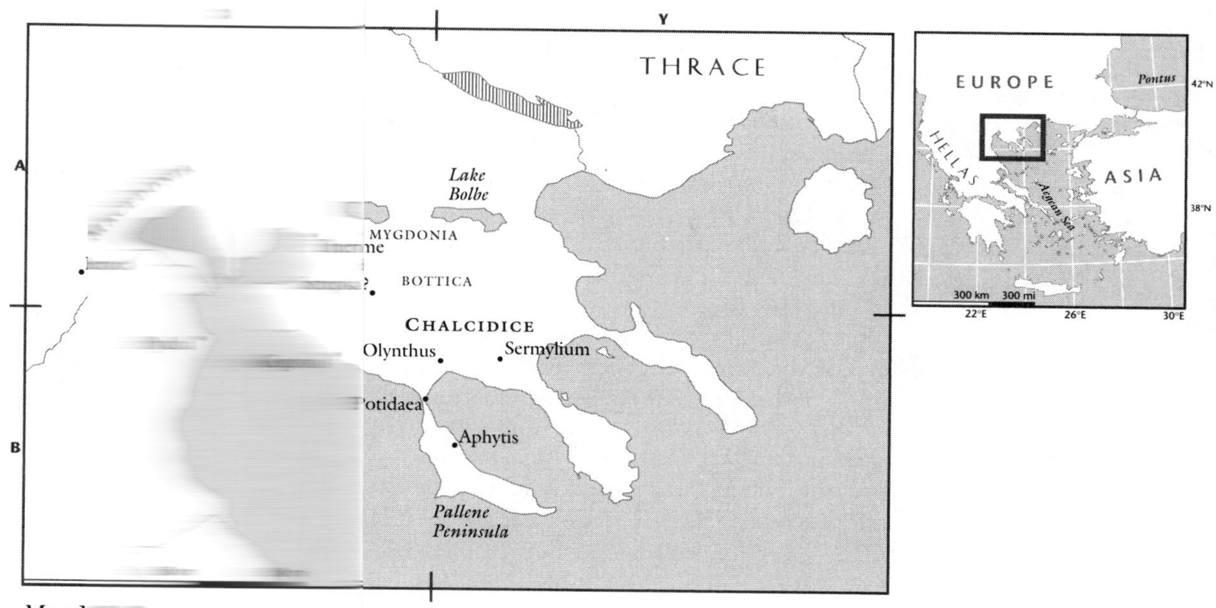

MAP

1.61
432
CHALCIDICE
The Athenians force Perdiccas to return to his alliance with them, and then march against Potidaea.

Th diately received the news of the revolt of the cities. hat Aristeus and his reinforcements were on their sand hoplites of their own citizens and forty ships lt, under the command of Callias son of Calliades] They arrived in Macedonia first, and found the fo that had been first sent out just become masters o g Pydna.[2c] [3] Accordingly they also joined in the in Pydna for a while. Subsequently they came to terms alliance with Perdiccas, hastened by the calls of Po val of Aristeus at that place. They withdrew from Beroea[4a] and thence to Strepsa,[4b] and, after a futile ce, they pursued by land their march to Potidaea lites of their own citizens, besides a number of th ed Macedonian horsemen, the followers of Philip these sailed seventy ships along the coast. Advar on the third day they arrived at Gigonus,[4c] where

1.61.2a were

1.61.2b

1.61.2c

1.61.4a

1.61.4b .60, AX.
s text

1.61.4c

1.62
432
CHALCIDICE
An indecisive battle occurs near Potidaea. Most Potidaeans retire inside their walls.

Meanwhile the Potidaeans and the Peloponnesians with Aristeus were encamped on the Olynthian[1a] side of the city on the isthmus, in expectation of the Athenians, and had established a market outside the city.[1b] [2] The allies had chosen Aristeus general of all the infantry; while the command of the cavalry was given to Perdiccas, who had now left the alliance of the Athenians and gone back to that of the Potidaeans, having deputed Iolaus as his general. [3] The plan of Aristeus was to keep his own force on the isthmus, and await the attack of the Athenians; leaving the Chalcidians and the allies outside the isthmus, and the two hundred cavalry from Perdiccas in Olynthus to act upon the Athenian rear, on the occasion of their advancing against him; and thus to place the enemy between two fires. [4] While Callias the Athenian general and his colleagues despatched the Macedonian horse and a few of the allies to Olynthus, to prevent any movement being made from that quarter, the Athenians themselves broke up their camp and marched against Potidaea. [5] After they had arrived at the isthmus, and saw the enemy preparing for battle, they formed against him, and soon afterwards engaged. [6] The wing of Aristeus, with the Corinthians and other picked troops round him, routed the wing opposed to it, and followed for a considerable distance in pursuit. But the rest of the army of the Potidaeans and of the Peloponnesians was defeated by the Athenians, and took refuge within the fortifications.

1.63
432
CHALCIDICE
Potidaean troops break through the Athenian lines and enter their city. Olynthian forces retire. Losses are enumerated.

Returning from the pursuit, Aristeus perceived the defeat of the rest of the army. Being at a loss which of the two risks to choose, whether to go to Olynthus or to Potidaea, he at last determined to draw his men into as small a space as possible, and force his way with a run into Potidaea. Not without difficulty, through a storm of missiles, he passed along by the breakwater through the sea, and brought off most of his men safe, though a few were lost. [2] Meanwhile the auxiliaries of the Potidaeans from Olynthus, which is about seven miles off, and in sight of Potidaea, when the battle began and the signals were raised, advanced a little way to render assistance; and the Macedonian horse formed against them to prevent it. But on victory speedily declaring for the Athenians and the signals being taken down, they retired back within the wall; and the Macedonians returned to the Athenians. Thus there were no cavalry present on either side. [3] After the battle the Athenians set up a trophy, and gave back their dead to the Potidaeans under truce.[3a] The Potidaeans and their allies had close upon three hundred killed; the Athenians a hundred and fifty of their own citizens, and Callias their general.

1.62.1a The northern side, toward Olynthus: Map 1.60, BX.

1.62.1b Greek soldiers and sailors at this time were expected to purchase their food from local markets with their own money, which made prompt disbursement of adequate military pay quite important. For a city to offer a special market at a convenient location for foreign military personnel was a polite and presumably profitable amenity, and it also helped to keep such "visitors" out of the city.

163.3a After a battle in ancient Greece, the victors would gather up their own dead, strip those of the enemy, and raise a trophy. The defeated would collect the bodies of their fallen during a truce that they explicitly requested and were granted for that purpose. In this way, appropriate reverence was shown and proper burial was accorded to all war dead. See Appendix F, Land Warfare, §6.

1.64
432
CHALCIDICE
Athenian reinforcements under Phormio complete the investment of Potidaea.

Th[illegible] the isthmus now had works at once raised agains[illegible] Athenians. That on the side of Pallene[1a] had no wo[illegible]y did not think themselves strong enough at once t[illegible]e isthmus, and to cross over to Pallene and raise w[illegible]raid that the Potidaeans and their allies might take a[illegible]n to attack them. [2] Meanwhile the Athenians at [illegible]e were no works at Pallene, sometime afterwards [illegible]d hoplites of their own citizens under the comm[illegible]Asopius. Arrived at Pallene, he fixed his headquarte[illegible] his army against Potidaea by short marches, ravagi[illegible]anced. No one venturing to meet him in the field, [illegible] the wall on the side of Pallene. [3] So at length [illegible]nvested on either side, and from the sea by the shi[illegible]ockade.

1.65
432
CHALCIDICE
The siege of Potidaea commences.

Ari[illegible]ent complete, and having no hope of its salvation [illegible] some movement from the Peloponnesus, or of son[illegible]ntingency, advised all except five hundred to watch [illegible]t of the place, in order that their provisions might [illegible]as willing to be himself one of those who remai[illegible]e them, and desirous of acting on the next altern[illegible]ngs outside in the best posture possible, he elude[illegible]e Athenians and sailed out. [2] Remaining amon[illegible]ntinued to carry on the war; in particular he set up [illegible]ty of the Sermylians,[2a] and cut off many of them; [illegible]with the Peloponnesus, and tried to contrive some [illegible]night be brought. Meanwhile, after the completio[illegible]Potidaea, Phormio next employed his sixteen hundr[illegible]alcidice and Bottica;[2b] some of the cities also were t[illegible]

1.66
432
HELLAS
Athens and Corinth complain much about Potidaea, yet there is still peace.

Th[illegible]onnesians had these antecedent grounds of compl[illegible]r: the complaint of Corinth was that her colon[illegible]nthian and Peloponnesian citizens within it, was b[illegible]Athens against the Peloponnesians that they had i[illegible] in their alliance and liable for tribute, to revolt[illegible]ne and were openly fighting against her on the si[illegible]r all this, war had not yet broken out: there was st[illegible] this was a private enterprise on the part of Corint[illegible]

1.64.1a [illegible]e the [illegible]ıla, Map [illegible]
1.64.2a [illegible]
1.65.2a [illegible]
1.65.2b [illegible]

1.67
432/1[1a]
SPARTA
Many cities denounce Athens to the allies assembled at Sparta. The Corinthians speak last.

But the siege of Potidaea put an end to her inaction; she had men inside it: besides, she feared for the place. Immediately summoning the allies to Sparta, she came and loudly accused Athens of breach of the treaty and aggression on the rights of the Peloponnesus. [2] With her, the Aeginetans, formally unrepresented from fear of Athens, in secret proved not the least urgent of the advocates for war, asserting that they had not the independence guaranteed to them by the treaty. [3] After extending the summons to any of their allies and others who might have complaints to make of Athenian aggression, the Spartans held their ordinary assembly,[3a] and invited them to speak. [4] There were many who came forward and made their several accusations; among them the Megarians, in a long list of grievances, called special attention to the fact of their exclusion from the ports of the Athenian empire and the market of Athens, in defiance of the treaty.[4a] [5] Last of all the Corinthians came forward, and having let those who preceded them inflame the Spartans, now followed with a speech to this effect:

1.68
432/1
SPARTA
The Corinthians complain of Athenian aggression against them at Corcyra and Potidaea, and also of Spartan inaction, which both injures Sparta's allies and strengthens Sparta's rival.

"Spartans! the confidence which you feel in your constitution and social order inclines you to receive any reflections of ours on other powers with a certain skepticism. Hence springs your moderation, but hence also the rather limited knowledge which you betray in dealing with foreign politics. [2] Time after time was our voice raised to warn you of the blows about to be dealt us by Athens, and time after time, instead of taking the trouble to ascertain the worth of our warnings, you contented yourselves with suspecting the speakers of being inspired by private interest. And so, instead of calling these allies together before the blow fell, you have delayed to do so till we are smarting under it; and of the allies it is not unfitting that we make this speech for we have very great complaints of high-handed treatment by the Athenians and of neglect by you. [3] Now if these assaults on the rights of Hellas had been made in the dark you might be unacquainted with the facts, and it would be our duty to enlighten you. As it is, long speeches are not needed where you see servitude accomplished for some of us, meditated for others—in particular for our allies—and prolonged preparations by the aggressor for the hour of war. [4] Or what, pray, is the meaning of their reception of Corcyra by fraud, and their holding it against us by force? What of the siege of Potidaea?—places one of which lies most conveniently for any action against the Thracian cities; while the other would have contributed a very large navy to the Peloponnesians?"

1.67.1a The Hellenic year began in the middle of our calendar year, and so "432/1," for example, is used to cover the winter period comprising the latter part of the year 432 and the initial part of the year 431.

1.67.3a Assembly: see Appendix C, Spartan Institutions, §6.

1.67.4a The precise date of the Megara Decree is uncertain (see note at 1.42.2a), as also is the way in which it was thought to infringe the Thirty Years' Peace. See also Appendix B, The Athenian Empire, §10.

1.69
432/1
SPARTA
The Corinthians assert that Spartan inaction has permitted Athens to grow at the expense of the Hellenes, and that Athens' perception of Sparta's acquiescence encourages her to commit further aggression. Once the Spartans could have stopped her easily, but Athens has now become such a formidable adversary that Hellenic confidence in Sparta is shaken.

esponsible. You it was who first allowed
the after the Persian war,[1a] and afterwards to
ere who, then and now, are always depriving
of whom they have enslaved, but also those
wh allies. For the true author of the subjuga-
tio much the immediate agent, as the power
wh e means to prevent it; particularly if that
po of being the liberator of Hellas. We are at
las not been easy to assemble, nor even now
are 'e ought not to be still inquiring into the
fac into the means for our defense. For the
ag lans to oppose to our indecision have cast
thr themselves to action. [3] And we know
wh ch Athenian aggression travels, and how
ins degree of confidence she may feel from
the ess of perception prevents your noticing
her e impulse which her advance will receive
fro you see, but do not care to interfere. [4]
Yo Hellenes are alone inactive, and defend
you ything but by looking as if you would do
so till the power of an enemy is becoming
twi ead of crushing it in its infancy. [5] And
yet hat you were to be depended upon; but in
you more than the truth. The Mede,[5a] we our-
sel come from the ends of the earth to the
Pel y force of yours worthy of the name
adv ut this was a distant enemy. Well, Athens
at bor, and yet Athens you utterly disregard;
aga to act on the defensive instead of on the
off n affair of chances by deferring the struggle stronger than at first. And yet you know
tha on which the barbarian was wrecked was
hin present enemy Athens has not again and
aga we it more to her blunders than to your
pro xpectations from you have before now
bee hose faith induced them to omit prepara-
tio

you will consider these words of remon-
str of hostility; men remonstrate with friends
wh ons they reserve for enemies who have
wr

1.69.1a "let" er the

1.69.5a The Greeks regularly referred to the Persians as "the Mede"; see note 1.18.1c.

1.70
432/1
SPARTA
The Corinthians characterize the Athenians and the Spartans as opposites: where the Athenians are active, innovative, daring, quick, enterprising, acquisitive, and opportunistic, the Spartans are passive, cautious, conservative, timid, and slow. The Athenians take no rest and allow none to others.

"Besides, we consider that we have as good a right as anyone to point out a neighbor's faults, particularly when we contemplate the great contrast between the two national characters; a contrast of which, as far as we can see, you have little perception, having never yet considered what sort of antagonists you will encounter in the Athenians, how widely, how absolutely different from yourselves. [2] The Athenians are addicted to innovation, and their designs are characterized by swiftness alike in conception and execution; you have a genius for keeping what you have got, accompanied by a total want of invention, and when forced to act you never go far enough. [3] Again, they are adventurous beyond their power, and daring beyond their judgment, and in danger they are sanguine; your wont is to attempt less than is justified by your power, to mistrust even what is sanctioned by your judgment, and to fancy that from danger there is no release. [4] Further, there is promptitude on their side against procrastination on yours; they are never at home, you are most disinclined to leave it, for they hope by their absence to extend their acquisitions, you fear by your advance to endanger what you have left behind. [5] They are swift to follow up a success, and slow to recoil from a reverse. [6] Their bodies they spend ungrudgingly in their country's cause; their intellect they jealously husband to be employed in her service. [7] A scheme unexecuted is with them a positive loss, a successful enterprise a comparative failure. The deficiency created by the miscarriage of an undertaking is soon filled up by fresh hopes; for they alone are enabled to call a thing hoped for a thing got, by the speed with which they act upon their resolutions. [8] Thus they toil on in trouble and danger all the days of their life, with little opportunity for enjoying, being ever engaged in getting: their only idea of a holiday is to do what the occasion demands, and to them laborious occupation is less of a misfortune than the peace of a quiet life. [9] To describe their character in a word, one might truly say that they were born into the world to take no rest themselves and to give none to others."

1.71
432/1
SPARTA
The Corinthians conclude by blaming Sparta's old-fashioned ways for her failure to perceive the effectiveness of Athenian innovation. They beg Sparta "to assist Potidaea now as she had promised." They threaten to seek another alliance if the Spartans continue to fail them.

"Such is Athens, your antagonist. And yet, Spartans, you still delay, and fail to see that peace stays longest with those who are not more careful to use their power justly than to show their determination not to submit to injustice. On the contrary, your ideal of fair dealing is based on the principle that if you do not injure others, you need not risk your own fortunes in preventing others from injuring you. [2] Now you could scarcely have succeeded in such a policy even with a neighbor like yourselves; but in the present instance, as we have just shown, your habits are old-fashioned as compared with theirs. [3] It is the law, as in the arts so in politics, that improvements ever prevail; and though fixed usages may be best for undisturbed communities, co[illegible]tion must be accompanied by the constant in[illegible] Thus it happens that the vast experience of A[illegible]ther than you on the path of innovation."

[illegible] your procrastination end. For the present, as[illegible]idaea in particular, as you promised, by a sp[illegible] and do not sacrifice friends and kindred to th[illegible]nd drive the rest of us in despair to some o[illegible]a step would not be condemned either by th[illegible]our oaths, or by the men who witnessed th[illegible]reach of a treaty cannot be laid on the peo- p[illegible]pels to seek new relations, but on the power th[illegible]ederate. [6] But if only you will act, we will st[illegible] be unnatural for us to change, and never sh[illegible]ch a congenial ally. [7] For these reasons c[illegible] and endeavor not to let the Peloponnesus u[illegible]egenerate from the prestige that it enjoyed u[illegible]ors."

1.72
432/1
SPARTA
Some Athenian envoys at Sparta ask for permission to address the assembly; it is granted.

S[illegible]the Corinthians. There happened to be Athen- ian [illegible]a on other business. On hearing the speeches they[illegible]lled upon to come before the Spartans. Their inte[illegible] defense on any of the charges which the cities brou[illegible] show on a comprehensive view that it was not a ma[illegible]d on, but one that demanded further consider- atio[illegible] to call attention to the great power of Athens, and [illegible] of the old and enlighten the ignorance of the you[illegible] their words might have the effect of inducing the[illegible]to war. [2] So they came to the Spartans and said[illegible] was no objection, wished to speak to their asse[illegible]nviting them to come forward. The Athenians adv[illegible]ws:

1.73
432/1
SPARTA
The Athenians hope to show that their country merits consideration for its achievements, particularly in the Persian wars in which all Hellenes benefited from extraordinary and courageous Athenian efforts.

[illegible]ssion here was not to argue with your allies, b[illegible]ers on which our state despatched us. How- e[illegible]the outcry that we hear against us has pre- v[illegible]ward. It is not to combat the accusations of t[illegible]e not the judges before whom either we or t[illegible] prevent your taking the wrong course on r[illegible]nce by yielding too readily to the persuasions c[illegible]sh to show on a review of the whole indict- r[illegible] title to our possessions, and that our coun- t[illegible]leration. [2] We need not refer to remote a[illegible]l appeal to the voice of tradition, but not to t[illegible]dience. But to the Persian wars and contemporary history we must refer, although we are rather tired of continually bringing this subject forward. In our action during that war we ran great risk to obtain certain advantages: you had your share in the solid results, do not try to rob us of all share in the good that the glory may do us. [3] However, the story shall be told not so much to seek to be spared hostility as to testify against it, and to show, if you are so ill-advised as to enter into a struggle with Athens, what sort of an antagonist she is likely to prove. [4] We assert that at Marathon[4a] we were in the forefront of danger and faced the barbarian by ourselves. That when he came the second time, unable to cope with him by land we went on board our ships with all our people, and joined in the action at Salamis.[4b] This prevented his taking the Peloponnesians city by city, and ravaging them with his fleet; when the multitude of his vessels would have made any combination for self-defense impossible. [5] The best proof of this was furnished by the invader himself. Defeated at sea, he considered his power to be no longer what it had been, and retired as speedily as possible with the greater part of his army."

1.74
432/1
SPARTA
The Athenians claim to have provided the most powerful and essential contributions to the Hellenic success at Salamis, which proved to be the decisive blow to the Persian advance. They remind the Spartans that they courageously abandoned their homes and fought on even before the Peloponnesians arrived to help.

"Such, then, was the result of the matter, and it was clearly proved that it was on the fleet of Hellas that her cause depended. Well, to this result we contributed three very useful elements, namely, the largest number of ships, the ablest commander, and the most unhesitating patriotism. Our contingent of ships was little less than two-thirds of the whole four hundred; the commander was Themistocles, through whom chiefly it was that the battle took place in the straits,[1a] the acknowledged salvation of our cause. Indeed, this was the reason for your receiving him with honors such as had never been accorded to any foreign visitor. [2] While for daring patriotism we had no competitors. Receiving no reinforcements from behind, seeing everything in front of us already subjugated, we had the spirit, after abandoning our city, after sacrificing our property (instead of deserting the remainder of the league or depriving them of our services by dispersing), to throw ourselves into our ships and meet the danger, without a thought of resenting your having neglected to assist us. [3] We assert, therefore, that we conferred on you quite as much as we received. For you had a stake to fight for; the cities which you had left were still filled with your homes, and you had the prospect of enjoying them again; and your coming was prompted quite as much by fear for yourselves as for us; at all events, you never appeared till we had nothing left to lose. But we left behind us a city that was a city no longer, and staked our lives for a city that had an existence

1.73.4a The battle of Marathon in 490: Map 1.11, BX.
1.73.4b Salamis, site of the decisive naval battle between Greeks and Persians in 480: Map 1.11, BX.
1.74.1a The Straits of Salamis where the fighting took place: Map 1.11, BX. For more about Themistocles, see 1.90.3–1.93 and 1.135.2–1.138.6.

on[illegible]d so bore our full share in your deliverance anc[illegible] had copied others, and allowed fears for ou[illegible]o over to the Mede before you came, or if we[illegible] break our spirit and prevent us embarking in [illegible] inferiority would have made a sea fight un[illegible]s would have been peaceably attained."

1.75
432/1
SPARTA
The Athenians claim that Athens acquired her empire peacefully, honorably, and by the default of Sparta; now it cannot be given up without risk. No state can be faulted for pursuing its own interest.

[illegible]er by the patriotism that we displayed at tha[illegible]sdom of our counsels, do we merit our ext[illegible] the Hellenes, not at least unpopularity for ou[illegible]ipire we acquired not by violence, but be[illegible]g to prosecute to its conclusion the war aga[illegible] because the allies attached themselves to us [illegible]d us to assume the command. [3] And the na[illegible]ompelled us to advance our empire to its pr[illegible] our principal motive, though honor and int[illegible]. [4] And at last, when almost all hated us, wh[illegible]volted and had been subdued, when you ha[illegible]nds that you once were, and had become ob[illegible]slike, it appeared no longer safe to give up ou[illegible] who left us would fall to you. [5] And no on[illegible]ople for making, in matters of tremendous ris[illegible]t it can for its interest."

1.76
432/1
SPARTA
The Athenians argue that Athens acted normally within the common practices of mankind to maintain her empire; fear, honor, and interest motivate her as they would any others in her place. Indeed, she deserves praise for acting with greater justice and moderation than her power would require.

[illegible]rtans, have used your supremacy to settle th[illegible]esus as is agreeable to you. And if at the pe[illegible]speaking you had persevered to the end of th[illegible]red hatred in your command, we are sure th[illegible] yourselves just as galling to the allies, and wo[illegible] choose between a strong government and da[illegible]t follows that it was not a very remarkable ac[illegible] common practice of mankind, if we did ac[illegible]s offered to us, and refused to give it up un[illegible]e of the strongest motives, fear, honor, and int[illegible]we who set the example, for it has always be[illegible]eaker should be subject to the stronger. Be[illegible]elves to be worthy of our position, and so yo[illegible]hen calculations of interest have made you tal[illegible]—a consideration which no one ever yet br[illegible]er his ambition when he had a chance of ga[illegible]. [3] And praise is due to all who, if not so su[illegible] as to refuse dominion, yet respect justice m[illegible]ompels them to do."

[4] "We imagine that our moderation would be best demonstrated by the conduct of who should be placed in our position; but even our equity has very unreasonably subjected us to condemnation instead of approval."

1.77
432/1
SPARTA
The Athenians speculate that Sparta would be equally hated were she to take Athens' place, and perhaps more so, because her peculiar institutions render her people unfit to rule other Hellenes.

"Our abatement of our rights in the contract trials with our allies, and our causing them to be decided by impartial laws at Athens, have gained us the character of being litigious. [2] And none care to inquire why this reproach is not brought against other imperial powers, who treat their subjects with less moderation than we do; the secret being that where force can be used, law is not needed. [3] But our subjects are so habituated to associate with us as equals, that any defeat whatever that clashes with their notions of justice, whether it proceeds from a legal judgment or from the power which our empire gives us, makes them forget to be grateful for being allowed to retain most of their possessions, and more vexed at a part being taken, than if we had from the first cast law aside and openly gratified our covetousness. If we had done so, they would not have disputed that the weaker must give way to the stronger. [4] Men's indignation, it seems, is more excited by legal wrong than by violent wrong; the first looks like being cheated by an equal, the second like being compelled by a superior. [5] At all events they contrived to put up with much worse treatment than this from the Persians, yet they think our rule severe, and this is to be expected, for the present always weighs heavy on the conquered. This at least is certain. [6] If you were to succeed in overthrowing us and in taking our place, you would speedily lose the popularity with which fear of us has invested you, if your policy now were to be at all like the sample you gave during the brief period of your command against the Mede. Not only is your life at home regulated by rules and institutions incompatible with those of others, but your citizens abroad act neither on these rules nor on those which are recognized by the rest of Hellas."

1.78
432/1
SPARTA
In conclusion, the Athenians advise the Spartans to decide carefully, reminding them of the chances of war and noting that the treaty calls for disputes to be submitted to arbitration.

"Take time then in forming your resolution, as the matter is of great importance; and do not be persuaded by the opinions and complaints of others and so bring trouble on yourselves, but consider the vast influence of accident in war, before you are engaged in it. [2] As it continues, it generally becomes an affair of chances, chances from which neither of us is exempt, and whose event we must risk in the dark. [3] It is a common mistake in going to war to begin at the wrong end, to act first, and wait for disaster to discuss the matter. [4] But we are not yet by any means so misguided, nor, so far as we can see, are you; accordingly, while it is still open to us both to choose aright, we bid you not to dissolve the treaty, or to break your oaths, but to have our differences settled by arbitration according to our ag[illegible]e the gods who heard the oaths to witness, ar[illegible]es, whatever line of action you choose, we w[illegible]urselves against you.”

1.79
432/1
SPARTA
The Spartans declare the Athenians to be aggressors.

S[illegible]e Athenians. After the Spartans had heard the com[illegible]st the Athenians, and the observations of the latte[illegible], and consulted by themselves on the question befo[illegible]ns of the majority all led to the same conclusion; [illegible]pen aggressors, and war must be declared at once[illegible]partan king, who had the reputation of being at o[illegible]e man, came forward and made the following spee[illegible]

1.80
432/1
SPARTA
The Spartan king, Archidamus, warns the Spartans that Athens is a powerful adversary with many advantages in war. He advises them to prepare carefully for such a struggle and not to act rashly.

[illegible]ng, Spartans, without having had the experi[illegible] I see those among you of the same age as m[illegible]nto the common misfortune of longing for w[illegible]from a belief in its advantage and its safety. [[illegible]ch you are now debating, would be one of th[illegible]on a sober consideration of the matter. [3] I[illegible]onnesians and neighbors our strength is of th[illegible] is possible to move swiftly on the different p[illegible]h a people who live in a distant land, who h[illegible] familiarity with the sea, and who are in the h[illegible]on in every other department; with wealth p[illegible]hips, and horses, and hoplites, and a population [illegible]ther Hellenic place can equal, and lastly a la[illegible] allies—what can justify us in rashly beginn[illegible]erein is our trust that we should rush on it u[illegible]ur ships? There we are inferior; while if we a[illegible]e a match for them, time must intervene. Is it[illegible]ve have a far greater deficiency. We neither h[illegible]nor are we ready to contribute it from our p[illegible]

1.81
432/1
SPARTA
Archidamus points out that Sparta can only devastate Attica, which will not harm Athens materially. He warns that the war will not be short, and wonders aloud how Sparta can win.

[illegible]ossibly be felt in our superiority in hoplites a[illegible]will enable us to invade and devastate their l[illegible]enians have plenty of other land in their e[illegible]what they want by sea. [3] Again, if we are t[illegible]n of their allies, these will have to be supp[illegible]of them being islanders. [4] What then is to b[illegible]we can either beat them at sea, or deprive t[illegible]ich feed their navy, we shall meet with little b[illegible]hile our honor will be pledged to keeping c[illegible]he opinion that we began the quarrel. [6]

For let us never be elated by the fatal hope of the war being quickly ended by the devastation of their lands. I fear rather that we may leave it as a legacy to our children; so improbable is it that the Athenian spirit will be the slave of their land, or Athenian experience be cowed by war."

1.82
432/1
SPARTA
Archidamus advises Sparta to continue discussions with Athens and to use the time thus gained to gather allies and to develop its resources for war. Such preparations might induce the Athenians to submit, but if not, Sparta will enter the war much strengthened.

"Not that I would bid you be so unfeeling as to suffer them to injure your allies, and to refrain from unmasking their intrigues; but I do bid you not to take up arms at once, but to send and remonstrate with them in a tone not too suggestive of war, nor again too suggestive of submission, and to employ the interval in perfecting our own preparations. The means will be, first, the acquisition of allies, Hellenic or barbarian it matters not, so long as they are an accession to our strength naval or financial—I say Hellenic or barbarian, because the odium of such an accession to all who like us are the objects of the designs of the Athenians is taken away by the law of self-preservation[1a]—and secondly the development of our home resources. [2] If they listen to our embassy, so much the better; but if not, after the lapse of two or three years our position will have become materially strengthened, and we can then attack them if we think proper. [3] Perhaps by that time the sight of our preparations, backed by language equally significant, will have disposed them to submission, while their land is still untouched, and while their counsels may be directed to the retention of advantages as yet undestroyed. [4] For the only light in which you can view their land is that of a hostage in your hands, a hostage the more valuable the better it is cultivated. This you ought to spare as long as possible, and not make them desperate, and so increase the difficulty of dealing with them. [5] For if while still unprepared, hurried on by the complaints of our allies, we are induced to lay it waste, have a care that we do not bring deep disgrace and deep perplexity upon the Peloponnesus. [6] Complaints, whether of communities or individuals, it is possible to adjust; but war undertaken by a coalition for sectional interests, whose progress there is no means of foreseeing, may not be easily or creditably settled."

1.83
432/1
SPARTA
Archidamus asserts that Sparta must accumulate money for a war with Athens.

"And none need think it cowardice for a large number of confederates to pause before they attack a single city. [2] The Athenians have allies as numerous as our own, and allies that pay tribute, and war is a matter not so much of arms as of money, which makes arms of use. And this is more than ever true in a struggle between a continental and a maritime power. [3] First, then, let us provide money, and not allow ourselves to be carried away by the talk of our allies before we have done so: as we shall have the largest share of respon-

1.82.1a Archidamus here proposes an approach to Persia for aid against Athens. For more on early diplomatic contacts between Sparta and Persia, see 2.7.1, 2.67.1, and 4.50.2.

sil[illegible]ces be they good or bad, we have also a rig[illegible] respecting them.”

1.84
432/1
SPARTA
Archidamus tells Sparta to ignore her allies' impatient calls for action and to move slowly and moderately. He praises Spartan character, a product of practical, limited education, and adds that Sparta traditionally assumes that her adversaries will plan wisely and not blunder.

[illegible] procrastination, the parts of our character th[illegible]heir criticism, need not make you blush. If we[illegible]hout preparation, we should by hastening its [illegible]delay its conclusion: further, a free and a fa[illegible]all time been ours. [2] The quality which th[illegible]thing but a wise moderation; thanks to its po[illegible]ot become insolent in success and give way les[illegible]une; we are not carried away by the plea-su[illegible] cheered on to risks which our judgment co[illegible]ed, are we any the more convinced by att[illegible]by accusation. [3] We are both warlike and wi[illegible]of order that makes us so. We are warlike, be[illegible]ns honor as a chief constituent, and honor br[illegible], because we are educated with too little lea[illegible]s, and with too severe a self-control to dis-ob[illegible]ght up not to be too knowing in useless ma[illegible]wledge which can give a specious criticism of[illegible]ory, but fails to assail them with equal suc-ce[illegible]aught to consider that the schemes of our en[illegible] to our own, and that the freaks of chance ar[illegible]calculation. [4] In practice we always base ou[illegible]n enemy on the assumption that his plans ar[illegible]ht to rest our hopes not on a belief in his bl[illegible]dness of our provisions. Nor ought we to be[illegible] difference between man and man, but to th[illegible]lies with him who is reared in the severest sch[illegible]

1.85
432/1
SPARTA
Archidamus concludes that the Spartans must decide calmly. He reminds them that Athens offers arbitration, but asks them to continue to prepare for war.

[illegible] which our ancestors have delivered to us, an[illegible]ce we have always profited, must not be gi[illegible]ot be hurried into deciding in a day's brief sp[illegible]ncerns many lives and fortunes and many cit[illegible]r is deeply involved—but we must decide cal[illegible]peculiarly enables us to do. [2] As for the At[illegible] on the matter of Potidaea, send on the ma[illegible]ongs of the allies, particularly as they are pr[illegible]rs to arbitration, for one should not pro-ce[illegible] offers arbitration as one would against a wr[illegible] not omit preparation for war. This deci-sio[illegible] yourselves and the most terrible to your op[illegible]

[3] Such were the words of Archidamus. Last came forward Sthenelaidas, one of the *ephors*[3a] for that year, and spoke to the Spartans as follows:

1.86
432/1
SPARTA
The Spartan ephor Sthenelaidas demands a declaration of war against Athens.

"The long speech of the Athenians I do not pretend to understand. They said a good deal in praise of themselves, but nowhere denied that they are injuring our allies and the Peloponnesus. And yet if they behaved well against the Persians in the past, but ill toward us now, they deserve double punishment for having ceased to be good and for having become bad. [2] We meanwhile are the same then and now, and shall not, if we are wise, disregard the wrongs of our allies, or put off till tomorrow the duty of assisting those who must suffer today. [3] Others have much money and ships and horses, but we have good allies whom we must not give up to the Athenians, nor by lawsuits and words decide the matter, as it is anything but in word that we are harmed, but render instant and powerful help. [4] And let us not be told that it is fitting for us to deliberate under injustice; long deliberation is rather fitting for those who have injustice in contemplation. [5] Vote therefore, Spartans, for war, as the honor of Sparta demands, and neither allow the further aggrandizement of Athens, nor betray our allies to ruin, but with the gods let us advance against the aggressors."

1.87
432/1
SPARTA
The Spartans vote by acclamation to declare war and to convene a decisive meeting of all their allies.

With these words he, as ephor, himself put the question to the assembly of the Spartans. [2] He said that he could not determine which was the loudest acclamation (their mode of decision is by acclamation, not by voting); the fact being that he wished to make them declare their opinion openly and thus to increase their ardor for war. Accordingly he said, "All Spartans who are of opinion that the treaty has been broken, and that Athens is guilty, leave your seats and go there," pointing out a certain place; "all who are of the opposite opinion, there." [3] They accordingly stood up and divided; and those who held that the treaty had been broken were in a decided majority. [4] Summoning the allies, they told them that their opinion was that Athens had been guilty of injustice, but that they wished to convoke all the allies and put it to the vote; in order that they might make war, if they decided to do so, on a common resolution.[4a] [5] Having thus gained their point, the delegates returned home at once; the Athenian envoys a little later, when they had dispatched the objects of their mission. [6] This decision of the assembly[6a] judging that the treaty had been broken, was made in the fourteenth year of the Thirty Years' Peace,[6b] which was entered into after the affair of Euboea.[6c]

1.85.3a Spartan *ephors* were powerful government officials; see Appendix C, Sparta, §5–6.
1.87.4a See Appendix D, The Peloponnesian League, §5, for the League congress.
1.87.6a See Appendix C, Spartan Institutions, §6.
1.87.6b The Thirty Years' Peace was sworn in 446/5, which dates this assembly to 432/1.
1.87.6c The "affair" of Euboea refers to its revolt from Athens, described by Thucydides in 1.114.1. See Appendix K, Calendars and Dating Systems, §2–3.

T[illegible] the treaty had been broken, and that war must be d[illegible]cause they were persuaded by the arguments of the a[illegible]red the growth of the power of the Athenians, seei[illegible] subject to them.

1.88
431
SPARTA
Fearing Athen's growing power, Sparta votes for war.

T[illegible] came to be placed in the circumstances under whic[illegible]this. [2] After the Persians had returned from Eur[illegible] land by the Hellenes, and after those of them who[illegible] to Mycale[2a] had been destroyed, Leotychides, king[illegible]mmander of the Hellenes at Mycale, departed hom[illegible]he Peloponnesus. But the Athenians and the allies[illegible]spont,[2c] who had now revolted from the King, rema[illegible] Sestos,[2d] which was still held by the Persians. After[illegible]ey became masters of the place on its evacuation [illegible] after this they sailed away from Hellespont to their[illegible]eanwhile the Athenian people, after the departure [illegible]heir country, at once proceeded to bring over their[illegible] such property as they had left, from the places wher[illegible]em, and prepared to rebuild their city and their walls[illegible]ons of the circumference had been left standing, [illegible]were in ruins; though a few remained, in which the I[illegible]en up their quarters.

1.89
479/8
PENTECONTAETIA[1a]
HELLESPONT
Thucydides tells how Athens grew powerful after Persia's defeat.

P[illegible] going to do, the Spartans sent an embassy to Athe[illegible]emselves preferred to see neither her nor any othe[illegible] wall; though here they acted principally at the insti[illegible]o were alarmed at the strength of her newly acqu[illegible] which she had displayed in the war with the Persi[illegible]er not only to abstain from building walls for hers[illegible] in throwing down the remaining walls of the cities[illegible]us. They did not express openly the suspicious inten[illegible] Athenians that lay behind this proposal but urge[illegible]he barbarians, in the case of a third invasion, woul[illegible] place, such as in this invasion he had in Thet[illegible]ration; and that the Peloponnesus would suffice f[illegible] retreat and offense. [3] After the Spartans had thus [illegible] the advice of Themistocles, immediately dismiss[illegible]h the answer that ambassadors should be sent to Sp[illegible]tion. Themistocles told the Athenians to send him [illegible]edaemon, but not to despatch his colleagues as soon[illegible]em, but to wait until they had raised their wall to th[illegible]ense was possible. Meanwhile the whole popu-

1.90
479/8
ATHENS
Sparta asks Athens not to rebuild its city wall. Themistocles goes to Sparta to discuss the matter and to delay a Spartan response while the Athenians hastily build a new city wall.

1.89.1a [illegible] com- [illegible] contae- [illegible] ek for [illegible] period [illegible] Persians [illegible] nmence- [illegible] in 431.

1.89.2a The Greek victory at Mycale (near Mt. Mycale, Map 1.99, BY) took place in 479.
1.89.2b Ionia: Map 1.99, BY.
1.89.2c Hellespont: Map 1.99, AY.
1.89.2d Sestos: Map 1.99, AY.
1.90.2a Thebes: Map 1.99, BX.

lation in the city was to labor at the wall, the Athenians, their wives, and their children, sparing no edifice, private or public, which might be of any use to the work, but throwing all down. [4] After giving these instructions, and adding that he would be responsible for all other matters there, he departed. [5] Arrived at Sparta he did not seek an audience with the magistrates, but tried to gain time and made excuses. When any of the authorities asked him why he did not appear in the assembly, he would say that he was waiting for his colleagues, who had been detained in Athens by some engagement; however, that he expected their speedy arrival, and wondered that they were yet there.

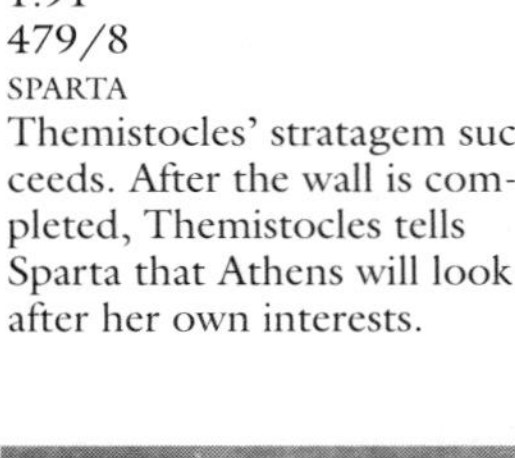

1.91
479/8
SPARTA
Themistocles' stratagem succeeds. After the wall is completed, Themistocles tells Sparta that Athens will look after her own interests.

At first the Spartans trusted the words of Themistocles, through their friendship for him; but when others arrived, all distinctly declaring that the work was going on and already attaining some elevation, they could not fail to believe them. [2] Aware of this, he told them that rumors are deceptive, and should not be trusted; they should send some reputable persons from Sparta to inspect, whose report might be trusted. [3] They despatched them accordingly. Concerning these Themistocles secretly sent word to the Athenians to detain them as far as possible without putting them under open constraint, and not to let them go until they had themselves returned. For his colleagues had now joined him, Abronichus son of Lysicles, and Aristides son of Lysimachus, with the news that the wall was sufficiently advanced; and he feared that when the Spartans heard the facts, they might refuse to let them go. [4] So the Athenians detained the envoys according to his message, and Themistocles had an audience with the Spartans and at last openly told them that Athens was now fortified sufficiently to protect its inhabitants; that any embassy which the Spartans or their allies might wish to send to them should in future proceed on the assumption that the people to whom they were going was able to distinguish both its own and the general interests; [5] that when the Athenians thought fit to abandon their city and to embark in their ships, they ventured on that perilous step without consulting them, and that on the other hand, wherever they had deliberated with the Spartans, they had proved themselves to be in judgment second to none; [6] and that they now thought it fit that their city should have a wall, and that this would be more for the advantage of both the citizens of Athens and the Hellenic confederacy, [7] for without equal military strength it was impossible to contribute equal or fair counsel to the common interest. It followed, he observed, either that all the members of the confederacy should be without walls, or that the present step should be considered a right one.[7a]

ILLUSTRATION 1.90
BUST OF THEMISTOCLES
(A ROMAN COPY, POSSIBLY OF A GREEK ORIGINAL)

1.91.7a It might be noted here that Sparta, alone among important Greek cities, had no defensive wall in 479.

1.92
478
SPARTA
Sparta accepts the Athenian wall with outward grace but secret annoyance.

Th[illegible]y any open signs of anger against the Athenians at [illegible] embassy, it seems, was prompted not by a
desire [illegible]de the counsels of their government: besides,
Sparta [illegible]ne very friendly toward Athens on account of
the pa[illegible] displayed in the struggle with the Mede. Still
the de[illegible]d not but cause them secret annoyance. The
envoy[illegible]home without complaint.

1.93
478
ATHENS
Themistocles fortifies the Piraeus, foreseeing that Athens would grow great through naval power.

In [illegible]walled their city in a short space of time. [2]
To thi[illegible] signs of the haste of its execution; the foundation[illegible]ll kinds, and in some places not wrought or
fitted, [illegible]rder in which they were brought by the different [illegible]nns, too, from tombs and sculptured stones
were [illegible]or the bounds of the city were extended at
every [illegible]ence; and so they laid hands on everything
witho[illegible]te. [3] Themistocles also persuaded them to
finish [illegible][a] which had been begun before, in his year of
office [illegible]enced alike by the fineness of a locality that
has th[illegible] by the great start which the Athenians would
gain i[illegible]ver by becoming a naval people. [4] For he
first v[illegible] stick to the sea and forthwith began to lay
the fo[illegible]e. [5] It was by his advice, too, that they
built t[illegible]ess which can still be discerned round the
Piraeu[illegible]ight up by two wagons meeting each other.
Betwe[illegible]d there was neither rubble nor mortar, but
great s[illegible]itted together, cramped to each other on the
outsid[illegible]out half the height that he intended was finished. [illegible]r size and thickness to keep off the attacks of
an ene[illegible]ey might be adequately defended by a small
garris[illegible]st be freed for service in the fleet. [7] For the
fleet c[illegible]ion. He saw, as I think, that the approach by
sea wa[illegible]rmy than that by land: he also thought the
Piraeu[illegible]e upper city; indeed, he was always advising
the At[illegible] come when they were hard pressed by land,
to go [illegible] and defy the world with their fleet. In this
way, t[illegible] completed their wall, and commenced their
other [illegible]ter the retreat of the Persians.[7a]

1.94
478
HELLESPONT
Pausanias leads a fleet against Cyprus and Byzantium.

Me[illegible]of Cleombrotus was sent out from Sparta as
comm[illegible]llenes, with twenty ships from the Peloponnesus. [illegible]henians with thirty ships, and a number of
the ot[illegible]de an expedition against Cyprus[2a] and sub-

1.93.2a [illegible]wall [illegible]ty con- [illegible]ydides [illegible]
1.93.3a [illegible]relation [illegible]
1.93.3b For *archon*, see Glossary and Appendix A, The Athenian Government, §6.
1.93.7a Thucydides recounts the end of Themistocles' career in 1.135.2–38.6.
1.94.2a Cyprus: Map 1.99, locator.

duced most of the island, and afterwards against Byzantium,[2b] which was in the hands of the Persians, and compelled it to surrender. This event took place while the Spartans were still supreme. [1.95.1] But the violence of Pausanias had already begun to be disagreeable to the Hellenes, particularly to the Ionians and the newly liberated populations. These resorted to the Athenians and requested them as their kinsmen to become their leaders, and to stop any attempt at violence on the part of Pausanias. [2] The Athenians accepted their overtures, and determined to put down any attempt of the kind and to settle everything else as their interests might seem to demand. [3] In the meantime the Spartans recalled Pausanias for an investigation of the reports which had reached them. Manifold and grave accusations had been brought against him by Hellenes arriving in Sparta; and, to all appearance, his conduct seemed more like that of a despot than of a general. [4] As it happened, his recall came just at the time when the hatred which he had inspired had induced the allies to desert him, the soldiers from the Peloponnesus excepted, and to range themselves by the side of the Athenians. [5] On his arrival at Lacedaemon, he was censured for his private acts of oppression, but was acquitted on the heaviest counts and pronounced not guilty; it must be known that the charge of Medism formed one of the principal, and to all appearance one of the best-founded, articles against him.[5a] [6] The Spartans did not, however, restore him to his command, but sent out Dorkis and certain others with a small force; who found the allies no longer inclined to concede to them the command. [7] Perceiving this they departed, and the Spartans did not send out any to succeed them. They feared for those who went out a deterioration similar to that observable in Pausanias; besides, they desired to be rid of the war against the Persians, and were satisfied of the competency of the Athenians for the position, and of their friendship at the time toward themselves.

1.95
478
HELLESPONT
Pausanias grows arrogant and unpopular. Spartan leadership at sea is rejected by the allies in favor of Athens. Sparta accepts this decision.

The Athenians having thus succeeded to the supremacy by the voluntary act of the allies through their hatred of Pausanias, determined which cities were to contribute money against the barbarian, and which ships; their professed object being to retaliate for their sufferings by ravaging the King's country. [2] Now was the time that the office of "Treasurers for Hellas" was first instituted by the Athenians. These officers received the tribute, as the money contributed was called. The tribute was first fixed at four hundred and sixty talents.[2a] The common treasury was at

1.96
478
DELOS
Athens forms a new anti-Persian alliance.

1.94.2b Byzantium: Map 1.99, locator.

1.95.5a Greeks who submitted to the Persians, or who otherwise joined or assisted them, were accused of "Medism." Thucydides describes the end of Pausanias' career in 1.128–34.

1.96.2a Treasurers for Hellas, *Hellenotamiai;* see Appendix B, The Athenian Empire, §10. For the initial tribute, see Appendix B, §2. A talent is a unit of weight and money; see Appendix J, Classical Greek Currency, §5.

Delc[illegible] were held in the temple.

1.97 477–31 HELLAS Thucydides describes the growth of Athenian power, noting that no other historian has covered this topic adequately.

I[illegible] commanded autonomous allies and made their decis[illegible]ses. Their supremacy grew during the interval betw[illegible]d the Persian wars, through their military and polit[illegible]elow against the barbarians, against their own allies[illegible] the Peloponnesians whom they encountered on va[illegible] reason for relating these events, and for venturin[illegible] that this passage of history has been omitted by al[illegible] have confined themselves either to Hellenic histo[illegible]rs, or to the Persian wars itself. Hellanicus, it is true,[illegible]nts in his Athenian history;[2a] but he is somewhat[illegible]ate in his dates. Besides, the history of these event[illegible]n of the growth of the Athenian empire.

1.98 476–67[1a] AEGEAN AREA Athens' new alliance attacks Eion, Scyros, and Carystus, and defeats a revolt by Naxos.

Fi[illegible]d of Cimon son of Miltiades, the Athenians besie[illegible][1b] on the Strymon[1c] from the Persians, and made[illegible]s. [2] Next they enslaved Scyros[2a] the island in the [illegible]olopian population, and colonized it themselve[illegible] by a war against Carystus,[3a] in which the rest of Eu[illegible]l, and which was ended by surrender on conditio[illegible][4a] left the confederacy, and a war ensued, and she h[illegible]e; this was the first instance of the confederation [illegible]te an allied city,[4b] a precedent which was followe[illegible]e order which circumstances prescribed.

1.99 AEGEAN AREA Athens grows less popular as it strictly requires military and monetary contributions to the alliance.

O[illegible]ction, that connected with arrears of tribute and [illegible] of service, was the chief; for the Athenians were [illegible]g, and made themselves offensive by applying the s[illegible]n who were not used to and in fact not disposed[illegible]or. [2] In some other respects the Athenians were [illegible]ulers they had been at first; and if they had more[illegible] service, it was correspondingly easy for them to re[illegible]eave the confederacy. [3] For this the allies had t[illegible] wish to get off service making most of them arran[illegible] the expense in money instead of in ships, and so to [illegible]eir homes. Thus while Athens was increasing her n[illegible]ich they contributed, a revolt always found them[illegible]perience for war.

1.96.2b [illegible]
1.97.2a [illegible]fter 406, [illegible]en seen [illegible]rs on the [illegible]rom 480 [illegible] written [illegible]ile in [illegible]
1.98.1a [illegible]taetia is [illegible]n to [illegible]ord [illegible]
1.98.1b [illegible]
1.98.1c Strymon River: Map 1.99, AX.
1.98.2a Scyros: Map 1.99, AY.
1.98.3a Carystus: Map 1.99, BY.
1.98.3b Euboea: Map 1.99, AX.
1.98.4a Naxos: Map 1.99, BY.
1.98.4b Dates here are very difficult to establish, but one would not be far wrong to place the capture of Eion in 476; the campaign against Carystus in 474 (?); and the revolt of Naxos and its suppression in 471–70 (though some have assigned it to 468–67).

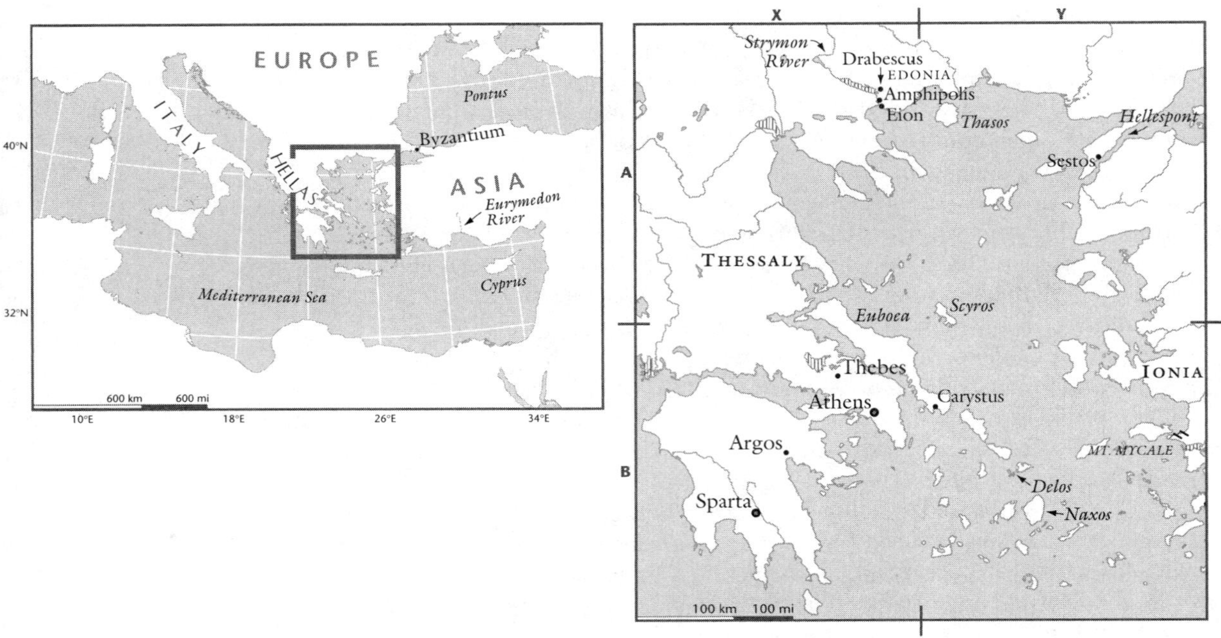

MAP 1.99 DELIAN LEAGUE OPERATIONS

1.100
467?
ASIA
The Persians are defeated on the Eurymedon River.
465?
THRACE
Thasos revolts. The Athenians are defeated at Amphipolis.

Next we come to the actions by land and by sea at the river Eurymedon,[1a] between the Athenians with their allies, and the Persians, when the Athenians won both battles on the same day under the leadership of Cimon son of Miltiades, and captured and destroyed the whole Phoenician fleet, consisting of two hundred vessels. [2] Some time afterwards occurred the defection of the Thasians, caused by disagreements about the markets on the opposite coast of Thrace, and about the mine in their possession. Sailing with a fleet to Thasos,[2a] the Athenians defeated them at sea and effected a landing on the island. [3] About the same time they sent ten thousand settlers of their own citizens and the allies to settle the place then called Ennea Hodoi (or Nine Ways), now Amphipolis.[3a] They succeeded in gaining possession of Ennea Hodoi from the Edonians, but on advancing

1.100.1a The battles on the Eurymedon River (Map 1.99, locator), can be dated no closer than the years 469–66.

1.100.2a The secession of Thasos (Map 1.99, AY) is estimated to have taken place in 466–5 and to have ended three years later in 463–2.

1.100.3a Ennea Hodoi: Amphipolis on Map 1.99, AX. This failure to establish a colony at Ennea Hodoi probably occurred in 465–64.

into [illegible] ere cut off in Drabescus,[3b] a city of the Edonians [illegible] racians, who regarded the settlement of the place [illegible] of hostility.

1.101
466–62?
SPARTA
Promised Spartan aid to Thasos is prevented by earthquake and Helot revolt. Thasos surrenders on terms.

M[illegible] being defeated in the field and suffering siege, appe[illegible] ed her to assist them by an invasion of Attica. [2] U[illegible] ans, she promised and intended to do so, but was p[illegible] ence of the earthquake, accompanied by the seces[illegible] d the Thuriats[2b] and Aethaeans[2c] of the *perioikoi* [illegible] the Helots were the descendants of the old Mess[illegible] ed in the famous war;[2e] and so all of them came [illegible] s. [3] The Spartans thus being engaged in a war w[illegible] e, the Thasians in the third year of the siege obtai[illegible] henians by razing their walls, delivering up their [illegible] pay the moneys demanded at once, and tribute i[illegible] possessions on the mainland together with the m[illegible]

1.102
462–61?
MESSENE
Athens sends troops to help the Spartans fight the Helots. When they are rudely dismissed, Athens renounces her alliance with Sparta.

Th[illegible] finding the war against the rebels in Ithome was li[illegible] nvoked the aid of their allies, and especially of the A[illegible] ome force under the command of Cimon. [2] The r[illegible] summons lay in their reputed skill in siege opera[illegible] ught the Spartans their own deficiency in this art, e[illegible] ken the place by assault. [3] The first open quarr[illegible] and Athenians arose out of this expedition. The S[illegible] failed to take the place, apprehensive of the enter[illegible] character of the Athenians, and further looking u[illegible] raction, began to fear that if they remained, they m[illegible] e besieged in Ithome to attempt some political ch[illegible] dismissed them alone of the allies, without declar[illegible] merely saying that they had now no need of them. [illegible], aware that their dismissal did not proceed from t[illegible] on of the two, but from suspicions which had been c[illegible] eply offended, and conscious of having done nothi[illegible] ent from the Spartans; and the instant that they r[illegible] ke off the alliance[4a] which had been made agains[illegible] hemselves with Sparta's enemy Argos;[4b] each of the [illegible] king the same oaths and making the same allianc[illegible]

1.100.3b [illegible] n of [illegible]
1.101.2a [illegible] ous [illegible] 65–64. [illegible] rtan [illegible] C, [illegible]
1.101.2b [illegible] X.
1.101.2c [illegible] nably [illegible]
1.101.2d Mount Ithome, site of the ancient capital of Messenia: Map 1.107, BX.
1.101.2e The Messenian war, about 720 B.C.? See Appendix C, Spartan Institutions §3.
1.102.4a The "alliance" in this case is the Hellenic Alliance against Persia, not the Peloponnesian League.
1.102.4b Argos: Map 1.107, BY.
1.102.4c Thessaly: Map 1.99, AX.

1.103
457–56
MESSENE
Given permission to leave Laconia, the Helots surrender and are settled in Naupactus by the Athenians.
MEGARA
A dispute with Corinth leads Megara to ally herself with Athens.

Meanwhile the rebels in Ithome, unable to prolong further a ten[1a] years' resistance, surrendered to Sparta; the conditions being that they should depart from the Peloponnesus under safe conduct, and should never set foot in it again: [2] anyone who might hereafter be found there was to be the slave of his captor. It must be known that the Spartans had an old oracle from Delphi,[2a] to the effect that they should let go the suppliant of Zeus at Ithome.[2b] [3] So they went forth with their children and their wives, and being received by Athens because of the hatred that she now felt for the Spartans, were located at Naupactus,[3a] which she had lately taken from the Ozolian Locrians.[3b] [4] The Athenians received another addition to their confederacy in the Megarians;[4a] who left the Spartan alliance, annoyed by a war about boundaries forced on them by Corinth.[4b] The Athenians occupied Megara and Pegae,[4c] and built for the Megarians their long walls from the city to Nisaea,[4d] in which they placed an Athenian garrison. This was the principal cause of the Corinthians conceiving such a deadly hatred against Athens.

1.104
460?
EGYPT
An Athenian fleet sails to Egypt to assist a revolt there against the Persians.

Meanwhile Inaros son of Psammetichus, a Libyan king of the Libyans on the Egyptian border, having his headquarters at Marea,[1a] the city above Pharos, caused a revolt of almost the whole of Egypt[1b] from King Artaxerxes, and placing himself at its head, invited the Athenians to his assistance. [2] Abandoning a Cyprian[2a] expedition upon which they happened to be engaged with two hundred ships of their own and their allies, the Athenians arrived in Egypt and sailed from the sea into the Nile,[2b] made themselves masters of the river and two-thirds of Memphis,[2c] and addressed themselves to the attack of the remaining third, which is called White Castle. Within it were Persians and Medes who had taken refuge there, and Egyptians who had not joined the rebellion.

1.105
459?
TROEZEN
An Athenian attack on Halieis is repelled, but the Peloponnesian fleet is defeated off Cecryphalia.
458?
AEGINA
Athens defeats the Aeginetans at sea and besieges their city.
MEGARID
A Corinthian attack on Megara is stopped by a reserve Athenian army.

At this time, other Athenians, making a descent from their fleet upon Halieis,[1a] were engaged by a force of Corinthians and Epidaurians;[1b] and the Corinthians were victorious. Afterwards the Athenians engaged the Peloponnesian fleet off Cecryphalia;[1c] and the Athenians were victorious. [2] Subsequently, war broke out between Aegina[2a] and Athens, and there was a great battle at sea off Aegina between the Athenians and Aeginetans, each being aided by their allies; in which victory remained with the Athenians, who took seventy of the enemy's ships, and landed in the country and commenced a siege under the command of Leocrates son of Stroebus. [3] Upon this the Peloponnesians,[3a] desirous of aiding the Aeginetans, threw

1.103.1a Thucydides is thought by many to have written here "four" instead of "ten."
1.103.2a Delphi: Map 1.107, AY.
1.103.2b Mt. Ithome: Map 1.107, BX.
1.103.3a Naupactus: Map 1.107, AX.
1.103.3b Ozolian Locris: Map 1.107, AX.
1.103.4a Megara: Map 1.107, AY.
1.103.4b Corinth: Map 1.107, AY.
1.103.4c Pegae: Map 1.107, AY.
1.103.4d Nisaea: Map 1.107, AY.
1.104.1a Marea, Egypt: Map 1.110.
1.104.1b Egypt: Map 1.110.
1.104.2a Cyprus: Map 1.110.
1.104.2b Nile River: Map 1.110.
1.104.2c Memphis on the Nile: Map 1.110.
1.105.1a Halieis: Map 1.107, BY.
1.105.1b Epidaurus: Map 1.107, BY.
1.105.1c Cecryphalia: Map 1.107, AY. This action (in 459?) was apparently the initial hostility of what is now called the "First Peloponnesian War" between Sparta and Athens.
1.105.2a Aegina: Map 1.107, AY.
1.105.3a The "Peloponnesians" in this case is probably the Peloponnesian League. See Appendix D, The Peloponnesian League.

into A[illegible]ndred hoplites, who had before been serving
with t[illegible]aurians. Meanwhile the Corinthians and their
allies [illegible]f Geraneia,[3b] and marched down into the
Megar[illegible]h a large force absent in Aegina and Egypt,
Athen[illegible]lp the Megarians without raising the siege of
Aegin[illegible]ns, instead of moving the army at Aegina,
raised [illegible]oung men that had been left in the city, and
march[illegible]der the command of Myronides. [5] After a
drawn [illegible]hians, the rival hosts parted, each with the
impres[illegible]d the victory. [6] The Athenians, however, if
anythi[illegible]tage, and on the departure of the Corinthians se[illegible]y the taunts of the elders in their city, the
Corint[illegible]rations, and about twelve days afterwards
came [illegible] as victors. Sallying out from Megara, the
Atheni[illegible] that was employed in erecting the trophy,
and en[illegible]rest.

1.106 458? MEGARID A division of Corinthians is destroyed.

In [illegible]ished army, a considerable division, pressed
by the [illegible]the road, dashed into a field on some private
proper[illegible] all round it and no way out. [2] Being
acquai[illegible]Athenians hemmed their front with hoplites,
and pl[illegible]und in a circle, stoned all who had gone in.
Corint[illegible] blow. The bulk of her army continued its
retreat [illegible]

1.107 457 ATHENS Athens begins work on the Long Walls. PHOCIS A Spartan army rescues Doris from Phocis but retires to Boeotia when the routes home are blocked. BOEOTIA The Athenian army advances to engage the Peloponnesians; Thessalian cavalry joins them but defects during the battle.

Ab[illegible]ns began to build the long walls to the sea,
that to[illegible]t toward the Piraeus.[1a] [2] Meanwhile the
Phocia[illegible] against Doris,[2b] the old home of the Spartans, c[illegible]Boeum,[2c] Cytinium,[2d] and Erineum.[2e] They
had tak[illegible]when the Spartans under Nicomedes son of
Cleom[illegible] King Pleistoanax son of Pausanias, who was
still a [illegible]of the Dorians with fifteen hundred hoplites
of thei[illegible]d of their allies. After compelling the Phocians t[illegible]nditions, they began their retreat. [3] The
route [illegible]n gulf[3a] exposed them to the risk of being
stoppe[illegible]t; that by land across Geraneia[3b] seemed
scarcel[illegible]s holding Megara and Pegae,[3c] for the pass
was a [illegible]ways guarded by the Athenians; and in the
present[illegible]had information that they meant to dispute

1.105.3b [illegible]
1.107.1a [illegible] and [illegible] 1.107,
1.107.2a [illegible]
1.107.2b [illegible]
1.107.2c [illegible]07,
1.107.2d [illegible]
1.107.2e [illegible]107,
1.107.3a [illegible]
1.107.3b Mount Geraneia: Map 1.107, AY.
1.107.3c Pegae: Map 1.107, AY.

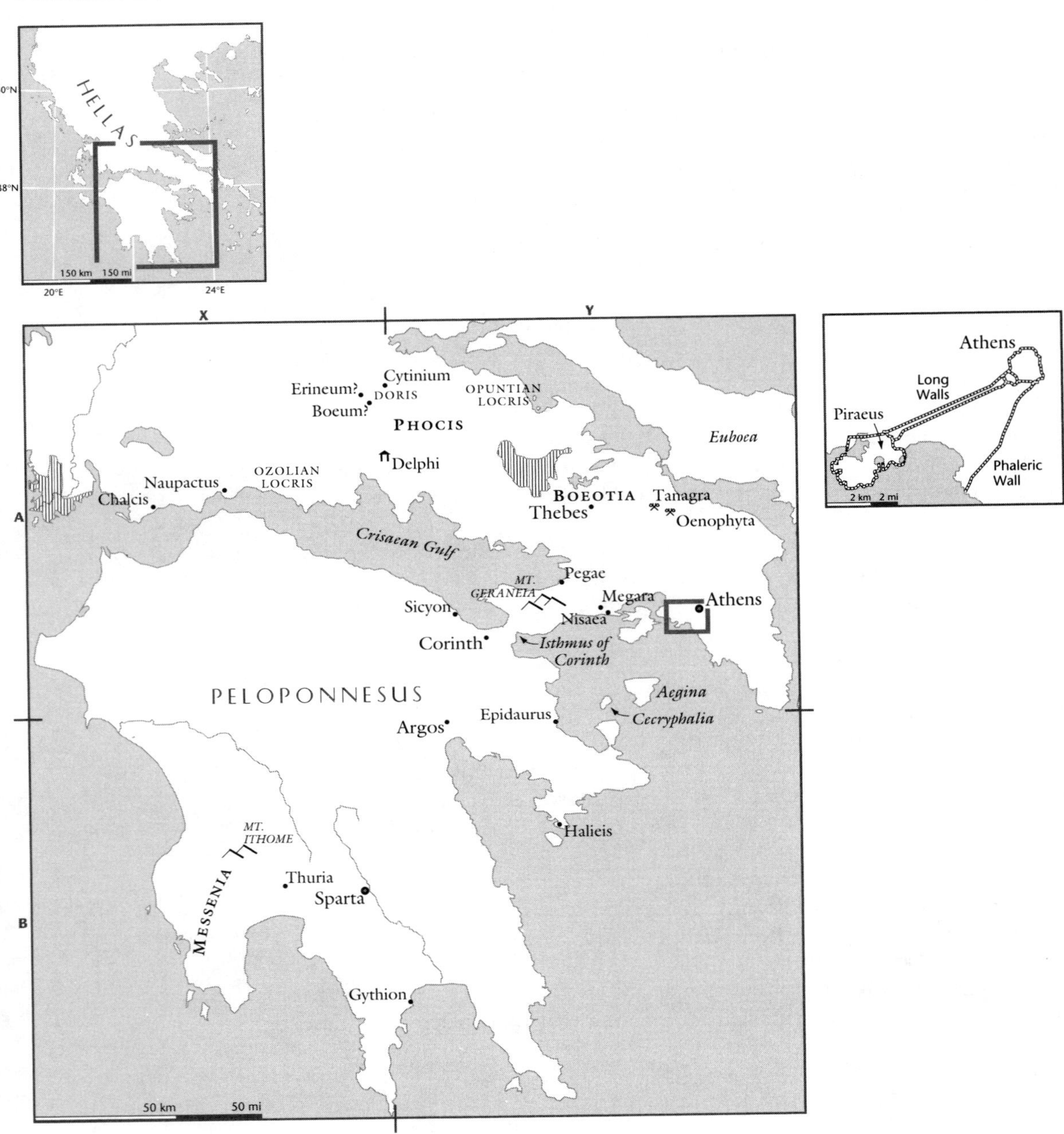

MAP 1.107 THE "FIRST PELOPONNESIAN WAR"

their [illegible] solved to remain in Boeotia,[4a] and to consider
whic[illegible] ne of march. They had also another reason for
this [illegible] gement had been given them by a party in
Athe[illegible] an end to the reign of democracy[4b] and the
build[illegible] 5] Meanwhile the Athenians marched against
them [illegible] nd a thousand Argives and the respective con-
tinge[illegible] llies. Altogether they were fourteen thousand
stron[illegible] prompted by the notion that the Spartans were
at a l[illegible] passage, and also by suspicions of an attempt
to ov[illegible]. [7] Some cavalry also joined the Athenians
from [illegible] but these went over to the Spartans during the
battl[illegible]

Th[illegible] Tanagra[1a] in Boeotia. After heavy loss on both
sides [illegible] Spartans and their allies. [2] After entering
the M[illegible] wn the fruit trees, the Spartans returned home
acros[illegible] nus. Sixty-two days after the battle the Athenians m[illegible] der the command of Myronides, [3] defeated
the B[illegible] nophyta,[3a] and became masters of Boeotia and
Phoc[illegible] e walls of the Tanagraeans, took a hundred of
the ri[illegible] tian Locrians[3c] as hostages, and finished their
own [illegible] followed by the surrender of the Aeginetans[4a]
to At[illegible] y pulled down their walls, gave up their ships,
and a[illegible] future. [5] The Athenians sailed round the
Pelop[illegible] es son of Tolmaeus, burnt the arsenal of
Spart[illegible] y of the Corinthians, and in a descent upon
Sicyo[illegible] ns in battle.

1.108
457
BOEOTIA
The Spartans defeat the Athenians at Tanagra and go home. Later the Athenians defeat the Boeotians at Oenophyta and become masters of Boeotia.
AEGINA
Aegina surrenders. The Athenians raid the Peloponnesus.

M[illegible] s in Egypt and their allies stayed on and
encou[illegible] s of war. [2] First the Athenians were masters
of Eg[illegible] Megabazus, a Persian, to Sparta with money to
bribe [illegible] invade Attica and so draw off the Athenians
from [illegible] t the matter made no progress, and that the
mone[illegible] d, he recalled Megabazus with the remainder
of the [illegible] byzus son of Zopyrus, a Persian, with a large
army [illegible] by land he defeated the Egyptians and their
allies [illegible] he Hellenes out of Memphis,[4a] and at length
shut t[illegible] f Prosopitis,[4b] where he besieged them for a
year a[illegible], draining the canal of its waters, which he
divert[illegible], he left their ships high and dry and joined

1.109
454?
EGYPT
The Persians defeat the Egyptians and their Athenian allies.

1.107.4a [illegible]
1.107.4b [illegible] cracy, see [illegible] rnment, [illegible]
1.108.1a [illegible]
1.108.3a [illegible]
1.108.3b [illegible]
1.108.3c [illegible].
1.108.4a Aegina: Map 1.107, AY.
1.108.5a Presumably the shipyard at Gythion on the coast of Laconia: Map 1.107, BY.
1.108.5b Chalcis of the Corinthians: Map 1.107, AX.
1.108.5c Sicyon: Map 1.107, AY.
1.109.4a Memphis, Egypt: Map 1.110.
1.109.4b Prosopitis, Egypt: location unknown.

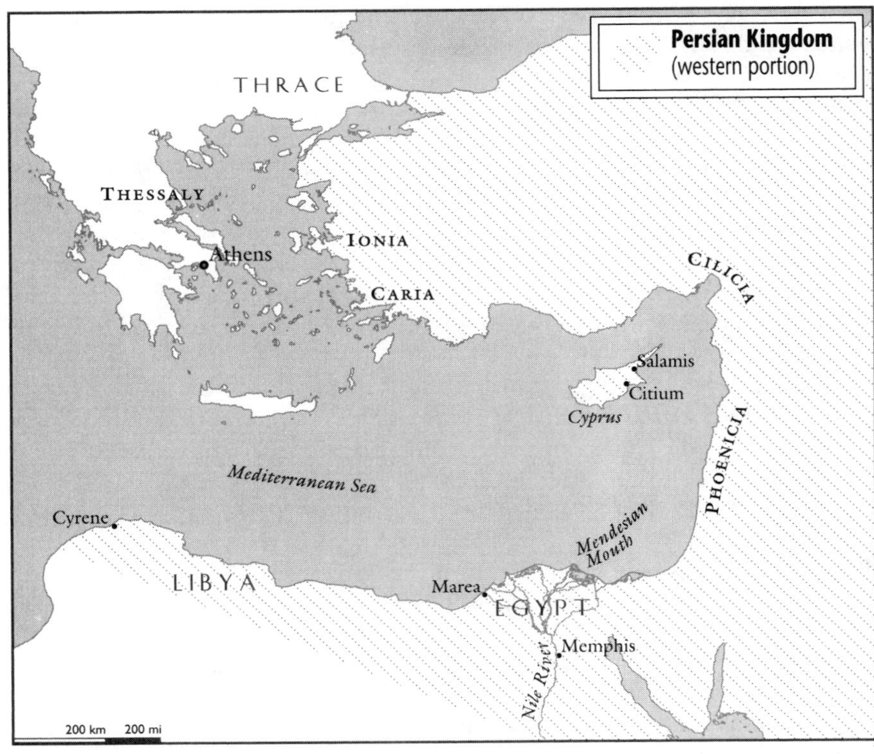

MAP 1.110 THE CAMPAIGN IN EGYPT

most of the island to the mainland, and then marched over on foot and captured it.

1.110 454? EGYPT Most of Athens' fleet in Egypt is lost. An Athenian relief fleet, unaware of the defeat, is surprised and destroyed.

Thus the enterprise of the Hellenes came to ruin after six years of war. Of all that large host a few traveling through Libya[1a] reached Cyrene[1b] in safety, but most of them perished. [2] And thus Egypt returned to its subjection to the King, except Amyrtaeus, the king in the marshes, whom they were unable to capture from the extent of the marsh; the marshmen being also the most warlike of the Egyptians. [3] Inaros, the Libyan king, the sole

1.110.1a Libya: Map 1.110.
1.110.1b Cyrene, Libya: Map 1.110.

autho olt, was betrayed, taken, and crucified. [4]
Mean ron of fifty triremes had sailed from Athens
and t acy for Egypt. They put in to shore at the
Menc e,[4a] in total ignorance of what had occurred.
Attac the troops, and from the sea by the Phoenician r ere destroyed; the few remaining being saved
by ret of the great expedition of the Athenians and
their

1.111 454?
THESSALY
Athens attempts to restore Orestes in Thessaly but fails.
SICYON
Pericles' fleet defeats the Sicyonians but fails to take Oeniadae.

M f the Thessalian king Echecratides, being an
exile ed the Athenians to restore him. Taking with
them Phocians[1c] their allies, the Athenians marched
to Ph hey became masters of the country, though
only i of the camp; beyond which they could not
go fo cavalry. But they failed to take the city or to
attain of their expedition, and returned home with
Orest ed anything. [2] Not long after this a thousand ed in the vessels that were at Pegae[2a] (Pegae,
it mu now theirs), and sailed along the coast to
Sicyor of Pericles son of Xanthippus. Landing in
Sicyor onians who engaged them, [3] they immediately t eans[3a] and sailing across, marched against and
laid si carnania.[3c] Failing however to take it, they
return

1.112 451?
HELLAS
Sparta and Athens sign a five-year truce.
CYPRUS
Athens defeats the Persians at Cyprus; Cimon dies.
DELPHI
Athens and Sparta vie for control of Delphi.

Th ruce was made between the Peloponnesians
and A 2] Released from Hellenic war, the Athenians m prus[2a] with two hundred vessels of their own
and th mmand of Cimon. [3] Sixty of these were
detach uest of Amyrtaeus, the king in the marshes;
the re from which, however, [4] they were compelled of Cimon and by scarcity of provisions. Sailing of ey fought with the Phoenicians,[4b] Cyprians,
and C ea, and being victorious on both elements
depart em the squadron that had returned from
Egypt. artans marched out on a sacred war, and
becom le at Delphi,[5a] placed it in the hands of the
Delphi their retreat, the Athenians marched out,
becam e, and placed it in the hands of the Phocians.[5b]

1.110.4a r: Map
1.111.1a
1.111.1b
1.111.1c
1.111.1d AY.
1.111.2a
1.111.2b
1.111.3a
1.111.3b
1.111.3c Acarnania: Map 1.112, AX.
1.112.2a Cyprus: Map 1.110.
1.112.3a Egypt: Map 1.110.
1.112.3b Citium, Cyprus: Map 1.110.
1.112.4a Salamis, Cyprus: Map 1.110.
1.112.4b Phoenicia: Map 1.110.
1.112.4c Cilicia: Map 1.110.
1.112.5a Delphi: Map 1.112, AY.
1.112.5b Phocis: Map 1.112, AY.

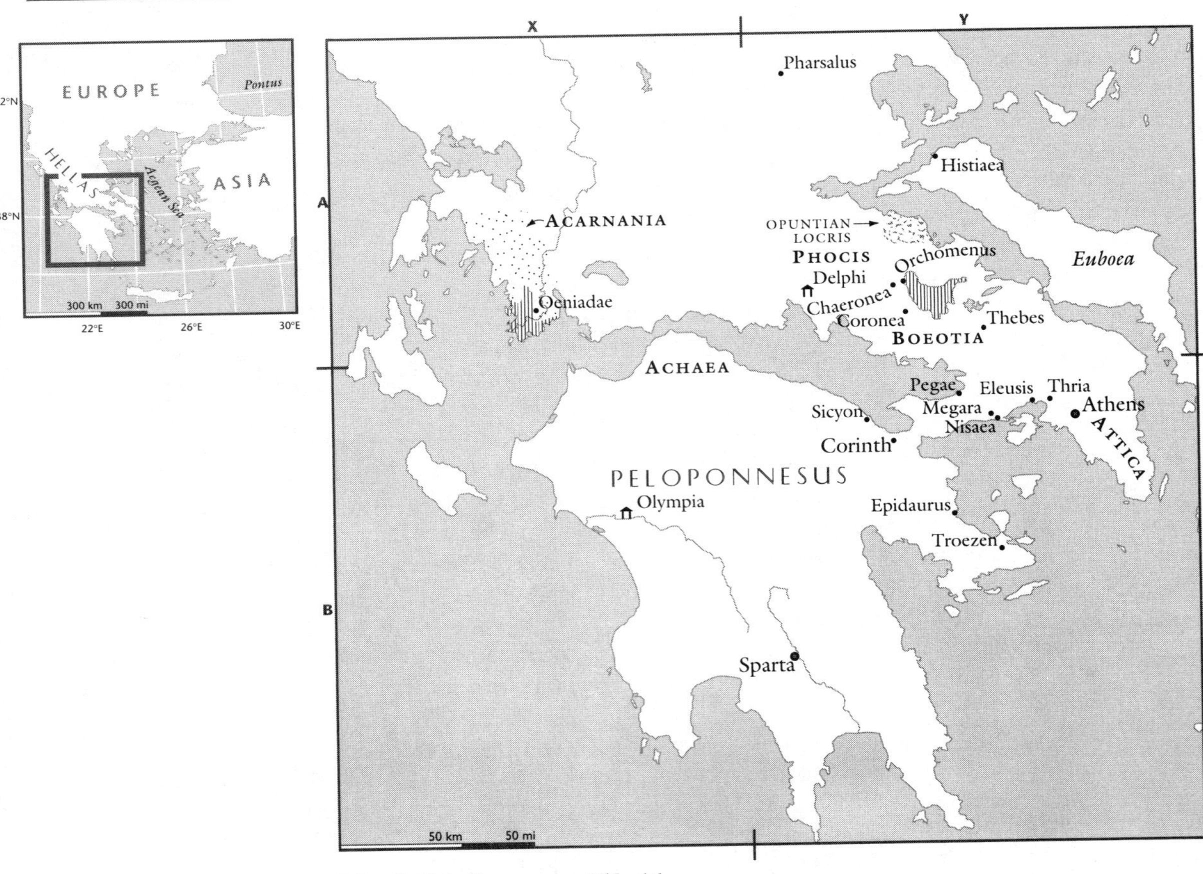

MAP 1.112 EVENTS OF 451–46

1.113
447
BOEOTIA
Boeotia defeats Athens at Coronea and regains her independence.

Some time after this, a thousand Athenians with allied contingents under the command of Tolmides son of Tolmaeus, marched against Orchomenus,[1a] Chaeronea,[1b] and some other places in Boeotia[1c] that were in the hands of the Boeotian exiles. They took Chaeronea, made slaves of the inhabitants, and leaving a garrison, commenced their return. [2] On their way they were attacked at Coronea[2a] by the Boeotian exiles from Orchomenus, with some Locrians[2b] and Euboean[2c] exiles, and others who were of the same way of thinking. The Athenians were defeated in battle

1.113.1a Orchomenus: Map 1.112, AY.
1.113.1b Chaeronea: Map 1.112, AY.
1.113.1c Boeotia: Map 1.112, AY.
1.113.2a Coronea: Map 1.112, AY.
1.113.2b Locris (Opuntian): Map 1.112, AY.
1.113.2c Euboea: Map 1.112, AY.

and s… taken captive. [3] The Athenians evacuated all
Boeo… g for the recovery of the men; [4] and the
exiled … nd with all the rest regained their independence

1.114
446
ATTICA
Euboea and Megara revolt. Athens recaptures Euboea but not Megara. A Peloponnesian army invades Attica but turns back.

Th… followed by the revolt of Euboea from Athens.
Pericl… over with an army of Athenians to the island,
when … m that Megara[1a] had revolted, that the Pelo-
ponn… t of invading Attica,[1b] and that the Athenian
garris… the Megarians, with the exception of a few
who … Nisaea.[1c] The Megarians had introduced the
Corin… nd Epidaurians[1f] into the city before they
revolt… brought his army back in all haste from
Eubo… Peloponnesians, under the command of King
Pleist… marched into Attica as far as Eleusis[2a] and
Thria, … y and without advancing further returned
home. … en crossed over again to Euboea under the
comm… dued the whole of the island. While they settled al… by means of agreed terms, they expelled the
peopl… ied their territory themselves.

1.115
446
PELOPONNESUS
Athens gives up bases in the Megarid and Peloponnesus to secure the Thirty Years' Peace.
441/0
SAMOS
Samos and Byzantium revolt; Persian troops assist Samos.

No… from Euboea, they made a peace treaty with
the Sp… r thirty years, giving up the posts which they
occup… s, Nisaea, Pegae,[1a] Troezen,[1b] and Achaea.[1c]
[2] In … ce, war broke out between the Samians[2a] and
Milesi… Worsted in the war, the Milesians came to
Athen… against the Samians. In this they were joined
by cer… m Samos itself, who wished to change the
consti…] Accordingly the Athenians sailed to Samos
with f… emocracy;[3a] took hostages from the Samians,
fifty b… odged them in Lemnos,[3b] and after leaving a
garris… l home. [4] Some of the Samians, however,
had n… d, but had fled to the continent. Making an
agreem… erful of those in the city, and an alliance with
Pissut… who at that time controlled Sardis[4a] for the
Persia… force of seven hundred mercenaries, and
under … over to Samos. [5] Their first step was to rise
against … whom they secured, their next to steal their
hostag… which they revolted, gave up the Athenian
garriso… ts commanders to Pissuthnes, and instantly

1.114.1a …
1.114.1b …
1.114.1c …
1.114.1d …
1.114.1e …
1.114.1f …
1.114.2a …
1.114.2b …
1.114.3a …
1.115.1a …
1.115.1b Troezen: Map 1.112, BY.
1.115.1c Achaea: Map 1.112, BX.
1.115.2a Samos: Map 1.115.
1.115.2b Miletus: Map 1.115.
1.115.2c Priene: Map 1.115.
1.115.3a See Appendix B, The Athenian Empire, §4.
1.115.3b Lemnos: Map 1.115.
1.115.4a Sardis: Map 1.115. See Appendix E, The Persians, §3, 7.

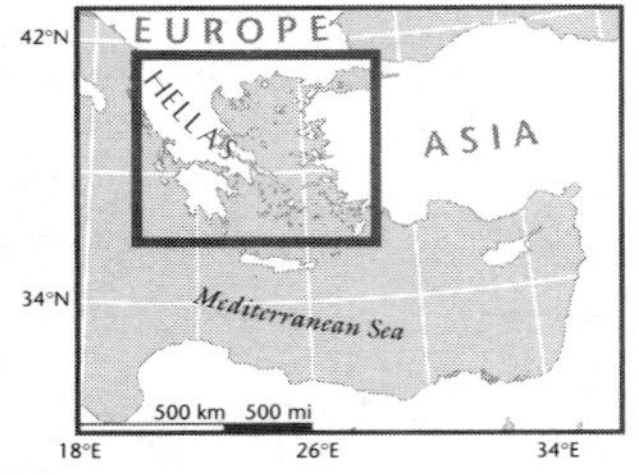

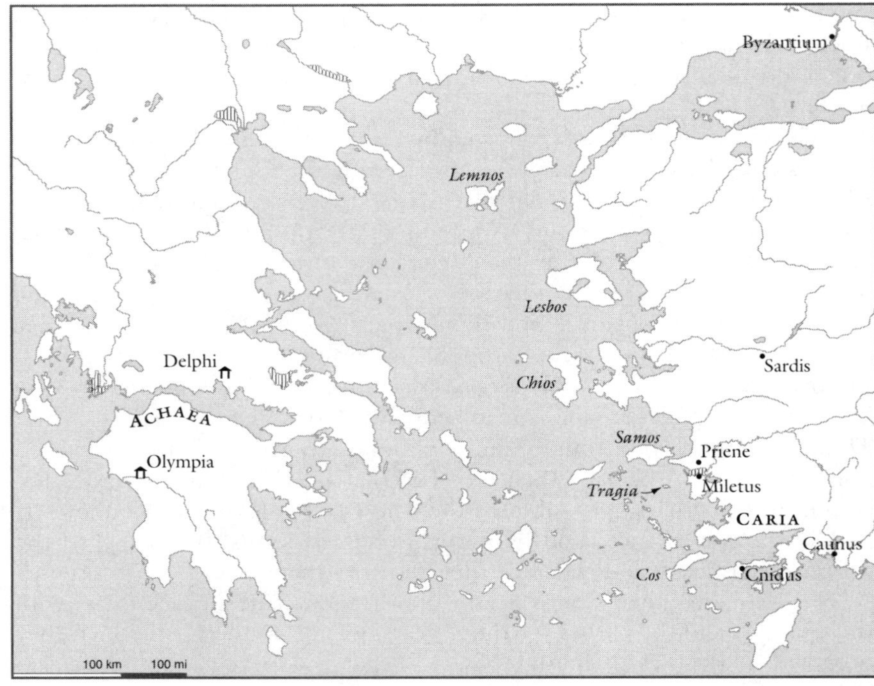

MAP 1.115 REVOLT OF SAMOS

prepared for an expedition against Miletus. The Byzantians[5a] also revolted with them.

1.116
441/0
SAMOS
The Athenians win a battle off Samos and prepare to engage the Phoenician fleet.

As soon as the Athenians heard the news, they sailed with sixty ships against Samos. Sixteen of these went to Caria[1a] to look out for the Phoenician fleet, and to Chios[1b] and Lesbos[1c] carrying round orders for reinforcements, and so never engaged; but forty-four ships under the command of Pericles and nine colleagues gave battle off the island of Tragia[1d] to seventy Samian vessels—of which twenty were transports—as they were sailing from Miletus. Victory remained with the Athenians. [2] Reinforced afterwards by forty ships from Athens, and twenty-five Chian and Lesbian vessels, the Athenians landed, and having the superiority by land besieged the city with three walls and also blockaded it from the sea. [3] Meanwhile Pericles took sixty ships from the blockading squadron and departed in haste for Caunus[3a] and Caria, intelligence having been brought in of the approach of the Phoenician fleet to the aid of the Samians; indeed Stesago-

1.115.5a Byzantium: Map 1.115.
1.116.1a Caria: Map 1.115.
1.116.1b Chios: Map 1.115.
1.116.1c Lesbos: Map 1.115.
1.116.1d Tragia: Map 1.115.1.
1.116.3a Caunus: Map 1.115.

1.117
440
SAMOS
Samos resists for nine months but finally surrenders to Athens.

ras an [illegible] and with five ships to bring them. [1.117.1] But i [illegible] mians made a sudden sally, and fell on the camp [illegible] ortified. Destroying the lookout vessels, and engag [illegible] as were being launched to meet them, they remai [illegible] n seas for fourteen days, and carried in and carrie [illegible]. [2] But on the arrival of Pericles, they were once [illegible] einforcements afterwards arrived—forty ships from [illegible] s,[2a] Hagnon, and Phormio; twenty with Tlepolen [illegible] irty vessels from Chios and Lesbos. [3] After a brie [illegible] ne Samians, unable to hold out after a nine-mont [illegible] surrender on terms; they razed their walls, gave [illegible] eir ships, and arranged to pay the expenses of the w [illegible] Byzantians also agreed to be subject as before.

1.118
432
HELLAS
Thus in the fifty years after the defeat of Persia, the power of Athens grew until Sparta felt compelled to oppose it. This chapter concludes the Pentecontaetia.

Af [illegible] ny years later, we at length come to what has been [illegible] s of Corcyra and Potidaea and the events that serve [illegible] sent war. [2] All these actions of the Hellenes again [illegible] barbarian occurred in the fifty years' interval betw [illegible] and the beginning of the present war. During this i [illegible] ucceeded in placing their empire on a firmer basis, [illegible] d their own power to a very great height. The Spart [illegible] of it, opposed it only for a little while, but remai [illegible] t of the period, being of old slow to go to war excep [illegible] necessity, and in the present instance being hamp [illegible] Finally, the growth of the Athenian power could [illegible] s their own confederacy became the object of its en [illegible] felt that they could endure it no longer, but that t [illegible] hem to throw themselves heart and soul upon the h [illegible] it, if they could, by commencing the present war.[2a] [illegible] partans had made up their own minds on the fact c [illegible] y and the guilt of the Athenians, yet they sent to D [illegible] he god whether it would be well with them if they [illegible] reported, received from him the answer that if they [illegible] into the war, victory would be theirs, and the prom [illegible] uld be with them, whether invoked or uninvoke [illegible]

1.119
432/1
SPARTA
The Corinthians speak at a meeting of the Spartans and their allies.

St [illegible] on their allies again, and to take their vote on the p [illegible] [a] After the ambassadors from the confederates had [illegible] ad been convened, they all spoke their minds, most [illegible] the Athenians and demanding that the war shoul [illegible] Corinthians. They had before on their own accou [illegible] eparately to induce them to vote for the war, in

1.117.2 [illegible] the [illegible] s the [illegible]

1.118.2 [illegible]

1.118.3a Delphi: Map 1.115.

1.119.1a See Appendix D, The Peloponnesian League, §5.

the fear that it might come too late to save Potidaea; they were present also on this occasion, and came forward the last, and made the following speech:

1.120
432/1
SPARTA
Corinth applauds Sparta's vote for war and urges all states in the Peloponnesian League to recognize their common interests and potential for injury, and to vote for war.

"Fellow allies, we can no longer accuse the Spartans of having failed in their duty: they have not only voted for war themselves, but have assembled us here for that purpose. We say their duty, for supremacy has its duties. Besides equitably administering private interests, leaders are required to show a special care for the common welfare in return for the special honors accorded to them by all in other ways. [2] All of us who have already had dealings with the Athenians require no warning to be on their guard against them. The states more inland and away from the main routes should understand that if they omit to support the coast powers, the result will be to injure the transit of their produce for exportation and the reception in exchange of their imports from the sea; and they must not be careless judges of what is now said, as if it had nothing to do with them, but must expect that the sacrifice of the powers on the coast will one day be followed by the extension of the danger to the interior, and must recognize that their own interests are deeply involved in this discussion. [3] For these reasons they should not hesitate to exchange peace for war. If wise men remain quiet while they are not injured, brave men abandon peace for war when they are injured, returning to an understanding on a favorable opportunity. In fact, they are neither intoxicated by their success in war nor disposed to take an injury for the sake of the delightful tranquillity of peace. [4] Indeed, to falter for the sake of such delights is, if you remain inactive, the quickest way of losing the sweets of repose to which you cling; while to conceive extravagant pretensions from success in war is to forget how hollow is the confidence by which you are elated. [5] For if many ill-conceived plans have succeeded through the still greater lack of judgment of an opponent, many more, apparently well laid, have on the contrary ended in disgrace. The confidence with which we form our schemes is never completely justified in their execution; speculation is carried on in safety, but, when it comes to action, fear causes failure."

1.121
432/1
SPARTA
The Corinthians optimistically assert that the Peloponnesians can raise enough money by contributions and by loans from Delphi and Olympia to finance a fleet and to subvert that of Athens; they say that the Peloponnesians with practice will soon equal the Athenians at sea.

"To apply these rules to ourselves, if we are now kindling war it is under the pressure of injury, and with adequate grounds of complaint; and after we have chastised the Athenians we will in season desist. [2] We have many reasons to expect success—first, superiority in numbers and in military experience, and secondly our general and unvarying obedience in the execution of orders. [3] The naval

st ss shall be raised by us from our respective
pr m the moneys at Olympia and Delphi.[3a] A
lo s to seduce their foreign sailors by the offer
of power of Athens is more mercenary than
na not be exposed to the same risk, as its
st than in money. [4] A single defeat at sea is
in n: should they hold out, in that case there
w r us to exercise ourselves in naval matters;
ar arrived at an equality in science, we need
sc shall be their superiors in courage. For the
ac y nature they cannot acquire by education;
w science must be removed by our practice.
[5 for these objects shall be provided by our
co deed could be more monstrous than the
su ir allies never tire of contributing for their
ov d refuse to spend for vengeance and self-
pr which by such refusal we shall forfeit to
A employed for our own ruin."

1.122
432/1
SPARTA
The Corinthians add that the Peloponnesians can suborn Athenian allies and establish fortified posts in Attica. They call for unity in the face of Athenian aggression since the alternative is slavery. They assert that the Peloponnesians must prevent Athens from ruling all Hellas as a tyrant state just as they have put down tyrants in individual states.

ays of carrying on the war, such as revolt of
th thod of depriving them of their revenues,
w heir strength, and establishment of fortified
po , and various operations which cannot be
fo ar of all things proceeds least upon definite
ru ly upon itself for contrivances to meet an
en cases the party who faces the struggle and
ke ts with most security, and he who loses his
te respondent disaster. [2] Let us also reflect
th mber of disputes of territory between rival
ne rne; but here we have in Athens an enemy
th hole coalition, and more than a match for
an t unless as a body and as individual national s we make a unanimous stand against her,
sh divided and city by city. That conquest, ter-
ri uld, it must be known, have no other end
th mple; [3] a word which the Peloponnesus
ca d without disgrace, or without disgrace see
sc y one. Meanwhile the opinion would be
ei y so used, or that we put up with it from
co ving degenerate sons in not even securing
fo which our fathers gave to Hellas; and in
al t in Hellas of a tyrant state, though in indi-

1.121.3a Offerings
her valu-
jor tem-
e that
e and
tempting repositories of ready capital in ancient Greece. In 2.13.4–5, Pericles lists the vast wealth lying in Athenian temples and shrines that could be called upon—if necessary—to support the war.

vidual states we think it our duty to put down sole rulers. [4] And we do not know how this conduct can be held free from three of the gravest failings, want of sense, of courage, or of vigilance. For we do not suppose that you have taken refuge in that contempt of an enemy which has proved so fatal in so many instances—a feeling which from the numbers that it has ruined has come to be thought not to express contempt but to deserve it."

1.123
432/1
SPARTA
The Corinthians claim that the god of Delphi sanctions war, which proves that the treaty has already been violated by Athens.

"There is, however, no advantage in reflections on the past further than may be of service to the present. For the future we must provide by maintaining what the present gives us and redoubling our efforts; it is hereditary to us to win virtue as the fruit of labor, and you must not change the habit, even though you should have a slight advantage in wealth and resources; for it is not right that what was won in want should be lost in plenty. No, we must boldly advance to the war for many reasons; the god has commanded it and promised to be with us, and the rest of Hellas will all join in the struggle, part from fear, part from interest. [2] You will not be the first to break a treaty which the god, in advising us to go to war, judges to be violated already, but rather to support a treaty that has been outraged: indeed, treaties are broken not by resistance but by aggression."

1.124
432/1
SPARTA
The Corinthians conclude with an appeal to their allies to vote for war in order to deny Athens her goal of universal empire.

"Your position, therefore, from whatever quarter you may view it, will amply justify you in going to war; and this step we recommend in the interests of all, bearing in mind that identity of interests is the surest of bonds whether between states or individuals. Delay not, therefore, to assist Potidaea,[1a] a Dorian city besieged by Ionians,[1b] which is quite a reversal of the order of things; nor to assert the freedom of the rest. [2] It is impossible for us to wait any longer when waiting can only mean immediate disaster for some of us and, if it comes to be known that we have conferred but do not venture to protect ourselves, likely disaster in the near future for the rest. Delay not, fellow allies, but convinced of the necessity of the crisis and the wisdom of this counsel, vote for the war, undeterred by its immediate terrors, but looking beyond to the lasting peace by which it will be succeeded. Out of war peace gains fresh stability, but to refuse to abandon repose for war is not so sure a method of avoiding danger. [3] We must believe that the tyrant city that has been established in Hellas has been established against

1.124.1a Potidaea: Map 1.129, AX.
1.124.1b For the Dorians and the Ionians, see Appendix H, Dialects and Ethnic Groups, §7–8.

all [illegible] of universal empire, part fulfilled, part in
co[illegible]n attack and reduce it, and win future
sec[illegible] freedom for the Hellenes who are now
en[illegible]

Su[illegible]e Corinthians. [1.125.1] The Spartans having
now h[illegible]n, took the vote of all the allied states present
in orc[illegible]e; and the majority voted for war.[1a] [2] This
decid[illegible]e for them to commence at once, from their
want [illegible]s resolved that the means requisite were to be
procu[illegible]tes, and that there was to be no delay. And
indeec[illegible]ccupied with the necessary arrangements, less
than a[illegible]ca was invaded, and the war openly begun.

1.125 432/1 SPARTA The Peloponnesians vote for war; less than one year later Attica is invaded.

Th[illegible] sending embassies to Athens charged with
compl[illegible] as good a pretext for war as possible, in the
event [illegible]tion to them. [2] The first Spartan embassy
was tc[illegible] drive out the curse of the goddess;[2a] the history c[illegible]] In former generations there was an Athenian of[illegible]victor at the Olympic games,[3a] of good birth
and p[illegible] had married a daughter of Theagenes, a
Megar[illegible]of Megara.[3b] [4] Now this Cylon was inquiring at [illegible] told by the god to seize the Acropolis of
Athen[illegible] of Zeus. [5] Accordingly, procuring a force
from [illegible]ling his friends to join him, he seized the
Acrop[illegible] festival in the Peloponnesus began with the
intent[illegible]yrant, thinking that this was the grand festival
of Ze[illegible]on appropriate for a victor at the Olympic
games[illegible] festival that was meant was in Attica or elsewhere[illegible]e never thought of, and which the oracle did
not of[illegible]henians also have a festival which is called the
grand [illegible]ios or Gracious, namely, the Diasia. It is cele-
bratec[illegible]e whole people sacrifice not real victims but a
numb[illegible] peculiar to the country. However, fancying
he ha[illegible], he made the attempt. [7] As soon as the
Athen[illegible]ocked in, one and all, from the country, and
sat do[illegible]e citadel. [8] But as time went on, weary of
the lal[illegible] them departed; the responsibility of keeping

1.126 432/1 ATHENS As a pretext for war, Sparta tells Athens to drive out the curse of the goddess. Thucydides describes Cylon's attempted coup, from which the curse derived.

1.124.3a [illegible]or a dis- [illegible]s.

1.125.1a [illegible]sian [illegible]

1.126.2a [illegible]o drive [illegible] (by foul [illegible]a god or [illegible]

1.126.3a [illegible]npic-vic- [illegible] 640 [illegible]ny was [illegible]e Appendix K, Classical Greek Calendars and Dating Systems, §4, and Appendix I, Classical Greek Religious Festivals, §5. For the location of Olympia, see Map 1.129, BX.

1.126.3b Megara: Map 1.129, BX.

1.126.4a Delphi: Map 1.129, BX.

1.126.4b The Acropolis of Athens was a steep hill on the top of which stood the city's most ancient religious shrines and temples. At one time it constituted the entire city, as Thucydides notes in 2.15.3–6.

guard being left to the nine archons, with plenary powers to arrange everything according to their good judgment. It must be known that at that time most political functions were discharged by the nine archons.[8a] [9] Meanwhile Cylon and his besieged companions were distressed for want of food and water. [10] Accordingly Cylon and his brother made their escape; but the rest being hard pressed, and some even dying of famine, seated themselves as suppliants at the altar in the Acropolis. [11] The Athenians who were charged with the duty of keeping guard, when they saw them at the point of death in the temple, raised them up on the understanding that no harm should be done to them, led them out, and slew them. Some who as they passed by took refuge at the altars of the awful goddesses were dispatched on the spot. From this deed the men who killed them were called accursed and guilty against the goddess, they and their descendants.[11a] [12] Accordingly these cursed ones were driven out by the Athenians, and driven out again by Cleomenes of Sparta and an Athenian faction; the living were driven out, and the bones of the dead were taken up; thus they were cast out. For all that, they came back afterwards, and their descendants are still in the city.

1.127
432/1
ATHENS
Thucydides reports that the Spartan aim was to discredit Pericles, a powerful Athenian who opposed concessions to Sparta and was one of "the accursed."

This, then, was the curse that the Spartans ordered them to drive out. They were actuated primarily, as they pretended, by care for the honor of the gods; but they also knew that Pericles son of Xanthippus was connected with the curse on his mother's side, and they thought that his banishment would materially advance their designs on Athens. [2] Not that they really hoped to succeed in procuring this; they rather thought to create a prejudice against him in the eyes of his countrymen from the feeling that the war would be partly caused by his misfortune. [3] For being the most powerful man of his time, and the leading Athenian statesman, he opposed the Spartans in everything, and would have no concessions, but ever urged the Athenians on to war.

1.128
432/1
SPARTA
Athens in turn tells Sparta to drive out the curse of Taenarum and the curse of the goddess of the Bronze House, the latter involving Pausanias' attempt to betray the Greeks to Xerxes.

The Athenians retorted by ordering the Spartans to drive out the curse of Taenarum. The Spartans had once raised up some Helot[1a] suppliants from the temple of Poseidon at Taenarum,[1b] led them away, and slain them; for which they believe the great earthquake at Sparta to have been a retribution.[1c] [2] The Athenians also ordered them to drive out the curse of the goddess of the Bronze House; the history of which is as follows. [3] After Pausanias the Spartan had been recalled by the Spartans from his command in the Hellespont[3a] (this is his first recall),[3b] and had been tried by them and acquitted, not being again sent out in a public capacity, he

1.126.8a When Thucydides wrote this, the archons at Athens had become officials with no real powers; see Appendix A, The Athenian Government, §6.

1.126.11a Those who sought protection at the altar of a god could not be harmed without risk of sacrilege. See the supplication of the Helots (1.128.1), of the servant of Pausanias (1.133.1), of Themistocles (1.136.1), and of the Mytilenians (3.28.2); also the excesses of the Corcyraean revolution (3.81.5); and the flights of Thrasyllus (5.60.6) and Astyochus (8.84.3).

1.128.1a For more on the Helots, see Appendix C, Spartan Institutions, §3–4.

1.128.1b Taenarum: Map 1.129, BX.

1.128.1c See note 1.126.11a.

1.128.3a Hellespont: Map 1.129. AY. This picks up the career of Pausanias from 1.95.

1.128.3b For Pausanias' first recall, See 1.95.5.

took [illegible]e[3c] on his own responsibility, without the autho[illegible] arrived as a private person in the Hellespont. He c[illegible] Hellenic war, but really to carry on his intrigu[illegible]n he had begun before his recall, being ambitious [illegible]s. [4] The circumstance which first enabled him t[illegible] obligation, and to make a beginning of the whole[illegible]me connections and kinsmen of the King had been [illegible]n its capture from the Persians, when he was first t[illegible]m Cyprus.[5b] These captives he sent off to the King [illegible] of the rest of the allies, the account being that t[illegible] him. [6] He managed this with the help of Gong[illegible]m he had placed in charge of Byzantium and the pr[illegible]ongylus a letter for the King, the contents of which [illegible]s afterwards discovered: [7] "Pausanias, the gener[illegible] do you a favor, sends you these his prisoners of wa[illegible]our approval, to marry your daughter, and to make [illegible]Iellas subject to you. I may say that I think I am ab[illegible] cooperation. Accordingly if any of this please you, [illegible]ea through whom we may in future conduct our c[illegible]

1.129
HELLESPONT
The account of the curse of the goddess of the Bronze House begins with Xerxes' favorable response to Pausanias' letter.

Th[illegible]aled in the writing, and Xerxes was pleased with [illegible] Artabazus son of Pharnaces to the sea with order[illegible]es, the previous governor in the province of Dascy[illegible]over as quickly as possible to Pausanias at Byzan[illegible] entrusted to him; to show him the royal signe[illegible]ommission which he might receive from Pausanias[illegible], with all care and fidelity. [2] Artabazus on his ar[illegible] orders into effect, and sent over the letter, [3] w[illegible]lowing answer: "Thus saith King Xerxes to Pausa[illegible]om you have saved for me from Byzantium acros[illegible] laid up to you in our house, recorded forever; [illegible]ls I am well pleased. Let neither night nor day s[illegible]y performing any of your promises to me, neith[illegible] of silver let them be hindered, nor yet for numb[illegible] it may be that their presence is needed; but with [illegible]e man whom I send you, boldly advance my objec[illegible] be most for the honor and interest of us both."

1.128.3 [illegible]
1.128.5 [illegible]
1.128.5 [illegible]campaign [illegible]3.
1.128.6 [illegible]X.
1.129.1 [illegible] Appen- [illegible]
1.129.3 [illegible]Iellespont [illegible]gh a nar- [illegible]the Per- [illegible]

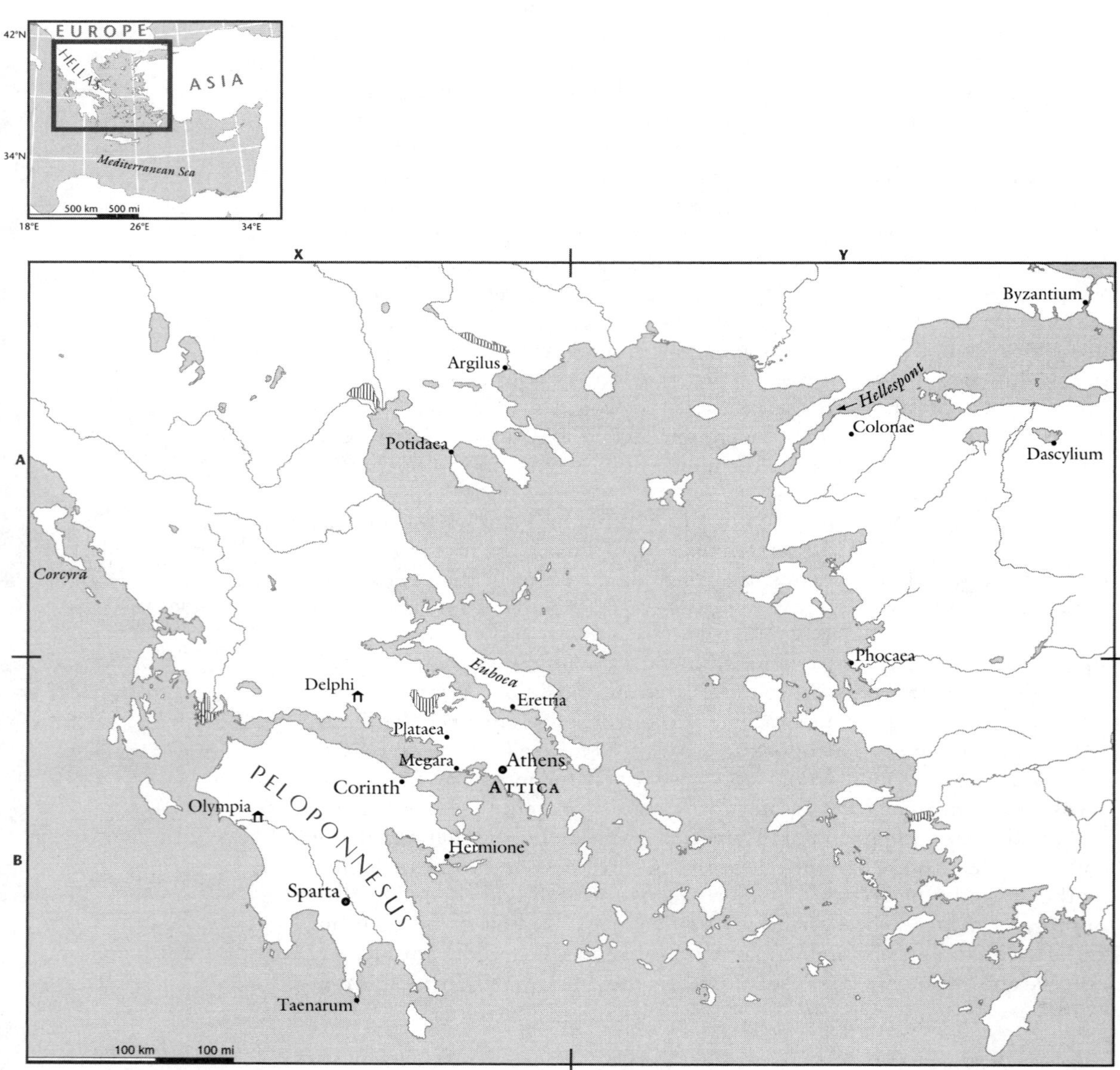

MAP 1.129 PRETEXTS FOR WAR—THE DEATH OF PAUSANIAS

1.130
HELLESPONT
Pausanias adopts Persian ways and antagonizes the Greeks.

Pr onor by the Hellenes as the hero of Plataea,[1a]
Paus of this letter, became prouder than ever, and
coul usual style, but went out of Byzantium in a
Medi on his march through Thrace by a bodyguard
of M t a Persian table, and was quite unable to contain trayed by his conduct in trifles what his ambition on a grander scale. [2] He also made himself
diffic yed so violent a temper to everyone without
excep come near him. Indeed, this was the principal
reaso ent over to the Athenians.

1.131
SPARTA
Suspecting treachery, the ephors recall Pausanias.

Th nduct, coming to the ears of the Spartans,
occas nd after his second voyage out in the ship of
Hern orders, he gave proofs of similar behavior.
Besie Byzantium[1b] by the Athenians, he did not
retur came that he had settled at Colonae[1c] in the
Troa th the barbarians, and that his stay there was
for n ephors,[1d] now no longer hesitating, sent him
a her orders to accompany the herald or be declared
a pub above everything to avoid suspicion, and con-
fiden he charge by means of money, he returned a
secon irst thrown into prison by the ephors (whose
powe s to the king), he soon compromised the matter a offered himself for trial to any who wished to
instit g him.

1.132
SPARTA
The ephors suspect Pausanias but they lack proof, until one of his servants betrays him.

N tangible proof against him—neither his enemies —of that indubitable kind required for the pun-
ishm oyal family, and at that moment in high office;
he be cousin King Pleistarchus, Leonidas' son, who
was s contempt of the laws and imitation of the bar-
baria for much suspicion of his being discontented
with the occasions on which he had in any way
depa customs were passed in review, and it was
reme en upon himself to have inscribed on the tripod dedicated by the Hellenes, as the first-fruits of
the sp llowing couplet:

> ated, great Pausanias raised
> it, that Phoebus might be praised.

1.130.1 ias led
ver the

1.131.1
1.131.1
1.131.1 29, AY.
1.131.1 e-ranging
Institu-

1.131.1 coding

secret messages, was a staff around which was rolled a strip of leather so that its edges always met. This surface was then written on crosswise, unrolled, and sent to its destination. It could only be read again when it was wound around an exactly similar staff that was given to an official when going abroad on public service.

1.131.2a Sparta: Map 1.129, BX.

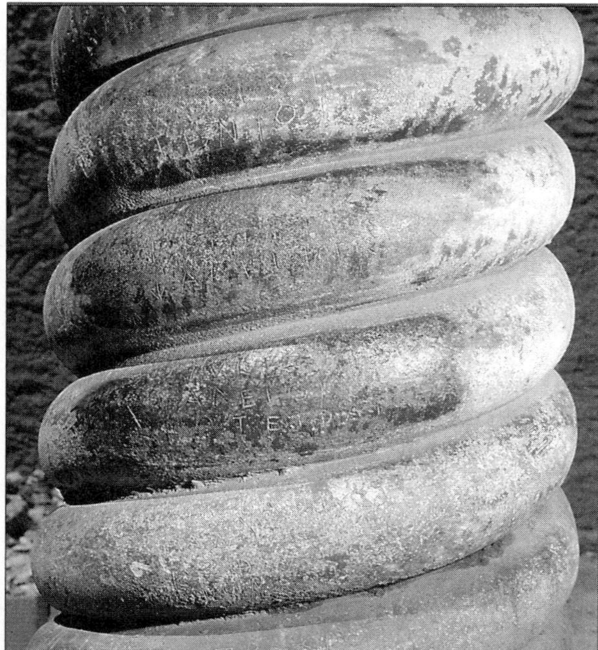

ILLUSTRATION 1.132 SERPENT COLUMN ERECTED AFTER THE BATTLE OF PLATAEA AS IT IS FOUND TODAY IN THE SITE OF THE HIPPODROME IN ISTANBUL; AND DETAIL (RIGHT) OF ITS INSCRIPTION.

[3] At the time the Spartans had at once erased the couplet, and inscribed the names of the cities that had aided in the overthrow of the barbarian and dedicated the offering.[3a] Yet it was considered that Pausanias had here been guilty of a grave offense, which, interpreted by the light of the attitude which he had since assumed, gained a new significance, and seemed to be quite in keeping with his present schemes. [4] Besides, they were informed that he was even intriguing with the Helots;[4a] and such indeed was the fact, for he was promising them freedom and citizenship if they would join him in insurrection, and would help him to carry out his plans to the end. [5] Even now, mistrusting the evidence even of the Helots themselves, the ephors would not consent to take any decided step against him; in accordance with their regular custom toward themselves, namely, to be slow in taking any irrevocable resolve in the matter of a Spartan citizen, without indisputable proof. At last, it is said, the person who was going to carry to Artabazus the last letter for the King, a man of Argilus, once the favorite and most trusty servant of Pausanias, turned

1.132.3a Remains of this tripod, and its inscription, can be seen today in Istanbul; see illustration 1.132.

1.132.4a For more on the Helots, see Appendix C, Spartan Institutions, §3–4.

inforr[illegible]flection that none of the previous messengers
had e[illegible]nterfeited the seal, in order that, if he found
himse[illegible]ses, or if Pausanias should ask to make some
corre[illegible]iscovered, he undid the letter, and found the
posts[illegible]d, namely, an order to put him to death.

1.133 471? SPARTA Posing as a suppliant at Taenarum, the servant tricks Pausanias into disclosing his crimes to the ephors in hiding.

O[illegible] the ephors now felt more certain. Still, they
wishe[illegible] hear Pausanias commit himself. Accordingly
the m[illegible]nt to Taenarum as a suppliant,[1a] and there
found[illegible] hut divided into two by a partition; within
which[illegible]e ephors and let them hear the whole matter
plainl[illegible] him and asked him the reason of his suppliant p[illegible]roached him with the order that he had written c[illegible]ne by one declared all the rest of the
circun[illegible]ad never yet brought him into any danger,
while[illegible]een him and the King, was yet just like the
mass[illegible]ewarded with death. Admitting all this, and
telling[illegible]out the matter, Pausanias gave him guarantee
of saf[illegible]ve the temple, and begged him to set off as
quickl[illegible] hinder the business in hand.

1.134 471? SPARTA Pausanias takes sanctuary in the temple of the goddess of the Bronze House. The ephors shut him in there and he starves to death, causing the curse.

Th[illegible]lly, and then departed, taking no action for
the m[illegible]st reached certainty, were preparing to arrest
him i[illegible] that, as he was about to be arrested in the
street,[illegible]f one of the ephors what he was coming for;
anoth[illegible]et signal, and betrayed it to him from kindness.[illegible] the temple of the goddess of the Bronze
Hous[illegible]h was near at hand, he succeeded in taking
sanctu[illegible]n, and entering into a small chamber, which
forme[illegible]o avoid being exposed to the weather, he
remai[illegible]rs, for the moment distanced in the pursuit,
afterw[illegible]f the chamber, and having made sure that he
was in[illegible]aded the doors, and staying before the place,
reduc[illegible]] When they found that he was on the point
of exp[illegible] the chamber, they brought him out of the
templ[illegible]ill in him, and as soon as he was brought out
he die[illegible] to throw him into the Kaiadas, where they
cast c[illegible]ded to inter him somewhere near. But the
god at[illegible]red the Spartans to remove the tomb to the
place[illegible] now lies in the consecrated ground, as an
inscrip[illegible]eclares—and, as what had been done was a
curse t[illegible]o bodies instead of one to the goddess of the
Bronz[illegible]o bronze statues made, and dedicated them

1.132.5a [illegible]lcidice [illegible]nown [illegible]

1.133.1a Taenarum: Map 1.129, BX. Suppliant: see note 1.126.11a.

ILLUSTRATION 1.135 OSTRAKA

1.135
471?
ATHENS
The investigation of Pausanias implicates Themistocles, who had been ostracized from Athens.

as a substitute for Pausanias. [1.135.1] Accordingly the Athenians retorted by telling the Spartans to drive out what the god himself had pronounced to be a curse.

[2] To return to the Medism of Pausanias, matter was found in the course of the inquiry to implicate Themistocles[2a]; and the Spartans accordingly sent envoys to the Athenians and required them to punish him as they had punished Pausanias. The Athenians consented to do so. [3] He had, as it happened, been *ostracized*[3a] and, from a residence at Argos,[3b] was in the habit of visiting other parts of the Peloponnesus. So they sent with the Spartans, who were ready to join in the pursuit, persons with instructions to take him wherever they found him.

1.136
470?
MOLOSSIA
Unable to remain at Corcyra, Themistocles flees to Molossia, to whose king, Admetus, a former adversary, he now becomes a suppliant.

Themistocles became aware of their intentions, however, and fled from the Peloponnesus to Corcyra,[1a] which was under obligations toward him. But the Corcyraeans alleged that they could not venture to shelter him at the cost of offending Athens and Sparta, and they conveyed him over to the continent opposite. [2] Pursued by the officers who hung on the report of his movements, and at a loss where to turn, he was compelled to stop at the house of Admetus, the Molossian[2a] king, though they were not on friendly terms. [3] Admetus happened not to be indoors, but his wife, to whom he made himself a suppliant, instructed him to take their child in his

1.135.2a Thucydides has already described Themistocles' role in persuading the Athenians to build a fleet (1.14.3), in the victory over the Persians at Salamis, (1.74.1), and in rebuilding Athens' walls, (1.89.3–1.93).

1.135.3a Themistocles is thought to have been ostracized no earlier than 472–1. *Ostracism* was a procedure by which an Athenian citizen could be honorably banished from Athens and her possessions for ten years without loss of property or citizenship if, after the Athenians had chosen to hold such a vote, he received the most votes out of a total of at least six thousand votes cast (votes were noted on shards of pottery called ostraka). See also 8.74.3; Appendix A, The Athenian Government, §8; and Illustration 1.135.

1.135.3b Argos: Map 1.137, BX.

1.136.1a Corcyra: Map 1.137, AX.

1.136.2a Molossia: Map 1.137, AX.

arms [illegible] earth.[3a] [4] Soon afterwards Admetus came in,
and [illegible] who he was, and begged him not to take
reve[illegible] exile for any opposition which his requests
migh[illegible] Themistocles at Athens. Indeed, he was now
far t[illegible]ge; retaliation was only honorable between
equa[illegible]n to the king had only affected the success of a
requ[illegible] person; if the king were to give him up to the
purs[illegible] and the fate which they intended for him, he
woul[illegible] to certain death.

T[illegible] and raised him up with his son, as he was sitting [illegible]ter the most effectual method of supplication,
and [illegible]rtans not long afterwards, refused to give him
up f[illegible]ay, but sent him off by land to the other sea to
Pydn[illegible]nions, as he wished to go to the Persian King.
[2] T[illegible]chant ship on the point of starting for Ionia.[2a]
Goin[illegible]ed by a storm to the Athenian squadron which
was [illegible]his alarm—he was luckily unknown to the people i[illegible] master who he was and what he was flying for,
and [illegible]o save him, he would declare that the captain
had [illegible]him. Meanwhile their safety consisted in letting
no o[illegible] a favorable time for sailing should arise. If he
com[illegible]emistocles promised him a proper recompense.
The [illegible]ed, and, after lying at anchor for a day and a
nigh[illegible] squadron, at length arrived at Ephesus.[2c]

[[illegible]d him with a present of money, as soon as he
recei[illegible]nds at Athens and from his secret hoards at
Argo[illegible]nland with a Persian from the coast, and sent a
lette[illegible]rxes' son, who had just come to the throne.[3a]
Its c[illegible] [4] "I, Themistocles, am come to you, who
did y[illegible]han any of the Hellenes, when I was compelled
to d[illegible]ur father's invasion—harm, however, far surpass[illegible]did him during his retreat, which brought no
dang[illegible] him. For the past, you owe me a good turn"—
here [illegible]ng sent to Xerxes from Salamis[4a] to retreat, as
well [illegible]ges unbroken, which, as he falsely pretended,
was [illegible]esent, able to do you great service, I am here,
purs[illegible] my friendship for you. However, I desire a
year'[illegible] able to declare in person the objects of my
comi[illegible]

1.137
471/0?
MOLOSSIA
Admetus protects Themistocles and sends him to Pydna.
NAXOS
Sailing to Ionia, his boat is forced to Naxos, a city besieged by Athenians. He avoids discovery and reaches Ephesus.
IONIA
He writes to Xerxes, describing his past services to the Persians and offering future ones.

1.136.[illegible]
1.137.[illegible], AX. [illegible]cedonia. [illegible] opposes [illegible]) to the [illegible]
1.137.[illegible]
1.137.[illegible]dides men-[illegible].
1.137.2c Ephesus: Map 1.137, BY.
1.137.3a. The date of the accession of Artaxerxes is 465/4. On any chronology of Themistocles, there is an awkward hiatus between the siege of Naxos (and Themistocles' arrival in Asia) and his meeting with Artaxerxes.
1.137.4a Salamis by Athens: Map 1.137, BX.

MAP 1.137 THE FLIGHT OF THEMISTOCLES

1.138
461?
PERSIAN ASIA
Themistocles is well received by Xerxes. Thucydides applauds Themistocles' extraordinary ability to foresee events and make decisions. Xerxes appoints him a governor.

It [illegible] proved his intention, and told him to do as he
said. [illegible] val in making what progress he could in the
study [illegible] and of the customs of the country. [2] Arrived
at co[illegible], he attained to very high consideration there,
such [illegible] possessed before or since; partly from his splendid r[illegible] the hopes which he held out of effecting the
subju[illegible] principally by the proof which experience daily
gave [illegible] For Themistocles was a man who exhibited the
most [illegible] ius; indeed, in this particular he has a claim on
our a[illegible] rdinary and unparalleled. By his own native
capac[illegible] shaped by education nor developed by later
traini[illegible] best judge in those sudden crises which admit
of litt[illegible] and the best prophet of the future, even to its
most [illegible] n able theoretical expositor of all that came
withi[illegible] ice, he was not without the power of passing
an ad[illegible] ters in which he had no experience. He could
also [illegible] ood and evil which lay hidden in the unseen
futur[illegible] we consider the extent of his natural powers,
or th[illegible] ation, this extraordinary man must be allowed
to ha[illegible] n the faculty of intuitively meeting an emergency[illegible] l cause of his death; though there is a story of
his ha[illegible] poison, on finding himself unable to fulfill his
prom[illegible] owever this may be, there is a monument to
him i[illegible] agnesia.[5a] He was governor of the district, the
King [illegible] esia, which brought in fifty talents[5b] a year for
bread[illegible] as considered to be the richest wine country,
for w[illegible] er provisions. [6] His bones, it is said, were
conve[illegible] es in accordance with his wishes, and interred
in At[illegible] one without the knowledge of the Athenians;
as it i[illegible] y in Attica an outlaw for treason. So ends the
histor[illegible] mistocles, the Spartan and the Athenian, the
most [illegible] e in Hellas.

1.139
432/1
ATHENS
Sparta also demands that Athens raise the siege of Potidaea, restore independence to Aegina, and rescind the Megarian Decree. A final ultimatum orders Athens to let the Hellenes be independent. As the Athenians debate these demands, Pericles rises to speak.

To [illegible] The history of their first embassy, the injunc-
tions [illegible] the rejoinder which it provoked concerning
the e[illegible] persons, have been related already. It was followe[illegible] dered Athens to raise the siege of Potidaea,[1a]
and t[illegible] nce of Aegina.[1b] Above all, it made very clear
to th[illegible] ght be prevented if they revoked the Megara

1.138.5a [illegible] Map [illegible] "Asiatic" [illegible] strip of [illegible] agnesia [illegible] s a classi- [illegible] its [illegible] d politi- [illegible]

1.138.5b The talent is a unit of weight and money. See Appendix J, Classical Greek Currency, §5.

1.138.5c Lampsacus: Map 1.137, AY.

1.138.5d Myos: Map 1.137, BY.

1.139.1a Potidaea: Map 1.137, AX.

1.139.1b Aegina: Map 1.137, BX.

decree,[1c] excluding the Megarians from the use of Athenian harbors and of the market of Athens. [2] But Athens was not inclined either to revoke the decree, or to entertain their other proposals; she accused the Megarians of pushing their cultivation into the consecrated ground and the unenclosed land on the border, and of harboring her runaway slaves. [3] At last an embassy arrived with the Spartan ultimatum. The ambassadors were Ramphias, Melesippus, and Agesander. Not a word was said on any of the old subjects; there was simply this: "Sparta wishes the peace to continue, and there is no reason why it should not, if you would let the Hellenes be independent." Upon this the Athenians held an assembly,[3a] and laid the matter before their consideration. It was resolved to deliberate once and for all on all their demands, and to give them an answer. [4] There were many speakers who came forward and gave their support to one side or the other, urging the necessity of war, or the revocation of the decree and the folly of allowing it to stand in the way of peace. Among them came forward Pericles son of Xanthippus, the first man of his time at Athens, ablest alike in counsel and in action, and gave the following advice:

1.140
432/1
ATHENS
Pericles demands no concession to Sparta because she has not offered or accepted arbitration, as called for in the treaty, and her demands have grown more dictatorial and threatening. He says the Megarian Decree is not a trifle, but a symbol of Athenian response to Spartan pressure.

"There is one principle, Athenians, which I hold to through everything, and that is the principle of no concession to the Peloponnesians. I know that the spirit which inspires men while they are being persuaded to make war is not always retained in action, that as circumstances change, resolutions change. Yet I see that now as before the same, almost literally the same, counsel is demanded of me; and I put it to those of you who are allowing yourselves to be persuaded, to support the decisions of the assembly even in the case of reverses, or to forfeit all credit for their wisdom in the event of success. For sometimes the course of things is as arbitrary as the plans of man; indeed this is why we usually blame chance for whatever does not happen as we expected. [2] Now it was clear before that Sparta entertained designs against us; it is still more clear now. The treaty provides that we shall mutually submit our differences to arbitration, and that we shall meanwhile each keep what we have. Yet the Spartans never yet made us any such offer, never yet would accept from us any such offer; on the contrary, they wish complaints to be settled by war instead of by negotiation; and in the end we find them here dropping the tone of protest and adopting that of command.[2a] [3] They order us to raise the siege of Potidaea, to let Aegina be independent, to revoke the Megara decree; and they conclude with an ultimatum warning us to leave the Hellenes indepen-

1.139.1c Athens' Megara decree was apparently a powerful sanction. See Appendix B, The Athenian Empire, §10. Megara: Map 1.137, BX.

1.139.3a Assembly: see Appendix A, The Athenian Government, §5, 8.

1.140.2a Failure to offer or to accept Athenian offers of arbitration did have adverse effects upon Spartan morale during the first phase of the Peloponnesian War, as we learn in 7.18.

d[illegible]u will none of you think that we shall be
g[illegible] if we refuse to revoke the Megara decree,
w[illegible]f their complaints, and the revocation of
w[illegible]ar, or let any feeling of self-reproach linger
in[illegible]vent to war for slight cause. [5] Why, this
tr[illegible]eal and trial of your resolution. If you give
w[illegible]e to meet some greater demand, as having
b[illegible]dience in the first instance; while a firm
re[illegible]arly understand that they must treat you as
ec[illegible]

[illegible]herefore at once, either to submit before
yo[illegible] are to go to war, as I for one think we
ou[illegible]aring whether the ostensible cause be great
or[illegible]making concessions or consenting to a pre-
ca[illegible]essions. For all claims from an equal, urged
up[illegible]ands, before any attempt at arbitration, be
th[illegible]l, have only one meaning, and that is slav-
er[illegible]

1.141
432/1
ATHENS
Pericles says that to heed Sparta's demands can lead only to slavery. He points out that the Peloponnesians lack funds to sustain conflicts and, being farmers, they will not be able to mobilize for long campaigns; that they cannot threaten Athens at sea; and, as a league of states with divergent interests, they will find it hard to act quickly or decisively.

[illegible]d the resources of either party, a detailed
co[illegible] you the inferiority of Athens. [3] Person-
all[illegible]ation of their land, without funds either
pr[illegible]ponnesians are also without experience in
lo[illegible] the strict limit which poverty imposes on
th[illegible]other. [4] Powers of this description are
qu[illegible]manning a fleet or often sending out an
ar[illegible]the absence from their homes, the expen-
di[illegible]ds; and besides, they have not command
of[illegible]t must be remembered, maintains a war
m[illegible]tions. Farmers are a class of men that are
al[illegible]e in person than in purse. Confident that
th[illegible]e dangers, they are by no means so sure
th[illegible] prematurely exhausted, especially if the
w[illegible]expect, which it very likely will. [6] In a
sir[illegible]esians and their allies may be able to defy
all[illegible]apacitated from carrying on a war against
a [illegible]acter from their own, by the want of the
sir[illegible]quisite to prompt and vigorous action, and
th[illegible]gress composed of various peoples,[6a] in
wh[illegible]s an equal vote, and each presses its own
en[illegible]gs which generally results in no action at

1.141.6a [illegible]ership of [illegible]

all. [7] The great wish of some is to avenge themselves on some particular enemy, the great wish of others to save their own pocket. Slow in assembling, they devote a very small fraction of the time to the consideration of any matter of common concern, most of it to the prosecution of their own affairs. Meanwhile each fancies that no harm will come of his neglect, that it is the business of somebody else to look after this or that for him; and so, by the same notion being entertained by all separately, the common cause imperceptibly decays."

1.142
432/1
ATHENS
Pericles argues that the enemy's principal handicap will be lack of money; that Athenian sea power will be more effective against them on land than their land power against Athens at sea; and that they will not easily acquire the skill to challenge Athens at sea, especially if Athenian fleets limit their opportunities to practice.

"But the principal point is the hindrance that they will experience from want of money. The slowness with which it comes in will cause delay; but the opportunities of war wait for no man. [2] Again, we need not be alarmed either at the possibility of their raising fortifications in Attica, or at their navy.[2a] [3] It would be difficult for any system of fortifications to establish a rival city, even in time of peace, much more, surely, in an enemy's country, with Athens just as much fortified against it, as it against Athens; [4] while a mere post might be able to do some harm to the country by incursions and by the facilities which it would afford for desertion, it can never prevent our sailing into their country and raising fortifications there, and making reprisals with our powerful fleet. [5] For our naval skill is of more use to us for service on land, than their military skill for service at sea. [6] Familiarity with the sea they will not find an easy acquisition. [7] If you who have been practicing at it ever since the Persian invasion have not yet brought it to perfection, is there any chance of anything considerable being effected by an agricultural, unseafaring population, who will besides be prevented from practicing by the constant presence of strong squadrons of observation from Athens? [8] With a small squadron they might hazard an engagement, encouraging their ignorance by numbers; but the restraint of a strong force will prevent their moving, and through want of practice they will grow more clumsy, and consequently more timid. [9] It must be kept in mind that seamanship, just like anything else, is a matter requiring skill, and will not admit of being taken up occasionally as an occupation for times of leisure; on the contrary, it is so exacting as to leave leisure for nothing else."

1.142.2a Here and in the points below concerning moneys from Delphi and Olympia, the suborning of Athens' foreign sailors with high pay, and the training of a Peloponnesian fleet to match Athens, Thucydides seems to have Pericles respond directly to points made by the Corinthians in their speech to the Spartans and their allies reported in 1.121–22.

[illegible] ouch the moneys at Olympia[1a] or Delphi,[1b] an[illegible] gn sailors by the temptation of higher pay, th[illegible] us danger if we could not still be a match for[illegible] our own citizens and the resident aliens.[1c] Bu[illegible] we are always a match for them; and, best of [illegible] and higher class of native coxswains and sai[illegible] zens than all the rest of Hellas. [2] And to say[illegible] of such a step, none of our foreign sailors wo[illegible] n outlaw from his country, and to take ser- vic[illegible] pes, for the sake of a few days' high pay."

[illegible] olerably fair account of the position of the Pel[illegible] hens is free from the defects that I have crit[illegible] other advantages of its own, which they car[illegible] [4] If they march against our country we wil[illegible] t will then be found that the desolation of the[illegible] the same as that of even a fraction of the Pel[illegible] ill not be able to supply the deficiency exc[illegible] e have plenty of land both on the islands anc[illegible] rule of the sea is indeed a great matter. Co[illegible] ppose that we were islanders: can you con- cei[illegible] position? Well, this in future should, as far as [illegible] on of our position. Dismissing all thought of [illegible] must vigilantly guard the sea and the city. No[illegible] feel for the former must provoke us to a bat[illegible] uperiority of the Peloponnesians. A victory wo[illegible] y another battle against the same superior- ity:[illegible] ss of our allies, the source of our strength, wh[illegible] a day after we become unable to march aga[illegible] not over the loss of houses and land but of me[illegible] nd land do not gain men, but men them. An[illegible] could persuade you, I would have bid you go [illegible] with your own hands, and show the Pelo- po[illegible] rate will not make you submit."

1.143
432/1
ATHENS
Pericles asserts that Sparta, even if she obtains funds, will never match Athens at sea, for Athens has enough citizen-sailors to match all of Hellas. Athens has lands across the sea that Sparta cannot harm. "Thus we must forgo our properties in Attica and, viewing ourselves as islanders, value most our sea power and its ability to provide us resources from our empire."

[illegible] sons to hope for a favorable outcome, if you[illegible] nbine schemes of fresh conquest with the co[illegible] will abstain from willfully involving your- sel[illegible] deed, I am more afraid of our own blun-

1.144
432/1
ATHENS
Pericles concludes his speech by advising the Athenians to accept this war as inevitable, and to avoid any new conquests or unnecessary risks until the war is over. He suggests that they let the Peloponnesians commence hostilities and reminds the Athenians of their glorious past.

1.143.1a [illegible]
1.143.1b [illegible]
1.143.1c Athenian resident aliens (*metics*) had both rights and obligations but were not citizens. See Appendix A, The Athenian Government, §2.

ILLUSTRATION 1.144
MARBLE HERM OF PERICLES; A ROMAN COPY OF AN ORIGINAL OF PERHAPS 430 B.C.

ders than of the enemy's devices. [2] But these matters shall be explained in another speech, as events require; for the present dismiss these men with the answer that we will allow Megara the use of our market and harbors when the Spartans suspend their alien acts against us and our allies, there being nothing in the treaty to prevent either one or the other; that we will leave the cities independent, if independent we found them when we made the treaty, and when the Spartans grant to their cities an independence not involving subservience to Spartan interest, but such as each severally may desire;

th[illegible]ve the legal satisfaction which our agreem[illegible]e shall not commence hostilities, but shall re[illegible]nence them. This is an answer agreeable at o[illegible]e dignity of Athens. [3] It must be thoro[illegible]var is a necessity, and that the more readily w[illegible]be the ardor of our opponents, and that out of[illegible] communities and individuals acquire the gr[illegible]ur fathers resist the Persians not only with re[illegible]n ours, but even when those resources had be[illegible]ore by wisdom than by fortune, more by da[illegible] did not they beat off the barbarian and ad[illegible]eir present height? We must not fall behind th[illegible] enemies in any way and in every way, and at[illegible] power to our posterity unimpaired."

1.145 432/1 ATHENS The Athenians vote as Pericles advises and the Spartan envoys return home.

Su[illegible]Pericles. The Athenians, persuaded of the wisdom [illegible]he desired, and answered the Spartans as he recon[illegible]eparate points and in general: they would not respo[illegible]vere ready to have the complaints settled in a fair a[illegible] arbitration, which the terms of the truce prescribe[illegible]d home, and did not return again.

1.146 432/1 HELLAS Thus the stage was set for war, though it did not yet begin.

Th[illegible]nd differences existing between the rival powers be[illegible]mediately from the affair at Epidamnus[1a] and Corcy[illegible]ntinued in spite of them, and mutual communicati[illegible]ithout heralds, but not without suspicion, as event[illegible] were equivalent to a breach of the treaty and matte[illegible]

1.146.1a [illegible]
1.146.1b [illegible]

BOOK TWO

The war between the Athenians and Pelop[illegible] on either side now really begins. For now all interc[illegible]ne medium of heralds[1a] ceased, and hostilities were [illegible]ted without intermission. The history follows the ch[illegible]nts by summers and winters. 2.1 431 1st Year/Summer HELLAS The war begins.

Th[illegible]which was entered into after the conquest of Eubo[illegible][1a] In the fifteenth year, the forty-eighth year of the[illegible]s at Argos,[1b] during the ephorate[1c] of Aenesias at Spa[illegible]h but two of the archonship[1d] of Pythodorus at Ath[illegible]ne battle of Potidaea[1e] and just at the beginning [illegible]rce a little over three hundred strong, under the c[illegible]*archs*,[1g] Pythangelus son of Phyleides, and Diem[illegible], about the first watch of the night, made an armed[illegible] city of Boeotia in alliance with Athens.[1i] [2] The g[illegible]m by a Plataean called Naucleides, who, with his pa[illegible], meaning to put to death the citizens of the oppos[illegible] city to Thebes, and thus obtain power for thems[illegible] arranged through Eurymachus son of Leontiades.[illegible]nce at Thebes. For Plataea had always been at varian[illegible]he latter, foreseeing that war was at hand, wishe[illegible]my in time of peace, before hostilities had ac- 2.2 431 1st Year/Summer PLATAEA In the fifteenth year of the Thirty Years' Peace, Thebes attacks Plataea.

2.1.1a [illegible]k insti- [illegible]ed [illegible]Hermes, [illegible]staff they [illegible]nmo- [illegible]ring [illegible]ges, take [illegible]y [illegible]

2.2.1a [illegible]s re- [illegible]

2.2.1b [illegible] and the [illegible]tess- [illegible]sumably, [illegible]ning of [illegible]ncident [illegible]described in 4.133.

2.2.1c For the Spartan ephorate, see Appendix C, Spartan Institutions, §5–6.

2.2.1d For a discussion of the Athenian eponymous archon, see Appendix A, The Athenian Government, §6; and for the problem of dating events in classical times, see Appendix K, Calendars and Dating Systems, §2–3.

2.2.1e This battle is described in 1.62–63.

2.2.1f Thebes: Map 2.5.

2.2.1g *Boeotarchs* were chief magistrates of the Boeotian federal government.

2.2.1h Plataea: Map 2.5.

2.2.1i Athens, in relation to Plataea and Thebes: Map 2.5.

tually broken out. Indeed this was how they got in so easily without being observed, as no guard had been posted. [4] After the soldiers had taken up positions in the *agora*[4a] those who had invited them in wished them to set to work at once and go to their enemies' houses. This, however, the Thebans refused to do, but determined to make a conciliatory proclamation, and if possible to come to a friendly understanding with the citizens. Their herald accordingly invited any who wished to resume their old place in the federation of all the Boeotians[4b] to take up positions beside them, for they thought that in this way the city would readily join them.

2.3
431
1st Year/Summer
PLATAEA
After perceiving the weakness of the occupying enemy force, the Plataeans counterattack.

On becoming aware of the presence of the Thebans within their gates, and of the sudden occupation of the city, the Plataeans concluded in their alarm that more had entered than was really the case, the night preventing their seeing them. They accordingly came to terms, and accepting the proposal, made no movement; especially as the Thebans offered none of them any violence. [2] But somehow or other, during the negotiations, they discovered the scanty numbers of the Thebans, and decided that they could easily attack and overpower them; the mass of the Plataeans being averse to revolting from Athens. [3] At all events they resolved to attempt it. Digging through the common walls of the houses, they thus managed to join each other without being seen going through the streets, in which they placed wagons without the beasts in them, to serve as a barricade, and arranged everything else as seemed suitable for the occasion. [4] When everything had been done that circumstances permitted, they watched their opportunity and went out of their houses against the enemy. It was still night, though daybreak was at hand: in daylight it was thought that their attack would be met by men full of courage and on equal terms with their assailants, while in darkness it would fall upon panic-stricken troops, who would also be at a disadvantage from their enemy's knowledge of the locality. So they made their assault at once, and came to close quarters as quickly as they could.

2.4
431
1st Year/Summer
PLATAEA
The Thebans are defeated; many surrender.

The Thebans, finding themselves outwitted, immediately closed up to repel all attacks made upon them. [2] Twice or thrice they beat back their assailants. But the men shouted and charged them, the women and slaves screamed and yelled from the houses and pelted them with stones and tiles; besides, it had been raining hard all night; and so at last their courage gave way, and they turned and fled through the city. Most of the fugitives were quite ignorant of the right ways out, and this, with the mud, and the darkness caused by the moon being in her last quarter, and the fact that their pursuers knew their way about and could easily stop their escape, proved

2.2.4a *Agora:* the marketplace and the social center of a classical Greek city.

2.2.4b For more on the constitution of the Boeotian Federation, see note 5.38.2a.

fatal [illegible] gate open was the one by which they had entere[illegible] one of the Plataeans driving the spike of a javeli[illegible] of the bolt; so that even here there was no longe[illegible] They were now chased all over the city. Some got [illegible]emselves over, in most cases with a fatal result. One [illegible] a deserted gate, and obtaining an axe from a wom[illegible];[4a] but as they were soon observed only a few succe[illegible]hers, scattered about in different parts of the city, [illegible]e most numerous and compact body rushed into [illegible] the city wall: the doors on the side of the stree[illegible] and the Thebans fancied that they were the gates [illegible]re was a passage right through to the outside. [6] T[illegible]ir enemies in a trap, now consulted whether they [illegible]uilding and burn them just as they were, or whet[illegible]lse that they could do with them; [7] until at lengt[illegible] the Theban survivors found wandering about the c[illegible]itional surrender of themselves and their arms to th[illegible]ch was the fate of the party in Plataea, [2.5.1] the r[illegible] were to have joined them with all their forces befor[illegible]ything miscarrying with the body that had entered [illegible]he affair while on the road, and pressed forward [illegible]Now Plataea is nearly eight miles from Thebes, and t[illegible]by the rain that had fallen in the night, for the river [illegible]was not easy of passage; [3] and so, having to marcl[illegible]hindered in crossing the river, they arrived too late, [illegible]party either slain or captive. [4] When they learn[illegible], they at once formed a design against the Plata[illegible] the attack had been made in time of peace, and w[illegible], there were of course men and stock in the fields[illegible]ed if possible to have some prisoners to exchang[illegible]men in the city, should any chance to have been [illegible]s their plan. But the Plataeans suspected their intent[illegible] formed, and becoming alarmed for their fellow c[illegible] sent a herald to the Thebans, reproaching them [illegible]ttempt to seize their city in time of peace, and warni[illegible]rage on those outside. Should the warning be disreg[illegible] to put to death the men they had in their hands[illegible]e Thebans retiring from their territory, they woul[illegible]s to their friends. [6] This is the Theban ac-

2.5
431
1st Year/Summer
PLATAEA
Theban reinforcements arrive too late. When the Plataeans threaten to harm the prisoners, the Thebans retire without taking hostages; but the Plataeans execute the prisoners anyway.

2.4.4a [illegible] wooden [illegible]l bolts. [illegible] release [illegible]en. [illegible]ld only open the gate by cutting through the bar, a noisy and lengthy process. See also 4.111.2.

2.5.2a Asopus river: Map 2.5.

count of the matter, and they say that they had an oath given them. The Plataeans, on the other hand, do not admit any promise of an immediate surrender, but make it contingent upon subsequent negotiation: the oath they deny altogether. [7] Be this as it may, upon the Thebans retiring from their territory without committing any injury, the Plataeans hastily got in whatever they had in the country and immediately put the men to death. The prisoners were a hundred and eighty in number; Eurymachus, the person with whom the traitors had negotiated, being one.

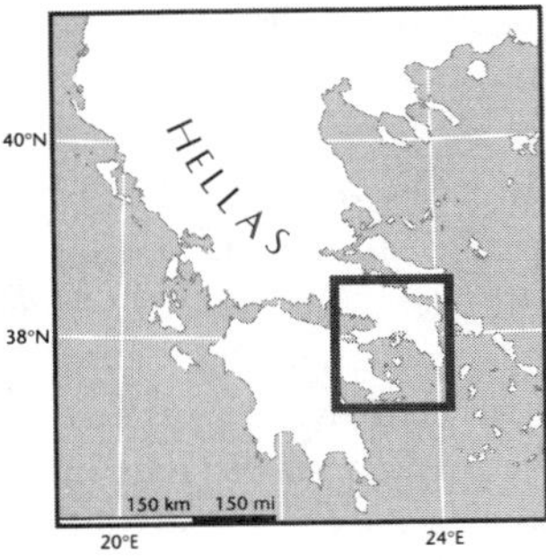

MAP 2.5 PLATAEA AND THEBES

2.6
431
1st Year/Summer
PLATAEA
Athenian instructions to preserve the prisoners arrive too late. Athens sends supplies and a garrison, and gives refuge to Plataean noncombatants.

This done, the Plataeans sent a messenger to Athens, gave back the dead to the Thebans under a truce,[1a] and arranged things in the city as seemed best to meet the present emergency. [2] The Athenians meanwhile, having had word of the affair sent them immediately after its occurrence, had instantly seized all the Boeotians in Attica, and sent a herald to the Plataeans to forbid their proceeding to extremities with their Theban prisoners without instructions from Athens. The news of the men's death had of course

2.6.1a This truce is granted according to the accepted ritual of hoplite warfare. See Appendix F, Land Warfare, §6.

not a[illegible]senger having left Plataea just when the Thebans [illegible]st after their defeat and capture; so there was no la[illegible]enians sent their orders in ignorance of the facts; [illegible]rrival found the men slain. After this the Athenians [illegible] brought in provisions, and left a garrison in the pl[illegible]e women and children and such of the men as were [illegible]

2.7
431
1st Year/Summer
HELLAS
Both sides prepare for war. Sparta sends embassies to neutrals and barbarians, and asks her Italian and Sicilian allies to build triremes.

W[illegible]the treaty had been broken by an overt act,[1a] and A[illegible]for war, as did also Sparta and her allies. They resolv[illegible] the King and to such other of the barbarian power[illegible]ook to for assistance, and tried to ally themselves [illegible]states at home.[1b] [2] Sparta, in addition to the existir[illegible]ders to the states that had declared for her in Italy [illegible]els up to a grand total of five hundred, the quota [illegible]mined by its size, and also to provide a specified s[illegible] were ready they were to remain neutral and to adr[illegible]s into their harbors. [3] Athens on her part review[illegible]racy, and sent embassies to the places more imme[illegible]nnesus, Corcyra, Cephallenia, Acarnania, and Zacyn[illegible]f these could be relied upon she could carry the w[illegible]nesus.

2.8
431
1st Year/Summer
HELLAS
Enthusiasm for war among young men runs high. Most Hellenes hope for Sparta to win, fearing absorption in Athens' empire or desiring liberation from it.

An[illegible]d the boldest hopes and put forth their utmost [illegible]s was only natural. Zeal is always at its height at the [illegible] undertaking; and on this particular occasion the P[illegible]ns were both full of young men whose inexpe[illegible]r to take up arms, while the rest of Hellas stood [illegible]ent at the conflict of its leading cities. [2] Every[illegible]being recited and oracles being chanted by such p[illegible]and this not only in the contending cities. [3] Furthe[illegible]s there was an earthquake at Delos,[3a] for the first ti[illegible]e Hellenes.[3b] This was said and thought to be omino[illegible]ding; indeed, nothing of the kind that happened [illegible]without remark. [4] Men's feelings inclined much [illegible]especially as they proclaimed themselves the liberat[illegible]te or public effort that could help them in speech[illegible] each thinking that the cause suffered wherever h[illegible]to it. [5] So general was the indignation felt against[illegible]ose who wished to escape from her empire,

2.6.3a [illegible] is con-[illegible]

2.7.1a [illegible]ies with [illegible] some [illegible]e, as we [illegible]

2.7.1b [illegible]this is [illegible]damus [illegible]

2.7.3a Corcyra, Cephallenia, Acarnania, Zacynthus, in relation to the Peloponnesus: Map 2.9, AX, BX.

2.8.3a Delos: Map 2.9, BY.

2.8.3b Since Herodotus (Book 6.98) mentions an earthquake on Delos in 490, this remark has caused some amazement.

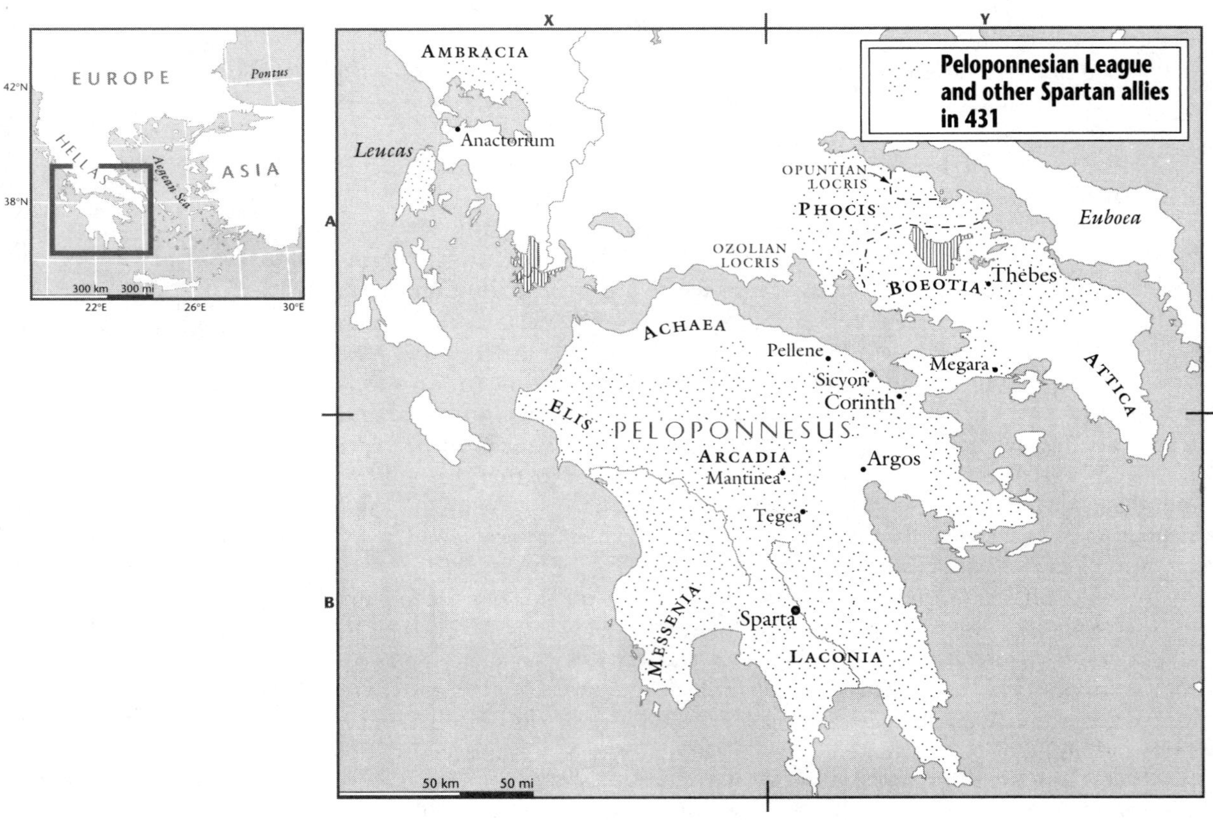

MAP 2.8 PELOPONNESIAN LEAGUE AND OTHER SPARTAN ALLIES

2.9
431
1st Year/Summer
HELLAS
The allies of the two belligerents are listed.

or were apprehensive of being absorbed by it. [2.9.1] Such were the preparations and such the feelings with which the contest opened. The allies of the two belligerents were the following. [2] These were the allies of Sparta: all the Peloponnesians within the Isthmus[2a] except the Argives[2b] and Achaeans,[2c] who were neutral; Pellene[2d] being the only Achaean city that first joined in the war, though her example was afterwards followed by the rest. Outside the Peloponnesus the Megarians,[2e] Locrians,[2f] Boeotians,[2g]

2.9.2a The Isthmus of Corinth, Corinth: Map 2.8, AY.
2.9.2b Argos: Map 2.8, BY.
2.9.2c Achaea: Map 2.8, AX.
2.9.2d Pellene in Achaea: Map 2.8, AY.
2.9.2e Megara, Map 2.8: AY
2.9.2f Presumably he means the Opuntian Locrians (Map 2.8, AY), not the Ozolian Locrians who were allied to Athens (see 3.95.3), or the Italian (Epizephyrian) Locrians.
2.9.2g Boeotia: Map 2.8, AY.

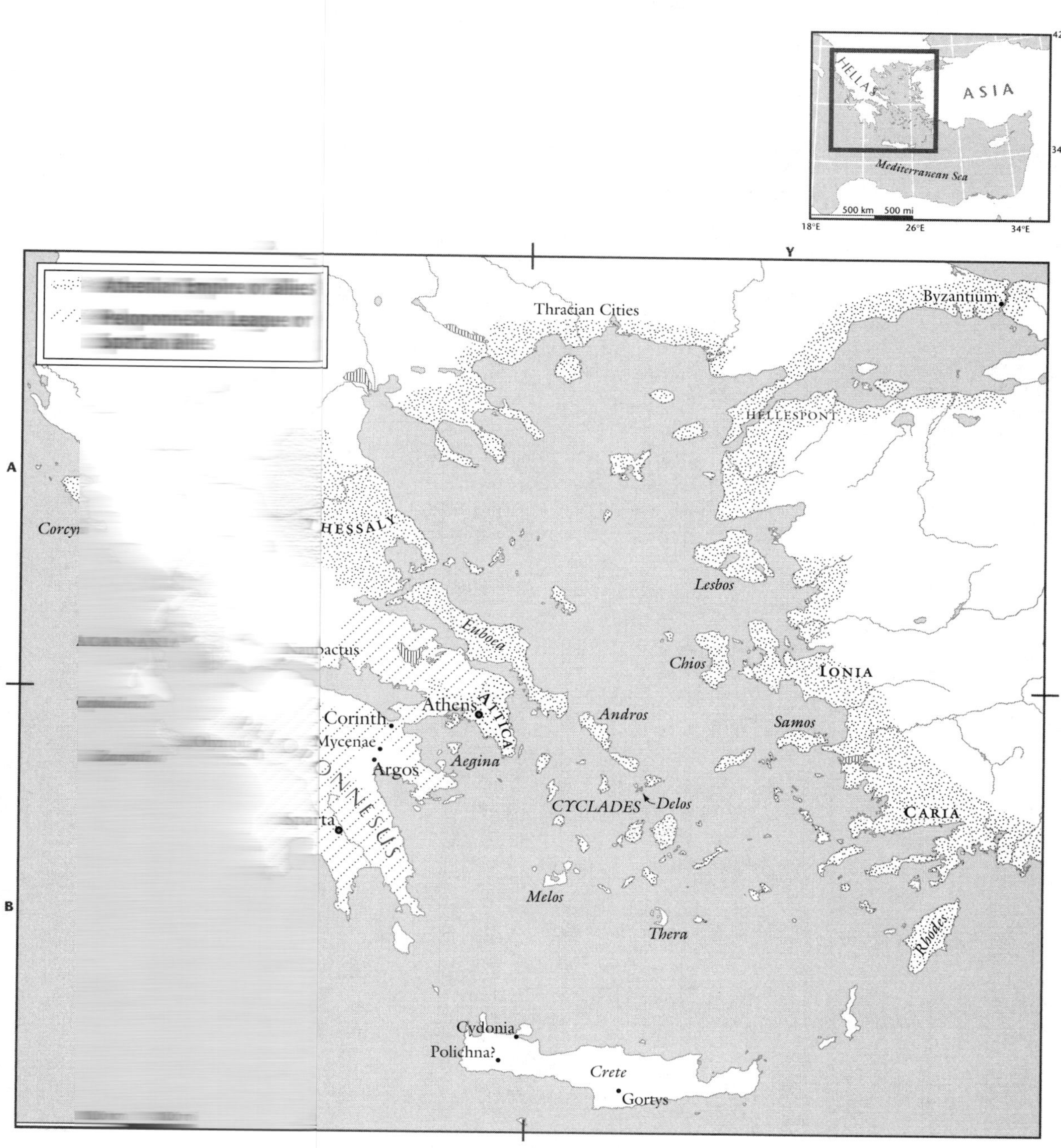

Map 2 t States and Allies

Phocians,[2h] Ambraciots,[2i] Leucadians,[2j] and Anactorians.[2k] [3] Of these, ships were furnished by the Corinthians, Megarians, Sicyonians,[3a] Pellenians, Eleans,[3b] Ambraciots, and Leucadians; and cavalry by the Boeotians, Phocians, and Locrians. The other states sent infantry. This was the Spartan confederacy.[3c] [4] That of Athens comprised the Chians,[4a] Lesbians,[4b] Plataeans, the Messenians in Naupactus,[4c] most of the Acarnanians,[4d] the Corcyraeans,[4e] Zacynthians,[4f] and some tributary cities in the following countries, namely, the seaboard part of Caria[4g] with its Dorian neighbors, Ionia,[4h] the Hellespont,[4i] the Thracian cities,[4j] the islands lying between the Peloponnesus and Crete[4k] toward the east, and all the Cyclades[4*l*] except Melos[4m] and Thera.[4n] [5] Of these, ships were furnished by Chios, Lesbos, and Corcyra, infantry and money by the rest. Such were the allies of either party and their resources for the war.

2.10
431
1st Year/Summer
ISTHMUS
Sparta and her allies assemble forces at the Isthmus.

Immediately after the affair at Plataea, Sparta sent round orders to the cities in the Peloponnesus and the rest of her confederacy to prepare troops and the provisions requisite for a foreign campaign, in order to invade Attica. [2] The several states were ready at the time appointed and assembled at the Isthmus; the contingent of each city being two-thirds of its whole force. [3] After the whole army had mustered, the Spartan king, Archidamus, the leader of the expedition, called together the generals of all the states and the principal persons and officers, and exhorted them as follows:

2.11
431
1st Year/Summer
ISTHMUS
Archidamus, Sparta's king, speaks to the army, calling for caution, vigilance, and discipline.

"Peloponnesians and allies, our fathers made many campaigns both within and without the Peloponnesus, and the elder men among us here are not without experience in war. Yet we have never set out with a larger force than the present; and if our numbers and efficiency are remarkable, so also is the power of the state against which we march. [2] We ought not then to show ourselves inferior to our ancestors, or unequal to our own reputation. For the hopes and attention of all Hellas are bent upon the present effort, and its sympathy is with the enemy of the hated Athens. [3] Therefore, numerous as the invading army may appear to be, and certain as some may think it that our adversary will not meet us in the field, this is no

2.9.2h Phocis: Map 2.8, AY.
2.9.2i Ambracia: Map 2.8, AX.
2.9.2j Leucas: Map 2.8, AX.
2.9.2k Anactorium: Map 2.8, AX.
2.9.3a Sicyon: Map 2.8, AY.
2.9.3b Elis: Map 2.8, BX.
2.9.3c The "confederacy" here includes both the Peloponnesian League and the wider Spartan alliance; see Appendix D, The Peloponnesian League, §3.
2.9.4a Chios: Map 2.9, AY.
2.9.4b Lesbos: Map 2.9, AY.
2.9.4c These "Messenians" lived now at Naupactus (Map 2.9, AX), where Athens settled them after they surrendered to Sparta from Ithome and were forced to leave the Peloponnesus; see 1.103.1–3.
2.9.4d Acarnania: Map 2.9, AX.
2.9.4e Corcyra: Map 2.9, AX.
2.9.4f Zacynthus: Map 2.9, BX.
2.9.4g Caria: Map 2.9, BY.
2.9.4h Ionia: Map 2.9, AY. See Appendix H, Dialects and Ethnic Groups, §7–8, for the Ionians and the Dorians.
2.9.4i Hellespont: Map 2.9, AY.
2.9.4j The region here called the Thracian cities: Map 2.9, AY.
2.9.4k Peloponnesus: Map 2.9, BX. Crete: Map 2.9, BY.
2.9.4*l* The Cyclades, islands in the Aegean Sea southeast of Attica: Map 2.9, BY.
2.9.4m Melos: Map 2.9, BY.
2.9.4n Thera: Map 2.9, BY.

sor [illegible] least negligence upon the march; but the off [illegible] articular city should always be prepared for the [illegible] ir own area. [4] The course of war cannot be [illegible] s are generally dictated by the impulse of the [illegible] overweening self-confidence has despised pre [illegible] ension has often been able to make head aga [illegible] [5] Not that confidence is out of place in an [illegible] an enemy's country it should also be accon [illegible] ions of apprehension: troops will by this com [illegible] red for dealing a blow, and best secured aga [illegible] In the present instance, the city against wh [illegible] om being powerless to defend itself, is on the [illegible] ly equipped at all points; so that we have eve [illegible] t they will take the field against us, and tha [illegible] ut already before we are there, they will cer [illegible] see us in their territory wasting and destr [illegible] For men are always exasperated at suffering [illegible] are not accustomed, and on seeing them infl [illegible] eyes; and where least inclined for reflection [illegible] heat to action. [8] The Athenians are the ver [illegible] do this, as they aspire to rule the rest of the [illegible] the habit of invading and ravaging their nei [illegible] f seeing their own treated in the like fashion [illegible] fore, the power of the state against which we [illegible] greatness of the reputation which, according [illegible] in or lose for our ancestors and ourselves, ren [illegible] here you may be led to regard discipline and [illegible] importance, and to obey with alacrity the ord [illegible] as nothing contributes so much to the cre [illegible] as when its soldiers, although numerous, qui [illegible] ansmitted to them."

2.12
431
1st Year/Summer
ATTICA
After the final herald sent by Archidamus to the Athenians is rebuffed, the Peloponnesians invade Attica.

Dis [illegible] er this brief speech, Archidamus first sent off Melesi [illegible] a Spartan, to Athens, in case she should be more [illegible] seeing the Peloponnesians actually on the march. [illegible] did not admit him into the city or to their assembly [illegible] y carried a motion against admitting either herald [illegible] artans after they had once marched out. The herald [illegible] ay without an audience, and ordered to be beyond [illegible] day; in future, if those who sent him had a propos [illegible] retire to their own territory before they dispatche [illegible] An escort was sent with Melesippus to prevent h [illegible] on with anyone. [3] When he reached the frontie [illegible] be dismissed, he departed with these words: "This [illegible] g of great misfortunes to the Hellenes." [4]

As soon as he arrived at the camp, and Archidamus learnt that the Athenians had still no thoughts of submitting, he at length began his march, and advanced with his army into their territory. [5] Meanwhile the Boeotians, sending their contingent and cavalry to join the Peloponnesian expedition, went to Plataea with the remainder and laid waste the country.

2.13
431
1st Year/Summer
ATHENS
Pericles donates his country estate to the city and describes Athens' best war strategy to the assembly, listing the city's financial and military resources.

While the Peloponnesians were still mustering at the Isthmus, or on the march before they invaded Attica, Pericles son of Xanthippus, one of the ten generals of the Athenians, finding that the invasion was to take place, conceived the idea that Archidamus, who happened to be his guest-friend,[1a] might possibly pass by his estate without ravaging it. This he might do, either from a personal wish to oblige him, or acting under instructions from Sparta for the purpose of creating a prejudice against him, as had been before attempted in the demand for the expulsion of the accursed family. He accordingly took the precaution of announcing to the Athenians in the assembly[1b] that, although Archidamus was his guest-friend, yet this friendship should not extend to the detriment of the state, and that in case the enemy should make his houses and lands an exception to the rest and not pillage them, he at once gave them up to be public property, so that they should not bring him into suspicion. [2] He also gave the citizens some advice on their present affairs in the same strain as before.[2a] They were to prepare for the war, and to carry in their property from the country. They were not to go out to battle, but to come into the city and guard it, and get ready their fleet, in which their real strength lay. They were also to keep a tight rein on their allies—the strength of Athens being derived from the money brought in by their payments, and success in war depending principally upon conduct and capital. [3] Here they had no reason to be despondent. Apart from other sources of income, an average revenue of six hundred *talents*[3a] of silver was drawn from the tribute of the allies; and there were still six thousand talents of coined silver in the Acropolis, out of nine thousand seven hundred that had once been there, from which the money had been taken for the Propylaea,[3b] the other public buildings, and for Potidaea.[3c] [4] This did not include the uncoined gold and silver in public and private offerings, the sacred vessels for the processions and games,[4a] the Median spoils,[4b] and

2.13.1a Such a relation of "guest-friendship" (*xenia*) was common between eminent citizens of different states; sometimes it was between an individual and a whole state (in which case the term *proxenia*, denoting a formalized relationship, was used; see 2.29.1, 2.85.5, 4.78.1, etc.). Such relationships were often hereditary (see 5.43.2, 6, and 6.89 for Alcibiades and Sparta).

2.13.1b The Athenian assembly; see Appendix A, The Athenian Government, §5, §7–9.

2.13.2a Pericles' strategy is set out in his reply to the Spartan envoys (1.144.1); see 2.65.7.

2.13.3a The *talent* was a large unit of weight and money. See Appendix J, Classical Greek Currency, §5.

2.13.3b The Propylaea, through the remains of which one still enters the Acropolis at Athens, was the costly and special pride of Pericles' building program. For financial reasons, the work on it was halted when the Peloponnesian War began and was never thereafter resumed.

2.13.3c For the campaign at Potidaea, which began in 432, see 1.56–65. For the costs of the siege there, see 2.70.2 and 3.17.4.

2.13.4a See Appendix I, Greek Religious Festivals, which notes that religious festivals often included athletic and cultural contests.

2.13.4b Booty taken from the Persians, whom the Greeks regularly referred to as "the Mede" or "the Medes," although the Medes and Persians were two distinct peoples.

simi[illegible]ount of five hundred talents. [5] To this he
add[illegible]her temples. These were by no means inconsid-
erab[illegible]sed. Nay, if they were ever absolutely driven to
it, th[illegible]gold ornaments of Athena herself; for the statue
cont[illegible]ure gold and it was all removable.[5a] This might
be u[illegible]n, and must every penny of it be restored. [6]
Such[illegible]ition—surely a satisfactory one. Then they had
an a[illegible]nd *hoplites*,[6a] besides sixteen thousand more in
the [illegible]tlements at Athens. [7] This was the number of
men[illegible]f the first invasion: it was composed of the oldest a[illegible] the resident aliens[7a] who had heavy armor. The
Phal[illegible] miles before it joined the wall that ran round
the [illegible]arly five miles had a guard, although part of it
was [illegible]y, that between the Long Wall and the Phaleric.
The[illegible] Walls to the Piraeus,[7c] a distance of some four
mile[illegible]of which was manned. Lastly, the circumference
of t[illegible]ia[7d] was nearly seven miles and a half; only half
of t[illegible]ed. [8] Pericles also showed them that they had
twel[illegible]uding mounted archers, with sixteen hundred
arch[illegible]ee hundred *triremes*[8a] fit for service. Such were
the [illegible] the different departments when the Peloponnesi[illegible]ng and hostilities were being commenced. Pericles[illegible]uments to show that they would survive in the
war.

[illegible]o his advice, and began to bring in their wives
and[illegible]ntry, and all their household furniture, even to
the [illegible]ses[1a] which they removed. Their sheep and cattle [illegible]a[1b] and the adjacent islands. But they found it
hard[illegible]em had always been used to living in the country.

2.14
431
1st Year/Summer
ATTICA
The Athenians move inside the city walls.

[illegible]his had been more the case with the Athenians
than[illegible]ecrops and the first kings, down to the reign of
The[illegible] consisted of a number of independent cities,

2.15
431
1st Year/Summer
ATTICA
Thucydides tells how the cities of Attica became politically united.

2.13[illegible]he Acropo-[illegible]e, accumu-[illegible]tals and[illegible] used for the[illegible]of Athena.[illegible]

2.13[illegible] a heavily[illegible]sary and Ap-[illegible]

2.13[illegible]*ics*) had both[illegible]re not citi-[illegible]thenian[illegible]

2.13[illegible]t.

2.13[illegible]and the Pi-[illegible]

2.13.7d The city of the Piraeus, the hill of Munychia: Map 2.19, inset.

2.13.8a *Triremes* were the standard warship of this period; see Appendix G, Trireme Warfare, §4–7.

2.14.1a Wooden doors, sills, window frames, shutters, and the like were valuable and so were built to be easily removed. See in 3.68.3 how the Thebans salvaged such items from Plataea when they destroyed that city.

2.14.1b Euboea: Map 2.9, AX, and Map 2.19.

each with its own town hall and magistrates. Except in times of danger the king of Athens was not consulted; in ordinary seasons they carried on their government and settled their affairs without his interference; sometimes they even waged war against him, as in the case of the Eleusinians with Eumolpus against Erechtheus. [2] In Theseus, however, they had a king whose intelligence matched his power; and one of the chief features in his organization of the country was to abolish the council chambers and magistrates of the petty cities, and to merge them in the single council chamber and town hall of the present capital. Individuals might still enjoy their private property just as before, but they were henceforth compelled to have only one political center, namely, Athens; which thus counted all the inhabitants of Attica among her citizens, so that when Theseus died he left a great state behind him. Indeed, from him dates the Synoecia, or Feast of Union,[2a] which is paid for by the state, and which the Athenians still keep in honor of the goddess. [3] Before this the city consisted of the present Acropolis and the district beneath it looking rather toward the south. [4] This is shown by the fact that the temples of the other deities, besides that of Athene, are in the Acropolis; and even those that are outside it are mostly situated in this quarter of the city, as that of the Olympian Zeus, of the Pythian Apollo, of Earth, and of Dionysus in the Marshes, the same in whose honor the older Dionysia are to this day celebrated in the month of Anthesterion not only by the Athenians but also by their Ionian[4a] descendants. [5] There are also other ancient temples in this quarter. The fountain too, which, since the alteration made by the tyrants,[5a] has been called Enneacrounos, or Nine Pipes, but which, when the spring was open, went by the name of Callirhoe, or Fairwater, was in those days, from being so near, used for the most important offices. Indeed, the old fashion of using the water before marriage and for other sacred purposes is still kept up. [6] Again, from their old residence in that quarter, the Acropolis is still known among Athenians as the *city*.

2.16
431
1st Year/Summer
ATTICA
The Athenians are greatly distressed at having to abandon their country homes.

The Athenians thus long lived scattered over Attica in independent cities. Even after the centralization of Theseus, old habit still prevailed; and from the early times down to the present war most Athenians still lived in the country with their families and households, and were consequently not at all inclined to move now, especially as they had only just restored their establishments after the Persian invasion.[1a] [2] Deep was their trouble and discontent at abandoning their houses and the hereditary temples of the ancient state, and at having to change their habits of life and to bid farewell to what each regarded as his native city.

2.15.2a See Appendix I, Greek Religious Festivals, §8.

2.15.4a See Appendix H, Dialects and Ethnic Groups, §3–4, 7–8, for more on the Ionians.

2.15.5a Thucydides refers here to the tyrant Pisistratus and his son Hippias, whose rule ended at Athens in 510. They are mentioned above in 1.20.2, and below in 3.104.1 and 6.53.3–59.4.

2.16.1a The Persian invasion of 480–79, when Athens and Attica were pillaged by the Persians. See Appendix E, The Persians, §4.

2.17
431
1st Year/Summer
ATHENS
Rural Athenians settle wherever they can within the city walls. Athens prepares a fleet of one hundred triremes to raid the Peloponnesus.

W[illegible]ens, though a few had houses of their own to go to [illegible]m with friends or relatives, by far the greater numb[illegible] dwelling in the parts of the city that were not built [illegible] and chapels of the heroes, except the Acropolis an[illegible]sinian Demeter and such other places as were alway[illegible]pation of the plot of ground lying below the Acro[illegible] had been forbidden by a curse; and there was also a[illegible]a Pythian oracle which said—

[illegible]e to leave the Pelasgian unworked

[2[illegible]uilt over in the necessity of the moment. And in m[illegible] proved true, it was in the opposite sense to what [illegible]misfortunes of the state did not arise from the unlaw[illegible] necessity of the occupation from the war; and thoug[illegible]tion this, he foresaw that it would be an evil day f[illegible]plot came to be inhabited. [3] Many also took up th[illegible]s of the walls or wherever else they could. For when[illegible]n, the city proved too small to hold them; thoug[illegible]ed the long walls and a great part of the Piraeus [illegible]ere. [4] All this took place while great attention [illegible]war; the allies were being mustered, and an arma[illegible] equipped for the Peloponnesus. [5] Such was the st[illegible]ens.

2.18
431
1st Year/Summer
ATTICA
The Peloponnesians besiege Oenoe. Archidamus' slow pace is criticized, but he hopes the Athenians will give in before their property is ravaged.

M[illegible]e Peloponnesians was advancing. The first city they [illegible]Oenoe,[1b] where they were to enter the country. Halti[illegible]red to assault the wall with siege engines and other[illegible]ng upon the Athenian and Boeotian border, was [illegible]nd was used as a fortress by the Athenians in time [illegible]nesians prepared for their assault, and wasted some[illegible] place. This delay brought the gravest censure upon[illegible]ng the levying of the war he had gained credit for w[illegible]ympathies by the half measures he had advocated[illegible]d assembled he had further injured himself in publi[illegible]ering at the Isthmus and the slowness with which[illegible]had been conducted. But all this was as nothing to[illegible]uring this interval the Athenians were carrying in th[illegible] the belief of the Peloponnesians that a quick adva[illegible]erything still out, had it not been for his pro-

2.18.1a [illegible] to [illegible]d Map [illegible]

2.18.1b [illegible]

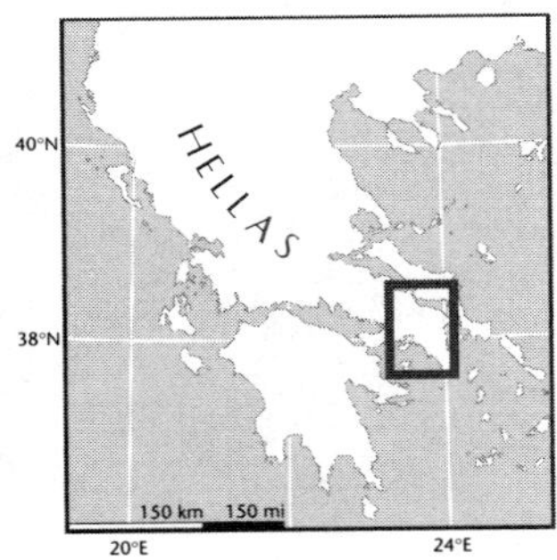

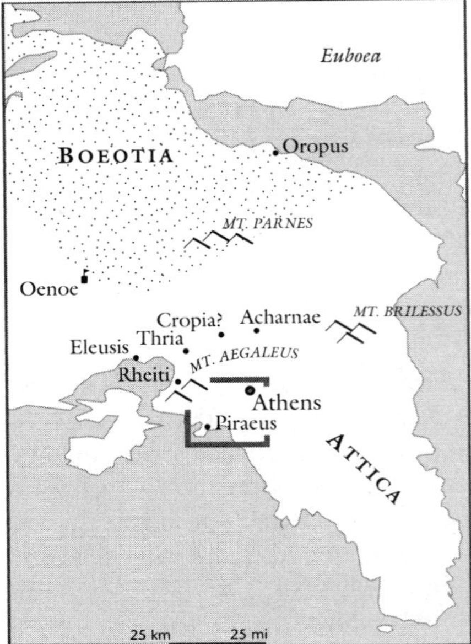

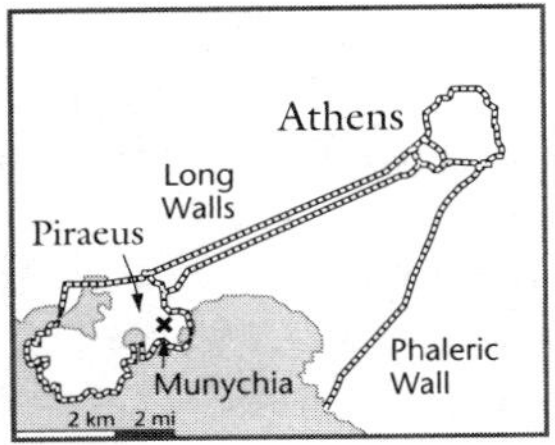

MAP 2.19 ATHENS AND ITS DEFENSES

crastination. Such was the feeling of the army toward Archidamus during the siege. But he, it is said, expected that the Athenians would shrink from letting their land be wasted, and would make their submission while it was still uninjured; and this was why he waited.

2.19
431
1st Year/Summer
ATTICA
Failing to take Oenoe, Archidamus marches into Attica to Acharnae. It is midsummer and the corn is ripe.

But after he had assaulted Oenoe, and every possible attempt to take it had failed, as no herald came from Athens, he at last broke up his camp and invaded Attica. This was about eighty days after the Theban attempt upon Plataea, just in the middle of summer, when the corn was ripe, and Archidamus son of Zeuxis, king of Sparta, was in command. Encamping in Eleusis[1a] and the Thriasian plain,[1b] they began their ravages, and putting to flight some Athenian horse at a place called Rheiti, or the Brooks,[1c] they then advanced, keeping Mount Aegaleus on their right, through Cropia,[1d] until they reached Acharnae,[1e] the largest of the Athenian *demes,* or townships. Sitting down before it, they formed a camp there, and continued their ravages for a long while.

2.19.1a Eleusis: Map 2.19.
2.19.1b Thria in the Thriasian plain: Map 2.19.
2.19.1c Rheiti is thought to be at the southeast corner of the Thriasian plain, at the foot of Mount Aegaleus; see Map 2.19 (A. W. Gomme, *A Historical Commentary on Thucydides,* ii [Oxford, 1956], 71).
2.19.1d Cropia, possible location: Map 2.19, BY.
2.19.1e Acharnae: Map 2.19.

Th[illegible] nus remained in order of battle at Acharnae durin[illegible] of descending into the plain, is said to have been [illegible] the Athenians might possibly be tempted by the n[illegible] and by their unprecedented preparedness for war t[illegible] and attempt to stop the devastation of their lands[illegible] y had not met him at Eleusis or the Thriasian plain[illegible] ould be provoked to a sally by the spectacle of a can[illegible] hought the place itself a good position for encamp[illegible] y that such an important part of the state as the t[illegible] of the Acharnians would refuse to submit to the r[illegible] d would force a battle on the rest of the citizens.[illegible] ould the Athenians not take the field during this i[illegible] fearlessly ravage the plain in future invasions, and e[illegible] the very walls of Athens. After the Acharnians had l[illegible] ney would be less willing to risk themselves for that [illegible] so there would be division in the Athenian coun[illegible] ne motives of Archidamus for remaining at Acha[illegible]

2.20
431
1st Year/Summer
ATTICA
Archidamus hopes that Athens will now give battle, since the Acharnaean hoplites might not fight for the property of others after their own had been destroyed.

In[illegible] as the army was at Eleusis[1a] and the Thriasian plain[illegible] tained of its not advancing any nearer. It was reme[illegible] son of Pausanias, king of Sparta, had invaded Attic[illegible] army fourteen years before, but had retreated with[illegible] an Eleusis and Thria, which indeed proved the cause[illegible] , as it was thought he had been bribed to retreat.[illegible] v the army at Acharnae,[2a] barely seven miles from[illegible] tience. The territory of Athens was being ravaged[illegible] the Athenians, a sight which the young men had r[illegible] e old only in the Persian wars;[2b] and it was naturall[illegible] ılt, and the determination was universal, especially[illegible] , to sally forth and stop it. [3] Knots were form[illegible] ngaged in hot discussion; for if the proposed sally [illegible] ed, it was also in some cases opposed. Oracles of th[illegible] vere recited by the collectors, and found eager listen[illegible] e disputants. Foremost in pressing for the sally were[illegible] tituting no small part of the army of the state, and [illegible] vas being ravaged. In short, the whole city was in a [illegible] cles was the object of general indignation; his previ[illegible] y forgotten; he was abused for not leading out the a[illegible] ed, and was made responsible for the whole of the p[illegible]

2.21
431
1st Year/Summer
ATTICA
Outraged by the sight of the enemy ravaging their land, the Athenians wish to sally out to attack. They turn against Pericles, whose past advice they now forget.

2.21.1a [illegible]
2.21.1b [illegible] p 2.19.
2.21.2a [illegible]
2.21.2b [illegible] espoiled [illegible]

2.22
431
1st Year/Summer
ATTICA
Pericles, certain that the Athenians should avoid a land battle, refuses to call an assembly or a meeting of the people. A cavalry skirmish takes place between Athenians and Thessalians against the Boeotians.

He, meanwhile, seeing anger and poor judgment just now in the ascendant, and confident of his wisdom in refusing a sally, would not call either an assembly or a meeting of the people,[1a] fearing the fatal results of a debate inspired by passion and not by prudence. Accordingly, he attended to the defense of the city, and kept it as quiet as possible, [2] though he constantly sent out cavalry to prevent raids on the lands near the city from flying parties of the enemy. There was a trifling affair at Phrygia[2a] between a squadron of the Athenian horse with the Thessalians against the Boeotian cavalry; in which the former had rather the best of it, until the hoplites advanced to the support of the Boeotians, when the Thessalians and Athenians were routed and lost a few men, whose bodies, however, were recovered the same day without a truce. The next day the Peloponnesians set up a trophy.[2b] [3] Ancient alliance brought the Thessalians to the aid of Athens; those who came being the Larissaeans, Pharsalians, Cranaeans, Pyrasians, Gyrtonians, and Pheraeans.[3a] The Larissaean commanders were Polymedes and Aristonus, two party leaders in Larissa; the Pharsalian general was Menon; each of the other cities had also its own commander.

2.23
431
1st Year/Summer
ATTICA
After Athens sends a fleet to raid Peloponnesus, the Peloponnesian army returns home.

In the meantime the Peloponnesians, as the Athenians did not come out to engage them, broke up from Acharnae and ravaged some of the *demes*[1a] between Mounts Parnes[1b] and Brilessus.[1c] [2] While they were in Attica, the Athenians sent off the hundred ships which they had been preparing round the Peloponnesus, with a thousand hoplites and four hundred archers on board,[2a] under the command of Carcinus son of Xenotimus, Proteas son of Epicles, and Socrates son of Antigenes. [3] This armament weighed anchor and started on its cruise, and the Peloponnesians, after remaining in Attica as long as their provisions lasted, retired through Boeotia by a different road to that by which they had entered. As they passed Oropus[3a] they ravaged the territory of Graea which is held by the Oropians from Athens, and reaching the Peloponnesus broke up to their respective cities.

2.24
431
1st Year/Summer
ATTICA
Athens sets aside a reserve of one thousand talents and one hundred triremes for defense against a naval attack.

After they had retired the Athenians set guards by land and sea at the points at which they intended to have regular stations during the war. They also resolved to set apart a special fund of a thousand talents[1a] from the moneys in the Acropolis. This was not to be spent, but the current expenses of the war were to be otherwise provided for. If anyone should

2.22.1a As a general, Pericles was expected to convene an extraordinary assembly, but it is unclear how he was able to prevent an assembly from being held. See Appendix A, The Athenian Government, §7.
2.22.2a Phrygia: the location of Phrygia in Attica is unknown.
2.22.2b After a battle in ancient Greece, the victorious side raised a trophy, usually a set of captured armor arranged on a pole, at or near the battlefield; see Appendix F, Land Warfare, §6.
2.22.3a Ancient alliance, yes, but some Thessalian cavalry betrayed the Athenians and went over to the enemy at the battle of Tanagra, in 457 (see 1.107.7). For the locations of Thessalian Larissa, Pharsalus, Cranon, Pyrasus, Gyrtone, and Pherae, see Map 2.24, inset.
2.23.1a For an explanation of Athenian *demes*, see Appendix A, The Athenian Government, §4.
2.23.1b Mount Parnes: Map, 2.19.
2.23.1c Mount Brilessus, more generally known as Mount Pentelikos: Map 2.19.
2.23.2a That is, manned with ten hoplites and four archers per trireme, a standard Athenian complement at this time; see Appendix G, Trireme Warfare, §5.
2.23.3a Oropus: Map 2.24.
2.24.1a See Appendix J, Classical Greek Currency, §5.

ILLUS[illegible] CAVALRY RECRUITS ON PARADE, AS REPRESENTED IN THE [illegible]

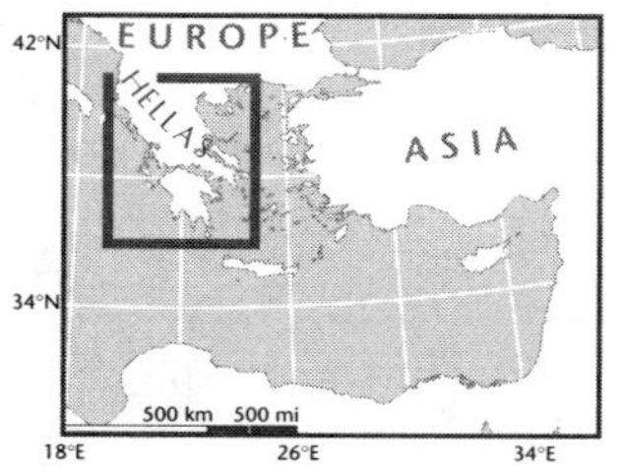

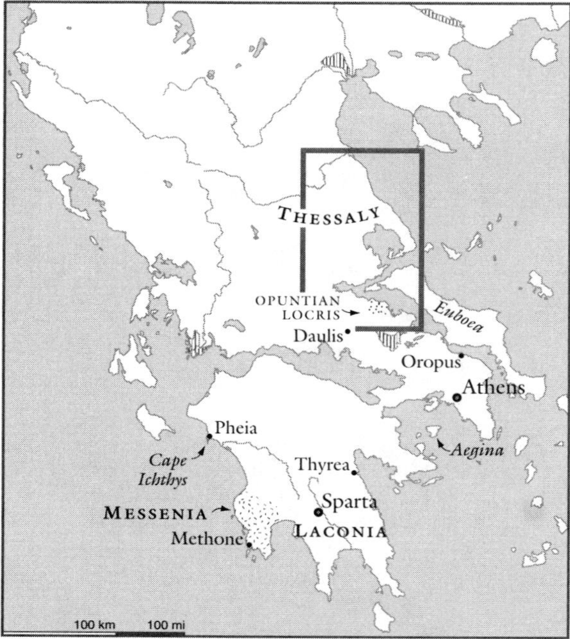

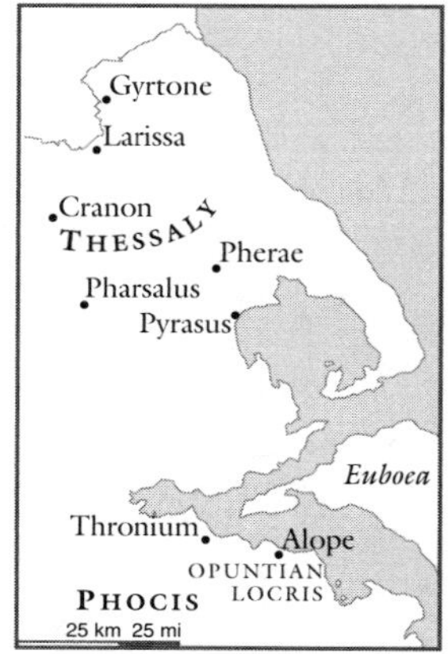

MAP 2.24
ATHENIAN NAVAL RAIDS IN 431; THESSALIANS WHO ASSISTED ATHENS IN 431

move or put to the vote a proposition for using the money for any purpose whatever except that of defending the city in the event of the enemy bringing a fleet to make an attack by sea, it should be a capital offense. [2] With this sum of money they also set aside a special fleet of one hundred triremes, the best ships of each year,[2a] with their captains. None of these was to be used except with the money and against the same peril, should such peril arise.

2.25
431
1st Year/Summer
PELOPONNESUS
The Athenian fleet, reinforced by allies, raids the coast of the Peloponnesus.

Meanwhile the Athenians in the hundred ships round the Peloponnesus, reinforced by a Corcyraean squadron of fifty vessels and some others of the allies in those parts, cruised about the coasts and ravaged the country. Among other places they landed in Laconia[1a] and made an assault upon Methone;[1b] there being no garrison in the place, and the wall being weak. [2] But it so happened that Brasidas son of Tellis, a *Spartiate*,[2a] was in command of a guard for the defense of the district. Hearing of the attack, he

2.24.2a New triremes were built every year to replace those that had been lost, worn out, or retired. Although the trireme design was standardized, some were judged to be better built, or proved to be better or faster sailers, than others. These were "the best ships of each year."

2.25.1a Laconia: Map 2.24.

2.25.1b Methone, Messenia: Map 2.24. Methone was a city of the Messenian *perioikoi;* see Appendix C, Spartan Institutions, §9.

2.25.2a A *Spartiate* was a full citizen of Sparta and a member of the highest Spartan military caste.

hurri[illegible]tes to the assistance of the besieged, and dashing th[illegible]Athenians, which was scattered over the country a[illegible]ned to the wall, threw himself into Methone. He l[illegible]g good his entrance, but saved the place and won [illegible]his exploit, being thus the first officer who obtaine[illegible]war.[2b] [3] The Athenians at once weighed anchor [illegible]ise. Touching at Pheia in Elis,[3a] they ravaged the c[illegible]defeated a picked force of three hundred men that [illegible] of Elis and the immediate neighborhood to the r[illegible]all came down upon them, and not liking to face i[illegible] was no harbor, most of them got on board their [illegible]pe Ichthys[4a] sailed into the port of Pheia. In the m[illegible]s,[4b] and some others who could not get on board[illegible]d and took Pheia. [5] The fleet afterwards sailed[illegible] up and then put to sea; Pheia being evacuated, [illegible]e Eleans had now come up. The Athenians conti[illegible]aged other places on the coast.

2.26 431 1st Year/Summer LOCRIS An Athenian fleet attacks Locris.

Ab[illegible] Athenians sent thirty ships to cruise round Locri[illegible]boea;[1b] Cleopompus son of Clinias being in comm[illegible]ts with the fleet he ravaged certain places on the se[illegible]um,[2a] and took hostages from it. He also defeate[illegible] that had assembled to resist him.

2.27 431 1st Year/Summer AEGINA After Athens expels the Aeginetans Sparta gives them refuge at Thyrea.

D[illegible]Athenians also expelled the Aeginetans with their [illegible] Aegina,[1a] on the ground of their having been the ch[illegible]e war upon them. Besides, Aegina lies so near the P[illegible]med safer to send colonists of their own to hold i[illegible]s the settlers were sent out. [2] The banished Aegin[illegible] in Thyrea,[2a] which was given to them by Spart[illegible]of her quarrel with Athens, but also because the A[illegible]nder obligations at the time of the earthquake and t[illegible] The territory of Thyrea is on the frontier of Argol[illegible]g down to the sea. Those of the Aeginetans who [illegible]cattered over the rest of Hellas.

2.28 431 1st Year/Summer HELLAS An eclipse of the sun.

Th[illegible] beginning of a new lunar month, the only time, [illegible] appears possible, the sun was eclipsed after noon.[illegible]e form of a crescent and some of the stars had come [illegible]tural shape.[1a]

2.25.2b [illegible] Spartan [illegible] next [illegible]he Pelo-[illegible]
2.25.3a [illegible]
2.25.4a [illegible]
2.25.4b [illegible] Nau-[illegible]3.1–3.
2.26.1a [illegible]
2.26.1b [illegible]
2.26.2a [illegible]
2.26.2b [illegible]
2.27.1a Aegina: Map 2.24.
2.27.2a Thyrea: Map 2.24. Thucydides describes what happened to the Aeginetans at Thyrea in 4.56.
2.27.2b The earthquake in Laconia and the revolt of the Helots (thought to have taken place in 465) is described by Thucydides in 1.101–3. For a discussion of the Spartan Helots, see Appendix C, Spartan Institutions, §3–4, 8.
2.28.1a This partial eclipse took place at Athens on August 3, 431, about 5:22 P.M.

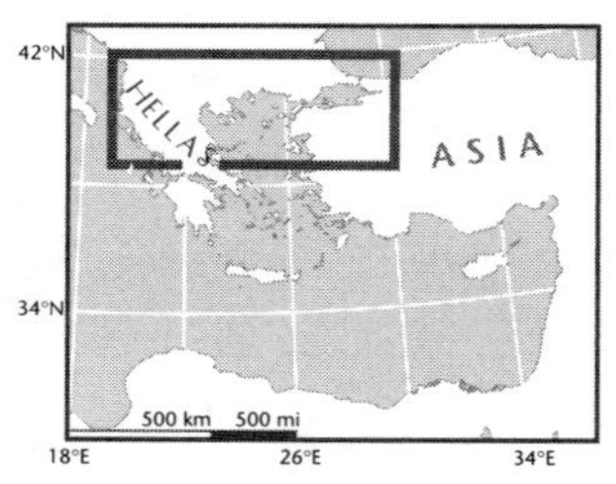

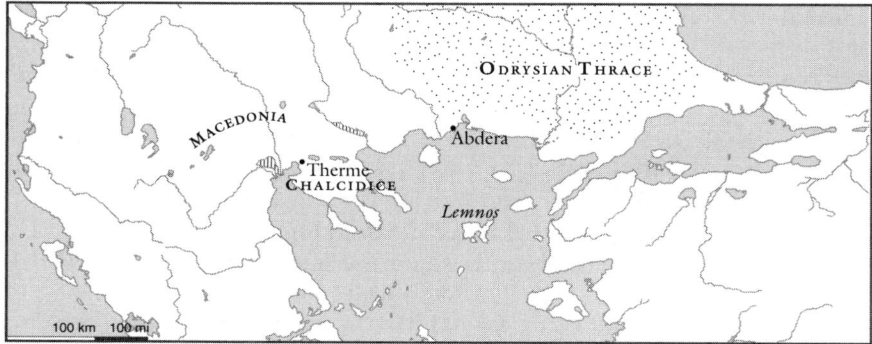

MAP 2.29 MACEDONIA AND THRACE

2.29
431
1st Year/Summer
THRACE
Athens concludes alliances with Sitalces, king of Thrace, and Perdiccas, king of Macedonia.

During the same summer Nymphodorus son of Pythes, an Abderite[1a] whose sister Sitalces had married, was made their *proxenus*[1b] by the Athenians and sent for to Athens. They had hitherto considered him their enemy; but he had great influence with Sitalces, and they wished this prince to become their ally. Sitalces was the son of Teres and king of the Thracians. [2] Teres, the father of Sitalces, was the first to establish the great kingdom of the Odrysians on a scale quite unknown to the rest of Thrace,[2a] a large portion of the Thracians being independent. [3] This Teres is in no way related to Tereus who married Pandion's daughter Procne from Athens; nor indeed did they belong to the same part of Thrace. Tereus lived in Daulis,[3a] part of what is now called Phocis,[3b] but which at that time was inhabited by Thracians. It was in this land that the women perpetrated the outrage upon Itys;[3c] and many of the poets when they mention the nightingale call it the Daulian bird. Besides, Pandion in contracting an alliance for his daughter, would consider the advantages of mutual assistance, and would naturally prefer a match at the above moderate distance to the journey of many days which separates Athens from the Odrysians. Again the names are different; and this Teres was king of the Odrysians, the first by the way who attained to any real power. [4] Sitalces, his son, was now sought as an ally by the Athenians, who desired his aid in the reduction of the Thracian cities and of Perdiccas.[4a] [5] Coming to Athens, Nymphodorus concluded the alliance with Sitalces, made his son Sadocus an Athenian citizen, and promised to finish the war in Thrace by persuading Sitalces to send the Athenians a force of Thracian horse and *peltasts*.[5a] [6] He also reconciled them with Perdiccas,

2.29.1a Abdera: Map 2.29.
2.29.1b A *proxenus,* although a citizen and resident of his own state, served as a "friend or representative" (much like a modern honorary consul) of a foreign state.
2.29.2a Odrysian Thrace: Map 2.29.
2.29.3a Daulis: Map 2.24.
2.29.3b Phocis: Map 2.24, inset.
2.29.3c When Procne discovered that Tereus had raped and mutilated her sister, Philomela, she took revenge by serving him a meal that included the flesh of their child, Itys. The gods prevented him from punishing her by turning him into a hoopoe, Philomela into a swallow, and Procne into a nightingale.
2.29.4a Perdiccas was king of Macedonia (Map 2.29). His devious role in the Potidaea affair is described above in 1.56–62.
2.29.5a *Peltasts* were troops armed only with a small light shield, a javelin, and a short sword. Unhinderd by body armor, they could move much more quickly than the fully armed hoplite, whose equipment was both far more heavy and far more expensive than theirs.

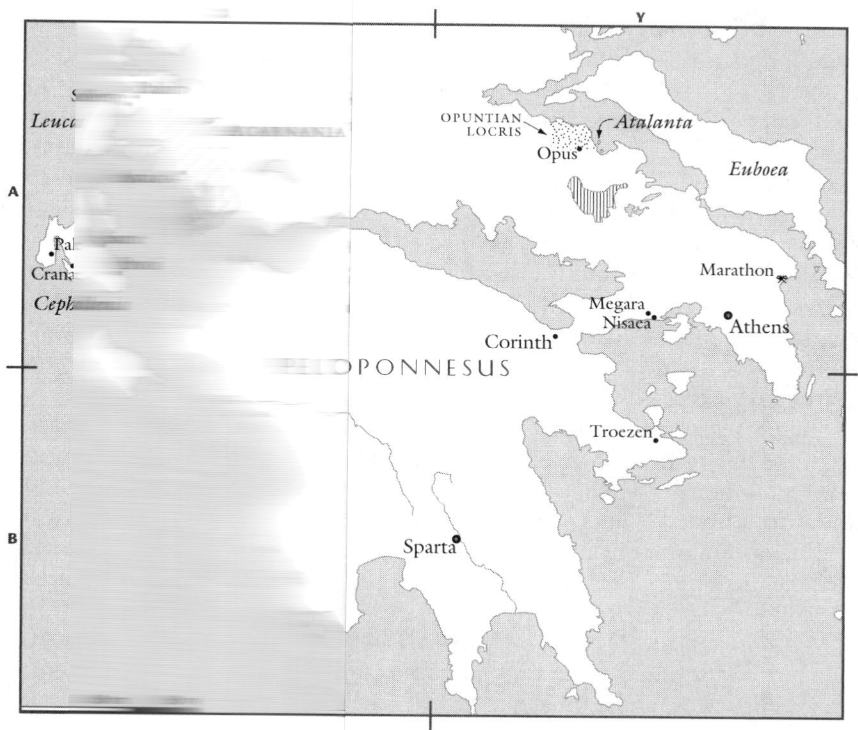

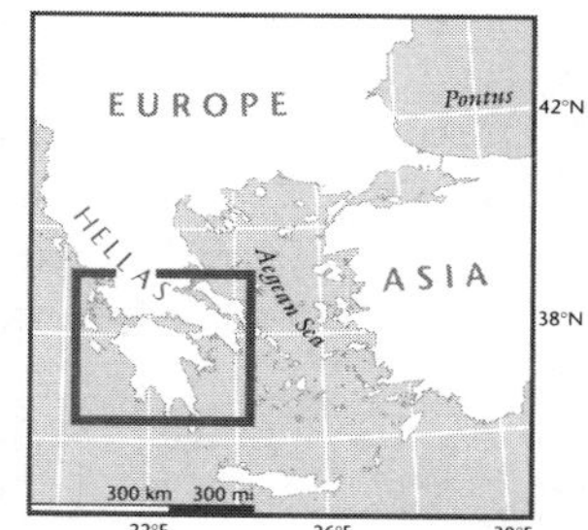

MAP PEDITIONS OF 431

and re Therme[6a] to him; upon which Perdiccas at once nd Phormio in an expedition against the Chalcidia son of Teres, king of the Thracians, and Perdiccas f the Macedonians, became allies of Athens.[7a]

2.30 431 1st Year/Summer ACARNANIA The Athenian fleet conducts operations in Acarnania. CEPHALLENIA Cephallenia joins the Athenians.

ns in the hundred vessels were still cruising rou After taking Sollium,[1a] a city belonging to Cor the city and territory to the Acarnanians of Pala us,[1d] expelled its tyrant Evarchus, and gained the plac 2] Next they sailed to the island of Cephallenia[2a] and using force. Cephallenia lies off Acarnania[2b] and Leu r states, the Paleans, Cranaeans, Samaeans, and Pro wards the fleet returned to Athens.

2.31 431 1st Year/Summer MEGARA An army under Pericles ravages Megara.

this year the Athenians invaded the Megarid[1a] with nt aliens[1b] included, under the command of Per-

2.29.
2.29.
2.29. 7, and of
2.30.
2.30.
2.30. AX.
2.30. hus returns pport in
2.30.
2.30.2b Acarnania: Map 2.31, AX. Events in Acarnania will appear next in 2.33.
2.30.2c Leucas: Map 2.31, AX.
2.30.2d Pale, Cranae, Same, Proni, of Cephallenia: Map 2.31, AX.
2.31.1a Megara: Map 2.31, AY.
2.31.1b Athenian resident aliens (*metics*) had both rights and obligations but were not citizens. See Appendix A, The Athenian Government, §2, 4.

icles son of Xanthippus. The Athenians in the hundred ships round the Peloponnesus on their journey home had just reached Aegina, and hearing that the citizens at home were in full force at Megara, now sailed over and joined them. [2] This was without doubt the largest army of Athenians ever assembled, the state being still in the flower of her strength and yet unvisited by the plague. Full ten thousand hoplites were in the field, all Athenian citizens, besides the three thousand before Potidaea. Then the resident aliens who joined in the incursion were at least three thousand strong; besides which there was a multitude of light troops. They ravaged the greater part of the territory, and then retired. [3] Other incursions into the Megarid were afterwards made by the Athenians annually during the war, sometimes only with cavalry, sometimes with all their forces. This went on until the capture of Nisaea.[2b]

2.32
431
1st Year/Summer
OPUNTIAN LOCRIS
The Athenians fortify a base on Atalanta.

Atalanta[1a] also, the deserted island off the Opuntian coast, was toward the end of this summer converted into a fortified post by the Athenians, in order to prevent privateers issuing from Opus[1b] and the rest of Locris[1c] and plundering Euboea.[1d] Such were the events of this summer after the return of the Peloponnesians from Attica.

2.33
431/0
1st Year/Winter
ACARNANIA
A Corinthian fleet retakes Astacus, raids Acarnania, and is repulsed at Cephallenia.

In the ensuing winter the Acarnanian[1a] Evarchus wishing to return to Astacus,[1b] persuaded the Corinthians to sail over with forty ships and fifteen hundred hoplites and restore him; himself also hiring some mercenaries. In command of the force were Euphamidas son of Aristonymus, Timoxenus son of Timocrates, and Eumachus son of Chrysis, [2] who sailed over and restored him, and after failing in an attempt on some places on the Acarnanian coast which they were desirous of gaining, began their voyage home. [3] Coasting along shore they touched at Cephallenia[3a] and made a descent on the Cranian[3b] territory, and losing some men in a surprise attack by the Cranians, put to sea somewhat hurriedly and returned home.

2.34
431/0
1st Year/Winter
ATHENS
The Athenian procedure for burying their war dead is described. Pericles is chosen to deliver this war's first funeral oration.

In the same winter the Athenians gave a funeral at the public cost to those who had first fallen in this war. It was a custom of their ancestors, and the manner of it is as follows. [2] Three days before the ceremony, the bones of the dead[2a] are laid out in a tent which has been erected; and their friends bring to their relatives such offerings as they please. [3] In the funeral procession cypress coffins are borne in carts, one for each tribe; the bones of the deceased being placed in the coffin of their tribe.[3a] Among these is carried one empty bier decked for the missing, that is, for those whose bodies could not be recovered. [4] Any citizen or stranger who pleases joins in the procession: and the female relatives are there to wail at the burial. [5] The dead are laid in the public sepulcher in the most beautiful suburb of the city, in which those who fall in war are always buried; with

2.31.2b Nisaea: Map 2.31, AY. The capture of Nisaea by the Athenians in 424 is described in 4.69.
2.32.1a Atalanta: Map 2.31, AY.
2.32.1b Opus: Map 2.31, AY.
2.32.1c Locris (Opuntian): Map 2.31, AY.
2.32.1d Euboea: Map 2.31, AY.
2.33.1a Acarnania: Map 2.31, AX.
2.33.1b Astacus: Map 2.31, AX.
2.33.3a Cephallenia: Map 2.31, AX.
2.33.3b Cranae on Cephallenia: Map 2.31, AX.
2.34.2a The Greek custom at this time was to burn the bodies of the dead and then to gather up the bones and bury them.
2.34.3a For more on Athenian "tribes," see Appendix A, The Athenian Government, §3–5.

the e[illegible]t Marathon,[5a] who for their singular and extraordi[illegible] on the spot where they fell. [6] After the bodies h[illegible]rth, a man chosen by the state, of approved wisd[illegible]ion, pronounces over them an appropriate eulogy[illegible] [7] Such is the manner of the burying; and thro[illegible] war, whenever the occasion arose, the establishe[illegible] [8] Meanwhile these were the first that had falle[illegible]anthippus was chosen to pronounce their eulogy.[illegible] arrived, he advanced from the sepulcher to an eleva[illegible] be heard by as many of the crowd as possible, and [illegible]

[illegible]ssors in this place have commended him w[illegible]rt of the law, telling us that it is well that it sh[illegible] burial of those who fall in battle. For myse[illegible]nt that the worth which had displayed itself in[illegible]iently rewarded by honors also shown by d[illegible]see in this funeral prepared at the people's co[illegible]wished that the reputations of many brave m[illegible]riled in the mouth of a single individual, to st[illegible] he spoke well or ill. [2] For it is hard to sp[illegible]bject where it is even difficult to convince y[illegible] speaking the truth. On the one hand, the fr[illegible]th every fact of the story may think that so[illegible]set forth with that fullness which he wishes a[illegible] on the other, he who is a stranger to the m[illegible]vy to suspect exaggeration if he hears anyth[illegible]ture. For men can endure to hear others p[illegible]they can severally persuade themselves of th[illegible]l the actions recounted: when this point is p[illegible]d with it incredulity. [3] However, since our a[illegible]his custom with their approval, it becomes m[illegible]and to try to satisfy your several wishes and o[illegible]

2.35
431/0
1st Year/Winter
ATHENS
Pericles begins his Funeral Oration by noting how difficult it is to properly praise the dead, but, since it is the law, offers to do his duty and make the attempt.

[illegible]ur ancestors: it is both just and proper that t[illegible]nor of the first mention on an occasion like t[illegible]in the country without break in the succes-s[illegible]generation, and handed it down free to the p[illegible]r. [2] And if our more remote ancestors des[illegible]do our own fathers, who added to their in-

2.36
431/0
1st Year/Winter
ATHENS
After Pericles praises all those who contributed to Athens' acquisition of its empire he describes the form of government under which the city grew great.

2.34.[illegible]where the [illegible]g force of [illegible]

heritance the empire which we now possess, and spared no pains to be able to leave their acquisitions to us of the present generation. [3] Lastly, there are few parts of our dominions that have not been augmented by those of us here, who are still more or less in the vigor of life; while the mother country has been furnished by us with everything that can enable her to depend on her own resources whether for war or for peace. [4] That part of our history which tells of the military achievements which gave us our several possessions, or of the ready valor with which either we or our fathers stemmed the tide of Hellenic or foreign aggression, is a theme too familiar to my hearers for me to dwell upon, and I shall therefore pass it by. But what was the road by which we reached our position, what the form of government under which our greatness grew, what the national habits out of which it sprang; these are questions which I may try to solve before I proceed to my eulogy upon these men; since I think this to be a subject upon which on the present occasion a speaker may properly dwell, and to which the whole assemblage, whether citizens or foreigners, may listen with advantage."

2.37
431/0
1st Year/Winter
ATHENS
Praising Athens' unique democratic institutions, Pericles says equality before the law leads to rewards based on merit and creates a society both free and law-abiding.

"Our constitution does not copy the laws of neighboring states; we are rather a pattern to others than imitators ourselves. Its administration favors the many instead of the few; this is why it is called a democracy. If we look to the laws, they afford equal justice to all in their private differences; if to social standing, advancement in public life falls to reputation for capacity, class considerations not being allowed to interfere with merit; nor again does poverty bar the way, if a man is able to serve the state, he is not hindered by the obscurity of his condition. [2] The freedom which we enjoy in our government extends also to our ordinary life. There, far from exercising a jealous surveillance over each other, we do not feel called upon to be angry with our neighbor for doing what he likes, or even to indulge in those injurious looks which cannot fail to be offensive, although they inflict no real harm. [3] But all this ease in our private relations does not make us lawless as citizens. Against this fear is our chief safeguard, teaching us to obey the magistrates and the laws, particularly such as regard the protection of the injured, whether they are actually on the statute book, or belong to that code which, although unwritten, yet cannot be broken without acknowledged disgrace."

2.38
431/0
1st Year/Winter
ATHENS
Pericles notes that Athens provides means for pleasure and recreation.

"Further, we provide plenty of means for the mind to refresh itself from business. We celebrate games and sacrifices all the year round, and the elegance of our private establishments forms a daily source of pleasure and helps to distract us from what causes us distress; [2] while the magnitude of our city draws the produce of the

v[illegible] so that to the Athenian the fruits of other
c[illegible] luxury as those of his own."
[illegible]ilitary policy, there also we differ from our
a[illegible]pen our city to the world, and never by
a[illegible]ners from any opportunity of learning or
o[illegible]e eyes of an enemy may occasionally profit
b[illegible] less in system and policy than to the native
s[illegible]le in education, where our rivals from their
v[illegible]discipline seek after manliness, at Athens we
li[illegible] and yet are just as ready to encounter every
le[illegible] proof of this it may be noticed that the
S[illegible]ur country alone, but bring with them all
t[illegible] we Athenians advance unsupported into
t[illegible]or, and fighting upon a foreign soil usually
v[illegible] who are defending their homes. [3] Our
u[illegible]et encountered by any enemy, because we
h[illegible] our marine and to despatch our citizens by
la[illegible]rent services; so that, wherever they engage
w[illegible]of our strength, a success against a detach-
m[illegible]victory over the nation, and a defeat into a
r[illegible]ds of our entire people. [4] And yet if with
h[illegible] ease, and courage not of art but of nature,
w[illegible]ounter danger, we have the double advan-
ta[illegible]ships before we need to, and of facing them
ir[illegible]earlessly as those who are never free from
th[illegible]

2.39
431/0
1st Year/Winter
ATHENS
Pericles says that Athens is open to the world, relying upon its citizens' natural capacity, not special training, to meet any challenge.

[illegible]ly points in which our city is worthy of ad-
m[illegible]

[illegible]ent without extravagance and knowledge
w[illegible]h we employ more for use than for show,
a[illegible]e of poverty not in owning to the fact but
in[illegible]against it. [2] Our public men have, besides
p[illegible]rs to attend to, and our ordinary citizens,
th[illegible] pursuits of industry, are still fair judges of
p[illegible]e any other nation, we regard the citizen
w[illegible]e duties not as unambitious but as useless,
a[illegible]proposals even if we cannot originate them;
in[illegible]cussion as a stumbling-block in the way of
ac[illegible]spensable preliminary to any wise action at
al[illegible]rprises we present the singular spectacle of
d[illegible]each carried to its highest point, and both
u[illegible]s; although with the rest of mankind deci-

2.40
431/0
1st Year/Winter
ATHENS
Pericles applauds Athens' concern for culture, her sensible use of wealth, her inclusion of all citizens in politics, her combination of daring and deliberation in action, and her liberal generosity.

2.39.1a [illegible]; see
[illegible]an Insti-
[illegible]

sion is the fruit of ignorance, hesitation of reflection. But the prize for courage will surely be awarded most justly to those who best know the difference between hardship and pleasure and yet are never tempted to shrink from danger. [4] In generosity we are equally singular, acquiring our friends by conferring not by receiving favors. Yet, of course, the doer of the favor is the firmer friend of the two, in order by continued kindness to keep the recipient in his debt; while the debtor feels less keenly from the very consciousness that the return he makes will be a payment, not a free gift. [5] And it is only the Athenians who, fearless of consequences, confer their benefits not from calculations of expediency, but in the confidence of liberality."

2.41
431/0
1st Year/Winter
ATHENS
Pericles says Athens is a model for Hellas, a city worthy to rule others, and worthy of the devotion of the men who died in her cause.

"In short, I say that as a city we are the school of Hellas; while I doubt if the world can produce a man, who where he has only himself to depend upon, is equal to so many emergencies, and graced by so happy a versatility as the Athenian. [2] And that this is no mere boast thrown out for the occasion, but plain matter of fact, is proved by the power of the state acquired by these habits. [3] For Athens alone of her contemporaries is found when tested to be greater than her reputation, and alone gives no occasion to her assailants to blush at the antagonist by whom they have been worsted, or to her subjects to question her title to rule by merit. [4] Rather, the admiration of the present and succeeding ages will be ours, since we have not left our power without witness, but have shown it by mighty proofs; and far from needing a Homer for our eulogist, or other of his craft whose verses might charm for the moment only for the impression which they gave to melt at the touch of fact, we have forced every sea and land to be the highway of our daring, and everywhere, whether for evil or for good, have left imperishable monuments behind us. [5] Such is the Athens for which these men, in the assertion of their resolve not to lose her, nobly fought and died; and well may every one of their survivors be ready to suffer in her cause."

2.42
431/0
1st Year/Winter
ATHENS
Pericles asserts that these men died gloriously, preferring death to submission or dishonor.

"Indeed if I have dwelt at some length upon the character of our country, it has been to show that our stake in the struggle is not the same as theirs who have no such blessings to lose, and also that the eulogy of the men over whom I am now speaking might be by definite proofs established. [2] That eulogy is now in a great measure complete; for the Athens that I have celebrated is only what the heroism of these and their like have made her, men whose fame, unlike that of most Hellenes, will be found to be no greater than what they deserve. And if a test of worth be wanted, it is to be found in their closing scene, and this not only in the cases in which it set the final seal upon their merit, but also in those in which it gave the first int[illegible] any. [3] For there is justice in the claim tha[illegible] country's battles should be as a cloak to co[illegible] fections; since the good action has blotted ou[illegible] as a citizen more than outweighed his de- me[illegible]] But none of these allowed either wealth wi[illegible] re enjoyment to unnerve his spirit, or po[illegible] day of freedom and riches to tempt him to shr[illegible] olding that vengeance upon their enemies wa[illegible] han any personal blessings, and reckoning thi[illegible] us of hazards, they joyfully determined to acc[illegible] sure of their vengeance and to let their wis[illegible] mmitting to hope the uncertainty of final suc[illegible] fore them they thought fit to act boldly and[illegible] hus choosing to die resisting, rather than to [illegible] l only from dishonor, but met danger face to [illegible] moment, while at the summit of their for- tur[illegible] their fear, but their glory."

2.43
431/0
1st Year/Winter
ATHENS
Pericles calls upon those who survive to emulate the war dead's valor and patriotism, saying that they risked all and lost their lives, but the renown of their deeds will last forever.

[illegible] became Athenians. You, their survivors, mu[illegible] as unaltering a resolution in the field, tho[illegible] it may have a happier outcome. And not co[illegible] ved only from words of the advantages wh[illegible] he defense of your country, though these wo[illegible] ext to a speaker even before an audience so [illegible] present, you must yourselves realize the po[illegible] your eyes upon her from day to day, till lov[illegible] ts; and then when all her greatness shall bre[illegible] t reflect that it was by courage, sense of dut[illegible] honor in action that men were enabled to wir[illegible] rsonal failure in an enterprise could make the[illegible] eir country of their valor, but they laid it at [illegible] orious contribution that they could offer. [2] [illegible] eir lives, made in common by them all, the[illegible] ually received that renown which never gro[illegible], not so much that in which their bones hav[illegible] hat noblest of shrines wherein their glory is la[illegible] membered upon every occasion on which dee[illegible] mmemorated. [3] For heroes have the wh[illegible]; and in lands far from their own, where the[illegible] h declares it, there is enshrined in every bre[illegible] with no monument to preserve it, except tha[illegible] take as your model, and judging happi- nes[illegible] dom and freedom of valor, never decline the[illegible] r it is not the miserable that would most

ILLUSTRATION 2.44 ATTIC MARBLE RELIEF OF C. 430 B.C. COMMEMORATING THE ATHENIANS WHO DIED IN THE FIRST YEAR'S FIGHTING OF THE PELOPONNESIAN WAR

j[illegible]eir lives; these have nothing to hope for: it
is[illegible]ontinued life may bring reverses as yet un-
k[illegible] fall, if it came, would be most tremendous
in[illegible] And surely, to a man of spirit, the degrada-
ti[illegible]e immeasurably more grievous than the un-
f[illegible] him in the midst of his strength and
p[illegible]

2.44
431/0
1st Year/Winter
ATHENS
Pericles comforts the parents of the war dead while acknowledging their grief. He advises those who can to have more children and those past child-bearing age to ease their years with the knowledge that their sons died with honor.

[illegible] not condolence, is what I have to offer to
th[illegible]l who may be here. Numberless are the
c[illegible] know, the life of man is subject; but fortu-
n[illegible]o draw for their lot a death so glorious as
th[illegible]ur mourning, and to whom life has been so
e[illegible]erminate in the happiness in which it has
b[illegible] know that this is a hard saying, especially
w[illegible] be reminded by seeing in the homes of oth-
e[illegible]ce you also enjoyed; for grief is felt not so
m[illegible]at we have never known, as for the loss of
th[illegible]een long accustomed. [3] Yet you who are
st[illegible]hildren must bear up in the hope of having
o[illegible]t only will they help you to forget those
w[illegible] will be to the state at once a reinforcement
a[illegible] can a fair or just policy be expected of the
ci[illegible] his fellows, bring to the decision the inter-
e[illegible] a father. [4] While those of you who have
p[illegible] congratulate yourselves with the thought
th[illegible]r life was fortunate, and that the brief span
th[illegible]red by the fame of the departed. For it is
o[illegible]hat never grows old; and honor it is, not
g[illegible] it, that rejoices the heart of age and help-
le[illegible]

2.45
431/0
1st Year/Winter
ATHENS
He says that the sons and brothers of the dead may seek to equal their renown, but that their widows should best seek to avoid notice of any sort.

[illegible] or brothers of the dead, I see an arduous
st[illegible]n a man is gone, all are wont to praise him,
a[illegible] ever so transcendent, you will still find it
d[illegible]ertake, but even to approach their renown.
T[illegible]ontend with, while those who are no longer
in[illegible] with a goodwill into which rivalry does not
e[illegible]and if I must say anything on the subject of
fe[illegible] of you who will now be in widowhood, it
w[illegible] this brief exhortation. Great will be your
g[illegible] of your natural character; and greatest will
b[illegible]d of among the men whether for good or
fo[illegible]

2.46
431/0
1st Year/Winter
ATHENS
Pericles concludes by reminding those present that Athens will pay for the upbringing of the children of the dead.

"My task is now finished. I have performed it to the best of my ability, and in words, at least, the requirements of the law are now satisfied. If deeds be in question, those who are here interred have received part of their honors already, and for the rest, their children will be brought up till manhood at the public expense: the state thus offers a valuable prize, as the garland of victory in this race of valor, for the reward both of those who have fallen and their survivors. And where the rewards for merit are greatest, there are found the best citizens."

[2] "And now that you have brought to a close your lamentations for your relatives, you may depart."[2a]

2.47
430
2nd Year/Summer
ATHENS
The Spartans invade Attica again. Plague appears in Athens.

Such was the funeral that took place during this winter, with which the first year of the war came to an end. [2] In the first days of summer the Spartans and their allies, with two-thirds of their forces as before, invaded Attica, under the command of Archidamus son of Zeuxidamus, king of Sparta, and established themselves and laid waste the country. [3] Not many days after their arrival in Attica the plague first began to show itself among the Athenians. It was said that it had broken out in many places previously in the neighborhood of Lemnos[3a] and elsewhere; but a pestilence of such extent and mortality was nowhere remembered. [4] Neither were the physicians at first of any service, ignorant as they were of the proper way to treat it, but they died themselves the most thickly, as they visited the sick most often; nor did any human art succeed any better. Supplications in the temples, divinations, and so forth were found equally futile, till the overwhelming nature of the disaster at last put a stop to them altogether.

2.48
430
2nd Year/Summer
ATHENS
Thucydides describes the origin and progress of the plague. He himself was stricken by it.

It first began, it is said, in the parts of Ethiopia above Egypt, and thence descended into Egypt and Libya[1a] and into most of the King's country. [2] Suddenly falling upon Athens, it first attacked the population in the Piraeus, which was the occasion of their saying that the Peloponnesians had poisoned the reservoirs, there being as yet no wells there, and afterwards appeared in the upper city, when the deaths became much more frequent. [3] All speculation as to its origin and its causes, if causes can be found adequate to produce so great a disturbance, I leave to other writers, whether lay or professional; for myself, I shall simply set down its nature, and explain the symptoms by which perhaps it may be recognized by the student, if it should ever break out again. This I can the better do, as I had the disease myself, and watched its operation in the case of others.[3a]

2.49
430
2nd Year/Summer
ATHENS
Symptoms of the plague and its progression through the body are described.

That year then is agreed to have been otherwise unprecedentedly free from sickness; and such few cases as occurred, all turned into this. [2] As a

2.46.2a See the Introduction (sec. II.v) for a discussion of speeches in Thucydides.
2.47.3a Lemnos: Map 2.29.
2.48.1a Ethiopia is "above" Egypt—up the Nile River and further away from the sea—from a point of view centered in the Mediterranean Sea; see Map 2.56, locator.
2.48.3a See the Introduction (sec. I) for a discussion of what is known about Thucydides' life.

rule, [illegible] ostensible cause; but people in good health were [illegible] by violent heats in the head, and redness and infla[illegible]e inward parts, such as the throat or tongue, beco[illegible]ing an unnatural and fetid breath. [3] These symp[illegible] sneezing and hoarseness, after which the pain soon [illegible] produced a hard cough. When it fixed in the stom[illegible]charges of bile of every kind named by physicians [illegible]y very great distress. [4] In most cases also an ineff[illegible]d, producing violent spasms, which in some cases [illegible]thers much later. [5] Externally the body was not [illegible]or pale in its appearance, but reddish, livid, and breal[illegible]les and ulcers. But internally it burned so that the [illegible]o have on him clothing or linen even of the very [illegible]ndeed to be otherwise than stark naked. What they [illegible]ould have been to throw themselves into cold wate[illegible] some of the neglected sick, who plunged into the r[illegible]es of unquenchable thirst; though it made no diffe[illegible]k little or much. [6] Besides this, the miserable feelir[illegible]est or sleep never ceased to torment them. The body [illegible]ste away so long as the distemper was at its heigh[illegible]rvel against its ravages; so that when they succumb[illegible] the seventh or eighth day, to the internal inflamm[illegible]me strength in them. But if they passed this stage [illegible]ded further into the bowels, inducing a violent ulcer[illegible] by severe diarrhea, this brought on a weakness [illegible]l. [7] For the disorder first settled in the head, ran it[illegible]rough the whole of the body, and even where it dic[illegible]l left its mark on the extremities; [8] for it settled i[illegible]gers and the toes, and many escaped with the loss [illegible] that of their eyes. Others again were seized with [illegible]y on their first recovery, and did not know either [illegible]ds.[8a]

2.50 430 2nd Year/Summer ATHENS Birds of prey abstained from eating plague victims or were poisoned. Such birds actually vanished from the area.

Bu[illegible]he distemper was such as to baffle all description, [illegible]o grievous for human nature to endure, it was still i[illegible]ance that its difference from all ordinary disorders [illegible] All the birds and beasts that prey upon human bodie[illegible] touching them (though there were many lying unbu[illegible]ng them. [2] In proof of this, it was noticed that b[illegible] disappeared; they were not about the bodies, or in[illegible] But of course the effects which I have mentione[illegible]n a domestic animal like the dog.

2.49.8a [illegible]not agree [illegible]ilence.

2.51
430
2nd Year/Summer
ATHENS
Strong and weak alike succumbed to the illness. Despair robbed the afflicted of resistance. Those who nursed the sick were stricken in turn. Only people who had survived the plague could show compassion with impunity.

Such then, if we pass over the varieties of particular cases, which were many and peculiar, were the general features of the distemper. Meanwhile the city enjoyed an immunity from all the ordinary disorders; or if any case occurred, it ended in this. [2] Some died in neglect, others in the midst of every attention. No remedy was found that could be used as a specific; for what did good in one case, did harm in another. [3] Strong and weak constitutions proved equally incapable of resistance, all alike being swept away, although dieted with the utmost precaution. [4] By far the most terrible feature in the malady was the dejection which ensued when anyone felt himself sickening, for the despair into which they instantly fell took away their power of resistance, and left them a much easier prey to the disorder; besides which, there was the awful spectacle of men dying like sheep, through having caught the infection in nursing each other. This caused the greatest mortality. [5] On the one hand, if they were afraid to visit each other, they perished from neglect; indeed many houses were emptied of their inmates for want of a nurse: on the other, if they ventured to do so, death was the consequence. This was especially the case with such as made any pretensions to goodness: honor made them unsparing of themselves in their attendance in their friends' houses, where even the members of the family were at last worn out by the moans of the dying, and succumbed to the force of the disaster. [6] Yet it was with those who had recovered from the disease that the sick and the dying found most compassion. These knew what it was from experience, and had now no fear for themselves; for the same man was never attacked twice—never at least fatally. And such persons not only received the congratulations of others, but themselves also, in the elation of the moment, half entertained the vain hope that they were for the future safe from any disease whatsoever.

2.52
430
2nd Year/Summer
ATHENS
The crowded and poor housing of the refugees aggravated the calamity. Burial and cremation rites were upset due to the large number of victims.

An aggravation of the existing calamity was the influx from the country into the city, and this was especially felt by the new arrivals. [2] As there were no houses to receive them, they had to be lodged at the hot season of the year in stifling cabins, where the mortality raged without restraint. The bodies of dying men lay one upon another, and half-dead creatures reeled about the streets and gathered round all the fountains in their longing for water. [3] The sacred places also in which they had quartered themselves were full of corpses of persons that had died there, just as they were; for as the disaster passed all bounds, men, not knowing what was to become of them, became utterly careless of everything, whether sacred or profane. [4] All the burial rites before in use were entirely upset, and they buried the bodies as best they could. Many from want of the proper appliances through so many of their friends having died already, had recourse to the most shameless modes of burial: sometimes getting in first before those [illegible], they threw their own dead body upon the strang[illegible] it; sometimes they tossed the corpse which they [illegible] p of another that was burning, and so went off.

2.53
430
2nd Year/Summer
ATHENS
Obsessed by death, men sought pleasure with no respect for honor, law, or the gods.

N[illegible] n of lawless extravagance which owed its origin to[illegible] did just what they pleased, cooly venturing on what [illegible] only in a corner, seeing the rapid transitions produ[illegible] perity suddenly dying and those who before had n[illegible] heir property. [2] So they resolved to spend quick[illegible] regarding their lives and riches as alike things of a [illegible] n what men called honor was popular with none, [illegible] ether they would be spared to attain the object; b[illegible] resent enjoyment, and all that contributed to it, wa[illegible] seful. [4] Fear of gods or law of man there was n[illegible] s for the first, they judged it to be just the same [illegible] d them or not, as they saw all alike perishing; and f[illegible] cted to live to be brought to trial for his offenses [illegible] ar severer sentence had been already passed upon [illegible] over their heads, and before this fell it was only r[illegible] little.

2.54
430
2nd Year/Summer
ATHENS
The Athenians argued about ancient prophecies and oracles. The plague struck Athens most severely and never entered the Peloponnesus.

Su[illegible] e calamity, and heavily did it weigh on the Athen[illegible] hin the city and devastation without. [2] Amon[illegible] hey remembered in their distress was, very natura[illegible] which the old men said had long ago been uttere[illegible]

[illegible] shall come and with it pestilence.

[3] S[illegible] hether dearth and not death[3a] had not been the w[illegible] he present juncture, it was of course decided in fav[illegible] eople made their recollection fit in with their sufferi[illegible], that if another Dorian war should ever afterwar[illegible] famine should happen to accompany it, the verse [illegible] ordingly. [4] The oracle also which had been given [illegible] w remembered by those who knew of it. When [illegible] her they should go to war, he answered that if they [illegible] victory would be theirs, and that he would himsel[illegible] h this oracle events were supposed to tally.[5a] For th[illegible] soon as the Peloponnesians invaded Attica, and n[illegible] onnesus (not at least to an extent worth noticin[illegible] t ravages at Athens, and next to Athens, at the m[illegible] cities. Such was the history of the plague.

2.54.3a [illegible] e,"

2.54.5a For Thucydides' attitude toward oracles, see the Introduction (sec. IV.i).

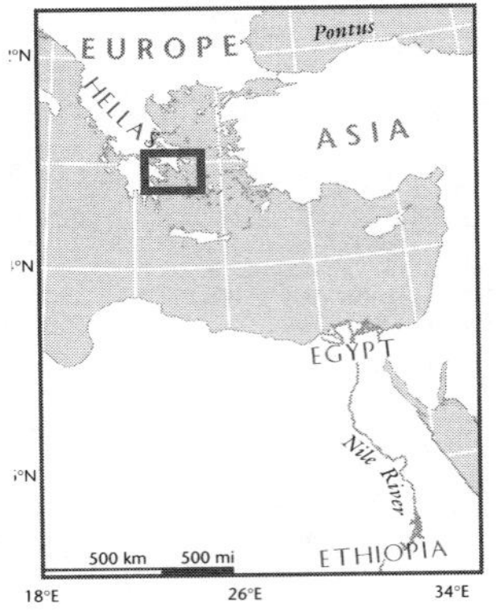

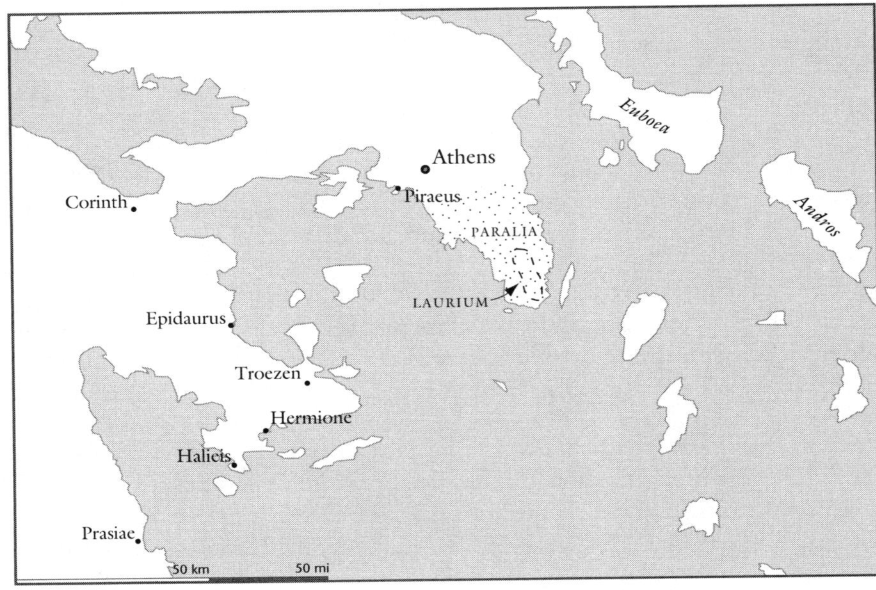

MAP 2.56 ORIGINS OF THE PLAGUE; ATHENIAN RAIDS IN THE PELOPONNESUS, 430

2.55
430
2nd Year/Summer
ATTICA
Attica is ravaged, but Pericles again restrains the Athenians.

After ravaging the plain the Peloponnesians advanced into the Paralian region as far as Laurium,[1a] where the Athenian silver mines are, and first laid waste the side looking toward the Peloponnesus, next that which faces Euboea and Andros.[1b] [2] But Pericles, who was still general, held the same opinion as in the former invasion, and would not let the Athenians march out against them.

2.56
430
2nd Year/Summer
PELOPONNESUS
Pericles leads an expedition to raid Epidaurus and nearby cities.

However while they were still in the plain, and had not yet entered the Paralian land, he had prepared an armament of a hundred ships for the Peloponnesus, and when all was ready put out to sea. [2] On board the ships he took four thousand Athenian heavy infantry, and three hundred cavalry in horse transports, then for the first time made out of old triremes; fifty Chian and Lesbian vessels also joining in the expedition. [3] When this Athenian armament put out to sea, they left the Peloponnesians in Attica in the Paralian region. [4] Arriving at Epidaurus[3a] in the Peloponnesus they ravaged most of the territory, and even had hopes of taking the city by an assault: in this however they were not successful. [5] Putting out from Epidaurus, they laid waste the territory of Troezen, Halieis, and Hermione,[5a] all cities on the coast of the Peloponnesus, and thence sailing to Prasiae,[5b] a maritime city in Laconia, ravaged part of its territory, and took and sacked the place itself; after which they returned home, but

2.55.1a Paralia, Laurium: Map 2.56.
2.55.1b Euboea, Andros: Map 2.56.
2.56.3a Epidaurus: Map 2.56. The unusually large size of this expedition under Pericles is mentioned in 6.31.2.
2.56.5a Troezen, Halieis, Hermione: Map 2.56.
2.56.5b Prasiae: Map 2.56.

four[illegible]one and no longer in Attica.

2.57
430
2nd Year/Summer
ATTICA
This longest invasion of Attica lasted forty days.

D[illegible]hat the Peloponnesians were in Attica and the Athe[illegible] in their ships, men kept dying of the plague both[illegible] Athens. Indeed it was actually asserted that the depa[illegible]sians was hastened by fear of the disorder; as they[illegible]at it was in the city, and also could see the burials g[illegible]nvasion they remained longer than in any other, and [illegible]ry, for they were about forty days in Attica.

2.58
430
2nd Year/Summer
POTIDAEA
Athenian reinforcements accomplish nothing at Potidaea and suffer heavy losses from the plague.

T[illegible]non son of Nicias, and Cleopompus son of Clini[illegible]ericles, took the armament of which he had lately[illegible]f upon an expedition against the Chalcidians in the [illegible]inst Potidaea,[1a] which was still under siege. As soon[illegible]rought up their siege engines against Potidaea and t[illegible]ng it, [2] but did not succeed either in capturing t[illegible]hing else worthy of their preparations. For the plagu[illegible]also, and committed such havoc as to cripple them[illegible]reviously healthy soldiers of the former expedition [illegible]rom Hagnon's troops; while Phormio and the sixte[illegible] he commanded[2a] only escaped by being no long[illegible] of the Chalcidians. [3] The end of it was that Hag[illegible]hips to Athens, having lost one thousand and fifty [illegible]plites in about forty days; though the soldiers statio[illegible]ned in the country and carried on the siege of Potid[illegible]

2.59
430
2nd Year/Summer
ATHENS
Oppressed by invasion and plague, Athens rejects Pericles and sends peace envoys to Sparta; after they fail, Pericles speaks to the Athenian assembly.

A[illegible] of the Peloponnesians a change came over the spirit[illegible] land had now been twice laid waste; and war and [illegible]d heavy upon them. [2] They began to find fault [illegible]hor of the war and the cause of all their misfortunes[illegible] come to terms with Sparta, and actually sent amba[illegible] not however succeed in their mission. Their despa[illegible]d all vented itself upon Pericles. [3] When he saw t[illegible]present turn of affairs and acting exactly as he had a[illegible] assembly, being (it must be remembered) still gener[illegible]bject of restoring confidence and of leading them[illegible]s to a calmer and more hopeful state of mind. He ac[illegible] and spoke as follows:

2.60
430
2nd Year/Summer
ATHENS
Pericles rebukes the Athenians, calling upon them to hold the good of the state above private concerns; he describes himself as a wise and honest patriot.

[illegible] for the indignation of which I have been th[illegible]uses; and I have called an assembly for the pu[illegible]of certain points, and of protesting against yo[illegible]rritated with me, or cowed by your suffer-

2.58.1a [illegible]y of the [illegible]ast de[illegible] of Chal[illegible]2, AY. [illegible]ntioned [illegible]

2.58.2a Phormio and his force of 1,600 citizen hoplites was last mentioned in 1.65.

2.58.3a The end of the siege of Potidaea is described in 2.70.

2.59.3a For the office of Athenian general, see Appendix A, The Athenian Government, §7.

ings. [2] I am of the opinion that national greatness is more to the advantage of private citizens than any individual well-being coupled with public humiliation. [3] A man may be personally ever so well off, and yet if his country be ruined he must be ruined with it; whereas a flourishing commonwealth always affords chances of salvation to unfortunate individuals. [4] Since then a state can support the misfortunes of private citizens, while they cannot support hers, it is surely the duty of everyone to be forward in her defense, and not like you to be so confounded with your domestic afflictions as to give up all thoughts of the common safety, and to blame me for having counseled war and yourselves for having voted it. [5] And yet if you are angry with me, it is with one who, as I believe, is second to no man either in knowledge of the proper policy, or in the ability to expound it, and who is moreover not only a patriot but an honest one. [6] A man possessing that knowledge without that faculty of exposition might as well have no idea at all on the matter: if he had both these gifts, but no love for his country, he would be but a cold advocate for her interests; while were his patriotism not proof against bribery, everything would go for a price. [7] So that if you thought that I was even moderately distinguished for these qualities when you took my advice and went to war, there is certainly no reason now why I should be charged with having done wrong."

2.61
430
2nd Year/Summer
ATHENS
Pericles asserts that Athens has no choice between war or submission, and that his policy remains correct except for the weakness of the Athenians themselves, who must overcome private griefs caused by the unforeseeable plague.

"For those of course who have a free choice in the matter and whose fortunes are not at stake, war is the greatest of follies. But if the only choice was between submission with loss of independence, and danger with the hope of preserving that independence—in such a case it is he who will not accept the risk that deserves blame, not he who will. [2] I am the same man and do not alter, it is you who change, since in fact you took my advice while unhurt, and waited for misfortune to repent of it; and the apparent error of my policy lies in the infirmity of your resolution, since the suffering that it entails is being felt by everyone among you, while its advantage is still remote and obscure to all, and a great and sudden reverse having befallen you, your mind is too much depressed to persevere in your resolves. [3] For before what is sudden, unexpected, and least within calculation the spirit quails; and putting all else aside, the plague has certainly been an emergency of this kind. [4] Born, however, as you are, citizens of a great state, and brought up, as you have been, with habits equal to your birth, you should be ready to face the greatest disasters and still to keep unimpaired the luster of your name. For the judgment of mankind is as relentless to the weakness that falls short of a recognized renown, as it is jealous of the arrogance that aspires higher than its due. Cease then to grieve for your private af-

fli[illegible]selves instead to the safety of the common-
w[illegible]

[illegible] the exertions which the war makes neces-
sa[illegible]ll they may not have a happy result, you
kn[illegible]ch I have often demonstrated to you the
gr[illegible]prehension. If those are not enough, I will
no[illegible]arising from the greatness of your domin-
io[illegible]ever yet suggested itself to you, which I
ne[illegible]revious speeches, and which has so bold a
so[illegible] adventure it now were it not for the un-
na[illegible] I see around me. [2] You perhaps think
th[illegible] only over your allies; I will declare to you
th[illegible] of action has two parts, land and sea. In
th[illegible] you are completely supreme, not merely as
fa[illegible], but also to what further extent you may
th[illegible]al resources are such that your vessels may
go[illegible]thout the King[2a] or any other nation on
ea[illegible]em. [3] So that although you may think it
a [illegible]he use of your land and houses, still you
m[illegible] something widely different; and instead of
fr[illegible] you should really regard them in the light
of[illegible] accessories that embellish a great fortune,
an[illegible] little moment. You should know too that
lib[illegible] efforts will easily recover for us what we
ha[illegible] once bowed, even what you have will pass
fro[illegible]ceiving these possessions not from others,
bu[illegible]not let slip what their labor had acquired,
bu[illegible] you; and in this respect at least you must
pr[illegible]ls, remembering that to lose what one has
go[illegible]n to be thwarted in getting, and you must
co[illegible]t merely with spirit but with disdain. [4]
C[illegible]lissful ignorance impart, ay, even to a cow-
ar[illegible] the privilege of those who, like us, have
be[illegible] of their superiority to their adversary. [5]
An[illegible] the same, knowledge fortifies courage by
th[illegible] consequence, its trust being placed, not
in [illegible]op of the desperate, but in a judgment
gr[illegible]sources, whose anticipations are more to
be [illegible]

[illegible]as a right to your services in sustaining the
gl[illegible]ese are a common source of pride to you
all, [illegible] the burdens of empire and still expect to
sh[illegible]ld remember also that what you are fight-

2.62
430
2nd Year/Summer
ATHENS
Pericles argues that the Athenians' naval supremacy permits them to go wherever they wish at sea; that the loss of land and houses is trivial; and that they may face the war with confidence based on a true assessment of their resources.

2.63
430
2nd Year/Summer
ATHENS
Pericles points out that the Athenian empire is a tyranny that cannot be given up without risk.

2.62.2a [illegible]

ing against is not merely slavery as an exchange for independence, but also loss of empire and danger from the animosities incurred in its exercise. [2] Besides, to recede is no longer possible, if indeed any of you in the alarm of the moment has become enamored of the honesty of such an unambitious part. For what you hold is, to speak somewhat plainly, a tyranny; to take it perhaps was wrong, but to let it go is unsafe. [3] And men of these retiring views, making converts of others, would quickly ruin a state; indeed the result would be the same if they could live independent by themselves; for the retiring and unambitious are never secure without vigorous protectors at their side; indeed, such qualities are useless to an imperial city, though they may help a dependency to an unmolested servitude."

2.64
430
2nd Year/Summer
ATHENS
Pericles concludes that all has gone according to plan except for the plague. He calls on the Athenians to cease parleying with the Spartans and to redouble their efforts to win the war.

"But you must not be seduced by citizens like these, nor be angry with me who, if I voted for war, only did as you did yourselves, in spite of the enemy having invaded your country and done what you could be certain that he would do if you refused to comply with his demands; and in addition to what we expected, the plague has come upon us—the only point indeed at which our calculation has been at fault. It is this, I know, that has had a large share in making me more unpopular than I should otherwise have been, quite undeservedly, unless you are also prepared to give me the credit for any success with which chance may present you. [2] Besides, the hand of Heaven must be borne with resignation, that of the enemy with fortitude; this was the old way at Athens, and do not you prevent it being so still. [3] Remember, too, that if your country has the greatest name in all the world, it is because she never bent before disaster; because she has expended more life and effort in war than any other city, and has won for herself a power greater than any hitherto known, the memory of which will descend to the latest posterity; even if now, in obedience to the general law of decay, we should ever be forced to yield, still it will be remembered that we held rule over more Hellenes than any other Hellenic state, that we sustained the greatest wars against their united or separate powers, and inhabited a city unrivaled by any other in resources or magnitude. [4] These glories may incur the censure of the slow and unambitious; but in the breast of the energetic they will awake emulation, and in those who must remain without them an envious regret. [5] Hatred and unpopularity at the moment have fallen to the lot of all who have aspired to rule others; but where hatred must be incurred, true wisdom incurs it for the highest objects. Hatred also is short-lived; but that which makes the splendor of the present and the glory of the future remains forever unforgotten. [6] Make your decision, therefore, for glory then

a[illegible]n both objects by instant and zealous effort: d[illegible]parta, and do not betray any sign of being o[illegible]nt sufferings, since they whose minds are le[illegible], and whose hands are most quick to meet it[illegible]d the greatest communities."

2.65
430
2nd Year/Summer
ATHENS
Thucydides gives an account of Pericles' character, accomplishments, and leadership; and then offers an analysis of why Athens, by failing to follow Pericles' advice, ultimately lost the war.

S[illegible] by which Pericles tried to cure the Athenians of th[illegible]d to divert their thoughts from their immediate a[illegible]nunity he succeeded in convincing them; they not [illegible]ending to Sparta, but applied themselves with incre[illegible] still as private individuals they could not help smar[illegible]gs, the common people having been deprived of th[illegible]ossessed, while the higher orders had lost fine prop[illegible]ishments and buildings in the country, and, wors[illegible] of peace. [3] In fact, the public feeling against him [illegible]e had been fined.[3a] [4] Not long afterwards, howe[illegible]vay of the multitude, they again elected him gene[illegible]heir affairs to his hands, having now become less s[illegible] and domestic afflictions, and understanding that [illegible]ll for the needs of the state. [5] For as long as he w[illegible]ate during the peace, he pursued a moderate and [illegible] in his time its greatness was at its height. Whe[illegible]ere also he seems to have rightly gauged the powe[illegible] outlived its commencement two years and six mont[illegible] of his foresight concerning the war became bette[illegible] [7] He told them to wait quietly, to pay attentio[illegible]ttempt no new conquests, and to expose the city t[illegible] war, and doing this, promised them a favorable r[illegible]s the very contrary, allowing private ambitions and p[illegible]rs apparently quite foreign to the war, to lead them[illegible]th to themselves and to their allies—projects whos[illegible]nduce to the honor and advantage of private perso[illegible]ntailed certain disaster on the country in the war. [[illegible]e not far to seek. Pericles indeed, by his rank, abilit[illegible] was enabled to exercise an independent control [illegible] short, to lead them instead of being led by them[illegible]power by improper means, be was never compelle[illegible]n the contrary, enjoyed so high an estimation that h[illegible] them by contradiction. [9] Whenever he saw them [illegible]ently elated, he would with a word reduce them [illegible]hand, if they fell victims to a panic, he could at once [illegible]nce. In short, what was nominally a democracy was becoming in his hands government by the first citizen.[9a] [10] With his successors it was different. More on a level with one another, and each grasping at supremacy, they ended by committing even the conduct of state affairs to the whims of the multitude. [11] This, as might have been expected in a great and sovereign state, produced a host of blunders, and amongst them the Sicilian expedition;[11a] though this failed not so much through a miscalculation of the power of those against whom it was sent, as through a fault in the senders in not taking the best measures afterwards to assist those who had gone out, but choosing rather to occupy themselves with private squabbles for the leadership of The People, by which they not only paralyzed operations in the field, but also first introduced civil discord at home. [12] Yet after losing most of their fleet besides other forces in Sicily, and with faction already dominant in the city, they could still for three years make head against their original adversaries, joined not only by the Sicilians, but also by their own allies nearly all in revolt, and at last by the King's son, Cyrus,[12a] who furnished the funds for the Peloponnesian navy. Nor did they finally succumb till they fell the victims of their own intestine disorders. [13] So excessively abundant were the resources from which the genius of Pericles foresaw an easy triumph in the war over the unaided forces of the Peloponnesians.

2.66
430
2nd Year/Summer
ZACYNTHUS
The Peloponnesians send a fleet to Zacynthus.

During the same summer the Spartans and their allies made an expedition with a hundred ships against Zacynthus,[1a] an island lying off the coast of Elis, peopled by a colony of Achaeans from the Peloponnesus, and in alliance with Athens. [2] There were a thousand Spartan hoplites on board, and Cnemus, a Spartiate, as admiral. They made a descent from their ships, and ravaged most of the country; but as the inhabitants would not submit, they sailed back home.

2.67
430
2nd Year/Summer
THRACE
With the help of Sadocus, Sitalces' son, Athenians in Thrace capture Spartan envoys to the Persian king. Sent to Athens, the envoys are executed without trial.

At the end of the same summer the Corinthian Aristeus, with the envoys from Sparta Aneristus, Nicolaus, and Protodamus, and Timagoras from Tegea, and a private individual named Pollis from Argos, came to Sitalces son of Teres, king of Thrace,[1a] on their way to Asia to persuade the King to supply funds and join in the war.[1b] They hoped to induce Teres, if possible, to forsake the alliance of Athens and to march on Potidaea[1c] which was then beseiged by an Athenian force. They also hoped to persuade Teres to

2.65.9a Pericles was an elected general who could be deposed at any time by popular vote, as he was in 430 (see above, 2.65.3). The only passage where he seems to act, as it were, above the constitution is in 2.22.1, when he is said to have refused to call an assembly or a meeting, and this has caused comment. But whatever is said of that, it is clear that Pericles was at all times fully subject to the will of the assembly. See Appendix A, The Athenian Government, §7.

2.65.11a This Athenian expedition to Sicily is described in Books 6 and 7, below. This chapter was clearly written after the end of the war (see section 12 of the chapter) and scholars have debated whether this statement represents a major change of mind about the Sicilian Expedition or only a shift of emphasis.

2.65.12a The intervention of Cyrus is described in Xenophon's account of the end of the Peloponnesian war. Xenophon joined Cyrus' army of mercenaries for the expedition that became the subject of his book *Anabasis*. This passage is one of many that must have been written late by Thucydides. See the Introduction (sec. II.ii) on the composition of Thucydides' text.

2.66.1a Zacynthus: Map 2.72, BX.

2.67.1a Sitalces was last mentioned in 2.29, and will appear next in 2.95.

2.67.1b Spartan contacts with Persia recall Archidamus' speech; see note 1.82.1a.

2.67.1c Potidaea: Map 2.72, AY.

conv[illegible] llespont[1d] to Pharnabazus,[1e] who was to send
then[illegible] ng. [2] But there chanced to be with Sitalces
som[illegible] Learchus son of Callimachus, and Ameiniades
son [illegible] aded Sitalces' son, Sadocus, the new Athenian
citiz[illegible] their hands and thus prevent their crossing
over[illegible] their part to injure his city. [3] He accordingly
had [illegible] ere traveling through Thrace to the vessel in
whic[illegible] Hellespont, by a party whom he had sent on
with[illegible] des, and gave orders for their delivery to the
Athe[illegible] whom they were brought to Athens. [4] On
their[illegible] afraid that Aristeus,[4a] who had been notably
the p[illegible] ous affairs of Potidaea and their Thracian possessi[illegible] em still more mischief if he escaped, slew them
all th[illegible] ing them a trial or hearing the defense which
they[illegible] st their bodies into a pit; thinking themselves
justif[illegible] on the same mode of warfare which the Spartans [illegible] slew and cast into pits all the Athenian and allied [illegible] ught on board the merchantmen round the
Pelo[illegible] outset of the war, the Spartans butchered as
enem[illegible] on the sea, whether allies of Athens or neutrals.

2.68
430
2nd Year/Summer
AMPHILOCHIAN ARGOS
The Ambraciots and their allies attack Amphilochian Argos, but fail to take the city. The history of enmity between these two peoples is described.

A[illegible] ward the close of the summer, the Ambraciot[1a]
force[illegible] barians that they had raised, marched against
the A[illegible] nd the rest of that country. [2] The origin of
their[illegible] ives was this. [3] This Argos and the rest of
Amp[illegible] by Amphilochus son of Amphiaraus. Dissatis-
fied [illegible] t home on his return after the Trojan war, he
built[illegible] cian gulf,[3a] and named it Argos after his own
coun[illegible] rgest city in Amphilochia, and its inhabitants
the m[illegible] der the pressure of misfortune many generations[illegible] n the Ambraciots, their neighbors on the Amphilo[illegible] eir colony; and it was by this union with the
Amb[illegible] their present Hellenic speech, the rest of the
Amp[illegible] ans. [6] After a time the Ambraciots expelled
the A[illegible] themselves. [7] Upon this the Amphilochians
gave [illegible] Acarnanians;[7a] and the two together called the
Athe[illegible] Phormio as general and thirty ships. Upon his
arriva[illegible] orm, and made slaves of the Ambraciots; and
the A[illegible] d Acarnanians inhabited the city in common.

2.67.1d [illegible]
2.67.1e [illegible] vernor [illegible] (Map [illegible] The Per- [illegible]
2.67.4a [illegible] d the [illegible]).2–1.65.
2.68.1a [illegible]
2.68.1b [illegible] ocation: [illegible]
2.68.3a Ambracian gulf: Map 2.72, BX.
2.68.7a Acarnania was last mentioned in 2.33. Acarnania: Map 2.72, BX.

[8] After this began the alliance between the Athenians and Acarnanians. [9] The enmity of the Ambraciots against the Argives thus commenced with the enslavement of their citizens; and afterwards during the war, the Ambraciots collected this armament among themselves and the Chaonians,[9a] and other of the neighboring barbarians. Arrived before Argos, they became masters of the country; but not being successful in their attacks upon the city, returned home and dispersed among their different peoples.[9b]

2.69
430/29
2nd Year/Winter
NAUPACTUS
Phormio's ships are at Naupactus.
CARIA, LYCIA
Athens' squadron to collect tribute and put down privateers in Caria and Lycia suffers a defeat.

Such were the events of the summer. The ensuing winter the Athenians sent twenty ships round the Peloponnesus, under the command of Phormio, who stationed himself at Naupactus[1a] and kept watch against anyone sailing in or out of Corinth[1b] and the Crisaean gulf.[1c] Six others went to Caria and Lycia[1d] under Melesander, to collect tribute[1e] in those parts, and also to prevent the Peloponnesian privateers[1f] from taking up their station in those waters and molesting the passage of the merchantmen from Phaselis and Phoenicia[1g] and the adjoining continent. [2] However, Melesander, going up the country into Lycia with a force of Athenians from the ships and the allies, was defeated and killed in battle, with the loss of a number of his troops.

2.70
430/29
2nd Year/Winter
POTIDAEA
Potidaea surrenders on terms. Athens criticizes its generals for granting terms and sends settlers to colonize the site.

The same winter the Potidaeans[1a] at length found themselves no longer able to hold out against their besiegers. The inroads of the Peloponnesians into Attica had not had the desired effect of making the Athenians raise the siege. There were no provisions left; and so far had distress for food gone in Potidaea that, besides a number of other horrors, instances had even occurred of the people having eaten one another. So in this extremity they at last made proposals for capitulating to the Athenian generals in command against them, Xenophon son of Euripides, Hestiodorus son of Aristocleides, and Phanomachus son of Callimachus. [2] The generals accepted their proposals, seeing the sufferings of the army in so exposed a position; besides which the state had already spent two thousand talents[2a] upon the siege. [3] The terms of the capitulation were as follows: a free passage out for themselves, their children, wives, and auxiliaries, with one garment apiece, the women with two, and a fixed sum of money for their journey. [4] Under this treaty they went out to Chalcidice[4a] and other places, according as was in their power. The Athenians, however, blamed the gener-

2.68.9a Chaonia: Map 2.72, AX.
2.68.9b The history of the conflict between Amphilochian Argos and the Acarnanians on one side, and the Ambraciots on the other, is resumed in 2.80.
2.69.1a Naupactus: Map 2.72, BY.
2.69.1b Corinth: Map 2.72, BY.
2.69.1c Crisaean gulf, now called the Corinthian Gulf: Map 2.72, BY.
2.69.1d Caria and Lycia: Map 2.72, locator.
2.69.1e It is generally believed that when Thucydides reports such collections of money, it is a sign that the tribute has been increased in the course of the preceding summer. See note 4.75.1b; Appendix B, The Athenian Empire, §2, 10; and Illustration 2.69.
2.69.1f Privateers were privately owned boats licensed by the belligerents to attack enemy shipping.
2.69.1g Phaselis and Phoenicia: Map 2.72, locator. Some scholars believe that the region of Phoenicia is not meant here, but some port like Phaselis on the Lycian coast that was called Phoenike.
2.70.1a This picks up the Potidaean narrative from 2.58. For Potidaea, see Map 2.72, AY.
2.70.2a Talent: see Appendix J, Classical Greek Currency, §5.
2.70.4a Chalcidice: Map 2.72, AY. Events in Chalcidice are next mentioned in 2.79.

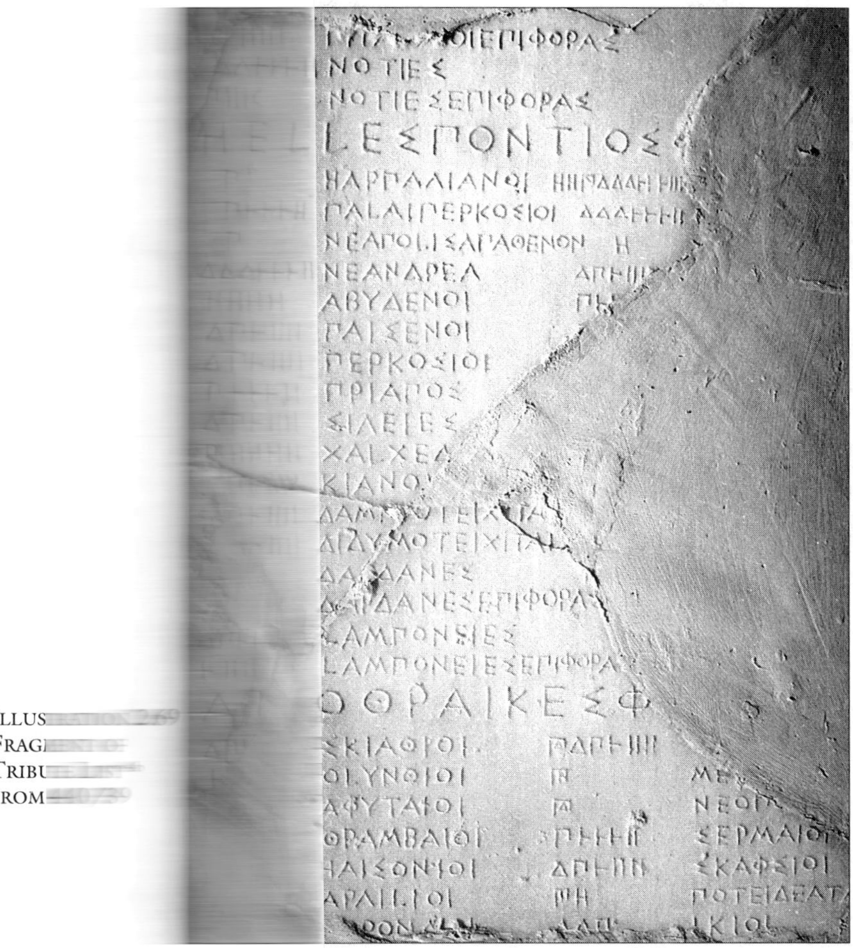

ILLUS[illegible]
FRAG[illegible]
TRIBU[illegible]
FROM [illegible]

als fo[illegible]ut instructions from home, being of opinion that [illegible] control of the city without granting terms. They [illegible] of their own to Potidaea, and colonized it. Such [illegible] winter, and so ended the second year of this war o[illegible] the historian.

2.71
429
3rd Year/Summer
PLATAEA
The Peloponnesians attack Plataea instead of Attica this year, despite Plataean appeals and protests.

Th[illegible]oponnesians and their allies, instead of invading A[illegible]Plataea,[1a] under the command of Archidamus son o[illegible]he Spartans. He had encamped his army and was a[illegible]ountry, when the Plataeans hastened to send envoy[illegible]follows: [2] "Archidamus and Spartans, in invadin[illegible] you do what is wrong in itself, and worthy neithe[illegible] the fathers who begot you. Pausanias son of

2.70.4b [illegible]e lists, [illegible]mpire in [illegible]

2.71.1a This picks up the narrative about Plataea (Map 2.72, BY) from 2.6.

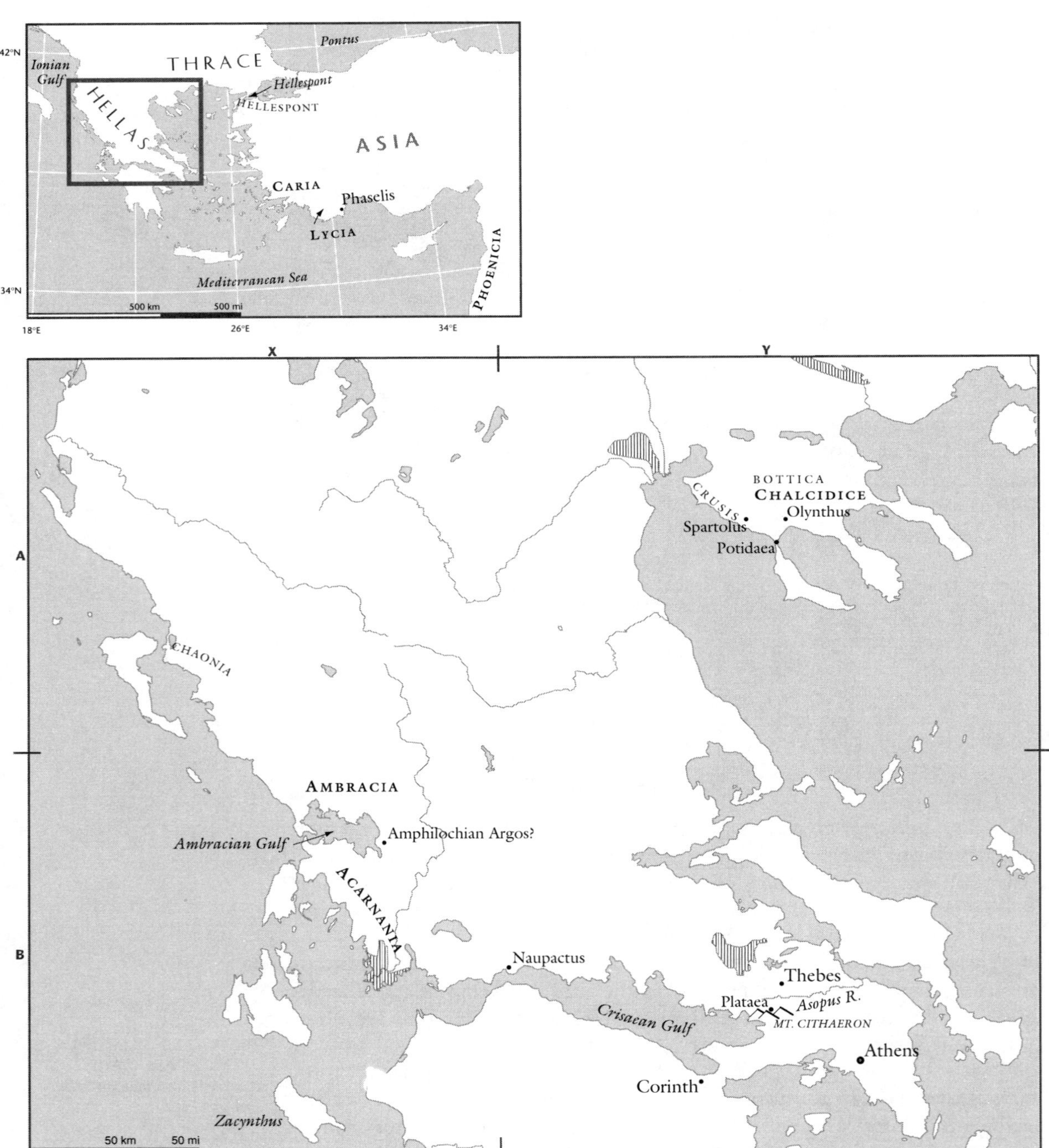

MAP 2.72 OPERATIONS IN ASIA, PLATAEA, AND CHALCIDICE

Cleo[illegible] yman, after freeing Hellas from the Medes
with [illegible] nes who were willing to undertake the risk of
the [illegible] ity, offered sacrifice to Zeus the Liberator in
the [illegible] calling all the allies together restored to the
Plata[illegible] ory, and declared it independent and inviolate
again[illegible] est. Should any such be attempted, the allies
prese[illegible] g to their power. [3] Your fathers rewarded us
thus [illegible] atriotism that we displayed at that perilous
epoc[illegible] ntrary, coming with our bitterest enemies, the
Theb[illegible] We appeal, therefore, to the gods to whom
the [illegible] to the gods of your ancestors, and lastly to
those [illegible] l upon you to refrain from violating our territory [illegible] s, and to let us live independent, as Pausanias
decre[illegible]

2.72
429
3rd Year/Summer
PLATAEA
Archidamus offers neutrality to Plataea, with guarantees of protection and restitution after the war.

Th[illegible] s far when they were cut short by Archidamus
sayin[illegible] aeans, in what you say, if you act up to your
word[illegible] nt of Pausanias, continue to be independent
yours[illegible] g those of your fellow countrymen who, after
shari[illegible] eriod, joined in the oaths to you, and are now
subje[illegible] t is to free them and the rest that all this provision [illegible] de. I could wish that you would share our
labor[illegible] yourselves; if this is impossible, do what we
have [illegible]—remain neutral, enjoying your own; join neither s[illegible] friends and neither as allies for the war. With
this [illegible]] Such were the words of Archidamus. The
Plata[illegible] he had to say, went into the city and ac-
quain[illegible] at had passed, and presently returned for answer [illegible] for them to do what he proposed without
consu[illegible] h whom their children and wives now were;
besid[illegible] ears for the city. After his departure, what was
to pr[illegible] coming and taking it out of their hands, or
the T[illegible] included in the oaths, from taking advantage
of the [illegible] make a second attempt to seize the city? [3]
Upon [illegible] reassure them by saying: "You have only to
delive[illegible] es to us Spartans, to point out the boundaries
of you[illegible] our fruit trees, and whatever else can be nu-
meric[illegible] es to withdraw wherever you like as long as
the w[illegible] over we will restore to you whatever we received [illegible] d it in trust and keep it in cultivation, paying
you a [illegible]

2.73
429
3rd Year/Summer
PLATAEA
Plataea consults Athens, which asks her to honor their alliance.

Wh[illegible] t he had to say, they reentered the city, and
after [illegible] le said that they wished first to acquaint the

2.71.2a [illegible] es to [illegible] attle of [illegible] and [illegible] es in [illegible]

2.71.2b Agora: the marketplace and social center of a classical Greek city.

2.71.3a Thebes, in relation to Plataea: Map 2.72, BY.

Athenians with this proposal, and in the event of their approving to accede to it; in the meantime they asked him to grant them a truce and not to lay waste their territory. He accordingly granted a truce for the number of days requisite for the journey, and meanwhile abstained from ravaging their territory. [2] The Plataean envoys went to Athens,[2a] and consulted with the Athenians, and returned with the following message to those in the city: [3] "The Athenians say, Plataeans, that they have never, since we became their allies, on any occasion abandoned you to an enemy, nor will they now neglect you, but will help you according to their ability; and they solemnly call upon you by the oaths which your fathers swore, to keep the alliance unaltered."

2.74
429
3rd Year/Summer
PLATAEA
Plataea decides to remain with Athens. Archidamus offers prayers to justify an assault on Plataea.

On the delivery of this message by the envoys, the Plataeans resolved not to be unfaithful to the Athenians but to endure, if it must be, seeing their lands laid waste and any other trials that might come to them, and not to send out again, but to answer from the wall that it was impossible for them to do as the Spartans proposed. [2] As soon as be had received this answer, King Archidamus proceeded first to make a solemn appeal to the gods and heroes of the country in the following words: "Ye gods and heroes of the Plataean territory, be my witnesses that not as aggressors originally, nor until these had first departed from the common oath, did we invade this land, in which our fathers offered you their prayers before defeating the Medes, and which you made favorable to the Hellenic arms; nor shall we be aggressors in the measures to which we may now resort, since we have made many fair proposals but have not been successful. Graciously accord that those who were the first to offend may be punished for it, and that vengeance may be attained by those who would righteously inflict it."

2.75
429
3rd Year/Summer
PLATAEA
Thucydides describes the Peloponnesian siege operations and the Plataean counterworks.

After this appeal to the gods Archidamus put his army in motion. First he enclosed the city with a palisade formed of the fruit trees which they cut down, to prevent further exit from Plataea; next day they threw up a mound against the city, hoping that the largeness of the force employed would insure the speedy reduction of the place. [2] They accordingly cut down timber from Cithaeron,[2a] and built it up on either side, laying it like latticework to serve as a wall to keep the mound from spreading abroad, and carried to it wood and stones and earth and whatever other material might help to complete it. [3] They continued to work at the mound for seventy days and nights without intermission, being divided into relief parties to allow some to be employed in carrying while others took sleep and refreshment; the Spartan officer attached to each contingent keeping the men to the work. [4] But the Plataeans, observing the progress of the mound, constructed a wall of wood and fixed it upon that part of the city wall against which the mound was being erected, and built up bricks inside it which they took from the neighboring houses. [5] The timbers served to bind the building together, and to prevent its becoming weak as it ad-

2.73.2a Athens, in relation to Plataea: Map 2.72, BY.
2.75.2a Mount Cithaeron: Map 2.72, BY.

vanc a covering of skins and hides, which protected
the w tacks of burning missiles and allowed the men
to w the wall was raised to a great height, and the
mou s rapid progress. The Plataeans also thought of
anot d out part of the wall upon which the mound
abutt into the city.

2.76 429 3rd Year/Summer PLATAEA A siege warfare of moves and countermoves is described.

D ponnesians twisted up clay in wattles of reed
and t formed in the mound, in order to give it con-
siste carried away like the soil. [2] Stopped in this
way their mode of operation, and digging a mine
from way under the mound, and began to carry off
its m went on for a long while without the enemy
outsi at for all they threw on the top their mound
made on, being carried away from beneath and constant acuum. [3] But the Plataeans fearing that even
thus to hold out against the superior numbers of
the e invention. They stopped working at the large
build nd, and starting at either end of it inside from
the c one in the form of a crescent running in toward n the event of the great wall being taken this
migh y have to throw up a fresh mound against it,
and might not only have their trouble over again,
but a s on their flanks. [4] While raising the mound
the I ght up siege engines against the city, one of
whic the mound against the great building and
shoo it, to the no small alarm of the Plataeans. Others w fferent parts of the wall but were lassoed and
brok also hung up great beams by long iron chains
from poles laid on the wall and projecting over it,
and le whenever any point was threatened by the
engi d let the beam go with its chains slack, so that
it fell he nose of the battering ram.

2.77 429 3rd Year/Summer PLATAEA Unable to take the city by assault, the Peloponnesians plan to besiege it. A last attempt to burn out the defenders fails.

A ians, finding that their siege engines effected
noth nd was met by the counterwork, concluded
that offense were unequal to the taking of the city,
and allation.[1a] [2] First, however, they determined
to tr see whether they could not, with the help of a
wind not a large one; indeed they thought of every
possi the place might be reduced without the ex-
pens cordingly brought bundles of brushwood and
threv l, first into the space between it and the wall;
and t from the number of hands at work, they next
heap into the city as they could reach from the top,

2.77.1 f a wall to
d.

and then lighted the wood by setting fire to it with sulfur and pitch. [4] The consequence was a fire greater than anyone had ever yet seen produced by human agency, though it could not of course be compared to the spontaneous conflagrations known to occur sometimes through the wind rubbing the branches of a mountain forest together. [5] And this fire was not only remarkable for its magnitude, but was also, at the end of so many perils, within an ace of proving fatal to the Plataeans; a great part of the city became entirely inaccessible, and had a wind blown upon it, in accordance with the hopes of the enemy, nothing could have saved them. [6] As it was, there is also a story of heavy rain and thunder having come on by which the fire was put out and the danger averted.[6a]

2.78
429
3rd Year/Summer
PLATAEA
The Peloponnesians build a siege wall around Plataea. The defenders are described.

Failing in this last attempt the Peloponnesians left a portion of their forces on the spot, dismissing the rest, and built a wall of circumvallation round the city, dividing the ground among the various cities present; a ditch being made within and without the lines, from which they got their bricks. [2] All being finished by about the rising of Arcturus,[2a] they left men enough to man half the wall, the rest being manned by the Boeotians, and drawing off their army dispersed to their several cities. [3] The Plataeans had before sent off their wives and children and oldest men and the mass of the noncombatants to Athens; so that the number of the besieged left in the place comprised four hundred of their own citizens, eighty Athenians, and a hundred and ten women to bake their bread. [4] This was the sum total at the commencement of the siege, and there was no one else within the walls, bond or free.[4a] Such were the arrangements made for the blockade of Plataea.[4b]

2.79
429
3rd Year/Summer
CHALCIDICE
Athenian forces win an initial success at Spartolus but then suffer heavy losses when defeated by peltasts and cavalry.

The same summer and simultaneously with the expedition against Plataea, the Athenians marched with two thousand hoplites and two hundred horse against the Chalcidians[1a] in the Thracian region and the Bottiaeans,[1b] just as the corn was getting ripe, under the command of Xenophon son of Euripides,[1c] with two colleagues. [2] Arriving before Spartolus[2a] in Bottiaea, they destroyed the corn and had some hopes of the city coming over through the intrigues of a faction within. But those of a different way of thinking had sent to Olynthus;[2b] and a garrison of hoplites and other troops arrived accordingly. These issuing from Spartolus were engaged by the Athenians in front of the city: [3] the Chalcidian hoplites, and some auxiliaries with them, were beaten and retreated into Spartolus; but the Chalcidian horse and light troops defeated the horse and light troops of the

2.77.6a Is Thucydides being skeptical about stories of divine intervention? See the Introduction (sec. IV.ii) for a discussion of Thucydides' attitude toward religion.

2.78.2a The reference is to the Heliacal rising of Arcturus when it first becomes visible after the forty days of invisibility owing to the fact that it rises after the sun; this occurs on approximately September 20.

2.78.4a This is one of the few occasions on which Thucydides mentions women, who in this case might have been slaves. See Appendix A, The Athenian Government, §2.

2.78.4b The narrative of the siege of Plataea is continued in 3.20.

2.79.1a This picks up the narrative of Chalcidice from 2.70.4, which Thucydides continues next in 2.95. Chalcidice: Map 2.72, AY.

2.79.1b Bottica (Bottike), the "current" location of the Bottiaeans: Map 2.72, AY.

2.79.1c Xenephon son of Euripides was one of the Athenian commanders at Potidaea; see 2.70.1.

2.79.2a Spartolus, approximate location: Map 2.72, AY.

2.79.2b Olynthus: Map 2.72, AY.

Ath dians already had a few peltasts from Crusis,[4a]
and e were joined by some others from Olynthus;
[5] ght troops from Spartolus, emboldened by this
extr vious success, with the help of the Chalcidian
hors just arrived again attacked the Athenians, who
retir ns which they had left with their baggage. [6]
Wh vanced, their adversary gave way, pressing them
with ey began to retire. The Chalcidian horse also,
ridir m just as they pleased, at last caused a panic
amo nd pursued them to a great distance. [7] The
Ath Potidaea, and afterwards recovered their dead
und o Athens with the remnant of their army; four
hun l all the generals having fallen. The Chalcidians
and phy, took up their dead, and dispersed to their
seve

2.80 429 3rd Year/Summer ACARNANIA At Ambraciot invitation, a Peloponnesian expedition sails to the Ambracian Gulf and launches an attack on Acarnania.

T long after this, the Ambraciots[1a] and Chaonians, cing the whole of Acarnania[1c] and detaching it
fron Spartans to equip a fleet from their confederacy
and tes to Acarnania, arguing that if a combined
mov nd and sea, the coastal Acarnanians would be
unal nquest of Zacynthus[1d] and Cephallenia[1e] would
follo ssion of Acarnania. Thus, the cruise round the
Pelo ger be so convenient for the Athenians. Besides
whic king Naupactus.[1f] [2] The Spartans accordingly
at o with Cnemus,[2a] who was still admiral, and the
hopl round orders for the fleet to equip as quickly as
poss [3] The Corinthians were the most forward in
the being a colony of theirs. While the ships from
Cori neighborhood were getting ready, and those
from and Ambracia, which had arrived before, were
wait [4] Cnemus and his thousand hoplites had run
into to Phormio, the commander of the Athenian
squa pactus, and began at once to prepare for the
land llenic troops with him consisted of the Ambraciots orians, and the thousand Peloponnesians with
who nd barbarian Chaonians, who, belonging to a
nati re led by Photys and Nicanor, the two mem-

2.79.4 were
, light
ord. Un-
ast could
the fully
nt was
ore expen-

2.80.1 events in
2.68. Am-

2.80.1

2.80.1

2.80.1d Zacynthus: Map 2.80, BX.
2.80.1e Cephallenia: Map 2.80, BX.
2.80.1f Naupactus: Map 2.80, BY.
2.80.2a Cnemus was the Spartiate commander of the Peloponnesian fleet that attacked Zacynthus in 2.66.
2.80.3a Corinth: Map 2.80, BY.
2.80.3b Sicyon: Map 2.80, BY.
2.80.3c Leucas: Map 2.80, AX.
2.80.3d Anactorium: Map 2.80, AX.
2.80.4a Crisaean gulf, now called the Corinthian Gulf: Map 2.80, BY.

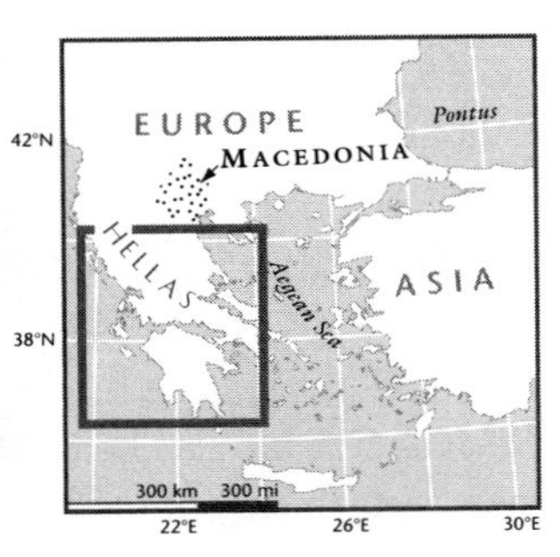

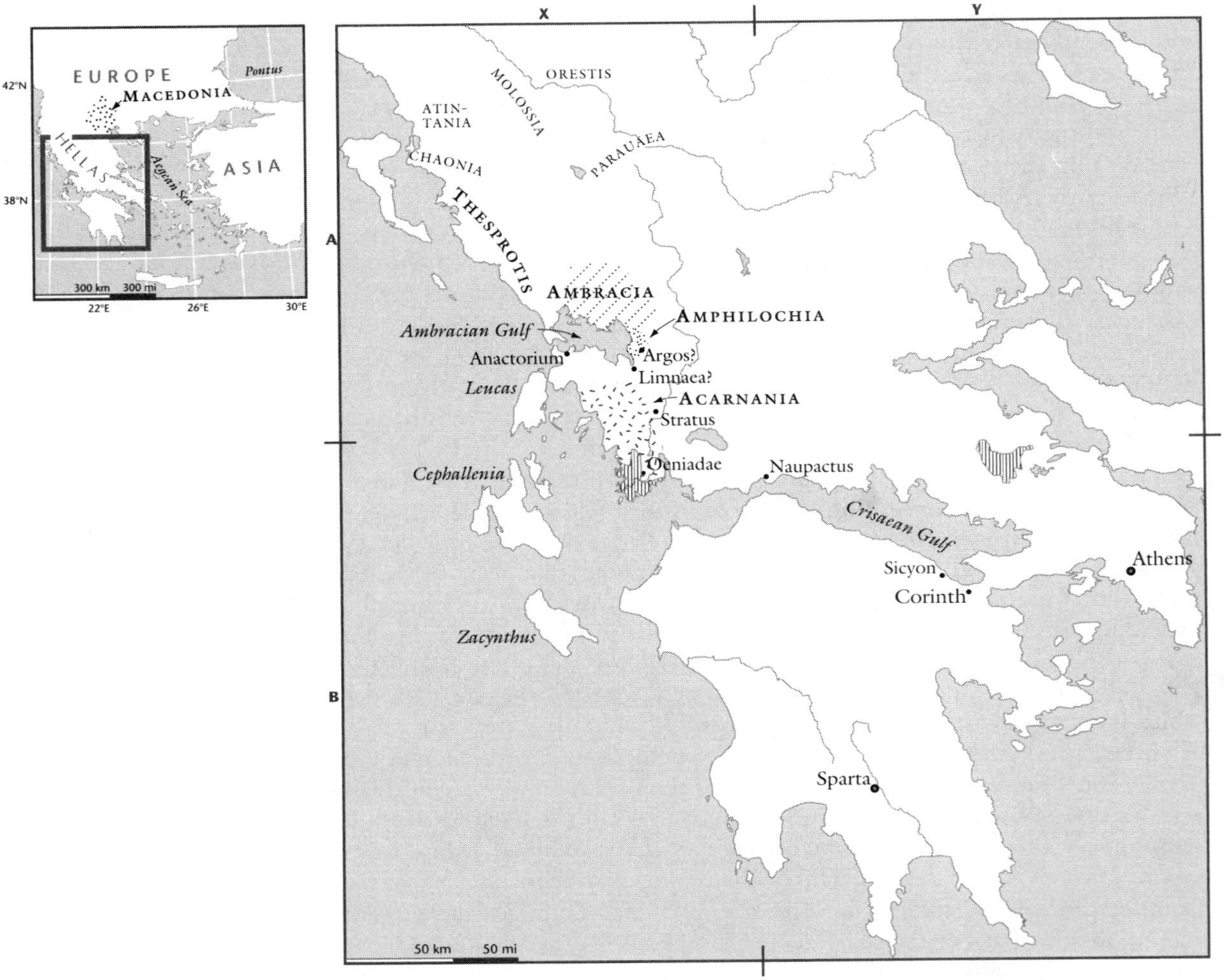

MAP 2.80 AMBRACIAN-PELOPONNESIAN OPERATIONS IN ACARNANIA[5a]

bers of the royal family to whom the chieftainship for that year had been assigned. With the Chaonians came also some Thesprotians,[5b] like them without a king, [6] some Molossians[6a] and Atintanians[6b] led by Sabylinthus, the guardian of King Tharyps who was still a minor, and some Parauaeans[6c] under their king Oroedus, accompanied by a thousand Orestians,[6d] subjects of king Antiochus and placed by him under the command of Oroedus. [7] There were also a thousand Macedonians[7a] sent by Perdic-

2.80.5a The source for the possible sites of Amphilochian Argos and Limnaea, shown in Map 2.80, is N.G.L. Hammond, "The Campaign in Amphilochia during the Archidamian War," *The Annual of the British School at Athens*, 1937, 128–40.

2.80.5b Thesprotis: Map 2.80, AX.

2.80.6a Molossia: Map 2.80, AX.

2.80.6b Atintania: Map 2.80, AX.

2.80.6c Parauaea: Map 2.80, AX.

2.80.6d Orestis: Map 2.80, AX.

2.80.7a The Macedonian king Perdiccas was last mentioned in 2.29.6 and will next appear in 2.95. Macedonia: Map 2.80, locator.

cas [illegible] of the Athenians, but they arrived too late. With [illegible] et out, without waiting for the fleet from Cori[illegible] e territory of Amphilochian Argos,[7b] and sacking t[illegible] aea,[7c] they advanced to Stratus[7d] the Acarnanian [illegible] once this was taken, the rest of the country woul[illegible]

2.81 429 3rd Year/Summer ACARNANIA The Acarnanians ambush and defeat the barbarian division of the Peloponnesian army in front of Stratus.

T[illegible] themselves invaded by a large army by land, and [illegible] by a hostile fleet, made no combined attempt at re[illegible] to defend their homes, and sent for help to Phor[illegible] when a fleet was on the point of sailing from Cori[illegible] for him to leave Naupactus unprotected. [2] The [illegible] hile and their allies advanced upon Stratus in thre[illegible] ention of encamping near it and attempting the [illegible] d to succeed by negotiation. [3] The order of marc[illegible] nter was occupied by the Chaonians and the rest [illegible] the Leucadians and Anactorians and their followe[illegible] nemus with the Peloponnesians and Ambraciots [illegible] on being a long way off from, and sometimes even [illegible] others. [4] The Hellenes advanced in good orde[illegible] l they encamped in a good position; but the Cha[illegible] onfidence, and having the highest reputation for c[illegible] s of that part of the continent, without waiting t[illegible] ushed on with the rest of the barbarians, with the i[illegible] e the city by assault and obtain the sole glory of th[illegible] they were coming on, the Stratians becoming awar[illegible] nd thinking that the defeat of this division woul[illegible] en the Hellenes behind it, occupied the environs [illegible] scades, and as soon as they approached engage[illegible] rs from the city and the ambuscades. [6] A pani[illegible] s, great numbers of them were slain; and as soon [illegible] ive way the rest of the barbarians turned and fled. [illegible] nce by which their allies had preceded them, neit[illegible] ions knew anything of the battle, but fancied they [illegible] ncamp. [8] However, when the flying barbarians [illegible] they opened their ranks to receive them, brou[illegible] ther, and stopped quiet where they were for the [illegible] ering to engage them, as the rest of the Acarnani[illegible], but contenting themselves with slinging at them [illegible] h distressed them greatly as they could not mov[illegible] The Acarnanians are thought to excel in this mod[illegible]

2.80.7[illegible] ocation:

2.80.7[illegible] p 2.80,

2.80.7[illegible]

2.82
429
3rd Year/Summer
ACARNANIA
Cnemus withdraws through Oeniadae.

As soon as night fell, Cnemus hastily drew off his army to the river Anapus,[1a] about nine miles from Stratus, recovering his dead next day under truce, and being there joined by the friendly Oeniadae,[1b] fell back upon their city before the enemy's reinforcements came up. From hence each returned home; and the Stratians set up a trophy for the battle with the barbarians.[1c]

2.83
429
3rd Year/Summer
OFF PATRAE
A Peloponnesian fleet carrying troops is attacked in open water by Phormio's triremes. The Peloponnesians form a defensive circle.

Meanwhile the fleet from Corinth and the rest of the confederates in the Crisaean gulf,[1a] which was to have cooperated with Cnemus and prevented the coastal Acarnanians from joining their countrymen in the interior, was stopped from doing so by being compelled about the same time as the battle at Stratus to fight with Phormio and the twenty Athenian vessels stationed at Naupactus. [2] For they were watched, as they coasted along out of the gulf, by Phormio, who wished to attack in the open sea. [3] But the Corinthians and allies had started for Acarnania without any idea of fighting at sea, and with vessels more like transports for carrying soldiers; besides which, they never dreamed of the twenty Athenian ships venturing to engage their forty-seven. However, while they were coasting along their own shore, there were the Athenians sailing along in line with them; and when they tried to cross over from Patrae[3a] in Achaea to the mainland on the other side, on their way to Acarnania, they saw them again coming out from Chalcis[3b] and the river Evenus[3c] to meet them. They slipped from their moorings in the night, but were observed, and were at length compelled to fight in midpassage. [4] Each state that contributed to the armament had its own general; the Corinthian commanders were Machaon, Isocrates, and Agatharchidas. [5] The Peloponnesians ranged their vessels in as large a circle as possible without leaving an opening, with the prows outside and the sterns in; and placed within all the small craft in company and their five best sailers[5a] to move out at a moment's notice and strengthen any point threatened by the enemy.

2.84
429
3rd Year/Summer
OFF PATRAE
Phormio skillfully waits for dawn winds to disturb the enemy formation and then attacks, routing the enemy and capturing twelve triremes.

The Athenians, formed in line, sailed round and round them, and forced them to contract their circle, by continually brushing past and making as though they would attack at once, having been previously cautioned by Phormio not to do so till he gave the signal. [2] His hope was that the Peloponnesians would not retain their order like a force on shore, but that the ships would fall foul of one another and the small craft cause confusion; and if the wind which usually rose toward morning should blow from the gulf (in expectation of which he kept sailing round them), he felt sure they would not remain steady an instant. He also thought that it rested with him to attack when he pleased, as his ships were better sailers, and that an attack

2.82.1a Anapus river, possible location: Map 2.86, AX.
2.82.1b Oeniadae: Map 2.80, BX. Pericles had failed to capture this city in 1.111.2–3.
2.82.1c The narrative of events in Acarnania is continued in 2.102.
2.83.1a Crisaean gulf, today called the Corinthian Gulf: Map 2.86, BY.
2.83.3a Patrae: Map 2.86, BX.
2.83.3b For the location of this Chalcis, see Map 2.86, BX.
2.83.3c Evenus river: Map 2.86, AX.
2.83.5a The trireme's design was standardized, but evidently some ships excelled in speed due to superior construction, age, condition, the training and vigor of crews, or some combination of these factors.

ILL
THE *AS* AT
SEA, SAIL

timed by the coming of the wind would tell best. [3] When the wind came up, the enemy's ships were now in a narrow space, and what with the wind and the small craft dashing against them, at once fell into confusion: ship fell foul of ship, while the crews were pushing them off with poles, and by their shouting, swearing, and struggling with one another, made captains' orders and boatswains' cries alike inaudible, and through being unable for want of practice to clear their oars in the rough water, prevented the vessels from obeying their helmsmen properly. At this moment Phormio gave the signal, and the Athenians attacked. Sinking first one of the commanders' ships, they then disabled all they came across, so that no one thought of resistance for the confusion, but all fled for Patrae and Dyme[3a] in Achaea. [4] The Athenians gave chase and captured twelve ships, and taking most of the men out of them[4a] sailed to Molycrium,[4b] and after setting up a trophy on the promontory of Rhium and dedicating a ship to Poseidon, returned to Naupactus. [5] As for the Peloponnesians, they at once sailed with their remaining ships along the coast from Dyme and Patrae to Cyllene,[5a] the Eleian arsenal where Cnemus and the ships from Leucas[5b] that were to have joined them also arrived after the battle of Stratus.[5c]

2.85
429
3rd Year/Summer
CYLLENE
Peloponnesian commissioners arrive to reorganize the fleet. The reinforcements requested by Phormio are diverted to Crete.

The Spartans now sent to the fleet of Cnemus three commissioners, Timocrates, Brasidas,[1a] and Lycophron, with orders to prepare to engage again with better fortune, and not to be driven from the sea by a few vessels. [2] For they could not at all explain their defeat, the less so as it was their first attempt at sea; and they fancied that it was not that their navy was so inferior, but that there had been misconduct somewhere, not considering the long experience of the Athenians as compared with the little practice which they had had themselves. The commissioners were accordingly sent in anger. [3] As soon as they arrived they set to work with Cnemus to order ships from the different states, and to put those which they already had in fighting order. [4] Meanwhile Phormio sent word to Athens of their preparations and his own victory, and desired as many ships as possible to be speedily sent to him, as he stood in daily expectation of a battle. [5] Twenty were accordingly sent, but instructions were given to their commander to go first to Crete.[5a] For Nicias, a Cretan of Gortys,[5b] who was proxenus[5c] of the Athenians, had persuaded them to sail against Cydonia,[5d] promising to procure the reduction of that hostile city; his real wish being to oblige the Polichnitans,[5e] neighbors of the Cydonians. [6] He accordingly went with the ships to Crete, and, accompanied by the Polichnitans, laid waste the lands of the Cydonians; and, what with adverse winds and stress of weather, wasted no little time there.

2.84.3a Dyme: Map 2.86, BX.
2.84.4a That is, "taking most of them prisoner."
2.84.4b Molycrium, possible location: Map 2.86, BX.
2.84.5a Cyllene: Map 2.86, BX.
2.84.5b Leucas: Map 2.86, AX.
2.84.5c Stratus: Map 2.86, AX. The battle of Stratus was described in 2.81. 5–8.
2.85.1a This is the same Brasidas who distinguished himself at Methone in 2.25.2. We shall next hear of him as an adviser to the Spartan admiral Alcidas, in 3.69.1.
2.85.5a Crete: Map 2.86, locator, and Map 2.9, BY.
2.85.5b Gortys, Crete: Map 2.9, BY.
2.85.5c *Proxenus:* see note 2.29.1b.
2.85.5d Cydonia, Crete: Map 2.9, BX.
2.85.5e Polichna, Crete, probable location: Map 2.9, BX.

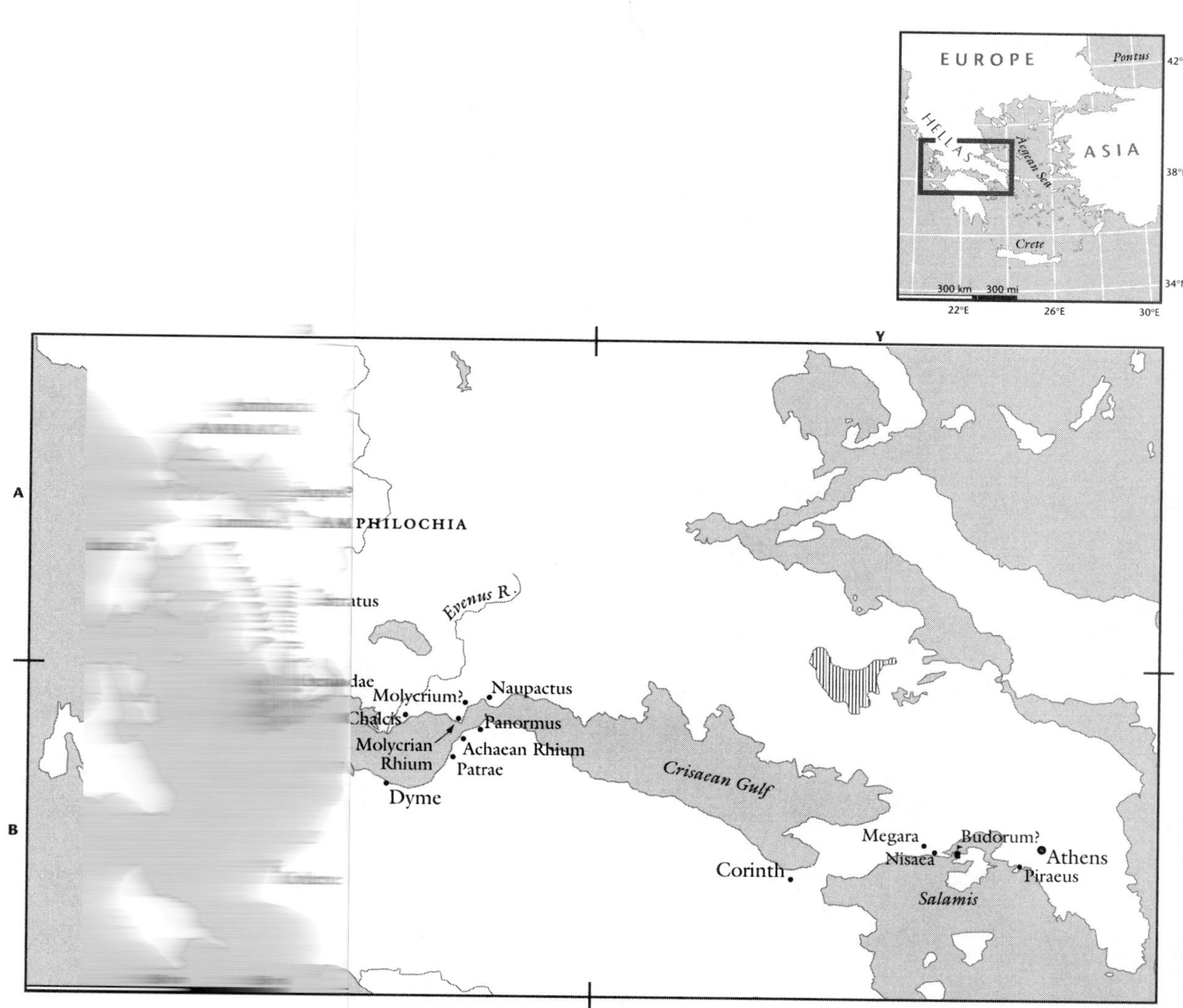

MAP ONS OFF NAUPACTUS; THE PELOPONNESIAN RAID ON THE PIRAEUS[6a]

2.86
429
3rd Year/Summer
ACHAEAN RHIUM
Both fleets maneuver to gain advantage. The Peloponnesian commanders decide to encourage their men with a speech.

While the Athenians were thus detained in Crete, the Peloponnesians in Cyllene[1a] got ready for battle, and coasted along to Panormus[1b] in Achaea, where their land army had come to support them. [2] Phormio also coasted along to Molycrian Rhium,[2a] and anchored outside it with twenty ships, the same as he had fought with before. [3] This Rhium was friendly to the Athenians. The other, in the Peloponnesus, lies opposite to it; the sea between them is about three-quarters of a mile broad, and forms the mouth of the Crisaean gulf. [4] At this, the Achaean Rhium,[4a] not far off Panormus, where their army lay, the Peloponnesians now cast anchor with seventy-seven ships, when they saw the Athenians do so. [5] For six or seven days they remained opposite each other, practicing and preparing for the battle; the one resolved not to sail out of the Rhia into the open sea, for fear of the disaster which had already happened to them, the other not to sail into the straits, thinking it advantageous to the enemy to fight in the narrows. [6] At last Cnemus and Brasidas and the rest of the Peloponnesian commanders, being desirous of bringing on a battle as soon as possible, before reinforcements should arrive from Athens, and noticing that the men were most of them cowed by the previous defeat and out of heart for the business, first called them together and encouraged them as follows:

2.87
429
3rd Year/Summer
ACHAEAN RHIUM
The Peloponnesian commanders call on their men to be brave despite their inexperience.

"Peloponnesians, the late engagement which may have made some of you afraid of the one now in prospect really gives no just ground for apprehension. [2] Preparation for it, as you know, there was little enough; and the object of our voyage was not so much to fight at sea as an expedition by land. Besides this, the chances of war were largely against us; and perhaps also inexperience had something to do with our failure in our first naval action. [3] It was not, therefore, cowardice that produced our defeat, nor ought the determination which force has not quelled, but which still has a word to say with its adversary, to lose its edge from the result of an accident; but admitting the possibility of a chance miscarriage, we should know that brave hearts must be always brave, and while they remain so can never put forward inexperience as an excuse for misconduct. [4] Nor are you so behind the enemy in experience as you are ahead of him in courage; and although the science of your opponents would, if valor accompanied it, have also the presence of mind to carry out in an emergency the lesson it has learnt, yet a faint heart will make all art powerless in the face of danger. For fear takes away presence of mind, and without valor art is useless. [5] Against their superior experience set your superior daring, and against the fear induced by defeat the fact of your having been then unprepared; [6] remember,

2.86.1a Cyllene: Map 2.86, BX.
2.86.1b Panormus: Map 2.86, BX.
2.86.2a Molycrian Rhium: Map 2.86, BX.
2.86.4a Achaean Rhium: Map 2.86, BX.

t… the advantage of superior numbers, and of
e… coast, supported by your hoplites; and as a
r… ment give victory. [7] At no point, there-
f… as for our previous mistakes, the very fact of
th… ch us better for the future. [8] Steersmen
a… , confidently attend to their several duties,
n… assigned to them; [9] as for ourselves, we
p… e engagement at least as well as your previ-
o… give no excuse for anyone misconducting
h… on doing so, he shall meet with the pun-
is… le the brave shall be honored with the ap-
p… ."

T… nanders encouraged their men after this fashion. … eing himself not without fears for the courage
of hi… at they were forming in groups among themselve… he odds against them, desired to call them to-
geth… ence and counsel in the present emergency. [2]
He … old them, and had accustomed their minds to
the i… numerical superiority that they could not face;
and … d long been persuaded that Athenians need
neve… ber of Peloponnesian vessels. [3] At the mo-
men… they were dispirited by the sight before them,
and … confidence, called them together and spoke as
follo…

2.88
429
3rd Year/Summer
MOLYCRIAN RHIUM
Phormio also encourages his men, seeing that they are frightened by the numerical odds they face.

… you are frightened by the number of the
e… ingly called you together, not liking you to
b… ally terrible. [2] In the first place, the Pelo-
p… ed, and not even themselves thinking that
th… have not ventured to meet us on equal
te… this multitude of ships against us. Next, as
t… most rely, the courage which they suppose
c… heir confidence here only arises from the
s… ence in land service usually gives them, and
w… the same for them at sea. [3] But this ad-
v… belong to us on this element, if to them on
th… ior to us in courage, but we are each of us
m… g to our experience in our particular de-
p… the Spartans use their supremacy over the
al… own glory, they are most of them being

2.89
429
3rd Year/Summer
MOLYCRIAN RHIUM
Phormio explains why his fleet, despite the odds, should face the coming battle with confidence.

brought into danger against their will, or they would never, after such a decided defeat, have ventured upon a fresh engagement. [5] You need not, therefore, be afraid of their dash. You, on the contrary, inspire a much greater and better founded alarm, both because of your late victory and also of their belief that we should not face them unless about to do something worthy of such an outstanding success. [6] An adversary numerically superior, like the one before us, comes into action trusting more to strength than to resolution; while he who voluntarily confronts tremendous odds must have very great internal resources to draw upon. For these reasons the Peloponnesians fear our irrational audacity more than they would ever have done a more commensurate preparation. [7] Besides, many armaments have before now succumbed to an inferior through want of skill or sometimes of courage; neither of which defects certainly are ours. [8] As to the battle, it shall not be, if I can help it, in the strait, nor will I sail in there at all; seeing that in a contest between a number of clumsily managed vessels and a small, fast, well-handled squadron, want of sea room is an undoubted disadvantage. One cannot run down an enemy properly without having a sight of him a good way off, nor can one retire at need when pressed; one can neither break the line nor return upon his rear, the proper tactics for a fast sailer; but the naval action necessarily becomes a land one, in which numbers must decide the matter.[8a] [9] For all this I will provide as far as can be. Do you stay at your posts by your ships, and be sharp at catching the word of command, the more so as we are observing one another from so short a distance; and in action think order and silence all important—qualities useful in war generally, and in naval engagements in particular[9a]—and behave before the enemy in a manner worthy of your past exploits. [10] The issues you will fight for are great—either you will destroy the naval hopes of the Peloponnesians or you will bring nearer to reality the Athenians' fear of losing control of the sea. [11] And I may once more remind you that you have defeated most of them already; and beaten men do not face a danger twice with the same determination."

2.90
429
3rd Year/Summer
NAUPACTUS
By sailing toward Naupactus, the Peloponnesians lure Phormio into following them into the straits where they successfully attack him, capturing nine triremes.

Such was the exhortation of Phormio. The Peloponnesians finding that the Athenians did not sail into the gulf and the narrows, in order to lead them in whether they wished it or not, put out at dawn, and forming four

2.89.8a See 7.36.4 and Appendix G, Trireme Warfare, §11.

2.89.9a Silence was particularly vital on warships so that rowers could hear the cadence, which was played on a shrill pipe, and the commands issued by the *keleustes*, the chief rowing officers. See also 2.84.3 and 7.70.6.

abre[illegible]lf in the direction of their own country, the right[illegible]ad lain at anchor. [2] In this wing were placed twen[illegible] so that in the event of Phormio thinking that their[illegible][a] and coasting along thither to save the place, the [illegible] able to escape their onset by getting outside their[illegible] off by the vessels in question. [3] As they expect[illegible]r the place at that moment emptied of its garrison[illegible]n put out, reluctantly and hurriedly embarked and [illegible] Messenian[3a] land forces moving along also to supp[illegible]onnesians seeing him coasting along with his ships[illegible]ly inside the gulf and close in shore as they so much[illegible]urned suddenly and bore down in line at their best [illegible], hoping to cut off the whole squadron. [5] The [illegible]however, escaped the Peloponnesian wing and its su[illegible]ached the more open water; but the rest were overt[illegible]n through, driven ashore and disabled; such of the c[illegible] not swum out of them. [6] Some of the ships the [illegible] their own, and towed off empty; one they took[illegible]ers were just being towed off, when they were saved[illegible]ing into the sea with their armor and fighting from[illegible] boarded.

2.91
429
3rd Year/Summer
NAUPACTUS
The fleeing Athenian ships reach Naupactus. One of them turns and sinks a pursuer, which causes the Peloponnesian vessels to halt. Some Peloponnesian ships run aground.

T[illegible] the Peloponnesians and the Athenian fleet destroy[illegible] the right wing being meanwhile in chase of the e[illegible]hat had escaped their sudden movement and reach[illegible]r. These, with the exception of one ship, all out-s[illegible] into Naupactus, and forming close in shore oppo[illegible]llo, with their prows facing the enemy, prepared[illegible]n case the Peloponnesians should sail in shore again[illegible]ile the Peloponnesians came up, chanting the *paea*[illegible]ey sailed on; the single Athenian ship remaining b[illegible]dian far ahead of the rest. [3] But there happene[illegible] lying at anchor in the roadstead, which the Athe[illegible]sail round, and struck the Leucadian in chase amid[illegible]] An exploit so sudden and unexpected produce[illegible]oponnesians; and having fallen out of order in the e[illegible]me of them dropped their oars and stopped their [illegible] main body come up—an unsafe thing to do consi[illegible]were to the enemy's prows; while others ran

2.90.2a [illegible]

2.90.3a [illegible]n Nau- [illegible]93.1–3.

2.91.2a [illegible]at the [illegible]ng as they [illegible] celebrated [illegible]

2.91.3a [illegible] and car- [illegible]t that they [illegible] the sea [illegible]nks were split by ramming. Instead, they filled with water—becoming unmaneuverable—and remained floating just at or below the surface of the sea, whence they were collected and towed back as booty to the victor's camp after battle. When Thucydides uses the word *kataduei* here (and at 3.78.1 and passim), which literally means "sink down," he must be referring to the partial sinking of the hulls as they filled with water.

aground in the shallows, in their ignorance of the localities.

2.92
429
3rd Year/Summer
NAUPACTUS
The Athenian ships counterattack, pursuing the Peloponnessans who flee in turn. The Athenians capture six of them and retake their own vessels lost earlier.

Elated at this incident, the Athenians at one word gave a cheer, and dashed at the enemy, who, embarrassed by his mistakes and the disorder in which he found himself, only stood for an instant, and then fled for Panormus,[1a] from which he had put out. [2] The Athenians following on his heels took the six vessels nearest them, and recovered those of their own which had been disabled close in shore and taken in tow at the beginning of the action; they killed some of the crews and took some prisoners. [3] On board the Leucadian which went down off the merchantman, was the Spartan Timocrates, who killed himself when the ship was sunk, and was cast up in the harbor of Naupactus. [4] The Athenians on their return set up a trophy on the spot from which they had put out and turned the day, and picking up the wrecks and dead that were on their shore, gave back to the enemy their dead under truce. [5] The Peloponnesians also set up a trophy as victors for the defeat inflicted upon the ships they had disabled in shore, and dedicated the vessel which they had taken at Achaean Rhium, side by side with the trophy. [6] After this, apprehensive of the reinforcement expected from Athens, all except the Leucadians sailed into the Crisaean gulf for Corinth. [7] Not long after their retreat, the twenty Athenian ships, which were to have joined Phormio before the battle,[7a] arrived at Naupactus.

2.93
429/8
3rd Year/Winter
MEGARA-PIRAEUS
The Peloponnesians plan to raid the Piraeus. They march their sailors by night to triremes at Megara. But instead of sailing to the Piraeus, they stop to pillage Salamis.

Thus the summer ended. Winter was now at hand; but before dispersing the fleet, which had retired to Corinth and the Crisaean gulf, Cnemus, Brasidas, and the other Peloponnesian captains allowed themselves to be persuaded by the Megarians[1a] to make an attempt upon the Piraeus,[1b] the port of Athens, which from her decided superiority at sea had been naturally left unguarded and open. [2] Their plan was as follows: the men were each to take their oar, cushion, and rowlock thong, and going overland from Corinth to the sea on the Athenian side, to get to Megara as quickly as they could, and launching forty vessels, which happened to be in the docks at Nisaea,[2a] to sail at once to the Piraeus. [3] There was no fleet on the lookout in the harbor, and no one had the least idea of the enemy attempting a surprise; while an open attack would, it was thought, never be deliberately ventured or if contemplated, would speedily be known at Athens. Their plan formed, the next step was to put it in execution. [4] Arriving by night, they launched the vessels from Nisaea but sailed not to the Piraeus as they had originally intended, being afraid of the risk (besides which there was some talk of a wind having stopped them), but to the point of Salamis[4a] that looks toward Megara. There the Athenians had

2.92.1a Panormus: Map 2.86, BX.
2.92.7a And which had sailed to Crete; 2.85.4–6.
2.93.1a Megara: Map 2.86, BY.
2.93.1b Piraeus: Map 2.86, BY.
2.93.2a Nisaea: Map 2.86, BY.
2.93.4a Salamis in relation to Nisaea: Map 2.86, BY, and Map 3.51, inset.

a fo… …ree triremes to prevent any vessels from sailing
in … …y assaulted this fort, towed off the triremes
emp… …nhabitants began to lay waste the rest of the is-
lanc…

… …ere raised to alarm Athens, and a panic ensued
ther… … occurred during the war. The idea in the city
was … …ady sailed into the Piraeus; in the Piraeus it was
tho… … Salamis and might at any moment arrive in the
por… … have been done if their hearts had been a little
firm… …ould have prevented them. [2] As soon as day
bro… …bled in full force, launched their ships, and em-
barl… …ar went with the fleet to Salamis, while their
sold… … the Piraeus. [3] The Peloponnesians, on becom… …g relief, after they had overrun most of Salamis,
hast… … plunder and captives and the three ships from
For… … the state of their ships also causing them some
anxi… …le since they had been launched, and they were
not … … at Megara, they returned back on foot to
Cor… … finding them no longer at Salamis, sailed back
ther… … made arrangements for guarding the Piraeus
mor… … closing the harbors, and by other suitable pre-
caut…

2.94
429/8
3rd Year/Winter
PIRAEUS
The Athenians, alarmed by fire signals from Salamis, rush to defend the Piraeus. The Peloponnesians hastily depart. Guards are set at the Piraeus to prevent future surprises.

… …t the beginning of this winter, Sitalces son of
Ter… … Thrace,[1a] made an expedition against Perdiccas
son … …acedonia,[1b] and the Chalcidians[1c] in the neigh-
borl… …ct being to enforce one promise and fullfil anoth… … Perdiccas had made him a promise, when hard
pres… …nent of the war, upon condition that Sitalces
shou… …nians to him and not attempt to restore his
brot… …tender Philip, but had not offered to fullfil his
eng… …he, Sitalces, on entering into alliance with the
Ath… …t an end to the Chalcidian war in Thrace. [3]
The… … of his invasion. With him he brought Amyntas
the … …e destined for the throne of Macedonia, and
som… … at his court on this business, and Hagnon as
gen… …ere to join him against the Chalcidians with a
fleet… … they could get together.

2.95
429/8
3rd Year/Winter
THRACE
Thucydides explains the reasons for the campaign of Sitalces of Thrace against Perdiccas of Macedon.

… …sians, he first called out the Thracian tribes subject … … Haemus[1a] and Rhodope[1b] and the Euxine[1c] and

2.96
429/8
3rd Year/Winter
THRACE
The peoples of Sitalces' empire and the forces available to him for this expedition are described.

2.94.… …lap 2.86,

2.94.… …regularly …in their …ppendix G, …sively dry …s had ab- …and close

2.95.1a Sitalces was last mentioned in 2.67. Odrysian Thrace: Map 2.97, BY.

2.95.1b Perdiccas was last mentioned in 2.80. Macedonia: Map 2.97, CX.

2.95.1c Chalcidean affairs were last mentioned in 2.79. Chalcidice: Map 2.97, CX.

2.96.1a Haemus mountains: Map 2.97, AY.

2.96.1b Rhodope mountains: Map 2.97, BY.

2.96.1c Euxine (Black Sea): Map 2.97, BZ.

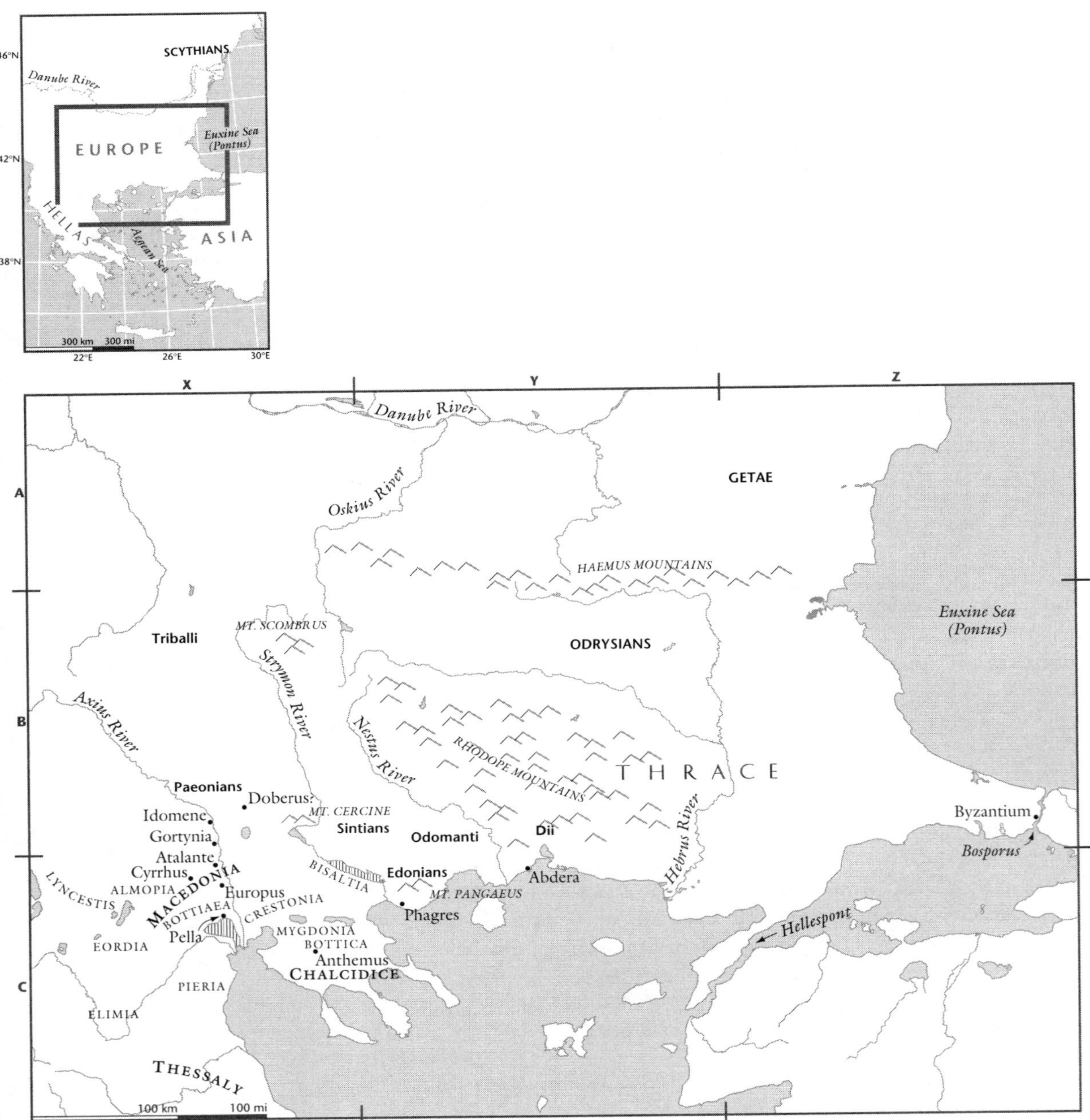

MAP 2.97 SITALCES' KINGDOM—ODRYSIAN THRACE

Hel[illegible]e[1c] beyond Haemus, and the other hordes settled[illegible] the neighborhood of the Euxine, who, like the
Get[illegible]ans[1g] and are armed in the same manner, being
all n[illegible]ides these he summoned many of the indepen-
den[illegible]ordsmen called Dii,[2a] mostly inhabiting Mount
Rho[illegible]me as mercenaries, others as volunteers; [3] also
the [illegible]nd the rest of the Paeonian[3a] tribes in his empire.[illegible] these lay, extending up to the Laeaean Paeonians [illegible] which flows from Mount Scombrus[3c] through
the [illegible] and Leaeans; there the empire of Sitalces ends
and [illegible]ependent Paeonians begins. [4] Bordering on
the [illegible]nt, were the Treres and Tilataeans, who dwell
to t[illegible]brus and extend toward the setting sun as far as
the [illegible] rises in the same mountains as the Nestus[4c] and
Heb[illegible]e range connected with Rhodope.

2.97
429/8
3rd Year/Winter
THRACE
A description of the immense size of Sitalces' empire, as well as its wealth and a few of its customs, illustrates its power.

T[illegible]sians extended along the seaboard from Abdera[illegible]Danube[1b] in the Euxine. The navigation of this
coas[illegible]akes a merchantman four days and four nights
with[illegible]e way: by land an active man, traveling by the
shor[illegible]Abdera to the Danube in eleven days. [2] Such
was [illegible]e. Inland from Byzantium[2a] to the Leaeans and
the [illegible]it of its extension into the interior, it is a journey [illegible]ctive man. [3] The tribute from all the barbarian [illegible]ic cities, taking what they brought in under
Seut[illegible]Sitalces, who raised it to its greatest height,
amo[illegible]ndred talents in gold and silver.[3a] There were
also [illegible]er to a no less amount, besides cloth, plain and
emb[illegible]cles, made not only for the king, but also for
the [illegible]es. [4] For there was here established a custom
opp[illegible] the Persian kingdom, namely, of taking rather
than[illegible]eing attached to not giving when asked than to
aski[illegible]d although this prevailed elsewhere in Thrace,
it w[illegible]ively among the powerful Odrysians, it being
imp[illegible]done without a present. [5] It was thus a very
pow[illegible]ue and general prosperity surpassing all in Europe[illegible]lf[5a] and the Euxine, and in numbers and mili-

2.96.1[illegible]
2.96.1[illegible] their terri-[illegible]
2.96.1[illegible]nd locator.
2.96.1[illegible]itory: Map[illegible]
2.96.2[illegible]eir terri-[illegible]appear in[illegible]gic fate of[illegible]
2.96.3[illegible]ocation of[illegible]
2.96.3[illegible]
2.96.3[illegible]BX.

2.96.4a Triballi, approximate location of their territory: Map 2.97, BX.
2.96.4b Oskius river: Map 2.97, AY.
2.96.4c Nestus river: Map 2.97, BX.
2.96.4d Hebrus river: Map 2.97, BY.
2.97.1a Abdera: Map 2.97, CY.
2.97.1b Danube river mouth in the Euxine (Black Sea): Map 2.97, AY, and locator.
2.97.2a Byzantium: Map 2.97, BZ.
2.97.3a Talents: see Appendix J, Classical Greek Currency, §5.
2.97.5a Ionian gulf (Adriatic Sea): Map 2.72, locator.

tary resources coming decidedly next to the Scythians, [6] with whom indeed no people in Europe can bear comparison, there not being even in Asia any nation singly a match for them if unanimous, though of course they are not on a level with other peoples in general intelligence and the arts of civilized life.

2.98
429/8
3rd Year/Winter
THRACE
Sitalces sets out for Macedon, his army increasing until it numbers perhaps 150,000, of which one-third is cavalry.

It was the master of this empire that now prepared to take the field. When everything was ready, he set out on his march for Macedonia, first through his own dominions, next over the desolate range of Cercine[1a] that divides the Sintians[1b] and Paeonians,[1c] crossing by a road which he had made by felling the timber on a former campaign against the latter people. [2] Passing over these mountains, with the Paeonians on his right and the Sintians and Maedians on the left, he finally arrived at Doberus,[2a] in Paeonia, [3] losing none of his army on the march except perhaps by sickness, but receiving some additional troops from many of the independent Thracians volunteering to join him in the hope of plunder; so that the whole is said to have formed a grand total of a hundred and fifty thousand. [4] Most of this was infantry, though there was about a third cavalry, furnished principally by the Odrysians[4a] themselves and next to them by the Getae.[4b] The most warlike of the infantry were the independent swordsmen who came down from Rhodope; the rest of the mixed multitude that followed him being chiefly formidable by their numbers.

2.99
429/8
3rd Year/Winter
THRACE
Thucydides offers a history of Macedon's foundation and growth.

Assembling in Doberus, they prepared to descend from the heights upon Lower Macedonia, where the dominions of Perdiccas lay; [2] for the Lyncestae,[2a] Elimiots,[2b] and other tribes more inland, though Macedonians by blood and allies and dependents of their kindred, still have their own separate governments. [3] The country on the seacoast, now called Macedonia,[3a] was first acquired by Alexander, the father of Perdiccas, and his ancestors, originally Temenids from Argos.[3b] This was effected by the expulsion from Pieria[3c] of the Pierians, who afterwards inhabited Phagres[3d] and other places under Mount Pangaeus[3e] along the sea beyond the Strymon[3f] (indeed the country between Pangaeus and the sea is still called the Pierian gulf), and also by the expulsion of the Bottiaeans, at present neighbors of the Chalcidians[3g] from Bottiaea.[3h] [4] They also acquired in Paeonia a narrow strip along the river Axius[4a] extending to Pella[4b] and the sea; and

2.98.1a Mount Cercine: Map 2.97, BX.
2.98.1b Sintians, approximate location of their territory: Map 2.97, BX.
2.98.1c Paeonians, approximate location of their territory: Map 2.97, BX.
2.98.2a Doberus, approximate location somewhere a little to the west of Mount Cercine: Map 2.97, BX.
2.98.4a Odrysian Thrace: Map 2.97, BY.
2.98.4b Getae, approximate location of their territory: Map 2.97, AZ.
2.99.2a Lyncestis: Map 2.97, CX.
2.99.2b Elimia, territory of the Elimiots: Map 2.97, CX.
2.99.3a Macedonia: Map 2.97, CX.
2.99.3b Fifth-century Greeks believed that the ruling house of Macedon originated in Argos in the Peloponnesus.
2.99.3c Pieria: Map 2.97, CX.
2.99.3d Phagres: Map 2.97, CY.
2.99.3e Mount Pangaeus: Map 2.97, CY.
2.99.3f Strymon river: Map 2.97, BX.
2.99.3g Chalcidice: Map 2.97, CX.
2.99.3h Bottiaea: Map 2.97, CX.
2.99.4a Axius river: Map 2.97, BX.
2.99.4b Pella: Map 2.97, CX.

havi[illegible]ns,[4c] they occupied Mygdonia[4d] between the Axiu[illegible] From Eordia[5a] also were driven the Eordians, mos[illegible]ough a few of them still live round Physca[5b]—and [illegible]nopia.[5c] [6] These Macedonians also conquered plac[illegible]ner tribes, which are still theirs—Anthemus,[6a] Cres[illegible]nuch of Macedonia proper. The whole is now calle[illegible]ne time of the invasion of Sitalces, Perdiccas, Alex[illegible]ning king.

2.100
429/8
3rd Year/Winter
MACEDONIA
The Macedonians, unable to oppose directly such large forces, withdraw to forts and occasionally harass the enemy with cavalry.

T[illegible]e to take the field against so numerous an invade[illegible] such strong places and fortresses as the country p[illegible]here was no great number, most of those now foun[illegible] been erected subsequently by Archelaus son of Perd[illegible]who also cut straight roads, and otherwise put the [illegible]ooting as regards horses, heavy infantry, and othe[illegible] been done by all the eight kings that preceded him. [illegible]Doberus,[3a] the Thracian host first invaded what had [illegible]nment, and took Idomene[3b] by assault, Gortynia,[3c] [illegible]other places by negotiation, these last coming over [illegible], Amyntas, then with Sitalces. Laying siege to Euro[illegible]ke it, [4] he next advanced into the rest of Mac[illegible]a[4a] and Cyrrhus,[4b] not proceeding beyond this into [illegible]but staying to lay waste Mygdonia, Crestonia, and [illegible]cedonians never even thought of meeting him with [illegible]ian host was, as opportunity offered, attacked by h[illegible]which had been reinforced from their allies in the i[illegible]eastplates, and excellent horsemen, wherever these [illegible]v all before them, but ran considerable risk in entar[illegible] masses of the enemy, and so finally desisted from [illegible] that they were not strong enough to venture agai[illegible]

2.101
429/8
3rd Year/Winter
MACEDONIA
Sitalces fails to reach his goals, runs out of provisions, and is persuaded by his nephew (who had been suborned by Perdiccas) to return to Thrace.

M[illegible]d negotiations with Perdiccas on the objects of his e[illegible]at the Athenians, not believing that he would come [illegible]heir fleet, though they sent presents and envoys, [illegible] of his army against the Chalcidians[1a] and Bot-

2.99.4c [illegible] of their [illegible] the [illegible]
2.99.4d [illegible]
2.99.5a [illegible]Map 2.97, [illegible]
2.99.5b [illegible]
2.99.5c [illegible] Map [illegible]
2.99.6a [illegible]
2.99.6b [illegible]: Map [illegible]
2.99.6c [illegible]Map 2.97, [illegible]
2.100.2 [illegible] reign of [illegible], but some scholars have found it hard to accept that he was still writing after 399; see the Introduction (sec. II.ii) for the date of composition of Thucydides' work.
2.100.3a Doberus, approximate location a little to the west of Mount Cercine: Map 2.97, BX.
2.100.3b Idomene: Map 2.97, BX.
2.100.3c Gortynia: Map 2.97, BX.
2.100.3d Atalante: Map 2.97, CX.
2.100.3e Europus: Map 2.97, CX.
2.100.4a Pella: Map 2.97, CX.
2.100.4b Cyrrhus: Map 2.97, CX.
2.100.4c Bottiaea: Map 2.97, CX.
2.100.4d Pieria: Map 2.97, CX.
2.101.1a Chalcidice: Map 2.97, CX.

tiaeans,[1b] and shutting them up inside their walls laid waste their country. [2] While he remained in these parts, the people farther south, such as the Thessalians,[2a] and the Hellenes as far as Thermopylae,[2b] all feared that the army might advance against them, and prepared accordingly. [3] These fears were shared by the Thracians beyond the Strymon to the north, who inhabited the plains, such as the Panaeans, the Odomanti,[3a] the Droi, and the Dersaeans, all of whom are independent. [4] It was even matter of conversation among the Hellenes who were enemies of Athens whether Sitalces might not be invited by his ally to advance against them also. [5] Meanwhile he held Chalcidice and Bottica[5a] and Macedonia, and was ravaging them all; but finding that he was not succeeding in any of the objects of his invasion, and that his army was without provisions and was suffering from the severity of the season, he listened to the advice of Seuthes son of Sparadocus, his nephew and highest officer, and decided to retreat without delay. This Seuthes had been secretly won over by Perdiccas by the promise of his sister in marriage with a rich dowry. [6] In accordance with this advice, and after a stay of thirty days in all, eight of which were spent in Chalcidice, he retired home as quickly as he could; and Perdiccas[6a] afterwards gave his sister Stratonice to Seuthes as he had promised. Such was the history of the expedition of Sitalces.[6b]

2.102
429/8
3rd Year/Winter
ACARNANIA
Phormio leads an army into Acarnania to ensure its political loyalty. He decides not to attack Oeniadae in winter. Thucydides describes the Achelous River, the Echinades Islands at its mouth, and the myth of Alcmaeon.

In the course of this winter, after the dispersion of the Peloponnesian fleet, the Athenians in Naupactus[1a] under Phormio coasted along to Astacus,[1b] disembarked, and marched into the interior of Acarnania[1c] with four hundred Athenian hoplites and four hundred Messenians.[1d] After expelling some suspected persons from Stratus,[1e] Coronta,[1f] and other places, and restoring Cynes son of Theolytus to Coronta, they returned to their ships, [2] deciding that it was impossible in the winter season to march against Oeniadae,[2a] a place which, unlike the rest of Acarnania, had been always hostile to them; for the river Achelous[2b] flowing from Mount Pindus[2c] through Dolopia[2d] and the country of the Agraeans[2e] and Amphilochians[2f] and the plain of Acarnania, past the city of Stratus in the upper part of its course, forms lakes where it falls into the sea round Oeniadae, and thus makes it impracticable for an army in winter by reason of the water.[2g] [3] Opposite to Oeniadae lie most of the islands called Echinades,[3a] so close to

2.101.1b They were now settled in Bottica: Map 2.97, CX.
2.101.2a Thessaly: Map 2.97, CX.
2.101.2b Thermopylae, the strategic pass where the Greeks fought the Persians in 480: Map 3.7, BX.
2.101.3a Odomanti, approximate location of their territory: Map 2.97, BY.
2.101.5a Bottica: Map 2.97, CX.
2.101.6a Perdiccas next appears in 4.79.
2.101.6b Sitalces, his nephew Seuthes, and events in Thrace are picked up again in 4.7.
2.102.1a Naupactus: Map 2.102.
2.102.1b Astacus: Map 2.102.
2.102.1c This picks up events in Acarnania from 2.82. Acarnania: Map 2.102.
2.102.1d These were the Messenians from Naupactus; see 1.103.1–3, and note 2.9.4a.
2.102.1e Stratus: Map 2.102.
2.102.1f Coronta: location unknown.
2.102.2a Oeniadae: Map 2.102.
2.102.2b Achelous river: Map 2.102.
2.102.2c Pindus mountain range: Map 2.102.
2.102.2d Dolopia: Map 2.102.
2.102.2e Agraea: Map 2.102.
2.102.2f Amphilochia: Map 2.102.
2.102.2g Thucydides returns to events in Acarnania in 3.7.
2.102.3a Echinades islands: Map 2.102.

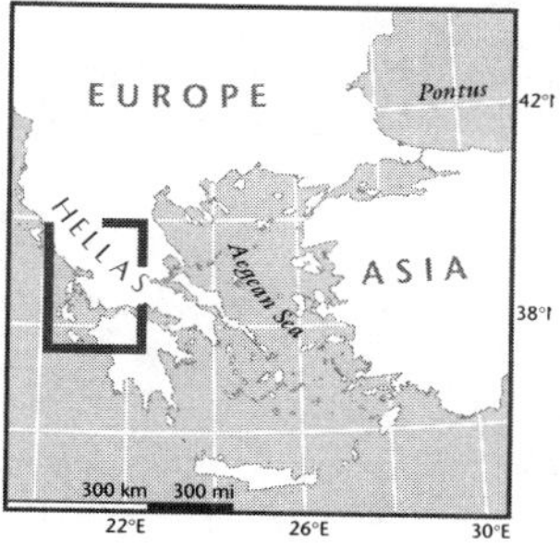

MAP
PHOR
TO A

the that that powerful stream is constantly forming depo has already joined some of the islands to the cont n no long while to do the same with the rest. [4] , deep, and turbid, and the islands are so thick toge nprison the alluvial deposit and prevent its dispersi ot in one line but irregularly, so as to leave no direc into the open sea. [5] The islands in question are reat size. There is also a story that Alcmaeon son is wanderings after the murder of his mother, was habit this spot, through an oracle which intimate release from his terrors until he should find a cour d not been seen by the sun; or existed as land at the time he slew his mother; all else being to him polluted ground. [6] Perplexed at this, the story goes on to say, he at last observed this deposit of the Achelous, and considered that a place sufficient to support life might have been thrown up during the long interval that had elapsed since the death of his mother and the beginning of his wanderings. Settling, therefore, in the district around Oeniadae, he founded a dominion and left the country its name from his son Acarnan. Such is the story we have received concerning Alcmaeon.

2.103
429/8
3rd Year/Winter
ATHENS
Phormio returns to Naupactus and Athens. His prisoners are exchanged.

The Athenians and Phormio putting back from Acarnania and arriving at Naupactus, sailed home to Athens in the spring, taking with them the ships that they had captured, and such of the prisoners made in the late actions as were freemen; who were exchanged, man for man. And so ended this winter, and the third year of this war, of which Thucydides was the historian.

BOOK THREE

3.1
428
4th Year/Summer
ATTICA
The Peloponnesians invade Attica again.

The next summer, just as the corn was getti[illegible]ians and their allies invaded Attica[1a] under the com[illegible]n of Zeuxidamus, king of Sparta, [2] and ravaged [illegible] horse as usual attacking them wherever it was prac[illegible] the mass of the light troops from advancing from [illegible]g the parts near the city. [3] After staying the time [illegible]n provisions, the invaders retired and dispersed to th[illegible]

3.2
428
4th Year/Summer
LESBOS
Lesbos revolts from Athens.

I[illegible]asion of the Peloponnesians all Lesbos,[1a] except Meth[illegible]the Athenians. The Lesbians had wished to revolt [illegible] the Spartans would not receive them; and yet now [illegible]hey were compelled to do so sooner than they had [illegible] were waiting until the moles for their harbors and [illegible] they were building should be finished, and for the a[illegible]in and other things that they were engaged in bring[illegible] [3] the Tenedians,[3a] with whom they were at enmi[illegible]s, and some dissident persons in Mytilene[3b] itself, [illegible]thens, informed the Athenians that the Mytilenians [illegible]he island under their sovereignty, and that the prep[illegible]ey were so active were all concerted with their kind[illegible] with the Spartans, with a view to a revolt, and that [illegible]ately prevented, Athens would lose Lesbos.

3.3
428
4th Year/Summer
MYTILENE
When negotiations fail, Athens sends a fleet to Mytilene.

H[illegible] distressed by the plague, and by the war that had [illegible] was now raging, thought it a serious matter to add [illegible] untouched resources to the list of their enemies; [illegible]believe the charge, giving too much weight to

3.1.1a [illegible]
3.2.1a [illegible]
3.2.1b [illegible]
3.2.2a [illegible]us (Eux-[illegible]n was ser-[illegible] through [illegible]d the [illegible]
3.2.3a [illegible]
3.2.3b Mytilene, Lesbos: Map 3.7, AY.
3.2.3c A *proxenus,* although a citizen and resident of his own state, served as a "friend or representative" (much like a modern honorary consul) of a foreign state.
3.2.3d Boeotia: Map 3.7, BX. The Lesbians were Aeolians, like their founders, the Boeotians; see 7.57.5.

their wish that it might not be true. But when an embassy which they sent had failed to persuade the Mytilenians to give up the union and the preparations complained of, they became alarmed, and resolved to strike the first blow. [2] Accordingly, they suddenly sent off forty ships that had been made ready to sail round the Peloponnesus, under the command of Cleippides son of Deinias, and two others; [3] word having been brought to them of a festival in honor of the Malean Apollo outside the city,[3a] which is celebrated by the whole people of Mytilene, and at which, if haste were made, they might hope to take them by surprise. If this plan succeeded, well and good; if not, they were to order the Mytilenians to deliver up their ships and to pull down their walls, and if they did not obey, to declare war. [4] The ships accordingly set out; the ten Mytilenian *triremes*[4a] present with the fleet according to the terms of the alliance, were detained by the Athenians and their crews placed in custody. [5] However, the Mytilenians were informed of the expedition by a man who crossed from Athens to Euboea, and going overland to Geraestus,[5a] sailed from thence by a merchant vessel which he found on the point of putting to sea, and so arrived at Mytilene the third day after leaving Athens. The Mytilenians accordingly refrained from going out to the temple at Malea, and moreover barricaded and kept guard round the half-finished parts of their walls and harbors.

3.4
428
4th Year/Summer
MYTILENE
During an armistice Mytilene sends a secret embassy to Sparta.

When the Athenians sailed in not long after and saw how things stood, the generals delivered their orders, and upon the Mytilenians refusing to obey, commenced hostilities. [2] The Mytilenians, thus compelled to go to war without notice and unprepared, at first sailed out with their fleet and made some show of fighting a little in front of the harbor; but being driven back by the Athenian ships, immediately offered to parley with the commanders, wishing, if possible, to get the ships away for the present upon any tolerable terms. [3] The Athenian commanders accepted their offers, being themselves fearful that they might not be able to cope with the whole of Lesbos; [4] and an armistice having been concluded, the Mytilenians sent to Athens one of the informers, already repentant of his conduct, and others with him, to try to persuade the Athenians of the innocence of their intentions and to get the fleet recalled. [5] In the meantime, having no great hope of a favorable answer from Athens, they also sent off a trireme with envoys to Sparta, unobserved by the Athenian fleet which was anchored at Malea to the north of the city.[5a]

[6] While these envoys, having reached Sparta after a difficult journey across the open sea, were negotiating for assistance to be sent them,

3.3.3a Cape Malea, Lesbos, probable location of the festival: Map 3.7, AY.
3.3.4a *Triremes* were the standard warship of this period; see Appendix G, Trireme Warfare, §4–7.
3.3.5a Cape Geraestus, Euboea: Map 3.7, BX.
3.4.5a The location of this Malea is unknown.

[3.5[illegible]om Athens returned without having effected anyt[illegible]e at once renewed by the Mytilenians and the rest [illegible]eption of the Methymnians, who came to the aid [illegible]he Imbrians and Lemnians[1a] and some few of the [illegible]ytilenians made a sortie with all their forces agai[illegible]and a battle ensued, in which they gained some sligh[illegible] notwithstanding, not feeling sufficient confidenc[illegible]d the night upon the field. After this they kept quie[illegible]he chance of reinforcements arriving from the Pelo[illegible]g a second venture; being encouraged by the arriv[illegible], and Hermaeondas, a Theban, who had been sent [illegible]ion but had been unable to reach Lesbos before [illegible]n, and who now stole in in a trireme after the battl[illegible] send another trireme and envoys back with them[illegible] accordingly did.[2a]

3.5 428 4th Year/Summer MYTILENE Hostilities resume. Mytilene sends more envoys to Sparta.

M[illegible]s, greatly encouraged by the inaction of the Myti[illegible]s to their aid, who came in all the quicker from seein[illegible]ed by the Lesbians, and bringing round their ships[illegible] south of the city, fortified two camps, one on each[illegible]ituted a blockade of both the harbors. [2] The sea w[illegible]he Mytilenians, who however commanded the whol[illegible] of the Lesbians who had now joined them; the Athe[illegible]nited area round their camps, and using Malea more[illegible]ships and their market.[2a]

3.6 428 4th Year/Summer MYTILENE Athens blockades Mytilene by sea.

W[illegible] this way at Mytilene, the Athenians, about the same[illegible]so sent thirty ships to the Peloponnesus under Asop[illegible]he Acarnanians insisting that the commander sent [illegible] relative of Phormio. [2] As the ships coasted along[illegible] seaboard of Laconia;[2a] [3] after which Asopius sent [illegible] and himself went on with twelve vessels to Nau[illegible]e whole Acarnanian[3b] population, he made an expe[illegible][3c] the fleet sailing along the Achelous,[3d] while the [illegible]ountry. [4] When the inhabitants, however, show[illegible]ng, he dismissed the land forces and himself sailed[illegible]king a descent upon Nericus,[4b] he was cut off durin[illegible] of his troops with him, by the people in those parts[illegible]ards; [5] after which the Athenians sailed away, recov[illegible]e Leucadians under truce.[5a]

3.7 428 4th Year/Summer PELOPONNESUS Asopius leads an Athenian fleet around Peloponnesus.

3.5.1a [illegible]
3.5.2a [illegible]rta are [illegible]
3.6.2a [illegible] and [illegible]e their [illegible]eir own [illegible]s at Myti- [illegible].
3.7.2a [illegible]
3.7.3a [illegible]
3.7.3b [illegible] dides here picks up the narrative of events in Acarnania from 2.102 and continues it next in 3.94.
3.7.3c Oeniadae: Map 3.7, BX.
3.7.3d Achelous river: Map 3.7, AX.
3.7.4a Leucas: Map 3.7, AX.
3.7.4b Nericus, Leucas: Map 3.7, AX.
3.7.5a This truce was granted according to the ritual of hoplite battle; see Appendix F, Land Warfare, §6.

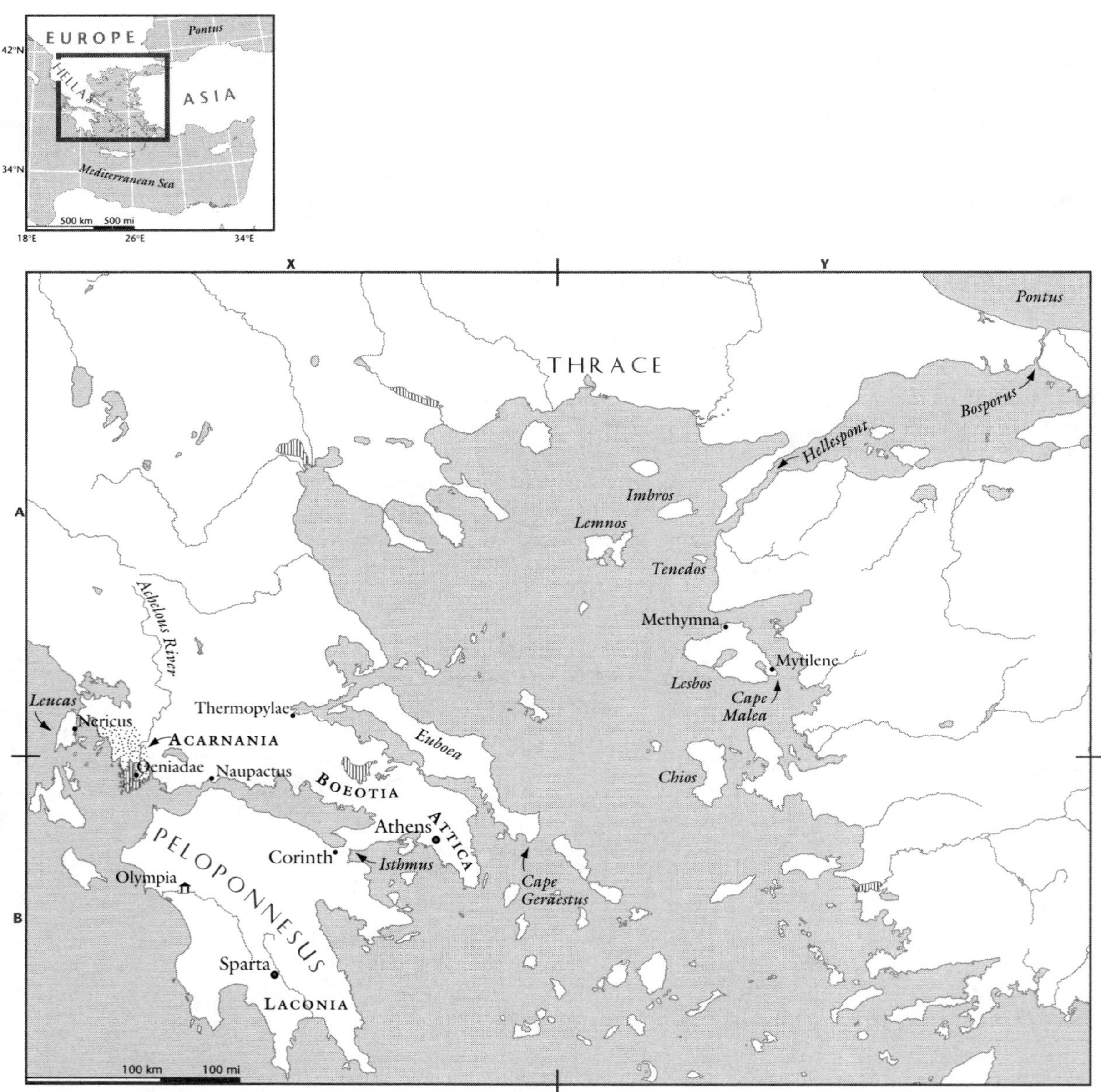

MAP 3.7 MYTILENIAN REVOLT; EXPEDITION OF ASOPIUS

N[illegible] the Mytilenians sent out in the first ship were
told [illegible]e to Olympia,[1a] in order that the rest of the allies[1b] [illegible]ecide upon their matter, and so they journeyed
thith[illegible]d[1c] in which the Rhodian Dorieus gained his
seco[illegible] envoys having been introduced to make their
spee[illegible]e as follows:

3.8 428 4th Year/Summer OLYMPIA Mytilenian envoys travel to Olympia.

[illegible]the rule established among the Hellenes is
n[illegible]se who revolt during a war and forsake their
f[illegible] favorably regarded by those who receive
t[illegible] of use to them, but otherwise are thought
l[illegible]g considered traitors to their former friends.
[[illegible] way of judging, where the rebels and the
p[illegible] secede are at one in policy and sympathy,
a[illegible]her in resources and power, and where no
r[illegible] for the rebellion. But with us and the Athe-
n[illegible]se; [3] and no one need think the worse of
u[illegible]m in danger, after having been honored by
t[illegible]

3.9 428 4th Year/Summer OLYMPIA The Mytilenians argue that their revolt is not dishonorable.

[illegible] will be the first topics of our speech, espe-
c[illegible]r alliance; because we know that there can
n[illegible]ship between individuals, or union between
c[illegible]h the name, unless the parties be persuaded
o[illegible] and be generally congenial the one to the
o[illegible]nce in feeling springs also difference in con-
d[illegible]etween ourselves and the Athenians began
w[illegible] the war against the Persians[2a] and they re-
n[illegible]iness. [3] But we did not become allies of
t[illegible]bjugation of the Hellenes, but allies of the
H[illegible]ion from the Mede; [4] and as long as the
A[illegible]e followed them loyally; but when we saw
t[illegible]to the Mede, and try to make the allies their
s[illegible]hensions began. [5] Unable, however, to
u[illegible]ves, on account of the number of confeder-
a[illegible]he allies were enslaved, except ourselves and
t[illegible]ued to send our contingents as independent
a[illegible] Given these examples, we could no longer
t[illegible], however, as it seemed unlikely that she

3.10 428 4th Year/Summer OLYMPIA The Mytilenians say they ceased to trust Athens when her allies were enslaved.

3.8.1a [illegible]are the en-
[illegible]ioned in
3.8.1b [illegible]ers to the
[illegible]pendix D,
[illegible]–4).
3.8.1c [illegible]s one of
[illegible]als which
[illegible]ontests
[illegible]eligious
[illegible] Calendars
and Dating Systems, §4.

3.10.2a Thucydides describes this withdrawal in 1.95.7. See Appendix E, The Persians, §4.

3.10.5a The Mytilenians here allude to votes of the council of the Delian League (see 1.96.2–1.97.1). See also Appendix B, The Athenian Empire, §2.

3.10.5b Chios: Map 3.7, BY. The Chians and the Lesbians were the only members of Athens' empire still contributing ships and men rather than money to the alliance.

would subject our fellow confederates and not do the same to us who were left, if ever she had the power."

3.11
428
4th Year/Summer
OLYMPIA
The Mytilenians say that their independence was a sham.

"Had we all been still independent, we could have had more faith in their not attempting any change; but the greater number being their subjects, while they were treating us as equals, they would naturally chafe under this solitary instance of independence as contrasted with the submission of the majority; particularly as they daily grew more powerful, and we more destitute. [2] Now the only sure basis of an alliance is for each party to be equally afraid of the other: he who would like to encroach is then deterred by the reflection that he will not have odds in his favor. [3] Again, if we were left independent, it was only because they thought they saw their way to empire more clearly by specious language and by the paths of policy than by those of force. [4] Not only were we useful as evidence that powers who had votes like themselves would not, surely, join them in their expeditions, against their will, without the party attacked being in the wrong; but the same system also enabled them to lead the stronger states against the weaker first, and so to leave the former to the last, stripped of their natural allies, and less capable of resistance. [5] But if they had begun with us, while all the states still had their resources under their own control and there was a center to rally round, the work of subjugation would have been found less easy. [6] Besides this, our navy gave them some apprehension: it was always possible that it might unite with you or with some other power, and become dangerous to Athens. [7] The respect which we paid to their community and its leaders for the time being also helped us to maintain our independence. [8] However, we did not expect to be able to do so much longer, if this war had not broken out, from the examples that we had of their conduct to the rest."

3.12
428
4th Year/Summer
OLYMPIA
The Mytilenians assert that their attempt to break such a relationship should not be condemned.

"How then could we put our trust in such friendship or freedom as we had here? We accepted each other against our inclination; fear made them court us in war, and us them in peace; sympathy, the ordinary basis of confidence, had its place supplied by terror, fear having more share than friendship in detaining us in the alliance; and the first party that should be encouraged by the hope of impunity was certain to break faith with the other. [2] So to condemn us for being the first to break off, because they delay the blow that we dread, instead of ourselves delaying to know for certain whether it will be dealt or not, is to take a false view of the case. [3] For if we were equally able with them to meet their plots and imitate their delay, we should be their equals and should be under no necessity of being their subjects; but the liberty of offense being always theirs, that of defense ought clearly to be ours."

3.13 428 4th Year/Summer OLYMPIA The Mytilenians ask Sparta to receive them as allies, to exploit Athenian weaknesses, and to show themselves as true liberators.

[illegible] lies, are the grounds and the reasons of our
re[illegible] convince our hearers of the fairness of our
co[illegible] o alarm ourselves and to make us turn to
so[illegible] is we wished to do long ago, when we sent
to[illegible] ile the peace yet lasted, but were prevented
by[illegible] e us; and now, upon the Boeotians inviting
us[illegible] to the call, and decided upon a twofold revo[illegible] nd from the Athenians, not to aid the latter
in[illegible] but to join in their liberation, and not to
al[illegible] the end to destroy us, but to act in time
ag[illegible] volt, however has taken place prematurely
an[illegible]—a fact which makes it all the more incum-
be[illegible] into alliance and to send us speedy relief, in
or[illegible] pport your friends, and at the same time do
ha[illegible] 3] You have an opportunity such as you
ne[illegible] and expenditure have wasted the Athenian[illegible] cruising round your coasts, or engaged in
bl[illegible] is not probable that they will have any to
sp[illegible] a second time this summer by sea and land.
E[illegible] resistance to your vessels, or withdraw from
bo[illegible] must it be thought that this is a case of
pu[illegible] nger for a country which is not yours. Les-
bo[illegible] but when help is wanted she will be found
ne[illegible] Attica that the war will be decided, as some
im[illegible] ries by which Attica is supported; [6] and
th[illegible] drawn from the allies, and will become still
la[illegible] not only will no other state revolt, but our
re[illegible] theirs, and we shall be treated worse than
th[illegible] before. [7] But if you will frankly support
us[illegible] side a state that has a large navy, which is
yo[illegible] smooth the way to the overthrow of the
At[illegible] em of their allies, who will be greatly en-
co[illegible] nd you will free yourselves from the accusa-
tio[illegible] not supporting insurrection. In short, only
sh[illegible] ors, and you may count upon having the
ad[illegible]

3.14 428 4th Year/Summer OLYMPIA The Mytilenians conclude with an appeal for help.

[illegible] th the hopes placed in you by the Hellenes,
an[illegible] ose temple we stand virtually as suppliants;
be[illegible] nders of the Mytilenians, and do not sacri-
fic[illegible] in jeopardy for a cause in which general
go[illegible] our success, and still more general harm if
we[illegible] ng to help us. [2] Be the men that the Hel-
le[illegible] ur fears desire."

3.15
428
4th Year/Summer
PELOPONNESUS
Sparta accepts Lesbos as an ally and prepares to invade Attica.

Such were the words of the Mytilenians.[1a] After hearing them out, the Spartans and their allies granted what they urged, took the Lesbians into alliance, and deciding in favor of the invasion of Attica, told the allies present to march as quickly as possible to the Isthmus with two-thirds of their forces. Arriving there first themselves, they prepared hauling machines to carry their ships across from Corinth to the sea on the side of Athens,[1b] in order to make their attack by sea and land at once. [2] However, the zeal which they displayed was not imitated by the rest of the allies, who came in but slowly, being both engaged in harvesting their grain and sick of making expeditions.

3.16
428
4th Year/Summer
ATHENS
Athens deploys one hundred triremes to counter the Spartan forty.

Meanwhile the Athenians, who were aware that the preparations of the enemy were due to his conviction of their weakness, wished to show him that he was mistaken, and that they were able, without moving their fleet off Lesbos, to repel with ease the one with which they were menaced from the Peloponnesus. They therefore manned a hundred ships by embarking the citizens of Athens, except the knights and *pentecosiomedimni,* and the resident aliens;[1a] and putting out to the Isthmus, displayed their power and made descents upon the Peloponnesus wherever they pleased. [2] So unexpected was this response that it made the Spartans think that the Lesbians had not spoken the truth; and embarrassed by the nonappearance of the allies, coupled with the news that the thirty ships round the Peloponnesus were ravaging the lands near Sparta, they went back home. [3] Afterwards, however, they prepared a fleet to send to Lesbos, and ordering a total of forty ships from the different cities in the League, appointed Alcidas to command the expedition in his capacity of admiral.[3a] [4] Meanwhile the Athenians in the hundred ships, upon seeing the Spartans go home, went home likewise.

3.17
428
4th Year/Summer
ATHENS
Athens has 250 triremes at sea, her largest naval deployment during the entire war.

If at the time that this fleet was at sea Athens had almost the largest number of first-rate ships in commission that she ever possessed at any one moment, she had as many or even more when the war began. [2] At that time one hundred guarded Attica, Euboea, and Salamis; a hundred more were cruising round the Peloponnesus, besides those employed at Potidaea and in other places; making a grand total of two hundred and fifty vessels employed on active service in a single summer. [3] It was this, with Potidaea, that most exhausted her revenues—[4] Potidaea being blockaded by a force of *hoplites*[4a] (each drawing two *drachmas*[4b] a day,

3.15.1a See the Introduction (sec. II.v) for a discussion of the speeches in Thucydides.

3.15.1b At the Isthmus of Corinth (Map 3.7, BX) remains of an ancient trackway on which specially made carts hauled ships across the Isthmus to avoid the long and sometimes difficult voyage around the Peloponnesus can still be seen today; see Illustration 8.8.

3.16.1a The knights and *pentecosiomedimni* were the two richest property classes at Athens and were most likely to serve as heavy infantry or cavalry. Resident aliens (*metics*) had rights and obligations but were not citizens. See Appendix A, The Athenian Government, §2.

3.16.3a Alcidas and his fleet are next mentioned in 3.26.

3.17.4a A *hoplite* is a heavily armed infantry man; see the Glossary or Appendix F, Land Warfare, §2.

3.17.4b *Drachmas:* see Appendix J, Classical Greek Currency, §3.

one [illegible] r for his servant), which amounted to three
thou[illegible] kept at this number down to the end of the
siege [illegible] ed with Phormio who went away before it was
over [illegible] paid at the same rate. In this way her money
was [illegible] was the largest number of ships ever manned
by h[illegible]

3.18 428 4th Year/Summer LESBOS The Athenians blockade Mytilene by land.

A[illegible] the Spartans were at the Isthmus, the Mytilenian[illegible] their mercenaries against Methymna,[1a] which
they [illegible] chery. After assaulting the city, and not meeting [illegible] they anticipated, they withdrew to Antissa,
Pyrr[illegible] king measures for the better security of these
citie[illegible] r walls, hastily returned home. [2] After their
depa[illegible] marched against Antissa, but were defeated in
a sor[illegible] their mercenaries, and retreated in haste after
losin[illegible]. [3] When word of this reached Athens, and
the [illegible] the Mytilenians were masters of the country
and [illegible] were unable to hold them in check, they sent
out, [illegible] of autumn, Paches son of Epicurus, to take
com[illegible] Athenian hoplites [4] who worked their own
pass[illegible] iving at Mytilene, built a single wall around it
with [illegible] rongest points. [5] Mytilene was thus blockaded [illegible], by land and by sea; and winter now drew
near.

3.19 428/7 4th Year/Winter ATHENS-CARIA Athens raises money for the siege.

A[illegible] first time raised a war tax of two hundred *talents*[1] [illegible] ns, the Athenians still needed money for the
siege [illegible] ips, under the command of Lysicles and four
other[illegible] m their allies.[1b] [2] After cruising to different
place[illegible] r contribution, Lysicles went up the country
from [illegible] ss the plain of the Meander[2c] as far as the hill
of Sa[illegible] ked by the Carians and the people of Anaia,[2e]
was s[illegible] diers.

3.17.4[illegible] er as not [illegible] ut from it [illegible] ilitary ex- [illegible] n trea- [illegible] es and [illegible] cost six [illegible] nt per day. [illegible] trireme's [illegible] drachma [illegible] nonth to [illegible] ent per [illegible] mes at [illegible] yed some [illegible] ships and [illegible] e cost her [illegible] per day.

3.18.1[illegible] s: Map [illegible] ns to mil- [illegible].

3.18.1[illegible] os: Map [illegible]

3.18.4a "Worked their own passage": the hoplites served as rowers in the triremes that carried them to Lesbos.

3.18.5a The narrative of Mytilene and Lesbos is continued in 3.25.

3.19.1a *Talent:* a unit of weight and money. See Appendix J, Classical Greek Currency, §5.

3.19.1b It is generally believed that when Thucydides reports such collections of money, it is a sign that the tribute has been increased in the course of the preceding summer. See Appendix B, The Athenian Empire, §2, 10, and note 4.75.1b.

3.19.2a Myos: Map 3.29, BY.

3.19.2b Caria: Map 3.29, BY.

3.19.2c Meander river: Map 3.29, BY.

3.19.2d Hill of Sandius, approximate location: Map 3.29, BY.

3.19.2e Anaia: Map 3.29, BY. Anaia was the base of Samian exiles hostile to Athens; see 3.32.2, 4.75.1.

3.20
428/7
4th Year/Winter
PLATAEA
The Plataeans decide to break out.

The same winter the Plataeans, who were still being besieged by the Peloponnesians and Boeotians, distressed by the failure of their provisions, and seeing no hope of relief from Athens, nor any other means of safety, formed a scheme with the Athenians besieged with them for escaping, if possible, by forcing their way over the enemy's walls. This attempt was suggested by Theaenetus son of Tolmides, a soothsayer, and Eupompides son of Daimachus, one of their generals. At first all were to join; [2] afterwards, half hung back, thinking the risk too great. About two hundred and twenty, however, voluntarily persevered in the attempt, which was carried out in the following way. [3] Ladders were made to match the height of the enemy's wall, which they measured by the layers of bricks, the side turned toward them not being thoroughly whitewashed. These were counted by many persons at once; and though some might miss the right calculation, most would hit upon it, particularly as they counted over and over again, and were no great way from the wall, but could see it easily enough for their purpose. [4] The length required for the ladders was thus obtained, being calculated from the breadth of the brick.

3.21
428/7
4th Year/Winter
PLATAEA
The Peloponnesian circumvallation works are described.

Now the wall of the Peloponnesians was constructed as follows: it consisted of two lines drawn round the place about sixteen feet apart, one against the Plataeans, the other against any attack on the outside from Athens. [2] The intermediate space was occupied by huts portioned out among the soldiers on guard, and built in one block, so as to give the appearance of a single thick wall with battlements on either side. [3] At intervals of every ten battlements were towers of considerable size, and the same breadth as the wall, reaching right across from its inner to its outer face, with no means of passing except through the middle. [4] Accordingly on stormy and wet nights the battlements were deserted and guard was kept from the towers, which were not far apart and roofed in above.

Such was the structure of the wall by which the Plataeans were blockaded.

3.22
428/7
4th Year/Winter
PLATAEA
The breakout begins.

When their preparations were completed, they waited for a stormy night of wind and rain without any moon and then set out, guided by the authors of the enterprise. Crossing first the ditch that ran round the city, they next reached the wall of the enemy unperceived by the sentinels, who did not see them in the darkness, or hear them, as the wind drowned with its roar the noise of their approach; [2] besides, they kept a good way off from each other so that they might not be betrayed by the clash of their weapons. They were also lightly equipped, and had only the left foot shod to preserve them from slipping in the mire. [3] They came up to the battlements at one of the intermediate spaces which they knew to be unguarded. Those who carried the ladders went first and planted them; next twelve light-armed soldiers with only a dagger and a breastplate mounted, led by

Am[illegible]who was the first on the wall), his followers getting [illegible] six to each of the towers. After these came anoth[illegible] armed with spears whose shields, that they mig[illegible]ere carried by men behind, who were to hand the[illegible]ound themselves in presence of the enemy. [4] Afte[illegible]unted they were discovered by the sentinels in the [illegible]nade by a tile knocked down by one of the Plat[illegible]hold of the battlements. [5] The alarm was instan[illegible] rushed to the wall, not knowing the nature of the [illegible]rk night and stormy weather. The Plataeans in the [illegible]ment to make a sortie against the wall of the Pelo[illegible]de opposite to that on which their men were gett[illegible]ert the attention of the besiegers. [6] Accordingl[illegible]ed at their several posts, without any venturing to s[illegible] own station, and at a loss to guess what was goin[illegible]e three hundred set aside for service on emergen[illegible]ll in the direction of the alarm. Fire-signals of an a[illegible]ward Thebes;[7a] [8] but the Plataeans in the city at o[illegible] of others, prepared beforehand for this very purp[illegible] the enemy's signals unintelligible, and to prevent [illegible] a true idea of what was happening and coming to h[illegible]des who had gone out should have made good thei[illegible]

3.23 428/7 4th Year/Winter PLATAEA The Plataeans cross over the wall and ditch.

M[illegible]e scaling-party that had got up, after carrying both [illegible] the sentinels to the sword, posted themselves insi[illegible]ning through against them; and rearing ladders fro[illegible]men up on the towers, and from their summit and [illegible]f the enemy that came up, with their missiles, whil[illegible]ed a number of ladders against the wall, and kno[illegible]ents, passed over between the towers. [2] Each as s[illegible] took up his station at the edge of the ditch, sho[illegible]g darts at any who came along the wall to stop the [illegible] [3] When all were over, the party on the towers [illegible]them not without difficulty, and proceeded to the [illegible] hundred came up carrying torches. [4] The Plat[illegible]dge of the ditch in the dark, had a good view of thei[illegible]ged their arrows and darts upon the unarmed part[illegible]hey themselves could not be so well seen in the obs[illegible]d thus even the last of them got over the ditch, thou[illegible]and difficulty; [5] as ice had formed in it, not stro[illegible]on, but of that watery kind which generally com[illegible]st than north, and the snow which this wind

3.22.7a [illegible]

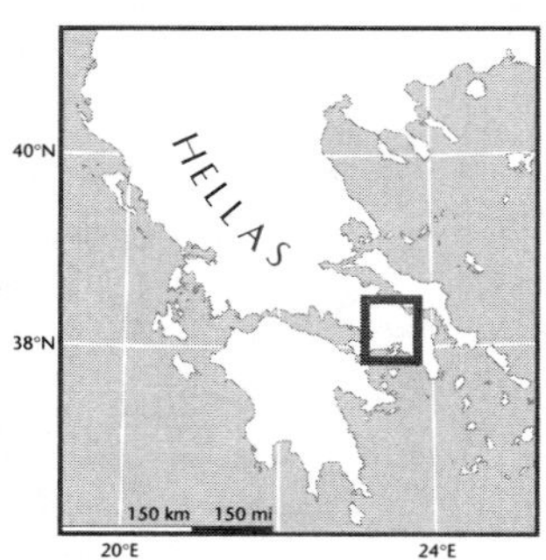

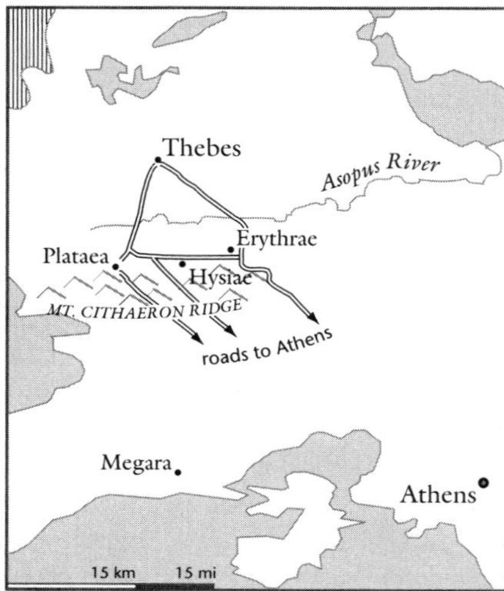

MAP 3.24 PLATAEAN ESCAPE

had caused to fall during the night, had made the water in the ditch rise, so that they could scarcely breast it as they crossed. However, it was mainly the violence of the storm that enabled them to escape at all.

3.24
428/7
4th Year/Winter
PLATAEA
The Plataeans evade pursuit and escape to Athens.

Starting from the ditch, the Plataeans went all together along the road leading to Thebes,[1a] keeping the chapel of the hero Androcrates upon their right, considering that the last road which the Peloponnesians would suspect them of having taken would be that toward their enemies' country. Indeed they could see them pursuing with torches upon the Athens road toward Cithaeron and Druoskephalai, or Oakheads. [2] After going for rather more than half a mile upon the road to Thebes, the Plataeans turned off and took that leading to the mountain, to Erythrae and Hysiae,[2a] and reaching the hills, made good their escape to Athens,[2b] two hundred and twelve men in all; some of their number having turned back into the outer ditch. [3] Meanwhile the Peloponnesians gave up the pursuit and returned to their posts; and the Plataeans in the city, knowing nothing of what had passed, and informed by those who had turned back that not a man had escaped, sent out a herald[3a] as soon as it was day to make a truce for the recovery of the dead bodies. Then, learning the truth, they desisted. In this way the Plataean party broke out and were saved.[3b]

3.24.1a For the roads from Plataea, see Map 3.24. This map is based in part on one in J. B. Bury, *A History of Greece* (New York: 1913), Map 51, p. 279.

3.24.2a Erythrae, Hisiae: Map 3.24.

3.24.2b Athens: Map 3.24

3.24.3a Heralds, already a venerable Greek institution in Thucydides' day, operated under the protection of the god Hermes, and were easily identified by the staff they carried. They alone could travel unmolested between states or armies at war in order to deliver messages, take back replies, and make perfunctory arrangements.

3.24.3b Events at Plataea are taken up again in 3.52.

3.25
428/7
4th Year/Winter
MYTILENE
The Spartan Salaethus arrives in Mytilene.

T[illegible] same winter, Salaethus, a Spartan, was sent out in a [illegible] Mytilene.[1a] Going by sea to Pyrrha,[1b] and from ther[illegible] along the bed of a torrent, where the line of circum[illegible]e, and thus entered unperceived into Mytilene. He [illegible]at Attica would certainly be invaded, that the fort[illegible]e them would arrive, and that he had been sent on t[illegible] superintend matters generally. [2] The Mytilenian[illegible]ge, and laid aside the idea of negotiating with the [illegible]s winter ended, and with it ended the fourth year[illegible]ucydides was the historian.

3.26
427
5th Year/Summer
ATTICA-AEGEAN
The Peloponnesians invade Attica and send a fleet to Mytilene.

T[illegible]eloponnesians sent off the forty-two ships for Myt[illegible]he admiral, and themselves and their allies invad[illegible] being to distract the Athenians by a double mov[illegible]ke it less easy for them to act against the fleet saili[illegible] commander in this invasion was Cleomenes, in the [illegible] son of Pleistoanax, his nephew, who was still a min[illegible]h laying waste whatever had grown up in the part[illegible]e devastated, the invaders now extended their rava[illegible] in their previous incursions; so that this invasion [illegible] by the Athenians than any except the second. [4] [illegible]until they had overrun most of the country, in the [illegible]om Lesbos of something having been achieved by t[illegible]ought must by now have got over. However, as non[illegible]ere realized, and their provisions began to run shor[illegible]persed to their different cities.

3.27
427
5th Year/Summer
MYTILENE
After Salaethus arms the Mytilenean commoners, they revolt.

I[illegible]tilenians, finding their provisions failing, while the [illegible]esus was loitering on the way instead of appearing [illegible]elled to come to terms with the Athenians in the [illegible] Salaethus, having himself ceased to expect the fleet [illegible] The People with heavy armor, which they had not [illegible] the intention of making a sortie against the Ath[illegible] however, no sooner found themselves in possessi[illegible]refused any longer to obey their officers and, mee[illegible] authorities to bring the grain reserve out in pub[illegible]st them all, or they would themselves come to term[illegible]d deliver up the city.

3.28
427
5th Year/Summer
MYTILENE
Mytilene surrenders to Athens.

T[illegible] of their inability to prevent this, and of the dan[illegible]f left out of the capitulation, publicly agreed

3.25.[illegible]rative of [illegible]9, AX.) [illegible]

3.25.[illegible]

3.25.[illegible] of a wall to [illegible]nd.

3.26.[illegible]16.3; it [illegible].

with Paches[1a] and the army to surrender Mytilene unconditionally and to admit the troops into the city upon the understanding that the Mytilenians should be allowed to send an embassy to Athens to plead their cause, and that Paches should not imprison, make slaves of, or put to death any of the citizens until its return. [2] Such were the terms of the capitulation; in spite of which the chief authors of the negotiation with Sparta were so completely overcome by terror when the army entered, that they went and seated themselves by the altars,[2a] from which they were raised up by Paches under promise that he would do them no wrong, and lodged by him in Tenedos,[2b] until he should learn the pleasure of the Athenians concerning them. [3] Paches also sent some triremes and seized Antissa,[3a] and took such other military measures as he thought advisable.

3.29
427
5th Year/Summer
ERYTHRAE
The Spartan fleet crosses the Aegean to Asia.

Meanwhile, the Peloponnesians in the forty ships,[1a] who ought to have made all haste to relieve Mytilene, lost time in coming round the Peloponnesus itself, and proceeding leisurely on the remainder of the voyage, made Delos[1b] without having been seen by the Athenians at Athens, and from thence arriving at Icarus and Myconus,[1c] there first heard of the fall of Mytilene. [2] Wishing to know the truth, they put into Embatum, in the territory of Erythrae,[2a] about seven days after the capture of the city. Here they learned the truth, and began to consider what they were to do; and Teutiaplus, an Elean, addressed them as follows:

3.30
427
5th Year/Summer
ERYTHRAE
Alcidas rejects a proposal to surprise the Athenians at Mytilene.

"Alcidas and Peloponnesians who share with me the command of this armament, my advice is to sail just as we are to Mytilene, before we have been heard of. [2] We may expect to find the Athenians as much on their guard as men generally are who have just taken a city: this will certainly be so by sea, where they have no idea of any enemy attacking them, and where our strength, as it happens, mainly lies; while even their land forces are probably scattered about the houses in the carelessness of victory. [3] If therefore we were to fall upon them suddenly and in the night, I have hopes, with the help of the well-wishers that we may have left inside the city, that we shall become masters of the place. [4] Let us not shrink from the risk, but let us remember that this is just the occasion for one of the baseless panics common in war; and that to be able to guard against these in one's own case, and to detect the moment when an attack will find an enemy at this disadvantage, is what makes a successful general."

3.28.1a Paches was sent to take command of the Athenian forces at Mytilene in 3.18.3.
3.28.2a It would have been sacrilege, an insult to the gods, to harm someone who had taken refuge at an altar; see note 1.126.11a.
3.28.2b Tenedos: Map 3.29, AX.
3.28.3a Antissa: Map 3.29 AX.
3.29.1a These are Alcidas and his forty (or forty-two) ships mentioned in 3.26.
3.29.1b Delos: Map 3.29, BX.
3.29.1c Myconus, Icarus: Map 3.29, BX.
3.29.2a The exact location of Embatum is not known, but it must have been near Erythrae; see Map 3.29, BY.

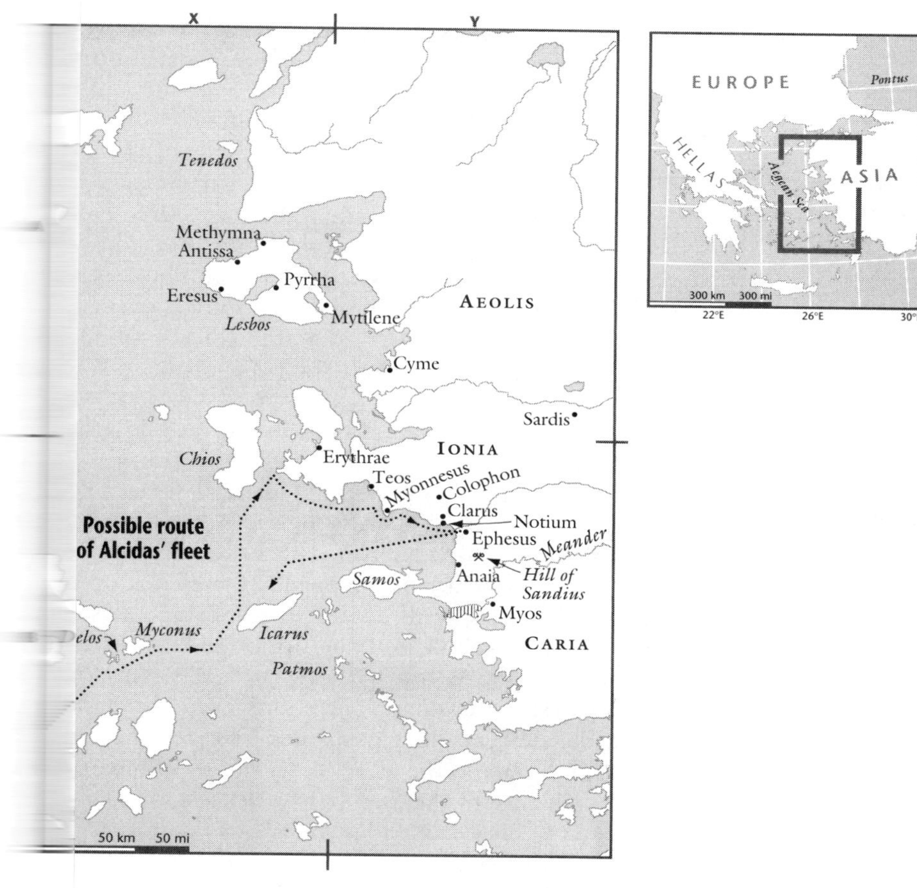

MA
ALC

us failing to move Alcidas, some of the Ionian exil h the expedition began to urge him, since this seer ize one of the Ionian cities or the Aeolic city of Cyn effecting the revolt of Ionia.[1a] This was by no mea e, as their coming was welcome everywhere; thei s move to deprive Athens of her chief source of reve me to saddle her with expense, if she chose to bloc ould probably induce Pissuthnes[1b] to join them in t lcidas gave this proposal as bad a reception as

3.31
427
5th Year/Summer
ERYTHRAE
Alcidas also rejects a proposal to foment revolt against Athens in Ionia.

3.31. Ionia: Map alects and rmation on

3.31. as the Per- 3.29, AY);

the other, being eager, since he had come too late for Mytilene, to find himself back in the Peloponnesus as soon as possible.

3.32
427
5th Year/Summer
AEGEAN
Before fleeing, Alcidas executes many prisoners. He is finally persuaded to release the rest.

Accordingly he put out from Embatum and proceeded along shore; and touching at the Teian city, Myonnesus,[1a] there butchered most of the prisoners that he had taken on his passage. [2] Upon his coming to anchor at Ephesus,[2a] envoys came to him from the Samians at Anaia,[2b] and told him that he was not going the right way to free Hellas in massacring men who had never raised a hand against him, and who were not enemies of his, but allies of Athens against their will, and that if he did not stop he would turn many more friends into enemies than enemies into friends. [3] Alcidas agreed to this, and let go all the Chians still in his hands and some of the others that he had taken, since the inhabitants, rather than fleeing, came up to him because they assumed his vessels were Athenian, and had no sort of expectation that Peloponnesian ships would venture over to Ionia while the Athenians commanded the sea.

3.33
427
5th Year/Summer
AEGEAN
Paches pursues Alcidas' fleet but fails to catch it.

From Ephesus Alcidas set sail in haste and fled. He had been seen while still at anchor off Clarus[1a] by the Athenian triremes the *Salaminia* and the *Paralus*,[1b] which happened to be sailing from Athens, and fearing pursuit he now made across the open sea, fully determined to touch nowhere, if he could help it, until he got to the Peloponnesus.[1c] [2] Meanwhile news of him had come in to Paches from the territory of Erythrae and indeed from all quarters. As Ionia was unfortified,[2a] great fears were felt that the Peloponnesians coasting along shore, even if they did not intend to stay, might make descents in passing and plunder the cities; and now the triremes *Salaminia* and the *Paralus*, having seen him at Clarus, themselves brought intelligence of the fact. [3] Paches accordingly gave hot chase, and continued the pursuit as far as the isle of Patmos,[3a] and then finding that Alcidas had got on too far to be overtaken, came back again. Meanwhile he thought it fortunate that, as he had not fallen in with them out at sea, he had not overtaken them anywhere where they would have been forced to encamp, and so give him the trouble of blockading them.

3.34
427
5th Year/Summer
NOTIUM
Paches tricks Hippias and captures Notium.

On his return along shore Paches touched, among other places, at Notium, the port of Colophon,[1a] where the Colophonians had settled after the capture of the upper city by Itamenes and the barbarians,[1b] who had been called in by certain individuals in a party quarrel. The capture of the

3.32.1a Teos and the Teian town Myonnesus: Map 3.29, BY.

3.32.2a Ephesus: Map 3.29, BY.

3.32.2b These were the Samian exiles hostile to Athens; see 3.19.2 and 4.75.1. Anaia, Samos: Map 3.29, BY.

3.33.1a Clarus: Map 3.29, BY.

3.33.1b The *Salaminia* and the *Paralus* were special state triremes used on sacred embassies and official business; see 3.77.3 in Corcyra, 6.53.1, and 6.61.4–7 in Sicily to fetch Alcibiades; 8.73.5–6 at Samos, and 8.74.1–2 in the revolution at Athens; and 8.86.9 at Argos and Samos.

3.33.1c The narrative of Alcidas' fleet continues at 3.69.

3.33.2a Some scholars hold that the cities of Ionia had been obliged by Athens to pull down their walls for the sake of imperial security. Others think that the measure was required by the terms of the "Peace of Callias," a treaty between the Athenians and the Persians; see Appendix E, The Persians, §5–6.

3.33.3a Patmos: Map 3.29, BX.

3.34.1a Notium, Colophon: Map 3.29, BY.

3.34.1b These barbarians are Persians. Itamenes is otherwise unknown, nor is it known whether he was acting under the orders of Pissuthnes, the Persian governor [satrap] at Sardis.

city [illegible]e of the second Peloponnesian invasion of Attica. [illegible]ees, after settling at Notium, again split up into facti[illegible]d in Arcadian and barbarian mercenaries from Pissu[illegible] these in a quarter apart, formed a new commun[illegible]ty of the Colophonians who joined them from the [illegible]ents had retired into exile, and now called in Pach[illegible]ppias, the commander of the Arcadians in the forti[illegible], upon condition that, if they could not agree, he w[illegible]and sound in the fortification. However, upon his c[illegible]es put him into custody, though not in chains, and [illegible] took by surprise the fortification, and putting the [illegible]rians found in it to the sword, afterwards took Hipp[illegible]romised, and, as soon as he was inside, seized him [illegible]4] Paches then gave up Notium to the Colopho[illegible]g party;[4a] and settlers were afterwards sent out from[illegible]colonized according to Athenian laws, after collecti[illegible] found in any of the cities.

3.35 427 5th Year/Summer MYTILENE Paches reconquers Lesbos.

A[illegible]hes reduced Pyrrha and Eresus;[1a] and finding the [illegible]iding in the city, sent him off to Athens, together[illegible] that he had placed in Tenedos,[1b] and any other pers[illegible]cerned in the revolt. [2] He also sent back the grea[illegible]aining with the rest to settle Mytilene and the rest [illegible] best.

3.36 427 5th Year/Summer ATHENS After first condemning the Mytilenians to death, the Athenians decide to vote again.

U[illegible]risoners with Salaethus, the Athenians at once put [illegible]ough he offered, among other things, to procure[illegible] Peloponnesians from Plataea, which was still und[illegible]eliberating as to what they should do with the form[illegible]oment determined to put to death not only the pris[illegible] whole adult male population of Mytilene, and to m[illegible]n and children. It was noted that Mytilene had revo[illegible]he same way as the rest, subjected to the empire; [illegible]elled the wrath of the Athenians was the fact of the [illegible]ng ventured over to Ionia to her support, a fact whic[illegible]ong-meditated rebellion. [3] They accordingly sent [illegible]ate the decree to Paches, commanding him to

3.34.4 [illegible]de in any [illegible]dized."

3.35.1 [illegible]

3.35.1 [illegible]re Paches [illegible]olt in [illegible]n 3.50.1.

3.36.2 [illegible]tilene was [illegible] money [illegible]

lose no time in despatching the Mytilenians. [4] The morrow brought repentance with it and reflection on the horrid cruelty of a decree which condemned a whole city to the fate merited only by the guilty. [5] This was no sooner perceived by the Mytilenian ambassadors at Athens and their Athenian supporters than they moved the authorities to put the question again to the vote;[5a] which they the more easily consented to do, as they themselves plainly saw that most of the citizens wished someone to give them an opportunity for reconsidering the matter. [6] An assembly was therefore at once called, and after much expression of opinion upon both sides, Cleon son of Cleaenetus, the same who had carried the former motion of putting the Mytilenians to death, the most violent man at Athens, and at that time by far the most powerful with The People, came forward again and spoke as follows:

3.37
427
5th Year/Summer
ATHENS
Cleon calls the Athenians inconstant and argues for the original decision to execute the Mytilenians.

"I have often before now been convinced that a democracy is incapable of empire, and never more so than by your present change of mind in the matter of Mytilene. [2] Fears or plots being unknown to you in your daily relations with each other, you feel just the same with regard to your allies, and never reflect that the mistakes into which you may be led by listening to their appeals, or by giving way to your own compassion, are full of danger to yourselves, and bring you no thanks for your weakness from your allies; entirely forgetting that your empire is a despotism and your subjects disaffected conspirators, whose obedience is insured not by your suicidal concessions, but by the superiority given you by your own strength and not their loyalty. [3] The most alarming feature in the case is the constant change of measures with which we appear to be threatened, and our seeming ignorance of the fact that bad laws which are never changed are better for a city than good ones that have no authority; that unlearned loyalty is more serviceable than quick-witted insubordination; and that ordinary men usually manage public affairs better than their more gifted fellows. [4] The latter are always wanting to appear wiser than the laws, and to overrule every proposition brought forward, thinking that they cannot show their wit in more important matters, and by such behavior too often ruin their country; while those who mistrust their own cleverness are content to be less learned than the laws, and less able to pick holes in the speech of a good speaker; and being fair judges rather than rival athletes, generally conduct affairs successfully. [5] These we ought to imitate, instead of being led on by cleverness and intellectual rivalry to advise the people against our real opinions."

3.36.5a To put an issue to the vote a second time in the Athenian assembly was not an easy or a trivial matter. See 6.14.1 and note 6.14.1a.

3.38
427
5th Year/Summer
ATHENS
Cleon criticizes the Athenians for permitting clever points of debate to distract them from obvious facts.

[illegible] to my former opinion, and wonder at those
v[illegible]pen the case of the Mytilenians, and who are
t[illegible]h is all in favor of the guilty, by making the
s[illegible] the offender with the edge of his anger
b[illegible] vengeance follows most closely upon the
w[illegible]d most amply requites it. I wonder also who
w[illegible] maintain the contrary, and will pretend to
s[illegible]he Mytilenians are of service to us, and our
m[illegible]he allies. [2] Such a man must plainly either
h[illegible]his rhetoric as to attempt to prove that what
h[illegible]ded is still undetermined, or be bribed to try
t[illegible] sophistic arguments. [3] In such contests the
s[illegible]others, and takes the dangers for herself. [4]
T[illegible] you who are so foolish as to institute these
c[illegible]an oration as you would to see a sight, take
y[illegible]ge of the practicability of a project by the wit
o[illegible] for the truth as to past events, not to the fact
w[illegible] to the clever strictures which you heard; [5]
t[illegible]gled arguments, unwilling to follow received
c[illegible]ry new paradox, despisers of the common-
p[illegible]f every man being that he could speak him-
s[illegible]e who can speak by seeming to keep up with
t[illegible] every hit almost before it is made, and by
b[illegible] an argument as you are slow in foreseeing its
c[illegible] if I may so say, for something different from
t[illegible]ich we live, and yet comprehending inade-
q[illegible]ions; very slaves to the pleasure of the ear,
a[illegible]e of a rhetorician than the council of a city."

3.39
427
5th Year/Summer
ATHENS
Cleon asserts that The People and the oligarchs of Mytilene are equally guilty.

[illegible] from this, I proceed to show that no one
s[illegible]u as much as Mytilene. [2] I can make al-
l[illegible]evolt because they cannot bear our empire,
o[illegible] to do so by the enemy. But for those who
p[illegible] fortifications; who could fear our enemies
o[illegible]had their own force of triremes to protect
t[illegible]ndent and held in the highest honor by
y[illegible] done, this is not revolt—revolt implies op-
p[illegible]and wanton aggression; an attempt to ruin
u[illegible]terest enemies; a worse offense than a war
u[illegible] account in the acquisition of power. [3]
T[illegible]ir neighbors who had already rebelled and
h[illegible] no lesson to them; their own prosperity

could not dissuade them from affronting danger; but blindly confident in the future, and full of hopes beyond their power though not beyond their ambition, they declared war and made their decision to prefer might to right, their attack being determined not by provocation but by the moment which seemed propitious. [4] The truth is that great good fortune coming suddenly and unexpectedly tends to make a people insolent: in most cases it is safer for mankind to have success in reason than out of reason; and it is easier for them, one may say, to stave off adversity than to preserve prosperity. [5] Our mistake has been to distinguish the Mytilenians as we have done: had they been long ago treated like the rest, they never would have so far forgotten themselves, human nature being as surely made arrogant by consideration, as it is awed by firmness. [6] Let them now therefore be punished as their crime requires, and do not, while you condemn the aristocracy, absolve the people. This is certain, that all attacked you without distinction, although they might have come over to us, and been now again in possession of their city. But no, they thought it safer to throw in their lot with the aristocracy and so joined their rebellion! [7] Consider therefore! if you subject to the same punishment the ally who is forced to rebel by the enemy, and him who does so by his own free choice, which of them, think you, is there that will not rebel upon the slightest pretext; when the reward of success is freedom, and the penalty of failure nothing so very terrible? [8] We meanwhile shall have to risk our money and our lives against one state after another; and if successful, shall receive a ruined city from which we can no longer draw the revenue upon which our strength depends; while if unsuccessful, we shall have an enemy the more upon our hands, and shall spend the time that might be employed in combating our existing foes in warring with our own allies."

3.40
427
5th Year/Summer
ATHENS
Cleon concludes that compassion is inappropriate for national foes, and that severe punishment is a necessary example.

"No hope, therefore, must be held out to the Mytilenians, that their rhetoric may inspire or money purchase the mercy due to human infirmity. Their offense was not involuntary, but of malice and deliberate; and mercy is only for unwilling offenders. [2] I therefore now as before persist against your reversing your first decision, or giving way to the three failings most fatal to empire—pity, sentiment, and indulgence. [3] Compassion is due to those who can reciprocate the feeling, not to those who will never pity us in return, but are our natural and necessary foes: the orators who charm us with sentiment may find other less important arenas for their talents, in the place of one where the city pays a heavy penalty for a momentary pleasure, themselves receiving fine acknowledgments for their fine phrases; while indulgence should be shown toward those who will be our friends in future, instead of toward men who will remain just what they were, and as much our enemies as before. [4] To sum up

s[illegible]ollow my advice you will do what is just to-
w[illegible]d at the same time expedient; while by a diffe[illegible] not oblige them so much as pass sentence
u[illegible] they were right in rebelling, you must be
w[illegible]r, if, right or wrong, you determine to rule,
y[illegible]principle and punish the Mytilenians as your
in[illegible]you must give up your empire and cultivate
h[illegible] [5] Make up your minds, therefore, to give
t[illegible] not let the victims who escaped the plot be
m[illegible]e conspirators who hatched it; but reflect
w[illegible]one if victorious over you, especially as they
w[illegible]t is they who wrong their neighbor without
a[illegible] victim to the death, on account of the dan-
g[illegible] letting their enemy survive; since the object
o[illegible]ore dangerous, if he escape, than an enemy
w[illegible]plain of. [7] Do not, therefore, be traitors
t[illegible]as nearly as possible the moment of suffer-
in[illegible]portance which you then attached to their
r[illegible]hem back in their turn, without yielding to
p[illegible]etting the peril that once hung over you.
P[illegible]erve, and teach your other allies by a strik-
in[illegible]alty of rebellion is death. Let them once un-
d[illegible]l not have so often to neglect your enemies
w[illegible]h your own confederates."

S[illegible] Cleon. After him Diodotus son of Eucrates, who[illegible] assembly spoken most strongly against putting the [illegible]ne forward and spoke as follows:

3.41 Diodotus speaks next.

[illegible]persons who have reopened the case of the
M[illegible]pprove the protests which we have heard
a[illegible]ons being frequently debated. I think the
t[illegible]d to good counsel are haste and passion;
h[illegible]in hand with folly, passion with coarseness
a[illegible] [2] As for the argument that speech ought
n[illegible] action, the man who uses it must be either
s[illegible]erested: senseless if he believes it possible to
d[illegible]ture through any other medium; interested
if[illegible]raceful measure and doubting his ability to
s[illegible], he thinks to frighten opponents and hear-
e[illegible]ny. [3] What is still more intolerable is to
a[illegible]g a display in order to be paid for it. If ig-
n[illegible]ted, an unsuccessful speaker might retire
w[illegible]esty, if not for wisdom; while the charge of
d[illegible]spected, if successful, and thought, if de-

3.42
427
5th Year/Summer
ATHENS
Diodotus argues for calm deliberation without haste or passion.

feated, not only a fool but a rogue. [4] The city is no gainer by such a system, since fear deprives it of its advisers; although in truth, if our speakers are to make such assertions, it would be better for the country if they could not speak at all, as we should then make fewer blunders. [5] The good citizen ought to triumph not by frightening his opponents but by beating them fairly in argument; and a wise city, without overdistinguishing its best advisers, will nevertheless not deprive them of their due, and far from punishing an unlucky counselor will not even regard him as disgraced. [6] In this way successful orators would be least tempted to sacrifice their convictions for popularity, in the hope of still higher honors, and unsuccessful speakers to resort to the same popular arts in order to win over the multitude."

3.43
427
5th Year/Summer
ATHENS
Diodotus declares that orators deserve respect and should be heeded.

"This is not our way; and, besides, the moment that a man is suspected of giving advice, however good, from corrupt motives, we feel such a grudge against him for the gain which after all we are not certain he will receive, that we deprive the city of its certain benefit. [2] Plain good advice has thus come to be no less suspected than bad; and the advocate of the most monstrous measures is not more obliged to use deceit to gain the people, than the best counselor is to lie in order to be believed. [3] The city and the city only, owing to these refinements, can never be served openly and without disguise; he who does serve it openly being always suspected of serving himself in some secret way in return. Still, considering the magnitude of the interests involved, and the position of affairs, we orators must make it our business to look a little further than you who judge offhand; especially as we, your advisers, are responsible, while you, our audience, are not so. [5] For if those who gave the advice, and those who took it, suffered equally, you would judge more calmly; as it is, you visit the disasters into which the whim of the moment may have led you, upon the single person of your adviser, not upon yourselves, his numerous companions in error."[5a]

3.44
427
5th Year/Summer
ATHENS
Diodotus argues that Athens' best interest, not justice, is the proper objective of the assembly.

"However, I have not come forward either to oppose or to accuse in the matter of Mytilene; indeed, the question before us as sensible men is not their guilt, but our interests. [2] Though I prove them ever so guilty, I shall not, therefore, advise their death, unless it be expedient; nor though they should have claims to indulgence, shall I recommend it, unless it be clearly for the good of the country. [3] I consider that we are deliberating for the future more than for the present; and where Cleon is so positive as to the useful deterrent effects that will follow from making rebellion a capital offense, I who consider the interests of the future quite as much as he, as positively maintain the contrary. [4] And I require you not to reject my useful considerations for his specious ones: his speech may have the attrac-

3.43.5a As they did to Pericles in 2.65.3.

[illegible] re just in your present temper against Myti-
[illegible] a court of justice, but in a political assembly;
[illegible] ustice, but how to make the Mytilenians use-
[illegible]

3.45
427
5th Year/Summer
ATHENS
Diodotus points out that some people will transgress regardless of the severity of punishments.

[illegible] munities have enacted the penalty of death
[illegible] ghter than this: still hope leads men to ven-
[illegible] yet put himself in peril without the inward
[illegible] d succeed in his design. [2] Again, was there
[illegible] id not believe that it possessed either in itself
[illegible] es adequate to the enterprise? [3] All, states
[illegible] prone to err, and there is no law that will
[illegible] ould men have exhausted the list of punish-
[illegible] ments to protect them from evildoers? It is
[illegible] imes the penalties for the greatest offenses
[illegible] at, as these were disregarded, the penalty of
[illegible] es in most cases arrived at, which is itself dis-
[illegible] [4] Either then some means of terror more
[illegible] discovered, or it must be admitted that this
[illegible] hat as long as poverty gives men the courage
[illegible] ls them with the ambition which belongs to
[illegible] each of the other conditions of life remains
[illegible] and master passion, so long will the impulse
[illegible] e men into danger. [5] Hope also and greed,
[illegible] e other following, the one conceiving the
[illegible] gesting the facility of succeeding, cause the
[illegible] gh invisible agents, are far stronger than the
[illegible] 6] Fortune, too, powerfully helps the delu-
[illegible] ected aid that she sometimes lends, tempts
[illegible] ferior means; and this is especially the case
[illegible] se the stakes played for are the highest, free-
[illegible] hen all are acting together, each man irra-
[illegible] n capacity. [7] In short, it is impossible to
[illegible] implicity can hope to prevent, human nature
[illegible] set its mind upon, by force of law or by any
[illegible] atsoever."

3.46
427
5th Year/Summer
ATHENS
Diodotus says that Athens' advantage here requires moderation.

[illegible] efore, commit ourselves to a false policy
[illegible] efficacy of the punishment of death, or ex-
[illegible] pe of repentance and an early atonement of
[illegible] a moment! At present, if a city that has al-
[illegible] hat it cannot succeed, it will come to terms
[illegible] und expenses, and pay tribute afterwards. In
[illegible] think you would not prepare better than is
[illegible] to the last against its besiegers, if it is all one

whether it surrender late or soon? [3] And how can it be otherwise than hurtful to us to be put to the expense of a siege, because surrender is out of the question; and if we take the city, to receive a ruined city from which we can no longer draw the revenue which forms our real strength against the enemy? [4] We must not, therefore, sit as strict judges of the offenders to our own prejudice, but rather see how by moderate chastisements we may be enabled to benefit in future by the revenue-producing powers of our dependencies; and we must make up our minds to look for our protection not to legal terrors but to careful administration. [5] At present we do exactly the opposite. When a free community, held in subjection by force, rises, as is only natural, and asserts its independence, it is no sooner reduced than we fancy ourselves obliged to punish it severely; [6] although the right course with freemen is not to chastise them rigorously when they do rise, but rigorously to watch them before they rise, and to prevent their ever entertaining the idea, and, the insurrection suppressed, to make as few responsible for it as possible."

3.47
427
5th Year/Summer
ATHENS
Diodotus argues that since the commons are friendly to Athens and delivered the city when they could, it would be a blunder to execute them.

"Only consider what a blunder you would commit in doing as Cleon recommends. [2] As things are at present, in all the cities The People is your friend, and either does not revolt with the oligarchy, or, if forced to do so, becomes at once the enemy of the insurgents; so that in the war with the hostile city you have the masses on your side. [3] But if you butcher The People of Mytilene, who had nothing to do with the revolt, and who, as soon as they got arms, of their own motion surrendered the city, first you will commit the crime of killing your benefactors; and next you will play directly into the hands of the higher classes, who when they induce their cities to rise, will immediately have The People on their side, through your having announced in advance the same punishment for those who are guilty and for those who are not. [4] On the contrary, even if they were guilty, you ought to seem not to notice it, in order to avoid alienating the only class still friendly to us. [5] In short, I consider it far more useful for the preservation of our empire to put up with injustice voluntarily, than to put to death, however justly, those whom it is our interest to keep alive. As for Cleon's idea that in punishment the claims of justice and expediency can both be satisfied, facts do not confirm the possibility of such a combination."

3.48
427
5th Year/Summer
ATHENS
Diodotus concludes with a plea for calm consideration.

"Confess, therefore, that this is the wisest course, and without conceding too much either to pity or to indulgence, by neither of which motives do I any more than Cleon wish you to be influenced, upon the plain merits of the case before you, be persuaded by me to try calmly those of the Mytilenians whom Paches sent off as guilty, and to leave the rest undisturbed. [2] This is at once best for the future, and most terrible to your enemies at the present moment; inas-

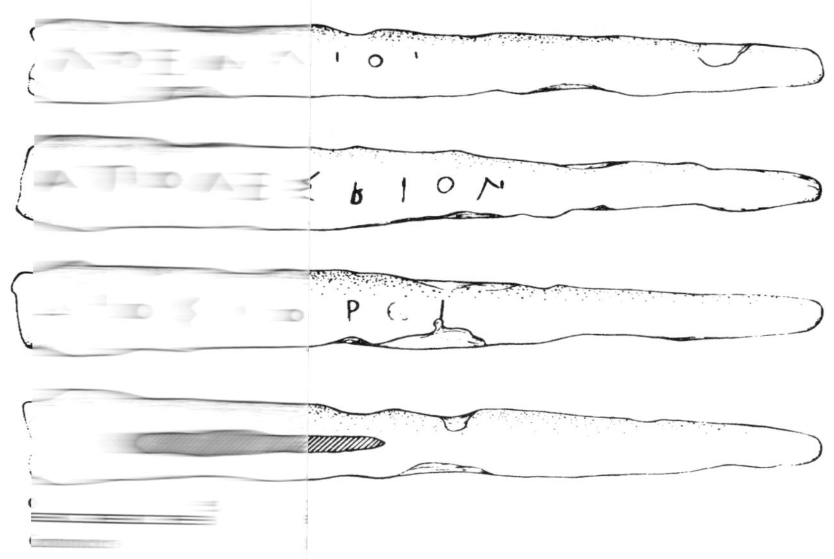

Illu[illegible]s of a bronze spear butt found at Athens sho[illegible]ying that it was taken from Lesbians and ded[illegible]undoubtedly when the Athenians put down the revo[illegible]s in 427

r[illegible]inst an adversary is superior to the blind at-t[illegible]

S[illegible] Diodotus. The two opinions thus expressed were[illegible]ectly contradicted each other; and the Athenians,[illegible] change of feeling, now proceeded to a vote in v[illegible]ds was almost equal, although the motion of Dio[illegible]] Another trireme was at once sent off in haste, for [illegible] reach Lesbos in the interval, and the city be foun[illegible]ip having about a day and a night's start. [3] Win[illegible] provided for the vessel by the Mytilenian ambass[illegible]es made if they arrived in time; which caused the [illegible]ce upon the voyage that they took their meals of b[illegible]n oil and wine as they rowed, and only slept by turn[illegible] at the oar. [4] Luckily they met with no contrary[illegible]p making no haste upon so horrid an errand, whil[illegible] in the manner described, the first arrived so little b[illegible]had only just had time to read the decree, and to p[illegible]ntence, when the second put into port and prevent[illegible]nger of Mytilene had indeed been great.

3.49
427
5th Year/Summer
ATHENS
Athens votes to spare Mytilene.
MITYLENE
The news arrives just in time to save the Mytilenians.

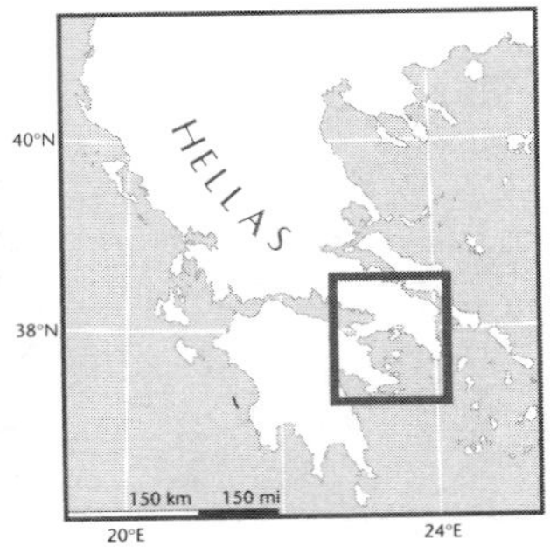

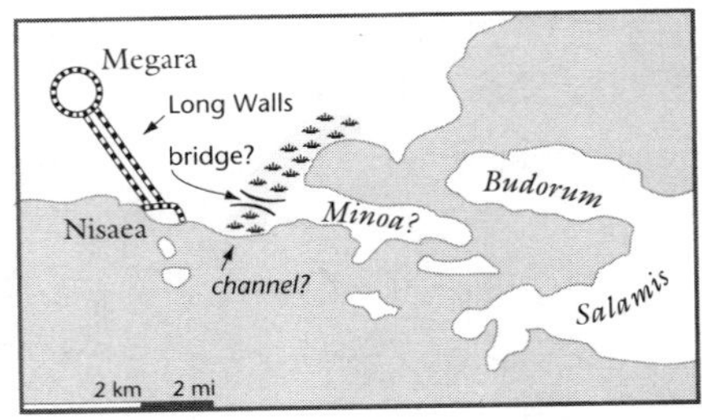

MAP 3.51 MEGARA, NISAEA, MINOA

3.50
427
5th Year/Summer
LESBOS
Mytilene is punished.

The other party whom Paches had sent off as the prime movers in the rebellion were, upon Cleon's motion, put to death by the Athenians, the number being rather more than a thousand. The Athenians also demolished the walls of the Mytilenians, and took possession of their ships. [2] Afterwards tribute was not imposed upon the Lesbians; but all their land, except that of the Methymnians, was divided into three thousand allotments, three hundred of which were reserved as sacred for the gods, and the rest assigned by lot to Athenian shareholders, who were sent out to the island. With these the Lesbians agreed to pay a rent of two *minae*[2a] a year for each allotment, and cultivated the land themselves. [3] The Athenians also took possession of the cities on the continent belonging to the Mytilenians, which thus became for the future subject to Athens. Such were the events that took place at Lesbos.[3a]

3.51
427
5th Year/Summer
MEGARA-MINOS
Nicias fortifies Minoa opposite Megara.

During the same summer, after the reduction of Lesbos, the Athenians under Nicias son of Niceratus made an expedition against the island of Minoa,[1a] which lies off Megara[1b] and was used as a fortified post by the Megarians, who had built a tower upon it. [2] Nicias wished to enable the Athenians to maintain their blockade from this nearer station instead of from Budorum and Salamis;[2a] to stop the Peloponnesian triremes and privateers sailing out unobserved from the island, as they had been in the habit of doing; and at the same time prevent anything from coming into

3.50.2a A *mina* was a unit of currency equal to one sixtieth of a *talent,* or one hundred *drachmae*. The 2,700 allotments renting for two minae each produced an annual rental of 5,400 minae or ninety talents. See Appendix J, Classical Greek Currency, §5. See also Appendix B, The Athenian Empire, §9, on Athenian *clerouchs*.

3.50.3a The story of Mytilene is resumed in 4.52.

3.51.1a Minoa: Map 3.51, inset, shows a possible location of the ancient island, which is no longer an island today. The map above is based in part on one in A.W. Gomme, *A Historical Commentary on Thucydides,* ii (Oxford, 1956), 334–36.

3.51.1b Megara: Map 3.51.

3.51.2a Budorum, possible location: Map 3.51, inset; Salamis: Map 3.51, and inset.

Meg ter taking two towers projecting on the side of Nisa om the sea, and clearing the entrance into the char and the shore, he next proceeded to cut off all com a wall on the mainland at the point where a brid ed reinforcements to be thrown into the island, whic the continent. [4] A few days sufficing to accom raised a fort on the island also, and leaving a garr n his forces.

3.52 427 5th Year/Summer PLATAEA Plataea surrenders.

A his summer, the Plataeans[1a] being now without prov ipport the siege, surrendered to the Peloponnesi nner. [2] An assault had been made upon the wall. ere unable to repel. The Spartan commander, perc ished to avoid taking the place by storm; his instruc g been so conceived, in order that if at any future nade with Athens, and they should agree each to re ey had taken in the war, Plataea might be held to h ly, and not be included in the list. He accordingly o ask if they were willing voluntarily to surrender , and accept them as their judges, upon the unde ty should be punished, but no one without form ns were now in the last state of weakness, and the l livered his message than they surrendered the city. d them for some days until the judges from Spar nber, arrived. [4] Upon their arrival no charge was lled up the Plataeans, and asked them whether they and allies any service in the war then raging. The speak at greater length, and deputed two of their em, Astymachus son of Asopolaus, and Lacon son *s* of the Spartans,[4a] who came forward and spok

3.53 427 5th Year/Summer PLATAEA The Plataeans complain of the unusual and summary form of their trial.

urrendered our city we trusted in you, and lo more agreeable to the forms of law than the p no idea of being subjected; the judges also in nted to place ourselves were you, and you o ught we were most likely to obtain justice), a is now the case. [2] As matters stand, we a en doubly deceived. We have good reason to the issue to be tried is the most terrible of al prove impartial; if we may argue from the

3.51.3a
3.52.1a tive from
3.52.4a

fact that no accusation was first brought forward for us to answer, but we had ourselves to ask leave to speak, and from the question being put so shortly, that a true answer to it tells against us, while a false one can be contradicted. [3] In this dilemma, our safest, and indeed our only course, seems to be to say something at all risks: placed as we are, we could scarcely be silent without being tormented by the damning thought that speaking might have saved us. [4] Another difficulty that we have to encounter is the difficulty of convincing you. Were we unknown to each other we might profit by bringing forward new matter with which you were unacquainted: as it is, we can tell you nothing that you do not know already, and we fear, not that you have condemned us in your own minds of having failed in our duty toward you, and make this our crime, but that to please a third party we have to submit to a trial the result of which is already decided."

3.54
427
5th Year/Summer
PLATAEA
The Plataeans claim to have helped Sparta against both the Persians and the Messenian Helots.

"Nevertheless, we will place before you what we can justly urge, not only on the question of the quarrel which the Thebans have against us, but also as addressing you and the rest of the Hellenes; and we will remind you of our good services, and endeavor to prevail with you. [2] To your short question, whether we have done the Spartans and allies any service in this war, we say, if you ask us as enemies, that to refrain from serving you was not to do you injury; if as friends, that you are more in fault for having marched against us. [3] During the peace, and against the Mede, we acted well: we have not now been the first to break the peace, and we were the only Boeotians who then joined in defending the liberty of Hellas against the Persian. [4] Although an inland people, we were present at the action at Artemisium;[4a] in the battle that took place in our territory we fought by the side of yourselves and Pausanias; and in all the other Hellenic exploits of the time we took a part quite out of proportion to our strength. [5] Besides, you, as Spartans, ought not to forget that at the time of the great panic at Sparta, after the earthquake, caused by the secession of the Helots to Ithome,[5a] we sent the third part of our citizens to assist you."

3.55
427
5th Year/Summer
PLATAEA
The Plataeans argue that since Sparta sent Plataea to Athens for alliance, Sparta must now accept Plataean loyalty to Athens.

"On these great occasions in the past such was the part that we chose, although afterwards we became your enemies. For this you were to blame. When we asked for your alliance against our Theban oppressors, you rejected our petition, and told us to go to the Athenians who were our neighbors, as you lived too far off. [2] In the war we never have done to you, and never would have done to you, anything unreasonable. [3] If we refused to desert the Athenians when you asked us, we did no wrong; they had helped us against the Thebans when you drew back, and we could no longer give them up

3.54.4a Artemisium: Map 3.93, AY; site of a naval battle between Persians and Greeks in 480.

3.54.5a For this earthquake and the revolt of the Helots, see 1.101 and 2.27.2.

we had obtained their alliance and had been …ship at our own request, and after receiving …but it was plainly our duty loyally to obey … the faults that either of you may commit in … laid, not upon the followers, but on the …ay."

3.56
427
5th Year/Summer
PLATAEA
The Plataeans call on Sparta to deny Theban wrath and to reward past Plataean help.

…Thebans, they have wronged us repeatedly, …, which has been the means of bringing us …n, is within your own knowledge. [2] In …of peace, and what is more at a holy time in …encountered our vengeance, in accordance …hich sanctions resistance to an invader; and …hat we should suffer on their account.[1a] [3] …mediate interest and their animosity as the … prove yourselves to be servants of expedi…of right; [4] although if they seem useful to …est of the Hellenes gave you much more …f greater need. Now you are the assailants, … at the crisis to which we allude, when the … with slavery, the Thebans were on his side. …o put our patriotism then against our error …een; and you will find the merit outweigh…ed at a juncture when there were few Hel…r valor against the strength of Xerxes,[5a] and … theirs who preferred the dangerous path of … of consulting their own interest with re…6] To these few we belonged, and highly … and yet we now fear to perish by having …e principles, and chosen to act well with …ly with Sparta. [7] Yet in justice the same … in the same way, and policy should not … lasting gratitude for the service of a good …oper attention to one's own immediate in…

3.57
427
5th Year/Summer
PLATAEA
The Plataeans say that Sparta's reputation will suffer if she permits Thebes to destroy Plataea.

… present the Hellenes generally regard you … honor; and if you pass an unjust sentence … no obscure cause—but one in which you, …ous as we, the prisoners, are blameless—take …not felt at an unworthy decision in the mat…ade by men yet more honorable than they, …n the national temples of spoils taken from …ctors of Hellas. [2] Shocking indeed will it …stroy Plataea, and for the city whose name

3.56.… Theban …2.6.

3.56.5a Xerxes was the Persian King who led the invasion of Greece in 480.

your fathers inscribed upon the tripod at Delphi[2a] for its good service, to be by you blotted out from the map of Hellas to please the Thebans. [3] To such a depth of misfortune have we fallen, that while the Medes' success had been our ruin, Thebans now supplant us in your once fond regards; and we have been subjected to two dangers, the greatest of any—that of dying of starvation then, if we had not surrendered our city, and now of being tried for our lives. [4] So that we Plataeans, after exertions beyond our power in the cause of the Hellenes, are rejected by all, forsaken and unassisted; helped by none of our allies, and reduced to doubt the stability of our only hope, yourselves."

3.58
427
5th Year/Summer
PLATAEA
The Plataeans contrast themselves, who care for the graves of Spartans who fell beside them fighting the Persians, with the Thebans, who fought against the Spartans with the Persians.

"Still, in the name of the gods who once presided over our confederacy, and of our own good service in the Hellenic cause, we appeal to you to relent; to rescind the decision which we fear that the Thebans may have obtained from you; to ask back the gift that you have given them, that they disgrace not you by slaying us; to gain a pure instead of a guilty gratitude, and not to gratify others to be yourselves rewarded with shame. [2] Our lives may be quickly taken, but it will be a heavy task to wipe away the infamy of the deed; as we are no enemies whom you might justly punish, but friends forced into taking arms against you. [3] To grant us our lives would be, therefore, a righteous judgment; if you consider also that we are prisoners who surrendered of their own accord, stretching out our hands for quarter, whose slaughter Hellenic law forbids, and who besides were always your benefactors. [4] Look at the tombs of your fathers, slain by the Persians and buried in our country, whom year by year we honored with garments and all other dues, and the first fruits of all that our land produced in their season, as friends from a friendly country and allies to our old companions in arms! Should you not decide aright, your conduct would be the very opposite to ours. Consider only: [5] Pausanias buried them thinking that he was laying them in friendly ground and among men as friendly; but you, if you kill us and make the Plataean territory Theban, will leave your fathers and kinsmen in a hostile soil and among their murderers, deprived of the honors which they now enjoy. What is more, you will enslave the land in which the freedom of the Hellenes was won, make desolate the temples of the gods to whom they prayed before they overcame the Persians, and take away your ancestral sacrifices from those who founded and instituted them."

3.59
427
5th Year/Summer
PLATAEA
The Plataeans conclude that they surrendered their city to Sparta, not to Thebes.

"It were not to your glory, Spartans, either to offend in this way against the common law of the Hellenes and against your own ancestors, or to kill us, your benefactors, to gratify another's hatred without

3.57.2a The Plataeans refer here to the tripod dedicated at Delphi in celebration of the victory over the Persians at Plataea (1.132.2–3.) Much of this tripod still exists in Istanbul and its inscription can still be read today. See Illustration 1.132.

h[illegible]urselves: it would be more to your glory to
sp[illegible]e impressions of a reasonable compassion; re-
fl[illegible]e awful fate in store for us, but also on the
ch[illegible] and on the impossibility of predicting how
so[illegible]even upon those who deserve it not. [2] We,
as[illegible]nd as our need impels us, entreat you, calling
al[illegible]hose common altar all the Hellenes worship,
to[illegible] not unmindful of the oaths which your fa-
th[illegible] now plead. We supplicate you by the tombs
o[illegible] to those that are gone to save us from falling
in[illegible]ebans and prevent the dearest friends of the
H[illegible]n up to their most detested foes. We also re-
m[illegible]hich we did the most glorious deeds by your
fa[illegible]ow on this day are likely to suffer the most
d[illegible]o do what is necessary and yet most difficult
fo[illegible]—that is, to make an end of speaking, since
w[illegible] of our lives draws near—[4] we say in con-
cl[illegible]urrender our city to the Thebans (to that we
w[illegible]orious starvation), but trusted in and capitu-
la[illegible] be just, if we fail to persuade you, to put us
b[illegible]n and let us take the chance that falls to us.
A[illegible] Plataeans, foremost among the Hellenic pa-
tr[illegible]ou, beseech you not to give us up out of your
h[illegible]st hated enemies, the Thebans, but to be our
sa[illegible] free the rest of the Hellenes, bring us to dest[illegible]

3.60
427
5th Year/Summer
PLATAEA
The Thebans ask to speak.

S[illegible] the Plataeans. The Thebans, afraid that the
Spar[illegible]y what they had heard, came forward and said
that [illegible]ess them, since the Plataeans had, against their
wish [illegible] at length instead of being confined to a simple
answ[illegible]e being granted, the Thebans spoke as follows:

3.61
427
5th Year/Summer
PLATAEA
The Thebans describe the origin of their quarrel with the Plataeans.

[illegible]e asked to make this speech if the Plataeans
o[illegible]nted themselves with briefly answering the
q[illegible]urned round and made charges against us,
c[illegible]nse of themselves upon matters outside the
p[illegible] even the subject of accusation, and with
p[illegible]ds fault with. However, since they have done
so[illegible]charges and refute their self-praise, in order
th[illegible]e nor their good may help them, but that
y[illegible]uth on both points, and so decide. [2] The

origin of our quarrel was this. We settled Plataea some time after the rest of Boeotia, together with other places out of which we had driven the mixed population. The Plataeans not choosing to recognize our supremacy, as had been first arranged, but separating themselves from the rest of the Boeotians, and proving traitors to their nationality, we used compulsion; upon which they went over to the Athenians, and with them did us much harm, for which we retaliated."

3.62
427
5th Year/Summer
PLATAEA
The Thebans say their government was a tyranny when it Medized, acting against the desires of the people. Now that they have recovered their constitution, Thebes is foremost in the fight against Athenian hegemony.

"Next, when the barbarian invaded Hellas, they say that they were the only Boeotians who did not Medize; and this is where they most glorify themselves and abuse us.[1a] We say that if they did not Medize, it was because the Athenians did not do so either; just as afterwards when the Athenians attacked the Hellenes they, the Plataeans, were again the only Boeotians who Atticized. [2] And yet consider the forms of our respective governments when we so acted. Our city at that juncture had neither an oligarchic constitution in which all the nobles enjoyed equal rights nor a democracy, but that which is most opposed to law and good government and nearest a tyranny—the rule of a close cabal. [3] These, hoping to strengthen their individual power by the success of the Persians, kept the people down by force, and brought them into the city. The city as a whole was not its own mistress when it so acted, and ought not to be reproached for the errors that it committed while deprived of its constitution. [4] Examine only how we acted after the departure of the Persians and the recovery of the constitution; when the Athenians attacked the rest of Hellas and endeavored to subjugate our country, of the greater part of which faction had already made them masters. Did we not fight and conquer at Coronea[4a] and liberate Boeotia, and do we not now actively contribute to the liberation of the rest, providing horses to the cause and a force unequaled by that of any other state in the confederacy?"

3.63
427
5th Year/Summer
PLATAEA
The Thebans criticize the Plataeans for helping the Athenians to subjugate other Hellenes.

"Let this suffice to excuse us for our Medism. We will now endeavor to show that you have injured the Hellenes more than we, and are more deserving of condign punishment. [2] It was in defense against us, say you, that you became allies and citizens of Athens. If so, you ought only to have called in the Athenians against us, instead of joining them in attacking others: it was open to you to do this if you ever felt that they were leading you where you did not wish to follow, as Sparta was already your ally against the Mede, as you so much insist; and this was surely sufficient to keep us off, and above all to allow you to deliberate in security. Nevertheless, of your own choice and without compulsion you chose to throw your lot in with Athens. [3] And you say that it had been base for you to betray your

3.62.1a See Appendix E, The Persians, §4.

3.62.4a Thucydides mentions the battle of Coronea in 1.113.2; for its location, see Map 4.5, BY.

b urely far baser and more iniquitous to sacri-
fi he Hellenes, your fellow confederates, who
w an the Athenians only, who were enslaving
it ou made them was therefore neither equal
n called them in, as you say, because you were
b s, and then became their accomplices in op-
p d indeed return like for like, but it is base to
d nt unjustly harms others."

3.64
427
5th Year/Summer
PLATAEA
The Thebans emphasize the willingness of the Plataeans to serve Athens, pointing out that they rejected an offer to remain neutral in the current struggle.

s plainly showing that it was not for the
sa you alone then did not Medize, but be-
ca not do so either, and you wished to side
w nst the rest; [2] you now claim the benefit
o ease your neighbors. This cannot be admit-
te ians, and with them you must stand or fall.
N eague then made and claim that it should
n ou abandoned that league, and offended
ag tead of hindering the subjugation of the
A its members, and that not under compul-
si ent of the same institutions that you enjoy
to no one forcing you as in our case. Lastly, an
in o you before you were besieged to be neu-
tr y: this you did not accept. [4] Who then
m he Hellenes more justly than you, you who
so he mask of honor? The former virtues that
yo not to be proper to your character; the real
b een at length damningly proved: when the
A f injustice you followed them."

Medism and your willful Atticizing this,
th

3.65
427
5th Year/Summer
PLATAEA
Though Theban Medizing was unwilling, Plataean Atticizing was willful. Some Plataean citizens acted honorably to help Thebes in the attack on their city to save it from its worst elements.

ich you complain consists in our having, as
yo d your city in time of peace and festival.
H nk that we were more in fault than your-
se proper motion we made an armed attack
up ed your territory, we are guilty; but if the
fir state and family, wishing to put an end to
th d to restore you to the common Boeotian
co ee will invited us, wherein is our crime?
W se who lead, as you say, are more to blame
th 3] Not that, in our judgment, wrong was
do us. Citizens like yourselves, and with more
at pened their own walls and introduced us
in as foes but as friends, to prevent the bad

among you from becoming worse; to give honest men their due; to reform principles without attacking persons, since you were not to be banished from your city, but brought home to your kindred, nor to be made enemies to any, but friends alike to all."

3.66
427
5th Year/Summer
PLATAEA
The Thebans say their intentions were not hostile, but that the Plataeans criminally violated their own agreement when they slew their prisoners.

"That our intention was not hostile is proved by our behavior. We did no harm to anyone, but publicly invited those who wished to live under a national, Boeotian government to come over to us; [2] which at first you gladly did, and made an agreement with us and remained tranquil, until you became aware of the smallness of our numbers. Now it is possible that there may have been something not quite fair in our entering without the consent of your People. At any rate you did not repay us in kind. Instead of refraining, as we had done, from violence, and inducing us to retire by negotiation, you fell upon us in violation of your agreement, and slew some of us in fight, of which we do not so much complain, for in that there was a certain justice; but others who held out their hands and received quarter, and whose lives you subsequently promised us, you lawlessly butchered. If this was not abominable, what is? [3] And after these three crimes committed one after the other—the violation of your agreement, the murder of the men afterwards, and the lying breach of your promise not to kill them, if we refrained from injuring your property in the country—you still affirm that we are the criminals and yourselves pretend to escape justice. Not so, if these your judges decide aright, but you will be punished for all together."

3.67
427
5th Year/Summer
PLATAEA
The Thebans conclude that the Plataeans are unworthy of pity, for they bear full responsibility for their plight after rejecting the Hellenes.

"Such, Spartans, are the facts. We have gone into them at some length both on your account and on our own, that you may feel that you will justly condemn the prisoners, and we, that we have given an additional sanction to our vengeance. [2] We would also prevent you from being melted by hearing of their past virtues, if any such they had: these may be fairly appealed to by the victims of injustice, but only aggravate the guilt of criminals, since they offend against their better nature. Nor let them gain anything by crying and wailing, by calling upon your fathers' tombs and their own desolate condition. [3] Against this we point to the far more dreadful fate of our youth, butchered at their hands; the fathers of whom either fell at Coronea,[3a] bringing Boeotia over to you, or seated, forlorn old men by desolate hearths, who with far more reason implore your justice upon the prisoners. [4] The pity which they appeal to is due rather to men who suffer unworthily; those who suffer justly, as they do, are on the contrary subjects for triumph. [5] For their present desolate condition they have themselves to blame, since they willfully rejected the better alliance. Their lawless act was not provoked by any

3.67.3a Thucydides mentions the battle of Coronea in 1.113.2; for its location, see Map 4.7, BY.

a[illegible]t justice, inspired their decision; and even n[illegible]ch they afford us is not adequate; they will s[illegible]e not, as they pretend, as suppliants asking f[illegible]t as prisoners who have surrendered upon a[illegible] trial. [6] Vindicate, therefore, the Hellenic l[illegible]en, Spartans, and grant to us, the victims of it[illegible] merited by our zeal. Nor let us be sup- p[illegible]their harangues, but offer an example to the H[illegible]s to which you invite them are of deeds, not w[illegible]e shortly stated, but where wrong is done a w[illegible]eded to veil its deformity. [7] However, if le[illegible]o what you are now doing, and putting one sh[illegible], were to decide accordingly, men would be le[illegible]phrases to cover bad actions."

S[illegible]the Thebans. The Spartan judges decided that the [illegible]had received any service from the Plataeans in the [illegible]em to put; as they had always invited them to be n[illegible] original covenant of Pausanias after the defeat of th[illegible]n definitely offered them the same conditions befo[illegible]fer having been refused, they were now, they conc[illegible] their intention released from their covenant; and [illegible]ed, suffered evil at the hands of the Plataeans, they [illegible] one by one and asked each of them the same ques[illegible]her they had done the Spartans and allies any servi[illegible] their saying that they had not, took them out and [illegible]xception. [2] The number of Plataeans thus mass[illegible]two hundred, with twenty-five Athenians who had s[illegible] women were taken as slaves. [3] The city the Theb[illegible]ear to some political emigrants from Megara, and t[illegible]s of their own party to inhabit, and afterwards razed[illegible] the very foundations, and built on to the preci[illegible] hundred feet square, with rooms all round abov[illegible] for this purpose of the roofs and doors of the Plata[illegible] materials in the wall, the brass and the iron, they [illegible]y dedicated to Hera, for whom they also built a sto[illegible] feet square. The land they confiscated and let out [illegible]Theban occupiers. [4] The adverse attitude of the S[illegible]ataean affair was mainly adopted to please the Theb[illegible]to be useful in the war at that moment raging. Such [illegible] in the ninety-third year after she became the ally o[illegible]

3.68
427
5th Year/Summer
PLATAEA
The Plataeans are executed and their city razed.

3.68.3a [illegible] Thucyd- [illegible]and sup- [illegible]eir allies, [illegible]

3.68.3b This is another instance of the salvage of woodwork; see note at 2.14.1a.

3.68.4a Plataea was restored in 386 B.C. under the "King's Peace"; see Epilogue, §4, and Appendix E, The Persians, §11.

3.69
427
5th Year/Summer
PELOPONNESUS
The Peloponnesian fleet returns to Cyllene.

Meanwhile, the forty ships of the Peloponnesians[1a] that had gone to the relief of the Lesbians, and which we left flying across the open sea, pursued by the Athenians, were caught in a storm off Crete, and scattering from thence made their way to the Peloponnesus, where they found at Cyllene[1b] thirteen Leucadian and Ambraciot triremes, with Brasidas son of Tellis lately arrived as counselor to Alcidas; [2] the Spartans, upon the failure of the Lesbian expedition, resolved to strengthen their fleet and sail to Corcyra, where a revolution had broken out, and to arrive there before the twelve Athenian ships at Naupactus could be reinforced from Athens. Brasidas and Alcidas began to prepare accordingly.

3.70
427
5th Year/Summer
CORCYRA
The Corcyraean oligarchs revolt.

The Corcyraean revolution began with the return of the prisoners taken in the sea fights off Epidamnus.[1a] These the Corinthians had released, nominally upon the security of eight hundred talents[1b] given by their *proxeni*[1c] but in reality upon their engagement to bring over Corcyra to Corinth. These men proceeded to canvass each of the citizens, and to intrigue with the aim of detaching the city from Athens. [2] Upon the arrival of an Athenian and a Corinthian vessel, with envoys on board, a conference was held in which the Corcyraeans voted to remain allies of the Athenians according to their agreement, but to be friends of the Peloponnesians as they had been formerly. [3] Meanwhile, the returned prisoners brought Peithias, a volunteer proxenus of the Athenians and leader of the commons, to trial, upon the charge of enslaving Corcyra to Athens. [4] He, being acquitted, retorted by accusing five of the richest of their number of cutting stakes in the ground sacred to Zeus and Alcinous; the legal penalty being a *stater*[4a] for each stake. [5] Upon their conviction, the amount of the penalty being very large, they seated themselves as suppliants in the temples, to be allowed to pay it by installments; but Peithias, who was one of the council, prevailed upon that body to enforce the law; [6] upon which the accused, rendered desperate by the law, and also learning that Peithias had the intention, while still a member of the council, to persuade the people to conclude a defensive and offensive alliance with Athens, banded together armed with daggers, and suddenly bursting into the Council killed Peithias and sixty others, council members and private persons; some few only of the party of Peithias taking refuge in the Athenian trireme, which had not yet departed.

3.69.1a This picks up the narrative of Alcidas' fleet from 3.33.
3.69.1b Cyllene: Map 3.76.
3.70.1a These sea battles were fought near Sybota, a long way from Epidamnus. They are described in 1.49–50. Thucydides last described events on Corcyra in 1.55.
3.70.1b Eight hundred talents was an enormous sum, more than Athens' annual tribute at that time. See A. W. Gomme, *A Historical Commentary on Thucydides,* iii (Oxford, 1956), 359, and Appendix J, Classical Greek Currency, §5.
3.70.1c *Proxeni*: see note 3.2.3c.
3.70.4a The *stater* was a unit of currency; probably in this case the Corinthian stater, almost equal to two Attic *drachmas;* see Appendix J, Classical Greek Currency, §4. According to A. W. Gomme, *A Historical Commentary on Thucydides,* iii (Oxford, 1956), 360, this fine seems too small to distress rich men, unless they had cut thousands of the stakes over many years. It was of course criminal sacrilege to touch land dedicated to a god. Athens based her Megarian Decree publicly on the grounds that the Megarians had cultivated consecrated ground (1.139.2).

A[illegible]onspirators summoned the Corcyraeans to an assem[illegible]ould turn out for the best and would save them fror[illegible]ens: for the future, they moved to receive neither[illegible] peacefully in a single ship, treating any larger num[illegible]otion made, they compelled it to be adopted, [2] [illegible]nvoys to Athens to justify what had been done and [illegible]es there from any hostile proceedings which mig[illegible]

3.71
427
5th Year/Summer
CORCYRA
The oligarchs declare Corcyra's neutrality.

U[illegible]embassy, the Athenians arrested the envoys and all w[illegible]revolutionists, and lodged them in Aegina.[1a] [2] Mea[illegible]eme arriving in the island with Spartan envoys, thos[illegible] attacked The People and defeated them in battle. [illegible]The People took refuge in the Acropolis and the high[illegible]nd concentrated themselves there, having also poss[illegible]arbor, their adversaries occupying the *agora*,[3b] whe[illegible] and the harbor adjoining, looking toward the mai[illegible]

3.72
427
5th Year/Summer
CORCYRA
Corcyraean oligarchs attack The People.

T[illegible]kirmishes of little importance, each party sending [illegible]r freedom to the slaves and to invite them to join[illegible]slaves answered the appeal of The People; their anta[illegible] by eight hundred mercenaries from the mainland

3.73
427
5th Year/Summer
CORCYRA
Both sides seek support from the slaves.

A[illegible]stilities recommenced, victory remaining with The[illegible]dvantage in numbers and position, the women also [illegible], pelting with tiles from the houses, and support[illegible]rtitude beyond their sex. [2] Toward dusk, the olig[illegible]g that the victorious commons might assault and [illegible]ut them to the sword, set fire to the houses roun[illegible]odging-houses, in order to bar their advance; spar[illegible]nor those of their neighbors; by which much stuff[illegible]onsumed and the city risked total destruction if a wi[illegible]e flame by blowing on it. [3] Hostilities now ceas[illegible]s kept quiet, passing the night on guard, the Cori[illegible] sea upon the victory of The People, and most of th[illegible]er secretly to the continent.

3.74
427
5th Year/Summer
CORCYRA
The oligarchs are defeated.

3.72.1[illegible]

3.72.3[illegible]cropolis [illegible]ity of Cor- [illegible]inset of [illegible]map and [illegible]*Historical* [illegible]Oxford, [illegible]

3.72.3[illegible] social [illegible]

3.75
427
5th Year/Summer
CORCYRA
The Athenian Nicostratus attempts to arrange a truce.

The next day the Athenian general, Nicostratus son of Diitrephes, came up from Naupactus with twelve ships and five hundred Messenian hoplites.[1a] He at once endeavored to bring about a settlement, and persuaded the two parties to agree together to bring to trial ten of the ringleaders, who were no longer in the city, while the rest were to live in peace, making terms with each other, and entering into an alliance with the Athenians. [2] This arranged, he was about to sail away, when the leaders of The People induced him to leave them five of his ships to make their adversaries less disposed to make trouble, while they manned and sent with him an equal number of their own. [3] He had no sooner consented, than they began to enroll their enemies for the ships; and these fearing that they might be sent off to Athens seated themselves as suppliants in the temple of the Dioscuri.[3a] [4] When an attempt by Nicostratus to reassure them and to persuade them to rise proved unsuccessful, The People armed upon this pretext, alleging the refusal of their adversaries to sail with them as a proof of the hollowness of their intentions, and took their arms out of their houses, and would even have killed some whom they fell in with if Nicostratus had not prevented it. [5] The rest of the party, being not less than four hundred in number, seeing what was going on, seated themselves as suppliants in the temple of Hera until The People, fearing that they might adopt some desperate resolution, induced them to rise, and conveyed them over to the island in front of the temple[5a] where provisions were sent across to them.

3.76
427
5th Year/Summer
CORCYRA
The Peloponnesian fleet arrives at Corcyra.

At this stage in the revolution, on the fourth or fifth day after the removal of the men to the island, the Peloponnesian ships arrived from Cyllene[1a] where they had been stationed since their return from Ionia, fifty-three in number, still under the command of Alcidas, but with Brasidas also on board as his adviser; and dropping anchor at Sybota,[1b] a harbor on the mainland, at daybreak made sail for Corcyra.

3.77
427
5th Year/Summer
CORCYRA
The Corcyraeans launch a disorganized naval attack.

The Corcyraeans in great confusion and alarm at the state of things in the city and at the approach of the invader, at once proceeded to equip sixty vessels, which they sent out, as fast as they were manned, against the enemy, in spite of the Athenians recommending them to let them sail out first, and to follow themselves afterwards with all their ships together. [2] Upon their vessels coming up to the enemy in this straggling fashion, two immediately deserted: in others the crews were fighting among themselves, and there was no order in anything that was done; [3] so that the Peloponnesians, seeing their confusion, placed twenty ships to oppose the Corcyraeans, and ranged the rest against the twelve Athenian ships, amongst which were the two vessels *Salaminia* and *Paralus*.[3a]

3.75.1a These "Messenians" now lived at Naupactus (Map 3.76), where Athens had settled them after they surrendered to Sparta at Ithome and were forced to leave the Peloponnesus (see 1.103.1–3).

3.75.3a No suppliant could be molested without insult to the gods, particularly that god or gods in whose temple or at whose altar the suppliant had taken refuge.

3.75.5a The temple of Hera and the island in front of it, possible location: Map 3.76, inset.

3.76.1a Cyllene: Map 3.76.

3.76.1b Sybota: Map 3.76.

3.77.3a The *Salaminia* and the *Paralus* were special state triremes used for official business.

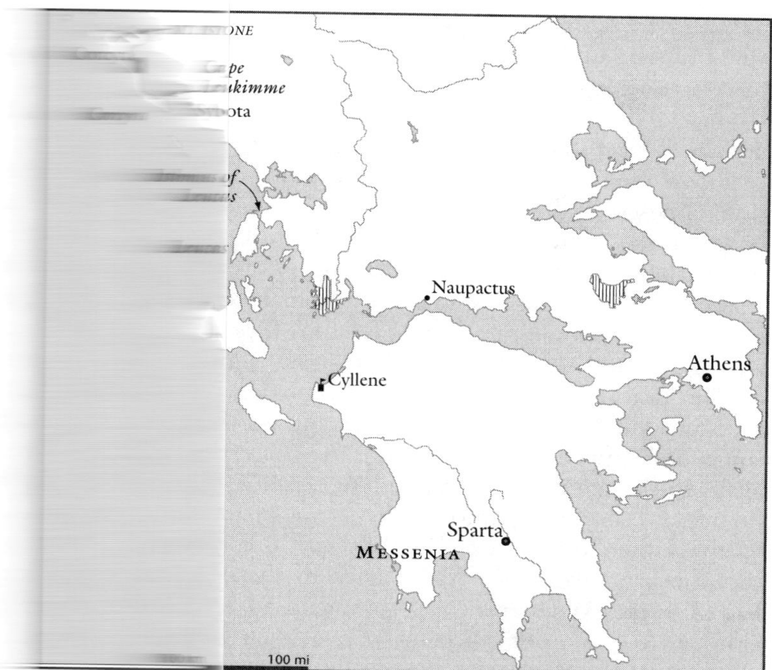

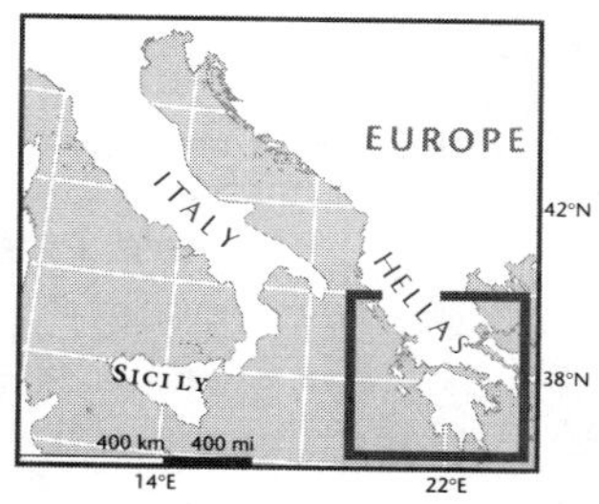

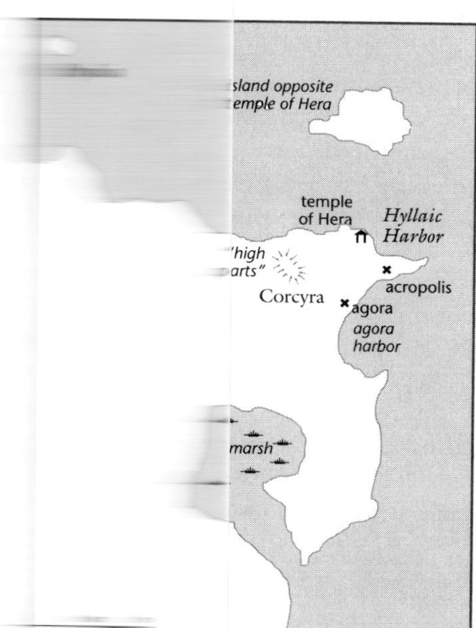

MAP[illegible]ITY: CITY OF CORCYRA

3.78
427
5th Year/Summer
CORCYRA
The Peloponnesians defeat the Corcyraeans at sea.

While the Corcyraeans, attacking without judgment and in small detachments, were already crippled by their own misconduct, the Athenians, afraid of the numbers of the enemy and of being surrounded, did not venture to attack the main body or even the center of the division opposed to them, but fell upon its wing and sank one vessel;[1a] after which the Peloponnesians formed in a circle, and the Athenians rowed round them and tried to throw them into disorder. [2] Perceiving this, the Peloponnesian division opposed to the Corcyraeans, fearing a repetition of the disaster of Naupactus,[2a] came to support their friends, and the whole fleet, now united, bore down upon the Athenians, [3] who retired before it, backing water, withdrawing as leisurely as possible in order to give the Corcyraeans time to escape while the enemy was thus kept occupied. [4] Such was the character of this sea fight, which lasted until sunset.

3.79
427
5th Year/Summer
CORCYRA
The Peloponnesians fail to exploit their victory.

The Corcyraeans now feared that the enemy would follow up their victory and sail against the city and rescue the men in the island, or strike some other equally decisive blow, and accordingly carried the men over again to the temple of Hera, and kept guard over the city. [2] The Peloponnesians, however, although victorious in the sea fight, did not venture to attack the city, but took the thirteen Corcyraean vessels which they had captured, and with them sailed back to the continent from whence they had put out. [3] The next day they again refrained from attacking the city, although the disorder and panic were at their height, and though Brasidas, it is said, urged Alcidas, his superior officer, to do so, but they landed upon the promontory of Leukimme and laid waste the country.[3a]

3.80
427
5th Year/Summer
CORCYRA
The Peloponnesians learn of the approach of a large Athenian fleet.

Meanwhile The People in Corcyra, being still in great fear of the fleet attacking them, came to a parley with the suppliants and their friends, in order to save the city; and prevailed upon some of them to go on board the ships, of which they still manned thirty, against the expected attack. [2] But the Peloponnesians after ravaging the country until midday sailed away, and toward nightfall were informed by beacon signals of the approach of sixty Athenian vessels from Leucas,[2a] under the command of Eurymedon son of Thucles; which had been sent off by the Athenians upon the news of the revolution and of the fleet with Alcidas being about to sail for Corcyra.

3.81
427
5th Year/Summer
CORCYRA
As the Peloponnesians flee, the Corcyraean popular faction massacres its domestic foes.

The Peloponnesians accordingly at once set off in haste by night for home, coasting along shore; and hauling their ships across the Isthmus of Leucas,[1a] in order not to be seen doubling it, so departed. [2] The Corcyraeans, made aware of the approach of the Athenian fleet and of the departure of the enemy, brought the Messenians[2a] from outside the walls into the city, and ordered the fleet which they had manned to sail round into the Hyllaic harbor;[2b] and while it was so doing, slew such of their enemies

3.78.1a On the "sinking" of triremes, see note 2.91.3a and Appendix G, Trireme Warfare, §9.
3.78.2a Thucydides refers here to the naval battle in 429 that took place in the sea off Patrae, and which he described in 2.83–84.
3.79.3a Cape Leukimme: Map 3.76.
3.80.2a Leucas: Map 3.76.
3.81.1a Isthmus of Leucas: Map 3.76.
3.81.2a These are the five hundred Messenian hoplites who had arrived with Nicostratus in 3.75.1.
3.81.2b Hyllaic harbor at Corcyra, probable location: Map 3.76, inset.

as th[illegible]g afterwards as they landed them, those whom
they[illegible]n board the ships. Next they went to the sanc-
tuar[illegible]ed about fifty men to take their trial, and con-
dem[illegible]3] The mass of the suppliants who had refused
to d[illegible]s taking place, slew each other there in the con-
secr[illegible]e hanged themselves upon the trees, and others
dest[illegible] were severally able. [4] During seven days that
Eur[illegible] sixty ships, the Corcyraeans were engaged in
butc[illegible]llow-citizens whom they regarded as their ene-
mie[illegible]e imputed was that of attempting to put down
the [illegible] slain also for private hatred, others by their
debt[illegible]neys owed to them. [5] Death thus raged in
ever[illegible] happens at such times, there was no length to
whic[illegible]sons were killed by their fathers, and suppliants
drag[illegible]ain upon it;[5a] while some were even walled up
in th[illegible]nd died there.

3.82 427 5th Year/Summer CORCYRA Thucydides describes the evils of revolution.

S[illegible] of the revolution, and the impression which it
mad[illegible]as one of the first to occur. Later on, one may
say, [illegible]rld was convulsed; struggles being everywhere
mad[illegible] to bring in the Athenians, and by the oligarchs
to in[illegible]n peace there would have been neither the pretext [illegible]ch an invitation; but in war, with an alliance alway[illegible]her faction for the hurt of their adversaries and
thei[illegible]vantage, opportunities for bringing in the foreign[illegible]o the revolutionary parties. [2] The sufferings
whic[illegible]pon the cities were many and terrible, such as
have[illegible]ill occur as long as the nature of mankind remai[illegible] a severer or milder form, and varying in their
sym[illegible]e variety of the particular cases. In peace and
pros[illegible]duals have better sentiments, because they do
not [illegible]ly confronted with imperious necessities; but
war [illegible]ply of daily wants and so proves a rough master
that [illegible]acters to a level with their fortunes. [3] Revolution [illegible] city to city, and the places which it arrived at
last, [illegible] had been done before, carried to a still greater
exce[illegible]eir inventions, as manifested in the cunning of
thei[illegible]ocity of their reprisals. [4] Words had to change
thei[illegible] to take that which was now given them. Reck-
less [illegible]nsidered the courage of a loyal supporter; prudent[illegible]wardice; moderation was held to be a cloak for

3.81.2[illegible]oximate

3.81.5[illegible]ken refuge [illegible]me.

unmanliness; ability to see all sides of a question incapacity to act on any. Frantic violence became the attribute of manliness; cautious plotting a justifiable means of self-defense. [5] The advocate of extreme measures was always trustworthy; his opponent a man to be suspected. To succeed in a plot was to have a shrewd head, to divine a plot a still shrewder; but to try to provide against having to do either was to break up your party and to be afraid of your adversaries. In short, to forestall an intending criminal, or to suggest the idea of a crime where it was lacking was equally commended, [6] until even blood became a weaker tie than party, from the superior readiness of those united by the latter to dare everything without reserve; for such associations sought not the blessings derivable from established institutions but were formed by ambition to overthrow them; and the confidence of their members in each other rested less on any religious sanction than upon complicity in crime. [7] The fair proposals of an adversary were met with jealous precautions by the stronger of the two, and not with a generous confidence. Revenge also was held of more account than self-preservation. Oaths of reconciliation, being only offered on either side to meet an immediate difficulty, only held good so long as no other weapon was at hand; but when opportunity arose, he who first ventured to seize it and to take his enemy off his guard, thought this perfidious vengeance sweeter than an open one since, considerations of safety apart, success by treachery won him the prize for superior intelligence. Indeed it is generally the case that men are readier to call rogues clever than simpletons honest, and are as ashamed of being the second as they are proud of being the first. [8] The cause of all these evils was the lust for power arising from greed and ambition; and from these passions proceeded the violence of parties once engaged in contention. The leaders in the cities made the fairest professions: on the one side with the cry of political equality of The People, on the other of a moderate aristocracy; but they sought prizes for themselves in those public interests which they pretended to cherish and, stopping at nothing in their struggles for ascendancy, engaged in direct excesses. In their acts of vengeance they went to even greater lengths, not limiting them to what justice or the good of the state demanded, but making the party caprice of the moment their only standard, and invoking with equal readiness the condemnation of an unjust verdict or the authority of the strong arm to glut the animosities of the hour. Thus religion was in honor with neither party; but the use of fair phrases to arrive at guilty ends was in high reputation. Meanwhile the moderate part of the citizens perished between the two, either for not joining in the quarrel, or because envy would not suffer them to escape.

3.83
427
5th Year/Summer
CORCYRA
Thucydides' description of the evils of revolution is continued.

Thus every form of iniquity took root in the Hellenic countries by reason of the troubles. The ancient simplicity into which honor so largely entered was laughed down and disappeared; and society became divided into camps in which no man trusted his fellow. [2] To put an end to this,

ther… to be depended upon, nor oath that could
com… arties dwelling rather in their calculation upon
the … anent state of things, were more intent upon
self… of confidence. [3] In this contest the blunter
wits … Apprehensive of their own deficiencies and of
the … agonists, they feared to be worsted in debate
and … e combinations of their more versatile oppo-
nen… dly had recourse to action: while their adver-
sari… that they should know in time, and that it was
unn… ction what policy could provide, often fell victim… tion.

3.84 … the first example of most of the crimes alluded
to; … by the governed who had never experienced eq-
uita… anything but insolence from their rulers—when
thei… quitous resolves of those who desired to get rid
of t… y and ardently coveted their neighbors' goods;
and … pitiless excesses into which men who had begun
the … but in a party spirit, were hurried by their un-
gov… the confusion into which life was now thrown
in t… e, always rebelling against the law and now its
mas… f ungoverned in passion, above respect for justice … periority; since revenge would not have been set
abo… ove justice, had it not been for the fatal power of
env… often take upon themselves in the prosecution of
the… ample of doing away with those general laws to
whi… salvation in adversity, instead of allowing them
to s… danger when their aid may be required.

427
5th Year/Summer
CORCYRA
Thucydides' description of the evils of revolution is concluded.

3.85 … passions thus for the first time displayed them-
selv… rcyra, Eurymedon and the Athenian fleet sailed
awa… five hundred Corcyraean exiles who had suc-
cee… ne forts on the mainland and, becoming masters
of t… on the mainland, made this their base to plunder … e island, and did so much damage as to cause a
sev… 3] They also sent envoys to Sparta and Corinth
to … on; but meeting with no success, afterwards got
tog… aries and crossed over to the island, being about
six … ning their boats so as to have no hope except in
bec… untry, went up to Mount Istone[3a] and fortifying
the… harm those in the city and obtain command of
the…

427
5th Year/Summer
CORCYRA
The Corcyraean revolution leads to famine and chronic civil strife.

3.86 … summer the Athenians sent twenty ships under
the … on of Melanopus, and Charoeades son of Eu-
phi… re the Syracusans[2a] and Leontines[2b] were at war.

427
5th Year/Summer
SICILY
The Athenians send a fleet to Sicily.

3.85… 3.76.
… to Corcyra

3.86.1a Sicily: Map 3.86.
3.86.2a Syracuse: Map 3.86.
3.86.2b Leontini: Map 3.86.

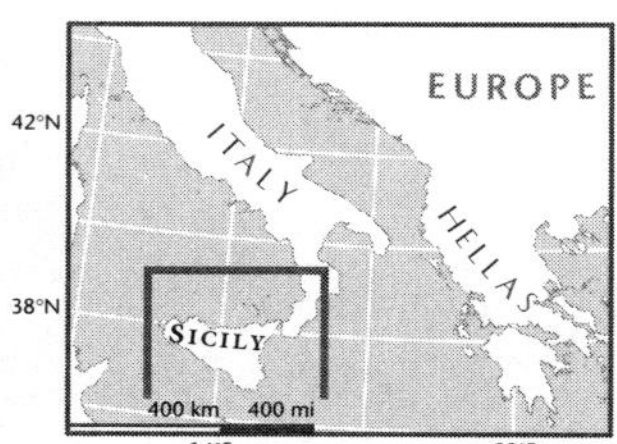

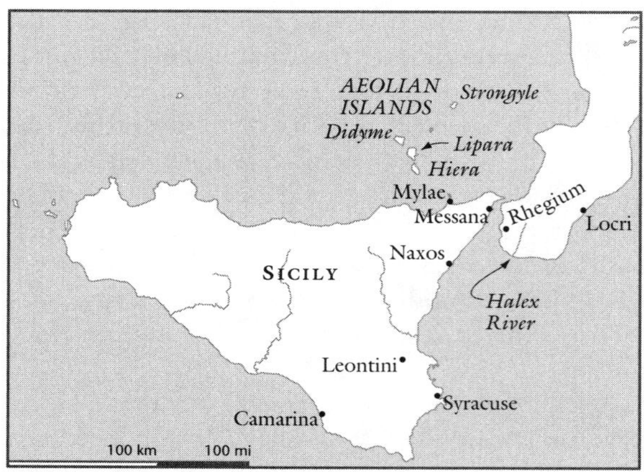

MAP 3.86 SICILIAN OPERATIONS IN 427

The Syracusans had for allies all the Dorian cities except Camarina[2c]—these had all been included in the Lacedaemonian confederacy from the commencement of the war, though they had not taken any active part in it—the Leontines had Camarina and the Chalcidian cities.[2d] In Italy the Locrians[2e] were for the Syracusans, the Rhegians[2f] for their Leontine kinsmen. [3] The allies of the Leontines now sent to Athens and appealed to their ancient alliance and to their Ionian origin, to persuade the Athenians to send them a fleet, as the Syracusans were blockading them by land and sea. [4] The Athenians sent it upon the plea of their common descent, but in reality to prevent the exportation of Sicilian corn to the Peloponnesus and to test the possibility of bringing Sicily into subjection. Accordingly they established themselves at Rhegium in Italy, and from thence carried on the war in concert with their allies.[4a]

3.87
427/6
5th Year/Winter
ATHENS
The plague returns to Athens.

Summer was now over. The winter following, the plague a second time attacked the Athenians; for although it had never entirely left them, still there had been a notable abatement in its ravages.[1a] [2] The second visit lasted no less than a year, the first having lasted two; and nothing distressed the Athenians and reduced their power more than this. [3] No less than four thousand four hundred hoplites in the ranks died of it and three hundred cavalry, besides a number of the multitude that was never ascertained. [4] At the same time took place the numerous earthquakes in Athens, Euboea, and Boeotia, particularly at Orchomenus[4a] in the last-named country.

3.86.2c Camarina: Map 3.86. For the Dorian cities, see Appendix H, Dialects and Ethnic Groups, §4–8.
3.86.2d Leontini, Naxos, and Rhegium (Map 3.86) were all founded by Chalcis of Euboea (Map 4.7, BY).
3.86.2e Locri (Epizephyrian, in Italy): Map 3.86.
3.86.2f Rhegium: Map 3.86.
3.86.4a Events in Sicily are continued at 3.88.
3.87.1a The first outbreak of plague in Athens was extensively described in 2.47–55.
3.87.4a Orchomenus, Boeotia, and Euboea: Map 3.93, AY.

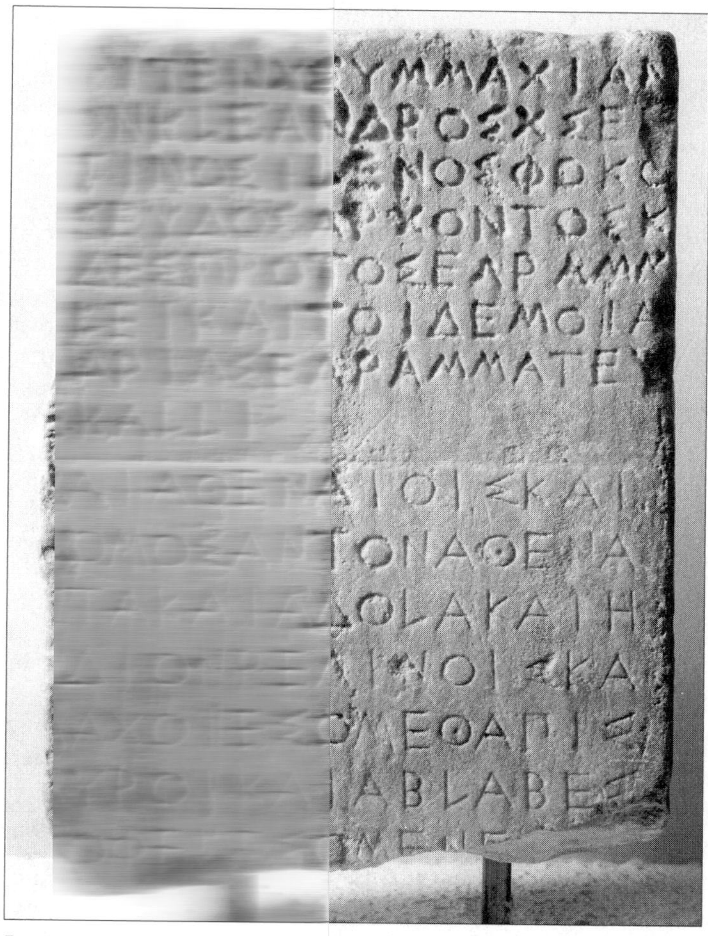

ILLU… OF A TREATY BETWEEN ATHENS AND RHE…

T… …henians in Sicily and the Rhegians, with thirty 3.88
ship… …gainst the islands of Aeolus:[1a] it being impossi- 427/6
ble t… …ner, owing to the want of water. [2] These is- 5th Year/Winter
land… …parians, a Cnidian[2a] colony, who live in one of SICILY
then… …d Lipara; and from this as their headquarters The Athenians raid the
culti… Strongyle, and Hiera.[2b] [3] In Hiera the peo- Aeolian islands.
ple i… …at Hephaestus has his forge, from the quantity

3.88.1 … s continues

3.88.2 …

3.88.2 … …era, Aeo-

of flame which they see it send out by night, and of smoke by day. These islands lie off the coast of the Sicels and Messanians, and were allies of the Syracusans. [4] The Athenians laid waste their land, and as the inhabitants did not submit, sailed back to Rhegium. Thus the winter ended, and with it ended the fifth year of this war, of which Thucydides was the historian.[4a]

3.89
426
6th Year/Summer
ATTICA-EUBOEA
The Peloponnesian invasion of Attica turns back due to earthquakes.

The next summer the Peloponnesians and their allies set out to invade Attica under the command of Agis son of Archidamus, and went as far as the Isthmus,[1a] but numerous earthquakes occurring, turned back again without the invasion taking place. [2] About the same time that these earthquakes were so common, the sea at Orobiae, in Euboea,[2a] retiring from the then line of coast, returned in a huge wave and invaded a great part of the city, and retreated leaving some of it still under water; so that what was once land is now sea; such of the inhabitants perishing as could not run up to the higher ground in time. [3] A similar inundation also occurred at Atalanta,[2b] the island off the Opuntian-Locrian[3a] coast, carrying away part of the Athenian fort and wrecking one of two ships which were drawn up on the beach. [4] At Peparethus[4a] also the sea retreated a little, without however any inundation following; and an earthquake threw down part of the wall, the city hall, and a few other buildings. [5] The cause, in my opinion, of this phenomenon must be sought in the earthquake. At the point where its shock has been the most violent the sea is driven back, and suddenly recoiling with redoubled force, causes the inundation. Without an earthquake I do not see how such an accident could happen.

3.90
426
6th Year/Summer
SICILY
Messana submits to the Athenians.

During the same summer different operations were carried on by the different belligerents in Sicily; by the Sicelians themselves against each other, and by the Athenians and their allies: I shall however confine myself to the actions in which the Athenians took part, choosing the most important. [2] The death of the Athenian general Charoeades, killed by the Syracusans in battle, left Laches in sole command of the fleet, which he now directed in concert with the allies against Mylae, a place belonging to the Messanians. Two Messanian battalions in garrison at Mylae[2a] laid an ambush for the party landing from the ships, [3] but were routed with great slaughter by the Athenians and their allies, who thereupon assaulted the fortification and compelled them to surrender the Acropolis and to march with them upon Messana.[3a] [4] This city afterwards also submitted upon the approach of the Athenians and their allies, and gave hostages and all other securities required.[4a]

3.91
426
6th Year/Summer
MELOS-BOEOTIA
Nicias' expedition to Melos and Tanagra is described.

The same summer the Athenians sent thirty ships round the Peloponnesus under Demosthenes son of Alcisthenes, and Procles son of Theodorus,[1a] and sixty others, with two thousand hoplites, against Melos,[1b] under Nicias son

3.88.4a Events in Sicily are continued at 3.90.
3.89.1a The Isthmus of Corinth: Map 3.93, BY.
3.89.2a Orobiae, in Euboea: Map 3.93, AY.
3.89.2b Atalanta: Map 3.93, AY; see 2.32.
3.89.3a Locris (Opuntian): Map 3.93, AY.
3.89.4a Peparethus: Map 3.93, AY.
3.90.2a Mylae: Map 3.86. This continues the narrative from 3.88.
3.90.3a Messana: Map 3.86.
3.90.4a Events in Sicily continue at 3.99.
3.91.1a The voyage of this fleet is described in 3.94ff.
3.91.1b Melos: Map 3.93, BY. A second Athenian assault on Melos is described in 5.84.

of N[illegible]hed to reduce the Melians, who, although islan[illegible]ects of Athens or even to join her confederacy. [3] [illegible]f their land failed to make the Melians submit, the [illegible]ed to Oropus[3a] in the territory of Graea where, lan[illegible]plites started at once from the ships by land for Tan[illegible] There they were met by the whole levy from Ath[illegible] prearranged signal, under the command of Hip[illegible] and Eurymedon son of Thucles. [5] They encam[illegible]ay in ravaging the Tanagran territory, remained the[illegible]t day, after defeating those Tanagrans who sallied [illegible] some Thebans who had come up to help the Tan[illegible]e arms, set up a trophy,[4a] and retired—one gro[illegible]ther to the ships. [6] Nicias with his sixty ships coa[illegible]vaged the Locrian seaboard, and so returned hon[illegible]

3.92
426
6th Year/Summer
HERACLEA IN TRACHIS
Sparta establishes the new polis of Heraclea in Trachis.

A[illegible]rtans founded their colony of Heraclea in Trachis[illegible]e following: [2] the Malians are divided into thre[illegible] the Hiereans, and the Trachinians. The last of thes[illegible]ly in a war with their neighbors the Oetaeans,[2a] at f[illegible]emselves up to Athens; but afterwards, fearing not [illegible]y that they sought, sent Tisamenus, whom they cho[illegible]rta. [3] The Dorians from the mother country of t[illegible] in this embassy with the same request, as they the[illegible]m the same enemy. [4] After hearing them, the Spa[illegible]d out the colony, wishing to assist the Trachinians [illegible] because they thought that the proposed city wou[illegible] for the purposes of the war against the Athenians. [illegible] ready there against Euboea,[4a] with the advantage[illegible]e island; and the city would also be useful as a stat[illegible]race.[4b] In short, everything made the Spartans eag[illegible]5] After first consulting the god at Delphi and rece[illegible], they sent off the colonists, Spartans and *Perioik*[illegible] the rest of the Hellenes who might wish to accom[illegible]ians, Achaeans, and certain other nationalities; thre[illegible]unders of the colony, Leon, Alcidas, and Damago[illegible] and fortified the city, now called Heraclea, on a new[illegible] and a half from Thermopylae[6a] and two miles and[illegible]; and commenced building docks, closing the side[illegible]st by the pass itself, in order that they might be easi[illegible]

3.91[illegible]
3.91[illegible]
3.91[illegible]d armor [illegible] at or near [illegible] See Appen- [illegible]
3.92[illegible]3, AX. The [illegible]es at 3.100.

3.92.2a Territory of the Malians: Map 3.93, AY. Territory of the Oetae: Map 3.93, AX.
3.92.4a Euboea: Map 3.93, AY.
3.92.4b Thrace: Map 3.93, locator.
3.92.5a For a description of the *perioikoi*, see the Glossary and Appendix C, Spartan Institutions, §9.
3.92.6a Thermopylae: Map 3.93, AY. See note 4.36.3a.

3.93
426
6th Year/Summer
HERACLEA IN TRACHIS
Heraclea does not thrive.

The foundation of this city, evidently meant to annoy Euboea (the passage across to Cenaeum in that island being a short one),[1a] at first caused some alarm at Athens, but in fact the city never caused them any trouble. [2] The reason for this was as follows: the Thessalians,[2a] who were sovereign in those parts and whose territory was menaced by its foundation, were afraid that it might prove a very powerful neighbor, and so they harassed and made war upon the new settlers continually until they at last wore them out in spite of their originally considerable numbers—people had flocked there from all quarters, believing that any place founded by the Spartans was sure to prosper. On the other hand the Spartans themselves, in the persons of their governors, did their full share toward ruining its prosperity and reducing its population, as they frightened away the greater part of the inhabitants by governing harshly and in some cases not fairly, and thus made it easier for their neighbors to prevail against them.

3.94
426
6th Year/Summer
LEUCAS
Demosthenes attacks Leucas.

The same summer, about the same time that the Athenians were detained at Melos, their fellow citizens in the thirty ships cruising round the Peloponnesus,[1a] after cutting off some guards in an ambush at Ellomenus[1b] in the territory of Leucas, subsequently went against Leucas[1c] itself with a large armament, having been reinforced by the whole levy of the Acarnanians[1d] except Oeniadae,[1e] and by the Zacynthians[1f] and Cephallenians[1g] and fifteen ships from Corcyra.[1h] [2] While the Leucadians witnessed the devastation of their land, without and within the isthmus upon which the city of Leucas and the temple of Apollo stand, without making any movement on account of the overwhelming numbers of the enemy, the Acarnanians urged Demosthenes, the Athenian general, to build a wall so as to cut off the city from the continent, a measure which they were convinced would secure its capture and rid them once and for all of a most troublesome enemy.

[3] Demosthenes however had in the meanwhile been persuaded by the Messenians[3a] that it was a fine opportunity for him, having so large an army assembled, to attack the Aetolians,[3b] who were not only the enemies of Naupactus,[3c] but whose reduction would further make it easy to gain the rest of that part of the mainland region for the Athenians. [4] The Aetolians, although numerous and warlike, dwelt in unwalled villages scattered far apart, had nothing but light armor, and might, according to the Messenians, be subdued without much difficulty before help could arrive. [5]

3.93.1a Cenaeum, western cape of Euboea: Map 3.93, AY.
3.93.2a Thessaly: Map 3.93, AY.
3.94.1a Operations at Melos were described in 3.91. These thirty ships were the fleet under Demosthenes and Procles mentioned in 3.91.1.
3.94.1b Ellomenus on Leucas: precise location unknown.
3.94.1c Leucas: Map 3.93, AX.
3.94.1d Acarnania: Map 3.93, AX. This briefly picks up the narrative of Acarnanian events from 3.7; it continues next in 3.102.
3.94.1e Oeniadae: Map 3.93, AX.
3.94.1f Zacynthus: Map 3.93, BX.
3.94.1g Cephallenia: Map 3.93, AX.
3.94.1h Corcyra: Map 3.93, AX
3.94.3a These were Messenians from Naupactus where Athens settled them; see 1.103.1–3 and note 3.75.1a.
3.94.3b Aetolia: Map 3.93, AX.
3.94.3c Naupactus: Map 3.93, AX, and Map 3.98, AX.

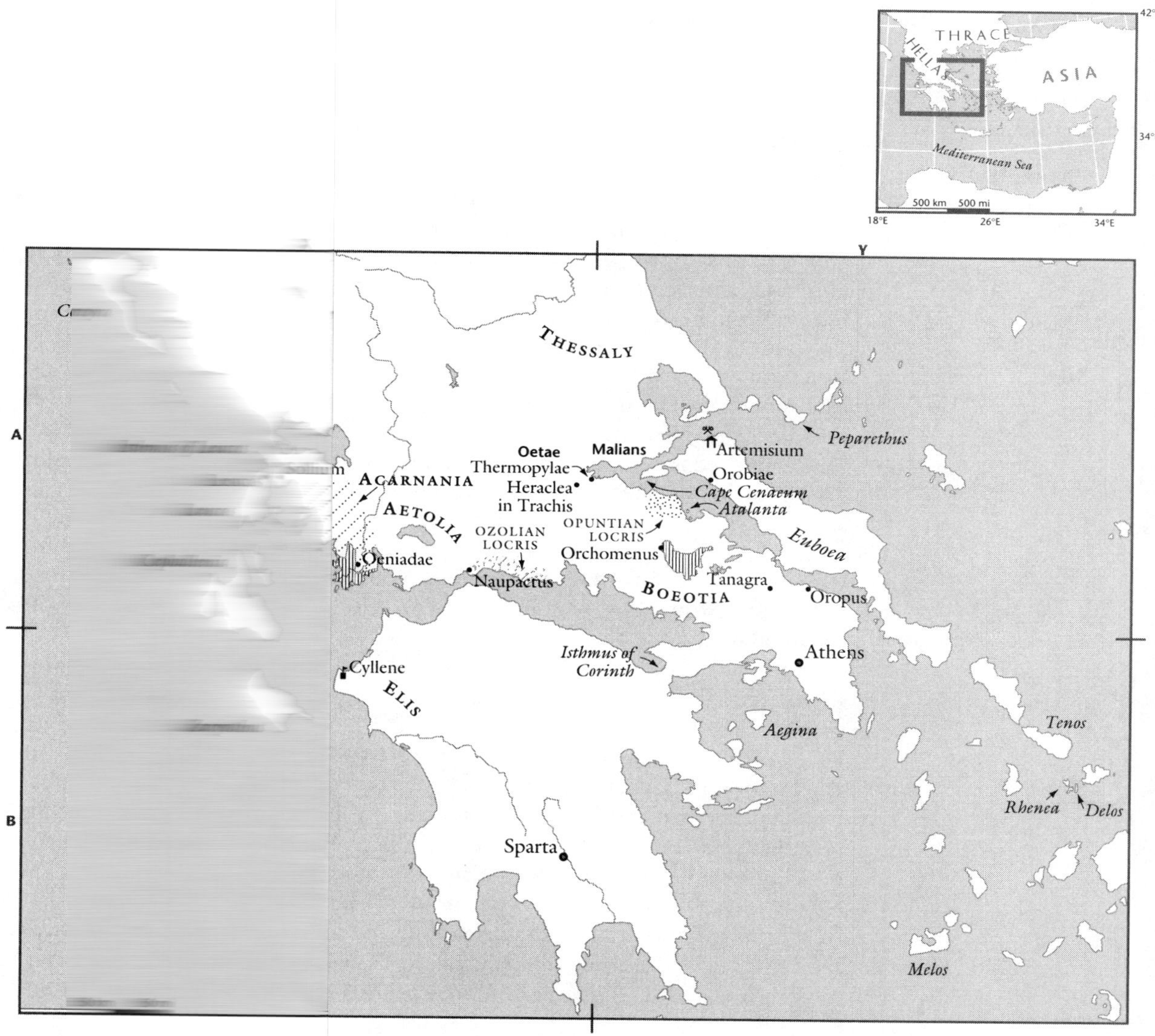

MAP IAS AND DEMOSTHENES, EARLY 426

The plan which they recommended was to attack first the Apodotians, next the Ophionians, and after these the Eurytanians.[5a] These last are the largest tribe in Aetolia. They speak, as is said, a language exceedingly difficult to understand and eat their flesh raw. Once these tribes were subdued, the rest would readily come over.

3.95
426
6th Year/Summer
AETOLIA
Demosthenes decides to attack Aetolia.

To this plan Demosthenes consented, not only to please the Messenians, but also in the belief that by adding the Aetolians to his other mainland allies he would be able, without aid from home, to march against the Boeotians[1a] by way of Ozolian Locris[1b] to Cytinium in Doris,[1c] keeping Parnassus[1d] on his right until he descended to the Phocians,[1e] whom he could force to join him if their ancient friendship for Athens did not, as he anticipated, at once persuade them to do so. Once in Phocis he would be upon the frontier of Boeotia. Accordingly, he sailed from Leucas against the wish of the Acarnanians, and with his whole armament cruised along the coast to Sollium[1f] [2] where he communicated to them his intention. When they refused to agree to his plan because he would not build the wall against Leucas, Demosthenes sailed against the Aetolians with the rest of the forces: the Cephallenians, the Messenians, the Zacynthians, and the three hundred Athenian marines from his own ships (the fifteen Corcyraean vessels having departed). [3] He established his base at Oeneon[3a] in Locris, as the Ozolian Locrians were allies of Athens and were to meet him with all their forces in the interior. Being neighbors of the Aetolians and armed in the same way, it was thought that they would be of great service upon the expedition, from their acquaintance with the localities and the warfare of the inhabitants.

3.96
426
6th Year/Summer
AETOLIA
Demosthenes invades Aetolia.

After bivouacking with the army in the precinct of Nemean Zeus—in which the poet Hesiod is said to have been killed by the people of the country, according to an oracle which had foretold that he should die in Nemea,[1a] Demosthenes set out at daybreak to invade Aetolia. [2] The first day he took Potidania, the next Krokyle, and the third Tichium,[2a] where he halted and sent back the booty to Eupalium[2b] in Locris, having determined to pursue his conquests as far as the Ophionians, and in the event of their refusing to submit, to return to Naupactus and make them the objects of a second expedition. [3] However, the Aetolians had been aware of his design from the moment of its formation, and as soon as the army invaded their country, had come up in great force with all their tribes; even the most remote Ophionians, the Bomiensians, and the Calliensians, whose

3.94.5a The boundaries of the territories of these peoples are unclear, but the territory of the Apodotians bordered Ozolian Locris (Map 3.93, AX) to the east, and the Ophionions and Eurytanions each lived successively further north.
3.95.1a Boeotia: Map 3.98, BY.
3.95.1b Locris (Ozolian): Map 3.93, AX.
3.95.1c Cytinium in Doris: Map 3.98, AY.
3.95.1d Mount Parnassus: Map 3.98, AY.
3.95.1e Phocis: Map 3.98, AY.
3.95.1f Sollium: Map 3.93, AX.
3.95.3a Oeneon in Ozolian Locris: Map 3.98, AX.
3.96.1a This religious precinct of Nemean Zeus must have been in Ozolian Locris (Map 3.98, AY), whereas the famous sanctuary of Nemea was situated in the Peloponnesus between Argos and Corinth. See Map 5.58, AY.
3.96.2a The locations of Potidania, Krokyle, and Tichium, all small unwalled places, have not been established.
3.96.2b Eupalium: Map 3.98, AX.

terr e Malian gulf,[3a] being among the number.

3.97
426
6th Year/Summer
AETOLIA
The Aetolians counterattack at Aegitium.

g to their original advice, assured Demosthenes tha easy conquest. They urged him to push on as rap take the villages as fast as he came up to them, wit hole nation should be in arms against him. [2] Lec trusting in his fortune—as he had met with no opp aiting for his Locrian reinforcements who were to h he light-armed darters in which he was most de- ficie rmed Aegitium,[2a] whose inhabitants fled before him upon the hills above the city, which stood on hig iles from the sea. [3] Meanwhile the Aetolians had and now attacked the Athenians and their allies, run s on every side and darting their javelins, falling bac my advanced, and coming on as it retired; and for was of this character, alternate advance and re- trea ations the Athenians had the worst.

3.98
426
6th Year/Summer
AETOLIA
The Athenians are routed with heavy losses.

hers had arrows left and were able to use them, the ed Aetolians retiring before the arrows; but after the d been killed and his men scattered, the soldiers, wor nt repetition of the same exertions and hard pres ith their javelins, at last turned and fled, and falli and places that they were unacquainted with, thu n Chromon, their guide, having also unfortu- nate eat many were overtaken in the pursuit by the swif d Aetolians, and fell beneath their javelins; the gre ssed their road and rushed into the wood, which had was soon ignited and burnt round them by the ene enian army fell victims to death in every form, and les of flight; the survivors escaped with difficulty to t ocris, whence they had set out. [4] Many of the allie one hundred and twenty Athenian hoplites, not a m ne of life. These were by far the best men in the city g this war. Among the slain was also Procles, the coll 5] Meanwhile the Athenians took up their dead und ians, and retired to Naupactus, and from thence wen ; Demosthenes staying behind in Naupactus and in t afraid to face the Athenians after the disaster.

3.96.
3.97. Map 3.98,

3.98. Aetolians
or the re-
granted ac-
plite battle;
, §6.

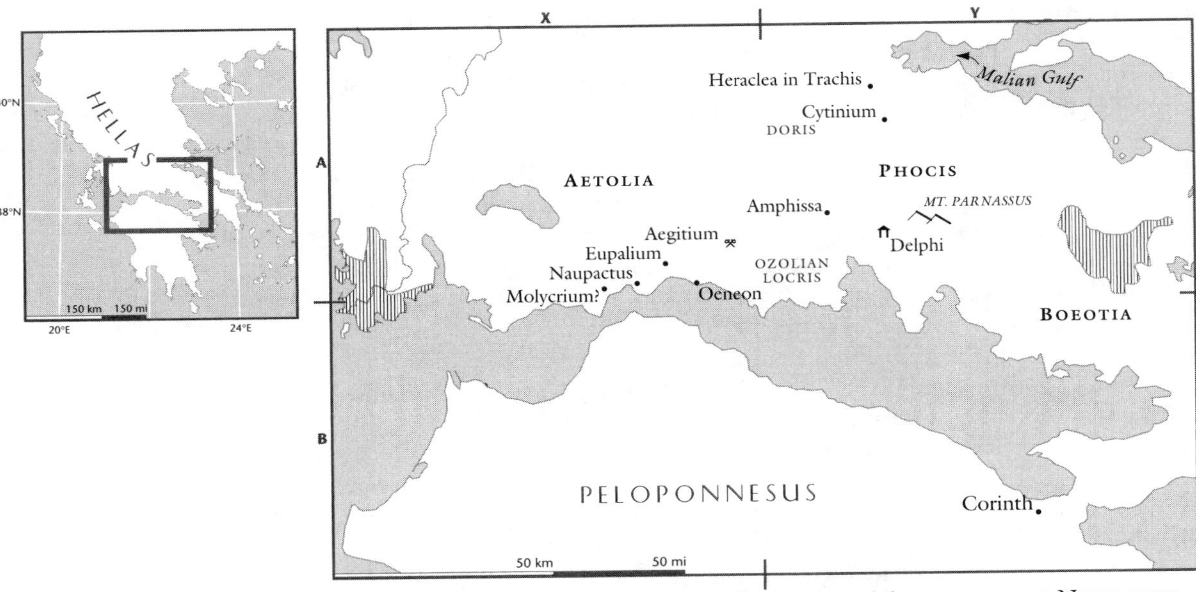

MAP 3.98 DEMOSTHENES IN AETOLIA; EURYLOCHUS' ATTACK AGAINST NAUPACTUS

3.99
SICILY
The Athenians attack Locris.

About the same time the Athenians on the coast of Sicily sailed to Locris, and in a descent which they made from the ships defeated the Locrians who came against them, and took a fort upon the river Halex.[1a]

3.100
426
6th Year/Summer
SPARTA
The Aetolians persuade the Spartans to attack Naupactus.

The same summer the Aetolians, who before the Athenian expedition had sent an embassy to Corinth and Sparta, composed of Tolophus, an Ophionian, Boriades, an Eurytanian, and Tisander, an Apodotian, persuaded them that an army should be sent to join them in an attack on Naupactus,[1a] which had prompted the Athenian invasion. [2] Accordingly, toward autumn, the Spartans sent out, under the command of the *Spartiates*[2a] Eurylochos, Macarius, and Menedaius, a force of three thousand hoplites of the allies, five hundred of whom came from the recently founded city of Heraclea[2b] in Trachis.

3.101
426
6th Year/Summer
DELPHI
The Spartan general Eurylochus prepares to attack Naupactus.

The army having assembled at Delphi,[1a] Eurylochus sent a herald to the Ozolian Locrians,[1b] as the road to Naupactus ran through their territory, and he had also conceived the idea of detaching them from Athens. [2] His chief abettors in Locris were the Amphissians,[2a] who were alarmed at the hostility of the Phocians.[2b] These first gave hostages themselves, and induced the rest to do the same for fear of the invading army; first, their

3.99.1a This chapter continues the Sicilian narrative from 3.90; it will be continued further at 3.103. The location of the fort on the river Halex is unknown (it is probably the same as the one mentioned in 3.116). For the Halex river and (Epizephyrian) Locri in Italy, see Map 3.86 or Map 3.115.
3.100.1a Naupactus: Map 3.98, AX.
3.100.2a A *Spartiate* is a full citizen of Sparta and a member of the highest Spartan military caste.
3.100.2b Heraclea in Trachis: Map 3.98, AY. The city's foundation is described in 3.92. It next appears in the narrative in 4.78.
3.101.1a Delphi: Map 3.98, AY.
3.101.1b Locris (Ozolian): Map 3.98, AY.
3.101.2a Amphissa: Map 3.98, AY.
3.101.2b Phocis: Map 3.98, AY.

neig[illegible]ho held the most difficult of the passes, and after[illegible]essapians, Tritaeans, Chalaeans, Tolophonians, Hes[illegible]all of whom joined in the expedition; the Olpaea[illegible]es with giving hostages, without accompanying the [illegible]ns[2c] refusing to do either, until the capture of Poli[illegible]

3.102
426
6th Year/Summer
NAUPACTUS
Eurylochus' attack on Naupactus is thwarted by the arrival of Acarnanian hoplites.

H[illegible]ted, Eurylochus lodged the hostages in Cytiniu[illegible]anced upon Naupactus through the country of the [illegible]his way Oeneon and Eupalium,[1b] two of their citie[illegible]m. [2] Having arrived in the Naupactian territory[illegible] joined by the Aetolians,[2a] the army laid waste the [illegible]rb of the city, which was unfortified; and after this [illegible]inthian colony subject to Athens.

[[illegible]ian Demosthenes, who since the affair in Aetolia h[illegible]actus, having had intelligence of the army's approa[illegible] city, went and persuaded the Acarnanians,[3a] altho[illegible]ulty because of his departure from Leucas,[3b] to go t[illegible]s. [4] They accordingly sent with him on board his [illegible]es, who threw themselves into the place and save[illegible]ll and the small number of its defenders otherwise[illegible]t danger.

[[illegible]us and his companions, finding that this force had [illegible] impossible to storm the city, withdrew, not to the [illegible] country once called Aeolis and now Calydon[5a] and [illegible]laces in that neighborhood and Proschium[5c] in Aeto[illegible]nbraciots[6a] had come and urged them to combine[illegible]g Amphilochian Argos[6b] and the rest of Amphilo[illegible]ffirming that the conquest of these countries wou[illegible]nt into alliance with Sparta. [7] To this Euryloch[illegible]issing the Aetolians, now remained quiet with his a[illegible]il the time should come for the Ambraciots to take[illegible] join them before Argos.[7a]

3.103
426/5
6th Year/Winter
SICILY
The Athenians attack Inessa and Locri.

S[illegible]The winter ensuing, the Athenians in Sicily with their[illegible]ch of the Sicel subjects or allies of Syracuse as had [illegible]oined their army, marched against the Sicel city

3.101[illegible]itaeans, [illegible]sians, [illegible]eans are [illegible]but the last [illegible]of their lo[illegible]rding to [illegible]*ntary on* [illegible]515.

3.102[illegible]AY.

3.102[illegible], AX.

3.102[illegible]

3.102[illegible]Map 3.98, [illegible]

3.102[illegible]his briefly picks up the Acarnanian narrative from 3.94; it will be continued next in 3.105.

3.102.3b For Demosthenes' departure from Leucas (Map 3.106, AX), see 3.94–95.

3.102.5a Calydon: Map 3.106, BY.

3.102.5b Pleuron: Map 3.106, BY.

3.102.5c Proschium: Map 3.106, BY.

3.102.6a Ambracia: Map 3.106, AX.

3.102.6b Amphilochia: Map 3.106, AY, and inset; Amphilochian Argos, possible location: Map 3.106, inset.

3.102.7a The narrative of events in the west of Hellas is continued at 3.105.

Inessa,[1a] the Acropolis of which was held by the Syracusans,[1b] and after attacking it without being able to take it, retired. [2] In the retreat, the allies marching behind the Athenians were attacked by the Syracusans from the fort, and a large part of their army was routed with great slaughter. [3] After this, Laches and the Athenians from the ships made some descents in Locri[3a] and, defeating the Locrians who came against them with Proxenus son of Capaton, upon the river Caicinus, took some arms and departed.[3b]

3.104
426/5
6th Year/Winter
DELOS
The Athenians purify Delos and celebrate the first Delian Games.

The same winter the Athenians purified Delos[1a] in compliance, it appears, with a certain oracle. It had been purified before by Pisistratus the tyrant; not indeed the whole island, but as much of it as could be seen from the temple. All of it was, however, now purified in the following way. [2] All the remains of those that had died in Delos were removed, and for the future it was commanded that no one should be allowed either to die or to give birth to a child in the island; but that they should be carried over to Rhenea,[2a] which is so near to Delos that Polycrates, tyrant of Samos, having added Rhenea to his other island conquests during his period of naval ascendancy, dedicated it to the Delian Apollo by binding it to Delos with a chain.

After the purification, the Athenians celebrated, for the first time, the quinquennial festival of the Delian games.[2b] [3] Once upon a time, indeed, there was a great assemblage of the Ionians and the neighboring islanders at Delos, who used to come to the festival, as the Ionians now do to that of Ephesus,[3a] and athletic and poetical contests took place there, and the cities brought choirs of dancers. [4] Nothing can be clearer on this point than the following verses of Homer, taken from a hymn to Apollo:—

Phoebus, where'er thou strayest, far or near,
Delos was still of all thy haunts most dear.
Thither the robed Ionians take their way
With wife and child to keep thy holiday,
Invoke thy favor on each manly game,
And dance and sing in honor of thy name.

[5] That there was also a poetical contest in which the Ionians went to contend is shown again by the following, taken from the same hymn. After celebrating the Delian dance of the women, he ends his song of praise with these verses, in which he also alludes to himself:—

3.103.1a Inessa: Map 3.115. This follows the last narrative concerning Sicily at 3.99.
3.103.1b Syracuse: Map 3.115.
3.103.3a Locri (Epizephyrian, in Italy): Map 3.115.
3.103.3b Caicinus river, probable course: Map 3.115. Events in Sicily are picked up again in 3.115.
3.104.1a Delos: Map 3.93, BY. This purification, and the Carian artifacts discovered when the graves were dug up, is mentioned in 1.8. Further purification steps are described in 5.1.
3.104.2a Rhenea: Map 3.93, BY.
3.104.2b See Appendix I, Classical Greek Religious Festivals, §5 and 8. These festivals often included athletic and cultural contests like those held every five years at Delos.
3.104.3a Ephesus: Map 4.44, AY.

[illegible] llo keep you all! and so,
[illegible] oodbye—yet tell me not I go
[illegible] hearts; and if in after hours
[illegible] anderer in this world of ours
[illegible] shores, and ask your maidens here
[illegible] songs the sweetest to your ear,
[illegible] hen, and answer with a smile,
[illegible] an of Scio's rocky isle.

[[illegible] that there was a great assembly and festival at Del[illegible] ter, although the islanders and the Athenians con[illegible] irs of dancers with sacrifices, the contests and mos[illegible] re abolished, probably through adversity, until the [illegible] e games upon this occasion with the novelty of hor[illegible]

3.105 426/5 6th Year/Winter AMPHILOCHIA Ambracia attacks Amphilochia; allies of both sides march to help.

[illegible] Ambraciots, as they had promised Eurylochus whe[illegible] y,[1a] marched out against Amphilochian Argos[1b] with [illegible] es, and invading the Argive territory occupied Olp[illegible] hill near the sea, which had been formerly fortified [illegible] nd used as the court of justice for their nation, and [illegible] miles and three-quarters from the city of Argos upo[illegible] nwhile the Acarnanians went with a part of their forc[illegible], and with the rest encamped in Amphilochia[2a] at t[illegible] or the Wells, to watch for Eurylochus and his Pel[illegible] vent their passing through and joining up with the [illegible] also sent for Demosthenes, the commander of the [illegible] o be their leader, and for the twenty Athenian ship[illegible] the Peloponnesus under the command of Aristotl[illegible] d Hierophon son of Antimnestus. [4] For their part [illegible] ae sent a messenger to their own city[4a] to beg ther[illegible] whole levy to their assistance, fearing that the arm[illegible] not be able to pass through the Acarnanians, and [illegible] lves be obliged to fight on their own, or be unable [illegible] d, without danger.

3.106 426/5 6th Year/Winter AMPHILOCHIA Eurylochus joins the Ambraciots at Olpae.

[illegible] nd his Peloponnesians, learning that the Ambraciot[illegible] set out from Proschium[1a] with all haste to join ther[illegible] elous[1b] advanced through Acarnania (which they

3.105[illegible] hat ended at [illegible]
3.105[illegible] location: [illegible]
3.105[illegible] 3.106, [illegible]
3.105[illegible]
3.105[illegible] and inset.
3.105[illegible] 3.106, [illegible]
3.105.3a For Demosthenes' Aetolian expedition, see 3.95–98.
3.105.4a Ambracia: Map 3.106, AX.
3.106.1a Proschium: Map 3.106, BY.
3.106.1b Achelous river: Map 3.106, BY.

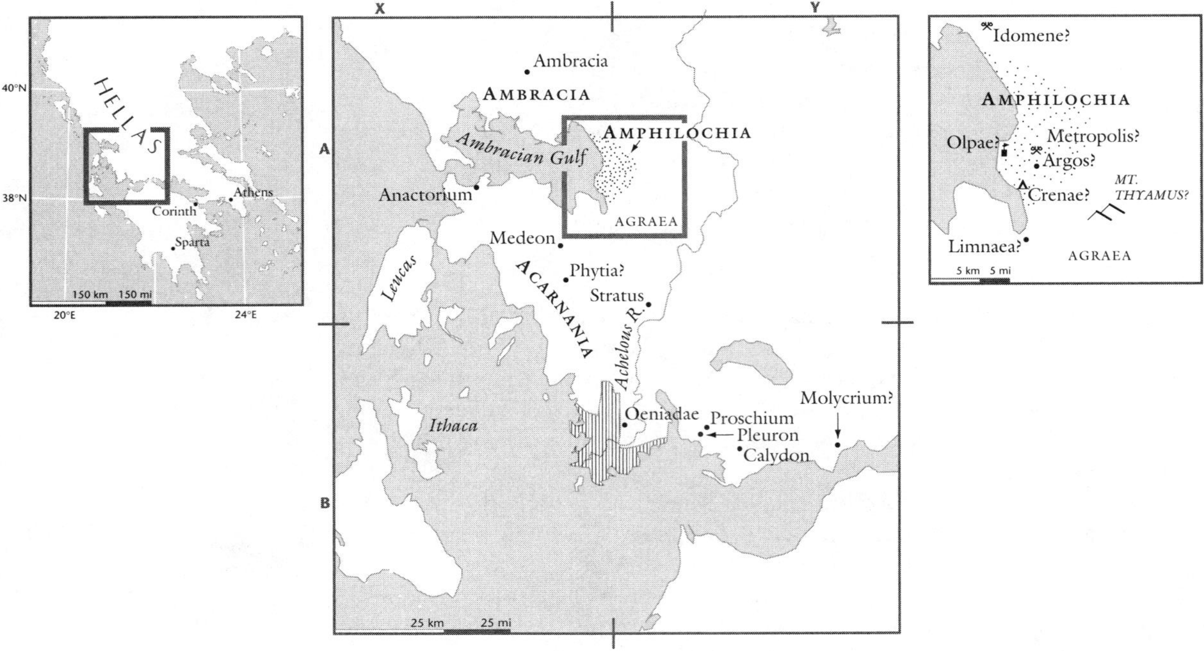

MAP 3.106 EURYLOCHUS' AND DEMOSTHENES' CAMPAIGN IN AMPHILOCHIA[1c]

found deserted by its population, who had gone to the relief of Amphilochian Argos);[1c] keeping on their right the city of Stratus[1d] and its garrison, and on their left the rest of Acarnania. [2] Traversing the territory of the Stratians, they advanced through Phytia, next, skirting Medeon, through Limnaea:[2a] after which they left Acarnania behind them and entered a friendly country, that of the Agraeans.[2b] [3] From thence they reached and crossed Mount Thyamus,[3a] which belongs to the Agraeans, and descended into the Argive territory after nightfall, and passing between the city of Argos and the Acarnanian posts at Crenae, joined the Ambraciots at Olpae.

3.107
426/5
6th Year/Winter
AMPHILOCHIA
Demosthenes plans an ambush.

Uniting here at daybreak, they halted at the place called Metropolis,[1a] and encamped. Not long afterwards the Athenians in the twenty ships came into the Ambracian gulf[1b] to support the Argives, with Demosthenes and two hundred Messenian hoplites, and sixty Athenian archers. [2] While the

3.106.1c The source of the possible sites of Amphilochian Argos, Limnaea, Crenae, Olpae, Metropolis, and Idomene is N.G.L. Hammond, "The Campaign in Amphilochia during the Archidamian War," *The Annual of the British School at Athens,* 1937, 128–40.
3.106.1d Stratus: Map 3.106, AX.
3.106.2a Phytia, Medeon, and Limnaea cannot be definitely located; possible sites for them are shown on Map 3.106, AX, and inset.
3.106.2b Agraea: Map 3.106, AY, and inset.
3.106.3a Mount Thyamus: Map 3.106, inset.
3.107.1a "Metropolis," possible location: Map 3.106, inset.
3.107.1b Ambracian gulf: Map 3.106, AX.

flee[illegible]ne hill from the sea, the Acarnanians and a few of t[illegible]nost of them were perforce detained by the Ambrac[illegible]d at Argos, and were preparing to give battle to the [illegible]Demosthenes to command the whole of the allied [illegible]their own generals. [3] Demosthenes led them near [illegible]ped, a great ravine separating the two armies. Dur[illegible]ned inactive; on the sixth both sides formed in ord[illegible]of the Peloponnesians was the largest and outflan[illegible]d Demosthenes, fearing that his right might be surr[illegible]ur hundred hoplites and light troops in ambush in a [illegible] with bushes. These were to rise up at the onset of b[illegible]ing left wing of the enemy, and to take them in the [illegible]les were ready they joined battle; Demosthenes bei[illegible]ith the Messenians and a few Athenians, while the [illegible]le up of the different divisions of the Acarnanians, [illegible]an dart throwers. The Peloponnesians and Ambra[illegible]xed together, except for the Mantineans, who wer[illegible]thout however reaching to the extremity of the win[illegible]nd his men confronted the Messenians and De[illegible]

[illegible]e now well engaged and with their outflanking win[illegible]of turning their enemy's right when the Acarnania[illegible]set upon them from behind, and broke them at the [illegible]ir staying to resist; while the panic into which they[illegible] most of their army, terrified beyond measure at seei[illegible]ochus and their best troops cut to pieces. Most of t[illegible] Demosthenes and his Messenians, who were pos[illegible]ld. [2] Meanwhile the Ambraciots (who are the bes[illegible], and the troops upon the right wing, defeated the [illegible]m and pursued it to Argos. [3] Returning from the [illegible]ir main body defeated and hard pressed by the Aca[illegible]od their passage to Olpae with difficulty, suffering [illegible] as they dashed on without discipline or order, exc[illegible], who kept their ranks better than any in the arm[illegible]e battle did not end until the evening.

3.108
426/5
6th Year/Winter
AMPHILOCHIA
The Peloponnesians and Ambraciots are defeated.

[illegible], who on the death of Eurylochus and Macarius had [illegible]command, being at a loss after so severe a defeat hov[illegible]ege, cut off as he was by land and by the Athenian [illegible] unable to retreat in safety, opened a parley with De[illegible]nanian generals for a truce and permission to re-

3.109
426/5
6th Year/Winter
AMPHILOCHIA
The Peloponnesians secretly request and receive permission to withdraw.

treat, and at the same time for the recovery of the dead. [2] The dead they gave back to him, and setting up a trophy[2a] took up their own also to the number of about three hundred. The requested retreat they refused publicly to the army; but permission to depart without delay was secretly granted to the Mantineans and to Menedaïus and the other commanders and principal men of the Peloponnesians by Demosthenes and his Acarnanian colleagues. They desired thus to strip the Ambraciots and their foreign mercenaries of their Peloponnesian supporters; and, above all, to discredit the Spartans and Peloponnesians with the Hellenes in those parts, as traitors and self-seekers. [3] While the enemy was taking up his dead and hastily burying them as he could, [and] those who obtained permission were secretly planning their retreat, [3.110.1] word was brought to Demosthenes and the Acarnanians that the Ambraciots from the city, in compliance with the first message from Olpae,[1a] were on the march with their whole levy through Amphilochia to join their countrymen at Olpae, knowing nothing of what had occurred. [2] Demosthenes prepared to march with his army against them, and meanwhile sent on at once a strong division to set ambushes on the roads and occupy the strong positions.

3.110
426/5
6th Year/Winter
AMPHILOCHIA
Demosthenes learns of the approach of another Ambraciot army.

3.111
426/5
6th Year/Winter
AMPHILOCHIA
The Peloponnesians attempt to leave their Ambraciot allies and escape.

In the meantime the Mantineans and others included in the agreement went out under the pretense of gathering herbs and firewood, and stole off by twos and threes, picking on the way the things which they professed to have come out for, until they had gone some distance from Olpae, when they quickened their pace. [2] The Ambraciots and such of the rest as had accompanied them in larger parties, seeing them going on, pushed on in their turn, and began running in order to catch up to them. [3] The Acarnanians at first thought that all alike were departing without permission, and began to pursue the Peloponnesians; and believing that they were being betrayed, even threw a dart or two at some of their own generals who tried to stop them and told them that leave had been given. Eventually, however, they let pass the Mantineans and Peloponnesians, and slew only the Ambraciots, [4] there being much dispute and difficulty in distinguishing whether a man was an Ambraciot or a Peloponnesian. The number thus slain was about two hundred; the rest escaped into the bordering territory of Agraea,[4a] and found refuge with Salynthius, the friendly king of the Agraeans.

3.112
426/5
6th Year/Winter
AMPHILOCHIA
Demosthenes routs the Ambraciot reinforcements in a dawn attack.

Meanwhile the Ambraciots from the city arrived at Idomene.[1a] Idomene consists of two lofty hills, the highest of which the troops sent on by Demosthenes succeeded in occupying after nightfall, unobserved by the Ambraciots, who had previously ascended the smaller and bivouacked upon it. [2] After supper Demosthenes set out with the rest of the army, as soon as it was evening; himself with half his force making for the pass, and the remainder going by the Amphilochian hills. [3] At dawn he fell upon the

3.109.2a Truce, return of the dead, and trophy, all according to the ritual of hoplite warfare; see Appendix F, Land Warfare, §6.

3.110.1a The message referred to can be found in 3.105.4.

3.111.4a Agraea: Map 3.106, AX, and inset.

3.112.1a Idomene, possible location: Map 3.106, inset.

Aml[illegible] still abed, ignorant of what had passed, and
fully [illegible]ir own countrymen—[4] Demosthenes having
purp[illegible]ns[4a] in front with orders to address them in the
Dor[illegible]inspire confidence in the sentinels who would
not [illegible]t was still night. [5] In this way he routed their
arm[illegible] it, slaying most of them where they were, the
rest [illegible]over the hills, [6] hindered by the fact that they
wor[illegible] light-armed foe. The roads, however, were al-
read[illegible]he Amphilochians knew their own country, the
Aml[illegible]f it and could not tell which way to turn, and
so fe[illegible]he ambushes which had been set for them, and
peris[illegible]manifold efforts to escape some even turned to
the s[illegible]f, and seeing the Athenian ships coasting along
shor[illegible]as going on, swam off to them, thinking it better i[illegible], to perish, if perish they must, by the hands of
the [illegible] of the barbarous and detested Amphilochians.
[8] [illegible] force destroyed in this manner, only a few
reacl[illegible]hile the Acarnanians, after stripping the dead
and [illegible]rned to Argos.

3.113
426/5
6th Year/Winter
AMPHILOCHIA
Thucydides offers the anecdote of the Ambraciot herald.

T[illegible]rived from the Ambraciots who had fled from
Olp[illegible]k leave to take up the dead that had fallen after
the [illegible] they left the camp with the Mantineans and
their [illegible]ike them, having had permission to do so. [2]
At tl[illegible]he Ambraciots from the city, the herald was as-
tonis[illegible]nowing nothing of the disaster and fancying
that [illegible]r own party. [3] Someone asked him what he
was [illegible]ow many of them had been killed, fancying in
his t[illegible]rald from the troops at Idomene. He replied,
"Ab[illegible]n which his interrogator took him up, saying,
[4] "[illegible]here are of more than a thousand." The herald
repli[illegible] the arms of those who fought with us?" The
othe[illegible]are, if at least you fought at Idomene yesterday."[illegible]o one yesterday; but the day before in the retreat[illegible]e, we fought yesterday with those who came
to re[illegible]ity of the Ambraciots." [5] When the herald
hear[illegible]e reinforcement from the city had been destroy[illegible]g, and stunned at the magnitude of the present
evils, [illegible]out having performed his errand, or again asking f[illegible]] Indeed, this was by far the greatest disaster
that [illegible] city in an equal number of days during this
war; [illegible] the number of the dead, because the amount
state[illegible]tion to the size of the city as to be incredible.

3.112.4[illegible]tled now [illegible], were [illegible]elopon- [illegible] the con- [illegible]k. See Appendix H, Ancient Greek Dialects and Ethnic Groups, §9.

3.113.5a The herald's errand: see Appendix F, Land Warfare, §6.

In any case I know that if the Acarnanians and Amphilochians had wished to take Ambracia as the Athenians and Demosthenes advised, they would have done so without striking a blow; as it was, they feared that if the Athenians had it they would be worse neighbors to them than the present.

3.114
426/5
6th Year/Winter
AMPHILOCHIA
Demosthenes returns to Athens. The Amphilochians and Ambraciots make peace.

After this the Acarnanians allotted a third of the spoils to the Athenians, and divided the rest among their own different cities. The share of the Athenians was captured on the voyage home; the arms now deposited in the Attic temples are three hundred panoplies, which the Acarnanians set apart for Demosthenes, and which he brought to Athens in person, his return to his country after the Aetolian disaster being rendered less hazardous by this exploit. [2] The Athenians in the twenty ships also went off to Naupactus. The Acarnanians and Amphilochians, after the departure of Demosthenes and the Athenians, granted the Ambraciots and Peloponnesians who had taken refuge with Salynthius and the Agraeans a free retreat from Oeniadae,[2a] to which place they had removed from the country of Salynthius, [3] and for the future concluded with the Ambraciots a treaty and alliance for one hundred years, upon the terms following. It was to be a defensive, not an offensive, alliance; the Ambraciots could not be required to march with the Acarnanians against the Peloponnesians, nor the Acarnanians with the Ambraciots against the Athenians; for the rest the Ambraciots were to give up the places and hostages that they held of the Amphilochians, and not to give help to Anactorium,[3a] which was at enmity with the Acarnanians. [4] With this arrangement they put an end to the war. After this the Corinthians sent a garrison of their own citizens to Ambracia, composed of three hundred hoplites, under the command of Xenocleides son of Euthycles, who reached their destination after a difficult journey across the continent. Such was the history of the affair of Ambracia.

3.115
426/5
6th Year/Winter
SICILY
The Athenians send reinforcements to Sicily.

The same winter the Athenians in Sicily[1a] made a descent from their ships upon the territory of Himera,[1b] in concert with the Sicels, who had invaded its borders from the interior, and also sailed to the islands of Aeolus.[1c] [2] Upon their return to Rhegium they found the Athenian general, Pythodorus son of Isolochus, come to supersede Laches in the command of the fleet. [3] The allies in Sicily had sailed to Athens and induced the Athenians to send out more vessels to their assistance, pointing out that the Syracusans who already commanded their land were making efforts to get together a navy, to avoid being any longer excluded from the sea by a few vessels. [4] The Athenians proceeded to man forty ships to send to them, thinking that the war in Sicily would thus be the sooner ended, and also

3.114.2a Oeniadae: Map 3.106, BX.
3.114.3a Anactorium: Map 3.106, AX.
3.115.1a This picks up the Sicilian narrative from 3.103.
3.115.1b Himera: Map 3.115.
3.115.1c Aeolian (Lipari) islands: Map 3.115.

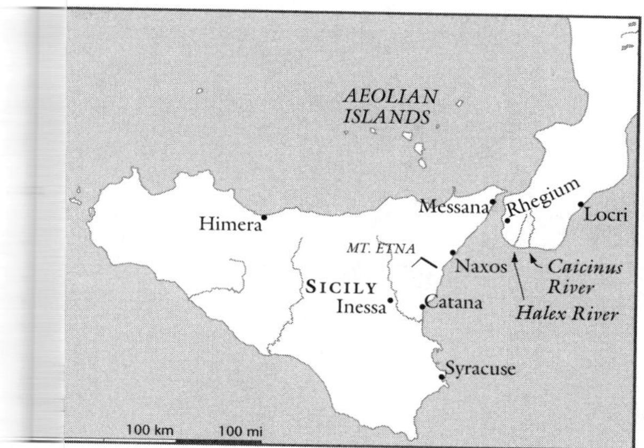

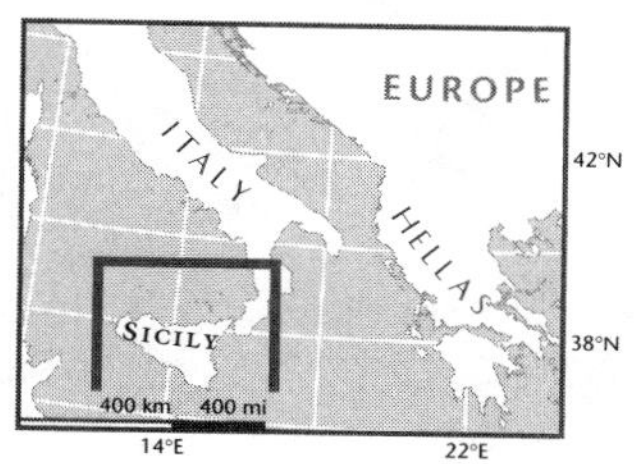

MAP [illegible]
SICI[illegible]
426/[illegible]

wish[illegible]vy.[4a] [5] One of the generals, Pythodorus, was acco[illegible] few ships; Sophocles son of Sostratides, and Eur[illegible] being destined to follow with the main body. [6] [illegible] had taken the command of Laches' ships, and tow[illegible]led against the Locrian fort, which Laches had form[illegible]ned after being defeated in battle by the Loc[illegible]

3.116
426/5
6th Year/Winter
SICILY
Mount Etna erupts.

I[illegible]pring, the stream of fire issued from Etna,[1a] as on f[illegible]stroyed some land of the Catanians,[1b] who live upo[illegible] the largest mountain in Sicily. [2] Fifty years, it is sa[illegible]e last eruption, there having been three in all sinc[illegible]abited Sicily. [3] Such were the events of this wint[illegible]e sixth year of this war, of which Thucydides was [illegible]

3.115.[illegible] contin-[illegible]

3.115.[illegible]own. It [illegible]ver Halex, [illegible] undoubtedly retaken by the Locrians. Locri (Epizephyrian): Map 3.115.

3.116.1a Mount Etna: Map 3.115.

3.116.1b Catana: Map 3.115.

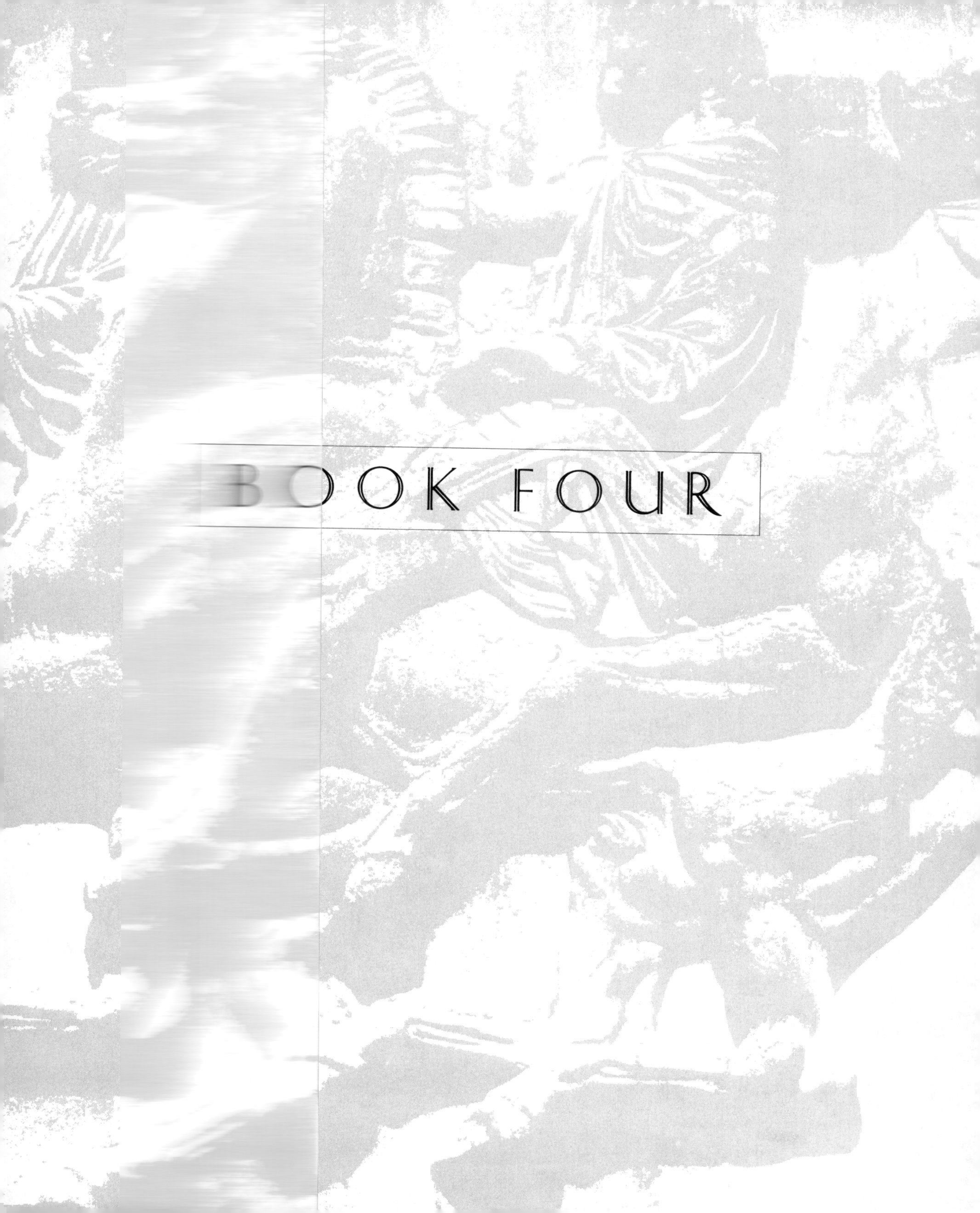

BOOK FOUR

Next summer, about the time of the
grai[illegible] Syracusan[1a] and as many Locrian[1b] vessels sailed
to M[illegible] occupied the city upon the invitation of the
inha[illegible] volted from the Athenians. [2] The Syracusans
cont[illegible] e they saw that the place afforded an approach
to S[illegible] Athenians might hereafter use it as a base for
atta[illegible] r force; the Locrians because they wished to
carr[illegible] h sides of the Strait[2a] and to reduce their ene-
mie[illegible] m.[2b] [3] Meanwhile, the Locrians had invaded
the [illegible] all their forces, to prevent their assisting Messana [illegible] t of some exiles from Rhegium who were with
ther[illegible] standing factions by which that city had been
torn [illegible] nent incapable of resistance, and thus furnished
an a[illegible] the invaders. [4] After devastating the country
the [illegible] red, their ships remaining to guard Messana,
whil[illegible] nned for the same destination to carry on the
war [illegible]

4.1
425
7th Year/Summer
SICILY
Messana invites occupation by Syracuse and Locris, and revolts from Athens.

A[illegible] the spring, before the corn was ripe, the Pelo-
pon[illegible] invaded Attica under Agis son of Archidamus,
king [illegible] stablished themselves there and laid waste the
cour[illegible] e Athenians sent off to Sicily the forty ships
whic[illegible] ring, with the remaining generals Eurymedon
and [illegible] olleague Pythodorus having already preceded
ther[illegible] instructions as they sailed by to assist the Corcyra[illegible] ere being plundered by the exiles in the mountain[illegible] xiles sixty Peloponnesian vessels had recently

4.2
425
7th Year/Summer
PELOPONNESUS
The Peloponnesians invade Attica again. An Athenian fleet leaves the Piraeus for Sicily.

4.1.1a [illegible]
4.1.1b [illegible] Map [illegible]
4.1.1c [illegible]
4.1.2a [illegible] the Strait [illegible] on the toe [illegible] near the [illegible] ap 3.115.
4.1.2b [illegible]
4.1.4a The narrative of Sicilian events will be continued in 4.24.
4.2.3a These preparations were mentioned in 3.115.
4.2.3b Corcyra: Map 4.5, AX.
4.2.3c Mount Istone: Map 4.5, AX. These oligarchic partisans were last mentioned in 3.85.

sailed, it being thought that the famine raging in the city would make it easy for them to reduce it. [4] Demosthenes also, who had remained without employment since his return from Acarnania,[4a] applied for and obtained permission to use the fleet, if he wished, upon the coast of the Peloponnesus.

4.3
425
7th year/Summer
PYLOS
A storm forces the Athenian fleet to put into Pylos. Demosthenes wants to fortify the place but the generals refuse.

Off Laconia they heard that the Peloponnesian ships were already at Corcyra, upon which Eurymedon and Sophocles wished to hasten to the island, but Demosthenes required them first to touch at Pylos and do what was wanted there, before continuing their voyage. While they were making objections, a squall chanced to come on and carried the fleet into Pylos.[1a] [2] Demosthenes at once urged them to fortify the place, as this was the reason why he had come on the voyage. He made them observe that there was plenty of stone and timber on the spot and that the place was strong by nature, and together with much of the country round unoccupied; Pylos, or Coryphasium, as the Spartans call it, lies about forty-five miles distant from Sparta in the former country of the Messenians. [3] The commanders told him that there was no lack of desert headlands in the Peloponnesus if he wished to put the city to expense by occupying them. He, however, thought that this place was distinguished from others of the kind by having a harbor close by; while the Messenians, the old natives of the country, speaking the same dialect as the Spartans,[3a] could do them the greatest harm by their incursions from it, and would at the same time be a trusty garrison.

4.4
425
7th year/Summer
PYLOS
The bored Athenian soldiers suddenly and impulsively decide to build a fort.

After speaking to the captains of companies on the subject, and failing to persuade either the generals or the soldiers, he remained inactive with the rest from stress of weather; until the soldiers themselves wanting occupation were seized with a sudden impulse to go round and fortify the place. [2] Accordingly they set to work in earnest, and having no iron tools,[2a] picked up stones, and put them together as they happened to fit, and where mortar was needed, carried it on their backs for want of hods, stooping down to make it stay on, and clasping their hands together behind to prevent it falling off; [3] sparing no effort to complete the most vulnerable points before the arrival of the Spartans, most of the place being sufficiently strong by nature without further fortification.

4.5
425
7th year/Summer
SPARTA
The Spartans make light of the news about Pylos and permit the Athenians to complete their fort.

Meanwhile the Spartans were celebrating a festival, and also at first made light of the news, thinking that whenever they chose to take the field the place would be immediately evacuated by the enemy or easily taken by force. The absence of their army before Athens also had something to do with their delay. [2] The Athenians fortified the place on the land side and where it most required it in six days, and leaving Demosthenes with five

4.2.4a Acarnania: Map 4.5, BX.
4.3.1a Pylos: Map 4.5, BX.
4.3.3a Originally Messenians, but now settled in Naupactus. For the Spartan (Dorian) dialect, see Appendix H, Dialects and Ethnic Groups, §7–9.
4.4.2a Literally, having no masonry tools (*lithourga*) for cutting and shaping stone.

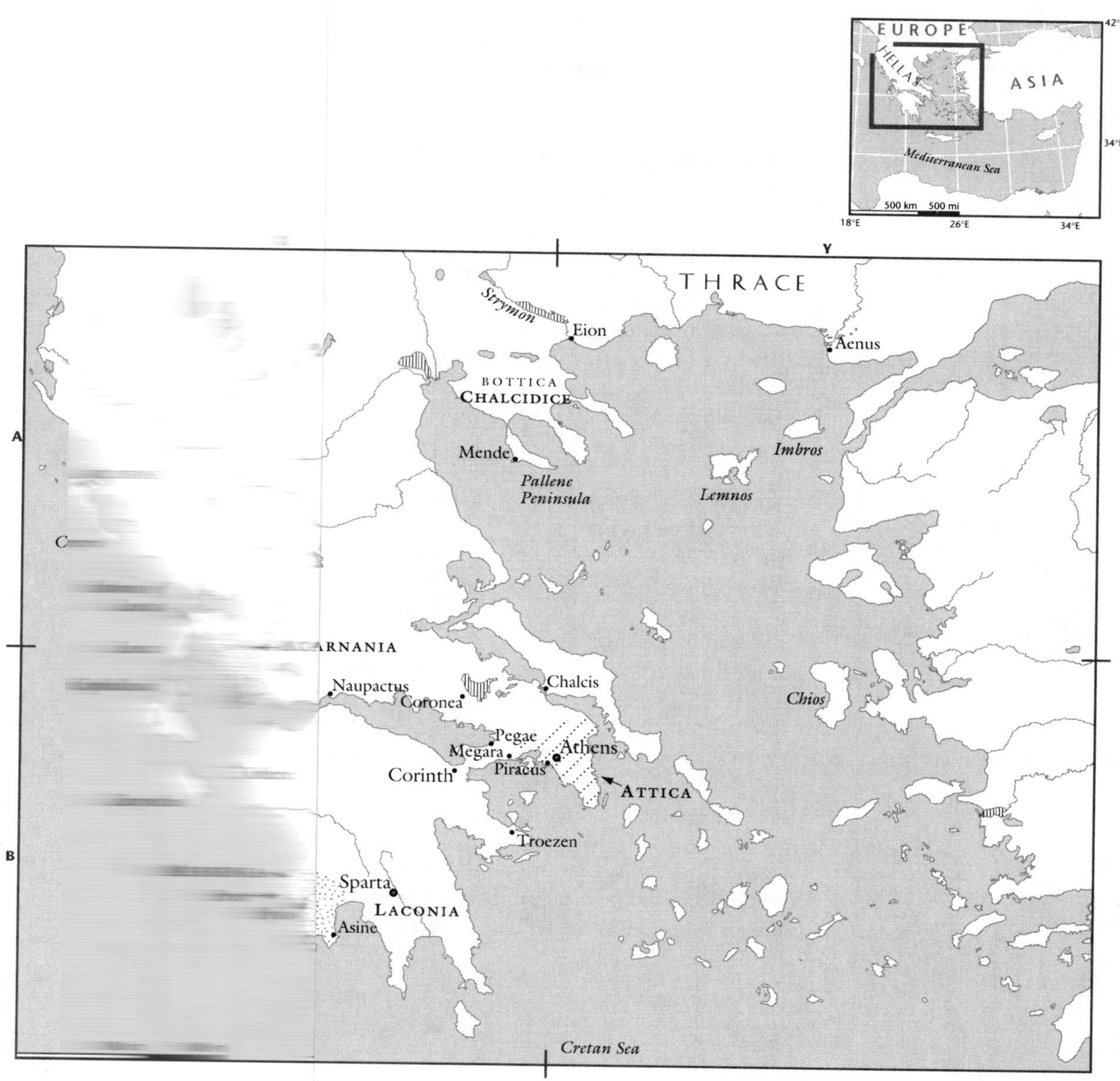

MA[illegible] PYLOS CAMPAIGN

ships to garrison it, hastened with the main body of the fleet on their voyage to Corcyra and Sicily.

4.6
425
7th year/Summer
ATTICA
But when Agis learns of the fort, he marches his army back to Sparta.

As soon as the Peloponnesians in Attica[1a] heard of the occupation of Pylos, they hurried back home, the Spartans and their king Agis thinking that the matter touched them nearly. Besides having made their invasion early in the season while the grain was still green, most of their troops were short of provisions: the weather also was unusually bad for the time of year, and greatly distressed their army. [2] Many reasons thus combined to hasten their departure and to make this invasion a very short one; indeed they stayed only fifteen days in Attica.

4.7
425
7th year/Summer
THRACE
The Athenians take but then fail to hold Mendaean Eion.

About the same time[1a] the Athenian general Simonides getting together a few Athenians from the garrisons, and a number of the allies in those parts, took by treachery the Mendaean[1b] colony of Eion[1c] in Thrace, which was hostile to Athens, but he had no sooner done so than the Chalcidians[1d] and Bottiaeans[1e] came up and beat him out of it, with the loss of many of his soldiers.[1f]

4.8
425
7th year/Summer
PYLOS
The Spartans concentrate land and sea forces to attack Pylos. Demosthenes sends for help from the Athenian fleet at Zacynthus. The Spartans plan to blockade Pylos and take it by siege. They occupy the island of Sphacteria.

On the return of the Peloponnesians from Attica the Spartans themselves and the nearest of the *perioikoi* at once set out for Pylos,[1a] the other Spartans following more slowly as they had just come in from another campaign. [2] Word was also sent round the Peloponnesus to come as quickly as possible to Pylos; while the sixty Peloponnesian ships were sent for from Corcyra,[2a] and being dragged by their crews across the isthmus of Leucas,[2b] passed unperceived by the Athenian squadron at Zacynthus,[2c] and reached Pylos, where the land forces had arrived before them. [3] Before the Peloponnesian fleet sailed in, Demosthenes found time to send out unobserved two ships to inform Eurymedon and the Athenians on board the fleet at Zacynthus of the danger to Pylos and to summon them to his assistance. [4] While the ships hastened on their voyage in obedience to the orders of Demosthenes, the Spartans prepared to assault the fort by land and sea, hoping to capture with ease a work constructed in haste, and held by a feeble garrison. [5] Meanwhile, as they expected the Athenian ships to arrive from Zacynthus, they intended, if they failed to take the place before, to block the entrances of the harbor to prevent their being able to anchor inside it. [6] For the island of Sphacteria[6a] stretches along in a line close in front of the harbor and at once makes it safe and narrows its entrances, leaving a passage for two ships on the side nearest

4.6.1a Attica: Map 4.5, BY.
4.7.1a This chapter deals with events in Thrace, which was last mentioned in 2.101.
4.7.1b Mende, on the Chalcidian peninsula of Pallene: Map 4.5, AX.
4.7.1c This Eion in Thrace, whose location is unknown, cannot be the more familiar Eion on the Strymon River (Map 4.5, AY), which had for some time now been subject to the Athenians.
4.7.1d Chalcidice: Map 4.5, AX.
4.7.1e Bottiaeans, living at that time in Bottica: Map 4.5, AX.
4.7.1f The narrative of events in Thrace is picked up again in 4.78.
4.8.1a Pylos: Map 4.5, BX. For information about the Spartan class of *perioikoi*, see the Glossary and Appendix C, Spartan Institutions, §9.
4.8.2a Corcyra: Map 4.5, AX.
4.8.2b Isthmus of Leucas: Map 4.5, AX.
4.8.2c Zacynthus: Map 4.5, BX.
4.8.6a Island of Sphacteria: Map 4.8.

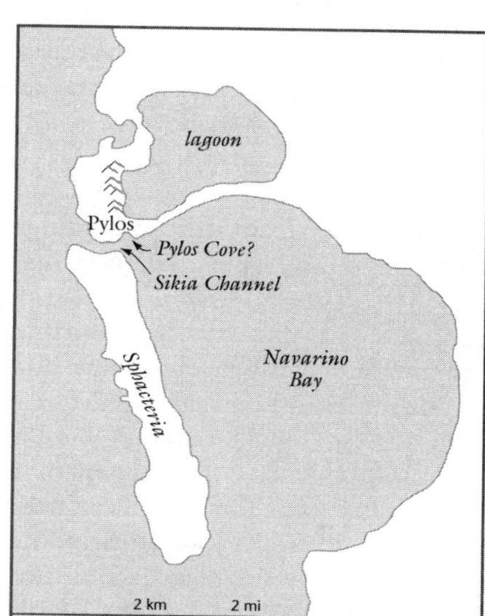

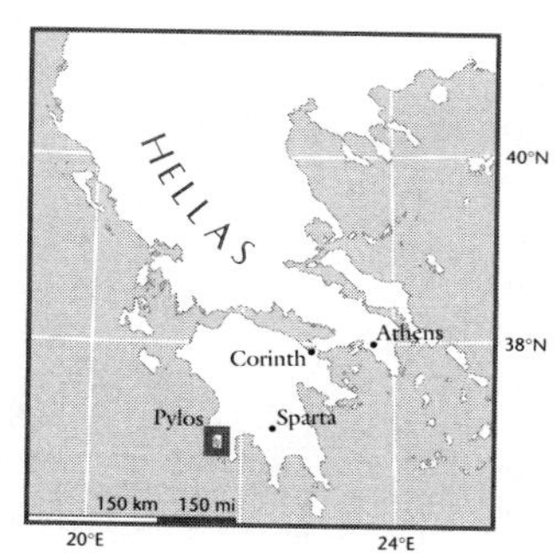

MA[illegible] FOR THE[illegible]

Pyl[illegible]rtifications, and for eight or nine ships on that ne[illegible] other side: for the rest, the island was entirely co[illegible]ithout paths through not being inhabited, and ab[illegible]ngth.[6b] [7] The Spartans meant to close the ent[illegible] ships placed close together with their prows tur[illegible] meanwhile, fearing that the enemy might make us[illegible] against them, carried over some *hoplites*[7a] to it, sta[illegible]e coast. [8] By this means both the island and the[illegible]stile to the Athenians, as they would be unable to [illegible]nce the shore of Pylos itself outside the inlet to[illegible] no harbor, there would be no point that the At[illegible] base from which to relieve their countrymen. Th[illegible] in all probability become masters of the place wi[illegible]k, as there had been little preparation for the

4.8.[illegible]es that [illegible] 15 *stades* (1.6 [illegible] closer to 24 [illegible]ttic stade was [illegible] 630.8 feet. [illegible]neasurements [illegible] rounded off [illegible]ley and to [illegible]

4.8[illegible]r a heavily [illegible]ssary and [illegible]

occupation and there was no food there.[8a] [9] This being decided, they carried the hoplites over to the island, drafting them by lot from all the companies. Some others had crossed over before in relief parties, but these last who were left there were four hundred and twenty in number, with their *Helot*[9a] attendants, and were commanded by Epitadas son of Molobrus.

4.9
425
7th year/Summer
PYLOS
Demosthenes, joined by some Messenians, prepares to defend Pylos and personally leads the defense against an anticipated Spartan amphibious attack.

Meanwhile Demosthenes, seeing that the Spartans were about to attack him by sea and land simultaneously, was himself not idle. He drew up under the fortification the *triremes*[1a] remaining to him of those which had been left him and enclosed them in a stockade, arming the sailors taken out of them with poor shields, most of them made of osier,[1b] it being impossible to procure arms in such a desert place. Indeed, even these were obtained from a thirty-oared Messenian privateer and a boat belonging to some Messenians who happened to have come to them. Among these Messenians were forty hoplites, whom he made use of with the rest. [2] Posting most of his men, unarmed and armed, upon the best fortified and strong points of the place facing the interior, with orders to repel any attack of the land forces, he picked sixty hoplites and a few archers from his whole force, and with these went outside the wall down to the sea, where he thought that the enemy would most likely attempt to land. Although the ground was difficult and rocky, looking toward the open sea, the fact that this was the weakest part of the wall would, he thought, encourage their ardor, [3] as the Athenians, confident in their naval superiority, had here paid little attention to their defenses, and the enemy, if he could force a landing, might feel sure of taking the place. [4] At this point, accordingly, going down to the water's edge, he posted his hoplites to prevent, if possible, a landing, and encouraged them in the following terms:

4.10
425
7th year/Summer
PYLOS
Demosthenes addresses his troops, advising them to offer firm resistance at the water's edge to repulse the enemy's amphibious assault.

"Soldiers and comrades in this adventure, I hope that none of you in our present strait will think to show his wit by exactly calculating

4.8.8a Thucydides' description of the Pylos campaign continues to be the subject of much debate; indeed, scholars have not yet reached a consensus even on such basic elements as the location of the harbor at the site. Most have identified Thucydides' harbor as the entire Bay of Navarino (Map 4.8), despite general recognition that it is much too large for an ancient "harbor," and that its wide and deep southern entrance could not have been blocked by Peloponnesian triremes. The Bay Harbor does, however, accord with important parts of the text, and would explain why the Spartans seem not to have carried out their blockade. I have argued that the harbor may best be located in a cove at the south end of Pylos itself, near the east end of the Sikia Channel (Map 4.8). The main virtue of the Cove Harbor is that it has narrow entrances that *could* be blocked (Thucydides says three times that this was the Spartan plan), and that the feasibility of this Spartan plan may provide an explanation for why the Spartans exposed their fleet at all here after avoiding naval battle for four years, why they placed troops on Sphacteria, and why the Athenian fleet went to Prote (Map 4.5, BX) and not to Pylos on the night before the naval battle (4.13.3). But while the Cove Harbor fits some parts of Thucydides' description of the site, and explains some parts of his story, it conflicts with others, and seems to be too small, in the opinion of many, for the action described to have taken place there. See A.W. Gomme, *A Historical Commentary on Thucydides,* iii (Oxford, 1956), 438–63, 466–89. See also R. B. Strassler, "The Harbor at Pylos: 425 B.C.," Note, *Journal of Hellenic Studies,* cviii (1988), 198.

4.8.9a For information on *Helots,* see Appendix C, Spartan Institutions, §3–4.

4.9.1a *Triremes* were the standard warship of the period; see Appendix G, Trireme Warfare, §4–7.

npass us, but that you will rather hasten to
vithout staying to weigh the odds, seeing in
safety. In emergencies like ours calculation is
r the danger is faced the better. [2] To my
chances are for us, if we will only stand fast
advantages, overawed by the numbers of the
points in our favor is the awkwardness of the
only helps us if we stand our ground. If we
it a defender, prove practicable enough, in
ulty, without a defender; and the enemy will
formidable from the difficulty he will have in
hat we succeed in repulsing him. Surely we
pel him while he is on board his ships, than
meets us on equal terms. [4] As to his num-
o much alarm you. Large as they may be he
detachments, from the difficulty of landing.
uperiority that we have to meet is not that of
verything else equal, but of troops on board
where many favorable accidents are required
therefore consider that his difficulties may be
merical deficiencies, and at the same time I
who know by experience what landing from
ory means, and how impossible it is to drive
ned enough to stand his ground and not to
ne surf and the terrors of the ships sailing in,
sent emergency, beat back the enemy at the
ourselves and the place."

4.11
425
7th year/Summer
PYLOS
The Spartans attack both by land and sea. Brasidas displays unusual zeal and bravery.

emosthenes, the Athenians felt more confident,
and e enemy, posting themselves along the edge of
the now put themselves in motion and simultaneous tion with their land forces and with their ships,
fort er their admiral, Thrasymelidas son of Cratesi-
cles de his attack just where Demosthenes expected.
[3] s to defend themselves on both sides, from the
lan enemy rowing up in small detachments, the one
reli g impossible for many to engage at once—and
sho eering each other on, in the endeavor to force a
lan tification. [4] He who most distinguished himself a trireme.[4a] Seeing that the captains and steers-
me culty of the position, hung back even where a
lan possible, for fear of wrecking their vessels, he

4.11. … Sparta and a … n military

4.11. … now a ship … reviously as a local commander at Methone (2.25.2), as a fleet commissioner (2.85.1), and then as adviser to the admiral (3.69.1).

shouted out to them that they must never allow the enemy to fortify himself in their country for the sake of saving timber, but must shiver their vessels and force a landing. He bade the allies, instead of hesitating in such a moment, to sacrifice their ships for Sparta in return for her many benefits, to run them boldly aground, land in one way or another, and make themselves masters of the place and its garrison.

4.12
425
7th year/Summer
PYLOS
Brasidas is wounded and faints. The Athenians recover his shield and use it for their victory trophy. Thucydides notes the irony of Athenians defending Spartan land against Spartans attacking from the sea.

Not content with this exhortation, he forced his own steersman to run his ship ashore, and stepping onto the gangway, was endeavoring to land when he was beaten back by the Athenians and after receiving many wounds fainted away. Falling into the bow, his shield slipped off his arm into the sea, and being thrown ashore was picked up by the Athenians and afterwards used for the trophy[1a] which they set up for this attack. [2] The rest also did their best, but were not able to land, owing to the difficulty of the ground and the unflinching tenacity of the Athenians. [3] It was a strange reversal of the order of things for Athenians to be fighting from the land and from Laconian land too, against Spartans coming from the sea; while Spartans were trying to land from shipboard in their own country, now become hostile, to attack Athenians, although the former were chiefly famous at the time as an inland people and superior by land, the latter as a maritime people with a navy that had no equal.[3a]

4.13
425
7th year/Summer
PYLOS
The Spartans attack Pylos for two days without success. The Athenian fleet from Zacynthus arrives and, unable to land at Pylos, camps for the night at Prote. The next morning it attacks the Spartans, who are taken by surprise.

After continuing their attacks during that day and most of the next, the Peloponnesians desisted, and the day after sent some of their ships to Asine[1a] for timber to make siege engines with which they hoped to take, in spite of its height, the wall opposite the harbor where the landing was easiest. [2] At this moment the Athenian fleet from Zacynthus[2a] arrived, now numbering fifty sail, having been reinforced by some of the ships on guard at Naupactus[2b] and by four Chian[2c] vessels. [3] Seeing both the coast and the island crowded with hoplites, and the hostile ships in the harbor showing no signs of sailing out, and at a loss where to anchor, they sailed for the moment to the desert island of Prote,[3a] not far off, where they passed the night. The next day they got under weigh in readiness to engage in the open sea if the enemy chose to put out to meet them, being determined in the event of his not doing so to sail in and attack him. [4] The Spartans did not put out to sea, and having omitted to close the entrances as they had intended, remained quiet on shore, engaged in manning their ships and getting ready, in the case of any one sailing in, to fight in the harbor, which is a fairly large one.

4.14
425
7th year/Summer
PYLOS
The Peloponnesian fleet is routed, but Spartan troops prevent the Athenians from dragging off their beached triremes. The Athenians cruise around Sphacteria to cut off the island's garrison.

Perceiving this, the Athenians advanced against them through both entrances and falling on the enemy's fleet, most of which was by this time

4.12.1a After a battle in ancient Greece, the victorious side raised a trophy, usually a set of captured armor on a pole at or near the battlefield, in thanks to the god who had defeated the enemy. Brasidas reappears next in 4.70.

4.12.3a This text must have been written a good deal after the battle, as no readers in 425 B.C. would need to be reminded of Athenian supremacy on the sea or Spartan superiority on the land.

4.13.1a Asine: Map 4.5, BX.

4.13.2a Zacynthus: Map 4.5, BX.

4.13.2b Naupactus: Map 4.5, BX.

4.13.2c Chios: Map 4.5, BY.

4.13.3a Prote, an island about eight miles north of Pylos up the coast: Map 4.5, BX.

aflo[illegible]ice put it to flight, and giving chase as far as the
sho[illegible]abled a good many vessels and took five, one
wit[illegible]en, dashing in at the rest that had taken refuge
on [illegible]ome that were still being manned before they
cou[illegible]on to their own ships and towed off empty others [illegible]2] At this sight the Spartans, maddened by a dis-
aste[illegible]n on the island, rushed to the rescue, and going
int[illegible]y armor, laid hold of the ships and tried to drag
the[illegible]nking that success depended on his individual
exe[illegible]e mêlée, and quite in contradiction to the naval
tac[illegible]mbatants; the Spartans in their excitement and
dis[illegible]ged in a sea fight on land, while the victorious
Ath[illegible]ss to push their success as far as possible, were
car[illegible]from their ships. [4] After great exertions and
nu[illegible]n sides they separated, the Spartans saving their
em[illegible]rst taken; [5] and both parties returning to their
car[illegible]p a trophy, gave back the dead,[5a] secured the
wr[illegible] to cruise round and carefully watch the island,
wit[illegible]on, while the Peloponnesians on the mainland,
wh[illegible]w all come up, stayed where they were before
Pyl[illegible]

4.15 425 7th year/Summer PYLOS Worried Spartan authorities arrive at Pylos and quickly conclude an armistice.

[illegible] had happened at Pylos reached Sparta, the disast[illegible]us that the Spartans resolved that the authorities
sh[illegible]mp and decide on the spot what was best to be
do[illegible]hat it was impossible to help their men and not
wi[illegible] reduced by hunger or overpowered by numbers,
the[illegible]consent of the Athenian generals, to conclude an
arr[illegible] envoys to Athens to obtain a convention, and to
en[illegible] men as quickly as possible.

4.16 425 7th year/Summer PYLOS Thucydides lists the terms of the armistice.

[illegible] their offers, an armistice was concluded upon
the[illegible]

[illegible]d bring to Pylos and deliver to the Athenians the
shi[illegible]e late engagement, and all in Laconia[1a] that were
ve[illegible]make no attack on the fortification either by land
or [illegible]ans should allow the Spartans on the mainland to
se[illegible]land a certain fixed quantity of already kneaded
gr[illegible]uarts of barley meal, one pint of wine, and a piece
of[illegible]d half the same quantity for a servant. That this
all[illegible]in under the eyes of the Athenians, and that no

4.1[illegible]nd the return
[illegible]ere in accord
[illegible]plite warfare.
[illegible]are, §6.

4.1[illegible]

boat should sail to the island except openly. That the Athenians should continue to guard the island the same as before, without however landing upon it, and should refrain from attacking the Peloponnesian troops either by land or by sea. [2] That if either party should infringe any of these terms in the slightest particular, the armistice should be at once void. That the armistice should hold good until the return of the Spartan envoys from Athens—the Athenians sending them thither in a trireme and bringing them back again—and upon the arrival of the envoys should be at an end, and the ships be restored by the Athenians in the same state as they received them. [3] Such were the terms of the armistice, and the ships were delivered over to the number of sixty, and the envoys sent off accordingly.[3a] When they arrived at Athens they spoke as follows:

4.17
425
7th year/Summer
ATHENS
Addressing the Athenian Assembly, Spartan envoys convey their wish to settle the war in a manner consistent with Athenian interests and Spartan dignity in its time of misfortune.

"Athenians, the Spartans sent us to try to find some way of settling the affair of our men on the island, that shall be at once satisfactory to your interests, and as consistent with our dignity in our misfortune as circumstances permit. [2] We can venture to speak at some length without any departure from the habit of our country. Men of few words where many are not wanted, we can be less brief when there is a matter of importance to be discussed and an end to be served by its illustration.[2a] [3] Meanwhile we beg you to take what we may say, not in a hostile spirit, nor as if we thought you ignorant and wished to lecture you, but rather as a suggestion on the best course to be taken, addressed to intelligent judges. [4] You can now, if you choose, employ your present success to advantage, so as to keep what you have got and gain honor and reputation besides, and you can avoid the mistake of those who meet with an extraordinary piece of good fortune, and are led on by hope to grasp continually at something further, through having already succeeded without expecting it. [5] While those who have known most vicissitudes of good and bad, have also and rightly, least confidence in their prosperity; and experience has not been wanting to teach your city and ours this lesson."

4.18
425
7th year/Summer
ATHENS
The Spartan envoys blame Sparta's current troubles on errors of judgment, not loss of power, and urge the Athenians to use their success wisely and moderately.

"To be convinced of this you have only to look at our present misfortune. What power in Hellas stood higher than we did? And yet we have come to you, although we formerly thought ourselves more able to grant what we are now here to ask. [2] Nevertheless, we have not been brought to this by any decay in our power, or through having our heads turned by aggrandizement; no, our resources are what they have always been, and our error has been an error of judgment, to which all are equally liable. [3] Accordingly the prosperity which your city now enjoys, and the accessions that it has lately received,

4.16.3a The narrative of events at Pylos will be taken up again in 4.23.

4.17.2a The Spartans here acknowledge their reputation for speaking "laconically"—that is, bluntly, ungraciously, and with as few words as possible. See Appendix C, Spartan Institutions, §2, and Appendix H, Dialects and Ethnic Groups, §8.

[illegible] pose that fortune will be always with you. [4]
[illegible] prudent enough to treat their gains as pre-
[illegible] uld also keep a clear head in adversity, and
[illegible] om staying within the limit to which a com-
[illegible] nfine it, will run the course that its chances
[illegible] t being puffed up by confidence in military
[illegible] ely to come to grief and most ready to make
[illegible] their fortune lasts. [5] This, Athenians, you
[illegible] y to do now with us, and thus to escape the
[illegible] h may follow upon your refusal, and the
[illegible] of having owed to accident even your present
[illegible] might have left behind you a reputation for
[illegible] ch nothing could endanger."

4.19
425
7th year/Summer
ATHENS
The Spartan envoys offer Athens a treaty of peace and alliance, pointing out that real peace must arise through generosity, not through military success that spawns a desire for revenge.

[illegible] dingly invite you to make a treaty and to end
[illegible] e and alliance and the most friendly and inti-
[illegible] way and on every occasion between us; and in
[illegible] on the island, thinking it better for both par-
[illegible] the end, hoping that some favorable accident
[illegible] force their way out, or of their being com-
[illegible] der the pressure of blockade. [2] Indeed if
[illegible] to be really settled, we think it will be, not by
[illegible] and military success, and by forcing an oppo-
[illegible] aty to his disadvantage; but when the more
[illegible] aives his privileges and, guided by gentler feel-
[illegible] al in generosity and accords peace on more
[illegible] han expected. [3] From that moment, instead
[illegible] which violence must entail, his adversary owes
[illegible] be paid in kind, and is inclined by honor to
[illegible]. [4] And men more often act in this manner
[illegible] nemies than where the quarrel is of less impor-
[illegible] nature as glad to give way to those who first
[illegible] are apt to be provoked by arrogance to risks
[illegible] wn judgment."

4.20
425
7th year/Summer
ATHENS
The Spartan envoys conclude by saying that Athens will receive credit for the ensuing peace, which will endure, since no one in Hellas could challenge the combined hegemony of Athens and Sparta.

[illegible] ourselves: if peace was ever desirable for both
[illegible] t the present moment, before anything irreme-
[illegible] rce us to hate you eternally, personally as well
[illegible] to miss the advantages that we now offer you.
[illegible] still in doubt, and you have reputation and our
[illegible], and we the compromise of our misfortune
[illegible] occur, let us be reconciled, and for ourselves
[illegible] of war, and grant to the rest of the Hellenes a
[illegible] ufferings, for which be sure they will think they

have chiefly you to thank. They know not who began this war, but their gratitude for concluding it, as it depends on your decision, will surely be laid at your door. [3] By such a decision you can become firm friends with the Spartans at their own invitation, which you do not force from them, but oblige them by accepting. [4] And from this friendship consider the advantages that are likely to follow: when Attica and Sparta are in concord, the rest of Hellas, you may be sure, will remain in respectful inferiority before its heads."

4.21
425
7th year/Summer
ATHENS
The Athenians, swayed by the demagogic Cleon, refuse Sparta's offer of peace and alliance, and instead "grasp for something more."

Such were the words of the Spartans, their idea being that the Athenians, already desirous of a truce and only kept back by their opposition, would joyfully accept a peace freely offered, and give back the men.[1a] [2] The Athenians, however, having the men on the island, thought that the treaty would be ready for them whenever they chose to make it, and grasped at something further. [3] Foremost to encourage them in this policy was Cleon son of Cleaenetus, a popular leader of the time and very powerful with the multitude, who persuaded them to answer as follows: First, the men in the island must surrender themselves and their arms and be brought to Athens. Next, the Spartans must restore Nisaea,[3a] Pegae,[3b] Troezen,[3c] and Achaea,[3d] all places acquired not by arms, but by the previous convention, under which they had been ceded by Athens herself at a moment of disaster, when a truce was more necessary to her than at present.[3e] This done they might take back their men, and make a truce for as long as both parties might agree.

4.22
425
7th year/Summer
ATHENS
When Cleon attacks a Spartan proposal to confer in private with Athenian commissioners, the Spartan envoys recognize that Athens will not negotiate moderately, and return to Sparta.

To this answer the envoys made no reply, but asked that commissioners might be chosen with whom they might confer on each point, and quietly talk the matter over and try to come to some agreement. [2] Hereupon Cleon violently assailed them, saying that he knew from the first that they had no right intentions, and that it was clear enough now by their refusing to speak before the people, and wanting to confer in secret with a committee of two or three. No! if they meant anything honest let them say it out before all. [3] The Spartans, however, seeing that whatever concessions they might be prepared to make in their misfortune, it was impossible to express them before the multitude and lose credit with their allies for a negotiation which might after all miscarry, and on the other hand, that the Athenians would never grant what they asked upon moderate terms, returned from Athens without having effected anything.

4.23
425
7th year/Summer
PYLOS
War resumes at Pylos; the Athenians refuse to return the Peloponnesian ships, and they reinforce the blockade of Sphacteria.

Their arrival at once put an end to the armistice at Pylos, and the Spartans asked for the return of their ships according to the truce.[1a] The Athenians, however, alleged an attack on the fort in violation of the truce, and other grievances seemingly not worth mentioning, and refused to give

4.21.1a Spartan confidence that Athens would welcome peace derived probably from the fact that Athens had sent ambassadors to Sparta to obtain peace in 430 (2.59.2).
4.21.3a Nisaea: Map 4.21.
4.21.3b Pegae: Map 4.21.
4.21.3c Troezen: Map 4.21.
4.21.3d Achaea: Map 4.21.
4.21.3e Thucydides refers here to the Thirty Years' Peace Treaty of 446, mentioned in 1.115.
4.23.1a This continues the narrative of events at Pylos from 4.16.

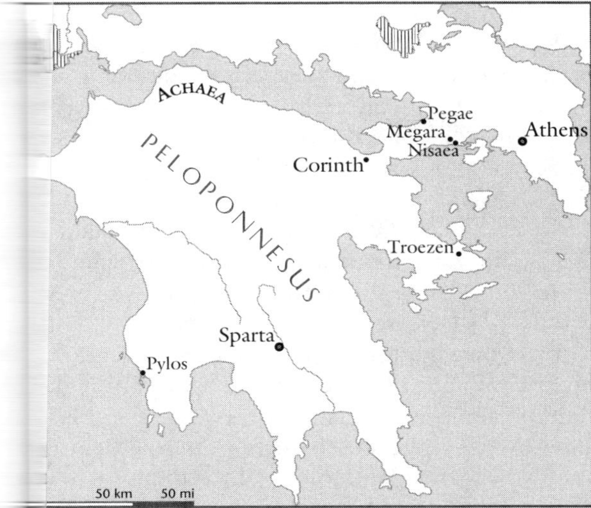

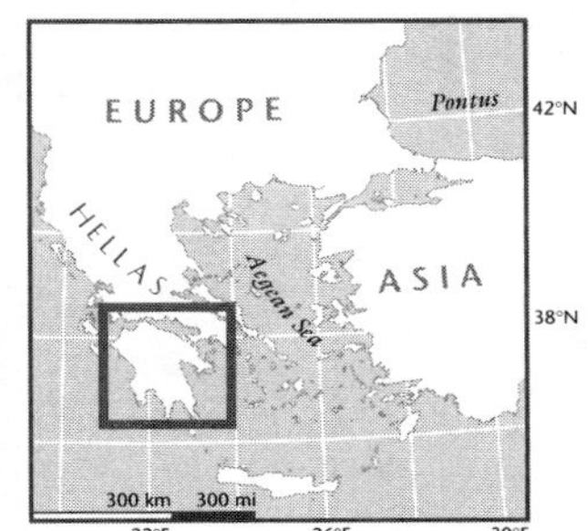

Ma[illegible]
Lo[illegible]
Pea[illegible]

the[illegible] the clause by which the slightest infringement ma[illegible] The Spartans, after denying the violation and pro[illegible]d faith in the matter of the ships, went away and ear[illegible]lves to the war. [2] Hostilities were now carried on[illegible] with vigor. The Athenians cruised round the isl[illegible]ps going different ways; and by night, except on the[illegible]y weather, anchored round it with their whole fle[illegible]einforced by twenty ships from Athens come to aid[illegible]numbered seventy sail; while the Peloponnesians re[illegible]e mainland, making attacks on the fort, and on the[illegible]tunity which might offer itself for the deliverance of[illegible]

4.24
425
7th Year/Summer
SICILY
The Syracusans reinforce their fleet at Messana and prepare to attack the Athenians at Rhegium to take control of the strait between the two cities.

[illegible]ans[1a] and their allies in Sicily had brought up to th[illegible]essana[1b] the reinforcement which they had been pr[illegible]n the war from there, [2] incited chiefly by the Lo[illegible]ed of the Rhegians,[2b] whose territory they had in[illegible]ces. [3] The Syracusans also wished to try their fo[illegible]t the Athenians had only a few ships actually at Rh[illegible]hat the main fleet destined to join them was en[illegible] island. [4] A naval victory, they thought, would en[illegible] Rhegium by sea and land, and to reduce it easily; a [illegible] once place their affairs upon a solid basis, as the pr[illegible] in Italy and Messana in Sicily are so near each

4.[illegible] Pylos is [illegible]

4.[illegible] continues the [illegible] from 4.1.

4.[illegible]

4.24.1c For these preparations, see 4.1.4.

4.24.2a Locri (Epizephyrian): Map 4.25.

4.24.2b Rhegium: Map 4.25.

other that it would be impossible for the Athenians to cruise against them and command the strait. [5] The strait in question consists of the sea between Rhegium and Messana, at the point where Sicily approaches nearest to the continent, and is the Charybdis through which the story makes Odysseus sail;[5a] and the narrowness of the passage, and the strength of the current that pours in from the vast Tyrrhenian and Sicilian mains,[5b] have rightly given it a bad reputation.

4.25
425
7th Year/Summer
SICILY
Fighting on land and sea between Athenians, Naxians, Rhegians, Sicels, and Leontines, on one side, and Syracusans, Locrians, and Messanians, on the other, is inconclusive.

In this strait the Syracusans and their allies were compelled to engage, late in the day, about a merchant ship sailing through, putting out with rather more than thirty ships against sixteen Athenian and eight Rhegian vessels. [2] Defeated by the Athenians they hastily set off, each for himself, to their own stations at Messana and Rhegium, with the loss of one ship; night coming on before the battle was finished. [3] After this the Locrians retired from the Rhegian territory, and the ships of the Syracusans and their allies united and came to anchor at Cape Pelorus,[3a] in the territory of Messana, where their land forces joined them. [4] Here the Athenians and Rhegians sailed up, and seeing the ships unmanned made an attack, in which they in their turn lost one vessel, which was caught by a grappling iron,[4a] the crew saving themselves by swimming. [5] After this the Syracusans got on board their ships, and while they were being towed along shore to Messana, were again attacked by the Athenians, but suddenly headed out to sea and became the assailants, and caused the Athenians to lose another vessel. [6] After thus holding their own in the voyage along shore and in the engagement as above described, the Syracusans sailed on into the harbor of Messana.

[7] Meanwhile the Athenians, having received warning that Camarina[7a] was about to be betrayed to the Syracusans by Archias and his party, sailed to that place; and the Messanians took this opportunity to attack their Chalcidian neighbor, Naxos[7b] by sea and land with all their forces. [8] The first day they forced the Naxians to stay within their walls, and laid waste their country; the next they sailed round with their ships, and laid waste their land on the river Akesines,[8a] while their land forces menaced the city. [9] Meanwhile the Sicels came down from the high country in great numbers to aid against the Messanians; and the Naxians, elated at the sight, and animated by a belief that the Leontines[9a] and their other Hellenic allies were coming to their support, suddenly sallied out from the city, and attacked and routed the Messanians killing more than a thousand of them; while the remainder suffered severely in their retreat home, being attacked

4.24.5a Thucydides refers to the monster whirlpool Charybdis of Homer's *Odyssey*, Book 12.
4.24.5b Tyrrhenian Sea, Sicilian Sea: Map 4.25.
4.25.3a Cape Pelorus: Map 4.25.
4.25.4a Grappling irons were large metal hooks with attached lines that were designed to be thrown so as to catch at the bulwarks (railings) of enemy ships; the lines were then used to pull the hostile ships alongside one another so that crews could engage in hand-to-hand combat. See 7.62.3a and Appendix G, Trireme Warfare, §11.
4.25.7a Camarina: Map 4.25.
4.25.7b Naxos: Map 4.25.
4.25.8a Akesines river: Map 4.25.
4.25.9a Leontini: Map 4.25.

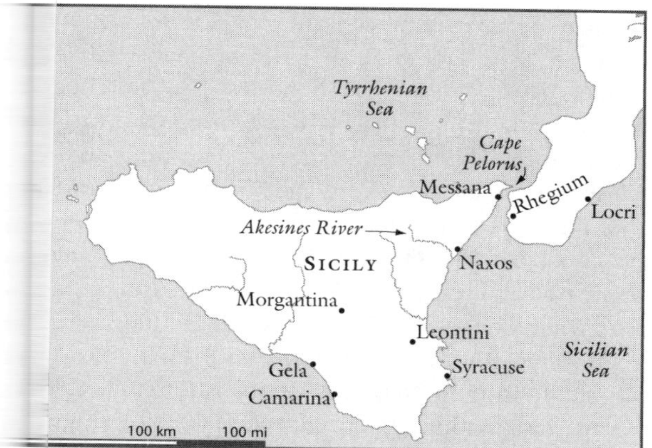

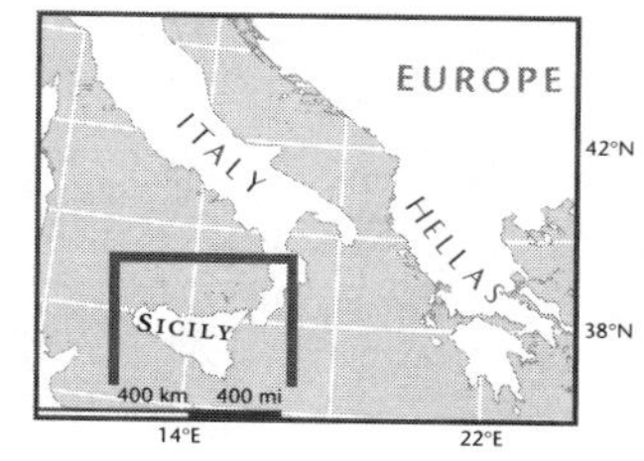

MA
EVE
ITA

by ad, and most of them cut down. [10] The ships put erwards dispersed to their different homes. The Le with the Athenians, upon this at once turned the weakened Messana, and attacked, the Athenians wit of the harbor, and the land forces on that of the city however, sallying out with Demoteles and some Lo t to garrison the city after the disaster, suddenly att of the Leontine army, killing a great number; up henians landed from their ships, and falling on the chased them back into the city, and setting up a tro . [12] After this the Hellenes in Sicily continued to by land, without the Athenians.[12a]

4.26
425
7th year/Summer
PYLOS
The hardships of the blockading Athenians are described. Spartan Helots risk their lives to bring food to the Sphacteria garrison, and thus win their freedom.

ns at Pylos[1a] were still besieging the Spartans in the an forces on the continent remaining where they we s very laborious for the Athenians from want of foo no spring except one in the citadel of Pylos itself, an nd most of them were obliged to scrape away the gra d drink such water as they could find. [3] They als room, being encamped in a narrow space; and as the or the ships, some took their meals on shore in the s were anchored out at sea.[3a] [4] But their greatest rom the unexpectedly long time which it took to re t up in a desert island, with only brackish water

4.2 Sicily is con-

4.2 narrative of

4.2 for the w had to be Trireme

to drink, a matter which they had imagined would take them only a few days. [5] The fact was, that the Spartans had made advertisement for volunteers to carry into the island flour, wine, cheese, and any other food useful in a siege; high prices being offered, and freedom promised to any of the Helots[5a] who should succeed in doing so. [6] The Helots accordingly were most forward to engage in this risky traffic, putting off from this or that part of the Peloponnesus, and running in by night on the seaward side of the island. [7] They were best pleased, however, when they could catch a wind to carry them in. It was more easy to elude the triremes on guard, when it blew from the seaward, as it then became impossible for them to anchor round the island; while the Helots had their boats valued at their worth in money, and ran them ashore without caring how they landed, being sure to find the soldiers waiting for them at the landing places. But all who risked it in fair weather were taken. [8] Divers also swam in under water from the harbor, dragging by a cord in skins poppyseed mixed with honey, and bruised linseed; these at first escaped notice, but afterwards a lookout was kept for them. [9] In short, both sides tried every possible contrivance, the one to throw in provisions, and the other to prevent their introduction.[9a]

4.27
425
7th Year/Summer
ATHENS
The Athenians begin to regret not making peace with the Spartans and blame Cleon, who in turn blames the general Nicias for not attacking and capturing the Spartans on Sphacteria.

At Athens, meanwhile, the news that the army was in great distress and that grain found its way in to the men in the island caused no small perplexity; and the Athenians began to fear that winter might come on and find them still engaged in the blockade. They saw that the convoying of provisions round the Peloponnesus would be then impossible. The country offered no resources in itself, and even in summer they could not send round enough. The blockade of a place without harbors could then no longer be kept up; and the men would either escape by the siege being abandoned, or would watch for bad weather and sail out in the boats that brought in their grain. [2] What caused still more alarm was the attitude of the Spartans, who must, it was thought by the Athenians, feel themselves on strong ground not to send them any more envoys; and they began to repent having rejected the treaty. [3] Cleon, perceiving the disfavor with which he was regarded for having stood in the way of the convention, now said that their informants did not speak the truth; and upon the messengers recommending that, if they did not believe them, they send some commissioners to see, Cleon himself and Theagenes were chosen by the Athenians as commissioners. [4] Aware that he would now be obliged either to say what had been already said by the men whom he was slandering, or be proved a liar if he said the contrary, he told the Athenians, whom he saw to be not altogether disinclined for a fresh expedition, that instead of sending commissioners and wasting their time and opportunities, if they believed what was told them, they ought to sail against the men. [5] And pointing

4.26.5a Spartan Helots; see Appendix C, Spartan Institutions, §3–4.

4.26.9a The narrative of events at Pylos is resumed in 4.30.

at [illegible]then general, whom he hated, he tauntingly said tha[illegible]y had men for generals, to sail with a force and tak[illegible]d that if he had himself been in command, he wo[illegible]

[illegible]nians murmuring against Cleon for not sailing no[illegible]o easy, and further seeing himself the object of att[illegible]ll that the generals cared, he might take what for[illegible]he attempt. [2] At first Cleon fancied that this resi[illegible]gure of speech, and was ready to go, but finding tha[illegible] he drew back, and said that Nicias, not he, was ger[illegible]ened, and having never supposed that Nicias wo[illegible]e in his favor. [3] Nicias, however, repeated his off[illegible]mand against Pylos, calling upon the Athenians to [illegible]And as the multitude is wont to do, the more Cle[illegible]pedition and tried to back out of what he had saic[illegible]raged Nicias to hand over his command, and cla[illegible]4] At last, not knowing how to get out of his wo[illegible]xpedition, and came forward and said that he was[illegible]ans, but would sail without taking anyone from the[illegible]e Lemnians and Imbrians[4a] that were at Athens, wit[illegible]d come up from Aenus,[4b] and four hundred arc[illegible]ith these and the soldiers at Pylos, he would wit[illegible]ring the Spartans alive, or kill them on the spot. [5][illegible]t help laughing at his empty words, while sensible [illegible]lves with the reflection that they must gain in eith[illegible]they would be rid of Cleon, which they rather hop[illegible] this expectation, would reduce the Spartans.

4.28
425
7th Year/Summer
ATHENS
Nicias withdraws from the command. The Athenian People now insist that Cleon take it and he does so, asking only for peltasts and archers, and promising to return victorious in twenty days.

[illegible]rything in the assembly, and the Athenians had vot[illegible]of the expedition, he chose as his colleague De[illegible]enerals at Pylos, and pushed forward the preparati[illegible]His choice fell upon Demosthenes because he hea[illegible]lating a descent on the island and because the sol[illegible]ifficulties of the position and feeling more like bes[illegible]re eager to fight it out. Moreover, the firing of the[illegible] confidence of the general. [3] At first he had bee[illegible]abited island's pathless woods would favor the ene[illegible]large force and yet suffer losses from an attack fro[illegible]He thought the woods would in great measure con[illegible]kes and forces of the enemy, while the blunders of [illegible] quickly detected by the enemy who, retaining alw[illegible]would fall upon his troops unexpectedly wherever[illegible]on the other hand, he should force them to

4.29
425
7th Year/Summer
ATHENS-PYLOS
Cleon chooses Demosthenes as his partner in command and prepares to depart. Thucydides lists the reasons why Demosthenes feared the Spartans on the island, although his forces far outnumbered them.

4.28.[illegible]Y.
4.28.[illegible]ly with a [illegible]nd a short sword. Unhindered by body armor, they could move much more quickly than the fully armed hoplite. Aenus: Map 4.5, AY.

engage in the thicket, the smaller number who knew the country would, he thought, have the advantage over the larger who were ignorant of it, and thus his own army might be imperceptibly destroyed in spite of its numbers, as his men would not be able to see where to support each other.

4.30
425
7th Year/Summer
PYLOS
A fire burns off the brush cover on the island, permitting Demosthenes to see the enemy and better plan his attack. Cleon arrives with his force. A herald is sent to demand the Spartans' surrender.

The Aetolian disaster,[1a] which had been mainly caused by the wood, had not a little to do with these reflections. [2] Meanwhile, one of the soldiers who were compelled by want of room to land on the extremities of the island and take their dinners, with outposts fixed to prevent a surprise, set fire to a little of the wood without meaning to do so; and as it came on to blow soon afterwards, almost the whole was consumed before they were aware of it. [3] Demosthenes was now able for the first time to see how numerous the Spartans really were, having up to this moment been under the impression that they took in provisions for a smaller number; he also saw that the Athenians thought success important and were anxious about it, and that it was now easier to land on the island, and accordingly got ready for the attempt, sending for troops from the allies in the neighborhood, and pushing forward his other preparations. [4] At this moment Cleon arrived at Pylos with the troops which he had asked for, having sent on word to say that he was coming. The first step taken by the two generals after their meeting was to send a herald[4a] to the camp on the mainland, to ask if they were disposed to avoid all risk and to order the men on the island to surrender themselves and their arms, to be kept in gentle custody until some general settlement should be concluded.

4.31
425
7th Year/Summer
PYLOS
The Athenians embark at night and land on Sphacteria just before dawn. Spartan troops are divided into three unequal forces.

On the rejection of this proposition the generals let one day pass, and the next embarking all their hoplites on board a few ships, put out by night, and a little before dawn landed on both sides of the island from the open sea and from the harbor, being about eight hundred strong, and advanced with a run against the first post in the island. [2] The enemy had distributed his force as follows: In this first post there were about thirty hoplites; the center and most level part, where the water was, was held by the main body, and by Epitadas their commander; while a small party guarded the very end of the island, toward Pylos, which was precipitous on the sea side and very difficult to attack from the land, and where there was also a sort of old fort of stones rudely put together, which they thought might be useful to them, in case they should be forced to retreat. Such was their disposition.[2a]

4.32
425
7th Year/Summer
PYLOS
The Spartan advance post is taken by surprise, and the rest of the Athenians land. Demosthenes' plan to refuse close combat and to attack the Spartans from all sides with missiles is described.

The advanced post thus attacked by the Athenians was at once put to the sword, the men being scarcely out of bed and still arming, the landing having taken them by surprise, as they fancied the ships were only sailing as usual to their stations for the night. [2] As soon as day broke, the rest of

4.30.1a For the Aetolian disaster, see 3.94–98.
4.30.4a Heralds, already a venerable Greek institution in Thucydides' day, operated under the protection of the god Hermes, and were easily identified by the staff they carried. They alone could travel unmolested between states or armies during wartime in order to deliver messages, take back replies, and make perfunctory arrangements.
4.31.2a Sphacteria and its features are described in Map 4.35.

the[illegible]o say, all the crews of rather more than seventy
shi[illegible]nk of oars,[2b] with the arms they carried, eight
hu[illegible]any peltasts, the Messenian reinforcements, and
all [illegible]ty round Pylos, except the garrison in the fort.
[3] [illegible]henes had divided them into companies of two
hu[illegible] made them occupy the highest points in order
to [illegible] surrounding him on every side. By refusing to
en[illegible]ns would leave him without any tangible adver-
sar[illegible] cross-fire of their host; plied by those in his rear
if h[illegible] by those on one flank if he moved against those
on [illegible]t, wherever he went he would have assailants
be[illegible]-armed attackers would prove the most difficult
to [illegible]darts, stones, and slings making them formidable
at [illegible]ing no means of getting at them at close quarter[illegible]pursued, and the moment their pursuer turned
the[illegible]Such was the idea that Demosthenes had in the
firs[illegible]nning the landing and so he arranged its execu-
tio[illegible]

4.33
425
7th Year/Summer
PYLOS
The main Spartan force advances but is thwarted by Demosthenes' tactics.

[illegible]dy of the troops in the island (that under Epi-
tad[illegible]t cut off and an army advancing against them,
ser[illegible]sed forward to close with the Athenian hoplites
in [illegible]t troops being upon their flanks and rear. [2]
H[illegible]le to engage or to profit by their superior skill,
the[illegible]hem in check on either side with their missiles,
an[illegible] stationary instead of advancing to meet them;
an[illegible] the light troops wherever they ran up and
ap[illegible] they retreated fighting, being lightly equipped,
an[illegible]heir flight, from the difficult and rugged nature
of [illegible] hitherto uninhabited, over which the Spartans
co[illegible]heir heavy armor.

4.34
425
7th Year/Summer
PYLOS
As the Spartans tire, the Athenians grow more confident. Blinded by dust and deafened by the noise of battle, the Spartans find it impossible either to attack or to defend themselves effectively.

[illegible]ad lasted some little while, the Spartans became
un[illegible] the same rapidity as before upon the points
att[illegible]ps, finding that they now fought with less vigor,
be[illegible]ey could see with their own eyes that they were
ma[illegible]s than the enemy; they were now more familiar
wit[illegible] him less terrible, the event not having justified
the[illegible]ey had suffered when they first landed in slavish
dis[illegible]king Spartans; and accordingly their fear changing[illegible]ushed upon them all together with loud shouts,
an[illegible]es, darts, and arrows, whichever came first to

4.32[illegible]hacteria: [illegible]

4.32[illegible]" see Appen-[illegible] 12.

hand. [2] The shouting accompanying their onset confounded the Spartans, unaccustomed to this mode of fighting; dust rose from the newly burnt wood, and it was impossible to see in front of one with the arrows and stones flying through clouds of dust from the hands of numerous assailants. [3] The Spartans had now to sustain a difficult conflict; their caps would not keep out the arrows, and darts had broken off in the bodies of the wounded. They themselves were unable to retaliate, being prevented from using their eyes to see what was before them, and unable to hear the words of command for the hubbub raised by the enemy; danger encompassed them on every side, and there was no hope of any means of defense or safety.

4.35
425
7th Year/Summer
PYLOS
After many Spartans are wounded, they retire to an old fort at the end of the island, and the Athenians pursue them. There the ground favors defense and prevents encirclement. Both sides endure the torments of sun and thirst.

At last, after many had been already wounded in the confined space in which they were fighting, they formed in close order and retired to the fort at the end of the island, which was not far off, and to their friends who held it.[1a] [2] The moment they gave way, the light troops became bolder and pressed upon them, shouting louder than ever, and killed as many as they caught up with in their retreat, but most of the Spartans made good their escape to the fort, and with the garrison in it ranged themselves all along its whole extent to repulse the enemy wherever it was assailable. [3] The Athenians pursuing, unable to surround and hem them in, owing to the strength of the ground, attacked them in front and tried to storm the position. [4] For a long time, indeed for most of the day, both sides held out against all the torments of the battle, thirst, and sun, the one endeavoring to drive the enemy from the high ground, the other to maintain himself upon it, it being now more easy for the Spartans to defend themselves than before, as they could not be surrounded upon the flanks.

4.36
425
7th Year/Summer
PYLOS
The Messenian commander leads a force by a hidden route to a position above and behind the Spartans, surprising them and forcing them to give way.

The struggle began to seem endless, when the commander of the Messenians came to Cleon and Demosthenes, and told them that they were wasting their efforts but that if they would give him some archers and light troops to go round on the enemy's rear by a way he would undertake to find, he thought he could force the approach. [2] Upon receiving what he asked for, he started from a point out of sight in order not to be seen by the enemy, and creeping on wherever the precipices of the island permitted, and where the Spartans, trusting to the strength of the ground, kept no guard, succeeded after the greatest difficulty in getting round without their seeing him, and suddenly appeared on the high ground in their rear, to the dismay of the surprised enemy and the still greater joy of his expectant friends. [3] The Spartans thus placed between two fires, and in the same dilemma, to compare small things with great, as at Thermopylae,[3a] where the defenders were cut off through the Persians getting round by the path, being now attacked in front and behind, began to give way, and overcome

4.35.1a Fort at the north end of Sphacteria. Map 4.35.

4.36.3a Thermopylae (Map 4.52, AX) was the site of a heroic battle in 480 B.C. A small Spartan-led force of Greeks occupied a narrow pass and held off a huge Persian army for several days until they were outflanked and surrounded. Even then the Greeks fought to the last man. See Appendix E, The Persians, §4.

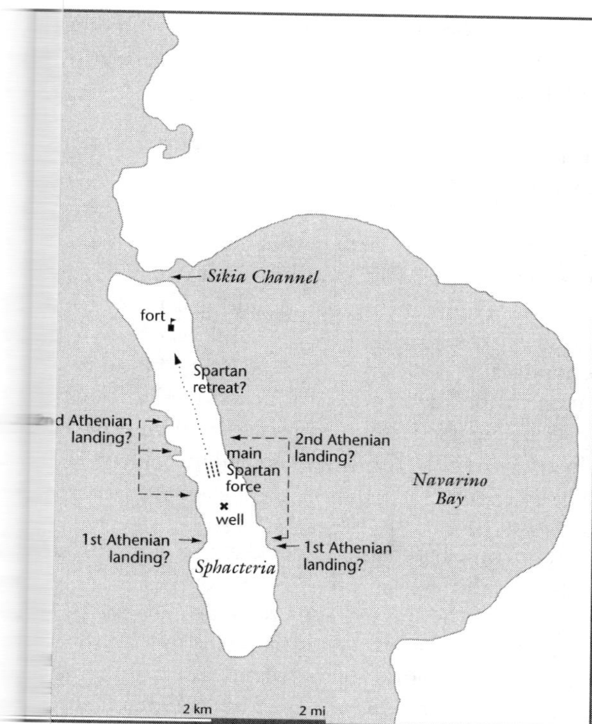

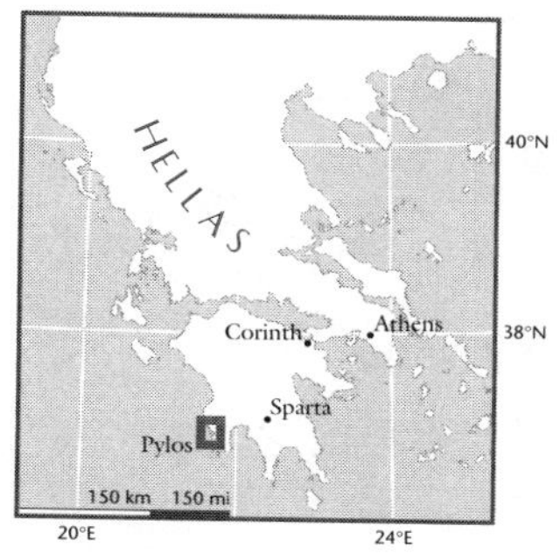

MA[illegible]
TH[illegible]
ON [illegible]

by [illegible]nd exhausted from want of food, retreated.

[illegible]eady masters of the approaches [4.37.1] when Cle[illegible]erceiving that the enemy, should he give way a sin[illegible]e destroyed by their soldiery, put a stop to the bat[illegible]back. They wished to take the Spartans alive to Ath[illegible]r stubbornness might relax on hearing the offer of [illegible]ight surrender and yield to the present overwh[illegible]clamation was accordingly made, to determine wh[illegible]der themselves and their arms to the Athenians to [illegible]retion.

4.37
425
7th Year/Summer
PYLOS
Demosthenes and Cleon halt the advance and ask the Spartans if they will now surrender.

[illegible]d this offer, most of them lowered their shields and [illegible] show that they accepted it. Hostilities now cea[illegible]eld between Cleon and Demosthenes, and Styph[illegible] other side; since Epitadas, the first of the previous [illegible] killed, and Hippagretas, the next in command, left [illegible]n, though still alive; and thus the command had dev[illegible]ording to the law in case of anything happening

4.38
425
7th Year/Summer
PYLOS
The Spartans surrender after consulting their forces on the mainland. The Spartans have lost about 130 men. Athenian losses are small, as there was no fighting at close quarters.

to his superiors. [2] Styphon and his companions said they wished to send a herald to the Spartans on the mainland, to know what they were to do. [3] The Athenians would not let any of them go, but themselves called for heralds from the mainland, and after questions had been carried backwards and forwards two or three times, the last man that passed over from the Spartans on the continent brought this message: "The Spartans bid you to decide for yourselves so long as you do nothing dishonorable"; upon which after consulting together they surrendered themselves and their arms. [4] The Athenians, after guarding them that day and night, the next morning set up a trophy in the island, and got ready to sail, giving their prisoners in batches to be guarded by the captains of the triremes; and the Spartans sent a herald and took up their dead. [5] The number of the killed and prisoners taken in the island was as follows: of the four hundred and twenty hoplites who had passed over originally, two hundred and ninety-two were taken alive to Athens; the rest were killed. About a hundred and twenty of the prisoners were Spartiates. The Athenian loss was small, the battle not having been fought at close quarters.

4.39
425
7th Year/Summer
PYLOS
The blockade lasted seventy-two days. Cleon returns to Athens with the prisoners, his promise fulfilled

The blockade lasted seventy-two days in all, counting from the naval fight to the battle on the island. [2] For twenty of these, during the absence of the envoys sent to negotiate for peace, the men had provisions given them; for the rest they were fed by the smugglers. Grain and other victuals were found in the island, the commander Epitadas having kept the men upon half rations. [3] The Athenians and Peloponnesians now each withdrew their forces from Pylos, and went home, and mad as Cleon's promise was, he fulfilled it, by bringing the men to Athens within the twenty days as he had pledged himself to do.

4.40
425
7th Year/Summer
PYLOS
All Greece is amazed that the Spartans at Sphacteria surrendered. Thucydides' recounts the anecdote of the clever arrows.

Nothing that happened in the war surprised the Hellenes so much as this. It was the general opinion that no force or famine could make the Spartans give up their arms, but that they would fight on as they could, and die with them in their hands: [2] indeed people could scarcely believe that those who had surrendered were of the same stuff as the fallen; and an Athenian ally, who some time after insultingly asked one of the prisoners from the island if those that had fallen were noble and good men, received for answer that the *atraktos*—that is, the arrow—would be worth a great deal if it could pick out noble and good men from the rest; in allusion to the fact that the killed were those whom the stones and the arrow happened to hit.

4.41
425
7th Year/Summer
PYLOS-ATHENS
The captured Spartans are imprisoned at Athens. The Messenians launch effective raids on Laconia. The Spartans send envoys to Athens to negotiate a peace, but the Athenians reject their proposals, "always grasping for more."

Upon the arrival of the men the Athenians determined to keep them in prison until the peace, and if the Peloponnesians invaded their country in the interval, to bring them out and put them to death. [2] Meanwhile the defense of Pylos was not forgotten; the Messenians from Naupactus[2a] sent to their old country, to which Pylos formerly belonged, some of the most suitable of their number, and began a series of incursions into Laconia, which their common dialect[2b] rendered most destructive. [3] The Spartans,

4.41.2a Naupactus: Map 4.44, locator.

4.41.2b For the Dorian dialect see Appendix H, Dialects and Ethnic Groups, §9.

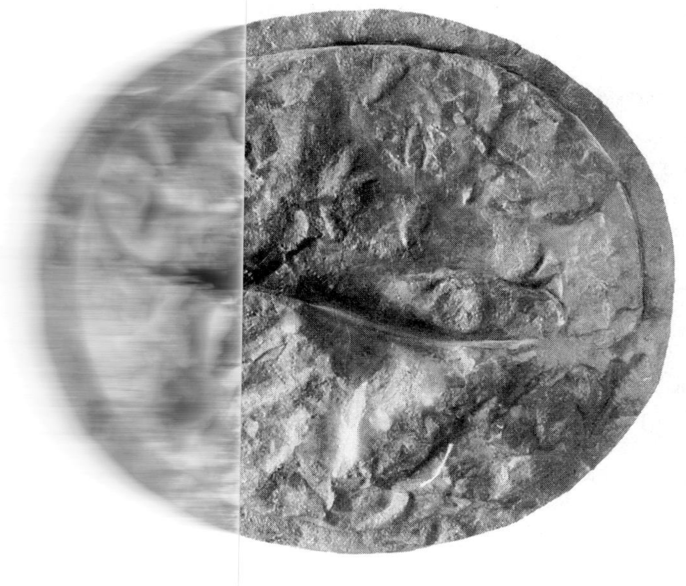

ILL[illegible]
SHI[illegible]E INSCRIPTION READS THAT IT WAS TAKEN BY THE ATH[illegible]S (LACEDAIMONIANS) AT PYLOS

hitherto without experience of incursions or a warfare of the kind, finding the Helots deserting, and fearing the march of revolution in their country, began to be seriously uneasy, and in spite of their unwillingness to betray this to the Athenians began to send envoys to Athens, and tried to recover Pylos and the prisoners. [4] The Athenians, however, kept grasping at more, and dismissed envoy after envoy without their having effected anything. Such was the history of the affair of Pylos.

4.42
425
7th Year/Summer
CORINTH
An Athenian expedition under Nicias attacks Corinthian territory near the Isthmus. Warned from Argos, Corinth prepares to meet the invaders.

The same summer, directly after these events, the Athenians made an expedition against the territory of Corinth[1a] with eighty ships and two thousand Athenian hoplites and two hundred cavalry on board horse transports, accompanied by the Milesians,[1b] Andrians,[1c] and Carystians[1d] from the allies; under the command of Nicias son of Niceratus, with two colleagues. [2] Putting out to sea they made land at daybreak between Chersonese and Rheitus,[2a] at the beach of the country underneath the Solygian hill, upon which the Dorians in old times established themselves and carried on war against the Aeolian inhabitants of Corinth, and where a village now stands called Solygia.[2b] The beach where the fleet put in is about a mile and a half from the village, seven miles from Corinth, and two and a quarter from the Isthmus.[2c] [3] The Corinthians had heard from Argos[3a] of the coming of the Athenian armament, and had all come up to the Isthmus long before, with the exception of those who lived beyond it, and also of five hundred who were away in garrison in Ambracia and Leucas;[3b] and they were there in full force watching for the Athenians to land. [4] These last, however, gave them the slip by coming in the dark; and being informed by signals of the fact, the Corinthians left half their number at Cenchreae,[4a] in case the Athenians should go against Crommyon,[4b] and marched in all haste to the rescue.

4.43
425
7th Year/Summer
CORINTH
The Corinthians attack the Athenians just after they land and a hard-fought battle at close quarters takes place.

Battus, one of the two generals present at the action, went with a company to defend the village of Solygia, which was unfortified; Lycophron remaining to give battle with the rest. [2] The Corinthians first attacked the right wing of the Athenians, which had just landed in front of Chersonese, and afterwards the rest of the army. The battle was an obstinate one, and fought throughout hand to hand. [3] The right wing of the Athenians and Carystians, who had been placed at the end of the line, received and with some difficulty repulsed the Corinthians, who thereupon retreated to a wall upon the rising ground behind, and throwing down the stones upon them, came on again singing the *paean*[2a] and being received by the Atheni-

4.42.1a Corinth: Map 4.44, AX.
4.42.1b Miletus: Map 4.44, locator.
4.42.1c Andros: Map 4.44, locator.
4.42.1d Carystus, Map 4.44, locator.
4.42.2a Chersonese, Rheitus in Corinthian territory, possible locations: Map 4.44, AX.
4.42.2b Solygia, possible location: Map 4.44, AX. For the Dorians and Aeolians, see Appendix H, Dialects and Ethnic Groups, §6–8.
4.42.2c Isthmus of Corinth: Map 4.44, AX.
4.42.3a Argos: Map 4.44, BX.
4.42.3b Three hundred of these Corinthians are mentioned in 3.114 as being sent to Ambracia. For the locations of Ambracia and Leucas, see Map 4.52, AX.
4.42.4a Cenchreae: Map 4.44, AX.
4.42.4b Crommyon: Map 4.44, AX.
4.43.2a The *paean* was a ritual chant that the men of classical Greek armies sang as they advanced into battle, rallied, or celebrated victory.

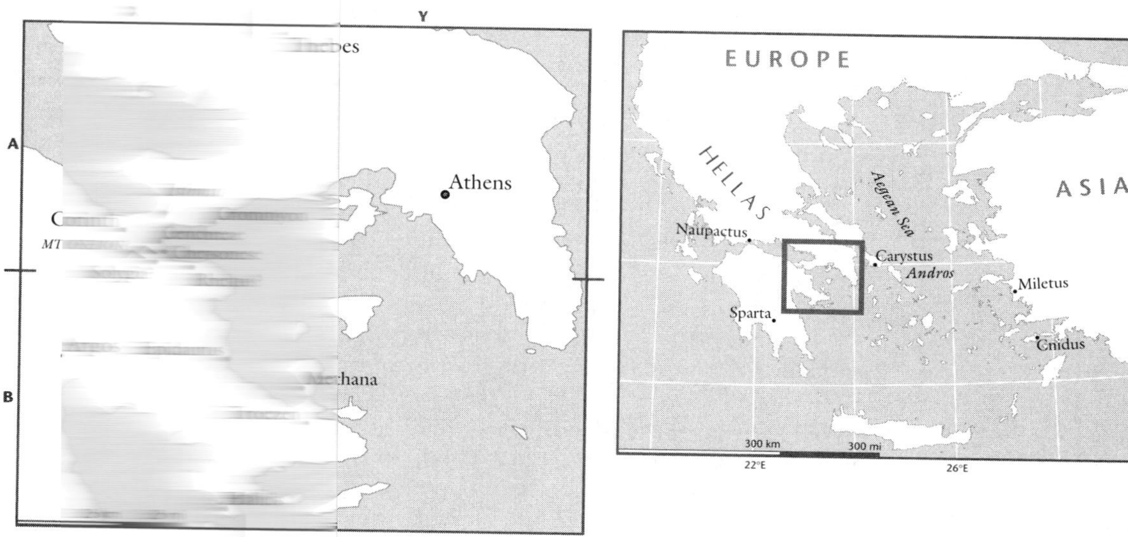

MA[illegible] ON CORINTH AND[illegible]

ans. [illegible] close quarters. [4] At this moment a Corinthian con[illegible]e relief of the left wing, routed and pursued the Ath[illegible] whence they were in their turn driven back by the [illegible]s from the ships. [5] Meanwhile the rest of the arm[illegible] on tenaciously, especially the right wing of the Co[illegible]ron sustained the attack of the Athenian left, whi[illegible]tempt the village of Solygia.

[illegible]ng while without either giving way, the Atheni- ans [illegible]f which the enemy had none, at length routed the [illegible]d to the hill and halting remained quiet there, wit[illegible]. [2] It was in this rout of the right wing that they [illegible]ycophron their general being among the num- ber. [illegible] broken and put to flight in this way without bei[illegible] hurried, retired to the high ground and there too[illegible]e Athenians, finding that the enemy no longer offe[illegible]tripped his dead and took up their own and

4.44
425
7th Year/Summer
CORINTH
The Corinthians are finally routed, but the Athenians, seeing other enemy forces approaching, withdraw by ship to nearby islands.

immediately set up a trophy. [4] Meanwhile, the half of the Corinthians left at Cenchreae to guard against the Athenians sailing on Crommyon, although unable to see the battle for Mount Oneion,[4a] found out what was going on by the dust, and hurried up to the rescue; as did also the older Corinthians from the city, upon discovering what had occurred. [5] The Athenians seeing them all coming against them, and thinking that they were reinforcements from the neighboring Peloponnesians, withdrew in haste to their ships with their spoils and their own dead, except two that they left behind, not being able to find them, [6] and going on board crossed over to the islands opposite and from thence sent a herald, and took up under truce the bodies which they had left behind. Two hundred and twelve Corinthians fell in the battle, and rather less than fifty Athenians.

4.45
425
7th Year/Summer
CORINTH
The Athenians ravage Crommyon and fortify Methana as a base for future raids

Weighing from the islands, the Athenians sailed the same day to Crommyon in the Corinthian territory, about thirteen miles from the city, and coming to anchor laid waste the country, and passed the night there. [2] The next day, after first coasting along to the territory of Epidaurus[2a] and making a descent there, they came to Methana[2b] between Epidaurus and Troezen,[2c] and drew a wall across and fortified the isthmus of the peninsula, and left a post there from which incursions were henceforth made upon the country of Troezen, Halieis,[2d] and Epidaurus. After walling off this spot the fleet sailed off home.

4.46
425
7th Year/Summer
CORCYRA
The Athenian fleet from Pylos sails to Corcyra; attacks and secures the surrender of the Corcyraeans from Mount Istone; and imprisons them on the island of Ptychia. The Corcyraean People plot to kill the prisoners.

While these events were going on, Eurymedon and Sophocles had put to sea with the Athenian fleet from Pylos on their way to Sicily, and arriving at Corcyra, joined the townsmen in an expedition against the party established on Mount Istone[1a] who, as I have mentioned, had crossed over after the revolution, and become masters of the country, to the great hurt of the inhabitants. [2] Their stronghold having been taken by an attack, the garrison took refuge in a body upon some high ground and there capitulated, agreeing to give up their mercenary auxiliaries, lay down their arms, and commit themselves to the discretion of the Athenian people. [3] The generals carried them across under truce to the island of Ptychia,[3a] to be kept in custody until they could be sent to Athens, upon the understanding that if any were caught running away, all would lose the benefit of the treaty. [4] Meanwhile the leaders of the Corcyraean commons, afraid that the Athenians might spare the lives of the prisoners, had recourse to the following stratagem. [5] They gained over some few men on the island by secretly sending friends with instructions to provide them with a boat, and to tell them, as if for their own sakes, that they had best escape as quickly as

4.44.4a Mount Oneion, possible location: Map 4.44, AX.
4.45.2a Epidaurus: Map 4.44, BX.
4.45.2b Methana: Map 4.44, BY.
4.45.2c Troezen: Map 4.44, BY.
4.45.2d Halieis: Map 4.44, BX.
4.46.1a These partisans were mentioned in 3.85 and 4.2. Mount Istone: Map 4.47.
4.46.3a Ptychia: Map 4.47.

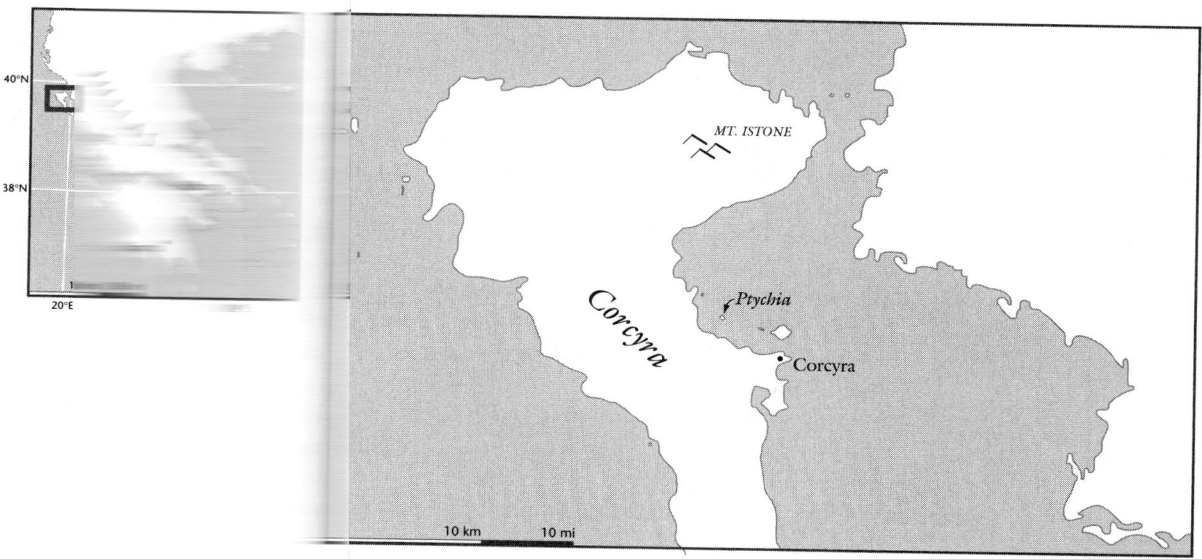

[illegible]AP 4.47 ATHENIANS IN CORCYRA

poss[illegible]nerals were going to give them up to the Corcyra[illegible]

T[illegible]ceeding, it was so arranged that the men were caug[illegible]oat that was provided, and the treaty became void[illegible]ole were given up to the Corcyraeans. [2] For this [illegible]erals were in a great measure responsible; their evid[illegible] for Sicily, and thus to leave to others the honor

4.47
425
7th Year/Summer
CORCYRA
Caught trying to escape, the prisoners are executed by the Corcyraean People. The Athenian generals bear much responsibility for this massacre.

of conducting the men to Athens, encouraged the intriguers in their design and seemed to affirm the truth of their representations. [3] The prisoners thus handed over were shut up by the Corcyraeans in a large building, and afterwards taken out by twenties and led past two lines of hoplites, one on each side, being bound together, and beaten and stabbed by the men in the lines whenever any saw pass a personal enemy; while men carrying whips went by their side and hastened on the road those that walked too slowly.

4.48
425
7th Year/Summer
CORCYRA
Civil strife now ends in Corcyra because the oligarchic faction has been annihilated.

As many as sixty men were taken out and killed in this way without the knowledge of their friends in the building, who fancied they were merely being moved from one prison to another. At last, however, someone opened their eyes to the truth, upon which they called upon the Athenians to kill them themselves, if such was their pleasure, and refused any longer to go out of the building, and said they would do all they could to prevent anyone coming in. [2] The Corcyraeans, not wishing themselves to force a passage through the doors, got up on the top of the building, and breaking through the roof, threw down the tiles and let fly arrows at them, from which the prisoners sheltered themselves as well as they could. [3] Most of their number, meanwhile, were engaged in killing themselves by thrusting into their throats the arrows shot by the enemy, and hanging themselves with the cords taken from some beds that happened to be there, and with strips made from their clothing; adopting, in short, every possible means of self-destruction, and also falling victims to the missiles of their enemies on the roof. Night came on while these horrors were taking place, and most of it had passed before they were concluded. [4] When it was day the Corcyraeans threw them in layers upon wagons and carried them out of the city. All the women taken in the stronghold were sold as slaves. [5] In this way the Corcyraeans from the mountain were destroyed by the People; and so after terrible excesses the party strife came to an end, at least as far as the period of this war is concerned, for of one party there was practically nothing left. Meanwhile the Athenians sailed off to Sicily, their primary destination, and carried on the war with their allies there.

4.49
425
7th Year/Summer
ANACTORIUM
The Athenians take Anactorium by treachery.

At the close of the summer, the Athenians at Naupactus[1a] and the Acarnanians[1b] made an expedition against Anactorium,[1c] the Corinthian city lying at the mouth of the Ambracian gulf, and took it by treachery; and the Acarnanians themselves sending settlers from all parts of Acarnania occupied the place.

4.50
425/4
7th Year/Winter
THRACE
The Athenians capture a Persian ambassador to Sparta and return him, with their own envoys, to Ephesus. There they learn that King Artaxerxes has died.

Summer was now over. [4.50.1] During the following winter Aristides son of Archippus, one of the commanders of the Athenian ships sent to collect money from the allies,[1a] arrested at Eion on the Strymon[1b] Arta-

4.49.1a Naupactus: Map 4.52, AX.
4.49.1b The enmity between Anactorium and Acarnania was mentioned in 3.114. Acarnania: Map 4.52, AX.
4.49.1c Anactorium: Map 4.52, AX.
4.50.1a For Athenian collections of tribute, see note 4.75.1b; also Appendix B, The Athenian Empire, §2, 10.
4.50.1b Eion, on the Strymon River in Thrace: Map 4.52, AX. Thucydides describes an Athenian siege of the Persians in this city in 1.98.

ph… way from the King to Sparta. [2] He was con- du… he Athenians had his dispatches translated from the … d read them. With numerous references to other sub… told the Spartans that the King did not know wh… e many ambassadors they had sent him no two eve… f however they were prepared to speak plainly the… e envoys with this Persian. [3] The Athenians afte… hernes in a trireme to Ephesus,[3a] and ambas- sad… d there of the death of King Artaxerxes son of Xer… about that time, and so returned home.

4.51
425/4
7th Year/Winter
CHIOS
The Chians dismantle their new wall.

…hians[1a] pulled down their new wall at the com- ma… o suspected them of meditating an insurrection, afte… g pledges from the Athenians, and security as far as t… r continuing to treat them as before. Thus the win… ended the seventh year of this war of which Th…

4.52
424
8th Year/Summer
LESBOS
Thucydides notes an eclipse of the sun, and describes the maneuvers and plans of the Mytilenian exiles.

…ext summer there was an eclipse of the sun[1a] at the …, and in the early part of the same month an ear…, the Mytilenian[2a] and other Lesbian exiles set out … n the continent, with mercenaries hired in the Pel… levied on the spot, and took Rhoeteum,[2b] but rest… on the receipt of two thousand Phocaean *stat…* marched against Antandrus[3a] and took the city by … g to free Antandrus and the rest of the Actaean citi… Mytilene but now held by the Athenians. Once fort… have every facility for shipbuilding from the vici… nd the consequent abundance of timber, and ple… nd might from this base easily ravage Lesbos, whi… make themselves masters of the Aeolian cities on the …

4.50.… e Appendix

4.50.… he message … neiform, but

4.50.…

4.50.… e part in … ns with … een the two … e Appendix … ting of the … s largely on … Babylon- … e curious … error), all … s that Dar- …, did not … east four- … ucydides … s mention … 4.52.1) … . Can … signed the incident to the wrong winter? Or does his use of the word "afterwards" cover quite a long delay before Artaphernes was escorted to Ephesus? Both alternatives have caused scholars discomfort.

4.51.1a Chios: Map 4.52, AY.

4.52.1a This eclipse took place on March 21, 424 B.C.; see A. W. Gomme, *A Historical Commentary on Thucydides,* iii (Oxford, 1956), 505.

4.52.2a This picks up the story of Mytilene from 3.50. Mytilene, Lesbos: Map 4.52, AY.

4.52.2b Rhoeteum: Map 4.52, AY.

4.52.2c Phocaean *staters* were a unit of currency thought to be worth twenty-four Attic drachmas, which would make the above sum equal to eight talents. See Appendix J, Classical Greek Currency, §4.

4.52.3a Antandrus: Map 4.52, AY.

4.52.3b Mount Ida: Map 4.52, AY.

4.52.3c We next hear of these Mytilenian exiles in 4.75.1.

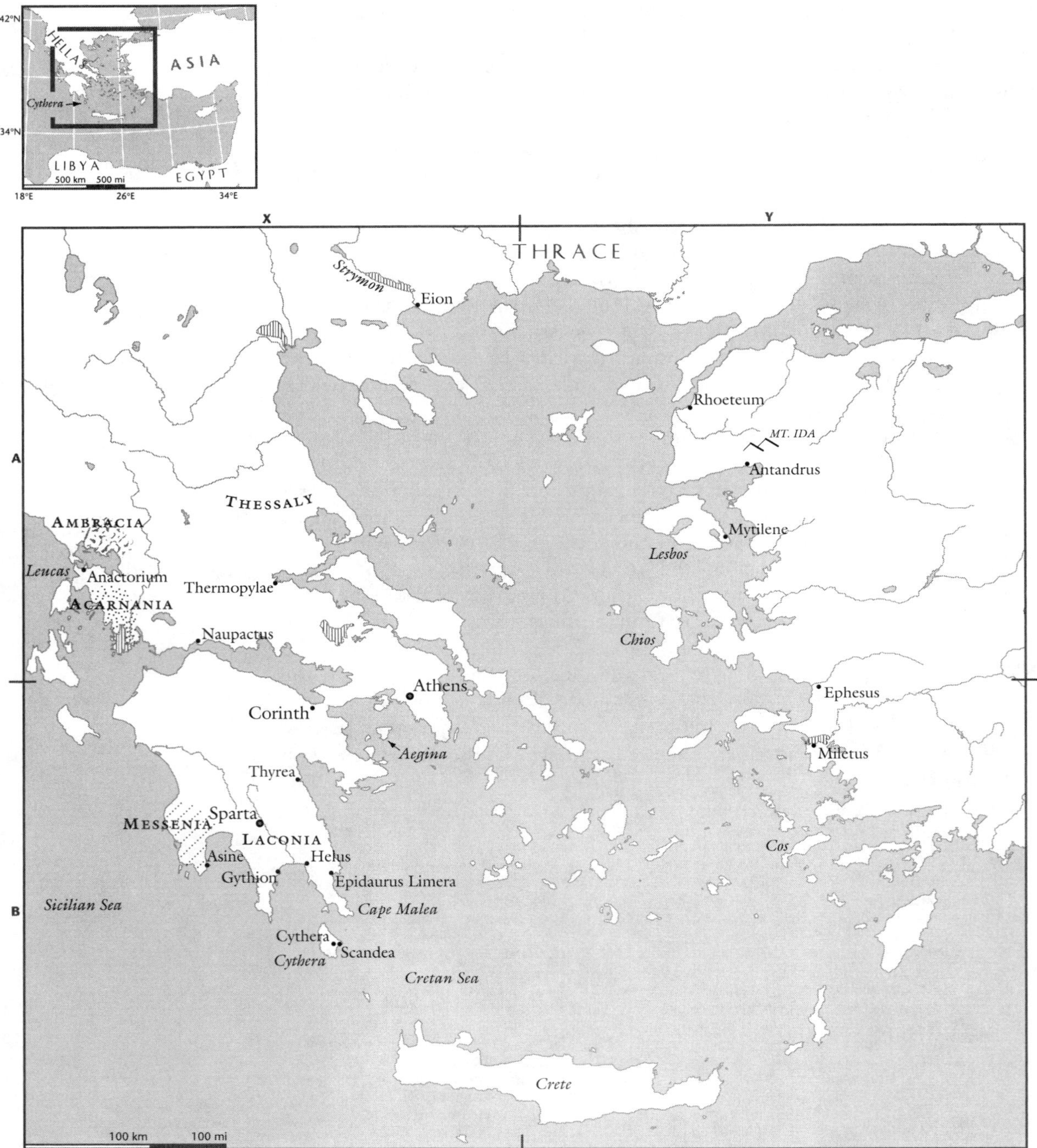

MAP 4.52 EVENTS IN LESBOS AND CHIOS; NICIAS' CYTHERAN CAMPAIGN

4.53
424
8th Year/Summer
CYTHERA
Athens sends an expedition against Cythera. Thucydides describes the island, its inhabitants, and its importance to Sparta.

[illegible]chemes of the exiles, [4.53.1] the Athenians in the [illegible] an expedition with sixty ships, two thousand hop[illegible]d some allied troops from Miletus[1a] and other par[illegible]der the command of Nicias son of Niceratus, Nic[illegible]hes, and Autocles son of Tolmaeus. [2] Cythera is a[illegible]a, opposite Malea;[2a] the inhabitants are Spartans of [illegible]*i*;[2b] and an officer called the Judge of Cythera wer[illegible]ally from Sparta. A garrison of hoplites was also reg[illegible]eat attention paid to the island, [3] as it was the lan[illegible]hant ships from Egypt and Libya,[3a] and at the sam[illegible] from the attacks of privateers[3b] from the sea, at the [illegible]sailable, as the whole coast rises abruptly toward the [illegible].[3c]

4.54
424
8th Year/Summer
CYTHERA
The Athenians under Nicias defeat the Cytherans who surrender on terms.

[illegible]th their armament, the Athenians with ten ships and [illegible] hoplites took the city of Scandea,[1a] on the sea; and [illegible]orces landing on the side of the island looking tow[illegible] the lower city of Cythera,[1b] where they found all t[illegible]d. [2] A battle ensuing, the Cytherans held their gro[illegible]e, and then turned and fled into the upper city, wh[illegible] capitulated to Nicias and his colleagues, agreeing [illegible]the decision of the Athenians, their lives only bei[illegible]ndence had previously been going on between Nic[illegible]nhabitants, which caused the surrender to be effe[illegible]l upon terms more advantageous, present and futu[illegible]who would otherwise have been expelled by the Ath[illegible]eir being Spartans and their island being so near to l[illegible]capitulation, the Athenians occupied the city of Sca[illegible]nd appointing a garrison for Cythera, sailed to Asi[illegible] of the places on the sea, and making descents and [illegible]ore at such spots as were convenient, continued rava[illegible]out seven days.

4.55
424
8th Year/Summer
LACONIA
Unnerved by its losses at Pylos and Cythera, Sparta organizes cavalry and archers and disperses hoplites to provide a mobile coast defense.

[illegible] Athenians masters of Cythera, and expecting des[illegible]eir coasts, nowhere opposed them in force, but sent [illegible]re through the country, consisting of as many hop[illegible]ed seemed to require, and generally stood very

4.53.[illegible]
4.53.[illegible]o Laconia [illegible]X.
4.53.[illegible]artan Insti-[illegible]
4.53.[illegible] Cythera: [illegible]
4.53.[illegible]d boats [illegible] attack [illegible]
4.53.[illegible] and Cre-[illegible], see Map [illegible]

4.54.1a Scandea, on the island of Cythera: Map 4.52, BX.
4.54.1b City of Cythera, on the island of Cythera: Map 4.52, BX.
4.54.3a The terms of this agreement are described in 4.57.4.
4.54.4a Asine in Messenia: Map 4.52, BX. This Asine seems too far away from Cythera to be raided from there, so Thucydides may have been referring here to another Asine located near Gythion: Map 4.52, BX.
4.54.4b Helus: Map 4.52, BX.

much upon the defensive. After the severe and unexpected blow that had befallen them in the island, the occupation of Pylos and Cythera, and the apparition on every side of a war whose rapidity defied precaution, they lived in constant fear of internal revolution, [2] and now took the unusual step of raising four hundred horse and a force of archers, and became more timid than ever in military matters, finding themselves involved in a maritime struggle, which their organization had never contemplated, and that against Athenians, with whom an enterprise unattempted was always looked upon as a success sacrificed. [3] Besides this, their late numerous reverses of fortune, coming close one upon another without any reason, had thoroughly unnerved them, and they were always afraid of a second disaster like that on the island, [4] and thus scarsely dared to take the field, but fancied that they could not stir without a blunder, for being new to the experience of adversity they had lost all confidence in themselves.

4.56
424
8th Year/Summer
LACONIA
Sparta cannot defend its coasts from naval raids like the one against Thyrea, a district occupied by Aeginetan exiles.

Accordingly they now allowed the Athenians to ravage their seaboard, without making any movement, the garrisons in whose neighborhood the descents were made always thinking their numbers insufficient, and sharing the general feeling. A single garrison which ventured to resist, near Cotyrta and Aphrodisia,[1a] struck terror by its charge into the scattered mob of light troops, but retreated, upon being received by the hoplites, with the loss of a few men and some arms, for which the Athenians set up a trophy, and then sailed off to Cythera. [2] From thence they sailed round to Epidaurus Limera,[2a] ravaged part of the country, and so came to Thyrea[2b] in the Cynurian territory, upon the Argive and Laconian border. This district had been given by its Spartan owners to the expelled Aeginetans[2c] to inhabit, in return for their good offices at the time of the earthquake and the rising of the Helots;[2d] and also because, although subjects of Athens, they had always sided with Sparta.

4.57
424
8th Year/Summer
LACONIA
The Athenians capture Thyrea. Aeginetan prisoners are executed. A few Cytherans are sent to Athens as hostages.

While the Athenians were still at sea, the Aeginetans evacuated a fort which they were building upon the coast, and retreated into the upper city where they lived, rather more than a mile from the sea. [2] One of the Spartan district garrisons which was helping them in the work refused to enter here with them at their entreaty, thinking it dangerous to shut themselves up within the wall, and retiring to the high ground remained quiet, not considering themselves a match for the enemy. [3] Meanwhile the Athenians landed, and instantly advanced with all their forces and took Thyrea. The city they burnt, pillaging what was in it; the Aeginetans who were not slain in action they took with them to Athens, with Tantalus son of Patrocles, their Spartan commander, who had been wounded and taken

4.56.1a Cotyrta, Aphrodisia: locations unknown.
4.56.2a Epidaurus Limera: Map 4.52, BX.
4.56.2b Thyrea: Map 4.52, BX.
4.56.2c Aegina: Map 4.52, BX. Thucydides mentions the expulsion of the Aeginetans from their island by the Athenians in 2.27.
4.56.2d The earthquake and the Helot revolt that followed it are described in 1.101–3.

pris[illegible]ok with them a few men from Cythera whom they [illegible]nove. These the Athenians decided to lodge in the [illegible]ytherans were to retain their lands and pay four *tale*[illegible]inetans captured were all to be put to death on acc[illegible]eterate feud between Athens and Aegina; and Tan[illegible]prisonment of the Spartans taken on the island.

[illegible] inhabitants of Camarina[1b] and Gela[1c] in Sicily first [illegible] each other, after which embassies from all the oth[illegible]ed at Gela to try to bring about a pacification. Aft[illegible]pinion on one side and the other, according to the [illegible] of the different parties complaining, Hermocrate[illegible]acusan,[1d] the most influential man among them, add[illegible]rds to the assembly:

4.58 424 8th Year/Summer SICILY Hermocrates addresses the Sicilians at Gela.

[illegible]ou, Sicilians, it is not because my city is the [illegible]test sufferer by the war, but in order to state [illegible]o me to be the best policy for the whole [illegible]n evil is a proposition so familiar to everyone [illegible] to develop it. No one is forced to engage in [illegible] out of it by fear, if he fancies there is any[illegible] To the former the gain appears greater than [illegible]tter would rather stand the risk than put up [illegible]rifice. [3] But if both should happen to have [illegible]nent for acting in this way, advice to make [illegible] and this, if we did but see it, is just what we [illegible] the present juncture."

4.59 424 8th Year/Summer SICILY Hermocrates begins his speech by declaring Sicily's need for peace.

[illegible]ne will dispute that we went to war at first in [illegible] individual interests, and that we are now, in [illegible]rests, debating how we can make peace; and [illegible]out having reached a fair agreement, we shall [illegible]

[illegible]of sense, we ought to see that our separate [illegible]at stake in the present congress: there is also [illegible]e have still time to save Sicily, the whole of [illegible] is menaced by Athenian ambition; and we [illegible]me of that people more imperious arguments [illegible]h I can advance, when we see the first power [illegible] mistakes with the few ships[1a] that she has at [illegible]nd under the fair name of alliance speciously

4.60 424 8th Year/Summer SICILY Hermocrates argues that war among Sicilians will only weaken them all and render them vulnerable to subjugation by Athens.

4.5[illegible]nd/or [illegible]sical Greek
4.5[illegible]f events in
4.5[illegible]
4.58.1c Gela: Map 4.25.
4.58.1d Syracuse: Map 4.25.
4.60.1a "Few ships"? At that time Athens had sixty triremes in Sicilian waters, no mean fleet. Was this written after the Sicilian expedition of 415?

seeking to exploit the natural hostility that exists between us. [2] If we go to war, and call in to help us a people that are ready enough to carry their arms even where they are not invited; and if we injure ourselves at our own expense, and at the same time serve as the pioneers of their dominion, we may expect when they see us worn out, that they will one day come with a larger armament, and seek to bring all of us into subjection."

4.61
424
8th Year/Summer
SICILY
Hermocrates claims that Athens is the common enemy of all Sicilians.

"And yet as sensible men, if we call in allies and court danger, it should be in order to enrich our different countries with new acquisitions, and not to ruin what they possess already; and we should understand that the internal discords which are so fatal to communities generally will be equally so to Sicily if we, its inhabitants, absorbed in our local quarrels, neglect the common enemy. [2] These considerations should reconcile individual with individual, and city with city, and unite us in a common effort to save the whole of Sicily. Nor should anyone imagine that the Dorians only are enemies of Athens, while the Chalcidian race is secured by its Ionian blood; [3] the attack in question is not inspired by hatred of one of two nationalities, but by a desire for the good things in Sicily, the common property of us all. [4] This is proved by the Athenian reception of the Chalcidian invitation: an ally who has never given them any assistance whatever, at once receives from them almost more than the treaty entitles him to. [5] That the Athenians should cherish this ambition and practice this policy is very excusable; and I do not blame those who wish to rule, but those who are too ready to serve. It is just as much in men's nature to rule those who submit to them, as it is to resist those who molest them. [6] Meanwhile all who see these dangers and refuse to provide for them properly, or who have come here without having made up their minds that our first duty is to unite to get rid of the common peril, are mistaken. [7] The quickest way to be rid of it is to make peace with each other; since the Athenians menace us not from their own country, but from that of those who invited them here. In this way instead of war resulting in war, peace quietly ends our quarrels; and the guests who come hither under fair pretenses for bad ends, will have good reason for going away without having attained them."

4.62
424
8th Year/Summer
SICILY
Hermocrates argues that regardless of the Athenian menace, peace itself is a blessing well worth seeking.

"So far as regards the Athenians such are the great advantages proved inherent in a wise policy. [2] Independently of this, in the face of the universal consent that peace is the first of blessings, how can we refuse to make it amongst ourselves; or do you not think that the good which you have, and the ills that you complain of, would be better preserved and cured by quiet than by war; that peace has its honors and splendors of a less perilous kind, not to mention the

gs that one might expand on, with the not
of war? These considerations should teach
words, but rather for everyone to look into
[3] If there be any here who feels certain
to effect his object, let not this surprise be
nent to him. Let him remember that many
chastise a wrongdoer, and failing to punish
en saved themselves; while many who have
an advantage, instead of gaining anything
ed to lose what they had. [4] Vengeance is
l because wrong has been done, or strength
dent; but the incalculable element in the
est influence, and is the most treacherous,
st useful of all things, as it frightens us all
us consider before attacking each other."

4.63
424
8th Year/Summer
SICILY
Hermocrates asserts that peace will leave Sicilians free, while continued war will lead to dependence on others.

w allow the undefined fear of this unknown
te terror of the Athenians' presence to pro-
ssion, and let us consider any failure to carry
e may each have sketched out for ourselves
for by these obstacles, and send away the
try; and if everlasting peace be impossible
events make a treaty for as long a term as
r private differences to another day. [2] In
hat the adoption of my advice will leave us
ate, and as such arbiters of our own destiny,
ad deeds with equal effect; while its rejection
on others, and thus not only impotent to
e most favorable supposition, friends to our
d with our natural friends."

4.64
424
8th Year/Summer
SICILY
Hermocrates concludes by arguing that Sicilians should always unite against any foreign invader.

as I said at first, the representative of a great
defending myself than of attacking others, I
something in anticipation of these dangers. I
nyself for the sake of hurting my enemies, or
as to think myself equally master of my own
ich I cannot command; but I am ready to
on. [2] I call upon the rest of you to imitate
free will, without being forced to do so by
no disgrace in connections giving way to one
orian, or a Chalcidian to his brethren; above
neighbors, live in the same country, are girt
by the same name of Sicilians. We shall go to
hen the time comes, and again make peace
ns of future congresses; [4] but the foreign

invader, if we are wise, will always find us united against him, since the hurt of one is the danger of all; and we should never, in future, invite into the island either allies or mediators. [5] By so acting we shall at the present moment do for Sicily a double service, ridding her at once of the Athenians, and of civil war, and in future shall live in freedom at home, and be less menaced from abroad."

4.65
424
8th Year/Summer
SICILY-ATHENS
The Sicilians make peace among themselves. The Athenians return home, where their generals are prosecuted for bribery.

Such were the words of Hermocrates. The Sicilians took his advice, and came to an understanding among themselves to end the war, each keeping what they had—the Camarinaeans taking Morgantina[1a] at a fixed price to be paid to the Syracusans—[2] and the allies of the Athenians called the officers in command, and told them that they were going to make peace and that they would be included in the treaty. The generals assenting, the peace was concluded, and the Athenian fleet afterwards sailed away from Sicily.[2a] [3] Upon their arrival at Athens, the Athenians banished Pythodorus and Sophocles, and fined Eurymedon for having taken bribes to depart when they might have subdued Sicily.[3a] [4] So thoroughly had the present prosperity persuaded the Athenians that nothing could withstand them, and that they could achieve what was possible and what was impracticable alike, with means ample or inadequate it mattered not. The reason for this was their general extraordinary success, which made them confuse their strength with their hopes.

4.66
424
8th Year/Summer
MEGARA
The Megarian popular party plots with Athens to open their gates to a surprise attack against Nisaea and Megara.

The same summer the Megarians[1a] in the city, pressed by the hostilities of the Athenians, who invaded their country twice every year with all their forces, and harassed by the incursions of their own exiles at Pegae,[1b] who had been expelled in a revolution by the popular party, began to ask each other whether it would not be better to receive back their exiles, and free the city from one of its two scourges. [2] The friends of the exiles perceiving the agitation, now more openly than before demanded the adoption of this proposition; [3] and the leaders of The People, seeing that the sufferings of the times had worn down the determination of their supporters, entered in their alarm into correspondence with the Athenian generals, Hippocrates son of Ariphron, and Demosthenes son of Alcisthenes, and resolved to betray the city, thinking this less dangerous to themselves than the return of the party which they had banished. It was accordingly arranged that the Athenians should first take the long walls extending for nearly a mile from the city to the port of Nisaea[3a] to prevent the Peloponnesians coming to the rescue from that place, where they formed the sole garrison to secure the fidelity of Megara; and that after this the attempt

4.65.1a Morgantina: Map 4.25.
4.65.2a The story of Athenian activity in Sicily is continued in 5.5.
4.65.3a It was not all that unusual for Athenians to punish statesmen or generals with whom they were angry or disappointed by fines or exile. Note also the fining of Pericles (2.65.3), as well as the banishment of Thucydides himself (5.26.5).
4.66.1a Megara: Map 4.69.
4.66.1b Pegae: Map 4.69.
4.66.3a Nisaea: Map 4.69.

sho… ontrol of the upper city which, it was thought,
wo… less difficulty.

…ns had been arranged between themselves and
the… as to words and actions, sailed by night to
Mi… gara, with six hundred hoplites under the comma… took a position in a ditch not far off, out of
wh… aken for the walls; while [2] Demosthenes, the
oth… detachment of Plataean light troops and another
of … in ambush in the precinct of Enyalius,[2b] which
was… ew of it, except those whose business it was to
kn… e before daybreak, the traitors in Megara began
to … ng time back, under pretense of marauding, and
in … of opening the gates, they had been used, with
the… command, to carry by night a rowboat upon a
car… sea and to sail out, bringing it back again before
day… ng it within the wall through the gates in order,
as … fle the Athenian blockade from Minoa, there
bei… in the harbor. [4] On the present occasion the
car… s, which had been opened in the usual way for
the… ans, with whom this had been arranged, saw it,
and… the ambush in order to reach the gates before
the… while the cart was still there to prevent their
bei… moment their Megarian accomplices killed the
gu… he first to run in was Demosthenes with his
Pla… where the trophy now stands; and he was no
soo… n the Plataeans engaged and defeated the nearest… who had taken the alarm and come to the rescue… for the approaching Athenian hoplites.

4.67
424
8th Year/Summer
MEGARA
The Athenians attack from ambush and gain entrance by a gate that has been opened by a stratagem of their Megarian confederates.

…thenians as fast as they entered went against the
wal… ponnesian garrison stood their ground at first,
and… lt, and some of them were killed, but the main
bo… the night attack and the sight of the Megarian
tra… m making them think that all Megara had gone
ove… o happened also that the Athenian herald of his
ow… vited any of the Megarians to join the Athenian
ran… oner heard by the garrison than they gave way
and… were the victims of a prearranged attack, took
ref… daybreak, the walls being now taken and the
Me… reat agitation, the persons who had negotiated

4.68
424
8th Year/Summer
MEGARA
The Athenians capture the long walls but the popular party's plot to open the city gates is betrayed to their Megarian opponents, who prevent its execution.

4.67… land's cap-
…1, and Map

4.67… for buildings

4.67… *ipoli*. They
…ile force of young recruits serving as a frontier guard; see A.W. Gomme, *A Historical Commentary on Thucydides*, iii (Oxford, 1956), 529.

4.67.2b The location of this sanctuary or shrine of Enyalius has not been identified.

with the Athenians, supported by the rest of the popular party which was privy to the plot, said that they ought to open the gates and march out to battle. [5] It had been agreed between them that the Athenians should rush in the moment that the gates were opened, and that the conspirators were to be distinguished from the rest by being anointed with oil, and so avoid being hurt. They could open the gates with more security, as four thousand Athenian hoplites from Eleusis,[5a] and six hundred horse, had marched all night according to plan and were now close at hand. [6] The conspirators were all anointed and at their posts by the gates when one of their accomplices denounced the plot to the opposite party, who gathered together and came in a body, and roundly said that they must not march out—a thing they had never yet ventured on even when they were in greater force than at present—or wantonly compromise the safety of the city; and that if what they said was not heeded the battle would have to be fought in Megara. For the rest, they gave no sign of their knowledge of the intrigue, but stoutly maintained that their advice was the best, and meanwhile kept close by and watched the gates, making it impossible for the conspirators to effect their purpose.

4.69
424
8th Year/Summer
MEGARA
The Athenians invest Nisaea and its garrison surrenders.

The Athenian generals seeing that some obstacle had arisen, and that the capture of the city by force was no longer practicable, at once proceeded to invest Nisaea, thinking that if they could take it before relief arrived, the surrender of Megara would soon follow. [2] Iron, stonemasons, and everything else required quickly coming up from Athens, the Athenians started from the wall which they occupied, and from this point built a cross wall looking toward Megara down to the sea on either side of Nisaea;[2a] the ditch and the walls being divided among the army, stones and bricks taken from the suburb, and the fruit trees and timber cut down to make a palisade wherever this seemed necessary; the houses also in the suburb with the addition of battlements sometimes became part of the fortification. The whole of this day the work continued, [3] and by the afternoon of the next the wall was all but completed, when the garrison in Nisaea, alarmed by the absolute want of provisions, which they used to take in for the day from the upper city, not anticipating any speedy relief from the Peloponnesians, and supposing Megara to be hostile, capitulated to the Athenians on condition that they should give up their arms, and should each be ransomed for a stipulated sum; their Spartan commander, and any others of his countrymen in the place, being left to the discretion of the Athenians. [4] On these conditions they surrendered and came out, and the Athenians broke down the long walls at their point of junction with Megara, took possession of Nisaea, and went on with their other preparations.

4.68.5a Eleusis: Map 4.69.
4.69.2a Presumably "looking toward Megara" from Nisaea. See the scheme of the Athenian siege walls of Nisaea in Map 4.69.

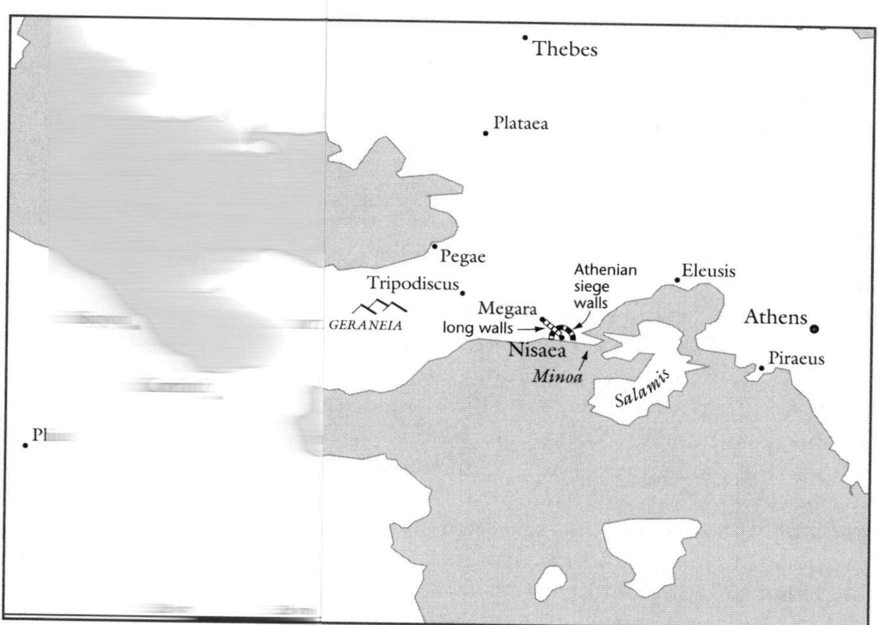

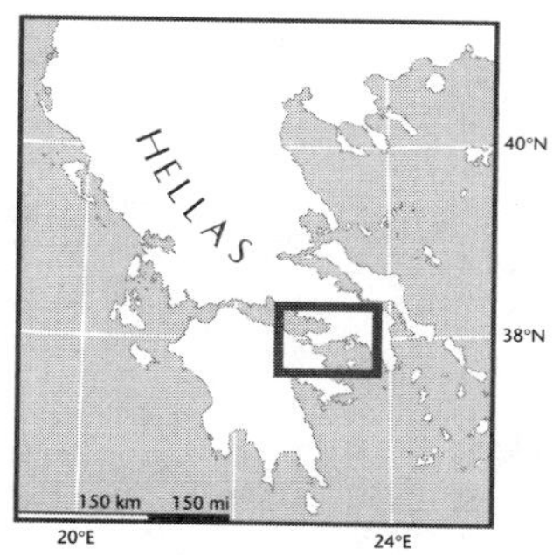

MA ACK ON MEGARA

rtan Brasidas son of Tellis happened to be in the 4.70 424 8th Year/Summer MEGARA The Spartan Brasidas, calling for Boeotian help, marches with local allied forces to Megara, hoping to rescue Nisaea and at the least to occupy Megara before it falls.
nei d Corinth,[1a] getting ready an army for Thrace.[1b]
As capture of the walls, fearing for the Pelopon-
nes safety of Megara, he sent to the Boeotians to
me ible at Tripodiscus,[1c] a village of the Megarid on
the eia.[1d] He then went himself, with two thousand
sev hoplites, four hundred Phliasians,[1e] six hundred
Sic s of his own as he had already levied, expecting
to . [2] Hearing of its fall (he had marched out by
nig ook three hundred picked men from the army,
wit ing should be known, and came up to Megara
unc ns, who were down by the sea, ostensibly, and
real t Nisaea, but above all to get into Megara and
sec ngly invited the townspeople to admit his party,
say recovering Nisaea.

garian factions feared that he might expel them 4.71 424 8th Year/Summer MEGARA The Megarians decide to see which side will win before admitting anyone into their city.
and he other that the popular party, apprehensive of

4.70 Brasidas last his shield ship at

4.70 ch of Brasidas and his army to Thrace (Map 4.78, AY) in 4.78.

4.70.1c Tripodiscus: Map 4.69.

4.70.1d Mount Geraneia: Map 4.69.

4.70.1e Phlius: Map 4.69.

this very danger, might set upon them, and that the city would be thus destroyed by a battle within its gates under the eyes of the Athenians lying in ambush. He was accordingly refused admittance, both parties electing to remain quiet and await the event; [2] each expecting a battle between the Athenians and the relieving army, and thinking it safer to see their friends victorious before declaring in their favor.

Unable to get his way, Brasidas went back to the rest of the army.

4.72
424
8th Year/Summer
MEGARA
The Boeotians arrive; their cavalry attacks the Athenian light troops and are countered by the Athenian cavalry.

[4.72.1] At daybreak the Boeotians joined him. Having determined to relieve Megara, whose danger they considered their own, even before hearing from Brasidas, they were already in full force at Plataea[1a] when his messenger arrived to add spurs to their resolution; and they at once sent on to him two thousand two hundred hoplites, and six hundred horse, returning home with the main body. [2] The whole army thus assembled numbered six thousand hoplites. The Athenian hoplites were drawn up by Nisaea and the sea; but the light troops being scattered over the plain were attacked by the Boeotian horse and driven to the sea, being taken entirely by surprise, as on previous occasions no relief had ever come to the Megarians from any quarter. [3] Here the Boeotians were in their turn charged and engaged by the Athenian horse, and a cavalry action ensued which lasted a long time, and in which both parties claimed the victory. [4] The Athenians killed and stripped the leader of the Boeotian horse and some few of his comrades who had charged right up to Nisaea, and remaining masters of the bodies gave them back under truce, and set up a trophy; but regarding the action as a whole the forces separated without either side having gained a decisive advantage, the Boeotians returning to their army and the Athenians to Nisaea.

4.73
424
8th Year Summer
MEGARA
The Peloponnesians offer battle but do not attack. The Athenians also hold back, unwilling to risk defeat. The Megarians view the failure to fight as a Spartan victory and open their gates to Brasidas.

After this Brasidas and the army came nearer to the sea and to Megara, and taking up a convenient position, remained quiet in order of battle, expecting to be attacked by the Athenians and knowing that the Megarians were waiting to see which would be the victor. [2] This attitude seemed to present two advantages. Without taking the offensive or willingly provoking the hazards of a battle, they openly showed their readiness to fight, and thus without bearing the burden of the day would fairly reap its honors; while at the same time they effectually served their interests at Megara. [3] For if they had failed to show themselves, they would not have had a chance, but would have certainly been considered vanquished, and have lost the city. As it was, the Athenians might possibly not be inclined to accept their challenge, and their object would be attained without fighting. [4] And so it turned out. The Athenians formed outside the long walls, and the enemy not attacking, there remained motionless; their generals having decided that the risk was too unequal. In fact most of their objects had been already attained; and they would have to begin a battle against supe-

4.72.1a Thebes and Plataea, in relation to Megara: Map 4.69. The occupation of Megara by the Athenians would have cut Boeotian land communications with the Peloponnesus.

rio[illegible]orious could only gain Megara, while a defeat wo[illegible]f their hoplite forces. For the enemy it was different[illegible]tually represented in his army risked each only a par[illegible]night well be more audacious. Accordingly after wai[illegible]hout either side attacking, the Athenians withdre[illegible]oponnesians after them to the point from which the[illegible]ds of the Megarian exiles now threw aside their hes[illegible]gates to Brasidas and the commanders from the diff[illegible]pon him as the victor and upon the Athenians as hav[illegible]—and receiving them into the city proceeded to dis[illegible]the party in correspondence with the Athenians bei[illegible] things had taken.

4.74 424 8th Year/Summer MEGARA Both sides return home, leaving Megara firmly in the hands of the oligarchs, who then execute one hundred of their foes.

[illegible]the allies go home, and himself went back to Co[illegible] expedition to Thrace, his original destination. [2][illegible]turning home, the Megarians in the city most imp[illegible]an negotiation, knowing that they had been det[illegible]ared; while the rest conferred with the friends of the[illegible]he party at Pegae, after binding them under sol[illegible]ngeance for the past, and only to consult the real int[illegible]wever, as soon as they were in office, they held a rev[illegible]d separating the battalions, picked out about a hu[illegible] and of those who were thought to be most inv[illegible]ence with the Athenians, brought them before the[illegible]g the vote to be given openly, had them conde[illegible] established a close oligarchy in the city—[4] a rev[illegible]ery long while, although effected by a very few par[illegible]

4.75 424 8th Year/Summer LESBOS-PONTUS Athenians prevent the Mytilenian exiles from fortifying Antandrus. Lamachus loses his ships in Pontus and marches home by land.

[illegible]Mytilenians were about to fortify Antandrus[1a] as the[illegible] Demodocus and Aristides, the commanders of the[illegible]ngaged in collecting tribute,[1b] heard on the He[illegible] being done to the place (Lamachus their colleag[illegible]en ships into the Pontus[1d]) and conceived fears of i[illegible]Anaia,[1c] the place in which the Samian exiles had est[illegible] annoy Samos,[1f] helping the Peloponnesians by sen[illegible], and keeping the city in agitation and receiving

4.73[illegible]plites and six [illegible]2). The [illegible] hoplites [illegible]eusis (4.68), [illegible]l arrived [illegible]sthenes' [illegible] (4.67).

4.75[illegible]iles hostile [illegible]ytilene,

4.75[illegible] missions of [illegible]ribute in [illegible] (Winter [illegible]), and here in Summer 424. For various reasons these notices have been thought to signify reassessments of tribute in 430, 428, and 425, for which last a large inscription survives indicating great increases all around and including cities in the Pontus (Map 4.75), to which Lamachus had now gone, as described in 4.75.2. See Appendix B, The Athenian Empire, §2, 10.

4.75.1c Hellespont: Map 4.75.

4.75.1d Pontus (the Euxine or Black Sea): Map 4.75.

4.75.1e Anaia: Map 4.75.

4.75.1f Samos: Map 4.75.

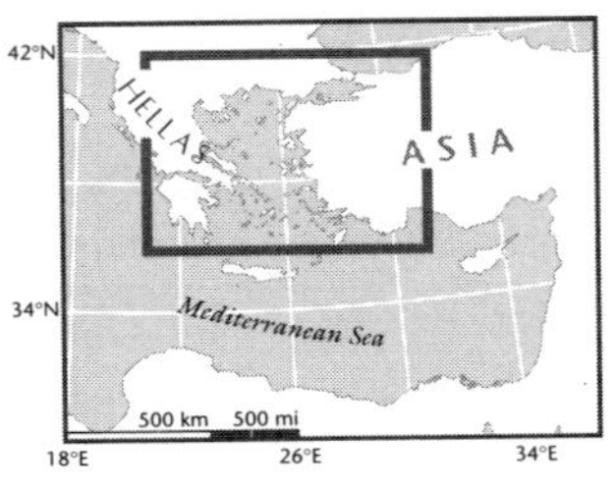

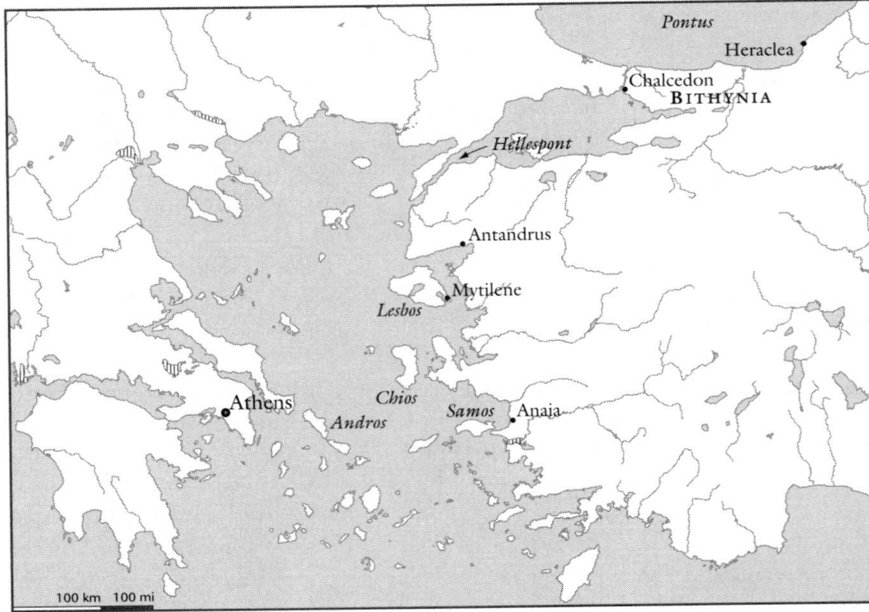

MAP 4.75 THE NORTH AEGEAN THEATER, 424

all its outlaws. They accordingly got together a force from the allies and set sail, defeated in battle the troops that met them from Antandrus, and retook the place. [2] Not long after, Lamachus, who had sailed into the Pontus, lost his ships at anchor in the river Calex, in the territory of Heraclea, rain having fallen in the interior and the flood coming suddenly down upon them; and himself and his troops passed by land through the Bithynian Thracians on the Asiatic side, and arrived at Chalcedon,[2a] the Megarian colony at the mouth of the Pontus.

4.76
424
8th Year/Summer
BOEOTIA
Athens plans a series of simultaneous attacks in Boeotia.

The same summer immediately after his return from the Megarid, the Athenian general Demosthenes arrived at Naupactus[1a] with forty ships. [2] He and Hippocrates had had overtures made to them by certain men in the cities in Boeotia[2a] who wished to change the constitution and introduce a democracy as at Athens.[2b] Ptoeodorus, a Theban exile, was the chief mover in this intrigue. [3] The seaport city of Siphae,[3a] on the bay of Crisae[3b] in the territory of Thespiae,[3c] was to be betrayed to them by one party; and Chaeronea[3d] (a dependency of what was formerly called the Minyan, but now the Boeotian, Orchomenus[3e]) was to be put into their hands by

4.75.2a Heraclea, Bithynia, Chalcedon: Map 4.75.
4.76.1a Naupactus: Map 4.77, AX.
4.76.2a Boeotia: Map 4.77, BY.
4.76.2b For the Boeotian constitution, see 5.38 and note 5.38.2a.
4.76.3a Siphae: Map 4.77, BY.
4.76.3b Bay of Crisae: Map 4.77, BY.
4.76.3c Thespiae: Map 4.77, BY.
4.76.3d Chaeronea: Map 4.77, AY.
4.76.3e Orchomenus: Map 4.77, AY.

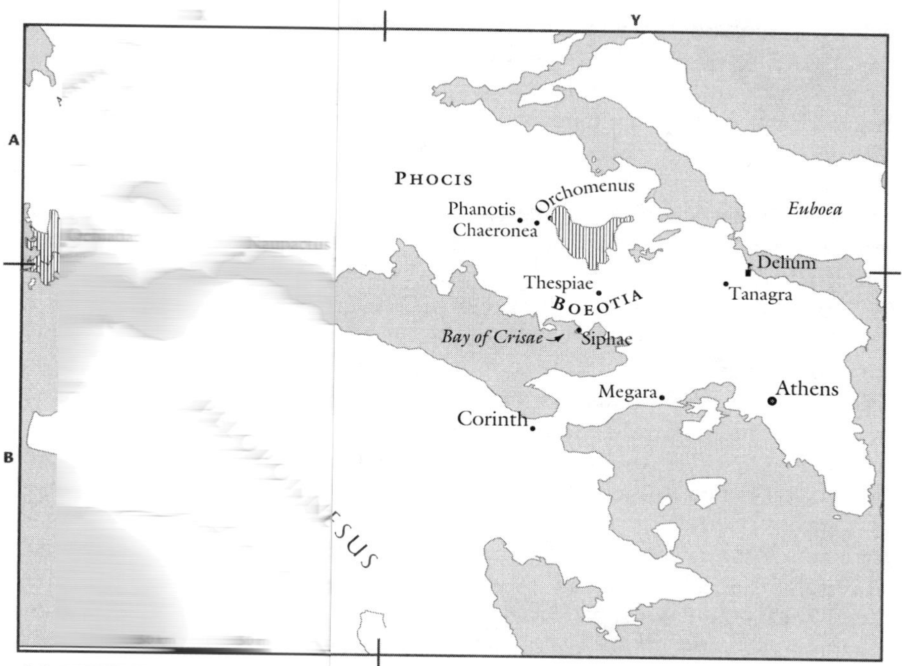

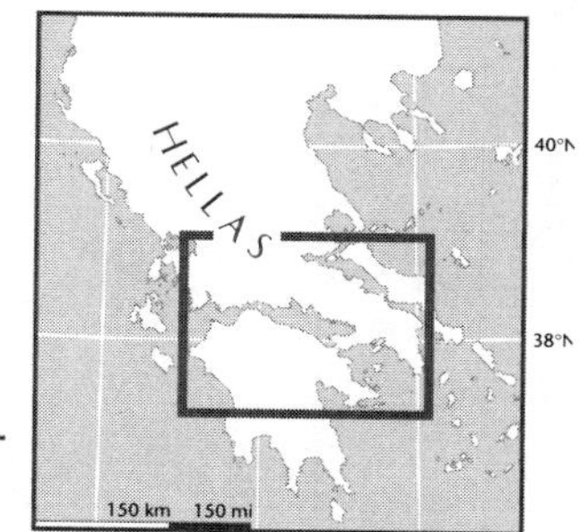

MA AN TO ATTACK BOEOTIA

an ose exiles were very active in the business, hiring me Some Phocians also were in the plot, Chaeronea bei Boeotia and close to Phanotis in Phocis.[3f] [4] At th ians were to seize the sanctuary of Apollo at De of Tanagra[4a] looking toward Euboea;[4b] and all th place simultaneously upon an appointed day in or might be unable to unite to oppose them at De detained by disturbances at home. [5] Should th nd Delium be fortified, its authors confidently ex evolution should immediately follow in Boeotia, yet heir hands, and the country being harassed by in each instance nearby for the partisans engaged in remain as they were, but that the rebels being su ns, and the forces of the oligarchs divided, it w hile to settle matters according to their wishes.

preparation. Hippocrates, with a force raised at ho moment to take the field against the Boeotians,

4.77
424
8th Year/Summer
ACARNANIA
The Acarnanians compel Oeniadae to join the Athenians; Demosthenes enlists allies and conquers Salynthius of Agrae.

4.7 cis: Map

4.7 , BY.
4.7

while he sent on Demosthenes with the forty ships above mentioned to Naupactus to raise in those parts an army of Acarnanians and other allies, and sail for Siphae, expecting that it would be betrayed; a day having been agreed on for the simultaneous execution of both these operations. [2] Demosthenes on his arrival found Oeniadae[2a] already compelled by the united Acarnanians to join the Athenian confederacy, and himself raising all the allies in those countries, marched against and subdued Salynthius and the Agraeans;[2b] after which he devoted himself to the preparations necessary to enable him to be at Siphae on the appointed day.[2c]

4.78
424
8th Year/Summer
THESSALY
Brasidas marches his Peloponnesian army through Thessaly to Macedonia so rapidly that the Thessalians are unable to stop him.

About the same time in the summer, Brasidas set out on his march for the Thracian region with seventeen hundred hoplites, and arriving at Heraclea in Trachis,[1a] sent on from there a messenger to his friends at Pharsalus[1b] to ask them to conduct himself and his army through the country. Accordingly there came to Melitia in Achaea[1c] Panaerus, Dorus, Hippolochidas, Torylaus, and Strophacus, the Chalcidian *proxenus*,[1d] under whose escort he resumed his march. [2] He was also accompanied by other Thessalians, among whom was Niconidas from Larissa,[2a] a friend of Perdiccas. It was never very easy to traverse Thessaly[2b] without an escort; and throughout all Hellas for an armed force to pass without leave through a neighbor's country was a delicate step to take. Besides this the Thessalian people had always sympathized with the Athenians. [3] Indeed if instead of the customary close oligarchy there had been a constitutional government in Thessaly, he would never have been able to proceed; since even as it was, he was met on his march at the river Enipeus[3a] by certain of the opposite party who forbade his further progress, and complained of his making the attempt without the consent of the nation. [4] To this his escort answered that they had no intention of taking him through against their will; they were only friends in attendance on an unexpected visitor. Brasidas himself added that he came as a friend to Thessaly and its inhabitants; his arms not being directed against them but against the Athenians, with whom he was at war, and that although he knew of no quarrel between the Thessalians and Spartans to prevent the two nations having access to each other's territory, he neither would nor could proceed against their wishes; he could only beg them not to stop him. [5] With this answer they went away, and he took the advice of his escort, and pushed on without halting, before a greater force might gather to prevent him. Thus in the day that he set out from Melitia he performed the whole distance to Pharsalus, and encamped

4.77.2a Oeniadae: Map 4.77, AX.
4.77.2b Agraea, a pro-Peloponnesian state in 425 (see 3.106.2): Map 4.77. AX.
4.77.2c The narrative of this planned attack on Boeotia is continued in 4.89.
4.78.1a Heraclea in Trachis: Map 4.78, BX. This city was last mentioned in 3.100 and appears again in 5.12.
4.78.1b Pharsalus: Map 4.78, BX.
4.79.1c Melitia in Achaea: Map 4.78, BX.
4.78.1d A *proxenus,* though a citizen and resident of his own state, served as a "friend or representative" (much like a modern honorary consul) of a foreign state.
4.78.2a Larissa: Map 4.78, BX.
4.78.2b Thessaly: Map 4.78, BX.
4.78.3a The Enipeus river runs near to Melitia: Map 4.78, BX.

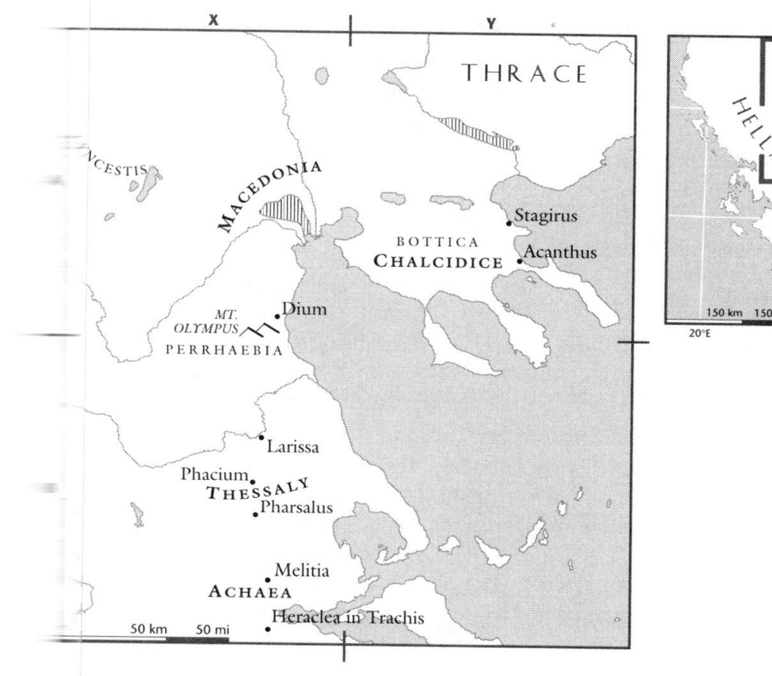

MA
BR
TH

on nd so to Phacium,[5b] and from there to Perrhaebia an escort went back and the Perrhaebians, who are ought him to Dium,[6a] a Macedonian city on the slo [6b] looking toward Thessaly in the dominions of Pe

urried through Thessaly and reached Perdiccas an y armed force could be assembled to stop him. [2 army from the Peloponnesus had been obtained by were in revolt against Athens and by Perdiccus, wh successes of the Athenians. The Chalcidians th the first objects of an Athenian expedition (not th which had not yet revolted did not also secretly joi Perdiccas, although not openly at war with the

4.79
424
8th Year/Summer
THRACE
Brasidas had been invited by Perdiccas of Macedonia and by Chalcidian and Thracian cities who had revolted, or wished to revolt, from Athens.

4.78 Pharsalus:
4.78
4.78
4.78
4.78 AX.
4.79

Athenians, also had his apprehensions on account of his old quarrels with them, and above all wished to subdue Arrhabaeus king of the Lyncestians.[2a] [3] It had been less difficult for them to get an army to leave the Peloponnesus, because of the ill fortune of the Spartans at the present moment.

4.80
424
8th Year/Summer
SPARTA
Wishing to retaliate somehow against Athens, Sparta was happy to send warlike Helots out of Laconia. A Spartan atrocity against the Helots is described.

The attacks of the Athenians upon the Peloponnesus, and in particular upon Laconia, might, it was hoped, be diverted most effectively by annoying them in return, and by sending an army to their allies, especially as they were willing to maintain it and asked for it to aid them in revolting. [2] The Spartans were also glad to have an excuse for sending some of the Helots[2a] out of the country, for fear that the present aspect of affairs and the occupation of Pylos might encourage them to revolt. [3] Indeed fear of their numbers and obstinacy even persuaded the Spartans to the action which I shall now relate, their policy at all times having been governed by the necessity of taking precautions against them.[3a] The Helots were invited by a proclamation to pick out those of their number who claimed to have most distinguished themselves in the wars, in order that they might receive their freedom; the object being to test them, as it was thought that the first to claim their freedom would be the most high-spirited and the most apt to rebel. [4] As many as two thousand were selected accordingly, who crowned themselves and went round the temples, rejoicing in their new freedom. [5] The Spartans, however, soon afterwards did away with them, and no one ever knew how each of them perished. The Spartans now therefore gladly sent seven hundred Helots as hoplites with Brasidas,[5a] who recruited the rest of his force by means of money in the Peloponnesus.

4.81
424
8th Year/Summer
THRACE
Brasidas captures some cities and his just and moderate conduct induces others to revolt. The memory of his wise conduct helped Sparta years later.

Brasidas himself was sent out by the Spartans mainly at his own desire, although the Chalcidians also were eager to have a man so energetic as he had shown himself whenever there was anything to be done at Sparta, and whose later service abroad proved of the utmost use to his country. [2] At the present moment his just and moderate conduct toward the cities generally succeeded in persuading many to revolt, besides the places which he managed to take by treachery; and thus when the Spartans desired to negotiate, as they ultimately did, they had places to offer in exchange, and the burden of war meanwhile shifted from the Peloponnesus. Later on in the war, after the events in Sicily,[2a] the present valor and conduct of Brasidas, which was known by experience to some, by hearsay to others, was what mainly created an esteem for the Spartans among the allies of Athens. [3] He was the first who went out and showed himself so good a man at all points as to leave behind him the conviction that the rest were like him.

4.82
424
8th Year/Summer
THRACE
Athens declares war on Perdiccas.

Meanwhile his arrival in the Thracian region no sooner became known

4.79.2a Two campaigns against Arrhabaeus in Lyncestis (Map 4.78, AX) are described in 4.83 and 4.124–28.

4.80.2a Helots of Sparta: See Appendix C, Spartan Institutions, §3–4.

4.80.3a This famous comment by Thucydides has also been taken in a more restricted sense, to wit, "their policy with regard to the Helots has been governed by the necessity of taking precautions."

4.80.5a The return, emancipation, and settlement of these Helots is described in 5.34; see Appendix C, Spartan Institutions, §9.

4.81.2a This remark sheds light on the date of the composition of this section of the history; see the Introduction (sect. II.ii).

to … ey declared war against Perdiccas, whom they
reg… he expedition, and kept a closer watch on their
alli…

4.83
424
8th Year/Summer
LYNCESTIS
Perdiccas and Brasidas march against Arrhabaeus, king of Lyncestis. Brasidas insists on parleying first, and agrees to withdraw without invading Lyncestis. Perdiccas is furious and thereafter reduces his subsidy to Brasidas.

… idas and his army, Perdiccas immediately set out
wit… n forces against his neighbor Arrhabaeus son of
Br… cestian Macedonians, with whom he had a quarrel … subdue. [2] However, when he arrived with his
arr… pass leading into Lyncestis,[2a] Brasidas told him
tha… stilities he wished to try to persuade Arrhabaeus
to … a, [3] as Arrhabaeus had already made overtures
inc… o let Brasidas arbitrate between them, and the
Ch… ccompanied Brasidas had warned him not to
rer… ons of Perdiccas, in order to insure his greater
zea… des, the envoys of Perdiccas had talked at Sparta
ab… f the places round him into alliance with them;
an… he might take a larger view of the question of
Ar… however retorted that he had not brought Brasi-
da… their quarrel but to subdue the enemies whom
he … and that while he, Perdiccas, was paying for half
of … of faith for Brasidas to parley with Arrhabaeus.
[6] … disregarded the wishes of Perdiccas and held the
pa… allowed himself to be persuaded to lead off the
arr… country of Arrhabaeus; after which Perdiccas,
ho… not kept faith with him, contributed only a third
ins… rt of the army.

4.84
424
8th Year/Summer
ACANTHUS
Brasidas threatens Acanthus just before the grape harvest. He enters the city alone to address the citizens.

… hout delay, Brasidas marched with the Chalcidian… ony of the Andrians,[1a] and arrived just before the
gr… habitants were divided into two parties on the
qu… those who had joined the Chalcidians in inviting
hi… . However, fear for their grapes, which were still
on … sidas to persuade the multitude to admit him
alc… d to say before making a decision; and he was
ad… appeared before the people and, not being a bad
sp… ressed them as follows:

4.85
424
8th Year/Summer
ACANTHUS
Brasidas speaks to the Acanthians, asking them to aid Sparta against Athens.

… rtans have sent me out with an army to make
… e gave for the war when we began it, namely,
… var with the Athenians in order to free Hellas.
… g has been caused by mistaken expectations

4.8…
4.8… ndros, Map
4.8… speaking
…, ungra-
… See Appen-
… Groups, §8,
… otypes con-
….

about the war in Greece which led us to hope that by our own unassisted efforts, and without your risking anything, we could effect the speedy downfall of the Athenians; and you must not blame us for this, as we have now come at the first moment we could, prepared with your aid to do our best to defeat them. [3] I am therefore astonished at finding your gates shut against me, and at not meeting with a better welcome. [4] We Spartans thought of you as allies eager to have us, to whom we should come in spirit even before we were with you in body; and in this expectation undertook all the risks of a march of many days through a strange country, so far did our zeal carry us. [5] It will be a terrible thing if after this you have other intentions, and mean to stand in the way of your own and Hellenic freedom. [6] It is not merely that you oppose me yourselves; but wherever I may go people will be less inclined to join me, on the score that you, to whom I first came—an important city like Acanthus, and prudent men like the Acanthians—refused to admit me. I shall have nothing to prove that the reason which I advance is the true one; it will be said either that there is something unfair in the freedom which I offer, or that I am here in insufficient force and unable to protect you against an attack from Athens. [7] Yet when I went with the army which I now have to the relief of Nisaea, the Athenians did not venture to engage me although in greater force than I;[7a] and it is not likely they will ever send by sea against you an army as numerous as they had at Nisaea."

4.86
424
8th Year/Summer
ACANTHUS
Brasidas guarantees that Sparta will respect Acanthus' independence and will not interfere in her affairs.

"And for myself, I have come here not to hurt but to free the Hellenes: witness the solemn oaths by which I have bound my government that the allies that I may bring over shall be independent; and besides my object in coming is not to obtain your alliance by force or fraud, but to offer you mine to help you against your Athenian masters. [2] I protest, therefore, against any suspicions of my intentions after the guarantees which I offer, and equally so against doubts of my ability to protect you, and I invite you to join me without hesitation."

[3] "Some of you may hang back because they have private enemies, and fear that I may put the city into the hands of a party: none need be more tranquil than they. [4] I am not come here to help this party or that; and I do not consider that I should be bringing you freedom in any real sense, if I should disregard your constitution, and enslave the many to the few or the few to the many. [5] This would be heavier than a foreign yoke; and we Spartans instead of being thanked for our pains, should get neither honor nor glory but,

4.85.7a As Thucydides comments in 4.108.5, Brasidas is lying, or at best stretching the truth, here. His forces at Nisaea, combined with the Boeotians present (4.70–72), were certainly more numerous than the Athenians on that occasion, at least according to Thucydides' account (4.67–68); see note 4.73.3a.

oaches. The charges which strengthen our
st the Athenians would on our own showing
s, and more hateful in us than in those who
honesty; [6] as it is more disgraceful for per-
e what they covet by fair-seeming fraud than
e aggression having for its justification the
ves, the other being simply a piece of clever

4.87
424
8th Year/Summer
ACANTHUS
Brasidas concludes by threatening to ravage Acanthian territory if Acanthus refuses to join his "Hellenic liberation."

cerns us greatly, we attend to it with great
nd the oaths that I have mentioned, what
you have that it is indeed in our interests to
than when you compare our words with our
nd that they are consistent."

nsiderations of mine you put in the plea of
t your friendly feeling should save you from
sal; if you say that freedom, in your opinion,
rs, and that it is right to offer it to those who
force it on any against their will, then I shall
es of your country to witness that I came for
cted, and shall do my best to compel you by
[3] I shall do so without scruple, being justi-
ich constrains me; first, to prevent the Spared by you, their friends, in the event of your
the moneys that you pay to the Athenians;
t the Hellenes from being hindered by you in
de. [4] Otherwise indeed we should have no
ose; except in the name of some public inter-
Spartans have to free those who do not wish
ot aspire to: it is what we are laboring to put
wrong the greater number if we allowed you
the independence that we offer to all. [6]
decide wisely, and strive to begin the work of
nes, and gain for yourselves endless renown,
e loss, and cover your commonwealth with

4.88
424
8th Year/Summer
ACANTHUS
The Acanthians decide to revolt from Athens.

Brasidas. The Acanthians, after much had been
sai estion, gave their votes in secret, and the majority. ctive arguments of Brasidas and by fear for their
vin from Athens; not however admitting the army
un sonal security for the oaths sworn by his govern-

4.8 I.ii) for a dis-
dides.

ment before they sent him out, assuring the independence of the allies whom he might bring over. [2] Not long after, Stagirus,[2a] a colony of the Andrians, followed their example and revolted. Such were the events of this summer.[2b]

4.89
424/3
8th Year/Winter
BOEOTIA
Athenian attacks at Delium, Siphae, and Chaeronea fail due to faulty timing and the betrayal of their plan to the Boeotians.

It was in the first days of the winter following that the places in Boeotia were to be put into the hands of the Athenian generals, Hippocrates and Demosthenes, the latter of whom was to go with his ships to Siphae, the former to Delium.[1a] A mistake, however, was made in the days on which they were each to start; and Demosthenes sailing first to Siphae, with the Acarnanians and many of the allies from those parts on board, failed to effect anything because the plot had been betrayed by Nicomachus, a Phocian from Phanotis,[1b] who informed the Spartans and they the Boeotians. [2] Help accordingly flocked in from all parts of Boeotia, and since Hippocrates had not yet entered the country to make his diversion, Siphae and Chaeronea[2a] were promptly secured and the conspirators, informed of the mistake, did not cause any trouble in the cities.

4.90
424/3
8th Year/Winter
DELIUM
The Athenian army under Hippocrates advances to Delium and fortifies it before marching back to Attica.

Meanwhile Hippocrates called out the Athenians in full force, citizens and resident aliens, and the foreigners in Athens,[1a] and arrived at his destination after the Boeotians had already come back from Siphae, and encamping his army began to fortify the sanctuary of Apollo at Delium,[1b] in the following manner. [2] A trench was dug all round the temple and the consecrated ground, and the earth thrown up from the excavation was made to do duty as a wall, in which stakes were also planted, the vines round the sanctuary being cut down and thrown in, together with stones and bricks pulled down from the houses near, using, in short, every means to build the rampart. Wooden towers were also erected where they were wanted, and where there was no part of the temple buildings left standing, as on the side where the gallery once existing had fallen in. [3] The work was begun on the third day after leaving home, and continued during the fourth till dinnertime on the fifth, [4] when most of it being now finished, the army marched about a mile and a quarter from Delium on its way home. From this point, most of the light troops went straight on, while the hoplites halted and remained where they were; Hippocrates stayed behind at Delium to arrange the posts and to give directions for the completion of such part of the outworks as had been left unfinished.

4.91
424/3
8th Year/Winter
DELIUM
The Boeotians advance upon the Athenians. Against the advice of the other boeotarchs, Pagondas urges an immediate attack.

During the days thus employed the Boeotians were mustering at Tanagra,[1a] and by the time that they had come in from all the cities, they found the Athenians already on their way home. The rest of the eleven *boeotarchs*[1b] were against giving battle, as the enemy was no longer in

4.88.2a Stagirus: Map 4.78, AY.
4.88.2b Thucydides' narrative returns to Thrace in 4.101.5.
4.89.1a Thucydides returns here to the Athenian plan to attack Boeotia described in 4.77. Siphae: Map 4.96, BY; Delium: Map 4.96, AY.
4.89.1b Phanotis (Panopeus) in Phocis: Map 4.96, AX.
4.89.2a Chaeronea: Map 4.96, AX.
4.90.1a Athens, in relation to Delium: Map 4.96, BY. For resident aliens (*metics*), see Appendix A, The Athenian Government, §2, 4.
4.90.1b Delium: Map 4.96, AY.
4.91.1a Tanagra: Map 4.96, AY.
4.91.1b *Boeotarchs* were chief magistrates of the Boeotian federal government; see note 5.38.2a.

Bo ing just crossed over the Oropian[1c] border when the s son of Aeolidas, one of the boeotarchs of Th of Lysimachidas, being the other), and then co ht it best to fight a battle. He accordingly called the after company, to prevent their all leaving their arr em to attack the Athenians, and face the hazards of ows:

4.92
424/3
8th Year/Winter
DELIUM
Pagondas speaks to the Boeotian army to encourage it to attack the Athenians; he calls the fortification of Delium an assault that must be repulsed.

that we ought not to give battle to the Athe- upon them in Boeotia is one which should the head of any of us, your generals. It was they crossed the frontier and built a fort in re therefore, I imagine, our enemies wherever em, wherever they may have come to act as anyone has taken up with the idea in question s high time for him to change his mind. The wn country is in danger, can scarcely discuss e calmness of men who are in full enjoyment are thinking of attacking a neighbor in order our national habit to resist a foreign invader, ne is in your country or not; and when that d lives upon your frontier as well, it is doubly 4] As between neighbors generally, freedom nation to hold one's own; and with neighbors ng to enslave near and far alike, there is noth- out to the last. Look at the condition of the t of the rest of Hellas and you will be con- s have to fight with their neighbors for this being conquered means one frontier for the which there will be no dispute, for they will by force what we have. [5] So much more is neighbor than from another. Besides, peo- nians in the present instance, are tempted by ck their neighbors, usually march most confi- ho keep still, and only defend themselves in think twice before they grapple with those de their frontier and strike the first blow if] The Athenians have shown us this them- we inflicted upon them at Coronea,[6a] at the

4.9 on the bor- tica.
4.9 the Boeotian te 5.38.2a
4.9 ery near to
4.9 at Coronea 1.113.

time when our quarrels had allowed them to occupy the country, has given great security to Boeotia until the present day. [7] Remembering this, the old must equal their ancient exploits, and the young, the sons of the heroes of that time, must endeavor not to disgrace their native valor; and trusting in the help of the god whose temple has been sacrilegiously fortified, and in the victims which, when we sacrificed, appeared propitious, we must march against the enemy and teach him that he must go and get what he wants by attacking someone who will not resist him, but that men whose glory it is to be always ready to give battle for the liberty of their own country and never unjustly to enslave that of others, will not let him go without a struggle."

4.93
424/3
8th Year/Winter
DELIUM
Persuaded to attack, the Boeotians advance late in the day; their numbers, types, and disposition are described.

By these arguments Pagondas persuaded the Boeotians to attack the Athenians, and quickly breaking up his camp led his army forward, it being now late in the day. On nearing the enemy, he halted in a position where a hill intervening prevented the two armies from seeing each other, and then formed and prepared for action. [2] Meanwhile Hippocrates at Delium, informed of the approach of the Boeotians, sent orders to his troops to throw themselves into line, and himself joined them not long afterwards, leaving about three hundred horse behind him at Delium to guard the place in case of attack, and at the same time to watch their opportunity and fall upon the Boeotians during the battle. [3] The Boeotians placed a detachment to deal with these, and when everything was arranged to their satisfaction appeared over the hill, and halted in the order which they had decided on, to the number of seven thousand hoplites, more than ten thousand light troops, one thousand horse, and five hundred peltasts.[3a] [4] On their right were the Thebans and those of their division,[4a] in the center the Haliartians, Coronaeans, Copaeans,[4b] and the other people around the lake, and on the left the Thespians, Tanagrans, and Orchomenians,[4c] the cavalry and the light troops being at the extremity of each wing. The Thebans formed twenty-five shields deep, the rest as they pleased.[4d] [5] Such was the strength and disposition of the Boeotian army.

4.94
424/3
8th Year/Winter
DELIUM
The Athenians form their battle line.

On the side of the Athenians, the hoplites throughout the whole army formed eight deep, being in numbers equal to the enemy, with the cavalry upon the two wings. Light troops regularly armed there were none in the army, nor had there ever been any at Athens. Those who had joined in the invasion, though many times more numerous than those of the enemy, had mostly followed unarmed, as part of the citizens and foreigners at Athens, and having started first on their way home were not present in any

4.93.3a Peltasts were troops armed only with a small, light shield, a javelin, and a short sword. Unhindered by body armor, they could move much more quickly than the fully armed hoplite. Aenus: Map 4.5, AY.

4.93.4a See note 5.38.2a for the "divisions" of the Boeotian Confederacy.

4.93.4b Haliartus: Map 4.96, AX; Coronea: Map 4.96, AX; Lake Copais: Map 4.96, AY.

4.93.4c Thespiae, Tanagra: Map 4.96, AY; Orchomenus: Map 4.96, AX.

4.93.4d This deep formation was peculiarly Theban; see Appendix F, Ancient Greek Land Warfare, §3.

nu[illegible] being now in line and upon the point of engaging [illegible] neral, passed along the Athenian ranks, and
enc[illegible]s:

[illegible] only say a few words to you, but brave men [illegible] ey are addressed more to your understanding [illegible] [2] None of you must suppose that we are [illegible] to run this risk in the country of another. [illegible] y the battle will be for ours: if we conquer, [illegible] ll never invade your country without the [illegible] one battle you will win Boeotia and in a man- [illegible] vance to meet them then like citizens of a [illegible] l glory as the first in Hellas, and like sons of [illegible] em at Oenophyta[3a] with Myronides and thus [illegible] eotia."[3b]

4.95
424/3
8th Year/Winter
DELIUM
Hippocrates encourages the Athenian army.

[illegible] lf through the army with his exhortation, when the [illegible] more hasty words from Pagondas, struck up the *pa*[illegible] them from the hill; the Athenians advancing to me[illegible] a run. [2] The extreme wing of neither army ca[illegible] the other being stopped by the water courses in the [illegible] with the utmost obstinacy, shield against shield. [3] [illegible] far as the center, was worsted by the Athenians. Th[illegible] of the field suffered most severely. The troops alo[illegible] en way, they were surrounded in a narrow space an[illegible] d to hand; some of the Athenians also fell into co[illegible] he enemy and mistook and so killed each other. [4] [illegible] the Boeotians were beaten, and retreated upon th[illegible] ut the right, where the Thebans were, got the be[illegible] d shoved them further and further back, though gr[illegible] so happened also that Pagondas, seeing the dis- tre[illegible] wo squadrons of horse, where they could not be see[illegible] their sudden appearance struck a panic into the vic[illegible] henians, who thought that it was another army co[illegible] At length in both parts of the field, disturbed by thi[illegible] ne broken by the advancing Thebans, the whole

4.96
424/3
8th Year/Winter
DELIUM
After a long struggle, the Athenians give way and retreat, pursued by the Boeotian cavalry. The onset of night limits the pursuit and many Athenians escape.

4.9[illegible] roops was [illegible] ucydides [illegible] light troops [illegible] lties in [illegible] Most poor [illegible] made up a [illegible] her state's [illegible] d Athens in

4.9[illegible] ap 4.96, BY) [illegible] in 1.108.

4.9[illegible]

4.9[illegible] that the men of classical Greek armies sang as they advanced into battle, rallied, or celebrated victory.

4.96.4a See Appendix F, Ancient Greek Land Warfare, for a discussion of such implications of this chapter as that these combatants wore no uniforms or national identifying emblems; that once the phalanx formation was broken, heavy casualties were inflicted; and that the depth of the Theban formation probably permitted them to "shove" the thinner Athenian lines backward.

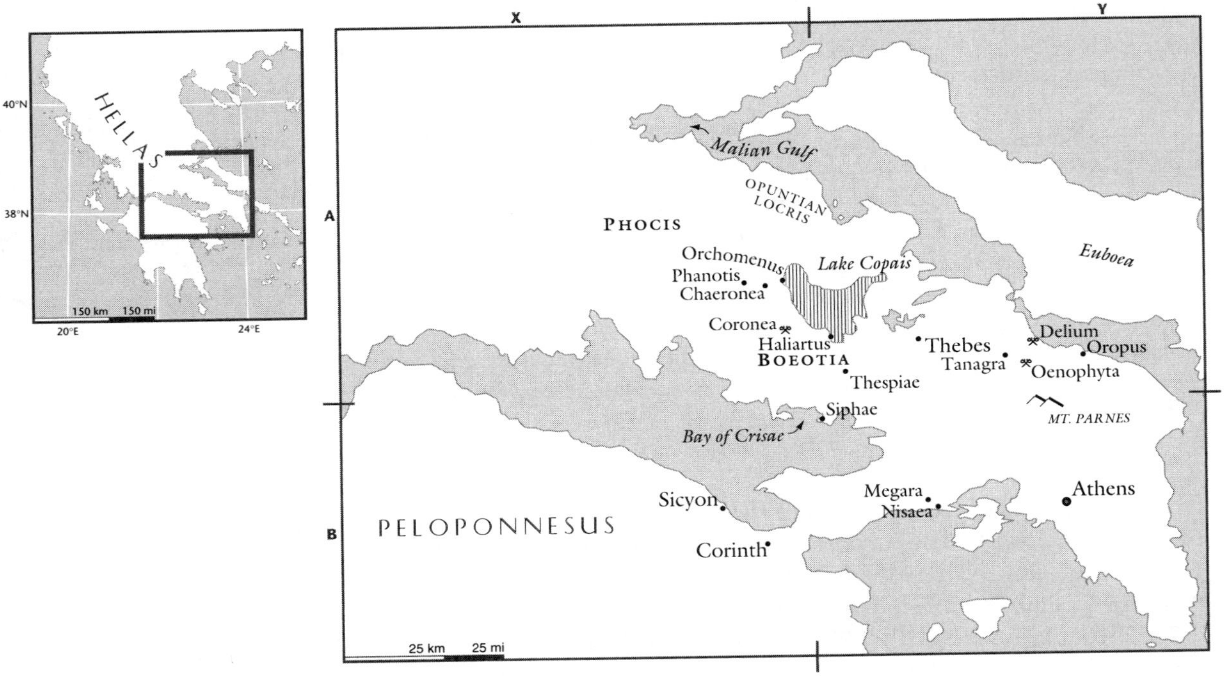

MAP 4.96 THE DELIUM CAMPAIGN

Athenian army took to flight. [7] Some made for Delium and the sea, some for Oropus, others for Mount Parnes,[7a] or wherever they had hopes of safety, [8] pursued and cut down by the Boeotians, and in particular by the cavalry, composed partly of Boeotians and partly of Locrians,[8a] who had come up just as the rout began. Night however coming on to interrupt the pursuit, the mass of the fugitives escaped more easily than they would otherwise have done. [9] The next day the troops at Oropus and Delium returned home by sea, after leaving a garrison in the latter place, which they continued to hold notwithstanding the defeat.

4.97
424/3
8th Year/Winter
DELIUM
The Boeotians refuse to return the Athenian dead until Athens evacuates Delium. They call the occupation of this shrine a sacrilegious violation of Hellenic law.

The Boeotians set up a trophy, took up their own dead, and stripped those of the enemy, and leaving a guard over them retired to Tanagra, there to take measures for attacking Delium. [2] Meanwhile a herald came from the Athenians to ask for the dead, but was met and turned back by a Boeotian herald, who told him that he would effect nothing until the return of himself (the Boeotian herald), and who then went on to the Athenians and told them on behalf of the Boeotians that they had done wrong in transgressing the law of the Hellenes. [3] Of what use was the

4.96.7a Delium Oropus: Map 4.96, AY; Mount Parnes: Map 4.96, BY.

4.96.8a The horsemen came from Opuntian Locris (Map 4.96, AX), which borders Boeotia on the northwest.

uni [illegible] the temples in an invaded country if the Athenia [illegible] n and live there, acting exactly as if they were on unc [illegible] drawing and using for their purposes the water wh [illegible] s, never touched except for sacred uses? [4] Ac [illegible] well as for themselves, in the name of the deities co [illegible] he Boeotians called on them first to evacuate the ten [illegible] e up the dead that belonged to them.

4.98
424/3
8th Year/Winter
DELIUM
Justifying their occupation of Delium, the Athenians call the Boeotian refusal to return their dead a greater sacrilege.

[illegible] the herald, the Athenians sent their own herald to [illegible] at they had not done any wrong to the temple, and [illegible] do it no more harm than they could help; not hav [illegible] lly for this purpose, but to defend themselves fro [illegible] were really wronging them. [2] The law of the He [illegible] t of a country, whether more or less extensive, car [illegible] f the temples in that country, with the obligation to [illegible] nonies, at least as far as possible. [3] The Boeotia [illegible] e who had turned out the owners of a country, and [illegible] r places by force, now held as of right the temple [illegible] entered as usurpers. [4] If the Athenians could hav [illegible] oeotia this would have been the case with them: as t [illegible] f it which they had got they should treat as their ow [illegible] bliged. [5] The water they had disturbed out of a n [illegible] not wantonly incurred, having been forced to use [illegible] ves against the Boeotians who had first invaded Att [illegible] ng done under the pressure of war and danger mig [illegible] ulgence even in the eye of the god; or why, pray, we [illegible] for involuntary offenses? Transgression also was a ter [illegible] ous offenders, not to the victims of adverse circu [illegible] which were most impious—the Boeotians who wis [illegible] es for holy places, or the Athenians who refused to [illegible] tain what was theirs by right? [8] The condition of [illegible] t therefore be withdrawn. They were no longer in [illegible] ere they stood by the right of the sword. All that the [illegible] was to tell them to take up their dead under a tru [illegible] onal custom.

4.99
424/3
8th Year/Winter
DELIUM
The Boeotians again refuse to give up the dead until the Athenians vacate Boeotian territory.

[illegible] hat if they were in Boeotia, they must evacuate tha [illegible] up their dead; if they were in their own territory, the [illegible] ed: for they knew that, although the territory of Or [illegible] as it chanced were lying (the battle having been fou [illegible] s subject to Athens, yet the Athenians could not get [illegible] ave. Besides, why should they grant a truce for Ath [illegible] at could be fairer than to tell the Athenians to evacuate Boeotia if they wished to get what they asked? The Athenian herald accordingly returned with this answer, without having accomplished his object.

4.100
424/3
8th Year/Winter
DELIUM
The Boeotians assault Delium and take it, setting fire to its wooden walls with an ingenious "flamethrower."

Meanwhile the Boeotians at once sent for darters and slingers from the Malian gulf,[1a] and with two thousand Corinthian hoplites who had joined them after the battle, the Peloponnesian garrison which had evacuated Nisaea, and some Megarians[1b] with them, marched against Delium, and attacked the fort, and after divers efforts finally succeeded in taking it by means of a device of the following description. [2] They sawed in two and scooped out a great beam from end to end, and fitting it nicely together again like a flute, hung by chains a cauldron at one extremity, from which there was free passage to an iron tube projecting from the beam, which was itself in great part plated with iron. [3] This they brought up from a distance upon carts to the part of the wall principally composed of vines and timber, and when it was near, inserted huge bellows into their end of the beam and blew with them. [4] The blast passing closely confined into the cauldron, which was filled with lighted coals, sulfur and pitch, made a great blaze, and set fire to the wall, which soon became untenable for its defenders, who left it and fled; and in this way the fort was taken.[4a] [5] Of the garrison some were killed and two hundred made prisoners; most of the rest got on board their ships and returned home.

4.101
424/3
8th Year/Winter
DELIUM
After the fall of Delium the Boeotians give up the Athenian dead. Thucydides recounts both sides' casualties.
SICYON
Demosthenes is repulsed at Sicyon with losses.
THRACE
Sitalces, king of Odrysiann Thrace, dies.

Soon after the fall of Delium, which took place seventeen days after the battle, the Athenian herald, without knowing what had happened, came again for the dead, which were now restored by the Boeotians, who no longer answered as at first. [2] Not quite five hundred Boeotians fell in the battle, and nearly one thousand Athenians, including Hippocrates the general, besides a great number of light troops and camp followers.[2a]

[3] Soon after this battle Demosthenes, after the failure of his voyage to Siphae and of the plot on the city, availed himself of the Acarnanian and Agraean troops and of the four hundred Athenian hoplites which he had on board, to make a descent on the Sicyonian coast.[3a] [4] Before all his ships had come to shore, however, the Sicyonians came up and routed those that had landed and chased them to their ships, killing some and taking others prisoner; after which they set up a trophy, and gave back the dead under truce.

[5] About the same time as the affair of Delium, Sitalces[5a] king of the Odrysians died, defeated in battle while campaigning against the Triballi; Seuthes son of Sparadocus, his nephew, succeeded to the kingdom of the Odrysians, and of the rest of Thrace ruled by Sitalces.

4.100.1a Malian Gulf: Map 4.96, AX.
4.100.1b Nisaea, Megara: Map 4.96, BY.
4.100.4a For the development of siege warfare, see Appendix F, Ancient Greek Land Warfare, §10.
4.101.2a Since few Athenian light troops were at the battle (4.94.1), we can only assume that such casualties were caused later by pursuing Boeotian cavalry, which caught up with these retreating Athenians.
4.101.3a Sicyon: Map 4.96, BX.
4.101.5a Sitalces and his nephew Seuthes were last mentioned in the Thracian campaign of 428, recounted in 2.95–101. Events in Thrace are resumed here from 4.88.

4.102
424/3
8th Year/Winter
AMPHIPOLIS
Brasidas marches against Amphipolis, whose history and geography is described.

[illegible]das, with his allies in Thrace, marched against Am[illegible] colony on the river Strymon.[1a] [2] Aristagoras the [illegible] establish a settlement upon the spot on which the [illegible]e fled from King Darius,[2a] but he was dislodged by [illegible]two years later the Athenians sent ten thousand of [illegible] whoever else chose to go) to settle the region, bu[illegible]t Drabescus[2c] by the Thracians. [3] Twenty-nine yea[illegible]eturned—Hagnon, son of Nicias, being sent out as [illegible]e drove out the Edonians and founded a city on the [illegible]rly called Ennea-hodoi, or Nine Ways. The base fro[illegible]as Eion,[3a] their commercial seaport at the mouth of [illegible] three miles from the present city, which Hagnon na[illegible]e the Strymon flows round it on two sides, and he [illegible]spicuous from the sea and land alike, running a lo[illegible] to river, to complete the circumference.

4.103
424/3
8th Year/Winter
AMPHIPOLIS
Brasidas, aided by Argilians and conspirators inside Amphipolis, marches quickly on a stormy night to the Strymon bridge and occupies it easily.

[illegible]d against this city, starting from Arne in Ch[illegible]t dusk at Aulon and Bromiscus, where the lake of [illegible][1b] he took supper there, and went on during the nig[illegible]vas stormy and it was snowing a little, which en[illegible] on in order, if possible, to take everyone at Am[illegible]xcept the party who were to betray it). [3] The pl[illegible] of Argilus,[3a] an Andrian[3b] colony, who resided in Am[illegible]ad also other accomplices won over by Perdiccas or [illegible]t the most active in the matter were the inhabitants [illegible]h is close by, who had always been suspected by the [illegible]esigns on the place. These men now saw their op[illegible]rasidas, and having for some time been in corresp[illegible]trymen in Amphipolis for the betrayal of the city, at [illegible] Argilus, and revolted from the Athenians. That sa[illegible] on to the bridge over the river, [5] where he fo[illegible] to oppose him, the city being at some distance fr[illegible] walls not reaching down to it as at present. He ea[illegible]gh this guard, partly through there being treason in [illegible] the stormy state of the weather and the sudden-ne[illegible] got across the bridge and immediately became m[illegible]y outside—the Amphipolitans having houses all ov[illegible]

4.104
424/3
8th Year/Winter
AMPHIPOLIS
Despite surprise and confusion, the gates of Amphipolis are secured and a message sent to Thucydides, general and author of this history, who after receiving it leaves immediately from Thasos with seven triremes.

[illegible]s was a complete surprise to the people in the cit[illegible]any of those outside, as well as the flight of the

4.1[illegible]mpt to found [illegible]phipolis, Stry-[illegible]
4.1[illegible] and the [illegible]e, see [illegible]6. See also [illegible]§2–3.
4.1[illegible]
4.1[illegible]; also see [illegible]

4.102.3a Eion: Map 4.106, AY.
4.103.1a Arne in Chalcidice: location unknown. For the location of Chalcidice, see Map 4.106, AX.
4.103.1b Aulon: location unknown. Bromiscus: Map 4.106, AY; Lake Bolbe: Map 4.106, AX.
4.103.3a Argilus: Map 4.106, AY.
4.103.3b Andros: Map 4.128, BY.

rest within the wall, combined to produce great confusion among the citizens; especially as they did not trust one another. [2] It is even said that if Brasidas, instead of stopping to pillage, had advanced straight against the city, he would probably have taken it. [3] Instead, however, he established himself where he was, overran the country outside, and for the present remained inactive, vainly awaiting a demonstration on the part of his friends within. [4] Meanwhile the party opposed to the traitors proved numerous enough to prevent the gates being immediately thrown open, and in concert with Eucles, the general, who had come from Athens to defend the place, sent to the other commander in Thrace, Thucydides son of Olorus, the author of this history,[4a] who was at the isle of Thasos,[4b] a Parian colony,[4c] half a day's sail from Amphipolis, to tell him to come to their relief. [5] On receipt of this message he at once set sail with seven ships which he had with him, in order, if possible, to reach Amphipolis in time to prevent its capitulation, or in any case to save Eion.

4.105
424/3
8th Year/Winter
AMPHIPOLIS
Brasidas, anxious to capture the place before Thucydides arrives, offers generous terms to the citizens.

Meanwhile Brasidas, afraid that help would arrive by sea from Thasos, and learning that Thucydides possessed the right of working the gold mines in that part of Thrace, and had thus great influence with the inhabitants of the mainland, hastened to gain the city, if possible, before the people of Amphipolis should be encouraged by his arrival to hope that he could save them by getting together a force of allies from the sea and from Thrace, and so refuse to surrender. [2] He accordingly offered moderate terms, proclaiming that any of the Amphipolitans and Athenians who so chose, might continue to enjoy their property with full rights of citizenship; while those who did not wish to stay had five days to depart, taking their property with them.

4.106
424/3
8th Year/Winter
AMPHIPOLIS
The Amphipolitans decide to capitulate. Thucydides arrives too late to save Amphipolis, but he does save Eion.

Upon hearing this, the bulk of the inhabitants began to change their minds, especially as only a small number of the citizens were Athenians, the majority having come from various places, and also because many of the prisoners Brasidas had taken outside had relatives within the walls. They found the proclamation a fair one in comparison to what their fears had suggested. The Athenians were glad to get out, as they thought they ran more risk than the rest, and did not expect any speedy relief. The multitude were generally content at being left in possession of their civic rights, and at such an unexpected reprieve from danger. [2] The partisans of Brasidas now openly advocated this course, seeing that the feeling of the people had changed, and that they no longer gave ear to the Athenian general present; and thus the surrender was made and Brasidas was admitted by them on the terms of his proclamation. [3] In this way they gave up the city, and late in the same day, Thucydides and his ships entered the harbor of Eion,[3a]

4.104.4a This statement, and that in 4.105.1 just below it, are two of Thucydides' rare and restrained remarks about himself. See the Introduction (sect. I) for what is known of the life of Thucydides.

4.104.4b Thasos: Map 4.106, AY.

4.104.4c Paros: Map 4.128, BY.

4.106.3a Eion: Map 4.106, AY.

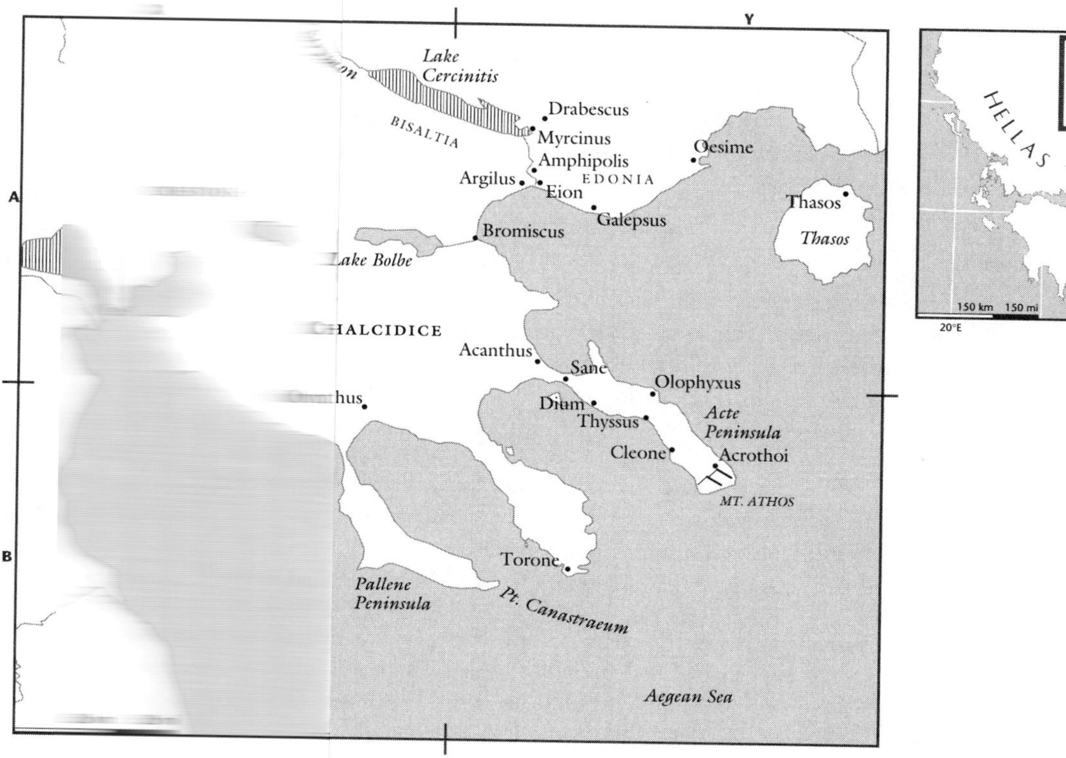

MA… RASIDAS AGAINST AMPHIPOLIS, ACTE, AND TORONE

[4] … t hold of Amphipolis, and having been within a nig… the ships been less prompt in relieving it, in the mo… n his.

4.107
424/3
8th Year/Winter
AMPHIPOLIS
Brasidas attacks Eion but is beaten off. Other nearby cities now revolt against Athens.

… put all in order at Eion to secure it against any pre… f Brasidas, and received such as had elected to co… rior according to the agreed-upon terms. [2] Me… ly sailed with a number of boats down the river to … not seize the point running out from the wall, an… nce; and at the same time he attacked the city by lan… on both sides and had to content himself with arr… ipolis and in the neighborhood. [3] Myrcinus,[3a] an … over to him (the Edonian king Pittacus having bee… Goaxis and his own wife Brauro); and Galepsus[3b]

4.1…
4.1…

and Oesime,[3c] which are Thasian colonies, followed its example not long afterward. Perdiccas too came up immediately after the capture and joined in these arrangements.

4.108
424/3
8th Year/Winter
ATHENS
Athens is alarmed by the fall of Amphipolis because all Thrace is now threatened and more revolts are feared. Indeed, many cities go over to Brasidas, for they believe revolt would be painless and underestimate Athens' power.

The news that Amphipolis was in the hands of the enemy caused great alarm at Athens. Not only was the city valuable for the timber it afforded for shipbuilding and the tribute money that it brought in; but it also was a barrier to movement across Thrace. The escort of the Thessalians had brought the Spartans within reach of the allies of Athens as far as the river Strymon, yet as long as they were not masters of the bridge and were blocked toward the sea by the Athenian triremes at Eion,[1a] and impeded on the inland side by a large and extensive lake formed by the waters of the river,[1b] they could not advance further. Now, however, their way forward seemed open. The Athenians also feared that more allies would revolt, [2] particularly because Brasidas displayed such moderation in all his conduct, and declared everywhere that he had been sent out to free Hellas. [3] The cities subject to the Athenians, hearing of the capture of Amphipolis and of the terms accorded to it, and of the gentleness of Brasidas, felt most strongly encouraged to change their condition, and sent secret messages to him, begging him to come to them; each wishing to be the first to revolt. [4] Indeed, there seemed to be no danger in so doing; their mistake in their estimate of the Athenian power was as great as that power afterwards turned out to be, and their judgment was based more upon blind wishing than upon any sound prediction; for it is a habit of mankind to entrust to careless hope what they long for, and to use sovereign reason to thrust aside what they do not desire. [5] Besides the late severe blow which the Athenians had met with in Boeotia,[5a] joined to the seductive, though untrue, statements of Brasidas, about the Athenians not having ventured to engage his single army at Nisaea,[5b] made the allies confident, and caused them to believe that no Athenian force would be sent against them. [6] Above all the wish to do what was agreeable at the moment, and the likelihood that they would find the Spartans full of zeal from the outset, made them eager to run the risk. Observing this, the Athenians sent garrisons to the different cities, as far as was possible at such short notice and in winter; while Brasidas sent dispatches to Sparta asking for reinforcements, and made preparations for building triremes in the Strymon. [7] The Spartans however did not support him, partly out of envy on the part of their chief

4.107.3c Oesime: Map 4.106, AY.
4.108.1a Eion: Map 4.106, AY.
4.108.1b Thucydides refers here to Lake Cercinitis; see Map 4.106, AX.
4.108.5a Boeotia: Map 4.118.
4.108.5b As Brasidas told the Acanthians in 4.85.7. Nisaea: Map 4.118.

me[illegible]ere more bent on recovering the prisoners from
the[illegible] war.

[illegible]egarians took and razed to the foundations the
lon[illegible] occupied by the Athenians;[1a] and Brasidas, after
the[illegible], marched with his allies against Acte,[1b] [2] a
pro[illegible]rom the King's canal[2a] with an inward curve and
en[illegible]mountain looking toward the Aegean sea. [3] In
it [illegible]s an Andrian[3a] colony lying close to the canal,
an[illegible] direction of Euboea;[3b] the others are Thyssus,
Cl[illegible]yxus, [4] and Dium.[4a] They are inhabited by
mi[illegible]peaking the two languages. There is also a small
Ch[illegible]e greater number are Tyrrheno-Pelasgians (forme[illegible] and Athens), and Bisaltians, Crestonians, and
Ed[illegible]ll small ones [5] and most of these came over to
Br[illegible]um held out and saw their land ravaged by him
an[illegible]

4.109
424/3
8th Year/Winter
MEGARA
The Megarians raze their long walls.
ACTE, THRACE
Brasidas secures most of the small non-Greek-speaking cities in Acte.

[illegible]ting, he at once marched against Torone[1a] in
Ch[illegible] by an Athenian garrison, having been invited by
a f[illegible]epared to hand over the city. Arriving in the dark
a l[illegible]e halted with his army near the temple of the
Di[illegible] a quarter of a mile from the city. [2] The rest of
the[illegible] Athenian garrison did not perceive his approach;
but[illegible] that he was coming (a few of them had secretly
go[illegible]ere on the watch for his arrival, and were no
soo[illegible]ey let in to them seven light armed men with
dag[illegible]nty men ordered on this service dared to enter),
co[illegible] an Olynthian. These passed through the sea wall
an[illegible]nt up and put to the sword the garrison of the
hig[illegible]ich stands on a hill, and broke open the postern
gat[illegible]aeum.[2a]

4.110
424/3
8th Year/Winter
TORONE
Brasidas sends a small party inside Torone with the help of conspirators. They occupy a high point in the city and open a gate.

[illegible]e a little nearer and then halted with his main
bo[illegible]dred peltasts[1a] to be ready to rush in first, the
mo[illegible]d be thrown open and the beacon lighted as
agr[illegible]e passed in waiting and wondering at the delay,
the[illegible] up close to the city. The Toronaeans inside who
we[illegible]rty that had entered, had by this time broken

4.111
424/3
8th Year/Winter
TORONE
Brasidas sends in peltasts and, the gates finally being opened, ignites a fire-signal to start the main assault.

4.10[illegible]en on the [illegible] see 4.31–39.
4.10[illegible]e Athenians [illegible]cribed in [illegible]3.
4.10[illegible]BY.
4.10[illegible]rsians at [illegible]ion for his [illegible]s construc- [illegible]us, Book 7, [illegible]rsians, §4.
4.10[illegible]Y.
4.10[illegible]ap 4.128, BY.
4.109.3b Euboea: Map 4.128, BY; in relation to Chalcidice, Map 4.128, AY.
4.109.4a Thyssus, Cleone, Acrothoi, Olophyxus, and Dium, all on the Acte Peninsula: Map 4.106, BY.
4.109.4b Lemnos: Map 4.128, AY.
4.109.4c Bisaltia, Crestonia: Map 4.106, AX; Edonia: Map 4.106, AY.
4.110.1a Torone: Map 4.106, BY.
4.110.2a The postern faced west, toward Point Canastraeum, the easternmost cape of the Pallene Peninsula: Map 4.106, BY
4.111.1a Peltasts: see note 4.93.3a.

down the postern and opened the gates leading to the marketplace by cutting through the bar.[2a] They first brought some men round and let them in by the postern in order to strike panic into the surprised townsmen by suddenly attacking them from behind and on both sides at once; after which they raised the fire-signal as had been agreed, and took in by the market gates the rest of the peltasts.

4.112
424/3
8th Year/Winter
TORONE
Brasidas' main force enters the city.

Brasidas seeing the signal told the troops to rise, and dashed forward amid the loud hurrahs of his men, which caused dismay among the astonished townspeople. [2] Some burst in straight by the gate, others over some square pieces of timber placed against the wall (which had fallen down and was being rebuilt) to draw up stones; [3] Brasidas and the greater number making straight uphill for the higher part of the city, in order to take it from top to bottom, once and for all, while the rest of the multitude spread in all directions.

4.113
424/3
8th Year/Winter
TORONE
The Athenian garrison and its local supporters escape to their ships and to Lecythus.

The capture of the city was effected before the great body of the Toronaeans had recovered from their surprise and confusion; [2] but the conspirators and the citizens of their party at once joined the invaders. About fifty of the Athenian hoplites happened to be sleeping in the marketplace when the alarm reached them. A few of these were killed fighting; the rest escaped, some by land, others to the two ships on the station, and took refuge in Lecythus, a fort garrisoned by their own men in the corner of the city running out into the sea at the end of a narrow isthmus. [3] There they were joined by the Toronaeans of their party.

4.114
424/3
8th Year/Winter
TORONE
The Athenians refuse to leave and are granted a truce. Both sides fortify their positions. Brasidas calms the Toronaeans and gains their support.

Day now arrived, and the city being secured, Brasidas made a proclamation to the Toronaeans who had taken refuge with the Athenians, to come out as many as chose, to their homes, without fearing for their rights or persons, and he sent a herald to invite the Athenians to accept a truce, and to evacuate Lecythus with their property, as being Chalcidian ground. [2] The Athenians refused this offer, but asked for a truce for a day to take up their dead. Brasidas granted it for two days, which he employed in fortifying the houses near the fort and the Athenians in doing the same to their positions. [3] Meanwhile he called a meeting of the Toronaeans, and said very much what he had said at Acanthus, namely, that they must not look upon those who had negotiated with him for the capture of the city as bad men or as traitors, as they had not acted as they had done from corrupt motives or in order to enslave the city, but for the good and freedom of Torone; nor again must those who had not shared in the enterprise suppose that they would not equally reap its fruits, as he had not come to destroy either the city or any individual in it. [4] This was the reason for his proclamation to those that had fled for refuge to the Athenians: he thought none the worse of them for their friendship for the Athenians; he believed that they had only to make trial of the Spartans to like them as well, or even

4.111.2a Cut through the bar of the gate: see note 2.4.4a.

mu[illegible]h more justly: it was for want of such a trial that
the[illegible]m. [5] Meanwhile he warned all of them to pre-
par[illegible]nd as such to be held responsible for all faults in
fut[illegible] had not wronged the Spartans but had been
wr[illegible]re too strong for them, and any opposition that
the[illegible]n could be excused.

4.115
424/3
8th Year/Winter
TORONE
Athenian efforts to thwart an enemy fire-throwing machine cause one of their own fortified posts to collapse; their men thereafter panic and flee.

[illegible]m with this address, he made his attack upon
Le[illegible]uce expired, and the Athenians defended them-
sel[illegible]d from some houses with parapets. [2] For one
day[illegible]the next the enemy were preparing to bring up a
sie[illegible] from which they meant to throw fire upon the
wo[illegible]he troops were already coming up to the point
wh[illegible] could best bring up the engine, and where the
pla[illegible] meanwhile the Athenians put a wooden tower
up[illegible] carried up a quantity of jars and casks of water
and[illegible] number of men also climbed up. [3] The house
thu[illegible]enly broke down with a loud crash; at which the
me[illegible]w it were more vexed than frightened; but those
no[illegible] those furthest off, thought that the place was
alr[illegible]and fled in haste to the sea and the ships.

4.116
424/3
8th Year/Winter
TORONE
Brasidas dashes forward to take the fort, and the Athenians escape to their ships.

[illegible]t they were deserting the parapet, and seeing
wh[illegible] forward with his troops, and immediately took
the[illegible]ord all whom he found in it. [2] In this way the
pla[illegible] Athenians, who went across in their boats and
shi[illegible]re is a temple of Athena in Lecythus, and Brasidas[illegible] moment of making the assault that he would
giv[illegible]o the man first on the wall. Being now of the
opi[illegible]vas scarcely due to human agency, he gave the
thi[illegible]dess for her temple, and razed and cleared
Le[illegible]ole of it consecrated ground. [3] The rest of the
wi[illegible] the places in his hands, and in making designs
up[illegible] expiration of the winter the eighth year of this
wa[illegible]

4.117
423
9th Year/Summer
ATHENS-SPARTA
Thucydides explains why the Athenians and Spartans entered into a one-year armistice.

[illegible]ummer following, the Spartans and Athenians
ma[illegible]r. The Athenians thought that they would thus
gai[illegible]ons before Brasidas could procure the revolt of
any[illegible]nd that they might also, if it suited them, con-
clu[illegible]Spartans suspecting the actual fears of the Athenia[illegible]ce they had enjoyed a respite from trouble and
mis[illegible] disposed to consent to a reconciliation, to give
bac[illegible] make a treaty for the longer period. [2] The
mo[illegible] the Spartans was to get back their men while

4.11[illegible]5, BX.
4.11[illegible]f currency [illegible]nt, or one hundred drachmas; see Appendix J, Classical Greek Currency, §5.

Brasidas' good fortune lasted; further successes might make the struggle a less unequal one in Chalcidice, but would leave them still deprived of their men, and even in Chalcidice not more than a match for the Athenians and by no means certain of victory. [3] An armistice was accordingly concluded by Sparta and her allies upon the terms following:

4.118
423
9th Year/Summer
ATHENS-SPARTA
The terms of the armistice are described.

• As to the temple and oracle of the Pythian Apollo,[1a] we are agreed that whoever so wishes shall have access to it, without fraud or fear, according to the usages of his forefathers. [2] The Spartans and the allies present agree to this, and promise to send heralds to the Boeotians and Phocians, and to do their best to persuade them to agree likewise.

• [3] As to the treasure of the god, we agree to exert ourselves to detect all wrongdoers, truly and honestly following the customs of our forefathers, we and you and all others willing to do so, all following the customs of our forefathers. [4] As to these points the Spartans and the other allies are agreed as has been said.

• As to what follows, the Spartans and the other allies agree, if the Athenians conclude a treaty, to remain, each of us in our own territory, retaining our respective acquisitions; the garrison in Coryphasium keeping within Buphras and Tomeus;[4a] that in Cythera[4b] attempting no communication with the Peloponnesian confederacy, neither we with them, or they with us; that in Nisaea and Minoa[4c] not crossing the road leading from the gates of the temple of Nisus to that of Poseidon and from thence straight to the bridge at Minoa;[4d] the Megarians and the allies being equally bound not to cross this road, and the Athenians retaining the island they have taken, without any communication on either side; as to Troezen,[4e] each side retaining what it has, and as was arranged with the Athenians.

• [5] As to the use of the sea, so far as refers to their own coast and to that of their confederacy, that the Spartans and their allies may voyage upon it in any vessel rowed by oars and of not more than five hundred talents' tonnage,[5a] not a vessel of war.

• [6] That all heralds and embassies, with as many attendants as they please, for concluding the war and adjusting claims, shall have free passage, going and coming, to the Peloponnesus or Athens by land and by sea.

4.118.1a For the temple and oracle of Pythian Apollo at Delphi, see Map 4.118.
4.118.4a "Coryphasium" is the Spartan name for Pylos (Map 4.118); the locations of Buphras and Tomeus are unknown.
4.118.4b Cythera: Map 4.118.
4.118.4c Nisaea, Minoa: Map 4.118.
4.118.4d The locations of the temple of Nisus and Poseidon are not known, but a possible site for the bridge to Minoa, if that is the island meant here, is shown on Map 3.51, BX.
4.118.4e Troezen: Map 4.118. We do not know the reason why Troezen is included here. It probably concerns territory on Methana which Athens captured in 4.45.2, and presumably still held, or about which she had made some arrangement with Troezen.
4.118.5a The talent is a unit of weight, whose value varied over time and place between sixty and eighty pounds. Hence these vessels would be limited to something between fifteen and twenty tons—quite small even then. The boat in 7.25.5 is twenty times larger.

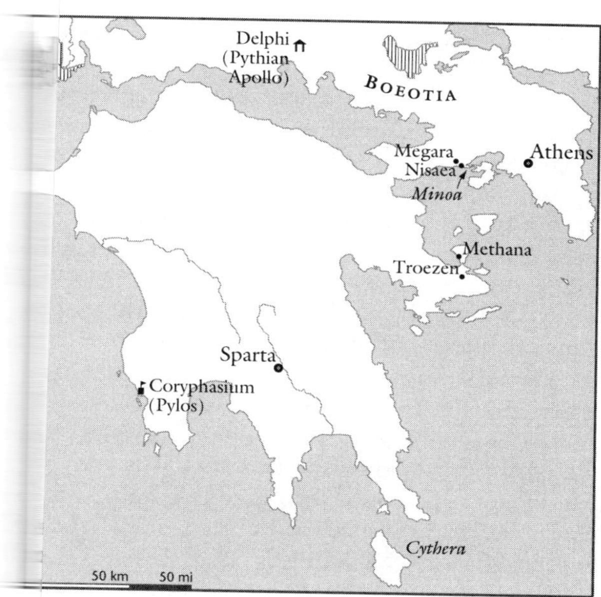

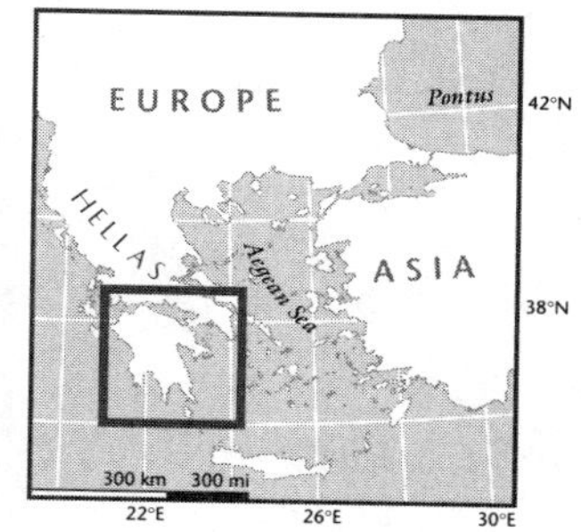

MA
LO
AR

he truce, deserters whether slave or free shall ou, nor by us.

atisfaction shall be given by you to us and by the public law of our several countries, [9] all y law without recourse to hostilities.

llies agree to these articles: but if you have just to suggest, come to Sparta and let us just will meet with no objection either from e allies.

se who come come with full powers, as you ice shall be for one year.

ople

Acamantis had the *prytany*,[11a] Phoenippus was rman. Laches moved that in the name of the thenians, they should conclude the armistice upon by the Spartans and the allies.

l accordingly in the popular assembly, that the one year, beginning that very day, the four- of Elaphebolion;[12a] [13] during which time ds should go and come between the two coun- of a peace. [14] That the generals and prytanes

4. see Appendix nent, §5.

4. see Appendix K, Classical Greek Calendars and Dating Systems, §1–3.

should call an assembly of the people, in which the Athenians should first consult on the peace, and on the mode in which the embassy for putting an end to the war should be admitted. And that the embassy now present should at once pledge on oath before the people to keep well and truly this truce for one year.

4.119
423
9th Year/Summer
ATHENS-SPARTA
Thucydides lists the signers of the armistice. Discussions on a general peace take place.

On these terms the Spartans concluded a truce with the Athenians and their allies on the twelfth day of the Spartan month Cerastius;[1a] [2] the allies also taking the oaths. Those who concluded and poured the libation[2a] were Taurus son of Echetimides, Athenaeus son of Pericleidas, and Philocharidas son of Eryxilaidas, Spartans; Aeneas son of Aeneas, and Euphamidas son of Aristonymus, Corinthians; Damotimus son of Naucrates, and Onasimus son of Megacles, Sicyonians; Nicasus son of Cecalus, and Menecrates son of Amphidorus, Megarians; and Amphias son of Eupaidas, an Epidaurian; and the Athenian generals Nicostratus son of Diitrephes, Nicias son of Niceratus, and Autocles son of Tolmaeus. [3] Such was the armistice, and during the whole of it conferences were held on the subject of a full peace.

4.120
423
9th Year/Summer
SCIONE
Scione, although isolated like an island, revolts from Athens after the armistice negotiations are concluded, but before that is known in Chalcidice. Brasidas sails there, welcomes the Scionaeans as allies, and praises their courage.

In the days in which they were going backwards and forwards to these conferences, Scione, a city in Pallene,[1a] revolted from Athens, and went over to Brasidas. The Scionaeans say that they are Pallenians from the Peloponnesus, and that their first founders settled the place when they were carried to it by the storm which caught the Achaeans on their return voyage from Troy. [2] The Scionaeans had no sooner revolted than Brasidas crossed over by night to Scione, with a friendly trireme ahead and himself in a small boat some way behind; his idea being that if he fell in with a vessel larger than the boat he would have the trireme to defend him, while a ship that was a match for the trireme would probably neglect the small vessel to attack the large one, and thus leave him time to escape. [3] When he had completed the crossing, he called a meeting of the Scionaeans and spoke to the same effect as at Acanthus[3a] and Torone,[3b] adding that they merited the utmost commendation in that, in spite of their insular position, located as they were on Pallene, an isthmus cut off from the mainland by the Athenian occupation of Potidaea,[3c] they had of their own free will gone forward to gain their liberty instead of timorously waiting until they had been by force compelled to accept their own manifest good. This was a sign that they would valiantly undergo any trial, however great; and if he were to order affairs as he intended, he would count them among the truest and sincerest friends of the Spartans, and would in every other way honor them.

4.119.1a By the Spartan calendar: see Appendix K, Classical Greek Calendars and Dating Systems, §1–3.
4.119.2a The pouring of the libations was ritually necessary to complete the agreement.
4.120.1a Scione, Pallene Peninsula: Map 4.122.
4.120.3a Acanthus: Map 4.122; see 4.84–87.
4.120.3b Torone: Map 4.122; see 4.114.3.
4.120.3c Potidaea: Map 4.122.

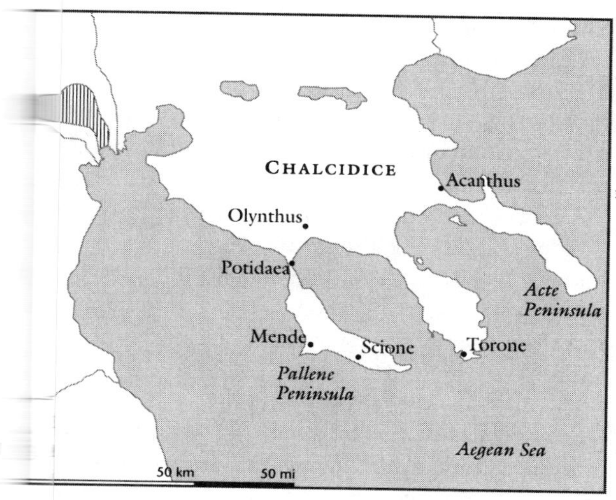

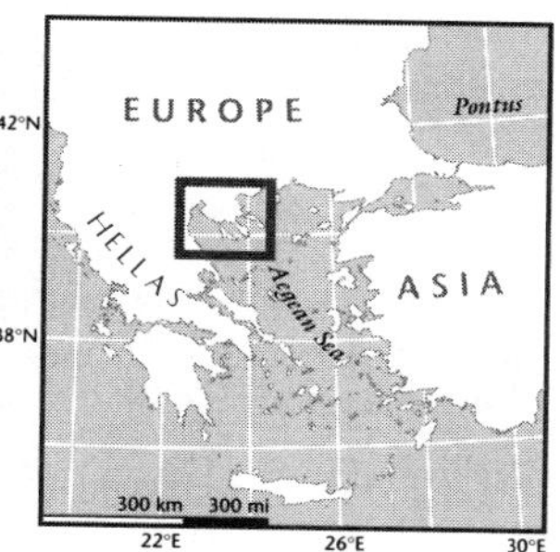

MA[illegible]
BR[illegible]
CH[illegible]

4.121
423
9th Year/Summer
SCIONE
Brasidas hopes to contrive the revolt of Mende and Potidaea to end Scione's isolation.

[illegible]ted by his language, and when even those who had [illegible] what was being done caught the general confi-der[illegible] vigorous conduct of the war. They welcomed Bra[illegible]onors, publicly crowning him with a wreath of gol[illegible]ellas; private persons crowded round him and dec[illegible] as though he had been an athlete.[1a] [2] Mean-wh[illegible] small garrison for the present and crossed back aga[illegible]ards sent over a larger force, intending with the hel[illegible]tempt Mende[2a] and Potidaea before the Atheni-ans [illegible] he felt, was too like an island for them not to att[illegible]ed, with regard to these cities, he was actively see[illegible]

4.122
423
9th Year/Summer
SCIONE
Commissioners arrive with news of the armistice. Brasidas falsely claims that Scione had revolted before the armistice. Athens prepares to attack Scione.

[illegible]gns upon the cities in question, a trireme arrived wit[illegible]rying round the news of the armistice, Aristony-mu[illegible] Athenaeus for the Spartans. [2] The troops now cro[illegible]d the commissioners gave Brasidas notice of the tru[illegible]s in Thrace accepted what had been done; [3] and [illegible] difficulty about the rest, but finding, on count-ing [illegible]aeans had revolted after the date of the conven-tio[illegible]hem in it. To this Brasidas earnestly objected, ass[illegible]ok place before, and would not give up the city. [4] [illegible]orted the case to Athens, the people at once pre-

4.12[illegible]endix I, [illegible]tivals, §5.

4.12[illegible]

pared to send an expedition to Scione. Upon this, envoys arrived from Sparta, alleging that this would be a breach of the truce, and laid claim to the city, trusting the word of Brasidas, and at the same time offering to submit the question to arbitration. [5] Arbitration, however, was what the Athenians did not choose to risk; they were determined to send troops at once to the place, and furious at the idea of even the islanders now daring to revolt, in a vain reliance upon the power of the Spartans by land. [6] Besides the facts of the revolt were rather as the Athenians contended, the Scionaeans having revolted two days after the convention. Cleon accordingly succeeded in carrying a decree to reduce and put to death the Scionaeans and the Athenians employed the leisure which they now enjoyed in preparing for the expedition.

4.123
423
9th Year/Summer
MENDE-SCIONE
Mende revolts after the armistice, but Brasidas sends troops and prepares both it and Scione for an anticipated Athenian attack.

Meanwhile the city of Mende in Pallene, a colony of the Eretrians,[1a] revolted and was received without scruple by Brasidas, in spite of its having evidently come over during the armistice, on account of certain infringements of the truce alleged by him against the Athenians. [2] This audacity of Mende was partly caused by seeing Brasidas so active in the matter and by the conclusions they drew from his refusal to betray Scione. Besides, the conspirators in Mende were few, and had carried on their practices too long not to fear detection for themselves, and had forced the multitude to go against their own inclination. [3] This news made the Athenians more furious than ever, and they at once prepared an expedition against both cities. [4] Expecting their arrival, Brasidas conveyed the women and children of the Scionaeans and Mendaeans away to Olynthus[4a] in Chalcidice, and sent over to them five hundred Peloponnesian hoplites and three hundred Chalcidian peltasts,[4b] all under the command of Polydamidas.

4.124
423
9th Year/Summer
LYNCESTIS
Brasidas and Perdiccas lead a second expedition against Arrhabaeus and rout the Lyncestians in battle. Perdiccas wants to advance but Brasidas needs to return to Chalcidice.

Leaving these two cities to prepare together against the speedy arrival of the Athenians, [4.124.1] Brasidas and Perdiccas started on a second joint expedition into Lyncestis[1a] against Arrhabaeus; the latter with the forces of his Macedonian subjects, and a corps of hoplites composed of Hellenes dwelling in his country; the former with the Peloponnesians whom he still had with him and the Chalcidians,[1b] Acanthians,[1c] and the rest in such force as they could muster. In all there were about three thousand Hellenic hoplites accompanied by all the Macedonian cavalry together with the Chalcidians, almost one thousand strong, besides an immense crowd of barbarians. [2] On entering the country of Arrhabaeus, they found the Lyncestians encamped and waiting for them, and themselves took up a position opposite. [3] The infantry on either side were upon a hill, with a plain between them, into which the horse of both armies first galloped

4.123.1a Eretria, a city on the island of Euboea: Map 4.128, BY.
4.123.4a Olynthus (Map 4.122), where Perdiccas had already (in 433) induced many of the Chalcidians to settle inland, abandoning and demolishing their cities on the seaboard, to make that one city a strong place; see 1.58.2.
4.123.4b Peltasts: see note 4.93.3a.
4.124.1a Lyncestis: Map 4.128, AX. Their previous attack against Lyncestis was described in 4.83.
4.124.1b Chalcidice: Map 4.128, AY.
4.124.1c Acanthus: Map 4.128, AY.

do[illegible]avalry action. After this the Lyncestian hoplites adv[illegible] join their cavalry and offered battle; upon which Br[illegible] came down to meet them, and engaged and rou[illegible]ss; the survivors taking refuge upon the heights and [illegible]ive. [4] The victors now set up a trophy and wai[illegible] for the Illyrian[4a] mercenaries who were to join Pe[illegible] wished to go on and attack the villages of Ar[illegible] no longer; but Brasidas, far from seconding this wis[illegible]xious to return, seeing that the Illyrians did not app[illegible] Athenians might sail up during his absence and att[illegible]

4.125 423 9th Year/Summer LYNCESTIS The defection of Illyrian allies to Arrhabaeus forces Perdiccas and Brasidas to retreat. During the night the Macedonians panic and flee; Brasidas arranges his force to repel attacks while retreating.

[illegible]isputing, the news arrived that the Illyrians had act[illegible] and had joined Arrhabaeus; and the fear inspired by [illegible]made both parties now think it best to withdraw. Ho[illegible]spute, nothing had been settled as to when they sho[illegible]ht came on, the Macedonians and the barbarian cro[illegible]nt in one of those mysterious panics to which gre[illegible]and persuaded that an army many times more nu[illegible] had really arrived was advancing and all but up[illegible]e and fled in the direction of home. This compel[illegible]st did not perceive what had occurred, to depart wit[illegible]e two armies being encamped at a considerable dis[illegible]2] At daybreak, Brasidas, seeing that the Macedo[illegible] that the Illyrians and Arrhabaeus were on the poi[illegible]rmed his hoplites into a square with the light tro[illegible]repared to retreat. [3] Posting his youngest soldie[illegible] the enemy should attack them, he himself with thr[illegible] in the rear intended to face about during the ret[illegible]ost forward of their assailants. [4] Meanwhile, bef[illegible]hed, he sought to sustain the courage of his soldie[illegible]sty exhortation:

4.126 423 9th Year/Summer LYNCESTIS Brasidas encourages his troops as the Lyncestians prepare to attack; he says that the barbarians, however numerous, cannot defeat a determined defense.

[illegible] I did not suspect you of being dismayed at [illegible]ain the attack of a numerous and barbarian [illegible]ve said a few words to you as usual without [illegible] it is, in the face of the desertion of our [illegible]s of the enemy, I have some advice and infor[illegible] brief as it must be, will, I hope, suffice for [illegible]nts. [2] The bravery that you habitually dis-

4.1[illegible]
4.1[illegible]the Athenians [illegible]

play in war does not depend on your having allies at your side in this or that encounter, but on your native courage; nor have numbers any terrors for citizens of states like yours, in which the many do not rule the few, but rather the few the many, owing their position to nothing else than to superiority in the field. [3] Inexperience now makes you afraid of barbarians; and yet the trial of strength which you had with the Macedonians among them, and my own judgment (confirmed by what I hear from others), should be enough to satisfy you that they will not prove formidable. [4] Where an enemy seems strong but is really weak, a true knowledge of the facts makes his adversary the bolder, just as a serious antagonist is encountered most confidently by those who do not know him. [5] Thus the present enemy might terrify an inexperienced imagination; they are formidable in outward bulk; their loud yelling is unbearable; and the brandishing of their weapons in the air has a threatening appearance. But when it comes to real fighting with an opponent who stands his ground, they are not what they seemed; they have no regular order that they should be ashamed of deserting their positions when hard pressed; flight and attack are equally honorable with them, and afford no test of courage; their independent mode of fighting never leaving anyone who wants to run away without a fair excuse for doing so. In short, they think frightening you at a secure distance a surer game than meeting you hand to hand; otherwise they would have done the one and not the other. [6] You can thus plainly see that the terrors with which they were at first invested are in fact trifling enough, though to the eye and ear very prominent. Stand your ground therefore when they advance, and wait your opportunity to retire in good order, and you will reach a place of safety all the sooner. Thus you will know forever afterwards that rabble such as these, to those who sustain their first attack, do but show off their courage by threats of the terrible things that they are going to do at a distance, but with those who give way to them are quick enough to display their heroism in pursuit when they can do so without danger."

4.127
423
9th Year/Summer
LYNCESTIS
After their attack is resolutely repulsed, the Lyncestian barbarians pursue the Macedonians and block Brasidas' route at a pass.

With this brief address Brasidas began to lead off his army. Seeing this, the barbarians came on with much shouting and hubbub, thinking that he was flying and that they would overtake him and cut him off. [2] But wherever they charged they found the young men ready to dash out against them, while Brasidas with his picked company sustained their onset. Thus the Peloponnesians withstood the first attack, to the surprise of the enemy, and afterwards received and repulsed them as fast as they came on, retiring as soon as their opponents became quiet. The main body of the barbarians ceased therefore to molest the Hellenes with Brasidas in the open country,

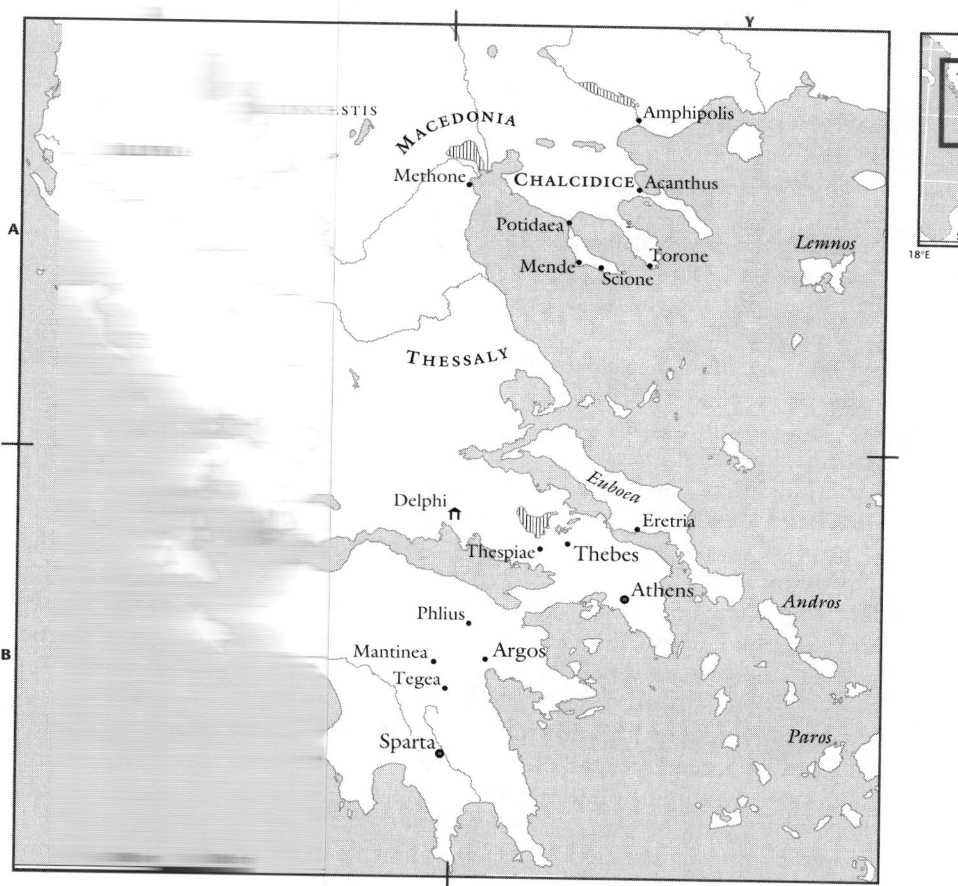

MA NG THE WINTER OF 423

an n number to harass their march, the rest went on aft ns, slaying those with whom they came up, and so py the narrow pass between two hills that leads int aeus.[2a] They knew that this was the only way by wh t, and now proceeded to surround him just as he en art of the road, in order to cut him off.

4.128 423 9th Year/Summer LYNCESTIS Brasidas drives the barbarians away. His enraged soldiers pillage the Macedonian baggage train and kill the oxen. From this moment, Perdiccas and Brasidas drift apart.

ir intention, told his three hundred to run on wi ckly as he could, to the hill which seemed easiest to lodge the barbarians already there, before they sh ain body closing round him. [2] These attacked an upon the hill, and the main army of the Hel- le ss difficulty toward it; the barbarians being terri-

4.1 mentioned sely deter-fied at seeing their men on that side driven from the height, and no longer following the main body who they considered had gained the frontier and made good their escape. [3] The heights once gained, Brasidas now proceeded more securely, and the same day arrived at Arnisa,[3a] the first city in the dominions of Perdiccas. [4] The soldiers, enraged at the desertion of the Macedonians, vented their rage on all their yokes of oxen which they found on the road, and on any baggage which had tumbled off (as might easily happen in the panic of a night retreat), by unyoking and cutting down the cattle and taking the baggage for themselves. From this moment [5] Perdiccas began to regard Brasidas as an enemy and to feel against the Peloponnesians a hatred which could not suit well the adversary of the Athenians. Indeed, he now departed from his natural interests and made it his endeavor to come to terms with the latter and to get rid of the former.

4.129
423
9th Year/Summer
MENDE
An Athenian attack on Mende is initially repulsed.

On his return from Macedonia to Torone,[1a] Brasidas found that the Athenians were already masters of Mende,[1b] and remained quiet where he was, thinking it now out of his power to cross over into Pallene and assist the Mendaeans, but he kept good watch over Torone. [2] For about the same time as the campaign in Lyncestis, the Athenians sailed upon the expedition which we left them preparing against Mende and Scione,[2a] with fifty ships (ten of which were Chians[2b]), one thousand Athenian hoplites and six hundred archers, one hundred Thracian mercenaries and some peltasts drawn from their allies in the neighborhood, under the command of Nicias son of Niceratus, and Nicostratus son of Diitrephes. [3] Departing from Potidaea,[3a] the fleet came to land opposite the temple of Poseidon, and proceeded against Mende; there they found the men of this city, reinforced by three hundred Scionaeans, with their Peloponnesian auxiliaries, seven hundred hoplites in all, under Polydamidas, encamped upon a strong hill outside the city. [4] These Nicias, with one hundred and twenty light-armed Methonaeans,[4a] sixty picked men from the Athenian hoplites, and all the archers, tried to reach by a path running up the hill, but he received a wound and found himself unable to force the position. Nicostratus, meanwhile, with all the rest of the army, advanced upon the hill, which was naturally difficult, by a different approach further off. His troops were thrown into utter disorder and the whole Athenian army narrowly escaped being defeated. [5] For that day, as the Mendaeans and their allies showed no signs of yielding, the Athenians retreated and encamped, and the Mendaeans at nightfall returned into the city.

4.130
423
9th Year/Summer
MENDE
The gates of Mende are opened after disputes between Mendaean and Peloponnesian troops; the Athenians take and sack the city.

The next day the Athenians sailed round to the Scione side[1a] and took the suburb there, and all day plundered the country, without anyone coming out against them, partly because of intestine disturbances in the city; and the following night the three hundred Scionaeans returned home. [2]

4.128.3a Arnisa: location unknown.
4.129.1a Torone: Map 4.128, AY.
4.129.1b Mende: Map 4.128, AY.
4.129.2a These Athenian preparations were mentioned in 4.122.6. Scione: Map 4.128, AY.
4.129.2b Island of Chios: Map 4.75, and Map 5.3.
4.129.3a Potidaea: Map 4.128, AY.
4.129.4a Methone in Macedonia: Map 4.128, AX.
4.130.1a The south side of Mende: Map 4.128, AY.

On[illegible]dvanced with half the army to the frontier of Sci[illegible] country; while Nicostratus with the remainder sta[illegible]e the city near the upper gate on the road to Po[illegible]he Mendaeans and of their Peloponnesian auxiliari[illegible]ned to be piled in that quarter, where Polydamidas[illegible] draw them up for battle, encouraging the Me[illegible]e. [4] At this moment one of the popular party ans[illegible] that they would not go out and did not want a wa[illegible] was dragged by the arm and knocked about by Po[illegible]e popular party at once seized their arms and rus[illegible]ns and at their allies of the opposite faction. [5] Th[illegible]were at once routed, partly from the suddenness of [illegible] through fear of the gates being opened to the At[illegible] imagined that the attack had been planned. [6] As [illegible]d on the spot took refuge in the citadel, which the[illegible]st; and the whole Athenian army, Nicias having by [illegible] being close to the city, now burst into Mende, wh[illegible] without any agreed terms, and sacked it just as if t[illegible]rm, the generals even finding some difficulty in res[illegible] massacring the inhabitants. [7] After this the At[illegible]ans that they might retain their civil rights, and the[illegible]sed authors of the revolt; and cut off the party in [illegible]ilt down to the sea on either side, appointing tro[illegible]ckade. Having thus secured Mende, they procee[illegible]

4.131
423
9th Year/Summer
SCIONE
The Athenians win a victory outside Scione and then besiege the city.

[illegible]oponnesians marched out against them, occupying [illegible] of the city, which had to be captured by the ene[illegible]nvest the place. [2] The Athenians stormed the hill[illegible]d its occupants, and having encamped and set up a t[illegible] work of circumvallation.[2a] [3] Not long after the[illegible]ations, the auxiliaries besieged in the citadel of Me[illegible]by the sea side and arrived by night at Scione, int[illegible] succeeded in entering, passing through the bes[illegible]

4.132
423
9th Year/Summer
THRACE
After making peace with Athens, Perdiccas prevents reinforcements from reaching Brasidas. Spartan commissioners do arrive, and bring young Spartans to take charge of the allied cities.

[illegible]f Scione was in progress, Perdiccas sent a herald to [illegible]nd made peace with the Athenians, through spite aga[illegible]eat from Lyncestis, from which moment indeed he [illegible]. [2] The Spartan Ischagoras was just then upon the[illegible]n army overland to join Brasidas; and Perdiccas, bei[illegible]ias to give some proof of the sincerity of his reconc[illegible]s, and being himself no longer disposed to let

4.13[illegible] of a wall to [illegible] land; see [illegible] Land War-[illegible]

the Peloponnesians into his country, put in motion his friends in Thessaly,[2a] with whose chief men he always took care to have relations, and so effectually stopped the army and its preparation that they did not even try the Thessalians. [3] Ischagoras himself, however, with Amaeinias and Aristeus, succeeded in reaching Brasidas; they had been commissioned by the Spartans to inspect the state of affairs, and in breach of the law brought out from Sparta some of their young men to put in command of the cities, to prevent their being entrusted to the persons upon the spot. Brasidas accordingly placed Clearidas son of Cleonymus in Amphipolis, and Pasitelidas son of Hegesander in Torone.[3a]

4.133
423
9th Year/Summer
BOEOTIA
Thebes dismantles the wall of Thespiae.
ARGOS
The temple of Hera at Argos burns down.
SCIONE
Scione is completely invested by the Athenians.

The same summer the Thebans[1a] dismantled the wall of the Thespians[1b] on the charge of Atticism, having always wished to do so, and now finding it an easy matter, as the flower of the Thespian youth had perished in the battle with the Athenians.[1c] [2] The same summer also the temple of Hera at Argos[2a] was burnt down, through Chrysis, the priestess, placing a lighted torch near the garlands and then falling asleep, so that they all caught fire and were in a blaze before she observed it. [3] Chrysis that very night fled to Phlius[3a] for fear of the Argives, who, following the law in such a case, appointed another priestess named Phaeinis. Chrysis at the time of her flight had been priestess for eight years of the present war and half the ninth.[3b] [4] At the close of the summer the siege works around Scione[4a] were completed and the Athenians, leaving a detachment to maintain the blockade, returned with the rest of their army.[4b]

4.134
423/2
9th Year/Winter
LAODICIUM
Mantinea and Tegea fight an indecisive battle at Laodicium.

During the following winter the Athenians and Spartans were kept quiet by the armistice; but the Mantineans and Tegeans,[1a] and their respective allies, fought a battle at Laodicium,[1b] in the territory of Oresthis. The victory remained doubtful, as each side routed one of the wings opposed to them, and both set up trophies and sent spoils to Delphi. [2] After heavy loss on both sides the battle was undecided, and night interrupted the action; yet the Tegeans passed the night on the field and set up a trophy at once, while the Mantineans withdrew to Bucolion and set up theirs afterwards.

4.132.2a Thessaly: Map 4.128, AX.
4.132.3a Amphipolis, Torone: Map 4.128, AY. Thucydides' meaning is not clear here, but a breach of the law could be found on two possible counts: (1) that it was not Spartan custom to send out young men of military age as governors of allied cities; and (2) that this move violated Brasidas' promise to the Chalcidian cities that the Spartans would not interfere in their governments but would leave them free.
4.133.1a Thebes: Map 4.128, BY.
4.133.1b Thespiae: Map 4.128, BY.
4.133.1c For the losses suffered by the Thespians in the battle of Delium, see 4.96.3.
4.133.2a Argos: Map 4.128, BY.
4.133.3a Phlius: Map 4.128, BY.
4.133.3b Chrysis must have been very old, for she had already served as priestess at the temple of Hera for forty-eight years some eight and one half years earlier when the war began; see 2. 2.1.
4.133.4a Scione: Map 4.128, AY.
4.133.4b For the end of the siege of Scione, see 5.32.1.
4.134.1a Mantinea, Tegea: Map 4.128, BX.
4.134.1b Laodicium: location unknown.

[illegible]e winter, in fact almost in spring, Brasidas made an [illegible][1a] He arrived by night, and succeeded in placing a l[illegible]thout being discovered, the ladder being planted jus[illegible]n the passing round of the bell and the return of the[illegible] back. Upon the garrison, however, taking the ala[illegible]rds, before his men came up, he quickly led off his[illegible] until it was day.[1b] So ended the winter and the nin[illegible]hich Thucydides is the historian.

4.135
423/2
9th Year/Winter
POTIDAEA
Brasidas' attempt to take Potidaea fails.

4.1[illegible]
4.1[illegible] Thrace con-[illegible]

BOOK FIVE

5.1 422 10th Year/Summer DELOS The truce ends. The Athenians expel the Delians from Delos; they settle at Atramyttium.

The next summer the truce for a year
en the Pythian games.[1a] During the armistice the
At elians from Delos,[1b] concluding that they must
ha e old offense at the time of their consecration,
an e omission in the previous purification of the
isl ted, had been thought to have been duly accom-
pli he graves of the dead. The Delians had Atramyt-
tiu by Pharnaces,[1d] and settled there when they left
De

5.2 422 10th Year/Summer THRACE Cleon leads an expedition to Thrace, going first to Scione and then to Torone, which he attacks.

ailed on the Athenians to let him set sail at the
ex e for the cities in the Thracian[1a] district with
tw and three hundred horse from Athens, a larger
fo ty ships. [2] First touching at the still-besieged
Sc hoplites from the army there, he next sailed into
C itory of Torone,[2b] which is not far from the city.
[3 learnt from deserters that Brasidas was not in
To on was not strong enough to give him battle, he
ad ainst the city, sending ten ships to sail round into
th first to the fortification recently built in front of
th der to take in the suburb, to do which he had
pu riginal wall and made it one city [5.3.1] Pasitel-
id der, with such garrison as there was in the place,
hu el the Athenian assault; but finding himself hard

5.3 422 10th Year/Summer THRACE The Athenians take Torone before Brasidas can come to its support. Torone's women and children are enslaved, and its men and garrison sent to Athens, from which they are later exchanged or freed by the peace. ATTICA The Boeotians capture Panactum by treachery.

5.1 letic and phi (Map . See Appen- als, §5.

5.1 purification 104.

5.1 : Map 5.3. In e Delians elos, but nained in ntions them ere.

5.1 ian governor of the Hellespontine region (Map 5.3), whom the Peloponnesian envoys to the Persian king were trying to reach in 2.67 when the Thracians detained them and turned them over to the Athenians.

5.2.1a Thrace: Map 5.3. This continues the narrative of events in Thrace from 4.135.

5.2.1b *Hoplites* were heavily armed Greek infantrymen. See Appendix F, Land Warfare, §2.

5.2.2a Scione: Map 5.3. The siege of Scione began in the summer of 423; see 4.131.

5.2.2b Torone: Map 5.3.

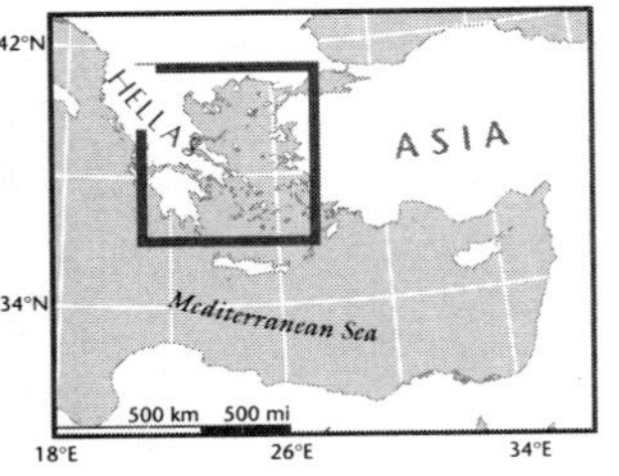

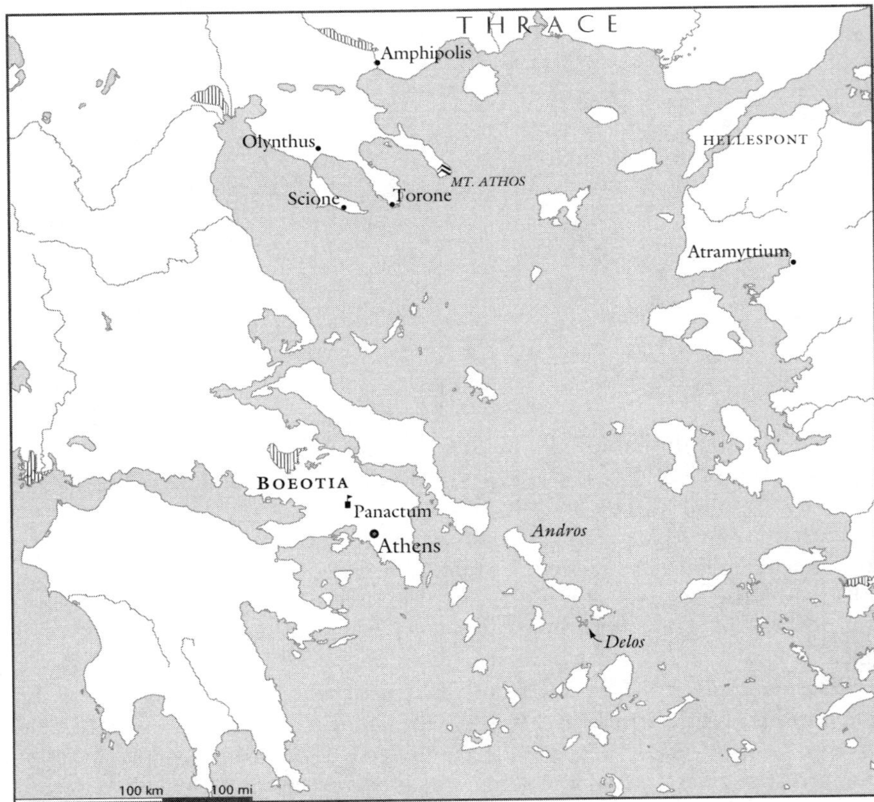

MAP 5.3 CLEON'S EXPEDITION TO THRACE

pressed, and seeing the ships that had been sent round sailing into the harbor, Pasitelidas began to be afraid that they might get up to the city before its defenders were there, and the fortification being also carried, he might be taken prisoner, and so abandoned the outer fortification and ran into the city. [2] But the Athenians from the ships had already taken Torone, and their land forces following at his heels burst in with him with a rush over the part of the old wall that had been pulled down, killing some of the Peloponnesians and Toronaeans in the mêlée, and making prisoners of the rest, and Pasitelidas their commander amongst them. [3] Brasidas meanwhile had advanced to relieve Torone, and had only about four miles more to go when he heard of its fall on the road and turned back again. [4] Cleon and the Athenians set up two trophies,[4a] one by the harbor, the

5.3.4a A trophy was set up by the victors after an ancient Greek battle. It usually consisted of a set of captured armor arranged on a pole that was raised on or near the battlefield.

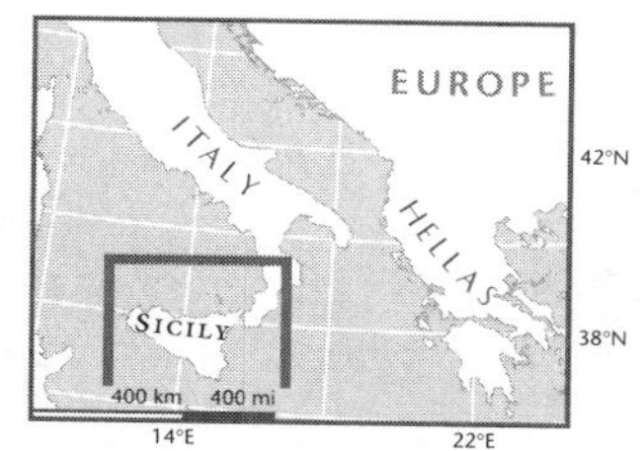

MA...
TR...
SI...

ot... and making slaves of the wives and children of
th... nen with the Peloponnesians and any Chalcidians
th... mber of seven hundred, to Athens; from which,
ho... ome afterwards, the Peloponnesians on the con-
cl... rest by being exchanged against other prisoners
wi... About the same time Panactum,[5a] a fortress on
th... taken by treachery by the Boeotians.[5b] [6] Mean-
wh... a garrison in Torone, weighed anchor and sailed
ro... to Amphipolis.[6b]

... Phaeax son of Erasistratus set sail with two col-
le... om Athens to Italy and Sicily.[1a] [2] The Leon-
ti... re of the Athenians from Sicily after the peace
ag... many new citizens and The People planned to
re... those in power, aware of their intention, called in
th... ed The People. [3] These last were scattered in
va... e upper classes came to an agreement with the
Sy... d laid waste their city, and went to live at Syracu... ade citizens. [4] Afterwards some of them were
di... yracuse occupied Phocaeae, a quarter of the city
of... e,[4a] a fortified place in the Leontine country, and
be... st of the exiled People carried on war from the
fo... henians hearing this, sent Phaeax to see if they
co... so convince their allies there and the rest of the
Si... designs of Syracuse, as to induce them to form a

5.4
422
10th Year/Summer
SICILY
The Athenians send Phaeax to Sicily to form a coalition against Syracuse and to rescue the exiled Leontines. Phaeax returns to Athens unsuccessful.

5.3...
5.3...
5.3...
5.3...
5.3... narrative of
... nued in 5.6.

5.4.1a This episode resumes the narrative of events in Sicily from 4.65.
5.4.2a Leontini: Map 5.4.
5.4.2b Thucydides is referring to the Peace of Gela; see 4.65.
5.4.4a Bricinniae, possible location: Map 5.4.

general coalition against her, and thus save The People of Leontini. [6] Arrived in Sicily, Phaeax succeeded at Camarina[6a] and Agrigentum,[6b] but meeting with a repulse at Gela[6c] did not go on to the rest, as he saw that he should not succeed with them, but returned through the country of the Sicels to Catana,[6d] and after visiting Bricinniae as he passed, and encouraging its inhabitants, sailed back to Athens.

5.5
422
10th Year/Summer
ITALY
Phaeax tries to secure the friendship of some Italian cities for Athens. Epizephyrian Locri, at war with its neighbors, makes peace with Athens.

During his voyage along the coast to and from Sicily, he talked with some cities in Italy on the subject of friendship with Athens, and also encountered some Locrian[1a] settlers exiled from Messana,[1b] who had been sent there when the Locrians were called in by one of the factions that divided Messana after the pacification of Sicily,[1c] and Messana came for a time into the hands of the Locrians. [2] These being met by Phaeax on their return home received no injury at his hands, as the Locrians had agreed with him for a treaty with Athens. [3] They were the only people of the allies of Syracuse who, when the reconciliation between the Sicilians took place, had not made peace with Athens; nor indeed would they have done so now, if they had not been pressed by a war with the Hipponians[3a] and Medmaeans[3b] who lived on their border, and were colonists of theirs. Phaeax meanwhile proceeded on his voyage, and at length arrived at Athens.

5.6
422
10th Year/Summer
THRACE
Cleon makes Eion his base and calls upon local allies for additional troops. Brasidas establishes a base at Amphipolis.

Cleon, having sailed round from Torone[1a] to Amphipolis,[1b] made Eion[1c] his base, and after an unsuccessful assault upon the Andrian[1d] colony of Stagirus,[1e] took Galepsus,[1f] a colony of Thasos,[1h] by storm. [2] He now sent envoys to Perdiccas to command his attendance with an army, as provided by the alliance; and others to Thrace, to Polles, king of the Odomantians,[2a] who was to bring as many Thracian mercenaries as possible; and himself remained inactive in Eion, awaiting their arrival. [3] Informed of this, Brasidas on his part took up a position of observation upon Cerdylium,[3a] a place situated in the Argilian[3b] country on high ground across the river, not far from Amphipolis, and commanding a view on all sides, and thus made it impossible for Cleon's army to move without his seeing it; for he fully expected that Cleon, contemptuous of the scanty numbers of his opponent, would march against Amphipolis with the force that he had with him. [4] At the same time Brasidas made his preparations, calling to his standard fifteen hundred Thracian mercenaries, and all the Edonians,[4a] horse and *peltasts*;[4b] he also had a thousand Myrcinian[4c] and Chalcidian peltasts,[4d]

5.4.6a Camarina: Map 5.4.
5.4.6b Agrigentum: Map 5.4.
5.4.6c Gela: Map 5.4.
5.4.6d Catana: Map 5.4.
5.5.1a Locri (Epizephyrian): Map 5.4.
5.5.1b Messana: Map 5.4.
5.5.1c The pacification, or "reconciliation between the Sicilians," took place in 424; see 4.65.
5.5.3a Hipponium: Map 5.4.
5.5.3b Medma: Map 5.4.
5.6.1a Torone, Map 5.7, BX. Cleon's voyage is continued from 5.3.
5.6.1b Amphipolis: Map 5.7, AX.
5.6.1c Eion: Map 5.7, AX.
5.6.1d Andros: Map 5.3.
5.6.1e Stagirus: Map 5.7, AX.
5.6.1f Galepsus: Map 5.7, AY.
5.6.1h Thasos: Map 5.7, AY.
5.6.2a Odomantian territory, approximate location: Map 5.7, AY.
5.6.3a Cerdylium, a hill near Amphipolis: exact location unknown.
5.6.3b Argilus: Map 5.7, AX.
5.6.4a Edonian territory, approximate location: Map 5.7, AX.
5.6.4b *Peltasts* were lightly armed troops; see note 4.111.1a.
5.6.4c Myrcinus: Map 5.7, AX.
5.6.4d Chalcidice, Map 5.7, AX.

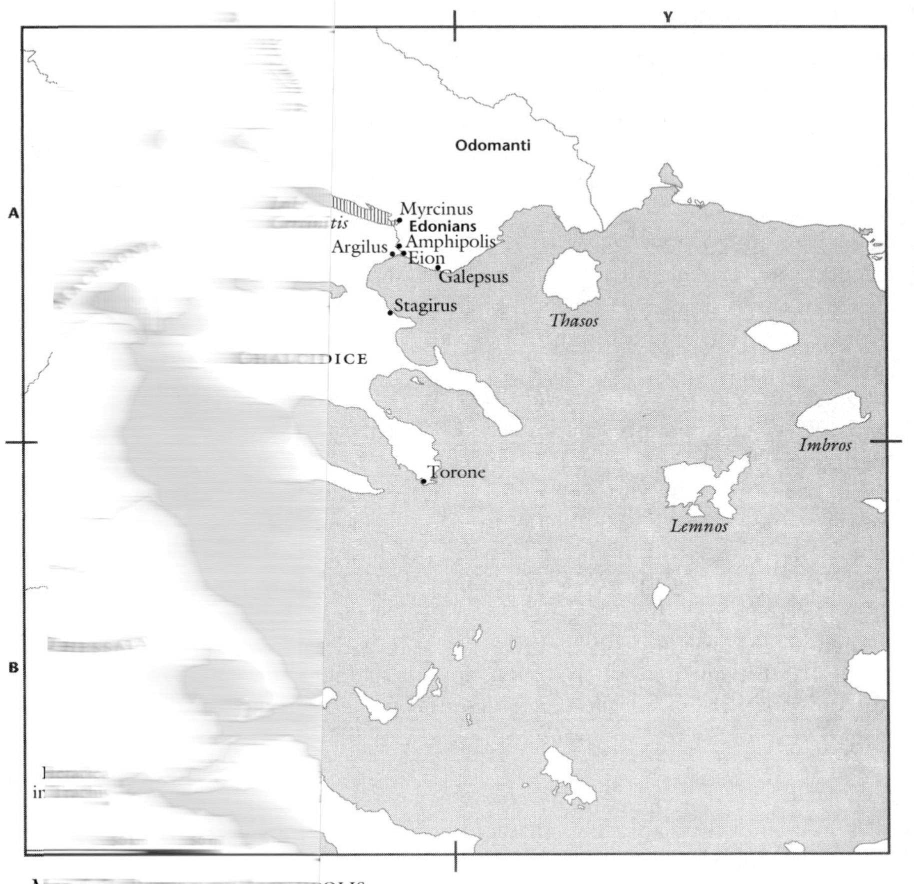

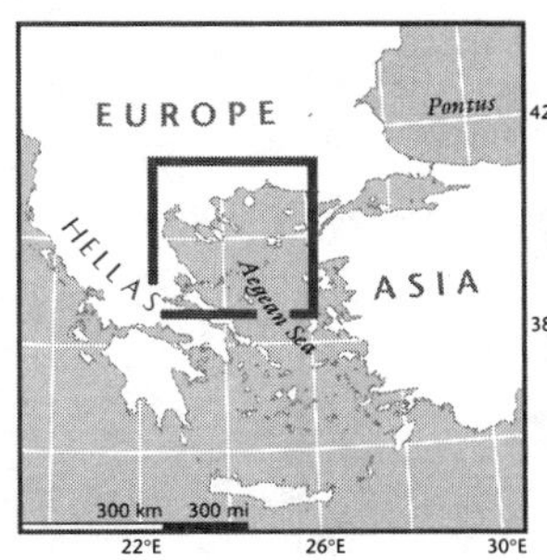

OLIS

olis, [5] and a force of hoplites numbering alto-
and, and three hundred Hellenic horse. Fifteen
with him upon Cerdylium; the rest were stationed
olis.

for some time, Cleon was at length obliged to do
] His soldiers, tired of their inactivity, began seri-
akness and incompetence of their commander and
ould be opposed to him, and on their own original
any him. These murmurs coming to the ears of
o disgust the army by keeping it in the same place,
and advanced. [3] The temper of the general was
os,[3a] his success on that occasion having given him
ty. He never dreamed of anyone coming out to
he was rather going up to view the place; and if he

5.7
422
10th Year/Summer
AMPHIPOLIS
In order to satisfy his men, Cleon makes a reconnaissance in force to Amphipolis. He does not expect to fight or to be attacked.

scribed in
begins at

waited for his reinforcements it was not in order to make victory secure in case he should be compelled to engage, but to be enabled to surround and storm the city. [4] He accordingly came and posted his army upon a strong hill in front of Amphipolis, and proceeded to examine the lake formed by the Strymon,[4a] and how the city lay on the side of Thrace. [5] He thought to retire when he chose without fighting, as there was no one to be seen upon the wall or coming out of the gates, all of which were shut. Indeed, it seemed a mistake not to have brought down siege engines with him; he could then have taken the city, there being no one to defend it.

5.8
422
10th Year/Summer
AMPHIPOLIS
Recognizing Cleon's ineptitude, Brasidas decides that this is an opportune moment to attack, and explains his plan to his troops.

As soon as Brasidas saw the Athenians in motion he descended himself from Cerdylium and entered Amphipolis. [2] He did not venture to go out in regular order against the Athenians: he mistrusted his strength, and thought it inadequate to the attempt; not in numbers—these were not so unequal—but in quality, the flower of the Athenian army being in the field, with the best of the Lemnians[2a] and Imbrians.[2b] He therefore prepared to assail them by stratagem. [3] For if he let the enemy see both the numbers of his men and the makeshift nature of their armament, he thought he was less likely to win than if the enemy did not have a view of them in advance and thus come rightly to despise them. [4] He accordingly picked out a hundred and fifty hoplites, and putting the rest under Clearidas, determined to attack suddenly before the Athenians retired; thinking that he should not again have such a chance of catching them alone if their reinforcements were once allowed to come up; and so calling all his soldiers together in order to encourage them and explain his intention, spoke as follows:

5.9
422
10th Year/Summer
AMPHIPOLIS
Brasidas says that the Athenians are careless and their advance to Amphipolis is a blunder. He divides his force and plans to launch a double surprise attack in order to panic the enemy. He promises to set an example by his own courage.

"Peloponnesians, the character of the country from which we have come, one which has always owed its freedom to valor, and the fact that you are Dorians and the enemy you are about to fight Ionians whom you are accustomed to beat, are things that do not need further comment.[1a] [2] But as for the plan of attack that I propose to pursue, this it is well to explain, in order that the fact of our adventuring with a part instead of with the whole of our forces may not damp your courage by the apparent disadvantage at which it places you. [3] I imagine it is the poor opinion that he has of us, and the fact that he has no idea of anyone coming out to engage him, that has made the enemy march up to the place and carelessly look about him as he is doing, without noticing us. [4] But the most successful soldier will always be the man who most happily detects a blunder like this, and who carefully consulting his own means makes his attack not so much by open and regular approaches, as by seizing the

5.7.4a The Strymon River (Map 5.7, AX) flowed through Lake Cercinitis (Map 5.7, AX).
5.8.2a Lemnos: Map 5.7, BY.
5.8.2b Imbros: Map 5.7, AY.
5.9.1a This is one of several manifestations in Thucydides of Dorian contempt for Ionian valor; see Appendix H, Dialects and Ethnic Groups, §8.

ent; [5] and these stratagems, which do the
iends by most completely deceiving our ene-
liant name in war. [6] Therefore, while their
tinues, and they are still thinking, as in my
doing, more of retreat than of maintaining
eir spirit is slack and not high-strung with
nen under my command will, if possible, take
ll with a run upon their center; [7] and do
ds, when you see me already upon them, and,
r among them, take with you the Amphipoli-
allies, and suddenly open the gates and dash
engage as quickly as you can. [8] That is our
ing a panic among them, as a fresh assailant
for an enemy than the one he is immediately
ow yourself a brave man, as a *Spartiate*[9a]
es, follow him like men, and remember that
nce mark the good soldier, and that this day
free men and allies of Sparta, or slaves of
cape without personal loss of liberty or life,
harsher terms than before, and you will also
the rest of the Hellenes. [10] Make no show
our part, seeing the greatness of the issues at
that what I preach to others I can practice

5.10
422
10th Year/Summer
AMPHIPOLIS
When Brasidas' preparations are observed by the Athenians, Cleon orders his army to return to Eion. Brasidas' sudden attack overwhelms the Athenians. Cleon is killed in the rout. Brasidas, however, is mortally wounded.

rasidas himself prepared for the sally, and placed
the the Thracian gates to support him as had been
agr had been seen coming down from Cerdylium
an is overlooked from the outside), sacrificing near
the hort, all his movements had been observed, and
wo on, who had at the moment gone on to look
ab of the enemy's force could be seen in the city,
an and men in great numbers were visible under the
ga nded. [3] Upon hearing this he went up to look,
an unwilling to venture upon the decisive step of a
ba nents came up, and thinking that he would have
tin eat be sounded and sent orders to the men to
ex e left wing in the direction of Eion,[3a] which was
in cable. [4] This however not being quick enough
fo reat in person and made the right wing wheel
ro armed side to the enemy. [5] It was then that

5.9 f Sparta and a
an military

5.1 I.v) for a dis-
dides.

5.10.3a Eion: Map 5.7, AX.

Brasidas seeing the Athenian force in motion and his opportunity come, said to the men with him and the rest, "Those fellows will never stand before us, one can see that by the way their spears and heads are going. Troops which do as they do seldom stand a charge. Quick, someone, open the gates I spoke of, and let us be out and at them with no fears for the result." [6] Accordingly moving out by the palisade gate and by the first gate in the long wall then existing, he ran at top speed along the straight road, where the trophy now stands as you go by the steepest part of the hill, and fell upon and routed the center of the Athenians, panic-stricken by their own disorder and astounded at his audacity. [7] At the same moment Clearidas in execution of his orders issued out from the Thracian gates to support him, and also attacked the enemy. [8] The result was that the Athenians, suddenly and unexpectedly attacked on both sides, fell into confusion; and their left toward Eion, which had already got on some distance, at once broke and fled. Just as it was in full retreat and Brasidas was passing on to attack the right, he received a wound; but his fall was not perceived by the Athenians, as he was taken up by those near him and carried off the field. [9] The Athenian right made a better stand, and though Cleon, who from the first had no thought of fighting, at once fled and was overtaken and slain by a Myrcinian peltast,[9a] his infantry forming in close order upon the hill twice or thrice repulsed the attacks of Clearidas, and did not finally give way until they were surrounded and routed by the missiles of the Myrcinian and Chalcidian[9b] horse and the peltasts. [10] Thus all the Athenian army was now in flight; and those who escaped being killed in the battle by the Chalcidian horse and the peltasts dispersed among the hills, and with difficulty made their way to Eion. [11] The men who had taken up and rescued Brasidas, brought him into the city with the breath still in him: he lived to hear of the victory of his troops, and not long after expired. [12] The rest of the army returning with Clearidas from the pursuit stripped the dead and set up a trophy.

5.11
422
10th Year/Summer
AMPHIPOLIS
The Amphipolitans bury Brasidas and honor him as if he were their city's founder. The Athenian casualties are very heavy.

After this all the allies attended in arms and buried Brasidas at the public expense in the city, in front of what is now the marketplace, and the Amphipolitans having enclosed his tomb, ever afterwards sacrifice to him as a hero and have given to him the honor of games and annual offerings. They constituted him the founder of their colony, and pulled down the Hagnonic erections and obliterated everything that could be interpreted as a memorial of his [Hagnon] having founded the place; for they considered that Brasidas had been their preserver and courting as they did the alliance of Sparta for fear of Athens, in their present hostile relations with the latter they could no longer with the same advantage or satisfaction pay Hagnon his honors.[1a] [2] They also gave the Athenians back their dead.[2a] About six

5.10.9a Myrcinus: Map 5.7, AX.
5.10.9b Chalcidice: Map 5.7, AX.
5.11.1a For Hagnon's foundation of Amphipolis in 437/6, see 4.102.3.
5.11.2a The return of the vanquished dead was part of the post-battle ritual of hoplite warfare. See Appendix F, Land Warfare, §6.

hu[illegible] fallen and only seven of the enemy, owing to the[illegible]lar engagement, but the affair of accident and pa[illegible]d. [3] After taking up their dead the Athenians sail[illegible]ridas and his troops remained to arrange matters at [illegible]

5.12 422 10th Year/Summer HERACLEA Spartan reinforcements for Thrace delay at Heraclea.

[illegible] three Spartans—Ramphias, Autocharidas, and Ep[illegible]ement of nine hundred hoplites to the cities in the [illegible] arriving at Heraclea in Trachis[1a] made changes an[illegible]thought best. [2] While they delayed there, this bat[illegible] summer ended.

5.13 422/1 10th Year/Winter THESSALY The Spartan reinforcements halt because of Thessalian opposition and Spartan desire for peace.

[illegible]winter Ramphias and his companions penetrated as [illegible]y;[1a] but as the Thessalians opposed their further adv[illegible]m they came to reinforce was dead, they turned bac[illegible] the moment had gone by, the Athenians being def[illegible]emselves not equal to the execution of Brasidas' de[illegible]e however of their return was because they knew tha[illegible]rtan opinion was really in favor of peace.

5.14 422/1 10th Year/Winter ATHENS-SPARTA Both sides now desire peace, and Thucydides explains why this is so.

[illegible] that directly after the battle of Amphipolis and the[illegible]om Thessaly, both sides ceased to prosecute the wa[illegible]tion to peace. Athens had suffered severely at De[illegible]y afterwards at Amphipolis, and had no longer tha[illegible]gth which had made her before refuse to accept the[illegible]elief of ultimate victory which her success at the mo[illegible]] besides, she was afraid of her allies being ter[illegible] rebel more generally, and repented having let go the[illegible]or peace which the affair of Pylos had offered. [3][illegible]hand, found the actuality of the war falsify her no[illegible]ir land for a few years would suffice for the overthr[illegible] Athenians. She had suffered on the island a disast[illegible] Sparta; she saw her country plundered from Py[illegible] *Helots*[3c] were deserting, and she was in constant app[illegible]who remained in the Peloponnesus would rely up[illegible]ke advantage of the situation to renew their old att[illegible] Besides this, as chance would have it, her thirty yea[illegible]ves[4a] was upon the point of expiring; and they ref[illegible]s Cynuria[4b] were restored to them; so that it see[illegible] Argos and Athens at once. She also suspected so[illegible] Peloponnesus of intending to go over to the en[illegible]ase.

5.15 422/1 10th Year/Winter ATHENS-SPARTA The Spartans are eager for peace in order to liberate the prisoners taken at Pylos, some of whom belonged to the first families of Sparta.

[illegible]ade both sides disposed for an accommodation; the[illegible]bly the most eager, as they ardently desired to

5.1[illegible]7, BX. This [illegible]78 and

5.1[illegible] but probably [illegible].7, BX.

5.1[illegible]cribed in

5.14.3a Pylos: Map 5.17, BX.
5.14.3b Cythera: Map 5.17, BY.
5.14.3c For information on Spartan *Helots*, see Appendix C, Spartan Institutions, §3–4.
5.14.4a Argos: Map 5.17, BY.
5.14.4b Cynuria: Map 5.17, BY.

recover the men taken on the island,[1a] the Spartiates among whom belonged to the first families and were accordingly related to leading men in Sparta.[1b] [2] Negotiations had been begun directly after their capture, but the Athenians in their hour of triumph would not consent to any reasonable terms; though after their defeat at Delium Sparta, knowing that they would now be more inclined to listen, at once concluded the truce for a year, during which they were to confer together and see if a longer period could not be agreed upon.

5.16
422/1
10th Year/Winter
ATHENS-SPARTA
With Brasidas and Cleon dead, new leaders (king Pleistoanax in Sparta and Nicias in Athens) come to prominence. They are eager for peace. The campaign behind Pleistoanax's return from exile is described.

Now, however, after the Athenian defeat at Amphipolis, and the death of Cleon and Brasidas, who had been the two principal opponents of peace on either side—the latter from the success and honor which war gave him, the former because he thought that, if tranquillity were restored, his crimes would be more open to detection and his slanders less credited—the foremost candidates for power in either city, Pleistoanax son of Pausanias, king of Sparta, and Nicias son of Niceratus, the most fortunate general of his time, each desired peace more ardently than ever. Nicias, while still happy and honored, wished to secure his good fortune, to obtain a present release from trouble for himself and his countrymen, and hand down to posterity a name as an ever-successful statesman, and thought the way to do this was to keep out of danger and commit himself as little as possible to fortune, and that peace alone made this keeping out of danger possible. Pleistoanax, on the other hand, was assailed by his enemies for his restoration, and regularly criticized by them in front of his countrymen for every reverse that befell them, as though his unjust restoration were the cause. [2] They accused him and his brother Aristocles of having bribed the prophetess of Delphi[2a] to tell the Spartan deputations which successively arrived at the temple to bring home the seed of the demigod son of Zeus[2b] from abroad, else they would have to plough with a silver share. [3] They insisted that in time, he had in this way induced the Spartans to restore him with the same dances and sacrifices with which they had instituted their kings upon the first settlement of Sparta. This they did in the nineteenth year of his exile to Lycaeum[3a] where he had gone when banished on suspicion of having accepted a bribe to retreat from Attica, and where he had built half his house within the consecrated precinct of Zeus for fear of the Spartans.

5.17
422/1
10th Year/Winter
ATHENS-SPARTA
As peace negotiations drag on, Sparta threatens to fortify a post in Attica. The final treaty involves compromises and is not approved by certain members of the Peloponnesian League.

The sting of this accusation, and the reflection that in peace no disaster could occur, and that when Sparta had recovered her men there would be nothing for his enemies to seize upon (whereas, while war lasted the highest station must always bear the scandal of everything that went wrong), made him ardently desire a settlement. [2] Accordingly this winter was employed in conferences; and as spring rapidly approached, the Spartans

5.15.1a Thucydides is referring to the men captured on the island of Sphacteria in the final action at Pylos; see 4.31–38.

5.15.1b The text of Thucydides is corrupt at this point. (Translators generally seek to reproduce the sense of Plutarch, *Nicias,* 10.8.) See note at 5.34 for the Spartan population problem.

5.16.2a Delphi: Map 5.17, BX.

5.16.2b The demigod son of Zeus referred to here is Heracles.

5.16.3a Lycaeum: Map 5.17, BX. Pleistoanax's withdrawal from Attica is described in 1.114.2.

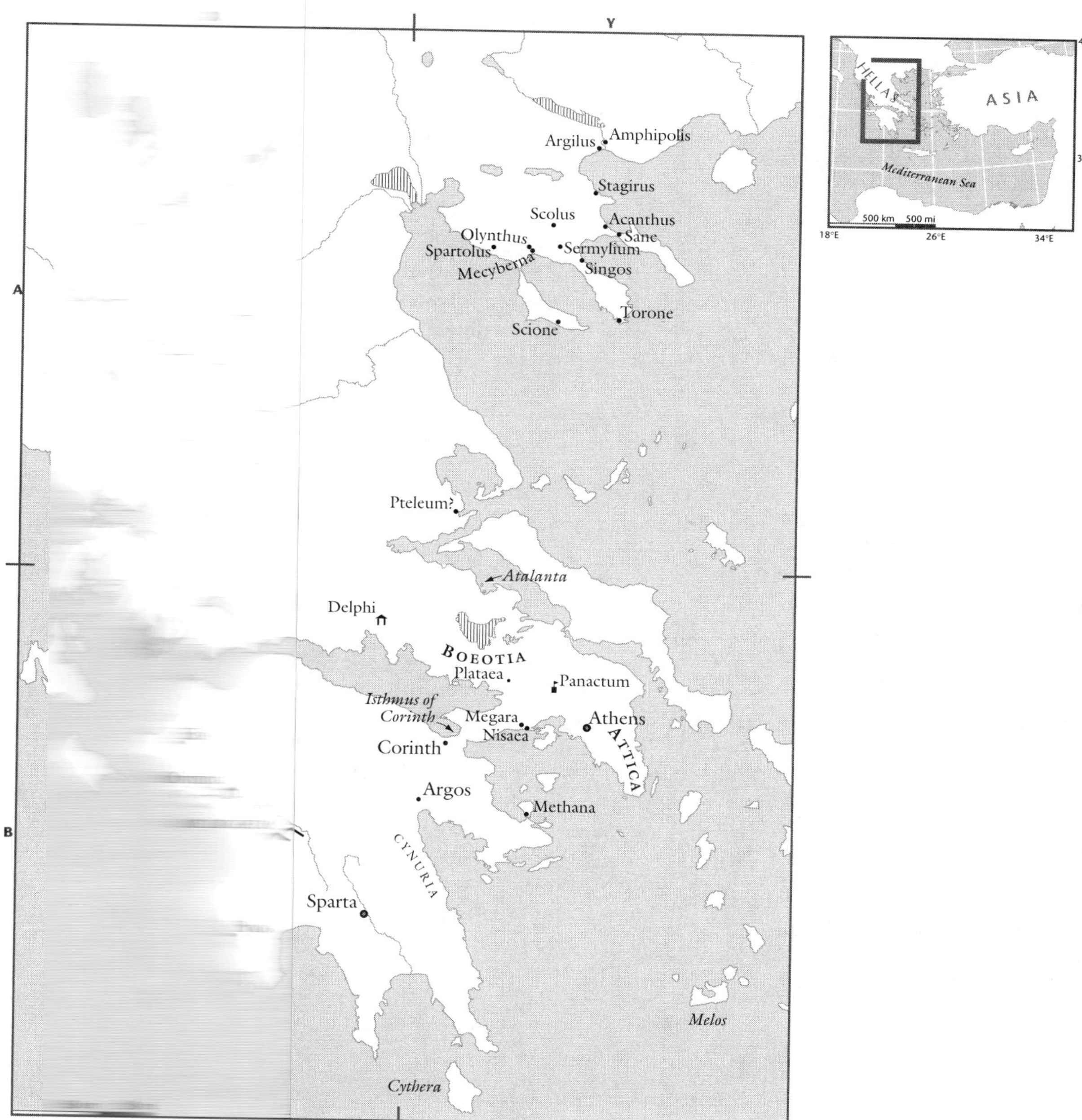

MA ONED IN THE FIFTY-YEAR TREATY OF PEACE

sent round orders to the cities to prepare for a fortified occupation of Attica,[2a] and held this as a sword over the heads of the Athenians to induce them to listen to their overtures; and at last, after many claims had been urged on either side at the conferences, a peace was agreed to upon the following basis: each party was to restore its conquests, but Athens was to keep Nisaea;[2b] her demand for Plataea[2c] being countered by the Thebans asserting that they had acquired the place not by force or treachery, but by the voluntary adhesion upon agreement of its citizens; and the same, according to the Athenian account, being the history of her acquisition of Nisaea. This arranged, the Spartans summoned their allies, and all voting for peace except the Boeotians,[2d] Corinthians,[2e] Eleans,[2f] and Megarians,[2g] who did not approve of these proceedings, they concluded the treaty and made peace, each of the contracting parties swearing to the following articles:

5.18
422/1
10th Year/Winter
ATHENS-SPARTA
Thucydides lists the articles of the treaty.

The Athenians and Spartans and their allies made a treaty, and swear to it, city by city, as follows:

• [2] Regarding the national temples, there shall be a free passage by land and by sea to all who wish it, to sacrifice, travel, consult, and attend the oracle or games, according to the customs of their countries.

• The temple and shrine of Apollo at Delphi[2a] and the Delphians shall be governed by their own laws, taxed by their own state, and judged by their own judges, the land and the people, according to the customs of their country.

• [3] The treaty shall be binding for fifty years upon the Athenians and the allies of the Athenians, and upon the Spartans and the allies of the Spartans, without fraud or harm by land or by sea.

• [4] It shall not be lawful to take up arms, with intent to do injury either for the Spartans and their allies against the Athenians and their allies, or for the Athenians and their allies against the Spartans and their allies, in any way or means whatsoever. But should any difference arise between them they are to have recourse to law and oaths, according as may be agreed between the parties.

• [5] The Spartans and their allies shall give back Amphipolis[5a] to the Athenians. Nevertheless, in the case of cities given up by the Spartans to the Athenians, the inhabitants shall be allowed to go where they please and to take their property with them; and the cities shall be independent, paying only the tribute of Aristides.[5b]

5.17.2a Attica: Map 5.17, BY. The "cities" Sparta called on here were the members of the Peloponnesian League; see Appendix D, The Peloponnesian League, §3–4.
5.17.2b Nisaea: Map 5.17, BY.
5.17.2c Plataea: Map 5.17, BY.
5.17.2d Boeotia: Map 5.17, BY.
5.17.2e Corinth: Map 5.17, BY.
5.17.2f Elis: Map 5.17, BX.
5.17.2g Megara: Map 5.17, BY.
5.18.2a Delphi: Map 5.17, BX.
5.18.5a Amphipolis: Map 5.17, AY.
5.18.5b By this clause the Spartans agree to return to Athens not only Amphipolis but certain other cities of the Thracian district of the Athenian Empire that had revolted. This involved not only the dissolution of the Chalcidian League, to which Thucydides refers by the term "Chalcidians," but also the physical return to their own cities of the people who had migrated to Olynthus, Acanthus, or other large cities. For the cities that were to be restored to Athens, Sparta secured a guarantee of autonomy, provided that they paid to Athens the tribute assessed by Aristides in 478/7 at the foundation of the Delian League. The peace proved largely abortive. Thucydides mentions Aristides in 1.91.3.

…l for the Athenians or their allies to carry on …he treaty has been concluded, so long as the …s referred to are Argilus, Stagirus, Acanthus, …partolus.[5c] These cities shall be neutral, allies …nor of the Athenians; but if the cities consent, …e Athenians to make them their allies, pro… cities wish it. [6] The Mecybernaeans, …s[6a] shall inhabit their own cities, as also the …ans; [7] but the Spartans and their allies shall … the Athenians.

… shall give back Coryphasium, Cythera, …and Atalanta[7d] to the Spartans, and also all … prison at Athens or elsewhere in the Athen… …all let go the Peloponnesians besieged in … Scione that are allies of the Spartans, and all …here, and any others of the allies of the Spar… …prison at Athens or elsewhere in the Athenian …

…their allies shall in like manner give back any … allies that they may have in their hands.

… Scione, Torone,[8a] and Sermylium[8b] and any …henians may have, the Athenians may adopt …ease.

… shall take an oath to the Spartans and their … man shall swear by the most binding oath of …om each city. The oath shall be as follows:— …greement and treaty honestly and without …y an oath shall be taken by the Spartans and …ans;

… shall be renewed annually by both parties. … at Olympia,[10a] Pythia,[10b] the Isthmus,[10c] at … and at Sparta in the temple at Amyclae.

… forgotten, whatever it be, and on whatever …nt with their oath for both parties the Athe…er it, according to their discretion.

…om the ephorate[1a] of Pleistolas in Sparta, on …onth of Artemisium, and from the archon-

5.19
422/1
10th Year/Winter
ATHENS-SPARTA
Thucydides gives the date of the treaty and names of the oath-takers who acted as the representatives for Sparta and Athens.

5.18… …Scolus, Olyn… …Y.
5.18… …ap 5.17, AY.
5.18…
5.18… …17, BX; …, BY.
5.18… …ap 5.17,
5.18…
5.18…
5.18…
5.18…
5.18…
5.18… …X.
5.18… …7, BY.

5.19.1a An ephor was one of the most powerful officials of the Spartan government; see Appendix C, Spartan Institutions, §5. See also Appendix K, Calendars and Dating Systems, §1–2.

ship[1b] of Alcaeus at Athens, on the 25th day of the month of Elaphebolion. [2] Those who took the oath and poured the libations for the Spartans were Pleistoanax, Agis, Pleistolas, Damagetus, Chionis, Metagenes, Acanthus, Daithus, Ischagoras, Philocharidas, Zeuxidas, Antippus, Tellis, Alcinadas, Empedias, Menas, and Laphilus; for the Athenians, Lampon, Isthmionicus, Nicias, Laches, Euthydemus, Procles, Pythodorus, Hagnon, Myrtilus, Thrasycles, Theagenes, Aristocrates, Iolcius, Timocrates, Leon, Lamachus, and Demosthenes.

5.20
422/1
10th Year/Winter
HELLAS
Thucydides explains his method of dating by annual summer and winter seasons rather than by referring to magistrates' names.

This treaty was made in the spring, just at the end of winter, directly after the city festival of Dionysus,[1a] just ten years, with the difference of a few days, from the first invasion of Attica and the commencement of this war. [2] This must be calculated by the seasons rather than by trusting to the enumeration of the names of the various magistrates or offices of honor that are used to mark past events. Accuracy is impossible where an event may have occurred in the beginning, or middle, or at any period in their tenure of office.[2a] [3] But by computing by summers and winters, the method adopted in this history, it will be found that, each of these amounting to half a year, there were ten summers and as many winters contained in this first war.

5.21
422/1
10th Year/Winter
HELLAS
The Spartans begin to carry out the treaty but find that they cannot deliver Amphipolis and other Chalcidian cities which refuse to return to Athenian rule.

Meanwhile the Spartans, to whose lot it fell to begin the work of restitution, immediately set free all the prisoners of war in their possession, and sent Ischagoras, Menas, and Philocharidas as envoys to the cities in the Thracian region, to order Clearidas to hand over Amphipolis[1a] to the Athenians, and the rest of their allies each to accept the treaty as it affected them. [2] The allies, however, did not like its terms, and refused to accept it; Clearidas also, wishing to oblige the Chalcidians, would not hand over the city, declaring he could not do so against their will. [3] Meanwhile he hastened in person to Sparta with envoys from the place, to defend his disobedience against the possible accusations of Ischagoras and his companions, and also to see whether it was too late for the agreement to be altered; and on finding the Spartans were bound, quickly set out back again with instructions from them to hand over the place, if possible, or at all events to bring out the Peloponnesians that were in it.

5.22
422/1
10th Year/Winter
ATHENS-SPARTA
When some of Sparta's allies refuse to accept the peace treaty, Sparta enters into an alliance with Athens.

The allies happened to be present in person at Sparta, and those who had not accepted the treaty were now asked by the Spartans to adopt it. This, however, they refused to do, for the same reasons as before, unless a fairer one than the present were agreed upon; [2] and remaining firm in their determination were dismissed by the Spartans, who now decided to

5.19.1b Archons were the chief administrative officers of the Athenian government. Alcaeus was the Eponymous archon for that year; see Appendix A, The Athenian Government, §6.

5.20.1a For the Festival of Dionysus, see Appendix I, Greek Religious Festivals, §8.

5.20.2a See Appendix K, Classical Greek Calendars and Dating Systems, §1–3, 8.

5.21.1a Amphipolis: Map 5.17, AY.

for ...Athenians, thinking that Argos, who had refused
the ...as and Lichas for a renewal of the treaty, would
wit... be formidable, and that the rest of the Pelopon-
ne... ...eep quiet if the desired alliance of Athens were
shu... ...ccordingly, after conference with the Athenian
am... ...as agreed upon and oaths were exchanged, upon
the...

... allies of the Athenians for fifty years.
...vade the territory of Sparta and injure the Spartan... ...elp them in such way as they most effectively can,
acc... But if the invader is no longer there after plun-
de... ...ty shall be the enemy of Sparta and Athens, and
sh... and one shall not make peace without the other.
Th... ...estly, loyally, and without fraud.

5.23
422/1
10th Year/Winter
ATHENS-SPARTA
Thucydides reports the text of the treaty of alliance between Athens and Sparta.

...y invade the territory of Athens and injure the
At... ...all help them in such way as they most effectively
ca... ...ower. But if the invader is no longer there after
pl... ...hat city shall be the enemy of Sparta and Athens,
an... both, and one shall not make peace without the
ot... ...d honestly, loyally, and without fraud.
... population rise,[3a] the Athenians shall help the
Sp... ...ht, according to their power.
...liance) shall be sworn to by the same persons on
ei... the other treaty. It shall be renewed annually by
th... ...ens for the Dionysia, and the Athenians to Sparta
fo... and a pillar shall be set up by either party; at
Sp... ...pollo at Amyclae, and at Athens on the Acropolis
ne... [6] Should the Spartans and Athenians see fit to
ad... the alliance in any particular, it shall be consistent
w... ...arties to do so, according to their discretion.
...ath for the Spartans were Pleistoanax, Agis, Pleis-
to... ...is, Metagenes, Acanthus, Daithus, Ischagoras,
Ph... ...ntippus, Alcinadas, Tellis, Empedias, Menas, and
La... ...s, Lampon, Isthmionicus, Laches, Nicias, Euthy-
de... ...rus, Hagnon, Myrtilus, Thrasycles, Theagenes,
A... ...ocrates, Leon, Lamachus, and Demosthenes.

5.24
422/1
10th Year/Winter
ATHENS-SPARTA
Thucydides lists the names of the oath-takers of the treaty of alliance. The Athenians return their Spartan prisoners. This ends the history of the "first war" that lasted ten years.

...made not long after the treaty; and the Athenians
ga... the island to the Spartans, and the summer of the

5.... ...ers to the Spar- ... 5.14.3 for ... elot revolt). ... later on in the ... are no indica- ... ne feared a ... always feared an uprising of the Helots. See 4.80.2–5, 5.14.3, and Appendix C, Spartan Institutions, §3–4.

5.23.4a The Dionysia at Athens and the Hyacinthia at Sparta were annual religious festivals; see Appendix I, Classical Greek Religious Festivals, §8.

eleventh year began.[2a] This completes the history of the first war, which occupied the whole of the ten previous years.

5.25
421
11th Year/Summer
HELLAS
The peace lasts almost seven years but is not accepted by all parties and proves unstable. Both sides continue to injure each other until they finally resume open hostilities.

After the treaty and the alliance between the Spartans and Athenians, concluded after the ten years' war (in the ephorate of Pleistolas at Sparta, and the archonship of Alcaeus at Athens), the states which had accepted these agreements were at peace; but the Corinthians and some of the cities in the Peloponnesus tried to disturb the settlement and immediately agitated against Sparta. [2] Moreover, the Athenians, as time went on, began to suspect the Spartans because they had not performed some of the provisions of the treaty; [3] and though for six years and ten months they abstained from invasion of each other's territory, yet abroad an unstable armistice did not prevent either party doing the other serious injury, until they were finally obliged to break the treaty made after the ten years' war and to have recourse to open hostilities.

5.26
421
11th Year/Summer
HELLAS
Thucydides argues that the peace was not a genuine peace between wars but merely an interval of limited hostility during a single long war.

The history of this period has also been written by the same Thucydides, an Athenian, in the chronological order of events by summers and winters, up to the time when the Spartans and their allies put an end to the Athenian empire, and took the Long Walls and the Piraeus. The war had then lasted for twenty-seven years in all.[1a] [2] Only a mistaken judgment can object to including the interval of treaty in the war. Looked at in the light of the facts it cannot, it will be found, be rationally considered a state of peace, as neither party either gave or got back all that they had agreed, apart from the violations of it which occurred on both sides in the Mantinean[2a] and Epidaurian[2b] wars and other instances, and the fact that the allies in the region of Thrace were in as open hostility as ever, and that the Boeotians had only a truce renewed every ten days. [3] So that the first ten years' war, the treacherous armistice that followed it, and the subsequent war will, calculating by the seasons, be found to make up the number of years which I have mentioned, with the difference of a few days, and to provide an instance of faith in oracles being for once justified by the event.[3a] [4] I certainly remember that all along from the beginning to the end of the war it was commonly declared that it would last thrice nine years. [5] I lived through the whole of it, being of an age to comprehend events, and giving my attention to them in order to know the exact truth about them. It was also my fate to be an exile from my country for twenty years after my command at Amphipolis;[5a] and being present with both parties, and more especially with the Peloponnesians by reason of my exile, I had leisure to observe affairs more closely. [6] I will accordingly now relate

5.24.2a Thucydides refers to the men captured on the island of Sphacteria in the final action at Pylos; see 4.31–38.

5.26.1a This comment was certainly written after the end of the war in 404, although Thucydides' narrative breaks off in 411; see the Introduction (sect. II. ii).

5.26.2a For the Mantinean War, see 5.64–74. Mantinea: Map 5.29.

5.26.2b For the Epidaurian War, see 5.53–80. Epidaurus: Map 5.29.

5.26.3a See the Introduction (sect. IV. i) for a discussion of Thucydides' attitude to oracles and to religion.

5.26.5a Amphipolis: Map 5.17, AY. Thucydides describes his role in Brasidas' attack on Amphipolis in 4.104.4–4.107.3.

the [illegible] after the ten years' war, the breach of the treaty,
and [illegible] owed.[6a]

[illegible] of the fifty years' peace and of the subsequent
alli [illegible] n the Peloponnesus which had been summoned
for [illegible] from Sparta. [2] Most of them went straight
ho [illegible] first turned aside to Argos and opened negotia-
tio [illegible] n in office there, pointing out that Sparta could
hav [illegible], but only the subjugation of the Peloponnesus,
or [illegible] entered into treaty and alliance with the once
det [illegible] hat the duty of consulting for the safety of the
Pe [illegible] en upon Argos,[2a] who should immediately pass a
dec [illegible] c state that chose (such state being independent
and [illegible] ellow powers upon the fair and equal ground of
law [illegible] defensive alliance with the Argives and appoint a
few [illegible] otentiary powers, instead of making the people
the [illegible], in order that, in the case of an applicant being
rej [illegible] rtures might not be made public. They said that
ma [illegible] m hatred of the Spartans. [3] After this explana-
tio [illegible] nthians returned home.

5.27 421 11th Year/Summer ARGOS Corinthian envoys visit Argos to express their fear that Sparta will use her alliance with Athens to dominate the Peloponnesus. They advise Argos to develop alliances to counter Sparta.

[illegible] n they had communicated reported the proposal
to [illegible] people, and the Argives passed the decree and
ch [illegible] iate an alliance for any Hellenic state that wished
it, [illegible] ta, neither of which should be able to join with-
ou [illegible] he Argive people. [2] Argos came in to the plan
all [illegible] e she saw that war with Sparta was inevitable, her
tre [illegible] on the point of expiring; and also because she
ho [illegible] acy of the Peloponnesus. For at this time Sparta
ha [illegible] ic estimation because of her disasters, while the
Ar [illegible] urishing condition, having taken no part in the
wa [illegible] having on the contrary profited largely by their
ne [illegible] accordingly prepared to receive into alliance any
of [illegible] d it.

5.28 421 11th Year/Summer ARGOS Argos follows the Corinthian envoys' advice, believing war with Sparta to be inevitable and hoping herself to gain Peloponnesian supremacy.

[illegible] their allies were the first to come over through
fea [illegible] ng taken advantage of the war against Athens to

5.29 421 11th Year/Summer PELOPONNESE Mantinea allies with Argos to protect her own recent conquests in Arcadia. Other Peloponnesian states, unhappy that Athens and Sparta can alter the treaty without the consent of Sparta's allies, begin to consider an Argive alliance.

5.2[illegible] [illegible] nfrequent [illegible] out himself. [illegible] I) for a dis- [illegible] out the life [illegible]

5.2[illegible] [illegible] "leadership" [illegible] "supremacy" [illegible] rd) came to [illegible] hen Sparta [illegible] battle of the [illegible] erodotus at i, [illegible] eek to revive [illegible] er threatened [illegible] 1.71.6ff.). [illegible] ll (5.28.2 and [illegible] e of Mantinea their army was urged to fight for their ancient "supremacy" (5.69.1). Some Argives even proposed that the dispute over the border territory of Cynuria (Map 5.29) should be settled by another battle of the Champions (see 5.41.2).

5.28.2a Perhaps Thucydides reflects a Peloponnesian point of view here when he calls the subject of his history the "war against Athens," as the Peloponnesians may well have done, instead of the "Peloponnesian War," as the Athenians called it, and as it has come down to us.

5.29.1a Mantinea: Map 5.29.

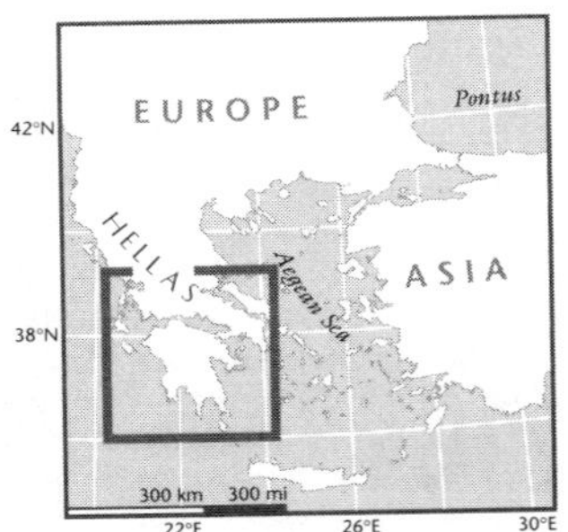

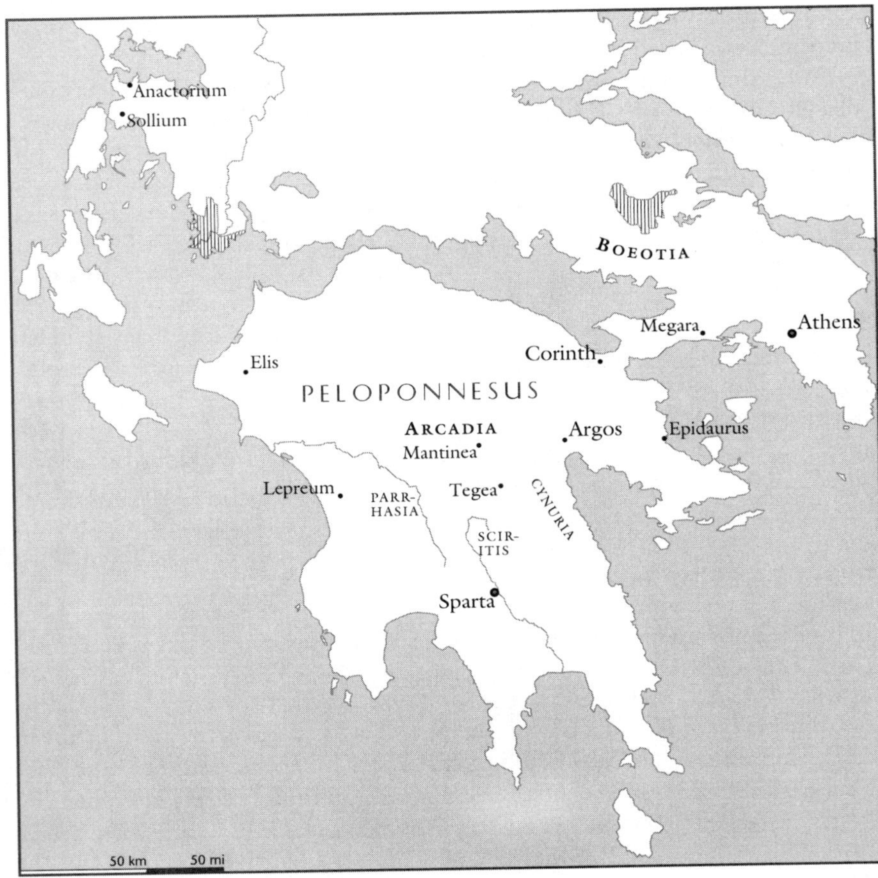

MAP 5.29 SUMMER OF 421, PELOPONNESUS

reduce a large part of Arcadia[1b] into subjection, they thought that Sparta would not leave them undisturbed in their conquests now that she had leisure to interfere,[1c] and consequently were glad to turn to a powerful city like Argos, the historical enemy of the Spartans, and a sister democracy. [2] Upon the defection of Mantinea the rest of the Peloponnesus at once began to consider following her example, thinking that the Mantineans would not have changed sides without good reason. Besides, they were angry with Sparta among other reasons for having inserted in the treaty with Athens that it should be consistent with their oaths for both parties, Spartans and Athenians, to add to or take away from it according to their discretion.[2a] [3]

5.29.1b Arcadia: Map 5.29.

5.29.1c These Mantinean fears were well founded; see 5.33.

5.29.2a The clause referred to was that of the peace treaty described in 5.18.11, not that of the Athens-Sparta alliance (5.23.6), which it seems to echo.

It [illegible]the real origin of the panic in the Peloponnesus,
by [illegible] Spartan and Athenian combination against their
libe[illegible]uld properly have been made conditional upon
the [illegible]ody of the allies. [4] Because of these apprehen-
sio[illegible]ral desire in each state to place itself in alliance
wit[illegible]

5.30
421
11th Year/Summer
CORINTH
Sparta tells Corinth to stay in the league and abide by the majority's decision to accept the treaty. The Corinthians respond that their oaths prevent acceptance of the treaty and that they would continue to discuss the Argive alliance with their friends.

[illegible]artans, perceiving the agitation going on in the
Pel[illegible]nth was the author of it and was herself about to
ent[illegible] Argives, sent ambassadors there in the hope of
pre[illegible]ontemplation. They accused Corinth of having
bro[illegible] told her that she could not desert Sparta and
bec[illegible]ithout adding violation of her oaths to the crime
whi[illegible]mitted in not accepting the treaty with Athens,
wh[illegible] agreed that the decision of the majority of the
allie[illegible]n all, unless the gods or heroes stood in the way.[1a]
[2] [illegible]which she delivered before those of her allies who
had [illegible]t the treaty, and whom she had previously invited
to [illegible]enly stating the injuries she complained of, such
as t[illegible] Sollium or Anactorium[2a] from the Athenians, or
any[illegible]he thought she had come off badly. Instead she
too[illegible]xt that she could not give up her Thracian[2c] allies,
to [illegible]vidual security had been given when they first
reb[illegible]s well as upon subsequent occasions. [3] She
den[illegible]committed any violation of her oaths to the allies
by [illegible]aty with Athens. Since she had sworn upon the
fait[illegible]racian friends, she could not honestly give them
up. [illegible]e treaty was, "unless the gods or heroes stand in
the [illegible] her in this case that the gods stood in the way.
[4] [illegible] on the subject of her former oaths. As to the
Arg[illegible]nfer with her friends, and do whatever was right.
[5] [illegible]rning home, some Argive ambassadors who happen[illegible]ed her to conclude the alliance without further
del[illegible]d at the next congress to be held at Corinth.

5.31
421
11th Year/Summer
PELOPONNESUS
Angered by Sparta's support of Lepreum, Elis allies with Corinth and Argos. Corinth and the Thracian Chalcidians also ally with Argos, but Boeotia and Megara remain quiet, finding Argos too democratic.

[illegible]an Elean[1a] embassy arrived, and first making an
allia[illegible] on from there to Argos, according to their
inst[illegible]ies of the Argives, their country being just then
at e[illegible]epreum.[1b] [2] Some time back there had been a
war[illegible]nd some of the Arcadians; and the Eleans being
call[illegible] the offer of half their lands, had put an end to
the [illegible]and in the hands of its Leprean occupiers had
imp[illegible]ute of a *talent*[2a] to the Olympian Zeus. [3] Till

5.30.[illegible]nesian [illegible]l heroes [illegible]eague.
5.30.[illegible]29.
5.30.[illegible]
5.30.[illegible]

5.31.1a Elis: Map 5.29.
5.31.1b Lepreum: Map 5.29.
5.31.2a A *talent* is a unit of weight and money. See Appendix J, Classical Greek Currency, § 5.

the war against Athens[3a] this tribute was paid by the Lepreans, who then took the war as an excuse for no longer doing so, and upon the Eleans using force appealed to Sparta. The case was thus submitted to her arbitration; but the Eleans, suspecting the fairness of the tribunal, abandoned the submission and laid waste the Leprean territory. [4] The Spartans nevertheless decided that the Lepreans were independent[4a] and the Eleans aggressors, and as the latter did not abide by the arbitration, sent a garrison of hoplites into Lepreum. [5] Upon this the Eleans, holding that Sparta had received one of their rebel subjects, put forward the agreement providing that each allied state should come out of the war against Athens in possession of what it had at the beginning, and considering that justice had not been done them, went over to the Argives and now made the alliance through their ambassadors, who had been instructed for that purpose. [6] Immediately after them the Corinthians and the Thracian Chalcidians[6a] became allies of Argos. Meanwhile the Boeotians and Megarians,[6b] who acted together, remained quiet, being left to do as they pleased by Sparta, and thinking that the Argive democracy would not agree so well with their aristocratic forms of government as the Spartan constitution.

5.32
421
11th Year/Summer
THRACE
The Athenians capture Scione.
DELOS
Athens permits the Delians to return to Delos.
TEGEA
Corinth and Argos fail to pry Tegea away from the Spartan alliance.
CORINTH
Corinth fails to persuade Boeotia to ally with Argos, and to secure for Corinth a ten-day truce with Athens.

About the same time in this summer Athens succeeded in reducing Scione,[1a] put the adult males to death and, making slaves of the women and children, gave the land to the Plataeans to live in. She also brought back the Delians to Delos,[1b] moved by her misfortunes in the field and by the commands of the god at Delphi.[1c] [2] Meanwhile the Phocians[2a] and Locrians[2b] commenced hostilities. [3] The Corinthians and Argives being now in alliance, went to Tegea[3a] to bring about its defection from Sparta, thinking that if so considerable a state could be persuaded to join, all the Peloponnesus would be on their side. [4] But when the Tegeans said that they would do nothing against Sparta, the hitherto zealous Corinthians relaxed their activity, and began to fear that none of the rest would now come over. [5] Still they went to the Boeotians and tried to persuade them to join the alliance and adopt common action generally with Argos and themselves, and also begged them to go with them to Athens and obtain for them[5c] a ten days' truce similar to that made between the Athenians and Boeotians not long after the fifty years' treaty, and in the event of the Athenians refusing, to renounce the armistice, and not make any truce in future without Corinth. These were the requests of the Corinthians. [6] The Boeotians refused them on the subject of the Argive alliance, but went with them to Athens where, however, they failed to obtain the ten days' truce; the Athenian answer being that the Corinthians had truce already, as allies of

5.31.3a For the "Attic war," see note 5.28.2a.
5.31.4a Being independent and paying tribute were not incompatible; see 5.18.5.
5.31.6a Chalcidice: Map 5.35, AY.
5.31.6b Megara: Map 5.29 and Map 5.35, BY.
5.32.1a This harsh punishment was carried out in accordance with the decree moved by Cleon in 4.122.6. Scione: Map 5.35, AY.
5.32.1b Delos: Map 5.35, BY. Some Delians must have remained in Atramyttium, however, where Thucydides describes them as residing in 8.108.4.
5.32.1c Delphi: Map 5.35, BX.
5.32.2a Phocis: Map 5.35, BY.
5.32.2b Locris (presumably Opuntian Locris): Map 5.35, BY.
5.32.3a Tegea: Map 5.29 and Map 5.35, BY.
5.32.5c I.e., for Corinth.

Sp… he Boeotians did not renounce their ten days' tru… ers and reproaches of the Corinthians for their bre… last had to content themselves with a de facto arr…

5.33 421 11th Year/Summer ARCADIA Sparta invades Parrhasia, a district subject to Mantinea, destroys the Mantinaean fort of Cypsela, and makes the Parrhasians independent.

… Spartans marched into Arcadia[1a] with their whole lev… n of Pausanias, king of Sparta, against the Parrha… ects of Mantinea, and a faction of whom had inv… so meant to demolish, if possible, the fort of Cy… eans had built and garrisoned in the Parrhasian ter… gainst the district of Sciritis[1c] in Laconia. [2] The Sp… aste the Parrhasian country, and the Mantineans, pla… ds of an Argive garrison, addressed themselves to the… deracy, but being unable to save Cypsela or the Pa… to Mantinea.[2a] [3] Meanwhile the Spartans made the… t, razed the fortress, and returned home.

5.34 421 11th Year/Summer SPARTA Helots among Spartan troops returning from Thrace are freed and allowed to live where they like. The disgraced Spartans captured at Sphacteria are at first restricted, but later restored to their full rights.

… soldiers from Thrace who had gone out with Br… g been brought from thence after the treaty by Cl… s decreed that the Helots who had fought with Br… d allowed to live where they liked, and not long aft… th the Neodamodeis[1a] at Lepreum,[1b] which is situa… nd Elean border; Sparta being at this time at en… e, however, of the Spartans who had been taken pri… and had surrendered their arms might, it was fea… vere to be subjected to some degradation in conse… ne, and so make some attempt at revolution, if lef… ull rights. These were therefore at once deprived of… hough some of them were in office at the time, an… l from taking office, or buying and selling anythi… wever, their rights were restored to them.[2b]

5.3…
5.3…
5.3…
5.3…
5.3… …n hundred …80) he inau- …ange at …ilitary pur- …em all in bit- …ots were not …as this chapter … Sparta had …y by creating …*is* whose num- …y in the suc- …19.3). Their …own, and …hat they were …dy, most …ee Appendix

5.3… …he settlement …*neodamodies* in Lepreum was undoubtedly connected with Sparta's contemporary difficulties with Elis (see 5.31.2ff.).

5.34.2a Thucydides refers to the men captured on the island of Sphacteria in the final action at Pylos; see 4.31–38.

5.34.2b Spartan concern to recover the 120 Spartiates taken prisoner on Sphacteria is evident (4.41.3, 4.108.7, 4.117.1, and 5.15.1). The reason may lie in the serious decline in the number of Spartiates—from eight thousand in 480 (Herodotus, 7.234.2) to about two thousand five hundred in 418, judging from Thucydides' comments in 5.68.3 (see note there), and to less than one thousand by 371 (according to Aristotle's *Politics,* 1270[a] 30ff.). To be taken prisoner of war was a dreadful disgrace at Sparta, and the lenient treatment of the survivors of Sphacteria shows that they were badly needed at home.

5.35
421
11th Year/Summer
THRACE
The Dians take Thyssus.
ATHENS-SPARTA
Athens and Sparta are still at peace, but Sparta's failure to fulfill her treaty obligations arouses Athenian suspicions. Athens holds onto Pylos and the other places she had agreed to give up, but does withdraw the Messenians and the Laconian deserters from Pylos.

The same summer the Dians[2c] took Thyssus,[2d] a city on Acte[2e] near Athos[1d] and in alliance with Athens. [2] During the whole of this summer, intercourse between the Athenians and Peloponnesians continued, although each party began to suspect the other immediately after the treaty, because of the places specified in it not being restored. [3] Sparta, to whose lot it had fallen to begin by restoring Amphipolis[3a] and the other cities, had not done so. She had equally failed to get the treaty accepted by her Thracian allies, or by the Boeotians or the Corinthians; although she was continually promising to unite with Athens in compelling their compliance, if it were longer refused. She also kept fixing a time at which those who still refused to come in were to be declared enemies to both parties, but took care not to bind herself by any written agreement. [4] Meanwhile the Athenians, seeing none of these promises actually fulfilled, began to suspect the honesty of her intentions, and consequently not only refused to comply with her demands for Pylos,[4a] but also repented having given up the prisoners from the island, and kept tight hold of the other places, until Sparta's part of the treaty should be fulfilled. [5] Sparta, on the other hand, said she had done what she could, having given up the Athenian prisoners of war in her possession, evacuated Thrace, and performed everything else in her power. Amphipolis, she said, it was out of her ability to restore; but she would endeavor to bring the Boeotians and Corinthians in to the treaty, to recover Panactum,[5a] and send home all the Athenian prisoners of war in Boeotia. [6] Meanwhile she insisted that Pylos should be restored, or at least that the Messenians and Helots should be withdrawn (as her troops had been from Thrace), and the place garrisoned, if necessary, by the Athenians themselves. [7] After a number of different conferences held during the summer she succeeded in persuading Athens to withdraw the Messenians from Pylos and the rest of the Helots and deserters from Laconia, who were accordingly settled by her at Cranae in Cephallenia.[7a] [8] Thus during this summer there was peace and intercourse between the two peoples.

5.36
421/0
11th Year/Winter
SPARTA
Two of the new Spartan ephors oppose the treaty with Athens and plot with Corinth and Boeotia to bring Argos into alliance with Sparta—even if that should cause a break with Athens. Sparta asks Boeotia for Panactum in order to exchange it for Pylos.

Next winter, however, the ephors under whom the treaty had been made were no longer in office, and some of their successors were directly opposed to it. Embassies now arrived from the Spartan confederacy, and the Athenians, Boeotians, and Corinthians also presented themselves at Sparta, and after much discussion and no agreement between them, were returning to their homes; when Cleobulus and Xenares, the two ephors who were the most anxious to terminate the treaty, took advantage of this

5.34.2c The Dians lived at Dium on the Acte Peninsula of Chalcidice (Map 5.35, AY).
5.34.2d Thyssus: Map 5.35, AY.
5.34.2e Acte Peninsula: Map 5.35, AY.
5.35.1d Mount Athos, on the Acte Peninsula: Map 5.35, AY.
5.35.3a Amphipolis: Map 5.35, AY.
5.35.4a Pylos: Map 5.35, BX.
5.35.5a Panactum (Map 5.35, BY) was the Athenian border fort captured by the Boeotians in 422; see 5.3.5.
5.35.7a Cranae, on the island of Cephallenia: Map 5.35, BX.

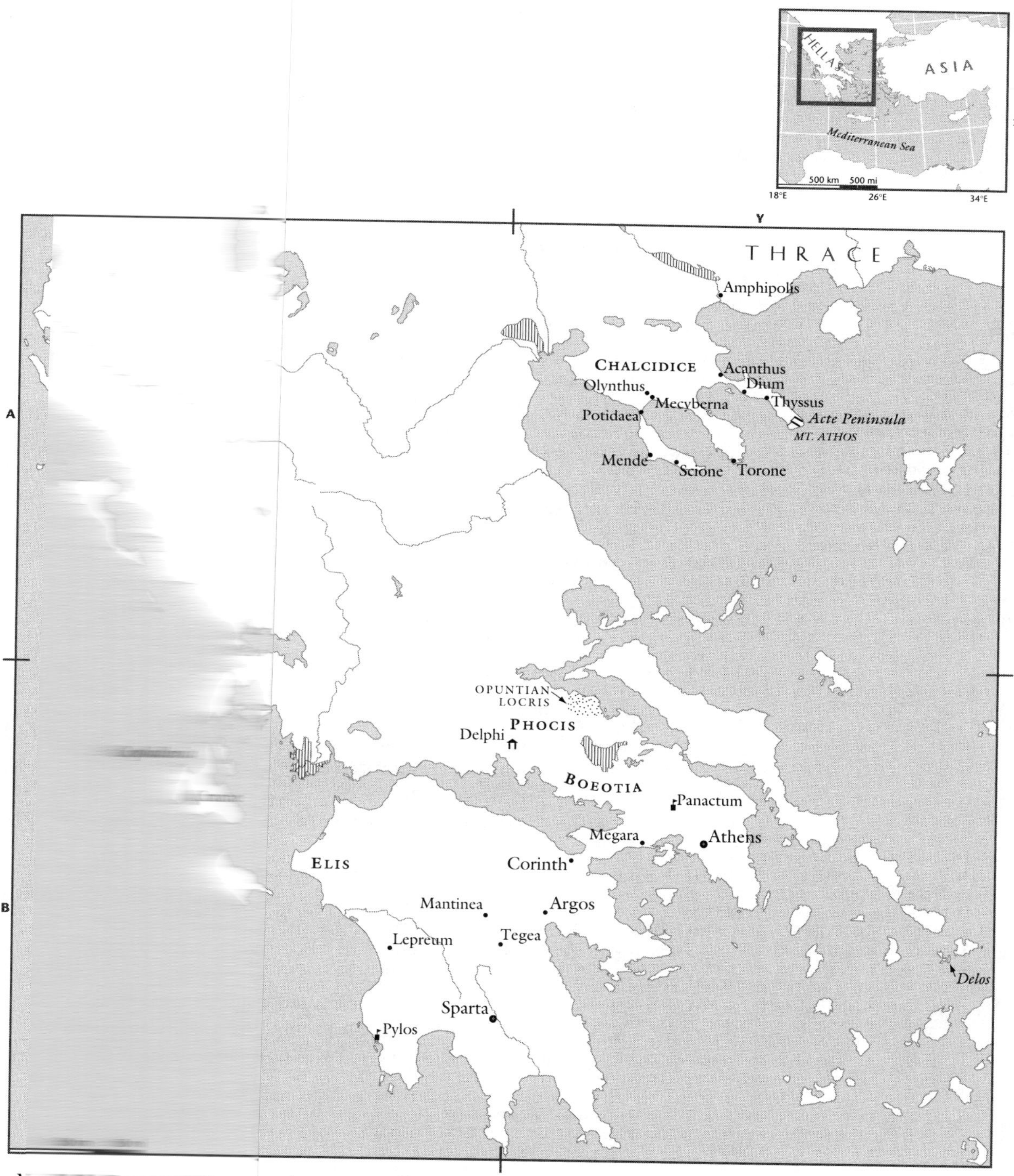

M[illegible]CE, ATTICA, AND PHOCIS, SUMMER 421

opportunity to communicate privately with the Boeotians and Corinthians, and advising them to act as much as possible together, instructed the former first to enter into alliance with Argos, and then to try and bring themselves and the Argives into alliance with Sparta. The Boeotians would thereby feel least compulsion to join the Attic treaty; and the Spartans would prefer to gain the friendship and alliance of Argos even at the price of the hostility of Athens and the rupture of the treaty. The Boeotians knew that an honorable friendship with Argos had long been the desire of Sparta; for the Spartans believed that this would considerably facilitate the conduct of the war outside the Peloponnesus. [2] Meanwhile they begged the Boeotians to place Panactum[2a] in Sparta's hands in order that she might, if possible, obtain Pylos[2b] in exchange for it, and so be in a better position to resume hostilities with Athens.

5.37
421/0
11th Year/Winter
BOEOTIA
Boeotia happily accepts Argos' invitation to join her alliance, as this is exactly what the Spartan ephors had advised Boeotia to do. Boeotia promises to send delegates to Argos to negotiate alliance terms.

After receiving these instructions for their governments from Xenares and Cleobulus and their other friends at Sparta, the Boeotians and Corinthians departed. [2] On their way home they were joined by two persons in high office at Argos who had waited for them on the road, and who now explored with them the possibility of the Boeotians joining the Corinthians, Eleans, and Mantineans in becoming the allies of Argos, thinking that if this could be effected they would be able, thus united, to make peace or war as they pleased either against Sparta or any other power. [3] The Boeotian envoys were pleased at thus hearing themselves accidentally asked to do what their friends at Sparta had told them; and the two Argives perceiving that their proposal was agreeable, departed with a promise to send ambassadors to the Boeotians. [4] On their arrival the Boeotians reported to the *boeotarchs*[4a] what had been said to them at Sparta and also by the Argives who had met them, and the boeotarchs, pleased with the idea, embraced it with all the more eagerness from the lucky coincidence of Argos soliciting the very thing wanted by their friends at Sparta. [5] Shortly afterwards ambassadors appeared from Argos with the proposals indicated; and the boeotarchs approved of the terms and dismissed the ambassadors with a promise to send envoys to Argos to negotiate the alliance.

5.38
421/0
11th Year/Winter
BOEOTIA
Boeotia, Corinth, Megara, and Thrace form a pact, and agree to ally with Argos. However, the Boeotian councils, unwilling to offend Sparta and ignorant of the Spartan ephors' wishes, refuse to ally with Argos.

In the meantime it was decided by the boeotarchs, the Corinthians, the Megarians, and the envoys from Thrace[1a] first to exchange oaths together to give help to each other whenever it was required and not to make war or peace except in common; after which the Boeotians and Megarians, who acted together, should make the alliance with Argos. [2] But before the oaths were taken the boeotarchs communicated these proposals to the four councils of the Boeotians, in whom the supreme power resides, and advised them to exchange oaths with all such cities as should be willing to enter into a

5.36.2a Panactum: Map 5.35, BY.
5.36.2b Pylos: Map 5.35, BX.
5.37.4a *Boeotarchs* were the chief magistrates of the Boeotian Federal government. See note 5.38.2a.
5.38.1a Thrace: Map 5.35, AY.

de Boeotians.[2a] [3] But the members of the Boeotian
co to the proposal, being afraid of offending Sparta
by ith the deserter Corinth; the boeotarchs not having hat had passed at Sparta and with the advice given
by nd the Boeotian partisans there, namely, that they
sh inth and Argos as a preliminary to joining up with
Sp ed that even if they should say nothing about all
thi t vote against what had been decided and recom-
me . [4] When this difficulty arose, the Corinthians
an ce departed without anything having been con-
clu , who had previously intended (after carrying this
po e alliance with Argos, now gave up bringing the
Ar councils, or sending to Argos the envoys whom
th neral coldness and delay ensued in the matter.

cyberna,[1a] which had an Athenian garrison inside 5.39 421/0 11th Year/Winter THRACE The Olynthians take Mecyberna from the Athenians.
it, by the Olynthians.[1b]

ations had been going on between the Athenians ATTICA Sparta allies with Boeotia to gain Panactum (to exchange for Pylos), but the Boeotians raze the fort before delivering it to them.
an nquests still retained by each, and Sparta hoping
th back Panactum[2a] from the Boeotians, she might
he w sent an embassy to the Boeotians and begged
th d their Athenian prisoners in her hands, in order
th hem for Pylos. [3] This the Boeotians refused to
do eparate alliance with them as she had done with
At this would be a breach of faith with Athens, as it
ha her of them should make peace or war without
th obtain Panactum which she hoped to exchange
fo who pressed for the dissolution of the treaty
str Boeotian alliance, she at length concluded the
all ve way to spring; and Panactum was instantly
ra year of the war ended.

following summer, the Argives, seeing that the 5.40 420 12th Year/Summer ARGOS The Argives misinterpret recent events and, fearful of being left isolated, send envoys to Sparta to negotiate as favorable a treaty as possible with her.
pr n Boeotia did not arrive, and that Panactum was
be t a separate alliance had been concluded between
th s, began to be afraid that Argos might be left iso-

5.3 Boeotia of Oxyrhynchus hor of a ten by a hucydides, of vere discov- nchus, here were eotarch for real power, ll divisions alry to the was divided hich in turn g business for the whole division; and each division sent sixty representatives to a central Boeotian council. The Oxyrhynchus History does not say that this central council was divided into four, and many scholars incline to the view that Thucydides has here erred.

5.39.1a Mecyberna, in Chalcidice: Map 5.35, AY.

5.39.1b Olynthus: Map 5.35, AY. Mecyberna was the port city for Olynthus. The Olynthians, by expelling the Athenian garrison from it, signified their rejection of the peace treaty described in 5.18.5.

5.39.2a Panactum: Map 5.35, BY.

5.39.2b Pylos: Map 5.35, BX.

lated, and all her allies would go over to Sparta. [2] They supposed that the Boeotians had been persuaded by the Spartans to raze Panactum and to enter into the treaty with the Athenians, and that Athens was privy to this arrangement, so that an alliance with Athens would no longer be open to her. This was a resource which she had always counted upon, by reason of the existing tensions, if her treaty with Sparta were not maintained. [3] In this crisis the Argives, afraid that, as the result of refusing to renew the treaty with Sparta and aspiring to the supremacy of the Peloponnesus,[3a] they would at the same time be at war with the Spartans, Tegeans, Boeotians, and Athenians, now hastily sent off Eustrophus and Aeson, who seemed the persons most likely to be acceptable as envoys to Sparta, with the goal of making as good a treaty as they could with the Spartans, upon such terms as could be obtained, and of being left in peace.

5.41
420
12th Year/Summer
SPARTA
Argos and Sparta agree on the terms for a treaty, including a prospective trial by battle to determine the ownership of Cynuria. The Argive delegates return home to secure the approval of the Argive people.

Having reached Sparta, their ambassadors proceeded to negotiate the terms of the proposed treaty. [2] What the Argives first demanded was that they might be allowed to refer to the arbitration of some state or private person the question of the Cynurian land,[2a] a piece of frontier territory about which they have always been disputing, which contains the cities of Thyrea and Anthene,[2b] and which is occupied by the Spartans. The Spartans at first said that they could not allow this point to be discussed, but were ready to conclude upon the old terms. Eventually, however, the Argive ambassadors succeeded in obtaining from them this concession:—For the present there was to be a truce for fifty years, but it should be competent for either party, there being neither plague nor war in Sparta or Argos, to give a formal challenge and decide the question of this territory by battle, as on a former occasion,[2c] when both sides claimed the victory; pursuit not being allowed beyond the frontier of Argos or Sparta. [3] The Spartans at first thought this mere folly; but at last, anxious at any cost to have the friendship of Argos, they agreed to the terms demanded, and committed them to writing. However, before any of this should become binding, the ambassadors were to return to Argos and communicate with their people, and in the event of their approval, to come at the feast of the Hyacinthia and take the oaths. The envoys returned accordingly.

5.42
420
12th Year/Summer
ATHENS
Sparta returns Athenian prisoners held by Boeotia and the razed fort of Panactum, but Athens responds indignantly to the razing of the fort, to the clauses of the treaty which the Spartans had not fulfilled, and to the alliance that Sparta had made with Boeotia.

In the meantime, while the Argives were engaged in these negotiations, the Spartan ambassadors, Andromedes, Phaedimus, and Antimenidas, who were to receive the prisoners from the Boeotians and restore them and Panactum[1a] to the Athenians, found that the Boeotians had themselves razed Panactum, upon the plea that oaths had been anciently exchanged between their people and the Athenians, after a dispute on the subject, to the effect

5.40.3a For details about Argive aspirations to the supremacy of the Peloponnesus, see note at 5.27.2e.
5.41.2a Cynuria: Map 5.45.
5.41.2b Thyrea and the possible location of Anthene: Map 5.45.
5.41.2c For the battle of the Champions in 546 B.C., see note at 5.27.2a.
5.42.1a Panactum, Boeotia: Map 5.45.

tha [illegible] the place, but that they should graze it in com-
mo [illegible] prisoners of war in the hands of the Boeotians,
the [illegible] to Andromedes and his colleagues, and by them
co [illegible] given back. The envoys at the same time
an [illegible] Panactum, which to them seemed as good as its
res [illegible] no longer lodge an enemy of Athens. [2] This
an [illegible] ed with great indignation by the Athenians, who
tho [illegible] had played them false, both in the matter of the
de [illegible] which ought to have been restored to them
sta [illegible] s they now heard, made a separate alliance with
the [illegible] their previous promise to join Athens in compel [illegible] those who refused to accede to the treaty. The
At [illegible] the other points in which Sparta had failed in her
co [illegible] t they had been deceived, gave an angry answer
to [illegible] nt them away.

[illegible] e Spartans and Athenians having gone thus far, the [illegible] ished to cancel the treaty immediately put them-
sel [illegible] nost amongst these was Alcibiades son of Clinias,
a [illegible] for any other Hellenic city, but distinguished by
the [illegible] ry. Alcibiades thought the Argive alliance really
pre [illegible] al pique had not also a great deal to do with his
op [illegible] ded with the Spartans for having negotiated the
tre [illegible] Laches, and having overlooked him on account
of [illegible] not having shown him the respect due to the
an [illegible] s family with them as their *proxenii*[2a] which,
re [illegible] her, he had himself recently attempted to renew
by [illegible] prisoners taken in the island.[2b] [3] Being thus, as
he [illegible] l, he had in the first instance spoken against the
tre [illegible] rtans were not to be trusted, but that they only
ne [illegible] enabled by this means to crush Argos, and after-
wa [illegible] ne; and now immediately upon the occurrence of
th [illegible] ly to the Argives, telling them to come as quickly
as [illegible] ompanied by the Mantineans and Eleans, with
pr [illegible] e moment was propitious and he himself would
do [illegible] m.

5.43
420
12th Year/Summer
ATHENS
Alcibiades, who feels personally slighted by the Spartans, leads the faction opposed to the treaty with Sparta. He sends hastily to Argos advising them to send envoys to Athens, for now conditions are favorable for an anti-Sparta alliance.

[illegible] nessage and discovering that the Athenians, far
fro [illegible] eotian alliance, were involved in a serious quarrel
wi [illegible] gives paid no further attention to the embassy
wh [illegible] to Sparta on the subject of the treaty, and began
to [illegible] ne Athenians, reflecting that, in the event of war,

5.44
420
12th Year/Summer
ATHENS
Argos drops negotiations with Sparta and moves to conclude an alliance with Athens. Spartan envoys come to Athens to explain their alliance with Boeotia and ask for the return of Pylos.

5.4 [illegible] en and resi- [illegible] d as a "friend [illegible] e a modern [illegible] n state.

5.4 [illegible] n captured on the island of Sphacteria in the final action at Pylos; see 4.31–38.

they would thus have on their side a city that was not only an ancient ally of Argos, but a sister democracy and very powerful at sea. [2] They accordingly at once sent ambassadors to Athens to negotiate for an alliance, accompanied by others from Elis and Mantinea.

[3] At the same time an embassy consisting of persons reputed to be well disposed toward the Athenians—Philocharidas, Leon, and Endius[3a]—arrived in haste from Sparta, out of fear that the Athenians in their irritation might conclude an alliance with the Argives. They also intended to ask for the return of Pylos in exchange for Panactum, and to defend their alliance with the Boeotians by pleading that it had not been made to hurt the Athenians.

5.45
420
12th Year/Summer
ATHENS
After Alcibiades persuades the Spartan envoys to deny before the Athenian assembly that they were fully empowered to negotiate, he attacks them and urges the assembly to choose alliance with Argos, Mantinea, and Elias.

When the envoys spoke in the council upon these points, stating that they had come with full powers to settle all others at issue between them, Alcibiades became afraid that if they were to repeat these statements to the popular assembly,[1a] they might gain the support of the multitude and cause the Argive alliance to be rejected, [2] so he resorted to the following stratagem. He persuaded the Spartans by a solemn assurance that if they would say nothing of their full powers in the assembly, he would give back Pylos[2a] to them (himself, the present opponent of its restitution, engaging to obtain this from the Athenians), and would settle the other points at issue. [3] His plan was to detach them from Nicias and to disgrace them before the people, as being without sincerity in their intentions, or even common consistency in their language, and so to get the Argives, Eleans, and Mantineans taken into alliance. [4] This plan proved successful. When the envoys appeared before the people, and upon the question being put to them, did not say as they had said in the council, that they had come with full powers, the Athenians lost all patience, and carried away by Alcibiades, who thundered more loudly than ever against the Spartans, were ready instantly to introduce the Argives and their companions and to take them into alliance. An earthquake, however, occurring before anything definite had been done, this assembly was adjourned.

5.46
420
12th Year/Summer
ATHENS-SPARTA
Nicias persuades the Athenians to delay the Argive alliance while he attempts to obtain Spartan fulfillment of the treaty. When he fails, however, Athens enters into alliances with Argos, Mantinea, and Elis.

In the assembly held the next day, Nicias, in spite of the Spartans having been deceived themselves, and having also allowed him to be deceived in not admitting that they had come with full powers, still maintained that it was best to be friends with the Spartans. He argued that they should postpone action on the Argive proposals and send once more to Sparta and learn her intentions. The postponement of the war could only increase their own prestige and injure that of their rivals; the excellent state of their affairs making it in their interest to preserve this prosperity as long as possible, while the affairs of Sparta were so desperate that the sooner she could try her fortune again the better. [2] He succeeded accordingly in persuading them to send ambassadors, himself being among them, to invite the Spar-

5.44.3a For the relationship between Endius and Alcibiades, see 8.6.3.

5.45.1a For the council and the assembly, see Appendix A, The Athenian Government.

5.45.2a Pylos: Map 5.45.

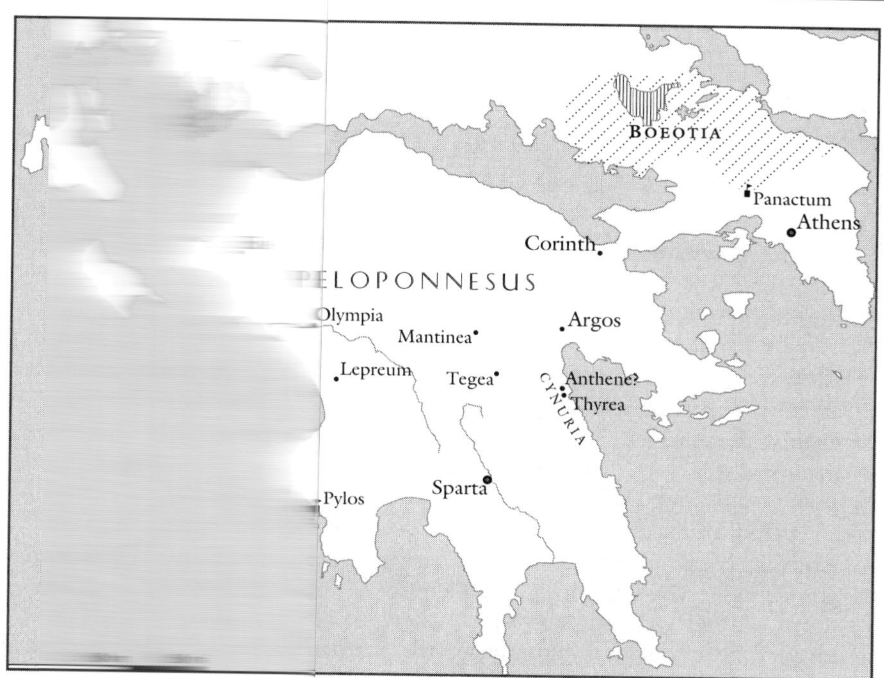

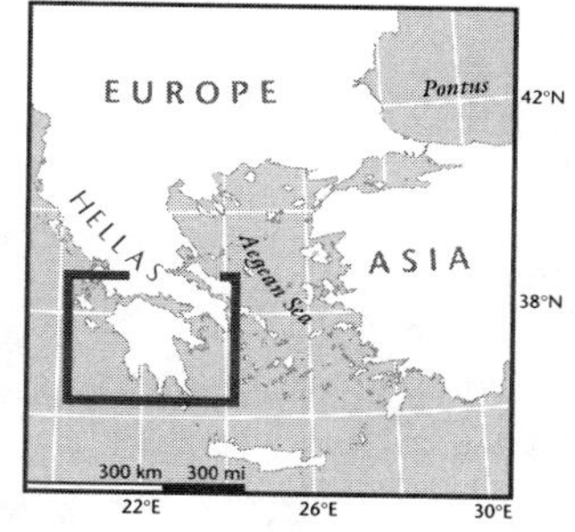

M[illegible]UMMER 420

ta[illegible]cere, to restore Panactum[2a] intact with Amphipolis[illegible]ir alliance with the Boeotians (unless they conse[illegible]treaty), in agreement with the stipulation which fo[illegible]egotiate without the other. [3] The ambassadors w[illegible]that the Athenians, had they wished to play false, m[illegible] alliance with the Argives, who had indeed come to[illegible]urpose, and they went off furnished with instructi[illegible]plaints that the Athenians had to make. [4] Havin[illegible]ommunicated their instructions, and concluded by te[illegible]unless they gave up their alliance with the Boeoti[illegible]fuse to accept their treaty, the Athenians for their p[illegible]s with the Argives and their friends. The Spartans, h[illegible]up the Boeotian alliance—the party of Xenares the e[illegible] shared their view, carrying the day upon this p[illegible] oaths at the request of Nicias, who feared to re[illegible]complished anything and to be disgraced; as was

5.[illegible]
5.[illegible]

indeed his fate, he being held the author of the treaty with Sparta. [5] When he returned, and the Athenians heard that nothing had been done at Sparta, they flew into a rage, and deciding that faith had not been kept with them, took advantage of the presence of the Argives and their allies, who had been introduced by Alcibiades, and made a treaty and alliance with them upon the terms following:

5.47
420
12th Year/Summer
ATHENS
Thucydides offers the text of the hundred-year treaty between Athens, Argos, Mantinea, and Elis.

The Athenians, Argives, Mantineans, and Eleans, acting for themselves and the allies in their respective empires, made a treaty for a hundred years, to be without fraud or injury by land and by sea.[1a]

• [2] It shall not be lawful to carry on war, either for the Argives, Eleans, Mantineans, and their allies, against the Athenians, or the allies in the Athenian empire; or for the Athenians and their allies against the Argives, Eleans, Mantineans, or their allies, in any way or means whatsoever. The Athenians, Argives, Eleans, and Mantineans shall be allies for a hundred years upon the terms following:—

• [3] If an enemy invade the country of the Athenians, the Argives, Eleans, and Mantineans shall go to the relief of Athens, according as the Athenians may require by message, in such way as they most effectively can, to the best of their power. But if the invader be gone after plundering the territory, the offending state shall be the enemy of the Argives, Mantineans, Eleans, and Athenians, and war shall be made against it by all these cities; and no one of the cities shall be able to make peace with that state, except all the above cities agree to do so.

• [4] Likewise the Athenians shall go to the relief of Argos, Mantinea, and Elis, if an enemy invade the country of Elis, Mantinea, or Argos, according as the above cities may require by message, in such way as they most effectively can, to the best of their power. But if the invader be gone after plundering the territory, the state offending shall be the enemy of the Athenians, Argives, Mantineans, and Eleans, and war shall be made against it by all these cities, and peace may not be made with that state except all the above cities agree to it.

• [5] No armed force shall be allowed to pass for hostile purposes through the country of the powers contracting, or of the allies in their respective empires, or to go by sea, except all the cities—that is to say, Athens, Argos, Mantinea, and Elis—vote for such passage.

• [6] The relieving troops shall be maintained by the city sending them for thirty days from their arrival in the city that has required them, and upon their return in the same way; if their services be desired for a longer period the city that sent for them shall maintain them, at the rate of three Aeginetan *obols* per day for a heavy-armed soldier, archer, or light soldier, and an Aeginetan *drachma*[6a] for a cavalryman.

5.47.1a The members of this alliance, Elis, Mantinea, Argos, and Athens, are shown on Map 5.45.

5.47.6a For the Aeginetan *obol* and the *drachma*, see Appendix J, Classical Greek Currency, §3.

IL
IN
PA
TR
EI
M

ding for the troops shall have the command own country; but in case of the cities resolving n the command shall be equally divided among

hall be sworn to by the Athenians for them- by the Argives, Mantineans, Eleans, and their ividually. Each shall swear the oath most bind- full-grown victims; the oath being as follows:

"I will stand by the alliance and its articles, justly, innocently, and sincerely, and I will not transgress the same in any way or means whatsoever."

• [9] The oath shall be taken at Athens by the council and the magistrates, the *prytaneis* administering it; at Argos by the council, the Eighty, and the artynae, the Eighty administering it; at Mantinea by the demiurgi,[9a] the council, and the other magistrates, the theori and polemarchs administering it; at Elis by the demiurgi, the magistrates, and the Six Hundred, the demiurgi and the thesmophylakes administering it. [10] The oaths shall be renewed by the Athenians going to Elis, Mantinea, and Argos thirty days before the Olympic games; by the Argives, Mantineans, and Eleans going to Athens ten days before the feast of the Great Panathenaea.[10a] [11] The articles of the treaty, the oaths, and the alliance shall be inscribed on a stone pillar by the Athenians in the Acropolis,[11a] by the Argives in the *agora,*[11b] in the temple of Apollo; by the Mantineans in the temple of Zeus, in the agora and a bronze pillar shall be erected jointly by them at the Olympic games now at hand. [12] Should the above cities see fit to make any addition to these articles, whatever all the above cities shall agree upon, after consulting together, shall be binding.

5.48
420
12th Year/Summer
CORINTH
Neither Athens nor Sparta renounce their treaty. Although allied with Argos, Corinth refuses to join the new alliance.

Although the treaty and alliances were thus concluded, still the treaty between the Spartans and Athenians was not renounced by either party. [2] Meanwhile Corinth, although the ally of the Argives, did not accede to the new treaty, any more than she had done to the defensive and offensive alliance formed before this between the Eleans, Argives, and Mantineans, when she declared herself content with the first alliance, which was defensive only, and which bound them to help each other, but not to join in attacking any. [3] The Corinthians thus stood aloof from their allies, and again turned their thoughts toward Sparta.

5.49
420
12th Year/Summer
OLYMPIA
Elis excludes Sparta from the Olympic festival, alleging that Sparta violated the Olympic truce when she invaded Lepreum. Elis offers relief if Sparta restores Lepreum. Sparta protests but to no avail.

At the Olympic games[1a] which were held this summer, and in which the Arcadian Androsthenes was victor the first time in the wrestling and boxing, the Spartans were excluded from the temple by the Eleans, and thus prevented from sacrificing or contending, for having refused to pay the fine specified in the Olympic law imposed upon them by the Eleans, who alleged that they had attacked Fort Phyrcus,[1b] and sent some of their hoplites into Lepreum[1c] during the Olympic truce. The amount of the fine

5.47.9a Demiurgi: the title of high officers in a number of states, most of them Dorian.

5.47.10a The Olympic games and the great feast of the Panathenaea were quadrennial religious festivals; see Appendix I, Classical Greek Religious Festivals, §5, 8.

5.47.11a A fragment of the Athenian copy of this treaty was found on the south slope of the Acropolis (IG i². 86 (GHI 72, not in ML)). There are only minor variations from the text given by Thucydides. See Illustration 5.47.

5.47.11b The *agora* was a city's main square for commercial, social, and political activity.

5.49.1a Olympia: Map 5.45. See Appendix I, Classical Greek Religious Festivals, §5.

5.49.1b Fort Phyrcus: site unknown.

5.49.1c Lepreum: Map 5.45.

wa two for each hoplite, as the law prescribes. [2]
Th and pleaded that the penalty was unjust; saying
th t been proclaimed at Sparta when the hoplites
we e Eleans affirmed that the armistice with them
ha roclaim it first among themselves), and that the
ag had taken them by surprise while they were liv-
in eace, and not expecting anything. [4] The Sparta Eleans really believed that Sparta had committed
an not have subsequently proclaimed the truce at
Sp aimed it notwithstanding (as if they had believed
no fter the proclamation, the Spartans had made no
att . [5] Nevertheless the Eleans adhered to what
th g would persuade them that an aggression had
no owever, the Spartans would restore Lepreum to
th their own share of the money and pay that of the
go

5.50
420
12th Year/Summer
OLYMPIA
The festival and games are conducted in the presence of Elean and allied armed forces to prevent a Spartan intrusion, which does not take place.
ARGOS
Argos invites Corinth to ally with her, but achieves nothing.

t accepted, the Eleans tried a second. Instead of
res was objected to, the Spartans should ascend the
alt s, as they were so anxious to have access to the
te e Hellenes that they would surely pay the fine at
a l ing refused, the Spartans were excluded from the
te the games, and sacrificed at home; the Lepreans
be nes who did not attend. [3] Still the Eleans were
af sacrifice by force, and kept guard with a heavy-
ar young men; being also joined by a thousand
Ar of Mantineans, and by some Athenian cavalry who
sta the feast. [4] Great fears were felt in the assembly
of arms, especially after Lichas son of Arcesilaus, a
Sp l on the course by the umpires because, upon his
ho nd the Boeotian people being proclaimed the vic-
to ing no right to enter, he came forward on the
co arioteer in order to show that the chariot was his.
Af e more afraid than ever, and expected a distur-
ba er, kept quiet and let the feast pass by, as we have
se ic games, the Argives and the allies repaired to
C me over to them. There they found some Spartan
en ssion ensued, which after all ended in nothing
be rred and they all dispersed to their homes.

5.4 this sum
-three tal-
al Greek

5.4 s that were
rtain great
dix I, Classi-
, §7.

5.5

5.51
420/9
12th Year/Winter
HERACLEA
The Heracleots are defeated by their neighbors; their Spartan general is killed.

Summer was now over. During the following winter a battle took place between the Heracleots in Trachinia and the Aenianians, Dolopians, Malians, and certain of the Thessalians,[1a] [2] all tribes bordering on and hostile to the city, which directly menaced their country. Accordingly, after having opposed and harassed it from its very foundation by every means in their power, they now in this battle defeated the Heracleots, Xenares son of Cnidis, their Spartan commander, being among the slain. Thus the winter ended and the twelfth year of this war ended also.

5.52
419
13th Year/Summer
HERACLEA
The Boeotians occupy Heraclea and offend Sparta.
PELOPONNESUS
Alcibiades leads a small Athenian force through the territories of the Peloponnesian allies.

After the battle Heraclea was so terribly reduced that in the first days of the following summer the Boeotians occupied the place and sent away the Spartan Agesippidas for misgovernment, fearing that the city might be taken by the Athenians while the Spartans were distracted with the affairs of the Peloponnesus. The Spartans, nevertheless, were offended with them for what they had done. [2] The same summer Alcibiades son of Clinias, now one of the generals at Athens, in concert with the Argives and the allies, went into the Peloponnesus with a few Athenian hoplites and archers, and some of the allies in those parts whom he gathered up as he passed, and with this army marched here and there through the Peloponnesus, and settled various matters connected with the alliance, and among other things induced the Patrians[2a] to carry their walls down to the sea, intending himself also to build a fort near the Achaean Rhium,[2b] but the Corinthians and Sicyonians,[2c] and all others who would have suffered by its being built, came up and hindered him.

5.53
419
13th Year/Summer
EPIDAURUS
Argos attacks Epidaurus to neutralize Corinth and shorten her communication route with Athens.

The same summer war broke out between the Epidaurians[1a] and Argives. The pretext was that the Epidaurians did not send an offering for their pasture land to Apollo Pythaeus, as they were bound to do, the Argives having the chief management of the temple; but, apart from this pretext, Alcibiades and the Argives were determined, if possible, to gain possession of Epidaurus, and thus to insure the neutrality of Corinth and give the Athenians a shorter passage for their reinforcement from Aegina[1b] than if they had to sail round Scyllaeum.[1c] The Argives accordingly prepared to invade Epidaurus by themselves, to exact the offering.

5.54
419
13th Year/Summer
SPARTA
The Spartans under Agis march out on a secret mission but turn back after unfavorable sacrifices.
EPIDAURUS
Argos invades Epidaurus during Carneia.

About the same time the Spartans marched out with all their people to Leuctra[1a] upon their frontier, opposite to Mount Lycaeum,[1b] under the command of Agis son of Archidamus, without anyone knowing their destination, not even the cities that sent the contingents.[1c] [2] The sacrifices,

5.51.1a Heraclea in Trachis was last mentioned in 5.12. For its location, and that of Aenis of the Aenianians, Malis, and Thessaly: Map 5.54, AY. Dolopia (possible location): Map 5.54, AX,

5.52.2a Patrae: Map 5.54, AX.

5.52.2b Achaean Rhium: Map 5.54, AX.

5.52.2c Sicyon: Map 5.54, AY.

5.53.1a Epidaurus: Map 5.54, BY.

5.53.1b Aegina: Map 5.54, BY.

5.53.1c Point Scyllaeum: Map 5.54, BY; the strategic position of Epidaurus across Athenian lines of communication with Argos and its other allies can also be seen on Map 5.58.

5.54.1a Leuctra: the site of this Leuctra in the Peloponnesus is unknown. There is another Leuctra in Boeotia which is the site of a famous defeat inflicted upon the Spartans by the Boeotians in 371.

5.54.1b Mount Lycaeum: Map 5.54, BX.

5.54.1c The cities that sent contingents were probably those of the *perioikoi,* not those of the Peloponnesian League; see Appendix C, Spartan Institutions, §9.

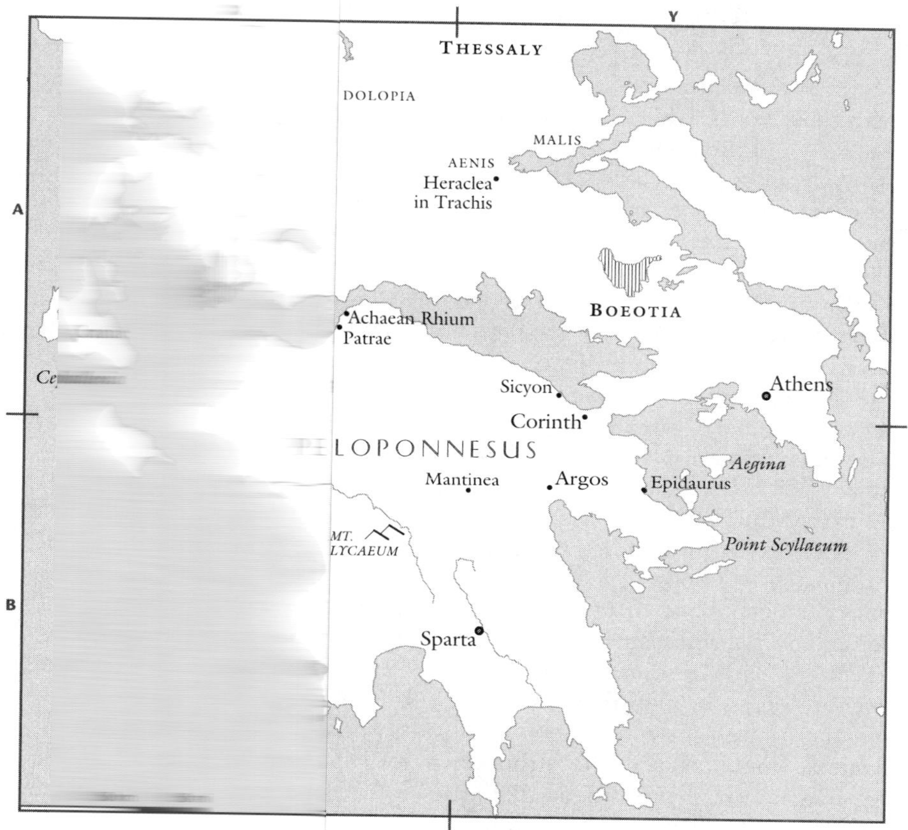

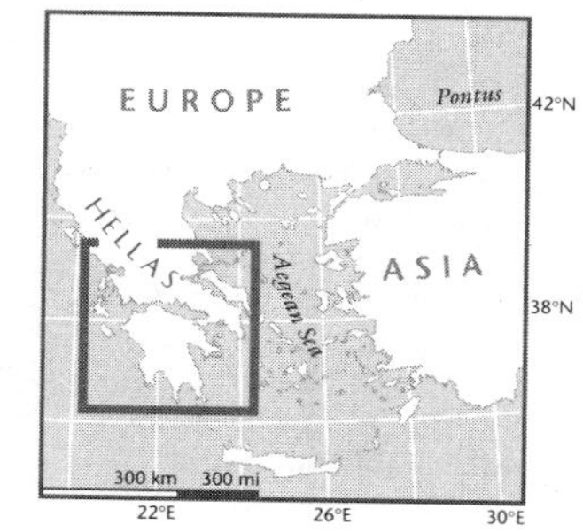

M[illegible] NARRATIVE FOR THE YEAR 419

h[illegible]e frontier not proving propitious, the Spartans re[illegible], and sent word to the allies to be ready to march af[illegible] which happened to be the month of Carneia, a h[illegible][2a] [3] Upon the retreat of the Spartans the Argives m[illegible] day but three of the month before Carneia, and k[illegible]ring the whole time that they were out,[3a] invaded a[illegible]. [4] The Epidaurians summoned their allies to th[illegible]pleaded the month as an excuse; others came as far as[illegible]s and there remained inactive.

5.5[illegible] he Greeks are [illegible] ritual sacrifices [illegible] f the gods to a [illegible]

5.5[illegible] is means that [illegible] umber of days before their Carneian truce by adding intercalated days; see Appendix K, Calendars and Dating Systems, §7.

5.55
419
13th Year/Summer
MANTINEA
Corinth commands Argos to leave Epidaurus. The Argives retire but reinvade after no agreements are reached. Athens and Sparta threaten to intervene but the Spartans return home after unfavorable sacrifices.

While the Argives were in Epidaurus embassies from the cities assembled at Mantinea, upon the invitation of the Athenians. The conference having begun, the Corinthian Euphamidas said that their actions did not agree with their words; while they were sitting deliberating about peace, the Epidaurians and their allies and the Argives were arrayed against each other in arms; deputies from each party should first go and separate the armies, and then the talk about peace might be resumed. [2] In compliance with this suggestion they went and made the Argives withdraw from Epidaurus, and afterwards reassembled, but without succeeding any better in coming to a conclusion; and the Argives a second time invaded Epidaurus and plundered the country. [3] The Spartans also marched out to Caryae;[3a] but the frontier sacrifices again proving unfavorable, they went back again, [4] and the Argives, after ravaging about a third of the Epidaurian territory, returned home. Meanwhile a thousand Athenian hoplites had come to their aid under the command of Alcibiades, but finding that the Spartan expedition was at an end, and that they were no longer wanted, went back again. So passed the summer.

5.56
419/8
13th Year/Winter
EPIDAURUS
After Sparta reinforces Epidaurus, Argos persuades Athens to return the Helots to Pylos. An Argive attempt to take Epidaurus fails.

The next winter the Spartans managed to elude the vigilance of the Athenians, and sent in a garrison of three hundred men to Epidaurus, under the command of Agesippidas. [2] Upon this the Argives went to the Athenians and complained of their having allowed an enemy to pass by sea, in spite of the clause in the treaty by which the allies were not to allow an enemy to pass through their country. Unless, therefore, the Athenians now put the Messenians and Helots in Pylos[2a] to harass the Spartans, they, the Argives, would consider that Athens had not kept faith with them. [3] The Athenians were persuaded by Alcibiades to inscribe at the bottom of the Laconian pillar that the Spartans had not kept their oaths, and to convey the Helots at Cranae[3a] to Pylos to plunder the country; but for the rest they remained quiet as before. [4] During this winter hostilities went on between the Argives and Epidaurians, without any pitched battle taking place, but only forays and ambushes, in which the losses were small and fell now on one side and now on the other. [5] At the close of the winter, toward the beginning of spring, the Argives went with scaling ladders to Epidaurus, expecting to find it left unguarded on account of the war and to be able to take it by assault, but returned unsuccessful. And the winter ended, and with it the thirteenth year of the war ended also.

5.57
418
14th Year/Summer
PELOPONNESUS
Sparta and her allies prepare a major effort against the Argive alliance.

In the middle of the next summer the Spartans, seeing the Epidaurians, their allies, in distress, and the rest of the Peloponnesus either in revolt or disaffected, concluded that it was high time for them to interfere if they wished to stop the progress of the evil, and accordingly with their full force, the Helots included, took the field against Argos, under the command of

5.55.3a Caryae: Map 5.58, BY.

5.56.2a Pylos: Map 5.58, BX. These Helots, of course, were those who had escaped from Spartan rule and had sought refuge with the Messenians at Pylos.

5.56.3a This Cranae was on the island of Cephallenia (Map 5.54, AX), to which the Helots who had escaped to Pylos had been transferred in 421, at Sparta's request; see 5.35.7.

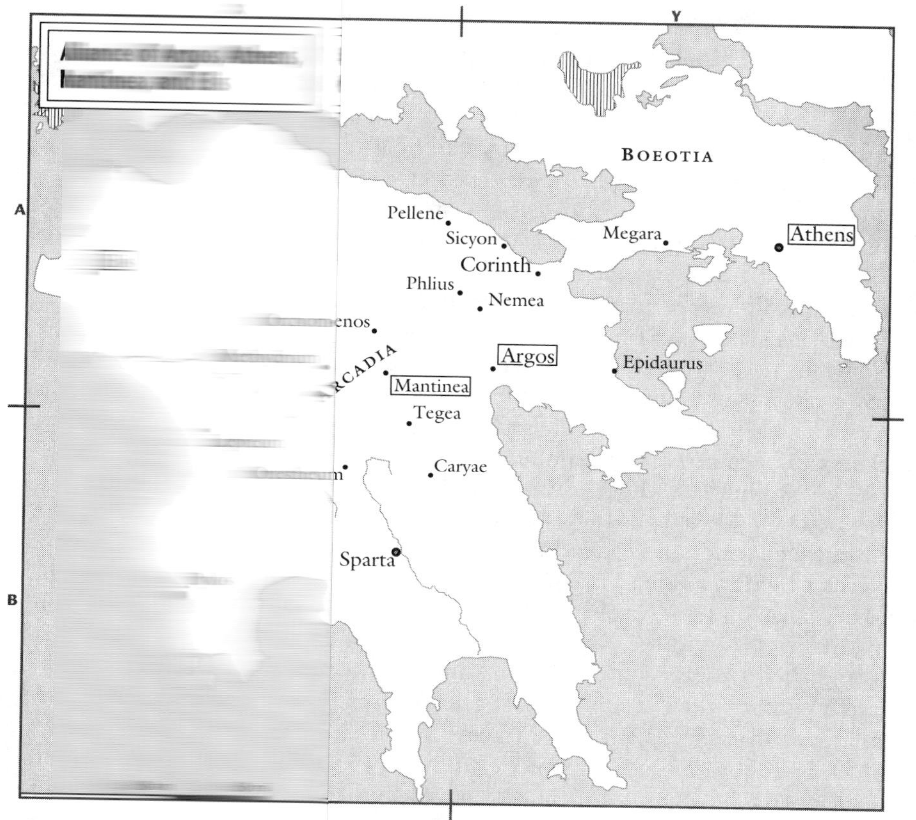

M... NVASION OF ARGOS

Ag... ing of the Spartans. [2] The Tegeans[2a] and the ot... parta joined in the expedition. The allies from th... sus and from outside mustered at Phlius;[2c] the Bo... nd hoplites and as many light troops, and five hu... same number of dismounted troopers; the Co... usand hoplites; the rest more or less as might ha... s with all their forces, the army being in their co...

... e Spartans had from the first been known to th... however, take the field until the enemy was on hi... t Phlius. Reinforced by the Mantineans with th... ousand Elean hoplites, [2] they advanced and

5.58
418
14th Year/Summer
ARGOS
The Argives confront the Spartans alone in Arcadia but Agis eludes them and joins his allies at Phlius. He advances by three roads toward Argos.

5.5...
5.5...
5.5...

fell in with the Spartans at Methydrium in Arcadia.[2a] Each party took up its position upon a hill, and the Argives prepared to engage the Spartans while they were alone; but Agis eluded them by breaking up his camp in the night, and proceeded to join the rest of the allies at Phlius. [3] The Argives discovering this at daybreak, marched first to Argos and then up the Nemean road,[3a] down which they expected the Spartans and their allies would come. [4] Agis, however, instead of taking this road as they expected, ordered the Spartans, Arcadians, and Epidaurians to descend into the plain of Argos by a different, difficult road. The Corinthians, Pellenians,[4a] and Phliasians marched by another steep road; while the Boeotians, Megarians, and Sicyonians[4b] had instructions to come down by the Nemean road where the Argives were posted, so that if the enemy advanced into the plain against the troops of Agis, they might fall upon his rear with their cavalry. [5] These dispositions concluded, Agis invaded the plain and began to ravage Saminthus[5a] and other places.

5.59
418
14th Year/Summer
ARGOS
The Argives and their allies are surrounded by the Spartans and their allies, but do not recognize their danger. Two Argive leaders offer to submit all problems to arbitration and to make peace with Sparta.

Discovering this, the Argives came down from Nemea,[1a] day having now dawned. On their way they fell in with the troops of the Phliasians and Corinthians, and killed a few of the Phliasians, and had perhaps a few more of their own men killed by the Corinthians. [2] Meanwhile the Boeotians, Megarians, and Sicyonians, advancing upon Nemea according to their instructions, found the Argives no longer there as they had gone down on seeing their property ravaged, and were now forming for battle, the Spartans imitating their example. [3] The Argives were now completely surrounded; from the plain the Spartans and their allies shut them off from their city; above them were the Corinthians, Phliasians, and Pellenians; and on the side of Nemea the Boeotians, Sicyonians, and Megarians. Meanwhile their army was without cavalry, the Athenians alone among the allies not having yet arrived. [4] Now the bulk of the Argives and their allies did not see the danger of their position, but thought that they could not have a fairer field, having intercepted the Spartans in their own country and close to the city. [5] Two men, however, in the Argive army, Thrasylus, one of the five generals, and Alciphron, the Spartan *proxenus,*[5a] just as the armies were upon the point of engaging, went and held a parley with Agis and urged him not to bring on a battle, as the Argives were ready to refer to fair and equal arbitration whatever complaints the Spartans might have against them, and to make a treaty and live in peace in future.

5.60
418
14th Year/Summer
ARGOS
Agis and the two Argives agree to a truce and, without consulting anyone else, Agis leads the Spartan forces away. Both sides attack the authors of this truce, thinking they had lost a favorable opportunity to defeat their opponents.

The Argives who made these statements did so upon their own authority, not by order of the people, and Agis on his accepted their proposals, and without himself either consulting the majority, simply communicated the matter to a single individual, one of the high officers accompanying the

5.58.2a Methydrium in Arcadia: Map 5.58, AX.
5.58.3a The road from Argos to Nemea: for Nemea's location, see Map 5.58, AY.
5.58.4a Pellene: Map 5.58, AX.
5.58.4b Sicyon, Megara: Map 5.58, AY.
5.58.5a Saminthus in the Argive plain: exact site unknown.
5.59.1a Nemea: Map 5.58, AY.
5.59.5a *Proxenus:* see note 5.43.2a or Glossary.

ex[illegible]e Argives a truce for four months, in which to ful[illegible] which he immediately led off the army without giv[illegible]ny of the other allies. [2] The Spartans and allies fol[illegible] of respect for the law, but amongst themselves lou[illegible]oing away from so fair a field (the enemy being he[illegible] by infantry and cavalry) without having done an[illegible]rength. [3] Indeed this was by far the finest Hel-len[illegible]t together; and it should have been seen while it wa[illegible], with the Spartans in full force, the Arcadians, Bo[illegible]cyonians, Pellenians, Phliasians and Megarians,[3a] an[illegible] their respective populations, thinking themselves a [illegible] Argive confederacy but for another added to it. [4[illegible] blaming Agis, and returned every man to his ho[illegible]wever blamed still more loudly the persons who ha[illegible]without consulting the people, themselves think-ing[illegible]e with the Spartans an opportunity such as they sh[illegible] the struggle would have been under the walls of th[illegible] of many and brave allies. [6] On their return ac[illegible] stone Thrasylus in the bed of the Charadrus,[6a] wh[illegible] cases before entering the city. Thrasylus fled to th[illegible]ife;[6b] his property however they confiscated.

5.61 418 14th Year/Summer ARGOS After Athenian troops arrive, Alcibiades denounces the Argive-Spartan truce and calls for a resumption of the war. The Argives agree and join the allied siege of Orchomenos, which then capitulates and joins the alliance.

[illegible]housand Athenian hoplites and three hundred ho[illegible]d of Laches and Nicostratus; whom the Argives, be[illegible]nt to break the truce with the Spartans, begged to[illegible] bring before the people, to whom they had a co[illegible]until compelled to do so by the entreaties of the M[illegible] who were still at Argos. [2] The Athenians, th[illegible] ambassador who was present there, told the Ar[illegible] they had no right to make a truce at all without th[illegible] confederates, and now that the Athenians had ar[illegible] war ought to be resumed. [3] These arguments pr[illegible] the allies, they immediately marched upon Or[illegible] the Argives, who, although they had consented lik[illegible]d at first, but eventually joined the others. [4] Th[illegible]rchomenos and made assaults upon it; one of th[illegible]o gain this place being that hostages from Arca-di[illegible]here by the Spartans. [5] The Orchomenians, ala[illegible]f their wall and the numbers of the enemy, and at [illegible]shing before relief arrived, capitulated upon con-dit[illegible]e, of giving hostages of their own to the Manti-

5.6[illegible] Map 5.58, [illegible]h, Sicyon, [illegible]

5.6[illegible]e bed of a [illegible]e [illegible]he north and [illegible]s.

5.60.6b It would have been sacrilege, an insult to the gods, to harm someone who had taken refuge at an altar.

5.61.3a Orchomenos: Map 5.58, AX.

5.61.4a Arcadia: Map 5.58, AX.

neans, and giving up those lodged with them by the Spartans.

5.62
418
14th Year/Summer
ORCHOMENOS
Because the allies vote to attack Tegea instead of Lepreum, the Eleans leave in anger.

Orchomenos thus secured, the allies now consulted as to which of the remaining places they should attack next. The Eleans were urgent for Lepreum;[1a] the Mantineans for Tegea; and the Argives and Athenians giving their support to the Mantineans, [2] the Eleans went home in a rage at their not having voted for Lepreum; while the rest of the allies made ready at Mantinea for going against Tegea, which a party inside had arranged to put into their hands.

5.63
418
14th Year/Summer
SPARTA
The loss of Orchomenos makes the Spartans furious at Agis; they threaten to punish him but relent when he promises to fight well. A new law attaches counselors to the king when he leads the army.

Meanwhile the Spartans, upon their return from Argos after concluding the four months' truce, vehemently blamed Agis for not having subdued Argos, after an opportunity such as they thought they had never had before; for it was no easy matter to bring so many allies, and such good ones, together. [2] But when the news arrived of the capture of Orchomenos,[2a] they became more angry than ever, and, departing from all precedent, in the heat of the moment had almost decided to raze his house, and to fine him ten thousand drachmas. [3] Agis however entreated them to do none of these things, promising to atone for his fault by good service in the field, failing which they might then do to him whatever they pleased; [4] and they accordingly abstained from razing his house or fining him as they had threatened to do, and now made a law, hitherto unknown at Sparta, attaching to him ten Spartiates as counselors, without whose consent he should have no power to lead an army out of the city.

5.64
418
TEGEA
The Spartans receive word of Tegea's peril and march out, summoning their allies to join them at Mantinea. The allies try to join them, but some are delayed by having to cross hostile territory.

At this juncture word arrived from their friends in Tegea that unless they speedily appeared, Tegea would go over from them to the Argives and their allies, if it had not gone over already. [2] Upon this news a force marched out from Sparta of Spartans and Helots and all their people immediately and upon a scale never before witnessed. [3] Advancing toward Orestheum in Maenalia,[3a] they directed the Arcadians[3b] in their league to follow close after them to Tegea, and going on themselves as far as Orestheum, from there sent back the sixth part of the Spartans, consisting of the oldest and youngest men, to guard their homes, and with the rest of their army arrived at Tegea; where their Arcadian allies soon after joined them. [4] Meanwhile they sent to Corinth, to the Boeotians, the Phocians,[4a] and Locrians,[4b] with orders to come up as quickly as possible to Mantinea. These had but short notice; and it was not easy except all together, and after waiting for each other, to pass through the enemy's country, which lay right across and blocked the line of march. Nevertheless they made what haste they could. [5] Meanwhile the Spartans, with the Arcadian allies that had joined them, entered the territory of Mantinea, and encamping near the temple of Heracles began to plunder the country.

5.62.1a Lepreum: Map 5.58, BX.
5.63.2a Orchomenos: Map 5.71, BX.
5.64.3a Maenalia, a district in Arcadia in which Orestheum was located. Orestheum: Map 5.58, BX.
5.64.3b Arcadia: Map 5.58, AX, and Map 5.71, BX.
5.64.4a Phocis: Map 5.71, AY.
5.64.4b Locris (Opuntian Locris): Map 5.71, AY.

y the Argives and their allies, who immediately
to difficult to approach, and formed up in order of
ba at once advanced against them, and came on
wi javelin's cast, when one of the older men, seeing
the a strong one, shouted to Agis that he must be
thi with another; meaning that he wished to make
am Argos, for which he had been so much blamed,
by ish to engage. [3] Meanwhile Agis, whether in
co age or of some sudden new idea of his own,
qu without engaging, [4] and entering the Tegean
ter into Mantinean land the water about which the
M are always fighting, on account of the extensive
da er of the two countries it flows into. [5] His pur-
po the Argives and their allies come down from the
hil of the water, as they would be sure to do when
the to fight the battle in the plain. He accordingly
sta was, engaged in changing the course of the water.
Th were at first amazed at the sudden retreat of the
en near, and did not know what to make of it; but
wh and disappeared, without their having stirred to
pu ew to find fault with their generals, who had not
on ff before, when they were so happily intercepted
be w again allowed them to run away, without any-
on escape at their leisure while the Argive army was
lei e generals, half-stunned for the moment, after-
wa the hill, and went forward and encamped in the
pla attacking the enemy.

5.65
418
14th Year/Summer
MANTINEA
Agis advances upon the Argive army's strong position but decides at the last minute to withdraw, to flood Mantinean territory, and thus to force the enemy to descend and fight in the plain. The Argives, after criticizing their generals for letting the enemy escape, do descend into the plain.

ves and their allies formed up in the order in
wh if they chanced to encounter the enemy; and the
Sp e water to their old encampment by the temple
of their adversaries close in front of them, all in
co nced from the hill. [2] A shock like that of the
pr ans do not ever remember to have experienced:
th preparation, as they instantly and hastily fell into
th g, directing everything, according to the law, [3]
fo eld all commands proceed from him: he gives the
wo ey to the *lochagoi*, these to the *pentecostyes*, these
ag and these last to the *enomoties*.[3a] [4] In short all
or in the same way and quickly reach the troops; as
alr army, save for a small part, consists of officers

5.66
418
14th Year/Summer
MANTINEA
Returning to camp, the Spartans discover the enemy close by in battle order. Agis quickly orders the Spartans into proper formation to face the enemy.

5.6 f the Spartan
an Institu-

under officers, and the care of what is to be done falls upon many.

5.67
418
14th Year/Summer
MANTINEA
Thucydides describes both sides' order of battle.

In this battle the left wing was composed of the *sciritae*,[1a] who in a Spartan army always have that post to themselves alone; next to these were the soldiers of Brasidas from Thrace,[1b] and the *neodamodeis* with them; then came the Spartans themselves, company after company, with the Arcadians of Heraea[1c] at their side. After these were the Maenalians,[1d] and on the right wing the Tegeans with a few of the Spartans at the extremity; their cavalry being posted upon the two wings. [2] Such was the Spartan formation. That of their opponents was as follows: On the right were the Mantineans, the action taking place in their country; next to them the allies from Arcadia; after whom came the thousand picked men of the Argives, to whom the state had given a long course of military training at the public expense;[2a] next to them the rest of the Argives, and after them their allies, the Cleonaeans;[2b] and Orneans;[2c] and lastly the Athenians on the extreme left, and their own cavalry with them.

5.68
418
14th Year/Summer
MANTINEA
The Spartan army appears larger than that of its opponent. Thucydides calculates its numbers.

Such were the order and the forces of the two combatants. The Spartan army looked the largest; [2] though as to putting down the numbers of either host, or of the contingents composing it, I could not do so with any accuracy. Owing to the secrecy of their government the number of the Spartans was not known, and men are so apt to brag about the forces of their country that the estimate of their opponents was not trusted. The following calculation, however, makes it possible to estimate the numbers of the Spartans present upon this occasion. [3] There were seven companies in the field without counting the *sciritae*, who numbered six hundred men: in each company there were four *pentecostyes*, and in the *pentecosty* four *enomoties*. The first rank of the *enomoty* was composed of four soldiers: as to the depth, although they had not been all drawn up alike, but as each captain chose, they were generally ranged eight deep; the first rank along the whole line, exclusive of the *sciritae*, consisted of four hundred and forty-eight men.[3a]

5.67.1a For the *sciritae*, see Appendix C, Spartan Institutions, §9.

5.67.1b The return of these troops, the granting of freedom to these Helots among them, and their settlement with the *neodamodeis* in Lepreum was mentioned in 5.34.

5.67.1c Heraea, in Arcadia: Map 5.71, BX.

5.67.1d Maenalia, in Arcadia: Map 5.71, BX.

5.67.2a For the Argive picked force trained at public expense, see Appendix F, Ancient Greek Land Warfare, §7.

5.67.2b Cleonae: Map 5.71, BY.

5.67.2c Orneae: Map 5.71, BX.

5.68.3a Taking into account the one sixth of the army sent home before the battle (5.64.3), and including the six hundred *sciritae*, one reaches by Thucydides' method of calculation a total Spartan army in 418 of about five thousand. If the numbers of Spartiates and *perioikoi* (see Glossary) in the "companies" (*lochoi*) were roughly equal, one arrives at a total of no more than two thousand five hundred Spartiates in all. But some have argued that Thucydides has made a serious mistake. His calculations are based on an army of seven "companies," but in Xenephon's *History of Greece,* which covers the period from the end of Thucydides to 362 B.C., one encounters a Spartan army of six "divisions" (*morae*) with two "companies" in each. Was Thucydides unaware that there had been by 418 a great reform of the army? The answer greatly affects both our understanding of the developing Spartan demographic problem (see note 5.34.1b and Appendix G, Spartan Institutions §7–9) and our estimate of Thucydides' credibility. Scholarly opinion is much divided.

5.69
418
14th Year/Summer
MANTINEA
Both sides now encourage their men to fight: the Argives and their allies with speeches, the Spartans with war songs and mutual reminders of their superior training.

… on the eve of engaging, each contingent received
so … ment from its own commander. The Mantineans
we … ere going to fight for their country and to avoid
ret … e of servitude after having tasted that of empire;
th … ld contend for their ancient supremacy, to regain
th … he Peloponnesus of which they had been so long
de … n enemy and a neighbor for a thousand wrongs;
th … y of gaining the honors of the day with so many
an … nd that a victory over the Spartans in the Pelopo … nd extend their empire, and would besides pre-
ser … sions in future. [2] These were the incitements
ad … nd their allies. The Spartans meanwhile, man to
ma … ongs in the ranks, exhorted each brave comrade
to … learnt before; well aware that the long training
of … for saving lives than any brief verbal exhortation,
th … ed.

5.70
418
14th Year/Summer
MANTINEA
The armies advance to battle.

… attle, the Argives and their allies advancing with
ha … s slowly and to the music of many flute players—
a s … heir army, that has nothing to do with religion,
bu … em advance evenly, stepping in time, without
bre … ge armies are apt to do in the moment of engaging …

5.71
418
14th Year/Summer
MANTINEA
Agis, concerned by the overlap of his left by the enemy's right, orders his left-most units to extend left and other units from the right to fill the gap thus opened in the line.

… joined, King Agis resolved upon the following
ma … like in this: on going into action they get forced
ou … wing, and one and the other overlap with this
th … se fear makes each man do his best to shelter his
un … eld of the man next him on the right, thinking
tha … are locked together the better will he be pro-
tec … responsible for this is the first upon the right
wi … g to withdraw from the enemy his unarmed side;
an … n makes the rest follow him. [2] On the present
oc … reached with their wing far beyond the *sciritae*,
an … eans still farther beyond the Athenians, as their
arm … Agis afraid of his left being surrounded, and
thi … ns outflanked it too far, ordered the sciritae and
Br … rom their place in the ranks and make the line
eve … and told the polemarchs Hipponoidas and Aris-
toc … us formed, by throwing themselves into it with
tw … n the right wing; thinking that his right would
stil … to spare, and that the line fronting the Mantinea … y.

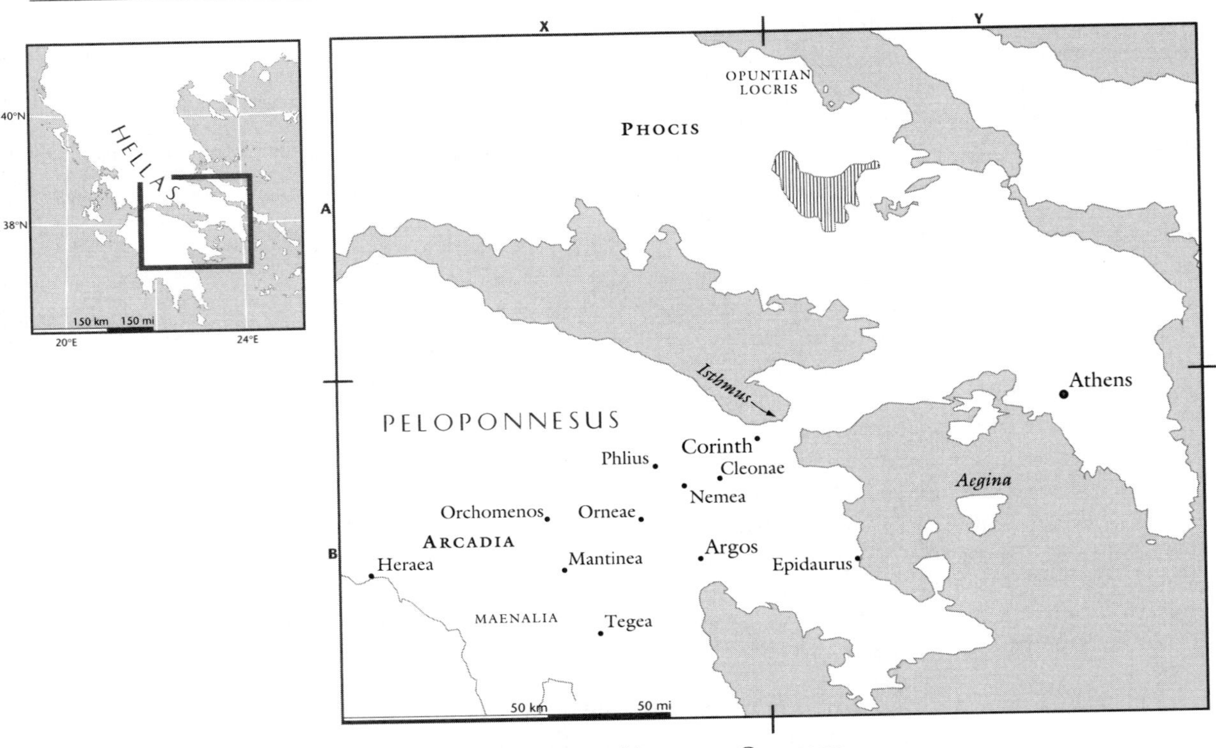

MAP 5.71 THE BATTLE OF MANTINEA CAMPAIGN

5.72
418
14th Year/Summer
MANTINEA
The polemarchs on the right refuse to move their units, and Agis rescinds his order. The Spartan left is defeated but the Spartan right easily routs its opponents.

However, as he gave these orders in the moment of the onset, and at short notice, Aristocles and Hipponoidas refused to move (for which offense they were afterwards found guilty of cowardice and banished from Sparta); and although Agis, when he saw that the two companies did not move, ordered the sciritae to return to their place in line, they did not have time to fill up the breach in question before the enemy closed. [2] Now it was, however, that the Spartans, utterly worsted in respect of skill, showed themselves as superior in point of courage. [3] As soon as they came to close quarters with the enemy, the Mantinean right broke the sciritae and Brasideans, and bursting in with their allies and the thousand picked Argives into the unclosed breach in their line cut up and surrounded the Spartans, and drove them in full rout to the wagons, slaying some of the ol[illegible] [4] But if the Spartans got the worst of it in this pa[illegible] so with the rest of their army, and especially the ce[illegible]ndred knights,[4a] as they are called, fought round Ki[illegible] older men of the Argives and the five companies so [illegible]eonaeans, the Orneans, and the Athenians next th[illegible]d them; the greater number not even waiting to str[illegible]vay the moment that they came on, some even be[illegible]ot, in their fear of being overtaken by their ass[illegible]

5.73
418
14th Year/Summer
MANTINEA
Agis orders his successful right wing to support the defeated left, and the Argive-allied force flees. Spartan pursuit is brief.

[illegible]s and their allies having given way in this quarter wa[illegible] two, and as the Spartan and Tegean right simultan[illegible]he Athenians with the troops that outflanked th[illegible]emselves placed between two fires, being surrou[illegible]lready defeated on the other. Indeed they would hav[illegible]ly than any other part of the army, but for the ser[illegible]h they had with them. [2] Agis also, on perceiving[illegible] opposed to the Mantineans and the thousand Ar[illegible]rmy to advance to the support of the defeated wi[illegible]ook place, as the enemy moved past and slanted aw[illegible]nians escaped at their leisure, and with them the be[illegible]eanwhile the Mantineans and their allies and the pic[illegible]es ceased to press the enemy and, seeing their fri[illegible]partans in full advance upon them, took to flight. [4[illegible]ns perished; but the bulk of the picked body of the[illegible]eir escape. The flight and retreat, however, were nei[illegible] the Spartans fighting long and stubbornly until the[illegible]ut that once accomplished, pursuing for a short tim[illegible]

5.74
418
14th Year/Summer
MANTINEA
The Spartans return the enemy dead under truce and bury their own. Losses on both sides are enumerated.

[illegible]s nearly as possible as I have described it; the gre[illegible] for a very long while among the Hellenes, and joi[illegible]rable states. [2] The Spartans took up a position in [illegible]d, and immediately set up a trophy and stripped the[illegible]eir own dead and carried them back to Tegea,[2a] wh[illegible]nd restored those of the enemy under truce. [3] Th[illegible]and Cleonaeans[3c] had seven hundred killed; the Ma[illegible] and the Athenians and Aeginetans[3d] also two hu[illegible]generals. On the side of the Spartans, the allies dic[illegible]rth speaking of: as to the Spartans themselves it wa[illegible]truth; it is said, however, that there were slain ab[illegible]m.

5.72[illegible]knights of [illegible]ng's body-[illegible]round him.

5.74[illegible]

5.74[illegible]

5.74[illegible]

5.74[illegible]

5.74.3d Aegina: Map 5.71, BY. These Aeginitan casualties were Athenian settlers; Thucydides mentions the expulsion of the Aeginetans from their island and its resettlement by Athenians in 2.27 and 7.57.2.

5.75
418
14th Year/Summer
MANTINEA
The Spartans dismiss their allies and celebrate the Carneia.
EPIDAURUS
Epidaurians plunder Argive territory. The Argives return and begin a circumvallation of Epidaurus.

While the battle was impending, Pleistoanax, the other king, set out with a reinforcement composed of the oldest and youngest men, and got as far as Tegea, where he heard of the victory and went back again. [2] The Spartans also sent a message to turn back the allies from Corinth and from beyond the Isthmus,[2a] and returning home themselves dismissed their allies, and celebrated the Carneian festival,[2b] which happened to be at that time. [3] The imputations cast upon them by the Hellenes at the time, whether of cowardice on account of the disaster in the island,[3a] or of mismanagement and slowness generally, were all wiped out by this single action: fortune, it was thought, might have humbled them, but the men themselves were the same as ever. [4] The day before this battle, the Epidaurians with all their forces invaded the deserted Argive territory, and killed many of the guards left there in the absence of the Argive army. [5] After the battle three thousand Elean hoplites arrived to aid the Mantineans, as well as a reinforcement of one thousand Athenians; all these allies marched at once against Epidaurus while the Spartans were keeping the Carneia and, dividing the work among themselves, began to build a wall round the city. [6] The rest left off; but the Athenians finished at once the part assigned to them round Cape Heraeum;[6a] and after all joined in leaving a garrison in the fortification in question, they returned to their respective cities. Summer now came to an end.

5.76
418/7
14th Year/Winter
ARGOS
Sparta, relying upon a strengthened antidemocratic party in Argos after the battle, offers to negotiate a peace. After much discussion, Argos accepts the Spartan proposal.

In the first days of the next winter, when the Carneian holidays were over, the Spartans took the field, and arriving at Tegea sent on to Argos proposals for an accommodation. [2] There had before been a party in the city desirous of overthrowing the democracy; and after the battle that had been fought, these were now in a far better position to persuade the people to listen to terms. Their plan was to make a treaty with the Spartans first, follow it with an alliance, and after this to fall upon the popular party. [3] Lichas son of Arcesilaus, the Argive *proxenus*,[3a] accordingly arrived at Argos with two proposals from Sparta, to regulate the conditions of war or peace, according to whichever one they preferred. After much discussion, Alcibiades happening to be in the city, the Spartan party, who now ventured to act openly, persuaded the Argives to accept the proposal for a peace treaty, which ran as follows:

5.77
418/7
14th Year/Winter
ARGOS-SPARTA
Thucydides presents the text of the peace proposal offered by Sparta to Argos.

The assembly of the Spartans agrees to negotiate with the Argives upon the terms following:

- The Argives shall restore to the Orchomenians[1a] their children,

5.75.2a Isthmus of Corinth: Map 5.71, AY.

5.75.2b For the Carneian festival, see Appendix I, Religious Festivals, §8, and Appendix H, Dialects and Ethnic Groups, §5.

5.75.3a The island referred to is Sphacteria at Pylos, where almost three hundred Spartans surrendered to Athenian forces in 425; see 4.31–40.

5.75.6a Cape Heraeum juts out northward into the sea from Old Epidaurus. Epidaurus: Map 5.71, BY.

5.76.3a *Proxenus:* see note 5.43.2a or Glossary. This Lichas may be remembered as the owner of victorious racehorces at Olympia; see 5.50.4.

5.77.1a Orchomenos: Map 5.71, BX.

[b] their men, and shall restore the men they Spartans.

acuate Epidaurus, and raze the fortification refuse to withdraw from Epidaurus, they shall the Argives and of the Spartans, and of the d the allies of the Argives.

have any children in their custody, they shall to his city.

ering to the god,[4a] the Argives, if they wish, pon the Epidaurians, but, if not, they shall

in the Peloponnesus, both small and great, cording to the customs of their country.

owers outside the Peloponnesus invade Pelo- parties contracting shall unite to repel them, may agree upon, as being most fair for the

e Spartans outside the Peloponnesus shall be the Spartans, and the allies of the Argives oting as the Argives, being left in enjoyment s.

ll be shown to the allies,[8a] and shall be con- if the allies think fit, they may send the treaty ne.

5.78 418/7 14th Year/Winter ARGOS Renouncing her pact with Athens, Elis, and Mantinea, Argos allies with Sparta.

accepting this proposal, and the Spartan army ret a. After this, normal intercourse was renewed be g afterwards the same faction contrived that the Ar alliance with the Mantineans, Eleans, and Athe- nia treaty of alliance with the Spartans; which was co e following terms:

5.79 418/7 14th Year/Winter ARGOS-SPARTA Thucydides offers the text of the treaty of alliance between Argos and Sparta.

rgives agree to a treaty and alliance for fifty lowing:

be decided by fair and impartial arbitration, oms of the two countries.

ties in the Peloponnesus may be included in as independent and sovereign, in full enjoy-

5.7 71, BX.

5.7 s here to the etween 53.1.

5.7 y the states , a Spartan- led coalition which Argos would not have been willing to join. See Appendix D, The Peloponnesian League, §3, 5–6.

ment of what they possess; all disputes being decided by fair and impartial arbitration, consistent with the customs of the said cities.

• [2] All allies of the Spartans outside the Peloponnesus shall be upon the same footing as the Spartans themselves, and the allies of the Argives shall be upon the same footing as the Argives themselves, continuing to enjoy what they possess.

• [3] If it shall be anywhere necessary to make an expedition in common, the Spartans and Argives shall consult upon it and decide, as may be most fair for the allies.

• [4] If any of the cities, whether inside or outside the Peloponnesus, have a question of frontiers or of other matters, it must be settled; but if one allied city should have a quarrel with another allied city, it must be referred to some third city thought impartial by both parties. Private citizens shall have their disputes decided according to the laws of their respective countries.

5.80
418/7
14th Year/Winter
ARGOS-SPARTA
Argos and Sparta fulfill the terms of their treaty and extend their alliance to Perdiccas and the Chalcidian cities.
EPIDAURUS
As ordered by Argos, the Athenians leave Epidaurus.

The treaty and above alliance concluded, each party at once released everything whether acquired by war or otherwise, and thereafter acting in common voted to receive neither herald nor embassy from the Athenians unless they evacuated their forts and withdrew from the Peloponnesus, and also to make neither peace nor war with anyone, except jointly. [2] Zeal was not wanting: both parties sent envoys to the Thracian district[2a] and to Perdiccas,[2b] and persuaded the latter to join their league. Still he did not at once break with Athens, although inclined to do so upon seeing the way shown him by Argos, the original home of his family. They also renewed their old oaths with the Chalcidians and took new ones: [3] the Argives, besides, sent ambassadors to the Athenians, bidding them evacuate the fort at Epidaurus. The Athenians, seeing their own men outnumbered by the rest of the garrison, sent Demosthenes to bring them out. This general, under color of a gymnastic contest which he arranged on his arrival, got the rest of the garrison out of the place and shut the gates behind them. Afterwards the Athenians renewed their treaty with the Epidaurians, and by themselves gave up the fortress.

5.81
418/7
14th Year/Winter
MANTINEA-SPARTA
Mantinea and Sparta make peace; a Spartan-Argive army strengthens the oligarchy at Sicyon and establishes an oligarchy at Argos.

After the defection of Argos from the league, the Mantineans, though they held out at first, in the end found themselves powerless without the Argives; they too came to terms with Sparta,[1a] and gave up their rule over the cities. [2] The Spartans and Argives, each a thousand strong, now took the field together, and the former first went by themselves to Sicyon[2a] and made the government there more oligarchic than before, and then both, uniting, put down the democracy at Argos and set up an oligarchy favorable to Sparta. These events occurred at the close of the winter, just before spring; and the fourteenth year of the war ended.

5.80.2a Thracian district, including Chalcidice: Map 5.82, AX, AY.

5.80.2b Perdiccas was the king of Macedonia (Map 5.82, AX).

5.81.1a This special treaty with Mantinea, now a Peloponnesian League ally (see Appendix D, The Peloponnesian League, §5), is also mentioned in what is probably a near-contemporary treaty between Sparta and Aetolian Erxadieis.

5.81.2a Sicyon: Map 5.82, BX.

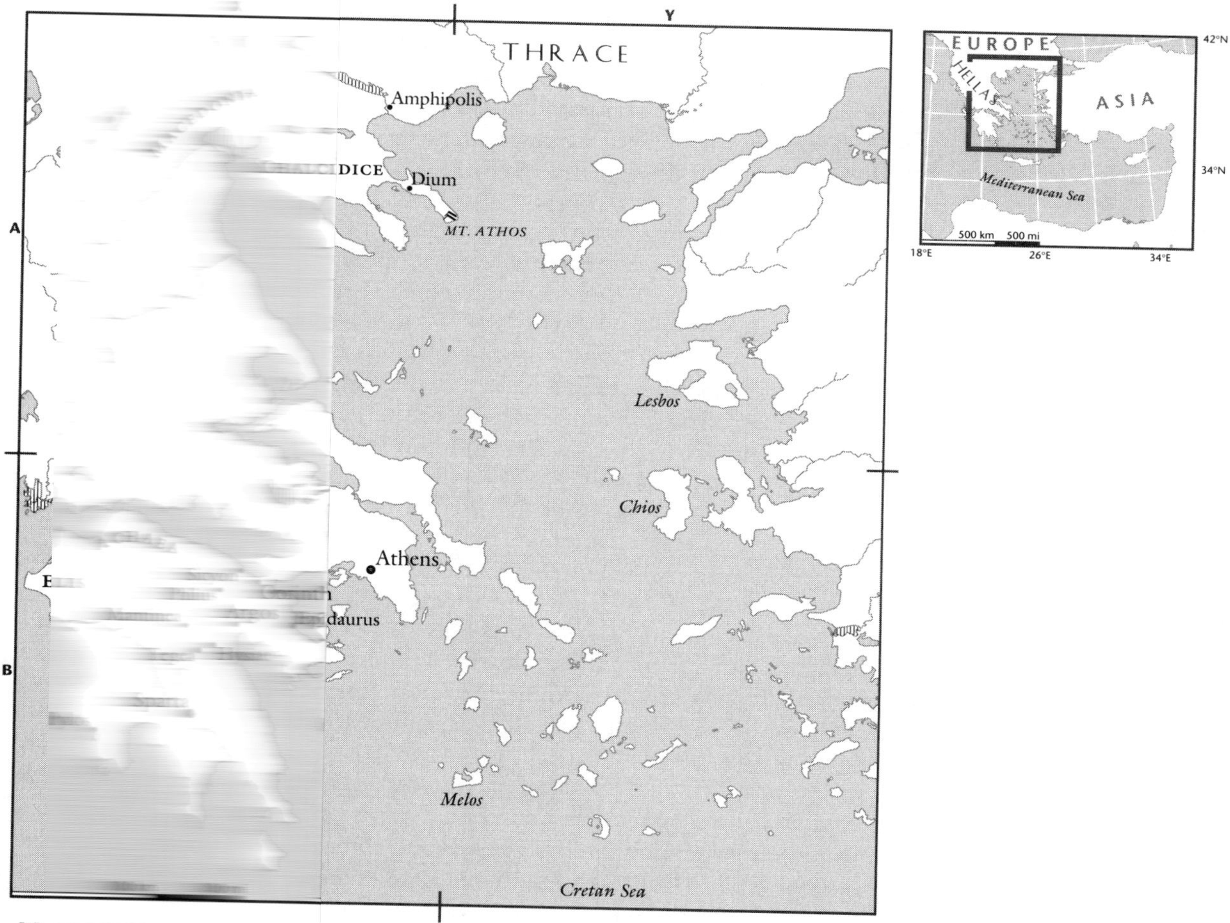

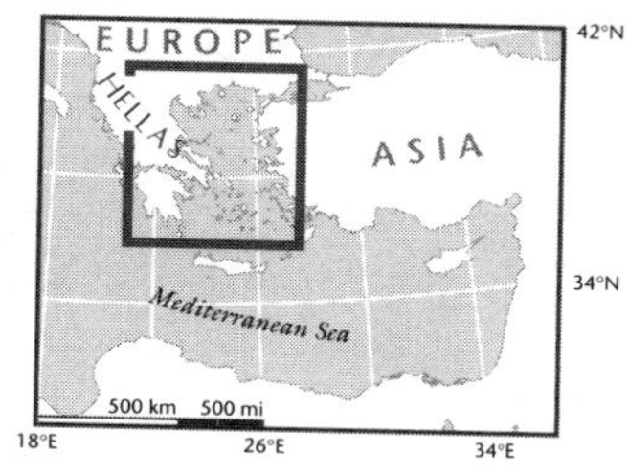

M ARS 417 AND 416

people of Dium, in Athos,[1a] revolted from the At ans,[1b] and the Spartans settled affairs in Achaea[1c] in o the interests of their country. [2] Meanwhile th s little by little gathering strength and courage, w the Gymnopaedic festival at Sparta and then fell up a fight in the city victory declared for the popu- la of their opponents and banished others. [3] The Sp e disregarded the messages of their friends at

5.82
417
15th Year/Summer
ARGOS
Argive democrats revive and overthrow the oligarchs, killing some and banishing others. Sparta resolves to attack Argos, but procrastinates. Argos renews ties with Athens and begins to build long walls to the sea.

5.8 the Acte

5.8 Chalcidian .18.5b; Chal-

5.82.1c Achaea: Map 5.82, BX.

Argos; at last they postponed the Gymnopaediae and marched to their assistance, but learning at Tegea of the defeat of the oligarchs, refused to go any further in spite of the entreaties of those who had escaped, and returned home and celebrated the festival. [4] Later on, envoys arrived with messages from the Argives in the city and from the exiles, when the allies were also at Sparta; and after much had been said on both sides, the Spartans decided that the party in the city had done wrong and resolved to march against Argos, but kept delaying and putting off the matter. [5] Meanwhile the popular party at Argos, in fear of the Spartans, began again to court the Athenian alliance, which they were convinced would be of the greatest service to them; and accordingly proceeded to build long walls to the sea, in order that in case of a blockade by land, with the help of the Athenians they might have the advantage of importing what they wanted by sea. [6] Some of the cities in the Peloponnesus were also privy to the building of these walls; and the Argives with all their people, women and slaves not excepted, applied themselves to the work, while carpenters and masons came to them from Athens. Summer was now over.

5.83
417/6
15th Year/Winter
ARGOS
Sparta invades Argos and destroys the long walls. Argos plunders Phlius for harboring Argive exiles.
MACEDONIA
Athens blockades Perdiccas because, by joining the Argive-Spartan alliance, he forced the Athenians to cancel their expedition against Chalcidice and Amphipolis.

The following winter the Spartans, hearing of the walls that were being built, marched against Argos with their allies (except for the Corinthians), under the command of their king Agis son of Archidamus. [2] They had intelligence of affairs in the city itself but this intelligence, which they counted upon, came to nothing; however, they took and razed the walls which were being built, and after capturing the Argive city Hysiae[2a] and killing all the freemen that fell into their hands, went back and dispersed every man to his city. [3] After this the Argives marched into Phlius[3a] and plundered it for harboring their exiles, most of whom had settled there, and so returned home. [4] The same winter the Athenians blockaded Macedonia[4a] in retaliation for the alliance entered into by Perdiccas with the Argives and Spartans, and also because of his breach of his engagements on the occasion of the expedition prepared by Athens against the Chalcidians in the Thracian region[4b] and against Amphipolis,[4c] under the command of Nicias son of Niceratus, which had to be abandoned mainly because of his desertion. He was therefore proclaimed an enemy. And thus the winter ended, and the fifteenth year of the war ended with it.

5.84
416
16th Year/Summer
ARGOS
Alcibiades seizes three hundred pro-Spartan Argives and lodges them in nearby islands.
MELOS
An Athenian expedition against Melos sends envoys to negotiate.

The next summer Alcibiades sailed with twenty ships to Argos and seized the suspected persons still left of the Spartan faction to the number of three hundred, whom the Athenians forthwith lodged in the neighboring islands of their empire.[1a] The Athenians also made an expedition against the isle of Melos[1b] with thirty ships of their own, six Chian,[1c] and two Les-

5.83.2a Hysiae: Map 5.82, BX.
5.83.3a Phlius: Map 5.82, BX.
5.83.4a Macedonia: Map 5.82, AX.
5.83.4b Chalcidice, Thrace: Map 5.82, AX, AY. "The Chalcidians" here are the members of the Chalcidian League; see note 5.18.5b.
5.83.4c Amphipolis: Map 5.82, AX.
5.84.1a For what happened to these unfortunate hostages, see 6.61.3.
5.84.1b Melos: Map 5.82, BY. An earlier Athenian expedition to Melos was described in 3.91, but the background to this invasion is not fully explained by Thucydides.
5.84.1c Chios: Map 5.82, BY.

bia[illegible]red hoplites, three hundred archers, and twenty mo[illegible]ns, and about fifteen hundred hoplites from the allie[illegible] The Melians are a colony of Sparta that would not[illegible]s like the other islanders, and at first remained neu[illegible] the struggle, but afterwards upon the Atheni- ans [illegible]ndering their territory, assumed an attitude of ope[illegible]des son of Lycomedes, and Tisias son of Tisi- mac[illegible]mping in their territory with the above arma- mer[illegible]m to their land, sent envoys to negotiate. These the[illegible]efore the people, but bade them state the object of t[illegible]gistrates and the few; upon which the Athenian env[illegible]

[illegible]e negotiations are not to go on before the [illegible] may not be able to speak straight on with- [illegible]ceive the ears of the multitude by seductive [illegible] pass without refutation (for we know that [illegible]ır being brought before the few), what if you [illegible]ırsue a method more cautious still! Make no [illegible]ıt take us up at whatever you do not like, and [illegible] any farther. And first tell us if this proposi- [illegible]

5.85
416
16th Year/Summer
MELOS
Noting that only the Few, not The People, are present, the Athenians offer to debate frankly and spontaneously.

[illegible]ers answered:

[illegible]ness of quietly instructing each other as you [illegible] to object; but your military preparations are [illegible]e with what you say, as we see you are come [illegible]n cause, and that all we can reasonably expect [illegible] war, if we prove to have right on our side [illegible] in the contrary case, slavery."

5.86
416
16th Year/Summer
MELOS
The Melians agree to talk, but feel that their only choices are war or slavery.

[illegible]ave met to reason about presentiments of the [illegible]lse than to consult for the safety of your state [illegible] see before you, we will cease talking; other- [illegible]

5.87
416
16th Year/Summer
MELOS

[illegible]al and excusable for men in our position to [illegible]ne both in thought and utterance. However, [illegible]ference is, as you say, the safety of our coun- [illegible] if you please, can proceed in the way which [illegible]

5.88
416
16th Year/Summer
MELOS

5.8[illegible]

5.89 416 16th Year/Summer MELOS The Athenians say that the strong do what they can and the weak suffer what they must.

Athenians: "For ourselves, we shall not trouble you with specious pretenses—either of how we have a right to our empire because we overthrew the Mede, or are now attacking you because of wrong that you have done us—and make a long speech which would not be believed; and in return we hope that you, instead of thinking to influence us by saying that you did not join the Spartans, although their colonists, or that you have done us no wrong, will aim at what is feasible, holding in view the real sentiments of us both; since you know as well as we do that right, as the world goes, is only in question between equals in power, while the strong do what they can and the weak suffer what they must."

5.90 416 16th Year/Summer MELOS The Melians point out how useful moral arguments could be to Athens if her empire fell.

Melians: "As we think, at any rate, it is expedient—we speak as we are obliged, since you enjoin us to let right alone and talk only of interest—that you should not destroy what is our common protection, namely, the privilege of being allowed in danger to invoke what is fair and right, and even to profit by arguments not strictly valid if they can be persuasive. And you are as much interested in this as any, as your fall would be a signal for the heaviest vengeance and an example for the world to meditate upon."

5.91 416 16th Year/Summer MELOS The Athenians reply that it is in their mutual interests for Melos to peacefully accept Athenian rule.

Athenians: "The end of our empire, if end it should, does not frighten us: a rival empire like Sparta, even if Sparta was our real antagonist, is not so terrible to the vanquished as subjects who by themselves attack and overpower their rulers.[1a] [2] This, however, is a risk that we are content to take. We will now proceed to show you that we have come here in the interest of our empire, and that we shall say what we are now going to say, for the preservation of your country; as we would desire to exercise that empire over you without trouble, and see you preserved for the good of us both."

5.92 *Melians:* "And how, pray, could it turn out as good for us to serve as for you to rule?"

5.93 *Athenians:* "Because you would have the advantage of submitting before suffering the worst, and we should gain by not destroying you."

5.94 *Melians:* "So you would not consent to our being neutral, friends instead of enemies, but allies of neither side."

5.95 *Athenians:* "No; for your hostility cannot so much hurt us as your friendship will be an argument to our subjects of our weakness, and your enmity of our power."

5.96 *Melians:* "Is that your subjects' idea of equity, to put those who have nothing to do with you in the same category with peoples that are most of them your own colonists, and some conquered rebels?"

5.97 416 16th Year/Summer MELOS The Athenians say that Athens must subdue Melos to keep the respect of its subjects.

Athenians: "As far as right goes they think one has as much of it as the other, and that if any maintain their independence it is because

5.91.1a Scholars have differed as to whether this statement could have been written only after 404, when Athens did get off more lightly than was to be expected. See the Introduction (sect. II.ii).

[illegible]at if we do not molest them it is because we [illegible]des extending our empire we should gain in [illegible]on; the fact that you are islanders and weaker [illegible] all the more important that you should not [illegible] masters of the sea."

5.98
416
16th Year/Summer
MELOS
The Melians argue that Athens' policy will only create more enemies for her.

[illegible]u consider that there is no security in the pol-[illegible] For here again if you debar us from talking [illegible]e us to obey your interest, we also must [illegible] persuade you, if the two happen to coincide. [illegible]king enemies of all existing neutrals who shall [illegible]onclude from it that one day or another you [illegible]what is this but to make greater the enemies [illegible]and to force others to become so who would [illegible]ought of it?"

5.99
416
16th Year/Summer
MELOS

[illegible]ie fact is that mainlanders generally give us [illegible]erty which they enjoy will long prevent their [illegible]nst us; it is rather islanders like yourselves, [illegible]nd subjects smarting under the yoke, who [illegible]y to take a rash step and lead themselves and [illegible]"

5.100
416
16th Year/Summer
MELOS

[illegible], if you risk so much to retain your empire, [illegible]t rid of it, it were surely great baseness and [illegible]e still free not to try everything that can be [illegible] to your yoke."

5.101
416
16th Year/Summer
MELOS

[illegible]ou are well advised, the contest not being an [illegible] as the prize and shame as the penalty, but a [illegible]ation and of not resisting those who are far [illegible]

5.102
416
16th Year/Summer
MELOS

[illegible]ow that the fortune of war is sometimes more [illegible]oportion of numbers might lead one to sup-[illegible]ve ourselves over to despair, while action still [illegible]that we may stand erect."

5.103
416
16th Year/Summer
MELOS
The Melians are advised to avoid hope, which deludes men and leads them to ruin.

[illegible] danger's comforter, may be indulged in by [illegible]nt resources, if not without loss, at all events [illegible]ature is to be extravagant, and those who go [illegible] all upon the venture see it in its true colors [illegible]ed; but so long as the discovery would enable [illegible]t, it is never found wanting. [2] Let not this [illegible]ho are weak and hang on a single turn of the [illegible] vulgar, who, abandoning such security as [illegible]ll afford, when visible hopes fail them in [illegible]nvisible, to prophecies and oracles, and other such inventions that delude men with hopes to their destruction."

5.104
416
16th Year/Summer
MELOS

Melians: "You may be sure that we are as well aware as you of the difficulty of contending against your power and fortune, unless the terms be equal. But we trust that the gods may grant us fortune as good as yours, since we are just men fighting against unjust, and that what we want in power will be made up by the alliance of the Spartans, who are bound, if only for very shame, to come to the aid of their kindred. Our confidence, therefore, after all is not so utterly irrational."

5.105
416
16th Year/Summer
MELOS
The Athenians also hope for the gods' favor, since they only do what is natural to both gods and men: "rule where they can." It is foolish to believe that the Spartans, who are moral hypocrites when the interests of others are concerned, will aid Melos because of sentiment or shame.

Athenians: "When you speak of the favor of the gods, we may as fairly hope for that as yourselves; neither our pretensions nor our conduct being in any way contrary to what men believe of the gods, or practice among themselves.[1a] [2] Of the gods we believe, and of men we know, that by a necessary law of their nature they rule wherever they can. And it is not as if we were the first to make this law, or to act upon it when made: we found it existing before us, and shall leave it to exist forever after us; all we do is to make use of it, knowing that you and everybody else, having the same power as we have, would do the same as we do. [3] Thus, as far as the gods are concerned, we have no fear and no reason to fear that we shall be at a disadvantage. But when we come to your notion about the Spartans, which leads you to believe that shame will make them help you, here we bless your simplicity but do not envy your folly. [4] The Spartans, when their own interests or their country's laws are in question, are the worthiest men alive; of their conduct toward others much might be said, but no clearer idea of it could be given than by shortly saying that of all the men we know they are most conspicuous in considering what is agreeable honorable, and what is expedient just. Such a way of thinking does not promise much for the safety which you now unreasonably count upon."

5.106
416
16th Year/Summer
MELOS

Melians: "But it is for this very reason that we now trust to their respect for expediency to prevent them from betraying the Melians, their colonists, and thereby losing the confidence of their friends in Hellas and helping their enemies."

5.107
416
16th Year/Summer
MELOS

Athenians: "Then you do not adopt the view that expediency goes with security, while justice and honor cannot be followed without danger; and danger the Spartans generally court as little as possible."

5.108
416
16th Year/Summer
MELOS

Melians: "But we believe that they would be more likely to face even danger for our sake, and with more confidence than for others, as our nearness to the Peloponnesus makes it easier for them to act; and our common blood insures our fidelity."

5.105.1a See the Introduction (sect. IV.i) for a discussion of Thucydides' view of religion.

t what an intending ally trusts to is not the
› ask his aid, but a decided superiority of
he Spartans look to this even more than oth-
eir distrust of their home resources that it is
llies that they attack a neighbor; now is it
masters of the sea they will cross over to an

5.109
416
16th Year/Summer
MELOS

would have others to send. The Cretan sea[1a]
more difficult for those who command it to
for those who wish to elude them to do so
the Spartans miscarry in this, they would
d upon those left of your allies whom Brasi-
instead of places which are not yours, you
your own country and your own confeder-

5.110
416
16th Year/Summer
MELOS

iversion of the kind you speak of you may
nly to learn, as others have done, that the
et withdrew from a siege for fear of any. [2]
fact, that after saying you would consult for
ry, in all this discussion you have mentioned
ght trust in and think to be saved by. Your
pend upon hope and the future, and your
o scanty, as compared with those arrayed
come out victorious. [3] You will therefore
judgment, unless, after allowing us to retire,
nsel more prudent than this. You will surely
lea of disgrace, which in dangers that are dis-
ne time too plain to be mistaken, proves so
in too many cases the very men that have
to what they are rushing into, let the thing
nere influence of a seductive name, lead them
they become so enslaved by the phrase as in
hopeless disaster, and incur disgrace more
panion of error, than when it comes as the
[4] This, if you are well advised, you will
will not think it dishonorable to submit to
as, when it makes you the moderate offer of
ally, without ceasing to enjoy the country
nor when you have the choice given you
ty, will you be so blinded as to choose the
that those who do not yield to their equals,
eir superiors, and are moderate toward their
succeed best. [5] Think over the matter,

5.111
416
16th Year/Summer
MELOS
The Athenians advise the Melians not to act from fear of dishonor or disgrace, saying that Melos lacks the resources for such concepts and that heeding them now will bring her to ruin.

5.11
5.11 's attitude
8.27.2–3.

therefore, after our withdrawal, and reflect once and again that it is for your country that you are consulting, that you have not more than one, and that upon this one deliberation depends its prosperity or ruin."

5.112
416
16th Year/Summer
MELOS
The Melians refuse to yield and offer the Athenians no more than friendly neutrality.

The Athenians now withdrew from the conference; and the Melians, left to themselves, came to a decision corresponding to what they had maintained in the discussion, and answered, [2] "Our resolution, Athenians, is the same as it was at first. We will not in a moment deprive of freedom a city that has been inhabited these seven hundred years; but we put our trust in the fortune by which the gods have preserved it until now, and in the help of men, that is, of the Spartans; and so we will try and save ourselves. [3] Meanwhile we invite you to allow us to be friends to you and foes to neither party, and to retire from our country after making such a treaty as shall seem fit to us both."

5.113
416
16th Year/Summer
MELOS
The Athenians predict ruin for Melos.

Such was the answer of the Melians. The Athenians now departing from the conference said, "Well, you alone, as it seems to us, judging from these resolutions, regard what is future as more certain than what is before your eyes, and what is out of sight, in your eagerness, as already coming to pass; and as you have staked most on, and trusted most in, the Spartans, your fortune, and your hopes, so will you be most completely deceived."

5.114
416
16th Year/Summer
MELOS
The Athenians begin their siege of Melos.

The Athenian envoys now returned to the army; and as the Melians showed no signs of yielding, the generals at once commenced hostilities, and built a wall around the Melians, dividing the work among the different states. [2] Subsequently the Athenians returned home with most of their army, leaving behind them a certain number of their own citizens and of the allies to keep guard by land and sea. The force thus left stayed on and besieged the place.

5.115
416
16th Year/Summer
PHLIUS
The Argives lose eighty men in an ambush.
PYLOS
Athenians from Pylos plunder so much from Sparta that she permits retaliation.
MELOS
The Melians sally out by night successfully

About the same time the Argives invaded the territory of Phlius[1a] and lost eighty men cut off in an ambush by the Phliasians and Argive exiles. [2] Meanwhile the Athenians at Pylos[2a] took so much plunder from the Spartans that the latter, although they still refrained from breaking off the treaty and going to war with Athens, yet proclaimed that any of their people that chose might plunder the Athenians. [3] The Corinthians also commenced hostilities with the Athenians for private quarrels of their own; but the rest of the Peloponnesians stayed quiet. [4] Meanwhile the Melians attacked by night and took the part of the Athenian lines near the market, and killed some of the men, and brought in corn and all else that they could find useful to them, and so returned and kept quiet, while the Athenians took measures to keep better guard in future.[4a] Summer was now over.

5.115.1a Phlius: Map 5.82, BX.
5.115.2a Pylos: Map 5.82, BX.
5.115.4a Melos: Map 5.82, BY.

5.116
416/5
16th Year/Winter
ARGOS
Sparta threatens Argos but withdraws.
MELOS
After some treachery, the Melians surrender. The men are executed, the women and children enslaved.

[illegible] partans intended to invade the Argive territory, bu[illegible] found the sacrifices for crossing unfavorable, and we[illegible] mpt of theirs made the Argives suspicious of certai[illegible], some of whom they arrested; others, however, es[illegible] the same time the Melians again took another pa[illegible] which were but feebly garrisoned. [3] Reinforceme[illegible] from Athens in consequence, under the comma[illegible] f Demeas, the siege was now pressed vigorously, an[illegible] place inside, the Melians surrendered at discretio[illegible] who put to death all the grown men whom they too[illegible] n and children for slaves, and subsequently sent ou[illegible] and settled the place themselves.

BOOK SIX

6.1
416/5
16th Year/Winter
ATHENS
The Athenians vote to attack Sicily, though most are ignorant of the island's size.

The same winter the Athenians resolved to [illegible] a greater armament than that under Laches and Eu[illegible]ible, to conquer the island; most of them being ign[illegible] the number of its inhabitants, Hellenic and barba[illegible] they were undertaking a war not much inferior to [illegible]onnesians. [2] For the voyage round Sicily in a me[illegible]hort of eight days; and yet, large as the island is, the[illegible] sea to prevent its being mainland.

6.2
SICILY
Thucydides describes the history of the settlement of barbarian peoples—Sicanians, Trojans, Sicels, and Phoenicians—in Sicily.

[illegible] as follows, and the peoples that occupied it are the[illegible]nts spoken of in any part of the country are the Cy[illegible]s; but I cannot tell of what race they were, or fro[illegible]o where they went, and must leave my readers to wh[illegible] them and to what may be generally known concer[illegible]anians appear to have been the next settlers, altho[illegible]ave been the first of all and aborigines; but the fac[illegible] Iberians, driven by the Ligurians from the river Sic[illegible]rom them that the island, before called Trinacria, too[illegible] and to the present day they inhabit the west of Sic[illegible] Ilium,[3a] some of the Trojans escaped from the Ac[illegible]o Sicily, and settled next to the Sicanians under the[illegible]i; their cities being called Eryx[3b] and Egesta.[3c] Wi[illegible] the Phocians carried on their way from Troy by a s[illegible]nd afterwards from there to Sicily. [4] The Sicels cro[illegible] their first home Italy,[4a] fleeing from the Opicans, as [illegible]ems not unlikely, upon rafts, having watched till the [illegible]he strait to make the passage; although perhaps

6.1[illegible]cator.
6.1[illegible].1, 3.90.2, [illegible] in Sicily, see [illegible]
6.2[illegible]

6.2.3a Ilium (Troy): Map 6.4, locator.
6.2.3b Eryx: Map 6.4, AX.
6.2.3c Egesta: Map 6.4, AX.
6.2.3d Libya: Map 6.4, locator.
6.2.4a Italy: Map 6.4, AY, locator.

they may have sailed over in some other way. Even at the present day there are still Sicels in Italy; and the country got its name of Italy from a king of the Sicels called Italus. [5] These went with a great host to Sicily, defeated the Sicanians in battle and forced them to withdraw to the south and west of the island, which thus came to be called Sicily instead of Sicania. After they crossed over, they continued to enjoy the richest parts of the country for nearly three hundred years before any Hellenes came to Sicily; indeed they still hold the center and north of the island. [6] There were also Phoenicians[6a] who had occupied promontories upon the sea coasts and nearby islands for the purpose of trading with the Sicels. But when the Hellenes began to arrive in considerable numbers by sea, the Phoenicians abandoned most of their stations, and drawing together took up their abode in Motya,[6b] Soloeis,[6c] and Panormus,[6d] near the Elymi, partly because they trusted in their alliance with them, and also because these are the nearest points for the voyage between Carthage[6e] and Sicily. These were the barbarians in Sicily, settled as I have said.

6.3
SICILY
The first Hellenes to settle in Sicily were Euboeans, who founded Naxos, Leontini, and Catana. The Dorians of Corinth settled Syracuse.

Of the Hellenes, the first to arrive were Chalcidians from Euboea[1a] with Thoucles, their founder. They founded Naxos[1b] and built the altar to Apollo Archegetes, which now stands outside the city, and upon which the deputies for the games sacrifice before sailing from Sicily. [2] Syracuse[2a] was founded the year afterwards by Archias, one of the Heraclids from Corinth,[2b] who began by driving out the Sicels from the island upon which the inner city now stands, though it is no longer surrounded by water: over time, the outer city also was enclosed within the walls and became populous. [3] Meanwhile Thoucles and the Chalcidians set out from Naxos in the fifth year after the foundation of Syracuse, and drove out the Sicels by arms and founded Leontini[3a] and afterwards Catana;[3b] the Catanians themselves choosing Evarchus as their founder.

6.4
SICILY
Thucydides reports the settlement of other principal Hellenic cities in Sicily: Thapsus, Hyblaean Megara, Selinus, Gela, Agrigentum, and Zancle which became Messana.

About the same time Lamis arrived in Sicily with a colony from Megara.[1a] He founded a place called Trotilus[1b] beyond the river Pantacyas,[1c] and afterwards left it and for a short while joined the Chalcidians at Leontini, but was driven out by them and founded Thapsus.[1d] After his death his companions were driven out of Thapsus, and founded a place called the Hyblaean Megara;[1e] Hyblon, a Sicel king, having given up the place and inviting them there. [2] Here they lived two hundred and forty-five years; after which they were expelled from the city and the country by the Syracusan tyrant Gelon. Before their expulsion, however, a hundred years after they had settled there, they sent out Pamillus and established Selinus;[2a] he

6.2.6a Phoenicia: Map 6.4, locator.
6.2.6b Motya: Map 6.4, AX.
6.2.6c Soloeis: Map 6.4, AX.
6.2.6d Panormus: Map 6.4, AX.
6.2.6e Carthage: Map 6.4, locator.
6.3.1a Chalcidians from Chalcis, Euboea: Map 6.4, Hellas.
6.3.1b Naxos, Sicily: Map 6.4, AY.
6.3.2a Syracuse: Map 6.4, BY.
6.3.2b Corinth: Map 6.4, Hellas.
6.3.3a Leontini: Map 6.4, BY.
6.3.3b Catana: Map 6.4, BY.
6.4.1a Megara: Map 6.4, Hellas.
6.4.1b Trotilus, possible location: Map 6.4, BY.
6.4.1c Pantacyas River, possible location: Map 6.4, BY.
6.4.1d Thapsus: Map 6.4, BY.
6.4.1e Megara Hyblaea: Map 6.4, BY.
6.4.2a Selinus: Map 6.4, AX.

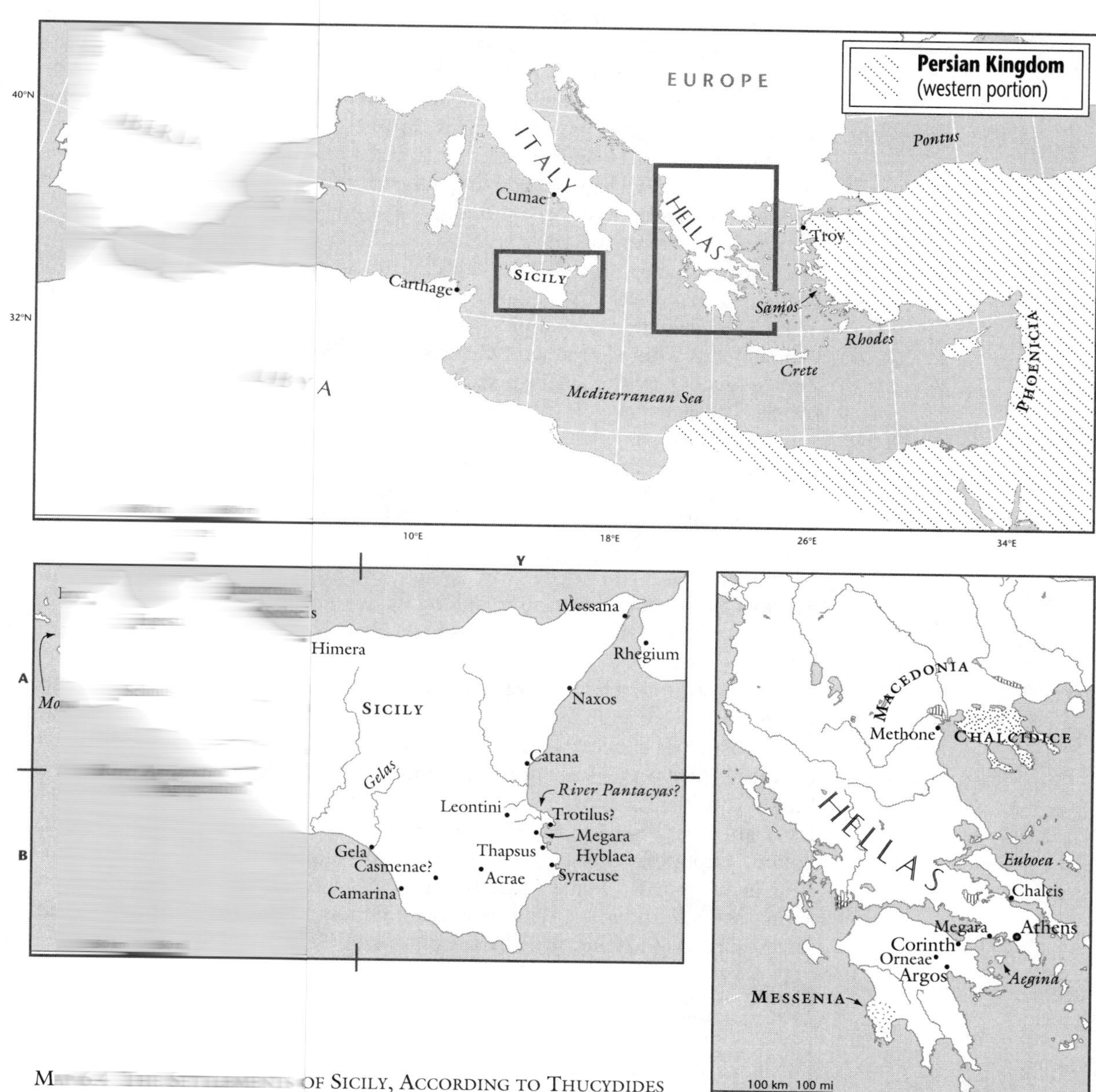

OF SICILY, ACCORDING TO THUCYDIDES

having come from their mother country Megara to join them in its foundation. [3] Gela[3a] was founded by Antiphemus from Rhodes[3b] and Entimus from Crete,[3c] who joined in leading a colony there, in the forty-fifth year after the foundation of Syracuse. The city took its name from the river Gelas,[3d] and the place which was first fortified, where the citadel now stands, was called Lindii. The institutions which they adopted were Dorian.[3e] [4] Nearly one hundred and eight years after the foundation of Gela, the Geloans founded Acragas[4a] (Agrigentum), so called from the river of that name, and made Aristonous and Pystilus their founders; giving their own institutions to the colony. [5] Zancle[5a] was originally founded by pirates from Cumae,[5b] the Chalcidian city in the country of the Opicans: afterwards, however, large numbers came from Chalcis and the rest of Euboea, and helped to people the place; the founders being Perieres and Crataemenes from Cumae and Chalcis respectively. It first had the name of Zancle given it by the Sicels, because the place is shaped like a sickle, which the Sicels call *zanclon*; but when the original settlers were later expelled by some Samians[5c] and other Ionians who landed in Sicily fleeing from the Persians,[5d] [6] and the Samians driven out in their turn not long afterwards by Anaxilas, tyrant of Rhegium,[6a] the city was by him colonized with a mixed population, and its name changed to Messana, after his old country.[6b]

6.5
SICILY
Thucydides recounts the founding of other Sicilian Greek cities: Himera, Acrae, Casmenae, and Camarina.

Himera[1a] was founded from Zancle by Euclides, Simus, and Sacon. Most of those who went to the colony were Chalcidians; though they were joined by some exiles from Syracuse who had been defeated in a civil war, called the Myletidae. The language was a mixture of Chalcidian and Doric, but the institutions which prevailed were the Chalcidian.[1b] [2] Acrae[2a] and Casmenae[2b] were founded by the Syracusans; Acrae seventy years after Syracuse, Casmenae nearly twenty after Acrae. [3] Camarina[3a] was first founded by the Syracusans, close upon a hundred and thirty-five years after the building of Syracuse; its founders being Dascon and Menecolus. But after the Camarinaeans were expelled by arms by the Syracusans for having revolted, Hippocrates, tyrant of Gela,[3b] who some time later received their land in ransom for some Syracusan prisoners, resettled Camarina, himself acting as its founder. Lastly, it was again depopulated by Gelon and settled once more for the third time by the people of Gela.

6.4.3a Gela: Map 6.4, BX.
6.4.3b Rhodes: Map 6.4, locator.
6.4.3c Crete: Map 6.4, locator.
6.4.3d Gelas River, Map 6.4, BX.
6.4.3e See Appendix H, Dialects and Ethnic Groups, for a brief description of the different ethnic and dialect groups into which the Greeks were divided.
6.4.4a Acragas (Agrigentum): Map 6.4, BX.
6.4.5a Zancle (Messana): Map 6.4, AY.
6.4.5b Cumae: Map 6.4, locator and Map 6.88.
6.4.5c Samos: Map 6.4, locator.
6.4.5d Persia, Map 6.4, locator. See Appendix E, The Persians, §3, for a description of Persia's expansion into Asian Ionia.
6.4.6a Rhegium: Map 6.4, AY.
6.4.6b His "old country" was Messenia in Peloponnesus (Map 6.4, Hellas).
6.5.1a Himera: Map 6.4, AX.
6.5.1b See Appendix H, Dialects and Ethnic Groups, §3, for a discussion of the Dorians.
6.5.2a Acrae: Map 6.4, BY.
6.5.2b Casmenae, possible location: Map 6.4, BY.
6.5.3a Camarina: Map 6.4, BX.
6.5.3b Gela: Map 6.4, BX.

eoples, Hellenic and barbarian, inhabiting Sicily,
an f the island which the Athenians were now bent
up itious in real truth[1a] of conquering the whole, al-
th specious design of aiding their kindred and other
all ut they were especially incited by envoys from
Eg to Athens and invoked their aid more urgently
th had gone to war with their neighbors the Selin-
un f marriage and disputed territory, and the Selin-
un alliance of the Syracusans,[2c] and pressed Egesta
ha Egestaeans now reminded the Athenians of the
all of Laches, during the former Leontine war,[2d] and
be eet to their aid. Their main argument, among a
nu ations urged, was that if the Syracusans were al-
lo for their depopulation of Leontini,[2e] to ruin the
all Sicily, and to get the whole power of the island
int uld be a danger of their one day coming with a
lar ne aid of their Dorian brethren,[2f] and as colonists,
to esians who had sent them out, and joining these
in nian empire. The Athenians would, therefore, do
we es still left to them, and to make a stand against
th as they, the Egestaeans, were prepared to furnish
m war. [3] The Athenians, hearing these arguments
co ir assemblies[3a] by the Egestaeans and their sup-
pc d envoys to Egesta, to see if there was really the
m f in the treasury and temples,[3b] and at the same
tir about the war with the Selinuntines.

6.6
416/5
16th Year/Winter
ATHENS
Egestan envoys seek help at Athens for their war with Selinus. They warn of potential Syracusan domination of Sicily and aid to Sparta, and promise to pay Athens' war expenses in Sicily. The Athenians send envoys to Egesta.

nians were accordingly dispatched to Sicily. That
sa s and their allies (except for the Corinthians),
m erritory,[1a] ravaged a small part of the land, took
so carried off some grain. They also settled the Ar-
gi d left them a few soldiers taken from the rest of

6.7
416/5
16th Year/Winter
ARGOS
The Spartans plunder Argos and settle exiles in Orneae. Reinforced by Athens, Argos demolishes Orneae.
MACEDONIA
The Athenians, joined by Macedonian exiles, ravage Macedonia. Sparta fails to persuade the Chalcidians to join Perdiccas against Athens.

6.6 n real truth"
hich he trans-

6.6
6.6
6.6
6.6 g to the
y in 427–26
in 3.86,
d 3.115–16.
n 3.86. The
aeans now re-
e alliance with
ng the former
ect transla-
envoys could
hat had been
, as some
Introduction

6.6.2e Leontini: Map 6.4, BY.

6.6.2f Dorian: see Appendix H, Dialects and Ethnic Groups, for a brief description of the groups into which the Greeks were divided.

6.6.3a Athenian assemblies are briefly discussed in Appendix A, The Athenian Government, §8.

6.6.3b Offerings of silver and gold objects and other valuable material accumulated at major temples and shrines to such a degree that these institutions became unique and tempting repositories of ready capital in ancient Greece. In 2.13.4–5, Pericles lists the vast wealth lying in Athenian temples and shrines that could be called upon, if necessary, to support the war.

6.7.1a Argos: Map 6.4, Hellas.

6.7.1b Orneae: Map 6.4, Hellas.

the army, and after making a truce for a certain period, according to which neither Orneatae nor Argives were to injure each other's territory, returned home with the army. [2] Not long afterwards the Athenians came with thirty ships and six hundred *hoplites*,[2a] and the Argives joining them with all their forces, marched out and besieged the men in Orneae for one day; but the garrison escaped by night, the besiegers having camped some way off. The next day the Argives, discovering this, razed Orneae to the ground, and went back again; after which the Athenians went home in their ships. [3] Meanwhile the Athenians took some cavalry of their own and the Macedonian exiles that were at Athens by sea to Methone[3a] on the Macedonian[3b] border and plundered the country of Perdiccas. [4] Upon this the Spartans sent to the Thracian Chalcidians,[4a] who had a truce with Athens from one ten days to another, urging them to join Perdiccas in the war, which they refused to do. And the winter ended, and with it ended the sixteenth year of this war of which Thucydides is the historian.

6.8
415
17th Year/Summer
ATHENS
Athenian envoys return from Egesta with favorable (but untrue) reports. Athens votes to send a fleet to Sicily to assist Egesta, restore Leontini, and order Sicilian affairs to suit Athens' interests.

Early in the spring of the following summer the Athenian envoys arrived from Sicily, and the Egestaeans[1a] with them, bringing the sixty *talents*[1b] of uncoined silver, as a month's pay for sixty ships, which they were to ask to have sent to them. [2] The Athenians held an assembly, and after hearing from the Egestaeans and their own envoys a report, as attractive as it was untrue, upon the state of affairs generally, and in particular as to the money, of which, it was said, there was abundance in the temples and the treasury, voted to send sixty ships to Sicily, under the command of Alcibiades son of Clinias, Nicias son of Niceratus, and Lamachus son of Xenophanes, who were appointed with full powers;[2a] they were to help the Egestaeans against the Selinuntines,[2b] to restore Leontini[2c] upon gaining any advantage in the war, and to order all other matters in Sicily as they should deem best for the interests of Athens. [3] Five days after this a second assembly was held, to consider the speediest means of equipping the ships, and to vote whatever else might be required by the generals for the expedition. [4] Nicias, who had been chosen to the command against his will, and who thought that the state was not well advised, but upon a slight and specious pretext was aspiring to the conquest of the whole of Sicily, a great matter to achieve, came forward in the hope of diverting the Athenians from the enterprise, and gave them the following counsel:

6.9
415
17th Year/Summer
ATHENS
Nicias speaks to Athens' assembly to dissuade the Athenians from the Sicilian expedition.

"Although this assembly was convened to consider the preparations to be made for sailing to Sicily, I think, notwithstanding, that we should still examine whether it be better to send out the ships at

6.7.2a *Hoplite* is the Greek word for a heavily armed infantryman. See Appendix F, Land Warfare, §2.
6.7.3a Methone in Macedonia: Map 6.4, Hellas. Perdiccas was the king of Macedonia.
6.7.3b Macedonia: Map 6.4, Hellas.
6.7.4a Chalcidice in Thrace: Map 6.4, Hellas.
6.8.1a Egesta: Map 6.4, AX.
6.8.1b The *talent* was a unit of weight and of money; see Appendix J, Classical Greek Currency, §5.
6.8.2a By "full powers" was meant that the generals could decide matters for themselves without referring back to Athens, but decide only within stated terms of reference. Cf. the situation in 5.45.
6.8.2b Selinus: Map 6.4, AX.
6.8.2c Leontini: Map 6.4, BY.

to give so little consideration to a matter of
selves be persuaded by foreigners into under-
we have nothing to do. [2] And yet, individ-
y such a course, and fear as little as other men
t I think a man need be any the worse citizen
ht for his person and estate; on the contrary,
his own sake desire the prosperity of his coun-
—nevertheless, as I have never spoken against
honor, I shall not begin to do so now, but
best. [3] Against your character any words of
nough; particularly if I were to advise you to
d not risk it for advantages which are dubious
ch you may or may not attain. I will, there-
ith showing that your ardor is untimely, and
y accomplished."

6.10
415
17th Year/Summer
ATHENS
Nicias argues that it is imprudent to attack Sicily while affairs nearer home are still precarious. He emphasizes the fragility of the current peace, since many enemies await an opportune moment to attack Athens again, and points out that rebels in Chalcidice have not yet been subdued.

t you leave many enemies behind you here to
bring more back with you. [2] You imagine,
y[2a] which you have made can be trusted; a
ue to exist nominally, as long as you keep
has become, owing to the practices of certain
a—but which in the event of a serious reverse
not delay our enemies a moment in attacking
onvention was forced upon them by disaster
to them than to us; and secondly, because in
ere are many points that are still disputed. [3]
st powerful states have never yet accepted the
ne of these are at open war with us; others (as
yet move) are restrained by truces renewed
it is only too probable that if they found our
re hurrying to divide it, they would attack us
eliots, whose alliance they would have in the
ould that of few others. [5] A man ought,
hese points, and not to think of running risks
so critically, or of grasping at another empire
d the one we have already; for in fact the
have been all these years in revolt from us
dued, and others on the mainland[5a] yield us
ence. Meanwhile the Egestaeans, our allies,
d we run to help them, while the rebels who

6.1 re is the fifty-
s and Sparta

6.1 t be referring

have so long wronged us still wait for punishment."

6.11
415
17th Year/Summer
ATHENS
Nicias says that Sicily is too far away to be permanently subdued, and that the Sicilians, even if united under Syracuse, are most unlikely to attack the Athenian empire. He argues that Athens' reputation is higher in Sicily because it is untested, and will decline immediately after the first reverse. He points out that Sparta is still the main threat to Athens.

"And yet the latter, if brought under might be kept under; while the Sicilians, even if conquered, are too far off and too numerous to be ruled without difficulty. Now it is folly to go against men who could not be kept under even if conquered, while failure would leave us in a very different position from that which we occupied before the enterprise. [2] The Sicilians, again, to take them as they are at present, in the event of a Syracusan conquest (which the Egestaeans most use to frighten us), would to my thinking be even less dangerous to us than before. [3] At present they might possibly come here as separate states for love of Sparta; in the other case one empire would scarcely attack another; for after joining the Peloponnesians to overthrow ours, they could only expect to see the same hands overthrow their own in the same way. [4] The Hellenes in Sicily would fear us most if we never went there at all, and next to this, if after displaying our power we went away again as soon as possible. We all know that which is farthest off and the reputation of which can least be tested, is the object of admiration; at the least reverse to us they would at once begin to look down upon us, and would join our enemies here against us. [5] You have yourselves experienced this with regard to the Spartans and their allies, whom your unexpected success, as compared with what you feared at first, has made you suddenly despise, tempting you further to aspire to the conquest of Sicily. [6] Instead, however, of being puffed up by the misfortunes of your adversaries, you ought to think of breaking their spirit before giving yourselves up to confidence, and to understand that the one thought awakened in the Spartans by their disgrace is how they may even now, if possible, overthrow us and repair their dishonor; inasmuch as they have for a very long time devoted themselves to the cultivation of military renown above all. [7] Our struggle therefore, if we are wise, will not be for the barbarian Egestaeans[7a] in Sicily, but to defend ourselves most effectively against the oligarchic machinations of Sparta."

6.12
415
17th Year/Summer
ATHENS
Nicias reminds the Athenians that having only recently suffered plague and war, they should use the respite properly and not be swayed by young hotbloods whose leader may be eager for command and desperate to cover the expenses of his private life.

"We should also remember that we are only now enjoying some respite from a great pestilence and from war, to the no small benefit of our estates and persons, and that it is right to employ these at home on our own behalf, instead of using them on behalf of these exiles[1a] whose interest it is to lie as well as they can, who do nothing but talk themselves and leave the danger to others, and who if they

6.11.7a It is only here and at 6.2.3 that it plainly emerges that the Egestaeans are not Greek.

6.12.1a Nicias refers to the Leontines exiled in 422; see 5.4.3 and 6.19.1.

roper gratitude, and if they fail will drag down [2] And if there be any man here, overjoyed mmand, who urges you to make the expedi- his own—especially if he is still too young to to be admired for his stud of horses, but on nses hopes for some profit from his appoint- h a one to maintain his private splendor at his ember that such persons injure the public for- er their own, and that this is a matter of im- a young man to decide or hastily to take in

6.13
415
17th Year/Summer
ATHENS
Nicias calls on the older men to curb the enthusiasm of the young, asserting that Athens should not help allies who could not help Athens in turn, and who did not consult Athens when they went to war with their neighbors.

persons now sitting here at the side of that mmoned by him, alarm seizes me; and I, in of the older men that may have such a person let himself be checked by shame, for fear of d if he does not vote for war, but, remember- is gained by wishing and how often by fore- he mad dream of conquest, and as a true lover eatened by the greatest danger in its history, the other side to vote that the Sicilians be left ng between us—limits of which no one can ea for the coasting voyage[1a] and the Sicilian —to enjoy their own possessions and to settle Let the Egestaeans, for their part, be told to war with the Selinuntines which they began Athenians; and that for the future we do not ve have been used to do, with people whom eed, and who can never help us in ours."

6.14
415
17th Year/Summer
ATHENS
Nicias concludes by asking for a second vote on the Sicilian expedition.

,[1a] if you think it your duty to care for the you wish to show yourself a good citizen, put e, and take a second time the opinions of the raid to move the question again, consider that cannot with so many abettors, incur any e the physician of your misguided city, and in office is briefly this, to do their country as or in any case no harm that they can avoid."

6.1 the narrowest Map 6.20. See e, §7, for an were forced y ventured to the open

6.1 est from the hant vessels.

6.1 ouncil who chairman.

He was normally termed the *Epistates*, not the *Prytanis*. He was a member of the *Prytaneis*, a group that acted as a standing committee for both the council and the assembly during the tenth of the year that it was each tribe's turn to "preside." (See Appendix A, The Athenian Government, §5.) Whether it was illegal for the *Epistates* to put to the vote a matter previously decided, as would seem to be the case here, has been disputed.

6.15
415
17th Year/Summer
ATHENS
How the character and habits of Alcibiades, who now comes forward to speak in favor of the expedition, caused Athens to distrust him as a potential tyrant and contributed to Athens' eventual ruin.

Such were the words of Nicias.[1a] Most of the Athenians who came forward spoke in favor of the expedition and of not annulling what had been voted, although some spoke on the other side. [2] By far the warmest advocate of the expedition was, however, Alcibiades son of Clinias, who wished to thwart Nicias both as his political opponent and also because of the attack he had made upon him in his speech, and who was, besides, exceedingly ambitious of a command by which he hoped to reduce Sicily[2a] and Carthage,[2b] and personally to gain in wealth and reputation by means of his successes. [3] For the position he held among the citizens led him to indulge his tastes beyond what his real means would bear, both in keeping horses and in the rest of his expenditure; and this later on had not a little to do with the ruin of the Athenian state. [4] Alarmed at the greatness of the license in his own life and habits, and at the ambition which he showed in all things whatsoever that he undertook, the mass of the people marked him as an aspirant to the tyranny and became his enemies; and although in his public life his conduct of the war was as good as could be desired, in his private life his habits gave offense to everyone, and caused them to commit affairs to other hands, and thus before long to ruin the city.[4a] [5] Meanwhile he now came forward and gave the following advice to the Athenians:

6.16
415
17th Year/Summer
ATHENS
Alcibiades speaks to the assembly, asserting his right to command the Sicilian expedition. He argues that the magnificence of his private life has added to Athens' prestige abroad, that his arrogance should be accepted as properly based on excellence, and that he deserves credit for having formed the recent coalition against Sparta.

"Athenians, I have a better right to command than others—I must begin with this as Nicias has attacked me—and at the same time I believe myself to be worthy of it. The things for which I am abused bring fame to my ancestors and to myself, and also profit to my country. [2] The Hellenes, after expecting to see our city ruined by the war, concluded it to be even greater than it really is, by reason of the magnificence with which I represented it at the Olympic games,[2a] when I sent into the lists seven chariots, a number never before entered by any private person, and won the first prize, and was second and fourth, and took care to have everything else in a style worthy of my victory. Custom regards such displays as honorable, and they cannot be made without leaving behind them an impression of power. [3] Again, any splendor that I may have exhibited at home in providing choruses or otherwise, is naturally envied by my fellow citizens, but in the eyes of foreigners has an air of strength as in the other instance. And this is no useless folly, when a man at his own private cost benefits not himself only, but his city: [4] nor is it unfair that he who prides himself on his position should refuse to be upon an equality with the rest. He who is badly off has his misfortunes all to

6.15.1a See the Introduction (sect. II.v) for a discussion of speeches in Thucydides.
6.15.2a Sicily: Map 6.20.
6.15.2b Carthage: Map 6.20. Regarding the plan to conquer it, see 6.90.2.
6.15.4a Since Thucydides seems here to refer Athens' defeat in the Peloponnesian War, it has been thought that 6.16.3 and 4 were inserted after 404 BC.
6.16.2a Alcibiades refers to the Olympic Games of 416 B.C. See Appendix I, Religious Festivals, §5, 8.

not see men courted in adversity, on the like
to accept the insolence of prosperity; or else,
qual measure to all, and then demand to have
] What I know is that persons of this kind and
ined to any distinction, although they may be
ime in their relations with their fellow men
r equals, leave to posterity the desire of claim-
em even without any ground, and are vaunted
h they belonged, not as strangers or evildoers,
nen and heroes. [6] Such are my aspirations,
sed for them in my private life, the question is
ges public affairs better than I do. Having
ful states of the Peloponnesus, without great
ou, I compelled the Spartans to stake their all
gle day at Mantinea;[6a] and although victorious
never since fully recovered confidence."

6.17
415
17th Year/Summer
ATHENS
Alcibiades bids the Athenians to make use of his youthful energy and Nicias' good fortune together in command. He argues that the Sicilians are politically weak and will be easily divided; that barbarians will help the Athenians, and that the Spartans, whose navy will remain inferior to the Athenian fleet left at home, will be unable to injure Athens during the Sicilian expedition.

h and so-called monstrous folly find fitting ar-
the power of the Peloponnesians, and by its
ence and prevail. And do not be afraid of my
I am still in its flower, and Nicias appears for-
to the utmost of the services of us both. [2]
nd your resolution to sail to Sicily, on the
d be going to attack a great power. The cities
y motley rabbles, and easily change their insti-
ones in their stead; [3] and consequently the
hout any feeling of patriotism, are not provided
rsons, and have not regularly established them-
ery man thinks that either by fair words or by
ain something at the public expense, and then
rophe settle in some other country, and makes
dingly. [4] From a mob like this you need not
nity in counsel or unity in action; but they will
come in as they get a fair offer, especially if they
as we are told. [5] Moreover, the Sicilians have
as they boast; just as the Hellenes generally did
ous as each state reckoned itself, but Hellas
their numbers, and has hardly had an adequate
ughout this war. [6] The states in Sicily, there-
can hear, will be found as I say, and I have not
dvantages, for we shall have the help of many

6 attle of Manti-

barbarians, who from their hatred of the Syracusans will join us in attacking them; nor will the powers at home prove any hindrance, if you judge rightly. [7] Our fathers with these same adversaries, which it is said we shall now leave behind us when we sail, and the Mede[7a] as their enemy as well, were able to win the empire, depending solely on their superiority at sea. [8] The Peloponnesians have never had so little hope against us as at present; and let them be ever so optimistic, although strong enough to invade our country even if we stay at home, they can never hurt us with their navy, as we leave one of our own behind us that is a match for them."

6.18
415
17th Year/Summer
ATHENS
Alcibiades argues that Athens must help its allies—if only to extend its empire further. He claims that to sit and enjoy what it has, as Nicias advises, will risk atrophy and the loss of her present empire. He concludes by urging the Athenians to unite in support of the Sicilian expedition which, if it should fail to achieve a permanent conquest, will certainly injure Syracuse, increase Athens' prestige, and incur little risk of loss due to Athens' naval superiority.

"In this state of affairs what reason can we give to ourselves for holding back, or what excuse can we offer to our allies in Sicily for not helping them? They are our confederates, and we are bound to assist them, without objecting that they have not assisted us. We did not take them into alliance to have them help us in Hellas, but that they might so annoy our enemies in Sicily as to prevent them from coming over here and attacking us. [2] It is thus that empire has been won, both by us and by all others that have held it, by a constant readiness to support all, whether barbarians or Hellenes, that invite assistance; since if all were to keep quiet or to pick and choose whom they ought to assist, we should make but few new conquests, and should imperil those we have already won. Men do not rest content with parrying the attacks of a superior, but often strike the first blow to prevent the attack being made. [3] Moreover, we cannot fix the exact point at which our empire shall stop; we have reached a position in which we must not be content with retaining what we have but must scheme to extend it for, if we cease to rule others, we shall be in danger of being ruled ourselves. Nor can you look at inaction from the same point of view as others, unless you are prepared to change your habits and make them resemble theirs."

[4] "Be convinced then that we shall augment our power at home by this adventure abroad, and let us make the expedition, and so humble the pride of the Peloponnesians by sailing off to Sicily, and letting them see how little we care for the peace that we are now enjoying. At the same time we shall either become masters, as we very easily may, of the whole of Hellas through the accession of the Sicilian Hellenes, or in any case ruin the Syracusans, to the no small advantage of ourselves and our allies. [5] Our ability to stay if successful, or to return if not, will be secured to us by our navy, as we shall be superior at sea to all the Sicilians put together. [6] And do not let the passive policy which Nicias advocates, or his setting of the

6.17.7a By "Mede," Alcibiades means here the Persians; see Appendix E, The Persians, §1.

urn you from your purpose, but in the good
ur fathers, old and young together, by their
t our affairs to their present height, do you
e them; understanding that neither youth nor
g the one without the other, but that levity,
judgment are strongest when united, and
action, the city, like everything else, will wear
n everything decay; while each fresh struggle
ence, and make it more used to defend itself
d. [7] In short, my conviction is that a city
could not choose a quicker way to ruin itself
ting such a policy, and that the safest rule of
haracter and institutions for better and for
them as closely as one can."

of Alcibiades. After hearing him and the Eges- 6.19
tae exiles, who came forward reminding them of 415
the their assistance, the Athenians became more 17th Year/Summer
ea than before. [2] Nicias, perceiving that it would ATHENS
no ter them by the old line of argument, but think- Nicias tries again to deter the Athenians from the Sicilian expedition.
ing alter their resolution by the extravagance of his
est second time and spoke as follows:

at you are thoroughly bent upon the expedi- 6.20
e that all will turn out as we wish, and I pro- 415
pinion at the present juncture. [2] From all 17th Year/Summer
g against cities that are great and not subject ATHENS
eed of change, so as to wish to pass from en- Nicias describes the Hellenic cities of Sicily as independent, politically stable, formidable powers that will resist Athenian forces.
asier condition, or be in the least likely to ac-
ge for freedom; and, to take only the Hellenic
nerous for one island. [3] Besides Naxos and
to join us from their connection with Leon-
thers armed in every way just like our own
nus and Syracuse,[3a] the main objectives of our
re full of hoplites, archers, and dart throwers,
ance and multitudes to man them; they also
he hands of private persons, partly in the tem-
yracuse tribute of first-fruits from some of the
their chief advantage over us lies in the num-
in the fact that they grow their grain at home
"

6.2 linus, Syra-

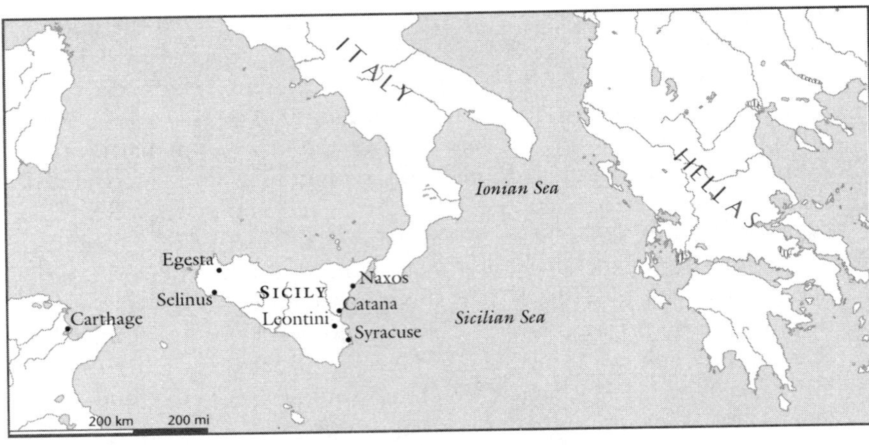

MAP 6.20 KEY SICILIAN CITIES

6.21
415
17th Year/Summer
ATHENS
Nicias argues that because of Sicily's strength and its great distance from Athens, the Athenian expedition must be very powerful in order to obviate the need to send more forces later or to avoid a disgraceful withdrawal.

"Against a power of this kind it will not do to have merely a weak naval armament, but we shall want also a large land army to sail with us, if we are to do anything worthy of our ambition and are not to be shut out from the country by a numerous cavalry; especially if the cities should take alarm and combine, and we should be left without friends (except the Egestaeans) to furnish us with cavalry with which to defend ourselves. [2] It would be disgraceful to have to retire under compulsion, or to send back for reinforcements, owing to want of reflection at first. We must therefore start from home with a competent force, seeing that we are going to sail far from our country, and upon an expedition not like any which you may have undertaken in the quality of allies. Among your subject states here in Hellas, any additional supplies needed are easily drawn from the friendly territory; but we are cutting ourselves off, and going to a land entirely strange, from which during four months in winter it is not even easy for a messenger to get to Athens."

6.22
415
17th Year/Summer
ATHENS
Nicias says the expedition should be strong in all arms, recruited from Athens as well as the empire, and include mercenary troops too. He demands that it be well provisioned and financed.

"I think, therefore, that we ought to take great numbers of hoplites, both from Athens and from our allies, and not merely from our subjects,[1a] but also any we may be able to get for love or for money in the Peloponnesus, and great numbers also of archers and slingers, to oppose the Sicilian horse. Meanwhile we must have an overwhelming superiority at sea to enable us the more easily to carry in what we want; and we must take our own grain in merchant vessels, that is to say, wheat and roasted barley, and bakers from the mills compelled to serve for pay in the proper proportion; so that if

6.22.1a See 7.57 for a list by status of the allies who came with the Athenians to Sicily. See 2.7.3.

und the armament may not lack provisions, as will be able to sustain numbers like ours. We elves with everything else as far as we can, so upon others; and above all we must take with money as possible, as the sums talked of as eadier, you may be sure, in talk than in any

leave Athens with a force not only equal to pt in the number of hoplites in the field, but or to him, we shall still find it difficult to con- selves. [2] We must not disguise from our- ind a city among strangers and enemies, and such an enterprise should be prepared to be- ntry the first day he lands, or failing in this to o him. [3] Fearing this, and knowing that we h good counsel and more good fortune—a men to aspire to—I wish as much as possible dent of fortune before sailing, and when I do rong force can make me. This I believe to be t large, and safest for us who are to go on the thinks differently I resign to him my com-

6.23 415 17th Year/Summer ATHENS Nicias reiterates how difficult and dangerous the expedition's mission will be and concludes that it must have overwhelming power in order to succeed.

ded, thinking that he should either put the Athe- nia of the undertaking or, if obliged to sail on the ex so in the safest way possible. [2] The Athenians, ho their enthusiasm for the voyage destroyed by the bu eparations, became more eager for it than ever; an place of what Nicias had thought, as it was held th vice, and that the expedition would be the safest in fell in love with the enterprise. The older men th ither subdue the places against which they were to so large a force, meet with no disaster; those in th ing for foreign sights and spectacles, and had no do me safe home again; while the idea of the com- m ry was to earn wages at the moment, and make co ly a never-ending fund of pay for the future. [4] Wi e majority, the few that did not like it feared to ap ng up their hands against it, and so kept quiet.

6.24 415 17th Year/Summer ATHENS Although Nicias intended to deter the Athenians from such a huge undertaking, his speech actually fuels enthusiasm for the expedition.

nians came forward and called upon Nicias and tol ot to make excuses or put them off, but say at on forces the Athenians should vote him. [2] Upon

6.25 415 17th Year/Summer ATHENS Nicias says Athens must send one hundred triremes, transports, five thousand hoplites, and other arms in proportion.

6.2

this he said, not without reluctance, that he would advise upon that matter more at leisure with his colleagues; as far however as he could see at present, they must sail with at least one hundred triremes—the Athenians providing as many transports as they might determine, and sending for others from the allies—not less than five thousand hoplites in all, Athenian and allied, and if possible more; and the rest of the armament in proportion; archers from home and from Crete, and slingers, and whatever else might seem desirable, being made ready by the generals and taken with them.

6.26
415
17th Year/Summer
ATHENS
Athens votes the generals full powers to recruit the force they deem necessary.

Upon hearing this the Athenians at once voted that the generals should have full powers[1a] in the matter of the numbers of the army and of the expedition generally, to do as they judged best for the interests of Athens. [2] After this the preparations began; messages being sent to the allies and the enlistment rolls drawn up at home. And as the city had just recovered from the plague and the long war, and a number of young men had grown up and capital had accumulated by reason of the peace, everything was the more easily provided.

6.27
415
17th Year/Summer
ATHENS
The city's Hermae are all mysteriously mutilated; this event is deemed ominous for the expedition to Sicily.

In the midst of these preparations all the stone Hermae in the city of Athens, that is to say the customary square figures so common in the doorways of private houses and temples, had in one night most of them their faces mutilated. [2] No one knew who had done it, but large public rewards were offered to find those responsible; and it was further voted that anyone who knew of any other act of impiety having been committed should come and give information without fear of consequences, whether he were citizen, alien, or slave. [3] The matter was taken up the more seriously, as it was thought to be ominous for the expedition, and part of a conspiracy to bring about a revolution and to upset the democracy.

6.28
415
17th Year/Summer
ATHENS
An inquiry into the blasphemy implicates Alcibiades. His enemies magnify his role, claiming that he is scheming to overthrow the democracy.

Information was accordingly given by some resident aliens and body servants, not about the Hermae but of some previous mutilations of other images perpetrated by young men in a drunken frolic, and of mock celebrations of the Mysteries,[1a] alleged to have taken place in private houses. [2] When Alcibiades was implicated in this charge, it was taken up by those who could least endure him, because he stood in the way of their obtaining the undisturbed leadership of The People, and who thought that if he were once removed the first place would be theirs. These accordingly magnified the matter and loudly proclaimed that the affair of the Mysteries and the mutilation of the Hermae were part and parcel of a scheme to overthrow the democracy, and that nothing of all this had been done without Alcibiades; the proofs alleged being the general and undemocratic license of his life and habits.

6.26.1a For the meaning of "full powers," see note 6.8.2a.

6.28.1a The Mysteries were religious ceremonies celebrated twice a year at Eleusis in Attica (Map 4.69). Only those who had been solemnly initiated were permitted to share the secret of what happened, and to profane these sacred rites by divulging their content or mocking them was a most grievous offense.

6.29
415
17th Year/Summer
ATHENS
Alcibiades demands a trial on all charges to clear his name before the expedition sails. His foes, fearing the army's support for him, succeed in postponing a trial though they plot to recall him later.

denied the charges in question, and also offered
to oing on the expedition (for which the prepara-
tio , so that it might be determined whether he was
gu to him; as he was willing to be punished if found
gu tted, to take the command. [2] Meanwhile he
pr ceiving slanders against him in his absence, and
be ut him to death at once if he were guilty, and
po ce of sending him out at the head of so large an
arı arge still undecided. [3] But his enemies feared
th: rmy's support if he were tried immediately, and
th: ent in favor of the man and protect him as the
cau ome of the Mantineans joining in the expedition,
an have this proposition rejected, putting forward
ot t he ought at present to sail and not delay the depa be tried on his return within a fixed number of
da ave him sent for and brought home for trial upon
so they would the more easily trump up in his ab-
ser decreed that he should sail.[3a]

6.30
415
17th Year/Summer
ATHENS
Their preparations now complete, the Athenian forces go to the Piraeus to man the ships. The citizenry bid farewell to the fleet. Many allies muster at Corcyra.

e for Sicily took place, it being now about mid-
su s, with the grain transports and the smaller craft
an tion, had already received orders to assemble at
Cc nian sea[1b] from there in a body to the Iapygian
pr thenians themselves, and such of their allies as
ha m, went down to the Piraeus[1d] upon a day ap-
po began to man the ships for putting out to sea.
[2 the whole population, one may say, of the city,
bc rs; the inhabitants of the country each escorting
th hem, their friends, their relatives, or their sons,
wi on upon their way, as they thought of the con-
qu to make, or of the friends whom they might
ne ng the long voyage which they were going to
m .31.1] Indeed, at this moment, when they were

6.31
415
17th Year/Summer
ATHENS
The Athenians now become aware of the danger and magnitude of their expedition, but they are comforted by the unprecedented wealth and magnificence of the fleet.

nc arting from one another, the danger came home
to they had voted for the expedition; although the
str , and the profuse provision which they observed
in a sight that could not but comfort them. As for
th t of the crowd, they simply went to see a sight
wc ing all belief. [2] Indeed this armament that first
sai most costly and splendid Hellenic force that had
ev single city up to that time. In mere number of

6.2 nd the affair
rmae in 6.53.
6.3
6.3
6.30.1c Iapygian promontory (Cape Iapygium): Map 6.38, AX.
6.30.1d Piraeus: Map 6.38, inset.

ships and hoplites that against Epidaurus[2a] under Pericles, and the same fleet when it was going against Potidaea[2b] under Hagnon, was not inferior; containing as it did four thousand Athenian hoplites, three hundred horse, and one hundred triremes accompanied by fifty Lesbian[2c] and Chian[2d] vessels and many allies besides. [3] But these were sent upon a short voyage and with scanty equipment. The present expedition was formed in contemplation of a long term of service by land and sea alike, and was furnished with ships and troops so as to be ready for either as required. The fleet had been elaborately equipped at great cost to the captains and the state; the treasury giving a *drachma*[3a] a day to each seaman, and providing empty ships, sixty warships and forty transports, and manning these with the best crews obtainable; while the captains gave a bounty in addition to the pay from the treasury to the *thranitae* and crews generally,[3b] besides spending lavishly upon figureheads and equipments, and one and all making the utmost exertions to enable their own ships to excel in beauty and fast sailing. Meanwhile the land forces had been picked from the best enlistment rolls, and vied with each other in attention to their arms and personal accouterments. [4] From this resulted not only a rivalry among themselves in their different departments, but an idea among the rest of the Hellenes that it was more a display of power and resources than an armament against an enemy. [5] For if anyone had counted up the public expenditure of the state, and the private outlay of individuals—that is to say, the sums which the state had already spent upon the expedition and was sending out in the hands of the generals, and those sums which individuals had expended upon their personal outfit, or as captains of triremes had laid out and were still to lay out upon their vessels; and if he had added to this the journey money which each was likely to have provided himself with, independently of the pay from the treasury, for a voyage of such length, and what the soldiers or traders took with them for the purpose of exchange—it would have been found that many talents in all were being taken out of the city. [6] Indeed the expedition became not less famous for its wonderful boldness and for the splendor of its appearance, than for its overwhelming strength as compared with the peoples against whom it was directed, and for the fact that this was the longest passage from home hitherto attempted, and the most ambitious in its objectives considering the resources of those who undertook it.

6.32
415
17th Year/Summer
ATHENS
The fleet departs with proper ceremony.
SYRACUSE
At Syracuse, many doubt the Athenian threat. Hermocrates rises to speak to the assembly.

The ships being now manned, and everything put on board with which they meant to sail, the trumpet commanded silence, and the prayers customary before putting out to sea were offered, not in each ship by itself, but by all together to the voice of a herald; and bowls of wine were mixed

6.31.2a Epidaurus: Map 6.38, inset. This expedition is mentioned in 2.56.3 and 2.58.3.
6.31.2b Potidaea: Map 6.38, AY.
6.31.2c Lesbos: Map 6.38, AY.
6.31.2d Chios: Map 6.38, AY.
6.31.3a The *drachma* is a unit of currency. See Appendix J, Classical Greek Currency, §3.
6.31.3b For the role of the captains and the skilled crewmen in the Athenian navy, and of the different classes of oarsmen, such as *thranitae,* see note 1.31.1a and Appendix G, Trireme Warfare, §5, 12.

thr[illegible] and libations made by the soldiers and their of-
fic[illegible] oblets. [2] They were joined in their prayers by
the[illegible] e citizens and all others who wished them well.
Th[illegible] ibations finished, they put out to sea, and first
sai[illegible] raced each other as far as Aegina,[2a] and so has-
ter[illegible] where the rest of the allied forces were also assem[illegible]

[illegible] use news of the expedition came in from many
qu[illegible] ile met with no credence whatsoever. Indeed, an
ass[illegible] n speeches, as will be seen, were delivered by differ[illegible] contradicting the report of the Athenian expedi-
tio[illegible] nocrates son of Hermon came forward, being
pe[illegible] he truth of the matter, and gave the following
co[illegible]

6.33 415 17th Year/Summer SYRACUSE Hermocrates warns that Athens is about to attack Syracuse, but stresses the difficulties they face and the favorable position Syracuse holds. The great size of their expedition, for example, will frighten other Sicilians and induce them to unite with Syracuse. Logistical difficulties alone may defeat them, without Syracusan effort, but to her ultimate renown.

[illegible] erhaps be no better believed than others have
[illegible] ut the reality of the expedition, and although
[illegible] either make or repeat statements thought not
[illegible] ly gain no converts, but are thought fools for
[illegible] ertainly not be frightened into holding my
[illegible] is in danger, and when I am persuaded that I
[illegible] uthority on the matter than other persons. [2]
[illegible] at it, the Athenians nevertheless have set out
[illegible] force, naval and military, professedly to help
[illegible] restore Leontini, but really to conquer Sicily,
[illegible] which once gained, the rest, they think, will
[illegible] up your minds, therefore, to see them speed-
[illegible] you can best repel them with the means at
[illegible] aken off guard through scorning the news, or
[illegible] good through disbelieving it. [4] Meanwhile
[illegible] need not be dismayed at the force or daring of
[illegible] ot be able to do us more hurt than we shall do
[illegible] ness of their armament altogether without ad-
[illegible] the greater it is the better, with regard to the
[illegible] hom dismay will make more ready to join us;
[illegible] ve them away, having failed in their ambition
[illegible] moment that they will get what they want), it
[illegible] is exploit for us, and in my judgment by no
[illegible] . [5] Few indeed have been the large arma-
[illegible] or barbarian, that have gone far from home

6.[illegible]
6.[illegible]

and been successful. They cannot be more numerous than the people of the country and their neighbors, whom fear unites; and if they fail for want of supplies in a foreign land, to those against whom their plans were laid they nonetheless leave renown, although they may themselves have been the main cause of their own discomfort. [6] Thus these very Athenians rose by the defeat of the Persians, in a great measure due to accidental causes, from the mere fact that Athens had been the object of his attack; and this may very well be the case with us also."

6.34
415
17th Year/Summer
SYRACUSE
Hermocrates advises the Syracusans to confirm old allies and seek new ones. He calls upon the Sicilians to unite their fleets and meet the Athenians at the Iapygian promontory. He concludes by begging the Syracusans, even if they will not adopt this proposal, to make preparations to defend themselves.

"Let us, therefore, confidently begin preparations here; let us send to and confirm the support of some of the Sicels, and obtain the friendship and alliance of others, and despatch envoys to the rest of Sicily to show that the danger is common to all, and to Italy to get them to become our allies, or at all events to refuse to receive the Athenians. [2] I also think that it would be best to send to Carthage[2a] as well; they are by no means without apprehension there, for it is their constant fear that the Athenians may one day attack their city, and they may perhaps think that they might themselves suffer by letting Sicily be sacrificed, and be willing to help us secretly if not openly, in one way if not in another. They are the best able to do so, if they will, of any of the present day, as they possess most gold and silver, by which war, like everything else, flourishes. [3] Let us also send to Sparta[3a] and Corinth,[3b] and ask them to come here and help us as soon as possible, and to keep alive the war in Hellas. [4] But in my opinion the most important thing to do at the present moment is what you, with your constitutional love of quiet, will be slow to see, and what I must nevertheless mention. If we Sicilians all together, or at least as many as possible besides ourselves, would only launch the whole of our present navy with two months' provisions, and meet the Athenians at Tarentum[4a] and the Iapygian promontory,[4b] and show them that before fighting for Sicily they must first fight for their passage across the Ionian sea,[4c] we would strike dismay into their army, and make them realize that we have a base for our defense—for Tarentum is ready to receive us—while they have a wide sea to cross with all their armament, which could with difficulty keep its order through so long a voyage, and would be easy for us to attack as it came on slowly and in small detachments. [5] On the other hand, if they were to lighten their vessels,[5a] and draw together their fast sailers and attack us with these, we could ei-

6.34.2a Carthage: Map 6.20.
6.34.3a Sparta: Map 6.38, BY.
6.34.3b Corinth: Map 6.38, inset.
6.34.4a Tarentum: Map 6.38, AX.
6.34.4b Iapygian promontory (Cape Iapygium): Map 6.38, AX.
6.34.4c Ionian sea: Map 6.38, AX.
6.34.5a Warships were "lightened" by being stripped of all nonessential equipment (such as masts and sails used for long-distance travel). This gear might be immediately jettisoned in an emergency but more often would be stored at a shore camp before the ships entered into battle. See 7.24.2, 8.28.1, 8.43.1, and Appendix G, Trireme Warfare, §8.

hen they were wearied with rowing or, if we tire to Tarentum; while they, having crossed t to give battle, would have a difficult time in ould either have to remain and be blockaded, the coast, abandoning the rest of their arma- er discouraged by not knowing for certain ld receive them. [6] In my opinion this con- be sufficient to deter them from putting out hat with deliberating and reconnoitering our outs, they would let the season go on until or, confounded by so unexpected a circum- the expedition, especially as their most expe- I hear, taken the command against his will, first excuse offered by any serious demonstra- ould also be reported, I am certain, as more ly are, and men's minds are affected by what first to attack, or to show that they mean to nst an attack, inspire greater fear because men for the emergency. [8] This would be pre- Athenians at present. They are now attacking shall not resist, having a right to judge us se- not help the Spartans to destroy them; but if owing a courage for which they are not pre- more dismayed by the surprise than they could power. [9] I could wish to persuade you to if this cannot be, at all events lose not a mo- erally for the war; and remember all of you sailant is best shown by bravery in action, but e best course is to accept the preparations ving the surest promise of safety, and to act as That the Athenians are coming to attack us, e voyage, and all but here—this is what I am

es. Meanwhile the people of Syracuse[1a] were at ves; some contending that the Athenians had no ere was no truth in what he said; some asking if they could do that would not be repaid them hers made light of the whole affair and turned it

6.35
415
17th Year/Summer
SYRACUSE
Many Syracusans do not agree with Hermocrates. Athenagoras, a leader of The People, rises to speak.

gr
ide
the
te

6.3
6.3

into ridicule. In short, there were few that believed Hermocrates and feared for the future. [2] Meanwhile Athenagoras, the leader of The People and very powerful at that time with the masses, came forward and spoke as follows:

6.36
415
17th Year/Summer
SYRACUSE
Athenagoras argues that men like Hermocrates spread alarm for their own political purposes. He says that the Athenians are unlikely to come to Sicily while the Peloponnesians so near them at home remain hostile.

"For the Athenians, he who does not wish that they may be as misguided as they are supposed to be, and that they may come here to become our subjects, is either a coward or a traitor to his country; while as for those who carry such tidings and fill you with so much alarm, I wonder less at their audacity than at their folly if they flatter themselves that we do not see through them. [2] The fact is that they have their private reasons to be afraid, and wish to throw the city into consternation to have their own terrors cast into the shade by the public alarm. In short, this is what these reports are worth; they do not arise of themselves, but are concocted by men who are always causing agitation here in Sicily. [3] However, if you are well advised, you will not be guided in your calculation of probabilities by what these persons tell you, but by what shrewd men and of large experience, as I esteem the Athenians to be, would be likely to do. [4] Now it is not likely that they would leave the Peloponnesians behind them, and before they have well ended the war in Hellas wantonly come in quest of a new war quite as arduous, in Sicily; indeed, in my judgment, they are only too glad that we do not go and attack them, being so many and so great cities as we are."

6.37
415
17th Year/Summer
SYRACUSE
Athenagoras argues that even a very large expedition would probably fail in a hostile Sicily, shut up in a camp near their ships by superior Sicilian cavalry. He doubts whether it could escape annihilation.

"However, if they should come as is reported, I consider Sicily better able to go through with the war than the Peloponnesus, being at all points better prepared, and our city by itself far more than a match for this alleged army of invasion, even were it twice as large again. I know that they will not have horses with them, or get any here (except a few perhaps from the Egestaeans) or be able to bring a force of hoplites equal in number to our own, in ships which will already have enough to do to come all this distance, however lightly laden, not to speak of the transport of the other stores required against a city of this magnitude, which will be no slight quantity. [2] In fact, so strong is my opinion upon the subject, that I do not well see how they could avoid annihilation if they brought with them another city as large as Syracuse, and settled down and carried on war from our frontier; much less can they hope to succeed with all Sicily hostile to them, as all Sicily will be, and with only a camp pitched from the ships, and composed of tents and bare necessaries, from which they would not be able to stir far for fear of our cavalry."

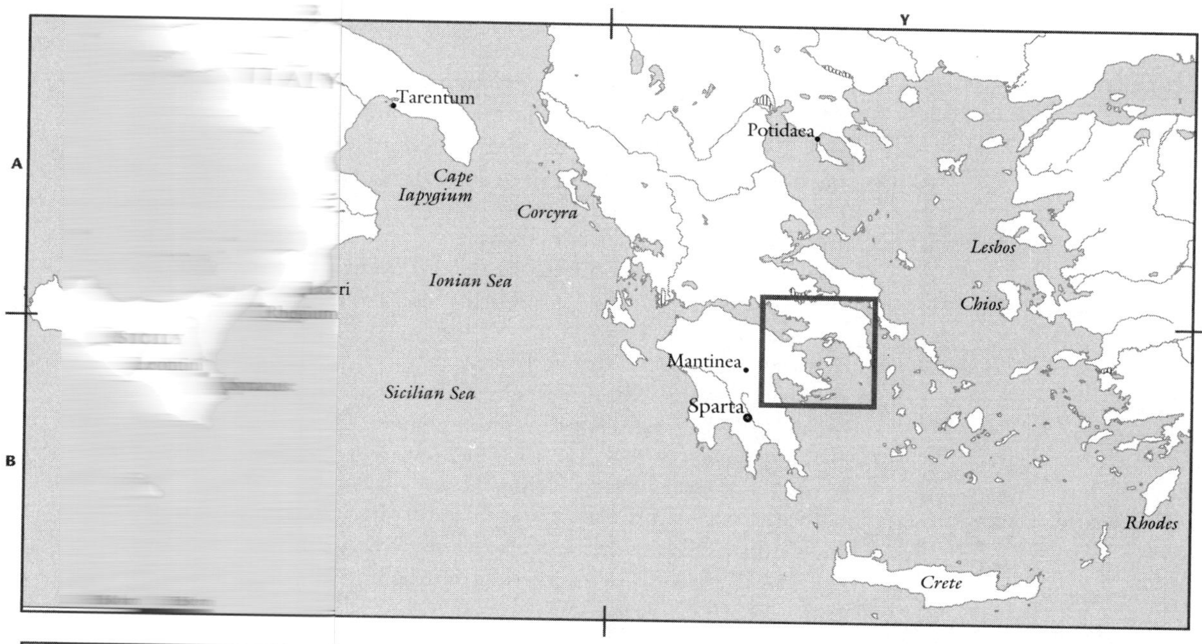

AP 6.38
LLIES OF THE ATHENIANS LISTED FOR THE EXPEDITION TO SICILY IN 415

ee this as I tell you, and as I have reason to
heir possessions at home, while persons here
er are true nor ever will be. [2] Nor is this
these persons, when they cannot resort to
ries and by others even more abominable to
l themselves take over the government: it is
cannot help fearing that trying so often they
nd that we, as long as we do not suffer, may
ask of prevention, or, when the offenders are
he result is that our city is rarely at rest, but

6.38
415
17th Year/Summer
SYRACUSE
Athenagoras argues that the Athenians are too smart to risk such an attempt. He warns against those who spread such rumors in hopes of seizing power from The People. He condemns the conspiracies that threaten Syracuse's government and advises the citizenry to remain vigilant against such plots.

is subject to constant troubles and to conflicts as frequent against herself as against the enemy, not to speak of occasional tyrannies and other infamous forms of government. [4] However, I will try, if you will support me, to let nothing of this happen in our time, by winning over you, the many, and by chastising the authors of such machinations, not merely when they are caught in the act—a difficult feat to accomplish—but also for what they have the wish though not the power to do; as it is necessary to punish an enemy not only for what he does, but also beforehand for what he intends to do, if the first to relax precaution would not also be the first to suffer. I shall also reprove, watch, and on occasion warn The Few—the most effective way, in my opinion, of turning them from their evil courses. [5] And after all, as I have often asked—What would you have, young men? Would you hold office immediately? The law forbids it, a law enacted rather because you are not competent than to disgrace you when competent. Meanwhile you wish not to be on a legal equality with the many! But how can it be right that citizens of the same state should be held unworthy of the same privileges?"

6.39
415
17th Year/Summer
SYRACUSE
Athenagoras contrasts the justice and utility of democracy with the wickedness and unfairness of oligarchy.

"It will be said, perhaps, that democracy is neither wise nor equitable, but that the holders of property are also the best fitted to rule. I say, on the contrary, first, that the word *demos*, or people, includes the whole state, oligarchy only a part; next, that if the best guardians of property are the rich, and the best counselors the wise, none can hear and decide so well as the many; and that all these talents, individually and collectively, have their just place in a democracy. [2] But an oligarchy gives the many their share of the danger, and not content with the largest part takes and keeps the whole of the profit; and this is what the powerful and young among you aspire to, but in a great city cannot possibly obtain."

"But even now, foolish men, most senseless of all the Hellenes that I know, if you have no sense of the wickedness of your designs, or most criminal if you have that sense and still dare to pursue them,

6.40
415
17th Year/Summer
SYRACUSE
Athenagoras asks the young oligarchs to give up their designs and again condemns those who spread rumors. He concludes by restating his belief that if Athens attacks, Syracuse will successfully defend herself.

[6.40.1] even now, if it is not a case for repentance, you may still learn wisdom, and thus advance the interest of the country, the common interest of us all. Reflect that in the country's prosperity the men of merit in your ranks will have a share and a larger share than the great mass of your fellow countrymen, but that if you have other designs you run a risk of being deprived of all; and cease to spread reports like these, as The People realize your purpose and will not put up with it. [2] If the Athenians arrive, this city will repulse them in a manner worthy of itself; we have generals who will see to this matter. And if nothing of this be true, as I incline to believe, the city

a panic by your reports, or impose upon it-
e by choosing you for its rulers; the city itself
r, and will judge your words as if they were
wing itself to be deprived of its liberty by lis-
e to preserve that liberty, by taking care to
means of making itself respected."

6.41
415
17th Year/Summer
SYRACUSE
A Syracusan general then speaks, affirming that the city should prepare its defense and scout the enemy's approach. The assembly ends.

Athenagoras. One of the generals now stood up
anc kers coming forward, adding these words of his
ow natter in hand:

r speakers to utter calumnies against one an-
s to entertain them; we ought rather to look
we have received, and see how each man by
a whole may best prepare to repel the in-
should be no need, there is no harm in the
ith horses and arms and all other accouter-
e will undertake to see to and order this, and
ties to reconnoiter and do all else that may
f this we have seen to already, and whatever
before you."

6.42
415
17th Year/Summer
CORCYRA
From Corcyra the Athenian expedition sends scouts to Italy and Sicily to test the cities there.

the general, the Syracusans departed from the
ass

thenians and all their allies had now arrived at
Co ls began by again reviewing the armament, and
ma he order in which they were to anchor and en-
can le fleet into three divisions, allotted one to each
of sailing all together and thus lacking sufficient
wat stations where they might land, and at the same
tim ordered and easier to handle, by each squadron
hav . [2] Next they sent three ships ahead to Italy[2a]
anc hich of the cities would receive them, with in-
stru the way and let them know before they put in
to l

6.43
415
17th Year/Summer
CORCYRA
The forces of the Athenian expedition are described.

sailed from Corcyra, and proceeded to cross to
Sici ow consisting of one hundred and thirty-four
tri Rhodian *penteconters*)[1a] of which one hundred
wer y men-of-war, and forty troopships—and the remai the other allies; five thousand and one hundred
hop teen hundred were Athenian citizens from the

6.42
6.42
6.42

6.43.1a Rhodes: Map 6.38, BY. *Penteconters*, 50-oared warships, were smaller than triremes, with 170 oars.
6.43.1b Chios: Map 6.38, AY.

rolls at Athens and seven hundred *Thetes* shipped as marines,[1c] and the rest allied troops, some of them Athenian subjects, and besides these five hundred Argives[1d] and two hundred and fifty Mantineans[1e] serving for hire; four hundred and eighty archers in all, eighty of whom were Cretans,[1f] seven hundred slingers from Rhodes, one hundred and twenty light-armed exiles from Megara,[1g] and one horse-transport carrying thirty horses.

6.44
415
17th Year/Summer
ITALY
Carrying abundant supplies, the Athenians were not distressed that most Italian cities refused to provide markets for them.
RHEGIUM
The Athenians stop at Rhegium, send to Egesta for support, and discuss their next move.

Such was the strength of the first armament that sailed over for the war. The supplies for this force were carried by thirty merchant ships laden with grain, which conveyed the bakers, stonemasons and carpenters, and the tools for raising fortifications, accompanied by one hundred boats, like the former conscripted into the service, besides many other boats and merchant ships which followed the armament voluntarily for purposes of trade; all of which now left Corcyra and struck across the Ionian sea[1a] together. [2] The whole force made land at the Iapygian promontory[2a] and Tarentum,[2b] with more or less good fortune. They then coasted along the shores of Italy,[2c] the cities shutting their markets and gates against them, and according them nothing but water and liberty to anchor (and Tarentum and Locri[2d] not even that), until they arrived at Rhegium,[2e] the extreme point of Italy. [3] Here at length they reunited, and not gaining admission within the walls, pitched a camp outside the city in the precinct of Artemis, where a market was also provided for them,[3a] and drew their ships on shore and kept quiet. Meanwhile they opened negotiations with the Rhegians, and called upon them as Chalcidians to assist their Leontine[3b] kinsmen; to which the Rhegians replied that they would not side with either party, but should await the decision of the rest of the Italians, and do as they did.[3c] [4] Upon this the Athenians now began to consider what would be the best action to take in the affairs of Sicily, and meanwhile waited for the ships sent on to come back from Egesta,[4a] in order to know whether there was really there the money mentioned by the messengers at Athens.

6.45
415
17th Year/Summer
SYRACUSE
Syracuse learns the Athenians are at Rhegium, and rushes to prepare her defense.

In the meantime reliable reports came in from all quarters to the Syracusans, as well as from their own officers sent to reconnoiter, that the fleet was at Rhegium; upon which they laid aside their incredulity and threw

6.43.1c The *thetes* were the poorest of the four property classes at Athens. Since they were unable to afford the cost of hoplite equipment, their principal military employment was to serve in the fleet as rowers. Their role as marines here is quite anomalous. Perhaps they had been equipped and armed at public expense. See Appendix G, Trireme Warfare, §8, 11, 14, and Appendix A, The Athenian Government, §2.
6.43.1d Argos: Map 6.38, inset.
6.43.1e Mantinea: Map 6.38, BY.
6.43.1f Crete: Map 6.38, BY.
6.43.1g Megara: Map 6.38, inset.
6.44.1a Ionian sea: Map 6.38, AX.
6.44.2a Iapygian promontory (Cape Iapygium): Map 6.38, AX.
6.44.2b Tarentum: Map 6.38, AX.
6.44.2c Italy: Map 6.38, AX.
6.44.2d Locri (Epizephyrian Locri, in Italy): Map 6.38, AX.
6.44.2e Rhegium: Map 6.38, AX.
6.44.3a Greek soldiers and sailors at this time were expected to purchase their food from local markets with their own money, which made prompt and adequate military pay quite important. For a city to offer a special market at a convenient and exterior location for foreign troops was a polite and presumably profitable amenity; and it also helped to keep such visitors out of the city.
6.44.3b Leontini: Map 6.38, BX.
6.44.3c See Illustration 3.86, of a fragment of a treaty between Athens and Rhegium dated from 433 B.C.
6.44.4a Egesta: Map 6.49.

the… e work of preparation. They sent round guards
or … be, to the Sicels, put garrisons into the posts of
the … y, reviewed horses and arms in the city to see
tha… and took all other steps to prepare for a war
wh… at any moment.

…hips that had been sent ahead returned from
Eg… at Rhegium, with the news that far from there
bei… ll that could be produced was thirty talents. [2]
Th… ttle disheartened at being thus disappointed at
the… usal of the Rhegians to join in the expedition,
the… they had tried to gain and had most reason to
cou… ationship to the Leontines and constant friend-
shi… was prepared for the news from Egesta, his two
col… pletely by surprise. [3] The Egestaeans had had
rec… stratagem when the first envoys from Athens
can… urces. They took the envoys in question to the
ten… yx[3a] and showed them the treasures deposited
the… censers, and a large number of other objects
wh… gave an impression of wealth quite out of pro-
por… value. They also privately entertained the ships'
cre… cups of gold and silver that they could find in
Eg… ow in the neighboring Phoenician and Hellenic
citi… em to the banquets as their own; [4] and as all
use… e, and everywhere a great quantity of silver was
sho… n was most dazzling upon the Athenian sailors,
and… of the riches they had seen when they got back
to … in question—who had in their turn persuaded
the … d by the soldiers when the news got abroad that
the… pposed at Egesta.

6.46
415
17th Year/Summer
RHEGIUM
The Athenians are dismayed to discover that Rhegium refuses to join them and that Egesta can provide only thirty talents. The Egestaean ruse that had duped the Athenian envoys is described.

… discussed what was to be done. [6.47.1] The
opi… ail with all the armament to Selinus,[1a] the main
obj… , and if the Egestaeans could provide money for
the … heir plans accordingly; but if they could not, to
req… visions for the sixty ships that they had asked for,
to … etween them and the Selinuntines either by force
or … to coast past the other cities and, after displaying … nd proving their zeal for their friends and allies,
to … they should have some sudden and unexpected
op… Leontines,[1b] or of bringing over some of the
oth… danger the state by wasting its home resources.

6.47
415
17th Year/Summer
RHEGIUM
Nicias proposes that with so little Egestaean support, they try to settle the war with Selinus, display their power, and then return home.

6.45… i in Athens … ormally em- … ntryside, … on the occa- … em (4.67.2 … ems to have been a similar institution at Syracuse. See 7.45.5 for these guardposts.

6.46.1a Egesta: Map 6.49.

6.46.3a Eryx: Map 6.49.

6.47.1a Selinus: Map 6.49.

6.47.1b Leontini: Map 6.49.

6.48
415
17th Year/Summer
RHEGIUM
Alcibiades suggests offering alliance to all Sicilian cities. Once Athens' allies are known, the expedition might then attack Syracuse and Selinus.

Alcibiades said that a great expedition like the present must not disgrace itself by going away without having accomplished anything; heralds must be sent to all the cities except Selinus and Syracuse, and efforts be made to make some of the Sicels revolt from the Syracusans, and to gain the friendship of others, in order to obtain grain and troops; and first of all to win over the Messanians,[1a] who lay right in the passage and entrance to Sicily, and would afford an excellent harbor and base for the army. Thus, after bringing over the cities and knowing who would be their allies in the war, they might then indeed attack Syracuse and Selinus—unless the latter came to terms with Egesta and the former ceased to oppose the restoration of Leontini.

6.49
415
17th Year/Summer
RHEGIUM
Lamachus advocates an immediate attack on Syracuse, thus exploiting surprise and the formidable reputation that unfamiliarity still accords them.

Lamachus, on the other hand, said that they ought to sail straight to Syracuse, and fight their battle at once under the walls of the city while the people were still unprepared, and the panic at its height. [2] Every armament was most terrible at first; if it allowed time to run on without showing itself, men's courage revived, and they saw it appear at last almost with indifference. By attacking suddenly, while Syracuse still trembled at their coming, they would have the best chance of gaining a victory for themselves and of striking a complete panic into the enemy by the aspect of their numbers—which would never appear so considerable as at present—by the anticipation of coming disaster, and above all by the immediate danger of the engagement. [3] They might also count upon surprising many in the fields outside, incredulous of their coming; and at the moment that the enemy was carrying in his property the army would not want for booty if it settled in force before the city. [4] The rest of the Sicilians would thus be immediately less disposed to enter into alliance with the Syracusans, and would join the Athenians, without waiting to see which were the strongest. They must make Megara[4a] their naval station as a place to retreat to and a base from which to attack: it was an uninhabited place at no great distance from Syracuse either by land or by sea.

6.50
415
17th Year/Summer
CATANA
Failing to secure Messanian alliance, the Athenians sail to Naxos, Catana, and Syracuse; they reconnoiter the harbor and nearby coast before returning to Catana.

Having spoken to this effect, Lamachus nevertheless gave his support to the opinion of Alcibiades. After this Alcibiades sailed in his own vessel across to Messana[1a] with proposals of alliance, but met with no success, the inhabitants answering that they could not receive him within their walls, though they would provide him with a market outside.[1b] Upon this he sailed back to Rhegium.[1c] [2] Immediately upon his return the generals manned and provisioned sixty ships out of the whole fleet and coasted along to Naxos,[2a] leaving the rest of the armament behind them at Rhegium with one of their number. [3] Received by the Naxians, they then coasted on to Catana,[3a] and being refused admittance by the inhabitants (there being a pro-Syracusan party in the city), went on to the river

6.48.1a Messana: Map 6.49.
6.49.4a Megara (Hyblaea): Map 6.49.
6.50.1a Messana: Map 6.49.
6.50.1b Markets for military forces: see note at 6.44.3a.
6.50.1c Rhegium: Map 6.49.
6.50.2a Naxos: Map 6.49.
6.50.3a Catana: Map 6.49.

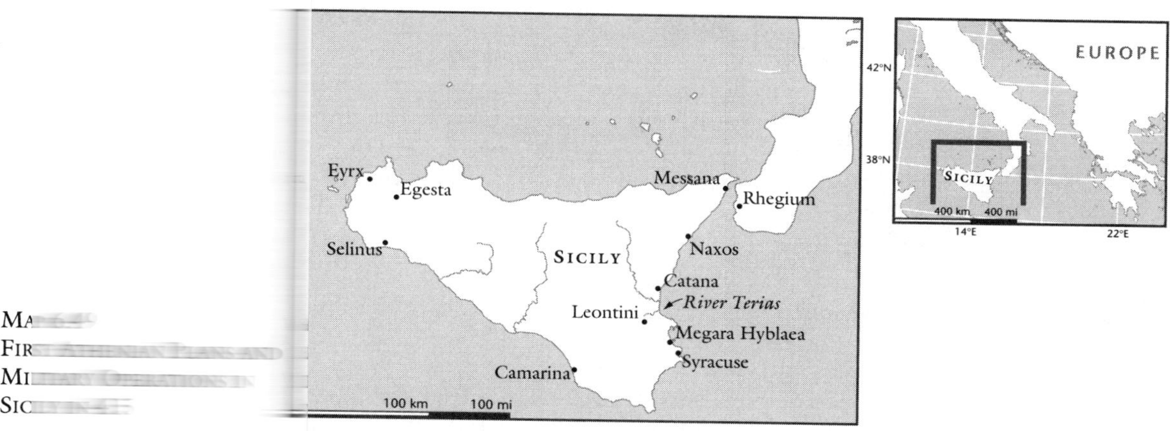

MA[illegible]
FIR[illegible]
MI[illegible]
SIC[illegible]

Te[illegible]ouacked, and the next day sailed in single file to Sy[illegible]ps except ten which they sent on in front to sail int[illegible] see if there was any fleet launched, and to pro-cla[illegible]oard that the Athenians had come to restore the Le[illegible]ry, as being their allies and kinsmen, and that suc[illegible]s were in Syracuse should leave it without fear anc[illegible]benefactors the Athenians. [5] After making this pro[illegible]tering the city and the harbors, and the features of [illegible] would have to make their base of operations in the[illegible] Catana.

[illegible] here, the inhabitants refused to receive the ar-ma[illegible]nerals to come in and say what they desired; and wh[illegible]ng and the citizens were intent on the assembly, the[illegible] badly walled-up postern gate without being ob-ser[illegible] the city, flocked into the marketplace. [2] The Sy[illegible]no sooner saw the army inside than they became frig[illegible]not being at all numerous; while the rest voted for[illegible]thenians and invited them to bring the rest of the[illegible]. [3] After this the Athenians sailed to Rhegium anc[illegible]h all the armament, for Catana,[3a] where they beg[illegible]ediately upon their arrival.

6.51
415
17th Year/Summer
CATANA
The Catanians refuse to receive the Athenians, but when the Athenians gain entrance to the city, they change their minds.

[illegible]rought them from Camarina[1a] that if they went the[illegible]ver to them, and also that the Syracusans were ma[illegible]nians accordingly sailed along shore with all their

6.52
415
17th Year/Summer
CAMARINA
When Camarina refuses to receive the Athenians, they return to Catana, raiding Syracusan territory on their way.

6.5C[illegible]
6.5C[illegible]
6.5C[illegible]
6.51[illegible]
6.52[illegible]

armament, first to Syracuse,[1b] where they found no fleet being manned, and then along the coast to Camarina, where they stopped at the beach and sent a herald to the people who, however, refused to receive them, saying that their oaths bound them to receive only a single vessel of the Athenians unless they themselves sent for more. [2] Disappointed here, the Athenians now sailed back again, and after landing on and plundering Syracusan territory and losing some stragglers from their light-armed troops through the coming up of the Syracusan horse, so got back to Catana.

6.53
415
17th Year/Summer
CATANA
Alcibiades is summoned home to face trial for his supposed role in the Hermae and the Mysteries affairs. Inquiry into these cases had become rabid as many Athenians feared an attempt to establish a tyranny.

There they found the *Salaminia*[1a] come from Athens for Alcibiades, with orders for him to sail home to answer the charges which the state brought against him, and for certain others of the soldiers who with him were accused of sacrilege in the matter of the Mysteries and of the Hermae.[1b] [2] For the Athenians, after the departure of the expedition, had continued as active as ever in investigating the facts of the Mysteries and of the Hermae, and, instead of testing the informers, in their suspicious temper welcomed all indifferently, arresting and imprisoning the best citizens upon the evidence of rascals, and preferring to sift the matter to the bottom sooner than to let an accused person of good character pass unquestioned, owing to the rascality of the informer. [3] The People had heard how oppressive the tyranny of Pisistratus and his sons had become before it ended, and further that his tyranny had been put down at last, not by themselves and Harmodius, but by the Spartans,[3a] and so were always in fear and took everything suspiciously.

6.54
514
ATHENS
To show that Athenians do not know their own history, Thucydides recounts the story of Aristogiton and Harmodius, and their true role in the fall of the Pisistratidean tyranny nearly one hundred years earlier.

Indeed, the daring action of Aristogiton and Harmodius was undertaken in consequence of a love affair, which I shall relate at some length, to show that the Athenians are no more accurate than the rest of the world in their accounts of their own tyrants and of the facts of their own history. [2] Pisistratus dying at an advanced age in possession of the tyranny, was succeeded by his eldest son, Hippias, and not Hipparchus, as is commonly believed.[2a] Harmodius was then in the flower of youthful beauty, and Aristogiton, a citizen in the middle rank of life, was his lover and possessed him. [3] Solicited without success by Hipparchus son of Pisistratus, Harmodius told Aristogiton, and the enraged lover, afraid that the powerful Hipparchus might take Harmodius by force, immediately formed a design, such as his condition in life permitted, for overthrowing the tyranny. [4] In the meantime Hipparchus, after a second solicitation of Harmodius met with no better success, unwilling to use violence, arranged to insult him in some covert way. [5] Indeed, generally their government was not grievous to the multitude, or in any way odious in practice; and these tyrants culti-

6.52.1b Syracuse: Map 6.49.

6.53.1a The *Salaminia* and her sister ship the *Paralus* were special state triremes used on sacred embassies and official business. Thucydides mentions them several times in his history (3.33.1, 3.77.3, 6.61.4–7, 8.73.5–6, and 8.74.1–2).

6.53.1b For Thucydides' account of the blasphemous affairs of the Mysteries and the Hermae, and their political effects, see 6.27–29 and note 6.28.1a.

6.53.3a Tyrannies overthrown by Sparta: see 1.18.1 and 1.122.3; also 6.59.4.

6.54.2a This common belief was first described by Thucydides in 1.20.

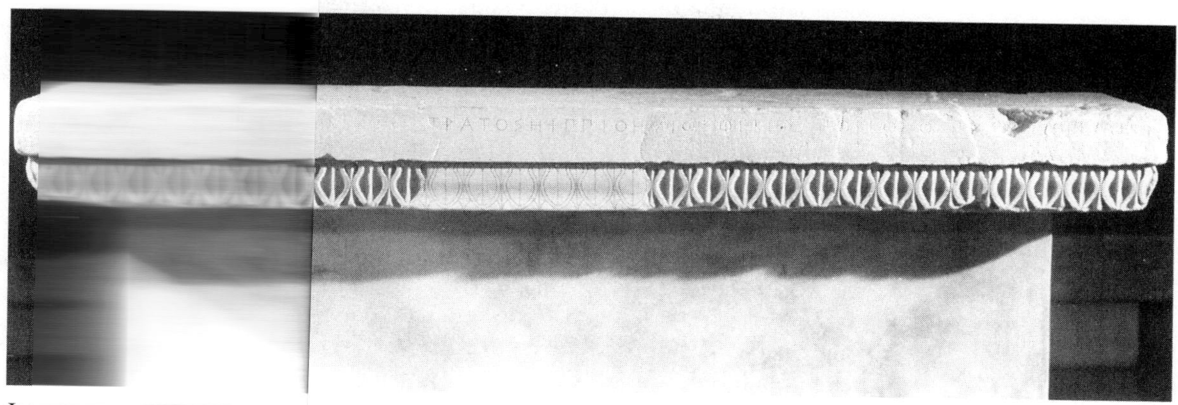

IL... AR STONE DESCRIBED BY THUCYDIDES IN 6.54 WITH THE IN... SISTRATUS THE SON OF HIPPIAS

va... as much as any, and without exacting from the At... entieth of their income, splendidly adorned their ci... wars, and provided sacrifices for the temples. [6] F... left in full enjoyment of its existing laws, except th... to have some one of the family among the *ar-ch*... ives that held the yearly archonship at Athens was P... nt Hippias, and named after his grandfather, who w... cated the altar to the twelve gods in the market-pl... in the Pythian precinct.[6c] [7] The Athenian peo-p... and lengthened the altar in the marketplace, and o...; but that in the Pythian precinct can still be seen, th... nd is to the following effect:

...atus, the son of Hippias,
... this record of his archonship
... precinct of Apollo Pythias.[7a]

... eldest son and succeeded to the government is w... a fact upon which I have had more exact accounts t... also ascertained by the following circumstance. He i... itimate brothers that appears to have had children; a... he pillar placed in the Athenian Acropolis,[1a] com-

6.55
514
ATHENS
Thucydides describes epigraphic and circumstantial evidence which proves that Hippias, not Hipparchus, became tyrant of Athens after Pisistratus.

6... of Athens; see ... n Government,

6... twelve gods ... henian *agora;*

6... n the Pythian ... been in the southeast part of the city, between the Athenian Olympieum sanctuary and the Ilissos river; see Map 6.56, inset.

6.54.7a This altar stone exists today and its inscription is still legible. See Illustration 6.54.

6.55.1a Acropolis of Athens: Map 6.56, inset.

memorating the crime of the tyrants, which mentions no child of Thessalus or of Hipparchus,[1b] but five of Hippias, which he had by Myrrhine, who was the daughter of Callias son of Hyperechides; and naturally the eldest would have married first. [2] Again, his name comes first on the pillar after that of his father, and this too is quite natural, as he was the eldest after him, and the reigning tyrant. [3] Nor can I ever believe that Hippias would have obtained the tyranny so easily, if Hipparchus had been in power when he was killed, and he, Hippias, had had to establish himself upon the same day; but he had no doubt been long accustomed to overawe the citizens, and to be obeyed by his mercenaries, and thus not only conquered, but conquered with ease, without experiencing any of the embarrassment of a younger brother unused to the exercise of authority. [4] It was the sad fate which made Hipparchus famous that got him also the credit with posterity of having been tyrant.

6.56
514
ATHENS
When Harmodius rejects his advances, Hipparchus insults Harmodius' sister. Outraged, Harmodius and Aristogiton plot to kill Hipparchus' brother, the tyrant Hippias, during the great Panathenaic festival.

To return to Harmodius: Hipparchus having been repulsed in his solicitations insulted him as he had resolved, by first inviting a sister of Harmodius, a young girl, to come and bear a basket in a certain procession, and then rejecting her, on the grounds that she had never been invited at all owing to her unworthiness. [2] If Harmodius was indignant at this, Aristogiton for his sake now became more exasperated than ever; and having arranged everything with those who were to join them in the enterprise, they only waited for the great feast of the Panathenaea,[2a] the sole day in which the citizens forming part of the procession could meet together in arms without suspicion. Aristogiton and Harmodius were to begin, but were to be supported immediately by their accomplices against the bodyguard. [3] The conspirators were not many, for better security, besides which they hoped that those not in the plot would be carried away by the example of a few daring spirits, and use the arms in their hands to recover their liberty.

6.57
514
ATHENS
Frightened that their plot had been discovered, they slew Hipparchus. Harmodius died immediately, Aristogiton was executed later.

At last the festival arrived; and Hippias with his bodyguard was outside the city in the Ceramicus,[1a] arranging how the different parts of the procession were to proceed. Harmodius and Aristogiton had already their daggers and were getting ready to act, [2] when seeing one of their accomplices talking familiarly with Hippias, who was easily accessible to everyone, they took fright and concluded that they had been discovered and were on the point of being arrested; [3] and eager if possible to be revenged first upon the man who had wronged them and for whom they had undertaken all this risk, they rushed, as they were, within the gates, and meeting with Hipparchus by the Leocorium[3a] recklessly fell upon him at once, infuriated, Aristogiton by love, and Harmodius by insult, and struck and killed him. [4] Aristogiton escaped the guards at the moment, through the crowd run-

6.55.1b Thessalus and Hipparchus were, with Hippias, the sons of Pisistratus the tyrant; see 1.20.2.

6.56.2a For the Feast of the Panathenaea, see Appendix I, Religious Festivals, §8.

6.57.1a The Ceramicus district of Athens, which lay both inside and outside the walls: Map 6.56, inset.

6.57.3a Leocorium, possible location: Map 6.56, inset.

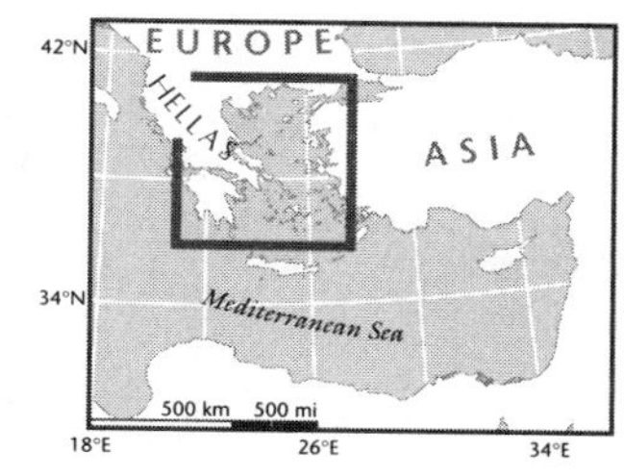

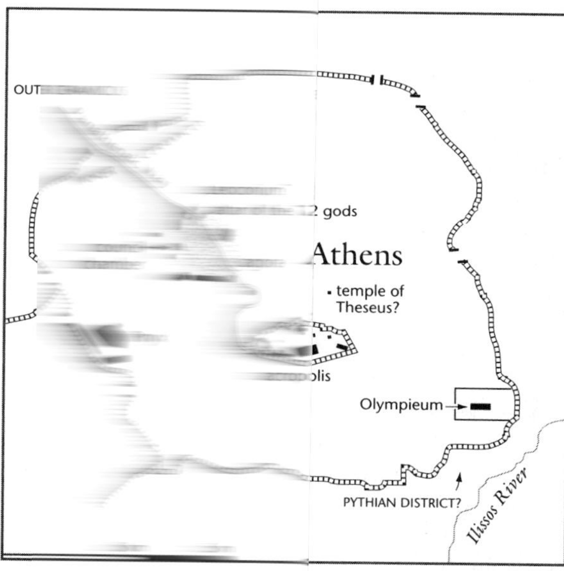

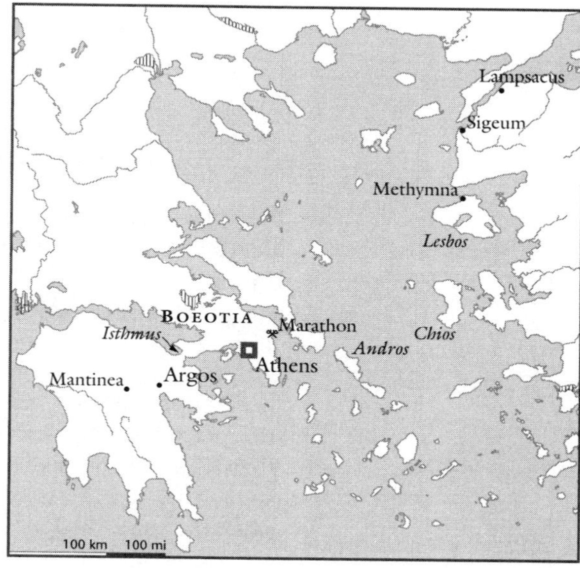

M MODIUS, AND ARISTOGITON

ni ds taken and executed in no merciful way: Har-
m pot.

rought to Hippias in the Ceramicus, he at once
pr e of action, but to the armed men in the proces-
si ome distance away, knew anything of the matter.
C or the occasion so as not to betray himself, he
p nd bade them assemble there without their arms.
[2 dingly, supposing that he had something to say;
w rcenaries to remove the arms, and then and there
pi ought guilty and all who were found with daggers
(t g the usual weapons for a procession).

6.58
514
17th Year/Summer
ATHENS
Hippias swiftly disarmed all Athenians in the procession.

6. ncluded a cer-
ie Panathenaic
ie temple of
Acropolis

6.59
514
17th Year/Summer
ATHENS
Hippias ruled harshly for four more years before the Spartans and exiled Alcmeonidae deposed him. He went into exile and later accompanied the Persian expedition to Marathon.

In this way offended love first led Harmodius and Aristogiton to conspire, and the alarm of the moment to commit the rash action recounted. [2] After this the tyranny pressed harder on the Athenians, and Hippias, now grown more fearful, put to death many of the citizens, and at the same time began to turn his eyes abroad for a refuge in case of revolution. [3] Thus, although an Athenian, he gave his daughter, Archedice, to a Lampsacene, Aeantides, son of the tyrant of Lampsacus,[3a] seeing that they had great influence with Darius.[3b] And there is her tomb in Lampsacus with this inscription:

Archedice lies buried in this earth,
Hippias her sire, and Athens gave her birth;
Unto her bosom pride was never known,
Though daughter, wife, and sister to the throne.

[4] Hippias, after reigning three years longer over the Athenians, was deposed in the fourth by the Spartans and the banished Alcmaeonidae,[4a] and went with a safe conduct to Sigeum,[4b] and to Aeantides at Lampsacus, and from thence to King Darius; from whose court he set out twenty years after, in his old age, and came with the Persians to Marathon.[4c]

6.60
415
17th Year/Summer
ATHENS
Memories of earlier tyranny convinced many at Athens that the Hermae and Mysteries affairs were connected to oligarchic plots. They grew savage in their search for the guilty. One imprisoned suspect accused some Athenians in exchange for immunity, and many of them were executed.

With these events in their minds, and recalling everything they knew by hearsay on the subject, the Athenian people grew uneasy and suspicious of the persons charged in the affair of the Mysteries, and became convinced that all that had taken place was part of an oligarchic and monarchical conspiracy. [2] In the state of agitation thus produced, many persons of considerable status had already been thrown into prison, and far from showing any signs of abating, public feeling grew daily more savage, and more arrests were made; until at last one of those in custody, thought to be the most guilty of all, was induced by a fellow prisoner to give information, whether true or not is a matter on which there are two opinions, no one having been able, either then or since, to say for certain who did the deed.[2a] [3] However this may be, the other found arguments to persuade him, that even if he had not done it, he ought to save himself by gaining a promise of impunity, and free the state of its present suspicions; as he would be surer of safety if he confessed after promise of impunity than if he denied and were brought to trial. [4] He accordingly made a confession implicating himself and others in the affair of the Hermae; and the Athenian people, glad at last to get at what they supposed was the truth, and furious until then at not being able to discover those who had conspired against the ma-

6.59.3a Lampsacus: Map 6.56.
6.59.3b Darius, King of Persia.
6.59.4a The Alcmeonidae was a powerful clan easier to banish because of its role in the curse of the goddess; see 1.126–7.
6.59.4b Sigeum: Map 6.56.
6.59.4c Marathon, the Attic site of a famous Athenian victory over the invading Persians in 490: Map 6.56. Also see Appendix E, The Persians, §4.
6.60.2a As Andocides' existing oration *On the Mysteries* shows, Andocides himself was the "one in custody."

jo informer and all the rest whom he had not de-
nc e accused to trial, executed as many as were ap-
pr d to death such as had fled and set a price upon
th was, after all, not clear whether the sufferers had
be nd in any case the rest of the city received imme-
di

s: public feeling was very hostile to him, being
w enemies who had attacked him before he went
ou enians fancied that they had got at the truth of
th , they believed more firmly than ever that the af-
fai in which he was implicated, had been contrived
by ion and was connected with the plot against the
de it so happened that, just at the time of this agi-
ta partans had advanced as far as the Isthmus,[2a] in
pu e with the Boeotians.[2b] It was now thought that
th rangement and at his instigation, and not on acco nd that if the citizens had not acted on the infor-
m stalled them by arresting the prisoners, the city
w d. [3] The citizens went so far as to sleep one
ni of Theseus within the walls.[3a] Also, and just at
th cibiades at Argos[3b] were suspected of a design to
at so the Argive hostages deposited in the islands[3c]
w enians to the Argive People to be put to death
up short, everywhere something was found to cre-
at biades. It was therefore decided to bring him to
tri d the *Salaminia*[4a] was sent to Sicily for him and
th nformation, with instructions to order him to re-
tu ges against him, [5] but not to arrest him, be-
ca d causing any agitation in the army or among the
er ve all to retain the services of the Mantineans[5a]
ar thought, had been induced to join by his influ-
er his own ship and his fellow accused, accordingly
sa *inia* from Sicily, as though to return to Athens,
ar s Thurii,[6a] and there they left the ship and disap-
pe o home for trial with such a prejudice existing
ag w of the *Salaminia* stayed some time looking for
A nions, and at length, as they were nowhere to be
fo ed. Alcibiades, now an outlaw, crossed in a boat
n i to the Peloponnesus; and the Athenians passed

6.61
415
17th Year/Summer
ITALY
These investigations and other developments convince many Athenians that Alcibiades has plotted against the democracy. He is recalled to stand trial. He sails for home in his own ship but disappears at Thurii in Italy, and later reaches the Peloponnesus. He is condemned to death in absentia at Athens.

6.(6.56.
6.(
6.(heseus is un-
says it lay
6.56, inset,

6.(
6.(me hostages
nty ships
various is-
lands of the empire, as described in 5.84.

6.61.4a The *Salaminia* and her sister ship the *Paralus* were special state triremes used on sacred embassies and official business. Thucydides mentions them several times in the course of his narrative. See note 6.53.1a.

6.61.5a Mantinea: Map 6.56.

6.61.6a Thurii: Map 6.64, locator.

ILLUSTRATION 6.61 FRAGMENT OF AN ATTIC STELA WITH AN INSCRIBED NOTICE OF SALE OF ALCIBIADES' PROPERTY AFTER HIS CONDEMNATION IN CONNECTION WITH THE MOCK MYSTERIES AND THE MUTILATION OF THE HERMAE

sentence of death by default upon him and those in his company.

6.62
415
17th Year/Summer
SICILY
The Athenians accomplish little while sailing along the coast of Sicily. Hyccara is taken and its people sold as slaves, but Himera refuses them entrance and they fail to take Hybla.

The Athenian generals left in Sicily now divided the armament into two parts, and each taking one by lot, sailed with the whole for Selinus and Egesta,[1a] wishing to know whether the Egestaeans would give the money, and to look into the question of Selinus and ascertain the state of the quarrel between her and Egesta. [2] Coasting along Sicily, with the shore on their left, on the side toward the Tyrrhenian Sea,[2a] they touched at Himera,[2b] the only Hellenic city in that part of the island, and being refused admission resumed their voyage. [3] On their way they took Hyccara,[3a] a petty Sicanian seaport nevertheless at war with Egesta, and making slaves of the inhabitants gave up the city to the Egestaeans, some of whose horse had joined them; after which the army proceeded through the territory of the Sicels until it reached Catana,[3b] while the fleet sailed along the coast with the slaves on board. [4] Meanwhile Nicias sailed straight from Hyccara along the coast and went to Egesta, and after transacting his other

6.62.1a Selinus, Egesta: Map 6.64.
6.62.2a Tyrrhenian sea: Map 6.64.
6.62.2b Himera: Map 6.64.
6.62.3a Hyccara: Map 6.64.
6.62.3b Catana: Map 6.64.

bu ... irty talents, rejoined the forces. They now sold
th ... one hundred and twenty talents, [5] and sailed
ro ... o urge them to send troops; and meanwhile went
wi ... to the hostile city of Hybla in the territory of
G ... d in taking it.

6.63
415/4
17th Year/Winter
SICILY
Athenian inactivity for the rest of the summer leads the Syracusans to despise them and to beg their generals to lead them against the invaders.

... the Athenians at once began to prepare for mov-
in ... Syracusans on their side for marching against
th ... ent when the Athenians failed to attack them inst ... ed and expected, every day that passed did some-
th ... ge; and when they saw them sailing far away from
th ... Sicily, and going to Hybla only to fail in their at-
te ... thought less of them than ever, and called upon
th ... itude is apt to do in moments of confidence, to
le ... ce the enemy would not come to them. [3] Par-
ti ... horse employed in reconnoitering constantly rode
up ... ament, and among other insults asked them
w ... lly come to settle alongside the Syracusans in a
fo ... n to resettle the Leontines in their own.

6.64
415/4
17th Year/Winter
CATANA
The Athenian generals employ a strategem to trick the Syracusans into marching to Catana.

... enian generals determined to draw them out in
m ... n the city, and themselves in the meantime to sail
b ... d take up at their leisure a convenient position.
T ... d not do so well if they had to disembark from
th ... orce prepared for them, or to go by land openly.
T ... the Syracusans (a force which they were themse ... en be able to do the greatest harm to their light
tr ... followed them; but this plan would enable them
to ... which the horse could do them no hurt worth
sp ... san exiles with the army having told them of the
sp ... ,[1a] which they afterwards occupied. In pursuance
o ... devised the following stratagem. [2] They sent to
S ... to them, and by the Syracusan generals thought
to ... est; he was a native of Catana,[2b] and said he came
fr ... e, whose names the Syracusan generals were ac-
q ... n they knew to be among the members of their
p ... [3] He told them that the Athenians passed the
n ... distance from their arms, and that if the Syracu-
sa ... d come with all their people at daybreak to attack
th ... friends, would close the gates upon the troops in
th ... he vessels, while the Syracusans would easily take

6. ... ap 6.64) can ... territory of ... ps Thucydides ... o another town ... ocation is un-

6.63.2a Catana: Map 6.64.
6.64.1a Olympieum, a temple built on the heights southwest of Syracuse: Map 6.68.
6.64.2a Syracuse: Map 6.64.
6.64.2b Catana: Map 6.64.

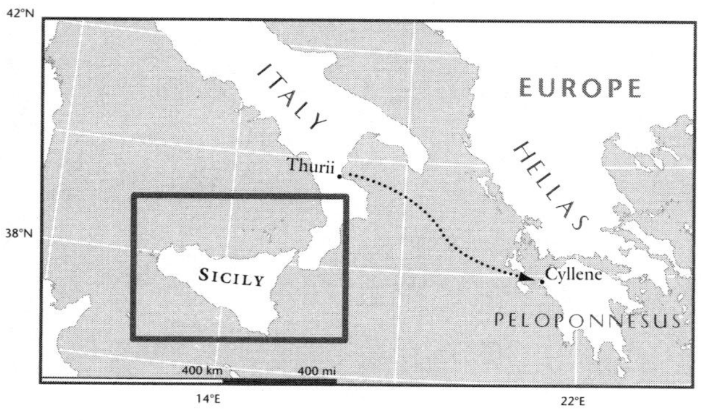

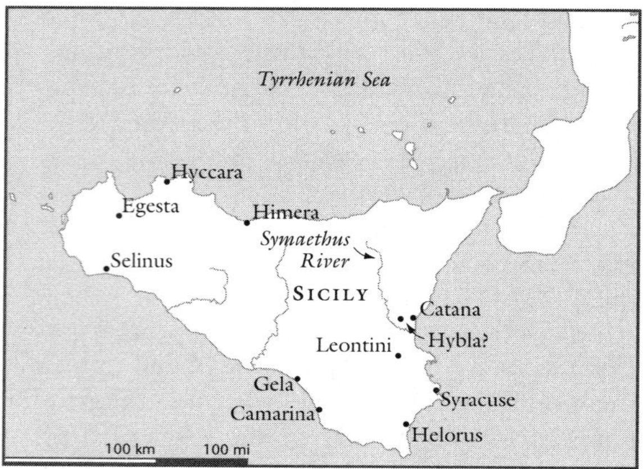

MAP 6.64
LATER ATHENIAN MILITARY OPERATIONS IN 415 AND IN THE WINTER OF 415/4

the camp by an attack upon the stockade. In this they would be aided by many of the Catanians, who were already prepared to act, and from whom he himself came.

6.65
415/4
17th Year/Winter
SYRACUSE
As the Syracusans approach Catana by land, the Athenians sail off to Syracuse. Finding the Athenians gone, the Syracusans have to hurry back to their city.

The generals of the Syracusans, who did not lack confidence, and who had intended even without this information to march on Catana, believed the man without any sufficient inquiry, fixed at once a day upon which they would be there, and dismissed him; and the Selinuntines[1a] and others of their allies having now arrived, they gave orders for all the Syracusans to march out in full force. Their preparations completed, and the time fixed for their arrival being at hand, they set out for Catana, and passed the night upon the river Symaethus,[1b] in the Leontine[1c] territory. [2] Meanwhile the Athenians no sooner knew of their approach than they took all their forces and such of the Sicels or others as had joined them, put them on board their ships and boats, and sailed by night to Syracuse. [3] Thus, when morning broke the Athenians were landing opposite the Olympieum[3a] ready to seize their camping ground, and the Syracusan horse having ridden up first to Catana and found that all the armament had put to sea, wheeled back and told the infantry, and then all turned back together and went to the relief of the city.

6.66
415/4
17th Year/Winter
SYRACUSE
The Athenians occupy favorable positions near Syracuse and await the Syracusans who return and camp for the night.

In the meantime, as the march before the Syracusans was a long one, the Athenians quietly established their army in a convenient position, where they could begin an engagement when they pleased, and where the Syracusan cavalry would have least opportunity of harassing them, either before or during the action, being flanked on one side by walls, houses, trees, and by

6.65.1a Selinus: Map 6.64.
6.65.1b Symaethus river: Map 6.64.
6.65.1c Leontini: Map 6.64.
6.65.3a Olympieum sanctuary: Map 6.68.

a … r by cliffs. [2] They also felled the neighboring
tr… wn to the sea, and formed a palisade alongside of
th… s (which they picked up) and wood, hastily raised
a … ost vulnerable point of their position, and broke
do… Anapus.[2b] [3] These preparations were allowed to
go… uption from the city; the first hostile force to appe… cavalry, followed afterwards by all the infantry toge… l close up to the Athenian army and then, finding
th… gage, crossed the Helorine road[3a] and camped for
th…

6.67 415/4 17th Year/Winter SYRACUSE The battle order of both armies is described. Nicias speaks to his army.

…nians and their allies prepared for battle, their dis-
po… :—Their right wing was occupied by the Argives
an… er by the Athenians, and the rest of the field by
th… r army was drawn up eight deep in advance, half
cl… ollow square, formed also eight deep, which had
o… ready to go to the support of the troops hardest
p… ers were placed inside this reserve. [2] The Syracu… ed their hoplites sixteen deep, consisting of the
m… people, and such allies as had joined them, the
st… g that of the Selinuntines; next to them the cav-
al… nbering two hundred in all, with about twenty
h… om Camarina.[2a] The cavalry, full twelve hundred
st… eir right, and next to it the darters. [3] As the
A… begin the attack, Nicias went along the lines, and
a… encouragement to the army and the nations com-
p…

6.68 415/4 17th Year/Winter SYRACUSE After deprecating the enemy, Nicias warns that Athens and her allies must win a place in Sicily by the sword, and that the enemy's superior cavalry will make retreat impossible.

… exhortation is little needed by men like our-
… fight in the same battle, the force itself being,
… fit to inspire confidence than a fine speech with
… ere we have Argives, Mantineans, Athenians,
… anders in the ranks together, it were strange in-
… nd so brave companions in arms, if we did not
… ory; especially when we have mass levies op-
… oops, and what is more, Sicilians, who may dis-
… stand against us, their skill not being at all
… r rashness. [3] You may also remember that we
… d have no friendly land near, except what your
… you; and here I put before you a motive just
… which the enemy are appealing; their cry being
… or their country, mine that we shall fight for a

…
…
… connecting
… ap 6.68.
… Map 6.64.

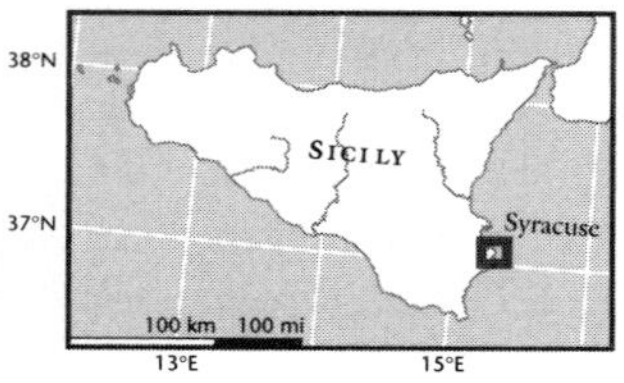

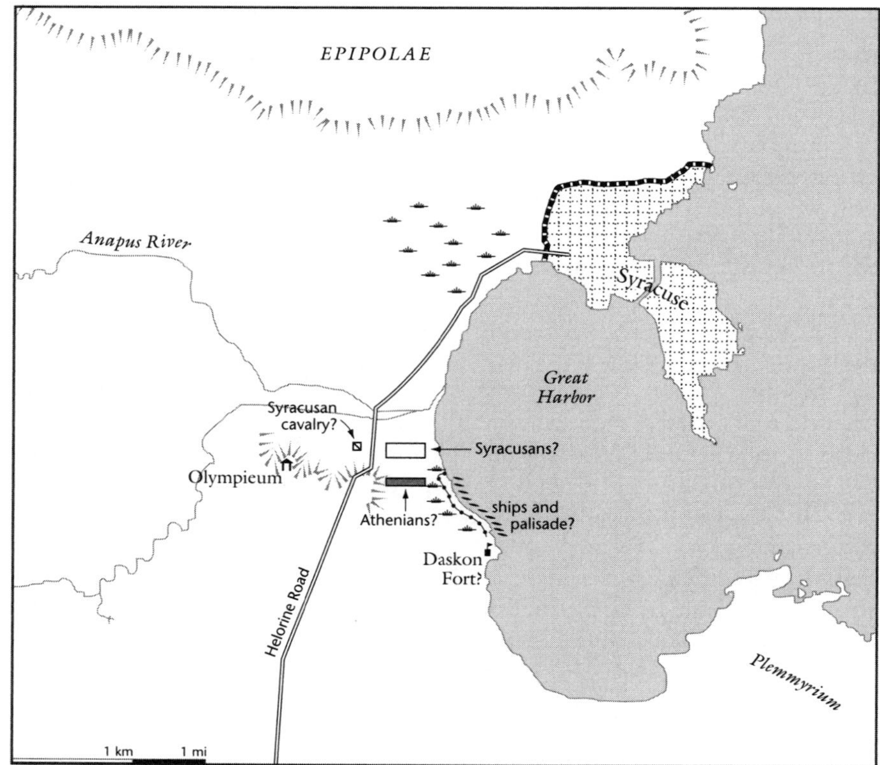

MAP 6.68 THE BATTLE AT THE ANAPUS RIVER

country that is not ours, where we must conquer or hardly get away, as we shall have their horse upon us in great numbers. [4] Remember, therefore, your renown, and go boldly against the enemy, thinking the present difficulty and necessity more terrible than they."

6.69
415/4
17th Year/Winter
SYRACUSE
An Athenian advance takes the Syracusans by surprise but they form lines to meet it. They lack practice but not zeal or courage. Thucydides describes the motivations of both forces.

After this address Nicias at once led on the army. The Syracusans were not at that moment expecting an immediate engagement, and some had even gone away to the city, which was close by; these now ran up as fast as they could, and though late, took their places here or there in the main body as they joined it. Lack of zeal or daring was certainly not the fault of the Syracusans, either in this or the other battles, but although not inferior in courage for as long as their military science proved adequate, when this failed them, they were compelled to give up their resolution also. On the present occasion, although they had not supposed that the Athenians

w[illegible] and although constrained to stand upon their de-
fe[illegible] ey at once took up their arms and advanced to
m[illegible] e stone-throwers, slingers, and archers of either
ar[illegible] and routed or were routed by one another, as
m[illegible] een light troops; next, soothsayers brought for-
w[illegible] and trumpeters urged on the hoplites to the
c[illegible] advanced, the Syracusans to fight for their countr[illegible] or his safety that day and liberty hereafter. In the
e[illegible] ians sought to make another's country theirs and
t[illegible] uffering by their defeat; the Argives and indepen-
d[illegible] them in getting what they came for, and to earn
b[illegible] of the country they had left behind; while the subje[illegible] their ardor to the desire for self-preservation,
w[illegible] ope for if victorious and, as a secondary motive,
f[illegible] on easier terms after helping the Athenians to a
fr[illegible]

[illegible] e to close quarters, and for a long while fought
w[illegible] ound. Meanwhile there occurred some claps of
th[illegible] nd heavy rain, which did not fail to add to the fears
o[illegible] the first time, and very little acquainted with war;
w[illegible] rienced adversaries these phenomena appeared to
b[illegible] of year, and much more alarm was felt at the con-
t[illegible] nemy. [2] At last the Argives drove in the Syracu-
s[illegible] he Athenians routed the troops opposed to them,
a[illegible] was thus cut in two and betook itself to flight. [3]
T[illegible] pursue far, being held in check by the numerous
a[illegible] n horse, who attacked and drove back any of their
h[illegible] pursuing in advance of the rest; in spite of which
t[illegible] r as was safe in a body, and then went back and set
u[illegible] while the Syracusans rallied at the Helorine road,[4a]
w[illegible] well as they could under the circumstances, and
e[illegible] heir own citizens to the Olympieum,[4b] fearing that
t[illegible] hands on some of the treasures there. The rest re-
t[illegible]

6.70
415/4
17th Year/Winter
SYRACUSE
The battle goes evenly until a thunderstorm disconcerts the inexperienced Syracusans, who are pushed back and then routed. Syracusan cavalry prevents pursuit.

[illegible] ver, did not go to the temple, but collected their
c[illegible] n a pyre, and passed the night upon the field. The
n[illegible] nemy back their dead under truce,[1a] to the number

6.71
415/4
17th Year/Winter
CATANA
After returning the enemy dead under truce, the Athenians sail to Catana and make preparations for a spring campaign against Syracuse.

6[illegible] e victors after [illegible] t usually con- [illegible] armor arranged [illegible] on or near the [illegible]

6[illegible] connecting [illegible] ap 6.68.

6[illegible] ap 6.68.

6[illegible] Greece, the victors would gather up their dead, strip those of the enemy, and raise a trophy. The defeated would collect the bodies of their fallen during a truce that they would explicitly request and be granted for that purpose. In this way, appropriate reverence was shown and proper burial was accorded to all war dead. See Appendix F, Land Warfare, §6.

of about two hundred and sixty, Syracusans and allies, and gathered together the bones of their own, some fifty, Athenians and allies, and taking the spoils of the enemy, sailed back to Catana.[1b] [2] It was now winter; and it did not seem possible for the moment to carry on the war so near Syracuse[2a] until cavalrymen had been sent for from Athens[2b] and levied among the allies in Sicily[2c]—to do away with their utter inferiority in cavalry—and money had been collected in the country and received from Athens; and until some of the cities, which they hoped would now be more disposed to listen to them after the battle, had been brought over, and grain and all other necessities provided for a campaign in the spring against Syracuse.

6.72
415/4
17th Year/Winter
SYRACUSE
Speaking to a Syracusan assembly, Hermocrates says the army had done unexpectedly well against the Athenians, and will improve with better arms and training. He calls for a reform of the army's command structure.

With this intention they sailed off to Naxos and Catana[1a] for the winter. Meanwhile the Syracusans burned their dead, and then held an assembly, [2] in which Hermocrates son of Hermon, a man who with a general ability of the first order had given proofs of military capacity and brilliant courage in the war, came forward and encouraged them, and told them not to let what had occurred make them give way, [3] since their spirit had not been conquered, but their want of discipline had done the mischief. Still they had not been beaten by so much as might have been expected, especially as they were, one might say, novices in the art of war, an army of artisans opposed to the most experienced soldiers in Hellas. [4] What had also done great harm was the number of the generals (there were fifteen of them) and the quantity of orders given, combined with the disorder and insubordination of the troops. But if they were to have a few skillful generals, and used this winter in preparing their hoplites, finding arms for such as had not got any so as to make them as numerous as possible, and forcing them to attend to their training generally, they would have every chance of beating their adversaries, courage being already theirs and discipline in the field having thus been added to it. Indeed, both these qualities would improve, since danger would exercise them in discipline, while their courage would be led to surpass itself by the confidence which skill inspires. [5] The generals should be few and elected with full powers, and an oath should be taken to leave them entire discretion in their command: if they adopted this plan, their secrets would be better kept, all preparations would be properly made, and there would be no room for excuses.

6.73
415/4
17th Year/Winter
SYRACUSE
Syracuse requests aid from Corinth and Sparta.

The Syracusans heard him, and voted everything as he advised, and elected three generals, Hermocrates himself, Heraclides son of Lysimachus, and Sicanus son of Execestes. [2] They also sent envoys to Corinth and

6.71.1b Catana, Sicily: Map 6.75.
6.71.2a Syracuse, Sicily: Map 6.75 and inset.
6.71.2b Athens: Map 6.75.
6.71.2c Sicily: Map 6.75.
6.72.1a Naxos and Catana, Sicily: Map 6.75.

S[illegible] of allies to join them, and to induce the Spartans
f[illegible] themselves more seriously to the war against the
A[illegible]t either have to leave Sicily or be less able to send
r[illegible]my there.

[illegible]t Catana now at once sailed against Messana[1a] in
th[illegible]ould be betrayed to them. The intrigue, however,
c[illegible]ibiades, who had known the secret when he left
h[illegible]ummons from home, foreseeing that he would be
o[illegible]on about the plot to the friends of the Syracusans
in[illegible] once put to death its authors, and now rose in
a[illegible]pported them against the opposing faction and
s[illegible] the admission of the Athenians. [2] The latter
w[illegible] and then, as they were exposed to the weather
a[illegible]and met with no success, went back to Naxos,[2a]
w[illegible]for their ships to lie in, erected a palisade round
th[illegible]to winter quarters; meanwhile they sent a trireme
t[illegible]money and cavalrymen be sent to them in the
s[illegible] the winter the Syracusans built a wall onto the
c[illegible]e statue of Apollo Temenites,[1b] all along the side
f[illegible]r to make the task of circumvallation[1d] longer and
m[illegible] their being defeated. They also erected a fort at
M[illegible] the Olympieum,[1f] and stuck palisades along the
s[illegible] landing place. [2] Meanwhile, as they knew that
th[illegible]ring at Naxos,[2a] they marched with all their peo-
p[illegible]ed the land and set fire to the tents and encamp-
m[illegible]nd so returned home. [3] Learning also that the
A[illegible]emissaries to Camarina[3a] on the strength of the alli[illegible]cluded in the time of Laches,[3b] in order to gain
th[illegible] also sent envoys from Syracuse to oppose them.
T[illegible]ion that the Camarinaeans had not provided the
ai[illegible]e first battle very willingly; and they now feared
th[illegible]o assist them at all in future, after seeing the suc-
c[illegible]n the action, and would join the latter on the
st[illegible]ndship. [4] Hermocrates, with some others, ac-
c[illegible]arina from Syracuse, and Euphemus and others
fr[illegible] an assembly of the Camarinaeans having been
c[illegible]poke as follows, in the hope of prejudicing them
a[illegible]

6.74
415/4
17th Year/Winter
MESSANA
A plot to betray Messana to the Athenians is revealed by Alcibiades, and fails. The Athenians winter in Naxos and send to Athens for cavalry and money.

6.75
415/4
17th Year/Winter
SYRACUSE
The Syracusans extend their city walls and fortify key places.
CAMARINA
Learning that the Athenians are sending envoys to Camarina, the Syracusans send Hermocrates there to speak on their behalf to the assembly.

6.[illegible]: Map 6.75.
6.[illegible]
6.[illegible]ew wall built in [illegible] 6.75, inset.
6.[illegible]use: Map 6.75, [illegible]
6.[illegible]oking Syracuse: [illegible]
6.[illegible]ing of a wall to [illegible]y land.
6.[illegible]ap 6.75.
6.75.1f Olympieum sanctuary: Map 6.75, inset.
6.75.2a Naxos, Sicily: Map 6.75.
6.75.2b Catana, Sicily: Map 6.75.
6.75.3a Camarina, Sicily: Map 6.75.
6.75.3b For operations while Laches was in Sicily, see 3.86.1, 3.90.2, and 3.115.2; Thucydides mentions no treaties of alliance, although he writes in 5.5.3 that all the allies of Syracuse, except the Locrians, made peace with Athens when the reconciliation between the Sicilians took place.

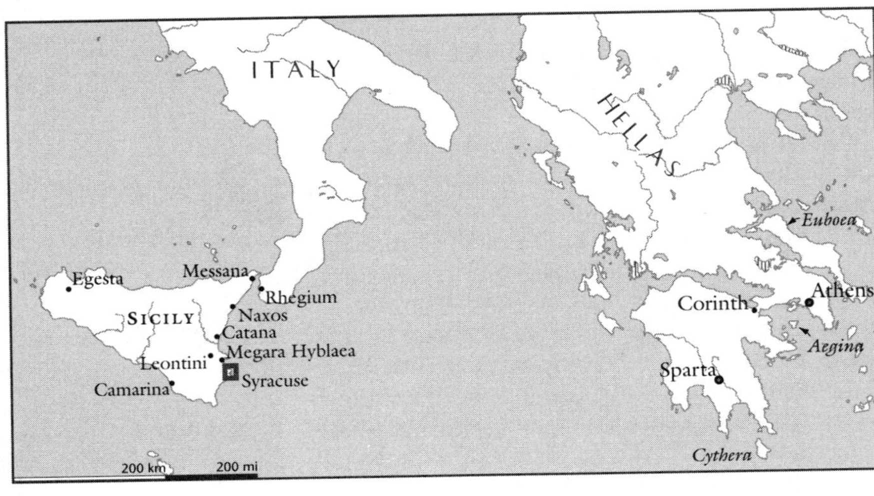

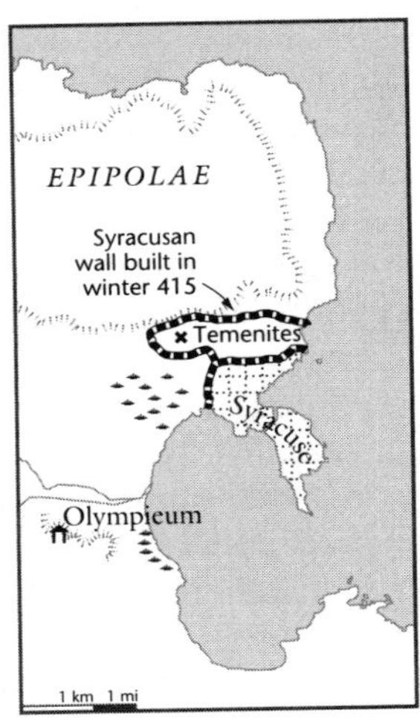

MAP 6.75 FURTHER MILITARY OPERATIONS, WINTER OF 415/4[4a]

6.76
415/4
17th Year/Winter
CAMARINA
Hermocrates warns the Camarinaeans that the Athenians are not in Sicily to return the Leontines as they say, but to expand their rule in the west by the same methods they employed to develop their empire in Ionia and Hellas.

"Camarinaeans, we did not come on this embassy because we were afraid of your being frightened by the actual forces of the Athenians, but rather of your being won over by what they would say to you before you heard anything from us. [2] They have come to Sicily with the pretext that you know, and the intention which we all suspect, in my opinion less to restore the Leontines[2a] to their homes than to oust us from ours; as it is beyond all reason that they should restore in Sicily the cities that they lay waste in Hellas, or should cherish the Leontine Chalcidians because of their Ionian blood, and keep in servitude the Euboean[2b] Chalcidians, of whom the Leontines are a colony. [3] No; it is the very same policy which has proved so successful in Hellas that is now being tried in Sicily. After being chosen as the leaders of the Ionians and of the other allies of Athenian origin in the struggle to punish the Persians, the Athenians accused some allies of failure in military service, some of fighting against each other, and others, as the case might be, upon any specious pretext that could be found, until they thus subdued them all. [4] In short, in the struggle against the Persian, the Athenians did not fight for the liberty of the Hellenes, or the Hellenes for their own liberty, but the former to make their countrymen serve them instead of him, the

6.75.4a The new Syracusan wall in Map 6.75, inset, basically follows the interpretation of Peter Green in *Armada from Athens* (Hodder and Stoughton, 1971), passim. The reader should be aware that many scholars follow the quite different views expressed in A.W. Gomme, A. Andrewes, and K.J. Dover, *A Historical Commentary on Thucydides*, iv (Oxford, 1970), 466 ff.

6.76.2a Leontini, Sicily: Map 6.75.

6.76.2b Euboea, Map 6.75.

aster for another, wiser indeed than the first,

6.77
415/4
17th Year/Winter
CAMARINA
Hermocrates blames the Sicilians for not uniting against an obvious foreign threat, and thus permitting Athens to hope to conquer them one by one.

now come to declare to an audience familiar
ds of a state so open to accusation as is the
rather to blame ourselves, who, with the
n the Hellenes in those parts that have been
supporting each other, and seeing the same
ried upon ourselves—such as restorations of
support of Egestaean[1a] allies—do not stand
ly show them that here are no Ionians, or
anders, who change continually, but always
imes the Mede[1b] and sometimes some other,
the independent Peloponnesus, dwelling in
waiting until we be taken in detail, one city
as we do that in no other way can we be con-
t they turn to this plan, so as to divide some of
some by the bait of an alliance into open war
o ruin others by such flattery as different cir-
r acceptable? And do we suppose when de-
s a distant fellow countryman that the danger
of us also, or that he who suffers before us will

6.78
415/4
17th Year/Winter
CAMARINA
Addressing those Camarinaeans who envy or resent Syracuse, Hermocrates points out that by aiding Syracuse against the Athenians, Camarina will be defending itself against the same enemy, who if strengthened by the fall of Syracuse will soon come against them.

aean who says that it is the Syracusan, not he,
e Athenian, and thinks it awful to have to en-
of my country, I would have him bear in mind
country not more for mine than for his own,
ore safely in that he will enter the struggle not
s been cleared by my ruin, but with me as his
t of the Athenian is not so much to punish the
an as to use me as an excuse to secure the
arinaean. [2] As for him who envies or even
nd feared great powers must always be), and
ishes Syracuse to be humbled to teach us a les-
ve her survive in the interest of his own secu-
indulges is not humanly possible. A man can
but he cannot likewise control circumstances;
calculations proving mistaken, he may live to
une, and wish to be again envying my prosper-
he now sacrifice us and refuse to take his share
same in reality, though not in name, for him

6.
6. rsians; see Ap-

6. rians, see Ap-
nic Groups,

as for us; what is nominally the preservation of our power being really his own salvation. [4] It was to be expected that you, of all people in the world, Camarinaeans, being our immediate neighbors and the next in danger, would have foreseen this, and instead of supporting us in the lukewarm way that you are now doing, would rather have come to us of your own accord and be now offering at Syracuse the aid which you would have asked of us for Camarina[4a] (if the Athenians had first come to Camarina), in order to encourage us to resist the invader. Neither you, however, nor the rest have as yet bestirred yourselves in this direction."

6.79
415/4
17th Year/Winter
CAMARINA
Hermocrates says it would be unnatural for Camarina to support Chalcidians when other Sicilian Chalcidians will not do so, and to maintain a neutrality harmful to Syracuse. He reminds them that last year Syracuse beat off the Athenians by herself.

"Fear perhaps will make you seek to do right both by us and by the invaders, and plead that you have an alliance with the Athenians. But you made that alliance, not against your friends, but against the enemies that might attack you, and to help the Athenians when they were wronged by others, not when as now they are wronging their neighbors. [2] Even the Rhegians,[2a] Chalcidians though they be, refuse to help to restore the Chalcidian Leontines;[2b] and it would be strange if, while they suspect the truth behind this fine pretense and are wise without reason, you, with every reason on your side, should yet choose to assist your natural enemies, and should join with their direst foes in undoing those whom nature has made your own kinsfolk. [3] This is not right; you should help us without fear of their armament, which has no terrors if we hold together, but only if we let them succeed in their endeavors to separate us; indeed, even after attacking us by ourselves and being victorious in battle, they had to go off without accomplishing their purpose."

6.80
415/4
17th Year/Winter
CAMARINA
Hermocrates concludes by saying that a neutrality that harms one side is not necessarily a fair or safe policy; that Camarina's failure to help Syracuse will lead to permanent Syracusan enmity; and that continued neutrality will result in Camarina's submission to Athenian rule. He entreats the Camarinaeans to assist Syracuse now.

"United, therefore, we have no cause to despair, but rather new encouragement to league together; especially as help will come to us from the Peloponnesians, who are in military matters the undoubted superiors of the Athenians. And you need not think that your prudent policy of taking sides with neither, because allies of both, is either safe for you or fair to us. [2] Practically it is not as fair as it pretends to be. If the vanquished be defeated, and the victor conquer, through your refusing to join, what is the effect of your abstention but to leave the former to perish unaided, and to allow the latter to offend unhindered? And yet it were more honorable to join those who are not only the injured party, but your own kindred, and by doing so to defend the common interests of Sicily and save your friends the Athenians from doing wrong."

"[3] In conclusion, we Syracusans say that it is useless for us to demonstrate either to you or to the rest what you know already as

6.78.4a Camarina, Sicily: Map 6.75.
6.79.2a Rhegium, Sicily: Map 6.75.
6.79.2b Leontini, Sicily: Map 6.75.

entreat, and if our entreaty fail, we protest that
eternal enemies the Ionians, and are betrayed
ans.[3a] [4] If the Athenians reduce us, they will
our decision, but in their own name will reap
eive as the prize of their triumph the very men
gain it. On the other hand, if we are the con-
to pay for having been the cause of our dan-
re; and now make your choice between the
servitude offers and the prospect of conquer-
y escaping disgraceful submission to an Athen-
g the lasting enmity of Syracuse."

of Hermocrates; after whom Euphemus, the 6.81
At ke as follows:

6.82 415 17th Year/Winter CAMARINA The Athenian Euphemus responds to Hermocrates by describing the Athenian empire as an Ionian defense against a stronger Dorian confederacy. He defends Athens' hegemony as a just reward for having risked all against Persia.

here only to renew the former alliance,[1a] the
s compels us to speak of our empire and of the
it. [2] The best proof of this the speaker him-
called the Ionians eternal enemies of the Do-
nd since the Peloponnesian Dorians are our
nd near neighbors, we Ionians looked out for
ping their domination. [3] After the Persian
so got rid of the empire and the supremacy of
no right to give orders to us more than we to
being the strongest at that moment; and we
s of the King's[3a] former subjects, and continu-
we are least likely to fall under the dominion
if we have sufficient force with which to de-
strict truth having done nothing unfair in re-
he Ionians and islanders, the kinsfolk whom
have enslaved. [4] They, our kinsfolk, came
ountry, that is to say against us, together with
of having the courage to revolt and sacrifice
id when we abandoned our city, chose to be
o try to make us slaves too."

6.83 415/4 17th Year/Winter CAMARINA Euphemus says Athens has come to Sicily to increase its security, which coincides with Camarina's interests; and argues that fear of domination has led Athens to empire and to Sicily, not a desire to enslave others.

rve to rule because we placed the largest fleet
riotism at the service of the Hellenes, and be-
ts, did us harm by their ready subservience to
e apart from that we seek to strengthen our-
onnesians. [2] We make no fine professions of
because we overthrew the barbarian single-

6.8 to suggest
division
th Athens al-
use allied with
er (7.57–58) emphasize the ethnic paradoxes of the contending armies in Sicily. See Appendix H, Dialects and Ethnic Groups, §7, 9.

6.82.1a Former alliance: see note 6.75.3b.

6.82.3a The Persian King: see Appendix E, §2.

handed, or because we risked what we did risk for the freedom of the subjects in question any more than for that of all, and for our own: no one can be censured for providing for his own safety. If we are now here in Sicily, it is equally in the interest of our security, with which we perceive that your interest also coincides. [3] We prove this from the conduct which the Syracusans cast against us and which you somewhat too fearfully suspect; knowing that those whom fear has made suspicious, may be carried away by the charm of eloquence for the moment, but when they come to act follow their interests."

[4] "Now, as we have said, fear makes us hold our empire in Hellas, and fear makes us now come, with the help of our friends, to safely order matters in Sicily, and not to enslave any but rather to prevent any from being enslaved. [6.84.1] Meanwhile, let no one imagine that it is none of our business to be interested in you, seeing that if you are preserved and able to hold out against the Syracusans, they will be less likely to harm us by sending troops to the Peloponnesians. [2] In this way you have everything to do with us, and on this account it is perfectly reasonable for us to restore the Leontines,[2a] and to make them, not subjects like their kinsmen in Euboea,[2b] but as powerful as possible, to help us by causing trouble for the Syracusans from their frontier. [3] In Hellas we are alone a match for our enemies; and as for the assertion that it is beyond all reason that we should free the Sicilian, while we enslave the Chalcidian, the fact is that the latter is useful to us by being without arms and contributing money only; while the former, the Leontines and our other friends, cannot be too independent."

6.84
415/4
17th Year/Winter
CAMARINA
Euphemus asserts that Athens supports all Sicilians hostile to Syracuse because their independence will preoccupy her and prevent her from aiding the Peloponnesians.

"Besides, for tyrants and imperial cities nothing is unreasonable if expedient, no one a kinsman unless sure; but friendship or enmity is everywhere a matter of time and circumstance. Here, in Sicily, our interest is not to weaken our friends, but by means of their strength to cripple our enemies. Why doubt this? In Hellas we treat our allies as we find them useful. [2] The Chians[2a] and Methymnians[2b] govern themselves and furnish ships; most of the rest have harder terms and pay tribute in money; while others, although islanders who would be easy for us to take, are free altogether, because they occupy convenient positions round the Peloponnesus.[2c] [3] In our settlement of the states here in Sicily, we should, therefore, naturally be guided by our interest, and by fear, as we say, of the Syracusans.[3a] Their ambition is to rule you, their plan is to use the suspicions that we excite to

6.85
415/4
17th Year/Winter
CAMARINA
Euphemus insists that expedience determines friendship for hegemonic powers. As she does in Hellas, Athens will build up independent states here to prevent Syracuse from achieving hegemony.

6.84.2a Leontini: Map 6.88.
6.84.2b Euboea: Map 6.91.
6.85.2a Chios: Map 6.56.
6.85.2b Methymna, a city on the island of Lesbos: Map 6.56. The other cities on the island of Lesbos revolted from Athens in 428, were conquered, and reduced to subject status; see 3.2–19, 3.26–50.
6.85.2c Peloponnesus: Map 6.91. The free islands mentioned here are Zacynthus, Cephallenia, and Corcyra, Map 6.95, Hellas inset.
6.85.3a Syracuse: Map 6.88.

hen we have gone away without effecting any-
ugh your isolation, to become the masters of
y must become, if you unite with them; as a
e would no longer be easy for us to deal with
d be more than a match for you as soon as we

the case is condemned by the facts. When you
e fear which you held out was that of danger
u come under the dominion of Syracuse; [2]
to mistrust the very same argument by which
ce us, or to give way to suspicion because we
er force against the power of that city. Those
ly distrust are the Syracusans. [3] We are not
ut you, and if we proved perfidious enough to
tion, we should be unable to keep you in
e length of the voyage and the difficulty of
a military sense mainland, cities. The Syracu-
not in a camp, but in a city greater than the
They plot always against you, never let slip an
ed, [4] as they have shown in the case of the
and now they have the effrontery just as if you
ou to aid them against the power that hinders
far maintained Sicily independent. [5] We, as
ou to a much more real safety, when we beg
t common security that we provide for each
t they, even without allies, will, by their num-
ay open to you, while you will not often have
ending yourselves with such numerous auxil-
suspicions, you once let us go away unsuccess-
ll wish to see us back again, if only a handful,
n which our presence could do anything for

6.86
415/4
17th Year/Winter
CAMARINA
Euphemus points out that Athens is far from Sicily and would be unable to hold Sicilian cities subject, whereas Syracuse is a near, powerful, and constant threat. Thus alliance with Athens is the natural and correct course for Camarina, despite the large force that Athens has sent to Sicily.

arinaeans,[1a] that the calumnies of the Syracu-
d to succeed either with you or with the rest:
whole truth upon the things we are suspected
recapitulate, in the hope of convincing you.
re rulers in Hellas in order not to be subjects;
we may not be harmed by the Sicilians; that
terfere in many things, because we have many

6.87
415/4
17th Year/Winter
CAMARINA
Euphemus concludes that Athens' actions are defensive only—intended to guard and protect itself—and that this policy is in the interest of free Greeks everywhere as it restrains aggression by such potential hegemonists as Syracuse.

6.8…
6.8…

things to guard against; and that now, as before, we are come as allies to those of you who suffer wrong in this island, not without invitation but upon invitation. [3] Accordingly, instead of making yourselves judges or censors of our conduct, and trying to turn us (which it were now difficult to do), so far as there is anything in our interfering policy or in our character, that accords with your interest, this take and make use of it; and be sure that far from being injurious to all alike, to most of the Hellenes that policy is even beneficial. [4] Thanks to it, all men in all places, even where we are not, who either fear or plan aggression, from the near prospect before them, in the one case, of obtaining our intervention in their favor, in the other, of our arrival making the venture dangerous, find themselves constrained, respectively, to be moderate against their will, and to be preserved without effort of their own. [5] Do not you reject this security that is open to all who desire it, and is now offered to you; but do like others, and instead of being always on the defensive against the Syracusans, unite with us, and in your turn at last threaten them."

6.88
415/4
17th Year/Winter
CAMARINA
Camarina decides to remain neutral, but to give limited aid to Syracuse in fear that she is nearby and will win.
CATANA
The Athenians obtain support and some new allies among the Sicels. They transfer their winter base to Catana.
PELOPONNESUS
The Syracusans send for help to the Italians, the Corinthians, and the Spartans. Corinth responds enthusiastically but Sparta refuses aid. Alcibiades, having just arrived, speaks to the Spartans to urge them to act.

Such were the words of Euphemus. What the Camarinaeans felt was this. They sympathized with the Athenians, except insofar as they might be afraid of their subjugating Sicily, and they had always been at enmity with their neighbor Syracuse. From the very fact, however, that they were their neighbors, they feared the Syracusans most of the two, and being apprehensive that the Syracusans might win even without their help, both sent them in the first instance the few horsemen mentioned[1a] and for the future determined to support them most in fact, although as sparingly as possible; but for the moment in order not to seem to slight the Athenians, especially as they had been successful in the engagement, to answer both alike. [2] In accordance with this resolution they answered that as both the contending parties happened to be allies of theirs, they thought it most consistent with their oaths, at present, to side with neither; with which answer the ambassadors of each party departed.

[3] In the meantime, while Syracuse pursued her preparations for war, the Athenians were encamped at Naxos,[3a] and tried by negotiation to gain as many of the Sicels as possible. [4] Those more in the lowlands, and subjects of Syracuse, mostly held aloof; but the peoples of the interior who had never been otherwise than independent, with few exceptions, at once joined the Athenians, and brought down grain to the army, and in some cases even money. [5] The Athenians marched against those who refused to join, and forced some of them to do so; in the case of others they were stopped by the Syracusans sending garrisons and reinforcements. Mean-

6.88.1a Thucydides wrote in 6.67.2 that Camarina had sent about twenty horse and fifty archers to Syracuse.

6.88.3a Naxos: Map 6.88.

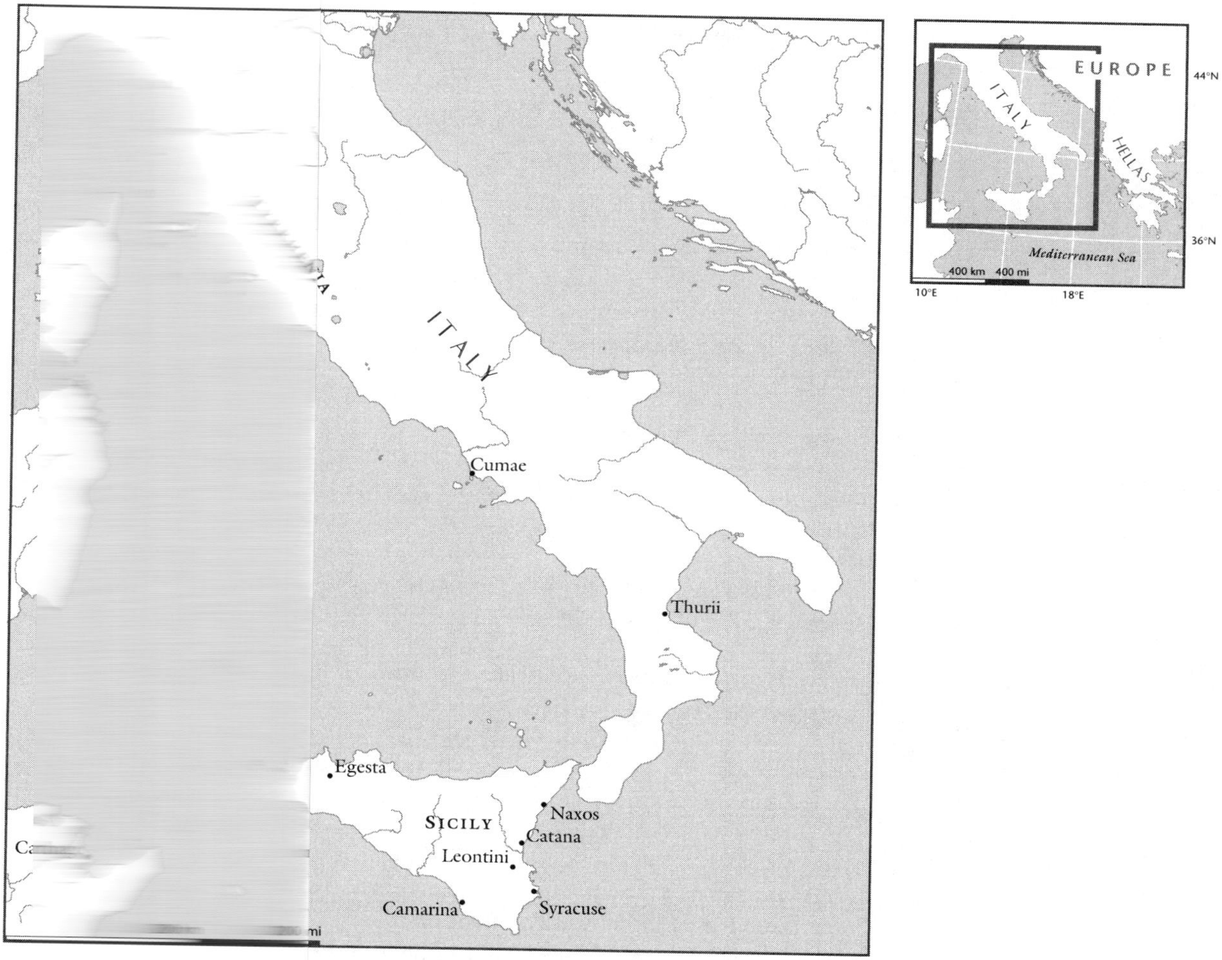

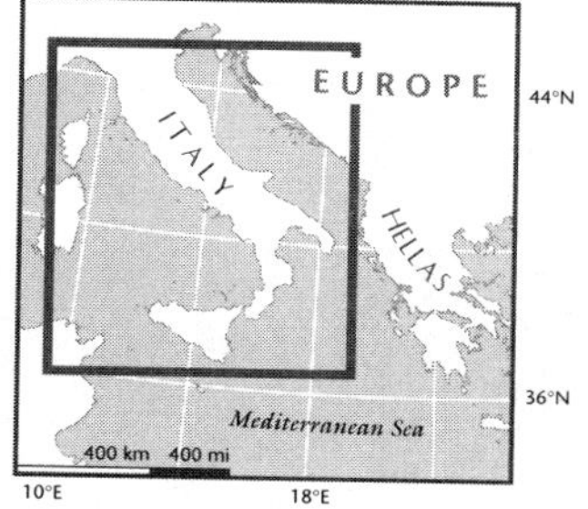

M... PERATIONS, WINTER OF 415/4

wh... d their winter quarters from Naxos to Catana,[5a] an... p burnt by the Syracusans, and stayed there the re... y also sent a trireme to Carthage,[6a] with offers of fri... ce of obtaining assistance, and another to Ty... cities there having spontaneously offered to join th... sent round to the Sicels and to Egesta,[6c] desiring th... any horses as possible, and meanwhile prepared br... r things necessary for the work of circumvalla- tio... ring to begin hostilities.

6.8...
6.8...
6.8... 88.

6.88.6c Egesta: Map 6.88.
6.88.6d Circumvallation: the building of a wall to surround or isolate a city by land.

[7] In the meantime the Syracusan envoys that had been dispatched to Corinth and Sparta[7a] tried as they passed along the coast to persuade the Italians to interfere with the proceedings of the Athenians which, they argued, threatened Italy quite as much as Syracuse, and having arrived at Corinth made a speech calling on the Corinthians to assist them on the ground of their common origin. [8] The Corinthians voted at once to aid them unstintingly themselves, and then sent on envoys with them to Sparta, to help them to persuade her also to prosecute the war with the Athenians more openly at home and to send assistance to Sicily. [9] The envoys from Corinth having reached Sparta found Alcibiades there with his fellow refugees, who had without delay crossed over in a trading vessel from Thurii, first to Cyllene in Elis,[9a] and afterwards from there to Sparta; upon the Spartans' own invitation, after first obtaining a safe conduct, as he feared them for the part he had taken in the affair of Mantinea.[9b] [10] The result was that the Corinthians, Syracusans, and Alcibiades, all pressing the same request in the assembly of the Spartans, succeeded in persuading them; but as the *ephors* and the authorities,[10a] although resolved to send envoys to Syracuse to prevent them surrendering to the Athenians, showed no inclination to send them any assistance, Alcibiades now came forward and inflamed and stirred the Spartans by speaking as follows:

6.89
415/4
17th Year/Winter
SPARTA
Alcibiades addresses his Spartan critics and justifies his past actions against Sparta. He explains his role in Athenian politics. He agrees that democracy is absurd, but that it was successful at Athens, that he had inherited it there, and that it could not be altered in the face of Spartan pressure.

"I am forced first to speak to you of the prejudice with which I am regarded, in order that suspicion may not make you disinclined to listen to me upon public matters. [2] The connection with you as your *proxeni*[2a] which the ancestors of our family by reason of some discontent renounced, I personally tried to renew by my good offices toward you, in particular upon the occasion of the disaster at Pylos.[2b] But although I maintained this friendly attitude, you yet chose to negotiate the peace with the Athenians through my enemies, and thus to strengthen them and to discredit me. [3] You had therefore no right to complain if I turned to the Mantineans and Argives, and seized other occasions of thwarting and injuring you; and the time has now come when those among you, who in the bitterness of the moment may have been then unfairly angry with me, should look at the matter in its true light, and take a different view. Those again who judged me unfavorably, because I leaned rather to the side of The People must not think that their dislike is any better founded. [4] We have always been hostile to tyrants, and all who oppose arbitrary power are called The People; hence we continued to act as

6.88.7a The dispatch of these envoys was mentioned in 6.73.2.

6.88.9a He sailed from Thurii, Italy (Map 6.88) to Cyllene in Elis (Map 6.91). See also Map 6.64, locator.

6.88.9b Mantinea: Map 6.91. The "affair" is the campaign and battle described by Thucydides in 5.61–75.

6.88.10a For the Spartan assembly and *ephors,* see Appendix C, Spartan Institutions, §5–6.

6.89.2a A *proxenus,* although a citizen and resident of his own state, served as a "friend or representative" (much like a modern honorary consul) of a foreign state.

6.89.2b Pylos: Map 6.91. The Spartan "disaster at Pylos" is described by Thucydides in 4.2–41.

[illegible] e; besides which, as democracy was the gov-
[illegible] vas necessary in most things to conform to es-
[illegible] [5] However, we endeavored to be more
[illegible] ntious temper of the times; and while there
[illegible] s now, who tried to lead the multitude astray
[illegible] d me), [6] our party was that of the whole
[illegible] g to do our part in preserving the form of
[illegible] ch the city enjoyed the utmost greatness and
[illegible] e had found existing. As for democracy, the
[illegible] s knew what it was, and I perhaps as well as
[illegible] se to complain of it; but there is nothing new
[illegible] bsurdity—meanwhile we did not think it safe
[illegible] ssure of your hostility."

[illegible] the prejudices with which I am regarded: I
[illegible] tion to the questions you must consider, and
[illegible] nowledge perhaps permits me to speak. [2]
[illegible] to conquer, if possible, the Sicilians, and after
[illegible] and finally to assail the empire and city of
[illegible] vent of all or most of these schemes succeed-
[illegible] ttack the Peloponnesus, bringing with us the
[illegible] enes lately acquired in those parts, and taking
[illegible] into our pay, such as the Iberians[3a] and others
[illegible] gnized as the most warlike known, and build-
[illegible] in addition to those which we had already
[illegible] in Italy); and with this fleet blockading the
[illegible] sea and assailing it with our armies by land,
[illegible] es by storm, and besieging others, we hoped
[illegible] feat them completely and after this to rule the
[illegible] orld. [4] Money and grain for the better exe-
[illegible] ere to be supplied in sufficient quantities by
[illegible] ces in those countries, independently of our
[illegible]"

6.90
415/4
17th Year/Winter
SPARTA
Alcibiades says that Athens' true purpose in Sicily is the conquest of all the Hellenes. She intends to use the resources gained by the conquest of Sicily and Italy, and from alliances with others, to return to the Peloponnesus in overwhelming force to reduce it city by city.

[illegible] d the history of the present expedition from
[illegible] ctly knows what our intentions were; and the
[illegible], if they can, carry these out just the same.
[illegible] cily must succumb if you do not help them, I
[illegible] ough the Sicilians, with all their inexperience,
[illegible] ed if their forces were united, the Syracusans
[illegible] n one battle with all their people and block-

6.91
415/4
17th Year/Winter
SPARTA
Alcibiades reiterates that Sparta should act for Peloponnesian interests by preventing the fall of Syracuse. He urges the Spartans to fortify Decelea in Attica and to send troops and a general to Syracuse to lead a professional defense.

6.9[illegible]
6.9[illegible]

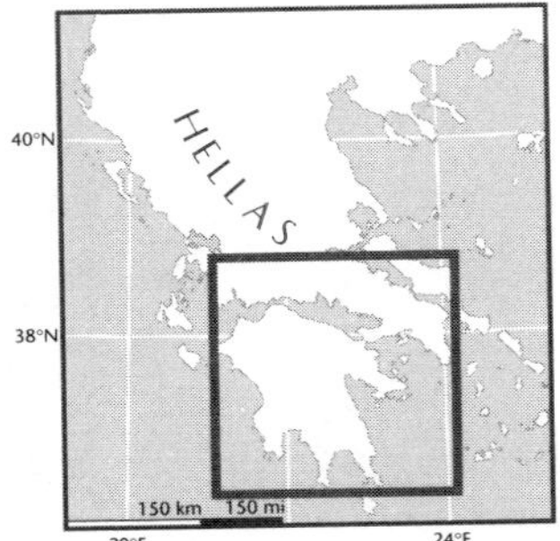

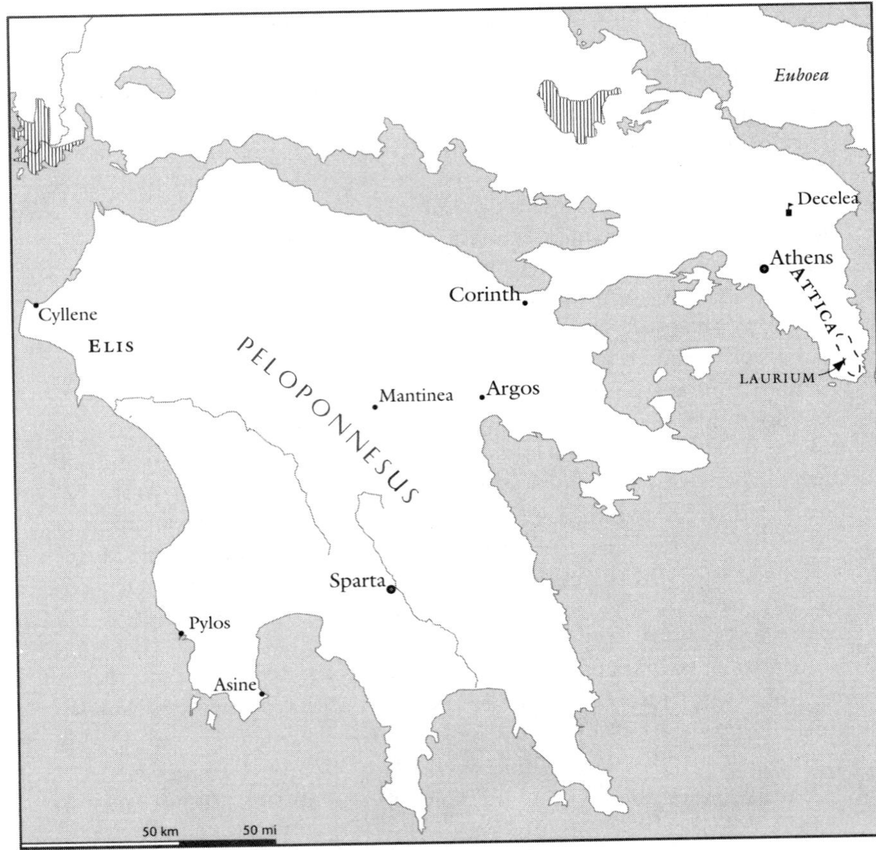

MAP 6.91 ALCIBIADES' FLIGHT AND SPEECH

aded from the sea, will be unable to withstand the Athenian armament that is now there. [3] But if Syracuse falls, all Sicily falls also, and Italy immediately afterwards; and the danger which I just now spoke of from that quarter will before long be upon you. [4] None need therefore imagine that only Sicily is in question; the Peloponnesus will be so also, unless you speedily do as I tell you, and send on board ship to Syracuse troops that shall be able to row their ships themselves,[4a] and serve as hoplites the moment that they land; and what I consider even more important than the troops, a *Spartiate*[4b] as commanding officer to discipline the forces already on foot and to compel shirkers to serve. The friends that you have already will thus

6.91.4a Oarsmen were not often soldiers also, but sometimes (see 3.18.4) it made economic and/or military sense to man a ship with those who could both row at sea and fight as hoplites on land.

6.91.4b A *Spartiate* is a full citizen of Sparta and a member of the highest Spartan military caste.

, and the waverers will be encouraged to join
i must carry on the war here more openly, so
eing that you do not forget them, may put
ce, and that the Athenians may be less able to
nt. [6] You must fortify Decelea in Attica,[6a]
Athenians are always most afraid and the only
have not experienced in the present war; the
ng an enemy being to find out what he most
means of attacking him, since everyone nat-
n weak points and fears accordingly. [7] The
, while it benefits you, will create difficulties
which I shall pass over many, and shall only
atever property there is in the country will
rs, either by capture or surrender; and the
be deprived of their revenues from the silver
their present gains from their land and from
ve all of the revenue from their allies, which
ly, as they lose their awe of Athens and see
es with vigor to this war. [6.92.1] The zeal
ll this shall be done depends, Spartans, upon
ibility, I am quite confident, and I have little

pe that none of you will think any the worse
herto passed as a lover of my country, I now
nemies in attacking it, or will suspect what I
itlaw's enthusiasm. [3] I am an outlaw from
o drove me forth, not, if you will be guided
ce: my worst enemies are not you who only
hey who forced their friends to become ene-
country is what I do not feel when I am
lt when secure in my rights as a citizen. In-
that I am now attacking a country that is still
g to recover one that is mine no longer; and
untry is not he who consents to lose it unit, but he who longs for it so much that he
recover it. [5] For myself, therefore, Spar-
ne without scruple for danger and trouble of
ember the argument in everyone's mouth,
harm as an enemy, I could likewise do you
inasmuch as I know the plans of the Atheni-
d yours. For yourselves I entreat you to be-

6.92
415/4
17th Year/Winter
SPARTA
Alcibiades argues that he is not a traitor because he cannot betray a country from which he was wrongfully driven and which is no longer his. Moreover, he adds, a true patriot will go to any length, even to aid his country's enemies, in order to recover it. He concludes by asking the Spartans to use his knowledge of Athens and Athenian plans to their best advantage.

6.91 [illegible]
6.91 [illegible]

lieve that your most vital interests are now under consideration; and I urge you to send without hesitation the expeditions to Sicily and Attica; by the presence of a small part of your forces you will save important cities in that island, and you will destroy the power of Athens both present and prospective; after this you will dwell in security and enjoy the supremacy over all Hellas, resting not on force but upon consent and affection."

6.93
415/4
17th Year/Winter
SPARTA
Moved by Alcibiades, the Spartans vote to aid the Sicilians and send Gylippus to take command there. They prepare to fortify Decelea in Attica.
ATHENS
Athens votes to send funds and reinforcements to their forces in Sicily.

Such were the words of Alcibiades. The Spartans, who had previously intended to march against Athens themselves, but were still waiting and looking about them, at once became much more serious when they received this particular information from Alcibiades, and considered that they had heard it from the man who best knew the truth of the matter. [2] Accordingly they now turned their attention to fortifying Decelea[2a] and sending immediate aid to the Sicilians; and naming Gylippus son of Cleandridas to the command of the Syracusans, instructed him to consult with that people and with the Corinthians[2b] and arrange for help to reach the island in the best and speediest way possible under the circumstances. [3] Gylippus requested the Corinthians to send him at once two ships to Asine,[3a] and to prepare the rest that they intended to send, and to have them ready to sail at the proper time. Having settled this, the envoys departed from Sparta.

[4] In the meantime the Athenian trireme from Sicily sent by the generals for money and cavalry arrived at Athens; and the Athenians, after hearing what they wanted, voted to send the supplies for the armament and the cavalry. And the winter ended, and with it ended the seventeenth year of the present war of which Thucydides is the historian.

6.94
414
18th Year/Summer
SICILY
The Athenians in early spring pillage some cities and coerce others to join them. At Catana, they find reinforcements of funds and horsemen sent from Athens.

The next summer, at the very beginning of the season, the Athenians in Sicily put out from Catana,[1a] and sailed along shore to Megara in Sicily, from which, as I have mentioned above, the Syracusans expelled the inhabitants in the time of their tyrant Gelon,[1b] themselves occupying the territory. [2] Here the Athenians landed and laid waste the country, and after an unsuccessful attack upon a fort of the Syracusans, went on with the fleet and army to the river Terias,[2a] and advancing inland laid waste the plain and set fire to the grain; and after killing some of a small Syracusan party which they encountered, and setting up a trophy, went back again to their ships. [3] They now sailed to Catana and took in provisions there, and going with their whole force against Centoripa,[3a] a city of the Sicels, acquired it by capitulation, and departed, after also burning the grain of the Inessaeans and Hybleans.[3c] [4] Upon their return to Catana they found the horsemen arrived from Athens, to the number of two hundred and fifty (with their

6.93.2a Decelea, in Attica: Map 6.91.
6.93.2b Corinth: Map 6.91.
6.93.3a Asine, probably in Messenia: Map 6.91.
6.94.1a Catana: Map 6.95, Sicily.
6.94.1b This expulsion by Gelon is mentioned in 6.4.2. Megara (Hyblaea): Map 6.95, Sicily.
6.94.2a Terias river: Map 6.95, Sicily.
6.94.3a Centoripa: Map 6.95, Sicily.
6.94.3c Inessa, Hybla, possible location: Map 6.95, Sicily.

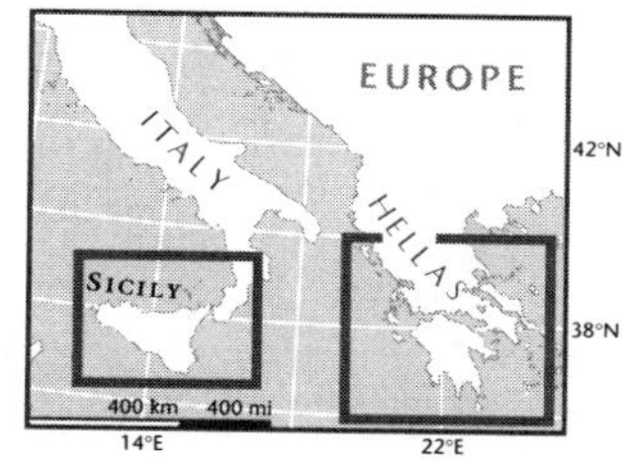

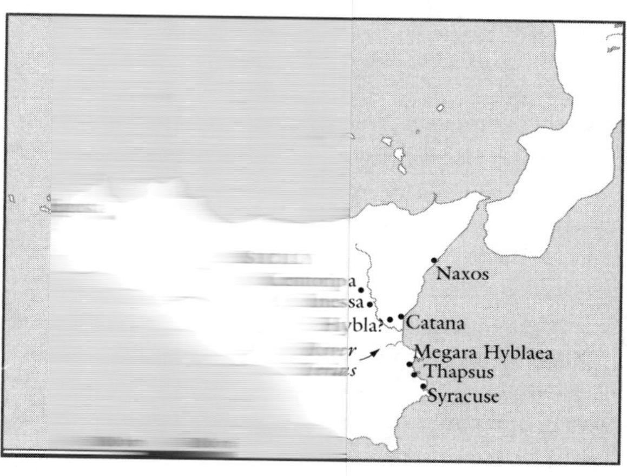

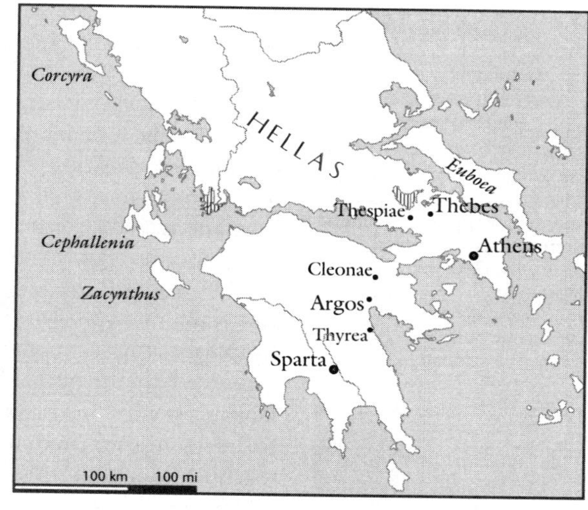

MA ONS IN SPRING 414

eq eir horses which were to be procured upon the sp archers and three hundred talents of silver.[4a]

artans marched against Argos and went as far as Cl uake occurred and caused them to return. After thi e territory of Thyrea,[1b] which is on their border, an n the Spartans, which was sold for no less than tw same summer, not long after, the popular party in upon the party in office, which was not successful. hebes, and some were caught, while others took ref

6.95
414
18th Year/Summer
HELLAS
Thucydides reports military raids and uprisings in Argos, Thyrea, and Boeotia.

Syracusans learned that the Athenians had been joi d were on the point of marching against them; an coming masters of Epipolae,[1a] a precipitous spot sit y, the Athenians could not, even if victorious in bat hey determined to guard its approaches in order

6.96
414
18th Year/Summer
SYRACUSE
Syracuse decides that control of Epipolae is vital to its defense and selects six hundred picked troops to guard it.

6.94 ht and of sical Greek

6.95 Hellas.

6.95

6.95.2a Thespiae, Thebes, Athens: Map 6.95, Hellas.

6.96.1a Epipolae: Map 6.99, AX.

that the enemy might not ascend unobserved by these, the only ways by which ascent was possible, [2] as the remainder is lofty ground, and falls right down to the city, and can all be seen from inside; and as it lies above the rest the place is called by the Syracusans Epipolae, or Overtown.

[3] They accordingly went out in mass at daybreak into the meadow along the river Anapus,[3a] their new generals, Hermocrates and his colleagues, having just come into office, and held a review of their hoplites, from whom they first selected a picked body of six hundred, under the command of Diomilus, an exile from Andros,[3b] to guard Epipolae, and to be ready to muster at a moment's notice to help wherever help should be required.

6.97
414
18th Year/Summer
SYRACUSE
The Athenians sail to Leon and occupy Epipolae from there before the picked Syracusan force arrives. The Syracusans are defeated as they come up and the Athenians build a fort on the plateau at Labdalum.

Meanwhile the Athenians, the very same morning, were holding a review, having already made land unobserved with all the armament from Catana,[1a] opposite a place called Leon,[1b] not much more than half a mile from Epipolae,[1c] where they disembarked their army. They anchored their fleet at Thapsus,[1d] a peninsula running out into the sea with a narrow isthmus, and not far from the city of Syracuse either by land or water. [2] While the naval force of the Athenians threw a stockade across the isthmus and remained quiet at Thapsus, the army immediately went on at a run to Epipolae, and succeeded in getting up by Euryelus[2a] before the Syracusans perceived them, or could come up from the meadow and the review. [3] Diomilus with his six hundred and the rest advanced as quickly as they could, but they had nearly three miles to go from the meadow before reaching them. [4] Attacking in this way in considerable disorder, the Syracusans were defeated in battle at Epipolae and retired to the city, with a loss of about three hundred killed, and Diomilus among the number. [5] After this the Athenians set up a trophy and restored to the Syracusans their dead under truce, and next day descended to Syracuse itself; and no one coming out to meet them, reascended and built a fort at Labdalum,[5a] upon the edge of the cliffs of Epipolae, looking toward Megara,[5b] to serve as a storehouse for their baggage and money, whenever they advanced to give battle or to work at the lines.

6.98
414
18th Year/Summer
SYRACUSE
The Athenians start to build a wall of circumvallation around Syracuse. The Syracusans try to attack but cannot organize their lines properly and retreat without offering battle.

Not long afterwards three hundred cavalry came to them from Egesta,[1a] and about a hundred from the Sicels, Naxians,[1b] and others; and thus, with the two hundred and fifty from Athens, for whom they had got horses from the Egestaeans and Catanians,[1c] besides others that they bought, they now mustered six hundred and fifty cavalry in all. [2] After posting a garrison in Labdalum,[2a] they advanced to Syca,[2b] where they halted and quickly built the Circle[2c] or center of their wall of circumvallation. The Syracusans,

6.96.3a Anapus river: Map 6.99, BX.
6.96.3b Andros: Map 6.56.
6.97.1a Catana: Map 6.95, Sicily.
6.97.1b Leon: Map 6.99, AX.
6.97.1c Epipolae: Map 6.99, AX.
6.97.1d Thapsus: Map 6.95, Sicily.
6.97.2a Euryelus: Map 6.99, AX.
6.97.5a Labdalum: Map 6.99, AX.
6.97.5b Megara (Hyblaea): Map 6.95, Sicily.
6.98.1a Egesta: Map 6.95, Sicily.
6.98.1b Naxos: Map 6.95, Sicily.
6.98.1c Catana: Map 6.95, Sicily.
6.98.2a Labdalum: Map 6.99, AX.
6.98.2b Syca, possible location: Map 6.99, AY.
6.98.2c Circle fort: Map 6.99, AX.

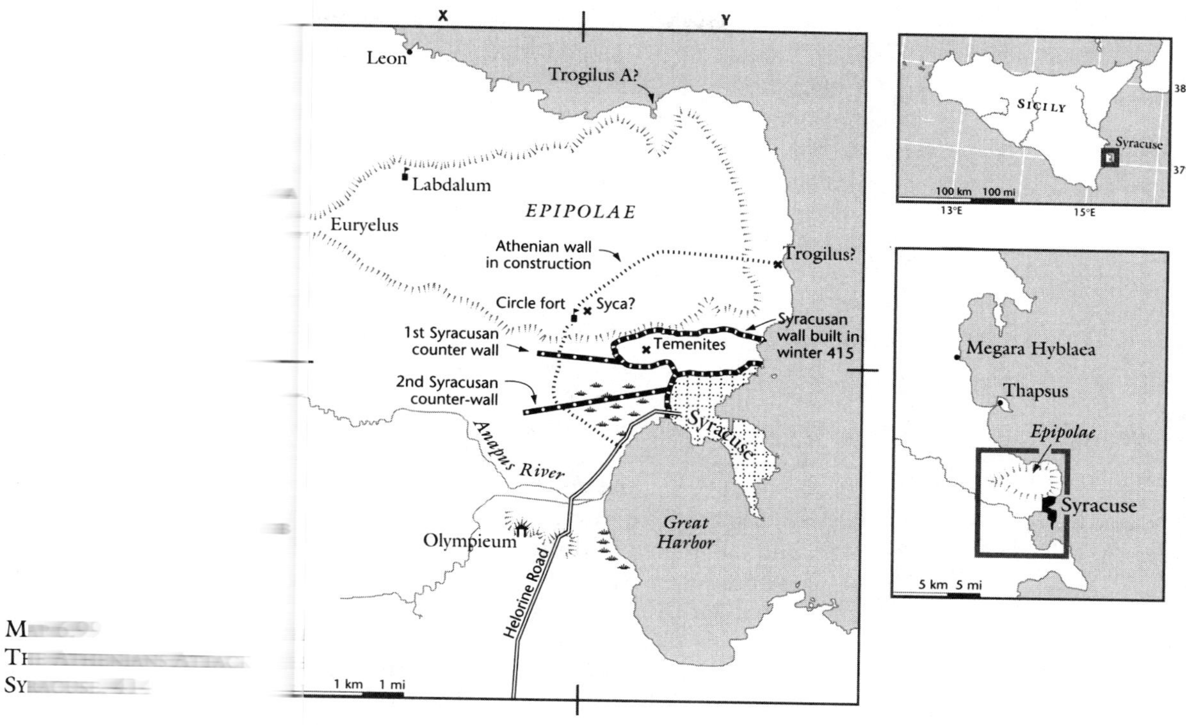

M
Tr
Sy

ap ith which the work advanced, determined to go
ou battle and interrupt it; [3] and the two armies
w when the Syracusan generals observed that their
tr ty in getting into line, and were in such disorder,
th nto the city, except part of the cavalry. These re-
m Athenians from carrying stones or dispersing to
an til a tribe[4a] of the Athenian hoplites, with all the
ca d the Syracusan horse with some loss; after which
th e cavalry action.

nians began building the wall to the north of the
Ci ollecting stone and timber, which they kept laying
do along the shortest line for their works from the
G 2] while the Syracusans, guided by their generals,

6.99 414 18th Year/Summer SYRACUSE Athenian wall construction proceeds rapidly from the Circle fort on Epipolae. The Syracusans build a counter-wall to cut the line of the enemy's wall.

6.9 ten tribes at
rmy was also
s. This was also
see 6.100.1.

6.9 Map 6.99, AY.
he interpreta-
ada from
nd Stoughton,
n the location of Trogilus and the Lysimeleia marsh (Map 7.39). The reader should be aware, however, that many scholars follow the view adopted by K. J. Dover, as described in A.W. Gomme, A. Andrewes, and K.J. Dover, *A Historical Commentary on Thucydides,* iv (Oxford, 1970), 466 ff., which locates Trogilus in a more northerly cove shown as "Trogilus A?" on Map 6.99, AY.

and above all by Hermocrates, instead of risking any more general engagements, determined to build a counterwall in the direction in which the Athenians were going to carry their wall. If this could be completed in time the enemy's lines would be cut; and meanwhile, if he were to attempt to interrupt them by an attack, they would send a part of their forces against him, and would secure the approaches beforehand with their stockade, while the Athenians would have to leave off working with their whole force in order to attend to them. [3] They accordingly sallied forth and began to build, starting from their city, running a cross wall below the Athenian Circle,[3a] at the same time cutting down the olive trees and erecting wooden towers. [4] As the Athenian fleet had not yet sailed round into the Great Harbor,[4a] the Syracusans still commanded the sea coast, and the Athenians brought their provisions by land from Thapsus.[4b]

6.100
414
18th Year/Summer
SYRACUSE
In a surprise attack, the Athenians take the Syracusan counterwall and destroy it.

The Syracusans now thought the stockades and stonework of their counterwall sufficiently far advanced; and as the Athenians, afraid of being divided and so fighting at a disadvantage, and intent upon their own wall, did not come out to interrupt them, they left one tribe to guard the new work and went back into the city. Meanwhile the Athenians destroyed the underground pipes that carried drinking water into the city; and watching until the rest of the Syracusans were in their tents at midday (and some even gone away into the city), and those in the stockade keeping but indifferent guard, they appointed three hundred picked men of their own, and some men selected from the light troops who were appropriately armed for the purpose to run suddenly as fast as they could to the counterwall, while the rest of the army advanced in two divisions, one with one of the generals to the city in case of a sortie, the other with the other general to the stockade by the postern gate. [2] The three hundred attacked and took the stockade, abandoned by its garrison, who took refuge in the outworks round the statue of Apollo Temenites.[2a] Here the pursuers burst in with them, and after getting in were beaten out by the Syracusans, and some few of the Argives and Athenians slain; [3] after which the whole army retired, and having demolished the counterwall and pulled up the stockade, carried away the stakes to their own lines, and set up a trophy.

6.101
414
18th Year/Summer
SYRACUSE
A second Syracusan counterwall is also captured by the Athenians. In a confused battle the Syracusans are defeated but the Athenian general Lamachus is killed.

The next day the Athenians from the Circle[1a] proceeded to fortify the cliff above the marsh which on this side of Epipolae looks toward the Great Harbor; this being also the shortest line for their wall to go down across the plain and the marsh to the harbor. [2] Meanwhile the Syracusans marched out and began a second stockade, starting from the city, across the middle of the marsh, digging a trench alongside to make it impossible for the Athenians to carry their wall down to the sea. [3] As soon as the Athenians had finished their work at the cliff they again attacked the stockade

6.99.3a Circle fort: Map 6.99, AX.
6.99.4a Great Harbor: Map 6.99, BY.
6.99.4b Thapsus: Map 6.95, Sicily.
6.100.2a Temenites district: Map 6.99, AY.
6.101.1a Circle fort: Map 6.99, AX.

an s. Ordering the fleet to sail round from Thapsus[3a] int Syracuse,[3b] they descended at about dawn from Ep nd laying doors and planks over the marsh where it crossed over on these, and by daybreak took the dit cept for a small portion which they captured af- te ensued, in which the Athenians were victorious, th usans fleeing to the city and the left to the river. Th d Athenians, wishing to cut off their passage, pr bridge, [5] when the alarmed Syracusans, who ha ir cavalry, closed and routed them, hurling them ba ight wing, the first tribe[5a] of which was thrown int [6] Seeing this, Lamachus came to their aid from th ew archers and with the Argives, and crossing a dit a few that had crossed with him, and was killed wi . These the Syracusans managed immediately to sn t across the river into a place of security, them- sel of the Athenian army now came up.

6.102
414
18th Year/Summer
SYRACUSE
The Syracusans attack the enemy in the plain and at the Circle fort on Epipolae. Nicias saves the Circle by burning timber and war engines so that the fire holds off the enemy until reinforcements arrive. The defeated Syracusans return to their city.

had at first fled for refuge to the city, seeing the tu ow rallied from the city and formed against the At , sending also a part of their number to the Cir- cle ey hoped to take while denuded of its defenders. [2 yed the Athenian outwork of a thousand feet, the Ci y Nicias, who happened to have been left in it th now ordered the servants to set fire to the ma- ch been thrown down before the wall; lack of men, as other means of survival impossible. [3] This step wa as the Syracusans came no further on account of th anwhile help was coming up from the Athenians be ght the troops opposed to them; and the fleet als was sailing from Thapsus[3a] into the Great Har- bo Syracusan troops on the heights retired in haste, an tered the city, thinking that with their present fo be able to hinder the wall reaching the sea.

6.103
414
18th Year/Summer
SYRACUSE
The Athenians extend their wall against the city. Provisions are secured from Italy. Some Tyrrhenians and many Sicels now join their forces. The Syracusans despair, divide into factions, replace their generals, and begin to discuss surrender terms.

s set up a trophy and restored to the Syracusans th ceiving in return Lamachus and those who had fal e of their forces, naval and military, being now wi om Epipolae[1a] and the cliffs and enclosed the Sy wall down to the sea. [2] Provisions were now br nt from all parts of Italy; and many of the Sicels, wh oking to see how things went, came as allies to th rrived three ships of fifty oars from Tyrrhenia.[2a]

6.1
6.1 Y.
6.1
1.1 f the Athen-

6.102.1a Circle fort: Map 6.99, AX.
6.102.3a Thapsus: Map 6.95, Sicily.
6.102.3b Great Harbor: Map 6.99, BY.
6.103.1a Epipolae: Map 6.99, AX.
6.103.2a Tyrrhenia: Map 6.104, locator.

Meanwhile everything else progressed favorably for their hopes. [3] The Syracusans began to despair of finding safety in arms, no relief having reached them from the Peloponnesus, and were now proposing terms of capitulation among themselves and to Nicias, who after the death of Lamachus was left sole commander. [4] No decision was reached, but as was natural with men in difficulties and besieged more severely than before, there was much discussion with Nicias and still more in the city. Their present misfortunes had also made them suspicious of one another; and the blame of their disasters was thrown upon the ill-fortune or treachery of the generals under whose command they had happened; and these were deposed and others, Heraclides, Eucles, and Tellias, elected in their stead.

6.104
414
18th Year/Summer
ITALY
Gylippus leaves Leucas, believing that Syracuse was lost. He hopes to save Italy. Tarentum receives him but Thurii rejects his plea. Nicias hears of his approach but, despising the smallness of his force, takes no precautions.

Meanwhile the Spartan Gylippus and the ships from Corinth[1a] were now off Leucas,[1b] intent upon going with all haste to the relief of Sicily. The news that reached them being of an alarming kind, and all agreeing in a false report that the siege line around Syracuse was already complete. Gylippus abandoned all hope for Sicily, and wishing to save Italy, rapidly crossed the Ionian Sea[1c] to Tarentum[1d] with the Corinthian, Pythen, in two Laconian, and two Corinthian vessels, leaving the Corinthians to follow him after manning, in addition to their own ten, two Leucadian and two Ambraciot[1e] ships. [2] From Tarentum Gylippus first went on a mission to Thurii,[2a] and claimed anew the rights of citizenship which his father had enjoyed, but failing to bring over the townspeople, he weighed anchor and coasted along Italy. Opposite the Terinaean gulf[2b] he was caught by the wind which blows violently and steadily from the north in that quarter, and was carried out to sea; and after experiencing very rough weather, made it back to Tarentum where he hauled ashore and refitted such of his ships as had suffered most from the tempest. [3] Nicias heard of his approach, but, like the Thurians, scorned the scanty number of his ships, and set down piracy as the only probable purpose of the voyage, and so took no precautions for the present.

6.105
414
18th Year/Summer
ARGOS-LACONIA
Sparta invades Argos, and Athenian forces sent in response conduct raids against Peloponnesian territories, providing a pretext for the initiation of Spartan hostilities against Athens.

About the same time in this summer, the Spartans invaded Argos[1a] with their allies, and laid waste most of the country. The Athenians went with thirty ships to the relief of the Argives, thus breaking their treaty with the Spartans in the most overt manner. [2] Up to this time incursions from Pylos[2a] and descents on the coasts of the rest of the Peloponnesus, instead of on the Laconian, had been the extent of their cooperation with the Ar-

6.104.1a Corinth: Map 6.104.
6.104.1b Leucas: Map 6.104.
6.104.1c Ionian sea: Map 6.104, locator.
6.104.1d Tarentum: Map 6.104, locator.
6.104.1e Ambracia: Map 6.104.
6.104.2a Thurii: Map 6.104, locator.
6.104.2b Terinaean gulf, possible location: Map 6.104, locator. Perhaps Thucydides makes a geographic error here. The city of Terina is located on the west coast of Bruttium (as shown in Map 6.104, locator), but a north wind there would hardly blow a ship out to sea, nor would Gylippus' ships be likely to return to Tarentum from the Tyrrhenian Sea west of Italy. A location on the south coast of Italy between Croton and Rhegium is certainly a more plausible location for this possibly misnamed gulf.
6.105.1a Argos: Map 6.104.
6.105.2a Pylos: Map 6.104.

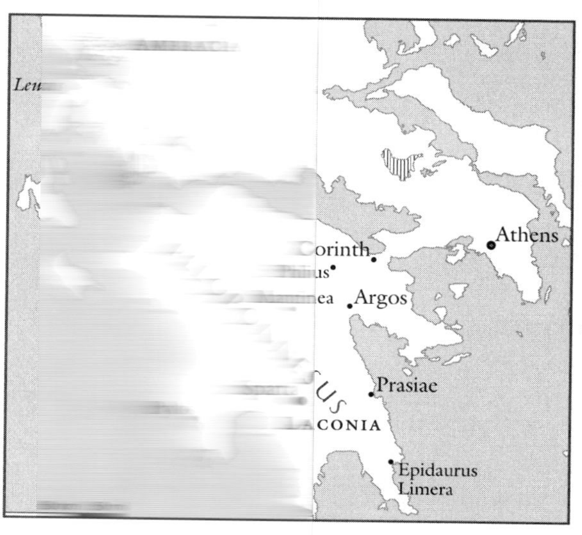

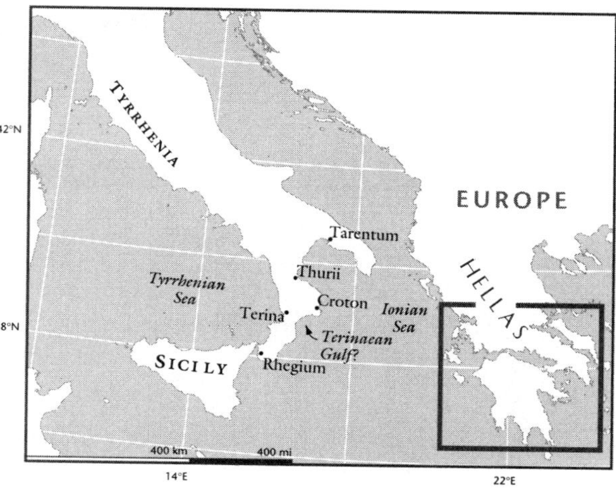

M… TIONS IN SUMMER, 414

gi… nd although the Argives had often begged them to… nent, with their hoplites in Laconia,[2c] lay waste ev… m, and depart, they had always refused to do so. N… command of Pythodorus, Laespodius, and Dem… idaurus Limera,[2d] Prasiae,[2e] and other places, and pl… d thus furnished the Spartans with a better prete… Athens. [3] After the Athenians had retired from Ar… the Spartans also, the Argives made an incursion int… is,[3a] and returned home after ravaging the land an… abitants.

6.1…
6.1…
6.1… 04.
6.1…
6.1…

BOOK SEVEN

7.1
414
18th Year/Summer
SICILY
Hearing that Syracuse might still be saved, Gylippus sails to Himera where he gathers allies before marching overland to Syracuse.

After refitting their ships, Gylippus
an [illegible] from Tarentum[1a] to Epizephyrian Locri.[1b] They
nc [illegible] rect information that the siege works at Syracuse[1c]
w [illegible] d that it was still possible for an army arriving by
Ep [illegible] ntrance; they considered, accordingly, whether
th [illegible] their right and risk sailing in by sea, or leaving
it [illegible] rst sail to Himera,[1e] and taking with them the
H [illegible] rs that might agree to join them, go to Syracuse
by [illegible] decided to sail for Himera, especially as the four
A [illegible] as had at last sent off, on hearing that they were
at [illegible] rrived at Rhegium.[2a] Accordingly, before these
re [illegible] loponnesians crossed the strait and after touching
at [illegible] [2b] came to Himera. [3] There they persuaded the
H [illegible] war, and not only to go with them themselves
bu [illegible] the seamen from their vessels which they had
dr [illegible] and they sent and appointed a place for the Selin-
ur [illegible] with all their forces. [4] A few troops were also
pr [illegible] [a] and by some of the Sicels, who were now ready
to [illegible] greater alacrity, owing to the recent death of
A [illegible] Sicel king in that neighborhood and friendly to
A [illegible] o the vigor shown by Gylippus in coming from
Sp [illegible] ow took with him about seven hundred of his
sa [illegible] number only having arms), a thousand *hoplites*[5a]
ar [illegible] mera with a body of a hundred horse, some light
tr [illegible] Selinus, a few Geloans, and Sicels numbering a
th [illegible] it on his march for Syracuse.

7. [illegible]
7. [illegible]: Map 7.1.
7. [illegible]
7. [illegible]
7. [illegible]
7. [illegible]
7. [illegible]
7. [illegible]

7.1.4a Gela: Map 7.1.
7.1.4b Sparta: Map 7.1.
7.1.5a *Hoplite* is the Greek word for a heavily armed infantryman. See Glossary and Appendix F, Land Warfare, §2. Marines were hoplites trained to fight from the decks of triremes; see Appendix G, Trireme warfare, §8, §11, §14.

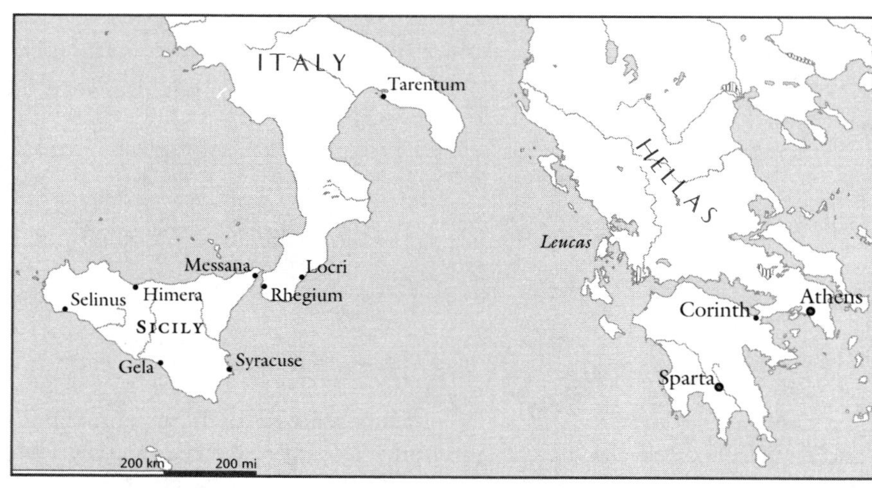

MAP 7.1 REINFORCEMENTS FOR SYRACUSE

7.2
414
18th Year/Summer
SYRACUSE
Just as the Athenians are about to close their siege walls, and the Syracusans are losing hope, Gongylus arrives with news that reinforcements from the Peloponnesus are coming. The arrival of Gylippus restores Syracusan morale.

Meanwhile the Corinthian[1a] fleet from Leucas[1b] made all haste to arrive; and one of their commanders, Gongylus, starting last with a single ship, was the first to reach Syracuse, a little before Gylippus. Gongylus found the Syracusans on the point of holding an assembly to consider whether they should not put an end to the war. This he prevented, and reassured them by telling them that more vessels were still to arrive, and that Gylippus son of Cleandridas had been despatched by the Spartans to take the command. [2] Upon this the Syracusans took courage, and immediately marched out with all their forces to meet Gylippus, who they found was now close at hand. [3] Meanwhile Gylippus, after taking Ietae,[3a] a fort of the Sicels, on his way, formed his army in order of battle, and so arrived at Epipolae, and ascending by Euryelus,[3b] as the Athenians had done at first, now advanced with the Syracusans against the Athenian lines. [4] By chance, he had arrived at a critical moment. The Athenians had already finished a double wall of almost a mile[4a] to the Great Harbor, with the exception of a small portion next to the sea, which they were still engaged upon; and in the remainder of the circle toward Trogilus[4b] on the other sea, stones had been laid ready for building for the greater part of the distance, and some points had been left half finished, while others were entirely completed. The danger of Syracuse had indeed been great.

7.2.1a Corinth: Map 7.1.
7.2.1b Leucas: Map 7.1.
7.2.3a Ietae: site unknown.
7.2.3b Euryelus on Epipolae: Map 7.4, AX.
7.2.4a Thucydides actually wrote six or seven *stades:* the Attic stade was 607 feet, the Olympic stade 630.8 feet. Complete and incomplete Athenian walls: Map 7.4.
7.2.4b Trogilus: Map 7.4, AY. For another theory as to its location, see note 6.99.1a.

ans, recovering from the confusion into which 7.3 414 18th Year/Summer EPIPOLAE The two armies form up but neither will attack. While they confront each other, Gylippus sends out a force that captures the Athenian fort of Labdalum.
th own by the sudden approach of Gylippus and the
Sy der of battle. Gylippus halted at a short distance
of [a] to tell them that if they would evacuate Sicily
wi hin five days' time, he was willing to make a truce
ac nians treated this proposition with contempt, and
di out an answer. After this both sides began to prepa pus, observing that the Syracusans were in disor-
de into line, drew off his troops more into the open
gr not lead on the Athenians but lay still by his own
wa that they did not come on, he led off his army to
th of Apollo Temenites,[3a] and passed the night there.
[4 he led out the main body of his army, and draw-
in attle before the walls of the Athenians to prevent
th of any other quarter, dispatched a strong force
ag nd took it, and put all whom he found in it to the
sw g within sight of the Athenians. [5] On the same
da that lay moored off the harbor was captured by
th

ns and their allies began to build a single wall, 7.4 414 18th Year/Summer SYRACUSE The Syracusans begin to construct a counterwall. Nicias fortifies Plemmyrium and other sites, and dispatches a squadron to intercept the approaching Corinthian ships.
st a slanting direction up Epipolae, in order to pre-
ve they could hinder the work, from extending and
co l. [2] Meanwhile the Athenians, having now fin-
is the sea, had come up to the heights; and part of
th ippus drew out his army by night and attacked it.
[3 ns who happened to be bivouacking outside real-
iz and came out to meet him, upon seeing which he
qu again. The Athenians now built their wall higher,
an at this point themselves, disposing their confeder-
at of the works, at the stations assigned to them. [4]
N fortify Plemmyrium,[4a] a promontory opposite the
ci narrows the mouth of the Great Harbor. He
th ion of this place would make it easier to bring in
su e able to carry on their blockade from a shorter
di port used by the Syracusans; instead of being
ob ement of the enemy's navy, to sail out against
th the Great Harbor. Besides this, he now began to
pa war by sea, seeing that the coming of Gylippus
ha s by land. [5] Accordingly, he conveyed over his

7.3 ... Greek institu- ... ated under ... rmes, and ... staff they car- ... unmolested ... ng wartime in ... ke back replies, ... ements.

7.3.3a Temenites district of Syracuse: Map 7.4, AY.

7.3.4a Fort Labdalum: Map 7.4, AX.

7.3.5a *Triremes* were the standard warship of this period; see Appendix G, §4–7.

7.4.4a Plemmyrium: Map 7.4, BY.

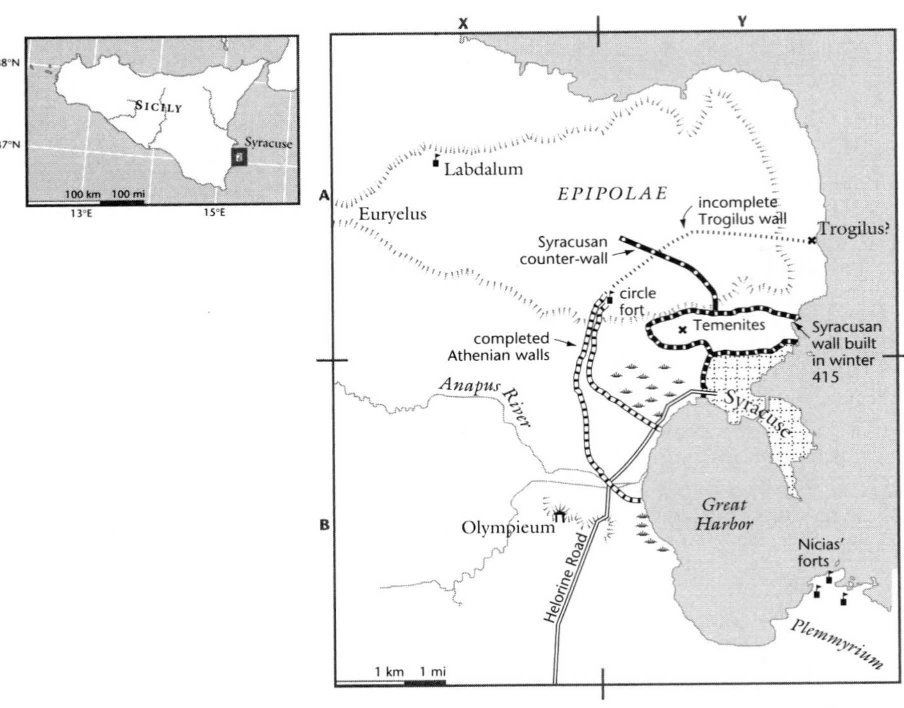

MAP 7.4 GYLIPPUS' FIRST BATTLES AT SYRACUSE[5a]

ships and some troops, and built three forts in which he placed most of his baggage, and moored there for the future the larger craft and warships. [6] This was the first and chief occasion of the losses which the crews experienced. The water which they used was scarce and had to be fetched from far away, and the sailors could not go out for firewood without being cut off by the Syracusan horse, who were masters of the country; a third of the enemy's cavalry being stationed at the little town of Olympieum,[6a] to prevent plundering incursions on the part of the Athenians at Plemmyrium. [7] Meanwhile Nicias learned that the rest of the Corinthian fleet was approaching, and sent twenty ships to watch for them, with orders to be on the lookout for them in the vicinity of Locri and Rhegium[7a] and the approaches to Sicily.

7.4.5a Map 7.4 basically follows the interpretation of Peter Green in *Armada from Athens* (London: Hodder and Stoughton, 1971), passim, particularly regarding the locations of Trogilus (Map 7.4, AY) and the Lysimeleia marsh (Map 7.41, BY). The reader should be aware, however, that many scholars follow the views of K. J. Dover as set out in A.W. Gomme, A. Andrewes, and K.J. Dover, *A Historical Commentary on Thucydides*, iv (Oxford, 1970), 466 ff. See note 6.99.1a.

7.4.6a Olympieum: Map 7.4, BX.

7.4.7a Locri (Epizephyrian) and Rhegium: Map 7.1.

went on with the wall[1a] across Epipolae, using the
st ns had laid down for their own wall, and at the
sa out the Syracusans and their allies, and formed
th front of the lines, the Athenians forming against
hi ht that the moment had come, and began the atta fight ensued between the lines, where the Syracu-
sa use; [3] and the Syracusans and their allies were
d r dead under truce,[3a] while the Athenians erected
a pus called the soldiers together, and said that the
fa his; he had kept their lines too much within the
w prived them of the services of their cavalry and
d ow, therefore, lead them on a second time. He
b per that in material force they would be fully a
m s, while with respect to moral advantages, it were
in sians and Dorians should not feel confident of
o islanders with the motley rabble that accompanied
t n out of the country.[4a]

7.5
414
18th Year/Summer
EPIPOLAE
Because Gylippus orders an attack in a constricted area where the Syracusan cavalry cannot be used, the Syracusans are defeated. Gylippus accepts blame for the defeat and promises a second effort with better results.

d the first opportunity that arose of again leading
t Now Nicias and the Athenians were of the opinion
t ns should not wish to offer battle, it was necessary
f building of the cross wall, as it already almost over-
l of their own, and if it went any further it would
f no difference whether they fought ever so many
s ver fought at all. They accordingly came out to
r Gylippus led out his hoplites further from the for-
t ormer occasion, and so joined battle; posting his
h he flank of the Athenians in the open space, where
t ls terminated. [3] During the engagement the cav-
a the left wing of the Athenians, which was opposed
t the Athenian army was in consequence defeated by
t en headlong within their lines. [4] The night fol-
l xtended their wall up to the Athenian works and
p ng it out of their power any longer to stop them,
a n if victorious in the field, of all chance of investing

7.6
414
18th Year/Summer
EPIPOLAE
Gylippus orders another attack. This time he uses his cavalry effectively and defeats the Athenians. The Syracusans then carry their counterwall past the Athenian works and prevent Athenian investment of the city.

ng twelve vessels of the Corinthians, Ambraciots,[1a]
d into the harbor under the command of the
having eluded the Athenian ships on guard, and
n completing the remainder of the cross wall. [2]

7.7
414
18th Year/Summer
SYRACUSE
Eluding the Athenians, the Corinthian ships arrive safely. Gylippus leaves to raise Sicilian forces. Both sides request reinforcements and the Syracusans begin to exercise their fleet.

Map 7.4, AY.
of hoplite warfare;
arfare, §6.
n of Dorian con-
s; see Appendix
Groups, §8.

Meanwhile Gylippus went into the rest of Sicily to raise land and naval forces, and also to bring over any of the cities that either were lukewarm in the cause or had until then kept out of the war altogether. [3] Syracusan and Corinthian envoys were also dispatched to Sparta and Corinth to get a fresh force sent over, in any way possible, either in merchant vessels or transports, or in any other manner likely to prove successful, as the Athenians too were sending for reinforcements; [4] while the Syracusans proceeded to man and train a fleet,[4a] intending to try their fortune in this way also, and generally became exceedingly confident.

7.8
414
18th Year/Summer
SYRACUSE
Nicias, feeling that his force must immediately depart or be strongly reinforced, sends a letter to Athens that frankly describes the situation. While awaiting their response, he adopts a defensive posture.

Nicias perceiving this, and seeing the strength of the enemy and his own difficulties daily increasing, himself also sent to Athens. He had before sent frequent reports of events as they occurred, and felt it especially incumbent upon him to do so now, as he thought that they were in a critical position, and that unless speedily recalled or strongly reinforced from home, they had no hope of safety. [2] He feared, however, that the messengers, either through inability to speak, or through failure of memory, or from a wish to please the multitude, might not report the truth, and so thought it best to write a letter, to insure that the Athenians should know his own opinion without its being lost in transmission, and be able to decide upon the real facts of the case. [3] His emissaries, accordingly, departed with the letter and the requisite verbal instructions; and he attended to the affairs of the army, making it his aim now to keep on the defensive and to avoid any unnecessary danger.

7.9
414
18th Year/Summer
AMPHIPOLIS
The Athenians fail to take Amphipolis.

At the close of the same summer the Athenian general Euetion marched in concert with Perdiccas[1a] with a large body of Thracians against Amphipolis,[1b] and failing to take it brought some triremes round into the Strymon,[1c] and blockaded the city from the river, having his base at Himeraeum.[1d]

7.10
414/3
18th Year/Winter
ATHENS
Nicias' letter arrives at Athens.

Summer was now over.

The winter ensuing, the persons sent by Nicias, reaching Athens, gave the verbal messages which had been entrusted to them, and answered any questions that were asked them, and delivered the letter. The secretary of the city now came forward and read out to the Athenians the letter, which was as follows:

7.11
414/3
18th Year/Winter
ATHENS
Nicias describes the recent defeat, the arrival of Gylippus and reinforcements to the enemy, and the success of the enemy's counterwall which, given his superiority in cavalry, has forced the Athenians to remain on the defensive.

"Our past operations, Athenians, have been made known to you by many other letters; it is now time for you to become equally familiar with our present condition, and to take your measures accordingly. [2] We had defeated the Syracusans, against whom we were sent, in most of our engagements with them, and we had built

7.7.4a For training a fleet, see Appendix G, Trireme Warfare, §11–15.

7.9.1a Perdiccas was the king of nearby Macedonia, Map 7.9.

7.9.1b Amphipolis: Map 7.9. The previous attempt by Athens to capture Amphipolis had been organized in the winter of 417/6, and was to have been led by Nicias, but was aborted when Perdiccas joined the Spartan-Argive alliance and refused to assist Athens; see 5.83.

7.9.1c Strymon river: Map 7.9.

7.9.1d Himeraeum: location unknown.

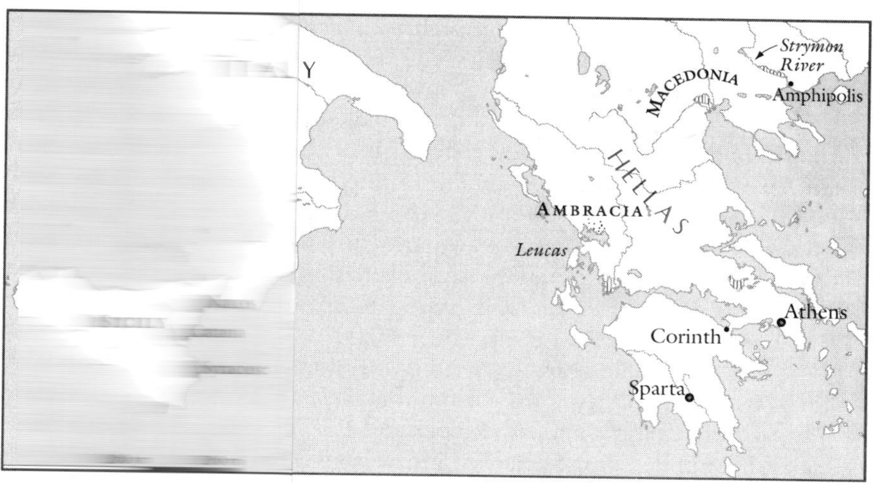

N 414

ow occupy, when Gylippus arrived from Sparta
d from the Peloponnesus and from some of the
first battle with him we were victorious; in the
g day we were overpowered by a multitude of
nd compelled to retire within our lines. [3] We
been forced by the numbers of those opposed
he work of circumvallation,[3a] and to remain in-
make use even of all the force we have, since a
oplites are absorbed in the defense of our lines.
have carried a single wall past our lines, thus
for us to invest them in future, until this cross
strong force and captured. [4] So that the become, at least from the land side, the besieged
prevented by their cavalry from even going for
country."

embassy has been dispatched to the Pelopon-
forcements, and Gylippus has gone to the cities
hope of inducing those that are at present neu-
e war, partly of bringing from his allies addi-
the land forces and material for the navy. [2]
they contemplate a combined attack upon our

7.12
414/3
18th Year/Winter
ATHENS
Nicias warns that the enemy is raising larger forces and is preparing to fight at sea, exploiting the deterioration that time has wreaked on Athenian ships and crews.

7 ling of a wall to
y land.

lines with their land forces and with their fleet by sea. [3] You must none of you be surprised that I say by sea also. They have discovered that the length of time we have now been in commission has rotted our ships and wasted our crews, and that with the completeness of our crews and the soundness of our ships the pristine efficiency of our navy has departed. [4] For it is impossible for us to haul our ships ashore and dry them out[4a] because the enemy's vessels being as many or more than our own, we are constantly anticipating an attack. [5] Indeed, they may be seen exercising, and it lies with them to take the initiative; and not having to maintain a blockade, they have greater facilities for drying their ships."

7.13
414/3
18th Year/Winter
ATHENS
Nicias elaborates on the reasons for the decline of his fleet's strength and efficiency.

"This we should scarcely be able to do, even if we had plenty of ships to spare, and were freed from our present necessity of exhausting all our strength upon the blockade. For it is already difficult to carry in supplies past Syracuse; and were we to relax our vigilance in the slightest degree it would become impossible. [2] The losses which our crews have suffered and still continue to suffer arise from the following causes. Expeditions for fuel and for forage, and the distance from which water has to be fetched, cause our sailors to be cut off by the Syracusan cavalry; the loss of our previous superiority emboldens our slaves to desert; our foreign seamen are impressed by the unexpected appearance of a navy against us, and the strength of the enemy's resistance; such of them as were pressed into the service take the first opportunity of departing to their respective cities; such as were originally seduced by the temptation of high pay, and expected little fighting and large gains, leave us either by desertion to the enemy or by availing themselves of one or other of the various facilities of escape which the magnitude of Sicily affords them. Some even engage in trade themselves and prevail upon the captains to take Hyccaric[2a] slaves on board in their place; thus they have ruined the efficiency of our navy."

7.14
414/3
18th Year/Winter
ATHENS
Nicias reports that he can neither remedy these problems nor recruit local reinforcements. If Italian markets are closed to the Athenians, which might occur in the absence of further support, the Athenians will have to evacuate Sicily. Nicias emphasizes that his report offers the unvarnished truth.

"Now I need not remind you that the time during which a crew is in its prime is short, and that the number of sailors who can start a ship on her way and keep the rowing in time is small.[1a] [2] But by far my greatest trouble is that holding the post which I do, I am prevented by the natural indiscipline of the Athenian seaman from putting a stop to these evils; and that meanwhile we have no source from which to recruit our crews, which the enemy can do from many quarters, but are compelled to depend both for supplying the crews in service and for making good our losses upon the men whom we

7.12.4a For the importance of regularly beaching triremes to dry their hulls, see Appendix G, Trireme Warfare, §6.

7.13.2a The capture of Hyccara and the enslavement of its inhabitants was described in 6.62.

7.14.1a For the significance of crew discipline and efficiency, see Appendix G, Trireme Warfare, §11–15 and the speech of the Athenian Phormio to his troops before battle in 2.89.9.

ur present allies, Naxos and Catana,[2a] are inca-
3] There is only one thing more that our op-
he loss of our Italian markets. If the Italians
to relieve us from our present condition, and
enemy, famine would compel us to evacuate,
sh the war without a blow."
rue, have written to you something different
n this, but nothing certainly more useful, if it
now the real state of things here before taking
I know that it is your nature to love to be told
, and then to blame the teller if the expecta-
ed in your minds are not answered by the re-
ought it safest to declare to you the truth."

o think that either your generals or your sol- 7.15 414/3 18th Year/Winter ATHENS Nicias closes by asking that the Athenian response, whether to recall or to reinforce the expedition, be made rapidly. He also asks to resign his command for reasons of health.
a match for the forces originally opposed to
eflect that a general Sicilian coalition is being
a fresh army is expected from the Pelopon-
we have here is unable to cope even with our
d you must promptly decide either to recall us
other fleet and army as numerous again, with
and someone to succeed me, as a disease in
unfit to retain my post. [2] I have, I think,
dulgence, as while I was in my prime I did you
ny commands. But whatever you mean to do,
cement of spring and without delay as the
Sicilian reinforcements shortly, those from the
onger interval; and unless you attend to the
be here before you, while the latter will elude
before."

tents of Nicias' letter. When the Athenians had 7.16 414/3 18th Year/Winter ATHENS The Athenians want Nicias to retain his command. They decide to send new generals to assist him and a new expedition to reinforce the Athenians at Syracuse.
he accept his resignation, but chose him two col-
le r and Euthydemus, two of the officers in Sicily,
to eir arrival, that Nicias might not be left alone in
hi ole weight of affairs. They also voted to send out
an drawn partly from the Athenians on the muster
ro es. [2] The colleagues chosen for Nicias were
D isthenes, and Eurymedon son of Thucles. Eu-
ry once, about the time of the winter solstice, with
te wenty *talents* of silver, and instructions to tell the

7.1 .
7.1 and money.
reek Cur-

army that reinforcements would arrive, and that care would be taken of them; [7.17.1] but Demosthenes stayed behind to organize the expedition, meaning to start as soon as it was spring, and sent for troops to the allies, and meanwhile got together money, ships, and hoplites at home.

7.17
414/3
18th Year/Winter
ATHENS
The Athenians decide to send the expedition in the spring. Athenian triremes are sent to block enemy reinforcements from reaching Sicily. The Corinthians plan to challenge the Athenian squadron at Naupactus.

[2] The Athenians also sent twenty vessels round the Peloponnesus to prevent anyone crossing over to Sicily from Corinth or the Peloponnesus. [3] For the Corinthians, filled with confidence by the favorable alteration in Sicilian affairs which had been reported by the envoys upon their arrival, and convinced that the fleet which they had before sent out had not been without use, were now preparing to despatch a force of hoplites in merchant vessels to Sicily, while the Spartans did the same for the rest of the Peloponnesus. [4] The Corinthians also manned a fleet of twenty-five vessels, intending to try the result of a battle with the squadron on guard at Naupactus,[4a] and meanwhile to make it less easy for the Athenians there to hinder the departure of their merchant vessels by obliging them to keep an eye upon the triremes thus arrayed against them.

7.18
414/3
18th Year/Winter
SPARTA
The Spartans prepare to invade Attica, to fortify Decelea (as Alcibiades advised), and thus to force a second front upon the Athenians. They were encouraged by their perception that they no longer carried the legal and moral opprobrium of refusing arbitration which they had borne when the war began.

In the meantime the Spartans prepared for their invasion of Attica,[1a] in accordance with their own previous resolve, and at the instigation of the Syracusans and Corinthians, who wished for an invasion to prevent the reinforcements which they heard that Athens was about to send to Sicily. Alcibiades also urgently advised the fortification of Decelea,[1b] and a vigorous prosecution of the war. [2] But the Spartans derived most encouragement from the belief that Athens, with two wars on her hands, against themselves and against the Sicilians, would be more easy to subdue, and from the conviction that she had been the first to violate the truce. In the former war, they considered that the offense had been more on their own side, both on account of the attack of the Thebans on Plataea[2a] in time of peace, and also of their own refusal to listen to the Athenian offer of arbitration, in spite of the clause in the former treaty that where arbitration[2b] should be offered there should be no appeal to arms. For this reason they thought that they deserved their misfortunes, and took to heart seriously the disaster at Pylos[2c] and whatever else had befallen them. [3] But when, besides the ravages from Pylos,[3a] which went on without any intermission, the thirty Athenian ships came out from Argos[3b] and wasted part of Epidaurus,[3c] Prasiae,[3d] and other places; when upon every dispute that arose as to the interpretation of any doubtful point in the treaty, their own offers of arbitration were always rejected by the Athenians—the Spartans at length decided that Athens had now committed the very same offense as they had before

7.17.4a Naupactus: Map 7.18, AX.
7.18.1a Attica: Map 7.18, AX.
7.18.1b Decelea: Map 7.18, AX.
7.18.2a Thucydides describes the Theban assault on Plataea in 2.2–6.
7.18.2b Pericles appeals to the arbitration clause in the treaty establishing the Thirty Years' Peace in 1.144.2, and the Athenians formally challenge the Spartans to submit their complaint to arbitration in 1.145.
7.18.2c Pylos: Map 7.18, BX. Thucydides describes the Spartan defeat at Pylos in 4.2–6, 4.8–23, and 4.26–41.
7.18.3a For the incursions from Pylos, see 6.105.2.
7.18.3b Argos: Map 7.18, BX.
7.18.3c Epidaurus: Map 7.18, BX.
7.18.3d Prasiae: Map 7.18, BX.

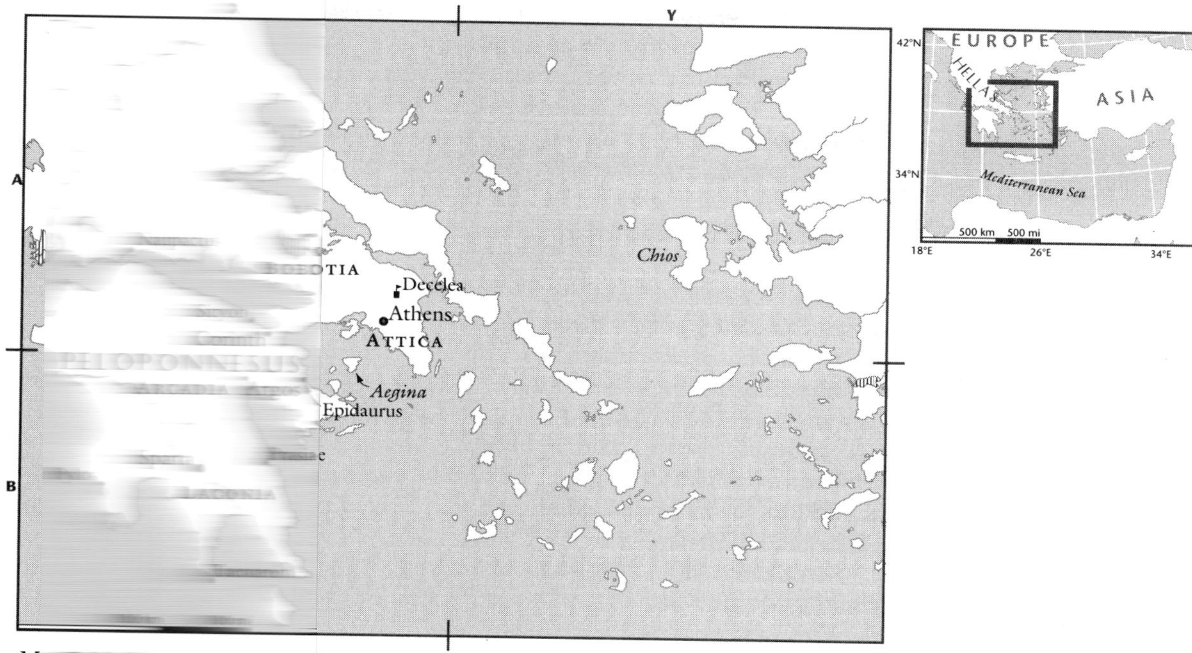

e guilty party; and they began to be full of enthusiasm … y spent this winter in sending round to their allies … eady the other implements for building their fort; … sing at home, and also by forced requisitions in … sus, a force to be sent out in the merchant ships … nter thus ended, and with it the eighteenth year of … des is the historian.

7.19 413 19th Year/Summer ATTICA The Spartans invade Attica and fortify Decelea. PELOPONNESUS Peloponnesian reinforcements leave for Sicily. A Corinthian squadron successfully prevents intervention by the Athenian ships at Naupactus.

following spring, at an earlier period than usual, … ies invaded Attica, under the command of Agis … of the Spartans. They began by devastating the … plain, and next proceeded to fortify Decelea, di… e different cities. [2] Decelea is about thirteen or … ty of Athens, and the same distance or not much … d the fort was intended to damage the plain and … ountry, being in sight of Athens. [3] While the

Peloponnesians and their allies in Attica were engaged in the work of fortification, their countrymen at home sent off, at about the same time, the hoplites in the merchant vessels to Sicily; the Spartans furnishing a picked force of Helots[3a] and *neodamodeis*,[3b] six hundred hoplites in all, under the command of Eccritus, a *Spartiate*; and the Boeotians three hundred hoplites, commanded by two Thebans, Xenon and Nicon, and by Hegesander, a Thespian. [4] These were among the first to put out into the open sea, starting from Taenarum[4a] in Laconia.[4b] Not long after their departure the Corinthians sent off a force of five hundred hoplites, consisting partly of men from Corinth[4c] itself, and partly of Arcadian[4d] mercenaries, placed under the command of Alexarchus, a Corinthian. The Sicyonians[4e] also sent off two hundred hoplites at the same time as the Corinthians, under the command of Sargeus, a Sicyonian. [5] Meantime the five-and-twenty vessels manned by Corinth during the winter lay confronting the twenty Athenian ships at Naupactus[5a] until the hoplites in the merchant ships were fairly on their way from the Peloponnesus; thus fulfilling the object for which they had been manned originally, which was to divert the attention of the Athenians from the merchant ships to the triremes.

7.20
413
19th Year/Summer
ATHENS
Athenian hoplites are joined by Argives and other allies. As Demosthenes prepares to leave, another squadron departs to raid the Peloponnesus.

During this time the Athenians were not idle. Simultaneously with the fortification of Decelea,[1a] at the very beginning of spring, they sent thirty ships round the Peloponnesus, under Charicles son of Apollodorus, with instructions to call at Argos[1b] and demand a force of their hoplites for the fleet, in agreement with the alliance. At the same time they dispatched Demosthenes to Sicily, [2] as they had intended, with sixty Athenian and five Chian[2a] vessels, twelve hundred Athenian hoplites from the enlistment roll, and as many of the islanders as could be raised in the different quarters, drawing upon the other subject allies for whatever they could supply that would be of use for the war. Demosthenes was instructed first to sail round with Charicles and to operate with him upon the coasts of Laconia, [3] and accordingly sailed to Aegina[3a] and there waited for the remainder of his force, and for Charicles to fetch the Argive troops.

7.21
413
19th Year/Summer
SYRACUSE
Gylippus urges the Syracusans to build and man a fleet to challenge the Athenians at sea. Hermocrates supports him, saying that such audacity will unnerve the Athenians and lead to victory. The Syracusans agree to try.

In Sicily about the same time in this spring, Gylippus came to Syracuse with as many troops as he could bring from the cities which he had persuaded to join. [2] Calling the Syracusans together, he told them that they must man as many ships as possible, and try their hand at a sea fight, by

7.19.3a For a discussion of Sparta's Helots, see Appendix C, Spartan Institutions, §3.
7.19.3b The first mention of the class of *neodamodeis* is in 4.21 when they are settled on the border of Elis alongside the Helots which Brasidas took to Thrace. The name would appear to signify "newly put in the damos" ("newly made citizens") but their precise status is still debated. They were used by Sparta more and more as the war progressed; see 5.67.1 (at the battle of Mantinea), 7.58.3 (in Sicily), and frequently in large numbers in the early decades of the fourth century. A *Spartiate* is a full citizen of Sparta, a member of its highest military caste.
7.19.4a Taenarum: Map 7.18, BX.
7.19.4b Laconia: Map 7.18, BX.
7.19.4c Corinth: Map 7.18, AX.
7.19.4d Arcadia: Map 7.18, BX.
7.19.4e Sicyon: Map 7.18, AX.
7.19.5a Naupactus: Map 7.18, AX.
7.20.1a Decelea: Map 7.18, AX.
7.20.1b Argos: Map 7.18, BX.
7.20.2a Chios: Map 7.18, AY.
7.20.3a Aegina: Map 7.18, BX. The narrative of Demosthenes' expedition continues in 7.26.

w ve an advantage in the war not unworthy of the
ris ocrates actively joined in trying to encourage his
co Athenians at sea, saying that the latter had not in-
he s nor would they retain it forever; they had been
la er degree than the Syracusans, and had only beco when obliged by the Mede.[3a] Besides, to daring
sp a daring adversary would seem the most formida-
bl n of paralyzing by the boldness of their attack a
ne inferior in strength, could now be used against
th by the Syracusans. [4] He was convinced also that
th e of Syracusans daring to face the Athenian navy
w e enemy, the advantages of which would far out-
w ian science might inflict upon their inexperience.
H m to throw aside their fears and to try their for-
tu Syracusans, under the influence of Gylippus and
H s some others, made up their minds for the sea
fi eir vessels.

dy, Gylippus led out the whole army by night; his
pl person the forts of Plemmyrium[1a] by land, while
th nes sailed according to an agreed plan against the
er arbor,[1b] and the forty-five remaining came round
fr where they had their arsenal, in order to join up
w nultaneously to attack Plemmyrium, and thus to
di assaulting them on two sides at once. [2] The
At d sixty ships, and with twenty-five of these en-
ga he Syracusans in the Great Harbor, sending the
re round from the arsenal; and an action now en-
su he mouth of the Great Harbor, maintained with
ec sides; the one wishing to force the passage, the
ot

7.22
413
19th Year/Summer
SYRACUSE
Gylippus plans a combined land and sea attack on Plemmyrium. His fleet attempts to unite in the Great Harbor and the Athenians man ships to engage them.

the Athenians in Plemmyrium were down at the
se agement, Gylippus made a sudden attack on the
fo and took the largest first, and afterwards the two
sn did not wait for him, seeing the largest so easily
ta he first fort, the men from it who succeeded in
ta ats and merchant ships, found great difficulty in
re Syracusans were having the best of it in the en-
ga Harbor, and sent a fast sailing trireme to pursue
th others fell, the Syracusans were now being de-

7.23
413
19th Year/Summer
SYRACUSE
As the naval battle develops, a surprise attack by the Syracusan land forces captures the Athenian forts at Plemmyrium. Confusion among the inexperienced Syracusan ships finally permits the Athenians to gain a naval victory.

7.2 des means the
nd Appendix

7.2 set.
7.2 nset.
7.2 nset.

feated; and the fugitives from these sailed along shore with more ease. [3] The Syracusan ships fighting off the mouth of the harbor forced their way through the Athenian vessels and sailing in without any order fell foul of one another, and transferred the victory to the Athenians; who not only routed the squadron in question, but also that by which they were at first being defeated in the harbor, [4] sinking eleven of the Syracusan vessels and killing most of the men, except the crews of three ships whom they made prisoners. Their own loss was confined to three vessels; and after hauling ashore the Syracusan wrecks and setting up a trophy upon the islet in front of Plemmyrium, they retired to their own camp.

7.24
413
19th Year/Summer
SYRACUSE
Athens' naval victory is outweighed by the Syracusan capture of Plemmyrium, due to high casualties, loss of stores and equipment, and damaged Athenian morale.

Unsuccessful at sea, the Syracusans had nevertheless the forts in Plemmyrium,[1a] for which they set up three trophies. One of the two last taken they razed, but put in order and garrisoned the two others. [2] In the capture of the forts a great many men were killed and made prisoners, and a great quantity of property was taken in all. As the Athenians had used them as warehouses, there was a large stock of goods and grain of the merchants inside, and also a large stock belonging to the captains; the masts and other equipment of forty triremes being taken,[2a] besides three triremes which had been drawn up on shore. [3] Indeed the first and foremost cause of the ruin of the Athenian army was the capture of Plemmyrium; even the entrance of the harbor being now no longer safe for carrying in provisions, as the Syracusan vessels were stationed there to prevent it, and nothing could be brought in without fighting; besides the general impression of dismay and discouragement produced upon the army.

7.25
413
19th Year/Summer
ITALY
A Syracusan squadron intercepts Athenian supply vessels and destroys stores gathered for the Athenians in Italy. The Athenians fail to block enemy reinforcements from the Peloponnesus. The Syracusans redouble their efforts to destroy the Athenians already in Sicily before the reinforcements arrive.

After this the Syracusans sent out twelve ships under the command of Agatharchus, a Syracusan. One of these went to the Peloponnesus with ambassadors to describe the hopeful state of their affairs, and to incite the Peloponnesians to prosecute the war there even more actively than they were now doing, while the eleven others sailed to Italy, hearing that vessels laden with stores were on their way to the Athenians. [2] After falling in with and destroying most of the vessels in question, and burning in the Caulonian territory[2a] a quantity of timber for shipbuilding, which had been gathered for the Athenians, [3] the Syracusan squadron went to Locri,[3a] and while they were at anchor there, one of the merchant ships from the Peloponnesus came in, carrying Thespian[3b] hoplites; [4] these they took on board and sailed along shore toward home. The Athenians were on the lookout for them with twenty ships at Megara,[4a] but were only able to take one vessel with its crew; the rest getting clear off to Syracuse. [5] There was also some skirmishing in the harbor about the piles which the Syracusans had driven in the sea in front of the old docks, to allow their ships to

7.24.1a Plemmyrium and Nicias' forts: Map 7.4, BY, and Map 7.25, inset.
7.24.2a Regarding the loss of "masts and other equipment," see note 6.34.5a, 8.28.1, and 8.43.1, and Appendix G, Trireme Warfare, §8.
7.25.2a Caulonia: Map 7.25, BX.
7.25.3a Locri (Epizephyrian): Map 7.25, BX.
7.25.3b Thespiae: Map 7.25, BY.
7.25.4a Megara (Hyblaea), Sicily: Map 7.25, BX.

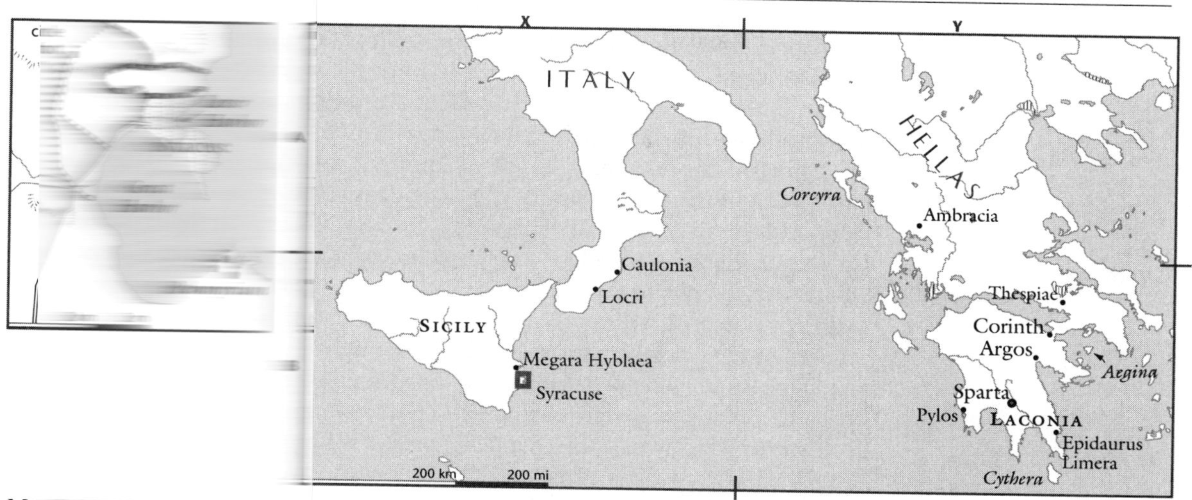

MA[illegible]F THE SUMMER OF 413

lie [illegible] out being hurt by the Athenians sailing up and ru[illegible] The Athenians brought up to them a ship of ten th[illegible] furnished with wooden turrets and screens, and fas[illegible] piles from their boats, wrenched them up and br[illegible] and sawed them in two. Meanwhile the Syracu- sa[illegible]les from the docks, to which they replied from the[illegible]ast most of the piles were removed by the Athe- nia[illegible]fficult part of the stockade was the part out of sig[illegible]hich had been driven in did not appear above wa[illegible]erous to sail up, for fear of running the ships up[illegible] reef, through not seeing them. However divers we[illegible] even these for reward; although the Syracusans dr[illegible]d there was no end to the contrivances to which the[illegible]other, as might be expected between two hostile ar[illegible]her at such a short distance; skirmishes and all kin[illegible]were constant occurrences. [9] Meanwhile the Sy[illegible] composed of Corinthians, Ambraciots,[9a] and Sp[illegible]l them of the capture of Plemmyrium, and that the[illegible] was due less to the strength of the enemy than to [illegible] generally, to let them know that they were full of [illegible] to come to their help with ships and troops, as

7.25[illegible] varied over [illegible] and eighty [illegible]he burden of [illegible]n three and [illegible]

7.25[illegible]

the Athenians were expected with a fresh army, and if the one already there could be destroyed before the other arrived, the war would be at an end.

7.26
413
19th Year/Summer
PELOPONNESUS
The Athenians sail round the Peloponnesus, fortifying a Laconian isthmus opposite Cythera and pillaging while on their way to Corcyra and Sicily.

While the contending parties in Sicily were thus engaged, Demosthenes, having now got together the armament with which he was to go to that island, put out from Aegina,[1a] and making sail for the Peloponnesus, joined Charicles and the thirty ships of the Athenians. Taking on board the hoplites from Argos[1b] they sailed to Laconia,[1c] [2] and after first plundering part of Epidaurus Limera,[2a] landed on the coast of Laconia, opposite Cythera,[2b] where the temple of Apollo stands, and laying waste part of the country, fortified a sort of isthmus,[2c] to which the Helots[2d] of the Spartans might desert, and from which plundering raids might be made as from Pylos.[2e] [3] Demosthenes helped to occupy this place, and then immediately sailed on to Corcyra[3a] to take up some of the allies in that island, and so to proceed without delay to Sicily; while Charicles waited until he had completed the fortification of the place, and leaving a garrison there, returned home subsequently with his thirty ships and the Argives also.

7.27
413
19th Year/Summer
ATTICA
The Thracian Dii arrive too late to join the Syracusan expedition. They are too expensive to maintain, especially since the permanent occupation of Decelea has deprived the Athenians of their land and cattle, and caused many valuable slaves to escape.

This same summer thirteen hundred *peltasts,* Thracian swordsmen of the tribe of the Dii,[1a] who were to have sailed to Sicily with Demosthenes, arrived at Athens. [2] Since they had come too late, the Athenians determined to send them back to Thrace, from where they had come; to keep them for the Decelean war seemed too expensive, as the pay of each man was a *drachma* a day.[2a] [3] Indeed since Decelea[3a] had been first fortified by the whole Peloponnesian army during this summer, and then occupied for the continuous harassment of the country—the garrisons from the cities relieving each other at stated intervals—it had been causing great harm to the Athenians. In fact this occupation, by the destruction of property and loss of men which resulted from it, was one of the principal causes of their ruin. [4] Previously the invasions were short, and did not prevent them from making use of their land during the rest of the time: the enemy was now permanently fixed in Attica; at one time it was an attack in force, at another it was the regular garrison overrunning the country and making forays for its subsistence, and the Spartan king, Agis, was in the field and diligently prosecuting the war; great damage was therefore done to the Athenians. [5] They were deprived of their whole country: more than twenty thousand slaves had deserted,[5a] a great part of them artisans, and all their sheep and beasts of burden were lost; and as the cavalry rode out daily upon ex-

7.26.1a Aegina: Map 7.25, BY, and Map 7.29.
7.26.1b Argos: Map 7.25, BY.
7.26.1c Laconia: Map 7.25, BY.
7.26.2a Epidaurus Limera: Map 7.25, BY.
7.26.2b Cythera: Map 7.25, BY.
7.26.2c Isthmus opposite Cythera: site unknown.
7.26.2d For more on the Spartan Helots, see Appendix C, Spartan Institutions, §3–4.
7.26.2e Pylos: Map 7.25, BY.
7.26.3a Corcyra: Map 7.25, AY.
7.27.1a Territory of the Dii: Map 7.29, locator. *Peltasts* were lightly armed troops who could move much more quickly than the heavily and expensively armed hoplites.
7.27.2a For the *drachma,* See Appendix J, Classical Greek Currency, §3.
7.27.3a Decelea: Map 7.29.
7.27.5a Presumably Thucydides refers not just to the losses of slaves in the first few months of the Decelean War but to losses sustained during the whole Decelean War. The figure of twenty thousand may have been a "late" addition. For slavery in Athens, see Appendix A, The Athenian Government, §2.

cu to guard the country, their horses were either
la y worked upon rocky ground, or wounded by the
er

7.28
413
19th Year/Summer
ATTICA
All Athenian provisions now had to come by sea. The stresses of the double war at home and at Syracuse began to exhaust the Athenians, whose endurance had thus far exceeded earlier estimates. They now replaced the tribute system with taxes on imports and exports to increase revenues.

of provisions from Euboea,[1a] which had before
b a more quickly over land by Decelea from Oro-
p t great cost by sea round Cape Sunium;[1c] every-
th ad to be imported from abroad, and instead of a
ci [2] Summer and winter the Athenians were worn
o ard on the fortifications, during the day by turns,
b cavalry excepted, at the different military posts or
u hat most oppressed them was that they had two
w is reached a pitch of frenzy which no one would
h ne had heard of it before it had come to pass. For
c ined that even when besieged by the Pelopon-
n ica, they would still, instead of withdrawing from
Si ging in like manner Syracuse, a city (taken as a
ci o Athens, or would so thoroughly upset the Hel-
le ength and audacity, as to give the spectacle of a
p nning of the war, some thought might hold out
o e more than three, if the Peloponnesians invaded
th een years after the first invasion, after having al-
re e evils of war, going to Sicily and undertaking a
n to that which they already had with the Pelopon-
n s, the great losses from Decelea, and the other
h on them, produced their financial distress; and it
w imposed upon their subjects, instead of the trib-
u h upon all imports and exports by sea, which they
th e money for them; their expenditure being now
n t having grown with the war while their revenues
d

7.29
413
19th Year/Summer
MYCALLESUS
On their return to Thrace, the Dii stop in Boeotia to launch a surprise dawn attack on the city of Mycalessus. They sack the city and massacre its inhabitants—a disaster unsurpassed in suddenness and horror.

ing to incur expense in their present want of
m once the Thracians who came too late for Demos-
th t of Diitrephes, who was instructed, as they were
to us,[1a] to make use of them if possible in the voyage
al enemy. [2] Diitrephes first landed them at Tana-
g some booty; he then sailed across the Euripus in
th s in Euboea[2b] and disembarking in Boeotia led
th [2c] [3] He passed the night unobserved near the
te uite two miles from Mycalessus, and at daybreak
as y, which is not a large one; the inhabitants being

7.
7.
7.
7. bute that
ect states, see
Empire, §2,
–5, 2.69.1,
and 3.19.1.

7.29.1a Euripus, the narrowest portion of the strait lying between Euboea and the mainland: Map 7.29.
7.29.2a Tanagra: Map 7.29.
7.29.2b Chalcis, Euboea: Map 7.29.
7.29.2c Mycalessus: Map 7.29.

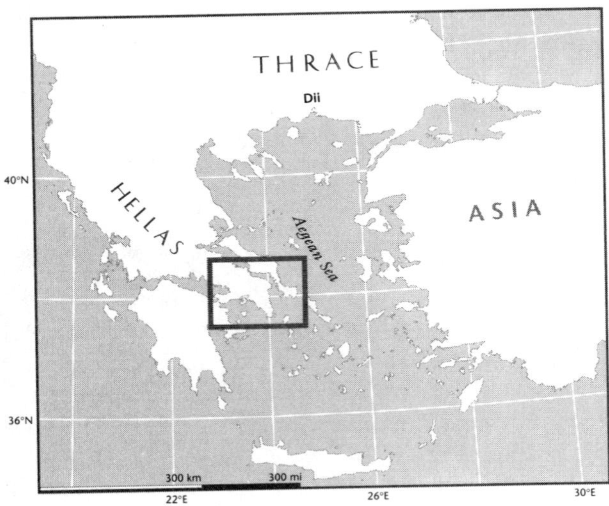

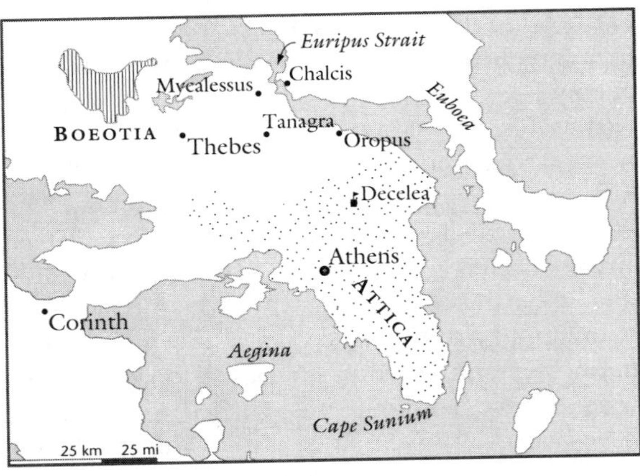

MAP 7.29 MYCALESSUS

off their guard and not expecting that anyone would ever come up so far from the sea to molest them, the wall too being weak, and in some places having tumbled down, while in others it had not been built to any height, and the gates also being left open through their feeling of security. [4] The Thracians bursting into Mycalessus sacked the houses and temples, and butchered the inhabitants, sparing neither youth nor age but killing all they fell in with, one after the other, children and women, and even beasts of burden, and whatever other living creatures they saw; the Thracian people, like the bloodiest of the barbarians, being ever most murderous when it has nothing to fear. [5] Everywhere confusion reigned and death in all its shapes; and in particular they attacked a boys' school, the largest that there was in the place, into which the children had just gone, and massacred them all. In short, the disaster falling upon the whole city was unsurpassed in magnitude, and unapproached by any in suddenness and in horror.

7.30
413
19th Year/Summer
MYCALESSUS
Theban cavalry drive the Dii to their ships, inflicting casualties. Mycalessus loses a large proportion of its population.

Meanwhile the Thebans[1a] heard of it and marched to the rescue, and overtaking the Thracians before they had gone far, recovered the plunder and drove them in panic to the Euripus and the sea, where the vessels which brought them were lying. [2] The greatest slaughter took place while they were embarking, as they did not know how to swim, and those in the vessels on seeing what was going on shore moored them out of bowshot: in the rest of the retreat the Thracians made a very respectable defense against the Theban horse, by which they were first attacked, dashing out and closing their ranks according to the tactics of their country, and lost only a few men in that part of the affair. A good number who were after plunder were actually caught in the city and put to death. [3] Alto-

7.30.1a Thebes: Map 7.29.

ge... two hundred and fifty killed out of thirteen hundr... he rest who came to the rescue about twenty,
tr... h Scirphondas, one of the *boeotarchs*.[3a] The Mycale... tion of their population.
... experienced a calamity, for its extent, as lamenta-
bl... in the war, [7.31.1] Demosthenes, who was at
th... ra[1a] after building the fort in Laconia,[1b] found a
m... heia in Elis,[1c] in which the Corinthian hoplites
w... he ship he destroyed, but the men escaped and
su... in which they pursued their voyage.[1d] [2] After
th... s[2a] and Cephallenia,[2b] he took a body of hoplites
or... for some of the Messenians from Naupactus,[2c]
cr... te coast of Acarnania,[2d] to Alyzia,[2e] and to Anac-
to... y the Athenians. [3] While he was in these parts
he... n returning from Sicily, where he had been sent
du... ne money for the army, who told him the news,
an... rd, while at sea, that the Syracusans had taken
Pl... so, Conon the commander at Naupactus came to
th... wenty-five Corinthian ships stationed opposite to
hi... om war, were meditating an engagement; and he
th... send him some ships, as his own eighteen were
nc... emy's twenty-five. [5] Demosthenes and Eu-
ry... t ten of their fastest triremes with Conon to reinfo... pactus, and meanwhile prepared for the assembly
of... n, who was now the colleague of Demosthenes,
an... onsequence of his appointment, sailed to Corcyra
to... n ships and to enlist hoplites while Demosthenes
rai... from the parts about Acarnania.[5a]
... [a] who had gone from Syracuse to the cities after
th... n had succeeded in their mission, and were about
to... ney had collected to Syracuse, when Nicias got
wi... the Centoripae and Alicyae[1b] and other friendly
Si... , not to let the enemy through, but to combine
to... there being no other way by which they could
ev... Agrigentines[1c] would not give them a passage
th... In response to this request the Sicels laid a triple

7.31
413
19th Year/Summer
ACARNANIA
Demosthenes sails to Acarnania, gathering forces along the way. Eurymedon and Conon join him there, the latter requesting more triremes for Naupactus with which to face the threatening Corinthian fleet.

7.32
413
19th Year/Summer
SICILY
Hearing that reinforcements were approaching Syracuse by land, Nicias asks friendly Sicels for help. They ambush the enemy and inflict large casualties.

7.3... rates of the ... t. See note ...
7.3...
7.3... nstruction of ... .26.3.
7.3... .
7.3... es blown by a ... in Syracuse
7.3...
7.3...
7.3...

7.31.2d Acarnania: Map 7.32, AY.
7.31.2e Alyzia: Map 7.32, AY.
7.31.2f Anactorium: Map 7.32, AY.
7.31.5a Thucydides apparently omitted reporting that Eurymedon was ordered in 7.16 to return to the main force after delivering the money, but it must be so.
7.32.1a These envoys went to the cities in 7.25.9.
7.32.1b Alicyae and Centoripae: the latter presumably inhabiting the territory around Centoripa (Map 7.32, BX).
7.32.1c Agrigentum: Map 7.32, BX.

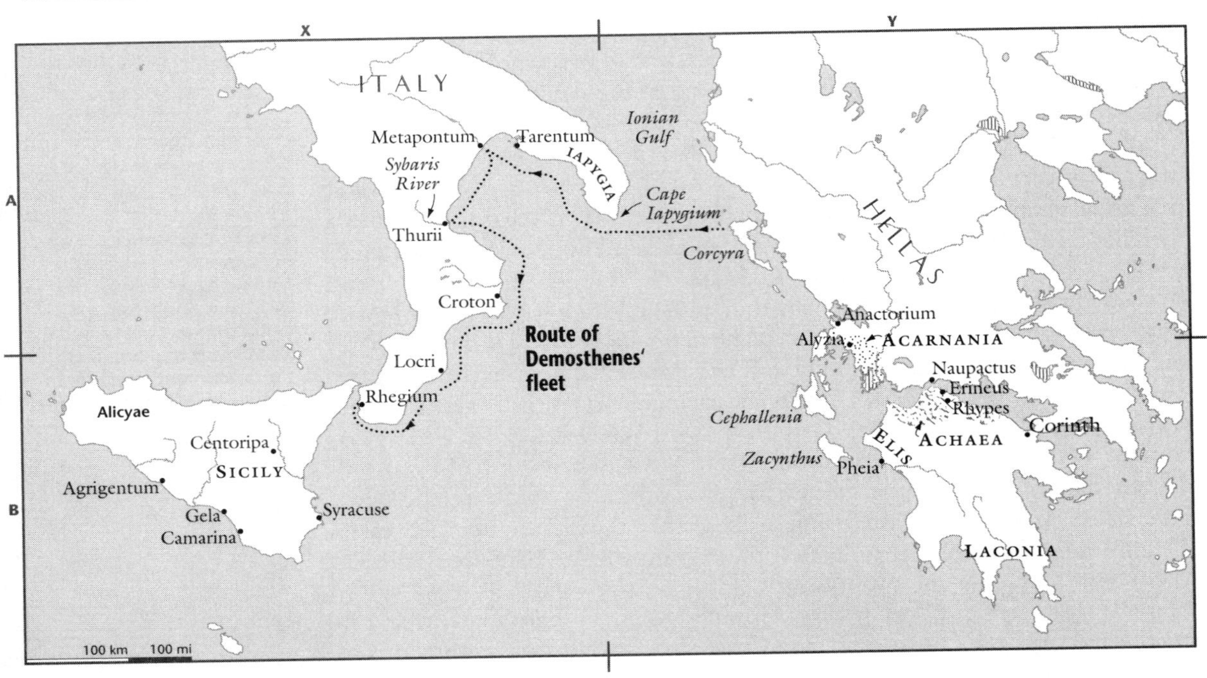

MAP 7.32 OPENING MOVES AND COUNTERMOVES IN 413

ambush for the Sicilians on their march, and attacking them suddenly, while off their guard, killed about eight hundred of them and all the envoys except the Corinthian by whom fifteen hundred who escaped were conducted to Syracuse.

7.33
413
19th Year/Summer
SICILY-ITALY
While all Sicily (except for Agrigentum) now actively sends assistance to Syracuse, Demosthenes and his expedition cross to Italy and advance via Metapontum to Thurii.

About the same time the Camarinaeans[1a] also came to the assistance of Syracuse with five hundred hoplites, three hundred darters, and as many archers, while the Geloans[1b] sent crews for five ships, four hundred darters, and two hundred horse. [2] Indeed almost the whole of Sicily, except the Agrigentines, who were neutral, now ceased merely to watch events as it had previously been doing, and actively joined Syracuse against the Athenians.

[3] While the Syracusans after the Sicel disaster put off any immediate attack upon the Athenians, Demosthenes and Eurymedon, whose forces from Corcyra[3a] and the mainland were now ready, crossed the Ionian gulf[3b] with all their armament to the Iapygian promontory,[3c] [4] and starting from thence touched at the Choerades Isles[4a] lying off Iapygia,[4b] where

7.33.1a Camarina: Map 7.32, BX.
7.33.1b Gela: Map 7.32, BX.
7.33.3a Corcyra: Map 7.32, AY.
7.33.3b Ionian gulf: Map 7.32, AY.
7.33.3c Iapygian promontory (Cape Iapygium): Map 7.32, AY.
7.33.4a Choerades Isles, thought to be small islands lying off the harbor of Tarentum, Italy: Map 7.32, AX. See A. W. Gomme, A. Andrewes, and K.J. Dover, *A Historical Commentary on Thucydides,* iv (Oxford, 1970), 413.
7.33.4b Iapygia: Map 7.32, AX.

the[illegible]dred and fifty Iapygian darters of the Messapian trib[illegible]n old friendship with Artas the chief, who had fur[illegible]rters, arrived at Metapontum[4c] in Italy. [5] Here the[illegible] the Metapontines to send with them three hundre[illegible]mes, and with this reinforcement coasted on to Th[illegible] the party hostile to Athens recently expelled by a r[illegible]dingly remained there to muster and review the wh[illegible] had been left behind, and to prevail upon the Th[illegible] them in their expedition, and in the circumsta[illegible]d themselves to conclude a defensive and offensiv[illegible]ians.

7.34 413 19th Year/Summer ACHAEA In an inconclusive naval battle off Erineus structurally braced Corinthian triremes cause extensive damage to seven Athenian ships, while losing three of their own number. Both sides erect trophies but the Corinthians claim victory for having avoided defeat and the Athenians are reluctant to claim victory for not having won decisively.

[illegible]he Peloponnesians in the twenty-five ships statio[illegible]adron at Naupactus in order to protect the passag[illegible]cily, had prepared for battle, and manning some ad[illegible] be numerically little inferior to the Athenians, an[illegible]chaea in the Rhypic[1a] country. [2] The place off wh[illegible] form of a crescent, the land forces furnished to th[illegible]nd their allies on the spot came up and ranged th[illegible]cting headlands on either side, while the fleet, un[illegible]olyanthes the Corinthian, held the intervening sp[illegible]ntrance. [3] The Athenians under Diphilus now sai[illegible]h thirty-three ships from Naupactus [4] and the C[illegible]oving, at length thought they saw their opportunit[illegible] advanced and engaged the Athenians. [5] After an[illegible] Corinthians lost three ships, and without sinking an[illegible]even of the enemy, which were struck prow to pr[illegible]ggers smashed by the Corinthian vessels, whose ca[illegible]hened for this very purpose.[5a] [6] After an action of[illegible] which either party could claim the victory (although[illegible]came masters of the wrecks through the wind dr[illegible] the Corinthians not putting out again to meet th[illegible]s parted. No pursuit took place, and no prisoners we[illegible]; the Corinthians and Peloponnesians who were fig[illegible]aping with ease, and none of the Athenian vessels ha[illegible]e Athenians now sailed back to Naupactus, and th[illegible]ely set up a trophy as victors, because they had di[illegible]r of the enemy's ships. Moreover they held that th[illegible]d, for the very same reason that their opponent he[illegible] victorious; the Corinthians considering that they we[illegible]ecidedly conquered, and the Athenians thinking

7.3[illegible].32, AX.
7.3[illegible].
7.3[illegible]a: Map 7.32,
[illegible]
7.3[illegible]e topmost [illegible]cted out from [illegible] were very vul[illegible]nthians seem to have reinforced at least the front faces of their own outriggers with strong bow timbers ("catheads"). This allowed them to ram their opponents' ships head on, thereby smashing the enemy's outriggers without causing damage to their own. See 7.36.1a and Appendix G, Trireme Warfare, §14.

themselves vanquished, because not decidedly victorious. [8] However, when the Peloponnesians sailed off and their land forces had dispersed, the Athenians also set up a trophy as victors in Achaea, about two miles and a quarter from Erineus, the Corinthian station. This was the termination of the action at Naupactus.

7.35
413
19th Year/Summer
ITALY
Demosthenes' force, reinforced by Thurian hoplites, sails along the Italian coast to Petra in Rhegian territory.

To return to Demosthenes and Eurymedon: the Thurians[1a] having now got ready to join in the expedition with seven hundred hoplites and three hundred darters, the two generals ordered the ships to sail along the coast to the Crotonian[1b] territory, and meanwhile held a review of all the land forces upon the river Sybaris,[1c] and then led them through the Thurian country. [2] Arrived at the river Hylias,[2a] they here received a message from the Crotonians, saying that they would not allow the army to pass through their country; upon which the Athenians descended toward the shore, and bivouacked near the sea and the mouth of the Hylias, where the fleet also met them, and the next day embarked and sailed along the coast touching at all the cities except Locri,[2b] until they came to Petra in the Rhegian territory.[2c]

7.36
413
19th Year/Summer
SYRACUSE
Following the Corinthian model, the Syracusans strengthen their ships to prepare them for head on ramming. They intend to engage the Athenians again, counting on the lack of room in the harbor and their control of the shore to prevent the Athenians from exploiting their superior maneuvering skills.

Meanwhile the Syracusans hearing of their approach resolved to make a second attempt with their fleet and their other forces on shore, which they had been collecting for this very purpose in order to do something before their arrival. [2] In addition to other improvements suggested by the recent sea fight which they now adopted in the equipment of their navy, they cut down their prows to a smaller compass to make them more solid and made their catheads stronger, and from these let support beams into the vessel's sides for a length of six cubits within and without, in the same way as the Corinthians had altered their prows before engaging the squadron at Naupactus.[2a] [3] The Syracusans thought that they would thus have an advantage over the Athenian vessels, which were not constructed with equal strength, but were slight in the bows, from their being more used to sail round and charge the enemy's side than to meet him prow to prow, and that the battle being in the Great Harbor, with a great many ships in not much room, was also a fact in their favor. Charging prow to prow, they would stave in the enemy's bows, by striking with solid and stout beaks against hollow and weak ones; [4] and secondly, the Athenians for want of room would be unable to use their favorite maneuver of breaking the line or of sailing round, as the Syracusans would do their best not to let them do the one, and want of room would prevent their doing the other.[4a] [5] This charging prow to prow which had up till then been thought lack of skill in a helmsman, would be the Syracusans' chief maneuver, as being that which they should find most useful, since

7.35.1a Thurii, Italy: Map 7.32, AX.
7.35.1b Croton, Italy: Map 7.32, AX.
7.35.1c Sybaris river: Map 7.32, AX.
7.35.2a Hylias river: site unknown.
7.35.2b Locri (Epizephyrian), Italy: Map 7.32, BX.
7.35.2c Petra, in Rhegian territory: site unknown. Rhegium: Map 7.32, BX.
7.36.2a See note 7.34.5a and Appendix G, Trireme Warfare, §14.
7.36.4a For these maneuvers, see Phormio's speech on naval tactics in 2.89, and Appendix G, Trireme Warfare, §11–14.

the [illegible] would not be able to back water in any direc-
tio[illegible]re, and that only for a little way, and in the little
spa[illegible]n camp. The rest of the harbor would be comma[illegible]s; [6] and the Athenians, if hard pressed and
cro[illegible]ll space, would run foul of one another and fall
int[illegible]n fact what did the Athenians most harm in all
the[illegible]had not, like the Syracusans, the whole harbor
ava[illegible]their sailing round into the open sea, this would
be [illegible]acusans in possession of the way in and out, es-
pec[illegible]would be hostile to them and the mouth of the
har[illegible]

7.37
413
19th Year/Summer
SYRACUSE
The Syracusan army advances against the Athenian walls while their fleet deploys in the harbor. The Athenians man their walls and ships to confront this double attack.

[illegible]s to suit their skill and ability, and now more
co[illegible]s sea fight, the Syracusans attacked by land and
sea[illegible]ed out the city force a little before and brought
it [illegible]thenians, where it looked toward the city, while
the[illegible]eum,[2a] that is to say, the hoplites that were there
wit[illegible]t troops of the Syracusans, advanced against the
wa[illegible]e; the ships of the Syracusans and allies sailing
ou[illegible]s. [3] The Athenians at first supposed that they
we[illegible]nd only, and it was not without alarm that they
sav[illegible]roaching as well; and while some were forming
up[illegible]ont of them against the advancing enemy, and
so[illegible]aste against the numbers of horse and darters
co[illegible]um and from outside, others manned the ships
or [illegible]each to oppose the enemy, and when the ships
we[illegible]th seventy-five sail against about eighty of the
Sy[illegible]

7.38
413
19th Year/Summer
SYRACUSE
After much skirmishing and maneuvering, the Syracusans retire. Nicias, anticipating more attacks, prepares harbor defenses for his fleet.

[illegible] part of the day in advancing and retreating and
ski[illegible]er, without either being able to gain any advan-
tag[illegible]cept that the Syracusans sank one or two of the
At[illegible]ed, the land force at the same time retiring from
th[illegible]ay the Syracusans remained quiet, and gave no
sig[illegible]oing to do; but Nicias, seeing that the battle had
be[illegible]pecting that they would attack again, compelled
th[illegible]f the ships that had suffered, and moored mer-
ch[illegible]stockade which they had driven into the sea in
fr[illegible]o serve instead of an enclosed harbor,[3a] at about
tw[illegible]ach other, in order that any ship that was hard
pr[illegible]etreat in safety and sail out again at leisure. These
pr[illegible] Athenians all day until nightfall.

7.3[illegible]r mouth: Map [illegible]

7.3[illegible]

7.3[illegible]losed harbor, [illegible]4, BY.

7.39
413
19th Year/Summer
SYRACUSE
The Syracusans attack again, planning to surprise the Athenians by a second, sudden attack after breaking off for a hasty meal.

The next day the Syracusans began operations at an earlier hour, but with the same plan of attack by land and sea. [2] A great part of the day the rivals spent as before, confronting and skirmishing with each other; until at last Ariston son of Pyrrhicus, a Corinthian, the ablest helmsman in the Syracusan service, persuaded their naval commanders to send to the officials in the city, and tell them to move the market as quickly as they could down to the sea, and oblige everyone to bring whatever edibles he had and sell them there, thus enabling the commanders to land the crews and dine at once close to the ships,[2a] and shortly afterwards, the same day, to attack the Athenians again when they were not expecting it.

7.40
413
19th Year/Summer
SYRACUSE
The Syracusans retire to their docks, where the market has been relocated so that they may eat quickly and attack again. Taken by surprise, the Athenians man their ships and advance. The reinforced Syracusan ships stave in the bows of many of the Athenian vessels.

In compliance with this advice a messenger was sent and the market got ready, upon which the Syracusans suddenly backed water and withdrew to the city, and immediately landed and took their dinner upon the spot; [2] while the Athenians, supposing that they had returned to the city because they felt they were beaten, disembarked at their leisure and set about getting their dinners and about their other occupations, under the impression that they had done with fighting for that day. [3] Suddenly the Syracusans manned their ships and again sailed against them; and the Athenians, in great confusion and most of them hungry, got on board, and with great difficulty put out to meet them. [4] For some time both parties remained on the defensive without engaging, until the Athenians at last resolved not to let themselves be worn out by waiting where they were, but to attack without delay, and giving a cheer, went into action. [5] The Syracusans received them, and charging prow to prow as they had intended, stove in a great part of the Athenian outriggers by the strength of their beaks; the darters on the decks also did great damage to the Athenians, but still greater damage was done by the Syracusans who went about in small boats, ran in upon the oars of the Athenian triremes, and sailed against their sides, and from there threw their javelins at the sailors.

7.41
413
19th Year/Summer
SYRACUSE
The Athenians flee to their harbor, pursued by the victorious and now confident Syracusans.

At last, fighting hard in this fashion, the Syracusans gained the victory, and the Athenians turned and fled between the merchant ships to their own station. [2] The Syracusan ships pursued them as far as the merchant ships, where they were stopped by the beams armed with dolphins suspended from those vessels over the passage.[2a] [3] Two of the Syracusan vessels went too near in the excitement of victory and were destroyed, one of them being taken with its crew. [4] After sinking seven of the Athenian ves-

7.39.2a Greek soldiers and sailors at this time had to purchase their food from local markets, so the speed with which a trireme crew's meal could be prepared and eaten would be significantly effected by the proximity of markets to the boat. See also 8.95.4, where the Athenians had to disperse to the outskirts of Eretria to purchase food because nothing was for sale in the *agora*, and thus were unable to quickly man and deploy their ships to meet an enemy attack.

7.41.2a These "dolphins" were heavy lead weights which were suspended from the main yardarms of the merchant ships that had been anchored to form a stockade harbor and refuge for the Athenians. The sail of an ancient ship was suspended from a long spar that, when squared (set perpendicular to its axis), extended far beyond its hull. Dolphins heavy enough to pierce a ship's deck and hull were hung from the end of the spar and dropped on any enemy boat that ventured too close.

sel [illegible] nd taking most of the men prisoners and killing
ot [illegible] ired and set up trophies for both the engage-
me [illegible] nt of having a decided superiority by sea, and by
no [illegible] ial success by land.

[illegible] le the Syracusans were preparing for a second
att [illegible] sea, Demosthenes and Eurymedon arrived with
th [illegible] Athens, consisting of about seventy-three ships,
in [illegible] early five thousand hoplites, Athenian and allied;
a l [illegible] Hellenic and barbarian, and slingers and archers
an [illegible] a corresponding scale. [2] The Syracusans and
th [illegible] oment not a little dismayed at the idea that there
wa [illegible] to their dangers, seeing, in spite of the fortifica-
tio [illegible] army arrive nearly equal to the former, and the
po [illegible] so great in every quarter. On the other hand, the
fir [illegible] regained a certain confidence in the midst of its
m [illegible] henes, seeing how matters stood, felt that he
co [illegible] fare as Nicias had done, who by wintering in
C [illegible] e attacking Syracuse had allowed the terror of his
fir [illegible] n contempt, and had given time to Gylippus to
ar [illegible] the Peloponnesus, which the Syracusans would
ne [illegible] had attacked immediately; for they thought that
th [illegible] n by themselves, and would not have discovered
th [illegible] were already under siege, and even if they then
se [illegible] no longer have been equally able to profit by its
ar [illegible] and well aware that it was now on the first day
af [illegible] like Nicias was most formidable to the enemy,
D [illegible] l to lose no time in drawing the utmost profit
fr [illegible] the moment inspired by his army; [4] and seeing
th [illegible] the Syracusans,[4a] which hindered the Athenians
fr [illegible] s a single one, and that he who should become
m [illegible] Epipolae,[4b] and afterwards of the camp there,
w [illegible] n taking it, as no one would even wait for his atta [illegible] tempt the enterprise. [5] This he took to be the
sh [illegible] e war, as he would either succeed and take Syra-
c [illegible] the armament instead of frittering away the lives
o [illegible] in the expedition and the resources of the countr [illegible]

7.42
413
19th Year/Summer
SYRACUSE
Demosthenes' relief expedition arrives, dismaying the Syracusans and raising the spirits of the Athenians. Demosthenes decides to attack and either achieve decisive success immediately or to withdraw the Athenians from their present difficult position.

7 [illegible] .29.
7 [illegible] 1 for the [illegible] r at Catana in [illegible]
7 [illegible] ble location: [illegible]
7 [illegible]

[6] First therefore the Athenians went out and laid waste the lands of the Syracusans about the Anapus[6a] and carried all before them as at first by land and by sea, the Syracusans not offering to oppose them upon either element, unless it were with their cavalry and darters from the Olympieum.[6b]

7.43
413
19th Year/Summer
SYRACUSE
After failing to take the Syracusan counterwall by seige engine and assault, Demosthenes attempts a night attack on Epipolae. It proves initially successful, but increasing Athenian disorganization and a determined stand by the Boeotians turn victory into defeat.

Next Demosthenes resolved to make an attempt on the counterwall first by means of siege engines. As however the engines that he brought up were burnt by the enemy fighting from the wall, and the rest of the forces repulsed after attacking at many different points, he determined to delay no longer, and having obtained the consent of Nicias and his fellow commanders, proceeded to put into execution his plan of attacking Epipolae. [2] As by day it seemed impossible to approach and get up without being observed, he ordered provisions for five days, took all the masons and carpenters, and other things such as arrows, and everything else that they could want for the work of fortification if successful; and after the first watch set out with Eurymedon and Menander and the whole army for Epipolae, Nicias being left behind in the lines. [3] Having come up by the hill of Euryelus[3a] (where the former army had ascended at first), unobserved by the enemy's guards, they went up to the fort which the Syracusans had there, and took it, and put to the sword part of the garrison. [4] The greater number, however, escaped at once and gave the alarm to the camps, of which there were three upon Epipolae, defended by outworks, one of the Syracusans, one of the other Sicilians, and one of the allies; and also to the six hundred Syracusans forming the original garrison for this part of Epipolae. [5] These at once advanced against the assailants, and encountering Demosthenes and the Athenians, were routed by them after a sharp resistance, the victors immediately pushing on, eager to achieve the objects of the attack without giving time for their ardor to cool; meanwhile others from the very beginning were taking the counterwall of the Syracusans, which was abandoned by its garrison, and pulling down the battlements. [6] The Syracusans and the allies, and Gylippus with the troops under his command, advanced to the rescue from the outworks, but engaged with some consternation (a night attack being a piece of audacity which they had never expected), and were at first compelled to retreat. [7] But while the Athenians, flushed with their victory, now advanced with less order, wishing to make their way as quickly as possible through the whole force of the enemy not yet engaged, without relaxing their attack or giving them time to rally, the Boeotians[7a] made the first stand against them, attacked them, routed them, and put them to flight.

7.42.6a Anapus River: Map 7.44, BX.
7.42.6b Olympieum: Map 7.44, BX.
7.43.3a Euryelus: Map 7.44, AX.
7.43.7a Boeotia: Map 7.29.

7.44
413
19th Year/Summer
SYRACUSE
Despite bright moonlight, the participants could perceive little of the battle. Athenian forces became scattered; they were confused by the *paean* of their Dorian allies, which was so like that of their Dorian foes. Many Athenians became lost in the rout that followed.

[illegible] into great disorder and perplexity, so that it was
nc [illegible] de or the other any detailed account of the affair.
By [illegible] atants have a clearer notion, though even then by
nc [illegible] place, no one knowing much of anything that
dc [illegible] n immediate neighborhood; but in a night en-
ga [illegible] ne only one that occurred between great armies
du [illegible] ld anyone know anything for certain? [2] Al-
th [illegible] moon they saw each other only as men do by
m [illegible] they could distinguish the form of the body, but
co [illegible] whether it was a friend or an enemy. Both had
gr [illegible] moving about in a small space. [3] Some of the
At [illegible] feated, while others were coming up yet uncon-
qu [illegible] k. A large part also of the rest of their forces eith [illegible] or were still ascending, so that they did not know
wh [illegible] ng to the rout that had taken place all in front
wa [illegible] d the noise made it difficult to distinguish anyth [illegible] Syracusans and allies were cheering each other on
wi [illegible] the only possible means of communication, and
m [illegible] no came against them; while the Athenians were
se [illegible] taking all in front of them for enemies, even
th [illegible] ne of their now flying friends; and by constantly
ask [illegible] which was their only means of recognition, not
on [illegible] on among themselves by asking all at once, but
als [illegible] enemy, [5] whose own they did not so readily
dis [illegible] were victorious and not scattered, and thus less
ea [illegible] was that if the Athenians fell in with a party of
th [illegible] er than they, it escaped them through knowing
th [illegible] hey themselves failed to answer they were put to
th [illegible] urt them as much, or indeed more than anything
els [illegible] *paean*,[6a] from the perplexity which it caused by
be [illegible] either side: the Argives and Corcyraeans and any
ot [illegible] e [Athenian] army struck terror into the Athenian [illegible] heir paean, no less than did the enemy. [7] Thus,
aft [illegible] nto disorder, they ended by coming into collision
wi [illegible] arts of the field, friends with friends, and citizens
wi [illegible] y terrified one another, but even came to blows
an [illegible] with difficulty. [8] In the pursuit many perished
by [illegible] own the cliffs, the way down from Epipolae being
na [illegible] got down safely into the plain, although many,

7.4 [illegible] t sung by [illegible] parently, [illegible] l elements, there was a distinctive Dorian paean, see Appendix H, Dialects and Ethnic Groups, §9.

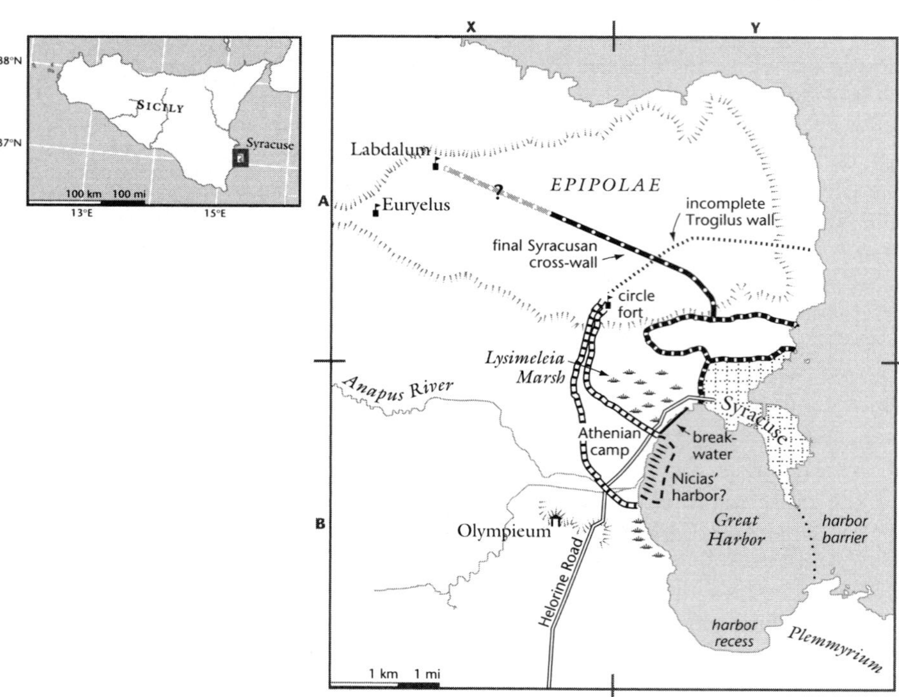

MAP 7.44 FIGHTING AT SYRACUSE IN 413[8a]

especially those who belonged to the first armament, escaped through their better acquaintance with the locality, some of the newcomers lost their way and wandered over the country, and were cut off in the morning by the Syracusan cavalry and killed.

7.45
413
19th Year/Summer
SYRACUSE
The Syracusans erect trophies and return the dead. Athenian losses are high.

The next day the Syracusans set up two trophies, one upon Epipolae where the ascent had been made, and the other on the spot where the first check was given by the Boeotians; and the Athenians took back their dead under truce. [2] A great many of the Athenians and allies were killed, although still more arms were taken than could be accounted for by the number of the dead, as some of those who were obliged to leap down from the cliffs without their shields escaped with their lives and did not perish like the rest.

7.46
413
19th Year/Summer
SYRACUSE
Their victory restores Syracusan morale.

After this the Syracusans, recovering their old confidence at such an unexpected stroke of good fortune, despatched Sicanus with fifteen ships to Agrigentum[1a] where there was a revolution, to induce if possible the city to join them; while Gylippus again went by land into the rest of Sicily to bring up reinforcements, being now in hope of taking the Athenian lines by storm, after the result of the affair on Epipolae.

7.44.8a Map 7.44 follows the interpretation of Peter Green in *Armada from Athens;* see note 7.4.7c.

7.46.1a Agrigentum: Map 7.49.

7.47
413
19th Year/Summer
SYRACUSE
Demosthenes urges an immediate withdrawal while his expedition's forces maintain their naval superiority, arguing that Athens had greater need of them at home.

Athenian generals consulted upon the disaster
wh d the general weakness of the army. They saw
th their enterprises, and the soldiers disgusted with
th g rife among them owing to its being the sickly
se the marshy and unhealthy nature of the spot in
wh ed; and the state of their affairs generally being
th cordingly, Demosthenes was of opinion that they
ou ger; but consistent with his original idea[3a] in risk-
in polae, now that this had failed, he gave his vote
fo urther loss of time, while the sea might yet be
cr nforcement might give them the superiority at all
ev 4] He also said that it would be more profitable
fo he war against those who were building fortifica-
tio st the Syracusans whom it was no longer easy to
su was not right to squander large sums of money to
no ith the siege.

7.48
413
19th Year/Summer
SYRACUSE
Nicias disagrees, arguing from information received from Syracusan informants that the enemy is running out of funds with which to pay mercenaries and sailors, and may soon financially collapse. He also fears Athenian blame for defeat and prefers a soldier's honorable death in the field to dishonorable execution in Athens.

f Demosthenes. Nicias, without denying the bad
sta unwilling to admit their weakness, or to have it
re at the Athenians in full council were openly vot-
in t case they would be much less likely to accom-
pl ed without discovery. [2] Moreover, his own
pa l gave him reason to hope that the affairs of the
er a worse state than their own, if the Athenians
pe s they would wear out the Syracusans by lack of
m e more extensive command of the sea now given
th y. Besides this, there was a party in Syracuse who
w to the Athenians, and kept sending him messages
ar se the siege.[2a] [3] Accordingly, knowing this and
re hesitated between the two courses and wished to
se n his public speech on this occasion he refused to
le he was sure the Athenians would never approve of
th vote of theirs. Those who would vote upon their
co ng the facts as eyewitnesses like themselves and
no hear from hostile critics, would simply be guided
by rst clever speaker; [4] while many, indeed most, of
th who now so loudly proclaimed the danger of their
po ned Athens would proclaim just as loudly the oppo at their generals had been bribed to betray them
an therefore, who knew the Athenian temper, sooner
th honorable charge and by an unjust sentence at
th ns, he would rather take his chance and die, if die
h at the hand of the enemy. [5] Besides, after all, the
S e case than themselves. What with paying merce-

7. n was described

7.48.2a For the pro-Athenian faction in Syracuse, see 6.103.3–4 and 7.73.3.

naries, spending upon fortified posts, and now for a full year maintaining a large navy, they were already at a loss and would soon be at a standstill: they had already spent two thousand talents and incurred heavy debts besides, and could not lose even ever so small a fraction of their present force through not paying it, without ruin to their cause; depending as they did more upon mercenaries than upon soldiers obliged to serve, like their own. [6] He therefore said that they ought to stay and carry on the siege, and not depart defeated in point of money, in which they were much superior.

7.49
413
19th Year/Summer
SYRACUSE
Demosthenes insists that they at least withdraw to some more favorable location from which to carry on the war. Nicias refuses, arousing suspicions that he knows more than he is telling, and no action is taken.

Nicias spoke positively because he had exact information of the financial distress at Syracuse, and also because of the strength of the pro-Athenian party there which kept sending him messages not to raise the siege; besides which he had more confidence than before in his fleet, and felt sure at least of its success. [2] Demosthenes, however, would not hear for a moment of continuing the siege, but said that if they could not lead off the army without a decree from Athens, and if they were obliged to stay on, they ought to remove to Thapsus[2a] or Catana;[2b] where their land forces would have a wide extent of country to overrun, and could live by plundering the enemy, and would thus do them damage; while the fleet would have the open sea to fight in, that is to say, instead of a narrow space which was all in the enemy's favor, a wide sea room where their skills would be of use, and where they could retreat or advance without being confined or circumscribed either when they put out or put in. [3] In any case he was altogether opposed to their staying on where they were, and insisted on removing at once, as quickly and with as little delay as possible; and in this judgment Eurymedon agreed. [4] Nicias however still objecting, a certain diffidence and hesitation came over them, with a suspicion that Nicias might have some further information to make him so positive.

7.50
413
19th Year/Summer
SYRACUSE
After Gylippus returns to Syracuse with reinforcements, the Athenians finally decide to leave Syracuse. An eclipse of the moon changes their minds, however, and Nicias insists that they wait at least twenty-seven days, as prescribed by the soothsayers.

While the Athenians lingered on in this way without moving from where they were, Gylippus and Sicanus now arrived at Syracuse. Sicanus had failed to win over Agrigentum, the party friendly to the Syracusans having been driven out while he was still at Gela; but Gylippus was accompanied not only by a large number of troops raised in Sicily, but by the hoplites sent off in the spring from the Peloponnesus in the merchant vessels that had arrived at Selinus[1a] from Libya.[1b] [2] They had been carried to Libya by a storm, and having obtained two triremes and pilots from the Cyrenians,[2a] on their voyage along shore had taken sides with the Euesperitae[2b] and had defeated the Libyans who were besieging them, and from thence coasting on to Neapolis,[2c] a Carthaginian[2d] trading post, and the nearest point to Sicily, from which it is only two days' and a night's voyage, there crossed over and came to Selinus. [3] Immediately upon their arrival the Syracusans prepared to attack the Athenians again by land

7.49.2a Thapsus: Map 7.49.
7.49.2b Catana: Map 7.49.
7.50.1a Syracuse, Agrigentum, Gela, and Selinus: Map 7.49.
7.50.1b Libya: Map 7.49. These hoplites were possibly the Corinthian hoplites mentioned in 7.31.1.
7.50.2a Cyrene, in Libya: Map 7.49.
7.50.2b Euesperides, in Libya: Map 7.49.
7.50.2c Neapolis: Map 7.49.
7.50.2d Carthage: Map 7.49.

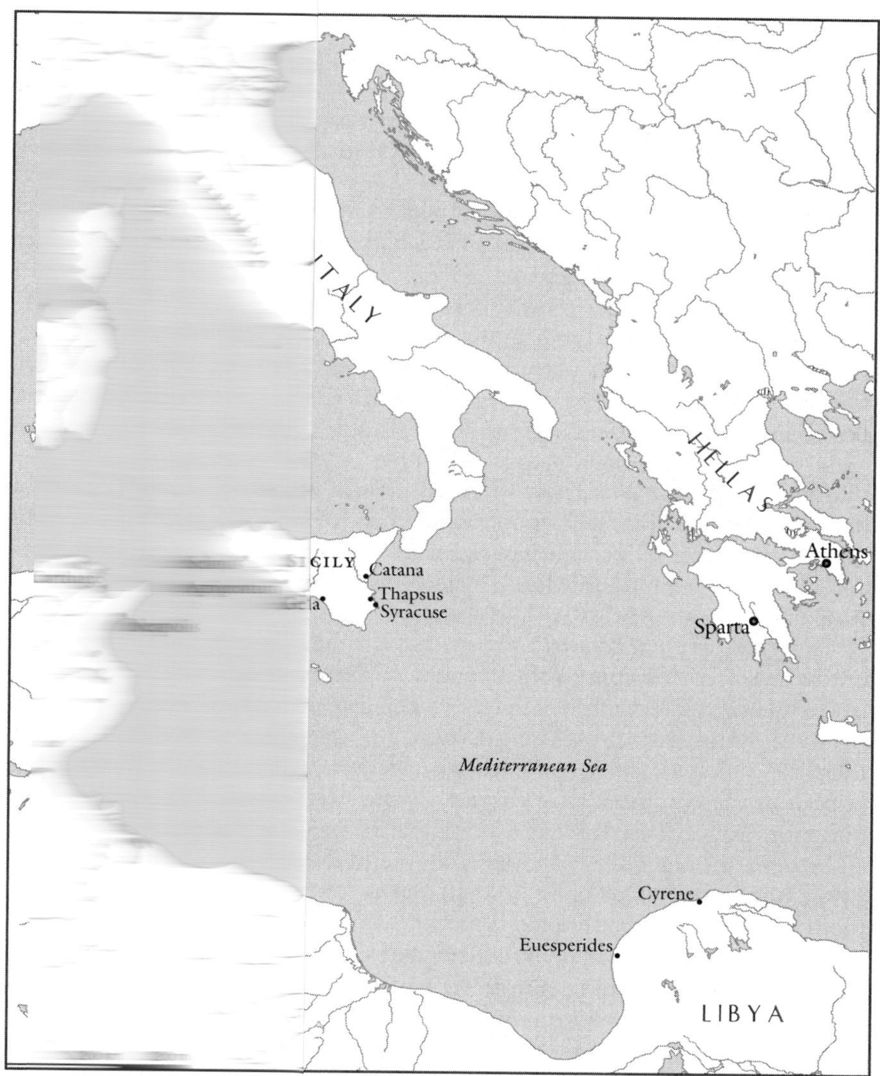

M MENTS FOR SYRACUSE

ar enian generals seeing a fresh army come to the ai at their own circumstances, far from improving, w se, and above all distressed by the sickness of the so epent of not having departed before; and Nicias n same opposition, except by urging that there sh g, they gave orders as secretly as possible for all to t from the camp at a given signal. [4] All was at la on the point of sailing away when an eclipse of the moon,[4a] which was then at the full, took place. Most of the Athenians, deeply impressed by this occurrence, now urged the generals to wait; and Nicias, who was somewhat overaddicted to divination and practices of that kind, refused from that moment even to take the question of departure into consideration, until they had waited the thrice nine days prescribed by the soothsayers.

7.51
413
19th Year/Summer
SYRACUSE
The Syracusans, eager to deal with the Athenians in their present location, renew their training at sea and attack the Athenians on land.

The besiegers were thus condemned to stay in the country; [7.51.1] and the Syracusans getting wind of what had happened, became more eager than ever to press the Athenians, who had now themselves acknowledged that they were no longer their superiors either by sea or by land, as otherwise they would never have planned to sail away. Besides which the Syracusans did not wish them to settle in any other part of Sicily, where they would be more difficult to deal with, but desired to force them to fight at sea as quickly as possible, in a position favorable to themselves. [2] Accordingly they manned their ships and practiced for as many days as they thought sufficient. When the moment arrived they assaulted on the first day the Athenian lines, and upon a small force of hoplites and horse sallying out against them by certain gates, cut off some of the former and routed and pursued them to the lines, where, as the entrance was narrow, the Athenians lost seventy horses and a few hoplites.

7.52
413
19th Year/Summer
SYRACUSE
The Syracusans decisively win a naval battle in the harbor. Eurymedon is killed.

Drawing off their troops for this day, on the next the Syracusans went out with a fleet of seventy-six sail, and at the same time advanced with their land forces against the lines. The Athenians put out to meet them with eighty-six ships, came to close quarters, and engaged. The Syracusans and their allies first defeated the Athenian center, [2] and then caught Eurymedon, the commander of the right wing, who was sailing out from the line more toward the land in order to surround the enemy, in the hollow and recess of the harbor,[2a] and killed him and destroyed the ships accompanying him; after which they now chased the whole Athenian fleet before them and drove them ashore.

7.53
413
19th Year/Summer
SYRACUSE
Gylippus attempts to capture some Athenian ships but is thwarted by the Athenians, who also stop a Syracusan fireship before it causes harm.

Gylippus seeing the enemy's fleet defeated and carried ashore beyond their stockades and camp, ran down to the breakwater[1a] with some of his troops, in order to cut off the men as they landed and make it easier for the Syracusans to tow off the vessels by the shore being friendly ground. [2] The Tyrrhenians[2a] who guarded this point for the Athenians seeing them come on in disorder, advanced out against them and attacked and routed their van, hurling it into the marsh of Lysimeleia.[2b] [3] Afterwards the Syracusan and allied troops arrived in greater numbers, and the Athenians fearing for their ships came up also to the rescue and engaged them, and defeated and pursued them for some distance and killed a few of their

7.50.4a This eclipse took place on August 27, 413.

7.52.2a Recess of the great harbor, probable location: Map 7.44, BY.

7.53.1a The "breakwater" was probably a narrow spit of high ground lying north of the Athenian camp between the waters of the great harbor and the marsh of Lysimeleia; see Map 7.44, BY.

7.53.2a "Tyrrhenians" is Thucydides' name for the Etruscans from Etruria (Thucydides' Tyrrhenia) in central Italy; see Map 7.49.

7.53.2b Marsh of Lysimeleia, probable location: Map 7.44, BY; see note 6.99.1a.

ho[illegible] n rescuing most of their ships and brought them
do[illegible] teen however were taken by the Syracusans and
th[illegible] n killed. [4] The rest the enemy tried to burn by
me[illegible] o which they filled with brush and pinewood, set
on [illegible] the wind which blew full on the Athenians. The
At[illegible] ed for their ships, contrived means for stopping
it [illegible] checking the flames and the nearer approach of
th[illegible] caped the danger.

7.54 413 Each side erects trophies.

[illegible] ns set up a trophy for the sea fight and for the
ho[illegible] ut off up at the lines, where they took the horses;
an[illegible] rout of the foot driven by the Tyrrhenians into
th[illegible] vn victory with the rest of the army.

7.55 413 19th Year/Summer SYRACUSE Naval defeat causes despair among the Athenians, who realize that they had never fought a city like Syracuse, which could not be suborned, overpowered, or persuaded to ally.

[illegible] ow gained a decisive victory at sea, where until
no[illegible] reinforcement brought by Demosthenes, and
de[illegible] s the despondency of the Athenians, and great
th[illegible] greater still their regret for having come on the
ex[illegible] e the only cities that they had yet encountered,
si[illegible] racter, under democracies like themselves, which
ha[illegible] were of considerable magnitude. They had been
un[illegible] ng them over by holding out the prospect of
ch[illegible] nts, or to crush them by their great superiority in
fo[illegible] ost of their attempts, and being already in per-
pl[illegible] eated at sea, where defeat could never have been
ex[illegible] lunged deeper into bewilderment than ever.

7.56 413 19th Year/Summer SYRACUSE The Syracusans perceive their superiority, and begin to close the harbor mouth to prevent an Athenian escape. They are now ambitious to win glory from the defeat and capture of such an expedition, and the consequent liberation of Hellas.

[illegible] sans immediately began to sail freely along the
ha[illegible] close up its mouth, so that the Athenians might
no[illegible] future, even if they wished. [2] Indeed, the Syracu[illegible] only of saving themselves, but also how to hinder
th[illegible] hinking, and thinking rightly, that they were now
m[illegible] hat to conquer the Athenians and their allies by
la[illegible] hem great glory in Hellas. The rest of the Hel-
le[illegible] ately be either freed or released from apprehen-
si[illegible] rces of Athens would be henceforth unable to
su[illegible] d be waged against her; while they, the Syracu-
sa[illegible] as the authors of this deliverance, and would be
he[illegible] not only with all men now living but also with
po[illegible] hese the only considerations that gave dignity to
th[illegible] thus conquer not only the Athenians but also
th[illegible] conquer not alone, but with their companions-
in[illegible] by side with the Corinthians and Spartans, havin[illegible] tand in the van of danger, and having been in a
gr[illegible] s of naval success.

[illegible] never so many peoples assembled before a single
ci[illegible] and total gathered together in this war under
At[illegible]

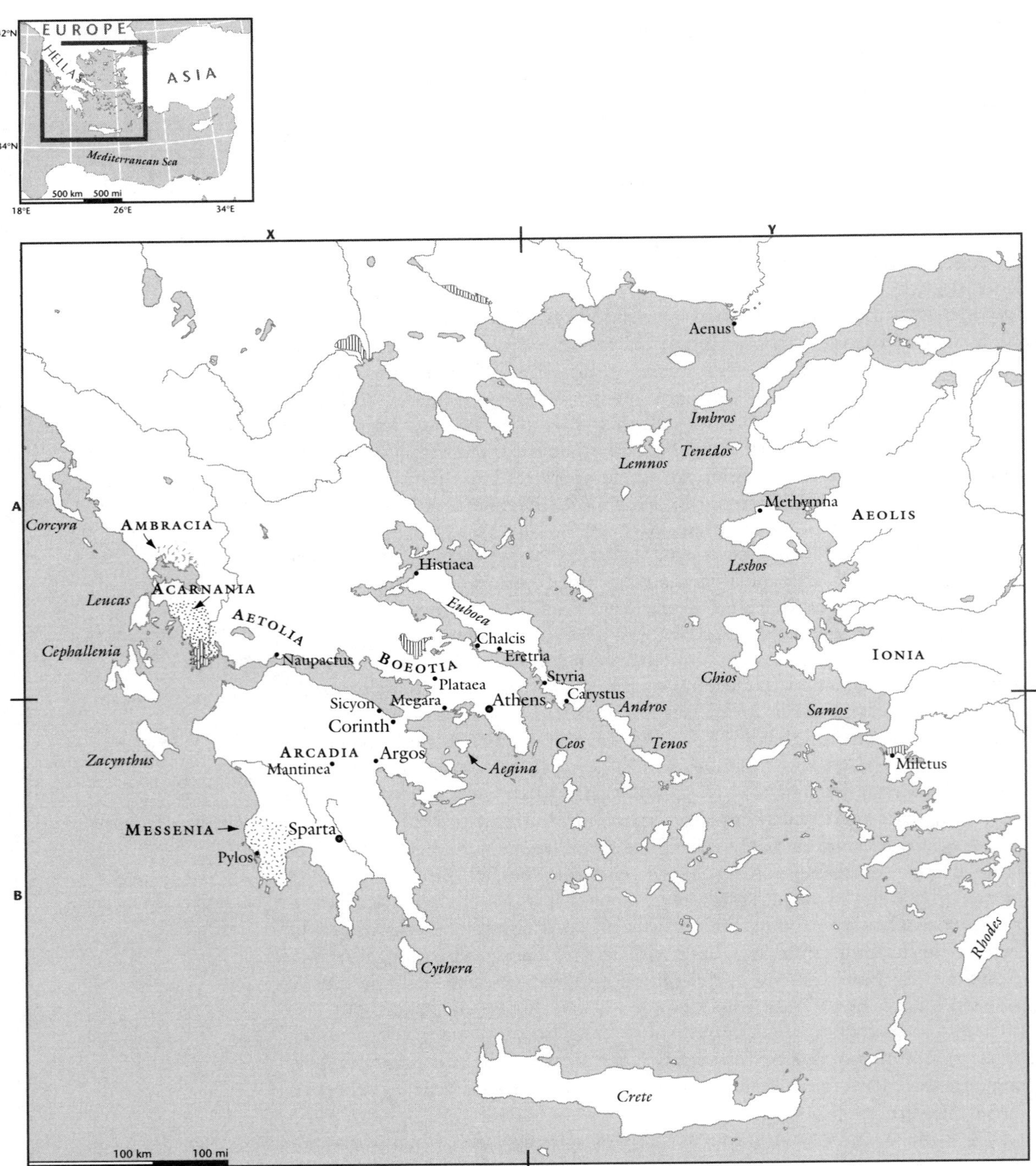

MAP 7.56 EASTERN CONTRIBUTORS TO ATHENIAN FORCES AT SYRACUSE

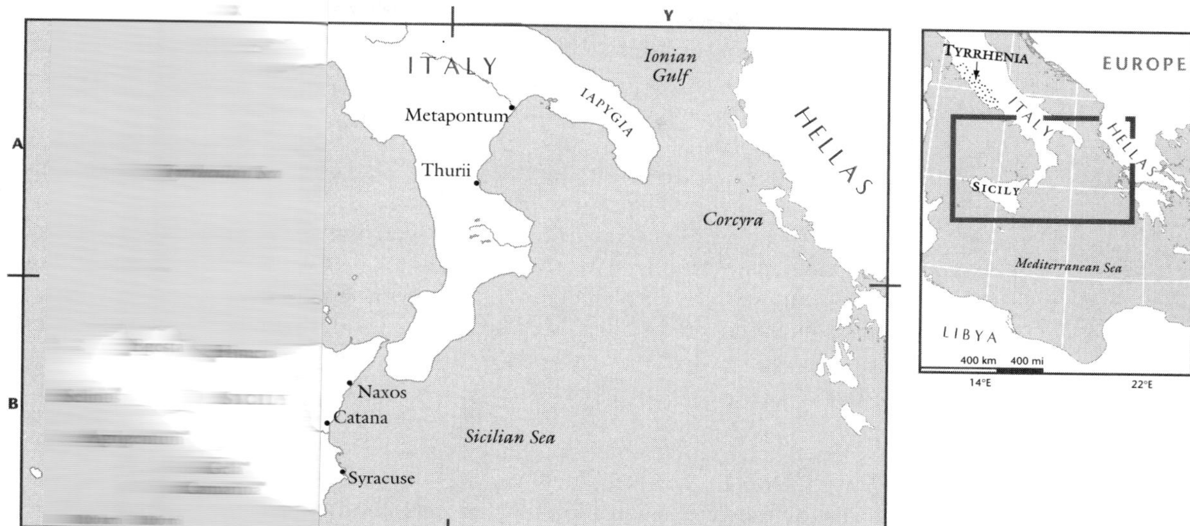

M BUTORS TO ATHENIAN AND SYRACUSAN FORCES

7.57
413
19th Year/Summer
SYRACUSE
Thucydides lists all participants in the Athenian force, recounting their ethnicity, their status, and the circumstances that led to their inclusion in the expedition.

e states on either side who came to Syracuse to
fi to help to conquer or defend the island. Right or
c not the bond of union between them, so much as
in the case might be. [2] The Athenians themselves
b st the Dorians of Syracuse of their own free will;
a ing Attic and using the Athenian laws, the Lemni-
a etans, that is to say, the then occupants of Aegina,
b with them. To these must be also added the His-
ti a in Euboea.[2b] [3] Of the rest some joined in the
e he Athenians, others as independent allies, others
a e number of the subjects paying tribute belonged
t s, Styrians, and Carystians[4a] from Euboea; the
C ans[4b] from the islands; and the Milesians, Samians,
a The Chians, however, joined as independent allies,
p nishing ships. Most of these were Ionians and de-
s ans, except the Carystians, who are Dryopes, and
a liged to serve, were still Ionians fighting against
D there were men of Aeolic race, the Methymnians,[5a]

7. 7.56, AY. For e Appendix H, s, §8.

7. s colonized by Histiaea, Eu- colonized in ve argued from pants" that ords after 404.

7. 7.56, AX; Styria and Carystus: Map 7.56, AY; all are cities in Euboea.

7.57.4b Ceos, Andros, and Tenos: Map 7.56, BY.

7.57.4c Chios, in Ionia: Map 7.56, AY; Miletus and Samos: Map 7.56, BY.

7.57.5a Methymna, on Lesbos: Map 7.56, AY. Methymna was the only city of Lesbos not involved in the revolt of 427; see 3.2.1, 3.5.1, and 3.18.1.

subjects who provided ships, not tribute, and the Tenedians and Aenians who paid tribute. These Aeolians[5b] fought against their Aeolian founders, the Boeotians in the Syracusan army, because they were obliged, while the Plataeans,[5c] the only native Boeotians opposed to Boeotians, did so upon a just quarrel. [6] Of the Rhodians[6a] and Cytherians,[6b] both Dorians, the latter, Spartan colonists, fought in the Athenian ranks against their Spartan countrymen with Gylippus; while the Rhodians, Argives by race, were compelled to bear arms against the Dorian Syracusans and their own colonists, the Geloans,[6c] serving with the Syracusans. [7] Of the islanders round the Peloponnesus, the Cephallenians and Zacynthians[7a] accompanied the Athenians as independent allies, although their insular position really left them little choice in the matter, owing to the maritime supremacy of Athens, while the Corcyraeans,[7b] who were not only Dorians but Corinthians,[7c] were openly serving against Corinthians and Syracusans, although colonists of the former and of the same race as the latter, ostensibly under compulsion, but really out of free will through hatred of Corinth. [8] The Messenians, as they are now called in Naupactus and from Pylos,[8a] then held by the Athenians, were taken with them to the war. There were also a few Megarian[8b] exiles, whose fate it was to be now fighting against the Megarian Selinuntines.[8c]

[9] The engagement of the rest was more of a voluntary nature. It was less the alliance than hatred of the Spartans and the immediate private advantage of each individual that persuaded the Dorian Argives to join the Ionian Athenians in a war against Dorians; while the Mantineans and other Arcadian[9a] mercenaries, accustomed to go against the enemy pointed out to them at the moment, were led by interest to regard the Arcadians serving with the Corinthians as just as much their enemies as any others. The Cretans[9b] and Aetolians[9c] also served for hire, and the Cretans who had joined the Rhodians in founding Gela thus came to consent to fight for pay against, instead of for, their colonists. [10] There were also some Acarnanians[10a] paid to serve, although they came chiefly for love of Demosthenes and out of goodwill to the Athenians whose allies they were. These all lived on the Hellenic side of the Ionian gulf.[10b] [11] Of the Italians, there were the Thurians and Metapontines,[11a] dragged into the quarrel by the stern necessities of a time of revolution; of the Sicilians, the Naxians and the Catanians;[11b] and of the barbarians, the Egestaeans,[11c] who called in the Athenians, most of the

7.57.5b Aenus, Tenedos, and Aeolis: Map 7.56, AY.
7.57.5c Plataea, in Boeotia: Map 7.56, AX. For the Aeolians from Boeotia and Lesbos, see Appendix H, Dialects and Ethnic Groups, §6.
7.57.6a Rhodes: Map 7.56, BY.
7.57.6b Cythera: Map 7.56, BX.
7.57.6c Gela: Map 7.57, BX.
7.57.7a Cephallenia: Map 7.56, AX; Zacynthus: Map 7.56, BX.
7.57.7b Corcyra: Map 7.56, AX, and Map 7.57, AY.
7.57.7c Corinth: Map 7.56, BX.
7.57.8a Messenia and Pylos: Map 7.56, BX; Naupactus: Map 7.56, AX.
7.57.8b Megara: Map 7.56, BX.
7.57.8c Selinus: Map 7.57, BX.
7.57.9a Argos, Mantinea, and Arcadia: Map 7.56, BX.
7.57.9b Crete: Map 7.56, BY.
7.57.9c Aetolia: Map 7.56, AX.
7.57.10a Acarnania: Map 7.56, AX.
7.57.10b Ionian gulf: Map 7.57, AY.
7.57.11a Thurii and Metapontum: Map 7.57, AY.
7.57.11b Naxos and Catana: Map 7.57, BX.
7.57.11c Egesta: Map 7.57, BX. See 6.2.3 and 6.11.7, where Egesta is declared to be an Elymian (i.e., non-Greek) city.

Si some Tyrrhenian[11d] enemies of Syracuse and Iapy-
gi were the peoples serving with the Athenians.

cusans had the Camarinaeans their neighbors, the
G em, and then passing over the neutral Agrigen-
ti ettled on the farther side of the island. [2] These
ir looking toward Libya;[2a] the Himeraeans[2b] came
fr Tyrrhenian sea,[2c] being the only Hellenic inhabi-
t the only people that came from thence to the aid
o the Hellenes in Sicily the above peoples joined in
t ndependent, and of the barbarians the Sicels only,
t d not go over to the Athenians. Of the Hellenes
o the Spartans, who provided a Spartan to take the
c *neodamodeis*[3a] and of Helots;[3b] the Corinthians,[3c]
v val and land forces, with their Leucadian and Am-
b mercenaries sent by Corinth from Arcadia;[3e] some
S ve, and from outside the Peloponnesus the Boeo-
t on, however, with these foreign auxiliaries, the
g nished more in every department—numbers of
h s, and an immense multitude besides having been
b in comparison, again, one may say, with all the
r was provided by the Syracusans themselves, both
f city and from the fact that they were in the great-

7.58 413 19th Year/Summer SYRACUSE Thucydides lists the nationality, tribe, status, and circumstances of all participants in the force defending Syracuse against the Athenians.

aries brought together on either side, all of which
ed, neither party receiving any further support. [2]
fore, if the Syracusans and their allies thought that
glory if they could follow up their recent victory in
ure of the whole Athenian armada, without letting
r by land. [3] They began at once to close up the
of boats, merchant vessels, and triremes moored
ith, which is nearly a mile wide,[3a] and made all their
the event of the Athenians again venturing to fight
, nothing small either in their plans or their ideas.

7.59 413 19th Year/Summer SYRACUSE The Syracusans begin to close the Great Harbor with moored boats, intending to capture the entire Athenian force.

g them closing up the harbor and informed of their
a council of war. [2] The generals and other com-
discussed the difficulties of the situation; the point

7.60 413 19th Year/Summer SYRACUSE Seeing the Syracusan efforts, the Athenians decide to reduce their lines to just a harbor fort, to man the largest fleet possible in order to defeat the enemy, and to withdraw to Catana. If defeated at sea, they plan to march to the nearest friendly city.

p 7.57, locator.
ntum, and Seli-
57, AX.
e note 7.19.3a.
lix C, Spartan In-
Map 7.56, AX.

7.58.3e Arcadia: Map 7.56, BX.
7.58.3f Sicyon: Map 7.56, BX.
7.58.3g Boeotia: Map 7.56, AX.
7.59.3a Syracusan harbor barrier, general location: Map 7.44, BY.

which pressed most being that they no longer had provisions for immediate use (having sent on to Catana[2a] to tell them not to send any, in the belief that they were going away), and that they would not have any in future unless they could command the sea. They therefore determined to evacuate their upper lines, to enclose with a crosswall and garrison a small space close to the ships, only just sufficient to hold their stores and sick, and manning all the ships, seaworthy or not, with every man that could be spared from the rest of their land forces, to fight it out at sea, and if victorious, to go to Catana, but if not, to burn their vessels, form in close order, and retreat by land to the nearest friendly place they could reach, Hellenic or barbarian. [3] This was no sooner settled than carried into effect: they descended gradually from the upper lines and manned all their vessels, compelling all to go on board who were of age to be in any way of use. [4] They thus succeeded in manning about one hundred and ten ships in all, on board of which they embarked a number of archers and darters taken from the Acarnanians[4a] and from the other foreigners, making all other provisions allowed by the nature of their plan and by the necessities which imposed it. [5] All was now nearly ready, and Nicias, seeing the soldiery disheartened by their unprecedented and decided defeat at sea, and by reason of the scarcity of provisions eager to fight it out as soon as possible, called them all together, and first addressed them speaking as follows:

7.61
413
19th Year/Summer
SYRACUSE
Nicias reminds his men that victory will permit them to see again their native cities. He calls upon them to act like veterans.

"Soldiers of the Athenians and of the allies, we have all an equal interest in the coming struggle, in which life and country are at stake for us quite as much as they can be for the enemy; since if our fleet wins the day, each can see his native city again, wherever that city may be. [2] You must not lose heart, or be like men without any experience, who fail in a first attempt, and ever afterwards fearfully expect a future as disastrous. [3] But let the Athenians among you who have already had experience of many wars, and the allies who have joined us in so many expeditions, remember the surprises of war, and with the hope that fortune will not be always against us, prepare to fight again in a manner worthy of the number which you see yourselves to be."

7.62
413
19th Year/Summer
SYRACUSE
Nicias lists the many steps they have taken in order to win the upcoming naval battle, which should give them confidence.

"Now, whatever we thought would be of service against the crush of vessels in such a narrow harbor, and against the force upon the decks of the enemy, from which we suffered before, has all been considered with the helmsmen, and, as far as our means allowed, provided. [2] A number of archers and darters will go on board, and a multitude that we should not have employed in an action in the open sea, where our science would be crippled by the weight of the vessels; but in the present land fight that we are forced to make from shipboard all this will be useful. [3] We have also discovered the changes

7.60.2a Catana: Map 7.57, BX.
7.60.4a Acarnania: Map 7.56, AX.

ve must make to meet theirs; and against the
ks, which did us the greatest mischief, we have
ons,[3a] which will prevent an assailant backing
f the marines on deck here do their duty; [4]
ly compelled to fight a land battle from the
e our interest neither to back water ourselves,
o so, especially as the shore, except so much of
ir troops, is hostile ground."

ber this and fight on as long as you can, and
es be driven ashore, but once alongside must
not to part company until you have swept the
ny's deck. [2] I say this more for the hoplites
as it is more the business of the men on deck;
re even now on the whole the strongest. [3]
and at the same time implore, not to be too
r misfortunes, now that we have our decks bet-
er number of vessels. Bear in mind how well
ne pleasure felt by those of you who through
r language and imitation of our manners were
ienians, even though not so in reality, and as
oughout Hellas, and had your full share of the
oire, and more than your share in the respect of
otection from ill treatment. [4] You, therefore,
freely share our empire, we now justly require
pire in its extremity, and in scorn of Corinthi-
often conquered, and of Sicilians, none of
sumed to stand against us when our navy was
u to repel them, and to show that even in sick-
skill is more than a match for the fortune and

7.63
413
19th Year/Summer
SYRACUSE
Nicias begs the seamen not to be daunted by recent reverses; he reminds them of the many privileges they enjoy under the empire; and he calls upon them to fight now in order to preserve themselves and it.

s among you I add once more this reflection:
no more such ships in your docks to compare
hoplites in their flower; if you do other than
here will immediately sail thither, and those
Athens will become unable to repel their home
by these new allies. Here you will fall at once
Syracusans—I need not remind you of the in-
you attacked them—and your countrymen at
ose of the Spartans. [2] Since the fate of both
single battle—now, if ever, stand firm, and re-
, that you who are now going on board are the
Athenians, and all that is left of the state and
hens, in whose defense if any man has any ad-

7.64
413
19th Year/Summer
SYRACUSE
Nicias tells the Athenians that Athens has no military resources in reserve and concludes that failure here will lead to Athens' quick defeat by Syracuse and Sparta.

7 ons, the Atheni-
he tactics of
o counteract
the enemy's new battle strategies (see 7.34.5a). See 4.25.4a and Appendix G, Trireme Warfare, §14.

vantage in skill or courage, now is the time for him to show it, and thus serve himself and save all."

7.65
413
19th Year/Summer
SYRACUSE
Gylippus and the Syracusan generals address their forces.

After this address[1a] Nicias at once gave orders to man the ships. Meanwhile Gylippus and the Syracusans could perceive by the preparations which they saw going on that the Athenians meant to fight at sea. They had also received intelligence of the grappling irons, [2] against which they specially provided by stretching hides over the prows and much of the upper part of their vessels, in order that the irons when thrown might slip off without taking hold. [3] All being now ready, the generals and Gylippus addressed them in the following terms:

7.66
413
19th Year/Summer
SYRACUSE
Gylippus speaks to his troops, recalling Athens' plan to first subdue Sicily and then the Peloponnesus. He asserts that the recently defeated Athenians are unlikely to recover their spirits.

"Syracusans and allies, the glorious character of our past achievements and the no less glorious results at issue in the coming battle are, we think, understood by most of you, or you would never have thrown yourselves with such ardor into the struggle; and if there be anyone not as fully aware of the facts as he ought to be, we will declare them to him. [2] The Athenians came to this country first to conquer Sicily, and after that, if successful, the Peloponnesus and the rest of Hellas, possessing already the greatest empire yet known, of present or former times, among the Hellenes. Here for the first time they found in you men who faced their navy which made them masters everywhere; you have already defeated them in the previous sea fight, and will in all likelihood defeat them again now. [3] When men are once checked in what they consider their special excellence, their whole opinion of themselves suffers more than if they had not at first believed in their superiority, the unexpected shock to their pride causing them to give way more than their real strength warrants; and this is probably now the case with the Athenians."

7.67
413
19th Year/Summer
SYRACUSE
Gylippus asserts that the Syracusans' superior morale, resulting from recent successes, will overcome Athenian desperation and numbers. He points out that the Athenians will be forced to use unfamiliar tactics.

"With us it is different. The original estimate of ourselves which gave us courage in the days of our unskillfulness has been strengthened, while the conviction added to it that we must be the best seamen of the time, if we have conquered the best, has given a double measure of hope to every man among us; and, for the most part, where there is the greatest hope, there is also the greatest ardor for action. [2] The means to combat us which they have tried to find in copying our armament are familiar to our warfare, and will be countered by appropriate measures; while they will never be able to have a number of hoplites on their decks, contrary to their custom, and a number of darters—born landsmen, one may say, Acarnanians and others, embarked afloat, who will not know how to discharge their weapons when they have to keep still, without hampering their vessels and falling all into confusion among themselves through fighting

7.65.1a See the Introduction (sect. II.v) for a discussion of the speeches in Thucydides.

own tactics.[2a] [3] For they will gain nothing … ships—I say this to those of you who may be … ight against odds—as a quantity of ships in a … ly be slower in executing the movements re- … sed to injury from our means of offense. [4] … know the plain truth, as we are credibly in- … their sufferings and the necessities of their … ade them desperate; they have no confidence … to try their fortune in the only way they can, … ir passage and sail out, or after this to retreat … sible for them to be worse off than they are."

7.68
413
19th Year/Summer
SYRACUSE
Gylippus urges the Syracusans to take revenge and accept nothing less than total victory, asserting that failure will bring little loss and success great advantage.

… r greatest enemies having thus betrayed itself, … ng what I have described, let us engage in … othing is more legitimate between adversaries … the whole wrath of one's soul in punishing … hing more sweet, as the proverb has it, than … enemy which it will now be ours to take. [2] … and mortal enemies you all know, since they … ur country, and if successful had in reserve for … st dreadful, and for our children and wives all … ble, and for the whole city the name which … proach. [3] None should therefore relent or … away without further danger to us. This they … even if they get the victory; while if we suc- … , in chastising them, and in handing down to … eedom strengthened and confirmed, we shall … triumph. And the rarest dangers are those in … le loss and success the greatest advantage."

7.69
413
19th Year/Summer
SYRACUSE
After both sides manned their ships, Nicias, feeling the crisis keenly, continued to speak, calling on captains by name and tribe to remember their ancestors, country, families, and gods, in hope of inciting them to greater efforts.

… s to the soldiers on their side, the Syracusan gen- er… erceived that the Athenians were manning their sh… oceeded to man their own also. [2] Meanwhile N… te of affairs, realizing the greatness and the near- ne… hat they were on the point of putting out from sh… en are apt to think in great crises, that when all ha… still something left to do, and when all has been sa… said enough, again called on the captains one by o… his father's name and by his own, and by that of hi… hem not to be false to their own personal renown, o… ary virtues for which their ancestors were illustri- o… f their country, the freest of the free, and of the u… wed to all in it to live as they pleased; and added o… en would use at such a crisis, and which, with lit-

7.… efer here to … or trireme … e ship was

7.69.4a Syracusan harbor barrier, general location: Map 7.44, BY.

tle alteration, are made to serve on all occasions alike—appeals to wives, children, and national gods—without caring whether they are thought commonplace, but loudly invoking them in the belief that they will be of use in the consternation of the moment. [3] Having thus admonished them, not, he felt, as he would, but as he could, Nicias withdrew and led the troops to the sea, and arranged them in as long a line as he was able, in order to sustain as far as possible the courage of the men afloat; [4] while Demosthenes, Menander, and Euthydemus, who took the command on board, put out from their own camp and sailed straight to the barrier across the mouth of the harbor and to the passage left open, to try to force their way out.[4a]

7.70
413
19th Year/Summer
SYRACUSE
The Syracusans take stations around the harbor as the Athenians charge the barrier at its mouth. After the first shock a general mêlée occurs in which crowding prevents maneuver, so that much chaotic fighting amid noise and confusion takes place, with both sides displaying great zeal for battle.

The Syracusans and their allies had already set out with about the same number of ships as before, a part of which kept guard at the outlet, and the remainder all round the rest of the harbor, in order to attack the Athenians on all sides at once; while the land forces held themselves in readiness at the points at which the vessels might put into the shore. The Syracusan fleet was commanded by Sicanus and Agatharchus, who each had a wing of the whole force, with Pythen and the Corinthians in the center. [2] When the rest of the Athenians came up to the barrier, with the first shock of their charge they overpowered the ships stationed there, and tried to undo the fastenings; after this, as the Syracusans and allies bore down upon them from all quarters, the action spread from the barrier over the whole harbor, and was more obstinately disputed than any of the preceding ones. [3] On either side the rowers showed great zeal in bringing up their vessels at the boatswains' orders, and the helmsmen great skill in maneuvering, and great emulation one with another; and once the ships were alongside each other, the marines on board did their best not to let the service on deck be outdone by the others; in short, every man strove to prove himself the first in his particular department. [4] And as many ships were engaged in a small compass (for these were the largest fleets fighting in the narrowest space ever known, being together little short of two hundred), the regular attacks with the beak were few, there being no opportunity of backing water or of breaking the line; while the collisions caused by one ship chancing to run foul of another, either in flying from or attacking a third, were more frequent. [5] So long as a vessel was coming up to the charge the men on the decks rained darts and arrows and stones upon her; but once alongside, the marines tried to board each other's vessel, fighting hand to hand. [6] In many quarters also it happened, by reason of the narrow room, that a vessel was charging an enemy on one side and being charged herself on another, and that two, or sometimes more ships, had perforce got entangled round one, obliging the helmsmen to attend to defense here, offense there, not to one thing at once, but to many on all sides; while the huge din caused by the number of ships crashing together not only spread terror, but made the orders of the boatswains inaudible. [7] The boatswains on either side in the

7.69.4a Syracusan harbor barrier, general location: Map 7.44, BY.

di[illegible]d in the heat of the conflict incessantly shouted or[illegible] men; the Athenians they urged to force the passa[illegible] to show their mettle and lay hold of a safe return to[illegible]yracusans and their allies they cried that it would be[illegible]e escape of the enemy, and conquering, to exalt th[illegible]eirs. [8] The generals, moreover, on either side, if th[illegible]e battle backing ashore without being forced to do[illegible]captain by name and asked him—the Athenians, wh[illegible]ing because they thought the thrice hostile shore m[illegible] sea which had cost them so much labor to win—th[illegible] they were fleeing from the fleeing Athenians, wh[illegible]e eager to escape in whatever way they could.

7.71
413
19th Year/Summer
SYRACUSE
Thucydides describes the varied emotions, cries, exaltation, and anguish of the armies watching from shore as the sea battle rages. Finally as the Athenian ships are routed, the Athenians give way to panic and despair, with many wondering how they will save themselves.

[illegible]nies on shore, while victory hung in the balance, we[illegible] agonizing and conflicting emotions; the natives th[illegible] than they had already won, while the invaders fe[illegible]in even worse plight than before. [2] The fate of th[illegible]ed in their fleet, their fear for the event was like no[illegible]; while their view of the struggle was necessarily as[illegible] itself. [3] Close to the scene of action and not all lo[illegible]t at once, some saw their friends victorious and to[illegible]calling upon heaven not to deprive them of salvati[illegible]d their eyes turned upon those who were losing, w[illegible] and, although spectators, were more overcome th[illegible]nts. Others, again, were gazing at some spot w[illegible]ly disputed; as the strife was protracted without de[illegible]odies reflected the agitation of their minds, and th[illegible]gony of all, ever just within reach of safety or just o[illegible]on. [4] In short, in that one Athenian army as lo[illegible]ined doubtful there was every sound to be heard at[illegible] "We win," "We lose," and all the other manifold ex[illegible] host would necessarily utter in great peril; [5] ar[illegible]fleet it was nearly the same; until at last the Syracu[illegible]after the battle had lasted a long while, put the A[illegible]with much shouting and cheering chased them in o[illegible]6] The naval force, one one way, one another, as m[illegible]afloat, now ran ashore and rushed from on board th[illegible]; while the army, no more divided, but carried av[illegible] with shrieks and groans deplored the event, and ra[illegible] the ships, others to guard what was left of their w[illegible] and most numerous part already began to consi[illegible]ve themselves. [7] Indeed, the panic of the prese[illegible] been surpassed. They now suffered very nearly w[illegible]at Pylos;[7a] as then the Spartans with the loss of

7.[illegible]a description of [illegible]2–41.

their fleet lost also the men who had crossed over to the island, so now the Athenians had no hope of escaping by land, without the help of some extraordinary accident.

7.72
413
19th Year/Summer
SYRACUSE
The defeated Athenians are so stunned that they forget to ask for their dead. Demosthenes and Nicias agree to mount a second attack, but the demoralized Athenian sailors refuse to man the triremes.

The sea fight having been a severe one, and many ships and lives having been lost on both sides, the victorious Syracusans and their allies now picked up their wrecks and dead, and sailed off to the city and set up a trophy. [2] The Athenians, overwhelmed by their misfortune, never even thought of asking leave to take up their dead or wrecks, but wished to retreat that very night. [3] Demosthenes, however, went to Nicias and gave it as his opinion that they should man the ships they had left and make another effort to force their passage out next morning; saying that they had still left more ships fit for service than the enemy, the Athenians having about sixty remaining as against less than fifty of their opponents. [4] Nicias was quite in agreement; but when they wished to man the vessels, the sailors refused to go on board, being so utterly overcome by their defeat as no longer to believe in the possibility of success.

7.73
413
19th Year/Summer
SYRACUSE
The Athenians now plan to retreat by land this very night. Hermocrates, afraid they might escape, sends messengers to deceive the Athenian generals by warning them not to leave immediately because the roads are guarded. The Athenians follow this advice.

Accordingly they all now made up their minds to retreat by land. Meanwhile the Syracusan Hermocrates, suspecting their intention and impressed by the danger of allowing a force of that magnitude to retire by land, establish itself in some other part of Sicily, and from there to renew the war, went and stated his views to the authorities, and pointed out to them that they ought not to let the enemy get away by night, but that all the Syracusans and their allies should at once march out and block up the roads and seize and guard the passes. [2] The authorities were entirely of his opinion, and thought that it ought to be done, but on the other hand felt sure that the people, who had given themselves over to rejoicing and were taking their ease after a great battle at sea, would not be easily brought to obey; besides, they were celebrating a festival, having on that day a sacrifice to Heracles, and most of them in their rapture at the victory had fallen to drinking at the festival, and would probably consent to anything sooner than to take up their arms and march out at that moment. [3] For these reasons the thing appeared impracticable to the magistrates; and Hermocrates, finding himself unable to do anything further with them, had now recourse to the following stratagem of his own. What he feared was that the Athenians might quietly get ahead of them by passing the most difficult places during the night; and he therefore sent, as soon as it was dusk, some friends of his own to the camp with some horsemen who rode up within earshot and called out to some of the men, as though they were well-wishers of the Athenians, and told them to tell Nicias (who had in fact some contacts who informed him of what went on inside the city),[3a] not to lead off the army by night as the Syracusans were guarding the roads, but to make his preparations at his leisure and to retreat by day. [4] After saying this they departed; and their hearers informed the Athenian generals,

7.73.3a For Nicias' Syracusan contacts, see 6.103.3–4 and 7.49.1.

7.74
413
19th Year/Summer
SYRACUSE
The Athenians allow their soldiers one day to pack, and the Syracusans use this time to occupy strategic points on possible escape routes, and to tow off Athenian ships without opposition.

[7 [illegible] g for that night on the strength of this message, no [illegible]

[illegible] not set out at once, they now determined to stay als [illegible] give time to the soldiers to pack up as well as they co [illegible] cles, and, leaving everything else behind, to start or [illegible] tly necessary for their personal subsistence. [2] M [illegible] s and Gylippus marched out and blocked the ro [illegible] by which the Athenians were likely to pass, and ke [illegible] the streams and rivers, posting themselves so as to [illegible] the army where they thought best; while their fle [illegible] n and towed off the ships of the Athenians. Some fe [illegible] thenians themselves as they had intended; the rest th [illegible] to their own at their leisure as they had been th [illegible] out anyone trying to stop them, and conveyed to th [illegible]

7.75
413
19th Year/Summer
SYRACUSE
Saddened and shamed by the necessity to leave the unburied dead and their sick and wounded comrades, the forty thousand Athenians finally march out. Having already absorbed reverses greater than those suffered by any Hellenic army, they march in fear of capture and enslavement, their initial glory turned to humiliation.

[illegible] Demosthenes now thinking that enough had been do [illegible] ation, the departure of the army took place upon th [illegible] sea fight. [2] It was a lamentable scene, not m [illegible] cumstance that they were retreating after having lo [illegible] eat hopes gone, and themselves and their state in pe [illegible] the camp there were things most grievous for ev [illegible] ntemplate. [3] The dead lay unburied, and each m [illegible] iend among them shuddered with grief and horro [illegible] m they were leaving behind, wounded or sick, w [illegible] e shocking than the dead, and more to be pitied th [illegible] shed. [4] These fell to entreating and bewailing un [illegible] not what to do, begging them to take them and lo [illegible] ividual comrade or relative whom they could see, h [illegible] of their tent-fellows in the act of departure, and fo [illegible] ould, and when their bodily strength failed them, ca [illegible] pon heaven and shrieking aloud as they were left be [illegible] e army being filled with tears and in a distraught st [illegible] go, even from an enemy's land, where they had al [illegible] great for tears and in the unknown future before th [illegible] e. [5] Dejection and self-condemnation were also ri [illegible] l they could only be compared to a starved-out ci [illegible] e, escaping; the whole multitude upon the march b [illegible] thousand men. All carried anything they could w [illegible] and the hoplites and troopers, contrary to their cu [illegible] s, carried their own provisions, in some cases for la [illegible] rs through not trusting them; as they had long b [illegible] did so in greater numbers than ever. Yet even thus th [illegible] h, as there was no longer food in the camp. [6]

Moreover their disgrace generally, and the universality of their sufferings, although to a certain extent alleviated by being borne in company, were still felt at the moment a heavy burden, especially when they contrasted the splendor and glory of their setting out with the humiliation in which it had ended. [7] For this was by far the greatest reverse that ever befell an Hellenic army. They had come to enslave others, and were departing in fear of being enslaved themselves: they had sailed out with prayer and paeans, and now started to go back with omens directly contrary; traveling by land instead of by sea, and trusting not in their fleet but in their hoplites. Nevertheless the greatness of the danger still impending made all this appear tolerable.

7.76
413
19th Year/Summer
SYRACUSE
Nicias tries to encourage his men.

Nicias seeing the army dejected and greatly altered, passed along the ranks and encouraged and comforted them as far as was possible under the circumstances, raising his voice still higher and higher as he went from one company to another in his earnestness, and in his anxiety that the benefit of his words might reach as many as possible:

7.77
413
19th Year/Summer
SYRACUSE
Nicias argues that others have survived worse straits, and that the gods may now find them more an object of pity than of jealousy and stop tormenting them. He points out that they are still a formidable force, may still find friends among the Sicels, and may hope to raise Athens' power again.

> "Athenians and allies, even in our present position we must still hope on, since men have before now been saved from worse straits than this; and you must not condemn yourselves too severely either because of your disasters or because of your present unmerited sufferings. [2] I myself who am not superior to any of you in strength—indeed you see how I am in my sickness—and who in the gifts of fortune am, I think, whether in private life or otherwise, the equal of any, am now exposed to the same danger as the meanest among you; and yet my life has been one of much devotion toward the gods, and of much justice and without offense toward men. [3] I have, therefore, still a strong hope for the future, and our misfortunes do not terrify me as much as they might. Indeed we may hope that they will be lightened: our enemies have had good fortune enough; and if any of the gods was offended at our expedition, we have already been amply punished. [4] Others before us have attacked their neighbors and have done what men will do without suffering more than they could bear; and we may now justly expect to find the gods more kind, for we have become fitter objects for their pity than their jealousy. And then look at yourselves, mark the numbers and efficiency of the hoplites marching in your ranks, and do not give way too much to despondency, but reflect that you are yourselves at once a city wherever you sit down, and that there is no other in Sicily that could easily resist your attack, or expel you when once established. [5] The safety and order of the march is for yourselves to attend to; the one thought of each man being that the spot on which he may be forced to fight must be conquered and held as his country and stronghold. [6] Meanwhile we shall hasten on our

e, as our provisions are scanty; and if we can
ce of the Sicels, whom fear of the Syracusans
you may from then on consider yourselves
n sent on to them with directions to meet us
[7] To sum up, be convinced, soldiers, that
there is no place near for your cowardice to
if you now escape from the enemy, you may
r hearts desire, while those of you who are
again the great power of the state, fallen
e the city and not walls or ships without men

s, Nicias went along the ranks, and brought back
to ... oops that he saw straggling out of the line; while
De ... h for his part of the army, addressing them in
wc ... e army marched in a hollow square, the division
un ... d that of Demosthenes following, the hoplites
be ... ggage carriers and the bulk of the army in the
mi ... rived at the ford of the river Anapus[3a] they there
fo ... of the Syracusans and allies, and routing these,
ma ... and pushed on, harassed by the charges of the
Sy ... e missiles of their light troops. [4] On that day
the ... miles and a half, halting for the night upon a certai ... started early and got on about two miles further,
an ... e in the plain and there encamped[4a] in order to
pr ... n the houses, as the place was inhabited, and to
ca ... m there, as for many miles in front, in the direc-
tio ... going, it was not plentiful. [5] The Syracusans
me ... ortified the pass in front, where there was a steep
hil ... each side of it, called the Acraean cliff.[5a] [6] The
ne ... dvancing found themselves impeded by the mis-
sil ... rse and darters, both very numerous, of the Syracu ... fighting for a long while, at length retired to the
sa ... longer had provisions as before, it being impos-
sib ... by reason of the cavalry.

7.78
413
19th Year/Summer
SYRACUSE
The Athenians make slow progress on the march, crossing the Anapus and camping where they hope to find food. Halted by the Syracusans and prevented from foraging by enemy cavalry, they begin to run low on provisions.

y started afresh and forced their way to the hill,
wh ... where they found before them the enemy's in-
fa ... ields deep to defend the fortification, the pass
be ... enians assaulted the work, but were greeted by a
sto ... hill, which told with the greater effect through
its ... unable to force the passage, retreated again and
re ... curred some claps of thunder and rain, as often

7.79
413
19th Year/Summer
SYRACUSE
The Athenians fail to pierce the Syracusan defense and a thunderstorm is seen by them as an omen of ruin. The next day they are attacked on every side by cavalry and infantry, and make very little progress.

7.7 ... e site of the ... unknown.

7.7 ... le location:

7.78.5a Acraean cliff and pass, possible location: Map 7.81.

happens toward autumn, which still further disheartened the Athenians, who thought all these things to be omens of their approaching ruin.[3a] [4] While they were resting Gylippus and the Syracusans sent a part of their army to throw up works in their rear on the way by which they had advanced; however, the Athenians immediately sent some of their men and prevented them; [5] after which they retreated more toward the plain and halted for the night. When they advanced the next day the Syracusans surrounded and attacked them on every side, and disabled many of them, falling back if the Athenians advanced and coming on if they retired, and in particular assaulting their rear, in the hope of routing them in detail, and thus striking a panic into the whole army. [6] For a long while the Athenians persevered in this fashion, but after advancing for about a half a mile, halted to rest in the plain,[6a] the Syracusans also withdrawing to their own camp.

7.80
413
19th Year/Summer
SYRACUSE
Because the troops' condition is deteriorating, the Athenians try to escape by secretly leaving their camp at night and marching south toward the sea. The army's two divisions become separated but both reach the Helorine Road and cross the Erineus River.

During the night Nicias and Demosthenes, seeing the wretched condition of their troops, now in want of every kind of necessity, and numbers of them disabled in the numerous attacks of the enemy, determined to light as many fires as possible, and to lead off the army, no longer by the same route as they had intended, but toward the sea in the opposite direction to that guarded by the Syracusans. [2] This route led the army not to Catana but to the other side of Sicily, toward Camarina, Gela,[2a] and the other Hellenic and barbarian cities in that quarter. [3] They accordingly lit a number of fires and set out by night. Now all armies, and the greatest most of all, are liable to fears and alarms, especially when they are marching by night through an enemy's country and with the enemy near; and the Athenians now fell into one of these panics,[3a] [4] the leading division, that of Nicias, kept together and got on a good way in front, while that of Demosthenes, comprising rather more than half the army, became separated and marched on in some disorder. [5] By morning, however, they reached the sea, and getting onto the Helorine road,[5a] pushed on to reach the river Cacyparis[5b] in order to follow that stream up into the interior, where they hoped to be met by the Sicels whom they had sent for. [6] When they arrived at the river, they found there also a Syracusan party engaged in barring the passage of the ford with a wall and a palisade, and forcing this guard, crossed the river and went on to another called the Erineus,[6a] according to the advice of their guides.

7.81
413
19th Year/Summer
SYRACUSE
The Syracusans pursue the Athenians and overtake the division of Demosthenes; that of Nicias is some miles ahead. Demosthenes' men are soon surrounded and assaulted with missiles. Now certain of victory, the Syracusans become unwilling to risk close combat.

Meanwhile, when day came and the Syracusans and allies found that the Athenians were gone, most of them accused Gylippus of having let them escape on purpose, and hastily pursuing by the road that they had taken (which they had no difficulty finding), overtook them about dinnertime. [2] They first came up with the troops under Demosthenes, who were be-

7.79.3a Compare this reaction with the impact of a thunderstorm on the Syracusans in 6.70.1.
7.79.6a Second Athenian camp, possible location: Map 7.81.
7.80.2a Catana, Camarina, and Gela: Map 7.81, locator.
7.80.3a Compare this panic with the panic of the Macedonians in 4.125.1.
7.80.5a Helorine road: Map 7.81.
7.80.5b Cacyparis river: Map 7.81.
7.80.6a Erineus river, possible location: Map 7.81.

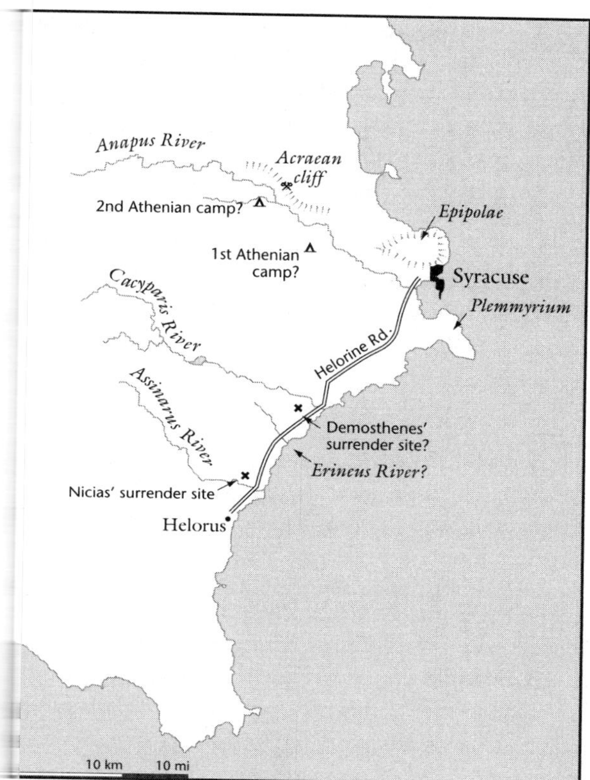

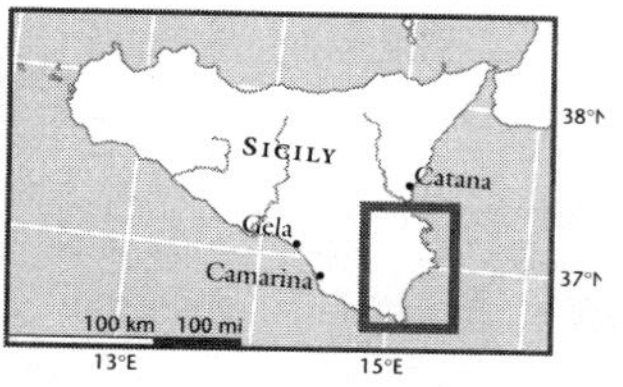

M…
T…
A…

hi… what slowly and in disorder, owing to the night pa… nd at once attacked and engaged them, the Syracu… them with more ease now that they were separa… hemming them in on one spot. [3] The division of N… s on in front, as he led them more rapidly, thinkin… stances their safety lay not in staying and fighting, u… eating as fast as possible, and only fighting when fo… he other hand, Demosthenes was, generally speakin… antly, as his post in the rear left him the first exp… he enemy; and now, finding that the Syracusans w… d to push on, in order to form his men for battle, a… was surrounded by his pursuers and himself and

7. … based primarily … *ce of Nicias* … (Ithaca, N.Y.: …981), Map 12,

the Athenians with him placed in the most distressing position, being huddled into an enclosure with a wall all round it, a road on this side and on that, and olive trees in great number, where missiles were showered in upon them from every quarter.[4a] [5] This mode of attack the Syracusans had with good reason adopted in preference to fighting at close quarters, as to risk a struggle with desperate men was now more to the advantage of the Athenians than to their own; besides, their success had now become so certain that they began to spare themselves a little in order not to be killed in the moment of victory, thinking too that they would in any case be able in this way to subdue and capture the enemy.

7.82
413
19th Year/Summer
SYRACUSE
The Syracusans offer liberty to islanders who surrender, but only a few go over. Then Demosthenes agrees to capitulate on condition that no one will be killed; six thousand Athenians surrender.

In fact, after plying the Athenians and allies all day long from every side with missiles, they at length saw that they were worn out with their wounds and other sufferings; and Gylippus and the Syracusans and their allies made a proclamation, offering their liberty to any of the islanders who chose to come over to them; and some few cities went over. [2] Afterwards a capitulation was agreed upon for all the rest with Demosthenes, to lay down their arms on condition that no one was to be put to death either by violence or imprisonment or want of the necessaries of life.[2a] [3] Upon this they surrendered to the number of six thousand in all, laying down all the money in their possession, which filled the hollows of four shields, and were immediately conveyed by the Syracusans to the city.[3a]

Meanwhile Nicias with his division arrived that day at the river Erineus, crossed over, and posted his army upon some high ground upon the other side. [7.83.1] The next day the Syracusans overtook him and told him that the troops under Demosthenes had surrendered, and invited him to follow their example. Incredulous of the fact, Nicias asked for a truce to send a horseman to see, [2] and upon the return of the messenger with the tidings that they had surrendered, sent a herald to Gylippus and the Syracusans, saying that he was ready to agree with them on behalf of the Athenians to repay whatever money the Syracusans had spent upon the war if they would let his army go; and offered until the money was paid to give Athenians as hostages, one for every talent. [3] The Syracusans and Gylippus rejected this proposition, and attacked this division as they had the other, standing all round and plying them with missiles until the evening. [4] Food and necessaries were as miserably wanting to the troops of Nicias as they had been to their comrades; nevertheless they watched for the quiet of the night to resume their march. But as they were taking up their arms the Syracusans perceived it and raised their paean, [5] upon which the Athenians, finding that they were discovered, laid them down again, except about three hundred men who forced their way through the guards and went on during the night as they were able.

7.83
413
19th Year/Summer
SYRACUSE
When the Syracusans inform Nicias of Demosthenes' surrender, Nicias offers to pay for his army's liberty. The Syracusans refuse his offer and attack his men from all sides with missiles. An attempt by Nicias to march off by night is thwarted.

7.81.4a The plight of the Athenians here parallels that of the Corinthians in 1.106.

7.82.2a Terms that the Syracusans did not carry out, see 7.86–7.

7.82.3a Possible site of Demosthenes' surrender: Map 7.81.

Nicias put his army in motion, pressed as before,
by ir allies, pelted from every side by their missiles,
ar javelins. [2] The Athenians pushed on for the
As ne attacks made upon them from every side by a
nu swarm of other arms, supposing that they should
br e across the river, and driven on also by their ex-
ha vater. [3] Once there they rushed in, and all order
wa vanting to cross first, and the attacks of the enemy
m at all; forced to huddle together, they fell against
ar , some dying immediately upon the javelins, other ther and stumbling over the articles of baggage,
wi again. [4] Meanwhile the opposite bank, which
wa e Syracusans, who showered missiles down upon
th em drinking greedily and heaped together in dis-
or of the river. [5] The Peloponnesians also came
do n, especially those in the water, which was thus
im which they went on drinking just the same, mud
ar nost even fighting to have it.

7.84
413
19th Year/Summer
SYRACUSE
Under attack all the way, the Athenians march to the Assinarus river, driven by thirst and the hope that they would be safe there. When they arrive, they find the Syracusans waiting for them. All order is lost as men rush to drink even the foul water in which they are being butchered.

ad now lay piled one upon another in the stream,
ar been destroyed at the river, and the few that es-
ca n cut off by the cavalry, Nicias surrendered himse e trusted more than he did the Syracusans, and
to s to do what they liked with him, but to stop the
sl [2] Gylippus, after this, immediately gave orders
to hich the rest were assembled alive, except a large
nu he soldiery, and a party was sent in pursuit of the
th ot through the guard during the night, and who
we rest. [3] The number of the enemy collected as
pu considerable; but that taken privately[3a] was very
la led with them, no agreement having been made
in aken with Demosthenes. [4] Besides this, a large
po ght, the carnage being very great, and not exce ian war. In the numerous other encounters upon
th had fallen. Nevertheless many escaped, some at
th d as slaves, and then ran away subsequently. These
fo

7.85
413
19th Year/Summer
SYRACUSE
Nicias surrenders to Gylippus, who then orders that prisoners be taken. Although more men died on this march than in any action of the Sicilian war, many escaped or were enslaved and escaped later to Catana.

ir allies now mustered and took up the spoils and
as could, and went back to the city. [2] The rest of
th captives were deposited in the quarries, this seem-
in eping them; but Nicias and Demosthenes were
bu l of Gylippus, who thought that it would be the

7.86
413
19th Year/Summer
SYRACUSE
The Athenian and allied prisoners are held in quarries. Demosthenes and Nicias are executed. Thucydides remarks that Nicias did not deserve this fate.

7.8
7.8 y taken in war
the state, not

7.85.4a Catana: Map 7.81, locator.

crown of his triumph if he could take the enemy's generals to Sparta. [3] One of them, as it happened, Demosthenes, was one of her greatest enemies, on account of the affair of the island and of Pylos;[3a] while the other, Nicias, was for the same reasons one of her greatest friends, owing to his exertions to procure the release of the prisoners by persuading the Athenians to make peace. [4] For these reasons the Spartans felt kindly toward him; and it was in this that Nicias himself mainly confided when he surrendered to Gylippus. But some of the Syracusans who had been in correspondence with him were afraid, it was said, of his being put to the torture and troubling their success by his revelations; others, especially the Corinthians, of his escaping by means of bribes (as he was wealthy), and living to do them further harm; and these persuaded the allies and put him to death. [5] This or the like was the cause of the death of a man who, of all the Hellenes in my time, least deserved such a fate, seeing that the whole course of his life had been regulated with strict attention to virtue.

7.87
413
19th Year/Summer
SYRACUSE
Thucydides describes the torments of the seven thousand or more captives who endured the crowded quarries for eight months before being sold as slaves. Many died. Thucydides calls the Syracusan victory the greatest of the war, and the Athenian defeat the most calamitous and total.

The prisoners in the quarries were at first harshly treated by the Syracusans. Crowded in a narrow hole, without any roof to cover them, the heat of the sun and the stifling closeness of the air tormented them during the day, and then the nights which came on autumnal and chilly made them ill by the violence of the change; [2] besides, as they had to do everything in the same place for want of room, and the bodies of those who died of their wounds or from the variation in the temperature, or from similar causes, were left heaped together one upon another, intolerable stenches arose; while hunger and thirst never ceased to afflict them, each man during eight months having only half a pint of water and a pint of grain given him daily. In short, no single suffering to be apprehended by men thrust into such a place was spared them. [3] For some seventy days they thus lived all together, after which all, except the Athenians and any Siceliots or Italians who had joined in the expedition, were sold. [4] The total number of prisoners taken it would be difficult to state exactly, but it could not have been less than seven thousand.

[5] This was the greatest Hellenic achievement of any in this war, or, in my opinion, in Hellenic history; at once most glorious to the victors, and most calamitous to the conquered. [6] They were beaten at all points and altogether; all that they suffered was great; they were destroyed, as the saying is, with a total destruction, their fleet, their army—everything was destroyed, and few out of many returned home. Such were the events in Sicily.

7.86.3a Pylos: Map 7.56, BX. For a description of the Pylos campaign, see 4.2–41.

BOOK EIGHT

8.1
413
19th Year/Summer
ATHENS
The Athenians are shocked by the disaster in Sicily and discouraged by their lack of resources with which to carry on the war. Yet they decide to resist and take steps to build ships and secure their hold on their allies.

When the news was brought to
Ath[illegible]y disbelieved even the most respectable of the soldie[illegible]aped from the scene of action and clearly reported
the[illegible] complete not being thought credible. When the
co[illegible] them, they were angry with the orators who had
joi[illegible]pedition, just as if they had not themselves voted
it, [illegible]ith the reciters of oracles and soothsayers, and all
oth[illegible]ime who had encouraged them to hope that they
sh[illegible]Already distressed at all points and in all quarters,
afte[illegible]ed they were seized by a fear and consternation
qui[illegible] was grievous enough for the state and for every
ma[illegible]o lose so many *hoplites,*[2a] cavalry, and able-bodied
tro[illegible]t to replace them; but when they saw, also, that
the[illegible] in their docks, or money in the treasury, or crews
for[illegible] despair of salvation. They thought that their ene-
mi[illegible]diately sail with their fleet against the Piraeus,[2b]
infl[illegible]ry; while their adversaries at home, redoubling all
the[illegible]igorously attack them by sea and land at once,
aid[illegible] confederates. [3] Nevertheless, with such means
as t[illegible]ed to resist to the last, and to provide timber and
mo[illegible] as they best could, to take steps to secure their
co[illegible]uboea,[3a] to reform things in the city upon a more
eco[illegible] elect a board of elders to advise upon the state of
affa[illegible]ise. [4] In short, as is the way of a democracy, in
the[illegible]ey were ready to be as prudent as possible. These
res[illegible]ect at once. Summer was now over.

8.1.[illegible]
8.1.[illegible] a heavily [illegible]ndix F, [illegible]
8.1.2b Piraeus: Map 8.3, AY.
8.1.3a Euboea: Map 8.3, AY.

8.2
413/2
19th Year/Winter
HELLAS
Peloponnesians, neutrals, and restive Athenian subjects plan a decisive effort, confident now that Athens cannot long resist their combined forces. The Spartans look forward to securing hegemony in Hellas.

The following winter saw all Hellas stirring under the impression of the great Athenian disaster in Sicily. Neutrals now felt that even if uninvited they no longer ought to stand aloof from the war, but should volunteer to march against the Athenians, who, as each city reflected, would probably have come against them if the Sicilian campaign had succeeded. Besides, they believed that the war would now be short, and that it would be creditable for them to take part in it. Meanwhile the allies of the Spartans felt all the more anxious than ever to see a speedy end to their heavy labors. [2] But above all, the subjects of the Athenians showed a readiness to revolt even beyond their ability, judging the circumstances with passion and refusing even to hear of the Athenians being able to last out the coming summer. [3] Beyond all this, Sparta was encouraged by the near prospect of being joined in great force in the spring by her allies in Sicily, lately forced by events to acquire their navy. [4] With these reasons for confidence in every quarter, the Spartans now resolved to throw themselves without reserve into the war considering that, once it was happily terminated, they would be finally delivered from such dangers as that which would have threatened them from Athens, if she had become mistress of Sicily, and that the overthrow of the Athenians would leave them in quiet enjoyment of the supremacy over all Hellas.

8.3
413/2
19th Year/Winter
HELLAS
Agis takes hostages and secures funds in the Malian Gulf area. Sparta allots quotas of ships to be built by various allies for the creation of a new fleet.

Their king, Agis, accordingly set out at once during this winter with some troops from Decelea,[1a] and levied from the allies contributions for the fleet, and turning toward the Malian gulf[1b] exacted a sum of money from the Oetaeans[1c] by carrying off most of their cattle in reprisal for their old hostility, and, in spite of the protests and opposition of the Thessalians,[1d] forced the Achaeans of Phthiotis[1e] and the other subjects of the Thessalians in those parts to give him money and hostages, and deposited the hostages at Corinth,[1f] and tried to bring their countrymen into the confederacy. [2] The Spartans now issued a requisition to the cities[2a] for building a hundred ships, fixing their own quota and that of the Boeotians at twenty-five each; that of the Phocians and Locrians[2b] together at fifteen; that of the Corinthians at fifteen;[2c] that of the Arcadians,[2d] Pellenians,[2e] and Sicyonians[2f] together at ten; and that of the Megarians, Troezenians, Epidaurians, and Hermionians[2g] together at ten also; and meanwhile made every other preparation for commencing hostility by the spring.

8.3.1a Decelea: Map 8.3, AY.
8.3.1b Malian Gulf: Map 8.3, AX.
8.3.1c Oetae, general location of their territory: Map 8.3, AX.
8.3.1d Thessaly: Map 8.3, AX.
8.3.1e Phthiotis: Map 8.3, AX.
8.3.1f Corinth: Map 8.3, AX.
8.3.2a The "cities" in this case, as in 5.17.2, are the members of the Peloponnesian League; see Appendix D, The Peloponnesian League, §3.
8.3.2b Boeotia: Map 8.3, AY; Phocis and Opuntian Locris: Map 8.3, AX.
8.3.2c This requisition, when compared to the seventy-five triremes launched by Corinth in 435 (1.29.1), may indicate how severely Corinth had been impoverished by the war.
8.3.2d Arcadia: Map 8.3, BX.
8.3.2e Pellene: Map 8.3, AX.
8.3.2f Sicyon: Map 8.3, AX.
8.3.2g Megara: Map 8.3, AY; Troezen, Epidaurus, and Hermione: Map 8.3, BY.

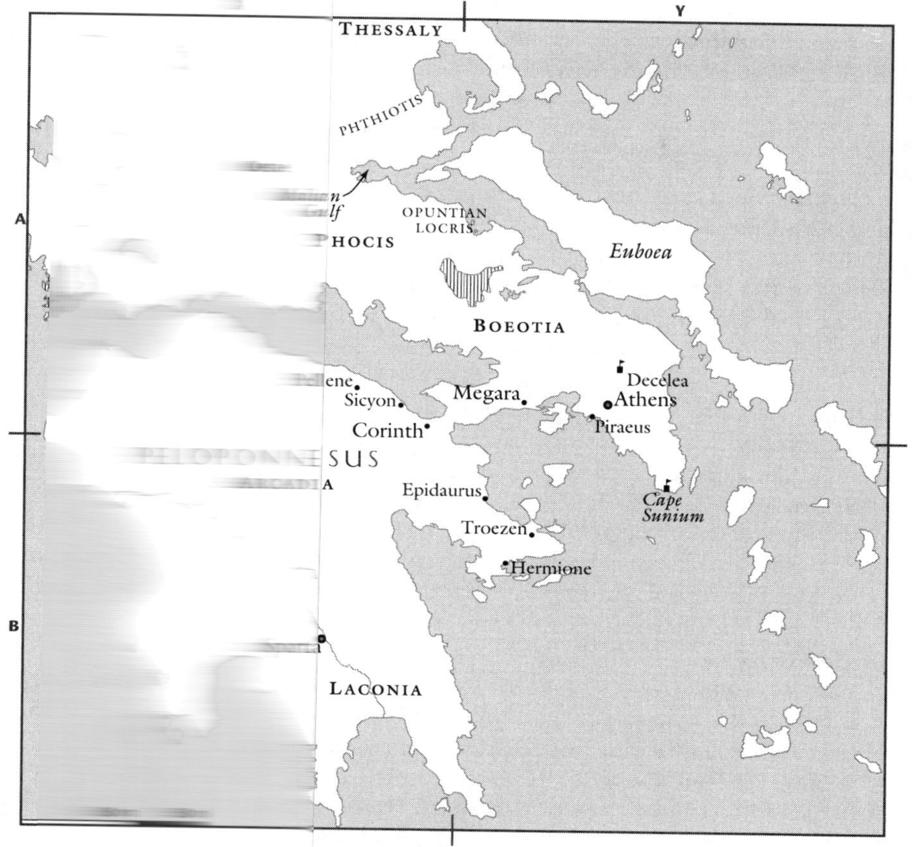

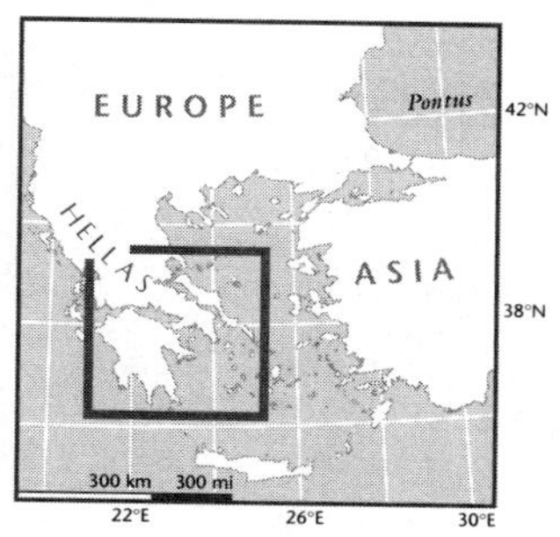

M RE FOR RENEWED WARFARE

Athenians were not idle. During this same winter, ey contributed timber and got on with their ship- unium[1a] to enable their grain ships to round it in fort in Laconia[1b] which they had built on their also, for economy, reduced any other expenses that above all kept a careful lookout against the revolt

8.4
413/2
19th Year/Winter
ATHENS
Athens also builds ships and prepares to carry on the war.

BY.
he exact location uction was known.

8.5
413/2
19th Year/Winter
EUBOEA
Agis at Decelea agrees to support a Euboean uprising but delays action because . . .
LESBOS
The Lesbians, with Boeotian support, convince Agis to assist their revolt first.
CHIOS
The Chians, supported by the Persian Tissaphernes, apply at Sparta for aid for their prospective revolt.

While both parties were thus engaged, and were as intent upon preparing for the war as they had been at the outset, the Euboeans first of all sent envoys during this winter to Agis to consult about their revolting from Athens. Agis accepted their proposals, and sent for Alcamenes son of Sthenelaidas,[1a] and Melanthus from Sparta to take the command in Euboea.[1b] These accordingly arrived with some three hundred *neodamodeis,*[1c] and Agis began to arrange for their crossing over. [2] But in the meantime some Lesbians[2a] arrived who also wished to revolt; and these being supported by the Boeotians,[2b] Agis was persuaded to defer acting in the matter of Euboea, and made arrangements for the revolt of the Lesbians, giving them Alcamenes, who was to have sailed to Euboea, as governor, and himself promising them ten ships, and the Boeotians the same number. [3] All this was done without instructions from home, as Agis while at Decelea[3a] with the army that he commanded had power to send troops to whatever quarter he pleased, and to levy men and money. During this period, one might say, the allies obeyed him much more than they did the Spartans in the city, as the force he had with him made him feared at once wherever he went. [4] While Agis was engaged with the Lesbians, the Chians and Erythraeans,[4a] who were also ready to revolt, applied not to him but at Sparta; where they arrived accompanied by an ambassador from Tissaphernes, the commander of King Darius son of Artaxerxes, [5] in the maritime districts,[5a] who invited the Peloponnesians to come over, and promised to maintain their army. The King had lately called upon him for the tribute from his province, for which he was in arrears, because the Athenians prevented him from collecting it from the Hellenic cities. He therefore calculated that by weakening the Athenians he could better obtain that tribute, and would also draw the Spartans into alliance with the King; and by this means, as the King had commanded him, take dead or alive Amorges the bastard son of Pissuthnes,[5b] who was in rebellion on the coast of Caria.[5c]

8.5.1a This may be the same Sthenelaidas who as ephor spoke so strongly for war twenty years earlier in 1.86.
8.5.1b Euboea: Map 8.3, AY.
8.5.1c When Brasidas took the 700 helots to fight in Thrace (4.80) he inaugurated the radical policy change at Sparta of using helots for military purposes rather than keeping them all in bitter subjection. Sparta further developed that policy by creating a special class of Neodamodeis whose numbers seem to increase steadily in the succeeding half century (cf. 7.19.3). Their precise status remains unknown, and although the name implies that they were made part of the citizen body, most scholars reject this notion. See Appendix C, §9.
8.5.2a Lesbos: Map 8.7, Asia.
8.5.2b Boeotia: Map 8.3, AY, and Map 8.7, Hellas.
8.5.3a Decelea: Map 8.3, AY, and Map 8.7, Hellas.
8.5.4a Chios and Erythrae: Map 8.7, Asia.
8.5.5a Tissaphernes, Persian satrap (governor) of the "maritime districts," governed his large province from Sardis (Map 8.7, Asia), the capital of the province or satrapy of Lydia.
8.5.5b This Pissuthnes, son of Hystaspes, is mentioned by Thucydides as supporting the Samian Revolt of 440 (see 1.115). Pissuthnes had revolted from Darius II—precisely when or why is not known—and had been brutally executed. The rebellion of his son, Amorges, may have followed shortly after, though the date is quite unsure—415/4 is possible. He appears to have requested and received Athenian help, which, if true, may prove to be another event of perhaps great importance that is entirely omitted by Thucydides, although we can indirectly infer the existence of an alliance between Amorges and the Athenians from his text at 8.19.1, 8.28.2, and especially 8.54.3.

(continued on next page)

8.6
413/2
19th Year/Winter
SPARTA
Envoys from the Persian satrap Pharnabazus arrive at Sparta to request that a fleet be sent to the Hellespont, not to Chios. Sparta decides to send forces to Chios but due to an earthquake and other problems sends only five triremes.

[illegible] Tissaphernes thus joined to effect a common pu[illegible] time Calligeitus son of Laophon, a Megarian,[1a] an[illegible]thenagoras, a Cyzicene,[1b] both of them exiles fr[illegible]ving at the court of Pharnabazus son of Pharna[illegible]upon a mission from Pharnabazus to procure a fle[illegible] by means of which, if possible, he might himse[illegible]rnes' ambition, and cause the cities in his pr[illegible] the Athenians, and thereby receive the tribute fr[illegible]n agency obtain for the King the alliance of the Sp[illegible]

[illegible]f Pharnabazus and Tissaphernes negotiated separa[illegible] now ensued at Sparta as to whether a fleet and ar[illegible] to Ionia[2a] and Chios, or to the Hellespont. [3] Th[illegible]decidedly favored the Chians and Tissaphernes, wh[illegible]Alcibiades, the family friend of Endius who was or[illegible]t year.[3a] Indeed, this is how their house got its La[illegible] being the family name of Endius. [4] Neverthe-les[illegible] to Chios Phrynis, one of the *perioikoi*,[4a] to see wh[illegible] ships as they said, and whether their city generall[illegible]reported; and upon his bringing word that they ha[illegible]mmediately entered into alliance with the Chians an[illegible]ted to send them forty ships, there being already, ac[illegible]t of the Chians, not less than sixty in the island. [5[illegible]meant to send ten of these forty themselves, with M[illegible]iral; but afterwards, an earthquake having oc[illegible]ideus instead of Melanchridas, and instead of the te[illegible]ve in Laconia.[5a] And the winter ended, and with it [illegible]nth year of this war of which Thucydides is the hi[illegible]

(co[illegible]
[illegible]morges may [illegible] between [illegible] the Persian [illegible]ltimately [illegible] Thucydides' [illegible] scholarly [illegible]me scholars [illegible]at the omis-[illegible] lack of [illegible] part than it is [illegible]ess of his [illegible]ioned in [illegible]e Persians,

8.[illegible]
8.[illegible]
8.[illegible]
8.[illegible]Pharnabazus [illegible]sian governor
8.[illegible]aphernes, [illegible] Sardis (Map 8.7, Asia), and Pharnabazus, Persian governor of the Hellespont (Map 8.7, Asia), see 8.109.1 and Appendix E, The Persians, §7.
8.6.2a Ionia: Map 8.7, Asia.
8.6.3a Endius was one of the three envoys sent to Athens eight years earlier who were then "known to be well disposed to the Athenians" (5.44.3), and who were duped by Alcibiades in the assembly (5.45). As a Spartan ephor, Endius was now a powerful government official. See Appendix C, Spartan Institutions, §5–6.
8.6.4a For *perioikoi*, see the Glossary and Appendix C, Spartan Institutions, §9.
8.6.4b Erythrae: Map 8.7, Asia.
8.6.5a Laconia: Map 8.3. BX.

ILLUSTRATION 8.7
COINS WITH PORTRAIT HEADS OF PHARNABAZUS (LEFT) AND TISSAPHERNES

ILLUSTRATION 8.8
TRACKWAY FOR CARTS (*DIOLKOS*) FOR HAULING BOATS ACROSS THE ISTHMUS OF CORINTH

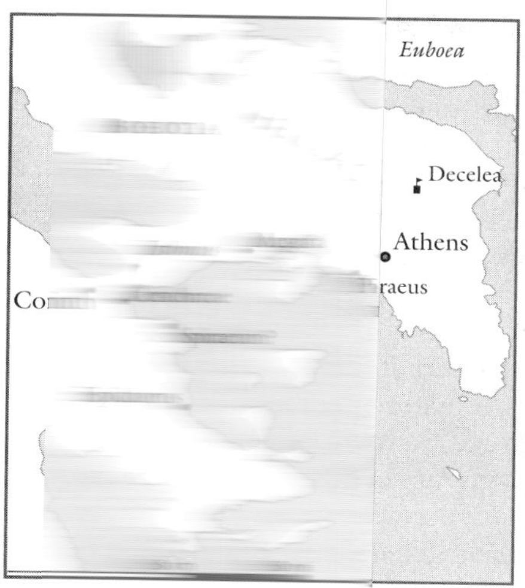

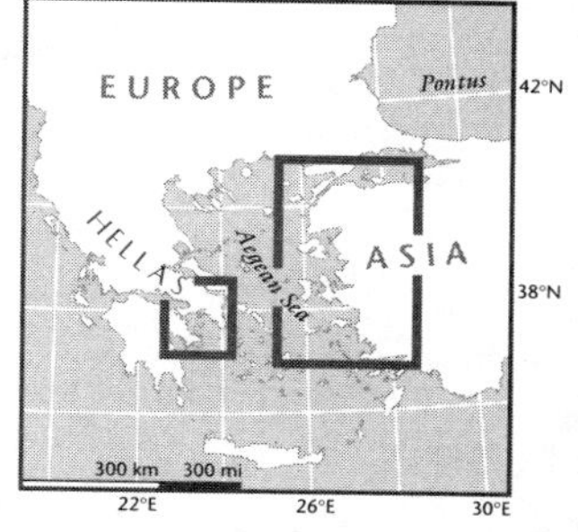

M OLTS OF
E S

he next summer the Chians were urging that the f being afraid that the Athenians, from whom all t t a secret, might find out what was going on, and t three *Spartiates*[1a] to Corinth to haul the ships as c the Isthmus[1b] from the other sea to that on the s order them all to sail to Chios,[1c] including those v g for Lesbos[1d] not excepted. The number of ships f thirty-nine in all.

8.7
412
20th Year/Summer
CORINTH
Sparta plans to haul thirty-nine Peloponnesian warships across the Isthmus and to send them to Chios.

s and Timagoras did not join on behalf of Pharn- to Chios or give the money—twenty-five *talents*[1a]— t with them to help in dispatching a force, but vards with another force by themselves. [2] Agis, ng the Spartans bent upon going to Chios first, ne view; and the allies assembled at Corinth and they decided to sail first to Chios under the com- o was equipping the five vessels in Laconia, then mmand of Alcamenes, the same whom Agis had o to the Hellespont,[2a] where the command was

8.8
412
20th Year/Summer
CORINTH
In assembly at Corinth, the Peloponnesians agree to send a fleet first to Chios, then to Lesbos, and finally to the Hellespont. Twenty-one triremes are prepared for immediate departure. Athens as yet has no fleet at sea.

n of Sparta and
Spartan military

n, (Map 8.7,
ent trackway on
hauled ships
d the long and
e around the
Peloponnesus can still be seen today; see Illustration 8.8.

8.7.1c Chios: Map 8.7, Asia.

8.7.1d Lesbos: Map 8.7, Asia.

8.8.1a A *talent* is a large unit of money; see Appendix J, Classical Greek Currency, §5.

8.8.2a Hellespont: Map 8.7, Asia. Alcamenes' selection by Agis was mentioned in 8.5.1.

given to Clearchus son of Ramphias. [3] Meanwhile they would take only half the ships across the Isthmus first, and let these sail off at once, in order that the Athenians might less notice this departing squadron than those who would be taken across afterward, [4] for no care had been taken to keep this voyage secret through contempt of the impotence of the Athenians, who had as yet no fleet of any account upon the sea. In accordance with this decision, twenty-one vessels were conveyed across the Isthmus at once.

8.9
412
20th Year/Summer
CORINTH-CHIOS
Corinth's determination to celebrate the Isthmian festival delays the fleet's departure. The Athenians become suspicious and demand that Chios send ships to Athens, and seven are sent, since most Chians were ignorant of the negotiations with the Spartans.

They were now impatient to set sail, but the Corinthians were not willing to accompany them until they had celebrated the Isthmian festival,[1a] which fell at that time. Upon this Agis proposed to them to respect their scruples about breaking the Isthmian truce by taking the expedition upon himself. [2] The Corinthians did not consent to this, and a delay ensued, during which the Athenians began to suspect what was being prepared at Chios,[2a] and sent Aristocrates, one of their generals, who accused them of planning to revolt and, upon the denial of the Chians, ordered them as faithful allies to send with them a contingent of ships. Seven Chian ships were sent accordingly. [3] The reason for the dispatch of the ships was that the mass of the Chians were not privy to the negotiations, while the few who were in on the secret did not wish to break with the multitude until they had something positive to lean upon, and no longer expected the Peloponnesians to arrive by reason of their delay.

8.10
412
20th Year/Summer
CORINTH
After learning more at the Isthmian Games about Chian intrigues, the Athenians man their fleet and, intercepting the twenty-one enemy triremes, force them into port. The Athenians attack the enemy ships there and disable most of them.

In the meantime the Isthmian games took place, and the Athenians, who had also been invited, went to attend them, and there perceiving more clearly the designs of the Chians, took measures as soon as they returned to Athens to prevent the enemy fleet from setting out from Cenchreae[1a] without their knowledge. [2] After the festival the Peloponnesians set sail with twenty-one ships for Chios, under the command of Alcamenes. The Athenians first sailed against them with an equal number, drawing off toward the open sea. When the enemy, however, turned back before he had followed them far, the Athenians turned back also, not trusting the seven Chian ships which formed part of their number, [3] and afterwards manned thirty-seven vessels in all and chased the enemy fleet as it passed along shore into Spiraeum,[3a] a deserted Corinthian port on the edge of the Epidaurian[3b] frontier. After losing one ship out at sea, the Peloponnesians got the rest together and brought them to anchor. [4] The Athenians now attacked not only from the sea with their fleet, but also disembarked upon the coast; and a mêlée ensued of the most confused and violent kind, in which the Athenians disabled most of the enemy's vessels and killed Alcamenes their commander, losing also a few of their own men.

8.9.1a The Isthmian festival was one of the main ceremonies involving all Greeks. A general truce was declared so that all Greeks could travel to and participate in the festival. See 5.49, for a description of Sparta's alleged violation of the Olympic truce, and Appendix I, Religious Festivals, §5–7.

8.9.2a Chios: Map 8.7, Asia. For the fate of these ships, see 8.15.2.

8.10.1a Cenchreae: Map 8.7, Hellas.

8.10.3a Spiraeum: Map 8.7, Hellas.

8.10.3b Epidaurus: Map 8.7, Hellas.

8.11
412
20th Year/Summer
SPIRAEUM
The Athenians blockade the Peloponnesian fleet, whose ships are now drawn up on shore and guarded. News of the defeat discourages the Spartans.

[illegible] d, and the Athenians, detaching a sufficient num- [illegible] hose of the enemy, anchored with the rest at the [illegible] n which they proceeded to encamp, and sent to [illegible]; [2] the Peloponnesians having been joined on [illegible] the Corinthians, who came to help the ships, and [illegible] n the vicinity not long afterwards. These saw the [illegible] d in a desert place, and in their perplexity at first [illegible] ips, but finally resolved to haul them up on shore [illegible] them with their land forces, until a convenient [illegible] should present itself. Agis also, on being informed [illegible] a Spartiate by the name of Thermon. [3] The [illegible] news of the fleet having put out from the Isth- [illegible] been ordered by the ephors to send off a horse- [illegible], and immediately resolved to dispatch their own [illegible] eus, and Alcibiades with him. But while they were [illegible] e the second news of the fleet having taken refuge [illegible] ened at their first step in the Ionian war proving a [illegible] idea of sending the ships from their own country, [illegible] some that had already sailed.

8.12
412
20th Year/Summer
SPARTA
Alcibiades persuades Endius and the other ephors to let him sail with five ships to Chios so that it will be Endius and not Agis who starts the revolt and thus brings Persia into alliance with Sparta.

[illegible] ades again persuaded Endius and the other ephors [illegible] edition, saying that the voyage would be made [illegible] of the fleet's misfortune, and that as soon as he set [illegible], by assuring them of the weakness of the Atheni- [illegible] rta, have no difficulty in persuading the cities to [illegible] dily believe his testimony. [2] He also represented [illegible] vate that it would be glorious for him to be the [illegible] revolt and the King become the ally of Sparta, [illegible] ing left to Agis, for Agis (it must be remembered) [illegible] ades;[2a] and [3] Endius and his colleagues thus per- [illegible] he five ships and the Spartan Chalcideus, and made [illegible].[3a]

8.13
412
20th Year/Summer
LEUCAS
There is a naval skirmish off Leucas.

[illegible] the sixteen Peloponnesian ships from Sicily, which [illegible] war with Gylippus, were caught on their return off [illegible] ndled by the twenty-seven Athenian vessels under [illegible] pus, on the lookout for the ships from Sicily. After [illegible] ber the rest escaped from the Athenians and sailed [illegible]

8.14
412
20th Year/Summer
CHIOS
Alcibiades arrives in Chios. Saying nothing of the recent Peloponnesian defeat, he persuades Chios, Erythrae, and Clazomenae to revolt from Athens.

[illegible] us and Alcibiades seized all they met with on their [illegible] s of their coming, and let them go at Corycus,[1a] [illegible] y touched at on the mainland. Here they were vis-

[illegible] p 8.7, Hellas.
[illegible]
[illegible] "Alcibiades," 23), [illegible] by Agis' wife.
[illegible] rently seen and [illegible] Strombichides, but not overtaken; see 8.15.1.
8.13.1a Leucas: Map 8.15, Hellas.
8.14.1a Corycus, presumably near Mount Corycus: Map 8.15, Asia.

ited by some of their Chian correspondents, and being urged by them to sail up to the city without announcing their coming, arrived suddenly before Chios.[1b] [2] The multitude were amazed and confounded, while The Few had so arranged it that the council should be sitting at the time; and after speeches from Chalcideus and Alcibiades stating that many more ships were sailing up, but saying nothing of the fleet being blockaded in Spiraeum,[2a] the Chians revolted from the Athenians, and the Erythraeans[1b] immediately afterwards. [3] After this three vessels sailed over to Clazomenae,[3a] and made that city revolt also; and the Clazomenians immediately crossed over to the mainland and began to fortify Polichna,[3b] in order to retreat there in case of necessity, from the island where they dwelt.

8.15
412
20th Year/Summer
ATHENS
The Athenians, alarmed by news of the Chian revolt, employ their emergency funds to assemble a fleet to send to Chios.

While the places that had revolted were all engaged in fortifying and preparing for the war, news of Chios speedily reached Athens. The Athenians thought the danger by which they were now menaced was great and unmistakable, and that the rest of their allies would not consent to keep quiet after the secession of the greatest of their number. In the consternation of the moment they at once canceled the penalty imposed on whoever proposed or put to the vote a proposal for using the thousand talents which they had jealously avoided touching throughout the whole war,[1a] and voted to employ them to man a large number of ships, and to send off at once under Strombichides son of Diotimus the eight vessels that formed part of the blockading fleet at Spiraeum,[1b] but which had left the blockade and had returned after pursuing and failing to overtake the vessels with Chalcideus. These were to be followed shortly afterwards by twelve more under Thrasycles, also taken from the blockade. [2] They also recalled the seven Chian vessels forming part of their squadron blockading the fleet in Spiraeum, and giving the slaves on board their liberty,[2a] put the freemen in confinement, and speedily manned and sent out ten fresh ships to blockade the Peloponnesians in the place of all those that had departed, and decided to man thirty more. Zeal was not lacking, and no effort was spared to send relief to Chios.

8.16
412
20th Year/Summer
TEOS
The Peloponnesian fleet sails from Chios to Teos, chasing away an Athenian squadron. Teos accepts the Peloponnesians.

In the meantime Strombichides with his eight ships arrived at Samos,[1a] and taking one Samian vessel, sailed to Teos[1b] and required the Teians to remain quiet. Chalcideus also set sail for Teos from Chios[1c] with twenty-three ships, the land forces of the Clazomenians[1d] and Erythraeans[1e] moving along shore to support him. [2] Informed of this in time, Strombichides put out from Teos before their arrival, and while out at sea, seeing the number of the ships from Chios, fled toward Samos, chased by the enemy. [3] The Teians at first would not receive the land forces, but upon the flight of the Athenians took them into the city. There they waited

8.14.1b Chios: Map 8.15, Asia.
8.14.2a Spiraeum: Map 8.15, Hellas.
8.14.1b Erythrae: Map 8.15, Asia.
8.14.3a Clazomenae: Map 8.15, Asia.
8.14.3b Polichna: exact site unknown.
8.15.1a This fund was set aside in 431; see 2.24.1.
8.15.1b Spiraeum: Map 8.15, Hellas.
8.15.2a These were the Chian vessels demanded in 8.9.2–3. The Chians apparently used slaves in the crews of these ships. See note 1.55.1b, 7.13.2, and Appendix G, Trireme Warfare, §12.
8.16.1a Samos: Map 8.15, Asia.
8.16.1b Teos: Map 8.15, Asia.
8.16.1c Chios: Map 8.15, Asia.
8.16.1d Clazomenae: Map 8.15, Asia.
8.16.1e Erythrae: Map 8.15, Asia.

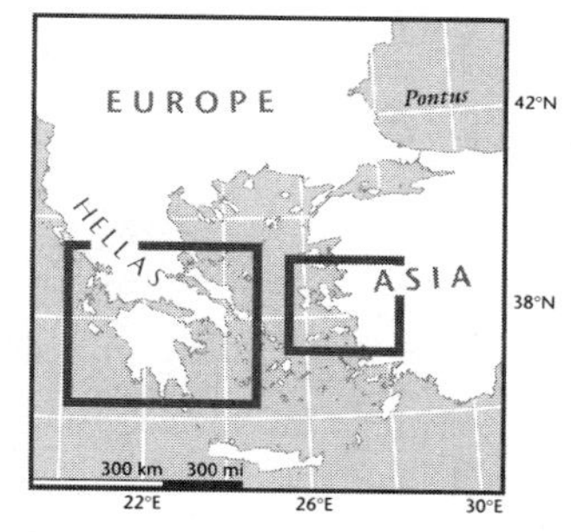

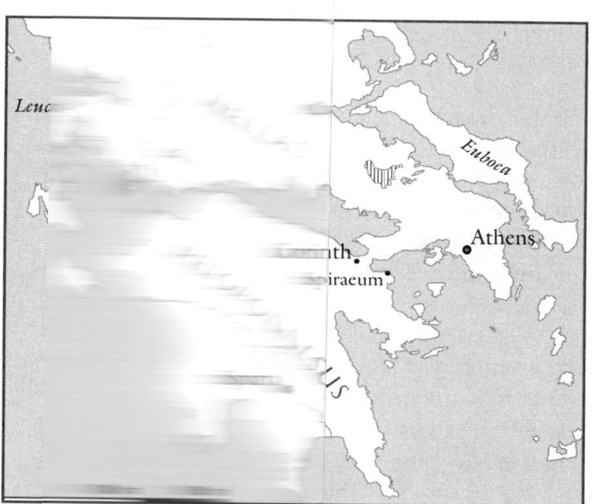

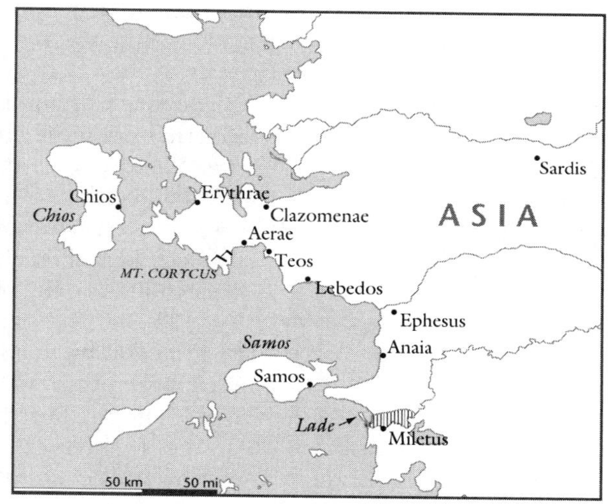

M… F LEUCAS; PELOPONNESIAN FLEET SAILS TO CHIOS

fo… eus to return from the pursuit, and as time went o… began themselves to demolish the wall which the A… e land side of the city of the Teians, being assisted b… ns[3a] who had come up under the command of St… issaphernes.

… and Alcibiades, after chasing Strombichides into S… f the ships from the Peloponnesus[1a] and left them at… places with substitutes from Chios and manning tw… to bring about the revolt of Miletus.[1b] [2] The w… had friends among the leading men of the Mile- si… the city before the arrival of the ships from the

8.17
412
20th Year/Summer
MILETUS
Led by Alcibiades, the Peloponnesians reach Miletus just ahead of an Athenian fleet. The ensuing revolt of Miletus is followed by an alliance between the Persians and the Peloponnesians.

8.… are Persians.
8.… Hellas.
8.…

Peloponnesus, and thus, by causing the revolt of as many cities as possible with the help of the Chian power and of Chalcideus, to secure the honor for the Chians and himself and Chalcideus, and, as he had promised, for Endius who had sent them out. [3] Not discovered until their voyage was nearly completed, they arrived a little before Strombichides and Thrasycles (who had just come with twelve ships from Athens, and had joined Strombichides in pursuing them), and brought about the revolt of Miletus. The Athenians sailing up close on their heels with nineteen ships found Miletus closed against them, and took up their station at the adjacent island of Lade.[3a] The first alliance between the King and the Spartans[4a] was now concluded immediately upon the revolt of the Milesians, by Tissaphernes and Chalcideus, and was as follows:

8.18
412
20th Year/Summer
MILETUS
Thucydides offers the text of the first treaty of alliance between the Persians and the Peloponnesians.

The Spartans and their allies made a treaty with the King and Tissaphernes upon the terms following:

• Whatever country or cities the King has, or the King's ancestors had, shall be the King's; and whatever came in to the Athenians from these cities, either money or any other thing, the King and the Spartans and their allies shall jointly hinder the Athenians from receiving either money or any other thing.

• [2] The war with the Athenians shall be carried on jointly by the King and by the Spartans and their allies; and it shall not be lawful to make peace with the Athenians unless both agree, the King on his side and the Spartans and their allies on theirs.

• [3] If any revolt from the King they shall be the enemies of the Spartans and their allies. And if any revolt from the Spartans and their allies they shall be the enemies of the King in like manner.

8.19
412
20th Year/Summer
IONIA
A Chian squadron is chased into Teos and four of its ships are taken by an Athenian flotilla. More cities revolt from Athens.

This was the alliance. After this the Chians immediately manned ten more vessels and sailed for Anaia,[1a] in order to gain intelligence of those in Miletus,[1b] and also to make the cities revolt. [2] A message, however, reaching them from Chalcideus to tell them to go back again, and that Amorges was near at hand with an army by land, they sailed to the temple of Zeus,[2a] and there sighting ten more ships sailing up with which Diomedon had started from Athens after Thrasycles,[2b] [3] they fled, one ship to Ephesus,[3a] the rest to Teos.[3b] The Athenians took four of their ships empty, the men finding time to escape ashore; the rest took refuge in the city of

8.17.3a Lade: Map 8.15, Asia. This force is next mentioned in 8.24.1.

8.17.4a This "First Alliance" is probably the first of three drafts (see 8.37 and 8.58) of the eventual alliance agreement; see note 8.57.2a.

8.19.1a Anaia: Map 8.15, Asia. Anaia was the base of anti-Athenian Samian exiles; see 3.19.2, 3.32.2, and 4.75.1.

8.19.1b Miletus: Map 8.15, Asia.

8.19.2a The location of this temple is not known. Amorges was the bastard son of Pissuthnes, the previous Persian governor at Sardis (Map 8.15, Asia), who was now in rebellion against Tissaphernes and the Persians. He had probably received assistance from the Athenians, although Thucydides does not directly say so. See 1.115.4, 8.5.5, 8.28.2, and 8.54.3. Also see Appendix E, The Persians, §7–8.

8.19.2b For Thrasycles, see 8.15.1 and 8.17.3.

8.19.3a Ephesus: Map 8.15, Asia.

8.19.3b Teos: Map 8.15, Asia.

th[illegible] Athenians sailed off to Samos,[3c] [4] while the Ch[illegible]eir remaining vessels, accompanied by the land for[illegible]s[4a] and after it Aerae[4b] to revolt. After this both th[illegible]rned home.

8.20
412
20th Year/Summer
SPIRAEUM
The Peloponnesian ships defeat the blockaders and escape. Astyochus takes command.
TEOS
Tissaphernes demolishes the Teian wall.

[illegible] the twenty ships of the Peloponnesians in Spirae[illegible]hased to land and blockaded by an equal number of [illegible]llied out and defeated the blockading squadron, too[illegible]d, sailing back to Cenchreae,[1b] prepared again for th[illegible] Ionia.[1d] Here they were joined by Astyochus as ad[illegible]ceforth invested with the supreme command at se[illegible] now withdrawing from Teos,[2a] Tissaphernes m[illegible]with an army, completed the demolition of anyth[illegible]e wall, and left. Not long after his departure Di[illegible]n Athenian ships, and having made a convention by[illegible]ted him as they had the enemy, coasted along to Ae[illegible]empt upon the city, sailed back again.

8.21
412
20th Year/Summer
SAMOS
The Samian People, with some Athenians, overthrow the upper classes and take over the government.

[illegible]place the rising of The People at Samos[1a] against th[illegible]t with some Athenians who were there in three ve[illegible]ar party put to death some two hundred in all of th[illegible]ed four hundred more, and themselves took their lan[illegible]hich the Athenians decreed their independence, be[illegible]delity, and the popular party henceforth governed th[illegible]dholders from all share in affairs, and forbidding an[illegible]e his daughter in marriage to them or to take a wi[illegible]

8.22
412
20th Year/Summer
IONIA
The Chians and Peloponnesians incite the revolt of Methymna and Mytilene on Lesbos. Peloponnesian troops march against Clazomenae and Cyme.

[illegible]ame summer, the Chians,[1a] whose zeal continued as[illegible] even without the Peloponnesians found themse[illegible] bring about the revolt of the cities and who also wi[illegible]companions in peril as possible, made an expediti[illegible] their own to Lesbos;[1b] following the instructions fr[illegible]to go to that island next, and from there to the H[illegible]the land forces of the Peloponnesians who were wi[illegible]se of the allies on the spot, moved along shore to[illegible] Cyme,[1c] under the command of Eualas, a Spartiat[illegible] fleet under Diniades, one of the *perioikoi*,[1f] [2] fi[illegible]a[2a] and caused it to revolt, and, leaving four ships th[illegible]ed the revolt of Mytilene.[2b]

8.[illegible]
8.[illegible]
8.[illegible]
8.[illegible]s; Map 8.25, [illegible]
8.[illegible]las.
8.[illegible]
8.[illegible]
8.[illegible]
8.[illegible]
8.[illegible]
8.[illegible]

8.22.1c Hellespont: Map 8.25, AX. For Spartan instructions, see 8.8.2.
8.22.1d Clazomenae: Map 8.25, BY.
8.22.1e Cyme: Map 8.25, BY.
8.22.1f *Perioikoi:* see the Glossary and Appendix C, Spartan Institutions, §9.
8.22.2a Methymna, Lesbos: Map 8.25, AX.
8.22.2b Mytilene, Lesbos: Map 8.25, AY.

8.23
412
20th Year/Summer
LESBOS-CHIOS
The Spartan Astyochus reaches Lesbos too late to save the island from an Athenian counterattack. The Peloponnesians retire to Chios.

In the meantime Astyochus, the Spartan admiral, set sail from Cenchreae[1a] with four ships, as he had intended, and arrived at Chios.[1b] On the third day after his arrival the Athenian ships, twenty-five in number, sailed to Lesbos under Diomedon and Leon, who had recently arrived with a reinforcement of ten ships from Athens. [2] Late in the same day Astyochus put to sea, and taking one Chian vessel with him sailed to Lesbos to render what assistance he could. Arrived at Pyrrha,[2a] and from there the next day at Eresus,[2b] he there learned that Mytilene had been taken, almost without a blow, by the Athenians, [3] who had sailed up and unexpectedly entered the harbor, had beaten the Chian ships, and landing and defeating the troops opposed to them, had become masters of the city. [4] Informed of this by the Eresians and the Chian ships, which had been left with Eubulus at Methymna and which had fled upon the capture of Mytilene, and three of which he now fell in with (one having been taken by the Athenians), Astyochus did not go on to Mytilene, but raised and armed Eresus; and sending the hoplites from his own ships by land under Eteonicus to Antissa[4a] and to Methymna, he himself proceeded there along shore with the ships which he had with him and with the three Chians, in the hope that the Methymnians upon seeing them would be encouraged to persevere in their revolt. [5] As, however, everything went against him in Lesbos, he took up his own force and sailed back to Chios; the land forces which were to have gone to the Hellespont being also conveyed on board back to their different cities. After this six of the allied Peloponnesian ships at Cenchreae joined the forces at Chios. [6] The Athenians, after restoring matters to their former state in Lesbos, set sail from there and took Polichna,[6a] the place that the Clazomenians were fortifying on the continent, and carried the inhabitants back to their city upon the island, except for the authors of the revolt, who withdrew to Daphnus;[6b] and thus Clazomenae became once more Athenian.

8.24
412
20th Year/Summer
CHIOS
Leaving a squadron to blockade Miletus, the Athenians sail to Chios. They defeat the Chians several times and force them to retire behind their walls. Thucydides praises the prudence and wisdom of the Chians, but admits that they, like many others, underestimated the ability of Athens to carry on the war.

The same summer the Athenians in the twenty ships at Lade[1a] blockading Miletus[1b] made a descent at Panormus[1c] in the Milesian territory, and killed Chalcideus the Spartan commander, who had come with a few men against them, and the third day after sailed over and set up a trophy,[1d] which, as they were not masters of the country, was however pulled down by the Milesians. [2] Meanwhile Leon and Diomedon with the Athenian fleet from Lesbos[2a] sailed out from the Oenoussae,[2b] the islands off Chios, and from their forts of Sidoussa and Pteleum in the territory of Erythrae,[2c] and from Lesbos, and carried on the war against the Chians from their ships, having on board hoplites from the enlistment rolls required to

8.23.1a Cenchreae: Map 8.25, Hellas.
8.23.1b Chios: Map 8.25, BX.
8.23.2a Pyrrha, Lesbos: Map 8.25, AX.
8.23.2b Eresus, Lesbos: Map 8.25, AX.
8.23.4a Antissa, Lesbos: Map 8.25, AX.
8.23.6a Polichna: exact location unknown.
8.23.6b Daphnus: exact location unknown.
8.24.1a Lade: Map 8.25, BY. This force took up station at Lade in 8.17.3.
8.24.1b Miletus: Map 8.25, BY.
8.24.1c Panormus: Map 8.25, BY.
8.24.1d A trophy was a set of captured armor arranged on a pole and raised at or near the battlefield by the victors.
8.24.2a Lesbos: Map 8.25, AX.
8.24.2b Oenoussae Islands: Map 8.25, BX.
8.24.2c The locations of Sidoussa and Pteleum are unknown. For the location of Erythrae, see Map 8.25, BY.

[illegible] Landing in Cardamyle[3a] and in Bolissus[3b] they [illegible] the Chians that took the field against them, and [illegible] in that neighborhood, defeated the Chians again [illegible]ae,[3c] and in a third at Leuconium.[3d] After this the [illegible]em in the field, while the Athenians devastated the [illegible]ifully stocked and had remained undamaged ever [illegible] [4] Indeed, after the Spartans, the Chians are the [illegible]nown who knew how to be wise in prosperity, and [illegible]e more securely the greater it grew. [5] Nor was [illegible] might seem to have erred on the side of rashness, [illegible] had numerous and gallant allies to share the dan[illegible] they perceived that the Athenians after the Sicilian [illegible] no longer denying the thoroughly desperate state [illegible]ey were tripped up by one of the surprises which [illegible], they found out their mistake in company with [illegible]elieved, like them, in the speedy collapse of the [illegible]ile they were thus blockaded from the sea and [illegible] of the citizens undertook to bring the city over to [illegible] of this, the authorities took no action themselves, [illegible]e admiral from Erythrae,[6a] with four ships that he [illegible]dered how they could most quietly, either by tak[illegible]other means, put an end to the conspiracy.

8.25
412
20th Year/Summer
MILETUS
The Athenians, with Argive support, engage the Milesian and Peloponnesian forces. Ionians defeat Dorians on both sides; the Athenians drive the enemy within their walls and consider mounting a siege against Miletus.

[illegible]e thus engaged, a thousand Athenian hoplites and [illegible] (five hundred of whom were *peltasts*[1b] furnished [illegible]ians), and one thousand of the allies, toward the [illegible]r sailed from Athens in forty-eight ships, some of [illegible] under the command of Phrynichus, Onomacles, [illegible]ing in to Samos[1c] crossed over and encamped at [illegible]e Milesians came out to the number of eight hun[illegible]eloponnesians who had come with Chalcideus, and [illegible] of Tissaphernes, along with Tissaphernes himself [illegible]ged the Athenians and their allies. [3] While the [illegible]n their own wing with the careless disdain of men [illegible]s who would never stand their charge, and were [illegible] with a loss little short of three hundred men, [4] [illegible]ed the Peloponnesians, and driving before them the [illegible] of the army, without engaging the Milesians, who [illegible]es retreated into the city upon seeing their comrades

8[illegible].25, BX.
8[illegible], BX.
8[illegible] 8.25, BX.
8[illegible]nown.
8[illegible]ing in the term [illegible]nts of the Ion[illegible] See Appendix [illegible]
8[illegible] We next hear of [illegible]1.1.

8.25.1a Argos: Map 8.25, Hellas.
8.25.1b *Peltasts* furnished with hoplite armor: peltasts were normally armed only with a small, light shield, a javelin, and a short sword. Unhindered by body armor, they could move much more quickly than the fully armed hoplite.
8.25.1c Samos: Map 8.25, Hellas.

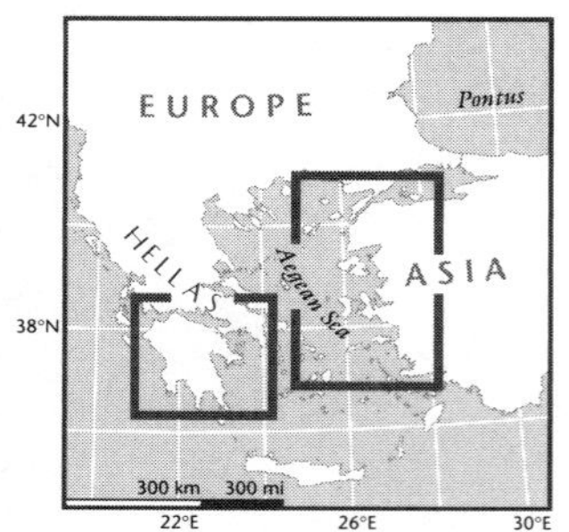

MAP 8.25
OPERATIONS IN LESBOS, CHIOS, SAMOS, AND MILETUS

defeated, crowned their victory by grounding their arms under the very walls of Miletus. [5] Thus, in this battle, the Ionians on both sides overcame the Dorians,[5a] the Athenians defeating the Peloponnesians opposed to them, and the Milesians the Argives. After setting up a trophy, the Athenians prepared to draw a wall round the place, which stood upon an isthmus; thinking that if

8.25.5a Thucydides obviously believed that a double victory of Ionians over Dorians was striking enough to warrant special mention. See Appendix H, Dialects and Ethnic Groups, §8.

the other cities also would easily come over to

word reached them that the fifty-five ships from
cily might be expected at any moment. Of these
ipally by the Syracusan Hermocrates[1a] to join in
to the power of Athens, furnished twenty-two—
nd two from Selinus;[1b] and the ships that were
nesus being now ready, both squadrons had been
, a Spartan, to take to Astyochus, the admiral.
eros,[1c] the island off Miletus, [2] and from there,
enians were before the city, sailed into the Iasic
how matters stood at Miletus. [3] Meanwhile
back to Teichioussa[3a] in the Milesian territory, the
they had put in for the night, and told them of
ad fought in person by the side of the Milesians
vised them, if they did not wish to sacrifice Ionia
to the relief of Miletus and hinder its investment.

8.26
412
20th Year/Summer
MILETUS
A combined Sicilian and Peloponnesian fleet now arrives at Miletus. Alcibiades advises them to quickly relieve the city.

lved to relieve it the next morning. Meanwhile
commander, had received precise intelligence of
when his colleagues expressed a wish to remain at
y refused either to stay himself or to let them or
ould help it. [2] Where they could hereafter con-
rbed preparation, with an exact knowledge of the
leet and of the force with which they could con-
r allow the reproach of disgrace to drive him into
ble. [3] It was no disgrace for an Athenian fleet to
em: put it as they would, it would be more dis-
nd to expose the city not only to disgrace but to
After its late misfortunes the city could hardly be
king the offensive even with the strongest force,
ute necessity: much less then without compulsion
of its own seeking. [4] He told them to take up
y as they could and the troops and stores which
em, and leaving behind what they had taken from
rder to lighten the ships, to sail off to Samos[4a] and
ir ships to attack as opportunity arose. [5] As he
thus not now more than afterwards, nor in this
ad to do with, did Phrynichus show himself to be a
s way that very evening the Athenians broke camp
ing their victory incomplete and the Argives, mor-
mptly sailed off home from Samos.

8.27
412
20th Year/Summer
MILETUS
Phrynichus, the Athenian commander, receives word of the enemy fleet's approach and prudently decides, against the objections of others, to avoid battle and retire immediately from Miletus to Samos, winning Thucydides' approval for his wisdom.

non is the states-
acuse (Map
6 and 7.
r.
forty miles from
but could be
described as "on the way" to Miletus.
8.26.2a Gulf of Iasus: Map 8.25, BY.
8.26.3a Teichioussa: Map 8.25, BY.
8.27.4a Samos: Map 8.25, BY.
8.27.5a Phrynichus reenters the narrative in 8.48.4.

8.28
412
20th Year/Summer
IASUS
At the request of the Persian Tissaphernes, the Peloponnesian fleet attacks Iasus and takes it, capturing the Persian rebel Amorges.

As soon as it was morning the Peloponnesians set out from Teichioussa and put into Miletus[1a] after the departure of the Athenians; they stayed one day, and on the next took with them the Chian vessels originally chased into port with Chalcideus,[1b] and resolved to sail back for the tackle[1c] which they had put on shore at Teichioussa. [2] Upon their arrival Tissaphernes came to them with his land forces and induced them to sail to Iasus,[2a] which was held by his enemy Amorges. Accordingly they suddenly attacked and took Iasus, whose inhabitants never imagined that the ships could be other than Athenian. The Syracusans distinguished themselves most in the action. [3] Amorges, a bastard of Pissuthnes and a rebel from the King, was taken alive and handed over to Tissaphernes, to carry to the King, if he chose, according to his orders: Iasus was sacked by the army, who found a very great booty there, the place being wealthy from ancient date. [4] The Peloponnesians received the mercenaries serving with Amorges and enrolled them in their army without doing them any harm, since most of them came from the Peloponnesus, and handed over the city to Tissaphernes with all the captives, bond or free, at the stipulated price of one Daric *stater*[4a] a head; after which they returned to Miletus. [5] Pedaritus son of Leon, who had been sent by the Spartans to take the command at Chios,[5a] they dispatched by land as far as Erythrae[5b] with the mercenaries taken from Amorges; appointing Philip to remain as governor of Miletus.

8.29
412/1
20th Year/Winter
MILETUS
Tissaphernes pays the Peloponnesian fleet as he had promised, but decides that future payments will be made at a lower scale.

Summer was now over. The following winter Tissaphernes put Iasus in a state of defense, and passing on to Miletus distributed a month's pay to all the ships as he had promised at Sparta, at the rate of an Attic drachma a day for each man. In future, however, he was resolved not to give more than three *obols*,[1a] until he had consulted the King when, if the King should so order, he would give, he said, the full drachma. [2] However, upon the protest of the Syracusan general Hermocrates (for as Therimenes was not admiral, but only accompanied them in order to hand over the ships to Astyochus, he made little difficulty about the pay), it was agreed that the amount of five ships' pay should be given over and above the three obols a day for each man; Tissaphernes paying thirty talents a month for fifty-five ships, and to the rest, for as many ships as they had beyond that number, at the same rate.

8.30
412/1
20th Year/Summer
MILETUS-CHIOS
The arrival of reinforcements permits the Athenians to blockade Miletus and to attack Chios.

The same winter the Athenians in Samos[1a] having been joined by thirty-five more vessels from home under Charminus, Strombichides, and Euctemon, called back their squadron at Chios[1b] and all the rest, intending to blockade Miletus[1c] with their navy, and to send a fleet and an army against

8.28.1a Teichioussa and Miletus: Map 8.31, BY.
8.28.1b For Chalcideus and the Chian ships' arrival at Miletus, see 8.17.
8.28.1c They had left the ships' tackle at Teichioussa in order to lighten their ships in preparation for battle off Miletus. See 6.34.5, 7.24.2, and Appendix G, Trireme Warfare, §8.
8.28.2a Iasus: Map 8.31, BY. The base of Amorges was last mentioned in 8.19.2; see also 8.5.5 (note 8.5.5b) and 8.54.3.
8.28.4a Doric *stater:* a unit of money; see Appendix J, Classical Greek Currency, §4.
8.28.5a Chios: Map 8.31, AX.
8.28.5b Erythrae: Map 8.31, BY. Pedaritus arrives here in 8.32.2.
8.29.1a This is a 50 percent reduction, as six obols equal one drachma; see Appendix J, Classical Greek Currency, §3. As we learn in 8.45.2, Alcibiades had advised Tissaphernes to reduce the pay.
8.30.1a Samos: Map 8.31, BY.
8.30.1b Chios: Map 8.31, AX.
8.30.1c Miletus: Map 8.31, BY.

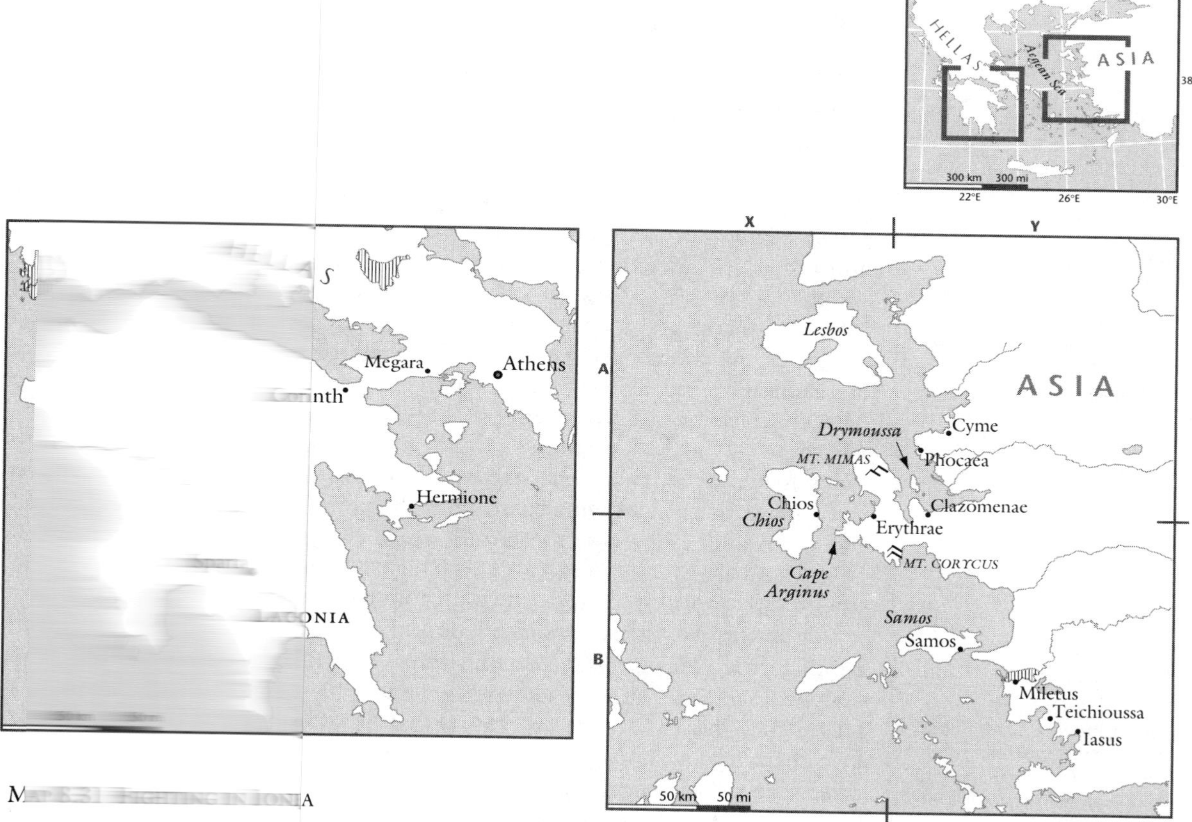

M… A

C… respective services. This intention they carried into e… Onomacles, and Euctemon sailing against Chios, w… h thirty ships and a part of the thousand hoplites w… in transports;[2a] while the rest remained masters of t… hips at Samos, and advanced upon Miletus.

8.31 412/1 20th Year/Winter IONIA The Spartan admiral Astyochus sails from Chios, attacks various places without success, and is blown to Phocaea by a gale.

…, who at that time was at Chios collecting the h… sequence of the conspiracy,[1a] stopped upon learn- i… herimenes had arrived, and that the affairs of the a… flourishing condition, and put out to sea with ten P… any Chian vessels. [2] After a futile attack upon P… to Clazomenae[2b] and ordered the pro-Athenian p… Daphnus,[2c] and to join the Peloponnesians—an

8… nd Athenian … 8.25.1.
8… 8.24.6, and per-…

8.31.2a Pteleum: location unknown.
8.31.2b Clazomenae: Map 8.31, AY.
8.31.2c Daphnus: location unknown.

order in which he was joined by Tamos, the King's lieutenant in Ionia. [3] This order being disregarded, Astyochus made an attack upon the city, which was unwalled, and having failed to take it was himself carried off by a strong gale to Phocaea and Cyme,[3a] while the rest of the ships put in at the islands adjacent to Clazomenae—Marathoussa, Pele,[3b] and Drymoussa.[3c] [4] Here they were detained eight days by the winds, and plundering and consuming all the property of the Clazomenians deposited there, put the rest on shipboard and sailed off to Phocaea and Cyme to join Astyochus.

8.32
412/1
20th Year/Winter
CHIOS
Envoys from Lesbos ask Astyochus to support a second revolt. He is willing but his Corinthian and Chian allies refuse to assist.

While he was there, envoys arrived from the Lesbians[1a] who wished to revolt again. With Astyochus they were successful; but the Corinthians[1b] and the other allies being averse to it by reason of their former failure, he weighed anchor and set sail for Chios,[1c] where they eventually arrived from different quarters, the fleet having been scattered by a storm. [2] After this Pedaritus, who was then marching along the coast from Miletus,[2a] arrived at Erythrae,[2b] and from there crossed over with his army to Chios, where he found also about five hundred soldiers with their arms who had been left there by Chalcideus from the five ships.[2c] [3] Meanwhile as some Lesbians made offers to revolt, Astyochus sought to persuade Pedaritus and the Chians that they ought to go with their ships and bring about a revolt of Lesbos and so increase the number of their allies or, if not successful, at all events harm the Athenians. The Chians, however, turned a deaf ear to this, and Pedaritus flatly refused to give up to him the Chian vessels.[3a]

8.33
412/1
20th Year/Winter
ERYTHRAE
Astyochus sails for Miletus, almost runs into the Athenian fleet at Corycus, returns to Erythrae in response to false reports of a plot there, and finally sails again to Miletus.

Upon this Astyochus took five Corinthian and one Megarian[1a] vessel, with another from Hermione,[1b] and the ships which had come with him from Laconia,[1c] and set sail for Miletus[1d] to assume his command as admiral; after telling the Chians[1e] with many threats that he would certainly not come and help them if they should be in need. [2] At Corycus[2a] in the territory of Erythrae,[2b] he went ashore for the night; the Athenian armament sailing from Samos[2c] against Chios being separated from him only by a hill, upon the other side of which it had stopped, so that neither perceived the other. [3] But when a letter arrived in the night from Pedaritus to say that some liberated Erythraean prisoners had come from Samos to betray Erythrae, Astyochus at once put back to Erythrae, and so just escaped falling in with the Athenians. [4] Here Pedaritus sailed over to join him; and after inquiry into the pretended treachery, finding that the whole story had been made up to procure

8.31.3a Phocaea and Cyme: Map 8.31, AY.
8.31.3b Marathoussa and Pele: locations unknown.
8.31.3c Drymoussa: Map 8.31, AX.
8.32.1a Lesbos: Map 8.31, AX.
8.32.1b Corinth: Map 8.31, Hellas.
8.32.1c Chios: Map 8.31, AX.
8.32.2a Miletus: Map 8.31, BY. Pedaritus set out from here in 8.28.5.
8.32.2b Erythrae: Map 8.31, BY.
8.32.2c These were the five ships that Alcibiades persuaded Endius and the other ephors to send in 8.12.1–3.
8.32.3a Pedaritus could refuse because he had been sent from Sparta to command at Chios (8.28.5).
8.33.1a Megara: Map 8.31, Hellas.
8.33.1b Hermione: Map 8.31, Hellas.
8.33.1c Laconia: Map 8.31, Hellas. Astyochus crossed over with four ships in 8.23.1.
8.33.1d Miletus: Map 8.31, BY.
8.33.1e Chios: Map 8.31, AX.
8.33.2a Mount Corycus: Map 8.31, BY.
8.33.2b Erythrae: Map 8.31, BY.
8.33.2c Samos: Map 8.31, BY.

th[illegible]om Samos, they acquitted them of the charge, an[illegible]s to Chios and Astyochus to Miletus, as he had in[illegible]

8.34
412/1
20th Year/Winter
CHIOS
An Athenian pursuit of three Chian ships in a gale leads to the shipwreck of three of their own ships.

[illegible]n armament sailing round Corycus[1a] fell in with th[illegible] Arginus,[1b] and gave immediate chase. A great st[illegible]ans with difficulty took refuge in the harbor; the th[illegible]ost forward in the pursuit being wrecked and bl[illegible] of Chios, and the crews slain or taken prisoners. T[illegible]leet took refuge in the harbor called Phoenicus,[1c] ur[illegible]d from there they later put into Lesbos[1e] and prepa[illegible]fication.

8.35
412/1
20th Year/Winter
CNIDUS
A Peloponnesian squadron at Cnidus is captured by Athenian ships, who then attack and almost succeed in taking the city before retiring to Samos.

[illegible] Spartan Hippocrates sailed out from the Pelopo[illegible]n[1a] ships (under the command of Dorieus son of D[illegible]gues), and one Laconian and one Syracusan vesse[illegible],[1b] which had already revolted at the instigation of [illegible]en their arrival was known at Miletus,[2a] orders ca[illegible]lf their squadron to guard Cnidus, and with the re[illegible]pium[2b] and seize all the merchant ships arriving fr[illegible]s a promontory of Cnidus and sacred to Apollo. [3[illegible] knowledge of the Athenians, they sailed from Sa[illegible] six ships on the watch at Triopium, the crews es[illegible]fter this the Athenians sailed into Cnidus and m[illegible] city, which was unfortified, and all but took it; [4[illegible]ulted it again, but with less effect, as the inhabita[illegible] defenses during the night, and had been reinfo[illegible]ped from the ships at Triopium. The Athenians n[illegible] plundering the Cnidian territory sailed back to Sa[illegible]

8.36
412/1
20th Year/Winter
MILETUS
Sparta concludes a new and more equitable treaty with Persia.

[illegible]styochus came to the fleet at Miletus.[1a] The Pelopo[illegible] plentifully supplied, being in receipt of sufficient pa[illegible]ng still in hand the large booty taken at Iasus.[1b] T[illegible]d great ardor for the war. [2] Nevertheless the P[illegible]he first agreement[2a] with Tissaphernes, made with C[illegible]d more advantageous to him than to them, and co[illegible]menes was still there concluded another, which w[illegible]

8.[illegible], BY.
8.[illegible]X.
8.[illegible]nknown.
8.[illegible]AX.
8.[illegible]
8.[illegible]
8.[illegible]
8.[illegible]
8.[illegible] BY.
8.[illegible]
8.[illegible]
8.[illegible]
8.36.1b Iasus: Map 8.37, BY. See 8.28.3–4.
8.36.2a Thucydides refers to the first of three agreements or three drafts of an agreement (8.18, 8.37, and 8.58); see note at 8.57.2.

8.37
412/1
20th Year/Winter
MILETUS
Thucydides offers the text of the new treaty between Sparta and Persia.

The agreement of the Spartans and the allies with King Darius and the sons of the King, and with Tissaphernes, for a treaty and friendship, as follows:

• [2] Neither the Spartans nor the allies of the Spartans shall make war against or otherwise injure any country or cities that belong to King Darius or did belong to his father or to his ancestors: neither shall the Spartans nor the allies of the Spartans exact tribute from such cities. Neither shall King Darius nor any of the subjects of the King make war against or otherwise injure the Spartans or their allies.

• [3] If the Spartans or their allies should require any assistance from the King, or the King from the Spartans or their allies, whatever they both agree upon they shall be right in doing.

• [4] Both shall carry on jointly the war against the Athenians and their allies; and if they make peace, both shall do so jointly.

• The expense of all troops in the King's country, sent for by the King, shall be borne by the King.

• [5] If any of the states which made this agreement with the King attack the King's country, the rest shall stop them and aid the King to the best of their power. And if any in the King's country or in the countries under the King's rule attack the country of the Spartans or their allies, the King shall stop it and help them to the best of his power.

8.38
412/1
20th Year/Winter
CHIOS
After an oligarchy is imposed upon the Chians, they fall out among themselves and, lacking confidence in their unity and power, request more aid from Astyochus. He refuses them.

After this convention Therimenes handed over the fleet to Astyochus, sailed off in a small boat, and was lost. [2] The Athenian armament had now crossed over from Lesbos[2a] to Chios,[2b] and being master on land and sea began to fortify Delphinium, a place naturally strong on the land side, provided with more than one harbor, and also not far from the city of Chios.[2c] [3] Meanwhile the Chians remained inactive. Already defeated in so many battles, they were now also at discord among themselves; the execution of the party of Tydeus son of Ion,[3a] by Pedaritus upon the charge of Atticism, followed by the forcible imposition of an oligarchy upon the rest of the city, having made them suspicious of one another; and they therefore thought neither themselves nor the mercenaries under Pedaritus a match for the enemy. [4] They sent, however, to Miletus[4a] to beg Astyochus to assist them, which he refused to do, and for which he was denounced at Sparta by Pedaritus as a traitor. [5] Such was the state of the Athenian affairs at Chios; while their fleet at Samos[5a] kept sailing out against the enemy in Miletus until they found that he would not accept their challenge, and then would retire again to Samos and remain quiet.

8.38.2a Lesbos: Map 8.37, AX; where the Athenian ships went to prepare for the work of fortification, 8.34.1.
8.38.2b Chios: Map 8.37, AX.
8.38.2c Delphinium and the city of Chios: Map 8.37, AX.
8.38.3a Party of Ion: probably the authors of the conspiracy on Chios mentioned in 8.24.6 and 8.31.1.
8.38.4a Miletus: Map 8.37, BY.
8.38.5a Samos: Map 8.37, BY.

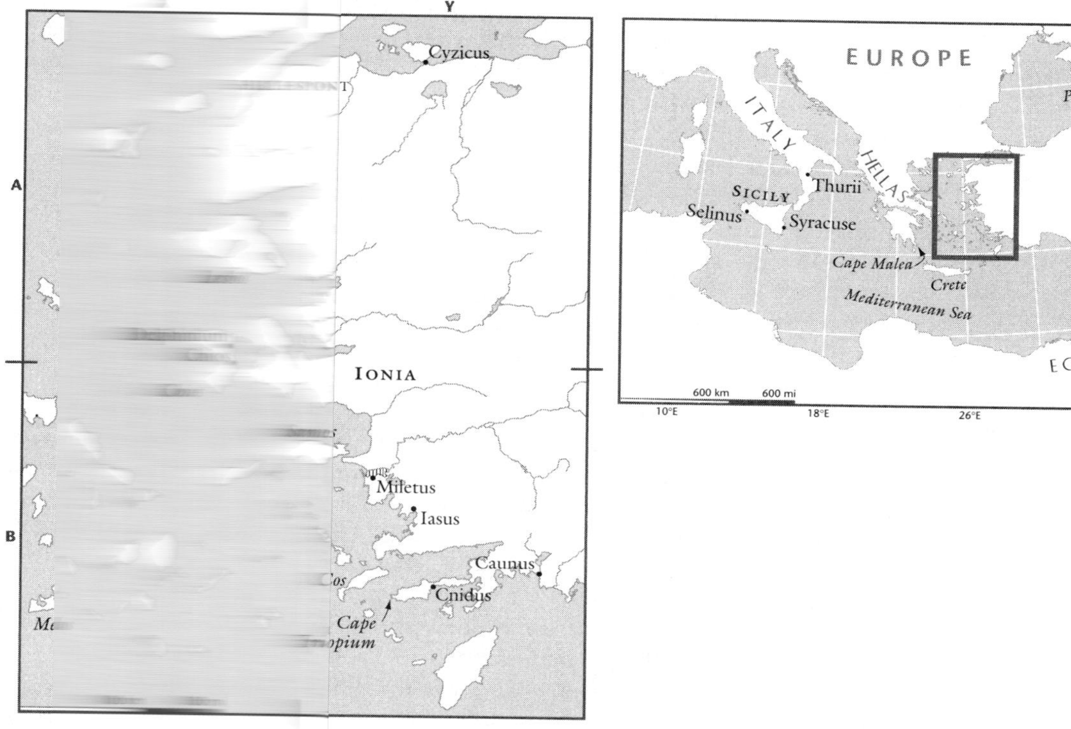

M… G IN THE WINTER OF 412/1

… twenty-seven ships equipped by the Spartans for Ph… e agency of the Megarian[1b] Calligeitus, and the Cy… ut out from the Peloponnesus and sailed for Io… the solstice, under the command of Antisthenes, a … the Spartans also sent eleven Spartiates as advis-er… son of Arcesilaus being among the number. Ar… orders were to aid in generally superintending th… war; to send off the above ships or a greater or les… espont to Pharnabazus, if they thought proper, ap… of Ramphias, who sailed with them, to the com-m… y thought proper, to make Antisthenes admiral, di… om the letters of Pedaritus had caused to be re… [3] Sailing accordingly from Malea[3a] across the

8.39
412/1
20th Year/Winter
AEGEAN
A fleet of Peloponnesian reinforcements for the Hellespont with new leaders sails to Miletus via Melos, Crete, and Caunus.

8.3… n governor … egion (Map … The Persians,

8.3… Calligeitus and … 6.1 and 8.8.1.

8.39.1c Cyzicus: Map 8.37, AY.
8.39.1d Ionia: Map 8.37, BY.
8.39.3a Cape Malea of the Peloponnesus: Map 8.37, locator, and Map 8.45, BX.

open sea, the squadron touched at Melos[3b] and there fell in with ten Athenian ships, three of which they took empty and burned. After this, being afraid that the Athenian vessels escaped from Melos might, as they in fact did, give information of their approach to the Athenians at Samos, they sailed to Crete,[3c] and having lengthened their voyage by way of precaution made land at Caunus[3d] in Asia [4] from where, considering themselves in safety, they sent a message to the fleet at Miletus for a convoy along the coast.

8.40
412/1
20th Year/Winter
CHIOS
The Chians continue to press Astyochus to help them, citing the desertion of their slaves and the impending completion of the Athenian siege works. Astyochus now prepares to go to their assistance.

Meanwhile the Chians[2a] and Pedaritus, undeterred by the delays of Astyochus, went on sending messengers pressing him to come with all the fleet to assist them against their besiegers, and not to leave the greatest of the allied states in Ionia to be shut up by sea and overrun and pillaged by land. [2] There were more slaves at Chios than in any one other city except Sparta,[2b] and being also by reason of their numbers punished more rigorously when they offended, most of them when they saw the Athenian armament firmly established in the island with a fortified position, immediately deserted to the enemy, and through their knowledge of the country did the greatest harm. [3] The Chians therefore urged upon Astyochus that it was his duty to assist them, while there was still a hope and a possibility of stopping the enemy's progress, while Delphinium[3a] was still in process of fortification and unfinished, and before the completion of a higher rampart which was being added to protect the camp and fleet of their besiegers. Astyochus now saw that the allies also wished it and prepared to go, in spite of his intention to the contrary owing to the threat already referred to.[3b]

8.41
412/1
20th Year/Winter
CARIA-LYCIA
Hearing of the new Peloponnesian fleet at Caunus, Astyochus postpones action at Chios and sails to Caunus, seeking an Athenian squadron off the coast of Lycia.

In the meantime news came from Caunus[1a] of the arrival of the twenty-seven ships with the Spartan commissioners; and Astyochus postponing everything to the duty of convoying a fleet of that importance, in order to be more able to command the sea, and to the safe conduct of the Spartans sent as spies over his behavior, at once gave up going to Chios[1b] and set sail for Caunus. [2] As he coasted along he landed at the Meropid Cos[2a] and sacked the city, which was unfortified and had been lately laid in ruins by an earthquake, by far the greatest in living memory, and, as the inhabitants had fled to the mountains, overran the country and made booty of all it contained, letting go, however, the free men. [3] From Cos arriving in the night at Cnidus[3a] he was compelled by the urgent pleas of the Cnidians not to disembark the sailors, but to sail immediately against the twenty Athen-

8.39.3b Melos: Map 8.37, BX.
8.39.3c Crete: Map 8.37, locator.
8.39.3d Caunus: Map 8.37, BY.
8.40.2a Chios: Map 8.37, AX.
8.40.2b Thucydides is probably thinking in terms of the proportion of slaves to free men in Chios in comparison to the ratio of Helots to free citizens in Sparta. Although a large and rich island, it is most unlikely that there would have been a larger absolute number of slaves at Chios than at Athens, or of Helots at Sparta.
8.40.3a Delphinium, Chios: Map 8.37, AX.
8.40.3b Astyochus had threatened to withhold aid from the Chians when they refused to assist the Lesbians; see 8.33.1.
8.41.1a Caunus: Map 8.45, BY. The departure and circuitous voyage of this fleet was described in 8.39.
8.41.1b Chios: Map 8.45, AY.
8.41.2a Cos: Map 8.45, BY.
8.41.3a Cnidus: Map 8.45, BY.

ian harminus, one of the commanders at Samos,[3b]
we very twenty-seven ships from the Peloponnesus[3c]
wh self sailing to join; [4] the Athenians in Samos
ha of their approach, and Charminus being on the
loc Rhodes, and Lycia,[4b] as he now heard that they
we

sailed as he was to Syme,[1a] before he was heard
of, the enemy somewhere out at sea. He encounter er, however, that caused his ships to straggle and
ge k. [2] In the morning his fleet had become sepa-
rat ill straggling round the island, so that as the left
wi f Charminus and the Athenians, they took it for
th were watching for from Caunus,[2a] and hastily put
ou rt of their twenty vessels. [3] Attacking immedi-
at s and disabled others, and had the advantage in
th ody of the fleet unexpectedly hove in sight, when
th every side. [4] Upon this they took to flight, and
aft st escaped to the island of Teutloussa[4a] and from
th After this the Peloponnesians put into Cnidus,[4c]
an enty-seven ships from Caunus, sailed all together
an e, and then returned to anchor at Cnidus.

8.42
412/1
20th Year/Winter
SYME
The Athenians attack the vanguard of Astyochus' fleet off Syme with success, but are driven off with losses when the rest of the Peloponnesian fleet joins the fray. Astyochus' ships and the new fleet from the Peloponnesus link up at Cnidus.

ns knew of the sea fight they sailed with all the
sh and without attacking or being attacked by the
fle e ships' tackle[1b] left at Syme, and touching at
L l sailed back to Samos. [2] Meanwhile the Pelopo w all at Cnidus, underwent such repairs as were
ne Spartan commissioners conferred with Tissaph meet them, upon the points which did not sat-
isf sactions, and upon the best and mutually most
ad conducting the war in future. [3] The severest
cr eding was Lichas, who said that neither of the
tr er that of Chalcideus, nor that of Therimenes; it
b King should at this date pretend to the possessi y ruled by himself or by his ancestors—a preten-
si back under the yoke all the islands, Thessaly,[3a]
L s far as Boeotia,[3c] and made the Spartans give to
th erty a Median[3d] master. [4] He therefore invited

8.43
412/1
20th Year/Winter
CNIDUS
Newly arrived Spartan commissioners reject the previous treaty as too generous to Persia and insist on a more equitable agreement. This demand angers Tissaphernes, who leaves in a rage.

8.4 X.
8.4 8.39.3.
8.4 Lycia: Map

8.4
8.4
8.4
8.4 Y.
8.4
8.4 5, BY.

8.43.1b Ships' tackle: see 6.34.5, 7.24.2, 8.28.1, and Appendix G, Trireme Warfare, §8.
8.43.1c Loryma: Map 8.45, BY.
8.43.3a Thessaly: Map 8.45, AX.
8.43.3b Locris (Opuntian): Map 8.45, AX.
8.43.3c Boeotia: Map 8.45, AX.
8.43.3d The Greeks regularly referred to the Persians as "the Mede," or "the Medes," and to the Persian wars as the "Median wars," although the Medes and Persians were distinct peoples. See Appendix E, §1.

Tissaphernes to conclude another and a better treaty, as they certainly would not recognize those existing and did not want any of his pay upon such conditions. This offended Tissaphernes so much that he went away in a rage without settling anything.

8.44
412/1
20th Year/Winter
RHODES
The Peloponnesian fleet sails to Rhodes and incites its cities to revolt from the Athenians, who arrive too late to prevent the uprising. The Spartans levy a contribution from Rhodes.

The Peloponnesians now determined to sail to Rhodes,[1a] upon the invitation of some of the principal men there, hoping to gain an island powerful by the number of its seamen and by its land forces, and also thinking that they would be able to maintain their fleet from their own allies without having to ask for money from Tissaphernes. [2] They accordingly at once set sail that same winter from Cnidus,[2a] and first put in with ninety-four ships at Camirus[2b] in the Rhodian country, to the great alarm of the mass of the inhabitants, who were not privy to the intrigue, and who consequently fled, especially as the city was unfortified. They were afterwards, however, assembled by the Spartans together with the inhabitants of the two other cities of Lindus and Ialysus;[2c] and the Rhodians were persuaded to revolt from the Athenians and the island went over to the Peloponnesians. [3] Meanwhile the Athenians had received the alarm and set sail with the fleet from Samos[3a] to forestall them, and came within sight of the island, but being a little too late sailed off for the moment to Chalce, and from thence to Samos, and subsequently waged war against Rhodes, sailing from Chalce, Cos,[3b] and Samos. [4] The Peloponnesians now levied a contribution of thirty-two talents from the Rhodians, after which they hauled their ships ashore and for eighty days remained inactive.

8.45
412/1
20th Year/Winter
MAGNESIA?
Alcibiades, already condemned to death by the Spartans, had joined Tissaphernes. He advises him to reduce the Spartan sailors' pay, to pay them irregularly, and to refuse to contribute to defending Chios and other cities that had revolted from Athens.

During this time, and even earlier, before they went to Rhodes, the following intrigues took place. After the death of Chalcideus and the battle at Miletus,[1a] Alcibiades began to be suspected by the Peloponnesians; and Astyochus received from Sparta an order from them to put him to death, he being the personal enemy of Agis,[1b] and in other respects thought unworthy of confidence. Alcibiades in his alarm first withdrew to Tissaphernes, and immediately began to do all he could with him to injure the Peloponnesian cause. [2] Henceforth becoming his adviser in everything, he cut down the pay from an Attic drachma to three obols a day,[2a] and even this not paid too regularly; and told Tissaphernes to say to the Peloponnesians that the Athenians, whose maritime experience was of an older date than their own, only gave their men three obols, not so much from poverty as to prevent their seamen being corrupted by being too well off, and spoiling their fitness by spending money upon enervating indulgences, and also paid their crews irregularly in order to have a security against their deserting in the arrears which they would leave behind them. [3] He also told Tissaphernes to bribe the captains and generals of the cities, and

8.44.1a Rhodes: Map 8.45, BY.
8.44.2a Cnidus: Map 8.45, BY.
8.44.2b Camirus, Rhodes: Map 8.45, BY.
8.44.2c Lindus and Ialysus on Rhodes: Map 8.45, BY.
8.44.3a Samos: Map 8.45, AY.
8.44.3b Chalce and Cos: Map 8.45, BY.
8.45.1a The battle at Miletus (Map 8.45, BY) was described in 8.25.
8.45.1b For Agis' enmity with Alcibiades, see note 8.12.2a.
8.45.2a Six *obols* equals one *drachma;* see Appendix J, Classical Greek Currency, §3.

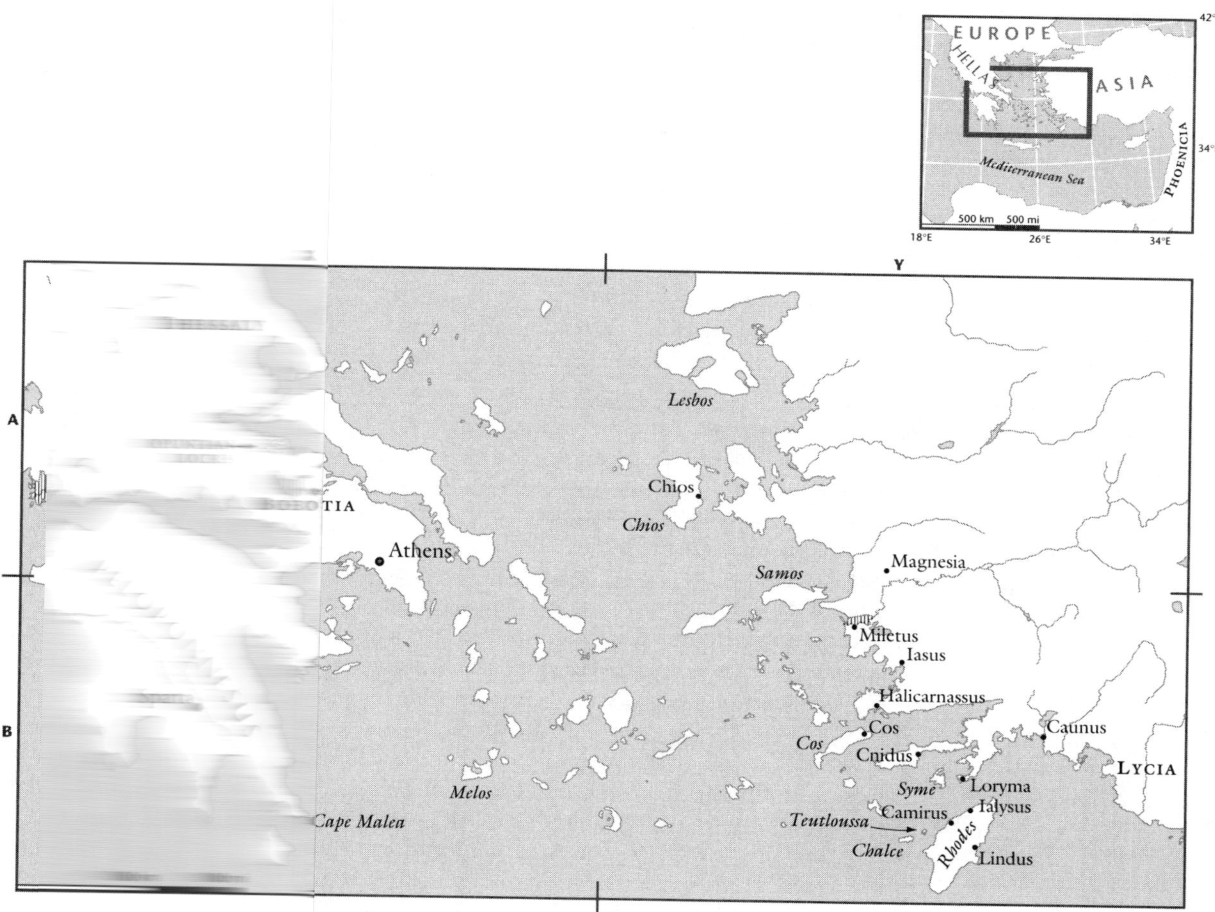

M… IA; ALCIBIADES LEAVES THE SPARTANS

s… ement—an expedient which succeeded with all e… Hermocrates alone opposing him on behalf of the w… anwhile Alcibiades sent away the cities that were a… them, in the name of Tissaphernes, that it was g… Chians,[4a] the richest people in Hellas, not content w… a foreign force, to expect others to risk not only t… ey as well on behalf of their freedom; [5] while

8… s to reduce the … sailors, and … o it, was previ- … —2.

8…

the other cities, he said, had to pay largely to Athens before their rebellion, and could not justly refuse to contribute as much or even more now for their own defense. [6] He also pointed out that Tissaphernes was at present carrying on the war at his own expense, and had good cause for economy, but that as soon as he received remittances from the King he would give them their pay in full, and do what was reasonable for the cities.

8.46
412/1
20th Year/Winter
MAGNESIA?
Alcibiades advises Tissaphernes that Persia's best policy is to let Sparta and Athens exhaust each other through prolonged warfare. He argues that Athens is a safer foe, since her power is only naval, whereas Spartan land power could menace interior Persian territory. Tissapherne's subsequent actions indicate his adoption of this policy.

Alcibiades further advised Tissaphernes not to be in too great a hurry to end the war, or to let himself be persuaded to bring up the Phoenician[1a] fleet which he was equipping, or to provide pay for more Hellenes, and thus put the power by land and sea into the same hands; but to leave each of the contending parties in possession of one element, thus enabling the King when he found one party troublesome to call in the other. [2] For if the command of the sea and land were united in one hand, he would not know where to turn for help to overthrow the dominant power; unless he at last chose to stand up himself and go through with the struggle at great expense and danger. The cheapest plan was to let the Hellenes wear each other out, at a small share of the expense and without risk to himself. [3] Besides, he would find the Athenians the most convenient partners in empire as they did not aim at conquests on shore, and carried on the war upon principles and with a practice most advantageous to the King; being prepared to combine to conquer the sea for Athens, and for the King all the Hellenes inhabiting his country, whom the Peloponnesians, on the contrary, had come to liberate. On the other hand, it was not likely that the Spartans would free the Hellenes from the Hellenic Athenians, without freeing them also from the barbarian Persians, unless overthrown by him in the meantime. [4] Alcibiades therefore urged him to wear them both out at first, and after reducing the Athenian power as much as he could, forthwith to rid the country of the Peloponnesians. [5] On the whole, Tissaphernes approved of this policy, at least so far as could be conjectured from his behavior; since he now gave his confidence to Alcibiades in recognition of his good advice, and kept the Peloponnesians short of money, and would not let them fight at sea, but ruined their cause by pretending that the Phoenician fleet would arrive, and that they would thus be enabled to wage war with the odds in their favor, and so made their navy lose its efficiency, which had been very remarkable, and generally betrayed a coolness in the war that was too plain to be mistaken.

8.47
412/1
20th Year/Winter
SAMOS
Alcibiades, hoping for recall to Athens, tells the Athenian generals at Samos that he can bring Tissaphernes to Athens' side if an oligarchy is installed at Athens.

Alcibiades gave this advice to Tissaphernes and the King, with whom he then was, not merely because he thought it really the best, but because he was seeking means to bring about his restoration to his country, well knowing that if he did not destroy it he might one day hope to persuade the Athenians to recall him, and thinking that his best chance of persuading them lay in letting them see that he possessed the favor of Tissaphernes. [2] The event

8.46.1a Phoenicia, Map 8.45, locator. The Phoenician fleet was a major component of Persian naval power.

pr[illegible]hen the Athenians at Samos[2a] found that he had in[illegible]s, principally of their own motion (though partly al[illegible]mself sending word to their chief men to tell the be[illegible] if only there were an oligarchy in the place of the co[illegible]d banished him, he would be glad to return to his co[illegible]phernes their friend), the captains and chief men in[illegible]nbraced the idea of subverting the democracy.

[illegible]d in the camp, and afterwards from there reached th[illegible]ssed over from Samos and had an interview with Al[illegible]ely offered to make first Tissaphernes, and afterw[illegible]end, if they would give up the democracy, and m[illegible]King to trust them. The most powerful citizens, wh[illegible]verely from the war, now had great hopes of getti[illegible] their own hands and of triumphing over the en[illegible]turn to Samos the emissaries formed their partisa[illegible]nly told the army generally that the King would be[illegible]d provide them with money if Alcibiades were re[illegible]acy abolished. [3] The multitude, if at first irrita[illegible]were nevertheless kept quiet by the advantageous pr[illegible] the King; and the oligarchic conspirators, after m[illegible]on to the people, now reexamined the proposals of[illegible]nselves, with most of their associates. [4] Unlike th[illegible]em advantageous and trustworthy, Phrynichus,[4a] wh[illegible] no means approved of the proposals. Alcibiades, he[illegible] no more for an oligarchy than for a democracy, an[illegible]ge the institutions of his country in order to get hi[illegible]sociates; while for themselves their one purpose sh[illegible]scord. He thought it would not be in the King's in[illegible]nnesians were now their equals at sea, and in posse[illegible]f cities in his empire, to go out of his way to side wi[illegible] he did not trust, when he might make friends of th[illegible]had never injured him. [5] And as for the allied st[illegible]was now offered, because the democracy was to be[illegible]e well knew that this would not make the rebels co[illegible]r, or confirm the loyal in their allegiance; as the all[illegible]ervitude with an oligarchy or democracy to freedo[illegible]n which they currently lived under, to whichever ty[illegible]des, the cities of the empire thought that the so-ca[illegible]d prove just as oppressive as The People, since it wa[illegible] proposed, and for the most part benefited from th[illegible] that were injurious to the allies. Indeed, if it de[illegible]eople," the citizens of the allied states would be pu[illegible] and with violence; while The People was their

8.48
412/1
20th Year/Winter
SAMOS
Alcibiades' ideas prove attractive to some Athenians at Samos, who form a cabal to promote them. The general Phrynichus opposes them, arguing that Alcibiades cares only for his own recall, the King wants only the restoration of his possessions, and the allies desire only freedom from subjection. He predicts that no allies will respond to the installation of an Athenian oligarchy with greater friendship for Athens.

8.4[illegible]

8.48.4a Phrynichus, the "man of sense," was last heard from in 8.27.

refuge and the chastiser of these men. [7] He was certain that the cities had learned this by experience, and that such was their opinion. The propositions of Alcibiades and the intrigues now in progress could therefore never meet with his approval.

8.49
SAMOS
The cabal prepares to send Pisander to Athens to argue for oligarchy.

However, the members of the cabal assembled in accordance with their original intention, accepted what was proposed, and prepared to send Pisander and others on an embassy to Athens to work for the restoration of Alcibiades and the abolition of the democracy in the city, and thus to make Tissaphernes the friend of the Athenians.

8.50
412/1
20th Year/Winter
SAMOS
To thwart Alcibiades, Phrynichus sends Astyochus a letter that accuses Alcibiades of injuring the Peloponnesian cause. Astyochus reveals this letter to Alcibiades, who quickly exposes Phrynichus' correspondence with the enemy to the Athenians at Samos. To save himself, Phrynichus writes again to Astyochus, describing the Athenian dispositions, and advising him when and how to attack the Athenian fleet.

Phrynichus now saw that there would be a proposal to restore Alcibiades, and that the Athenians would consent to it; and fearing after what he had said against it that Alcibiades, if restored, would revenge himself upon him for his opposition, had recourse to the following scheme. He sent a secret letter to the Spartan admiral, [2] Astyochus, who was still in the neighborhood of Miletus,[2a] to tell him that Alcibiades was ruining the Peloponnesian cause by making Tissaphernes the friend of the Athenians, and containing an explicit revelation of the rest of the intrigue, desiring to be excused if he sought to harm his enemy even at the expense of the interests of his country. [3] Astyochus, however, instead of thinking of punishing Alcibiades, who, besides, no longer ventured within his reach as formerly, went up to him and Tissaphernes at Magnesia,[3a] communicated to them the letter from Samos,[3b] and turned informer; and if report may be trusted, became the paid creature of Tissaphernes, undertaking to inform him about this and all other matters—which was also the reason why he did not object more strongly against the pay not being given in full. [4] Upon this Alcibiades instantly sent to the authorities at Samos a letter against Phrynichus, stating what he had done, and asking that he should be put to death. [5] Phrynichus distracted, and placed in the utmost peril by the denunciation, sent again to Astyochus, reproaching him with having so ill kept the secret of his previous letter, and saying that he was now prepared to give him an opportunity to destroy the whole Athenian armament at Samos, gave a detailed account of the means which he should employ—Samos being unfortified—and pleading that being in danger of his life on their account, he could not now be blamed for doing this or anything else to escape being destroyed by his mortal enemies. This also Astyochus revealed to Alcibiades.

8.51
412/1
20th Year/Winter
SAMOS
Phrynichus then orders the Athenians to prepare defenses against an enemy attack, which thwarts the intent of Alcibiades' letter to the Athenians that warns them of an attack and accuses Phrynichus of plotting with the enemy.

Meanwhile Phrynichus having had timely notice that Astyochus was playing him false, and that a letter on the subject was on the point of arriving from Alcibiades, himself anticipated the news, and told the army that the enemy, seeing that Samos was unfortified and the fleet not all stationed

8.50.2a Miletus: Map 8.45, BY, and Map 8.56.
8.50.3a Magnesia: Map 8.45, AY, and Map 8.56.
8.50.3b Samos: Map 8.45, AY, and Map 8.56.

wit o attack the camp; that he could be certain of
thi they must fortify Samos as quickly as possible,
anc r defenses. It will be remembered that he was
ge thority to carry out these measures. [2] According elves to the work of fortification, and Samos was
thu it would otherwise have been. Not long after-
wa iades arrived, saying that the army was betrayed
by emy about to attack it. [3] Alcibiades, however,
gai as it was thought that he was in on the secret of
the tried out of hatred to fasten them upon Phryn-
ich t he was their accomplice; and consequently far
fro er bore witness to what Phrynichus had said by
thi

to work to persuade Tissaphernes to become the
fri Tissaphernes, although afraid of the Pelopon-
ne more ships in Asia than the Athenians, was yet
dis if he could, especially after his quarrel with the
Pe [1a] about the treaty of Therimenes. The quarrel
ha the Peloponnesians were by this time actually at
Rh iginal argument of Alcibiades concerning the lib-
era he Spartans had been verified by the declaration
of ssible to submit to a convention which made the
Ki es at any former time ruled by himself or by his
fat

8.52 412/1 20th Year/Winter MAGNESIA Alcibiades tries to obtain Tissaphernes' friendship for the Athenians, which seems possible after his quarrel at Cnidus with the Spartans over the treaty.

soliciting the favor of Tissaphernes with an
ea o the greatness of the issue, [8.53.1] the Athen-
iar dispatched from Samos with Pisander arrived at
At h before the people, giving a brief summary of
th y insisting that if Alcibiades were recalled and the
de hanged, they could have the King as their ally,
an vercome the Peloponnesians. [2] A number of
sp n the question of the democracy, the enemies of
Al nst the scandal of a restoration to be brought
ab e constitution, and the *Eumolpidae* and *Ceryces*[2a]
pr Mysteries, the cause of his banishment, and called
up his recall; when Pisander, in the midst of much
op me forward, and taking each of his opponents
as wing question: In the face of the fact that the
Pe any ships as their own confronting them at sea,
m n them, and the King and Tissaphernes to supply

8.53 412/1 20th Year/Winter ATHENS Pisander and the envoys from Samos seek to persuade the Athenians to adopt an oligarchy, arguing that only by the restoration of Alcibiades and the establishment of an oligarchy can Athens hope to obtain the King's friendship and thereby the resources with which to resist and ultimately defeat the Spartans.

8.5
8.5 odes (Map
.
8.5 Lichas was
biades' prior
recounted in

8.5 *es* were the only two families from whom officials who led and conducted the Mystery rites at the shrine of Eleusis (Map 8.61, BX) could be selected. Since Alcibiades had been condemned for blaspheming against the "Mysteries" (see 6.27–29 and 6.61), they would naturally be concerned at his recall.

them with money, of which the Athenians had none left, had he any hope of saving the state unless someone could induce the King to come over to their side? [3] Upon their replying that they had not, he then plainly said to them: This we cannot have unless we have a more moderate form of government, and put the offices into fewer hands, and so gain the King's confidence, and forthwith restore Alcibiades, who is the only man living that can bring this about. The safety of the state, not the form of its government, is for the moment the most pressing question, as we can always change afterwards whatever we do not like.

8.54
412/1
20th Year/Winter
ATHENS
Bowing to necessity and hoping for a future return to democracy, the Athenians agree to alter the government, dismiss Phrynichus, and send Pisander to negotiate with Tissaphernes. Pisander solicits support for these moves from the political clubs.

The People were at first highly irritated at the mention of an oligarchy, but upon understanding clearly from Pisander that this was the only resource left, they took counsel of their fears, and promised themselves some day to change the government again, and gave way. [2] They accordingly voted that Pisander should sail with ten others and make the best arrangement that they could with Tissaphernes and Alcibiades. [3] At the same time The People, upon a false accusation of Pisander, dismissed Phrynichus from his post together with his colleague Scironides, sending Diomedon and Leon to replace them in the command of the fleet. The accusation was that Phrynichus had betrayed Iasus and Amorges;[3a] and Pisander asserted it because he thought him a man unfit for the business now in hand with Alcibiades. [4] Pisander also made the round of all the clubs[4a] already existing in the city for help in lawsuits and elections, and urged them to draw together and to unite their efforts for the overthrow of the democracy; and after taking all other measures required by the circumstances, so that no time might be lost, set off with his ten companions on his voyage to Tissaphernes.

8.55
412/1
20th Year/Winter
RHODES-CHIOS
The Athenians raid Rhodes. The Chians call on the Peloponnesians at Rhodes for help. A Chian attack against the Athenian siege works is initially successful, but is finally routed.

In the same winter Leon and Diomedon, who had by this time joined the fleet, made an attack upon Rhodes.[1a] The ships of the Peloponnesians they found hauled up on shore, and after making a descent upon the coast and defeating the Rhodians who appeared in the field against them, withdrew to Chalce[1b] and made that place their base of operations instead of Cos,[1c] as they could better observe from there if the Peloponnesian fleet put out to sea. [2] Meanwhile Xenophantes, a Laconian, came to Rhodes from Pedaritus at Chios,[2a] with the news that the fortification of the Athenians was now finished,[2b] and that, unless the whole Peloponnesian fleet came to the rescue, the cause in Chios must be lost. Upon this they

8.54.3a Iasus: Map 8.56. This statement indicates a relationship of some sort between Amorges and Athens that could be betrayed; see note 8.5.5b.

8.54.4a At Athens there were no political parties in the modern sense. Nonetheless, there were groups of citizens whose interests coincided. These groups even when ostensibly social in nature could be employed for political ends; indeed, they were constantly and lawfully active in the political life of the democracy. The "clubs" mentioned here are more sinister, as they are Crawley's translation of *synomosiai,* a word which shows that oaths were exchanged. They were not necessarily dedicated to the subversion of the democracy, but clearly could be so used. See Appendix A, The Athenian Government, §11.

8.55.1a Rhodes: Map 8.56.

8.55.1b Chalce: Map 8.56.

8.55.1c Cos: Map 8.56.

8.55.2a Chios: Map 8.56.

8.55.2b Progress on the Athenian fortifications on Chios at Delphinium (Map 8.37, AX) was mentioned in 8.38.2 and 8.40.3.

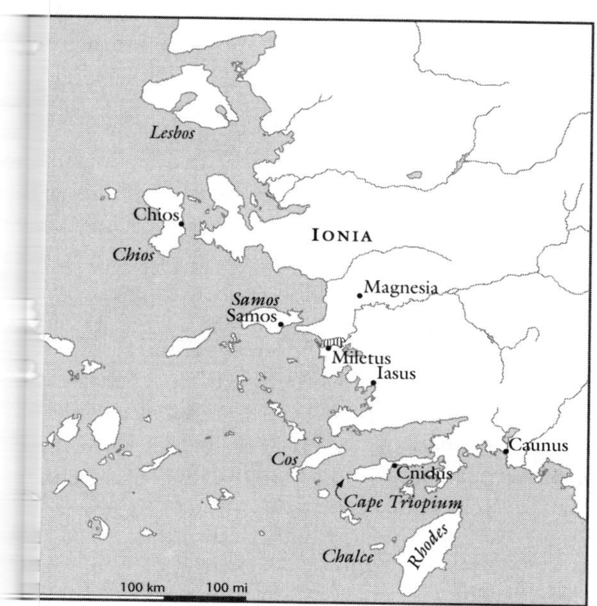

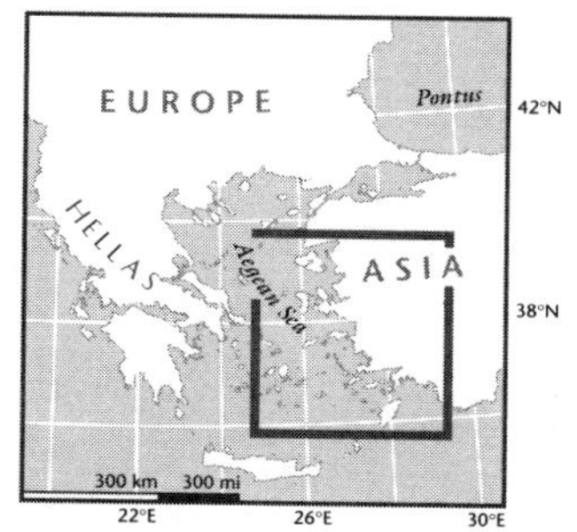

MA[illegible]
DI[illegible]
OF [illegible]

res[illegible] [3] In the meantime Pedaritus, with the mercenar[illegible]m and the whole force of the Chians, made an ass[illegible]round the Athenian ships and took a portion of it, [illegible]ome vessels that were hauled up on shore, when the[illegible]o the rescue, and first routing the Chians, next de[illegible]f the force round Pedaritus (who was himself kill[illegible]ians), and took a great quantity of arms.

8.56
412/1
20th Year/Winter
CHIOS
The siege of Chios continues.
MAGNESIA?
The Athenians begin discussions with Tissaphernes who, not wishing to conclude an agreement, makes unacceptable demands. The Athenians finally decide that Alcibiades has deceived them and that no agreement is possible, so they angrily break off negotiations.

[illegible]ere besieged even more tightly than before by lan[illegible]e in the place was great. Meanwhile the Athenian[illegible] arrived at the court of Tissaphernes, and confer[illegible] proposed agreement. [2] However, Alcibiades, no[illegible]of Tissaphernes (who feared the Peloponnesians m[illegible] and besides wished to wear out both parties, as Al[illegible]ommended), had recourse to the following stratag[illegible]etween the Athenians and Tissaphernes miscarry by[illegible]e of the latter's demands. [3] In my opinion Tissap[illegible]lt, fear being his motive; while Alcibiades, who no[illegible]s was determined not to treat on any terms, wi[illegible]hink, not that he was unable to persuade Tissaph[illegible]e latter had been persuaded and was willing to joi[illegible]onceded enough to him. [4] For the demands of

Alcibiades, speaking for Tissaphernes, who was present, were so extravagant that the Athenians, although for a long while they agreed to whatever he asked, yet had to bear the blame of failure: he required the cession of the whole of Ionia, next of the islands adjacent, besides other concessions, and these passed without opposition; at last, in the third interview, Alcibiades, who now feared a complete discovery of his inability, required them to allow the King to build ships and sail along his own coast wherever and with as many as he pleased.[4a] Upon this the Athenians would yield no further, and concluding that there was nothing to be done, but that they had been deceived by Alcibiades, went away in a rage and proceeded to Samos.[4b]

8.57
412/1
20th Year/Winter
CAUNUS-MILETUS
Tissaphernes now improves relations with the Spartans, giving pay to their sailors and concluding a new treaty with them.

Immediately after this, in the same winter, Tissaphernes proceeded along shore to Caunus,[1a] desiring to bring the Peloponnesian fleet back to Miletus, and to supply them with pay, making a fresh convention upon such terms as he could get, in order not to bring matters to an absolute breach between them. He was afraid that if many of their ships were left without pay they would be compelled to engage and be defeated, or that their vessels being left without hands, the Athenians would attain their objects without his assistance. Still more he feared that the Peloponnesians might ravage the continent in search of supplies. [2] Having calculated and considered all this, according to his plan of keeping the two sides equal, he now sent for the Peloponnesians and gave them pay, and concluded with them a third treaty[2a] in words following:

8.58
412/1
20th Year/Winter
MEANDER PLAIN
Thucydides offers the text of the third treaty between Sparta and the Persian Great King.

In the thirteenth year of the reign of Darius, while Alexipippidas was ephor at Sparta, a treaty was concluded in the plain of the Meander by the Spartans and their allies with Tissaphernes, Hieramenes, and the sons of Pharnaces, concerning the affairs of the King and of the Spartans and their allies.

• [2] The country of the King in Asia shall be the King's, and the King shall treat his own country as he pleases.

• [3] The Spartans and their allies shall not invade or injure the King's country; neither shall the King invade or injure that of the Spartans or of their allies. [4] If any of the Spartans or their allies

8.56.4a Many scholars have taken this last demand of Alcibiades to imply the existence of a treaty between Athens and Persia. The movement of the royal fleet may have been restricted by nothing more than fear of the Athenians, but what prevented the King from building ships if it was not some clause of a treaty? See Appendix B, The Athenian Empire, §8; Appendix E, The Persians, §5; and note E5c.

8.56.4b Samos: Map 8.56.

8.57.1a Caunus: Map 8.56.

8.57.2a Thucydides seems persuaded that there were three "treaties" between Sparta and Persia in 412/1 (8.18, 8.37, and here), but the truth seems to be that the first two were mere drafts of treaties and were rejected by one party, which is why only the third has a formal introduction with a date and the names of the Persians involved. It was negotiated in Caunus (8.57.1), but the introduction to the treaty says the agreement was made "in the plain of the Meander" (8.58.1), that is, there was an interval in which the text could be referred to both the King and to Sparta. It is to be noted, however, that only with this third "treaty" does Thucydides use the technical term (not reproduced in Crawley's translation) signifying, literally, the pouring of a libation which was necessary to complete the accord. So perhaps Thucydides was not deceived.

ng's country, the Spartans and their allies shall
rom the King's country invade or injure the
or of their allies, the King shall prevent it.
shall provide pay for the ships now present,
ment, until the arrival of the King's vessels;[5a]
l of the King's vessels the Spartans and their
wn ships if they wish it. If, however, they
pay from Tissaphernes, Tissaphernes shall fur-
s and their allies shall repay him at the end of
they shall have received.
g's vessels have arrived, the ships of the Spar-
and those of the King shall carry on the war
issaphernes and the Spartans and their allies
wish to make peace with the Athenians, they
intly.

fter this Tissaphernes prepared to bring up the
Ph ng to agreement, and to make good his other
pr vished to make it appear that he was so preparing.
ng to its close, when the Boeotians took Oropus
by was held by an Athenian garrison. Their accom-
pl ropians themselves, and some Eretrians who were
pl boea,[1a] as the place was exactly opposite Eretria,
ar nds was necessarily a great threat to Eretria and
th Oropus being in their hands, the Eretrians now
ca te the Peloponnesians into Euboea. The latter,
ho on the relief of the distressed Chians, and accord-
in sailed with all their ships from Rhodes. [3] Off
Tr Athenian fleet out at sea sailing from Chalce and
as he other, the Athenians went on to Samos, the
Pe s, seeing that it was no longer possible to relieve
C And this winter ended, and with it ended the
tw of which Thucydides is the historian.
he following summer Dercyllidas, a Spartiate, was
se land to the Hellespont to bring about the revolt
of ilesian[1b] colony; and the Chians, while Astyochus
w them, were compelled to fight at sea by the pres-
su e Astyochus was still at Rhodes they had received
fr nmander after the death of Pedaritus, a Spartiate
na come out with Antisthenes,[2a] and twelve vessels

8.59
Tissaphernes appears to fulfill his promises.

8.60
412/1
20th Year/Winter
OROPUS
The Boeotians take Oropus by treachery and plot a revolt of Euboea.
RHODES-MILETUS
The Peloponnesians sail toward Chios, but finding they cannot relieve it without a battle, they retire to Miletus.

8.61
411
21st Year/Summer
CHIOS
Pressed by the siege, the Chians decide to give battle at sea. Although they fight well, they are forced to retire inside their walls at the end of the day.

8. oenician fleet.
8. or.
8. 8.61, BX. Ere-
, AX. For the
see 8.95.
8.

8.60.3a Cape Triopium, Chalce, Samos, and Miletus: Map 8.61, BY; Chios, Map 8.61, AY.
8.61.1a Abydos: Map 8.61, AY.
8.61.1b Miletus: Map 8.61, BY.
8.61.2a For Antisthenes' arrival, see 8.39.2.

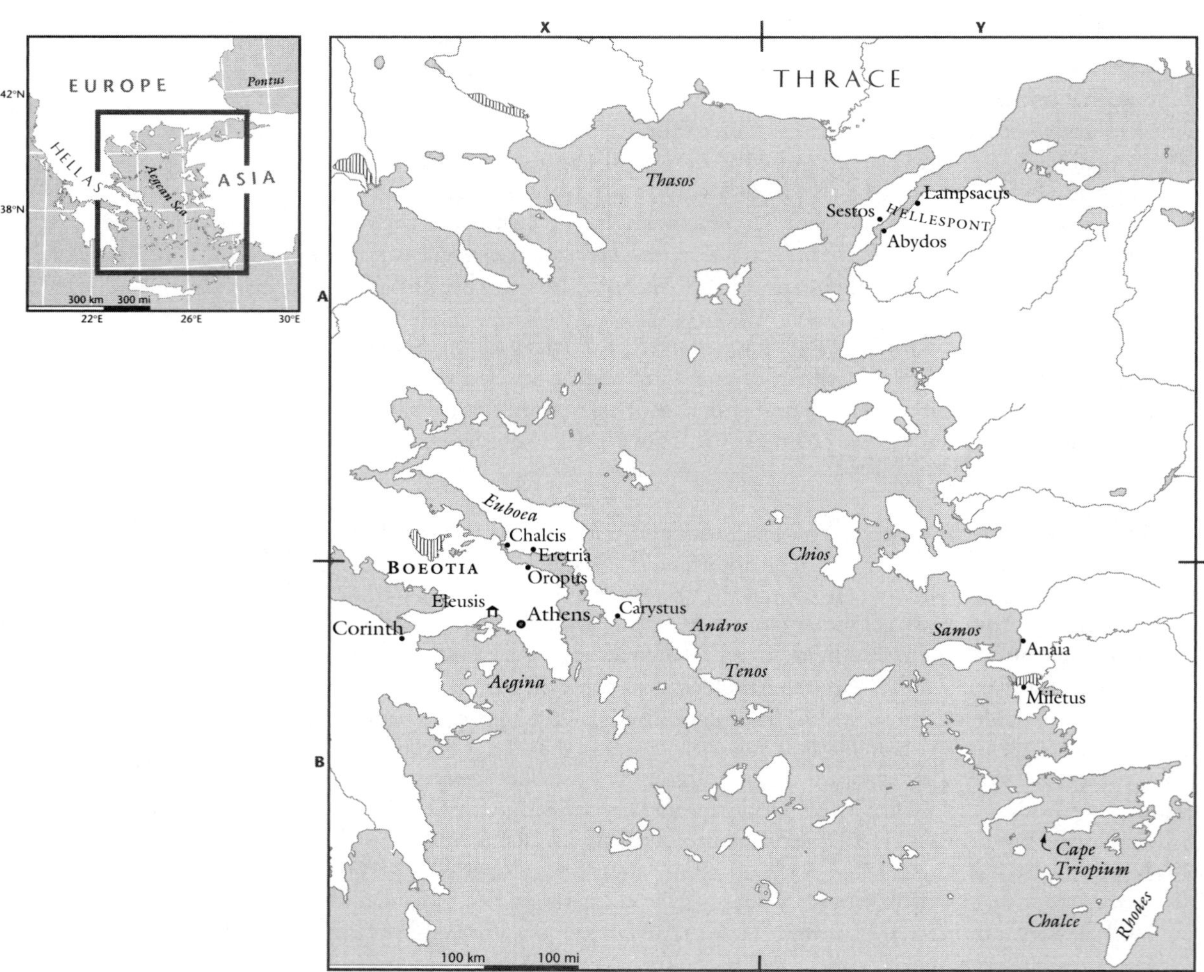

MAP 8.61 OPENING OF SUMMER 411

which had been on guard at Miletus, five of which were Thurian,[2b] four Syracusan, one from Anaia,[2c] one Milesian, and one Leon's own. [3] Accordingly the Chians marched out in mass and took up a strong position, while thirty-six of their ships put out and engaged thirty-two of the Athenians; and after a tough fight, in which the Chians and their allies had rather the best of it, as it was now late, they retired to their city.

8.61.2b Thurii: Map 8.37 locator.
8.61.2c Anaia: Map 8.61, BY. Anaia was the city from which the Samian exiles operated; see 4.75.1.

[illegible] Dercyllidas arrived by land from Miletus; and Abydo[illegible] olted to him (and to Pharnabazus),[1b] and Lampsac[illegible] Upon receipt of this news Strombichides hastily sai[illegible] venty-four Athenian ships, some transports carrying [illegible] umber, and defeating the Lampsacenes who came ou[illegible] psacus, which was unfortified, at the first assault, an[illegible] slaves and goods, restored the freemen to their ho[illegible] ydos. [3] The inhabitants there, however, refused to [illegible] assaults failed to take the place, he sailed over to th[illegible] ade Sestos,[3a] the city in the Chersonese once held by [illegible] for the defense of the whole Hellespont.

8.62
411
21st Year/Summer
HELLESPONT
When Peloponnesian land forces arrive, Abydos and Lampsacus revolt from Athens. The Athenians respond quickly and recover Lampsacus.

[illegible] Chians commanded the sea more than before; and th[illegible] etus[1a] and Astyochus, hearing of the sea fight and of [illegible] quadron with Strombichides, took fresh courage. [2[illegible] two vessels to Chios, Astyochus took the ships fr[illegible] moved with the whole fleet upon Samos,[2a] from wh[illegible] back to Miletus, as the Athenians did not put out ag[illegible] r suspicions of one another.

[illegible] his time, or even before, that the democracy was pu[illegible] en Pisander and the envoys returned from Tissaph[illegible] once strengthened still further their control in the ar[illegible] he upper class in Samos to join them in establishin[illegible] form of government which a party of them had re[illegible] 4] At the same time the Athenians at Samos, after a [illegible] mselves, determined to let Alcibiades alone, since he [illegible] nd besides was not the man for an oligarchy; and no[illegible] embarked on this course, to see for themselves ho[illegible] ent the ruin of their cause, and meanwhile to susta[illegible] ibute without stint money and all else that might be [illegible] n private estates, as they would henceforth labor fo[illegible]

8.63
411
21st Year/Summer
CHIOS-SAMOS
Gathering ships from Chios and Miletus, Astyochus challenges the Athenians at Samos. They refuse to fight, due to disunity caused by the fall of the democracy at Athens. The conspiracy at Samos begins to incite the local oligarchs to establish an oligarchy on Samos.

[illegible] other in these resolutions, they now at once sent of[illegible] sander to do what was necessary at Athens (with in[illegible] oligarchies on their way in all the subject cities w[illegible] at), and dispatched the other half in different di[illegible] pendencies. [2] Diitrephes[2a] also, who was in the ne[illegible] nd who had been elected to the command of the

8.64
411
21st Year/Summer
AEGEAN
Envoys from the Athenian army at Samos are sent to Athens and other places to abolish democracies and install oligarchies. At Thasos, the new oligarchy plots to join the Spartans. Thucydides says that Athen's allies were more interested in securing their freedom than in changes of constitution.

8.[illegible]
8.[illegible] aces was the [illegible] f the Helles- [illegible]).
8.[illegible]
8.[illegible] mbichides had [illegible] of Chios in [illegible]
8.[illegible] Athenian cap- [illegible] sians in 479/8 [illegible] his flotilla [illegible] tioned in 8.79.3.
8.63.1a Miletus: Map 8.61, BY.
8.63.2a Samos: Map 8.61, BY.
8.63.3a Thucydides describes the actual overthrow of the Athenian democracy below, in 8.65–69.
8.63.3b For the revolt at Samos in 412, see 8.21. The narrative of political events at Samos continues at 8.73.
8.64.2a Presumably this is the same Diitrephes who led the Dii in the massacre at Mycalessus in 413 (7.29).

Thracian district of the empire, was sent off to his command, and arriving at Thasos[2b] abolished the democracy there. [3] Within two months of his departure, however, the Thasians began to fortify their city, being quickly tired of an aristocracy allied to Athens when they daily expected to receive freedom from Sparta. [4] Indeed there was a party of them whom the Athenians had banished with the Peloponnesians, who with their friends in the city were already making every effort to bring up a squadron, and to bring about the revolt of Thasos; and this party thus saw exactly what they most wanted done, that is to say, the reformation of the government without risk, and the abolition of the democracy which would have opposed them. [5] Things at Thasos thus turned out just the contrary to what the oligarchic conspirators at Athens expected; and the same in my opinion was the case in many of the other dependencies; as the cities no sooner got a moderate government and liberty of action, than they went on to absolute freedom without being at all seduced by the show of reform offered by the Athenians.

8.65
411
21st Year/Summer
ATHENS
The envoys from the army at Samos find the overthrow of the Athenian democracy well under way. Gangs have already assassinated the leader of The People and others.

Pisander and his colleagues on their voyage along shore abolished, as had been determined, the democracies in the cities, and also took some hoplites from certain places as their allies, and so came to Athens. [2] Here they found most of the work already done by their associates. Some of the younger men had banded together and secretly assassinated one Androcles, the chief leader of The People, and the man mainly responsible for the banishment of Alcibiades; Androcles being singled out both because he was a popular leader, and because they sought by his death to recommend themselves to Alcibiades, who was, as they supposed, to be recalled, and to make Tissaphernes their friend. There were also some other obnoxious persons whom they secretly did away with in the same manner. [3] Meanwhile their cry in public was that no pay should be given except to persons serving in the war, and that not more than five thousand should share in the government, and those such as were most able to serve the state in person and in purse.

8.66
411
21st Year/Summer
ATHENS
The assembly and the council continue to meet but they are controlled by the conspirators. Open opponents of the oligarchy are murdered. The People are cowed because they cannot unite or speak openly to find out who among them are conspirators.

But this was merely a catchword for the multitude, as the authors of the revolution were really to govern. However, the assembly and the council[1a] still met notwithstanding, although they discussed nothing that was not approved of by the conspirators, who both supplied the speakers, and reviewed in advance what they were to say. [2] Fear, and the sight of the numbers of the conspirators, closed the mouths of the rest; or if any ventured to rise in opposition, he was promptly put to death in some convenient way, and there was neither search for the murderers nor justice to be had against them if suspected; but The People remained motionless, being so thoroughly cowed that men thought themselves lucky to escape violence, even when they held their tongues. [3] An exaggerated belief in the numbers of the conspirators also demoralized The People, rendered helpless by the magnitude of the city, and by their being

8.64.2b Thrace: Map 8.61, AY; Thasos: Map 8.61, AX.

8.66.1a For the assembly and council, see Appendix A, The Athenian Government, §5–8.

un ... r, and being without means of finding out what
th ... . [4] For the same reason it was impossible for
an ... d to a neighbor and to concert measures to
de ... ld have had to speak either to one whom he did
nc ... ew but did not trust. [5] Indeed all the popular
pa ... her with suspicion, each thinking his neighbor
in ... g on, the conspirators having in their ranks per-
sc ... d ever have believed capable of joining an oli-
g ... vho made the many so suspicious, and so helped
tc ... he few, by confirming the commons in their mis-
tr

8.67 411 21st Year/Summer ATHENS With the arrival of the envoys from Samos, the oligarchs led by Pisander change the constitution.

... der and his colleagues arrived, and lost no time in
c ... they assembled the people, and moved to elect
t ... ull powers to frame a constitution, and that when
t ... d on an appointed day lay before the people their
o ... node of governing the city. [2] Afterwards, when
t ... pirators enclosed the assembly in Colonus, a tem-
p ... nore than a mile outside the city;[2a] when the com-
r ... ht forward this single motion: that any Athenian
r ... unity whatever measure he pleased, and that heavy
p ... osed upon any who should indict for illegality, or
c ... r so doing.[2b] [3] The way thus cleared, it was now
p ... tenure of office and receipt of pay under the exist-
i ... an end, and that five men must be elected as presi-
... ir turn elect one hundred, and each of the hundred
... is body thus made up to four hundred should enter
... ith full powers and govern as they judged best, and
... thousand whenever they pleased.

8.68 411 21st Year/Summer ATHENS Thucydides describes the leaders of the oligarchs and comments that it was no small thing to deprive the Athenian people of their freedom after a century of democratic rule.

... d this resolution was Pisander, who was throughout
... nt in putting down the democracy. But he who con-
... and prepared the way for the catastrophe, and who
... thought to the matter, was Antiphon, one of the
... Athens; who, with a head to contrive measures and a
... them, did not willingly come forward in the assem-
... ic scene, being ill-looked upon by the multitude
... n for cleverness; and who yet was the one man best
... ts, or before the assembly, the suitors who required
... ed, when he was afterwards himself tried for his life
... ng been concerned in setting up this very govern-

... Hippios) in
... ation: Map 8.75,
... writes "ten
... was 607 feet long,
... 630.8 feet.

... ity from prosecu-
... sals to change the
... sary before any rev-
... uld be made.

8.67.3a Remains of this building (the Bouleuterion) have been located in the Athenian agora (Map 6.56, inset).

8.68.1a See Appendix A, The Athenian Government, §10, for some light on why citizens would require assistance from experts in the courts and the assembly.

ment, when the Four Hundred were overthrown and harshly dealt with by the commons, he made what would seem to be the best defense of any known up to my time.[2a] [3] Phrynichus also went beyond all others in his zeal for the oligarchy. Afraid of Alcibiades, and assured that he was no stranger to his intrigues with Astyochus at Samos, he held that no oligarchy was ever likely to restore him, and once embarked in the enterprise, proved, where danger was to be faced, by far the staunchest of them all. [4] Theramenes son of Hagnon was also one of the foremost of the subverters of the democracy—a man as able in council as in debate. Conducted by so many and by such sagacious heads, the enterprise, great as it was, not unnaturally went forward; although it was no light matter to deprive the Athenian people of its freedom, almost a hundred years after the deposition of the tyrants, when it had been not only not subject to any during the whole of that period, but accustomed during more than half of it to rule over subjects of its own.

8.69
411
21st Year/Summer
ATHENS
The assembly ratifies the new constitution unanimously and disbands. The council is driven out, intimidated by armed youths and foreigners.

The assembly ratified the proposed constitution, without a single opposing voice, and was then dissolved; after which the Four Hundred were brought into the council chamber[1a] in the following way. On account of the enemy at Decelea,[1b] all the Athenians were constantly on the wall or in the ranks at the various military posts. [2] On that day the persons not in on the secret were allowed to go home as usual, while orders were given to the accomplices of the conspirators to hang about, without making any demonstration, at some little distance from the posts,[2a] and in case of any opposition to what was being done, to seize the arms and put it down. [3] There were also some Andrians and Tenians,[3a] three hundred Carystians[3b] and some of the settlers in Aegina[3c] come with their own arms for this very purpose, who had received similar instructions. [4] These dispositions completed, the Four Hundred went, each with a dagger concealed about his person, accompanied by one hundred and twenty youths, whom they employed wherever violence was needed, and appeared before the councilors chosen by lot[4a] in the council chamber, and told them to take their pay and be gone; themselves bringing it for the whole of the residue of their term of office, and giving it to them as they went out.

8.70
411
21st Year/Summer
ATHENS
The council departs without objection by its members or other citizens. The Four Hundred now begin to rule arbitrarily by force, not by law. They inform Agis of their desire for peace.

Upon the council withdrawing in this way without venturing any objection, and the rest of the citizens making no movement, the Four Hundred entered the council chamber, and for the present contented themselves with drawing lots for their *prytanes*,[1a] and making their prayers and sacri-

8.68.2a A few fragments of this speech survive, but they are insufficient to assess Thucydides' judgment of it.
8.69.1a For the council chamber, see note 8.67.3a.
8.69.1b Decelea: Map 8.75.
8.69.2a By "posts" Thucydides means locations where arms were stored.
8.69.3a Andros and Tenos: Map 8.61, BX.
8.69.3b Carystus: Map 8.61, BX.
8.69.3c Aegina: Map 8.61, BX.
8.69.4a For an explanation of the "councilors chosen by lot," see Appendix A, The Athenian Government, §5.
8.70.1a The *prytanes* were a group who acted as a standing committee for both the council and the assembly during the tenth of the year when it was their tribe's turn "to preside"; see note at 6.14.1a and Appendix A, The Athenian Government, §5.

fi[illegible] entering office; but afterwards departed widely
fr[illegible] m of government, and except that on account of
Al[illegible] recall the exiles,[1b] ruled the city by force; [2]
pu[illegible] n, though not many, whom they thought it conve[illegible] prisoning and banishing others. They also sent to
A[illegible] Decelea,[2a] to say that they desired to make peace,
an[illegible] ably be more disposed to treat now that he had
th[illegible] of the inconstant People.

8.71
411
21st Year/Summer
ATHENS
Agis responds negatively to the Athenian oligarchs' first overtures with a show of force, marching his army to the walls of Athens. He finds the walls manned, and actively defended. When the oligarchs send a second embassy to him, he responds more positively.

[illegible] believe in the tranquillity of the city, or that the
co[illegible] a moment give up their ancient liberty, but
th[illegible] of a large Spartan force would be sufficient to
ex[illegible] not already in commotion, of which he was by
no[illegible] cordingly gave to the envoys of the Four Hun-
d[illegible] d out no hopes of an accommodation, and send-
in[illegible] nts from the Peloponnesus, not long afterwards,
w[illegible] on from Decelea, descended to the very walls of
A[illegible] at civil disturbances might help to subdue them
to[illegible] he confusion to be expected within and without
th[illegible] n surrender without a blow being struck; at all
e[illegible] uld succeed in seizing the Long Walls,[1a] bared of
th[illegible] wever, the Athenians saw him come close up,
w[illegible] t disturbance within the city; and sending out
th[illegible] ber of their hoplites, light troops, and archers,
sh[illegible] ldiers who approached too near, and got possessi[illegible] dead. Upon this Agis, at last convinced, led his
a[illegible] d remaining with his own troops in the old posi-
ti[illegible] reinforcement back home after a few days' stay
in[illegible] Four Hundred persevering sent another embassy
to[illegible] ng with a better reception, at his suggestion dis-
p[illegible] a to negotiate a treaty, being desirous of making
p[illegible]

8.72
411
21st Year/Summer
ATHENS
The oligarchs send envoys to the fleet at Samos to win acceptance for the new regime, fearing that failure to do so could lead to their overthrow.

[illegible] men to Samos[1a] to reassure the army, and to
e[illegible] y was not established to harm the city or the citi-
z[illegible] untry as a whole; and that there were five thou-
s[illegible] d only, concerned; although, what with their
e[illegible] yments abroad, the Athenians had never yet
a[illegible] uestion important enough to bring five thousand
o[illegible] he emissaries were also told what to say upon all

8[illegible] hat although
[illegible] government to
[illegible] ocracy and to
[illegible] hs did not now
[illegible] hey did not wish
[illegible] e city. It should
[illegible] himself at this
[illegible]

8[illegible]
8[illegible] ap 8.75, inset.

8.71.3a Attica: Map 8.75.
8.72.1a Samos: Map 8.75.

other points, and were sent off immediately after the establishment of the new government, which feared, as it turned out correctly, that the mass of seamen would not be willing to remain under the oligarchic constitution, and, the evil beginning there, might be the means of their overthrow.

8.73
411
21st Year/Summer
SAMOS
An oligarchic party is formed at Samos with the help of some Athenians, and it plots to overthrow Samos' democracy. The Samian democrats, learning of the plot, turn for help to various prodemocratic Athenian officers and the crew of the ship *Paralus*. They organize a force that helps the Samian democrats to defeat the coup.

Indeed at Samos the question of the oligarchy had already entered upon a new phase, the following events having taken place just at the time that the Four Hundred were conspiring.[1a] [2] That part of the Samian population which has been mentioned as rising against the upper class and as being the democratic party, had now turned round, and yielding to the solicitations of Pisander during his visit, and of the Athenians in the conspiracy at Samos, had bound themselves by oaths to the number of three hundred, and were about to fall upon the rest of their fellow citizens, whom they now in their turn regarded as the democratic party. [3] Meanwhile they put to death one Hyperbolus, an Athenian, a pestilent fellow who had been ostracized,[3a] not from fear of his influence or position, but because he was a scoundrel and a disgrace to the city; being aided in this by Charminus, one of the generals, and by some of the Athenians with them, to whom they had sworn friendship, and with whom they perpetrated other acts of the kind, and now determined to attack the majority. [4] The latter got wind of what was coming, and told two of the generals, Leon and Diomedon, who, on account of the credit which they enjoyed with The People, were unwilling supporters of the oligarchy; and also Thrasybulus and Thrasyllus, the former a captain of a trireme, the latter serving with the hoplites, besides certain others who had always been thought most opposed to the conspirators, appealing to them not to look on and see them destroyed, and Samos, the sole remaining stay of their empire, taken from the Athenians. [5] Upon hearing this, the persons whom they addressed now went round the soldiers one by one, and urged them to resist, especially the crew of the *Paralus*,[5a] which was made up entirely of Athenians and free men, and had always been enemies of oligarchy, even when there was no such thing existing; and Leon and Diomedon left behind some ships for their protection in case they had to sail away anywhere themselves. [6] Accordingly, when the Three Hundred attacked the people, all these came to the rescue, and foremost of all the crew of the *Paralus;* and the Samian majority gained the victory, and putting to death

8.73.1a This continues the narrative of political events at Samos from 8.63.3.

8.73.3a Hyperbolus was ostracized at some time before the Sicilian Expedition (the commonly cited date of 418/7 is ill-grounded). His was the last instance of a practice begun less than a century earlier whereby, if The People chose to have such a vote, the man who received the largest number of votes, provided that six thousand or more citizens voted, had to withdraw from Athens for ten years, though he retained his property; see Appendix A, The Athenian Government, §8. Small shards of pottery (*ostraka*) were used on which names were written; see Illustration 1.135. For the ostracism of Themistocles, see 1.135.3.

8.73.5a The *Paralus* and her sister ship the *Salaminia* were special state triremes used on sacred embassies and official business. They appear several times in Thucydides' narrative, see note 3.33.1a.

so undred, banishing three others of the ringleaders,
ac rest, and lived together under a democratic gov-
er

h Chaereas son of Archestratus on board, an
At n active part in the revolution, was now without
lo Samians and the army to Athens to report what
ha the Four Hundred were in power not being yet
kn led into harbor the Four Hundred immediately
ar the *Parali,* and taking the vessel from the rest,
sh hip and set them to keep guard round Euboea.[2a]
[3 nanaged to hide as soon as he saw how things
st amos, drew a picture to the soldiers of the horro ens, in which everything was exaggerated; saying
th th lashes, that no one could say a word against
th the soldiers' wives and children were outraged,
ar to seize and shut up the relatives of all in the
ar not of the government's way of thinking, to be
pu heir disobedience; and a host of other harmful
in

8.74
411
21st Year/Summer
ATHENS
Not yet aware of the coup at Athens, the *Paralus* arrives there with news of the failed coup at Samos; its crew is imprisoned or kept at sea. One escapes to Samos and gives an exaggerated account of events at Athens.

st thought of the army was to fall upon the chief
au nd upon all the rest concerned. Eventually, how-
ev is idea when the men of moderate views opposed
it nst ruining their cause with the enemy close at
ha e. [2] After this Thrasybulus son of Lycus, and
T ers in the revolution, now wishing in the most
pu the government at Samos to a democracy, bound
al st tremendous oaths, and those of the oligarchic
pa ccept a democratic government, to be united, to
pr against the Peloponnesians, and to be enemies of
th o hold no communication with them. [3] The
sa by all the Samians of full age; and the soldiers
as all their affairs and in the fruits of their dangers
ha t there was no way of escape for themselves or for
th ccess of the Four Hundred or of the enemy at
M in.

8.75
411
21st Year/Summer
SAMOS
The troops at Samos vow to remain united in support of democracy both at Samos and at Athens, to maintain the war against Sparta, and to have no relations with the oligarchs at Athens.

8. xt hear of the
5.9.
8.

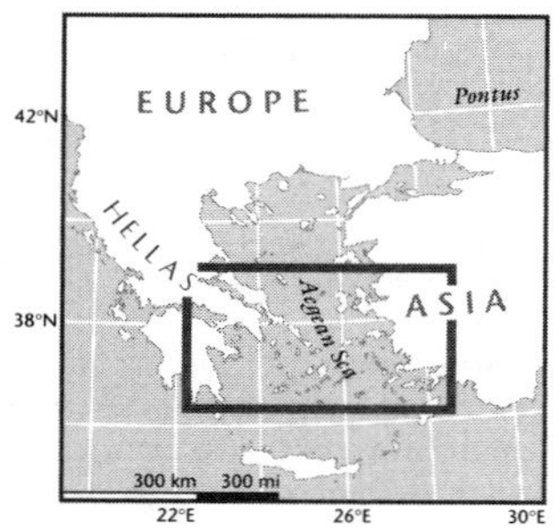

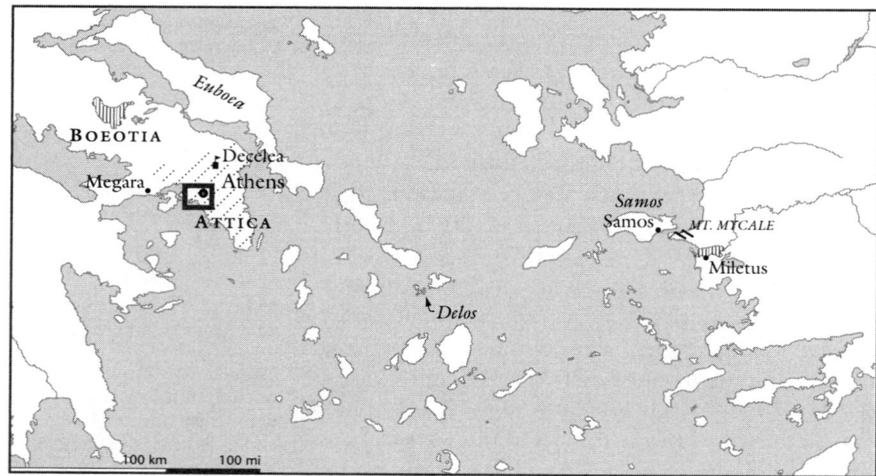

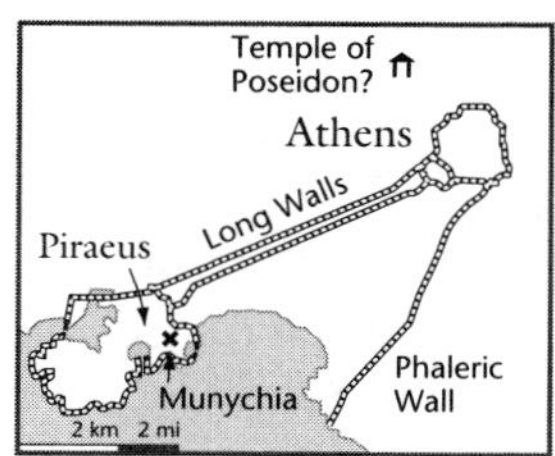

MAP 8.75 REVOLUTION IN ATHENS AND SAMOS

8.76
411
21st Year/Summer
SAMOS
Athenian forces on Samos choose new officers and agree to restore democracy at Athens. They realize that Athens no longer provides them with funds or counsel, that they can carry on the war alone and inflict more harm on Athens from Samos than the oligarchs can inflict on them. Moreover, their ships could carry them to refuge if they should fail.

The struggle was now between the army trying to force a democracy upon the city, and the Four Hundred an oligarchy upon the army. [2] Meanwhile the soldiers immediately held an assembly in which they deposed the former generals and any of the captains whom they suspected, and chose new captains and generals to replace them, in addition to Thrasybulus and Thrasyllus, whom they had already selected. [3] They also stood up and encouraged one another, and among other things urged that they ought not to lose heart because the city had revolted from them, as the party seceding was smaller and in every way poorer in resources than themselves. [4] They had the whole fleet with which to compel the other cities in their empire to give them money just as if they had their base in the capital, having a city in Samos[4a] which, far from lacking strength, had

8.76.4a Samos: Map 8.75.

wh [illegible] an inch of depriving the Athenians of the comma [illegible] far as the enemy was concerned they had the
sa [illegible] s before. Indeed, with the fleet in their hands,
th [illegible] rovide themselves with supplies than the govern-
m [illegible] s their advanced position at Samos which had
th [illegible] ome authorities to command the entrance into
Pi [illegible] used to give them back the constitution, they
w [illegible] rmy was more in a position to exclude them from
th [illegible] exclude the army. [6] Besides, the city was of little [illegible] them to overcome the enemy; and they had lost
n [illegible] o had no longer either money to send them (the
so [illegible] for themselves), or good counsel, which entitles
ci [illegible] the contrary, even in this the home government
ha [illegible] hing the institutions of their ancestors, while the
ar [illegible] stitutions, and would try to force the home gov-
er [illegible] So that even in point of good counsel the camp
ha [illegible] s the city. [7] Moreover, they had only to grant
A [illegible] person and his recall, and he would be only too
gl [illegible] alliance of the King. And above all, if they failed
c [illegible] which they possessed, they had numbers of places
t [illegible] would find cities and lands.

[illegible] d comforting themselves in this manner, they
p [illegible] ures as actively as ever; and the ten envoys sent to
S [illegible] red, learning how matters stood while they were
st [illegible] t there.

8.77 The envoys from Athens stop at Delos.

[illegible] rose among the soldiers in the Peloponnesian fleet
at [illegible] s and Tissaphernes were ruining their cause. Asty-
o [illegible] g to fight at sea—either before, while they were
st [illegible] fleet of the Athenians small, or now, when the
e [illegible] nformed, in a state of sedition and his ships not yet
u [illegible] m waiting for the Phoenician[1b] fleet from Tissa-
p [illegible] a nominal existence, at the risk of wasting away in
i [illegible] s not only did not bring up the fleet in question,
b [illegible] y by payments made irregularly, and even then not
m [illegible] herefore delay no longer, they insisted, but fight a
d [illegible] t. The Syracusans were the most urgent of all.

8.78 411 21st Year/Summer MILETUS The Peloponnesian sailors accuse Astyochus and Tissaphernes of ruining the fleet by refusing battle and by irregular and insufficient pay. They demand a decisive battle.

[illegible] us, aware of these murmurs, had already decided in
c [illegible] battle; and when the news reached them of the dis-
t [illegible] out to sea with all their ships, one hundred and ten
i [illegible] the Milesians to move by land to Mycale,[1a] set sail
f [illegible] henians with the eighty-two ships from Samos were
a [illegible] Glauce in Mycale,[2a] a point where Samos approaches
r [illegible] nd seeing the Peloponnesian fleet sailing against

8.79 411 21st Year/Summer MILETUS-SAMOS The Peloponnesian fleet sails to Samos seeking battle, but when they learn that Athenian reinforcements have arrived from the Hellespont, they retire to Miletus and refuse to engage the Athenians.

8 [illegible]
8 [illegible] patch of these [illegible] 8.72.
8 [illegible]

8.78.1b Phoenicia: Map 8.84, locator.
8.79.1a Mount Mycale: Map 8.75.
8.79.2a Glauce in Mycale: exact location unknown.

them, retired into Samos, not thinking themselves numerically strong enough to stake their all upon a battle. [3] Besides, they had intelligence from Miletus that the enemy wished to engage, and were expecting to be joined from the Hellespont[3a] by Strombichides (to whom a messenger had been already dispatched), with the ships that had gone from Chios[3b] to Abydos.[3c] [4] The Athenians accordingly withdrew to Samos, and the Peloponnesians put in at Mycale, and encamped with the land forces of the Milesians and the people of the neighborhood. [5] The next day they were about to sail against Samos when news reached them of the arrival of Strombichides with the squadron from the Hellespont, whereupon they immediately sailed back to Miletus. [6] The Athenians, thus reinforced, now in their turn sailed against Miletus with a hundred and eight ships, wishing to fight a decisive battle, but as no one put out to meet them, sailed back to Samos.

8.80
411
21st Year/Summer
HELLESPONT
The Peloponnesians send forty triremes to the Hellespont to Pharnabazus who had offered them pay, but a storm scatters the fleet and only ten arrive there. These incite Byzantium to revolt, which forces the Athenians to send a squadron north from Samos.

In the same summer, immediately after this, the Peloponnesians having refused to fight with their fleet united, through not thinking themselves a match for the enemy, and not knowing where to look for money for such a number of ships, especially as Tissaphernes proved so bad a paymaster, sent off Clearchus son of Ramphias with forty ships to Pharnabazus,[1a] in accordance with their original instructions from the Peloponnesus;[2a] [2] for Pharnabazus invited them and was prepared to furnish pay, and in addition Byzantium[2a] sent offers to revolt to them. [3] These Peloponnesian ships accordingly put out into the open sea, in order to escape the observation of the Athenians, and being overtaken by a storm, the majority with Clearchus put into Delos,[3a] and afterwards returned to Miletus,[3b] from which Clearchus proceeded by land to the Hellespont to take the command: ten of the ships, however, under the Megarian[3c] Helixus, made good their passage to the Hellespont, and brought about the revolt of Byzantium. [4] After this, the commanders at Samos[4a] were informed of it and sent a squadron against them to guard the Hellespont, and an encounter took place before Byzantium between eight vessels on either side.

8.81
411
21st Year/Summer
SAMOS
Thrasybulus persuades the Athenians on Samos to recall Alcibiades in order to win the friendship of Tissaphernes, their only hope for defeating Sparta. Alcibiades arrives and makes extravagant promises as to what he can accomplish for them with Tissaphernes if Athens only will reinstate him.

Meanwhile the leaders at Samos, and especially Thrasybulus, who from the moment that he had changed the government had remained firmly resolved to recall Alcibiades, at last in an assembly brought over the mass of the soldiery, and upon their voting for his recall and amnesty, sailed over to Tissaphernes and brought Alcibiades to Samos, being convinced that their only chance of salvation lay in his bringing over Tissaphernes from the Peloponnesians to themselves. [2] An assembly was then held in

8.79.3a Hellespont: Map 8.84, AY.
8.79.3b Chios: Map 8.84, BX.
8.79.3c Abydos: Map 8.84, AY. For Strombichides' triremes and mission from Chios to Abydos, see 8.62.2.
8.80.1a Pharnabazus was the Persian governor (satrap) of the Hellespont region (Map 8.84, AY). See Appendix E, The Persians, §2, 7.
8.80.2a The plan and instructions to send forces to Pharnabazus in the Hellespont after operations were begun in Chios and Lesbos was mentioned in 8.8.2 and 8.39.2.
8.80.2a Byzantium: Map 8.84, AY.
8.80.3a Delos: Map 8.84, BX.
8.80.3b Miletus: Map 8.84, BY.
8.80.3c Megara: Map 8.84, BX.
8.80.4a Samos: Map 8.84, BY.

w[illegible]ined of and deplored his private misfortune in
h[illegible]nd speaking at great length upon public affairs,
hi[illegible]s for the future, and extravagantly magnified his
o[illegible]phernes. His purpose in this was to make the oli-
g[illegible]thens afraid of him, to hasten the dissolution of
th[illegible]s influence with the army at Samos and heighten
th[illegible]nd lastly to prejudice the enemy as strongly as
p[illegible]ernes, and blast the hopes which they enter-
ta[illegible]cordingly held out to the army such extravagant
p[illegible]g: that Tissaphernes had solemnly assured him
th[illegible]t the Athenians they should never want for sup-
p[illegible]ng left, no, not even if he should have to coin his
o[illegible]at he would bring the Phoenician[3a] fleet now at
A[illegible]ans instead of to the Peloponnesians; but that he
c[illegible]enians if Alcibiades were recalled to be his secu-
ri[illegible]

[illegible]nd much more besides, the Athenians at once
el[illegible]her with the former ones, and put all their affairs
in[illegible]as now not a man in the army who would have
e[illegible]pes of safety and vengeance upon the Four Hun-
d[illegible]on whatever; and after what they had been told
th[illegible]o disdain the enemy before them, and to sail at
o[illegible]2] To the plan of sailing for the Piraeus, leaving
th[illegible]emies behind them, Alcibiades opposed the most
p[illegible]of the numbers that insisted upon it, saying that
n[illegible]lected general he would first sail to Tissaphernes
a[illegible]measures for carrying on the war. [3] Accordingly,
u[illegible]ly, he immediately took his departure in order to
h[illegible]re was a complete trust between them, and also
w[illegible]nding with Tissaphernes, and to show that he had
n[illegible]l and was in a position to do him good or evil as
h[illegible] to frighten the Athenians with Tissaphernes and
T[illegible]henians.

8.82
411
21st Year/Summer
SAMOS
The Athenian troops elect Alcibiades general. He insists on first consulting with Tissaphernes. Thucydides describes Alcibiades' policy as one of bluff and bluster to both the Athenians and Tissaphernes.

[illegible]ponnesians at Miletus[1a] heard of the recall of
A[illegible]eady distrustful of Tissaphernes, now became far
m[illegible]n than ever. [2] Indeed after their refusal to go
o[illegible]e Athenians when they appeared before Miletus,
T[illegible]n slacker than ever in his payments; and even

8.83
411
21st Year/Summer
MILETUS
After the Athenians recall Alcibiades, the Peloponnesians revile Tissaphernes and Astyochus all the more. They fear their sailors will desert unless they receive supplies or fight a decisive battle.

8[illegible] clubs, see note [illegible]
8[illegible]tor.
8[illegible]
8[illegible]
8[illegible]

before this, on account of Alcibiades, his unpopularity had been on the increase. [3] Gathering together, just as before, the soldiers and some persons of importance besides the soldiers began to reckon up how they had never yet received their pay in full; that what they did receive was small in quantity, and even that had been paid irregularly, and that unless they fought a decisive battle or moved away to some station where they could get supplies, the ships' crews would desert; and that it was all the fault of Astyochus, who humored Tissaphernes for his own private advantage.

8.84
411
21st Year/Summer
MILETUS
Sailors from Syracuse and Thurii demand their pay from Astyochus and attack him when he responds harshly, but he escapes to an altar. A Persian fort at Miletus is taken by the Milesians, with the approval of many Peloponnesians, but not of the Spartan Lichas.

The army was engaged in these reflections when the following disturbance took place about the person of Astyochus. [2] Most of the Syracusan and Thurian[2a] sailors were free men, and these the freest crews in the armament were likewise the boldest in setting upon Astyochus and demanding their pay. The latter answered somewhat stiffly and threatened them, and when Dorieus spoke up for his own sailors even went so far as to lift his baton against him; [3] upon seeing which the mass of the men, in sailor fashion, rushed in a fury to strike Astyochus. He, however, saw them in time and fled for refuge to an altar;[3a] and they were thus parted without his being struck. [4] Meanwhile the fort built by Tissaphernes in Miletus was surprised and taken by the Milesians, and the garrison in it expelled—an act which met with the approval of the rest of the allies, and in particular of the Syracusans, [5] but which found no favor with Lichas, who said moreover that the Milesians and others in the King's realm ought to show a reasonable submission to Tissaphernes and to pay him court until the war should be happily settled. The Milesians were angry with him for this and for other things of the kind, and upon his afterwards dying of sickness, would not allow him to be buried where the Spartans with the army desired.

8.85
411
21st Year/Summer
MILETUS
Mindarus, sent by the Spartans to take command of the fleet, arrives at Miletus. Astyochus, Hermocrates, and envoys of both Miletus and Tissaphernes all sail to Sparta to accuse each other.
SAMOS
Alcibiades returns to Samos.

The discontent of the army with Astyochus and Tissaphernes had reached this pitch when Mindarus arrived from Sparta to succeed Astyochus as admiral, and assumed the command. Astyochus now set sail for home; [2] and Tissaphernes sent with him one of his confidants, Gaulites, a Carian,[2a] who spoke the two languages, to complain about the Milesians for the affair of the fort, and at the same time to defend himself against the Milesians, who were, as he was aware, on their way to Sparta chiefly to denounce his conduct and had with them Hermocrates, who was to accuse Tissaphernes of joining with Alcibiades to ruin the Peloponnesian cause and of playing a double game. [3] Indeed Hermocrates had always been at enmity with him about the pay not being restored in full; and eventually when he was banished from Syracuse,

8.84.2a Syracuse, Sicily, and Thurii, Italy: Map 8.91. If *most* were free men, then *some* were not; see Appendix G, Trireme Warfare, §12.

8.84.3a It would have been sacrilege to harm someone who had taken refuge at an altar; see also the "curse of the goddess," 1.126.10–11; the supplication of the Mytilenians, 3.28.2; the excesses of the Corcyraean revolution, 3.81.5; and the flight of Thrasyllus, 5.60.6.

8.85.2a Caria: Map 8.84, BY.

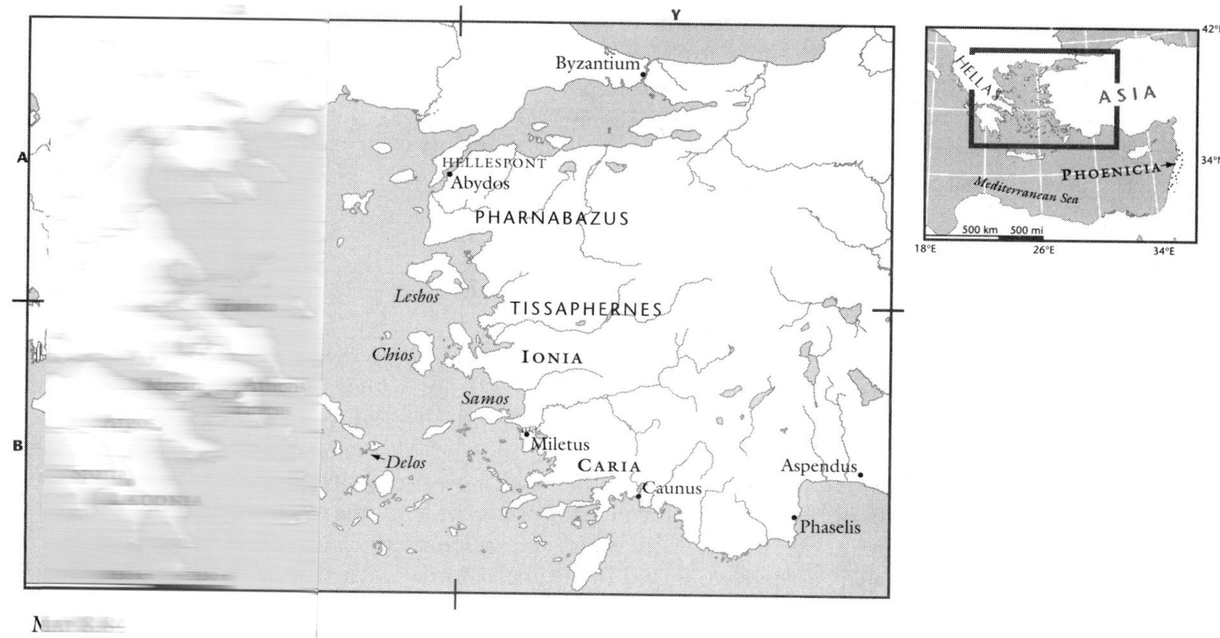

M...
A..., AND PERSIAN POLITICAL AND MILITARY MANEUVERS

...otamis, Myscon, and Demarchus, had come out to ...e Syracusans, Tissaphernes pressed harder than ever ...nd among other charges against him accused him of ...or money, and then pronounced himself his enemy ...n it.

...nd the Milesians and Hermocrates sailed for Sparta, ...ed back from Tissaphernes to Samos.[4a]

8.86 411 21st Year/Summer SAMOS Envoys from the Athenian oligarchs are received with anger and suspicion at Samos. Alcibiades serves Athens well by preventing the fleet from sailing to Piraeus, which would have abandoned Ionia and the Hellespont to the enemy. Alcibiades talks of reconciliation. Argive envoys arrive and promise support for democracy.

...nvoys of the Four Hundred who had been sent, as ...ove, to pacify and explain matters to the forces at ...elos;[1a] and an assembly was held in which they ...The soldiers at first would not hear them, and cried ...subverters of the democracy, but at last, after some ...and gave them a hearing. [3] Upon this the envoys

... from Syracuse ...o prominently in ...el with Tissa-...29. Except for ...cydides does not ...hment by the

8.85.4a Samos: Map 8.84, BY.

8.86.1a Delos: Map 8.84, BX. These ten envoys, whose dispatch was described in 8.72, had stopped at Delos (see 8.77.1) when they heard of the hostile reaction of the army at Samos to the Four Hundred's overthrow of the democracy at Athens.

proceeded to inform them that the recent change had been made to save the city, and not to ruin it or to deliver it over to the enemy, for they had already had an opportunity of doing this when he invaded the country during their government;[3a] that all the Five Thousand would have their proper share in the government; and that their hearers' relatives had neither outrage, as Chaereas had slanderously reported,[3b] nor other ill treatment to complain of, but were all in undisturbed enjoyment of their property just as they had left them. [4] Besides these they made a number of other statements which had no better success with their angry audience; and amid a host of different opinions the one which found most favor was that of sailing to the Piraeus.[4a] Now it was that Alcibiades for the first time did the state a service, and one of the most outstanding kind. For when the Athenians at Samos were bent upon sailing against their countrymen, in which case Ionia and the Hellespont would most certainly at once have passed into possession of the enemy, Alcibiades it was who prevented them. [5] At that moment, when no other man would have been able to hold back the multitude, he put a stop to the intended expedition, and rebuked and turned aside the resentment felt, on personal grounds, against the envoys; [6] he dismissed them with an answer from himself, to the effect that he did not object to the government of the Five Thousand, but insisted that the Four Hundred should be deposed and the Council of Five Hundred reinstated in power: meanwhile any retrenchments for economy, by which pay might be better found for military forces, met with his complete approval. [7] Generally, he told them to hold out and show a bold face to the enemy, since if the city was saved there was good hope that the two parties might some day be reconciled, whereas if either were once destroyed, that at Samos, or that at Athens, there would no longer be anyone to be reconciled to. [8] Meanwhile envoys arrived from the Argives,[8a] with offers of support to the Athenian democrats at Samos: these were thanked by Alcibiades, and dismissed with a request to come when called upon. [9] The Argives were accompanied by the crew of the *Paralus,* who had been placed in a troopship by the Four Hundred with orders to cruise round Euboea,[9a] and who when they were being employed to carry to Sparta some Athenian envoys sent by the Four Hundred—Laespodias, Aristophon, and Melesias—laid hands upon these envoys as they sailed by Argos, and delivering them over to the Argives as the chief subverters of the democracy; themselves, instead of returning to Athens, took the Argive envoys on board and came to Samos in the trireme which had been confided to them.

8.86.3a The recent invasion by forces under Agis: see 8.71.1–3.
8.86.3b Chaereas' reports were described in 8.74.3.
8.86.4a Piraeus: Map 8.84, BX.
8.86.8a Argos: Map 8.84, BX.
8.86.9a Euboea: Map 8.84, BX. See 8.74.2 for the previous mention of the crew of the *Paralus.*

8.87
411
21st Year/Summer
ASPENDUS
Tissaphernes goes to Aspendus ostensibly to bring on the Phoenician fleet. Thucydides reports that 147 Phoenician triremes definitely were at Aspendus, and that Tissaphernes did go there. Since the intervention of that force on either side would have been decisive, Tissaphernes was still following the policy of wearing out both sides, because he did not bring the fleet to the region and his explanation why was not credible.

e time that the return of Alcibiades coupled with
th saphernes had carried to its height the discontent
of o no longer entertained any doubt of his having
joi saphernes wishing, it would seem, to clear himsel ges, prepared to go to the Phoenician[1a] fleet at
As Lichas to go with him; saying that he would
ap enant to provide pay for the fleet during his own
ab er, and it is not easy to ascertain with what inten-
tic and did not bring the fleet after all. [3] That one
hu Phoenician ships came as far as Aspendus is cer-
ta t come further has been variously accounted for.
Sc way in pursuance of his plan of wasting the Pelo-
pc at any rate Tamos, his lieutenant, far from being
ar e paymaster than himself; others believe that he
br o Aspendus to exact money from them for their
di tended to employ them; others again think that it
w against him at Sparta, in order that it might be
sa lt, but that the ships were really manned and that
h fetch them. [4] To myself it seems only too evi-
d g up the fleet because he wished to wear out and
p es, that is, to waste their strength by the time lost
d endus, and to keep them evenly balanced by not
th either scale. Had he wished to finish the war, he
c ming of course that he made his appearance in a
w or doubt; as by bringing up the fleet he would in
al the victory to the Spartans, whose navy, even as it
w nore as an equal than as an inferior. [5] But what
c is the excuse which he put forward for not bring-
in at the number assembled was less than the King
h t would only have enhanced his credit if he spent
li y and accomplished the same end at less cost. [6]
I intention, Tissaphernes went to Aspendus and saw
t Peloponnesians at his request sent a Spartan called
F o bring the fleet.[6a]

8.88
411
21st Year/Summer
ASPENDUS
Alcibiades sails to Aspendus, promising to obtain favors from Tissaphernes for the Athenians at Samos.

vered that Tissaphernes had gone to Aspendus, he
s thirteen ships, promising to do a great and certain
s at Samos, as he would either bring the Phoenician
f or at all events prevent its joining the Pelopon-
n ty he had long known that Tissaphernes never

8 ator.
8
8 ponnesian fleet

meant to bring the fleet at all, and wished to compromise him as much as possible in the eyes of the Peloponnesians through his apparent friendship for himself and the Athenians, and thus in a manner to oblige him to join their side.

While Alcibiades weighed anchor and sailed eastward straight for Phaselis[1a] and Caunus,[1b] [8.89.1] the envoys sent by the Four Hundred to Samos[1a] arrived at Athens. Upon their delivering the message from Alcibiades, telling them to hold out and to show a firm front to the enemy, and saying that he had great hopes of reconciling them with the army and of overcoming the Peloponnesians, the majority of the members of the oligarchy, who were already discontented and only too much inclined to be quit of the business in any safe way that they could, were at once greatly strengthened in their resolve. [2] These now banded together and strongly criticized the administration, their leaders being some of the principal generals and men in office under the oligarchy, such as Theramenes son of Hagnon, Aristocrates son of Scellias, and others; who, although among the most prominent members of the government were afraid, as they said, of the army at Samos, and especially of Alcibiades, and also feared that the envoys whom they had sent to Sparta might do the state some harm without the authority of the majority. And so without insisting on their objections to the excessive concentration of power in a few hands, they nevertheless urged that the Five Thousand must be shown to exist not merely in name but in reality, and the constitution placed upon a fairer basis. [3] But this was merely their political cry; most of them were driven by private ambition into the line of conduct so surely fatal to oligarchies that arise out of democracies. For all at once pretend to be not only equals but each the chief and master of his fellows; while under a democracy a disappointed candidate accepts his defeat more easily, because he has not the humiliation of being beaten by his equals.[3a] [4] But what most clearly encouraged the malcontents was the power of Alcibiades at Samos, and their own conviction that the oligarchy was unstable; and that it was now a race among them as to who should first become the leader of The People.

8.89
411
21st Year/Summer
ATHENS
The oligarchy's envoys return from Samos and deliver Alcibiades' message. This leads discontented oligarchs, many now frightened of the army, to criticize the government. Now believing that the oligarchy would not last, they were maneuvering to establish themselves as leaders of The People.

Meanwhile the leaders and members of the Four Hundred most opposed to a democratic form of government—Phrynichus who had had the quarrel with Alcibiades during his command at Samos, Aristarchus the bitter and inveterate enemy of the democracy, and Pisander and Antiphon and others who were very powerful, and who already as soon as they entered upon power, and again when the army at Samos seceded from them and declared for a democracy, had sent envoys from their own body

8.90
411
21st Year/Summer
ATHENS
Alarmed by the antagonism of the army and of some in their own party, the oligarchs send a new delegation to Sparta with instructions to make peace on any tolerable terms. They also push forward work on the wall in Eetionia at the Piraeus, which would permit them to control the port, both to keep the fleet from Samos out and to permit an enemy fleet to enter.

8.88.1a Phaselis: Map 8.84, BY.
8.88.1b Caunus: Map 8.84, BY.
8.89.1a Samos: Map 8.91.
8.89.3a Thucydides means that indiscriminate and chance selection in a democratic drawing by rabble, where everyone votes, is not a valid measure of a man's worth, so defeat can cause no humiliation.

to [illegible] effort for peace, and were building the wall in Ee[illegible]d their efforts when their envoys returned from Sa[illegible]nly The People but their own most trusted associa[illegible]m. [2] Alarmed at the state of things at Athens an[illegible]nt off in haste Antiphon and Phrynichus and ten ot[illegible] make peace with Sparta upon any terms, no matte[illegible] at all tolerable. [3] Meanwhile they pushed on m[illegible]th the wall in Eetionia. Now the meaning of this wa[illegible]menes and his supporters, was not so much to ke[illegible]nos in case of its trying to force its way into the Pi[illegible] in, at pleasure, the fleet and army of the enemy. [4[illegible]water of the Piraeus, close alongside the entrance of[illegible]ow being fortified in connection with the wall al[illegible]nd side, so that a few men placed in it might be ab[illegible]ance; the old wall on the land side and the new o[illegible]n on the side of the sea both ending in one of the tw[illegible]he narrow mouth of the harbor. [5] They also wa[illegible]ch[5a] in the Piraeus which was connected to this wa[illegible] own hands, compelling all to unload there the gr[illegible]arbor, and what they had in stock, and to take it ou[illegible] sold it.

8.91
411
21st Year/Summer
ATHENS
Theramenes opposes the works at Eetionia and accuses the oligarchs of intending to invite a Peloponnesian squadron to join them in Piraeus. Indeed, the oligarchs preferred to lose empire and freedom rather than to fall victim to a restored democracy.

[illegible]ong provoked the murmurs of Theramenes, and wh[illegible]d from Sparta without having effected any gener[illegible] affirmed that this wall was likely to prove the ru[illegible]this moment forty-two ships from the Pelopon-ne[illegible]Sicilian[2b] and Italian[2c] vessels from Locri[2d] and Ta[illegible]vited over by the Euboeans[2f] and were already an[illegible]onia[2h] preparing for the voyage to Euboea, under th[illegible]ridas son of Agesander, a Spartiate. Theramenes no[illegible]adron was destined not so much to aid Euboea as th[illegible]nia,[2i] and that unless precautions were speedily ta[illegible]urprised and lost. [3] This was no mere calumny, th[illegible]uch plan entertained by the accused. Their first w[illegible]rchy without giving up the empire; failing this to ke[illegible]and be independent; while, if this also were denied th[illegible]first victims of the restored democracy, they were re[illegible]my and make peace, give up their walls and ships, an[illegible]session of the government, if only their lives were as[illegible]

8.9[illegible] Map. 8.92.
8.9[illegible] Greek word [illegible]g. This *stoa* [illegible]rehouse suit-[illegible]e city's grain [illegible] is shown on [illegible]
8.9[illegible]
8.9[illegible]
8.91.2c Italy: Map 8.91.
8.91.2d Locri (Epyzephyrian), in Italy: Map 8.91.
8.91.2e Tarentum, in Italy: Map 8.91.
8.91.2f Euboea: Map 8.91.
8.91.2g Las, in the Peloponnesus: Map 8.91. The route of Agesandridas' voyage to Euboea is shown on Map 8.96.
8.91.2h Laconia: Map 8.84, BX.
8.91.2i Eetionia, in Piraeus: Map 8.92, inset.

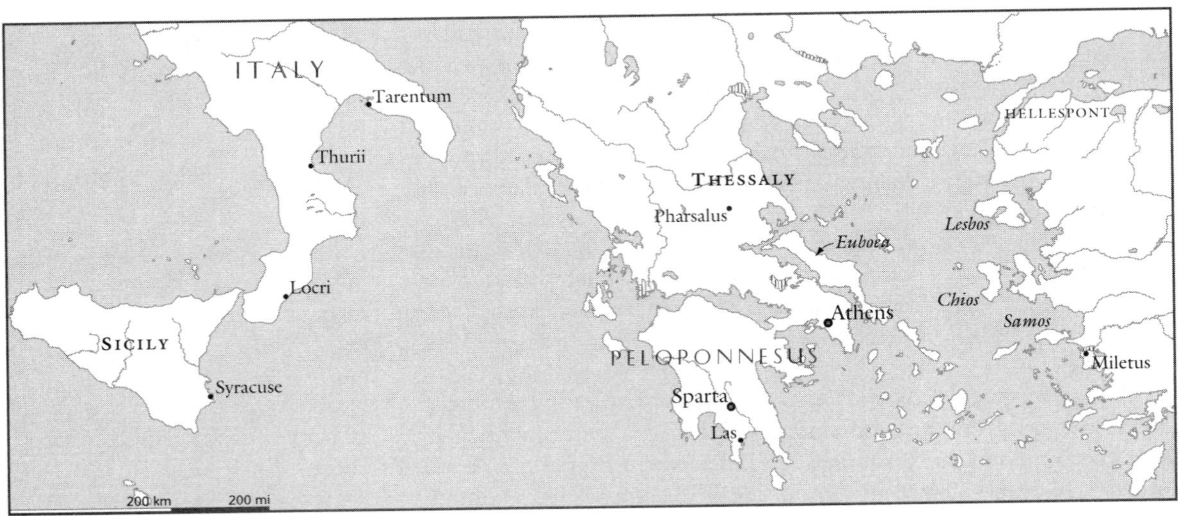

MAP 8.91 THE PELOPONNESIANS MOVE AGAINST EUBOEA

8.92
411
21st Year/Summer
ATHENS-PIRAEUS
Phrynichus is murdered. Failure to find the assassin encourages the regime's opponents, who also fear that a Spartan fleet will attack the Piraeus. When hoplites at Eetionia imprison a general, the Four Hundred send Theramenes to the Piraeus. He lets the hoplites destroy the wall. Many demand that the Five Thousand should rule, although no one knows if that body really exists.

For this reason they hastened the construction of their work with postern gates and entrances and means of introducing the enemy, being eager to have it finished in time. [2] Meanwhile the murmurs against them were at first confined to a few persons and went on in secret, until Phrynichus, after his return from the embassy to Sparta, was laid wait for and stabbed in the open market[2a] by one of the *peripoli*,[2b] and fell down dead before he had gone far from the council chamber.[2c] The assassin escaped; but his accomplice, an Argive,[2d] was taken and put to the torture by the Four Hundred, without their being able to extract from him the name of his employer, or anything further than that he knew of many men who used to assemble at the house of the commander of the *peripoli* and at other houses. Here the matter was allowed to drop. This so emboldened Theramenes and Aristocrates and the rest of their partisans in the Four Hundred and outside that body, that they now resolved to act. [3] For by this time the ships had sailed round from Las, and anchoring at Epidaurus had overrun Aegina;[3a] and Theramenes asserted that, being bound for Euboea, they would never have sailed in to Aegina and come back to anchor at Epidaurus, unless they had been invited to come to aid in the designs of which he had always accused the government.

8.92.2a Athenian market (*agora*): Map 8.92, inset, and Map 6.56, inset.

8.92.2b The *peripoli* were a special Athenian military unit, perhaps a mobile force of young recruits serving as frontier guards. They were used by Demosthenes in the surprise assault against Megara, described in 4.67.2. See note 4.67.2a.

8.92.2c Remains of this building (the council chamber, called the Bouleuterion) have been located in the Athenian *agora*, see Map 6.56, inset, and Map 8.92, inset.

8.92.2d Argos: Map 8.92.

8.92.3a Epidaurus, Aegina: Map 8.92. The route of this fleet's voyage to Euboea is shown on Map 8.96.

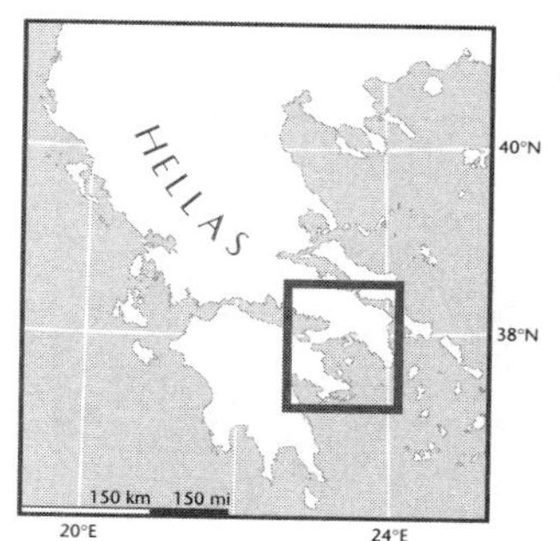

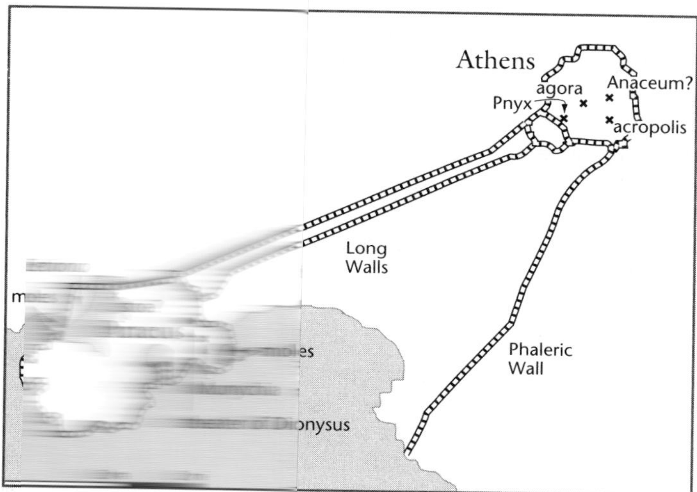

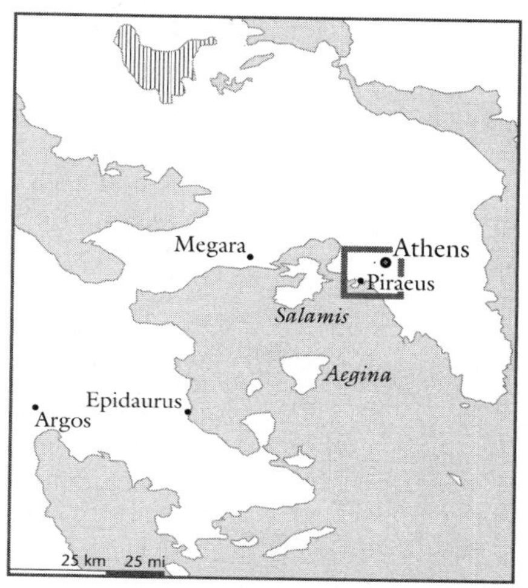

M[illegible]HE ATHENIAN OLIGARCHS

F[illegible]refore now become impossible. [4] In the end, a[illegible]ous harangues and suspicions, they set to work in r[illegible]s in the Piraeus who were building the wall in E[illegible] was Aristocrates, a commander having soldiers o[illegible] hands upon Alexicles, a general under the oli- g[illegible]herent of the cabal, and took him into a house a[illegible] [5] In this they were assisted by one Hermon, c[illegible]*oli* in Munychia,[5a] and others, and above all they h[illegible]reat bulk of the hoplites. [6] As soon as news of t[illegible]undred, who happened to be sitting in the coun-

8[illegible]2, inset.

[illegible]is map are [illegible] labeled 3. [illegible]me, A. [illegible]r, *A Historical* [illegible]*s*, v (Oxford, [illegible]

8[illegible]hought that troops of his own "tribe" would be more reliable for such work. See Appendix A, The Athenian Government, §3–5, 7, for a discussion of tribes in the Athenian constitution.

8.92.5a Munychia, a hill in the Piraeus: Map 8.92, inset.

cil chamber, all except the disaffected wished at once to go to the posts where the arms were and threatened Theramenes and his party. Theramenes defended himself, and said that he was ready immediately to go and help to rescue Alexicles; and taking with him one of the generals belonging to his party, went down to the Piraeus, followed by Aristarchus and some young men of the cavalry. [7] All was now panic and confusion. Those in the city imagined that the Piraeus was already taken and the prisoner put to death, while those in the Piraeus expected at every moment to be attacked by the party in the city. [8] The older men, however, stopped the persons running up and down the city and making for the stands of arms; and Thucydides the Pharsalian, *proxenus* of the city,[8a] came forward and threw himself between the rival factions, and appealed to them not to ruin the state while the enemy was still nearby waiting for his opportunity, and so at length succeeded in quieting them and in keeping them from attacking each other. [9] Meanwhile Theramenes came down to the Piraeus, being himself one of the generals, and raged and stormed against the hoplites, while Aristarchus and the opponents of The People were genuinely infuriated. [10] Most of the hoplites, however, went on with the business without faltering, and asked Theramenes if he thought the wall had been constructed for any good purpose, and whether it would not be better that it should be pulled down. To this he answered that if they thought it best to pull it down, he for his part agreed with them. Upon this the hoplites and a number of the people in Piraeus immediately got up on the fortification and began to demolish it. [11] Now their cry to the multitude was that all should join in the work who wished the Five Thousand to govern instead of the Four Hundred. For instead of saying in so many words "all who wished The People to govern," they still disguised themselves under the name of the Five Thousand; being afraid that these might really exist, and that they might be speaking to one of their number and get into trouble through ignorance. Indeed this was why the Four Hundred neither wished the Five Thousand to exist, nor to have it known that they did not exist; being of the opinion that to give themselves so many partners in empire would be downright democracy, while the mystery in question would make the people afraid of one another.

8.92.8a Pharsalus, in Thessaly: Map 8.91. A *proxenus* was the representative of a foreign state (much like a modern honorary consul) in another state of which he was a resident and citizen. This Thucydides was a citizen and resident of Pharsalia, who was the *proxenus* of Athens at Pharsalia, and happened to be in Athens during these events.

8.93
411
21st Year/Summer
ATHENS-PIRAEUS
While the oligarchs meet in Athens, the hoplites assemble in the Piraeus and march to Athens. They are met by envoys from the oligarchs who beg them to be calm and not to betray the city to its enemies. The hoplites agree to the convening of a new assembly to restore concord.

… Hundred, although alarmed, nevertheless assemble… …er[1a] while the hoplites in the Piraeus,[1b] after having… …r Alexicles and pulled down the fortification,
we… … the theater of Dionysus[1c] close to Munychia.
Th… …ly in which they decided to march into the city,
an… …gly halted in the Anaceum.[1d] [2] Here they were
joi… … from the Four Hundred, who reasoned with
the… …ersuaded those whom they saw to be the most
mo… … themselves, and to restrain the rest; saying that
the… …he Five Thousand, and have the Four Hundred
ch… …ion, as should be decided by the Five Thousand,
an… … them not to ruin the state or drive it into the
ar… …ter a great many had spoken and had been spoke… …f hoplites became calmer than before, absorbed
by… …ntry at large, and now agreed to hold upon an
ap… … in the theater of Dionysus for the restoration of
co…

8.94
411
21st Year/Summer
ATHENS-PIRAEUS
As the Athenians assemble, word arrives that a Spartan fleet is approaching the Piraeus from Megara. All hasten to the port to launch the remaining ships and man its defenses.

… the assembly in the theater, and they were upon
th… …ews arrived that the forty-two ships under Age-
sa… … Megara along the coast of Salamis.[1a] The people
to… …t it was just what Theramenes and his party had
so… …s were sailing to the fortification, and concluded
th… … demolish it. [2] But though it may possibly have
be… … Agesandridas hovered about Epidaurus[2a] and the
ne… … also naturally be kept there by the hope of an
op… … the troubles in the city. [3] In any case the Atheni… …ws, immediately ran down in mass to the Piraeus,
se… …ed by the enemy with a worse war than their war
an… … a distance, but close to the harbor of Athens.
So… … ships already afloat, while others launched fresh
ve… …e walls and the mouth of the harbor.

8.95
411
21st Year/Summer
EUBOEA
The Spartan fleet sails to Euboea, forcing Athens to send ships to protect that island. A battle takes place off Eretria in which the Spartans, aided secretly by the Eretrians, surprise the Athenians and gain a great victory. All Euboea, except for Oreus, which was settled by the Athenians, revolts from Athens.

… …nnesian vessels sailed by, and rounding Sunium
an… …us and Prasiae,[1a] and afterwards arrived at Oro-
pu… … with revolution in the city, and unwilling to lose
a … …e relief of their most important possession (for

8.9… …e note

8.9…

8.9… …iraeus: Map

8.9… … Dioscuri, in …ap 8.92,

8.94.1a Megara, Salamis: Map 8.96, BX. The voyage of Agesandridas' fleet to Euboea is shown in Map 8.96.

8.94.2a Epidaurus: Map 8.96, BX.

8.95.1a Cape Sunium, Thoricus, and Prasiae, in Attica: Map 8.96, BY.

8.95.1b Oropus: Map 8.96, AY.

Euboea[2a] was everything to them now that they were shut out from Attica), were compelled to put to sea in haste and with untrained crews, and sent Thymochares with some vessels to Eretria.[2b] [3] These upon their arrival, with the ships already in Euboea, made up a total of thirty-six vessels, and were immediately forced to engage. For Agesandridas, after his crews had taken their dinner, put out from Oropus, which is about seven miles[3a] from Eretria by sea; [4] and the Athenians, seeing him sailing up, immediately began to man their vessels. The sailors, however, instead of being by their ships, as they supposed, were gone away to purchase provisions[4a] for their dinner in the houses in the outskirts of the city; the Eretrians having so arranged that there should be nothing on sale in the *agora*,[4b] in order that the Athenians might be a long time in manning their ships, and the enemy's attack taking them by surprise, might compel them to put to sea just as they were. A signal also was raised in Eretria to give them notice in Oropus when to put to sea.[4c] [5] The Athenians, forced to put out so poorly prepared, engaged off the harbor of Eretria, and after holding their own for some little while notwithstanding, were at length put to flight and chased to the shore. [6] Such of their number as took refuge in Eretria, which they presumed to be friendly to them, found their fate in that city, being butchered by the inhabitants; while those who fled to the Athenian fort in the Eretrian territory, and the vessels which got to Chalcis,[6a] were saved. [7] The Peloponnesians, after taking twenty-two Athenian ships, and killing or making prisoners of the crews, set up a trophy, and not long afterwards effected the revolt of the whole of Euboea (except Oreus,[7a] which was held by the Athenians themselves) and made a general settlement of the affairs of the island.

8.96
411
21st Year/Summer
ATHENS
The loss of Euboea promotes panic at Athens. If the enemy besieges the Piraeus, the fleet from Samos would have to defend the city, exposing the rest of the empire. Thucydides notes that the Spartans were characteristically too slow to grasp or exploit this opportunity.

When the news of what had happened in Euboea reached Athens a panic ensued such as they had never before known. Neither the disaster in Sicily, great as it seemed at the time, nor any other, had ever so much alarmed them. [2] The fleet at Samos[2a] was in revolt; they had no more ships or men to man them; they were in conflict among themselves and might at any moment come to blows; and a disaster of this magnitude coming on top of everything else, by which they lost their fleet, and worst of all Euboea, which was of more value to them than Attica, could not occur without throwing them into the deepest despondency. [3] Meanwhile their greatest and most immediate trouble was the possibility that the enemy, emboldened by his victory, might make straight for them and sail

8.95.2a Euboea: Map 8.96, AY. For Euboea as a major source of supplies for Athens, see 7.28.1.
8.95.2b Eretria: Map 8.96, AY.
8.95.3a Thucydides writes "sixty stades"; the Attic stade was 607 feet long, the Olympic stade was 630.8 feet.
8.95.4a Greek soldiers and sailors at this time were expected to purchase their food from local markets with their own money. Triremes had no room or facilities for preparing food and had to put in to shore to feed the crew; see Appendix G, Trireme Warfare, §7.
8.95.4b The *agora* was a classical city's principal marketplace.
8.95.4c Boeotian plotting to take Euboea was mentioned in 8.60.1.
8.95.6a Chalcis: Map 8.96, AY.
8.95.7a Oreus is another name for Histiaea, in Euboea (Map 8.96, AY), and is so represented in the army in Sicily (7.57.2). Thucydides does not explain this, but perhaps the Athenians changed the name when they replaced the original inhabitants with their own colonists in 446 (1.116.3).
8.96.2a Samos: Map 8.96, locator.

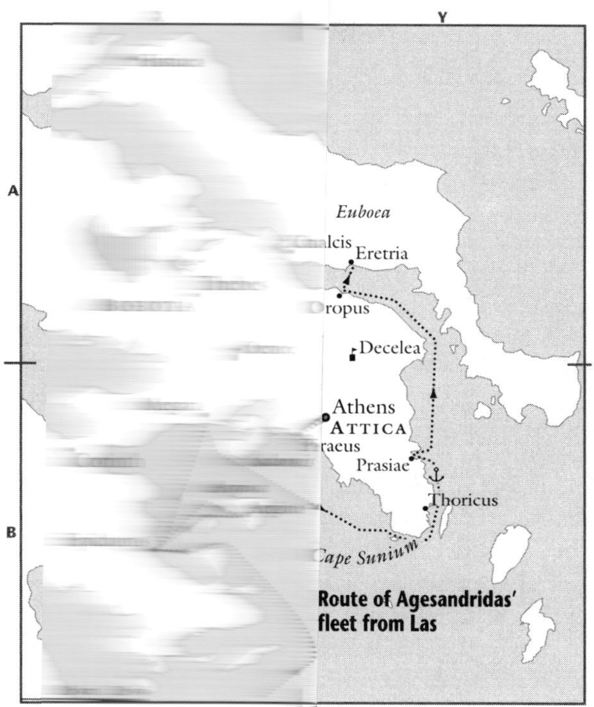

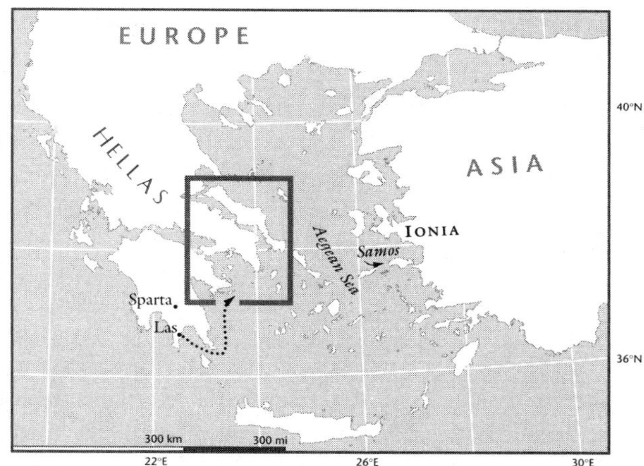

...VICTORY AT EUBOEA

...ch they no longer had ships to defend; and every ...he enemy to arrive. [4] This, with a little more ... have done, in which case he would either have ... of the city by his presence, or if he had stayed to ...d the fleet from Ionia,[4a] although opposed to the ... rescue of their country and of their relatives, and ...my would have become master of the Hellespont,[4b] ... everything as far as Euboea, or, to speak roundly, ...empire. [5] But here, as on so many other occasions, ...d the most convenient people in the world for the ...with. The wide difference between the two charac-...ant of energy of the Spartans as contrasted with the ...eir opponents, proved of the greatest service, espe-...re like Athens. Indeed this was shown by the Syra-... like the Athenians in character, and also most ...them.

8.96.4b Hellespont: Map 8.100, AY.

8.97
411
21st Year/Summer
ATHENS
The Athenians react to the Euboea disaster by deposing the oligarchy, installing a new regime of the Five Thousand, and enacting reforms. They also recall Alcibiades and other exiles and urge the army at Samos to vigorously carry on the war.

Nevertheless, upon receipt of the news, the Athenians manned twenty ships and immediately called a first assembly in the Pnyx,[1a] where they had been accustomed to meet formerly, and deposed the Four Hundred and voted to hand over the government to the Five Thousand, of which body all who furnished a suit of armor were to be members, decreeing also that no one should receive pay for the discharge of any office, [2] or if he did should be held accursed. Many other assemblies were held afterwards, in which lawmakers were elected and all other measures taken to form a constitution. It was during the first period of this constitution that the Athenians appear to have enjoyed the best government that they ever did, at least in my time.[2a] For the fusion of the high and the low was accomplished with judgment, and this was what first enabled the state to raise up her head after her manifold disasters. [3] They also voted for the recall of Alcibiades and of other exiles,[3a] and sent to him and to the camp at Samos, and urged them to devote themselves vigorously to the war.

8.98
411
21st Year/Summer
ATHENS
The chief oligarchs flee to the enemy at Decelea. Aristarchus, one of their generals, tricks the garrison of the Athenian fort at Oenoe into evacuating the fort, which is then occupied by the Boeotians.

Upon this revolution taking place, the party of Pisander and Alexicles and the chiefs of the oligarchs immediately withdrew to Decelea,[1a] with the single exception of Aristarchus, one of the generals, who hastily took some of the most barbarian of the archers and marched to Oenoe.[1b] [2] This was a fort of the Athenians upon the Boeotian[2a] border, at that moment besieged by the Corinthians[2b] who were responding to the loss of a party returning from Decelea, who had been cut off by the garrison. The Corinthians had volunteered for this service, and had called upon the Boeotians to assist them. [3] After communicating with them, Aristarchus deceived the garrison in Oenoe by telling them that their countrymen in the city had settled with the Spartans, and that one of the terms of the capitulation was that they must surrender the place to the Boeotians. The garrison believed him as he was general, and besides knew nothing of what had occurred owing to the siege, and so evacuated the fort under truce. [4] In this way the Boeotians gained possession of Oenoe, and the oligarchy and the troubles at Athens ended.

8.99
411
21st Year/Summer
MILETUS
Since the Peloponnesian fleet received no pay from Tissaphernes, who also did not bring up, as promised, the Phoenician fleet, Mindarus decides to take his fleet to Pharnabazus (who promised financial support) and, after diversion by a storm, arrives at Chios.

To return to the Peloponnesians in Miletus.[1a] No pay was forthcoming from any of the agents appointed by Tissaphernes for that purpose upon his departure for Aspendus;[1b] neither the Phoenician fleet nor Tissaphernes showed any signs of appearing; and Philip, who had been sent with him, and another Spartiate, Hippocrates, who was at Phaselis,[1c] sent word to Mindarus the admiral that the ships were not coming at all, and that they

8.97.1a The Pnyx, the traditional site for meetings of the assembly in Athens: Map 6.56, inset, and Map 8.92, inset.
8.97.2a The following alternative translation is more commonly accepted. "And in no little measure the Athenians for the first time, at least in my lifetime, appear to have enjoyed good government."
8.97.3a They recalled other exiles but not, presumably, Thucydides the author.
8.98.1a Decelea: Map 8.96, AY.
8.98.1b Oenoe: Map 8.96, AX. Oenoe was unsuccessfully besieged by the Peloponnesians under Archidamus during the first invasion of Attica in 431; see 2.18.1.
8.98.2a Boeotia: Map 8.96, AX.
8.98.2b Corinth: Map 8.96, BX.
8.99.1a Miletus: Map 8.100, BY. This picks up the Peloponnesian fleet narrative from 8.87.
8.99.1b Aspendus: Map 8.100, locator.
8.99.1c Phaselis: Map 8.100, locator.

by Tissaphernes. Meanwhile Pharnabazus[1d] was
nd making every effort to get the fleet and, like
revolt of the cities in his province that were still
ng great hopes on his success; until at length, at
mmer, Mindarus yielded to his requests and, with
ment's notice, in order to elude the enemy at
with seventy-three ships from Miletus and set sail
en vessels had already preceded him there in the
errun part of the Chersonese.[1g] Being caught in a
mpelled to run in to Icarus,[1h] and after being
ere by stress of weather, arrived at Chios.[1i]

8.100
411
21st Year/Summer
LESBOS
Learning of the Spartan move, the Athenian fleet leaves Samos for the Hellespont and takes station at Methymna on Lesbos. The general Thrasyllus decides to attack Eresus, a Lesbian city that has revolted and serves now as a base for Methymnian exiles.

had heard of his having put out from Miletus,[1a]
ith fifty-five ships from Samos, hurrying to arrive
ont. [2] But learning that he was at Chios, and
ay there, he posted scouts in Lesbos[2a] and on the
ent the fleet moving without his knowing it, and
oast to Methymna,[2b] and gave orders to prepare
necessaries, in order to attack them from Lesbos
ining for any length of time at Chios. [3] Mean-
against Eresus,[3a] a city in Lesbos which had
he could. For some of the principal Methymnian
bout fifty hoplites, their sworn associates from
from the mainland so as to make up three hun-
er, a Theban,[3c] to command them, on account of
existing between the Thebans and the Lesbians,
na. Thwarted in this attempt by the advance of
Mytilene,[3d] and repulsed a second time in a bat-
hen crossed the mountain and brought about the
syllus accordingly determined to go there with all
place. Meanwhile Thrasybulus had preceded him
Samos, as soon as he heard that the exiles had
too late to save Eresus, went on and anchored
they were joined also by two vessels on their way
t, and by the ships of the Methymnians, making a
vessels; and the forces on board now made ready
very other means available to do their utmost to

n governor
egion (Map
Map 8.100,

8.100.2b Methymna, on Lesbos: Map 8.100, AX.
8.100.3a Eresus, on Lesbos: Map 8.100, AX.
8.100.3b Cyme: Map 8.100, BY.
8.100.3c Thebes: Map 8.96, AX.
8.100.3d Mytilene, on Lesbos, Map 8.100, AX.

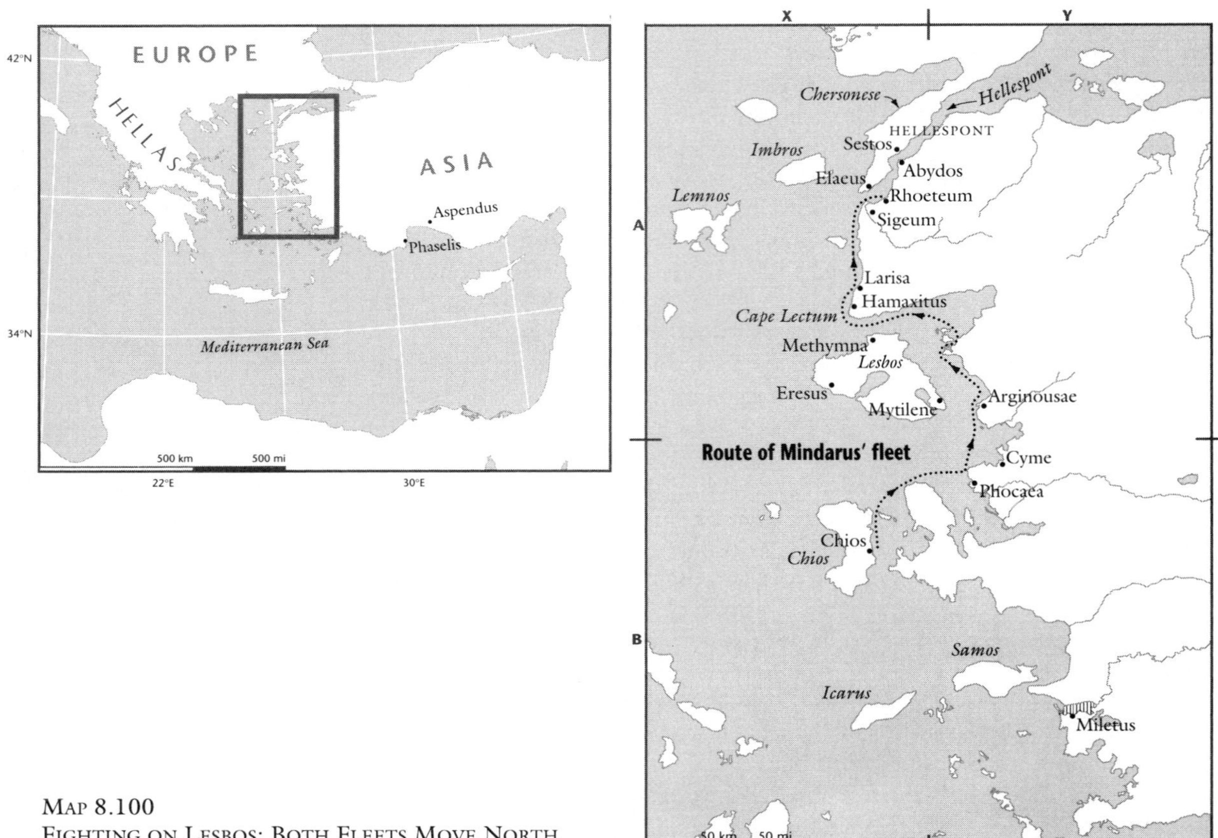

MAP 8.100
FIGHTING ON LESBOS; BOTH FLEETS MOVE NORTH

8.101
411
21st Year/Summer
LESBOS
After taking pay for its sailors from the Chians, the Peloponnesian fleet leaves Chios for Lesbos, sails north between Lesbos and the mainland, and arrives at the Hellespont without encountering the Athenian fleet.

In the meantime Mindarus and the Peloponnesian fleet at Chios,[1a] after taking provisions for two days and receiving three Chian pieces of money[1b] for each man from the Chians, on the third day sailed out in haste from the island; in order to avoid falling in with the ships at Eresus.[1c] They did not make for the open sea, but keeping Lesbos on their left, sailed for the mainland. [2] After touching at the port of Carteria, in the territory of

8.101.1a Chios: Map 8.100, BX.
8.101.1b Thucydides' word for these "pieces of money" is *tessarakontas,* literally, "a fortieth"; but scholars are not sure what these were "fortieths" of, or what three of them amounted to. See Appendix J, Classical Greek Currency, §3.
8.101.1c Eresus, on Lesbos: Map 8.100, AX.

Ph[illegible]ir dinner, they went on along the Cymaean[2b]
coa[illegible] Arginousae,[2c] on the mainland over against
My[illegible] they continued their voyage along the coast,
alt[illegible] night, and arriving at Harmatus[3a] on the conti-
ne[illegible] took a meal there; and swiftly passing Lectum,[3b]
La[illegible] the neighboring cities, arrived a little before
mi[illegible] Here they were now in the Hellespont.[3f] Some
of [illegible] Sigeum[3g] and at other places in the neighbor-
ho[illegible]

8.102
411
21st Year/Summer
HELLESPONT
Learning of the approach of the Spartan fleet, an Athenian squadron at Sestos attempts to flee. They are pursued, attacked, and lose four triremes off Elaeus.

[illegible]s of the fire signals and the sudden increase in the
nu[illegible]my's shore informed the eighteen Athenian ships
at [illegible] of the Peloponnesian fleet. That very night they
set [illegible]y were, and hugging the shore of the Chersonese[illegible]eus,[1c] in order to sail out into the open sea away
fro[illegible]ny. [2] After passing unobserved by the sixteen
shi[illegible]gh they had been warned by their approaching
fri[illegible]o prevent their sailing out), at dawn they sighted
th[illegible]h immediately gave chase. All had not time to get
aw[illegible]however escaped to Imbros[2b] and Lemnos,[2c] while
fo[illegible]were overtaken off Elaeus. [3] One of these was
str[illegible]ple of Protesilaus and taken with its crew, two
ot[illegible]s; the fourth was abandoned on the shore of
Im[illegible] enemy.

8.103
411
21st Year/Summer
HELLESPONT
The Athenians at Eresus finally learn of the nearby presence of the Peloponnesian fleet and leave for Elaeus, where they prepare for battle.

[illegible]nesians were joined by the squadron from Abydo[illegible]r fleet to a grand total of eighty-six vessels; they
sp[illegible]sfully besieging Elaeus,[1b] and then sailed back to
Ab[illegible]e Athenians, deceived by their scouts, and never
dr[illegible]'s fleet would go by undetected, were tranquilly
be[illegible]on as they heard the news they instantly aban-
do[illegible]ith all speed for the Hellespont, [3] and after tak-
in[illegible]sian ships which had been carried out too far into
th[illegible] of the pursuit and which now fell in their way,
dr[illegible] day at Elaeus. There they brought back the ships
th[illegible]mbros[3a] and for five days prepared for the coming
en[illegible]

8.[illegible]ory: precise [illegible]a: Map 8.100, [illegible]
8.[illegible]
8.[illegible]Y.
8.[illegible]wn.
8.[illegible] AX.
8.[illegible]
8.[illegible]X.
8.[illegible]X.
8.[illegible]Y. For the [illegible] described, see [illegible]
8.[illegible]
8.[illegible]stos was established as the Athenian naval base in the Hellespont by Strombichides in 8.62.3.
8.102.1b Chersonese (Hellespont): Map 8.100, AX, and Map 8.103, inset.
8.102.1c Elaeus: Map 8.100, AX.
8.102.2a Abydos: Map 8.100, AX. Abydos had revolted from Athens, as Thucydides writes in 8.62.1.
8.102.2b Imbros: Map 8.100, AX, and Map 8.103.
8.102.2c Lemnos: Map 8.100, AX and Map 8.103.
8.103.1a Abydos: Map 8.100, inset.
8.103.1b Elaeus: Map 8.100, inset.
8.103.2a Eresus: Map 8.100, AX.
8.103.3a Imbros: Map 8.103.

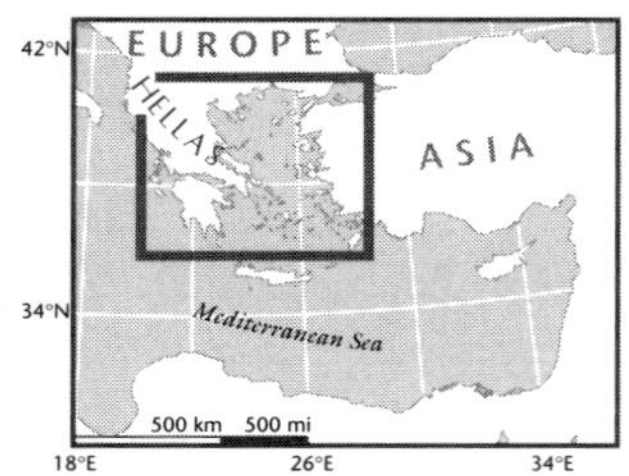

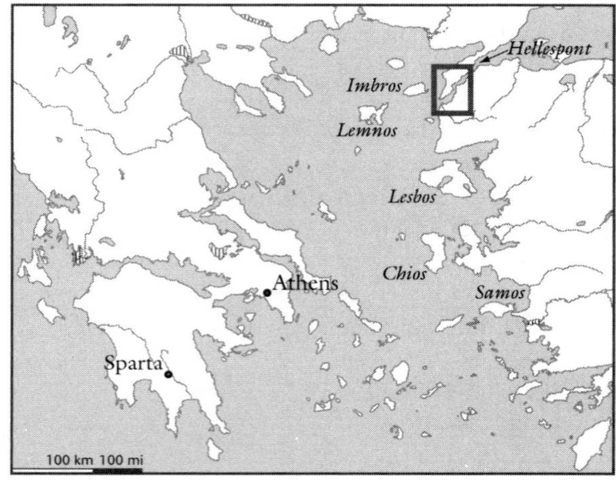

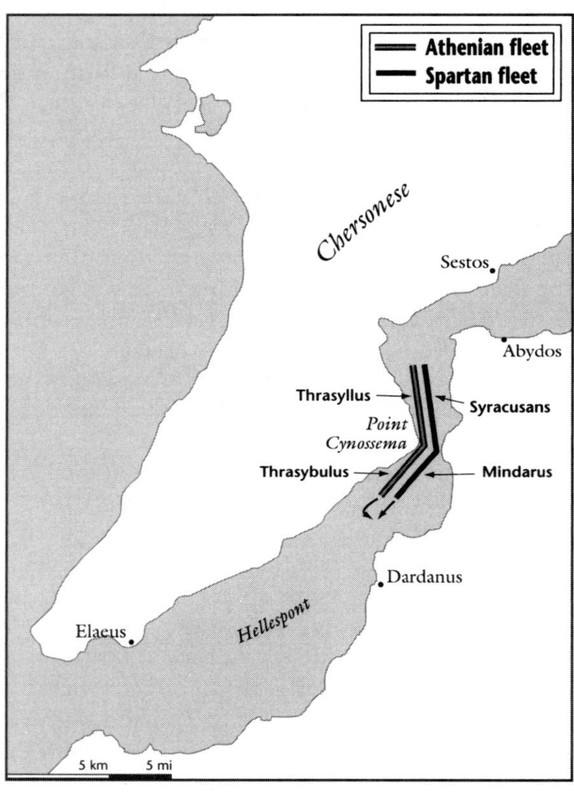

MAP 8.103
THE BATTLE IN THE HELLESPONT OFF POINT CYNOSSEMA

8.104
411
21st Year/Summer
HELLESPONT
The location, formations, and maneuvers of battle are described. The Athenian wings prevent the enemy's attempt to outflank them, but their center near Point Cynossema is thereby weakened.

After this they engaged in the following way. The Athenians formed in column and sailed close along shore to Sestos;[1a] upon perceiving which the Peloponnesians put out from Abydos to meet them. [2] Realizing that a battle was now imminent, both combatants extended their flank; the Athenians along the Chersonese[2a] from Idacus[2b] to Arrhiana[2c] with seventy-six ships; the Peloponnesians from Abydos to Dardanus[2d] with eighty-six. [3]

8.104.1a Sestos: Map 8.103, inset.
8.104.2a Chersonese (Hellespont): Map 8.103, inset.
8.104.2b Idacus: precise location unknown.
8.104.2c Arrhiana: precise location unknown.
8.104.2d Dardanus: Map 8.103, inset.

Th[illegible]ing was occupied by the Syracusans,[3a] their left
by [illegible] the best sailors in the navy; the Athenian left by
Th[illegible]hrasybulus, the other commanders being in dif-
fere[illegible]] The Peloponnesians hastened to engage first,
anc[illegible]eft the Athenian right sought to cut them off, if
pos[illegible]f the straits, and to drive their center upon the
sho[illegible] off. The Athenians perceiving their intention
ext[illegible]wing and outsailed them, [5] while their left had
by [illegible]nt of Cynossema.[5a] This, however, obliged them
to [illegible]enter, especially as they had fewer ships than the
ene[illegible]ound Point Cynossema formed a sharp angle
wh[illegible]g what was happening on the other side of it.

8.105
411
21st Year/Summer
HELLESPONT
Initial Peloponnesian victory in the center leads to disorder and then defeat when the Athenian wings attack and finally put their adversaries to flight.

[illegible] attacked their center and drove ashore the ships
of [illegible]nbarked to follow up their victory. [2] No help
co[illegible]er either by the squadron of Thrasybulus on the
rig[illegible]mber of ships attacking him, or by that of Thra-
syl[illegible]om the point of Cynossema hid what was going
on[illegible]ndered by his Syracusan and other opponents,
wh[illegible]equal to his own. At length, however, the Pelopo[illegible]nce of victory began to scatter in pursuit of the
shi[illegible]owed a considerable part of their fleet to get into
dis[illegible]s the squadron of Thrasybulus discontinued their
lat[illegible]ng about, attacked and routed the ships opposed
to [illegible]cely upon the scattered vessels of the victorious
Pe[illegible]d put most of them to flight without a blow. The
Sy[illegible] time given way before the squadron of Thrasyllus[illegible]o flight upon seeing the flight of their comrades.

8.106
411
21st Year/Summer
HELLESPONT
The completeness of the victory, although the Athenians only captured twenty-one triremes and lost fifteen of their own, restores Athenian confidence in their prowess at sea.

[illegible]plete. Most of the Peloponnesians fled for refuge
fir[illegible] and afterwards to Abydos.[1b] Only a few ships
we[illegible]enians; as owing to the narrowness of the
He[illegible]ad not far to go to be in safety. Nevertheless
no[illegible]more opportune for them than this victory. [2]
U[illegible]feared the Peloponnesian fleet, owing to a num-
be[illegible]disaster in Sicily; but they now ceased to mistrust
th[illegible]to think their enemies good for anything at sea.
[3[illegible]k from the enemy eight Chian[3a] vessels, five
C[illegible]iot,[3c] two Boeotian,[3d] one Leucadian,[3e] Spartan,
Sy[illegible]losing fifteen of their own. [4] After setting up a
tr[illegible]sema,[4a] securing the wrecks, and restoring to the
en[illegible]ice, they sent off a trireme to Athens with the
ne[illegible] The arrival of this vessel with its unhoped-for

8.1[illegible]
8.1[illegible]03, inset.
8.1[illegible]own.
8.1[illegible]
8.1[illegible], and Map [illegible]
8.1[illegible]

8.106.3b Corinth: Map 8.107, BX.
8.106.3c Ambracia: Map 8.107, AX.
8.106.3d Boeotia: Map 8.107, BX.
8.106.3e Leucas: Map 8.107, AX.
8.106.3f Pellene: Map 8.107, BX.
8.106.4a Point Cynossema: Map 8.103, inset.

good news, after the recent disasters of Euboea,[5a] and during the revolution at Athens, gave fresh courage to the Athenians, and caused them to believe that if they put their shoulders to the wheel their cause might yet prevail.

8.107
411
21st Year/Summer
HELLESPONT
The Athenians take Cyzicus and capture some triremes. The Spartans send for their squadron from Euboea.

On the fourth day after the sea fight the Athenians in Sestos[1a] having hastily refitted their ships, sailed against Cyzicus,[1b] which had revolted. Off Harpagium[1c] and Priapus[1d] they sighted at anchor the eight vessels from Byzantium,[1e] and sailing up and routing the troops on shore, took the ships, and then went on and recovered the city of Cyzicus, which was unfortified, and levied money from the citizens. [2] In the meantime the Peloponnesians sailed from Abydos[2a] to Elaeus,[2b] and recovered such of their captured triremes as were still uninjured, the rest having been burned by the Elaeusians, and sent Hippocrates and Epicles to Euboea to bring the squadron from that island.

8.108
411
21st Year/Summer
IONIA
Alcibiades returns to Samos, claiming to have prevented the Phoenician fleet from joining the enemy. He levies funds from Halicarnassus and fortifies Cos.
HELLESPONT
The Antandrians expel the Persian garrison because of Arsaces' ill treatment of the Delians.

About the same time Alcibiades returned with his thirteen ships from Caunus[1a] and Phaselis[1b] to Samos,[1c] bringing word that he had prevented the Phoenician[1d] fleet from joining the Peloponnesians, and had made Tissaphernes more friendly to the Athenians than before. [2] Alcibiades now manned nine more ships, and levied large sums of money from the Halicarnassians,[2a] and fortified Cos.[2b] After doing this and placing a governor in Cos, he sailed back to Samos, autumn being now at hand. [3] Meanwhile Tissaphernes, upon hearing that the Peloponnesian fleet had sailed from Miletus[3a] to the Hellespont,[3b] set off again back from Aspendus,[3c] and made all sail for Ionia.[3d]

[4] While the Peloponnesians were in the Hellespont, the Antandrians,[4a] a people of Aeolic[4b] extraction, conveyed by land across Mount Ida[4c] some hoplites from Abydos,[4d] and introduced them into the city; having been ill-treated by Arsaces, the Persian lieutenant of Tissaphernes. This same Arsaces had, upon pretense of a secret quarrel, invited the chief men of the Delians[4e] to undertake military service (these were Delians who had settled at Atramyttium[4f] after having been driven from their homes by the Athenians for the sake of purifying Delos);[4g] and after drawing them out from their city as his friends and allies, had laid wait for them at dinner, and surrounded them and caused them to be shot down by his soldiers. [5] This deed made the Antandrians fear that he might someday do them some mischief; and as he also laid upon them burdens too heavy for them to bear, they expelled his garrison from their citadel.

8.106.5a Euboea: Map 8.107, BX.
8.107.1a Sestos: Map 8.107, AY.
8.107.1b Cyzicus: Map 8.107, AY.
8.107.1c Harpagium: Map 8.107, AY.
8.107.1d Priapus: Map 8.107, AY.
8.107.1e Byzantium: Map 8.107, AY.
8.107.2a Abydos: Map 8.107, AY.
8.107.2b Elaeus: Map 8.107, AY.
8.108.1a Caunus: Map 8.107, BY.
8.108.1b Phaselis: Map 8.107, BY.
8.108.1c Samos: Map 8.107, BY.
8.108.1d Phoenicia: Map 8.107, locator.
8.108.2a Halicarnassus: Map 8.107, BY.
8.108.2b Cos: Map 8.107, BY.
8.108.3a Miletus: Map 8.107, BY.
8.108.3b Hellespont: Map 8.107, AY.
8.108.3c Aspendus: Map 8.107, BY.
8.108.3d Ionia: Map 8.107, BY.
8.108.4a Antandrus: Map 8.107, AY.
8.108.4b Aeolis: Map 8.107, AY.
8.108.4c Mount Ida: Map 8.107, AY.
8.108.4d Abydos: Map 8.107, AY.
8.108.4e Delos: Map 8.107, BY.
8.108.4f Atramyttium: Map 8.107, AY.
8.108.4g For this purification of Delos, see 3.104 and 5.1.

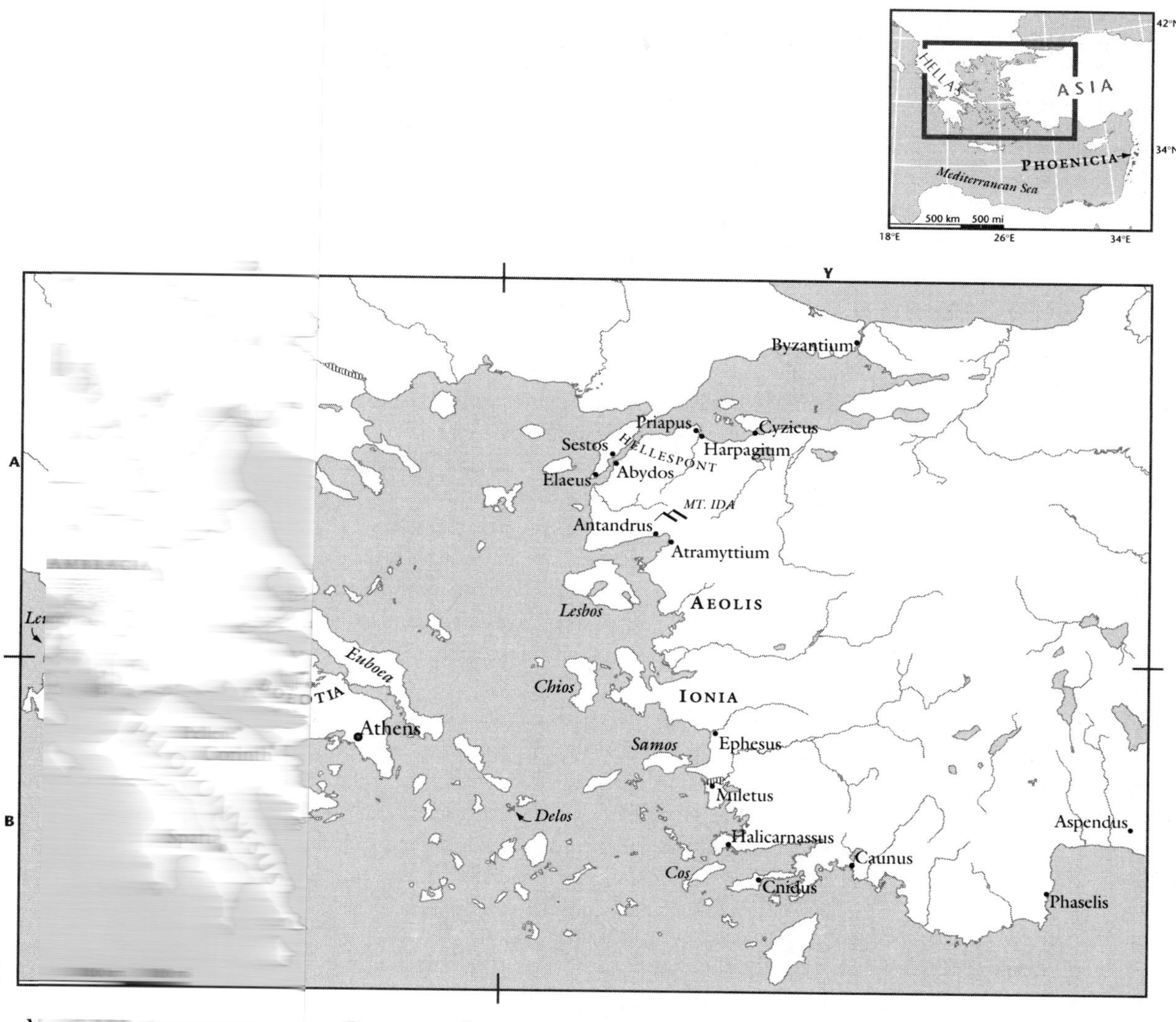

M[illegible] THE BATTLE OF CYNOSSEMA

8.109
411
21st Year/Summer
IONIA
Anxious to heal the breach between the Peloponnesians and himself, Tissaphernes hurries to the Hellespont to explain his actions and restore relations. He stops at Ephesus.

Tissaphernes[1a] upon hearing of this act of the Peloponnesians in addition to what had occurred at Miletus[1b] and Cnidus,[1c] where his garrisons had been also expelled, now saw that the breach between them was serious; and fearing further injury from them, and being also vexed to think that Pharnabazus[1d] should receive them, and in less time and at less cost perhaps succeed better against Athens than he had done, determined to rejoin them in the Hellespont, in order to complain of the events at Antandrus[1e] and excuse himself as best he could in the matter of the Phoenician[1f] fleet and of the other charges against him. Accordingly he went first to Ephesus[1g] and offered sacrifice to Artemis.

[When the winter after this summer is over the twenty-first year of this war will be completed.]

8.109.1a Tissaphernes was the Persian governor (satrap) of the "maritime provinces"; see note 8.5.5a and Map 8.84, BY.
8.109.1b Miletus: Map 8.107, BY.
8.109.1c Cnidus: Map 8.107, BY.
8.109.1d Pharnabazus was the Persian governor (satrap) of the Hellespont region (Map 8.107, AY, and Map 8.84, AY).
8.109.1e Antandrus: Map 8.107, AY. For the Aeolians, see Appendix H, Dialects and Ethnic Groups.
8.109.1f Phoenicia: Map 8.107, locator.
8.109.1g Ephesus: Map 8.107, BY.

EPILOGUE

narrative breaks off in the middle of the year 411, although he from exile after the war ended in 404 (5.26.5) and the last years id leave their mark on his final revisions of the text (e.g., 2.65, . Unfortunately, we lack what might have been his accounts of l military recovery—marked by her two great naval victories at d Arginousae[1b] (406)—and her final defeat at Aegospotami[1c] ed by obtuse and perhaps inexperienced Athenian commmanadmiral Lysander employed stealth and superior tactical skill to ach—almost the entire Athenian fleet in the Hellespont.[1e] After henians had no means left with which to prevent Lysander from y, starving her of the grain from the Black Sea region[1f] on which d, and ultimately forcing her to sue for peace. Victorious Sparta, nplating the total destruction of her defeated adversary, finally s would be allowed to continue to exist as a city, but demanded iat remained of her fleet, the demolition of the walls of Piraeus[1g] s, and the granting of complete freedom to the former subject oeen the Athenian Empire. Now supreme in Greece, Sparta thus a state of isolation, weakness, and dependency which must have d to the writer of Pericles' Funeral Oration.

ary of Pericles (2.65), which Thucydides wrote after the end of ledged the vital role of the Persian prince Cyrus the Younger in [2a] Yet he says little in the body of his text about the rising impor-ireek affairs. In truth, although the Persian governor at Sardis,[2b] did honor his promises to provide a fleet to assist Sparta, his ipport, along with that of Pharnabazus in the Hellespont, did iallenge Athens in the Aegean and to bring about the revolt of cities from Athenian allegiance. It was Cyrus the Younger,

), AY.
oilogue Map, AY.
e Map, AY.
ause most of the generals
ory at Arginousae had been
postbattle fit of fratricidal, if
ntagonism reminiscent of what
took place at Corcyra in 427 (3.69).

1e Hellespont: Epilogue Map, AY.
1f Black Sea: Epilogue Map, locator .
1g Piraeus: Epilogue Map, BX.
2a See 2.65.12.
2b Sardis: Epilogue Map, BY.

however, the successor to Tissaphernes, who demanded of his father, Darius II, that real naval support be provided to Sparta, and whose active assistance and collusion with Lysander encouraged the Spartans to persevere despite setbacks. Thus, even though Aegospotami was won without the help of a Persian fleet, Sparta found herself greatly indebted to Cyrus at the end of the war; and when Darius died in 404 and Cyrus began to assemble an army to support his claim to the throne, Sparta had no choice but to become involved, partly by her obligation of gratitude, and partly by the reflection that if Cyrus were to succeed without her aid, she would feel his wrath. So Sparta made her contribution to Cyrus' expedition and approved the creation of a mercenary force of Greek hoplites for his army. Their adventurous journey into and out of Mesopotamia was later made famous by one of its Athenian captains, Xenophon, in his book *Anabasis,* "The March of the Ten Thousand."

§3. Cyrus' army won the battle at Cunaxa near Babylon[3a] (401) but gained no victory, for Cyrus himself died on the field, and his death left Sparta, as far as the triumphant King Artaxerxes II was concerned, in an awkward position. Although efforts were made to restore amicable relations, the truth was inescapable. Alcibiades had been right when he predicted (8.46) that Sparta, having liberated the Greeks of Greece from Athens, could not refuse the entreaties of the Greeks of Asia to liberate them from Persia.[3b] When Sparta did go to their aid, she brought upon herself a war that was impossible for her to win and which irremediably damaged her supremacy and control over Greece itself; for Persia countered Sparta by encouraging (and in part financing) a new coalition of Athens, Thebes, Corinth, and Argos[3c] to oppose Spartan domination. This combined alliance waged the so-called Corinthian War (395–87) against Sparta, defeated her decisively at sea in 394—just ten years after Aegospotami—and ultimately forced her to abandon her attempt to liberate the Greeks of Asia.

§4. Certainly Sparta had no monopoly on folly. When the Athenians, bent on restoring their empire, chose to intervene in cities within the Persian King's domain, the King in turn allied with Sparta in order to thwart them, and the Athenians, faced again in 387 with the loss of their Black Sea grain supply, had to renounce their imperial goals. The general agreement of 386—known as the King's Peace—formalized the position. Both Sparta and her opponents in Greece undertook to leave the King in complete control of his domains and, with the threat of Persian support if it were needed, Sparta was established as the enforcer of the peace, the policeman of the Hellenes.

§5. In short, Sparta's total military victory over Athens in the Peloponnesian War gained her little more than a short-lived supremacy in Greece, one that ultimately could not be maintained without the support of Persia, who would not grant it to her unless she accepted conditions and limitations imposed by Persia. Thus it was the King of Persia who seems to have gained most from the war, for with the destruction of the Athenian Empire he recovered his territories in Asia at

3a Cunaxa and Babylon: Epilogue Map, locator.
3b Persia: Epilogue Map, locator.
3c Sparta, Athens, Thebes, Corinth, and Argos: Epilogue Map, BX.

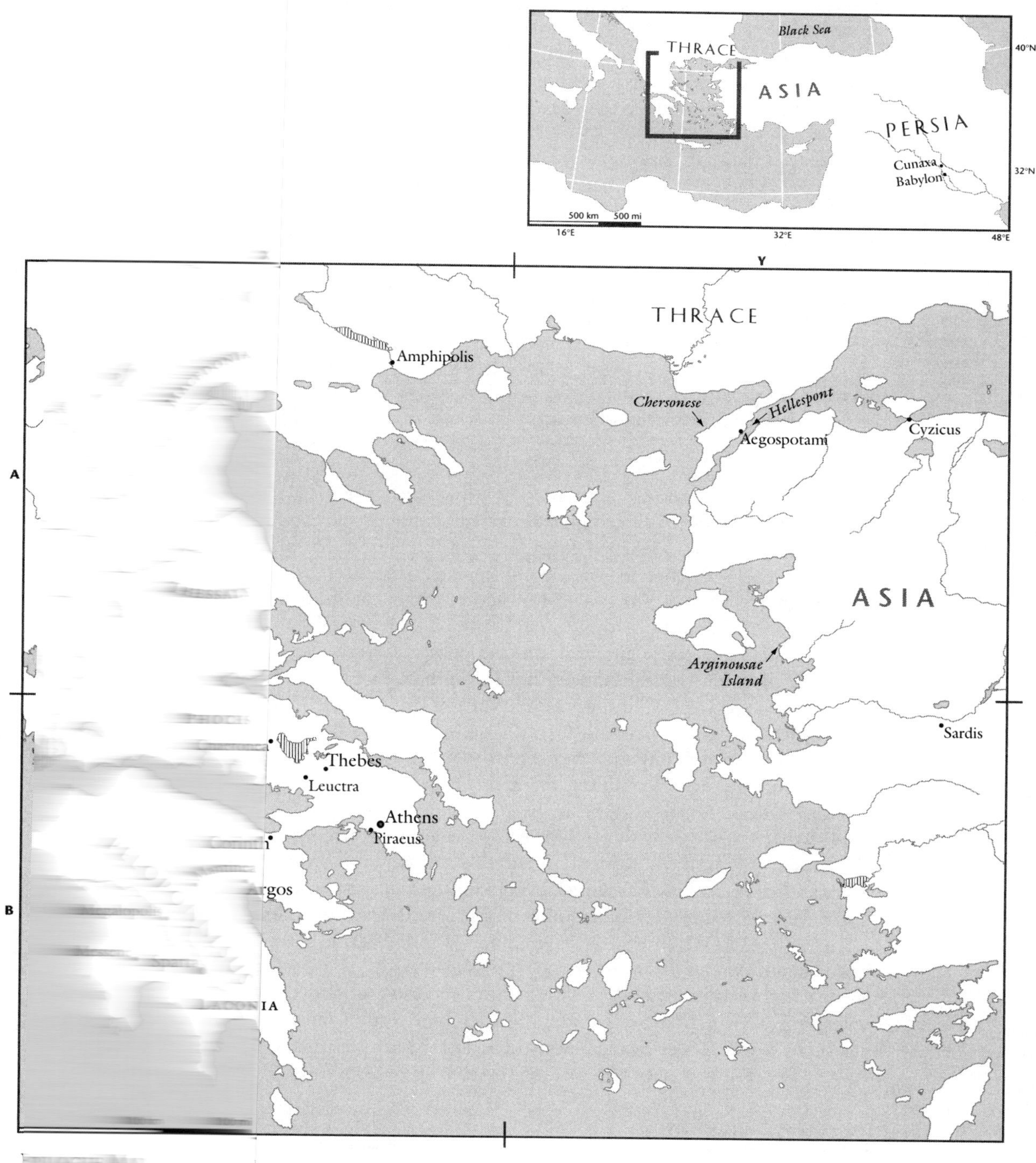
Black Sea
THRACE
ASIA
PERSIA
Cunaxa
Babylon
40°N
32°N
500 km
500 mi
16°E
32°E
48°E
Y
THRACE
Amphipolis
Chersonese
Hellespont
Aegospotami
Cyzicus
A
ASIA
Arginousae
Island
Sardis
Thebes
Leuctra
Athens
Piraeus
B

little cost to himself and was able to cheaply maintain his hold on them by playing off the always-contentious and now utterly disunited Greek *poleis* (city-states) against each other. Later Kings continued this policy with such success that none of them had to defend against invasion from the west until the Macedonians under Alexander the Great attacked Persia in 334.

§6. Persian dominance in Greece, exerted through, and made possible by, the continuous stalemate among Greek states—arrayed now in one, now in another balanced set of alliances—reveals the increasing inability of the traditional *polis* (city-state) to deal effectively with new problems of war, trade, and politics in a larger, Mediterranean framework. The polis, a uniquely Greek phenomenon, had developed and flowered in the particular circumstances of the eighth, seventh, and early sixth centuries when, as Thucydides noted (1.12–19), there were no great wars, powerful states, or large-scale enterprises in the Greek world. The key institutions of the polis—an agrarian economy, many owners of small plots of land, rule by a restricted list of citizen voters, and hoplite warfare—to which most Greeks remained deeply attached throughout the period—were not seriously challenged by the outside world until the encroachments and invasions of Persia in the late sixth and early fifth centuries. Although the Greeks threw back the Persians in the first half of the fifth century, they did so through leagues and alliances that proved inimical to the total autonomy, and incompatible with the local focus, that were so central to the classical polis. These inherent conflicts, perhaps first exposed in the fifth century by the Delian League's rapid transition to a tyrannous Athenian Empire, and then further revealed by Sparta's clumsy attempt to substitute her own domination for that of Athens, continued to manifest itself in the polis' essential political failure throughout the fourth century. In fact, the bankruptcy of the polis in the greater and more integrated world that was developing is nowhere more starkly revealed than in the narrow hegemonist goals that the leading Greek poleis continuously and unrealistically pursued during this period. Their myopic vision and sterile objectives embroiled the Greek cities in continuous and increasingly expensive warfare that not only impoverished them but that also allowed Persia to maintain sufficient control to neutralize, at little expense, what otherwise might have been a troublesome and dangerous region.

§7. Athens, for example, could not forego another attempt to recover her imperial assets from the fifth century. Although she was for a time checked by fear of Sparta and of provoking the Great King to intervene, she recognized and seized her opportunity when the Thebans inflicted a severe defeat upon Sparta at the battle of Leuctra[7a] in 371. When the decisive impact of that battle became clear, Athens set out to regain two of the most strategic of those assets, the city of Amphipolis[7b] (the loss of which was described by Thucydides in Book 4) and the Chersonese on the Hellespont,[7c] (which Athens under Pericles had settled, and which would protect her access to the Black Sea). When the Great King was distracted and temporarily paralyzed by the revolt of the satraps (provincial governors) of Asia[7d] between 366

7a Leuctra: Epilogue Map, BX.
7b Amphipolis: Epilogue Map, AX.
7c Chersonese on the Hellespont: Epilogue Map, AY.
7d Asia: Epilogue Map, AY.

attempt to recover her old empire became so offensive and f her main allies turned against her and stalemated her in what is l War of 357–55. Then, when the Great King, having restored atened Athens with another round of punitive action, the now y had no choice but to yield and finally to abandon her imperial .

rations to leadership in Greece were also dealt a fatal blow during he mass of Theban hoplites, arrayed in an extraordinary formation oke through their opposing phalanx at Leuctra, the Spartan army's ary invincibility was forever shattered; and the Thebans, led by the inondas, were not slow to exploit their new military advantage in rmanent. In 369, Epaminondas marched into the Peloponnesus and inviolate for centuries, and on its borders founded and fortified the atic bastions of Megalopolis and Ithome in Messenia[8b]—the inhabi- being given freedom from Sparta after centuries of degrading subjec- shment of these two states, he reduced Sparta in a flash from a world local wrangler intent for the rest of her independent existence on coverable Messene on which Spartan power had depended.

resounding victory at Leuctra, Thebes found herself the greatest f free Greece. The 380s and the 370s had been the decades of y; in the 360s Thebes sought to take Sparta's place, and for a brief spects seemed good. But with the death of Epaminondas on the ond Mantinea[9a] (362) and with the onset of the miserable Sacred iled Thebes with Phocis[9b] in a long and debilitating conflict, the power faded.

nenace to Greece now arose in Macedon, a kingdom that plays only in Thucydides' narrative, as it did in the Hellenic world before its , Philip II (reigned 359–36). Although the Macedonians spoke re considered boorish, primitive, and foreign by most Greeks of e. After all, they did not live in independent poleis like self-respect- Greeks; instead, they were citizens of loose and some of them petty owed loyalty to kings who ruled and played dynastic politics of ar in a style that must have reminded fifth-century Greeks of Homer's icated chieftains. Yet the Argeadae, the royal house of Macedon, cestry to Argos, and they demonstrated their Hellenic origin suffi- edonians to be allowed to participate in the Olympic Games. By the ry, they had become dominant in their region, and although Thu- them as weakly seeking help, now from Athens, now from Sparta, and restoring alliances with dizzying speed, their battles in Lyncestis, nse against overwhelming invasion from Odrysian Thrace, gained ce and stature. In the fourth century, under Philip II, they became a of Greece and indeed to much of the rest of the world also.

ue Map, BX.
d Messene: Epilogue Map, BX.
9a Mantinea: Epilogue Map, BX.
9b Phocis: Epilogue Map, BX.

§11. During the first part of his reign, Philip extended Macedonian power to Thrace,[11a] Thessaly,[11b] and the whole of northern Greece. From there, setting his eyes on the riches of Persia, he attempted to control and organize the many poleis of Greece so that they might assist him against Persia, but if they would not, to at least prevent them from joining with Persia against him when he moved east. In other words, he sought less to conquer the Greek cities than to render them impotent. He proved to be a skillful diplomat and an acute judge of his own interests. Above all, he was a resourceful general who commanded a large and superbly trained army. Although occasionally defeated in the field or checked by treaty, he tirelessly maneuvered by both war and diplomacy to increase his influence and power in Greece. The one Athenian political faction (led by the orator Demosthenes) which saw clearly that the huge Macedonian power posed a serious menace to Greek liberty achieved little more, for all its machinations and plots, than to cause Philip to delay his Asiatic plans for a few years. In the end, when Philip finally advanced into Greece proper, his opponents proved so incapable of uniting or otherwise seriously challenging him that he found himself opposed by the armies of only the two most directly threatened poleis: Athens and Thebes. When Philip defeated these armies in the decisive battle at Chaeronea[11c] in 338, all hopes of freedom for Greece from Macedonian dominion were extinguished.

§12. Philip settled affairs in Greece to his satisfaction by organizing a "League of Corinth" (337) and by establishing a few strategically placed garrisons throughout the country. Then, returning to Macedon, he prepared for his onslaught on Persia. In the spring of 336, the vanguard of his army crossed over to Asia, with Philip intending to follow shortly. By midsummer, however, he had been murdered. His son, Alexander III, succeeded him and, after a short interval, fulfilled and perhaps overfulfilled his father's ambitions. Crossing the Hellespont in 334, Alexander completely destroyed Persian military power in a series of brilliant victories in just three years. By 331, when the last Great King, Darius III, died ignominiously in flight, Alexander—known to us as Alexander the Great—began to rule over both Greece and Persia. Ten years later, when he died in Babylon, the independent polis was well on its way to oblivion, and the Hellenistic world was born.

R.B.S.

11a Thrace, now the area of modern Bulgaria and European Turkey: Epilogue Map, AY, and locator.

11b Thessaly: Epilogue Map, AX.

11c Chaeronea: Epilogue Map, BX.

THEATERS OF OPERATION IN THE PELOPONNESIAN WAR

Year/ Season	Attica-Euboea-Boeotia	Peloponnesus Megarid, Cephallenia, Zacynthus, Melos
BOOK ONE **Introduction** **The Archaeology**		
435		**1.24–29** Epidamnian affair. A Corinthian fleet is defeated by the Corcyraeans off Leukimme. **1.30** Corcyraeans raid Leucas and Cyllene. Corinth establishes bases at Actium and Thesprotis.
433	**1.31–45** Speeches by Corcyraeans (1.32) and Corinthians (1.37). **1.45** Athens makes a defensive alliance with Corcyra, sends 10 ships to the island. **1.50–51** Athenian ships at the battle of Sybota prevent a Corcyraean rout. **1.56** Suspicious of Potidaea, Athens prepares to send a fleet but is delayed by Potidaean envoys.	**1.31** Corinth prepares for more war with Corcyra; sends envoys to Athens to rebut the Corcyraeans. **1.37–43** Speech of the Corinthians at Athens. **1.46–55** Corinthian victory at Sybota. Corinthians take Anactorium. **1.58** Sparta promises to support a Potidaean revolt by invading Attica.
432	**1.59–65** The arriving Athenians find Potidaea already in revolt. They besiege the city.	**1.60** Corinthian volunteers go to Potidaea. **1.68** Speech of the Corinthians. **1.73** Speech of the Athenians. **1.80** Speech of Archidamus for caution and delay. **1.86** Speech of Sthenelaides. **1.87** The Spartans vote for war.
479–31 **Pentecontaetia**		
479–78 **Pentecontaetia**	**1.89** The Persians retreat; Athens rebuilds, and sends a fleet to the Hellespont. **1.90–92** Themistocles tricks the Spartans while Athens builds walls. **1.93** He fortifies the Piraeus.	**1.94** Pausanias leads an expedition against Cyprus and Byzantium.
478–77 **Pentecontaetia**	**1.95** The allies select Athens to lead; Sparta accepts this choice. **1.96** Delian league formed under Athenian leadership.	**1.95** Pausanias returns to Sparta; the allies choose Athens to lead them and Sparta accepts this choice.
476–67 **Pentecontaetia**	**1.98** The Delian League takes military actions against Scyros, Eion, Carystus, and Naxos.	
467–65? **Pentecontaetia**	**1.100–101** Persians defeated. Rebellion of Thasos put down. Athens' attempt to colonize Amphipolis fails.	
466–61 **Pentecontaetia**	**1.101–2** Athens sends troops to help Sparta defeat a Helot revolt. Sparta sends them home.	**1.101–2** An earthquake prevents Sparta from aiding Thasos and triggers a Helot revolt. Sparta requests, receives, and then rejects Athenian help. Athens renounces her alliance with Sparta.

We[illegible] Aca[illegible]ctus, Epi[illegible]	**Thrace** Chalcidice, Macedonia, Hellespont, Thessaly	**Other Regions** Asia, the Aegean, Italy-Sicily
		1.1–23 In his introduction, commonly known as "The Archaeology," Thucydides' discusses his aims and methods, traces human technical and political development, and compares the Peloponnesian War with earlier conflicts.
1.2[illegible]ds to wa[illegible]orcyra wi[illegible]mnus, rai[illegible]ablishes ba[illegible]		
1.[illegible]para-tio[illegible]s. **1.**[illegible]at At[illegible] **1.**[illegible]eated at Sy[illegible]ps and re[illegible]rout.	**1.57** Perdiccas schemes to organize the Chalcidians against the Athenians.	
	1.58 After receiving promises of Spartan support, Potidaea revolts. **1.61** Perdiccas allies with Athens. **1.65** A siege of the city begins.	
		1.89–1.118 Pentecontaetia. Thucydides describes Athens' growth in power during the fifty years following the defeat of the Persian invasion.
	1.95 The arrogance of Pausanias causes the allies to select Athens as leader; Sparta accepts this choice. **1.96** Delian league is formed under Athenian leadership.	**1.97** Thucydides describes his reasons for writing the Pentecontaetia.
	1.98 The Delian League takes military actions against Eion.	**1.98** The Delian League takes military actions against Scyros and Naxos.
	1.100–101 Rebellion of Thasos put down (465?). Athens' attempt to colonize Amphipolis fails.	**1.100** The Athenians defeat the Persians at the Eurymedon river (467?).
	1.101–2 An earthquake prevents Sparta from helping Thasos by invading Attica, as had been secretly promised.	

Year/ Season	Attica-Euboea-Boeotia	Peloponnesus Megarid, Cephallenia, Zacynthus, Melos
457–56? **Pentecontaetia**	**1.103** Athens resettles the Helot rebels in Naupactus. Megara allies herself with Athens.	**1.103** Megara quarrels with Corinth and allies with Athens.
460? **Pentecontaetia**	**1.104** Athens sends a fleet to aid an Egyptian rebellion against Persia.	
459–58? **Pentecontaetia**		**1.105–6** An Athenian fleet is repelled at Halieis; another defeats the Peloponnesian fleet at Cecryphalia and besieges Aegina. A reserve army defeats the Corinthians in the Megarid.
457 **Pentecontaetia**	**1.107** Athens begins the Long Walls. **1.108** A Peloponnesian army defeats the Athenians at Tanagra. Athens defeats the Boeotians at Oenophyta and becomes master of Boeotia. Aegina surrenders.	**1.108** An Athenian fleet raids the Peloponnesus.
454? **Pentecontaetia**	**1.109–10** Athens' fleet in Egypt is defeated and destroyed	**1.111** An Athenian fleet under Pericles raids Sicyon.
451? **Pentecontaetia**	**1.112** Athens and Sparta sign a five-year truce. Athens defeats the Persians at Cyprus.	**1.112** Athens and Sparta sign a five-year truce. Athens defeats the Persians at Cyprus.
447–46 **Pentecontaetia**	**1.113** The Boeotians defeat the Athenians at Coronea, and recover their independence. **1.114–15** Megara and Euboea revolt. A Peloponnesian army invades Attica but turns back.	**1.114–15** Megara revolts, joins Peloponnesian alliance.
446 **Pentecontaetia**	**1.115** Athens gives up bases in the Megarid and Peloponnesus and concludes a thirty-year peace with Sparta.	**1.115** Sparta and Athens conclude a thirty-year peace treaty.
441–40 **Pentecontaetia ends**	**1.115–17** Samos and Byzantium revolt. Athens forces Samos to surrender; Byzantium submits.	
432/1 **Winter**	**1.128** Athens tells the Spartans to drive out the curse of Taenarus. **1.135–38** Flight of Themistocles. **1.139** Further Spartan demands. **1.140–44** Speech of Pericles explains how Athens can win.	**1.119** Meeting of the allies at Sparta. **1.120** Speech of the Corinthians demands action. **1.126** Sparta tells the Athenians to drive out the curse of the Goddess. **1.129–34** The tale of Pausanias and the curse of the Goddess of the Bronze House.
BOOK TWO **431** **Summer**	**2.1–6** War begins when Thebes launches a surprise attack on Plataea. **2.9** Athenian allies listed. **2.12–17** Athenians abandon Attica and move inside the city walls. **2.18–21** The Peloponnesians invade Attica. **2.22** Pericles prevents the Athenians from sallying out. **2.23–25** An Athenian fleet raids the Peloponnesus. **2.24** Athens sets up an emergency war fund and a reserve fleet. **2.26** An Athenian fleet is sent to protect Euboea and raid Locris; (2.32) it fortifies Atalanta. **2.27** The Athenians expel the Aeginetans and occupy Aegina themselves. **2.32** The Athenians fortify the island of Atalanta.	**2.7–8** Preparing for war, Sparta sends envoys to Persia, asks allies to construct 500 triremes. **2.9** Spartan allies listed. **2.10–11** Speech of Archidamus to the Peloponnesian army assembled at the Isthmus. **2.23** The Peloponnesian army returns home. **2.25** An Athenian fleet raids Laconia, Methone (defended by Brasidas), and Pheia in Elis. **2.27** Exiled from Aegina, the Aeginetans are settled by Sparta in Thyrea. **2.31** Pericles commands the Athenians' first invasion of Megara.
431/0 **Winter**	**2.34–46** Pericles' funeral oration.	**2.33** Corinthian fleet raids Acarnania and Cephallenia.

We[illegible] Ac[illegible]ctus, Epi[illegible]	**Thrace** Chalcidice, Macedonia, Hellespont, Thessaly	**Other Regions** Asia, the Aegean, Italy-Sicily
		1.104 Athens sends a fleet to aid an Egyptian rebellion against Persia.
1.[illegible] from Ph[illegible]		
1.[illegible]les fails to[illegible]	**1.111** Athens' attempt to install a Thessalian king fails.	**1.109–10** Athens' fleet in Egypt is defeated and destroyed.
1.[illegible]trol of D[illegible]		**1.112** Athens defeats the Persians in Cyprus.
	1.115–17 Byzantium revolts, but later submits to Athens.	**1.115–17** Samos revolts, assisted by Persia, but is forced to surrender after an Athenian siege.
[illegible]nania and [illegible]an camp [illegible]	**2.29** The Athenians conclude alliances with Sitalces, king of Odrysian Thrace, and Perdiccas, king of Macedonia.	**2.7–8** Sparta orders contributions of money and ships from her allies in Sicily and Italy, and sends an embassy to the Persian King. **2.28** Eclipse of the sun occurs at the beginning of a new lunar month.
[illegible]re aided by [illegible]		

Year/ Season	Attica-Euboea-Boeotia	Peloponnesus Megarid, Cephallenia, Zacynthus, Melos
430 Summer	**2.47** The Peloponnesians invade Attica. **2.47–2.54** Plague strikes Athens. **2.55** Again, Pericles prevents the Athenians from sallying out. **2.56** An Athenian fleet raids the Peloponnesus. **2.58** Athenian reinforcements at Potidaea suffer losses from the plague. **2.59** Athenian envoys to Sparta fail to make peace. **2.60–64** Speech of Pericles urges Athens to continue the war. **2.65** Athenians fine Pericles but reelect him general. Thucydides appraises Pericles.	**2.47** The Peloponnesians invade Attica again, ravaging it extensively (2.55) for 40 days before returning (2.57). **2.66** Peloponnesian fleet raids Zacynthus.
430/29 Winter		
429 Summer	**2.71–78** The Peloponnesians assault Plataea. **2.72** Archidamus offers neutrality. **2.74** Plataea decides to remain with Athens. **2.75–78** The Peloponnesian assaults are described.	
429/8 Winter	**2.94** A Peloponnesian raid against Piraeus causes panic in Athens.	**2.93–94** A Peloponnesian fleet attempts a surprise attack against Piraeus, but stops at Salamis.
BOOK THREE 428 Summer	**3.1** The Peloponnesians invade Attica. **3.3** Athens sends a fleet to Lesbos in rebellion. **3.7** An Athenian fleet raids the Peloponnesus. **3.16–7** Athens deploys 100 triremes to deter the Spartans. At this time Athens has 250 triremes at sea. **3.18** Athens sends 1,000 hoplites to besiege Mytilene. **3.19** Athenians levy a special capital tax on themselves for the siege.	**3.1** The Peloponnesians invade Attica. **3.7** Athenian ships under Asopius, son of Phormio, raid the Peloponnesus. **3.8–14** Speech of the Mytilenians to the Peloponnesians at Olympia. **3.15** Sparta allies with Mytilene and prepares a fleet to help her.
428/7 Winter	**3.24** 212 Plataeans escape to Athens.	**3.25** Sparta sends Salaethus to encourage Mytilene.
427 Summer		**3.26** The Peloponnesians invade Attica and despatch a fleet under Alcidas to Lesbos.

We[illegible] Ac[illegible] ctus, Ep[illegible]	**Thrace** Chalcidice, Macedonia, Hellespont, Thessaly	**Other Regions** Asia, the Aegean, Italy-Sicily
2.[illegible] ochian A[illegible] on in the ar[illegible] en A[illegible]	**2.47** Plague appears in Lemnos before Athens. **2.58** Athenian reinforcements at Potidaea suffer losses from plague. **2.67** Peloponnesian envoys to the Persian King are captured in Thrace. They are executed without trial at Athens.	
2[illegible] upactus u[illegible]	**2.70** The Potidaeans surrender. They are expelled and replaced by settlers from Athens.	
[illegible] defeated [illegible] dron [illegible] trae. [illegible] Spartan [illegible] onnesian [illegible]	**2.79** An Athenian expedition in Chalcidice wins a victory at Spartolus but is then defeated by peltasts and cavalry.	
[illegible] ies in [illegible]		**2.95–101** Sitalces launches his Thracian army at Macedonia and Chalcidice.
[illegible] d leading a [illegible]		**3.2–6** Lesbos revolts. Mytilene sends envoys to Sparta for help. An Athenian fleet blockades Mytilene by sea. **3.18** Athenian hoplites arrive at Mytilene under Paches to blockade the city by land. **3.19** Troops from an Athenian squadron collecting tribute are defeated in Caria.
[illegible] it of Pelo- [illegible] Athens.		**3.25** The Spartan Salaethus arrives at Mytilene.
		3.27–28 The Mytilenian commons, armed by Salaethus, force him to surrender the city to the Athenians. **3.29–33** A Peloponnesian fleet reaches Ionia, learns of Mytilene's fall, and flees. **3.34–35** Paches takes Notium by trick, recaptures Lesbos.

Year/ Season	Attica-Euboea-Boeotia	Peloponnesus Megarid, Cephallenia, Zacynthus, Melos
427 **Summer *(cont'd)***	**3.36–50** Mytilenian debate. **3.37–40** Speech of Cleon. **3.41–48** Speech of Diodotus. **3.49** The Athenians vote to reduce the punishment of Mytilene. They send a boat which arrives (**3.50**) just in time to prevent a massacre.	
	3.51 The Athenians capture the island of Minoa near Megara. **3.52–68** Plataea surrenders. **3.53–60** Speech of the Plataeans. **3.61–67** Speech of the Thebans. **3.68** The Spartans condemn the Plataeans to death.	**3.51** The Athenians capture the island of Minoa near Megara.
		3.69 The Peloponnesian fleet arrives at Cyllene, is strengthened, and sails for Corcyra.
	3.86 Athens sends a squadron to Rhegium in Sicily.	
427/6 **Winter**	**3.87** Plague returns to Athens.	
426 **Summer**	**3.89** Earthquakes in the Isthmus turn back a Peloponnesian invasion of Attica. A tidal wave occurs near Euboea.	**3.89** Earthquakes in the Isthmus turn back a Peloponnesian invasion of Attica.
	3.91 After ravaging Melos, an Athenian fleet sails to Oropus from which its troops march to Tanagra to join other forces coming from Athens.	**3.91** An Athenian fleet raids Melos. **3.92** Sparta founds Heraclea.
		***3.100** The Aetolians send envoys to Corinth and Sparta to urge a combined attack on Naupactus.
426/5 **Winter**	**3.104** Athenians purify Delos.	
	3.114 Demosthenes returns from Amphilochia in triumph. **3.115** Athens votes to send reinforcements to Sicily.	

*Although the Aetolian-Peloponnesian assault on Naupactus (**3.101–2**) is preceded in the narrative by the description of Demosthenes' invasion of Aetolia (**3.94**), Thucydides makes it clear that the Aetolians had requested and persuaded the Peloponnesians to join in such an assault prior to Demosthenes' invasion (**3.100**). He also reports that the Aetolians were aware of Demosthenes' plan from its conception (**3.96.3**). Thus the text does not permit us to say which decision was made first; either side could plausibly have designed its move to preempt the other, and both plans could have been developed, whether independently or not, quite simultaneously.

We… Aca… tus, Epi…	**Thrace** Chalcidice, Macedonia, Hellespont, Thessaly	**Other Regions** Asia, the Aegean, Italy-Sicily
3.7… ks out in (… **3.7**… **3.7**… o arr… **3.7**… ives and def… **3.8**… when war… eet. **3.8**… e their dor… **3.8**… olution.		**3.49–50** The second boat reaches Mytilene in time to prevent execution of all adult males. Athens executes 1,000 revolt leaders, destroys city walls, allots Lesbian land to Athenian holders. **3.86** The Athenians establish themselves at Rhegium.
		3.88 The Athenians raid the Aeolian islands.
3.9… ctus. **3.9**… ***3.9**… ack Ae… **3.9**… at Ae… **3.**… elp the Ae… at De… **3.**… Nau- pa… assault.	**3.92–93** Heraclea in Trachis is founded by Sparta.	**3.90** Athenians capture Mylae and Messana in Sicily. **3.99** Athenians attack Locris in Italy.
3.… philochia, aic… **3.**… ns under De… and win ba… ae and Id… **3.**… racians ma…		**3.103** Athenians attack Inessa unsuccessfully. Later they raid Locris. **3.115** Athenians raid Himera and Locris. **3.116** Mount Etna erupts.

Year/ Season	Attica-Euboea-Boeotia	Peloponnesus Megarid, Cephallenia, Zacynthus, Melos
BOOK FOUR		
425 Summer	**4.2** Athens' fleet to Sicily departs with orders to stop at Corcyra and to allow Demosthenes to use the fleet as it rounds the Peloponnesus. **4.6** The Peloponnesian army in Attica marches home after learning of the Athenian fort at Pylos.	**4.2** Peloponnesians invade Attica. A Peloponnesian fleet sails to Corcyra. **4.3–5** The Athenian fleet destined for Sicily fortifies Pylos.
		4.8 Spartans arrive at Pylos to assault and blockade the fort. **4.9–12** Spartan assaults against Pylos from land and sea do not succeed. **4.13–14** The Athenian fleet returns to Pylos and routs the Peloponnesian fleet, marooning a Spartan force on Sphacteria. **4.15–16** Requesting and receiving a truce, Spartan envoys sail to Athens.
	4.17–22 Speech of the Spartan envoys from Pylos to the Athenians. **4.22** Led by Cleon, the Athenians turn down the Spartan offers.	**4.23** Negotiations fail; hostilities resume at Pylos.
		4.26 Helots bring food to the garrison.
	4.27–29 Cleon is chosen to command at Pylos.	**4.30–40** The Athenians invade Sphacteria and defeat the Spartans, forcing them to surrender.
	4.41 The Spartans fail to negotiate peace or the return of the men from Pylos. **4.42** An Athenian expedition under Nicias raids Corinth.	**4.41** Messenians raid Laconia from Pylos. Spartan attempts to negotiate peace fail. **4.42–45** Corinth defends against raid by an Athenian fleet.
425/4 Winter		
424 Summer		**4.53–57** An Athenian fleet under Nicias conquers Cythera and raids Thyrea. Sparta organizes defensive units of archers and cavalry.
	4.65 The Athenian generals returning from Sicily are punished.	**4.67–72** The Athenians attack Megara by surprise and occupy Nisea, but **(4.73)** fail to attack a rapidly assembled Peloponnesian and Theban force under Brasidas. **4.74** Megara remains a Peloponnesian ally; pro-Athenian Megarians flee. Some who do not are executed.
	4.76 Athenians plot with Boeotian factions to establish democracy in Boeotia.	
		4.80 Spartan atrocities against Helots are recounted.
	4.82 Athens declares war on Perdiccas.	
424/3 Winter	**4.89–90** Athens' assault against Boeotia is betrayed and goes awry, but they fortify Delium. **4.91–96** The Boeotians defeat the Athenians in the field. **4.100–101** The Boeotians retake Delium by storm.	**4.101** Demosthenes' raid on Sicyon fails.
	4.108 Athens is alarmed by the fall of Amphipolis.	**4.109** The Megarians recapture and raze their long walls.

We[illegible] Ac[illegible]ctus, Epi[illegible]	**Thrace** Chalcidice, Macedonia, Hellespont, Thessaly	**Other Regions** Asia, the Aegean, Italy-Sicily
4.2[illegible]ine in the[illegible]to Co[illegible] **4.8**[illegible]d from Co[illegible] **4.**[illegible]ylos, At[illegible]by help-ing[illegible]domestic fo[illegible]em. **4.**[illegible]ture A[illegible]	**4.7** An Athenian expedition takes an unknown Eion in Thrace but is soon driven out.	**4.1** Messana revolts and a Syracusan and Locrian fleet occupy the city. Locrian forces ravage Rhegium. **4.24–25** Indecisive fighting at Messana, Rhegium, and Naxos.
	4.50 A Persian envoy to Sparta is captured by Athenians at Eion in Thrace.	**4.51** Chios demolishes its new city wall at the command of Athens.
4[illegible]adae to jo[illegible]osthenes su[illegible]	**4.79–80** Brasidas marches rapidly through Thessaly to Macedonia and Thrace. **4.83** Brasidas makes peace in Lyncestis. **4.84–88** Brasidas persuades Acanthus to revolt from Athens.	**4.52** An eclipse of the sun occurs. Lesbian exiles capture Antandrus. **4.58** Sicilians assemble at Gela. **4.59–64** Speech of Hermocrates. The Sicilians decide to end the war in Sicily. **4.65** The Athenians sail home from Sicily. **4.75** An Athenian squadron collecting tribute prevents Lesbian exiles from fortifying Antandrus. Another squadron loses its ships at anchor to a river flood at Heraclea on Pontus. They return through Bythinia.
	4.101 Sitalces dies. **4.102–6** Brasidas captures Amphipolis. **4.107** Thucydides saves Eion. **4.109** The cities of Acte submit to Brasidas. **4.110–16** Brasidas takes Torone by treachery and audacity.	

Year/ Season	Attica-Euboea-Boeotia	Peloponnesus Megarid, Cephallenia, Zacynthus, Melos
423 **Summer**	**4.116–19** Athens and Sparta agree to a one-year truce. **4.129** Athens sends an expedition to retake Mende and Scione. **4.133** Thebes dismantles the walls of Thespiae.	**4.116–19** Sparta and Athens agree to a one-year truce. **4.133** The temple of Hera at Argos burns down.
423/2 **Winter**		**4.134** Mantineans and Tegeans fight at Laodicium.
BOOK FIVE **422** **Summer**	**5.1** The truce ends. Athens expels the Delians from Delos to Atramyttium. **5.2–3** Athens sends an expedition under Cleon to Thrace. **5.3** The Boeotians take Panactum in Attica by treachery.	**5.1** The truce ends.
422/1 **Winter**	**5.14–19** Sparta and Athens sign a treaty of peace. **5.21–24** Sparta and Athens sign a treaty of alliance.	**5.14–19** Sparta and Athens sign a treaty of peace. **5.21–24** Sparta and Athens sign a treaty of alliance.
421 **Summer**	**5.32** The Athenians retake Scione and resettle the Plataeans there. Obeying the god of Delphi, Athens permits the Delians to return to Delos. **5.35** At Spartan request, Athens withdraws the Messenians from Pylos.	**5.27–29** Reactions of Corinth, Argos, Mantinea, and Elis to Sparta's alliance with Athens. **5.30** Sparta complains to Corinth. **5.31** Elis allies with Corinth and Argos. **5.32** Tegea retains its Spartan alliance. Corinth fails to persuade Boeotia to ally with Argos. **5.33** Sparta liberates Arcadian subjects of Mantinea. **5.35** Athens withdraws the Messenians from Pylos.
421/0 **Winter**	**5.36–38** After Sparta and Boeotia fail to ally with Argos, they join in a separate alliance (**5.39**). **5.39** The Boeotians raze Panactum.	**5.36–38** After Sparta and Boeotia fail to ally with Argos, they join in a separate alliance (**5.39**).
420 **Summer**	**5.43–47** Alcibiades outwits the Spartan envoys and creates an alliance of Athens, Argos, Mantinea, and Elis.	**5.43–47** Spartan envoys are tricked by Alcibiades, who creates an anti-Spartan alliance in the Peloponnesus. **5.49–50** Elis excludes Sparta from Olympic games because of their quarrel over Lepreum.
420/19 **Winter**	**5.51** Heraclea-in-Trachis is defeated by its neighbors.	
419 **Summer**	**5.52** Boeotians occupy Heraclea-in-Trachis. Alcibiades marches a small force through the Peloponnesus.	**5.52** Alcibiades marches through the Peloponnesus. **5.53–55** War begins between Argos and Epidaurus.
419/8 **Winter**	**5.56** Athens returns the Messenians to Pylos at Argive request.	**5.56** The Messenians return to Pylos. Argos tries again to take Epidaurus.
418 **Summer**		**5.57-60** Spartans and allies surround the Argives near Argos, but grant them a truce and go home. **5.61–63** Alcibiades persuades Argos to renounce the truce and attack Orchomenos and Tegea. **5.64–75** Sparta defeats the Argive alliance in a battle at Mantinea.

We[illegible] Aca[illegible]tus, Epi[illegible]	**Thrace** Chalcidice, Macedonia, Hellespont, Thessaly	**Other Regions** Asia, the Aegean, Italy-Sicily
	4.120–1 Scione revolts, joins Brasidas before he knows of the truce. **4.123** Mende revolts, is received by Brasidas though he now knows of the truce. **4.124–28** Brasidas joins the Macedonians against Lyncestis. **4.129-31** Athenians retake Mende. They defeat the Scionaeans and besiege the city. **4.132** Macedonia makes peace with Athens and prevents Spartan reinforcements from marching through Thessaly.	
	4.135 Brasidas' attempt to recapture Potidaea fails.	
	5.2–3 Cleon takes an Athenian army to Thrace. He recaptures Torone. **5.6–11** Cleon advances to Amphipolis but is defeated by Brasidas' audacious attack. Both generals are killed. **5.12–13** Spartan reinforcements for Thrace delay at Heraclea.	**5.1** The Delians are expelled by Athens from Delos to Atramyttium. **5.4–5** Sicily-Italy; Phaeax, Athens' envoy to Sicily and Italy, fails to create an anti-Syracusan coalition. Locris makes peace with Athens.
		5.20 Thucydides discusses his method of dating by year and season rather than by magistrates' names.
5[illegible]ens to p[illegible]s.	**5.26** Thucydides describes how he continued to write his history from exile. **5.32** The Athenians retake Scione; they execute the adult males and enslave the women and children. The Plataeans settle Scione. **5.35** The Dians take Thyssus on Acte.	
	5.39 The Olynthians take Mecyberna from the Athenians.	
	5.52 Boeotians occupy Heraclea-in-Trachis.	

Year/ Season	Attica-Euboea-Boeotia	Peloponnesus Megarid, Cephallenia, Zacynthus, Melos
418/7 Winter	**5.80** Athenian forces withdraw from Epidaurus.	**5.76–80** Argos allies with Sparta. **5.81** Mantinea and Sparta make peace. An oligarchy is established at Argos.
417 Summer		**5.82** Argive democrats overthrow the oligarchy. They reestablish ties with Athens.
417/6 Winter		**5.83** Spartans destroy the new long walls at Argos.
416 Summer	**5.84** Athenians seize and exile 300 Argive oligarchs. Athens sends a fleet against Melos.	**5.84** Three hundred Argive oligarchs are exiled to islands by Athens. **5.85–111** The Melian Dialogue. **5.112–13** The Melians refuse to yield. **5.114** The Athenians besiege Melos. **5.115** Argos raids Phlius. Sparta is stung by raids on Laconia from Pylos.
416/5 Winter		**5.116** Melos surrenders. The Athenians execute the men and enslave the women and children. Athens sends settlers to the island.
BOOK SIX **416/5** Winter	**6.1** Athens votes to send a fleet to Sicily. **6.6** Egestan envoys request Athenian aid against Selinus. **6.7** An Athenian fleet raids Macedonia.	**6.7** Spartans ravage Argos and settle Argive exiles at Orneae. Argives, with Athenian help, raze Orneae.
415 Summer	**6.8–26** Athenians debate Sicily. **6.9–14** First speech of Nicias. **6.16–18** Speech of Alcibiades. **6.20–23** Second speech of Nicias. **6.24** Athens votes to send a huge force to Sicily. **6.27** Mutilation of the Hermae. **6.28–29** Alcibiades is suspected and attacked. **6.32** The Athenian expedition sails for Sicily. **6.53** Alcibiades is recalled home to face trial. **6.54–59** Digression on the tyrannicides Harmodius and Aristogiton. **6.60–61** Agitation in Athens arises from the affairs of the Mysteries and the Hermae. Alcibiades is recalled from Sicily to face charges but he sails to the Peloponnesus instead.	**6.61** Alcibiades sails to the Peloponnesus.
415/4 Winter		

Wes[illegible] Aca[illegible]tus, Epic[illegible]	**Thrace** Chalcidice, Macedonia, Hellespont, Thessaly	**Other Regions** Asia, the Aegean, Italy-Sicily
	5.83 An Athenian fleet blockades Macedonia.	
	6.7 The Athenians raid Macedonia.	**6.2–5** Thucydides describes the history of the Greek settlement of Sicily. **6.6** Egestan sends envoys to request Athenian help against Selinus.
6.4[illegible]ly ass[illegible] **6.4**[illegible]		**6.33–41** Hermocrates and Athenagoras and a Syracusan general give speeches at Syracuse discussing how their city should prepare for the approaching Athenian expedition. **6.44–51** Athenian fleet gets a cool reception in Italy. It stops at Rhegium, where the discovery of Egestan poverty leads to a policy debate. It finally finds a base at Catana. **6.60–61** Alcibiades is recalled from Sicily but escapes at Thurii. **6.62** Athenians take Hyccara and sell its inhabitants into slavery.
		6.63–70 The Syracusans are enticed to Catana while the Athenians sail to Syracuse. **6.70** The Athenian army wins the battle at the Anapus river that occurs when the Syracusans return, but not decisively. The Athenians send home for reinforcements. **6.73–75** Syracuse sends to Corinth and Sparta for help, and constructs new walls and forts. **6.74** An Athenian attack on Messana is betrayed by Alcibiades and fails. **6.75–88** After speeches by Hermocrates (**6.75–80**) and Euphemus (**6.82–87**) at Camarina, Camarina decides to remain neutral.

Year/ Season	Attica-Euboea-Boeotia	Peloponnesus Megarid, Cephallenia, Zacynthus, Melos
415/4 Winter *(cont'd)*	**6.93** Athens votes funds and reinforcements to Sicily.	**6.88–93** Syracusan requests for aid are approved at Corinth but initially rejected by Sparta. However, after Alcibiades' speech to them **(6.89–92),** the Spartans decide to send a general (Gylippus) to Syracuse and to renew the war with Athens by fortifying Decelea.
414 Summer	**6.95** A democratic uprising in Thespiae fails. **6.105** Athens joins the fighting between Argos and Sparta.	**6.95** Spartans invade Argos, but are turned back by an earthquake. The Argives plunder Thyrea. **6.105** Spartans invade Argos. The Athenians assist Argos by raiding Spartan territory, providing a pretext for Sparta to renew the war with Athens.
BOOK SEVEN		
414 Summer		
414/3 Winter	**7.10–15** Nicias' letter is received and debated at Athens. **7.16–17** The Athenians decide to send him large reinforcements and new generals. **7.20** As Demosthenes prepares to depart for Sicily with reinforcements, another Athenian fleet is sent to raid the Peloponnesus. **7.27–28** Athenian hardships are caused by Decelea. **7.29–30** Mycalessus is destroyed by Thracian Dii.	**7.18–19** Sparta prepares for war with Athens. Sparta invades Attica and fortifies Decelea. Peloponnesian reinforcements leave for Sicily. **7.26** Athenians fortify an isthmus of Laconia and pillage Spartan territory.
413 Summer		**7.34** An inconclusive naval battle takes place off Erineus in Achaea between a Peloponnesian fleet with reinforced prows and the Athenian squadron from Naupactus.
413 Winter		

W[illegible] Ac[illegible]ctus, Ep[illegible]	**Thrace** Chalcidice, Macedonia, Hellespont, Thessaly	**Other Regions** Asia, the Aegean, Italy-Sicily
6.[illegible]		**6.94** Operations of the Athenians in Sicily at Megara, Centoripa, Inessa, and Hybla. **6.96–103** The Athenians sail to Syracuse. They occupy Epipolae and construct circumvallation walls. Syracusan efforts to stop them or to build counterwalls are defeated. The Syracusans begin to despair. **6.104** Gylippus arrives in Italy.
	7.9 The Athenians and their allies attempt to take Amphipolis but fail.	**7.1–2** Gylippus marches from Himera to Syracuse, arriving just in time to save Syracuse. **7.3** The Syracusans capture Labdalum. **7.4–7** The Athenians fortify Plemmyrium. Gylippus and the Syracusans are defeated in the first of two battles, but by exploiting Syracusan cavalry in the second, he gains a victory. A Syracusan crosswall passes the Athenian wall and the Athenians are forced on the defensive. **7.8** Nicias writes home asking for large reinforcements or for permission to withdraw.
		7.21 Gylippus persuades the Syracusans to build and train a fleet. **7.22–25** While the Syracusan navy is fighting and losing its first battle **(7.23–24)**, the army takes the Athenian forts at Plemmyrium.
7.[illegible]thering fo[illegible]ce N[illegible]		**7.32** Sicels ambush the Syracusan reinforcements. **7.36–41** The Syracusans win a naval battle. **7.42–45** Athenian reinforcements arrive. Demosthenes' night assault on Epipolae fails. **7.47–49** Demosthenes wants an immediate withdrawal, but Nicias demurs. **7.50** An eclipse of the moon causes the Athenians to delay their withdrawal. **7.52** The Syracusans win another naval battle. **7.57–58** Thucydides lists the nationality and tribe of all the participants on either side, and describes how they became involved in the struggle.
		7.61–68 Speeches of Nicias and Gylippus in preparation for a final naval battle. **7.69–72** The Athenian fleet is decisively defeated. **7.73–85** An Athenian attempt to march north to Catana is blocked by the Syracusans. Returning south, the Athenians are pursued, harassed, and finally forced to surrender at the Assinarus river. **7.86–87** The prisoners are confined in quarries, where many die.

Year/ Season	Attica-Euboea-Boeotia Peloponnesus Western Hellas	Samos
BOOK EIGHT **413/2** **Winter**	**8.1–4** Though shocked by the Sicilian disaster, the Athenians vote to build more ships, secure their allies, and continue the war. The Peloponnesians plan a decisive effort against Athens. **8.5** The Spartan king Agis at Decelea receives envoys of Euboea and Lesbos who wish to discuss revolt. Chios and Tissaphernes sends envoys to Sparta to discuss aid for revolt against Athens. **8.6** Pharnabazus sends envoys to ask for a fleet to the Hellespont.	
412 **Summer**	**8.7–8** The Peloponnesians haul 21 triremes across the Isthmus to the Aegean. They make plans to conquer Athenian subjects in Asia. **8.10–11** An Athenian fleet drives a Peloponnesian fleet into Spiraeum and blockades it there. **8.13** A Peloponnesian squadron returning from Sicily loses one ship in battle with Athenian ships off Leucas. **8.15** Athens reacts strongly to the Chian revolt. The 1,000 talent reserve fund is used to equip a new fleet.	**8.16** The first Athenian forces arrive in the area.
	8.20 The Peloponnesian fleet at Spiraeum sails out, defeats the Athenians, and returns to Cenchreae.	**8.21** With Athenian help, the commons on Samos overthrow the upper classes.
	8.25 1,500 Argive hoplites participate with Athenians in a battle at Miletus.	**8.23–27** After the Athenians counter-attack at Lesbos, Chios, and Miletus, the arrival of a large enemy fleet causes the general Phrynichus to order his fleet to retire to Samos.
412/1 **Winter**		**8.30** Receiving reinforcements, the Athenians plan to blockade both Miletus and Chios.
	8.53–54 Pro-oligarch envoys from the army at Samos try to persuade the Athenian assembly to establish an oligarchy.	
	8.60 Boeotians capture Oropus by treachery. They ask the Peloponnesians at Rhodes to assist a revolt by Euboea but the latter decide to rescue Chios first.	

Chi[illegible]	Miletus and Asia South	Lesbos, Hellespont, Other
8.5 [illegible] ys to disc[illegible]		**8.6** Pharnabazus sends envoys to ask that a fleet be sent to the Hellespont.
8.1[illegible] in Ch[illegible] **8.1**[illegible] Chios inc[illegible]tus to rev[illegible] **8.**[illegible]olition of [illegible] **8.**[illegible]on ca[illegible]ne. **8.**[illegible]k and bl[illegible]	**8.16–17** As Athenian forces arrive in the area, a Peloponnesian fleet from Chios incites Miletus to revolt. **8.18** The Spartans and the Persians complete their first draft of a treaty of alliance. **8.25** The Athenians raid Milesian territory and win a battle there, but then retire to Samos when a large Peloponnesian fleet approaches.	**8.18** The Spartans and the Persians complete their first draft of a treaty of alliance. **8.22** A Chian-Peloponnesian squadron causes revolts at Clazomenae and Cyme. **8.23** The Athenians recover Lesbos. **8.28** At Tissaphernes' request, the Peloponnesian fleet from Miletus captures Iasus and the rebel Amorges.
8[illegible]ns on S[illegible]if Athens b[illegible]jects, and h[illegible]nd c[illegible] **8**[illegible]sent from t[illegible] the A[illegible]garchy.	**8.29** Tissaphernes pays the Peloponnesian fleet but decides in future to pay less. **8.35** An Athenian squadron captures six enemy triremes off Cnidus and almost takes the city before retiring to Samos. **8.36–37** Sparta and Persia conclude a second treaty draft. **8.39** 27 Peloponnesian triremes reach Miletus via Melos, Crete, and Caunus. **8.41–42** The Peloponnesian fleet under Astyochus sails from Miletus to Cnidus, from which he defeats an Athenian squadron near Syme. **8.43** The Spartan commissioners quarrel with Tissaphernes. **8.44** The Peloponnesian fleet sails to Rhodes, whose cities revolt. **8.45–6** Alcibiades escapes to Tissaphernes and advises him to let both sides exhaust each other. **8.56–58** Athenian negotiations with Tissaphernes fail. Sparta and Tissaphernes conclude their treaty of alliance. **8.60** The Boeotians ask the Peloponnesians at Rhodes to assist a revolt by Euboea but the Peloponnesians decide to rescue Chios first.	

Year/ Season	Attica-Euboea-Boeotia Peloponnesus Western Hellas	Samos
411 Summer		
		8.63–64 The main Athenian fleet remains at Samos. The pro-oligarchs in the army send envoys to create an oligarchy at subject cities and at Athens.
	8.64–70 Athenian democracy falls, weakened by assassination and intimidation. The new regime of the Four Hundred rules by force; it sends envoys to Agis with notice of its desire for peace, but they are rejected. **8.71** Agis responds negatively to the overtures of the Four Hundred.	
		8.73–76 At Samos, local democrats and pro-democratic Athenians from the army defeat an oligarchic plot. After learning of the fall of the democracy at Athens, the army chooses new generals and vows to fight both the Four Hundred and the Spartans.
		8.80 The Athenians send ships from Samos back to the Hellespont. **8.81–82** The Athenians on Samos recall Alcibiades and elect him general.
		8.88 Alcibiades sails for Caunus.
	8.89–94 Worried by opposition from the army in Samos, the Four Hundred send envoys to Sparta to make peace. Phrynichus is murdered in the agora. A faction of the Four Hundred led by Theramenes, fearing a betrayal to the Spartans, destroys the wall being built in Eetionia. Despite this civil strife, the Athenians unite against an approaching enemy fleet. **8.95–98** A hastily assembled Athenian fleet is defeated off Euboea by a Peloponnesian fleet assisted by Euboean treachery in Eritrea. Euboea revolts, causing panic at Athens, which leads to the restoration of the democracy. Some of the Four Hundred flee to Agis. One of them helps the Boeotians to capture the fort of Oenoe.	
		8.100 Learning of the departure of the Peloponnesian fleet, the Athenian fleet leaves Samos for the Hellespont.
		8.108 Alcibiades returns to Samos, claiming to have kept the Phoenician fleet from joining the enemy.

Chi[illegible]	Miletus and Asia South	Lesbos, Hellespont, Other
8.6[illegible] but fail t[illegible] **8.6**[illegible]chides leav[illegible]ians in the [illegible]		**8.62** A Peloponnesian army reaches the Hellespont and, with Pharnabazus, captures Abydos and Lampsacus. An Athenian fleet commanded by Strombichides retakes Lampsacus.
	8.78–79 Tissaphernes and Astyochus are strongly criticized by the Peloponnesian sailors at Miletus. The Peloponnesian fleet challenges the Athenians at Samos but draws back after learning Athenian reinforcements have arrived from the Hellespont.	
8.7[illegible]k to joi[illegible] **8.8**[illegible]o the He[illegible]s' offer to [illegible]		**8.80** The Peloponnesians send ships to the Hellespont in response to Pharnabazus' offer to pay them. Byzantium revolts.
	8.84 Thurian and Syracusan sailors demand their pay from Astyochus.	**8.87** The Phoenician fleet appears at Aspendus, where Tissaphernes joins it, promising to bring it into the struggle, but it advances no further.
	8.99 The Peloponnesian fleet leaves Miletus for the Hellespont.	
8.[illegible]s at C[illegible]		**8.100** The Athenian fleet sails from Samos to Lesbos but misses the Peloponnesian fleet. **8.102** The Peloponnesian fleet avoids the Athenian fleet at Lesbos. **8.103–7** The Athenian fleet sails to the Hellespont where the fleets join battle off Point Cynossema. The Peloponnesian fleet is defeated, but not decisively. **8.109** Tissaphernes hurries to the Hellespont.

APPENDIX A

…e Athenian Government in Thucydides

[illegible] the chief population center in Attica, an area about the size of [illegible] ıded east and south by the Aegean Sea, and north and west by [illegible] ·a. Other centers within the state included Piraeus (the chief [illegible] rnae, Rhamnous, Thoricus, and Marathon.[1a] Some three to four [illegible] ɔeople lived in Attica, most of them crowded behind the walls of [illegible] ʼeloponnesian War but otherwise spread out in lesser centers and [illegible] Of the total population, thirty thousand or so had full rights as [illegible] nning of the war, which is to say they were males over thirty [illegible] ˙ two Athenian parents.

[illegible] ·longed to one of the four classes defined and named by the law- [illegible] the sixth century: the criterion was annual income, expressed in [illegible] ıl units or other capabilities. At the top were the *pentacosiomed-* [illegible] ıd five hundred measures (wet or dry) of produce a year. Next [illegible] three hundred measures), who could afford to keep a horse. [illegible] the *zeugitai* or yokefellows (two hundred measures), and last [illegible] ɔ even into the fourth century endured certain limitations in the [illegible] ır civil status. The rest of the population consisted of women; [illegible] ıliens (*metics*), whose numbers fluctuated between ten and forty [illegible] ıg on how many foreigners happened to be in residence at a [illegible] ves, whose number has been estimated at 150,000. Women, even [illegible] identified as fully Athenian, had no vote in courts or assemblies. [illegible] women were not supposed to appear in public except in duly [illegible] ɔns.[2a] Only as an heiress could a woman in some sense control [illegible] ı she could not dispose of an estate. Metics could prosper in [illegible] omen they had to have a citizen represent them if they ever had [illegible] court or assembly. Despite their lack of citizenship, many metics [illegible] ommerce and some grew rich as manufacturers, merchants, and [illegible] almost every kind of work. Some wore out their lives in painful

[illegible] ıarnae, Rhamnous, Thoricus, [illegible] endix A Map.

A2a See Pericles' advice to war widows at 2.45.2.

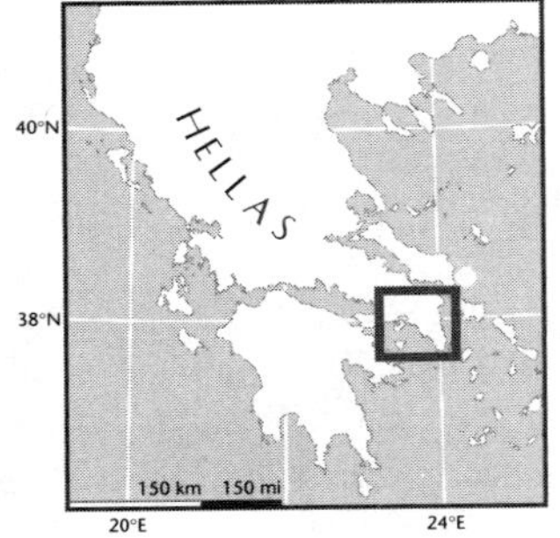

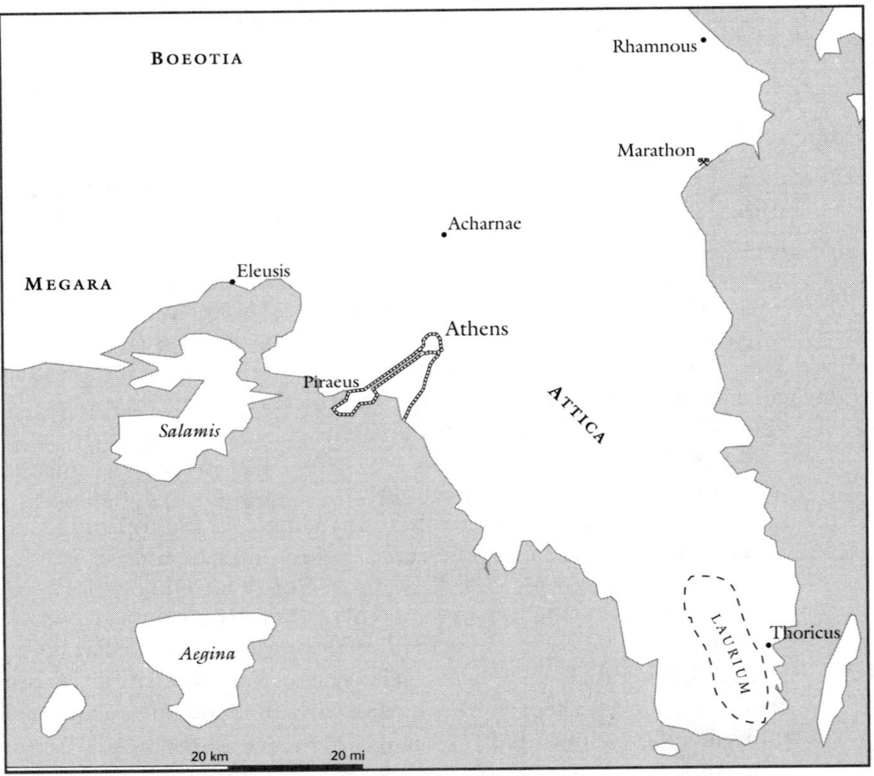

APPENDIX A MAP

iderground work in silver mines at Laurium,[2b] others labored in l others performed relatively light duties as household staff. Some onaries, prostitutes, or teachers; more than a few were skilled arti- ngs might someday permit them to purchase their freedom. When ted to a god, he became a free man.

terms the granting of full citizen rights to less than 10 percent of ould hardly qualify a constitution to be called democratic, but in world the extension of the franchise to that many adult males was mocratic. This "radical" democracy at Athens developed in the ifth century, after appointment by lot had been established for ouncil and (in 487/6) for the chief administrative officers of the n 462) popular courts, manned by citizens who were paid to pro- ad gained a wide jurisdiction. Kleisthenes, an aristocrat, prepared ocracy when in 507 he replaced a venerable aristocratic system of one based on a more or less arbitrarily defined set of ten tribes ymous heroes. By this constitutional reform, he increased the gen- ation and weakened the power of the few.

sthenes, an Athenian's civic identity was fixed in his *deme,* a geo- d administrative district, one of 140 in Attica. A father introduced o his fellow *demesmen* when the son reached eighteen years of age, asion the son was enrolled in the deme register as a citizen. An fficial name included his own name, his father's name, and his , Thucydides son of Oloros, of the deme Halimous). Besides be- e, he was a member of one of the ten tribes devised by Kleisthenes. a brotherhood called a *phratry* was desirable but probably not a on of citizenship. Citizens were landowners; resident aliens and A small landowner might nevertheless work his land alongside the o he could afford to own. Citizens likewise worked for equal pay nd metics on public construction projects.

s were the basis of civic administration at Athens, where a council g of five hundred citizens—fifty from each tribe chosen annually by are an agenda for the assembly (*ekklesia*). They served for one year, ot permitted to serve more than twice in that office. For thirty-five s, that is, one tenth of the civic year, each of these bodies of fifty s standing executive committee (the *prytany*). Each prytany was re- sacred treasuries and kept watch twenty-four hours a day in the building on the west side of the agora just south of the council *uleuterion*) where the council conducted its meetings.[5a] Every day a er of the prytany was chosen by lot to serve as its chairman es preparing an agenda for meetings of the assembly, the council foreign ambassadors, assign various tasks and contracts (for con- e like), and authorize pay for services and materials.

pendix A Map.
estimates in 7.27.5 that twenty
an slaves, many of whom were
nad deserted or escaped.

A5a The remains of the Tholos and the council chamber have been located in the Athenian *agora* (see Glossary), where they can be seen today.

§6. Generally speaking, whatever civic tasks Athenians assigned to a committee were performed by citizens who had been chosen by lot and not by special capacity or training to do that committee's work. The nine chief administrative officers (*archons*) of the city were (in the order in which they are usually listed): archon eponymous (who gives his name to the year), king, *polemarch,* and six *Thesmothetai.* The titles "king" and "polemarch," or "war magistrate," later prompted Greek writers to record tales about an early transfer of power from an attenuated line of kings to the aristocracy. The historicity of this transfer, however, is not clear. *Thesmothetai,* to judge from the name, were concerned initially with legislation and continued to act in the administration of justice. The underlying supposition behind the Athenians' unremitting use of the lot to assign tasks and responsibilities was that every citizen could do what was necessary. The tasks accordingly were made simple.

§7. Generals and treasurers, however, were appointed not by lot, but by election, as it was manifestly dangerous to simplify responsibilities so that persons of indifferent quality could be qualified to hold those offices. Ten generals, one from each tribe, were elected every year for annual terms, and they could be reelected without interruption. No order of precedence or assigned area of authority such as is attested for the fourth century is visible in the fifth century, but when two or more generals went along on an expedition, it would seem that one was designated as being in charge. A general had authority to convene extraordinary meetings of the assembly, and a decision to call or not call a meeting at critical times could be full of consequence. The means by which Pericles, for instance, prevented such a meeting from being called (2.22.1) is not clear; it may have had to do with his own personal authority.

§8. The assembly met regularly four times during each prytany,[8a] usually on a hillside called the Pnyx[8b] a little west of the agora. This gathering of six thousand or more citizens was the final arbiter of any and all business brought before it, and debated all major decisions of state such as whether or not to go to war, sign a treaty, embark on a new campaign, send an embassy, receive envoys, raise and assign forces, or levy or dispose of funds, with all that such decisions entail. One question that recurred during the fifth century at a regular interval, namely, during the sixth prytany of the year, was whether or not to hold an *ostracism.* The issue was private, personal power. A man who was felt to have amassed too much of it was "ostracized," that is, sent into honorable exile for ten years, after which he could return and reclaim his property and his political rights. Although the assembly was scheduled to meet at least four times a prytany, it could meet as often as was deemed necessary. A different president chaired the meeting every day. Motions were introduced, and speakers advocated, modified, or contested what was proposed. The speakers were citizens who for one reason or another—training, natural ability, political climate—could persuade their fellow citizens to vote as they recommended. Pericles was one such speaker, Cleon another. There was no authority higher than

A8a I.e., four times every five weeks or so, or at least forty times per year given one prytany per year for each of ten tribes.

A8b Pnyx: Map 6.56. See 8.97.1. Note, however, that certain assemblies were convened elsewhere; see 8.67.2, 8.93.3, and 8.97.1.

people voted by raising their hands, and their determinations s in the Mytilenian debate (3.36–50), they themselves reversed

ration of justice was likewise in the hands of citizens, who acted s *dikasts*[9a] in two separate and distinct systems. Certain officials l summary powers of judgment in some cases, and the assembly orm of prosecution called *eisangelia,* but for the most part citi- l trials in courts. A homicide might be tried in one of five differ- specially designated citizens judged. Most legal cases, however, the five popular (or *heliastic*) courts, which drew on a pool of citizens who were selected by lot, assigned to a single court for to judge in panels that numbered (according to the sums in- usness of the alleged offense) two hundred, four hundred, five sand, or even six thousand. Athenians saw these panels as repre- a whole; pay for service allowed poor citizens to participate, and t affirmed a random mix. The combination of selection by lot t ballot helped to keep bribes, threats, and other inappropriate ecting judicial decisions. Since the city was the ultimate judging form of appeal to a higher tribunal. As a corollary to this con- of prosecutions and convictions, such as that of Alcibiades .1,4;), may have reflected politics or public opinion more than rials might be won or lost by eloquence. Speeches for the prose- fense were carefully timed and limited so that no trial lasted Votes on verdict and (when required by the lack of a statutory ment were by secret ballot; a simple majority determined the favoring the defendant. Athenians were rightly proud of their ut, however, ignoring its defects and abuses.[9b] Any citizen could for wrongdoing, and there was no publicly appointed prosecutor. onists could threaten or initiate lawsuits against wealthy Atheni- ten settle for cash rather than expose themselves to the risky out- temperament. Or citizens could for whatever private reason take pular mood and indict someone for a real or a fancied wrong. es are famous examples of people so indicted.

and defendant alike were expected to speak for themselves, and citizen, whose real business might be running his small farm, rily know how to begin and end a speech. But length was tightly utcome might be literally life or death, since imprisonment was porary restraint, not for long-term punishment. Penalties were or death. As a result, skilled speakers who could help friends or ; them how to speak and how to behave in a court when under gation were highly prized resources. Antiphon, whom Thucydides

ganized in panels to hear nine guilt or innocence in cases n.

A9b See the speech of the Athenian emissaries to the Spartan assembly, 1.76.3–77.5.

calls "the one man best able to aid in the courts, or before the assembly, the suitors who required his opinion" (8.68.1), was one such speaker.[10a]

§11. There were some Athenians who persistently criticized and sometimes even physically attacked the Athenian democratic system. Many were powerful, educated, and articulate aristocrats who saw no virtue in entrusting power to a mass of base persons.[11a] These Athenians, who wanted a narrower base of power (and who tended to admire the Spartan way of life), were styled *oligarchs.*[11b] When they modified the constitution, as happened in 411,[11c] they limited the franchise and stopped pay for service in public offices. As a result, the number of citizens entitled to vote on major questions (ostensibly) shrunk from thirty thousand to five thousand, and the actual numbers present in any given assembly were accordingly greatly diminished. A council of four hundred actually governed. The popular courts of the democracy, whose panels required numerous citizens, could not function, and all the city's various councils and committees had to be manned (if they continued in existence at all) by men who could afford to serve.

§12. Despite the opposition of domestic and foreign oligarchs, the Athenian democracy proved a vigorous institution. For over one hundred forty years, during a period that extended approximately from 462 to 320, only two short-lived oligarchic regimes managed to seat themselves, namely, the ambiguous government of the Four Hundred in 411, and the oppressive rule of the Thirty in 404/3. Thucydides could well remark in 8.68.4 that "it was no light thing to deprive the Athenian people of its freedom a hundred years after the deposition of the tyrants."

Alan L. Boegehold
Brown University
Providence, Rhode Island

A10a But note that Thucydides also says that Antiphon never came forward to speak in the assembly or any other public forum, because he was not liked by the multitude owing to his reputation for cleverness.

A11a Note Athenagoras' criticism of the "young Syracusan aristocrats" in his speech at 6.36–40, and Alcibiades' antidemocratic remarks to the Spartans at 6.89–92.

A11b See note 8.54.4a on political clubs at Athens.

A11c The success of the oligarchs is described at 8.53ff.

APPENDIX B

The Athenian Empire in Thucydides

[illegible] Empire" is a phrase in conventional use, describing a system of [illegible] es who answered in varying ways to the authority of Athens. [illegible] e autonomous members of an alliance of Greek city-states and is- [illegible] 78 after the battles of Plataea[1a] and Mycale[1b] to defend Greeks [illegible] Persian invasions, and to avenge damage and injuries done by [illegible] recent past. This alliance came under Athenian military leader- [illegible] tan regent and general Pausanias disgraced himself and the Spar- [illegible] n further participation in the struggle against Persia.[1c] States from [illegible] ed Athens to lead them and Athens complied: she was in an ad- [illegible] n to command, employing as she did a large and active fleet and [illegible] d singular reputation for heroism gained by her triumph at the [illegible] n,[1d] her people's heroic evacuation of their city, and her role in the [illegible] y of Salamis.[1e]

[illegible] liance is known as the Delian League because its members at first [illegible] eliberations and established their treasury on the small centrally [illegible] Delos, an ancient Ionian sanctuary sacred to Apollo.[2a] Most of the [illegible] Aegean Sea and many coastal cities of Thrace and Asia Minor be- [illegible] recognizing that they were vulnerable to Persian forces and ex- [illegible] Greek fleet that could either support or harry them. When the [illegible] s, widely known as "the Just," took command, he designed a [illegible] which member states were to contribute money annually,[2c] with [illegible] nount determined more or less by its size and resources. It was [illegible] nautical cities, and the major islands of Chios, Lesbos, and

[illegible] B Map, BX. Site of a great land [illegible] ks over the Persians. See also [illegible]

[illegible] nt Mycale): Appendix B Map, [illegible] victory over the Persians men- [illegible] See also Appendix E, §4.

[illegible] bes the disgrace of Pausanias and [illegible] the Spartans in 1.95.

[illegible] dix B Map, BX. Site in Attica of a [illegible] the Athenians over a Persian ex- [illegible] Appendix E, §4.

[illegible] B Map, BX. Site of the first [illegible] by the combined Greek fleet [illegible] r Persian fleet in 480. See also [illegible]

B2a Delos: Appendix B Map, BY. For the religious significance of Delos, see Polycrates' consecration of Rhenea to Delos (1.13.6) and Athenian purifications of Delos (3.104.1).

B2b Melos: Appendix B Map, BX; Thera: Appendix B Map, BY. These islands in the southern Aegean, settled by Dorians, were however among the few Aegean islands that did not join the league (2.9.4).

B2c Thucydides says in 1.96.2 that the first year's tribute totaled 460 talents. The Athenian-Spartan peace treaty described by Thucydides in 5.18.5. refers to the tribute set by Aristides.

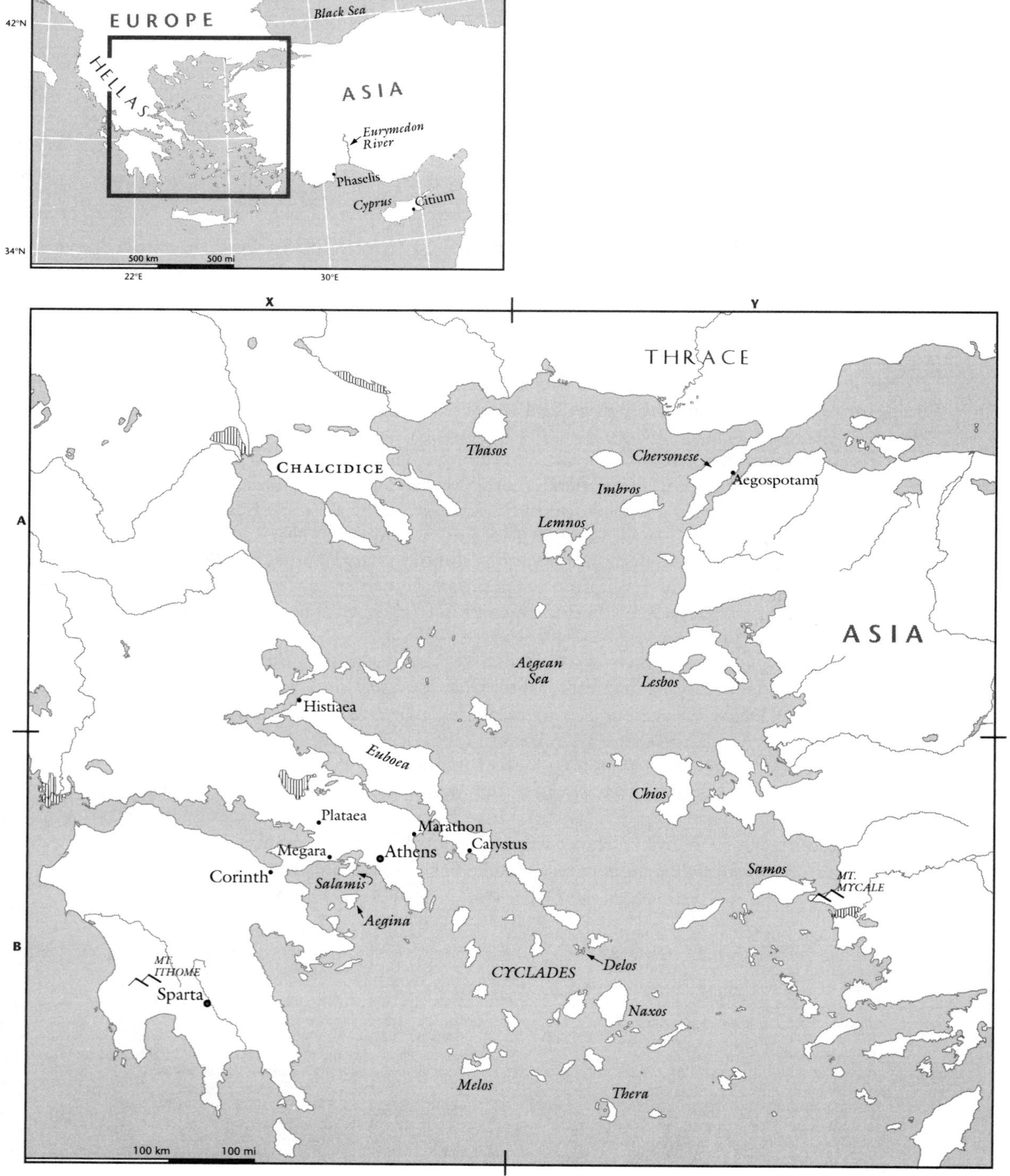

APPENDIX B MAP

ntribute ships and manpower in lieu of money. All member states ing them permanently to the alliance. Although each member n equal say in League matters, there was no major, counterbal- t that of Athens to attract clusters of votes in opposition. For this was great diversity of opinion among members, any few who weighted the balloting enough for Athens to prevail; and there ome who would cooperate with her. In time the restless energy lmost inevitably transformed their initial commanding position that of a ruling power.

s and duration of the Athenian Empire can be sketched in its om several ancient written sources. Thucydides' description years between the defeat of the Persians in 479 and the outbreak an War in 431—known as the "Pentecontaetia" by scholars, al- exactly comprise fifty years—is our most substantial account of some surprising omissions. Plutarch and Diodorus Siculus also information, and other details can be drawn from various surviv- nts inscribed on stone. And yet despite this comparative abun- for a short period of time, many elements of chronology and to resist satisfactory ordering. There can be no doubt, however, e ceased to exist when her fleet was defeated and captured by the Aegospotami in 405.[3a]

des came Cimon son of Miltiades, one of Athens' greatest gener- ommand of the Greek forces and vigorously and successfully set Persians out of the Aegean. By the early 460s (467?), when Cimon ous victory over the Persians in a combined land and sea battle at iver in Pamphylia,[4a] the Delian League comprised nearly two hun- es and controlled not only the entire Aegean Sea but also a broad stern Asia Minor. Many of these states benefited greatly from their alliance that suppressed piracy, encouraged trade and commerce, ployment for the poor as rowers in the fleet. Moreover, Athens democratic factions, and when oligarchs and democrats in a given equally matched in a struggle for dominance, Athenian support ve for the democrats. Democratic regimes that owed their estab- inued existence to Athens tended to be reliable and loyal subject have preferred autonomy, but, for many, answering to Athens was rnative to the rule of local oligarchs. Accordingly, despite the as- ch Corinth predicted uprisings,[4b] subject cities were slow to revolt ter the outbreak of the Peloponnesian War and only did so with the presence of Peloponnesian troops under Brasidas in Chal- thens' apparently crippling defeat in Sicily. Some states, however, Athens throughout the Peloponnesian War.

any members of the League found their contributions of military

B Map, AY; Chios and Samos: BY.

endix B Map, AY.

Appendix B Map, locator. Thucydides mentions this victory in 1.100.1.

B4b For Corinth's predicted uprisings, see 1.122.1.

B4c Chalcidice: Appendix B Map, AX.

service and ships onerous, and elected to pay a cash equivalent instead. Athens used these funds to improve her own properly equipped and well-trained fleet. As a result, Athens found herself in an even better position to collect tribute from reluctant allies, and such allies found themselves less able to offer serious resistance to Athenian demands. By 431, only Lesbos and Chios[5a] continued to supply ships of their own and to enjoy the status of privileged allies rather than subjects.

§6. States who sought to leave the alliance found early on that Athens would not permit them to do so. Naxos (before 467) and Thasos (465–62) tried to break away but were besieged, defeated, and compelled to remain as members.[6a] When the large island of Samos[6b] defied Athens in 440, a major military campaign was mounted to subdue and punish her. The revolts of Lesbos in 428 and of Chios and other states in 411 were more threatening still, because they took place during the Peloponnesian War. Athens responded to these uprisings with increasingly firm and harsh measures designed to maintain and even to increase the nature and extent of her rule. Opponents were exiled or executed. Fines were levied, and in some cases land was confiscated and allocated to Athenian citizens (see §10 below). Some states that refused to become members of the alliance were compelled to join it. This odious use of imperial power, perhaps based on the presumption that those who are not with us are against us, was first employed against Carystus in Euboea around 472; it culminated in the brutal conquest of Melos in 415,[6b] and collapsed in Athens' total and calamitous failure to subjugate Syracuse two years later.

§7. Relations with Sparta began to deteriorate when Cimon, in 462, persuaded the Athenians to help the Spartans, who were besieging Messenians and Helots at Mount Ithome.[7a] When the Spartans rudely sent the Athenians home soon after they had arrived, many Athenians were offended and blamed Cimon personally. Not long afterward they ostracized him (1.102), but they recalled him before his ten-year banishment was complete so that he could again command their forces against the Persians. He died while leading a Greek fleet at Citium on the island of Cyprus[7b] around 450. Cimon's death, together with the outbreak of open conflict with Sparta and the destruction by Persia of a large Greek fleet in Egypt[7c] in 454, may well have led Athens to increase her control over the League. In any case, she moved the League treasury from Delos to Athens in 454/3, and seems thereafter to have consulted less and less with the allies about questions of policy. In her official language, she began to refer to the allies as "all the cities that Athens rules." Pericles had reason to warn his fellow citizens in 429 that their rule over the empire was a tyranny, one that it may have been wrong to take, but which by that time was very dangerous to let go.[7d]

§8. For some reason, Athenian military activity against Persia ceased shortly after Cimon's death. There is a persistent tradition in the fourth century that the Athenian Callias, son of Hipponicus, secured a formal peace with Persia around this

B5a Lesbos: Appendix B Map, AY; Chios, Appendix B Map, BY. The Athenians were more acutely outraged by the revolt of Lesbos because of the island's privileged status (3.36.2).

B6a Naxos: Appendix B Map, BY; Thasos: Appendix B Map, AX.

B6b Samos: Appendix B Map, BY.

B6c For Thucydides' "Melian Dialogue," see 5.85–5.113. Carystus, Euboea, Melos: Appendix B Map, BX.

B7a Sparta, Mount Ithome: Appendix B Map, BX.

B7b Citium, Cyprus: Appendix B Map, locator.

B7c For the story of the loss of this Athenian expedition to Egypt, as well as the fleet sent by the Athenians to relieve it, see 1.104, 1.109–10.

B7d See Pericles' speech at 2.63.2 and the speech of the Athenians at Sparta, 1.75.3.

century. By the terms of that peace, it is thought that Persia s would not sail west of Phaselis or out of the Black Sea,[8a] and ernors of Persian provinces) would not attempt to force Athen- Persian rule. Thucydides, however, does not mention any such other fifth-century writers. As a result, there is wide disagree- a "Peace of Callias,"[8b] which occupies a key place in modern reconstruction of the course of the Athenian Empire, was actu-

exerted control over her subjects through judicial agreements. e required agreements between states—if only to determine ould be heard. Often more complex questions needed to be ad- e class of offense, the kind of court, and the citizenship of the normal for a state to enter into a formal agreement with another atters, and the two would publish their own particular rules of enians required that a larger number and variety of cases be tried usual in such agreements. They believed their courts were just ubjects, and indeed they complained that despite their superior by such agreements to their own disadvantage.[9a] It is relevant to , when Athenian popular courts entered a new era, one in which ated a vastly wider array of suits and prosecutions, their facilities , courts and personnel, functioned at a level of volume and com- anything that could be found anywhere else in the Aegean basin.

the allocation of legal business was consistent with perfect equity point. Certainly, Athens wielded various instruments of power ef- uring the first sixty years of its empire. An important control was ulate a robust flow of commercial traffic by sea and to pay for an ds, from basic foodstuffs to luxuries, all of which meant profit for siness with her. This power was used against Megara when Athens Megarians from conducting trade in any ports of the empire or the This particular prohibition proved so harmful to Megara and was rageous that its repeal was among the key Peloponnesian demands outbreak of war.[10a] In addition, the League treasurers (*helleno-* re all Athenians, collected the tribute and acted as enforcers when to pay. In some locations—for example, on Lemnos, Imbros, the ell as at Histiaea, Aegina, Lesbos and Melos[10b]—Athens settled her olonists or lot-holders (*clerouchs*) who turned their new land into s of Athens, and served, if only by their presence, as Athenian gar- the local citizens.[10c] In time, Athens also imposed on her tributary ver coinage and a system of standard weights and measures.

e Athenians moved the League treasury to Athens in 454/3, they

lack Sea: Appendix B Map, locator.
allias" is also discussed in Appen-
te E5c. See also note 8.56.4a.
1.77.
n Decree, see note 1.42.2a;
40.3; and 1.144.2.
s, Chersonese, and Lesbos: Appendix B Map, AY; Histiaea, Appendix B Map, AX; Aegina and Melos: Appendix B Map, BX. For the establishment of *clerouchs* on Lesbos, see 3.50.2.

B10c The taking of land by these *clerouchies* was deeply resented by the local citizens and was explicitly forbidden in the charter of a second Athenian confederacy formed briefly in the mid-fourth century.

consecrated a sum equal to one sixtieth of each year's tribute to Athena, tutelary goddess of Athens, and used that money in various ways to enhance their city; they could now pay citizens to hold many civic offices, and they could honor Athena on the Acropolis with magnificent new buildings such as the Parthenon and the Propylaia. A fragmentary record of these appropriated sums, published as lists inscribed on marble slabs, begins in 454/3 and ends possibly in 410/409.[11a] A 5 percent harbor tax imposed on the allies in 413 may have turned out to be more practicable. A major reassessment in 425, which substantially increased the annual tribute of the allies, and which is preserved on its own stele, is not mentioned at all by Thucydides.

§12. Plutarch wrote that Pericles had to respond to complaints that he should not use League contributions to beautify Athens. In reply, he said that the allies contributed nothing but money, and that as long as the Athenians did their job, which was to run the war against Persia, they did not need to present any accounting to those who gave the money. This cool assessment is in its tone quite in keeping with the chilling Athenian "realpolitik" of the Melian Dialogue:[12a] those who have power do what they like, those who do not, do what they must.

Alan L. Boegehold
Brown University
Providence, Rhode Island

B11a See Illustration 2.69, which shows a fragment of a tribute list.

B12a For the Melian Dialogue, see Thucydides, 5.85–113.

APPENDIX C

Spartan Institutions in Thucydides

[illegible]

[illegible] different, "other," almost un-Greek—or so it could be made to
[illegible] thenian side of the fifth-century B.C. "Great Powers" divide
[illegible]). Only a few favored non-Spartans knew Sparta well from the
[illegible] unwelcome foreign visitors might find themselves summarily ex-
[illegible] ut the experience of Thucydides was probably more typical. He
[illegible] eration of "the secrecy of their government" (5.68.2), and his
[illegible] emphasize the polar opposition between themselves and their
[illegible] aracter as in institutions (1.69.4–71; 2.39; 8.96.5). These funda-
[illegible] can almost all be traced to two Spartan peculiarities: their educa-
[illegible] heir relationship with the Helots of Laconia and Messenia.

[illegible] other Greek city-states, Sparta had a comprehensively, minutely,
[illegible] ized system of education that was prescribed as a condition of at-
[illegible] n adult citizen status. Its main emphasis was military. Boys were
[illegible] rom their mothers—indeed, from all females—and educated
[illegible] controlled packs divided and subdivided by age. Fighting, steal-
[illegible] en murdering (see §4) were enjoined as integral parts of the ed-
[illegible] asic literacy was apparently taught, so some Spartans at least could
[illegible] he few official documents their city chose to record and display
[illegible] (5.70) and dancing (5.16) were also part of the prescribed cur-
[illegible] y were crucial to performing the major religious festivals devoted
[illegible] the Carneia (5.54; 5.76.1), but they were also learned in signifi-
[illegible] heir military benefits.[2a] Hence, too, the conscious development of
[illegible] -style form of utterance (4.17.2; 4.84.2), which is still called by us
[illegible] ne Greek adjective meaning "Spartan"), just as we still speak of a
[illegible], a spare, austere, self-denying—mode of existence. Between the
[illegible] thirty Spartan males spent almost their entire lives in communal
[illegible] es, or barracks; even married men were required to make their
[illegible] tively, briefly, and under cover of darkness.

[illegible] ntinea, the Spartans advanced
[illegible] ably in unison) into battle to the
music of flute players (5.70). Mantinea: Appendix
D Map, AX.

§3. The Helots, especially the more numerous portion living in Messenia to the west of Sparta on the far side of the eight-thousand-foot Taygetus mountain range,[3a] were the Spartans' enemy within, not least because they always and appreciably outnumbered their masters. Most were farmers producing the food, drink, and other basics (especially barley, pork, wine, and olive oil) that enabled all Spartans to live a barrack-style military life in Sparta instead of working for a living. But the Helots, though native Greeks, farmed the Spartans' land under a harsh yoke of servitude, so that many of them vehemently opposed the Spartan regime, yearned to regain the liberty and autonomy they imagined they had lost through earlier defeats (their name probably means "captives"), and were prepared to stake all on revolt (1.101.2; 2.27.2; 4.56.2). Spartan policy, therefore, as Thucydides starkly and accurately asserts, was "at all times . . . governed by the necessity of taking precautions against them" (4.80.2; cf. 1.132.4–5; 5.23.3—"the slave population").

§4. Precautions might exceptionally be intensified, as in 425–24, when, in response to the Athenians' exploitation of Helot disaffection following the vital loss of Pylos and Cythera[4a] (4.3.3; 4.55.1; 5.35.7), some two thousand selected troublemakers were secretly liquidated (4.80.5). But Spartans were routinely brought up, within the normal framework of their educational curriculum, to put Helots to death in peacetime. This occurred under cover of a general proclamation, repeated every autumn by each new board of *ephors* (see below), declaring war on the Helots collectively and thereby exonerating their Spartan killers in advance from the ritual pollution of homicide. There could not be a more perfect illustration of the Spartans' intense religiosity bordering on superstition that was perhaps another by-product of their military style of life.

Government Institutions

§5. The five ephors, chosen by a curious form of election from any Spartans who wished to stand, were Sparta's chief executive officials. They possessed very extensive powers in both the formulation and the execution of foreign and domestic policy (1.85.3; 1.86; 1.131.1; 2.2.1; 6.88.10). Collegiality and the majority principle did impose some constraints, but the annual oath they exchanged with the two Spartan hereditary kings indicates where the balance of authority rested: the ephors swore on behalf of the Spartans collectively to uphold the kingship so long as the kings themselves observed the laws (which the ephors interpreted and applied).

§6. Ephors, though, were annual officials, and the office could apparently be held only once. The two kings, on the other hand, and the other members of the thirty-strong Gerousia (Sparta's senate, also curiously elected, but only from men aged sixty or over who probably also had to belong to certain aristocratic families), held office for life and partly for that reason enjoyed exceptional prestige and authority. However, not even the kings' supposed direct descent from Heracles, "the demigod son of Zeus" (5.16.2), nor their hereditary right to the overall command of any Spartan army or Spartan-led allied force, prevented them from being disci-

C3a Messenia and the Taygetus range in relation to Sparta: Appendix D Map, BY.

C4a Pylos: Appendix D Map, BX; Cythera: Appendix D Map, BY.

and sometimes deposed and exiled (5.16). An adroit king such ght seek to exploit his aura of prestige and abundant opportuni- to exercise a decisive and sometimes lasting influence on policy. ven Archidamus (1.80–85) and his supporters in the Gerousia assembly of citizen warriors, which had the final say in matters to vote against immediate war with Athens—in this one known al division rather than by its usual crude procedure of shouting

ation

unt of the great battle of Mantinea[7a] in 418, Thucydides provides se of Sparta's unique and complex military organization in deci- l action (esp. 5.66, 5.69.2–7; cf. 4.34.1; 5.9). The goal of the al system was to produce exceptionally disciplined and efficient n (see Appendix F, §7); the navy was very much an inferior Spar- .2). For almost two centuries, indeed, the Spartans suffered no any sort. Yet partly because of the constant internal Helot threat, not lightly undertake aggressive foreign wars (1.118.2; cf. 5.107), ly fought without large-scale allied support.

, the Spartans experienced a growing and increasingly critical n military manpower, caused basically by internal socioeconomic Spartan citizen had to contribute a minimum of natural produce orked for him by Helots toward the upkeep of the communal he lived and ate, and through which he exercised his military and sibilities. But in the period after the Persian Wars the number of who could contribute the required minimum declined, through a ely understood today, but which probably was the result of an in- ration of land in fewer hands. This socioeconomic manpower gravated by the catastrophic earthquake of the 460s (1.101.2; 4.56.2) and by important losses in the Peloponnesian War.

ans therefore drew ever more heavily on non-Spartan troops to ontline infantry force. In the first place, they had regular and in- to the hoplites of the *perioikoi* (literally, "dwellers around") whom ed in the same regiments as themselves. These perioikoi were free d in their own semiautonomous communities, mainly along the aconia (e.g., Epidaurus Limera and Thyrea [4.56.2]) and Messe- one [2.25.1]), but also along the vulnerable northern border with gos[9b] (e.g., the Sciritae [5.67.2; 5.68.3; 5.71.2–3; 5.73.1–2; perioikoi spoke the same dialect as the Spartans and resembled ltural ways, but they enjoyed no political rights at Sparta and so parta's foreign affairs (3.92.5; 4.8.1; 4.53.2; 5.54.1; 5.67.1; 8.6.4; ly, and paradoxically, the Spartans also had regular and increasing

dix D Map, AX.
: Thyrea: Appendix D Map, AY.
dix D Map, BX.

C9b Arcadia: Appendix D Map, AX; Argos: Appendix D Map, AY.

military recourse to Helots and various categories of liberated Helots, of which the most privileged but still awkwardly unassimilated were the *neodamodeis* (4.21; 5.67; 7.19.3; 7.58.3). All the same, the Peloponnesian War was decided not on land but at sea, and above all by Persian money, rather than by traditional Spartan military prowess.

Paul Cartledge
Clare College
Cambridge University
Cambridge, England

APPENDIX D

[illegible]e Peloponnesian League in Thucydides

[illegible]

[illegible] esian League," a modern term for the ancient formula "The Spar- [illegible] es," invites the Voltairean comment that it was actually neither [illegible] r a league (as the Holy Roman Empire was to Voltaire neither [illegible] nor an empire). It was not a "league" in our sense because the al- [illegible] individually by treaty to Sparta, not to each other, and indeed [illegible] against each other (4.134; 5.81.1). The official name is known to [illegible] rative sources such as Thucydides, who also abbreviates it to "the [illegible] alone (1.105.3), and from a tiny handful of documentary inscrip- [illegible]

[illegible] how Sparta's original military alliances with such Peloponnesian [illegible] (always her most important ally), Elis, and Tegea[2a] were translated [illegible] League is not known for certain, though the transformation had [illegible] d by the time of the Persian Wars of 480–79 and probably as many [illegible] before that. The turning point may well have been the fiasco of [illegible] Sparta under her wayward and autocratic king Cleomenes I lost [illegible] e majority of her allies on the very brink of a combined attack on [illegible] es' Spartan co-king led the defection at the prompting of the [illegible] reafter only one king at a time was empowered to lead a Spartan or [illegible] Sparta required the allies' formal consent before undertaking such a [illegible] n (see "Mechanisms," below).

[illegible]

[illegible] ties within the Peloponnese, most conspicuously Argos, were never [illegible] League, and some cities outside, above all Megara and those of the [illegible] ion,[3a] sometimes were. At its largest, within the half century follow- [illegible] nesian War, the League extended as far north as Chalcidice,[3b] but [illegible] ainland Greece. It is useful therefore to distinguish between the [illegible] liance (1.31.2; 2.9.3), on the one hand, and its inner core or circle

[illegible] ix D Map, AY; Elis, Tegea: Appen- [illegible]

D3a Argos, Megara, Boeotia: Appendix D Map, AY.

D3b Chalcidice: Appendix D Map, locator.

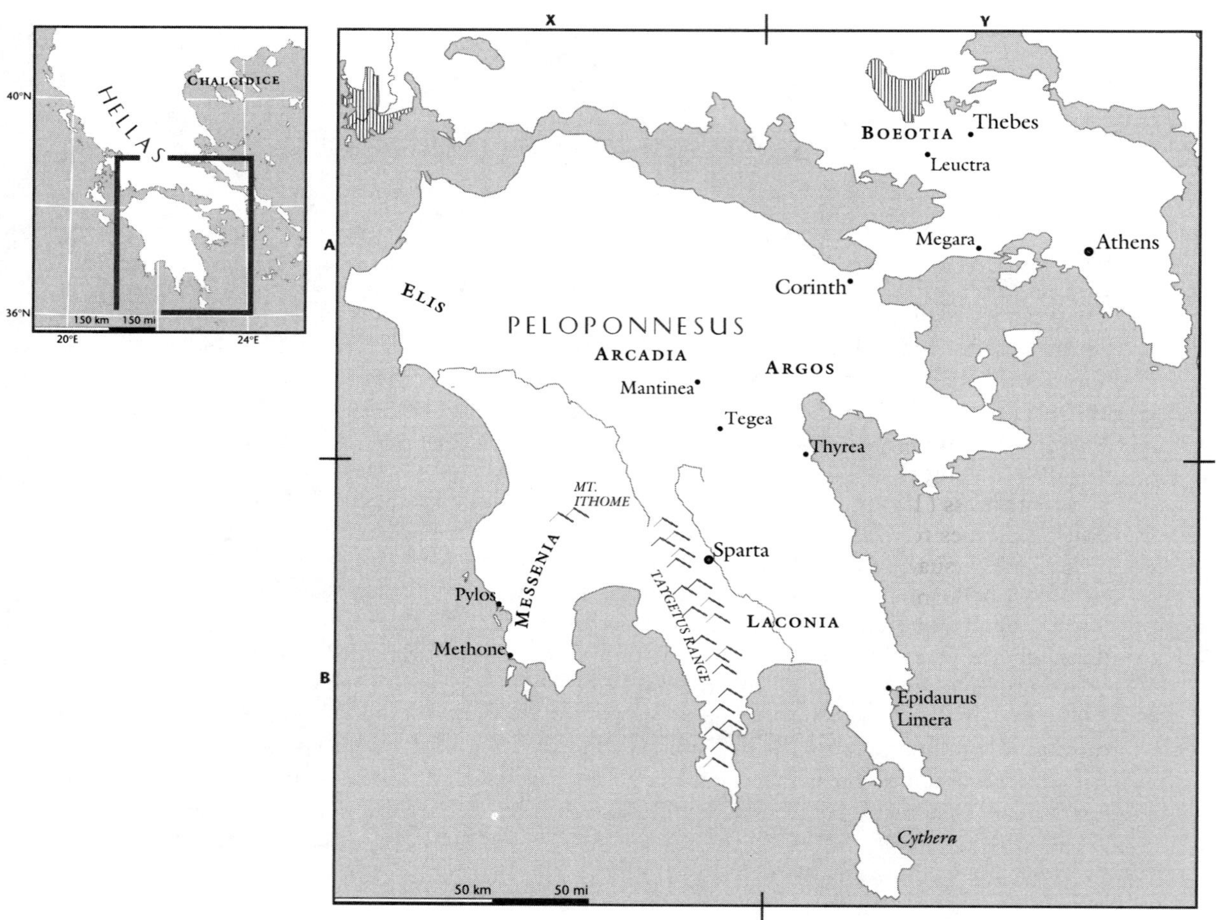

Appendix D Map

eloponnesian League members, on the other. Occasionally there status of an ally, most conspicuously in the case of Athens after War in the years 404 and immediately following. We know that use" (discussed below) was applied to Athens by Sparta, but it t Athens was incorporated fully within the League structure any d been after the battle of Mantinea (5.79–80.1).

there were episodes, indeed whole periods, in which a Pelopon- or allies defected from or even fought an outright war against iod was 421–18, when Corinth, Mantinea, and Elis[4a] revolted lied themselves with Argos. The Boeotians and the Megarians, tly refused to join the Argive-led coalition in the belief that "the would not agree so well with their aristocratic forms of govern- constitution" (5.31.6).

l language the Peloponnesian League was a hegemonic sym- arta's allies swore to have the same friends and enemies as their) and to follow the Spartans wherever they might lead them. In eadership was restricted by the obligation to persuade a majority at a duly constituted League congress to follow her in declaring eace, and to do so on her terms. But only Sparta could summon .67.3; 1.87.4; 1.119–125.1), so that she could never be commit- a policy she opposed (1.88.1; 1.118.2). On the other hand, she le a majority on more than one occasion (e.g., 1.40.5). Allies, important opt-out clause: they were obligated to obey a major- on "unless the gods or heroes stand in the way" (5.30.3)—unless, legitimately invoke a prior and overriding religious obligation.

ens, Sparta did not impose on her allies tribute in cash or kind use traditional hoplite-style warfare (see Appendix F) was much maintaining a large trireme navy (see Appendix G, §12 and 13, §6), but also because Sparta lacked the necessary administrative tructure (1.141.6). Allies were required by Sparta to contribute a proportion of their troops to a League force, and Sparta pro- both to levy and to command the contingents stipulated (2.75.3). of all, however, by a variety of informal means, and chiefly or covert support of favorable oligarchic regimes in the allied .2; cf. 1.18.1; 5.31.6), Sparta took great care to ensure that her d routinely fulfill her wishes.

150 years (c. 505–365), therefore, the Peloponnesian League realized the twin aims the *hegemon* set for it: to serve as the arta could behave on the international stage as one of the two (or powers, and to throw a protective cordon around the vulnerable

endix D Map, AX.

domestic basis of all Spartan life and policy, the Helots. In 371, however, the Spartans and their allies were decisively beaten at Leuctra in Boeotia by their former allies the Thebans;[7a] the now-undisguisable shortage of Spartan citizen manpower (see Appendix C, §8) was not the least cause of their disastrous defeat. In its wake the brilliant Theban commander Epaminondas conducted a massive invasion of Laconia, the first-ever invasion of Laconia by land by a foreign power since the formation of the Spartan state some three to four centuries earlier. By freeing the Helots of Messenia, and so destroying the economic basis of the Spartan army's superiority, and by fortifying the Messenians' old stronghold on Mt. Ithome[7b] (1.101.2–3; 1.102.1–3; 1.103.1; 3.54.5) to ensure the independence of their new (or reborn) city of Messene, Epaminondas put an end to Sparta's "Great Power" status for good. The Peloponnesian League was an early casualty of Sparta's enforced weakness, simply melting away into oblivion well before Sparta's second major defeat in hoplite battle at the hands of Epaminondas, at Mantinea in 362.

Paul Cartledge
Clare College
Cambridge University
Cambridge, England

D7a Boeotia, Leuctra, Thebes: Appendix D Map, AY.
D7b Messenia, Mt. Ithome (Ithome): Appendix D Map, BX.

APPENDIX E

The Persians in Thucydides

s the Great overthrew the kingdom of the Medes in 550 B.C. he been a Median empire into a Persian one. Since both Medes and n the same region—Iran—and Median nobles continued to be e empire of the Persians, Greeks often used the terms "Mede" or geably with "Persian" or "Persians." Those Greeks who took the y conflicts were said to have "Medized" or to be guilty of

nis successors vigorously expanded their empire until, under Darom 521 to 486 B.C., Persian dominion reached from Thrace in pe to parts of India, and from southern Egypt to the Caucasus.[2a] eeks referred to the Persian ruler simply as "the King," there out which monarch was thus signified. To govern so vast an emuthority had to be delegated to governors (called *satraps*) of *s*) who, in turn, exercised power through subordinate officials or system worked well when provincial governors, who were usuagents of the King, were loyal to him, but when central authorwhen problems occurred in the royal succession, they could be dependently or even to revolt. Satrapies were linked by imperial yal messenger post whose speed and efficiency amazed the con- Trade was facilitated by common official languages and a univerirrency. To a Greek of the fifth century, even a sophisticated one was not entirely limited to the borders and neighbors of his *polis* seemed immense in size, in wealth, and in power. It was largely with Persia that the Greeks became acquainted with the accumuof ancient Egypt, Mesopotamia, and even India, so that it is not most of the first Greek philosophers, poets, and historians came Asia Minor that had fallen under Lydian and later Persian rule. ns, the Greeks must have seemed a troublesome, if peripheral, set peoples with strange customs and enough military prowess to be

ppendix E Map, locator; Thrace:
Y.

dangerous—although fortunately self-neutralized by wars they constantly waged among themselves.

§3. In 546 B.C., Cyrus conquered Lydia[3a] in western Asia (Asia Minor), and thereby succeeded to the dominion over many Greek cities that had been earlier subdued and made tributary by the Lydians. Almost fifty years later, in 499 B.C., the Greeks of Ionia (in Asia Minor) revolted against Persian rule and requested their fellow Greeks to help them. Sparta refused, but Athens and Eretria (a city on Euboea),[3b] sent small squadrons of ships to assist them. Troops from their contingents joined a combined Greek assault against Sardis,[3c] the former capital of the kingdom of Lydia and now the seat of a Persian satrap. The Greeks captured the lower city and burned it, but thereafter Persian forces defeated them on both land and sea (the fighting spread as far away as Cyprus[3d]) and finally put down the Greek rebellion by 494.

§4. To punish the affront at Sardis, Darius sent a punitive expedition into Greece in 490 B.C., which, after sacking Eretria and carrying off its inhabitants, was defeated by the Athenians at Marathon[4a] in Attica (1.18.1; 1.73.4; 2.34.5). A decade later, a second and much larger Persian invasion of Greece was launched by Darius' successor Xerxes, who led the combined land and sea expedition in person, and clearly hoped to add the states of Greece permanently to his empire. The Persians crossed the Hellespont, advanced unhindered through Thrace and Thessaly, and met their first serious Greek opposition at the narrow pass of Thermopylae.[4b] Here a small Greek force fought effectively and checked the entire Persian army for several days; when it was finally outflanked, most of the Greeks withdrew, but a few, led by the Spartan king Leonidas with a unit of three hundred Spartan *hoplites* (see Appendix F), remained in the pass and fought gloriously until surrounded and annihilated. Xerxes then advanced through Boeotia—which Medized[4c]—crossed into Attica, and reached Athens itself. He occupied the city and destroyed it, but he captured few of the inhabitants because, in an unprecedented step, the Athenians had left their lands and hearths and evacuated by sea to the island of Salamis and other nearby parts of Greece (1.18.2; 1.73.4). Shortly thereafter, the combined Greek fleet, inspired by the leadership and stratagems of the Athenian general Themistocles, inflicted such a crushing defeat on the Persian navy at Salamis[4d] that Xerxes retired with what remained of his fleet to Persian territory. In the following year, the Persian army also withdrew from Greece after it was defeated at Plataea[4e] by the largest allied force ever assembled by the Greek city-states under the command of the Spartan Pausanias.[4f] Finally, the Persian fleet was again smashed by the Greeks at

E3a Lydia: Appendix E Map, AY.
E3b Eretria on Euboea: Appendix E Map, BX.
E3c Sardis: Appendix E Map, BY.
E3d Cyprus: Appendix E Map, locator.
E4a Marathon in Attica: Appendix E Map, BX.
E4b Hellespont, Thrace. Thessaly, Thermopylae: Appendix E Map, AX. Thucydides refers to the great Persian invasion at 1.18.2, and to the battle of Thermopylae at 4.36.3
E4c Boeotia: Appendix E Map, BX. The Plataeans remind the Spartans of the "Medism" of the Thebans in 3.56.4 and the Thebans in turn explain their defection in 3.62.
E4d Salamis: Appendix E Map, BX. Thucydides recounts Themistocles' role as both advocate for the construction of an Athenian fleet (1.14.3) and as a wily restorer of Athens' walls (1.90–3); he evaluates him as a statesman and describes his ultimate flight from Athens and reception by the Persian king in 1.135–38.
E4e Plataea: Appendix E, Map BX. See 2.71.2–4, where the Plataeans seek to halt the invading Spartans by invoking the memory of Pausanias' victory over the Persians at their city, and the oaths taken later by the Spartans in appreciation of Plataea's bravery in that struggle.
E4f Pausanias' subsequent arrogance, his alleged final treason, and his death are described in 1.94–95 and 1.128–34.

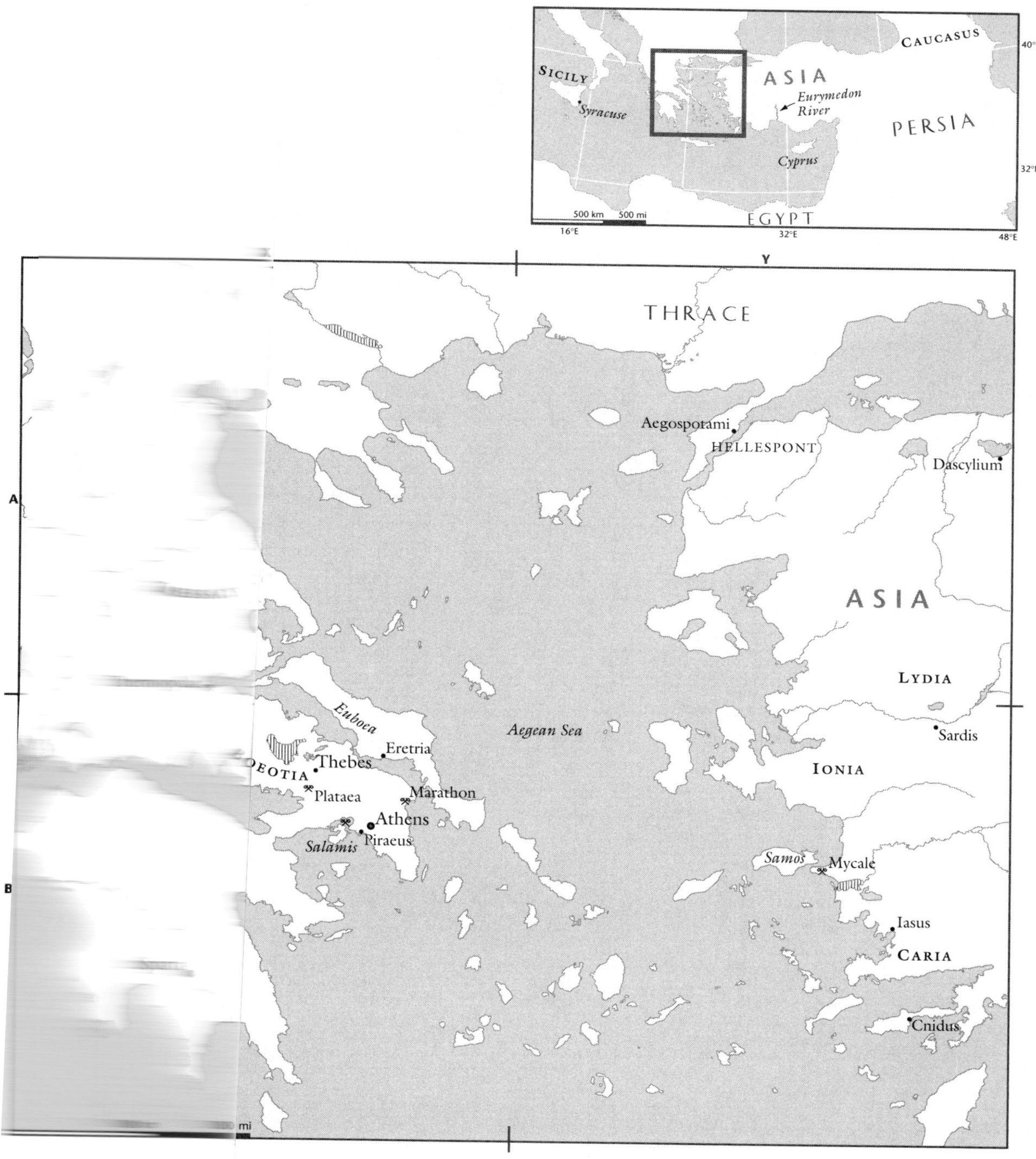
CAUCASUS
SICILY
ASIA
Syracuse
Eurymedon River
PERSIA
Cyprus
EGYPT
500 km
500 mi
40°N
32°N
16°E
32°E
48°E
Y
THRACE
Aegospotami
HELLESPONT
Dascylium
A
ASIA
LYDIA
Euboea
Aegean Sea
Sardis
Eretria
Thebes
IONIA
Plataea
Marathon
Athens
Salamis
Piraeus
Samos
Mycale
B
Iasus
CARIA
Cnidus

Mycale (1.89.2) on the coast of Ionia. The story of these events (and of many others) is told by Herodotus.[4g]

§5 Thucydides takes up the historical narrative after the Persian withdrawal from mainland Greece in a major digression in Book 1, beginning at chapter 1.89 and ending at 1.118. In these twenty-nine chapters[5a] he describes many but not all of the significant events that mark the growth of Athenian power in the Aegean in the fifty years (479–31) between the defeat of Xerxes' expedition and the outbreak of the Peloponnesian War. He briefly mentions, for example, the outstanding victory of the Athenians and their allies over Persian forces on both land and sea that took place about 467 B.C. at the Eurymedon River on the south coast of Asia Minor,[5b] but he says nothing at all about the very important peace between Athens and Persia negotiated in 449 by the Athenian Callias at the court of the Persian king.[5c] Yet that peace left Athens free to strengthen her power over the members of the Delian League and to turn that alliance further into an Athenian-controlled naval empire; it also ratified the withdrawal of Persian rule from the coastlands of western Asia Minor, and in effect ceded that region to the control of Athens. Finally, it left Athens free to confront Sparta, and it is not impossible that the Persian king realized, even at this early date, that his interest could best be served if the two leading states of Greece were to exhaust themselves in a struggle for dominance.

§6. The failure of Thucydides to mention the so-called Peace of Callias (or some treaty between Athens and Persia) either in the text at 1.112 or somewhere else, has led some scholars to question his reliability and others to infer that the historian had not yet worked out the earlier Greco–Persian diplomatic background to the struggle before he died. There can be no doubt that Thucydides had gathered much evidence concerning Persian diplomacy. He was certainly aware of the diplomatic exchanges between Pausanias and Artabazus, the Persian governor at Dascylium (1.129.1),[6a] and he was informed about the negotiations between the fugitive Themistocles and King Artaxerxes that took place soon after the accession of the latter in 464 (1.137.3). Thucydides also knew that even before hostilities broke out, the Spartans had intended to ask for Persian assistance against Athens (1.82.1; 2.7.1), that they sent at least one diplomatic mission for that purpose (2.67.1), and that on at least one occasion the Great King responded to their overtures by expressing his willingness to listen (4.50.1).

§7. Persian intervention in Aegean affairs did not become significant until after the crippling failure in 413 of the Athenian expedition to Sicily, and Athens' decision to support Amorges, the rebel governor of Caria[7a]. As Thucydides describes it,

E4g Mycale, Ionia: Appendix Map E, BY. Herodotus (who lived c. 484–25) is the author of a major history of the wars between the Persians and Greeks that includes much other interesting information. Thucydides criticizes him without naming him in 1.20. See introduction, II, i, ii, v and IV.ii.

E5a This section or excursus is often called the "Pentecontaetia" although the period it describes does not exactly cover fifty years. Despite Thucydides' treatment, there is much scholarly controversy over the detailed chronology of this period.

E5b Eurymedon River: Appendix E Map, locator.

E5c We lack definitive proof that this treaty really existed, but there is much circumstantial evidence. Thucydides provides indirect evidence for a treaty between Athens and Persia in 8.56.4, when he describes Alcibiades' demands that the King should have the right "to build ships and sail along his own coast wherever and with as many as he please." Why would these freedoms have been demanded unless they had been previously prohibited by treaty? See also Appendix B, The Athenian Empire, §8.

E6a Dascylium: Appendix E Map, AY.

E7a Caria: Appendix E Map, BY. Athens' relationship with Amorges is discussed in note 8.5.5b.

sian governors—Tissaphernes (8.5.5) at Sardis and Pharnabazus
n—began to compete with each other in obedience to a com-
ng to conclude an alliance with the Spartans. The Persians ex-
eir assistance the Spartans would drive the Athenians out of the
he Persian governors to regain the tribute from the cities which
ed them; Tissaphernes also hoped that the Spartans would help
(8.5.5).

er the annihilation of Athens' expedition in Sicily, Sparta re-
solicitation and Asian Greek entreaties by establishing a fleet in
commanders found it difficult to maintain their ships on Persian
nd supplies. Despite their success in capturing and delivering
rtan relationship with Tissaphernes did not run smoothly. The
urned out to be an unreliable and stingy paymaster, which led to
us disputes over his failure to supply sufficient pay for the sailors
.78; 8.80.1; 8.83.3). Three successive draft treaties between
had to be negotiated in 412 and 411 before agreement was
; 8.58). The Spartans rejected the first two of them as unaccept-
ichas objecting particularly to the Great King's implied claim to
formerly held, which would have required Sparta to recognize a
vern northern and central Greece (8.43.4; 8.52). Moreover, Tis-
ontend with a potentially dangerous division of opinion at Sparta
e who proposed sending troops and ships to him in Ionia, and
instead to dispatch those forces to Pharnabazus, his rival in the
. It is not surprising, then, that Tissaphernes may have come to
alings with the renegade Athenian aristocrat Alcibiades than with
(cf. 8.46.5).

1 a desperate Athens tried to renew her relationship with Persia,
and Pisander (8.53.3) argued, not quite disingenuously, that an
government would prove more acceptable to the Great King and
.53.3). It is clear, however, that Persia cared less about the Athe-
ernment than about Athenian activity in the eastern Aegean, and
n of democracy at Athens produced no perceptible impediment
ngs between them.

more important development, if Thucydides reports the affair ac-
ibiades' advice to Tissaphernes may have originated what was to
w long-term policy toward Greece: that of managing her support

established himself at Iasus in
Map, BY), where he was
ponnesians, who also sacked
d the inhabitants to replenish
ces.

so as to prevent either side from achieving victory (8.46.1–4). It is interesting to note that this policy was not followed by the Persian prince Cyrus the Younger, whose steadfast and generous assistance to the Spartans after 407 permitted the Peloponnesian fleet to recover from successive reverses until they were finally able to inflict a decisive defeat on the Athenian navy at Aegospotami in 405[10a]. Indeed, Thucydides, in a late passage written after the end of the war (2.65.12), characterized Cyrus' aid as the one cause of Sparta's success. Aegospotami led to the complete surrender of Athens and to a Spartan hegemony over Greece that proved unfavorable to Persian interests. So when Persia decided to limit Sparta's power, she financed an alliance of Greek states (including a democratic Athens) to oppose Sparta on land, and used her fleet, commanded by the Athenian Conon (see 7.31.4), to defeat the Spartan fleet at Cnidus in 394[10b]. Later, with Persian approval, Conon helped the Athenians to complete new Long Walls and to refortify Piraeus,[10c] thus restoring Athens to independence from Sparta.

§11. Ever since the peace of 449, the Aegean had been essentially a frontier problem for Persia—one of many frontier problems—and so it remained even in the time of Alcibiades' intrigues with Tissaphernes in 411. But Persia's policy in the region, which could be characterized as passive from 449 to 411, became more aggressive and interventionist thereafter. In the following decades, having learned from Prince Cyrus' error, she became adept at maneuvering politically among the Greeks, manipulating their governments, and keeping them divided into rival alliances so that, exhausted by constant warfare, they would pose no threat to herself. Finally, in 387 B.C., Persia dictated what was called the King's Peace, which ratified her reestablished control over the Greek cities of Asia Minor and effectively protected her from Greek attack for more than forty years.

R.B.S.

10a Aegospotami: Appendix E Map, AY.
10b Cnidus: Appendix E Map, BY.
10c Piraeus: Appendix E Map, BX.

APPENDIX F

Land Warfare in Thucydides

[illegible] reek infantry fighting in mass formation was hardly original— [illegible] ear Eastern armies had done the same for centuries. But the [illegible] y (700–500 B.C.) city-states refined the earlier loosely organized [illegible] es and files, with each propertied citizen now claiming an equal [illegible], a voice in the assembly, and a plot of land in the countryside.

[illegible] antrymen by the late eighth century B.C. had adopted sophisti- [illegible] nd armor to meet the new realities of formalized shock warfare. [illegible] reastplates, and greaves were constructed entirely of bronze, [illegible] ss of about a half inch, providing them with substantial protec- [illegible] ws of most swords, missiles, and spears. An enormous and heavy [illegible] or *hoplon*—some three feet in diameter covered half the body [illegible] e panoply. But the hoplite still depended on the man next to [illegible] own unprotected right side and to maintain the cohesion of the [illegible] hus military service now reinforced the egalitarian solidarity of [illegible] 126). The shield's unique double grip allowed its oppressive [illegible] by the left arm alone, and its concave shape permitted the rear [illegible] their shoulders. Because of the natural tendency of each hoplite [illegible] n for his unshielded right side behind the shield of his compan- [illegible] the entire phalanx often drifted rightward during its advance [illegible] of Sparta, the general—an amateur and elective public official— [illegible] oops on the right wing to spearhead the attack; in defeat he nor- [illegible] nong his men (4.44.2; 4.101.2; 5.74.3). Because of the limited [illegible] open to a phalanx once battle commenced, complex maneuvers [illegible] problematic (5.66.2; 5.72) and therefore rarely attempted. Usu- [illegible] nply tried to win the battle outright on the stronger right side [illegible] nferior left side collapsed and eroded the cohesion of the entire [illegible] –73).

[illegible] y, the hoplite depended on his eight-foot spear; should the shaft break, he might turn around what was left of its length to employ the reverse end, which was outfitted with a bronze spike.[3a] Each hoplite carried a small iron sword in case his spear was lost altogether. The phalanx usually stacked eight men deep (5.68.3), but only the spears of the first three rows could extend to the enemy—the rear five lines pushed on the men in front. If he kept his nerve and stayed in formation with his fellow fighters, the hoplite with his seventy pounds of armor and his long spear was practically invulnerable *on level ground* to cavalry charges and skirmishers alike—even in the most desperate circumstances impenetrable to any but other hoplites (1.63.1; 3.108.3). True, on rare occasions, heavy infantry could be defeated by mixed contingents (4.35.2–6), but almost always this turnabout was accomplished through ruse, manipulation of terrain, or ambush and encirclement (4.32.3–34.2; 5.10.3–8), not decisive engagement or shock tactics.

§4. This traditional practice of hoplite battle as Greek warfare persisted well into the fifth century B.C. Even then phalanxes continued to fight almost entirely over disputed land, usually border strips of marginal ground (1.15.2; 5.41.2), often more important to an agrarian community's national pride than to its economic survival. Preliminary devastation of fields and rural infrastructure was sometimes used to draw reluctant opponents onto the battlefield or to shame them into submission (1.82.3–6; 2.11.6–8; 4.84.1–2; 4.88.1–2). But inflicting permanent damage to agricultural land was difficult, laborious, and time-consuming (3.26.3; 7.27.4), and thus ravaging was more often a formalized part of the more general protocols between city-states that governed the time, location, and conduct of such one-day wars (5.41.2–3; 5.47) than a realistic means to starve an enemy community. Campaigning was confined to the late spring and summer months and thus synchronized with the slack periods in the agricultural year, when agrarian infantrymen and their servile attendants (3.17.3) might be free from their planting and harvesting labors (1.141.3, 5; 3.15.2; 4.6.1; cf. 4.84.1; 4.88.1–2).

§5. The contrived and ritualized nature of Greek infantry fighting should not suggest an absence of mayhem and savagery. Columns eyed each other formally across flat plains, with bronze glittering in the summer sun, and their generals shouting a few words of last-minute encouragement (4.92; 5.69.1). After divination and sacrifice by the seer (6.69.2), hoplites often advanced at a trot from about two hundred yards, singing the *paean* or war-chant (4.43.2; 4.96.1). The initial collision was horrific, as each side stumbled blindly ahead into the enemy mass, attempting to create some momentum that might shatter the opposing formation into fragments (4.96).

§6. Hearing and sight by those in the ranks was difficult if not nonexistent (4.34.2; 7.44.1). The din of clashing metal and screaming men must have been earsplitting; dust, the crowded conditions of the battlefield, and crested helmets with small eye slots would have limited vision severely—indeed, mistaken identity was commonplace as uniforms and national insignia were usually absent (4.96.3–6; 7.44.7–8). Reports of gaping wounds to the unprotected neck and groin, involun-

F3a Such a spear-butt spike, in this case taken as spoil from the defeated Lesbians and dedicated to the Dioscuri (whose temple at Athens is mentioned as the Anaceum in 8.93), is shown in Illustration 3.48.

[illegible] urination, and panic abound in battle descriptions in Greek lit- [illegible] d steadiness in formation were crucial to hoplite success: the [illegible] n and thrust of the column, the more likely it was for a phalanx [illegible] and through the enemy (5.10.5). Perhaps after not much more [illegible] pushing ceased as one side collapsed and fled the field, allowing [illegible] rs to gather up their own dead and to strip the armor from the [illegible] enemy. One set of captured armor would be arranged on a pole [illegible] r the battlefield as a trophy or monument to the victors' prowess [illegible] .74); the disputed territory would usually be annexed. The van- [illegible] nifest their defeat by sending a herald (whose distinctive herald's [illegible]) to request a truce in which they could return to the field to [illegible] ies of their own fallen (5.11; 5.74; 6.71.1). This request was [illegible] ed, for the bodies of all war dead had to be respected and ac- [illegible] eral rites according to Panhellenic custom. Any failure to carry [illegible] le rituals was a profound offense against both gods and man that [illegible] mned. Yet abandonment and desecration of the dead by both [illegible] did occur in extreme circumstances. The Thebans refused to [illegible] e defeated Athenians as long as they occupied and profaned the [illegible] (4.97–99); the Ambraciot herald was so shocked and appalled [illegible] the annihilation of his compatriots at Idomene that he forgot to [illegible] 13); and the demoralization of the Athenians during their retreat [illegible] exacerbated by their inability to care properly for their dead and [illegible] s (7.75).

[illegible] uniformity of weaponry and tactics there were qualitative differ- [illegible] k armies. The more professional hoplites of Sparta, notorious for [illegible] d deliberate advance at a walk to the music of flutes, gained a rep- [illegible] ferocity and consistently maintained military supremacy on land [illegible] 2–7). It was the agrarian hoplites of Boeotia, however, who char- [illegible] ed in deep columns who ultimately proved of all Greek armies the [illegible] on the battlefield (4.96). Argive, Corinthian, and Athenian hop- [illegible] ss well trained and often undependable, enjoyed mixed success [illegible] 5.73.1; 8.25). Gradually cities began to form elite corps to en- [illegible] -trained contingents with high morale who might form effective [illegible] e and offer examples for emulation by their amateur counterparts [illegible]

[illegible] Sparta during the fifth century managed to circumvent many of [illegible] e fighting. The presence of thousands of indentured agrarian ser- [illegible] and Messenia allowed Spartan infantry to be less worried over [illegible] s free to campaign year round if need be (see Appendix C, §3). [illegible] imperial infrastructure overseas (see Appendix B, §§ 10 and 11) [illegible] capital and food, lessening dependence on her native ground [illegible] 1; 2.14.1; 2.21–22) and all the traditional encumbrances to absolute warmaking that agrarianism had entailed (2.20.1–2.21.3; 2.59.1–2). During the Peloponnesian War (431–404 B.C.) the strategic limitations of war waged exclusively by phalanxes became unmistakable, and Thucydides clearly saw that the inevitable collision of Athens and Sparta—atypical poleis both—would have far-reaching effects on hoplite warfare in particular and the culture of the city-state in general (1.2–3). Capital, not courage alone, would prove the key to the victory (1.83.2; 1.141.5–143.2).

§9. In the new way of fighting of the Peloponnesian War battle was ubiquitous: in rough terrain, within mountain passes, during amphibious operations, and on long marches, cavalry, light-armed troops, and archers were needed to provide reconnaissance, cover, and pursuit against like kind (2.24–26; 3.1.2; 3.98; 6.21; 7.81–82). Peltasts (see Glossary) and other light troops—mostly highly mobile javelin throwers unencumbered by body armor—became especially prized once battle moved away from the plains and on to difficult ground (2.29.5; 2.79.4; 3.107–8; 4.11.1; 4.34.1–2; 4.123.4; 5.10.9). Horsemen, no longer mere ancillaries at the peripheries of hoplite battle (4.94.1; 5.67), often became critical to military success against a melange of enemies in a variety of locales (1.11.1; 2.31.3; 2.100; 4.44.1; 4.94.5; 6.70.2–3; 7.4.6; 7.6.2–3; 7.27.5). In the entire Peloponnesian War there were fewer than a half dozen battles decided by the traditional collision of phalanxes (4.43; 4.96; 4.134; 5.10–11; 5.66–73; 6.70). Far more Greeks were killed during sieges, mass executions, ambushes, cavalry pursuits, urban street fights, and night raids than in traditional hoplite battles.

§10. Just as often cities now chose to ride out a siege, so that the science of circumvallation—the construction of massive counterwalls to trap the citizenry within their own fortifications—became commonplace (1.64; 3.21; 5.114; 6.99). Athens enjoyed preeminence in storming fortifications (1.102.2) and expended enormous sums in lengthy though ultimately successful sieges (1.104.2; 1.65.3; 2.70.2; 3.17.3–4; 4.133.4; 5.116). So in the place of agrarian protocol and phalanx fighting, city-states in search of absolute victory applied capital and technology without ethical restraint and began to hire mercenaries, build engines, employ marines, and rely on missile troops (4.100; 7.29–30; 7.81–82). There was no longer a clear distinction between civilians and combatants (2.5.7; 3.50; 3.68; 5.32; 5.116). The census rubrics that had correlated civilian and military status were often ignored. Slaves, resident aliens, and foreigners entered battle side-by-side (2.13.6; 2.31.2; 4.28.4; 5.8.2; 7.57.2); the poor and rich citizenry themselves often were employed indistinguishably on land and sea with their participation determined solely on the basis of military expediency (3.16.1; 3.18.3–4; 6.43.1). But the breakdown of the old rituals—resulting in the enslavement of entire populations, the execution of captive adversaries and the enormous capital allotted to siege works and support troops—ensured the impoverishment of the victors and the defeated alike. Military efficacy came at the expense of increased barbarity (1.50.1; 2.90.5; 3.50.1; 5.32.1; 5.116.4; 7.29.3–5; 7.87.3).

§11 In a social sense, the growing importance during the Peloponnesian War of horsemen, archers, slingers, skirmishers, mercenaries, and naval forces in the city-state's front ranks was antithetical to the whole idea of an agrarian community defended by its middling hoplite citizenry. So gradually military service of all types became divorced from social status and the values of an agrarian citizenry, and the original idea of the hoplites' city-state was lost. No wonder that the nostalgic Thucydides could on occasion find poignancy in the destruction of hoplite infantry on both sides during the Peloponnesian War (3.98.4; 2.42–43; 4.40.2; 7.75; 7.87).

Victor Davis Hanson
Professor of Greek
Department of Foreign Languages
and Literatures
California State University, Fresno

APPENDIX G
Trireme Warfare in Thucydides

§1. Ships, sea battles, and naval policy are key features in Thucydides' account of the Peloponnesian War. Thucydides—who served as a general and commanded a squadron of *triremes* himself (4.104.4–5; 4.106.3)—clearly viewed naval power as the key to supremacy in the Aegean (1.15); Athens' rise to empire and fall from glory was inextricably bound up with her fortunes at sea.

§2. The opening years of the Peloponnesian War saw the Athenian navy at the height of its glory: her ships were the fastest and most efficient afloat, and her oarsmen were superior in executing the complicated maneuvers by which sea battles were fought and won. But by the end of the war, the Athenian navy had collapsed: her generals had been outsmarted, her men were exhausted or dead, her ships were outmoded and defeated more than once by new tactics of naval warfare. Thucydides had a dramatic story to tell.

§3. He told it in snapshots—a moment of battle, an orator's defense of a certain naval policy, the snippet of a commander's exhortation to his men—and wrote for an audience intimately familiar with the ships, men, and often the localities and the battles themselves. These factors sometimes make it difficult for us to understand the details of what he is describing, though the general outlines are clear.

§4. The building of specialized warships already had a long history by Thucydides' day, and both warship design and naval fighting tactics had evolved substantially over the centuries. In earliest times, when fleets were used primarily for transport and the battle itself took place on land, warships were built to quickly carry as many men as possible to battle. Eventually confrontations took place at sea, but at first these earliest naval skirmishes hardly differed from the kind of fighting done on land: ships served simply as vehicles to get soldiers within close range of their enemy. Archers, javelin throwers, and hand-to-hand combat decided the outcome of battle. Gradually the ships themselves began to be used as weapons, and speed, maneuverability, and hull strength superseded the importance of transport capacity in warship design. By the time of the Peloponnesian War, naval strategy centered on the offensive capabilities of the trireme, a warship

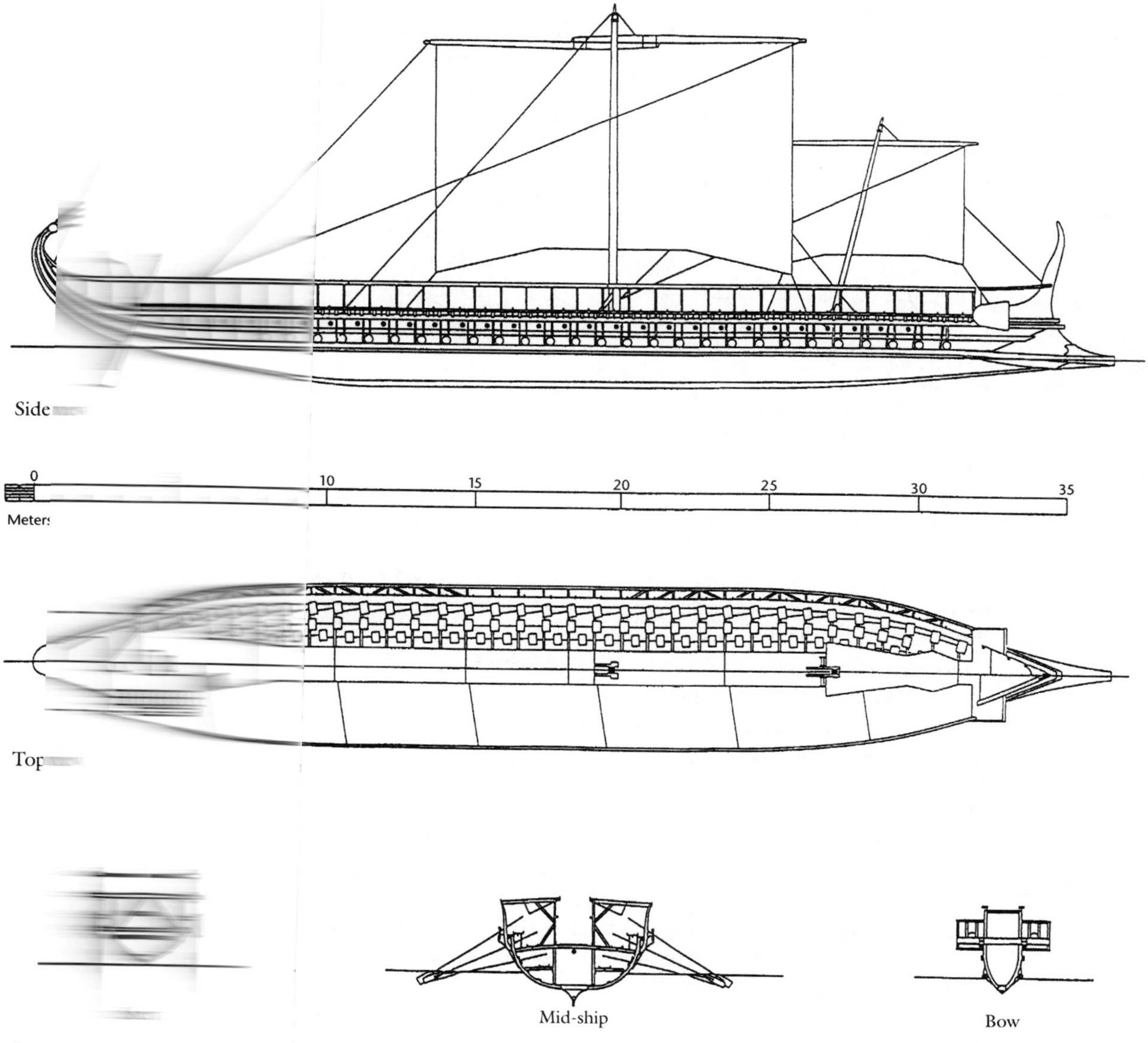

Side

0 10 15 20 25 30 35
Meters

Top

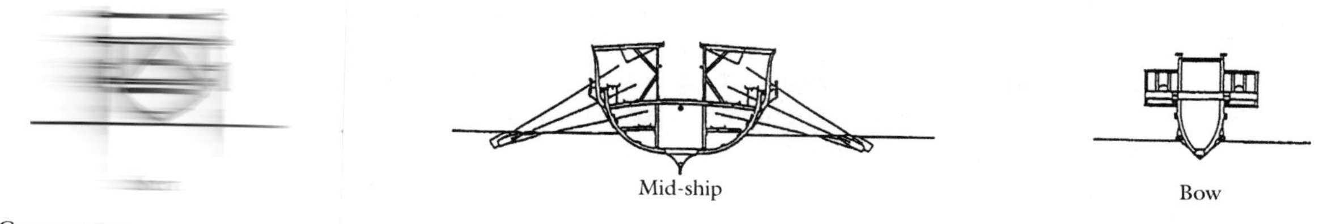

Cr

Appe
Dia eme Olympias

whose main weapon was the ram mounted upon her prow. Success at sea depended on a strong crew of rowers skilled in carrying out ramming tactics.

§5. Long and sleek, with a length-to-beam ratio of 9 to 1, the trireme took its name from the arrangement of rowers. The hull enclosed two levels of rowers: the *thalamites* in the depths of the hold and the *zygites* seated on the hull's crossbeams (thwarts). A third row of oarsmen, the *thranites,* sat in outriggers mounted along the topsides of the hull. Thranites were the key members of the crew, since only they were in a position to see the oar blades enter the water. For this reason each thranite was responsible for guiding the zygite and thalamite immediately next to and below him to adjust their stroke to fit the general cadence. Thus the trireme crew worked in teams of three, and this is why the Greeks referred to these warships as *trieres,* "three-fitted." (*Trireme* is an Anglicized and Latinized version of the Greek.) This configuration packed 170 rowers into a hull only about 120 feet long and 15 feet wide, and optimized the balance of power, speed, and maneuverability: a longer boat with more rowers would have been heavier and more difficult to maneuver without gaining much in the way of increased speed; a smaller boat with fewer rowers would have lacked speed and striking power. Since ramming was the primary offensive technique, and since lightness and speed were paramount, the rest of the crew was pared down to a bare minimum. In addition to the rowers, the standard complement for an Athenian trireme during the Peloponnesian War consisted of only ten *hoplites* (marines), four archers, and about sixteen other crew to sail the boat.

§6. Like the hulls of modern racing shells, the hull of a trireme was built to be as strong but light as possible, and this is reflected in its design as well as in the techniques and materials used in its construction. The elaborate shipsheds built around the Piraeus harbors to dry-dock warships also bear eloquent testimony to the Athenians' concern for light hulls. Since a dry ship was both faster and less apt to rot than a waterlogged one, crews regularly pulled their triremes out of the water when they weren't in use. The lightweight, shallow-drafted ships were relatively easy to beach and carried rollers to help haul them onto the shore and supports to stabilize them once there. During the Sicilian expedition, when the constant danger of attack required the Athenian fleet to be ever battle-ready, drying out the hulls was of paramount concern. A note of real desperation creeps into Nicias' letter to the Athenians as he describes the impossibility of pulling his sodden ships out of the water (7.12.3–5).

§7. Because triremes were designed to maximize speed and minimize weight, almost every inch of space was used to accommodate rowers. There was hardly room for stretching, much less for sleeping or preparing and serving food. Thus, in addition to the necessity of regular beaching, triremes were constrained to travel along the coast (and put in at night so that the crew could eat and rest (1.52; 4.26; 6.44).[7a] These logistical considerations affected the strategy and tactics, the pace, and sometimes even the outcome of battles. Fighting usually ceased at sunset—sometimes even at midday—in order to rest and feed crews quickly fatigued by their exertions in the stifling heat of cramped, closely packed quarters baked under the

G7a It was this constraint that made the nonstop voyage at the second trireme to Mytilene so remarkable that Thucydides felt the need to explain how the crew did it (3.49).

. In fact, several "naval" battles were won by one fleet surprising
ashore while they were on dinner break (7.40). Beaches where
and the crew could disembark for eating and sleeping were so
at that the Spartans at Pylos could plan to drive away the Athen-
denying it access to all local landing places (4.8).

p was also vital as a repository. Although a trireme carried masts
listance travel, as well as anchors, spare oars, cooking equipment,
when the ship entered combat all dead weight was left ashore or
ttisoned. Finally, the shore station served as both a refuge and a
organize a new attack in the event of defeat. For these reasons,
re often amphibious affairs that included fiercely fought battles
l of the shore (7.24). The loss of a base camp was a serious set-
t undefeated on the water.

's light and slender hull can be likened to the shaft of an arrow;
hip's offensive weapon, was the bronze-clad ram mounted on its
row—the only ancient ram ever found—has been excavated off
near Athlit. A warship with its buoyant wooden construction was
long after the battle had ended the victorious fleet scoured the
and capsized hulls to tow off as war booty (1.54). At the very
s and the bronze ram could be salvaged and reused. The Athlit
m a ship larger and later than the fifth-century triremes, provides
se into the engineering and cost invested in a Greek warship. The
v casing weighing half a ton, was cast in a single pouring—a feat
n modern bronzesmiths. Its tip flared into fins rather than coming
r to prevent it from getting wedged in the hull of its opponent,
at the bronze casing covered were carefully designed to distribute
ct over the entire length of the light hull. Like our sophisticated
y today, the ancient warship was an example of contemporary en-
hest level.

, then, with its ram and heavy buildup of timbers, was both the of-
d the best protected area of the ship. The stern and sides were her
s. As long as a warship kept her prow toward the enemy, she was
fensive and defensive action. Consequently, in the vicinity of land,
eous position was a battle line drawn up parallel to the shore with
ard against the enemy (2.90). This position also had the advantage
ace on the beach for the fleet to store all nonessential equipment
arship before going into battle. In open seas, a fleet achieved a de-
y forming a circle with sterns toward the center and prows bristling
3.78.1). A confrontation between two evenly matched fleets usu-
arships ranged in two parallel lines, prows facing one another.

mmander with fast ships and skilled rowers could successfully take
A commander less sure of his forces would simply wait for the at-

tack, hoping to escape by means of evasive action. If the attacker faltered within close range, marine hoplites threw grappling irons to secure the enemy ship alongside and close-range fighting commenced between the crews of the two ships. The skilled Athenians, however, had a reputation for aggressiveness and were particularly proficient at executing two standard attack maneuvers. In the *periplous* ("sailing around") the faster Athenian ships outflanked the enemy, turned quickly, and struck from behind. Alternately, in the *diekplous* ("sailing through"), the Athenian ships broke through gaps between the enemy ships and then either immediately rammed their sides or turned quickly and battered their sterns. Ramming itself required great skill, for the enemy hull had to be hit with enough force to cause significant damage but not so much as to entangle the attacking ship in the splintered hull, preventing its crew from backing their ship away to safety. The triremes of all navies were theoretically capable of these maneuvers, but at the outset of the Peloponnesian War it seems that only Athenian crews had the expertise and discipline necessary to execute such tactics effectively.

§12. Swift confusion could descend upon even well-trained rowers once an engagement commenced and more than once turned the tide of battle (2.91, 3.77). Therefore, skilled and experienced crews were a prime commodity and rival navies competed fiercely for personnel. Rowers were generally free men hired on at decent wages; slaves were employed only in unusual circumstances (1.55; 8.15). Thucydides tells us that Athenian (6.31) and Corinthian (1.31) *trierarchs* (trireme commanders) offered substantial bonuses in an effort to lure well-trained crews, and that desertion from one navy to another was frequent (7.13). In an effort to keep her crews intact, the Athenian custom was to pay half in advance and the remainder upon completion of the voyage (8.45). The going rate in Athens was one *drachma* per day—the standard workman's wage—to row in the lower two levels of a trireme (the thalamite and zygite positions). Thranites received an additional bonus. At these rates (along with the wages of the rest of the crew), it cost about one *talent* per month to operate each trireme (for *drachma* and *talent,* see Appendix J). One major advantage of Athens' imperial income was that it allowed her to maintain fleets at sea every year and thereby bring her crews to a decisively superior level of skill in relation to those of her opponents.

§13. Their navy was an evocative symbol of the power and discipline of the democratic state for all ranks of Athenians. Even members of the upper class actively participated in the maintenance and operation of her fleet. Wealthy and powerful individuals were assigned one-year commissions as commanders (*trierarchs*) of triremes. Their appointment served as a form of tax, for while the state provided an empty ship and the crew's wages, the trierarch was responsible for outfitting and maintaining the vessel with funds from his own pocket. Their financial investment gave the upper class a powerful voice in setting naval policy, and many decisions made by Athenian commanders had at least as much to do with domestic politics as with field strategies.

§14. Of course, Thucydides, an Athenian, wrote a history of Athens, and his story is clearest in its portrayal of Athenian policy. Yet many other states—Corinth, [illegible] yra, among others—had powerful navies and, like Athens, their [illegible] s the trireme. All triremes were basically alike in design, so that [illegible] ienian trireme could comfortably operate a Peloponnesian or a [illegible], and vice versa. But certainly the number of warships and skilled [illegible] d muster varied greatly. At least in the early decades of the war, [illegible] challenge the fleets and experienced crews of the Athenians. [illegible] descriptions give us an indication of the tactics developed by [illegible] o counteract her superior might at sea. For example, since the [illegible] aval maneuvers required plenty of sea room (2.89), one straight- [illegible] aken by her enemies was to avoid engaging in battle on the open [illegible] ossible, they took advantage of topography and challenged the [illegible] onfined waters such as the harbors of Pylos and Syracuse, where it [illegible] execute the periplous or diekplous. Confinement not only pre- [illegible] ans from employing their prowess at rowing but also increased [illegible] langer of ships running afoul of one another. Once fleets were [illegible] ill, fighting was reduced to hand-to-hand combat and tactics and [illegible] ittle from those used on land (1.48). The Corinthians (7.34) and [illegible] 36) carried this strategy one step further and rebuilt their navy to [illegible] ands of warfare based on strong hulls and brute force. Thucydides' [illegible] brief for us to understand the exact nature of the alterations, but [illegible] y redesigned their prows so that the force of collision would be [illegible] Athenians' unprotected outriggers. Rowers rather than hulls were [illegible] e effect was the same: with their wings clipped, the Athenian [illegible] sitting ducks and were easily overcome by the heavily manned [illegible] mies. Over the course of the war, tactics developed to counteract [illegible] prowess became standard battle strategy. For navies relying on [illegible] ull strength and capacity to carry marines became more important [illegible] naneuverability, and the design and operation of the classic Athen- [illegible] ventually superseded by the demands of new kinds of warfare.

[illegible] uled the sea during the period when she alone, due to her imperial [illegible] ance the training, manning, and sustained operation of large numbers [illegible] le of executing sophisticated maneuvers. Thucydides eloquently de- [illegible] ay of Athenian naval might. But as the war dragged on, Athens' op- [illegible] d new strategies and modified their ships to gain a major victory in [illegible] btained financial support from Persia with which to challenge Athen- [illegible] the Aegean, and ultimately to destroy it. Almost a century would [illegible] nal eclipse of the trireme, but Thucydides' account heralds the begin- [illegible]

Nicolle Hirschfeld
Department of Classics
University of Texas at Austin

APPENDIX H

Dialects and Ethnic Groups in Thucydides

§1. "Hellas," as the Greeks did and continue to refer to their land, was not a unified nation in Thucydides' time, but rather a country composed of hundreds of independent city-states, most of them very small. The citizens of these states all spoke Greek, but the Greek of each city-state was at least slightly different from the Greek speech of all other city-states. Athenian speech, for example, differed from that of neighboring Boeotia, and Spartan speech differed from both of these and also from that of nearby Arcadia.

§2. In general, Greeks made little comment about dialects. There was no ancient, common, Standard Greek, as there is a Modern Standard English, and it seemed natural to them that the people of different city-states had different accents. Every Greek could understand every other Greek regardless of dialect, although Thucydides does mention the Eurytanians of Aetolia whose speech was said to be exceedingly difficult to understand (3.94.5).[2a] Greek authors only occasionally took notice of dialectal differences. The Athenian comic poet Aristophanes brings Spartan, Megarian, and Boeotian characters on stage, each speaking in his native dialect[2b] to achieve comic effects; and Aeschylus, the tragic poet, has one character in the drama *The Libation Bearers* refer to speaking in "the Phocian manner"—the dialect spoken in the vicinity of Delphi. Thucydides mentions dialects several times. Although he himself writes in his native Attic with an admixture of a few Ionic forms, he does quote Dorian decrees in 5.77 and 5.79, and quotes them in a Doric dialect. The first decree must have been composed in Sparta, the second either in Sparta or in Argos. Though he might well have summarized the decrees or translated them into Attic if he had time to revise them, their presence in the text shows that he had access to Spartan decrees and could read them easily, and that later readers and scribes also could understand these dialects.

§3. Throughout antiquity the Greeks thought that all their dialects arose from three main roots: Doric, Ionic, and Aeolic. This concept must be an ancient one, for it is found in the work of the early epic poet Hesiod, who says (fragment 9) that

H2a These same people were said to eat their meat raw. Most likely Thucydides knew very little about them, but thinking them primitive, felt that their language must be primitive as well.

H2b Boeotian and Megarian characters appear in *The Acharnians,* and a Spartan woman plays an important role in *Lysistrata*. The broad use of dialect by these characters must have delighted Athenian audiences in much the same way that modern American writers employ "yankee" or a "southern" or "western" drawl, or modern British writers use Scots or Yorkshire dialects.

(= Greek) were born three sons, Dōros, Xouthos, and Aiolos. : ancestors of the later Dorians, Ionians, and Aeolians—Xouthos ɔ settled in Athens and was regarded as the ancestor of the Ioni- ars accept the ancient classification, but add a fourth grouping, te, a dialect spoken over much of the Peloponnese before the ar- ›orians.

of these dialectal differences is of course lost to us by time. Some :el that the Greeks migrated into Greece in three distinct waves: :hen the Aeolians, and finally the Dorians. And it is true at least l Ionic dialects must have become differentiated long before they sia Minor (Ionia, 1.2.6), perhaps around 1000 B.C. The Dorian ought to have taken place at the very end of the Bronze Age :r, and this date, at least for the Dorian settlement of the Pelopon- :re, must be about right. A later wave of Greek colonization :peakers of the various dialects to Sicily, southern Italy, and the

ɔ longer believe in this neat three-wave hypothesis of the arrival of assume rather that dialectal differences arose among Greeks in : Bronze Age (2200–1200 B.C.). There are, however, a number of :s that argue for some period of independent development of Do- s. The names of the Dorian tribes—Hylleis, Dumanes, Pam- mon to all states whose citizens speak the Dorian dialect, but are :rs. Each dialect group celebrates at least a few religious festivals to themselves and different from those of other groups. The :d by Thucydides (5.54; 5.75) was a uniquely Dorian festival, just nentioned by Herodotus (1.1.148) was a uniquely Ionic festival. ɪlso differ in characteristic ways, as in the names of the months. tagonist of many tales, was the Dorian hero par excellence, and the :d myths involving the Athenian Theseus in part so as to have a na- :rful as Heracles.[5a]

e dialect spoken in Boeotia, Thessaly, Lesbos and a small portion of a Minor coast, is of little importance in Thucydides, and he rarely ns (3.31.1; 8.108.4). He does say that the Lesbians are kin to the ; 7.57.5; 8.100.3), as indeed they are linguistically, but he also in- :d that Aeolians once lived in the area around Corinth (4.42.2) and :.5).

es does make frequent references to Ionians and Dorians, however, the war between Athens and Sparta was perceived by many as a dis- ɪese two distinct groups, with Athens and the Ionians of the Asia ted against the Dorian inhabitants of the Peloponnesus and else- w was maintained despite the fact that many Dorians fought with

Appendix E, §4.

Athens, and many Ionians, at least near the end of the war, fought against her. Thucydides provides a convenient list of the mixed dialectal allegiances in his description of the combatants at Syracuse (7.57–58). Rhetorically, at least, Dorians and Ionians were eternal enemies (6.80.3; 6.82.2).

§8. Thucydides makes abundantly clear that his contemporaries developed, used, and responded to distinct and pronounced stereotypes of Dorians and Ionians. Dorians were thought to be rough, hardy folk in habits—brave fighters to be sure, but rural, conservative, and a little slow. In speech they were spare, pithy, and blunt (4.17.2; 4.84.2). Ionians (and primarily Athenians), on the other hand, were cultivated in manner (1.6.3) and glib in language—clever, commercial, and adventurous: one may instance Pericles' Funeral Oration (2.36–46) as an example of Athenian developed oratory. Although some Ionians (but not Athenians) were scorned as all too ready to serve any master (6.77.2), the Athenian Ionians were feared as restless and aggressive. Many Greeks seem to have been surprised when Ionians defeated Dorians (8.25.5), as this outcome was contrary to the expectation often expressed (5.9.1; 7.5.4).

§9. The linguistic differences between the dialects were clear. Where Dorians said *dāmos* "people," as in the name of the Spartan king Archidamos, Ionians said *dēmos;* and when a Dorian said "he gives," he would say *didōti,* while an Ionian would say *didōsi.* These differences were slight, but they could sometimes be very significant. The Athenian general Demosthenes, for example, exploited the Dorian accent of the Messenians from Naupactus in order to deceive and surprise the Ambraciots at Idomene (3.112.4); and he later remarked that because their dialect was the same as that of Sparta, they would make particularly effective raiders against the Spartans (4.3.3). The Athenians, in their turn, were thrown into confusion in the night battle on Epipolae (7.44.6), when the *paean* (see Glossary) was simultaneously raised both by their Dorian allies, the Argives and Corcyraeans, and by their Dorian enemies, the Syracusans and Peloponnesians; since all these Dorians were chanting their paean in the same dialect but the Athenians could not distinguish friendly from hostile accents, the Athenians were unable to locate their allies and perceived their enemies to be on all sides, which contributed much to their bewilderment and ultimate panic.

§10. The ancients were generally more concerned with ethnic differences than with linguistic ones, and believed that language reflected character. Thucydides shared this focus, as his own interest in dialect was generally more cultural than linguistic. In this he proves a better guide to ancient attitudes toward language than to the facts of linguistic diversity.

William F. Wyatt
Classics Department
Brown University
Providence, Rhode Island

APPENDIX I

Religious Festivals in Thucydides

[illegible]gion in Thucydides is much like the famous dog in the Sherlock [illegible] provided a clue because he did *not* bark in the night: Thucydides' [illegible]ce on Greek religious practices and institutions dramatically illus- [illegible]lizing and secular nature of his work. Herodotus, for example, [illegible]us sanctuary of Apollo at Delphi more than five times as often as [illegible]

[illegible]because Thucydides' secular outlook anticipates modern inclina- [illegible]make an effort to understand how atypical this would have been: [illegible]course, executed for impiety, while the mutilation of the *Hermae* [illegible]he profanation of the Eleusinian Mysteries described in Book 6 of [illegible].1) brought down sentences of exile and death. An eclipse of the [illegible] the Athenians into delaying their retreat from Syracuse and led to [illegible] of the entire expedition (7.50). Thus the average fifth-century [illegible]ave been far more superstitious and intolerant than one might sus- [illegible] Thucydides' calm and rational narrative.

[illegible]ortant to bear in mind two key aspects of Greek religion. First, [illegible]eligious texts comparable to the Bible or the Koran. Their religion [illegible] ritual practice rather than doctrine: participation in communal ac- [illegible]e heart of Greek religion, while belief was less important. Second, [illegible]us actions were, to some measure, exclusive: some religious cults [illegible]o kinship groups, others were open only to citizens of a particular [illegible]he great "Panhellenic" events were restricted to those who could [illegible]s to be Greek. Participation in any Greek religious activity was a [illegible]hip in an exclusive group, whether small or large.

[illegible] as they were among hundreds of small city-states from the Crimea [illegible]eeks desperately needed a number of central locations in which they [illegible]change information, establish and strengthen personal contacts, and [illegible]restige that would transcend that which they had gained in their [illegible] Thucydides stresses at 1.3 that Homer has no word for the Greeks as a whole: the idea of Greece and a common Greek identity gained force only after the Greeks founded colonies throughout the Mediterranean world and came into contact with a number of different, often unfriendly, cultures.

§5. In the eighth century the local athletic contests at Olympia began to acquire an international character, as Greeks from outside the Peloponnese started competing for prizes and the admiration of their peers. The oracle of Apollo at Delphi also evolved into an international Greek institution: those who wished to found a new colony regularly consulted the god, and the oracle could, at the least, prevent two expeditions from accidentally setting off to colonize the same location. The popularity of the athletic contests at Olympia grew so great that in the first half of the sixth century games were added at Delphi (the so-called Pythian Games) as well as at Nemea and the Isthmus of Corinth. Alcibiades' speech at 6.16, which boasts of his victories at Olympia and of the credit that they conferred on Athens as a whole, provides an outstanding account of how Greeks viewed these games. Greek states took pride in the achievements of their citizens, and individual citizens could convert their athletic prestige into political power (witness the attempt by the Athenian Cylon at 1.126.3 to make himself tyrant after becoming an Olympic victor).

§6. The Greeks were extremely jealous of their independence and suspicious of any entity that acquired too much power. Panhellenic religious centers badly needed at least the appearance of neutrality if they were to maintain their authority. Unquestionably, the religious hub of the classical Greek world was the sanctuary of Apollo at Delphi. Located in the virtual center of the Greek world (it was, in fact, called the "navel of the world"), Delphi played a crucial role: it was militarily weak and thus could not translate any cultural prestige or moral authority into imperial power. Eventually, when the oracle of Apollo at Delphi took sides and reported that the god would aid the Peloponnesian side (1.118), it violated its apolitical status. Even Panhellenism had it limits: both sides assumed that the Peloponnesians would "borrow" the treasures accumulated at Delphi and Olympia (1.121; 1.143).

§7. Similarly, a universal truce was supposed to reign among Greeks during the Panhellenic athletic contests at Olympia, Delphi, Nemea, and Isthmia. When the people of Elis barred the Spartans from competing (5.49), it caused a major scandal that many feared would lead to war and undermine the cultural authority of the games. The people of Elis justified this action by accusing the Spartans of invading the territory of another Greek state during a previous Olympic truce. Thucydides reports that a truce for the Isthmian games delayed a Corinthian expedition to Chios (8.9), and that during the games themselves the Athenians gained knowledge of the Corinthian plan and were able to take preemptive action at Chios (8.10).

§8. By contrast, each Greek city-state and even many kinship groups had their own exclusive religious rituals. These included the Carneia (5.75.2) and the Hyacinthia (5.23.4) at Sparta and the Dionysia at Athens (5.23.4). Athens had pretensions to Panhellenic stature: the Eleusinian Mysteries (8.53) and the "Festival of All Athens" (Panathenaea, 6.56.2) had potential for Panhellenic stature, but the power of Athens, especially in the fifth century, made many Greeks leery of these religious institutions and limited their appeal. Contests at the religious festivals included cultural as well as athletic events—poetry, music, even orations—but it was the local festival of Dionysus at Athens that produced Greek drama, one of the most successful literary forms ever produced.

Gregory Crane
Classics Department
Tufts University
Medford, Massachusetts

APPENDIX J
Classical Greek Currency in Thucydides

§1. By the time of the Peloponnesian War, many Greek city-states, whether by themselves or organized into leagues, were minting their own coins, primarily in silver. They minted much less often in gold, a far more valuable metal, but the Persian Empire produced gold coins that the Greeks called "Daric staters."[1a] During the Peloponnesian War gold seems to have been worth about thirteen to fourteen times the value of silver. Bronze, an alloy of copper and tin, gradually became common for minting coins of small value. Most Greek coinages were used only in their own region. Only a handful of mints, Athens among them, produced coins that people were willing to accept internationally.

§2. The many different mints identified their coinages via designs and inscriptions, but they did not usually include an indication of a coin's value as money, as modern currency does. Users were expected to know how much a particular coin was worth. Greek silver and gold coinages derived perhaps as much as 95 percent of their monetary value from the intrinsic bullion value of the precious metal in each coin; the remaining value was added by the implicit guarantee that the authority issuing a coin would redeem it and thus prevent a consumer from winding up with worthless currency. Bronze coins constituted what today we call a "fiduciary coinage," whose value comes from the guarantee that its minting authority would redeem it rather than from any intrinsic value of the material from which it is made. (Almost all currency in use today is fiduciary.)

§3. Since intrinsic metallic value was so important in Greek coinages, the weight of a coin was directly related to its value. (For everyday purposes Greeks seem to have assumed that the purity of officially minted coins was essentially the same.) A Greek mint therefore produced its various denominations of coins corresponding to a system of weights. Numerous and different weight standards were in use in the Greek world. The most commonly mentioned Greek silver denomination, the *drachma* (plural = *drachmae*), weighed somewhat more than 4.3 grams as minted at Athens on the so-called Attic standard. The nearby mint of Aegina, by contrast, minted a drachma weighing 6.1 grams and therefore worth about 40 percent more

J1a See Thucydides 8.28.4. It was presumably named after the Persian king Darius I (521–485 B.C.). Some manuscripts of the text read "Doric stater," but this is an obvious mistake.

[illegible] drachma. Six *obols* equaled one drachma, and some mints, such [illegible] 5.47.6), produced obols and fractions of obols as smaller denom- [illegible] ence at Thucydides 8.101.1 to coins of Chios called "fortieths" [illegible] a small denomination, but we lack other evidence to clarify this [illegible]

[illegible] r than the drachma also existed; the largest denomination in each [illegible] known as a *stater.* Silver staters represented different multiples of [illegible] fferent weight standards. The mention of staters at Thucydides [illegible] le, is usually taken as referring to Corinthian staters, which were [illegible] ee-drachmae-each on the Corinthian standard (whose drachma [illegible] 9 grams). The staters of Phocaea mentioned in Thucydides 4.52.2 [illegible] ghing about 16.1 grams and minted from electrum, a naturally oc- [illegible] old and silver that only a few Greek mints used. A Phocaean elec- [illegible] robably worth about twenty-four Athenian drachmae (sometimes [illegible] etimes a few less as exchange rates fluctuated). As I mentioned [illegible] s also referred to Persian gold coins as "staters"; these coins [illegible] 4 grams.

[illegible] hing to exchange different currencies had to make careful calcula- [illegible] alues, and moneychangers charged a hefty fee of about 5–7 per- [illegible] rvices. As the text of Thucydides shows (e.g., 1.96.2; 3.50.2), [illegible] ulate large sums of money by using terms of Mesopotamian origin [illegible] red to weights and not to existing denominations. The largest such [illegible] *nt,* which meant a weight of just over twenty-six kilograms (about [illegible] s), or a value in Athenian coin equivalent to six thousand drach- [illegible] ural = *minae*) stood for one hundred drachmae (and therefore one- [illegible] nt). No mints produced coins that approached these values. Since [illegible]" and "mina" strictly speaking referred to weights, they could be [illegible] amounts of precious metal still in bullion form (see 6.8.1).

[illegible] meaningful way to measure the value of ancient money in its own [illegible] wages and prices. Before the inflation characteristic of the Pelopon- [illegible] d, an unskilled laborer could expect to earn two obols per day. To- [illegible] the fifth century that had risen to a drachma a day, which is what a [illegible] henian fleet was paid. Since a *trireme* (see Appendix G, Trireme [illegible] carried a crew of about two hundred men, it cost one talent per [illegible] e crew of a fully manned ship (i.e., six thousand drachmae, calcu- [illegible] x 200 men at 1 drachma per day). Therefore, Athens needed at [illegible] d talents to keep a fleet of one hundred triremes operational for six [illegible]

[illegible] 425 B.C. a citizen of Athens received three obols for each day spent [illegible] his payment seems to have been enough to make jury service attrac- [illegible] ho could use the money to supplement other income. It was not [illegible] however, to replace a day's pay for most workers. Food and clothing could be very expensive by modern Western standards. Enough barley to provide a day's porridge, the dietary staple, for a family of five cost only one-eighth of an obol, but a gallon of olive oil, another staple, cost three drachmas. A woolen cloak cost from five to twenty drachmae, while a pair of shoes could set a customer back from six to eight drachmae.

Thomas R. Martin
Classics Department
College of the Holy Cross
Worcester, Massachusetts

APPENDIX K

[illegible]endars and Dating Systems in Thucydides

[illegible]ern, Western, Christian system of indicating years by assigning [illegible]om a single point in time and then designating them consecutively [illegible]viously did not exist in the classical Greek world. Ancient Greek [illegible] completely different system based on local arrangements: each [illegible]d a particular year by the name of the person who held a specified [illegible]cal office in that particular city-state during that year. Therefore, [illegible] known by a different designation in every city-state.

[illegible]es illustrates the complexity of Greek dating systems with his famous [illegible] Book 2.2.1 to specify the date at which hostilities first broke out in [illegible]n War. The war began, he reports, when at Argos the priestess [illegible]ng in her forty-eighth year, when at Sparta the political office of [illegible]ry) was held by Aenesias, and when at Athens the office of *archon* [illegible]as held by Pythodorus (see §5 below for Thucydides' reference to [illegible]oint).[2a]

[illegible]es gave three different references to make the date of the first year [illegible]standable by as many people as possible; that is, he hoped that any [illegible] would be able to make sense of at least one of these three systems. [illegible]rse, a reader would have needed a list that recorded in chronologi[illegible]nes of the holders of the office being used as a standard of refer[illegible]h century B.C. city-states officially compiled lists of this sort, but [illegible] were unlikely to have had personal copies because they had no need [illegible]ryday purposes. Making correspondences between different local [illegible]ating years, as Thucydides did, required research. He expected his [illegible]e chronological fixed point of the first year of the war to calculate [illegible]er important events in his history, most notably the Thirty Years' [illegible]Athens and Sparta that he says (1.87.6; 2.2.1) had been negotiated [illegible]arlier.

[illegible] non-local Greek system for indicating the dates of years was based [illegible]on of the Olympic Games, which took place every four years. Each

[illegible]nine archons every year. The one [illegible] used to designate the year is known as *eponymous,* meaning "giving his name to."

period of four years (called an "Olympiad") was numbered consecutively, starting with Olympiad I, which was agreed to have begun in the year that we designate as 776 B.C. An individual year could then be specified as year one, two, three, or four of a certain Olympiad. As Thucydides' failure to give an Olympiad date for the opening of the Peloponnesian War implies, this system of reference seems not yet to have been in use at the time when he wrote.[4a] All he could probably do to derive chronological information from the Olympic record was to consult a list of victors in the games for a rough approximation of the time when someone like Cylon, whose victory he mentions at 1.126.3 as evidence of the man's eminence, had lived. As his imprecise dating of Cylon to "former generations" reveals, he could not hope for much precision from this source.

§5. In Book 2.2.1 Thucydides also mentions that Pythodorus's annual term as archon still had two months to run. Since Greeks divided the calendar of the year into twelve months, a reader who knew that the Athenians reckoned the year to begin around midsummer could deduce that the war had begun about two months before that season. To make matters more complicated, different city-states had different dates for New Year's and different names for the months. Thus, when in 423 B.C. the Athenians and the Spartans agreed on the date upon which an armistice was to begin, the same day had to be specified according to the differing calendars of the two city-states: the fourteenth day of the month Elaphebolion according to the Athenian calendar and the twelfth day of the month Cerastius according to the Spartan calendar.[5a]

§6. Greeks reckoned months according to observation of the changing phases of the moon, which meant their months were generally twenty-nine or thirty days long. Since twelve lunar months amounted to a smaller number of days than the slightly more than 365 days in a solar year, Greeks had to add extra days to the annual count to try to keep their cycle of months synchronized with the year and its seasons. Such days are said to be "intercalated," that is, inserted between other days.

§7. Since no uniform method existed for inserting extra days, sometimes officials would insert days into the calendar for religious or political reasons rather than merely to fill out the solar year. Thucydides reports (5.54.3), for example, that the Argives began a military expedition to invade their neighbor Epidaurus on the third day before the end of the month that preceded the month called Carneia by Dorian-speaking Greeks. Carneia was a month that Greeks of Dorian origin regarded as sacred and therefore off-limits for waging war. The Argives, who observed this custom, manipulated the calendar by repeatedly inserting another "third day before the end of the month" every day that they were in the field. That is, they kept designating each day of their expedition as the same day in the calendar. Since in this way they postponed the start of the month Carneia, they could continue to fight without committing any religious impropriety. When they returned home, they could then resume the regular progress of their calendar.

K4a The sophist Hippias, who lived from approximately 485 to 415 B.C., had compiled a list of Olympic victors, but numbering Olympiads to yield dates did not take place until the fourth century B.C.

K5a Thucydides, 4.118.12, 4.119.1.

68. Thucydides explains (5.20.2) that he devised his own system of time reckoning to use in his history because he wanted a greater precision than reference to the names of officeholders allowed. His system divided time into summers and winters. "Winter" referred to the period of several months each year when Greek armies and navies generally refrained from conducting military operations for fear of inclement weather. "Summer" referred to a longer period that more or less encompassed what we mean by the seasons of spring, summer, and fall, when war could for the most part be conducted at will. Thucydides' idiosyncratic system made sense for a narrative like his that was organized around the rhythm of the military campaigns of a protracted war.

Thomas R. Martin
Classics Department
College of the Holy Cross
Worcester, Massachusetts

GLOSSARY

of a city, its highest point. Typically, it was the site of temples, buildings. Enclosed by its own set of defensive walls, it served as of retreat when a city's outer walls were breeched.

reeks who spoke the Aeolian dialect: Boeotians, Thessalians, Les- nts of a small part of the adjacent coast of northern Asia Minor.

ty's marketplace, its center for commercial, social, and political

ate at Athens, chosen by lot in the later fifth century. The nine ar- rned with administering justice, overseeing foreign residents of ng family property disputes, and carrying out a variety of other ous archon gave his name to the civil year.

strict of Athens, both inside and outside the city wall, where the orked. It was also the site of an important and famous cemetery.

shrine to Apollo at Delphi where petitioners consulted the god the most important oracular shrine in the Greek world.

, those Greeks who lived in the villages (*demes*) of the land. In ancient Greek states the term "demos" came to mean the com- most numerous body of citizens of the state. They were often a ne People or The Many—in contrast to nobles, oligarchs, or ratic Athens, the word also stood for the citizen body as a whole.

reeks who spoke the Doric dialect and whose lives shared certain , governmental, and religious features. They were located mainly areas of Greek settlement: Sicily, Peloponnesus, Crete, Libya, y islands.

Drachma: a unit of Greek currency: Six **obols** equaled one drachma; one hundred drachmas equaled a **mina;** six thousand drachmas (or sixty minas) equaled a **talent.**

Hellenes: men of Hellas, of Greek descent and Greek speaking, i.e., the Greeks.

Helots: Although Helot-type unfree laborers are known elsewhere, in Thucydides these are the lowest class of the Spartan state who lived in oppressive, hereditary servitude, and who were for the most part engaged in agriculture. They lived throughout Laconia and also in adjacent Messenia, where the Helot system had been extended by Spartan conquest, and they apparently far outnumbered their masters, who feared as well as exploited them.

Hermes: messenger of the gods, escort of the dead, and a fertility figure. This last identity is clearly signified by Hermae, stone columns featuring a carved depiction of Hermes' head at their top and an erect penis at the column's midpoint. Hermae were placed in front of homes, apparently as good-luck charms.

Homer: a poet thought to have lived in the eighth century B.C., possibly on the Ionian coast. Greeks knew him as the author of the epics *Iliad* and *Odyssey.* These works were famous and familiar to almost all educated Greeks.

Hoplite: a heavily armed Greek foot soldier. Though not wealthy enough to maintain a horse, a hoplite could afford the expense of outfitting himself with bronze armor consisting of helmet, breastplate, and greaves, a heavy bronze shield, a spear, and a short iron sword. The hoplite fought in close rank and file with his fellows, both giving and receiving support.

Ionians: those Greeks who spoke the Ionic dialect and whose lives shared certain distinctive cultural, governmental, and religious features. The Athenians believed that the Ionians had originated in Athens and had spread from there by an early colonization to what came to be called Ionia on the central coast of Asia Minor; there they founded and formed a loose league of cities.

Knights: the second rank of Athenian citizens, whose annual income was between three and five hundred **medimnoi** of grain; see **pentecosiomedimnoi, zeugitae,** and **thetes.**

Lacedaemon: the region of southeastern Peloponnesus that was governed by Sparta. Thucydides used the terms "Lacedaemon," "Lacedaemonian," and "Lacedaemonians" almost interchangeably with those used exclusively in this edition: "Sparta," "Spartan," and "Spartans."

Mede: the Greeks regularly referred to the Persians as "the Mede," or "the Medes," and to the Persian Wars as the "Median Wars," although the Medes and the Persians were distinct, but related, peoples.

ic dry measure of approximately twelve gallons. The **penteco-** example, were Athenian citizens whose annual income equaled ndred medimnoi of grain.

eeks who submitted to the Persians, or who otherwise joined or accused of "Medism" or of having "Medized."

Aliens: inhabitants of Athens who were not citizens. They could were liable to special taxes and military services. Many were in- e.

currency worth one hundred **drachmas.** Sixty minae (plural) .

pecial military class created by Sparta whose numbers seem to in- he succeeding half century (Sec. 7.19.3). Their precise status re- nd although the name implies that they were made part of the scholars reject this notion.

of Greek currency; six obols equaled one **drachma.**

al procedure by which the Athenians could banish a citizen from Athenian controlled territory for ten years without his incurring citizenship. A citizen was "ostracized" if, after the Athenians had h a vote, he received the most votes, and a total of at least 6,000 ards of pottery called ostraka) were cast.

int that Greek soldiers and sailors sang as they advanced into bat- orated victory.

Athenian festival celebrating Athena's birthday with games, sacri- ions (along the Panathenaic Way from the **Ceramicus** to the s celebrated every year but with particular magnificence every reat Panathanaea).

wo special Athenian state triremes (the other was the *Salaminia*) bassies and for official business.

rmed soldiers who fought without formation from a distance by or other missiles. Their name derived from the small, light shield

noi: Athenian citizens of the highest economic class whose an- led or exceeded five hundred medimnoi of grain (see **medimnos**). **knights** whose annual income was between three and five hun- f grain, **zeugitae** whose annual income was between two and three hundred medimnoi of grain, and **thetes,** whose annual income was less than two hundred medimnoi of grain.

Perioikoi: In Thucydides these are people who "lived around Sparta." They paid taxes to the Spartan state and served in the Spartan army, but they did not participate in the Spartan government or enjoy the rights and privileges of Spartan citizens.

Peripoli: a special military corps, perhaps consisting of young recruits who served as a frontier guard.

Pnyx: the hill where the Athenian assembly met to conduct its deliberations.

Proxenus: a citizen and resident of his own state who served as a "friend or representative" (much like a modern honorary consul) of a foreign state.

Pythia: the priestess who conveyed Apollo's prophecies at Delphi.

Salaminia: one of two special Athenian state triremes (the other was the *Paralus*) used on sacred embassies and official business.

Spartiate: a full citizen of Sparta and a member of its highest citizen elite.

Stade: a unit of distance from which is derived our word *stadium;* the Attic stade was 607 feet long; the Olympic stade was 630.8 feet.

Stoa: a shedlike structure with one open side whose roof is supported by columns.

Talent: a large unit of currency equal to sixty **minae** or six thousand **drachmas.**

Thetes: the lowest rank of Athenian citizens, whose annual income was less than the two hundred **medimnoi** of grain; see **pentecosiomedimnoi, knights,** and **zeugitae.**

Thranitae: the uppermost bank of rowers in a trireme.

Zeugitae: the middle bank of rowers in a trireme; also Athenian citizens of middling status, whose annual income was between two and three hundred **medimnoi** of grain; see **pentecosiomedimnoi, knights,** and **thetes.**

BIBLIOGRAPHY OF ANCIENT SOURCES

[illegible] would like to explore additional ancient sources—some more or [illegible] with Thucydides whose writings were influenced by events of the [illegible]r, others who wrote about the war or events immediately before [illegible]ven some who lived and wrote much later than Thucydides [illegible]nple, worked in the second century A.D., five hundred years after [illegible]who wrote about the Peloponnesian War or some of its leading [illegible] sources that were subsequently lost and are unavailable to us [illegible]ng list of historians, philosophers, and playwrights may prove use-[illegible]e in English translation.

[illegible] 440–c. 390 B.C.): This is the very man whom Thucydides men-[illegible]t name in 6.60.2–4, who confessed to a role in the mutilation of [illegible]ne of three extant speeches, *On the Mysteries,* he describes his im-[illegible]e reasons for his decision to confess.

[illegible]80–411 B.C.): Several speeches and exercises survive. This is the [illegible]describes as "not liked by the multitude because of his reputation [illegible]d as being a man best able to help in the courts." Although a [illegible]r Hundred, he did not flee to Decelea with the other extreme oli-[illegible]egime fell, and remained to be tried, found guilty, and executed.

[illegible] (c. 450–385 B.C.): The greatest of Attic comic playwrights. Eleven [illegible]e; many speak directly of the Peloponnesian War, criticize Athen-[illegible]irize all parties, particularly contemporary Athenians.

[illegible]lus: He wrote a world history (c. 60–30 B.C.), some parts of which [illegible]ull, others lost or only fragmentary. The work is not of high qual-[illegible]terest to us for its reflection of other historical writers and sources [illegible] that are now lost. His section on the Peloponnesian War is com-[illegible]n his Books 12 and 13. While he clearly relies upon Thucydides for [illegible]ch of his account comes from others, presumably a great deal from [illegible]orus, whose work is lost.

[illegible]485–c. 406 B.C.): One of three outstanding Attic tragic playwrights and poets of the fifth century, some of whose surviving plays are clearly marked by events of and attitudes connected to the Peloponnesian War.

Herodotus (c. 485–c. 425 B.C.): A marvelous historian of the Persian Wars (who describes much else besides); his work was certainly known to Thucydides, and it is probably Herodotus whom Thucydides criticizes (without mentioning his name), in 1.20. See the Introduction to this volume, II.i, ii, v; IV.i, ii.

Hippocratic Writings: A compilation of medical writings, some more or less contemporaneous with Thucydides, which may well have influenced his extraordinary clinical description of the plague (2.47–53).

Lysias: A resident alien at Athens; a manufacturer of shields during the war who, when condemned to death by The Thirty tyrants in 404, managed to escape to Megara (although his brother Polemarchus was captured and executed). He returned later to write many legal speeches that have come down to us, many of which are informative about Athenian life at that time, and one of which (*Against Eratosthenes*) describes his own arrest and escape from the tyranny of The Thirty.

Old Oligarch: The name given by us to the author of a pamphlet titled *The Constitution of the Athenians* that describes and explains the Athenian democracy and the success of its navy while criticizing the system as unnatural. The unknown author is thought to have been a fifth-century Athenian with oligarchic views.

Oxyrhynchus Hellenica: Three separate papyri containing some nine hundred lines of an unknown Greek historian were found at the site of Oxyrhynchus in Egypt in 1906. This competent historian writes of Greek history in the period that immediately followed that covered by Thucydides, and like him he arranges his material by successive summers and winters. The best section of what survives deals with the Boeotian federal constitution of 396/5. See note 5.38.2a.

Plutarch (c. A.D. 50–c. 120): A Boeotian author who wrote comparative biographies of famous Romans and Greeks to illustrate morality and personal worth or failure. Despite this moral focus, and the fact that he wrote almost five hundred years after Thucydides died, he provides interesting information, some of it in the form of personal anecdotes, and much of it drawn from sources now lost. Among many biographical depictions, he wrote about such Athenians as Pericles, Alcibiades, and Nicias, and about the Spartan Lysander, all of whom were military and political leaders during the Peloponnesian War.

Xenophon (c. 428–c. 354 B.C.): As an Athenian of aristocratic background, Xenophon took part in and intentionally wrote about events that occurred just after Thucydides' narrative breaks off. His aristocratic background and connections with The Thirty in 404–3 forced him to leave Athens for most of his adult life. While not nearly as skillful a historian as Thucydides, he provides much useful information for which he is the only source.

R.B.S.

CONCISE BIBLIOGRAPHY OF MODERN SOURCES

All modern inquiry on Thucydides is based on A. W. Gomme, A. Andrewes, and K. J. Dover's five-volume *A Historical Commentary on Thucydides* (Oxford, 1945–1981). The *Commentary* is much more than a running guide to the Greek text of Thucydides; in addition it serves as a philologically based history of fifth-century Greece itself. More recently, Simon Hornblower has published the first installment (Oxford, 1991) of a proposed two-volume *A Commentary on Thucydides,* which is planned to update, but not to replace, Gomme et al., incorporating more recent advances in archaeological discovery and modern secondary historical and philological research. Hornblower has wisely designed his commentary to appeal to the growing number of introductory students working entirely from an English translation of Thucydides.

Both the most recent and the most accessible surveys of Thucydides in English are Simon Hornblower's *Thucydides* (Baltimore, 1986), and W. R. Connor's similarly entitled *Thucydides* (Princeton, N.J., 1984). Connor's book is the more approachable for the student, providing an empathetic and often moving account of the historian and his subject matter within a formal summary of the eight books of the history. Hornblower, in contrast, is concerned with introducing the scholarly problems that arise from the specialist's use of Thucydides. One finds within the latter's eight chapters an introduction to controversies over methodology, dating, the speeches, and Thucydides' own notion of history itself.

Literally hundreds of comprehensive articles and books have been written in the last two centuries on Thucydides in the modern European languages. Most are specialist studies of authorship, language, structure, and dating, and many of the best remain untranslated in German. However, some of this valuable work of K. von Fritz, O. Luschnat, E. Schwartz, and W. Schadewaldt can still be accessed in English through derivative criticism in F. Adcock's well-written *Thucydides and His History* (Cambridge, 1963); F. M. Cornford's widely speculative, but at times brilliant *Thucydides Mythistoricus* (London, 1907); J. de Romilly's *Thucydides and Athenian Imperialism*, trans. P. Thody (Oxford, 1963); and especially the essays by A.

Momigliano (*Studies in Historiography* [London, 1966]) and M. I. Finley (*Ancient History: Evidence and Models* [London, 1985]), which contain random though invaluable insights into Thucydides' place in the tradition of Greek historiography. Less detailed efforts also draw on the same material in placing the thought and language of Thucydides within the intellectual landscape of his times. The two best shorter summaries still remain J. H. Finley's *Three Essays on Thucydides* and K. J. Dover's brief *Thucydides* (Oxford, 1973).

Standard encyclopedias of Greek history and literature contain well-summarized entries on Thucydides as historian, philosopher, and literary artist. The four most useful and available articles are found in *The Cambridge History of Classical Literature, Vol. 1: Greek Literature,* ed. P. E. Easterling and B.M.W. Knox (Cambridge, 1985); *The Cambridge Ancient History, Vol. 5: The Fifth Century B.C.,* ed. D. M. Lewis, J. Boardman, J. K. Davies, and M. Ostwald (Cambridge, 1992); A. Lesky, *A History of Greek Literature,* trans. J. Willis-C. de Heer (London, 1966); and a brief sketch in W. K. C. Guthrie, *A History of Greek Philosophy,* 6 vols. (Cambridge, 1962–1980).

Finally, general accounts of the Peloponnesian War critique Thucydides' investigative accuracy and his overall value in reconstructing Greek history of the period. The two most engaging summaries of Thucydides as historian of the war between Athens and Sparta are found in D. Kagan's sober *The Archidamian War* (Ithaca, 1974), the first volume of a comprehensive and indispensable four-volume history of the Peloponnesian War, and G. E. M. de Ste. Croix's brilliant but often combative *The Origins of the Peloponnesian War* (London, 1972). G. B. Grundy's *Thucydides and the History of His Age* (Oxford, 1948) was written before many of the important fifth-century Attic inscriptions were published, but it remains a fascinating review of Thucydides' own knowledge about the military, economic, and social conditions of fifth-century Greece.

Victor Davis Hanson
Professor of Greek
Department of Foreign Languages
and Literatures
California State University, Fresno

ACKNOWLEDGMENTS

This edition could never have been completed without the assistance of a large number of colleagues and friends. Foremost among them is Alan Boegehold of Brown University, who not only submitted two appendices to this text, but has consistently supported my forays into the classics in many ways and for many years. Special thanks also go to Donald Kagan of Yale University, who provided encouragement at crucial moments and recommended me to others who became vitally important to the project. Among those was Glen Hartley, my agent for the book, who gave much helpful advice and introduced me to Adam Bellow, who seems unique among current trade editors for his interest in the classics. Glen also recommended Kim Llewellyn, who designed this book, and whose expertise is basically responsible for its lucid and tasteful presentation of text, notes, and maps. Stephen Morrow did the editorial trench work for The Free Press and deserves high praise for bringing the whole project together. Thanks also are due to Loretta Denner for her superb copyediting and proofing supervision.

Victor Davis Hanson of California State University, Fresno, has contributed the Introduction, an Appendix on hoplite warfare, and the modern bibliography to this volume. I am profoundly grateful for his invaluable support, advice, and counsel. George Cawkwell of University College, Oxford, also provided much indispensable counsel and assistance, particularly in examining and revising Crawley's text, but also in reviewing and commenting on other elements of the edition. Paul Cartledge of Clare College, Cambridge, contributed appendices on Sparta and the Peloponnesian League, gave much good advice, and greatly improved the many sections of text that he kindly reviewed.

Many thanks are owed to Anne Gibson, manager of the Clark University Cartography and Information Service, who drew the finished maps: her patience and professional skill were a tremendous help to me, and I believe the quality and clarity of her work is outstanding. I am also most grateful to Professor Richard Talbert, director and editor of the Classical Atlas Project, for his expert assistance in locating obscure classical sites and his general review of this edition's maps.

I wish also to express my appreciation to Simon's Rock College of Bard, its students, and its provost Bernard Rodgers; it was while teaching there that I first perceived the need for this volume. Elli Mylonas and Gregory Crane of the Perseus project gave freely of their time and educated me in the basic computer techniques that were so essential to my own preliminary design of the maps, the notes, and the text itself. My assistant Sandra Kleiner kept the project in order when I was not, conducted the search for illustration rights, and remained cool even when machine breakdowns at crucial moments threatened to overwhelm us.

I would like to acknowledge a debt to the History Department of Harvard University, which in 1958, when I was an undergraduate, set up a special tutorial course for me in ancient history. The man who tutored me, George Nadel, provided the stimulus and the scholarly background that I believe made it possible for me to return to the study of ancient history some twenty-five years later, after a career in business. In that context, I would also like to thank John B. Wilson of Oxford who provoked my interest in Thucydides' Pylos narrative and encouraged me to write about it, and Christopher B. R. Pelling of University College, Oxford, whose excellent and always sympathetic editorial assistance made it possible for me to complete the articles that marked my entry into the field.

Finally, I must acknowledge the assistance and support that I received at all times from my family. My daughter, Karen, reviewed Crawley's text and by noting terms, phrases, and constructions that seemed to her modern ear to be archaic, obscure, or awkward, provided an invaluable opening platform for revising his text. My son, Matthew, has always expressed interest in this edition and provided much assistance to my first efforts to return to the classics when I wrote articles on the Pylos campaign. My brother, David, who is also my partner in business, must be thanked for permitting me without comment or complaint to greatly reduce my time and attention to our business affairs in order to pursue this labor of love. Last but certainly not least, my greatest thanks go to my wife, Toni, who suffered through my occasional bouts of despair when I doubted whether this book would ever be completed, and endured my frequent bursts of obsessive attention to this six-year project. Her support through it all at no little personal sacrifice was more essential to the completion of this edition than any element of assistance that I received from anyone, anywhere. I am profoundly grateful to her.

R.B.S.

INDEX

…at this index treats only the English translation, not the Greek text. …bstractions, concepts, and images present in Thucydides' original …but absent in the translation are not cited.

REFERENCE MAPS

AX
BX

BX
BX
AY

BX
BX E
BX C
BX H

AY Ia
AY Ia
AY Io
AY Io
AY Ita

BX Le
BY Lo

BX Me
BY Me
AY Met

BX Nax

BY Rheg

BX Selin
BY Sicili
BX Syrac

AY Taren
AY Thuri
AX Tyrrh

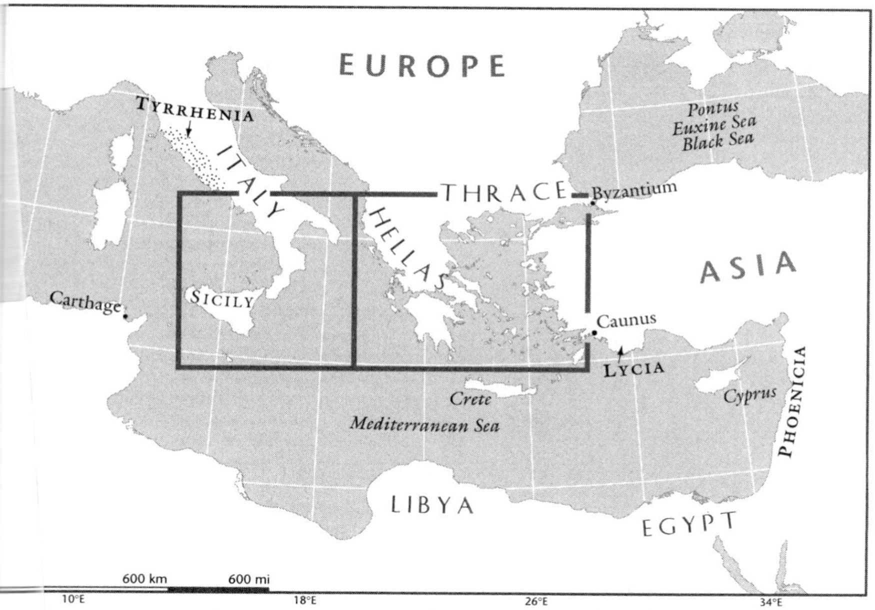

EUROPE
TYRRHENIA
ITALY
HELLAS
THRACE
Byzantium
Pontus
Euxine Sea
Black Sea
ASIA
Carthage
SICILY
Caunus
LYCIA
Crete
Mediterranean Sea
Cyprus
PHOENICIA
LIBYA
EGYPT
600 km
600 mi
10°E
18°E
26°E
34°E

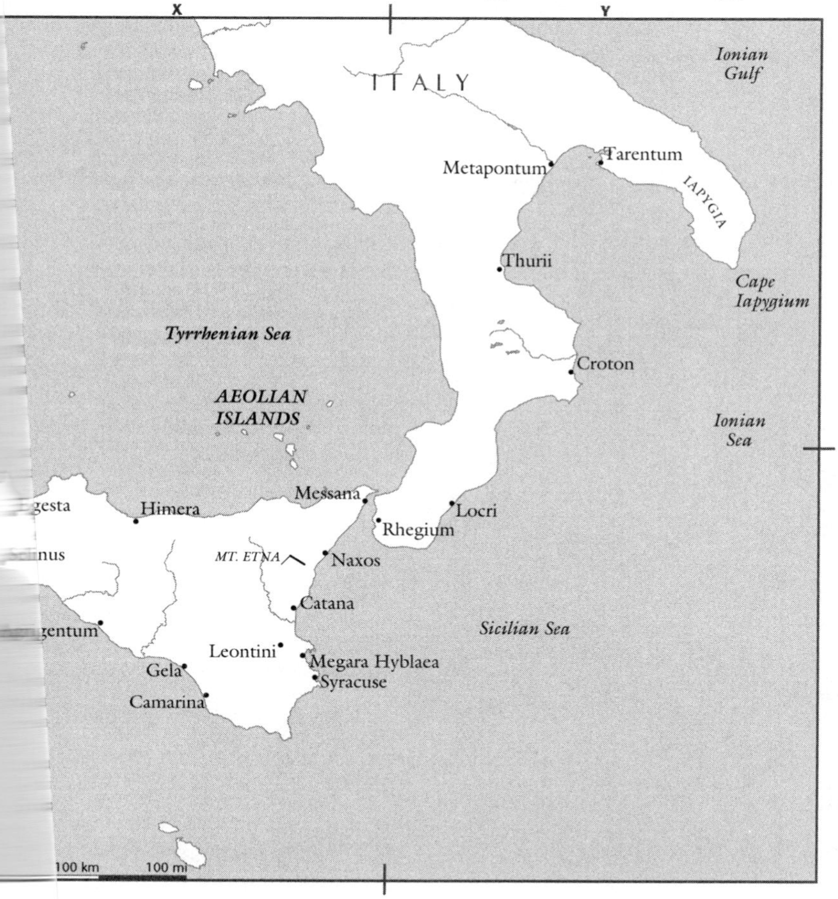

X
Y
ITALY
Ionian
Gulf
Metapontum
Tarentum
IAPYGIA
Thurii
Cape
Iapygium
Tyrrhenian Sea
Croton
AEOLIAN
ISLANDS
Ionian
Sea
Messana
Himera
Locri
Rhegium
MT. ETNA
Naxos
Catana
Sicilian Sea
Leontini
Megara Hyblaea
Gela
Syracuse
Camarina
100 km
100 mi

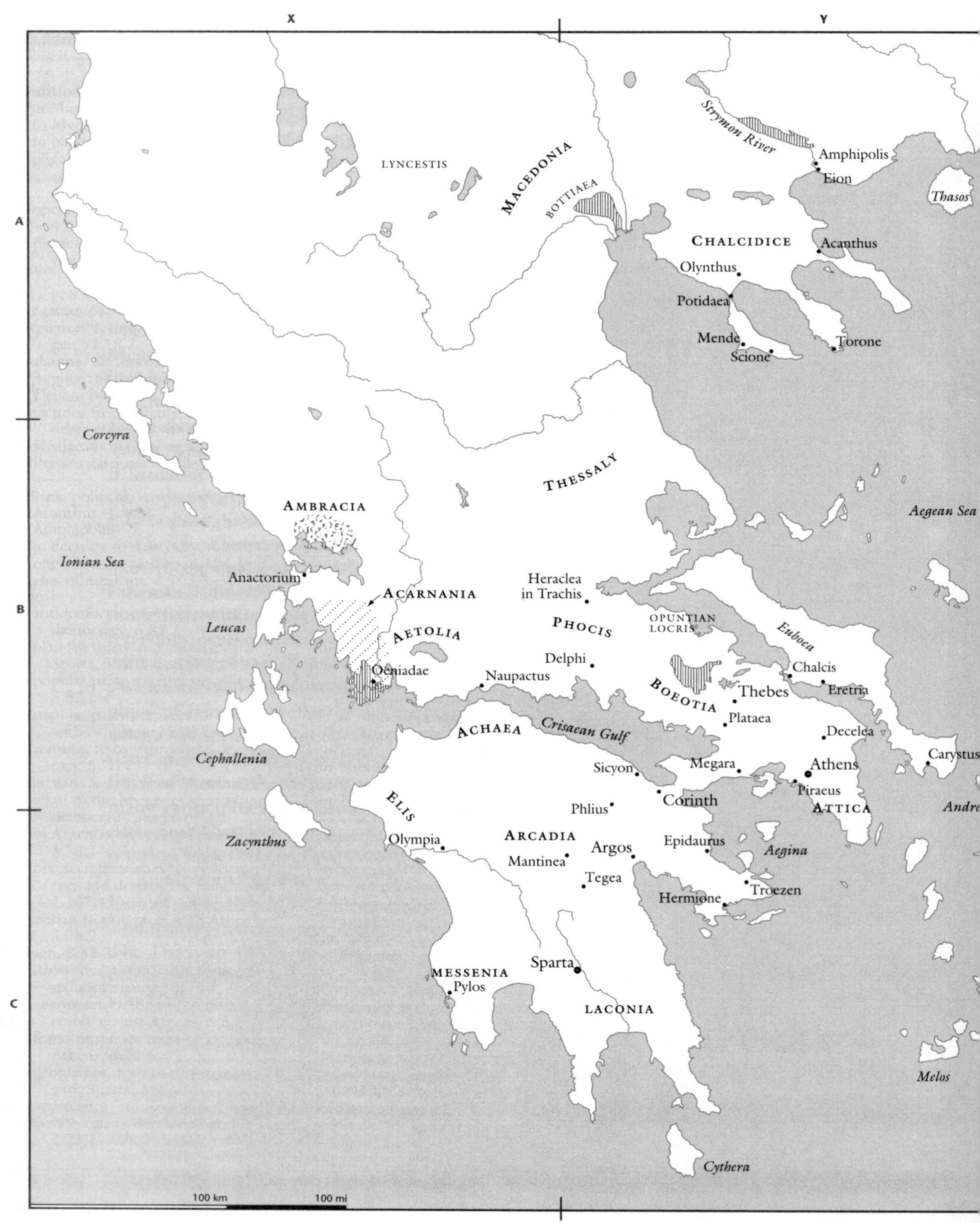
X
Y
A
B
C
Strymon River
Amphipolis
Eion
Thasos
LYNCESTIS
MACEDONIA
BOTTIAEA
CHALCIDICE
Acanthus
Olynthus
Potidaea
Mende
Scione
Torone
Corcyra
THESSALY
Aegean Sea
AMBRACIA
Ionian Sea
Anactorium
Heraclea
in Trachis
ACARNANIA
Leucas
PHOCIS
OPUNTIAN
LOCRIS
Euboea
AETOLIA
Delphi
Oeniadae
Naupactus
Chalcis
BOEOTIA
Thebes
Eretria
Plataea
ACHAEA
Crisaean Gulf
Decelea
Cephallenia
Sicyon
Megara
Athens
Carystus
Piraeus
Corinth
ELIS
Phlius
ATTICA
Zacynthus
Olympia
ARCADIA
Argos
Epidaurus
Aegina
Mantinea
Tegea
Troezen
Hermione
Sparta
MESSENIA
Pylos
LACONIA
Melos
Cythera
100 km
100 mi

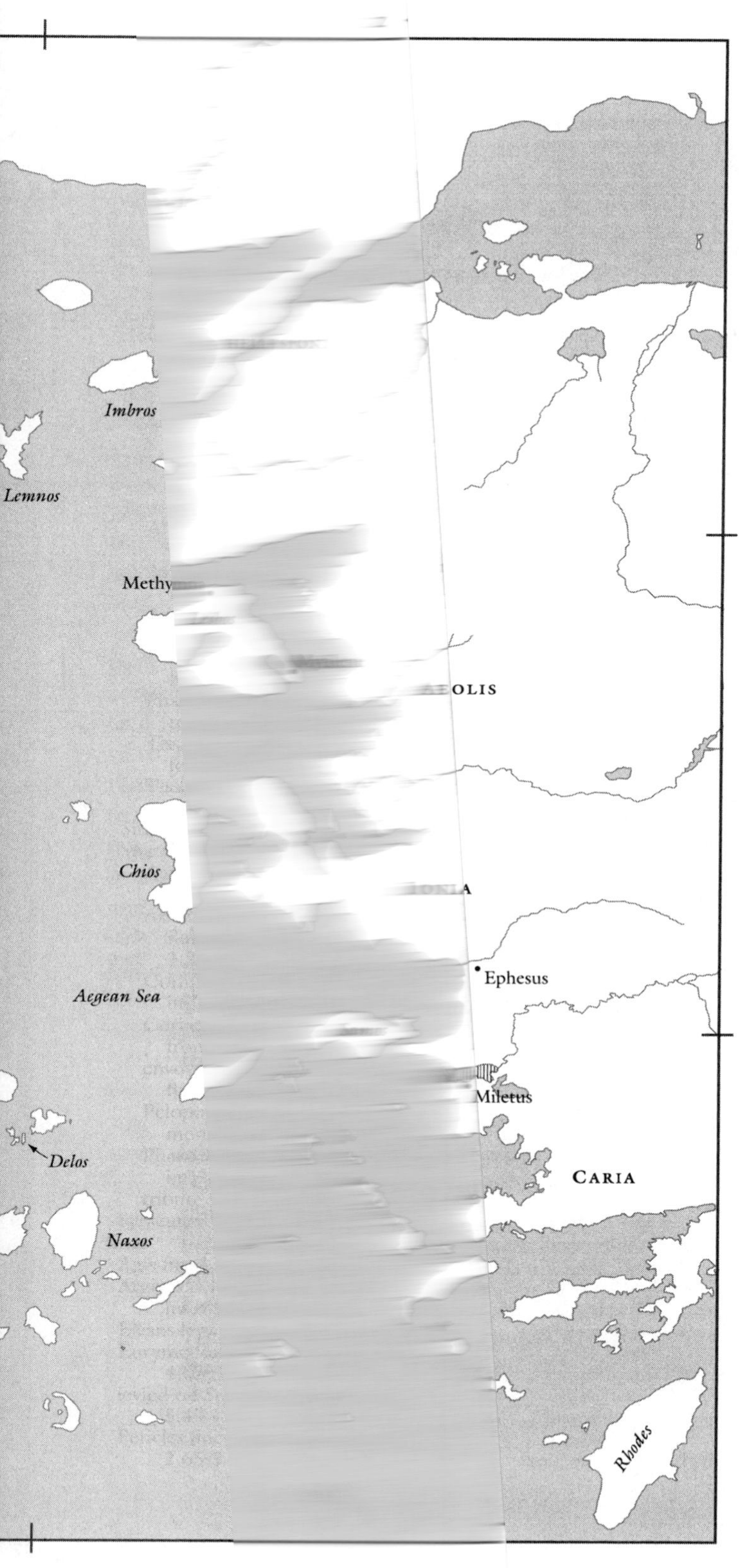

Imbros
Lemnos
Methy
AEOLIS
Chios
IONIA
Ephesus
Aegean Sea
Miletus
Delos
CARIA
Naxos
Rhodes